ACCOUNTING
PRACTICE
MANAGEMENT
HANDBOOK

EDITED BY JAMES H. MacNEILL, CPA, M.B.A.

PUBLISHED BY THE
AMERICAN INSTITUTE OF CERTIFIED PUBLIC ACCOUNTANTS
270 Madison Avenue, New York 16, New York

Contents

Section 7. Accounting Reports, Records, and Procedures

Appendix

Index

Foreword

■ THE ACCOUNTING PRACTICE MANAGEMENT HANDBOOK offers specific guides to the many different aspects of administering a public accounting practice. It replaces, and includes a considerable amount of material from, *The CPA Handbook,* which has been the most widely read reference work in this area for a decade.

Selections from the writings of dozens of different authors make up this book. They are individual practitioners, teachers, partners of small, medium-sized, and large accounting firms. Other sources include Institute committees, members of the Institute staff, and department editors and authors of *The Journal of Accountancy.*

Choice of material, organization and editing were by James H. MacNeill, CPA, Assistant Professor of Accounting at the Fordham University School of Business in New York City, who also has his own public accounting practice.

Preface

■ FOR MANY YEARS, practicing accountants have been swapping experiences and ideas in the management of their practices. While a great deal of this material has appeared in print, much of it has failed to reach the busy practitioner who has too little time to screen all of the numerous publications in order to locate the items in which he is specifically interested.

This book was, therefore, conceived for the purpose of bringing together in a single volume the suggestions, experiences, and comments of many accountants on a wide variety of practice management problems. At first glance, it might be thought of as a "how-to-do-it" book. Methods and procedures, however, are only part of the management story; our aspirations, the measurement of our progress, our very attitudes must necessarily be considered in such a volume. The editor hopes that this *Accounting Practice Management Handbook* will serve as a convenient reference manual in which the practitioner can benefit from the collective thinking of those who have dealt with many of the same problems that may beset him.

The material for this book was taken from American Institute publications and the unpublished reports of its committees. Among the most productive sources were the *CPA Handbook,* edited by Robert L. Kane, Jr., and the *Economics of Accounting Practice* series of bulletins. This series was inaugurated by Marquis G. Eaton, and edited and partially written by Roderic A. Parnell of the Institute staff, with the assistance of the advisory committee on economics of accounting practice.

The Practitioners Forum in *The Journal of Accountancy,* edited first by Dixon Fagerberg and then by Bernard B. Isaacson, was an important source, as were many individual articles from *The Journal*. Some material was also obtained from the Institute's membership publication, the *CPA*.

The results of numerous surveys and interviews which appeared in the original source material are referred to throughout this work. The extent of these surveys varies, as does the time when they were conducted. In some cases, there was no reason to believe that conditions had changed materially since the results were compiled. In this category are surveys on the prevalent use by accounting firms of various filing methods, grades of report paper, and the like. Since the passing of time has made the results of some surveys relatively meaningless, as in the case of fees charged and starting salaries for juniors, only recent studies have been included.

To those whose names appear on the list of contributing authors a word of explanation is offered. It will be noticed that no attempt has been made to identify specific material with the original contributor. Since the authors have so often treated a variety of subjects in a single work, the material was "dissected" so that it could be organized by subject. As a result, even a single page of this book may include the work of several authors. It was felt that repeated insertion of source references would impair the book's continuity, and be of little value to the reader.

Although there was little problem of availability of material, selecting the specific matter to be included required considerable thought. It was obvious at the outset that no one practitioner or firm would find the entire contents of this book of interest. The size of practice, the nature of clientele, and even location, all affect the needs of the reader. And, of course, attitudes and interests differ widely. One broad criterion was therefore chosen for the selection of material—would *some* practitioner find it useful in the management of his practice? Space limitations naturally dictated the omission of a great many items. An attempt was made to allot space to topics in some relation to their importance in the management of a practice and to avoid duplication wherever possible. Some overlapping was inevitable, however, because many of the topics are so interrelated. And since the finished product is a composite of the thoughts of many people, their views are sometimes in conflict. Where contrary views both seemed to have merit, both were included.

In such an undertaking, a number of special credits must always be extended. Many Institute committees helped to develop material included in this volume. Especially valuable was the work done by the Institute's committee on accounting and reporting for small business, the committee on data processing centers, the committee on accounting and office equipment, and the committee on management of accounting practice, including its special subcommittee which reviewed the organization of the book and the topics selected for inclusion.

Several members of the Institute's technical staff also helped to revise and update certain portions. I am particularly grateful to Charles E. Noyes, Loris Battin, S. L. Mason, and Ann O'Rourke of the Institute's publications division for their assistance and suggestions, as well as to Ida Hunt of the Institute library staff for preparing the index.

—*James H. MacNeill*

Contributing Authors

Paul J. Adam
Lee J. Adamson
Wilton T. Anderson

Jules Backman
Ralph H. Bearden, Jr.
Garret L. Bergen
John J. Bernard
Herman W. Bevis
Max Block
Milton Bogen
Frank W. Boydstun
Horace R. Brock
Robert Buchele
Douglas J. Burnett

John L. Carey
A. B. Carson
George R. Catlett
Stephen Chan
Nelson Conway
Edward A. Coughlan
Raymond A. Crovatto
Warren B. Cutting

Ernest Dale
W. Carl Dale

Dixon Fagerberg, Jr.
John Favaloro
Gordon Ford

Arthur B. Foye
Ira N. Frisbee
Bruce Futhey

Edward F. Gee
Richard C. Gerfen
Eli Gerver
Richard H. Goldberg
F. G. Gosling

Byron E. Haglund
Steven J. Halpern
William D. Hayes
James W. Heary
Leslie A. Heath
Samuel R. Hepworth
Sheldon Y. Howard
Robert R. Hudson
William P. Hutchison

Bernard B. Isaacson

Herbert L. Jamison
Charles E. Johnson

J. D. Kingsolver
Paul Kircher
J. T. Koelling
Stewart L. Kohn
John F. Kramer

John W. LaFrance
Arthur F. Lafrentz

Marcel Learned
James C. Leming
John E. Leslie
Ralph F. Lewis
Carl Lipoff
Edward O. Lutz

Robert E. Malesardi
S. Wesley Marcus
Ernest N. May
N. Loyall McLaren
Robert N. McMurry
Charles A. Meroney
Richard D. Metcalf
W. H. Middleton
Robert J. Murphey

Arthur P. Nash
Fred T. Neely
Robert E. Nelson
T. B. Noble
Carl B. Noyes

James P. Ould, Jr.
George A. Owen

Colin Park
Louis H. Penney
Kenneth W. Perry
Manfred E. Philip
Louis H. Pilié
Wayne E. Pollard

James W. Porter
William G. F. Price

George Rea
Richard C. Rea
Marion R. Reich
James A. Rennie
Charles S. Rockey
Charles P. Rockwood

Adrian F. Sanderbeck
L. Hartley Smith
Maurice H. Stans
Marvin L. Stone
Harry L. Stover
John M. Stoy
Rupert A. Stuart

Stephen D. Tanner
Roy E. Tuttle

Curtis C. Verschoor
Norman H. S. Vincent

Horace E. Weinstein
T. Dwight Williams
J. Frederick Witschey
Robert E. Witschey
Arthur E. Witte
Erwin Bud Wittus

L. C. J. Yeager
Harold M. Young

Fees

The Economic Background

The late Marquis G. Eaton, when president of the American Institute of Certified Public Accountants, talked often about the economics of an accounting practice. In one of his talks he said,

> Devotion to public service in a free economy obliges the professional man to have appropriate regard to the financial aspects of his work. Unless he maintains himself as a financially sound professional unit, he cannot serve the public. Instead, he simply disappears from public and professional view.

■   IT HAS BEEN shown in several surveys that a disturbing number of CPAs in public practice are deriving incomes from their practices which are below any reasonable standard.

For example, only a few years ago, statistics showed that roughly one out of five practitioners was receiving incomes which compared unfavorably with the salaries paid to staff accountants and accountants below the executive level in industry. An even higher proportion of the CPAs, moreover, were earning incomes which probably were not sufficient to permit them to discharge all the basic obligations imposed upon professional men as a group and as individuals.[1]

[1]*Incomes of Practicing Certified Public Accountants,* Economics of an Accounting Practice Bulletin 1, AICPA, 1957.

Since a professional man's income is a product of his fees, it is apparent that some CPAs must be charging rates for their services which do not accurately reflect the cost of performing those services.

This, in turn, raises some questions:

1. Do these practitioners include in their fees a reasonable amount for themselves as a legitimate expense in the conduct of a professional practice?

2. Do they maintain strict control over the time devoted to each engagement as a means of insuring that the proper levels of accounting skill are efficiently applied to it?

3. Do they lack a "resistance point" on fees—a constantly visible point at which a fee no longer recovers the full cost of an engagement?

4. Do they recognize that a professional fee can rarely be justified for nonprofessional work? And do they utilize nonprofessional assistants for work which cannot command professional fees?

5. Do they base their fee scale on a realistic estimate of the amount of "chargeable" time which can be expected of staff men and partners in a year?

If the approach of some CPAs to fee-setting is defective, it may well be due to the profession's reluctance to engage in open and candid discussions of the subject. To be sure, the old attitude of reserve is breaking down. Today, although a few CPAs still regard any outward expression of concern over fees as undignified, most members of the profession are ready to concede that a high quality of service cannot be provided unless the practice is functioning as an effective economic unit. Nonetheless, the old habit of reticence is not likely to be abandoned quickly.

This cannot, however, be held solely responsible for the fact that comparatively little has been written on fees. The complexity of the subject has also discouraged practitioners from freely discussing it. There are, unhappily, no simple formulas and no universal answers in the determination of a fair fee. Too many elements—including subjective ones which defy precise measurement—enter into the decision. But one conclusion seems inescapable: in the light of economic statistics, the difficult art of setting fees deserves far more attention than is generally accorded to it.

The CPA's Tentative Income Goal

■ BEFORE A TRULY effective fee structure can be developed, an objective should be established against which the day-to-day performance can be measured. This is represented by the practitioner's or partner's income target.

Some years ago a study was made of fees and their relationship to the cost of living. The purpose was to ascertain just how much net income was needed to yield an accountant the same standard of living as a given income supplied in 1939. The results of this study indicated that an accountant's *net* income would have had to rise two and one-half times since 1939 to yield a comparable standard of living after giving effect to differences in the cost-of-living index and to income-tax rates. By now, the ratio probably would exceed three times. Since the growth of labor costs has far outstripped the cost-of-living increase, gross fees should probably be four or five times as great as those charged in 1939 to keep the professional accountant in the same relative position in our economy. (See "The Effect of Inflation on the CPA," pages 81-82.)

Marquis G. Eaton expressed the CPA's income goal in terms of achievement rather than dollars:

> The financial resources available to the professional man from his practice must be sufficient to enable him to do these things, among others: to pay the compensation necessary to attract to the profession, in competition with others, the highest type of young people; to maintain the library and other equipment needed in his work; to pay the cost of a respectable and comfortable office; to afford the leisure necessary for thought and study of an advanced character; to render the public services which the community may ask of him; to provide for old age; to discharge family obligations; to maintain a standard of living that would contribute to a client's good opinion rather than detract from it; to provide for his participation in the affairs of professional societies and attendance at their meetings. The practice should yield financial returns to cover these things without the burden of excessively long hours devoted to work. . . .

One of the considerations mentioned by Mr. Eaton merits additional emphasis. In setting his income goal, the practitioner would be well advised to keep in mind that his own evaluation of his worth can have a strong effect upon the client's opinion of his value. If he consistently underestimates it, the client may well underrate his abilities. This is a truism which applies to almost any human relationship. One expert on professional fees has written:

> As a general rule, it is poor practice for the physician to undercharge. Certainly it is a psychological truth, evidenced in so many practical ways, that the man who undervalues himself loses caste in the eyes of the public. Often the large size of a man's fee increases his prestige and broadens his practice. If he charges an extremely moderate fee, however altruistic his underlying motive, the probability is that his patients will attribute it to

3

his own lack of experience and ineptness. This is, of course, no brief for exorbitant fees; hence the wisest policy, especially when the doctor is new to the community, and his capabilities are largely a matter of conjecture, is to emulate the majority of local physicians in the fixing of a set charge.[2]

The selection of an income target, of course, is a wholly personal matter.

Accountants, first of all, vary greatly in ability. The CPA has attained professional status because, in addition to other things, the certificate represents a high level of competence within his field. It does not, however, guarantee anything more than minimal acceptable competence. Some practitioners, either through inclination, ability, or circumstances, may reach a technical plateau during the course of their careers which is not appreciably higher than the knowledge necessary to obtain the certificate. On the other hand, many CPAs regard the certificate as a mere starting point; they continue to broaden their knowledge and, through its proper application, increase their usefulness to the business community. Those who fail to keep pace with these professional leaders can hardly hope to match them in compensation.

In establishing his income goal, the practitioner must also take into consideration the nature of his services. If he is largely preoccupied with routine tasks which require no great exercise of professional skill, he must realistically make an adjustment in his income expectations. But if his firm is primarily engaged in providing service at a truly professional level, he has a right to expect higher fees for its work. A professional service, after all, is a composite of many things. It is based on knowledge acquired through formal education, on experience gained in handling similar situations in the past, and on continual efforts to keep abreast of new developments. It demands an analytical ability which, combined with sound judgment, enables the practitioner to determine what work needs to be done and the most practical way of undertaking it. Such service quite properly carries a higher price tag.

As a guide in arriving at a reasonable figure, the practitioner must recognize that his net income should normally be composed of the following elements:

1. A realistic salary, equivalent perhaps to that required to hire someone to perform the practitioner's duties; or the salary the practitioner could expect to command if he were employed by another public accounting firm.

2. A return on the capital investment comparable to that which could be achieved if the money were otherwise invested.

3. A proprietary share—a reasonable amount which can be considered as the return to the principal for accepting the responsibility of conducting the practice. This represents the true profit of the accounting practice itself, for the other portions of the total net income generally can be realized without establishing or maintaining the practice.

[2]George D. Wolf, *The Physician's Business,* 2d ed., J. B. Lippincott & Co., Philadelphia, 1945, p. 115.

Finally, in deciding upon his income target, the practitioner should remember that clients expect a professional firm to be able to render competently any service within its acknowledged field. But the practitioner's level of fees affects his ability to render a variety of services of high quality. Consequently, if the fees charged by individual firms prevent its members from continuing to improve their capacities or interfere with the maintenance of an organization equipped to render effective services, the standards of the profession are lowered. Moreover, the fees of one firm are affected to some extent by the fees of others, with the quality of the services being determined, in part, by the extent to which the fee structure enables a firm to preserve high standards.

Probably the prevailing practice, in deciding upon hourly rates to be charged, is to find out what the other fellow is charging so as not to be too far out of line. Wouldn't it make more sense for the individual practitioner to start at the last line of his own profit-and-loss statement and work up from there? Such an approach would mean beginning with a realistic appraisal of one's own abilities, experience, and technical competence and an attempt to decide what ought to be a fair annual income under the circumstances.

Factors That Determine Fees

■ THE INCOME GOAL has an over-all effect upon the fee schedule; but a number of elements must always be weighed in establishing the charge for a particular engagement. Those most often mentioned by experienced CPAs and other professional men include:

1. Amount of time devoted to the engagement
2. Expense, including overhead and unusual expenses caused by the engagement
3. Skill and experience of the staff members who undertake the work
4. Technical importance of the work and amount of responsibility assumed by the CPA
5. Value to the client of the service rendered
6. Difficulty of the engagement
7. Established client vs. new or casual client
8. Size and character of the community
9. Inconvenience to the accounting firm
10. Ability of the client to pay
11. Acceptability of the fee to the client
12. Customary fees within the community
13. Reputation of the accounting firm

It is not necessary, of course, to consider every one of these factors anew every time a firm sets a fee. Some are fixed rather definitely with respect to all fees of a given firm. In this class, for instance, are those relating to skill and experience of the principal or firm and the size and character of the community. Others, such as those involving special consideration for a new client, difficulty of an engagement, and unusual overhead, have limited application and require attention only when involved specifically. However, there also are those that must be considered specially in every case. These are staff time and the degree of difficulty of the engagement.

The elements in setting fees fall into two basic groups:

1. Objective elements (direct expenses and time spent) which are the only ones capable of accurate measurement
2. Subjective elements (most of which have some "value" or "acceptability" characteristic) which cannot be measured precisely

In addition to the two basic categories, there are other factors which affect the upper and lower limits of the range of the fees which can be charged.

Opinion seems to be divided within the profession as to whether the first or second group should be emphasized in determining a fair fee for an engagement. Much of the literature in recent years has tended to dwell upon the "value" concept. No one, of course, would deny that a CPA's services have values which ought to be reflected in the fee. But a sound fee structure should be based on a hard core of measurable factors—and the "value" criterion is subject to a wide range of interpretations in any engagement. The "value" approach seems to have been advanced, in part, as an emulation of the practices of other professions. This, however, may have been the result of misunderstanding. While other professional men may seem to bill on the value of the work performed, they usually base their charges on an anticipated average hourly return. There is support for this view in the fact that articles have been appearing with increasing frequency in professional journals advocating the proper consideration of the measurable factor of time in order to practice on a sound financial basis.

It is perhaps fruitless to argue which set of elements—the objective or the subjective—generally deserves the heavier emphasis. A close examination of them reveals that they are closely interrelated, rather than in conflict with each other. Yet it is worth underscoring the point again that only the objective elements can be accurately measured and controlled.

THE OBJECTIVE ELEMENTS IN A FEE

A fee *must* recover the direct expenses of the engagement, reimburse the firm for a fair proportion of its general operating expenses, and provide some return for the principal or partners. Otherwise, the firm cannot long survive.

Time is usually the biggest single element of cost. The time cost of the staff can be accurately computed from their salaries, payroll taxes, insurance, and other employee expenses.

Time devoted to the work. In cases involving specialized ability, the weight given to the time factor is much less than for a routine audit engagement. This is consistent with the professional attitude that fees for such services should be determined on a basis clearly distinct from that applied in an employer-employee relationship in which time expended and an agreed rate are the sole factors. Staff time devoted to the work is the factor first considered in fixing fees. This is because it is definitely measurable and is usually the controlling fee factor in routine audit engagements. Despite the fact that greater weight is frequently given to the other factors in setting fees for the more important auditing, tax and consultation engagements, staff time given to the work is the basic yardstick employed for such engagements, for routine fees established according to it are upgraded in proportion to the special nature of the services rendered.

To accumulate the time factor, it is necessary for the people working on the engagement to report the time they have spent on it at least twice each month. The time devoted to the engagement will include all work done by the accountant and his staff in his own office, as well as in the client's office.

The determination of a *principal's time* cost is usually more arbitrary. Nonetheless, he should allocate a reasonable "salary" to himself as a basic cost of conducting a practice. The time and energy which he devotes to administering, planning and co-ordinating the staff operation is as much a cost of conducting a practice as staff salaries. The fact that he is the proprietor or a partner does not affect the validity of the cost. The practitioner is, in fact, one of his own most important creditors. A number of firms use the partners' drawing accounts as the cost figure and this, if set at a realistic level, seems to serve the purpose adequately.

How much of the time spent on an engagement should be charged to the client?

There is usually no question that the principals' and staff accountants' time should be included. Firms differ, however, in their treatment of their *office and clerical help*. Some regard typing and checking as a direct cost of the engagement and charge the client for them. Others absorb these costs in their overhead. According to recent surveys by several state societies, slightly more than half of the firms prefer the first method. The feeling seems to be that rising labor costs have made salaries of office help a significant item. Since the requirements of the clients vary, the cost should be distributed in proportion to the use of these employees.

Practically every engagement will require some *research* in the office of the accountant to determine either the generally accepted accounting principles, the auditing procedures pertaining to the engagement, or the rules and regulations of some governmental agency. Tax problems pertaining to the client's affairs may be the subject of considerable research. The time spent in such research is necessarily an element of the time factor of the engagement. Some firms make occasional adjustments in charging for these costs, when the knowledge gained might increase their capacity to serve other clients.

While the element of time is a fair starting point in determining the amount of the fee, the following statement of a practitioner illustrates the limitations of blindly adopting this single criterion:

> I called on a client who needed an audit and a partial revision of his accounting system. After the usual conversation as to what I thought would be necessary to give him what he wanted, the talk turned to the matter of my fee.
> I quoted him so much on a per-diem basis or on an hourly basis. His response was a question unique in my experience.
> "How do I know," he asked, "whether you are a fast or a slow worker?"
> I assured him that I was a worker of average speed. Privately, however, I felt that my answer was inadequate. I recognized that he had made a good point.

Expenses. Expenses incurred during the course of an engagement—for example, out-of-town travel expense and long-distance telephone calls—should be included in the bill. Most firms indicate major expenses as separate items on their invoices, feeling that they should be distinguished from "professional services rendered." A number of CPAs feel that all significant expenses which are directly related to an engagement should be charged to that particular client. This approach seems to be more in keeping with billing a client for work performed than it would if these items were included in overhead.

Overhead. Most of the expenses which are not directly charged to the client are usually classified as overhead. These include rent, taxes, telephone, insurance, library, supplies, depreciation of equipment, and salaries of "nonproductive" personnel. Ideally, the nonchargeable time of the principals, at their "salary" rate, should also be included in overhead. This overhead should be distributed among the clients as the cost of maintaining and keeping available an organization which can effectively render the services required of it.

The easiest method of allocating these expenses is derived from dividing the annual overhead expenses by the total number of hours charged to clients during the year by both staff and principals. This would give an hourly "burden" rate expressed in dollars which would be applied to each hour charged to a client during the course of an engagement. Like many simple methods, this one has its shortcomings. It enables the practitioner to recover his overhead costs; but those costs are not distributed among his clients according to the level of work performed for them. It follows that a client who is paying the same hourly burden rate, regardless of the staff grade employed, would be paying a much higher proportion of the overhead in a fee charged for the time of a junior than he would in the case of a partner.

Many firms believe that the amount of overhead charged to a client should vary in direct proportion to the level of work performed as well as to time. This is represented by the different grades of accountants used in the engagement. (The actual expense of a senior accountant is higher than that of a junior for several reasons—including the greater cost of the nonproductive time of the higher salaried man.) By dividing the amount of overhead expense for the year by the gross annual salary costs charged to clients (i.e., the sum of each staff member's chargeable time multiplied by his "direct labor" costs), the burden rate is then expressed as a percentage. Calculating the value of the percentage for each individual (or the average for each class of staff man) and adding to it the salary rate, will yield the basic cost per hour. The overhead can then be figured for each engagement from the number of hours which are charged for each grade or individual assigned to the job.

This approach is by no means universal. Some firms feel that overhead cannot be allocated on an hourly or job basis, since any rate employed would be based on last year's figures, rather than on current ones. The volume of billing varies, while overhead remains relatively fixed. Consequently, unless gross fees can be very closely estimated, a burden rate cannot be applied accurately. These firms, therefore, set their fees on a basis which, over a year's time, will recover the total overhead expenses without trying to allocate them to each engagement.

It is evident that the only way in which these costs can be effectively met is through the employment of basic time rates established in relation to the direct salary costs of the engagement, or direct salary and an allocated portion of the overhead.

How much should these costs be in relation to the total amount billed?

It is impossible to answer this specifically. It depends on a number of factors including size of firm, its location (affecting rents and salaries), the nature of the work performed and, to some extent, the type of client. Nonetheless, interviews with a number of firms indicated that certain ranges could be established. The consensus was that, except in highly unusual cases (e.g., a new client in an unfamiliar industry), direct salary costs should never exceed 50 per cent of the fee. In most cases, depending on the services performed, the firms felt that the direct salary cost should average somewhere around 40 per cent of the fee. Overhead expense exclusive of accountants' salary costs varied among them from a low of roughly 20 per cent to over 40 per cent of the gross fee. The most common range among these firms, as well as a number of other practitioners, seems to be 25 to 33 per cent, with the lower end of the scale prevailing.

THE SUBJECTIVE ELEMENTS IN A FEE

Where time is an important factor, it should be recognized that not all time is of equal value. Thus, time spent by an attorney in a courtroom will be valued at a higher rate than time in the office. The responsibility assumed will be an important factor in this connection. A doctor, accountant, or economist who testifies as an expert usually will make a higher charge for that service than for time spent in preparation. The reputation which enhances the value of the testimony means that such hours will carry a premium.

That actual time spent does not necessarily provide a basis for the fee in many instances, is well illustrated by the story of the surgeon who charged a patient $1,000 for an operation. The patient knew that the doctor had spent only about fifteen minutes in the operating room and had visited the hospital only twice. She was outraged by the bill and requested the doctor to provide a breakdown of the total. Whereupon she received the following detailed bill:

Time spent in operating room	$ 50
Visits to hospital	20
Knowing where to cut	930
Total	$1,000

James McNeill Whistler, the noted painter, also had an experience which illustrated this point. In 1877, he exhibited in London a picture called "The Falling Rocket, Nocturne in Black and Gold." It showed a splash of columns against a dark background and, like all of his nocturnes, which at the time were much ridiculed, but eventually became recognized as great works of art, showed to a superficial eye little detail and evidence of sustained work. The price marked on the picture was 200 guineas. Ruskin published an intemperate criticism of it, maintaining that it was an imposture on the public and should have never been admitted to the exhibition. "I have seen and heard much of cockney impudence before now, but never expected to hear a coxcomb ask 200 guineas for flinging a pot of paint in the public's face."

Whistler sued Ruskin for libel. At the trial the following exchange took place between the attorney general who acted for the defense and Whistler:

Attorney General: "Can you tell me how long it took you to knock off that Nocturne?"

Whister: "I beg your pardon?" (Laughter.)

Attorney General: "I am afraid that I am using a term that applies rather perhaps to my own work. . . ."

Whistler: "Let us say then, how long did I take to 'knock off'—I think that is it—to knock off that Nocturne; well, as well as I remember, about a day. . . . I may have still put a few more touches to it the next day if the painting were not dry. I had better say, then, that I was two days at work on it."

Attorney General: "The labor of two days then, is that for which you ask two hundred guineas?"

Whistler: "No, I ask it for the knowledge of a lifetime."[3]

It was "the knowledge of a lifetime" plus considerable preparation and study that went into the workmanship of every one of his pictures, not the actual time spent in painting. The same is true for many professional services. Clearly in connection with many services rendered by professional persons, the time spent may be no indication of the value of the service rendered.

[3]Elizabeth R. Pennell, *The Art of Whistler,* The Modern Library, New York, 1928, pp. 63-64.

Skill and experience of the staff members. Although the "value" elements within an engagement are almost impossible to measure, they remain in many cases important considerations in setting a fair fee.

They can include such things as amount of money involved, savings or convenience to the client, success or failure in attaining an objective, establishing a precedent or handling unusual problems. They are often closely related to the skill required to perform the work and the degree of responsibility assumed by the accountant. These elements of value to the client tend to fall into three groups:

1. Those that are reflected in a man's salary and receive proper consideration under a time-salary cost rate
2. Those arising from technical accomplishments which are only partially reflected in the accountant's salary
3. Those that bear little or no relation to the time involved

In seeking a fair gauge of value, it is sometimes necessary to consider several of the value components simultaneously. When the various levels of the work involved can be matched to the appropriate skill of the individual staff members, the problem is simplified and proper scheduling can often achieve the proper evaluation. When this can be done thoroughly, it is often adequate to multiply the salary and overhead cost by the time involved, plus a reasonable charge for supervision and a contribution toward the principals' return.

In many cases, however, the nature of the assignment or the limited size of the staff requires that each accountant perform duties which involve varying degrees of skill. Furthermore, as the scope of his talents broadens through experience, the accountant may be called upon to provide a wider range of services. Under these circumstances, an evaluation of the services based on the caliber of personnel assigned to perform them becomes more difficult. However, some of the firms interviewed did not consider this a serious problem. They usually do not make any downward adjustment in rates where a higher-grade staff member performs duties usually assigned to a lower grade. They believe that the greater skill of the higher-grade man enables him to do the job faster and better, thus offsetting the differential in rates. But it seems reasonable to assume that some routine assignments can be handled faster by a junior than by a partner because the junior has had more recent practice in repetitive tasks. A practitioner should be cautious, therefore, in billing for high-grade men on lower-grade work. In any case the client is likely to be more interested in what was done and how well it was done than in who did it.

Technical importance of the work. The factors relating to the technical importance of the work and the extent of responsibility assumed are:

1. Grade of work performed
2. Adequacy of the records on which the work is based

3. Intended uses of the reports rendered
4. Amounts involved
5. Obligations or responsibilities imposed by governmental regulations
6. Liability of the accountants to third parties

The evaluation of technical importance requires that due consideration be given to all of these factors.

Important accounting services, such as accounting reports in connection with the registration of securities with the Securities and Exchange Commission, merit a larger fee than routine auditing; and certain types of tax, advisory and specialist services justify charging more substantial fees.

The adequacy of the records, obligations, and responsibilities assumed by the accountant have a bearing on the risks involved. The intended use of the accountant's report, the amounts involved, and the possibility of liability to third parties are indications of the materiality of the services rendered. Logically, fees should have a direct relation to the degree of risk involved and to the materiality of the services. The risks involved in defending possible "strike" suits in the indefinite future in connection with public issues of securities must be given consideration in fixing a fee on such an engagement.

The liability of accountants to their clients for negligence is not considered as important by practitioners, probably because they believe it is a normal responsibility for which no additional charge is necessary. The general repute of the clients also is considered as of little importance for this purpose.

Value of services to client. The criterion of value of service rendered is closely related to ability to pay and in many instances the two are so closely interrelated as to be almost indistinguishable. A variety of evidence may be available to indicate the value of the service to the client. Perhaps the most obvious situation arises where savings can be effected: savings in taxes, savings attending the installation of a new accounting system, savings in costs of construction, savings in litigation, savings in operating costs, and so on. In these circumstances, there is a clear-cut measurement of the contribution made by the outside consultant.

In a complicated tax-settlement case, where thorough knowledge and judicious reasoning on the part of the accountant leads to substantial savings to the client, the accountant may well consider the amount of savings to be an important factor in setting his fee. As in all learned professions, circumstances arise where knowing what to do is of far greater significance than the physical execution of an act, which in itself might be relatively simple.

Under these conditions, the fee is often a result of personal judgment, weighing a number of factors, including the satisfaction of the client. For example:

A CPA represents two tax clients each requiring the same expenditure of time. One case results in a $5,000 tax refund and the other in a $50,000 refund. Some accountants may feel that one case is considerably more valuable than the other, while others hold that the value to the client lies not so much in the actual financial result as it does in having someone represent his rights. His rights exist, regardless of the point of view. It might then boil down to a question of how clearly the client was entitled to a refund and the accountant's ability to make a persuasive presentation. Any way it is approached, a "reasonable" fee becomes a matter of opinion.

The factors considered in estimating the value of the services to the client are:

1. The intrinsic value of the work performed to the client
2. The degree of success in attaining the purpose for which the work was required
3. The purpose itself

The intrinsic value of the services to a client might be greater in cases where a new issue of securities is contemplated or a reorganization effected than where the report is to be used in connection with casual borrowing.

The client's purpose and the degree of success in attaining it are of particular significance when substantial tax refunds are sought, or proposed tax deficiencies are materially reduced or eliminated.

Difficulty of engagement; skill applied. Practically all firms agree that higher fees are justified where difficult problems are present in the engagement. A few consider these factors when they are involved in only part of the services performed in a particular engagement.

Obviously, it is desirable to have a difficult engagement receive the attention of a highly competent principal and staff. It follows that a client should be willing to pay for the proper value of services under such conditions and to accept the fact that both the inherent difficulties of the engagement and the special competence of the principal and staff to deal with them are closely related to such value. What is not always understood so clearly, however, is that the client, in addition to the further safeguard of consideration by a particularly competent principal and staff, often obtains the definite advantage of a reduction in the time necessary for the engagement as compared with the time that would be necessary if a competent accountant, but not one specially qualified to handle the recognized difficulties, were to perform the engagement. It is quite possible, therefore, for a combination of greater experience, more specialized skill and the expenditure of less time to involve no greater financial outlay to a client than merely adequate experience, routine competence, and a greater time expenditure.

Special consideration to new clients. Established clients provide the main volume of regular business. The assurance of steady volume is just as worthy of favorable treatment in professional pricing as it is in the sale of goods. In many types of service organizations, the regular clients have paid, in part, for the experience acquired, or for research materials contained in the files. The new client, who has not contributed to this accumulation of research materials and experience, appropriately should pay something extra for "the key to the file." Or alternatively, he should pay as much as the regular client for the service rendered even though as a result of the earlier work, only a small fraction of the time was involved.

It should be noted that there are many circumstances under which the second client would receive more favorable treatment than the first one with a similar problem. The desire for future business, the tendency to emphasize the factor of time, and related factors could be significant.

Accountants generally tend to give special consideration to new clients only in exceptional cases. Usually, special consideration is given only to smaller businesses having prospects of future growth. The motive may be to aid them through a difficult period. When it is considered advisable to give a new client special consideration, he should be informed of that fact and advised that at a point in the future he will be charged the usual fee for the services performed. A minority of practitioners have no objection to charging a nominal fee on an initial engagement providing the client knows this fact, but most firms believe that the initial fee must never be less than a substantial portion of a normal fee. Some believe that a reduction of the fee has special justification on new engagements. In effect, obtaining familiarity with the affairs of the new client is considered an element of cost to be borne by the accountant. There may be occasions when this is warranted; but generally, and particularly when another accounting firm is being replaced, it may be difficult to distinguish such a practice from unethical competitive bidding.

A majority of firms extend the consideration in a different way to new clients of small size and means. Such new clients are charged the full amount for services rendered but are allowed to make monthly or other periodic payments in line with their financial situation.

Size and character of the community. Because living expenses and operating costs are often lower in the small cities, the general level of income might be somewhat lower. Smaller fees might therefore be appropriate. Opinions differ with regard to the population figure that should be chosen as the dividing line between low- and high-fee areas, but the differential diminishes rapidly when the community population is 100,000 or more.

If a smaller community has a number of independent businesses, or has diversified industry, the range of fees is apt to be somewhat higher than in a trading center primarily serving a farm area. These conditions are not absolute and tend to be localized without significant regional pattern. Furthermore, even though there may be a significant number of large local enterprises, there is no upward effect on fees when these enterprises are branches of national organizations which do not use local professional services. Some accountants have been able to overcome some of these limitations, as evidenced by the fact that a few small-town practices net as much as or more than successful firms in large cities.

Extra compensation for inconvenience. Convenience to the client or patient may also play a role in the determination of fees. Where consultations take place in the office the fee may be lower than where a trip must be made to the client's place of business or to his home. Perhaps the best-known illustration is found in the practice of doctors to charge higher fees for home visits than for office visits. The differential is designed to compensate the doctor for travel time, the cost of travel, and the inconvenience experienced. Similarly, the accountant may increase the standard charge for an engagement which demands priority during the busy period.

Conversely, an engagement that can be done during the accountant's slack season may permit retention of staff personnel who would otherwise be dropped, or require the hiring of added temporary staff members who need to be paid only for the period of the engagement. Again, an engagement may materially reduce idle time previously estimated for the period in which the engagement is to be performed. Consideration can be given to such favorable factors when fixing fees.

Ability to pay. In most professions, differential charges or sliding-scale fees are established, depending on the client's ability to pay. The fee charged for preparing an income-tax return usually rises as the income rises—without regard to the work that must be performed by the accountant. The wealthy patient pays more to the doctor than the poorer one. The same is true for charges made by dentists. Some obstetricians relate their fee to the type of hospital accommodations taken by the patient.

Studies of medical fees have shown that the size of the fee varies by size of family income and by size of community.

> Fees in large cities average higher than they do in small towns. Small-town fees vary far less according to income than those in big cities. Said one general practitioner: "In a small town, you can't charge a sliding scale based on income without everybody knowing—and complaining—about it."[4]

A precise gradation in fees is not generally feasible. In many instances, only rough approximations of the client's ability to pay are determinable. Moreover, the availability of other practitioners prevents the full realization of the ability-to-pay principle. Thus, a very rich man could afford to pay fabulous fees to doctors for their services. However, the actual fees usually fall far short of such sums because each doctor knows that at some point his services would be so costly that some other doctor might be called in.

During periods when income taxes are very high, that factor also influences ability to pay. This is particularly true in connection with fees that are deductible as business expenses. Since the government is paying for a substantial part of the fee (through foregone taxes), ability to pay is increased and unwillingness to pay tends to be less of a factor in many instances.

A number of practitioners contend that the CPA has an obligation to perform all of the services needed by small clients. However, if a client has a $2,000 limit on what he can fairly afford but the work required would cost $3,000 (including a fair return to the principals), the accountant would be operating at a loss if he undertook it for $2,000—or providing a disservice if he charged $3,000. Very small businesses, in fact, must recognize that they cannot afford the best of anything. They often cannot

---

[4]*Business Week,* March 1, 1952, pp. 78-80.

afford the best offices, legal counsel, equipment, or advertising media—nor the most comprehensive and expensive services a CPA can perform. A large company and a small one may have a problem whose solution requires substantially the same amount of work. In the first case, the solution may result in a $100,000 saving, in the second, $1,000. Because the costs of solving the problem may be well out of proportion to the results achieved in the latter case, the assignment ought not to be undertaken unless the CPA wishes to contribute a portion of his time for the welfare of the client, or can find a means of modifying his approach and still achieve the desired result. (He might, for example, set up the procedure to be used so that the client's own staff can perform the mechanics of the work.)

On the other hand, no business is so small or its ability to pay so limited that a careful diagnosis might not reveal opportunities for accounting services which could be useful at a fee scale which keeps in balance the value to the client, ability to pay and fair compensation for the time of the CPA. Some clients, for example, cannot afford to have a professional accountant keep their books. In many of these cases, an individual trained in bookkeeping can do an adequate job—and the client should pay no more than is justified by such work. If an accountant attempts to compete on a price basis under these conditions, he will doubtless fail to achieve a reasonable professional compensation. He might better devote his time to areas of greater usefulness. Nonetheless, rates at a professional level for some types of bookkeeping or write-up work can be justified if the accountant can do it faster and cheaper than a less skilled person—or the additional skill employed results in a better job which is worth more to the client. But this assumes that additional value is in keeping with the client's ability to pay for it.

Even if a CPA could charge whatever he wished and a client was willing to pay it, there is a self-imposed limit inherent in a professional fee. A professional man is not entitled to unlimited earnings, for at some point his own services, no matter how well performed, cease to have additional value. Although the point at which this may occur is nebulous (perhaps because so few CPAs may have reached it), there is at least a theoretical level in acquiring wealth through professional practice at which service gives way to profit as the primary consideration.

Having money and spending it are not always identical characteristics. Willingness to pay may be just as important as ability to pay. No one really likes to pay more for any service than he must. *Unwillingness to pay* may place an effective ceiling on fees far below the level suggested by ability to pay in any unrestrained meaning of that term. Thus, in practical terms, the ability-to-pay principle appears to mean that different fees will be charged for the same service to persons or companies of different economic means. It does not mean that the differentials in fees will be proportional to or closely related to varying abilities to pay.

Acceptability. Acceptability of the fee to the client is an important consideration. There is little point in rendering a bill unless the CPA can reasonably expect to collect it. The degree of acceptability, or satisfaction, can be influenced to a fairly large degree by the accounting firm itself, through continued high-quality service and proven value to the client. When client education has been effectively conducted, resistance to reasonable fees can be greatly diminished or completely eliminated.

Customary fees. Many types of service rendered in all professions are in effect routine. Customary fees develop within geographic areas for such services. Most young lawyers, accountants, doctors, and engineers give significant weight to this factor. Local bar associations and other professional groups often set up schedules of suggested fees for these typical situations. Lloyd K. Garrison has pointed out that:

> Minimum fee schedules set in an advisory way by a number of different bar associations constitute a fairly good guide as to what the going custom is or ought to be in charging for different matters, and no doubt help with varying degrees of success to promote a certain standardization. Essentially, however, the purpose of these schedules is to discourage competitive price-cutting and to check the practice some laymen have of shopping around among lawyers, telling each what the other said he would charge and thus trying to get the work done below what it ought to be done for.[5]

Hugh Cabot takes a dim view of the usefulness of minimum fees established by medical societies:

> The establishment of fee tables by medical societies has not served a very useful purpose, since they can at best only suggest the average fees which may properly be charged under average conditions to the patient in average circumstances. Obviously, they are likely to be wholly inapplicable to almost every individual circumstance.[6]

In many instances, such schedules may provide a list of *minimum* fees with the actual level determined by the various other factors. However, the customary fee is not necessarily the same for all practitioners since the level may be influenced by the group of patients or clients whom they serve, or by the level of economic conditions when they entered the profession. Thus, many lawyers and accountants who began to practice in the depressed thirties set their fees relatively low and undoubtedly lagged in raising them in the inflated forties.

Reputation of the accounting firm. Closely related to the factor of skill and experience of the staff members who perform the services is the reputation of the firm itself. It is not inconceivable that the services of an accounting firm would have greater than normal value to a client when that firm has established a reputation for a high degree of technical competence, expertness in a particular field, service to the community, contribution to the profession, and so on. A firm with a pre-eminent reputation may instill

[5]Lloyd K. Garrison et al., "The Economics of the Legal Profession," *American Bar Association Journal,* Chicago, June 1938, pp. 153-154.
[6]Hugh Cabot, *The Doctor's Bill,* Columbia University Press, New York, 1935, p. 122.

more confidence in a client than a relatively unknown one. The client may, therefore, rely more heavily on its recommendations and place greater value on them. Some businesses, especially small ones, may want to acquire prestige through employment of a CPA whose firm is highly regarded within the community. These variations tend to obviate adherence to the principle of "going rates" within a profession. Although going rates can affect accounting fees, their influence is less persuasive on firms of outstanding reputation. Truly professional fees should not, therefore, be fundamentally based on price competition.

LOWER LIMITS ON FEES

It is generally held that a laborer is worthy of his hire and that a professional man should expect and is entitled to a professional income for professional services.

As mentioned previously, a reasonable salary for the principals of a firm is as much an element of cost as those of the staff, rent, supplies, or equipment. On this basis it can be said that the bottom limit of a fee structure must be such that the annual fees cover annual costs.

There are several theories on the flow of costs, developed with varying degrees of logic. The common one seems to be that costs flow from one engagement to another. This, in turn, is usually based on one of two assumptions.

The simpler and probably the more widely employed is that costs become attached to an engagement by the number of man-hours (within each grade) assigned to the engagement. This method furnishes a control point in the management of the practice which serves as a guide in the day-to-day problems of practice. It is useful in making decisions on:

1. The work which a client can afford to have done for him, where there is a close limit on his ability to pay
2. The management of chargeable and nonchargeable time within the accounting firm
3. The minimum fees which can be accepted for any engagement for any client

The third area has special significance in that it provides a built-in "resistance point." The practitioner will know that if the fee for an engagement does not recover this amount, it will subtract from the proposed annual financial result. This doesn't mean that an engagement should never be undertaken for less. But by having what amounts to almost day-to-day control, this point is always visible to the practitioner. If he does not know where this point is, he will not know the level at which he should offer strong resistance to pressure for a lower fee. The use of the objectively measurable element of time is the only way in which this control can be maintained.

The other assumption, which is sometimes used, is that the cost flow is related to the value of each engagement. This requires that the fee involved be measured against the annual costs and fees, without any day-to-day control. The difficulty in this approach is that there is really no sound way (without the use of time) to determine how much a particular fee should be in relation to the total annual fees.

The Application of Cost Flow

■ HOW THEN IS the flow-of-costs principle applied to the fee to be rendered?

An annual-income result presupposes a certain number of hours which are to be charged to the clients. To these hours are applied the rates which will yield the desired return. The number of hours can be determined by the performance standard of the firm for the different grades of accountants employed.

Since practicing accountants seem to work longer hours than other occupational groups, an attempt was made to determine what number of chargeable hours was reasonable or desirable. Although no precise figure can be cited, some guides can be established.

An article in *Fortune* magazine[7] indicated that management-consulting firms base charges for their staffs on a supposition of 150 days (1,050 hours) a year. The nature of their services is often nonrepetitive and once a particular assignment is over, they must turn to new clients. It has also been said that 1,000 chargeable hours represents the optimum productive time in operating on patients (200 days at five productive hours per day) in a busy dental practice.[8]

Chargeable hours per year. Accounting firms, on the other hand, usually have a large portion of repetitive clients for whom the work remains relatively constant. Since they can forecast and plan their work more accurately, there are apt to be fewer and shorter gaps between assignments for the staff. Therefore, accounting firms can be expected to have a higher percentage of chargeable time than consultants. Assuming that overtime is undesirable, there may be about 1,800 hours a year (after deduction for vacations, holidays, sick time, etc.) which are theoretically available for each man. Since almost no one can be involved in chargeable work all of the time, the chargeable time standard should be less than this. Some firms, both large and small, feel that approximately 1,400 hours a year (200

---

[7] Perrin Stryker, "The Ambitious Consultants," *Fortune,* May 1954, p. 184.
[8] Meyer M. Silverman, "Fees that Are Fair to Your Patient and You," *Oral Hygiene,* January 1952.

seven-hour days) represent a sound estimate of a reasonable number of chargeable hours upon which to base staff rates (they felt possible overtime work should not be considered in the base)—with the partners having somewhat less, depending on their administrative and other duties. Other firms consulted for this study believed that 1,600 hours might be achieved without the use of overtime. A member of a large multi-office firm stated that, while 2,000 hours represented an ideal, the actual performance of the staff was about 80 per cent of the ideal—with roughly 60 per cent of the time for beginning juniors and partners being classified as chargeable. This situation was confirmed by several firms of comparable size, whose average of 1,600 annual chargeable hours included overtime.

Some variation also exists among firms due to the length of the work week. In large cities, a number of firms operate on a 35-hour week, others work 37½ or as much as 40 hours in a regular week.

After a realistic chargeable time standard is established (bearing in mind that sufficient time should be available for personal development, staff training, and other professional activities), salary and other costs can be computed and basic rates determined. There is evidence that some firms do not figure the direct salary cost in a way which lends itself to effective control. The hourly direct salary cost chargeable to a client for an $8,000-a-year man, for example, is not four dollars (based on the 2,000-hour year for which he is employed), but five dollars on the basis of his chargeable time (assumed to be 1,600 hours in this case). The firms who compute the salary cost on 2,000 hours usually allocate the nonchargeable time to general overhead; but in doing so they may lose control unless they recognize that nonchargeable time is a cost which should be recovered on a day-to-day basis.

Since the basic rates are established to achieve a particular income result over a given number of hours, a firm's income will be increased if its experience exceeds those hours—and if its basic rates were actually billed and costs did not rise (e.g., overtime pay). On the other hand, if the estimated financial result can be achieved only through exceptionally long hours, either the fee schedule or the expected income return requires some modifications.

A regular fee base is computed on several assumptions which, when not adhered to, may require some changes. These assumptions include:

1. That regular work is being performed for regular clients. When a nonrepetitive engagement from a casual client is accepted, a higher rate may be justified, since the flow of costs is different and the regular base rate may not have sufficiently allowed for such circumstances. On the other hand, experience with a regular client might suggest that economies could be instituted at times (e.g., a man might be assigned full time to a large client) which would permit the accountant to charge less per hour, without affecting the estimated annual income result. This doesn't imply that a lesser rate *should* be billed under these conditions, but only that it is possible, under certain circumstances, to charge a lesser rate which will not affect the annual income expectation.

2. That the work will be handled efficiently. If the costs are raised

through the accountant's fault, inexperienced help, inadequate supervision, false starts, or doing work which shouldn't have been done, he should bear the increased cost himself. This means the fee would be something less than the extension of the base rate.

3. That the various accountants involved in an engagement will be assigned "in grade." If a man is assigned to work which can be adequately handled by a lower-grade accountant, a downward adjustment might be in order. This, however, is not necessarily true. If a senior can do a job faster than a junior, the fee would be no more, even at higher rates. If he can do a better job and the additional value is significant, he might even justify a higher fee.

Methods Used to Determine Fees

■ OVER THE YEARS a number of articles have been written advancing the relative merits of per-diem (or hourly) fees and contract fees, represented by flat fees and retainers. Actually, their differences lie not so much in their being different *types* of fees but in their being different approaches to dealing with clients. Both are usually based on a computation of time. In the first case, the bill is figured from an extension of the time spent, multiplied by a standard rate. The latter is an attempt to estimate the time involved, applying the standard rate to the estimate, and quoting a fee to a client in advance of an engagement. In current practice, only a minority of the firms and practitioners seem to use one approach to the complete exclusion of the other or use either one in strict accordance to their traditional definitions. A third type of fee, also based on time, is some variation of a costing method.

In order to better understand the modifications which have evolved, a brief description of the merits of these approaches may be in order.

THE "COSTING" METHOD

One of the traditional methods of establishing a fee involves separate computations of the components of a fee and does not attempt to integrate them until the bill is prepared. In a simplified form it can be expressed as:

Fee $= A + B + C$, where $A =$ the product of the hours involved and the hourly salary cost (staff and principals); $B =$ an overhead allocation; and $C =$ principals' return, usually based on a percentage of the sum of A and B.

Although this method is still used by some firms, it involves extensive calculations in preparing bills. Many firms feel that this additional work is not necessary, for if the flow of costs is established by time spent, all costs (not just salary) should be applied when extending time. This gave rise to the use of hourly or per-diem rates, which give due consideration to most of the elements of a proper fee.

PER-DIEM RATES

These are charges made in direct proportion to the actual time (days or hours) spent on an engagement. The rates themselves usually vary according to the grade of the personnel who perform the work. In small offices, each accountant may have an individual rate, but a more common practice is to average them in accordance with the classifications of junior, semi-senior, senior, supervisor, manager, and principal. The rate is derived from the average salary cost for each classification, to which is added an amount to cover a proportion of the overhead and "principals' return" compensation for the partners. The client is billed on the basis of these rates multiplied by the amount of time spent by the accountants within each classification.

It has been found in practice that several formulas yield a return which adequately covers these factors in different practices. The most frequent ones mentioned range from two to three times the direct salary cost (based on the estimated annual chargeable time), with two and one half tending to predominate. Another method is to bill the daily rate at one per cent of the annual salary cost.

There has been a tendency on the part of some firms to accept one of these formulas as the "going" rate within the profession. The lack of comparability of these formulas lies in the failure to consider the varying methods used by different firms in considering the components of the rate. Twice the direct salary cost may be an entirely adequate rate for a firm which charges a client directly for the time of typists or other clerical help and other items which can be specifically associated with the engagement. But another firm which absorbs all clerical costs and other direct expenses as overhead might find that a rate of three times the direct salary cost is needed to achieve a satisfactory return. Variations in rent and other costs also affect the amount of overhead of different firms and thereby the size of the multiplier which is sufficient to consider them. In addition, different estimates of the number of chargeable hours per year are used to determine the salary cost. If the same formula was applied on an hourly or daily basis in these cases, therefore, the rates would be different. However, if two men in different firms at the same salary each met his performance standard, the amount of fee produced during the year would be identical—the difference being in the flow of costs, since one requires more chargeable time to produce the same annual results.

When rates of this type are employed, it is usually better to establish them on an hourly rather than daily basis for two reasons: the length of a day is often open to varying interpretations, and the charges for a fraction of a day are more difficult to distribute than smaller units of time.

The advantages of a straight-time rate, according to its advocates, are: (1) the client pays for exactly what he gets in the way of work performed, no more and no less; and (2) the accountant is assured of avoiding a loss on an engagement by receiving full payment for time devoted to work.

But this fee arrangement also has one important disadvantage: it places, under certain conditions, undue emphasis upon the time element, and is therefore suited primarily to more-or-less routine assignments. It may not be flexible enough, even with proper scheduling of staff grades, to consider the quality or value of the services. Nor does it always take into consideration the highest forms of professional service, where time has little significance as a measure of value.

A disadvantage of per-diem fees considered to be of less importance is that they give the client no definite way of estimating the cost of the work in advance. Where necessary to satisfy the client, this objection is usually met by guaranteeing that the total of the per-diem charges will not exceed a stipulated maximum fee. Under these conditions, the client may limit himself to the minimum service without realizing that additional service could be of greater value to him in the long run. Whenever this might be a problem, some firms keep their clients informed of the charges by advising them as the costs reach certain levels.

In fixing per-diem rates, the definition of "day" becomes an important factor. Most firms consider a standard working day to be seven hours. Some consider it as seven and one-half or eight hours. In comparing per-diem rates this variable must be kept in mind.

In having staff members record time spent on engagements or phases of engagements, firms usually do not require recording of time less than a specified minimum. Usually this minimum period is fifteen or thirty minutes. However, some firms add to recorded time an extra time allowance to cover units of fractional time devoted to engagements but unrecorded because less than the minimum unit. Most of the firms making such extra allowance figure it in definite relation to total time actually recorded. The extent of fractional time would depend greatly upon the length of the adopted minimum time unit recorded, but some firms are known to use 10 or 15 per cent of the total recorded time.

The objections to the per-diem basis are usually met by charging different rates for the various classes of personnel used and by increasing (upgrading) basic rates in proportion to the quality of services rendered. In some cases this remedy is not satisfactory because, in the highest forms of technical service, the time element may be wholly irrelevant in relation to the intrinsic value of the services. For example, discussion with a client of a proposed transaction may require only a small amount of time, but the advice given may be extremely advantageous to the client. It should be evident that the time element is relatively unimportant in fixing a fee in such a case. On the other hand, the intrinsic value of some services to the client may be less than the amount determined on a strict time basis, because staff members used are inexperienced or unfamiliar with the client's affairs, or because of inexpeditious over-all handling of the engagement.

When per-diem billing rates are fixed for each grade of staff personnel utilized, basic rates for each grade are those in effect for routine auditing and usually they are upgraded for other types of services by increasing them by a fixed percentage. But all rates, basic or upgraded, vary within fixed limits as to each classification of personnel and thus have a minimum-maximum range. Such flexibility has definite value in making it possible to relate charges even more closely to the nature and quality of services performed and the experience and ability of the personnel actually used.

Straight time with adjustments. A common practice is to extend the time of each class of accountant at basic rates and have the summary sheet examined by the principal most directly concerned with the engagement. The principal reviews the time and considers any extenuating circumstances. He may compare it with former bills to the client, if the services are similar, and attempt to account for discrepancies. He strives to assign a dollar value to the unusual elements of the work performed and the benefit to the client. He may then make some adjustment either upward (e.g., extensive contributions to improving internal procedures or large savings to the client in a complicated tax settlement) or downward (e.g., inexperienced personnel) to achieve what he feels is an equitable fee for "professional services rendered."

This method seems to be used by sole practitioners and large firms alike. In long, complex engagements, however, a number of valuable contributions may have been made in which the time involved bore no significant relation to the intrinsic value. The important reorganization conference appears on the time sheet as thirty minutes, the valuable piece of business advice delivered on the telephone appears as fifteen minutes (if it appears at all). Unless the "description" line on the time sheet is truly descriptive, it may be inadequate as a basis for determining the value of the work. Partially offsetting this, of course, is the fact that the greatest degree and variety of skill employed in the engagement and the major consultative contributions are often made by the man who makes the final billing decisions.

The variable scale. In an effort to keep the value of the time element in its proper perspective during the course of an engagement, a number of firms have adopted a *range* of rates within each classification of accountant. This differs from straight time with adjustments in that the adjustments take place during the course of the engagement and are considered in the hourly rate itself. Through the application of a rate most nearly related to the skill required of the individual, the firms which use this procedure believe that it reduces end-of-job adjustments and simplifies the billing process.

The higher the classification, the wider the range of possible rates, due to the wider range of abilities the accountant may be called upon to utilize.

In a letter to the AICPA advocating a variable-rate structure for most billing situations, Dixon Fagerberg[9] says:

[9]Mr. Fagerberg is the former editor of the Practitioner's Forum in *The Journal of Accountancy* and has made significant contributions to the field of practice management.

Averaging of rates is inevitable in both theory and practice, since the execution of virtually any engagement comprises a series of tasks calling for varying degrees of education, skill and experience. This is because, as a practical matter continuity of thought is required, so there are natural limits to the division of a five-task assignment among five persons so as to utilize the highest skill of each.

Notwithstanding, the larger the office staff and/or the engagement, the greater the possible subdivision of skill levels and the greater the potentialities of using lower skills on more routine phases and higher skills on more important and difficult phases of a given engagement. In general, the smaller the engagement the greater the averaging of the skills of the one man or two men performing it. The larger the engagement the less the overlapping of subdivided skills, hence the greater validity of fairly uniform standard rates (really average or composite-skill rates) by gradations from junior to light senior to heavy senior to supervisor to principal.

The closer the approach to the apex of the organization, the greater the possible variability in rates. There are many jobs or parts of jobs the young junior cannot be trusted with at all. On the other hand, circumstances (busy season, deadlines, etc.) not infrequently make it necessary for the top man to do work far below his highest skill, which he can do no better, and perhaps not as fast, as one of the semi-seniors, in which case the client can and should only be charged accordingly.

It is often difficult to determine which rate within a staff classification should apply, especially when the possible range is rather wide. The solution advanced by a number of firms is to establish some bench marks within the scale, resulting in perhaps several rates within a classification.

Sproull[10] suggests three scales which he calls the Simple Audit Scale, Others Audits and Tax Scale, and Complicated Scale. Regarding the Simple Audit Scale as the minimum rate within a staff classification, he establishes the rates for the Other Audits and Tax Scale and the Complicated Scale as 150 and 200 per cent and up, respectively, in their relation to the minimum rate.

T. Dwight Williams[11] reports the results of a survey on adjustments for types of services, as follows:

> To obtain upgraded rates for services of a nature other than routine auditing, most firms increase their basic rates by some percentage.
>
> For tax services, the reported percentage of increase ranges from 25 to 100 per cent and averages about 60 per cent. For systems installation, the percentage of increase varies from 10 to 100 per cent and averages about 40 per cent. For special investigations, the range of increase is from 10 to 100 per cent and averages about 50 per cent. For advisory and consultative services, the range is from 25 to 150 per cent and the average about 66 2/3 per cent.

It is impossible to define exactly the types of work which would fall within each rate when a variable scale is used, due to the variations inherent

[10]R. Sproull, *Accountants' Fees and Profits*, Professional & Trade Books, Ltd., London, 1951.
[11]T. Dwight Williams, *CPA Handbook*, AICPA, New York, 1952, Vol. I, Chap. 12.

in each assignment. The proponents of this method, however, feel that, with an understanding of the principles involved, a practitioner should be able to evaluate most assignments and assign a rate reflecting the average level of work performed. For engagements where time remains a major element, an increasing number of firms, especially the smaller ones, where each individual is called upon to handle a variety of assignments, have adopted some form of variable scale with which to evaluate their services.

If a firm employs a variable rate structure, it should still establish a "minimum" or "average" rate for each staff classification, designed to cover all costs (including a fair compensation to the principal). Unless such rates are set up, at least as a guide, the practitioner will not be able to relate his financial position to the specific engagements and will lose effective control over his efforts to achieve his desired annual-income result.

FIXED FEES

A fixed fee is an amount charged for an entire engagement as distinguished from charges for services by the hour or day. When used, it is fixed and quoted and arranged with the client in advance of the work. An agreement to perform any or all services for a specified fee has sometimes been represented as the truly professional basis for billing, for the client is aware of the cost before the engagement is undertaken.

The usual practice in setting a fixed fee is for the accountant to undertake the difficult task of estimating the time involved, apply per-diem rates and add a percentage for contingencies.

Advantages of fixed fees are that they enable the client to know the cost in advance, that they may relate the amount of the accountant's compensation more directly to the quality of the services than to time spent, and that they are representative of the professional attitude.

Disadvantages of fixed fees, in order of their apparent importance, are as follows:

1. The accountant may receive an inadequate return or suffer a loss if he underestimates his costs either by errors in considering the known facts at the beginning of the engagement or by not making proper allowance for new facts which may develop during the progress of the engagement.

2. It may be difficult to convince the client that higher fixed fees are justified for subsequent engagements involving further services and greater expenditure of time.

3. Fixed fees quoted to a client might be used by him to secure lower competitive bids.

4. Accountants may be tempted to cut corners to avoid losses when they realize that they have underestimated their costs.

5. Clients are subjected to excessive fees where the accountants overestimate their costs.

6. Clients might consider a fixed fee as a reduction of the amount that would be chargeable on a per-diem basis.

7. Misunderstandings may arise as to the exact services covered by the fixed fee.

To avoid or lessen the effect of some of the above disadvantages, a fixed-fee contract may be modified. The agreement may be that the fixed fee will not be less than a stated minimum, say $1,000, nor greater than a stated maximum, say $1,500; with the charge not to exceed the higher amount if normal and agreed conditions prevail. Some accountants make the stated minimum fee coincide with their estimate of the actual charge. In such cases, the clients get the benefit of the stated minimum unless unexpected difficulties develop.

On an initial engagement for a new client, a good plan is to conduct it on a per-diem basis, and thus gain a knowledge of the client's affairs which will serve as a basis for estimating fixed fees on subsequent engagements.

Some firms seek to avoid misunderstandings with the client by having a written agreement stipulating that the fixed fee covers only certain definitely stated arrangements and that additional charges will be made if (1) the records are not in a reasonably good condition, or (2) if there are unusual developments such as defalcations or substantial errors in the books. Other firms rely entirely upon a careful preliminary investigation of the work that will be required, the condition of the client's records, and the adequacy and enforcement of the system of internal control.

The possibility that clients may consider a fixed fee as a reduction in comparison with per-diem rates is not too serious. Many firms report that they set their fixed fees at little, if anything, under the total per-diem rates for the estimated duration of the engagement.

Firms differ in their views of the fixed fee. Some, especially those caught in the price squeeze arising from the spiraling costs since World War II, are adamantly opposed to them in any form. Yet a fairly recent survey by the AICPA of more than 2,100 firms and practitioners showed that over 75 per cent had *some* clients on a fixed-fee basis. This percentage remained fairly constant throughout the various regions of the country. The population of the community did not affect the results appreciably, although a slightly higher percentage of the firms in large cities indicated they had some clients in this category. Nor was the fixed fee characteristic of the smaller firm.

Most of those using fixed fees determine the amount by multiplying the estimated number of days of each staff classification required by the per-diem rates for the respective classifications. Seventy per cent base their fixed fees on rates varying directly in relation to (1) quality of services, and (2) classification and compensation of staff personnel. A negligible number use uniform rates for all work without regard to these factors or use on occasion rates higher or lower than their regular per-diem rates.

While the practice is doubtless quite rare, it seems that there are instances where clients are permitted to set the amount of a fixed fee. The main objections to such an obviously unwise procedure are (1) the client has no adequate or competent yardstick with which to measure the proper charge, (2) the relationship involved should be that of a professional man and client and not that of employer and employee, and (3) the basic cost which is a material element of the charge is known only to the accountant.

The widespread use of fixed fees, under certain circumstances, indicates that they can sometimes be effective if suitable precautions are taken.

RETAINER CONTRACTS

In the United States, a retainer fee paid to accountants usually means a fee paid for all services of whatever nature or for services of a specific nature rendered during a designated period. This definition differs from the English concept in requiring that services are to be performed for the fee. In England the fee is paid so that the accountant will be available if needed whether or not services are performed, and an additional fee is to be paid for whatever services are performed.

Under the American concept providing for payment for services over a specified period, retainers are usually on an annual basis with equal monthly payments at the end of each month, regardless of actual volume of service performed during each month. A monthly-retainer arrangement, which can be terminated at the end of any month, is reported as an occasional occurrence.

Types of work usually specified in these contracts are listed below in the order of their frequency:

1. Preparation of tax returns
2. Fiscal year-end work
3. Monthly and annual reports
4. Conferences on matters specified in the agreement
5. Periodic auditing
6. Attendance at revenue agent's examinations
7. Preparation of credit-agency statements

A few firms include additional classifications such as attendance at directors' meetings, conferences on management policies, supervision and training of bookkeeping personnel, conferences on accounting procedures, and handling of minor tax problems. Most firms favor the inclusion of advisory and consultative services in services covered by retainer agreements.

Retainer contracts provide the accountant with some assurance of retaining clients permanently and furnish steady periodic engagements. Also, where they are restricted as to scope, they frequently lead to additional engagements not contemplated in the original agreement. They also are advantageous to the client in that they assure the availability of the accountant and, when equal monthly payments are made, automatically spread accounting costs evenly over the year.

The principal disadvantage of a retainer agreement is that it may be necessary for the accountant to render a greater amount of service in the contractual period than was anticipated when the fee was set. Equally serious is the danger of a misunderstanding with the client as to the scope of services to be performed. The client may expect certain types of service not con-templated by the accountant at the time the agreement was entered into. This latter difficulty may be avoided by having a written agreement describing in detail the service to be furnished, thus assuring a clear understanding with the client which can be referred to when additional services are needed. Such agreements can be made more effective by specifying also any types of work which might be expected, but which are excluded by mutual consent. Many accountants find it advantageous to set out their understanding of an agreement by writing a letter to the client even though it is not formalized by having the client sign it. Others simply make a memorandum of the agreement for their files.

Many firms favor a reconsideration procedure to prevent inadequate return on retainers after the initial year. At the end of each retainer period, a review is made of the nature and extent of services rendered and the time expended. The result is compared with the retainer fee and discussed with the client. If the fee has been inadequate, the fee is increased for the ensuing year and, in some cases, it is found possible to secure a reasonable adjustment as to the period reviewed.

Disadvantages, other than those peculiarly applicable to fixed fees and the danger of misunderstandings with the client, are minor. Fees may be less than on a per-diem or fixed-fee basis, but this can be accounted for by the willingness of the accountant to accept a lower fee in order to obtain the advantages of the retainer contract. Commitments under retainer contracts sometimes cause an excessive volume of work at year-end and midyear periods, but this difficulty can be reduced by making specific arrangements with each client in such a manner as to stagger the load.

As a guide to the accepted procedure for operating on a retainer basis, the following outline is offered:[12]

1. The retainer when used should cover services that are reasonably pre-dictable as to volume and complexity. In this category, generally, are the following:
   a. Auditing
   b. Financial statement preparation
   c. Preparations of tax returns—covering routine business transactions
   d. Review of reports and tax returns with clients
2. By excluding the nonpredictable items, the retainer can be made less speculative . . .
3. Nonretainer items should be billed separately when, as, and if the services are performed. . . . Services included in this category, patently, are those not covered by the retainer. The following are illustrations of such services:
   a. Extraordinary tax planning
   b. Attendance at tax examinations except, perhaps, when only minor problems develop
   c. Conferences on a high level, not dealing directly with financial state-ments and tax returns prepared
   d. Special investigations, etc.

[12]Max Block, "Office and Staff Management," *The New York Certified Public Ac-countant,* March 1952, pp. 191-194.

4. In order that a client should not receive too many bills, nonretainer items might be billed semiannually, or even annually.
5. In any event, clients should be advised that it is not intended under a retainer arrangement that unlimited services be rendered for a limited fee. This should be understandable by a fair-minded businessman and, if necessary, his own business operations might be used for illustrating the propriety of this point. Thus, even where routine services are involved, should it happen that because of sharply increased business volume, or because of difficulties within the client's own organization, the annual retainer is substantially inadequate, "renegotiation" of the retainer should be possible and a year-end adjustment be provided for . . .

CONTINGENT FEES

A contingent fee is one which is payable only in case a certain event occurs. It may be a fixed amount or a percentage of amounts which the client hopes to receive as a result of the findings or work of the accountant.

Contingent fees are permissible only in connection with tax matters and should conform to:

1. The *Code of Professional Ethics* of the AICPA
2. The rules of the recognized professional society or board in the accountant's region
3. The regulations of the relevant governmental agency with respect to contingent fees

The applicable professional ethics rule of the AICPA states:

1.04. Professional service shall not be rendered or offered for a fee which shall be contingent upon the findings or results of such service. This rule does not apply to cases involving Federal, state or other taxes, in which the findings are those of the tax authorities and not those of the accountant. Fees to be fixed by courts or other public authorities, which are therefore of an indeterminate amount at the time when an engagement is undertaken, are not regarded as contingent fees within the meaning of this rule.

The Treasury Department requires the filing of a signed statement containing the terms of the compensation agreement if it is on a wholly or partially contingent basis. Section 10.37(b) of Treasury Department Circular No. 230 states:

An enrolled attorney or agent shall not enter into a wholly contingent fee agreement with a client for representation in any matter before the Internal Revenue Service unless the client is financially unable to pay a reasonable fee on any other terms. Partially contingent fee agreements are permissible where provision is made for the payment of a minimum, substantial in relation to the possible maximum fee, which minimum fee is to be paid and retained irrespective of the outcome of the proceeding.

Although it is generally recognized that a contingent-fee arrangement has no place in accounting and auditing work in general, it is sometimes difficult to determine the line of demarcation between contingent fees and fees which are justifiably determined after the work is completed and the benefits to the client are considered. "The test to apply is whether, by pre-arrangement, the CPA has what amounts to a financial interest in a venture of his client, in that the CPA may receive an *exceptional* financial reward, contingent upon the success of the venture."[13]

Contingent fees should not be used as a basis of compensation for accounting work not connected with taxes or court matters because:

1. They are incompatible with the obligation of public accountants to be independent and impartial in that they affect compensation to the extent of the direct benefit to the client.

2. They provide, in effect, for a profit-sharing basis between client and accountant inconsistent with the professional relationship of the accountant to the client.

3. They provide for a measure of compensation unrelated to the time spent, the nature and quality of the services, and the professional skill required and applied.

It is generally considered that a contingent fee is not involved where:

1. The fees for services engaged for are to be fixed by courts or other public authorities and are therefore indeterminate when the engagement is begun.

2. The fees are related to the amount of time devoted to the engagement, the nature and quality of the services rendered, the expected value of the services to the client, and the special experience and skill of the retained accountant and of his staff; and the expected value of the services to the client is not measured by the eventual degree of benefit actually derived by the client.

CONSULTING FEES

In certain cases none of the foregoing practices is really effective. These situations arise at the higher levels, generally in the case of a principal. Here the elements of value and the degree to which the practitioner must draw upon his professional training are often the only major considerations in determining the fee. Although some practitioners will bill these services at twice their "standard" rate, there are circumstances under which this is also inadequate. Conferences to which he has made substantial contributions; advice about complicated business problems; and negotiation of tax settlements are examples of this type of work. A "consulting" fee is mentioned not because it represents a method of setting fees, but it is indicative of

[13]John L. Carey, *Professional Ethics of Certified Public Accountants*, AICPA, New York, 1956.

situations occurring with varying frequency, for which a practitioner must make provision to arrive at a proper fee.

FEES SET BY CORRESPONDENTS

Correspondent accountants have the following methods of charging for their services:

1. A fixed fee at customary rates
2. A fixed fee at less than customary rates
3. Per-diem fees at customary rates
4. Per-diem fees at less than customary rates
5. A fee equal to the cost
6. A fee equal to the cost plus a nominal amount

Method 3 is employed by more than all of the others combined. Where the fee is less than the customary rate, the usual reduction is a flat 15 or 20 per cent.

ESTIMATING FEES FOR CLIENTS

In an effort to satisfy clients who insist on having an estimate of costs in advance of an engagement, some accountants will give a probable range.

After estimating the time involved at the rates usually charged for similar work, the accountant may present the total to the client as the minimum charge. To this he may add an amount which he feels is something in excess of all possible contingencies. He may bracket his estimate rather than use it as a minimum, but it is usually advisable to err on the high rather than the low side. Few clients have ever been known to complain if their bill runs less than the estimate. The more complex the engagement, the greater this amount should be. The estimate could then be presented as a bracket, wide enough to consider possible complications which may arise.

As is true with most compromises, this method leaves something to be desired. It does, however, provide the client with some idea of the probable fee, while furnishing the accountant with a hedge against unforeseen developments. When it is possible for the CPA to make a preliminary survey of the work to be performed, it reduces the amount of guesswork which would otherwise be involved. Some firms usually charge for such surveys.

An alternative to this procedure, used by some firms, is to tell the client the per-diem rates which would normally apply and then roughly approximate the time involved. This system enables the client to estimate, to a limited degree, the cost of other services which he might wish to add, but it makes it difficult for the accountant to vary rates to adjust for application of greater than "normal" skill within a staff classification which might be justified after the engagement is underway—or to give consideration to the additional value of the services which might be developed during the course of the engagement. Moreover, a number of successful firms object to this practice. They feel that quoting of hourly or daily rates is more in keeping with the relatively constant skill level of the artisan than the wide range of abilities required of the professional man. This approach, in their view, detracts from their status in the eyes of their clients.

When a CPA feels that it is necessary to make an estimate, other than for the limited services for which he may feel confident in quoting a fixed fee, the minimum-maximum dollar estimate seems to be the preferable choice.

It appears from the foregoing that there is no one right method of setting fees. It is entirely possible that each method might result in a proper fee, under certain circumstances, not only as they are applied by different firms, but within a single firm as well. Different situations may require different treatment, but the basic principle remains the same: although value of service rendered should be the criterion for any professional accounting fee, value itself is in large measure based on the costs of rendering the service.

Additional Fee When
Tax Returns Are Examined

■ EVERY YEAR MORE and more returns prepared for individual taxpayers are being examined by the Internal Revenue Service. Many of these individuals have never been examined before, and are apprehensive about coming into contact with the IRS. As a consequence, many of them contact their accountants to request their presence and assistance during the examination, or merely to give advice concerning points that may be questioned.

In this type of situation, the return is a fairly simple one and the examination is usually completed in an hour or two. However, in many instances the client feels that since the accountant prepared the return, he should be willing to "defend" it without further charge. The problem of how to go about charging for the service rendered is requiring serious attention from many practitioners.

One solution is to make a sufficient charge for the preparation of all returns so that an additional charge for assistance during the examination would not be necessary. However, this places all tax clients in the position of paying for examinations of the few, and therefore is not a completely satisfactory way to charge.

Another possibility would be to charge extra for the preparation of returns that are likely to be examined owing to large refunds, or some other reason. This involves trying to predict the actions of the IRS, and therefore is not desirable.

Another approach that one firm has considered is to devise some means of advising the client at the time of preparing the return that the fee does not take care of subsequent examination. A short, simple statement along this line might be used:

"Your fee covers preparation of your income-tax return. It does not cover assistance rendered during any examination of your return by the IRS. We will be happy to assist you should this occasion arise, and will make an additional charge based on the additional services rendered."

This could be placed on the invoice by means of a rubber stamp, or it could be printed on a small sheet which is attached to the client's copy of the return. It might be possible to include it on the client's instruction sheet, although it might be overlooked there.

Competitive Bidding

■ THE ATTITUDE OF the AICPA toward competitive bidding is expressed in Rule 3.03 of its *Code of Professional Ethics* as follows:

> A member or associate shall not make a competitive bid for professional engagements in any state, territory or the District of Columbia, if such bid would constitute a violation of any rule of the recognized society of certified public accountants or the official board of accountancy in that state, territory, or district.

The objections to competitive bidding are that it lowers the dignity and standing of the profession, tends to cause inadequate compliance with accepted auditing standards, and results in controversy and ill feeling within the profession.

One medium-sized firm reports that it invariably refuses to quote definite amounts to prospective clients. Engagements are accepted with the understanding that the necessary services will be performed, their value then discussed with the client and any difference of opinion adjusted to the satisfaction of the client. The firm states further that the plan has proved satisfactory. Few adjustments are found to be necessary. In cases where the client requests excessive downward adjustments, they are made, but no further assignments are accepted from that client.

The English writer, Sproull,[14] makes some interesting reflections upon "competition" and "quoting." One striking comment as to the former is that "the product delivered to the client in accounting is so individual and dif-

[14]R. Sproull, *Accountants' Fees and Profits,* Professional and Trade Books, Ltd., London, 1951.

ferent from time to time or case to case that trite comparisons between accountants' products are not possible by the layman and are almost equally difficult for accountants to make." As to "quoting," he thinks refusal to quote is the soundest policy as to both new and old clients. Where it is done, he feels that all that should be given is a rough guide to what the fee may be, together with a definite statement that the amount includes a margin (not specified) for contingencies and is conditioned also upon receipt of prompt and full data and records from the client and complete co-operation from all other parties with whom it may be necessary to deal.

Most of the firms covered in an AICPA survey stated that municipalities are now tending to abandon the practice of requesting competitive bids for accounting engagements, and are presently engaging accountants on a per-diem or fixed-fee basis. Most firms reporting considered that competitive bidding on municipal audits sometimes results in inadequate auditing. Some of those making this statement believe that such inadequate auditing leads frequently to bad publicity or even to suits by municipalities for losses claimed to be due to inadequate auditing. One firm highlighted its objection to competitive bidding by reference to an actual instance where a fee of $13,500 for a city audit was reduced gradually to $3,600.

Forwarding Fees and Commissions

■ ONLY A MINOR number of firms pay forwarding fees or commissions and then only to other accountants. This practice conforms to the following rule of professional ethics of the AICPA:

> 3.04. Commissions, brokerage or other participation in fees or profits of professional work shall not be allowed directly or indirectly to the laity by a member or associate.
>
> Commissions, brokerage, or other participation in the fees, charges or profits of work recommended or turned over to the laity as incident to services for clients shall not be accepted directly or indirectly by a member or associate.

Little information is readily available as to how much referral there is or as to the amount or method of computing the referral fees. In the legal profession, the usual referral fee is one-third the amount billed to the client. However, for accountants the rate appears to be much lower generally and, where there is a substantial amount of referral, it may be as low as 15 per cent.

The ethical principle involved is that the amount billed to the client must not exceed the amount that would have been billed had there been no referral. This means that the fee paid to the forwarder must be borne by the firm or practitioner performing the engagement, not by the client.

Commissions paid staff members for securing engagements vary in different circumstances and are usually a matter of individual arrangement.

Fees Charged Charitable Organizations

■ A MAJORITY OF firms and practitioners performing services for charitable organizations do so without charge or for substantially less than a normal fee. A minority charge standard fees, but make cash donations.

Where the services are performed at a reduced rate, the philanthropic organizations seldom list the accountants as donors, but they are more likely to do so when no charge is made. When there is no charge, some accountants bill the standard fee, attaching a notice that payment is not required because the invoiced amounts represent a donation to the organization.

Accountants generally do not consider the requests for special consideration by charitable organizations burdensome. In some communities, the possible burden is avoided by rotating charitable work among different firms on an equitable basis.

The subject is controversial, as indicated by the following comments based on opinions of practitioners and a layman:

One CPA suggests that if an accountant wants to make a contribution to a charitable endeavor in his community the best way is to do the work, evaluate his services, bill them, and then to give back some of it as a donation. On charitable boards and budget committees are people whom accountants serve in business from day to day (people with just as keen an analytical sense) and they measure what accountants do for these institutions in terms of what they presume to be their costs. On occasion some of them then turn around and apply leverage in the fixing of rates and fees for private engagements. This particular CPA is firmly convinced that the time has come when the accountant should no longer do free work or do work at nominal fees in these cases but, instead, should bill them on the basis of the value of services rendered and then make his contribution in a manner that will make it clear what contribution he is making to the cause.

While a substantial group of accountants nowadays disapprove of reduced bills for charitable organizations, many a CPA holds to the view that these groups merit special treatment. Typically, the CPA of this persuasion states that most charitable, religious, and educational institutions are of a worthy nature. The income of these institutions, small or large in size, private or public in nature, is very limited. Members and friends of members are constantly being tapped for funds and contributions. In turn, the expenses of the institutions go on with few reductions.

It is the feeling of these CPAs, as evidenced in action, that *those individuals closely connected and interested in the well-being of the institution* should, not only through right but by duty, contribute of their talents, capabilities, or funds so long as it does not interfere with their normal business practice. Thus, there are lawyers who have contributed their services, doctors who have examined campers free of charge, just as accountants have served those institutions in which they are interested. These gestures indicate that here is a profession the members of which are not mercenary, the members of which participate in community affairs, are selfless and give of themselves and of their talents to worthy and deserving causes. Perhaps not all professionals can contribute sizable funds, but many have time available equivalent to funds.

If more individuals, professions, and business concerns were to assume this attitude, the advocates of reduced fees conclude, we would find such institutions on a far sounder basis.

Another CPA describes his own definite policy in billing charitable groups and, equally interesting and important, reveals the personal philosophy and professional background underlying it.

Regarding reduced rates to charitable organizations, he votes yes. He believes all accountants have a duty to participate in community service just as do members of other professions. Accountants who give of themselves will gain in stature and in their perspective toward their fellow men. He feels their opinion of accountants also will be improved.

At the beginning of this CPA's fifteen years of practice, he accepted charitable engagements as a means of making favorable contacts with prospective clients—as do many young practitioners. Recently he has set lower rates in order to encourage all organizations to have periodic audits by CPAs, rather than by members of so-called "audit committees."

His policy in charging charitable organizations is to bill them at about 50 per cent of the usual rates, with the provision that all such work be done during the summer, if possible. If it is necessary to do such work during the busy season, he gives a smaller discount but still does not charge his regular rates. He extends the discount privilege whether or not he is personally connected with the organization. He adds:

> Some of my clients criticize me for giving discounts to charitable organizations, and tell me that they don't give discounts to anybody. But I do not consider that type of person in formulating my policies. Many individuals contribute their efforts to charitable organizations, and I want to be counted with them.
> Each of us has to make his own decision. I would be the last person to force a CPA to give a discount to anyone. However, I will continue to do work for charitable organizations and will welcome all those who choose to do likewise. I'm sure many CPAs have been following such a policy out of a sense of responsibility, and with no thought of publicity or reward.

An experienced layman's view was expressed as follows:

I am not an accountant, much less a CPA. I have, however, had a great deal of experience for twenty-five years in many subdivisions of charitable work; as trustee, treasurer, money raiser, committee chairman, just plain worker, and a contributor of more dollars than I like to think about. The causes have included hospitals, independent schools, war-time USO, Children's Bureau, Planned Parenthood, Community Chest, etc. In addition, I have had ample opportunity via my wife to observe the church.

Out of all this I am of the unqualified opinion that any charity large enough to require the services of a professional accountant is also large enough to be able to afford to pay for those services at the going rates—with no discount whatsoever.

To want to give to a charity is a very natural reaction and, on the surface, very laudable. When, however, a charity accepts a "gift" of services from a CPA, it should logically accept a "gift" of services or goods from anybody else. Most charities do.

Yet many such gifts all too frequently have many kinds of spoken or unspoken strings attached; favors of one kind or another. Charities being what they are, and charity management being what it probably always will be, the charity in the end loses on this barter.

The CPA loses too. He loses his fee in cash.

Much the cleaner policy—the policy open to much less abuse in the end— is for the charity to pay its own way at fair prices for all of its requirements, including CPA audits.[15]

Another CPA says:

There is no surer way to drive someone away than to charge nothing. Most people who are in poor financial position are proud and sensitive. Failure to charge will make them feel that they are being treated as charity cases, and they will be offended. If it is someone whom you feel obligated to help, then charge him something.

With regard to churches and other charitable organizations, never cut the rate. Always present your invoice for the work done at a fair value. If you feel that a special rate is justified, suggest to the clients that they pay you in full and you will return to them a check for whatever amount you consider advisable. If you make the mistake of rendering them an invoice for less than a fair value, you may find that this will some day work against you. Such organizations have a turnover in personnel and often the trustees and others active in these enterprises are businessmen. If they are not familiar with the circumstances, they may get the mistaken idea that your fees are in general that low.

---

[15]Letter sent to *The Journal of Accountancy,* November 1959, by Ernest R. May, President, Charitable Research Foundation, Inc., Wilmington, Del.

Current Practices in Fees

■   TO WHAT EXTENT is the profession as a whole giving the proper weight to realistic costs which include a fair "salary" to the principal, and a reasonable return on the proprietor's equity?

Too little statistical material has been compiled to justify many sound conclusions about the general practice of the profession in setting fees. From the available literature, however, several tentative generalizations may be attempted.

1.   Many firms rely heavily on billing at a rigid time rate or a lump sum based on such a rate, although some of them have not been based on a realistic evaluation of the factors involved.

2.   There is some trend, however, toward a more flexible fee structure, in an effort to give consideration to elements of value and the level of work performed.

3.   There is a tendency to use different rates for different types of services, notably auditing, tax work, and management services.

4.   There is less reluctance among accounting firms to have full and frank discussion with the client.

SURVEY RESULTS ON THE BASIS FOR SETTING FEES[16]

Eighty-five per cent of the over 2,100 accounting offices replying to a nationwide survey indicated that time spent was a fundamental consideration in setting their fees. (See Table 1 for analysis.) Of these offices about 52 per cent stated that their fee (with the exception of tax work) was usually an extension of a straight-time rate. Of this group more than half used special rates for tax work. The other 47 per cent of the offices where time was the primary factor indicated that the majority of their bills contained some sort of adjustment from a straight-time rate, for the circumstances surrounding the engagement.

[16]The statistics presented in this section are the results of a survey conducted by the AICPA in 1956.

Table I. Usual Basis for Setting Fees[17]

1 CPA No. of staff*	0-1	2-9	Total
Time spent	18.5%	23.5%	20.2%
Time spent with adjustments for circumstances	40.3	37.9	39.5
Special rates for tax work, time spent for most other	23.0	22.9	23.0
Depends on the engagement and the circumstances	18.2	15.7	17.3
Total	100.0	100.0	100.0

2-4 CPAs No. of staff*	0-1	2-4	5 or more	Total
Time spent	20.0%	20.0%	23.3%	20.4%
Time spent with adjustments for circumstances	43.7	38.0	36.4	39.9
Special rates for tax work, time spent for most other	23.7	25.7	30.2	25.6
Depends on the engagement and the circumstances	12.6	16.3	10.1	14.1
Total	100.0	100.0	100.0	100.0

5 and over CPAs No. of staff*	5-9 0-4	5-9 5 or more	5-9 Total	10 or more Total
Time spent	19.1%	21.5%	20.5%	21.2%
Time spent with adjustments for circumstances	47.9	45.4	46.5	40.4
Special rates for tax work, time spent for most other	18.1	20.8	19.6	28.8
Depends on the engagement and the circumstances	14.9	12.3	13.4	9.6
Total	100.0	100.0	100.0	100.0

*Refers to noncertified staff members.

The 15 per cent surveyed who did not feel that time was generally the primary consideration in their usual fee stated that the size of their fee depended on the nature of the engagement and its circumstances.

Since these figures may have been somewhat distorted by the high proportion of replies from small firms who were apt to limit their practices to auditing and tax work only, personal interviews were conducted with a number of representative firms, large multi-office organizations, and small

[17]The preceding tabulation, by office size, represents the distribution of the various criteria usually employed by 2,100 accounting offices in determining their fees, as per AICPA survey in 1956.

practitioners. Virtually all of them said that in engagements requiring a relatively constant level of ability by the men involved, or where the nature of the work lent itself to distribution among appropriate members of the staff according to the skill required, the fees did not vary materially from the basic rate for the classification involved. (See pages 48-49 for examples of conditions under which adjustments were made.)

THE LIMITATIONS OF FEE SURVEYS

The value of fee surveys as being indicative of general billing rates has been questioned by some practicing CPAs, while upheld by others. One of the arguments against such studies is that even if a "going" rate could be established for different services, it wouldn't be of too much help. They argue that accountants' fees are too low to start with and that these averages might tend to become the maximum fees in that area. They feel it is of more importance to know what the successful firms are charging, rather than the typical. The fact that different firms use different bases in determining their rates and that varying degrees of adjustments take place before the bill goes out, tend further to limit their value. Little control is usually exercised over the replies and the number of returns is generally not statistically valid in relation to the group it purports to study. On the other hand, proponents of such surveys feel that many practitioners have little or no idea of the rate structures within the other firms in the community. Therefore, they have difficulty in evaluating their own fees. Firms with the lowest rates, they say, are encouraged by these surveys to raise the level of their fees to a point which is more in keeping with the general practice in the locality. They also provide a guide for the use of new entrants into the profession, or the community.

Some state CPA societies and chapters have conducted fee surveys. While averages derived from them are of limited value, their most important contribution often lies in pointing up the extremely wide range of fees which exists among firms in similar locations, doing similar work. One study showed a range among principals of $5 to $25 an hour for similar work—under certain circumstances $50 an hour constituted the upper limit of the range for special engagements.

A certain amount of the spread can be attributed to varying degrees of ability, type of work, and the depth with which the CPA goes into a client's problems. The only answer, however, which can account for a good deal of it, is that the practitioners at the lower end of the scale are either grossly undervaluing their services, or are performing services which are of a clerical rather than professional nature.

Since fees are dependent on so many factors and computed from different bases, it is difficult to compare the fees of one firm with those of another.

However, if the practitioner is aware of the circumstances existing in other firms, their size and nature of practice, he is in a better position to make such a comparison. With this in mind, eighteen members of successful local firms were asked to describe the methods they use in arriving at their fees and the relationship of salaries and overhead expense to their gross billings. Their descriptions are not necessarily typical of general practices, but they are indicative of successful approaches which have been used by some highly regarded firms.

All of them stated that they use some sort of computation of time and rate as a foundation for their billing. However, the importance of straight time to the fee itself varied among the firms.

The value to the client of the services rendered and the type of work performed was almost universally regarded as an important element, but varying means of considering it were used. Some of the firms make rather arbitrary adjustments in the bill while others, especially those with large staffs, felt that they were able to weigh these factors sufficiently through the proper scheduling of work among the different grades of staff men, who in turn had different rates, depending on their experience and ability. In these cases rates for each grade of staff man tended to be somewhat flexible.

Case Studies in Fee-Setting[18]

■ THE FIVE CASE STUDIES outlined below are representative of the rate structures employed by twenty-two highly regarded firms who were personally interviewed about their fees.

These firms are located from coast to coast in communities ranging in population from less than 15,000 to the largest cities in the country. Although their fee practices are not necessarily representative of the profession, they are indicative of the situations existing in a number of successful firms.

No significant variations in rates among these firms could be attributed primarily to either the size of the firm or community. Although the upper range of partners' rates was higher in the major cities in some cases, the usual rates for both partners and staff were well distributed among all sizes. As a matter of fact, the lowest rates were charged by a three-partner firm in a large Eastern city, while the rates of an individual practitioner in a small Midwestern town were among the highest. This may seem to indicate that, among successful firms, the experience and ability of the individual and the reputation of the firm can enable a firm to overcome lower fee levels which may sometimes be associated with geography or the size of the city in which the practice is conducted.

[18]This section was also developed from data obtained from the AICPA 1956 survey.

A FIRM WHICH BILLS CLIENTS AT "COST"

Each individual in this firm of five partners and twenty-five staff men has his own rate and an extension of the time involved at the standard rate is usually the fee rendered. Except for tax work, adjustments, either up or down, are relatively rare and occur in less than 10 per cent of the cases.

This firm reasons that if a fair and reasonable compensation to the partners is acknowledged as a cost, their standard rates represent the cost of providing service. The client should pay these costs, unless the firm is at fault. If unnecessary time is consumed or poor scheduling of manpower is involved, this firm considers these conditions to be results of its inadequate management, and feels the additional costs should be absorbed by the firm. On the other hand, if a staff man makes a significant technical contribution not normally expected from his grade, an upward adjustment is sometimes made. In most cases, however, "value" is taken into consideration by taking pains to schedule the work so the staff men are engaged in work they normally perform within their respective grades.

The rates used are a product of twice the direct salary costs, which are figured on an annual chargeable time standard of 200 seven-hour days. Although the actual performance sometimes exceeds 1,400 hours, the firm feels this is a realistic yardstick to use. On this basis, the day rate works out to be 1 per cent of the annual salary, and the rate is easily applied to the salary with a minimum amount of computation. Close control is maintained to see that these rates are billed, on the average, during the course of the year.

Examples of the hourly rates within the firm derived from this and rounded off are: Junior (at $4,800), $7.00; Senior (at $8,000), $11.50. Rates for the partners, depending on their age and experience, range from about $15 to $25 an hour.

PER-DIEM RATE AFFECTED BY CLASS OF SERVICE

This individual practitioner bills basically from a standard per-diem rate for his six-man staff, but varies his own rate to some extent.

Engagements for almost all of his clients result in audit reports, but his practice also includes corporate tax work and a substantial amount of management service work incorporated in his long-form reports.

Although lump sum adjustments may occasionally be made (up or down), he averages the per-diem rate for work on which the standard rate would normally apply.

The normal hourly rates in this firm are:

Junior (beginner): $5 (business school or two years' college)
Junior (one to two years): $6
Senior: $8 (average)
Supervisor: $10
Principal: $10 (field work minimum); $15 (usual)

The time of the clerical staff is charged for at a rate of $3.50 an hour.

In addition to the above rates, the time involved in some types of work is usually billed at double the usual rates, including such things as corporate tax work (no individual returns are prepared except for officers of client companies), pension trusts, and profit sharing plans. (The practitioner devotes a substantial proportion of his 1,200 chargeable hours to work in such areas.)

The standard hourly rate for the accounting staff is established by taking the hourly salary being paid to the employee (i.e., 1/2,000 of the annual salary) to which is added an amount equal to 125 per cent of the salary for overhead, supervision, and salary for nonchargeable time. Then 20 per cent of the sum of the salary and overhead is added for firm income.

Irrespective of the rates, $25 is the minimum bill which the firm will render (e.g., a conference with a non-regular client). Also, the minimum fee for the preparation of a complete set of corporate tax returns is $250.

Once a bill is rendered, this firm will make no downward adjustments if the client complains about the size of the fee. Its members will take considerable pains to explain the fee, but will withdraw from the engagement if the client insists on the fee being reduced. This situation is minimized by the policy of the firm to give the client an idea of the rough range of the probable fee as soon as possible, and discussing the fee with the client on an interim basis, if the charges are running high.

UPWARD ADJUSTMENT FROM MINIMUM RATE

In deciding on an appropriate fee for an engagement, this firm, consisting of two partners, three staff members, and two clerks, attempts to weigh the value to the client and the amount of technical work involved as well as the amount of time spent. They use a calculated time rate as a minimum guide and adjust upward from it when circumstances warrant it. The firm confines its activities to auditing and tax work. Only in figuring fees for preparation of tax returns do they consciously take into account the client's ability to pay.

The firm's minimum hourly rate schedule, based on two times the labor cost, is: Juniors, $6; seniors, $8; partners, $10. The firm often bills 25 per cent higher and sometimes 50 per cent higher than the basic time-rate figure would indicate for some services with the greatest fluctuation at the partner level. These adjustments are based on the "in-charge" partner's evaluation of the work performed.

This firm has no fixed fee or retainer clients. Most bills are sent annually (e.g., for annual audits) or semiannually. Since more than 50 per cent of the firm's clients are on a well-distributed natural-business-year basis, the billing level remains fairly steady throughout the year.

Clerical help is charged to the client at $3 to $4 an hour and travel time is also added to the fee. Only the most extended telephone calls are billed.

The firm usually discusses fees in the initial engagement, especially if the job is comparable to work done for a previous client in a similar business.

FEES VARYING WITH THE LEVEL OF SERVICE

The hourly rates for the eight staff men in this five-partner office are established basically by class. These rates are: Juniors, $4 to $5; semi-seniors and seniors, $6 to $7; junior partners, $8; senior partners, $10. However, in setting rates, the ability of the individual staff man is taken into account.

The results of the job and financial position of the client are also considerations in setting fees. Although time spent serves as the foundation for calculating a fee, this firm generally makes adjustments from a straight-time basis.

Fees for various levels of services vary. Fees for tax work and more difficult assignments are adjusted upward in accordance with the level of the engagement. When a staff man does work normally handled by a lower grade, during periods when he would not be otherwise assigned, it is usually billed at the lower rate.

Fixed fees and retainers are rarely used. The firm attempts to give a client a very rough estimate of the fee or a maximum figure but very rarely mentions hourly rates. The bill is usually sent upon completion of a job. Audit work and tax work are usually billed separately.

Clerical time is not figured separately. Neither is travel time unless it occurs during regular working hours. Charges for business conferences and telephone conversations are determined by the partners for each job and usually only extended conversations are included in the fee.

Discussions of fees varies with clients and type of job. The firm tries to give a new client a rough minimum estimate or an idea of the maximum figure. Any major variations are discussed as the work progresses so the client is kept informed of the costs. The firm seldom mentions hourly rates in these discussions.

THREE DEPARTMENTS HAVE THREE RATE STRUCTURES

"It rarely happens that we bill strictly by accumulated time at the regular rate, except for auditing," says one of the nine partners of a firm which employs about forty staff men.

The firm operates with three distinct departments, each of which is directed by a senior partner. They are Auditing, Systems & Procedures, and the Tax Department.

The average basic per-diem (seven-hour) rates for auditing (juniors, $45; semi-seniors, $60; seniors, $75) are extended for each job but some adjustment for level of engagement and value of work performed is more the rule than the exception. For example, if time runs less than usual for a low level of work performed by a higher-grade staff man, the firm bills the higher rate. The partners' hourly charges range from $20 to as much as $50 for infrequent special engagements. The rate for systems specialists is $18 to $20 per hour and for tax specialists, $20 and up. The basic rates have been established at what the firm feels is the general practice in charging for staff time. Although no formula is applied, the rates are roughly between two and two-and-a-half times the average salary cost in each of the staff grades.

In pre-engagement discussions with a client, the firm gives him some idea of the per-diem rate structure and will give a very rough estimate of the total fee if the client insists upon it. If the firm feels that the fee is running higher than the estimate, it is brought to the client's attention early in the engagement.

The firm is retained for a fixed fee by some clients but does not like this practice. Clients for whom special work or systems work is being performed are billed once a month. Tax work is billed on completion. Some regular clients are billed when the report goes out and others are billed annually, although the firm dislikes this method of billing. (This seems to be the consensus of many successful CPA firms. One prominent practitioner in another firm says of annual billing, "I bill yearly only in the case of small audits where the fee is predetermined. I find that this practice minimizes any collection problems which may result from an annual bill where the amount involved is considerable.")

The firm uses a fifteen-minute billing unit. The decision to charge or not to charge for telephone calls is based on the subject discussed; travel time is charged for only if it occurs during working hours. Clerical time is usually absorbed in general overhead.

Table 2. Summary of Basic Hourly Rates Charged by Twenty-two Firms[19]

Staff class	Actual range	Usual practice
Juniors (0 to 2 years' experience)	$ 4.50- 7.00	$ 6.00
Semi-seniors (3 to 4 years' experience)	6.00- 8.00	7.00- 8.00
Seniors (5+ years' experience)	7.00-12.00	8.00-10.00
Supervisors	8.00-20.00	8.00-12.00
Principals*	10.00-25.00	15.00-20.00

*On certain engagements some firms report that the upper limits would be appreciably higher.

[19]These rates are based on AICPA data collected in 1956.

Modifications of "Standard" Fees[20]

■ FROM TIME TO TIME unusual elements are involved in engagements (other than taxes) where the practitioner should decide if some upward or downward adjustment to his usual fee is in order. He must then determine the amount of the adjustment to be applied if such a course is decided upon. One prominent CPA says, "I feel that every bill that goes out must have judgment applied to it after first noting what it might amount to at 'standard' billing rates." Policies of different firms vary in regard to adjusting their fees, but the firms interviewed felt that modifications might be warranted, under certain conditions, for the following reasons:

INCREASE IN FEE

1. An engagement is completed in less than the usual time, because of exceptional effort and familiarity with the problems involved.
2. The results achieved through the work of the firm are unusually good and the value to the client is enhanced.
3. Unusually skillful technical application may have to be employed to achieve the desired result.
4. Substantially increased costs may be anticipated. Some firms make some change to the current bill for repetitive clients so the entire increase will not be charged at one time.

DECREASE IN FEE

1. Time is lost breaking in inexperienced personnel on their assignments, or excessive time has been taken when compared to prior years and supervisor or partner feels it can be done in less time the following year.
2. Inadequate supervision or explanation may result in work which need not have been done.
3. Scheduling difficulties may require a higher-priced man to do work which he can do no better or faster than a lower-grade man.
4. Some firms may choose to defer or absorb some of the costs of becoming familiar with a new client's operation.
5. The charges are running higher than the firm led the client to expect and they cannot be satisfactorily explained to the client.

[20]Per AICPA survey referred to earlier.

CASES WHERE UPWARD ADJUSTMENTS WERE MADE

(a) The time spent for all personnel on an audit of a corporation selling contracting equipment at retail was 285 hours. In this case the time was slightly under that of the prior year but the business was larger and the work more difficult. The semi-senior who acted as a senior on the audit had been there twice before and is more than usually rapid. The total of $2,014.25 for time was increased by $189.25 to $2,203.50 to bring the semi-senior up to the $8.50 an hour senior rate. Our bill then went out as $2,225.00 for fee plus $346.93 for expenses, total $2,571.93.

(b) A highly unusual case in our practice is a situation where the client is a corporation doing about $2 million a year, and in which the entire stock ownership is held by one person who resides and spends most of his time a couple of thousand miles away from the site of the business operations. Our engagement was a continuous audit on a monthly basis. We felt the responsibility assumed by us because of the absence of adequate supervision by ownership warranted our billing at approximately four times our basic minimum rates.

(c) The audit of a retail store in a medium-size town resulted in a raw fee, at "standard" rates, of $1,581.50. The managing partner's long experience and special knowledge were used to work out a complicated employment agreement for the general manager. Accordingly his rate was increased to $25 (from the $20 standard) an hour, adding $105 to the total. The semi-senior conducted the work very well and did about as well as any senior would have done. His time was refigured at $8 an hour (two-thirds of the way from the semi-senior to the senior rate). That brought the total time charged to $1,747.25. The bill was made out for $1,750.00 for services plus $208.34 in expenses, total $1,958.34.

(d) The three stockholders of a client corporation had reached a point of violent disagreement as to how the provisions of an option agreement should be executed in order for one of them to acquire additional shares at what seemed to be bargain prices.

After interpreting the so-called accounting provisions of the agreement, I acted as referee in the negotiations for a compromise. After a continuous all-day session with the principals and their attorney, one of several suggestions was agreed upon.

I felt that in view of (1) my important contribution to the successful existence of the company, (2) the evident satisfaction of the principals with my efforts, and (3) the exhausting nature of the meeting, a bill based on double my usual hourly rate of $15 was in order.

CASES WHERE DOWNWARD ADJUSTMENTS WERE MADE

(a) The junior was slow on the audit of a charitable organization and took over twenty-five hours longer than any other man had. The work is quite uniform and the audit had been done annually for thirty years, without the fee exceeding $375. We refigured the three and a half hours of the senior partner's time at junior-partner field rates and the junior's on the basis of fifty hours instead of seventy-five. That left $432 out of the original figure of $618. This was arbitrarily cut another $22 and the invoice went out at $410. We felt that inflationary pressures justified about a 10 per cent increase over the previous year's invoice.

(b) The engagement was to prepare certified financial statements, for state security-registration purposes, for a newly formed life-insurance company about six months after it had started writing insurance policies.

The policies were very intricate, the client's accounting staff was inexperienced, records were inadequate, the company's actuaries were in a different city, and our firm was not very familiar with this field. Extraordinary care was required and exercised and, as a final precautionary measure, we asked an accounting firm experienced in the life-insurance field to review our work papers and proposed report. This resulted in several changes in accounting treatment and report presentation.

As we went along, we scaled down our rates as best we could to reflect our limited experience in this field and a certain amount of backing and filling. On the other hand, we felt that we had planned and carried on the work intelligently from beginning to end.

When all the charges were added up, the billable amount was about $2,800. We actually reduced our bill almost $800. We felt that on the next similar case, with our increased experience in this field, we could proceed with greater sureness and efficiency and that the reduced time, multiplied by our standard rates, would then be in the neighborhood of $2,000. We did not feel that the first client should pay us for acquiring the experience necessary to handle a similar engagement more efficiently.

(c) In an audit of an automobile dealer with a branch at a distant point, the books, particularly of the branch, were found to be in very bad condition. Because the work had taken much longer than anticipated, even though it was no fault of ours, the 156 hours of the semi-senior's time was figured at junior rates. Even so, the bill came to $4,720 (including expenses and referred work to other accountants near the branch office). This matter was discussed fully with the client before billing. The client had been with us a long time. He recognized the necessity and value of the work but had never had a bill larger than about $2,500 before and he felt it was just "too big" for his business after extended deliberation. We billed at $4,200, which was acceptable and paid. We continue with the client but are now in a position to require our regular rates.

Practitioners' Discussions of Fees

■ THE FOLLOWING EXCERPTS are taken from a variety of sources. Each selection expresses the particular view or approach of the practitioner involved.

None of us believes that our fees should be uniformly established on a basis comparable to union scales for trades, such as electricians, carpenters, and masons.

It seems that all of the factors involved in fee-setting are in some manner woven or merged into one determinate, namely, *service*. The CPA who serves best will profit most. If that be true, each of us should concentrate on the improvement and expansion of his services, and fees will then take care of themselves. Whether we are in practice for ourselves, in partnership with others, or in the employ of others, our fees or our share of the profits or compensation will be measured by the extent to which our services meet the needs of the clients. If our services are superior, our rewards will be comparably greater. If our services are average and routine, we deserve no more than average pay.

Let us then concentrate on the improvement and expansion of our own services and on raising the standards of practice throughout the country.

He profits most who serves best.

A suggestion that comes to me from time to time from the partner or accountant in charge of an engagement is that we should bill a lesser amount than the time calls for with the hope that we can make it up on later bills. Based upon a quarter of a century of experience, in 99 cases out of 100 this cannot be done. We are fortunate each year to collect each bill fully based upon the time as we go along, and it is almost impossible to catch up for underbilling in prior years.

Another point to be considered is that one-time engagements should not be billed at regular rates. We should get a premium for these jobs. It is not fair to our regular clients to bill one-time engagements at the same rates we bill a continuing client whom we have had for many years, and expect to continue to serve.

A third point that I think is important is not to have the idea that we should reduce our rates for work done in slack seasons. We are only cutting our own fees and standards, and will never be able to be on the right basis for fees with this particular client, as these things stick in his mind.

As our profession approaches maturity we are instinctively looking around us to see how we compare with other professions. We are rapidly becoming public relations conscious. It is almost axiomatic that public relations begin with client relations, and there is no more sensitive area in client relations than this matter of fees and billings.

There seems to be an increasing belief in some quarters that the time basis is unbecoming to the dignity of professional people. It is urged that we should abandon this customary practice, followed by tradesmen, in favor of something more in keeping with our stature as a profession. Before we go off the deep end, maybe we should take a second look at some fundamental differences between our profession and others following fee techniques which appear enviable.

Some of the contemporary professions apparently do pretty well by themselves in this matter of fees—at least at a first glance! We are all familiar with the surgeon's explanation that he charged $100 for his time plus $900 for knowing where to cut. Important criteria for legal fees are responsibility assumed, amount of money involved, and ability to pay. One successful practitioner in another profession once gave me the secret of his financial success in these words: "When you only get one swipe at a client, swipe all you can."

By contrast with other professions, ours is a continuing relationship with most of our clients. Normally, one suffers but one appendectomy in a lifetime, and leaves but one estate to be administered; but our clients seek professional assistance on their accounting, business, and tax matters continually. In our profession, a good client might be likened to an annuity, rather than a lump-sum settlement.

A more important contrast is the *nature* of our relationship with our clients. Ours is a privileged relationship; our clients cannot conceal their financial circumstances from us. We do not have to guess at what the traffic will bear—we know, because our clients let us count it. Therefore the fixing of our fees is something more sacred, more a matter of honor and good conscience, more to be justified on a factual basis than most other professional fees. Because of this privileged status, we must keep ourselves above any suspicion of avarice by having a basis which the client can understand and appreciate.

Our firm uses time as the basis for our fees. The time spent in behalf of each client, adequately described for the record, is extended at an applicable rate per hour which has been established for each of our partners and staff, based upon our own estimate of his ability and experience. This results in a "standard charge," but from this point forward the exercise of judgment and discretion plays an important part in the determination of our fee billings. In some cases, for the well-known reasons, the bill may be rendered at a discount from standard; for other well-known reasons, the bill may be rendered at a premium over standard. But in all cases of variation, whether discount or premium, the fee is a *percentage* of standard—50 (ouch!), 75, 90, 110, 133, 150, 200 per cent.

These procedures obviously result in odd-money billings except as a rare coincidence. While some may feel that this is unprofessional, it lets the client know that we have a *basis* for our charges other than some number picked out of the air. We are content to be considered undignified if our client relationships are maintained on a mutually satisfactory basis.

The accounting profession, as a whole, does not appear to be accused of larceny as frequently as are some of the other professions; this may be due to a general recognition that our charges are customarily based upon per-diem rates. It might be unfortunate for us to abandon this concept in our zeal to become more professional in this detail of billing our clients. We can fix our fees to provide us with proper compensation for the services rendered by using a combination of time and rate, divided or multiplied as the circumstances justify—and at the same time retain the confidence of our clients, which is the more important consideration in view of the privileged nature of our relationship with them.

The fee problem is something which we never seem to settle. Many CPAs may feel that the fee question is simple—keep track of hours, apply a rate, and that is it.

Let us take a fairly typical case in my own office. During one seven-week period I devoted my time almost equally between three jobs. One job was a small audit. I performed the job alone and it took me about thirteen days. I like to tell myself that my services are of considerable value and that I should earn a good hourly fee. On this job, however, I performed the junior work, the semi-senior work, and the senior work. Should I receive a senior's rates for junior work?

Another job that I worked on was a case involving a tax deficiency. There was a little less than ten days involved but because of the work a $21,000 deficiency was reduced to $6,000. Part of the deficiency was reduced by plain back work but mostly it was reduced by experience. Should I revise my fee upward to partly compensate for prior knowledge?

The third case took about eighteen working days. This client is a soft-drink bottler. He was called back to active duty and on his return home found that while his journals had been written up, the ledger hadn't been posted for two years and corporation income-tax returns hadn't been filed. The job was brought to me. The obvious procedure was to post the ledger and get returns filed. I looked around for one of the boys to handle the posting. But they were occupied on other jobs. Having some free time, I started into it myself and for the next couple of weeks I worked at it— telling myself all the while that I was too good a man to be doing that kind of work. A junior should have done the job. What should I charge—junior rates or the rates usually charged for my time?

A large firm can establish hourly or per-diem rates for various levels of performance and adhere closely to them. It is dealing with a clientele that is familiar with, and recognizes the value of, the accountant's service. Not so with the small office. Much of our work is in the nature of supervisory record-keeping and other types of work of a rather elementary nature so that our client may not make too much of a distinction between us and a good bookkeeper. It is difficult to extract a professional fee from him if he does not set us apart as professional men in his own mind. Then, too, many of our clients are close personal friends as well as clients. Frequently it is difficult to command a healthy respect for our ability from those close to us.

Add to these handicaps the fact that there is a very definite limit to the amount which the small client can pay. He may be able to afford more than he thinks, but very real limitations do exist. It is important, therefore, for us to carefully analyze each job so that the time which can be devoted to it is spent on the most important phases of the work.

My only suggestion is—in all possible cases bill for a sum commensurate with your professional ability even at the risk of losing clients. You will do a better job for those you retain and you will do something that is good for your own feeling of independence.

Our office has a total personnel of nine during the busy season, with two or three less during the remainder of the year, and its practice is almost exclusively with small and medium-sized businesses. Our policy is to bill regular clients at the close of each month; others when the engagement is completed. With very few exceptions, clients are billed an amount resulting from a multiplication of the hours involved in their work by standard rates for the various office personnel. An exception to this procedure is made in the case of income-tax returns for other than regular clients or their owners or officers. We have established standard minimums for the different classes of returns to which these clients are subject when time at regular rates fails to equal the established minimum for that type of return.

Our office, contrary to some offices, makes a universal practice of charging clients for all time consumed by any employee on work for that client, including time-typing, checking, and correcting reports. For this latter, we use a minimum rate which reduces materially, but does not obviate, net expense to the office for typists, etc. We feel this to be the fairest to the client, as it would appear only correct that the client furnished, for example, with a thirty-five-page report, many of the sheets of which require wide-carriage work, should pay the approximate cost of same. Spreading this cost over all clients by increasing the rates charged for staff men is unsatisfactory.

After reviewing the published material on fees, as well as the frank observations of a number of successful practitioners, several conclusions seem in order:

1. Although the setting of a proper professional fee is a difficult art, too many practitioners devote too little time to the task. They are inclined to rely upon formulas which seldom reflect all of the costs of operating a professional practice. One of the most significant of these costs is the annual income which a professional man has a right to expect from his practice. Yet relatively few CPAs—and the few are generally the successful ones—make a determined effort to establish this income goal and to design their fee schedule to produce it.

2. Time devoted to an engagement can be a useful gauge in setting a fee for it—if certain conditions are met. First of all, the men assigned to the engagement must be assigned "in grade"—that is, the salary cost of each of them should be closely related to the expected value of their contribution to the engagement. The work, too, must be closely supervised to avoid a dissipation of effort in the detours and dead ends which can occur in many engagements. Finally, the billing rates must be based on realistic estimates of the number of productive hours which can be expected of each man. If any of these conditions are not met, the "time" yardstick in billing can be a trap for the unwary—leading to one of two undesirable results: the client is overcharged, or the CPA is underpaid.

3. There are other circumstances, moreover, when time alone must be a highly defective measurement of service. In these cases, a reasonable fee can be determined only through a subjective evaluation of the skill and technical knowledge required to perform the needed services—and of the results to be attained in rendering them. Of course, this evaluation might occur when various levels of staff men were assigned to the engagement in grade—and thus the time factor could conceivably provide a fair standard for billing purposes. More often, however, the evaluation can be better undertaken at the completion of the engagement when all of the factors are clearly known.

4. As a matter of policy, some accounting firms decline any engagement which will not warrant charging rates which will at least recover their full

costs and thus enable them to maintain an office equipped to render high quality service. Although experiences with costs and chargeable time differ among firms, individual basic rates usually can be derived from the application of two propositions: (a) direct "labor" cost is the ratio between annual salary and annual chargeable hours; and (b) direct "labor" cost should not exceed 50 per cent of the fee (no firm interviewed felt it should be more, and some felt it normally should be less). Under these conditions, for example, a $6,000-a-year staff man who could be expected on the basis of experience to produce 1,600 hours of chargeable time would have a salary cost of $3.75 per hour, requiring an hourly billing rate of at least $7.50. If his record indicated that 1,400 chargeable hours was a more realistic estimate, the direct "labor" would cost $4.29 per hour with a minimum rate of $8.60.

5. Basic rates, when once established on a sound basis, provide a control point in the day-to-day management of a practice. Naturally, specific engagements may require adjustments from the rates; but the practitioner, knowing that he must average these rates over the year if he is to achieve his income goal, will be aware of the impact of every departure from his "standard" charges. He will, in other words, have built into his practice a "point of resistance" to the pressure for lower fees.

6. Since value to the client is a vital element in the acceptability of a fee, accountants cannot command a professional fee unless they render a truly professional service. The CPA certificate in itself cannot establish the level of fees. It merely indicates a certain degree of competence. The heart of the matter is whether that competence has been delivered to the client— and whether the client is fully aware of its delivery.

This section has tried to provide some guidance on many of the problems which arise in establishing reasonable fees. It has not answered one question: how much should a fee be? The reason for this is obvious: there simply is no single answer to that question.

Billings and Collections

INTRODUCTION

■ NO PROFESSIONAL SERVICE is complete until it has been satisfactorily performed and the fee for it has been determined, rendered, and collected.

Each of these elements is important. While the quality of the work is the primary consideration, quality is certain to suffer if a practitioner cannot obtain a reasonable fee for his efforts. Yet the billing of many accounting firms and practitioners is haphazard. It is frequently delayed until it cannot be put off any longer, if any fee at all is going to be collected.

The practitioner often approaches the billing task with distaste. He may feel that this chore, necessary as it is, somehow deprecates his ideal of dedicated professionalism and reduces him to the status of a vendor. He may hesitate to put a fair price on his services, fearing that such self-evaluation will appear immodest. He knows that he must recover his costs —although he is sometimes not sure what his true costs are; but how much can the fee exceed direct costs and still be fair to both his client and himself? The fact remains that, although profit cannot be his dominant motive, the CPA's professional practice is an economic unit. It can survive only if it is maintained on a financially sound basis.

The billing operation is an essential part of this effort to achieve fees which are consistent and equitable to all concerned. A well-planned system has four important advantages:

1. *To see that all services are adequately accounted for.* This requires that the proper records be maintained which show the time spent and on what, expenses, client "history," and special memoranda which may have a bearing on the fee. By reviewing these records at regular intervals, a bill can be prepared at a logical point.

2. *To establish and maintain adequate working capital.* With a planned program of billing, it is possible to predict income over the short term and to take into consideration the usual lag between the billing and collection of fees. The working capital can be minimized by keeping receivables and unbilled services current.

3. *To help insure full collection.* The key to this lies in prompt billing. A client is usually more willing to pay while the work is in progress or the results are still fresh in his mind. No one likes to pay for a "dead horse." A planned system of collection enables the firm to follow up outstanding accounts on a regular basis—for the older the debt, the less chance there is of collecting it.

4. *To systematize the internal operations of the accounting firm.* Establishing regularly followed procedures helps insure that all necessary time will be devoted to billing without wasting potential chargeable time. At billing time all pertinent records are available for evaluating the size of the fee.

The billing process cannot be isolated from other aspects of managing a practice. It is closely allied to and, in part, is determined by how the firm sets its fees and the manner in which it keeps its internal records. The degree to which the CPA has established effective relations with his client also plays an important role in the billing situation.

ESTABLISHING SOUND POLICIES AND PROCEDURES

Before a firm can set up an effective system for rendering and collecting its fees, it must resolve a number of questions. It must assign responsibility; it must determine the basis of fee-setting; it must decide upon the frequency and wording of the bills; and it must make provision for handling special cases. These and related questions are discussed in the following pages.

Who should handle billing? As is true with all aspects of practice, the practitioner or partners must bear the responsibility for the fee rendered and be prepared to justify it, if the need arises. Since the determination of the fee is so closely interwoven with the preparation of the bill, it is almost universally accepted that a principal of the organization should personally prepare or closely examine any bill submitted by the firm. This does not mean that a partner must personally handle the mechanical phases. Frequently a dollar extension of time spent by each staff member or partner, according to his "standard" billing rates, and a summary of expenses are supplied to the partner as a "raw" billing. This, together with the wording supplied by the partner, may well be the final amount rendered in many cases. However, this often constitutes merely a point of departure. The partner must then consider the numerous other factors which may have a bearing on a fair fee. Even in cases where fixed fees are employed for certain clients or other definite provisions have been made, a partner generally reviews the bills before they go out.

Some larger firms have a non-partner office manager who prepares "draft bills," including amounts and description of services, especially for repetitive work, for the consideration of the partner. In some other firms the supervisors prepare them.

Although there is general agreement that a partner should be intimately associated with the billing procedure, firms vary in their selection of the partner to handle it.

Billing responsibility breaks down into three basic approaches:

1. Partner directly in charge of the engagement
2. The managing or administrative partner
3. Partner committee, or a review by all partners

Partner-in-charge of engagement. He is more closely connected with the work performed than any other partner. He has more personal contact with the client and is probably a better judge of the client's attitudes, circumstances, and in some cases, idiosyncrasies. However, this approach can result in a diffusion of responsibility for billing throughout the firm. Because of the absence of central control, it is possible that varying evaluations of similar work may result in disparate bills to different clients for the same type and quality of work. Finally, different partners may vary widely in their aptitudes in dealing with clients over fee matters.

Managing or administrative partner. This practice is more usual in small firms dominated by one partner. He has ordinarily developed much of the clientele and is generally more experienced than his associates. However, this practice is by no means confined to this type of firm, especially if much of the practice is repetitive work on a monthly basis. This approach has two advantages: centralized control is being exercised by a man of considerable experience, and the same standards of evaluation are apt to be applied to all clients. On the other hand, the managing partner is often not in close day-to-day contact with clients and may not be in the best position to consider the "value" elements in determing the fee. He may not be in as good a position to insure collection as would be the case with the partner who deals directly with the client.

Partner committee or review by all partners. This procedure attempts to apply the "two-heads-are-better-than-one" concept to billing. It is especially effective where two or more partner-specialists have had direct dealings with clients in their particular area of specialization. The group-billing approach may often stiffen resistance to reducing the proposed fee by requiring an evaluation of the reasons for the reduction. It also promotes uniform treatment of all clients for similar work and provides an opportunity for all the partners to keep up to date on the firm's clientele. However, the method can be needlessly time-consuming on bills of relative simplicity. Moreover, in other cases, the partners must rely heavily on the partner who handled the engagement, since he is the only one who is familiar with the client and the work done.

The "best" method for the usual billing situation depends, to a large extent, on the firm organization, the type of clientele, and the work performed for them. These circumstances may indicate that a combination of these methods is most suitable for a particular firm.

Organization of the firm. Consideration should be given to the ratio of partners to staff members. As the number of staff members supervised by a single partner increases, it grows more difficult for him to remain completely informed on all aspects of the work. If a firm has developed "specialist" partners supervising different "departments" (audit, taxes, systems, etc.), there is often no longer a single partner in charge. The "field" partners may be less experienced in billing technique, but the managing partner may be familiar enough with all accounts to handle the billing after necessary consultation with his younger partners.

Type of clientele and work performed. When the clientele consists largely of small businesses which require repetitive monthly work, billing can more easily be centralized.

Once the nature of this work is established, fee variations are due mainly to changes in volume, as measured by time spent. However, if a substantial portion of the practice involves full-scale annual audits and special engagements, other factors assume considerable importance.

It is advisable to establish basic rates as a resistance point or guide, regardless of billing method. But mere extension of the basic rates is inadequate in some cases. Adjustments are frequently necessary to consider properly "value," responsibility assumed, and other factors. This requires intimate familiarity with the circumstances of the engagement. Therefore, many firms find it preferable to make the partner-in-charge of the client responsible for billing. A rather common modification of this approach is to have the in-charge partner prepare the bill, which is then reviewed by the managing partner. This is especially valid if there are any unusual circumstances. The extent to which the managing partner may question a fee is frequently determined by its relation to "standard" rates, the explanation for adjustments, and the experience of the partner who prepared the bill.

Some firms circulate a monthly "analysis of completed engagements" among all partners prior to billing. This includes the proposed bill, time extended by basic rates and the observations by the in-charge partner on his reasons for adjusting the fee for the job, either up or down. If no objection is raised by the remaining partners, the bill is rendered as proposed. These firms feel that this method, in addition to providing a billing review procedure, enables all partners to keep posted on the work being done throughout the firm.

Although a partner bears the responsibility for the billing, the senior staff member on the job frequently will be consulted if any questions arise. Usually this is limited to determining the nature and extent of work performed, but apparently an increasing number of firms permit staff members to suggest the fee to be charged. This is especially true where the firm has a large number of clients. Here is what a member of a four-partner firm has to say about his firm's policy in this respect:

> We have an arrangement with our seniors that compensates them on the basis of their annual production of fees rather than on a straight salary. Each man has a monthly drawing account and an annual bonus based on his percentage of production.
>
> Our firm has relatively few large audits and the large number of small accounts makes it difficult for the partners to give the same review to each client that they do on the larger audit accounts. In billing for tax work or for statements prepared without audit, a great deal of time used to be consumed by the partners in finding out as much about the job as is necessary to set a reasonable fee. However, the senior in charge is completely familiar with the account, and, we feel, is in a position to suggest what he thinks is a fair charge for the service. Accounts are permanently assigned to each senior staff member. He is anxious not to overcharge and jeopardize the good will of the client. He is equally anxious not to undercharge since his net compensation is based on his production of fees.
>
> We have attempted to create a considerable spirit of independence among our staff men, feeling that a profession calls for substantial individual initiative. This opportunity to suggest fees seems to have had a very favorable effect on the staff men. They feel a responsibility toward the client and the firm.
>
> We have been pleased by the very constructive suggestions we have had from the staff men, and we believe that it has, to a considerable degree, tended to stabilize the fees charged for various types of service.

Regardless of who has the responsibility for billing individual clients, it is most desirable to have a centralized control which measures performance in relation to basic rates. This usually takes the form of a summary of client billings, grouped according to the partners assigned to them. It shows actual billings and theoretical billings at "standard" rates. This report discloses weak spots and furnishes information on the firm's average "yield." In some firms it is prepared annually, but others require a monthly summary. The latter group feels that the extra time involved is more than offset by their ability to correct "trouble spots" as soon as they appear.

WHAT SHOULD BE BILLED?

A fee should recover all the direct expenses of an engagement, a proportionate amount of the general overhead, and include a "profit" factor. These three elements are usually included in a single time rate. The total overhead must be recovered during the course of the year, even if the fee for a few engagements does not recover the overhead "proportionate" to those engagements. However, the more the overhead factor can be reduced by isolating components which can be directly charged to specific clients, the more accurately the bills will apportion costs among the clients according to the services rendered. This may require more detailed record-keeping than some firms now employ, but many CPAs feel it is more equitable.

A brief word might be said about telephone calls and drop-in visits, because billing policies vary widely in charging clients for them.

Naturally, no practitioner wants the client to feel that the "meter is ticking" every time he contacts his CPA. But the practitioner is entitled to compensation for valuable assistance, even though the time consumed may be relatively insignificant. The intent and results of such calls or visits, it is generally agreed, are the primary considerations. If they are basically to make arrangements for future consultations or work, there is little point in charging for such time. However, a number of firms generally follow a policy of charging time, in the case of principals only, for these items, in addition to evaluating the results, when a call or visit lasts for more than a few minutes. Frequently a call of more than five or ten minutes will be charged out as fifteen minutes of time. This does not mean, however, that individual calls or visits will be identified in the bill.

One firm which found that a lot of potentially "chargeable" time was being absorbed, described its present policy as follows:

> The general rule in our office is that staff telephone calls are not charged because it would be quite difficult for them to put down the short time that they usually spend on the phone answering incidental questions for bookkeepers. However, telephone calls of partners are billed at regular rates and no phone call is considered to be less than a fifteen-minute time charge. Drop-in visits are also charged at the regular rates. Travel time is an area that is entirely up to the judgment of the partner and the man traveling. We try to give the client as little charge for travel time as possible. However, if it entails a considerable amount of time, we divide it in half and we pay part and the client pays part. Research time is definitely charged to the client, and the partner when he bills determines whether or not it should be at the full rate depending upon the item questioned. Typing, checking, and comparing time are also charged to the clients at our regular per-diem rates for these services.

TIMING THE BILL

Timeliness is an important consideration in billing policy. It helps insure full collection of all charges and leads to efficient billing practices. The three stages at which bills are commonly rendered are:

1. *Upon completion of the work.* Although some firms usually bill only after an engagement has been fulfilled, it is more common to bill on this basis only for small audits, tax-return preparation, short-term special engagements, or in other circumstances where the bill is relatively small.

2. *By period.* Billing a client regularly on a monthly or quarterly basis is especially suited to cases where regular monthly work is performed for the client or when a lengthy engagement would otherwise mean the build-up of substantial charges. When the client's ability to pay is limited, "installments" are helpful to both the client and the CPA. This has the effect of putting the CPA on the "payroll" in the sense that the client recognizes the fees of his CPA as a regular continuing expense. Prorating an annual "fixed" fee is not difficult, but some firms feel that evaluation of the over-all fee must await the completion of the job and billing in process work at the regular rates may not result in a fair total fee. However, this objection is usually overcome when the client understands that the regular payments are based on rough estimates and that necessary adjustments will be made in the final bill. This approach can also be effective when only annual or semiannual work is being performed, if the client realizes that he is paying "on account" for those months in which he has been billed, but no work has been performed.

3. *By client's annual cycle.* This involves the billing of completed and in-process work in such a way that all the client's expenses for his CPA are charged off during the fiscal year in which the work is performed. This is usually combined with some sort of period billing, differing only in that the fee adjustments are undertaken at the close of the client's year, rather than when the particular jobs are completed.

Although many firms may generally bill on one basis, the client's wishes must be considered. Some may prefer—and be able to pay—a single annual bill. Others, especially smaller businesses, may prefer other arrangements. As a general rule, however, it is most desirable to bill promptly—while the work is still fresh in the minds of the CPA and the client—and frequently to avoid building up extensive charges. Within limits, the client is less apt to question several small bills than one large one of an equivalent amount. Here is how one practitioner supports this view:

> We consider the ideal understanding with the client in the matter of fees to be such that we can bill monthly at standard rates for the hours on our books. This procedure accomplishes at least three desirable objectives:
> 1. The client spreads this item of overhead over the year instead of accumulating it in one month.
> 2. It keeps the client advised as to the amount of effort expended on his behalf currently instead of attempting to explain it at the end of the year.
> 3. It puts money in the bank for our payroll instead of forcing our partners to supply capital to carry the unbilled time.

For those who feel that monthly billings are only appropriate for write-up work or for small clients, this is what a partner of a national firm has to say:

I am a strong supporter of the practice of billing every month all time charges in excess of $100. At one time I sent a circular letter to all of our substantial clients stating that we proposed henceforth to send them monthly bills and asking for contrary instructions if they objected. As I recall, only two requested their bills once a year. Generally they preferred to pay for our services during the month following the rendering of the service. They didn't like the idea of having a creditor building up unbilled services not reflected in their books; at the same time, they did not like to set up a monthly accrual (and we also didn't like to have them make such an estimate —a round-figure guess). There is no logical reason why we should finance our clients—no more reason to defer our payments for services than for any supplier of materials or services to do so. Our staff men are paid their salaries promptly and almost any client will agree that there is no reason why we should defer billings. I see nothing unprofessional about this. In fact, I think the clients respect us more if we introduce a little bit of ordinary common-sense business practice into our relations with them.

A client should receive his bill as soon after the first of the month as possible. This should not be a problem in cases where an engagement is completed during the month or a client payment schedule is based on a fixed monthly payment with year-end adjustments. When work-in-process is charged out at an extension of billing rates, it becomes necessary to insist upon prompt submission of time sheets by the staff. Some firms find it easier to bill at the end of the month only for work performed through the 25th of the month, or thereabouts. "If a bill is to be dated the last day of the month," writes one practitioner, "it should be mailed within five days. I find it is very annoying to a client to receive such a bill late in the following month. It reflects on our business acumen."

DETERMINING THE BILL

One practitioner lists some hints which bear repeating:

1. Do your easy billings first. Then it's easier to deliberate on tough ones.
2. Never charge more than you would be willing to pay. If in serious doubt, err on the side of reasonableness. (Golden rule.)
3. Never charge more than you can collect. (This implies faulty arrangements with the client or failure to keep him posted. But this has happened once to every practitioner. When it does—well, reread the rule.)
4. Except for out-of-pocket expenses, do not use odd figures on invoices. Round them out.
5. Beware of establishing and publishing minimum rates. The minimums tend to become maximums.
6. Avoid "lapping." It has a backlash effect and will simultaneously destroy the fee structure and client good will. (New practitioners lacking the courage born of experience are likely to be vulnerable on this one. To be specific, suppose that for a new client you do work prudently worth $165

the first month, $110 the second, and $100 the third. The thing to do is to bill him just that. If you bill only $125 the first month, hoping to make up the $40 later, you are likely to be disappointed, and lose out all around, for the client is already conditioned to the wrong yardstick and with brute logic can complain when you bill him the correct $110 the second month, on the grounds that his bill was "nearly as high as the first month, but you didn't spend anywhere near the same time.")

SUPPORTING RECORDS

Before a bill can be intelligently prepared, certain basic information must be available to the partner handling it. This includes:

1. Time record for the client extended at a "basic" rate for each individual or grade of accountant who has been employed on the engagement.

2. Description of the work performed, preferably in relation to the various grades of accountants assigned to it.

3. Expense statement of all direct billable and nonbillable expenses incurred. This would include items such as postage and stationery for confirmations, long distance telephone calls, travel expenses, use of reproducing equipment, etc.

4. Basic information about the client, including the name and address, billing frequency, special instructions, and previous billings.

These four items form the basis for the "raw" billing and permit a comparison of the work done with the bills charged for prior work. All this information can be incorporated on a single "client card."

Although consideration is often given to the type and quality of service in establishing billing rates, the judgment factor must frequently be applied to these data in order to consider elements that may suggest an upward or downward adjustment from the "raw" billing. Much of this depends on familiarity with the client. But memory is often faulty and must be bolstered by written records. Other materials which are frequently helpful are:

1. Engagement memorandum; either the interoffice report or a copy of the confirmation sent to the client. This is helpful in measuring the results against the work agreed upon. Consideration can be given to special work beyond the limits of the original agreement, especially if some tentative fee arrangement had been made for the original engagement.

2. Conference reports or memoranda of lengthy telephone calls with clients which may well have a bearing on the value of the service and should be carefully read. They should consist of a brief summary of the nature and results of the conversation. The senior staff members should be trained to the habit of preparing these memoranda when necessary.

3. Correspondence, which should always be reviewed, prior to billing. Frequently important advice is given in a letter or references may be made to work, which might otherwise be overlooked.

THE ART OF PREPARING A BILL

There appears to be general agreement within the profession that "Accounting Services Rendered," without further amplification, is inadequate for most bills. But practitioners are divided as to the extent of itemization which is desirable.

Some prefer a highly itemized bill, in most cases, including a listing of the procedures and each schedule prepared for a tax return. They feel that a full explanation of all services mitigates against possible complaints about the fee by impressing upon the client the amount of work that has been undertaken on his behalf.

Other firms, probably a predominant number, prefer a brief description of major areas without extensive itemization. This description, they feel, should be sufficient to call the client's attention to significant items, without burdening him with a lot of detail. They recognize that different services may require descriptions of varying length, depending on the familiarity of the client with the work. But they find that overitemization can cause complaints because the client may attempt to assign dollar values to specific items, some of which might be relatively minor.

These firms list the following considerations as the most important to a well-written bill:

1. Be as brief as possible and confine the description to those significant items which would not be readily apparent to the client.

2. Do not show hours or rates on the bill.

3. Use a single round figure for the fee for all the services covered in the bill.

4. Adequately describe any item which has caused a significant increase in the bill.

Care should be taken to see that the bill specifies the period and the work covered, especially if more than one job is being done for the client. This is one advantage to period billing for all work being done for the client.

BILLING PITFALLS

A note of caution might be sounded here. Although the CPA would like the text of his bill to impress the client with the extent of his services, the wording should not imply a broader scope to the services than those actually rendered. A carelessly worded bill might have a bearing on the accountant's liability if it is admitted as evidence of the scope of the CPA's work. For example, a bill for an audit engagement which states *"Verification* of assets and liabilities . . ."* rather than *"Examination* of the financial statements . . ."* might be misleading even though the report was properly phrased.

EXAMPLES OF BILLING TEXTS

Since the need for description varies with the work performed, the following examples represent the varying treatment which might be given under certain circumstances:

Under many circumstances the descriptive text can and should be quite terse. *On repeat monthly work,* for instance, the text might be:

> Accounting and consulting services rendered during the month of September—$100.

On an annual audit, too, the text can be quite simple, even though the engagement was relatively large. This is so because the audit report speaks for itself as to what was done. Hence, the text might properly read:

> Examining and reporting upon the accounts for the year ended October 31, 19— per report transmitted December 8, including the review of the corporation's federal and state tax returns for the year—$3,000.

Similarly, *the billings for routine tax-return preparation* can be pretty well standardized, such as:

> Preparation of federal and state income-tax returns and declarations for 19—, including accounting analyses and tax research incidental thereto, and also incidental advisory service during the year—$85.

Under other circumstances, particularly on *new or special engagements,* considerable care should be exercised to make the text really descriptive. The description may be couched in general terms and yet be adequate. Example:

> Revision of the billing and collection procedures in the Title Department, including surveying and redesigning forms, testing and selection of new cash-registration equipment, preparation of a Manual of Operating Instructions for the new procedures, and complete installation of the forms, procedures and equipment to the point of satisfactory operation—$2,500.

In some cases, especially in *consulting work,* careful itemization may be in order. If small billheads are used, a letterhead might well be used to permit adequate description without crowding the space. The steps in the engagement, the phases of the work, the dates when conferences were held, or other services performed might be itemized. Thus, the billing might read:

> Accounting and auditing services rendered in the comprehensive Personnel Study completed April 15, as more fully described below—$2,000.

The itemization below will usually be under "Detail of Services" or "Memorandum of Services."

Within individual firms, over a period of time, certain fairly standard billing phraseology is developed to apply to various types of work. Some firms now employ a "billing instruction sheet" which includes a list of the standard billing phrases used by the firm in the more common cases, space for special wording to supplement or take the place of the "standard," and provision for inserting special instructions for filling out the bill. These firms have found this form to be highly effective. It saves time—the partner merely checks off the applicable statements and fills in the appropriate dates in many cases—and reduces the probability of clerical error.

SEPARATION OF EXPENSES

The majority of the firms and practitioners interviewed favor divorcing expenses from "services rendered" on their bills. A single lump sum is preferred. Although a few take pains to itemize virtually every item, the great majority find that a brief identification of the most significant expenses is completely adequate. However, where all out-of-pocket expenses represent only a small portion of the total bill, many of these firms include them in the "fee."

About a third of the firms do not favor segregating expenses from the fee, on the grounds that the fee plus expenses represent the total cost of the engagement—and that this is the client's most important interest. They supply details on out-of-pocket expenses only if requested. Such requests, they find, are relatively rare. One practical-minded practitioner pointed out that identification of out-of-town travel expense, in particular, works against the continued use of an out-of-town CPA.

PREPRINTED NOTATIONS ON BILLS

Almost without exception, the CPAs consulted in a survey on this subject were opposed to the commercial type of preprinted invoices. They favored the use of half-sized letterheads or facsimile letterheads; preprinted, in some cases, in "snap-apart" carbon form. Where special billheads were used, they contained no columnar delineations. Several of the firms numbered their bills, but the great majority felt that this practice was "too commercial."

Although one practitioner carries a statement on his bills to the effect that they are payable in ten days, special notations such as this were opposed by the others for similar reasons. Such notations might also include a reference to terms for prompt payment, or the right to charge interest on past due accounts.

COLLECTION AND FOLLOW-UP PROCEDURE

Generally favored practices relating to collections include the following:

1. Refraining from specifying on the bill when remittance is expected
2. Following up within thirty, sixty, or ninety days
3. Insisting on prompt payment when bills are overdue

4. Making no adjustment in charges to induce payment

5. Taking legal action only as a last resort and only in cases where the amount of the fee makes collection imperative

Perhaps the most important step in collecting the bill is a preventive one —an application of the principle that a client should never be unpleasantly surprised by a bill. If there is any reason to believe that the client will be unhappy, he should be contacted before the bill goes out. It is far easier to discuss it and reach an amicable solution while the work is still fresh in mind than to attempt to rehash it several months later, after no check has been forthcoming.

Every CPA wants to keep his receivables current. Some firms have stated that 10 to 15 per cent of annual billings should be the maximum for outstanding receivables, and that unbilled services should not represent more than 20 per cent. Of course, these figures are offered only as a rough guide, for each case is subject to individual judgment.

Almost all of the firms giving information in this area reported that they refrain from specifying on bills a period within which payment is expected. When payment is not received within a reasonable period, a follow-up by monthly statement or individual letter is made. A substantial number of firms do this within thirty days. An almost equal number prefer sixty days. A smaller group makes it ninety, and one firm sets it as low as twenty. Moreover, decisions as to when to send a reminder and how to word it are dependent upon such variable circumstances as (1) whether the client is new or old, (2) amount of fee due, (3) client's known financial condition, (4) whether services rendered are casual or periodically recurrent, (5) how close and friendly the tie with the client is, and so on.

Of the few who reported that they specify on their bills the period within which payment is expected, not one was a large firm. Further, only a few of the firms specifying a period indicate its length. However, one medium-sized firm states, "due when rendered," and two small firms stipulate ten and thirty days, respectively. When the stipulated period elapses without receipt of payment, the firms send discreet reminders which take, in general, the form of a monthly statement or an individual letter. When a letter is sent, it is dispatched usually from fifteen to thirty days after expiration of the period within which payment was required. One firm prefers, however, a personal call on the client instead of a letter, and another waits six months before supplementing monthly statements by a special letter.

Despite indications that some firms employ a "ten-day letter," the consensus appears to favor a thirty-day statement as the first step in the follow-up procedure. In many cases a sixty-day statement is sent and the partner does not personally enter the picture until ninety days have elapsed. Although this is common practice, ninety days seems to be too long a period before personal action is taken. By the time two months have elapsed, it is apparent that something is seriously wrong. Either the client is unhappy or he lacks the funds to pay. Possibly he may need some prodding, for the work has been done and he may decide he has more pressing creditors. In any event, a sixty-day lapse appears to warrant at least a telephone call.

The partner can then make definite arrangements for payment or get to the heart of the client's dissatisfaction.

There is understandable reluctance by all firms to remind a client that a payment due has been overlooked. However, the majority have had experience which indicates that prompt insistence on payment when overdue yields the best results and does not unduly irritate clients.

Incisive comment by Sproull as to the experiences of English practitioners deserves careful consideration. He breaks down slow payments into two groups. The first he terms "regular slow payers who are time wasters and, in common with would-be price cutters, are not only the least profitable but generally the most unproductive as to remunerative, desirable, extra assignments or the introduction of new clients to the accountant." The second type he labels "casual slow payers." The reason for their delinquency is usually defective control of their finances which makes them impecunious on occasions. As to them Sproull makes the apt professional observation that "they are often suitable to benefit from budget-installation work even if their businesses are small."[21]

CLIENT COMPLAINTS

Few firms receive complaints. Where they do, a definite connection seems to exist between complaints and the related invoice. Large and medium-sized firms believe this is because brevity in the invoice suggests lack of substantial value. Individual practitioners and small firms think that itemization strikes clients as constituting too much detail of little value. This phenomenon suggests that the extent of itemization might vary according to the size of the firm, but it is hardly a sound basis for a definite rule.

All firms reported a policy of giving careful consideration to reasonable complaints. When complaints are considered unreasonable, most firms take the precaution of making more specific any subsequent agreements with the client involved; other firms refuse subsequent engagements.

When a client is dissatisfied, how far should the CPA go in explaining the basis for his fee?

Although it may be necessary to go into considerable detail concerning the measurement of time and rates, it is usually not advisable to show the client the breakdown of hours and billings for the men used. Time spent is only one of several elements in a fee, and it often raises more questions than it answers. It is usually better to talk in general terms about the time and other factors involved. One practitioner described his approach in this way:

> Ordinarily, we do not show our time records to a client, but it is not good faith in some circumstances not to discuss details of the bill. It is generally best to talk on the basis of average billings per hour—preferably, merely in comparison with the previous year. In some instances I have discussed total hours for each year with explanations of differences and the average billing

[21]R. Sproull, *op. cit.*, pp. 126-132.

rates with considerable frankness. I have found that the clients are so conscious of inflationary trends in their own affairs that they are willing to recognize that we are subject to the same trends, and approve reasonable increases in the average billing rates per hour.

Another practitioner who keeps his account cards on IBM cards said:

I show the complaining client our machine installation. He usually doesn't understand it—but he is impressed.

This indicates that most clients are not so much interested in a blow-by-blow reconstruction of the fee as they are in being reassured that they are being treated fairly.

THE LAST RESORT

Unless there has been an honest misunderstanding about the scope of the work, the client is unable to pay, or the CPA plans to resign from the engagement, he should not permit any adjustments in his bill once it has been rendered. Presumably he feels that it is a reasonable charge and it should not be subject to later negotiation. If a client finds that he can "beat down the price," it undermines the whole billing structure. The obvious reaction of the client is that he was originally overcharged.

Most of the firms commenting on this were opposed in principle to making adjustments to induce payment where collection is difficult or long-delayed. One reason for their attitude is that adjustment downward may create an impression of deliberate overbilling originally. The few considering it expedient to make some adjustment in appropriate cases felt probably that the specific nature of the reason for the difficulty or delay and the extent of adjustment required are highly relevant factors.

Few things are more repugnant to professional men than to have to enforce collection by resort to lawsuits against clients. Regrettably, this aversion is so well recognized that advantage is taken of it occasionally. However, only a minority of the reporting firms have ever been compelled to take legal action. In the case of most of these firms, there has only been one such incident.

With only one exception, all firms reporting felt strongly that legal action should be taken only as a last resort and only in cases where the amount of the fee makes collection imperative. As a practical matter, suing a client for an accountant's fee usually involves time and expense equal to a large part—half or more—of the amount billed. Invariably the client is lost to the firm at this point and collection organizations are employed to salvage what they can from the engagement. Many firms prefer to sit down with the client and, if discussions prove fruitless, leave it up to the client to decide what he feels to be a fair fee. Then, after accepting the client's offer, the CPA will explain why he can no longer serve the client. Often this approach will yield as much or more to the firm than if an agency were retained, without the unpleasant effects a disgruntled former client may have on the rest of the practice. Some firms using this technique report that some of these clients, convinced of the firm's integrity, are subsequently recovered and become highly valued accounts.

PRACTITIONERS' DISCUSSIONS OF BILLING POLICIES AND PROCEDURES

Much has been said about billing for the value of the services rendered in preference to billing on the basis of time alone. Yet most accountants keep their records of productivity by time spent and think in terms of per-diem rates.

Convinced that "time alone should not measure the fee," and that "we should bill for the value of the services rendered," etc., a firm strove for a formula which would fuse measurement by time and measurement by value, and yield a fee which would be reasonable and easy to explain to the client.

Figure I

No. . . . .

ANALYSIS OF COMPLETED ENGAGEMENT

Based on per diem and expense

Initials	Hours	Rate	Ext.
. . . .	. . . .	. . . .	. . . .
. . . .	. . . .	. . . .	. . . .

Observations relative to charging more than per diem, based on value of unusual services

. . . .
. . . .

Observations relative to charging less than per diem due to persons at high rates doing low-rate work

. . . .
. . . .

Details of Bill

Client   Job Number

SERVICES BEYOND SCOPE OF ENGAGEMENT

. . . .
. . . .

Date   Signed

Figure 1 is the result of the firm's efforts. Each person has a "per-hour" rate. Upon completion of the engagement a tentative proposed billing is prepared on those rates. Then this form, together with the time ledger sheet, passes among the three partners, winding up in the hands of the partner who is in charge of that client. Each partner first writes down all the reasons he can think of to justify a billing at more than per-diem rates and writes these reasons in the second section of the form. He then takes the opposite and writes down all the reasons he can think of to justify a billing at less than per-diem rates.

Armed with these analyses the partner-in-charge of the engagement prepares the bill in pencil on the bottom of the form detailing the work performed and the total amount.

They do not bill expenses separately, but have the following printed on their billheads: "Unless Otherwise Stated, Billing Includes Travel and Other Expenses. Detail Breakdown Will Be Furnished on Request."

Even where an engagement has been undertaken at a fixed fee, this form is used. If it is an engagement that is continuous at the same fixed fee per month or per year, they can judge whether the amount they are charging is materially above or below a reasonable amount, and when they approach the client for renegotiation, they have the facts to support their position.

The following excerpts are taken from a variety of sources. Each expresses the particular view or approach of the practitioner involved:

> A recent engagement seemed never to arrive at a good billing point. The job was to supervise and improve the accounting methods for the client. Months passed. Finally, after ten months a bill for $850 was sent. The client "hit the ceiling." The bill remained unpaid for three months. The accountant was advised to appear less often. In fact, he wasn't called for four months.
>
> In this case, the accountant was at fault. In all probability, if ten monthly bills had been presented instead of one total bill for $850, $100 per month would have been paid readily for each of the ten months, and the work would have been appreciated.
>
> Some accountants have learned to bill monthly *always*. Yes, even on annual audits part of the total fee can be billed each month when interim work is being done.
>
> *Moral: Bill early and often.*
>
> A second fundamental rule is to talk freely with the client about the bill, particularly when it is larger than had been planned or estimated. Such a conversation must, of course, be interspersed with facts as to why additional time was required, what particular difficulties were encountered, the nature of the unusual services rendered, etc. Some clients may even be asked to suggest the proper fee under the circumstances, with gratifying results. For instance, one accountant asked his client a few years ago if $2,500 would be an agreeable amount for the engagement. The client replied that he had $3,000 in mind and would be glad to pay that amount. Since that time this particular client *always* sets the fee!

By the time all the service units and values are assembled, it is not unnatural for the practitioner to have grown slightly impatient with the tedium of the task. In such mood, it is all too easy to slight the job of preparing the bills. He is eager to get them in the mail and "get back to work." Yet here is the one point about which he should be unhurried and of judicial mien.

He should set aside an uninterrupted half-day for doing nothing else, consciously take plenty of time, and prepare the text of each bill as carefully as he would prepare an audit opinion. With more and more practice, smoothness (and hence speed) will develop.

There are, of course, different types of billings. The one essential common to all of them is that they be truly descriptive of the services rendered.

Many a practitioner has sat down at the end of the year to prepare a bill and has found it difficult to remember what he did for a particular client. Or he has taken over a case from another partner and found that many of his actions and recommendations are not on record in the files. A conference report is advantageous in these and many other cases.

A conference report, as the name implies, is a written memo of any kind of conference affecting a client. It could be prepared as the result of a phone conversation or a discussion with another partner or staff man. It is always prepared after a conference with the client or others representing him if any actions are taken or recommendations made. These reports are invaluable when a long project is going on, such as a tax case or a reorganization where a series of conferences is held over a relatively extended period. These reports in the file provide a running record of what is taking place so that any partner can take over the case right in the middle if necessary.

When originally adopted in one firm, the conference report was prepared as a printed form. Since the printed form was restricted as to space, they have since abandoned it and now require only that the conference report be prepared on work-sheet-size paper and contain the following information:

1. Client	6. Subject
2. Date of conference	7. Discussion
3. Time of conference	8. Recommendation
4. Place	9. Data promised, if any
5. Those present	10. Time spent
	11. Signature

The conference report is filed with the papers on the particular case or in the correspondence file.

When the time comes to make out the bill, it is a simple matter to review the file to see what has been done during the year, especially with regard to the many small but valuable tips which are given to the client by telephone or in his or the CPA's office, but which are often overlooked in a subsequent discussion of fees. Such a record also provides a ready answer when the client asks, "But what have you done for me lately?"

Perhaps, in preparing bills, accountants would like to consider giving first a broad description of all the work performed with wording similar to the following: "For accounting services rendered." It has been the experience of some that such wording lessens the likelihood of a possible challenge at a later date as to whether or not the invoice was all for accounting services rendered or whether possibly it was commingled with the billing of other kinds of professional services.

Usually an invoice is paid more promptly if it contains adequate description of the work performed. That eliminates questions in the mind of the client whose memory may be slightly rusty as to the services performed over a three- or four-month period. There is also the point that an invoice that is not clear on its face with respect to the work performed is apt to be delayed in payment and also challenged.

It is generally agreed that wherever feasible it is better to bill the work at the end of each month regardless of how much work is still in process. This monthly procedure, however, sometimes raises a question in the client's mind as to whether he is being billed twice for the same item, since identical descriptions of work performed may appear on several invoices. Wording to the following effect in small print at the bottom of the invoice, however, has solved this problem for one firm:

> Because of the nature of accounting services, it is not feasible to describe in detail all the work performed. In order to expedite our billing, a summary of certain major items only is shown. Won't you please review all invoices upon receipt and call us promptly if you have any questions? In general, invoices are forwarded at the end of each month whether or not the work is completed; this may result in identical wording appearing on more than one invoice; for example, if federal, state, and local tax returns were in the course of preparation at December 31, then identical wording would appear on the January invoice. We reserve the right, at any time, to charge interest at the legal rate on past-due accounts.

Measured by the number of returns prepared per accountant, the seasonal tax load probably falls heaviest on offices in the smaller towns throughout the country.

Bills for this class of service should be rendered at the same time the returns and declarations are submitted to clients.

One way to accomplish this easily is simply to drop in each tax client's file a copy of his bill as it is prepared. Then upon completion of the next year's return, the fee can be marked right on the return, and the bill typed at the same time that the return is typed. Thus the secretary, in typing the appropriate (form) transmittal letter, can refer therein to the fee payment due (per bill enclosed) as well as to the taxes due. This not only facilitates early finalization of the whole job, it also assures more uniform and equitable billings for each client from one year to the next because the amounts are determined at the very moment when the current year's work may be most fairly compared with the previous year's.

It is all too easy to let tax billings go until after the seasonal cleanup. Any accountant who does is in for a "three-day headache." And at least a few unintentional errors and even complete omissions are bound to occur, to say nothing of the delay in collections which is the result of such a course.

Once a bill has become past due, one practitioner states he does not hesitate to discuss it with the client. If the amount owed is substantial, he also asks the client for a judgment note, personally endorsed by an officer if the client is a corporation. He turns over accounts to attorneys or collection agencies if he feels a client is not giving him fair treatment.

Obviously, the best time to "collect" an account is before the accountant begins his work. By this is meant a frank discussion about fees with the client, even if the accountant has to admit that he does not know how much the fee will be. A frank discussion can go a long way toward prompt payment when the invoice finally is presented.

This practitioner deals frequently with the heads of small businesses. In his initial talk with such a client, he suggests that the client send him a check at the same time he makes out his payroll.

> We set a round amount which we feel will not be too much of a strain on the client, depending upon the circumstances he happens to be in, and we do not hesitate to bring up the matter if he should skip a payment. We have found from experience that this arrangement is highly acceptable. The client is paying us when he wants us most and when we are doing the most involved part of the work. If the original periodic payments turn out to be too small or too large, we change them. We send an invoice at the end of each month showing a credit for the amounts paid us, and noting the balance due.

Another technique favored by this accountant is enclosing a postage-paid envelope with his bills. He has learned that many of the small businessmen who are his clients find it quite a chore to write a check, hunt up an envelope, address it, and find a stamp. By furnishing a completed envelope, he accelerates payment.

A practitioner reports that he does not allow work to accumulate for billing at the end of a six-month or even a three-month period. Three invoices submitted at intervals seem to be paid with less question than one for the total of the three individual bills, or even one for 75 per cent of the three.

The practitioner further states that a CPA called in by a prospective client should determine whether the previous accountant has been paid in full for his past services, or whether arrangements to pay have been made. If a client leaves one accountant without paying him, he may be expected to do likewise to a new accountant.

Incomes of Practicing CPAs

■ AN ATTEMPT WILL be made here to help the practicing CPA measure his own economic well-being and answer some key questions about his own practice.

WHAT SHOULD A CPA's INCOME BE?

There is, of course, no formula which will yield a precise answer. The quality of service rendered is a principal factor. Bookkeeping, write-up work, and preparation of the usual tax returns will not command fees as high as professional service involving assumption of responsibility (as in "opinion" audits), representation of the client (as in tax controversies or business negotiations), or advice which the client can identify with production of profits. Nonetheless, the practitioner can roughly evaluate his own position by comparing his earnings with those of his colleagues and employees of private industry doing work comparable to his own.

WHAT ARE CPA INCOMES?

The available information on the income of the accounting profession is limited in scope and in statistical validity, but enough has been gathered to be indicative of general ranges. Much of the following information is taken from an AICPA study conducted in 1956 in which over 2,100 offices represented in the membership participated. The response from larger offices was not as great as from the medium-size and small ones, but the results are still helpful. These are the only income figures now available on anything approaching a national scale.

Practitioners and partners over the age of thirty-five indicated their median[22] income (before taxes) to be $12,716. Thirty-four per cent earned more than $15,000 but almost 49 per cent of the offices reported the income of their older principals was less than $12,500. (See Table 3.)

[22]The median is the midpoint (50th per cent point) of the distribution and is therefore not affected by the value of the extremes. Elsewhere in this section, where the average is specified, it refers to the arithmetic mean which is, of course, influenced by the values of each point in the distribution.

Table 3. National Income Distribution of Practitioners and Partners

Annual income	Under age 35 No. of offices	%	Over age 35 No. of offices	%
$ 5,000 to $ 7,500	197	25.2	166	9.3
7,500 to 10,000	247	31.6	348	19.5
10,000 to 12,500	170	21.7	353	19.7
12,500 to 15,000	101	12.9	301	16.9
15,000 to 20,000	45	5.8	316	17.7
Over $20,000	22	2.8	302	16.9
Total	782	100.0	1,786	100.0
25% pt.	$ 7,481		$ 9,515	
Median	9,460		12,716	
75% pt.	12,096		16,357	

Median income (before taxes) of partners and sole practitioners under the age of thirty-five was $9,460. Although 43 per cent of the younger men earned more than $10,000, the survey showed that 25 per cent of them were earning less than $7,500.

Perhaps one of the most significant facts revealed by the survey was the comparatively small differences among the median incomes reported for the four major regions of the country. As a matter of fact, less than $1,000 separated the median incomes of the older principals in any two regions and less than $500 for principals under thirty-five. This differential was appreciably less than existed within the legal, dental, and medical professions.[23]

Partners in offices with five or more accountants in cities with over 50,000 population seem more likely to earn incomes in excess of the median and a somewhat larger percentage of offices in the very large cities reported that their partners were in the over-$20,000 category. Despite this, there were indications that some practitioners and partners with smaller firms in small communities were able to earn incomes appreciably higher than the median for the whole profession. (See Table 4.)

To supplement this information, personal interviews were conducted in the spring of 1957 with twenty small and medium-size firms, ranging from individual practitioners to a firm of thirteen partners, in eight Midwestern, Eastern, and Southern cities. No attempt was made to select outstanding firms, but those interviewed were considered to be good examples of successful firms in their respective areas. Although the results have no statistical validity, they illustrate conditions within some smaller successful firms.

Annual incomes (before taxes) reported in these interviews ranged from $10,000 for a thirty-one-year-old junior partner in a small suburban office to $40,000 for the senior partners of two firms of moderate size. In addition to the fact that the incomes reported were generally higher than the national medians indicated above, the net income of the small-firm members

[23]Full details are available in Appendix A of Economics of an Accounting Practice Bulletin 1, *Incomes of Practicing Certified Public Accountants*, AICPA, 1957.

seemed to compare favorably with that of the larger local firms. For example, one individual practitioner earned about $25,000 per year and the members of a three-partner firm netted over $30,000 each.

MINIMUM INCOME REQUIREMENTS

While relatively small incomes may provide adequate satisfactions in unusual circumstances, it seems a reasonable generalization that CPAs in practice as partners or proprietors should earn more than bookkeepers employed by industry or noncertified staff accountants employed by other firms.

Bookkeepers in the New York metropolitan area averaged over $4,500 a year, with 25 per cent earning more than $5,200; in Houston, Texas, $5,200 was the average.[24] Annual salaries paid by public accounting firms, small and large, to inexperienced college graduates with a major in accounting frequently ranged from $4,200 to $4,800, and, at the time of the present writing, extend considerably higher. Many staff accountants with five years' experience were earning in the neighborhood of $7,000 a year with large firms. Most of the twenty smaller firms interviewed indicated that this was also true within their organizations. However, the AICPA study showed that principals under thirty-five in 25 per cent of the offices, and principals over thirty-five in 10 per cent of the offices averaged less than $7,500. (See Figure 2.)

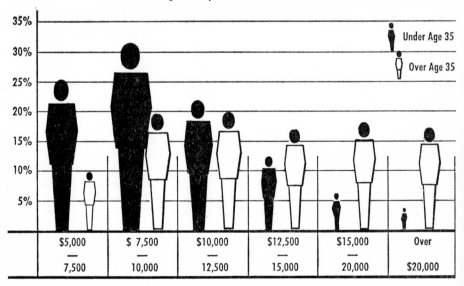

Figure 2. National Income Distribution of CPAs
Practicing as Proprietors or Partners—1955

[24]*Office Salaries: A Guide to 1957 Salary Rates,* National Office Management Association Survey Number 20.

Table 4. National Income Distribution of Practitioners and Partners According to Size of Office

Practitioners and partners under 35

Annual income $(000)	0-1 staff %	1 CPA 2-9 staff %	Total %	0-1 staff %	2-4 CPAs 2-4 staff %	2-4 CPAs 5+ staff %	Total %	0-4 staff %	5-9 CPAs 5+ staff %	Total %	10 or more CPAs %
5 to 7.5	41.7	23.3	36.9	37.0	17.4	10.5	23.7	8.2	5.9	7.0	7.7
7.5 to 10	32.5	31.5	32.3	29.4	36.0	29.8	32.6	32.7	27.5	30.0	30.8
10 to 12.5	14.2	26.0	17.2	20.3	25.9	24.6	23.7	26.5	23.5	25.0	19.2
12.5 to 15	8.7	15.1	10.4	9.8	13.8	19.3	13.1	16.3	19.6	18.0	15.4
15 to 20	1.9	1.4	1.8	2.8	2.1	14.0	4.1	14.3	17.6	16.0	11.5
Over 20	1.0	2.7	1.4	.7	4.8	1.8	2.8	2.0	5.9	4.0	15.4
Total	100.0	100.0	100.0	100.0	100.0	100.0	100.0	100.0	100.0	100.00	100.00
25% pt.	$ 6,485	$ 7,636	$ 6,634	$ 6,686	$ 8,024	$ 8,713	$ 7,603	$ 8,795	$ 9,241	$ 9,000	$ 8,906
Median	8,134	9,619	8,514	8,601	9,761	10,982	9,518	10,865	11,771	11,300	11,500
75% pt.	10,129	11,941	10,451	11,056	12,079	13,807	11,977	13,672	14,013	14,305	15,313

Practitioners and partners over 35

Annual income $(000)	0-1 staff %	1 CPA 2-9 staff %	Total %	0-1 staff %	2-4 CPAs 2-4 staff %	2-4 CPAs 5+ staff %	Total %	0-4 staff %	5-9 CPAs 5+ staff %	Total %	10 or more CPAs %
5 to 7.5	22.3	4.6	16.0	9.5	4.2	.8	5.7	—	—	—	—
7.5 to 10	29.2	26.4	28.3	25.5	10.9	4.1	15.4	4.6	3.1	3.7	3.8
10 to 12.5	21.3	22.9	21.8	22.0	21.2	9.1	19.6	10.3	13.1	12.0	—
12.5 to 15	13.5	21.5	16.3	18.0	20.1	14.9	18.5	20.7	15.4	17.5	7.5
15 to 20	9.2	14.8	11.2	14.2	24.3	28.9	21.2	25.3	25.4	25.3	22.7
Over 20	4.5	9.8	6.4	10.8	19.3	42.2	19.6	39.1	43.0	41.5	66.0
Total	100.0	100.0	100.0	100.0	100.0	100.0	100.0	100.0	100.0	100.0	100.0
25% pt.	$ 7,733	$ 9,433	$ 8,300	$ 9,038	$11,168	$14,340	$10,502	$13,715	$13,938	$13,832	$18,021
Median	9,866	12,077	10,661	11,724	14,201	18,643	13,759	17,841	18,636	18,318	20,000*
75% pt.	12,898	14,959	13,865	15,028	18,822	20,000*	18,430	20,000*	20,000*	20,000*	20,000*

*Indicates over 20,000.

A CPA in practice for himself or as a partner who, after the early years of establishing a practice, has been unable to command an income at least equal to that of experienced staff men might be wise to examine closely his own outlook for the future. What is his potential? Are his fees too low? Is he undervaluing his work? Can he justify professional fees for the type of work he currently does? Can he equip himself to render other services which will command higher fees? Is he personally constituted or experienced enough to administer an independent practice? If, upon examination, he is unable to make the necessary adjustments, he may find that his personal prospects are brighter as an employee of another firm or in a position with a business concern.

When the earnings of an individual practitioner or partner fall below the median for his group, he should make every effort to analyze the possible reasons and take whatever corrective action seems necessary.

CPA INCOME IN RELATION TO OTHER PROFESSIONS

Although comparisons between different professions are inconclusive, it is helpful to compare incomes of CPAs with others of roughly the same status in the community.

During the 1930's, surveys conducted by the U. S. Department of Commerce and analyzed by the National Bureau of Economic Statistics indicated that on a national basis, the practicing CPA led the other professions in net income.[25] Although the dollar differential was small, the rank of the professional practitioners at that time was: (1) CPAs; (2) lawyers; (3) physicians; (4) dentists.

Subsequently, physicians and dentists increased their earnings at such a rate that they came to hold first and second positions. By 1955, the mean average annual income of practicing physicians was over $18,000 and that of independent dentists about $12,500. Lawyers in practice averaged about $10,200 in 1954 and probably earned about $500 more in 1955. The mean average income of the more experienced CPA practitioners and partners could only be estimated from the AICPA study but it appeared to be on a par with, or slightly higher than, the dentist average. This would indicate that the mean average income of *all* practicing CPAs fell somewhere between that of the lawyers and the dentists, in the number three position.

Thus it appears that the incomes of CPAs and lawyers have not been increasing at a rate comparable to the other professions.

A CPA's earnings should follow the professional man's normal income pattern, which is characterized by a relatively low income during the early years of training and establishing a practice. It then rises at a rather steady rate, begins to level off during the forties and declines somewhat as he approaches retirement age.

[25]"Income of Independent Professional Practitioners," *Survey of Current Business,* April 1938. Milton Friedman and Simon Kuznets, *Income from Independent Professional Practice,* National Bureau of Economic Research, New York, 1945.

The pattern of distribution for the other professions, as illustrated in Figure 3, has an interesting implication. On the surface it appears that there may be a correlation between the age a professional man enters practice and the age at which he reaches his peak earnings. The bulk of the doctors and dentists are sole practitioners, who often start practicing shortly after they have met their formal educational and internship requirements. As the graph shows, dentists (whose training period is shorter) reach their peak five years earlier than physicians. On the other hand, law is frequently practiced in partnership form. Although medical training takes longer than law, a lawyer is more apt to spend a number of years as a staff man before being admitted as a partner.

As indicated by the graph, a lawyer's peak years seem to be his middle fifties. Of course, other factors have a strong effect, including the number of practitioners in the field (overcrowding tends to delay the peak period and reduce the over-all income level) and the differences in the type of services rendered. However, lacking information on the CPA pattern, it seems logical to assume that it more closely resembles that of the lawyers than that of the physicians or dentists. Accounting and law are usually practiced under the same type of organizational structure and their services bear more re-

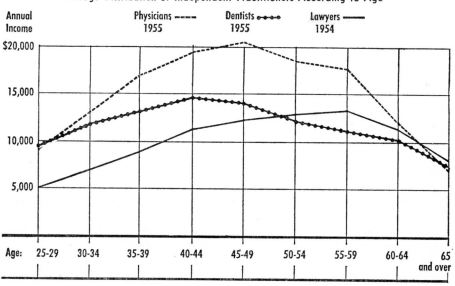

Figure 3. Incomes of Physicians,* Dentists,† and Lawyers‡
Average Distribution of Independent Practitioners According to Age

*This is a projection of the 1949 distribution published in *Survey of Current Business,* (July 1951) on the basis of the increased average incomes reported in the 1956 Survey by *Medical Economics* magazine.

†*1956 Survey of Dental Practice,* Bureau of Economic Research and Statistics, American Dental Association.

‡"Income of Lawyers in the Postwar Period," *Survey of Current Business,* December 1956.

semblance to each other than they do to the medical-dental field.

Incomes of the other professions can be found in Table 5 so that the reader can compare his earnings with those of the other professional men.

Table 5. Net Incomes of Other Professions in the United States*

Lawyers (1954)

Mean	$10,294
Median	7,554

Dentists (1955)

Mean	12,480
Median	11,533

Physicians (1955 median)

General practice	14,817
Specialty practice	18,010
All types of practice	16,017

*"Incomes of Lawyers in the Postwar Period," *Survey of Current Business,* December 1956. Survey conducted by the Office of Business Economics, U.S. Department of Commerce, in co-operation with the American Bar Association; *1956 Survey of Dental Practice,* American Dental Association, November 1956; "Yardsticks for Your Practice," based on *Medical Economics 8th Quadrennial Survey, Medical Economics,* October 1956.

COMPARISON WITH BUSINESS EXECUTIVES

Earnings of the business executive, with a background similar to that of the practicing accountant, can also be a valuable guide in trying to determine what a CPA should be worth.

The available studies have some shortcomings in that executives who have had accounting training but have assumed other duties within their organizations are difficult to identify. In addition to the variables affecting incomes in both the professions and industry, earnings of executives are affected by the type of industry with which they are associated. Size of the company is, however, probably the biggest single factor influencing the compensation of financial executives.

In small manufacturing companies, with sales under $2 million a year, the top financial executive averaged about $15,000 a year. When sales reached the $10 to $25 million bracket, his income just about doubled and continued to rise with the size of the company. As a general rule, the earnings of the chief financial officer, usually a vice-president, were from one-third to one-half of those of the company's chief executive.[26]

Between 1950 and 1954 compensation of the top financial executive seems to have increased by roughly 25 per cent. This same period saw a rise of more than one-third in the earnings of both the officer in the number two financial position and the internal auditor.[27]

[26]*Executive Compensation Service, Top Management Survey,* American Management Association, New York, 1955.
[27]*Executive Compensation, A Dartnell Survey,* The Dartnell Corporation, Chicago, 1955.

THE EFFECT OF INFLATION ON THE CPA

Everyone knows that the purchasing power of the dollar has been declining, but few people have a clear idea of the extent to which it actually affects their own *real* income. The worth of an employee in private industry is not wholly determined by the individual but is a reflection of what his company will pay for his services. This is, in part, determined by the competition for these services and the ability of the company to pay for them. During inflationary periods, as competition increases for most classes of workers and as the ability to pay rises with a company's increased dollar earnings, some adjustment in the income of the employee may take place almost automatically. The professional man, who generally sets his own rates, does not have a guide to his own value; to a large extent he can only estimate his worth to his client. As long as his personal tax return shows an increase in income from year to year, the professional man may often feel that he is making progress.

According to a number of economic indices, including the Consumer's Price Index, a man needed 20 per cent more income in 1957 (before taxes) than he required in the 1947-49 period to maintain the same standard of living. This figure rises even more if the increase in the personal tax rate is considered. The CPA who was earning $10,000 in 1949 (after taxes) would have had to earn more than $12,000 in 1957 (after taxes) before he could assume that he was making any financial progress. The extent to which the practicing CPA has been able to keep abreast of rising costs is not known, but the available evidence indicates that the net income of many firms is lagging behind inflation. One of the smaller firms interviewed reported that its gross income had increased by $50,000 from 1950 to 1957. On the surface, this certainly looks like progress. Further examination revealed, however, that overhead costs had risen by $40,000 over the same period. Rather than making progress, the members of this firm had barely maintained their 1949 position in terms of real income before taxes and had actually lost ground after taxes. None of the firms interviewed felt that they had kept ahead of their rising costs, despite the fact that some of them had increased their fee scales by 50 per cent since 1950.

Other professions have been more successful in solving this problem. The average lawyer's net income increased 28 per cent between 1949 and 1954, while that of the dentist rose by more than 62 per cent during the 1948-1955 period. Real income of physicians—that is, purchasing power—increased over 80 per cent between 1940 and 1954.

Part of this greater success may be due to the fact that these professions net a considerably higher percentage on their gross billing than does the accountant. Physicians average 64 per cent of their gross, lawyers 61 per cent, and dentists 57 per cent. Even the most successful CPA firms seem to run considerably less than this. (The highest figure given by the firms interviewed was 45 per cent. Some of the others indicated their net to be 35 to 40 per cent of their gross billings.[28] Although there are no current

[28]These net figures include the partners' draw or salary. The firms interviewed generally seemed to net 20 to 25% on work performed by staff members.

statistics on this subject, it is possible that the average for the profession is considerably less than this. Therefore, a doctor, dentist, or lawyer does not have to raise his fees as much as a practicing CPA in order to achieve the same net increase in personal income.

Much of the problem of the CPA's higher overhead lies in the fact that some of his costs have been increasing at a much faster rate than the general cost of living. This is especially true of staff salaries, which are usually not a major factor in the other professions. Beginning salaries of inexperienced college graduates increased approximately 75 per cent between 1950 and 1955. This has forced a rise in staff salaries generally and has narrowed the income differential between staff and partners or proprietors. It should not be regarded as satisfactory even to maintain a constant level of real income.

THE TIME ELEMENT IN EVALUATING INCOME

A professional practitioner may mislead himself if he believes his income to be satisfactory, but habitually puts in excessively long hours of "chargeable" time to produce it. This is especially true as the practice grows. Proper planning, administration, and supervision become even more necessary and

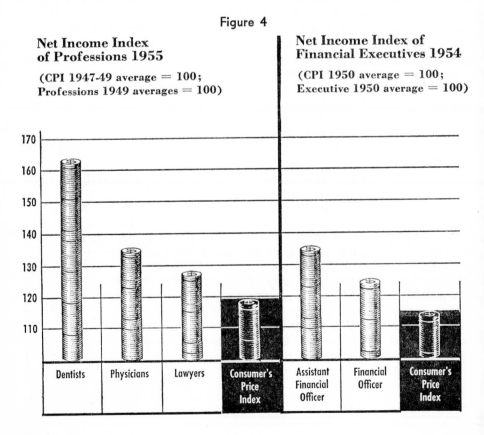

Figure 4

time consuming. Maintenance of satisfactory client relations, including a thorough understanding of their financial problems, becomes more difficult as their numbers increase. As a firm becomes established, it is expected that the principals will do their share in community service projects. In addition, with the complexities involved in modern accounting, a practitioner must keep abreast of current developments—studying technical journals, attending seminars, exchanging ideas with fellow practitioners, or engaging in other professional activities which will enable him to render the best possible service to his clients.

All of these things require time. With only twenty-four hours in a day, where can this time be found? In all too many cases it isn't found and the practitioner loses by it. Where it has been found, it has come either through sacrificing the portion of the day which ought to be devoted to rest and relaxation or a reduction in "chargeable" hours. The latter, of course, is more desirable—but to be accomplished effectively without a long-term reduction in income, it requires thoughtful planning and proper scheduling of work within the office. It may also necessitate adjustments in fees.

While most professional and business men put in more than forty hours a week on some aspects of their work, the most successful seem to devote a substantial portion of their time to the areas cited above. Some practicing CPAs feel that senior partners, depending on individual circumstances and the organization of the firm, should limit their "chargeable" time to roughly an average of twenty-six hours per week (1,300 hours a year). Dentists, as an example of other professions, average 39.4 hours a week of "productive" time (chairside and laboratory) and 3.8 other hours in the office for a total weekly average of 43.2 hours actually devoted to their practices.

There is some indication that the "chargeable" hours put in by the practicing CPA have declined somewhat during the past ten years, but the extent of this is not known.

Nevertheless, a practitioner may not truly be "keeping even" with the rest of the world if he commonly works fifty or more hours a week on billable engagements to produce annual income comparable to that of his contemporaries. Without giving sufficient attention to the other activities necessary for professional success, his future growth may be retarded.

It is evident—at least on the basis of the practitioner's income potential—that accounting has become a truly national profession. It wasn't too many years ago that the great majority of successful CPAs were concentrated in the East or in a few of the major cities in other parts of the country. Whatever the reason—decentralization of industry, the continuing westerly population shift, the general expansion of the economy, greater recognition of the value of professional accounting services, or a combination of these and other factors—the fact remains that geography, as such, is no longer a significant factor in the income differential which exists among practicing CPAs.

The incomes of CPA practitioners with several staff members or partners do, however, seem to be generally higher than those of sole practitioners.

There also seems to be a definite, but gradual, economic advantage to practices as they are located in larger communities, up to 100,000 population. From this point there is a definite leveling off and community size itself does not seem to have as much significance for practices in cities larger than this.

As far as the over-all income picture is concerned, CPAs in practice as principals do not compare as favorably with the other professions as they once did. In fact, the professional accountant, in many cases, does not seem to be keeping pace with inflation. The income level of not only the other professions but business executives as well, seems to be rising more rapidly than that of the CPA.

A large percentage of practicing CPAs (perhaps 20 per cent) are earning incomes which must be considered substandard for professional men, since they do not compare favorably with those of staff accountants of accounting firms, beginning college graduates, and in some cases bookkeepers.

Many CPAs, however, in small offices in small and large cities, have demonstrated their ability to earn incomes which are higher than the medians for CPAs, doctors, lawyers, and dentists. These practitioners demonstrate that the CPAs who operate small firms in small towns need not resign themselves to smaller incomes than those obtained by their big-firm, big-city colleagues.

The above material has merely been presented as a guide to what income can be reasonably expected today from the professional practice of accounting. It will have accomplished its purpose if it encourages readers to evaluate their own earning capacity and fix in their own minds, at least tentatively, figures which they believe to be reasonable income "targets" at the present stage of their professional careers.

Staff Personnel

A Practical Staff Program

■ MANY FIRMS HAVE their own particular ideas as to personnel practices. This is a natural result of variations in the size of the firms, the services rendered by them, their geographical location, and the personalities of the partners. It would be impractical, therefore, to suggest a detailed personnel program designed to meet the needs of every accounting firm.

But there are certain basic principles which characterize the approach of those who feel they have met with more than average success in coping with staff problems. Any firm, regardless of its size or special problems, ought to be able to test them against its own policies and practices.

These factors will be approached in a five-step program:

1. What do people expect—and need—to get from their work?
2. What objectives must an accounting firm establish to meet these needs and expectations, and thereby reach its own goals?
3. What policies with respect to pay, benefits, training, etc., should a firm establish to enable it to achieve those objectives?
4. How can a firm organize to put those policies into effect?
5. What specific practices, procedures, and techniques—based on the previous four points—would best implement a firm's program so that it gets results in terms of employing and keeping good staff men?

THE NEEDS AND EXPECTATIONS OF EMPLOYEES

Of course, any staff man expects not only a reasonable starting salary but a real opportunity to increase his earnings as he increases his value to the firm. Yet economic incentives are not all that matter. Sociologists in recent years have found other powerful social and psychological incentives. These incentives are particularly significant in a profession whose employees traditionally serve the public interest without an excessive concern for personal gain. Among these noneconomic motivations are:

Emotional security. An employee needs to feel that the partners are good managers; that if he does his work according to the standards of the firm, he will be reasonably secure in his employment; that he gets a fair break in terms of advancement; that he knows where he fits in, what is going on and why.

Belonging, sharing. A sense that one shares in the over-all activities of a firm, that one "belongs" to the organization for which he works is important to every individual. A man needs to feel that he is an accepted and trusted member of his firm. Even more than that, he wants to know that he pulls his own weight and shares in the over-all activities. He wants to be consulted about things that affect him; he wants to know that his ideas and the way he feels are taken into consideration.

Achievement. A man needs to know that he is doing important work which uses his training and challenges his ability; that his work is significant, interesting, varied; that he is making a professional contribution to his firm, to the client, and to the interests of the general public.

Recognition. It is important in terms of work motivation to give a man a word of appreciation or a sense of having done a creditable job. He wishes to be treated as an important person; one who can progress as far and as fast as his performance warrants; one who has status in the firm, in the profession, and in the community.

Provisions to satisfy these basic motivations contribute to a man's feeling of *self-respect and personal dignity.* A person likes to be treated as a mature individual; one who is respected; one who does not have to worry about saving face to protect his status.

These are the needs of grown men—not children. There are still some business and professional men who think these things are theoretical and impractical. Others admit their reality but feel "you can't afford to be soft in business." However, these needs are often more powerful incentives than material rewards.

It is admittedly difficult for the top executive to take these emotional forces into account in managing his organization. It requires constant self-discipline to keep in mind the importance to each staff member of his personal sense of security, achievement, belonging, and self-respect. It means thinking in another person's terms.

But the practical-minded executive knows that these needs and drives are essential elements in all business relationships involving people. It is not out of soft-heartedness that top managements in progressive corporations throughout the country make determined efforts to satisfy the emotional needs of their employees. It is just good business.

There seems little reason to doubt that it would be profitable for every accounting firm to check its personnel policies and practices against these work incentives, and to determine the extent to which it is satisfying them.

THE OBJECTIVES OF THE FIRM

Management, no less than its employees, must have a set of career goals. The accounting firm needs to know where it is going and how it is going to get there—and these questions of professional growth ought to concern every member of a firm, from the top partners down to the newest staff member.

One of the best ways for an organization to think through its objectives is to put down in writing a set of guideposts for all of its executives and employees. Here are a series of suggestions for the objectives that a progressive firm might include in its program:

1. The three chief aims of a firm are: (a) to serve clients effectively; (b) to protect the interests of the public; and (c) to earn a reasonable, satisfactory income.

2. To achieve these aims, it is necessary for a firm to satisfy the emotional and material needs of the people who share in its work.

3. There must be competent managerial direction for the firm to attract and retain qualified, ambitious people.

4. A firm must constantly improve its effectiveness. This can be done only through systematically developing the effectiveness of its professional staff. The proper development of staff will strengthen present and future performance, secure and develop the necessary number and quality of new employees for future needs, and guarantee each qualified individual the training and advancement essential to his growth.

This is only a suggested list. However, in one form or another, most of these ideas are reflected in the objectives of forward-looking business firms today. For a public accounting firm which has both professional responsibility and economic goals, most of these objectives would seem to be essential.

PERSONNEL POLICIES

The existence of an over-all management policy on personnel practices is inevitable. In some organizations these policies may be implicit, and evidenced only through the daily actions of the partners. In the long run, however, it will be more effective for a firm to be explicit about its personnel policies—to think through in written form its basic attitudes in these nine areas: general policies; employment; promotion and advancement; retirement and separation; pay; benefits; working conditions; training and development; communication.

Personnel policies are not developed in a vacuum. Before they are finally adopted, it is wise to check them against the needs of employees discussed above; to check them for consistency with the objectives of the firm; and to check them against each other for internal consistency.

THE ORGANIZATION OF THE FIRM

The pressure of client demands can result in situations where the task of staff development is either slighted or camouflaged under the assumption that "we are *all* responsible for developing staff people."

It is good practice for a firm to assign the function of professional staff development to a single individual, regardless of the size of the firm itself. In a large organization this may well be a full-time job. In a smaller firm, the person responsible for staff development may have other responsibilities as well. The important thing is to delegate the responsibility for staff development to someone so that it does not get fragmented or buried under the pressure of daily work.

The assignment of this responsibility to a specific individual does not necessarily release the other executives of the firm from considering it as their charge, too. But even in a firm with no more than two or three partners, it is important to clarify the responsibilities of all concerned with respect to development of the professional staff.

There are varying responsibilities for staff development at varying levels within the firm.

Partners. The chief function of the partners is to set the tone and create the climate in which staff development can best flourish. On the operative level, they determine the policies and needs of the firm; they establish or approve over-all plans of action for meeting these needs; they assign responsibility to senior members of the staff for carrying out the program; they follow up and monitor the results.

Partners demonstrate through their own behavior the high standards of performance and character required for advancement in the career of public accounting. Whether they realize it or not—and whether or not it may embarrass them personally—they can and do serve as a basic source of inspiration to the men who work for them.

Senior accountants and other supervisors. With the help of the executive who is in over-all charge of the training and development program, it is the function of the senior accountants and other supervisory staff members to set up the definite training plan for staff members. In addition to working with younger employees to train them in practical accounting work, supervisors should contribute personally something to the professional growth of the younger men.

It is the function of supervisory employees to see to it that the experience of staff members is gradually broadened. This can be done by delegating assignments and responsibilities of increasing difficulty to each staff member in order; or by arranging for special projects that will carry the staff member beyond the scope of his regular work.

Reasonable standards must be established against which the developing performance of a staff member can be measured. It is important for the staff member to understand these standards and know how he is progressing.

Finally, it should be the responsibility of supervisory employees to give whatever assistance may be necessary to staff members in solving problems arising from job experiences. This is only a small part of the supervisors' over-all responsibility to help each individual advance to the full limits of his potential.

The staff member himself. Every employee has responsibilities in connection with his own career development. He must, for example, determine for himself his goals in the firm and in the profession. This must be accompanied by a realistic self-appraisal that matches his own abilities against his desires. In doing so, the staff member will find it necessary to equate the two. It, therefore, becomes his responsibility to learn, practice, and work until he masters every aspect of each new assignment.

Finally, the individual staff member has a responsibility to undertake off-the-job activities, on his own initiative, which will contribute to his personal and professional growth.

PROCEDURES AND PRACTICES

Having examined the needs of the employees and the objectives of the firm, established its personnel policies, and assigned responsibilities for carrying them out, the firm is now ready to consider some of the specific methods by which it can get and keep competent personnel. Here is a partial list:

1. Take an inventory of:
   a. What the firm is doing now
   b. The talents of its people
   c. The future growth of the firm
2. Determine the present and long-range needs of the firm for professional staff via:
   a. A five- or ten-year plan, to the extent practicable
   b. In the framework of this plan, year-by-year needs
3. Examine exactly what the firm is in a position to offer a potential candidate in such areas as:
   a. Specific opportunity for advancement
   b. Reasonably competitive pay
   c. Fringe benefits in terms of financial security and professional advantages
   d. Pleasant working conditions
   e. A training plan which will help a staff member grow
   f. The reputation and growth potential of the firm itself
4. Establish a definite plan of action which will meet the firm's needs as determined in "2" above. The plan should be simple, direct, highly personal, and systematic. Recruiting and training activity goes on all the

time; the real question is whether the activity is effective or not. The removal of any barriers to the development of staff employees, and the establishment of an atmosphere conducive to an individual's progress and to the progress of the firm, can turn mere activity into purposeful growth.

5. Develop a definite plan for recruiting to fill the firm's needs at the beginning level. Such a plan begins with the decision on where and when the firm will concentrate its recruiting efforts. Firms successful in obtaining competent new employees maintain close personal contact with their sources of manpower—such as colleges—on a permanent basis, and do not come in and go out of the job market solely because of immediate needs. A firm that becomes known as an "in-and-outer" diminishes its chances of getting top-flight men in good times. Internship, part-time, and summer employment programs help cultivate sources of talent and serve as screening devices for future placement.

Next in the job program should be a systematic approach to the job interview. The good interviewer—as well as the interviewee—is aware not only of the importance of the interview but of its pitfalls for those who have not carefully prepared for it. The interviewer should realize that not only the candidate but the firm is "on trial" during the interview. The object of an interview is not to harry the applicant, but to obtain and to give information on a mature and friendly basis. It should be remembered that the interviewer represents the firm. He reflects the attitudes that the candidate should expect to face if he joins the firm.

The decision on a job applicant should not be made hastily. A "quick hire" is apt to get only average and below-average candidates. Good men come harder. A visit to the firm's office is becoming almost universal practice.

In making final selection of a candidate all available evidence should be used—interviews with more than one member of the firm; college and work references (worth investigating in person or by telephone rather than by mail, and before, not after hiring); college grades; test results where available.

6. Set up an adequate employee-orientation system, including employment records, which are prerequisites to a systematic approach to staff training and development. A new staff member should have information on the firm's objectives, policies, and the relationship between his productivity and compensation. It is wise to assign the new employee to a supervisor who is genuinely interested in and capable of helping him make a good start.

7. Set up an efficient program of staff training and development. This involves the training of seniors and supervisors in techniques of developing new employees and appraising their performance. It includes a planned approach to on-the-job training, and a consideration of special off-the-job courses both within and outside the firm. It also includes participation in civic and professional activities which not only adds to the staff members' status but furthers his training and development; giving him work which will tax his ability as early as possible; showing him how to look at each engagement as a whole; using the vacations or absences of others as an

opportunity to expose the junior to more responsible tasks; providing the opportunity for study to keep up with new developments; and giving him special or start-to-finish assignments on his own as soon as possible.

8. Maintain effective follow-up on new staff members. Not only top partners but the staff member himself should be kept in periodic touch with his development. A good supervisor discusses an individual's over-all performance with him both as a matter of keeping the staff man informed of his progress and as a means of improving his own ability to appraise personnel performance. This approach also makes possible two-way communication—an exchange of opinions between the firm and the staff member. There should be an early opportunity for staff men to sit in on conferences between partners and clients.

Salary reviews should be made at specific periods. Progress reviews should include not only what the firm thinks of the new man but what the staff member himself thinks about where he is going. Asking him to appraise himself and his progress sometimes brings to light stronger, sterner appraisal than if it is done by his supervisor. Finally, a follow-up program should allow for special attention to exceptionally talented people from whom the accounting firm expects unusual progress.

9. Establish various "status" considerations such as personal work areas, the use of business cards, memberships in professional societies, the solicitation of suggestions and ideas from the junior employees.

Other considerations include establishing professional titles equivalent to or comparable with supervisory titles in business; periodic reports to staff members on how the firm as a whole is doing; early profit-sharing participation in earnings of the firm; and reducing regimentation to a minimum.

The tasks assigned often have status significance. The intellectual capacity of the accounting graduate is substantially above average. The firm looks for intellectual competence as a major factor in selecting the candidate. However, to a degree beyond that experienced by his fellow graduates, the accountant often finds himself engaged in work of a clerical character without much opportunity to see the relationship between what he is doing and the professional contribution of the firm to the client.

The December 1956 issue of the *Journal of College Placement* contains a report by the University of Washington on "The Job Satisfactions of Business Administration Graduates" some seven years after graduation. Those in both public and industrial accounting were significantly less satisfied with current employment than those in other fields. "Graduates who have made careers in accounting work have not found their jobs to be turning out as they had expected at least with regard to the factors covered by this study." Accountants were most dissatisfied in areas of *advancement, interest* in work, *status* in the organization, and *working conditions.*

Organization of an Accounting Firm

ORGANIZATION CHART

■ THE SIZE OF an accounting firm often determines the degree to which a definite organization chart and outline of the functions of the personnel has been perfected. Nevertheless, a classifying of personnel and an outlining of the duties of each member of the staff are found in many small firms. The need for an organization chart or some similar outline of the duties and relationships of staff members is particularly evident in large firms having several offices. Even in a medium-sized firm, a chart of the organization will be particularly useful, especially if more than one office is maintained.

A chart, or other form of organization outline, is important chiefly as an aid to efficient management. Obviously, the majority of the staff members must be engaged mostly in carrying on the accounting work—making audits, preparing tax returns, assisting with systems and special problems, etc. But time must be spent by some one or more persons in administrative functions. For example, the extent and terms of engagements must be arranged with the clients. Assignments of staff to jobs must be made and the supervision of these jobs may need to be delegated. Working papers must be reviewed, as must the audit reports, tax returns, and other reports of the engagements. Responsibility for the prompt typing and preparing of the accounting reports for delivery cannot be entirely delegated to the typing department; even in this work the final decisions and responsibility for efficient results rest upon an administrative executive or executives of the accounting firm. Also, the authority and responsibility for many other duties of management must be assigned, such as: determining the fee to be charged for each completed engagement; purchasing supplies, equipment, books, tax, and other services; hiring staff and office assistants; developing staff-training methods and programs; engaging in research in accounting theory and auditing techniques in order to improve the practices and procedures of the firm. In an office having several partners, each partner undertakes part of the administrative functions. However, individual abilities will vary and it may be that there are partners who should be engaged chiefly in the accounting work rather than in administrative functions. Sometimes there are partners who are most able in supervising effectively the accounting engagements but who lack the ability and the desire to undertake any of the office work or the staff-management functions.

Even the sole practitioner operating without any permanent staff will find that he has both the functions of conducting his practice (that is, doing the work) and of administering his practice (making decisions not related to the work on individual engagements). Perhaps the administrative functions will be so intermingled with his work functions that he will fail to recognize and devote enough time to them. But, if his practice is to grow and if a staff of accountants and office people is to be acquired, he will find that more and more time must be spent in administrative work.

CLASSIFICATION OF THE STAFF

In classifying the accounting personnel of a public accounting office, five main groups or classes are usually recognized. These are: partners or principals; managers or supervisors; senior or in-charge accountants; semi-senior accountants; and junior accountants. In small firms and sometimes in medium-sized firms if there are many partners or principals there may be no need for "managers" or "supervisors." However, if there is only one principal (a sole practitioner) with a large staff, many managers and/or supervisors may be needed.

Within each main class there may be several grades. Often there are one or more senior partners, with junior partners varying in rank and in duties and authority. The sole practitioner and the partners are usually referred to as "principals," but some large firms have principals who are not partners. These principals have authority and internal responsibilities similar to partners. Although lacking ownership and the liabilities of partners, they usually share in profits under contractual arrangements, they are authorized to sign reports and other documents for the firm, and they act for and in place of the partners on many occasions.

Usually the majority of the functions of management are performed by the partners or principals, but some may be delegated to the managers or supervisors, such as interviewing and hiring staff assistants, making job assignments, and conducting staff-training programs. For the most part the managers and supervisors are in charge of engagements in the case of audits, or are in charge of separate departments such as the tax department or the systems department if separate departments are maintained for these services. In supervising engagements they usually plan the work to be performed and direct it either by calling frequently at the client's office during the engagement, or by staying on the job in the case of large audits, or by contacting frequently (by telephone or otherwise) the senior accountant who is in charge of the job. Also, they review the working papers and the report to determine that the work is complete and up to standard.

Seniors, semi-seniors, and juniors are the three customary classes of staff accountants who work under the managers, partners, and other principals in carrying out the audit engagements, preparing tax returns, etc. Actually there may be several grades in each classification, such as "top" senior, "medium" senior, "light" senior, and similar classifications for juniors and sometimes for semi-seniors. Inasmuch as continual advancement in position and responsibility is expected by both the employee and employer, there may be many more grades or stages of development within each group, particularly in the minds of their associates and superiors. These multiple or refined classifications are not usually formalized by a salary adjustment for each upgrading while the young man progresses. However, in a few instances, firms have formally classified their staff members as A, B, or C within each of these three major groups and apparently maintain these classes for salary purposes.

From the standpoint of management, an important reason for a chart or outline of the staff is the avoidance of situations that are embarrassing or discouraging to the individuals. Whether or not a formal chart exists, each staff member constantly makes his own mental chart and places himself on it, and each staff member is likely to have strong feelings of pride and jealousy. For instance, to assign a senior to work under another senior, unless the latter is recognized as being well above the former, is likely to result in mental anguish for the senior so assigned and may also give the second senior a false feeling of importance. This might be overcome in most instances if the reason for such assignment is explained to those involved at the time of making the assignment.

Staff Requirements

TYPES OF PERSONNEL

■ FUNDAMENTALLY, staff needs depend upon two factors. How much work can reasonably be estimated as in hand or in prospect? What is the nature of the work? The answers to these questions almost automatically reveal what grades of personnel are needed and the number of individuals in each classification.

Several national firms are continuing to recruit outstanding liberal arts graduates who agree to study accounting at night school. One of them is interviewing business school graduates who are not accounting majors but have taken courses in elementary, intermediate, and cost accounting. There is no indication of any significant increase in the hiring of women accounting majors for assignment to audit staffs.

Most new employees of accounting firms have had little or no previous accounting experience. The most common reason for a firm's preference for an inexperienced person is its desire to train new men in the firm's own practices. Another reason is the possibility of internal friction among present staff members if a new man is brought in "over their heads." However, some firms, particularly smaller ones, hire at all levels. There are three chief reasons for this:

1. Some firms have been expanding so rapidly that they have not had

time to train fully their less experienced men and have been obliged to hire semi-seniors and in-charge accountants in order to get the work done.

2. Because of the nature of their practices many smaller firms occasionally find it difficult to make a separate assignment of "junior work," and entire engagements are often handled by one man.

3. A few firms have felt it was more economical to hire men with some experience, since a beginner cannot always be fully occupied with chargeable work. With the narrowing differential between the salaries of inexperienced and trained men, these firms believe that they will do better to employ a man who can be productive in a minimum time, rather than a recent college graduate who cannot be expected to pay his way for some months or longer.

One firm prefers to hire somewhat older men without much public accounting experience. Its reason: The higher salaries are soon offset by fees because a more mature man can assume responsibility quicker, and the client is apt to have more confidence in him.

Typical attitudes of other firms:

> We used to hire men with little or no accounting training and be able to put them to work right away doing a lot of detail work. We don't have as much of that kind of work today. We need men who understand what accounting is all about, men who can assume responsibility quickly and justify the high salaries we have to pay now.

> Formerly we hired only juniors with one or two years of experience. Recently we have had to go after semi-seniors and seniors, because of the poor quality of younger men. It's not that most of the better men are going with the big firms; there just seem to be fewer choice beginners than we had in the late 1940's.

> There is no limit to the number of people we would take if we could get them. If we could keep more of them long enough so that we could have more in-charge accountants, we could take still more juniors. Growth possibilities in our profession are unlimited.

> I am losing men almost as fast as I can hire them. They quit as soon as they get a few years of experience and I can't bring the new men along fast enough to fill the gap.

These replies indicate the existence of four major problems concerning the staff needs of public accounting firms:

1. The demand for accounting graduates continues to be substantial, and in general exceeds the available supply of acceptable candidates.

2. The quality of applicants, in general, is not as high as most firms would like.

3. A large number of accounting majors are not interested in public accounting at all; many others regard it merely as a stepping stone to a position in private industry.

4. The increasing need for more accountants capable of providing a professional accounting service can be met only if an increasing number of young men with a high degree of ability can be attracted to and retained by the profession.

SEASONAL PROBLEMS

A particular condition has long existed that has made it very difficult for accounting firms to organize their arrangements as to compensation and utilization of staff members along regular and permanent lines. Twice a year they have been confronted with end-of-year and midyear peaks of business and in the intervals between these there are severe recessions from a normal tempo. During the rush periods it has been common not only to have permanent personnel work many extra hours under pressure but also to employ temporary and less-qualified, less-experienced assistants at special (sometimes per-diem) rates of pay who are rarely fully versed in the policies and practices of the firms taking them on. In the slack periods there has often been the equally disturbing problem of releasing some fairly well-skilled and specially trained staff members and of contending with excessive idle time for the irreducible staff nucleus retained.

Unless such prolonged and disruptive deviations can be reduced to a controllable and modest minimum, it is impossible to set up or to count upon orderly and effective personnel cost and utilization. Fortunately, the profession has made progress toward maintaining staff requirements on an even keel through the year.

Peak-season remedies. While semiannual concentrations of business constitute a major problem, firms have been able to reduce appreciably the intensity of these rush periods by spreading the work over longer periods.

Four specific measures are indicated to be most helpful. The two most effective and most widely used are (1) inducing clients to adopt their natural business year, and (2) doing a considerable amount of interim work. Also beneficial and employed to a lesser degree are (3) making quarterly or semiannual audits, and (4) making monthly interim examinations.

While firms may encourage their clients to adopt a natural business year, they frequently obtain an unfavorable reaction to the suggestion. This often represents the cases where there is no clearly marked natural business year. Probably another adverse factor is the definite tendency for single-product companies to seek the economic stability inherent in diversification by adding other products. In some of these instances the natural business year may be subject to change or the calendar year may seem to offer an easier choice. Nevertheless, the trend definitely is toward greater use of the natural business year. Where it is clearly advantageous to a client to change to a natural business year, reluctance to change is usually the only obstacle the accountant has to overcome. Where the client is a new concern and a natural fiscal year is logical, even this obstacle disappears.

Considered practically as important as the adoption of a natural business year, the doing of as much interim work as possible on year-end and midyear engagements is so generally accepted that in the planning of audits such preliminary work is usually outlined and scheduled as essential procedure.

Slack-season remedies. Decreasing the intensity of rush periods by spreading the work over more time lessens the slack periods to the extent to which the rearranged work can be allocated to the slack season. Further filling in of the slack season is possible in several ways.

Perhaps the most effective of these is the expansion of services to clients. A relatively high proportion of clients fail to use the services of their accountants to the most advantageous extent. It is always a legitimate and often a very vital part of accountants' formal or informal reports to clients to indicate areas of possible improvement in the clients' affairs through greater use of the accountant's skills. The most obvious instances of this type are, of course, the cases where clients stipulate limited services which are definitely inadequate to achieve the results they desire or require. Failure to point out such inadequacy is nothing less than dereliction of professional obligation on the part of the accountant.

Most of these possible additional services can be done readily in times of least activity. Some examples like these come easily to mind: (1) the preparation of manuals of procedure to improve the efficiency of a client's organization and implement control of principles governing operations; (2) the periodic review of all established control procedures from the handling of raw materials through all payroll phases, including billing and shipping; (3) the review and reclassification of factory burden rates; (4) the review of problems involved in personnel changes, including realignment and reallocation of duties; (5) the development and continued revision of reports to management from the client's internal accounting organization; and (6) the analyses of business trends and results, and comparison with trends of competitors. The development of management services as a regular function of the public accounting profession has expanded this area to the point where the slack season can now be most fruitfully utilized to the benefit of clients.

A certain amount of time of staff men during periods of slack business can be utilized for training and development of the staff. A staff member's usual work contributes materially to his training, but there are other phases of training, such as study, staff classes, reviews, reading of articles, and so on, that slack periods are best suited for from the important standpoint of available time. Slack periods comprise the ideal occasion for a critical examination of recent intensive activity with a view to extracting from such a survey ideas for improvement of performance in future periods of greater activity.

Another interesting possibility meriting consideration is the ever-present possibility of making available some staff members to certain clients for temporary use on special projects as to which such clients would normally neither require permanent personnel nor be in a position to refer the projects to their accountants for handling on a regular fee basis.

The problem presented by the alternating "feast-and-famine" aspects once distressingly common in the public accounting field cannot be said to have been cleared up completely. But there has been a distinctly noticeable flattening out of the sharp up-and-down curves representing deviation from normal activity within the year. This is due in good part to the measures just discussed.

Recruiting

SOURCES FROM WHICH TO OBTAIN STAFF MEMBERS

■ AS TO THE SOURCE of obtaining staff members, the most satisfactory is likely to be colleges. The success with any individual college may depend upon (1) whether its graduates are well trained, and (2) whether the public accounting firm has a contact or contacts with persons who are adept at placing graduates in the most suitable positions. Other sources used are:

1. Unsolicited applications
2. Recommendations of friends
3. Recommendations of clients
4. Private employment agencies
5. Newspaper advertising
6. Former temporary staff personnel
7. Business schools—commercial
8. Recommendations of other accounting firms
9. Professional accounting organizations (national, state, and local)
10. Former members of permanent staff
11. Federal and state employment services

As to the frequency of use of these sources, colleges and universities are rated highest and unsolicited applications, newspaper advertising, and private employment agencies follow in that order. Insertion of "Help-Wanted" advertisements in the newspapers is decidedly more useful than answering "Situation-Wanted" advertisements.

Employment agencies and newspaper advertising are sometimes used by a number of small firms, but generally prove unsatisfactory except in cases where specialists and men with experience are wanted. The weeding out of unqualified men is too time-consuming. Most firms find that friends of staff members and clients, and other personal contacts, rank second to the colleges as valuable sources of new employees.

COLLEGE RECRUITING

The manner in which college recruiting is conducted varies widely. At one end of the range is the firm which conducts extensive campus interviews and maintains close year-round personal contact with faculty members. For example:

We visit over 100 colleges every year, making two or three trips to some of them. Representatives of the firm attend the American Accounting Association conventions, and we participate in graduate study conferences.

At the other extreme is the firm which occasionally makes a phone call to a college placement office or to a friend on the faculty in search of a man to fill an actual vacancy. For example:

We don't keep in touch regularly with specific colleges, but call their placement offices when we have an opening.

You can't get much information from college placement people—so we deal mainly with employment agencies.

Many firms which confine their recruiting activities to these devices may be overlooking interested, qualified people. The head of the accounting department at a state university told a group of practitioners that he has had a number of students who would have preferred to start their careers in small local firms, but who so rarely saw representatives of such firms, and knew so little about them, that they ended up going elsewhere.

A firm in a small Midwestern city offers part-time employment and scholarships to a local college for one or two promising high school graduates each year.

One small firm recruits high school graduates, with some experience in business, who are willing to study at night. According to the firm the plan has been successful in adding ambitious, hard-working staff members of better than average ability.

A few accounting firms offer summer employment to students, generally at the completion of the junior year. Although the permanent staff is sometimes not fully occupied during this time of year, these firms feel it is a worth-while investment in introducing students to the profession and the firm.

Since we are not as seasonal as many other firms, we are in a position to bring in people for work during summer and at Christmas (we will have as many as five or six during the summer). We know that this costs a little money and that the people don't really have enough work to do at these times. But we find it is a valuable means of screening people whom we may want to employ later.

We don't have too much trouble in getting people because of our close relations with the local college and a few other places—also, people already with us help bring in their friends.

We don't solicit the big universities because we feel sure that the larger firms will get the good people there. We use agencies and get many people who start in private industry but who find later that they would prefer public accounting work.

COMPETITION FOR THE ACCOUNTING GRADUATE

CPA firms have said that they did not consider competition with industry for able graduates to be a very significant factor. Salary offers of both groups are comparable with very few exceptions. Firms agree that the chief competition is from other CPA firms.

Finding qualified candidates for staff positions is a major personnel problem. Even firms with elaborate recruiting programs are not entirely satisfied with their results. Starting salaries are by no means the fundamental problem. Young men and women with the qualities necessary for success in a profession do not base their choice primarily on what they can make when they first leave college, although they may be deterred if the prospect is too far out of line with what they could make in other fields.

The real attractions of any professional career are opportunities for constructive work, rapid advancement for those with exceptional ability, and assurance of a comfortable living for anyone who makes the grade.

Accounting, both in industry and public practice, offers all of these. As in other professions, the rewards are sufficient to attract too many average or below-average students who will never have the necessary combination of intelligence, perseverance and personality to make genuine success. But the competition between accounting and other professions (as well as with business and government) for the best brains grows tougher year by year.

No profession can solve its personnel problem merely by an increase in starting salaries—even if it were economically possible for one to outbid the others by a wide margin. Nor can public accounting fill its manpower needs by bidding higher against industry, or vice versa.

Rather, industry and public accounting must both redouble their efforts to present the opportunities and satisfactions of professional accountancy to the boys and girls who will soon be choosing their careers.

This cannot be done solely by writing or talking about prospects, though more educational work is needed. The opportunities and satisfactions must actually be in sight within a reasonable time after graduation. It is important to stress not only the chances for steady and fairly rapid increases in salary, but also the opportunities for practical, carefully supervised training which leads to professional competence.

The days when the professions could expect apprentices to spend long years of drudgery at low wages in the expectation of middle-aged success were doomed forever by the rapid growth of technology and need for professional skills. The accounting profession has recognized the change in most areas of practice, but the remarkable opportunities for outstanding young accountants are not yet well enough known. The best way to tell the story is to expand the opportunities even more rapidly.

WHEN TO RECRUIT—ONE PRACTITIONER'S VIEW

One of the greatest problems in staff selection (and the smaller the firm the greater the probability) is that men are employed because they happen to be needed at the particular moment. The time to make an addition to the staff is when the right man is available. If sometime within the coming year an employer plans an addition to his staff, he should not wait until he is swamped with work and his judgment is altered immeasurably by such pressure. The recruit should be sought right now, and while there is no pressure, intensive interviewing, testing, and investigating should be initiated.

When the studies are made and when our profession is really made aware of how much money has been thrown to the winds in attempting to develop good accountants out of men who had neither aptitude for nor interest in professional accountancy as a career, the cost of carrying a man an extra few months will look trivial. Moreover, the new man who comes in when there is no pressure on the office gets better adjusted; consequently, others in the office have more time, patience, and interest in getting him started off right.

In selecting a new staff addition, the first question is, "What is one looking for?" A worker whose services can be sold profitably, and one who will be content to continue in that capacity indefinitely? If that is the aim, the employer is certainly giving little thought to his own future security. Good accounting practices are hard to build, but fortunately they have a tendency to endure, once built. But in the years when the practitioner is making such an effort to build a sound practice, is it not just as important to be building for its vigorous continuation in the event he suffers ill-health or reaches the age when he must slow down? The smaller the practice, the more important it becomes to recruit strength. Each new man employed is possibly the future managing partner.

In addition to the time factor of need, consideration must be given to the proper time of year to begin recruiting. Competitive pressure has stimulated a trend toward visiting campuses earlier and increasing the number of schools visited. Several firms start making the rounds as early as October. One firm's personnel manager remarked that he hoped that it would not become necessary to sign up high school graduates.

RECRUITING FOR THE SMALL FIRM

Obviously, the larger firm with greater manpower needs will devote more effort to college recruiting. Yet some smaller firms have developed techniques or approaches which have proven successful in recruitment. Here are some examples:

We concentrate on the colleges in our vicinity, since the location of the applicant near home base seems to be important to him.

Although we don't do any campus interviewing—too much time for too little results—we are well known at the local colleges because of our activity in state-society work and speaking engagements before the accounting honor societies.

One of our six partners began visiting the universities in this state about three years ago. For the first two years, the results were almost nil, but this year we have been able to get all the men we need.

The key to our success is our close relation with the faculty at the local college—our own people do some teaching and in turn we use professors as part-time consultants.

We have the same man doing the recruiting each year. He gets to know the placement people and faculty.

One of our partners teaches a CPA review course at the university and therefore enjoys good relations with the placement office.

The small firm is frequently at a disadvantage in recruiting because, as a general rule, the larger firm is more in the public eye and is more likely to have better recruiting equipment and people with recruiting know-how.

In addition to being short on equipment, such as brochures and pamphlets depicting the advantages and opportunities in the firm, the small firm recruiter frequently has had little or no specialized training for recruiting and often has no special interest in the job. Last but not least, he usually has little or no time to devote to recruiting. If the latter is the case, much desirable recruiting activity may go by the board simply because the firm makes up time schedules only for direct responsibilities to clients. The small firm, as well as the large, must take the recruiting problem seriously enough to assign definite responsibility for it within the firm, with an appropriate spot on the time schedule, just as responsibility is assigned for carrying through an engagement for a client.

Recruiting staff for a small public accounting firm, as in any type of recruiting, is basically a matter of determining *where* the available supply is, and *how* to attract those with the proper qualifications. Although several sources are available, the primary source over the long run is new college graduates. That source is emphasized here.

If the small firm recruiter is sold on his profession and his firm and uses sound recruiting practices, he should be able to attract his share of the qualified personnel available. Like the recruiter for large firms, the man in the small firm to whom this responsibility is assigned should be aware of:

1. The advantages of employment by his firm. (These should be on the tip of his tongue—and in writing.)

2. Available aids for the selection and procurement of qualified men, and the avoidance of some common pitfalls that beset the inexperienced recruiter.

3. A need for a modest public relations program, so that students at a college or colleges where his firm recruits have an appropriate image of his firm.

Advantages of employment by a small firm. Today's young accountant entering public practice is primarily interested in the firm that offers members of its staff an opportunity for rapid development—both professional and personal. From a recruiting standpoint, this means that the successful firm must offer its new staff members the possibility of rapid professional growth through experience and training, and at the same time, an opportunity for a good personal life, which includes economic security and a sense of belonging.

While the following list is not exhaustive, it is indicative of the professional and personal advantages to be found in the good small firm. It should be emphasized that the mere listing of something as an advantage of a small firm does not necessarily imply that there is a corresponding disadvantage in a large firm; indeed, the advantages of one's own firm should never appear as an invidious attack on any other firm, large or small, or on employment by industry or government. The best salesmanship is positive. Also, there is no attempt to rank the advantages listed in order of importance. It is hoped that this list is suggestive, and that it will help the small firm recruiter to formulate his own "pitch."

1. *Professional Advantages*: *the new staff man—*
   a. *May move up fast in responsibility*
      Often the staff man *must* move up rapidly. There are fewer people to deal with the problems.
   b. *May acquire breadth of experience*
      Because of the firm's limited staff, the new staff member tends to generalize rather than specialize. As a consequence, he has an opportunity to develop himself not only in auditing but also in other areas such as taxes, systems, management services, and estate planning.
   c. *May grasp the big picture quickly*
      As a direct result of (a) and (b), the staff member has an excellent opportunity to see the big picture early. Since he is forced to move up in responsibility, he may work directly with partners and supervisors at an early stage in his development, and in many instances, directly with the client.
   d. *May acquire professional status early*
      If the staff member is successful in meeting the challenges inherent in (a), (b), and (c), he has an excellent opportunity of being recognized as a professional by both clients and community at an early date.
   e. *Must constantly improve himself*
      If the staff member is to make himself competent to fulfill (a), (b), (c), and (d), he must constantly study and continually improve himself, both technically and professionally. Participation in the AICPA's professional-development program would be of great value in this area.

2. *Personal Advantages*: *the new staff man—*
   a. *May live in a small community*
      This is sometimes desirable for personal reasons and it may occasionally cost less to live there.
   b. *May do little traveling*
      The small firm, as a general rule, requires little out-of-town work involving extended absences from home. In addition, little or no commuting is necessary in the smaller communities.
   c. *May quickly become part of the team*
      Although the team concept must be present in practically all successful business and professional organizations, it is particularly important in the successful public accounting firm. As a consequence, the new staff man is practically assured of rapidly becoming a member of the team.
   d. *May readily become part of the community*
      In many instances the small firm provides excellent opportunities

for the new staff member to enjoy an active and satisfying community life.

e. *May move into own practice if he so desires*

For the young accountant who is interested in eventually going into practice on his own, the small firm may provide excellent training.

Recruiting aids and pitfalls. Campus recruiting is not complicated. Yet proceeding in a professional manner can make it much more effective.

Furthermore, many large public accounting firms and industrial companies have specific aids for recruiting—brochures and other materials. The AICPA's advisory committee on recruiting personnel has developed similar aids for the use of small firms. These will be described below.

Initial contact. It would be difficult to overemphasize the importance of the initial contact with a potential staff member, whether it be in a group meeting, an interview room or a professor's office. As a general rule, the initial contact is prearranged with the placement director, department head, or other appropriate person. In each instance local ground rules, of course, are followed. Incidentally, a recruiter should not hesitate to become acquainted with, and wherever possible offer assistance to, college staffs and faculties.

The recruiter must remember that not only is he looking the prospect over but the prospect is also looking him over—and through him the profession and the firm. If the initial contact is an interview, both the recruiter and the interviewee are on the spot. The wise recruiter will remedy this immediately by putting the interviewee at ease. Frequently, referring to the interviewee by his first name and talking about something in which the interviewee is interested will help to do this. Information about his interests is usually available on the personal-data sheet which the college placement director has presented to the recruiter, who should have studied it *prior* to the interview.

1. Obviously, it is not worth the expense for a small accounting firm to print a brochure for students. The advisory committee on recruiting personnel offers a simple solution: the AICPA's pamphlet, *Accounting May Be the Right Field for You,* with an enclosed letter which relates the history and describes the advantages of employment with the firm of "Smith, Jones & Doe." With the help of this pattern letter or without, it should not be difficult for a firm to develop its own letter for this purpose (see page 783).

Since interviews are usually scheduled for only twenty to thirty minutes, maximum use must be made of the time allotted. The student should be sent the pamphlet and the firm's letter when the interview is arranged, so that he will have read them before he meets the firm's recruiter. Clearly, an interview devoted to discussion of matters that are easily explained in print will not bring the parties as close together as an interview in which both student and recruiter are prepared—the student with the letter, and the recruiter with the placement director's data sheet.

2. Since placement directors frequently do not provide some necessary

information, the student should have received, filled out, and returned the firm's own "Student Information" blank prior to the interview. The committee has provided a sample. (See Appendix, page 785.)

It is doubtful whether any set pattern of interviewing would ever be successful—the recruiter must feel his way along. However, he must take care not to monopolize all the time talking, thus leaving very little time for the interviewee to ask questions. Most students are interested in an informal interview with questions and answers coming from both sides. They are not interested in a formal presentation or "canned" speech from the recruiter.

Some recruiters have a tendency to use a "shock" approach with which they plan to put the interviewee on the defensive. If anything, the interviewee should be put on the offensive—not the defensive.

It must always be remembered that each student is an individual and should be so treated. A recruiter has nothing whatsoever to gain by being rude, crude, or unprofessional to a student, even though that student may not measure up scholastically or otherwise. Occasionally, when an interviewee does not measure up for one reason or another, the recruiter will try to rush him out of the interview or "brush him off." Although theoretically the recruiter may be justified, from a practical standpoint it only creates ill will and may hurt the firm with a subsequent prospect or prospects whom they would like to hire. This is especially true if the first prospect has time to pass the word around, and the recruiter should never be so naive as to think for a moment that the word does not get around. Almost every professor has observed how the reactions of one or two students who have been mishandled bias other students.

3. The committee has also developed a simple evaluation sheet. This should be filled out by the recruiter *immediately* after an interview—*before* he sees another interviewee. Without this simple element of system it is remarkable how easy it is to confuse the characteristics of four or five men, to say nothing of larger numbers. (See Appendix, page 786.)

4. Where the results of the testing program may be used in aiding a selection, the small-firm recruiter should read the explanation of the AICPA Personnel Testing Program.

5. Applicants should be notified promptly when they are rejected, in a letter that retains their good will for both the firm and the public accounting profession.

All of these aids may be useful in making selections for an internship program as well as for regular employment. More and more small firms are using such programs in obtaining and screening personnel.

Firm visits. After the initial contact, it is currently common practice to have the prospect in whom the firm is further interested visit the firm's office. This visit can be one of the best means of selling the firm to a given prospect, or it may boomerang and kill any chance the firm might have of landing the prospect.

Firm visits must be handled with care. Exposure of a prospect to any individual in the organization who displays a negative attitude or just happens to feel out of sorts may easily turn a prospect against the firm. Many a good prospect has been lost simply through one or two seemingly insignificant remarks. Again the word gets around, and what the student has heard may have campus-wide repercussions, thus automatically biasing others. Too many instances have been witnessed where a student has returned from a firm visit and related unfortunate experiences, ruining the organization's recruiting for that period, and, in some instances, subsequent periods.

During firm visits it should be remembered that although the prospective staff member is on trial, so is the firm. It is not a one-sided affair. Perhaps the simplest and certainly the best approach is to remember that the prospect is the firm's guest and should be treated accordingly.

The offer. Although the handling of the initial contact and the conduct of the firm visit (if used) are important to the recruiting process, the deciding factor is frequently the handling of the offer. Especially is this true if other offers appear to the prospect to be almost equal. The major problem in handling the offer appears to be one of timing. The timing must be just right and it must be flexible, dependent upon the individual prospect. Some students like to be rushed while others do not.

It is not uncommon for a firm to make an offer immediately after the initial contact and before leaving the campus. At first glance this might appear to be wise, assuming the firm can make a sound decision that quickly. However, different students react quite differently to this procedure. Although the firm might be (and frequently is) treating the student as a special case, the student may think that the firm is hard up for staff and as a consequence would hire just anyone, and that he is not actually a special case. Some students, particularly the good ones (and they, of course, are the ones normally rushed), question whether a firm can intelligently reach a decision regarding them and their future after seeing them for only twenty to thirty minutes. There are, however, students who are favorably impressed by this type of approach.

Although some students like to be rushed while others do not, under no circumstances should a student be kept waiting too long. Many a good student has changed his mind about a particular firm simply because the recruiter indicated that he would let him know within a week and made him wait two weeks or longer.

A public relations program. An accounting firm should assist recruiting for the profession as a whole, as well as follow a program to assure itself of qualified personnel. Indeed, the first activity may to some extent facilitate the second. However, recruiting for the profession as a whole is also a public relations opportunity for the firm. The quality—the richness and the depth—with which the recruiter speaks about his profession to students reflects on his firm. The business community generally manages to overhear. Most firms probably miss this opportunity to project a progressive image of themselves.

A program is needed, with someone in the firm responsible for its execution, and an appropriate allocation of time.

The objective of such a program might be defined, in public relations jargon, as building the image of a firm devoted to high standards of professional education and to obtaining highly qualified personnel. In general, a sound way to implement this program is to do things that tend to further these aims. Also, activity should be regular. Otherwise, the image won't last long enough in anybody's mind to register.

Obviously, the main targets of such campaigns are students and the academic community. However, the likelihood that the business community may come to see the same image may be regarded as a public relations bonus.

Activities need not be unduly time-consuming. The AICPA has provided a variety of aids, so that both time and money may well be regarded as almost negligible. Certainly, the outlay is small when compared with potential benefits to the firm. Following are some standard items, not an exhaustive list, for such a public relations program:

1. *Showing* the AICPA's recruiting film, *CPA,* to college preparatory high school students, and answering questions about the film and the profession.

2. *Speaking* to high school or college students, using or not using aids provided by the AICPA.

3. *Distributing* pamphlets. ("Young Eyes on Accounting" is appropriate as an elementary pamphlet for high school students, and can be distributed free in reasonable quantities. For very little expense, the AICPA's more advanced brochure emphasizing public accounting, *Accounting May Be the Right Field for You,* with the firm's letter included, may be distributed to new members of an accounting honor society or to some other group from which the firm's new staff members tend to be recruited.)

4. *Making use* of the AICPA's timesaving "Guide to Recruiting Activities in High Schools and Colleges," which provides patterns for the paper work in several activities for the use of state societies and chapter committees.

5. *Working* with a panel of representatives from the American Accounting Association, the Controllers Institute, the Institute of Internal Auditors, and the National Association of Accountants on information programs for high school students. (Joint Advisory Councils for Developing Student Interest in Accounting have been set up for this purpose.)

6. *Co-operating* with colleges in efforts to give students firsthand information about public accounting—by accepting formal teaching responsibilities or in other ways.

SALES APPEALS

Firms consider training and advancement opportunities as the most valuable things they can offer a prospective employee. Some firms, however, cite other sales appeals. For example: the firm's general reputation; little travel; the chance to work in one's home town; the wide variety of clients and experience; and individual treatment and close personal relationships.

One rarely mentioned sales appeal is the personal satisfaction to be derived from performing an important professional service. Many firms seem to feel that this is a less persuasive theme than the "what's-in-it-for-me?" approach. But the exclusive appeal to materialistic motives may detract from the significance of public accounting in the eyes of outstanding college students.

Some specific comments on sales appeals include:

> Our strongest sales appeals include our reputation; our policy of paying more than the market (and at the same time expecting more from the junior); our policy of movement of people so that holes *must* be opened up for advancement; opportunity to advance at as fast a rate as the individual demonstrates.

> Our major selling points are: we have topnotch clients who are just below the level of nationwide corporations; prestige of the firm in the community; a really close-knit family group; name your own starting drawing account; participation in profits immediately; opportunity for partnership (when ready, and four or five partners will be retiring soon); future growth.

> Our four most important sales appeals are: we're a growing firm; we can provide individualized treatment—you can move ahead as fast as you are able; we will subsidize you for a year or two; opportunity is unlimited.

> In a small firm like ours we can individualize—we don't have to follow a regimented pattern.

THE STUDENT'S REACTION TO THE INTERVIEW

Many accountants willingly admit that they have not had sufficient training in the fine points of recruiting. It is an activity which they undertake only at certain seasons of the year, and then only for brief periods. They feel that they might profit by some additional study of this subject.

Some accountants apparently are ill at ease while interviewing. One university placement officer has gone so far as to characterize several representatives of public accounting firms as "suffering from an apparent stiffness, an appearance of overpreciseness, and sometimes from an attitude of stooping to conquer."

A few years ago, students were surveyed in various sections of the country after being subjected to the recruiting interview. The findings can be summarized briefly as follows:

1. There is no pattern of excellence or of weakness in interviewing. Most students who had had interviews with several firms reported that not all were equally satisfactory. This reaction occurred regardless of the section of the country or the size of the firms involved.

2. The success of the interview apparently depended largely on the ability of the man who actually represented the firm and the way the interview was set up by the school. The same national firms were almost invaria-

bly rated differently by students in some areas than by students in others.

3. Students are alert to notice clues to the personality of the people with whom they are talking. Most interviewers were rated very high on such important qualities as professional bearing, appearance, and friendliness. However, they were rated lower on matters relating to their ability to handle the interview; for example, their manner of asking questions.

4. Frequently interviews did not appear to be carefully planned. When questions on a specific point about the firm were not readily answered, the recruiters seldom were able to explain why the firm had no fixed policy on the matter. Another student complaint was that sometimes they did not have a full opportunity to indicate their ability because too much of the conversation was centered in one or a few areas.

5. Many students felt that there was an overemphasis on grades. They said that the interviewers usually interpreted the grades properly. But although interviewers frequently talked about the need for all-round men, grades seemed to be the major criterion when it came to a showdown.

Some of the factors considered in this survey are noteworthy. Students were strongly interested in the following items:

Size of firm (CPA)	Transfers to other cities
Salary at start	Vacations
Training facilities	Salary after two years
Promotion policy	Load in busy season
Type of client	Why people leave
Overtime	Bonuses

Students were less interested in the following items:

| Number of partners | Mileage |
| Fringe benefits | Reliance on tests given by firm |

Bonus for securing clients

The following personality and other traits of the interviewer were considered important by the students:

Appearance	Mannerisms
Professional bearing of interviewer	Manner of asking questions
Friendliness	Interpretation of student's grades

Other factors considered embraced events taking place after the interview, namely consistency of the story told students by the interviewer, letters from the firm, and visit to the firm office.

The survey revealed that most recruiters seriously overrate the students' knowledge of the job situation. While students may know the techniques of accounting, they know little about the facts of life in public accounting firms.

This study clearly indicated that students felt they often did not obtain information on many important points during the interviews. The representative was either unwilling or unable to supply the answers. Sometimes this failure appeared to occur because the representative was himself not sure what the firm's policies were, or, in the smaller firm, the partner had not thought the matter out. Certainly partners have a responsibility to examine each of the major points and determine what position they wish to take. On some subjects it is possible that the decision will be to have no fixed policy. If that is the case, the interviewer should know the reasons so that he can provide a satisfactory answer when the point is raised.

This study revealed also that students frequently did not know enough to ask about certain things which would have a major influence on their later careers. The questionnaire was based on subjects raised by students. Obviously, they neglected certain important considerations.

For example, what is the firm's experience in the creation of new partners, and the status of these new partners? Merely knowing the number of partners gives little indication of this. In larger firms there may be a sizable number of junior partners whose status and income are little different from that of supervisors in another firm. Students should also want to know the extent to which partnerships are earned through competition, or through mere survival and seniority.

Another example would be the type of professional and social life engaged in by the partners. What is its relationship to business contacts which result in new clients and hold existing ones? To what extent are juniors invited to participate? The students' questions about "bonus for securing clients" show some awareness of this problem, but they were not directed to the heart of it.

A number of students showed an interest in the effect that possible military service might have on their chances of obtaining a position. There are so many facets to this question that it is difficult to evaluate the situation. Some firms will not interview students subject to draft, others interview them perfunctorily and immediately write letters explaining that they cannot hire the students. Still others promise to give the students consideration when they return from the service. And some hire immediately, regardless of draft status. In general, the students are apparently confused by this situation.

Still another problem is the relationship between the policies of the local office and the over-all firm policy.

HOW RECRUITING CAN BE IMPROVED

Clearly, it would be desirable for instructors and placement officials to give students a more realistic understanding of the major issues involved in choosing a firm. There are also certain things that the individual firm can do. It can set forth the facts in a letter, a mimeographed pamphlet, or a printed booklet. In this way it can give accurate, tangible data about the firm, its policies, its personnel, and its clients. While professional ethics prevent the publicizing of some points, there is much that can be put into such a publication that would help a student make an intelligent choice. Some national accounting firms have prepared excellent brochures for this purpose.

A clearly defined set of personnel policies is one of the strongest tools that a representative can use in attempting to attract a superior student. Any vagueness or hesitancy on the part of the recruiter, or any overselling in a booklet, will properly be interpreted by the student as a sign of weakness.

What the firm can do. What can the accounting firm do to improve recruiting practices? There are two approaches to the problem. The first is short term; it includes suggestions which the firm might adopt immediately. The second is concerned with the adoption of a long-range program which would involve co-operation with other firms to improve the general position of the profession. Essential points for a short-range program are:

1. Assignment of responsibility
2. Establishment and dissemination of personnel policies
3. Determination of criteria for hiring
4. Training of representatives, with special attention to interview techniques

Recruiting is an activity of sufficient importance to merit the attention of all the partners of a firm. In larger firms, however, it is advisable to centralize the responsibility. Someone should have definite authority to administer the program and be responsible for its success. But in both large and small firms, all partners should take an active interest in the subject.

In some firms it may be desirable to have someone below the partner level to choose the representatives who will do the recruiting, and to attend to other details. There is also an advantage in having students conducted on visits through the firm's office by younger staff men. These are the men with whom they will work and with whom they may feel more at ease. At the same time, however, the student should have an opportunity to meet some of the men who will set the policies that govern his activities. The over-all recruitment program should be designed and reviewed by one of the top partners, who should be expected to report to his associates periodically.

Determination of criteria for hiring. The criteria the representative is to use in choosing new employees should be clearly understood. If the firm wants to hire only students with outstanding grade records, it must recognize that there is stiff competition for these men. The firm must be prepared to demonstrate something extra in the way of incentives. Otherwise, it will find that its original decision is unrealistic, and it will have to make "on-the-spot" compromises in order to secure any new men at all.

After one drops below the top two or three men in grade standing, do the criteria change? What weight should be given to outside activities? What importance should be attached to the fact that the man had to work his way through college and got lower grades as a consequence?

How should previous work experience be evaluated? How does one distinguish between the student whose career has not been interrupted by military service and the one who has spent considerable time in the armed forces? Should age be a factor? Marriage? Dependents? Should average grades or improving grades be the proper criterion?

What personality traits are desired? At what point does an unprepossessing personality rule out a student with an excellent grade record? Or, conversely, to what extent will a weaker record be accepted in order to gain other abilities such as ambition, willingness to work hard, or steady character?

Training of representatives. Some accountants appear to assume that there is no organized information available on personnel selection techniques. As a result, they approach the task completely unprepared and just "do what comes naturally." They are victims of the false assumption that because a man is a successful public accountant, he somehow knows how to select men for a public accounting career. That is like assuming that a good ball-player is necessarily a good team manager, or that a skilled mathematician is necessarily an effective teacher of mathematics.

A few other accountants appear to go to the opposite extreme—they seem to feel that the process of personnel selection is too occult for non-psychologists, so they prefer to avoid trying to learn it.

Neither extreme assumption is valid. The study of personnel selection does lead one into realms of considerable difficulty. It is quite possible, however, for an intelligent layman to learn certain principles and techniques which will considerably improve his performance as a selector. It is *not* suggested that accountants become experts in selection; neither do firms have to turn over their selection work to nonaccountants.

It is suggested that public accounting firms: (a) confine recruitment and selection activities (except for a brief interview of the man by his prospective superiors) to a reasonably small number of persons within the firm, or, that the head of a smaller firm recognize his responsibility in this area; (b) see that these persons acquire some training and proficiency in employment interviewing and other aspects of recruitment and selection; and (c) make some provision for prompt "feedback," that is, some way of getting from job applicants their anonymous reactions to the interviewer and the interview.

Training in employment interviewing should cover the following main items:

1. The interviewer should have a sound and reasonably complete understanding of how personalities—that is, basic habit patterns such as self-reliance, industriousness, and the ability to get along with people—are formed in the early years of life and how they manifest themselves in adult activities.

It is an unfortunate fact that most persons have not given this subject systematic study. The result is that many otherwise well-educated and intelligent people, including some accountants, are quite confused in their evaluations of other individuals' personalities. They hold such invalid concepts as the idea that people with thin lips are not trustworthy, or that people who don't look you in the eye during an interview have weak characters. Some interviewers use pet questions or devise trick situations that they believe reveal important facts about the interviewee. The only fact revealed by such practices is that the interviewer does not understand employment interviewing.

2. The interviewer should plan a systematic coverage of the key areas in a person's history. He should seek evidence of the key personality traits in various phases of the student's personal history. Many recruiters make the

mistake of judging a candidate on one isolated incident, instead of developing a pattern of evidence drawn from the man's early home life, his school record, his service history, his social activities, his domestic life, and his work history.

3. The interviewer should attempt to make his judgment as objective as possible. There are two methods of doing this.

One method is to make notes during the interview. Such notes aid the interviewer in making more factual and less emotional judgments later. They also help compensate for the mental tiredness that often sets in at the end of a long interviewing day. In addition, some skilled interviewers have found that making notes, if properly explained, increases the student's respect as well as his belief that he will be graded objectively.

Another method of attaining objectivity is to relate the interview to a written list of criteria as soon as possible after the interview has been held. This practice insures that all pertinent points are noted.

4. The fact that the interviewer has planned his interview does not mean that his questions should be formal or stiff. He should have his topics in mind, but he should not prepare precisely worded questions. He should plan to open the interview with friendly comments designed to put the student at ease, and he should end on a friendly note. In short, he should feel—and show—a personal interest in people with whom he may work in the future.

He should be able to adjust his approach to the personality of the applicant. An extroverted or independent student may resent a highly directed and inquisitorial technique. On the other hand, an introverted or dependent student may respond only to that type of interview technique.

5. The interviewer should have a clear understanding of his firm's personnel policies. Furthermore, he should know how to present them in a setting which will enable the student to understand why they have been adopted.

6. The interviewer should plan to supplement his judgment with further meetings, investigations, or testing. Firms that interview on campus will find it helpful to invite the student to visit their offices. These visits should be carefully planned, with staff members briefed so that they can give the visitors a friendly reception. Student reaction to these visits is generally highly favorable.

How can a person acquire proficiency in personnel interviewing and selection? One way is to read the material that has been published on the subject. In addition, consulting firms which specialize in selection work may be used to train recruiters. Consultants sometimes offer general seminars of a few days' duration at which the salient points are covered. Many universities also offer courses in employment interviewing. The cost of such training, including the investment of time, may well be less than the cost of recruitment mistakes. A single poor selection may cost several thousand dollars. Failure to hire a good man, though less evident, may have even more serious results.

PROCEDURE FOR INTERVIEWING APPLICANTS

In the absence of psychological tests, and even with them, a personal interview with the applicant is an important means of evaluating his personality. The interview also may develop information as to the aptitude of the candidate, although it is to be noted that the testimony of the applicant seldom will erase the evidence of his scholastic attainment or the results of an orientation or other aptitude-testing procedure.

Most firms accomplish the personality evaluation of applicants through interviews based on informal "sizing up" of applicants. It is interesting to note that firms consider personality evaluation to be just as important and significant as aptitude testing.

Too few accountants realize that the interview should be planned carefully in advance and that considerable skill can be attained in conducting an interview. Interviews should be held upon appointment only and adequate time should be budgeted for the interview. Probably no interview with a candidate who has any possibility of qualifying for a position should be less than one-half hour. Also, the interviews should be dignified by promptness in meeting the applicant and he should be given every opportunity to present himself at his best. Interruptions should be avoided during the interview because they are certain to disturb one or both parties.

It is well to have the application form in advance of the interview. This enables the interviewer to plan the questions and to acquaint himself with information about the applicant to a considerable extent before the interview. (See sample on page 787.)

In the actual conduct of the interview, the employer should recognize as a primary purpose the obtaining of the confidence and co-operation of the party being interviewed. The interviewer himself must not be in a state of emotional upset and at no time should he betray disapproval of, or an adverse reaction to, the applicant. He must be natural and friendly in his attitude and seek to put the applicant at ease early in the interview. He should remember that his purpose is to get the party interviewed to do his share of the talking rather than spend the time in instructing the applicant.

A few suggestions as to the questions to be asked may be helpful. These are: questions evidencing interest in the applicant's home and family; questions about the school attended and how the applicant happened to choose the school and the course of study that he completed; questions as to the most valuable courses and why they were valuable; comments on the employment experiences of the applicant, if any, with particular questions as to how the applicant felt about a certain job, his reason for leaving employment with a certain company, etc. In asking about a specific job which the applicant has held it may be well to ask him just what he did on that job. Sometimes a discussion of hobbies, athletic activities, or similar items is particularly revealing.

An additional duty of the interviewer usually is to describe the position for which the applicant is being interviewed. Sometimes this subject can be introduced by asking the applicant just why he has applied, and why he believes he can be successful. Then, if the interviewer believes that the candidate is a good prospect, he should describe the position and the policies of the firm, particularly as to rates of pay, promotions, hours of work, requirements as to overtime, and opportunities for training. As a record of the interview many employment interviewers have a form which they utilize. (See the Appendix, page 790, for a sample.)

At the end of an interview the interviewer should know certain definite things about the applicant. He should have learned important and precise facts about the latter's accomplishments in the past, what his hopes and expectations are, why he is seeking the position, the real reasons for leaving past employment, how he regarded the working conditions and his immediate superiors on his former jobs, whether he has a happy family life, and whether his health is equal to the strain of public accounting. These are all fields in which the applicant's answers will reveal his personal qualifications and to some extent his aptitude for public accounting. Too often the interviewer relies only, or almost entirely, upon such matters as the appearance, dress, cleanliness, poise, self-assurance, and expressiveness of the candidate. Yet it is far more important for the interviewer to ascertain whether the applicant has qualities of initiative, imagination, leadership, and perseverance and whether he is capable of assuming responsibility. Also, evidence of his ambition and his comprehension of professional-service standards and aspirations will need to be observed. If the interviewer has been successful in drawing out the applicant, he will have some concept of the latter's outlook on life, his general culture, and seriousness of purpose.

In closing the interview, the applicant should be informed as to when the final employment decision will be made and when notification can be expected. Rarely can a decision be made by the interviewer as to the desirability of employing the applicant until after the close of the interview. Where such a decision is reached, the employment can be arranged for at that time. If the applicant has other prospects he should be given a reasonable time to come to a decision as to which position he will accept. Courtesy and respect for good will suggest that all unsuccessful applicants be notified promptly and tactfully, usually by letter.

Testing

THE AICPA PERSONNEL TESTING PROGRAM

■ THE PERSONNEL TESTING PROGRAM of the AICPA is offered to assist the practitioner. The tests provide a means of quickly identifying some of an individual's aptitudes and abilities for public accounting. Early identification of an employee's talents should permit the practitioner to reduce turnover. Having greater knowledge of the abilities of a new employee should permit making better use of his time, and thus provide a quicker recovery of the costs invested in him.

The tests can be obtained from the Project Director, Accounting Testing Program, American Institute of Certified Public Accountants, 21 Audubon Avenue, New York 32, New York. The cost is nominal.

It is generally agreed that to be successful in public accounting an individual must have a reasonably high intelligence level, must be well educated in accounting, and should have interests compatible with those of successful practitioners. Many other attributes contribute to success; however, procedures for measuring other attributes with reasonable certainty have not yet been developed. The tests offered in the AICPA's Personnel Testing Program provide comparisons of an individual's aptitude in accounting, knowledge of the field, and pattern of interests with those of others who have similar education and experience.

The Orientation Test. The Orientation Test is designed to measure aptitude for accounting. It is essentially a measure of intelligence slanted toward business. Three factors are tested: vocabulary, reading ability, and an understanding of quantitative relationships. This type of test has been found to be superior to a general intelligence test which measures only an individual's mental ability, because the Orientation Test measures an additional factor: the application of mental ability to business. The test may be used to measure aptitudes of high school students, college students, or other adults.

Only fifty minutes are required for taking the test. Three results are reported: a verbal score which is based on the ability to read and the extent of vocabulary; a score based on ability in quantitative relationships; and a total score. All three scores are important. The verbal score indicates the relative ability to understand written communication as well as ability to understand words. The quantitative score reports ability to handle numerical figures and mathematical relationships. The total score combines the two.

The scores of an individual are reported by means of a comparison to a group. The standard of comparison, referred to as a "norm," is based on the performance level attained by a group which has had the same type and amount of education and experience. The norms were developed scientifically by evaluating the test results of large numbers of accountants and students from all regions of the country, from large and small firms, and from large and small colleges. The best of the group is ranked in the 100th percentile; the poorest of the group is ranged in the 1st percentile. If an individual ranks at the 75th percentile it means that he has more ability than 74 out of 100 persons whose test results were used in establishing the norms and less ability than 25. When a percentile reporting system is used, the results on the test for one individual are compared to the results of others. The percentile rating does not indicate that a certain percentage of the questions were answered correctly nor does it indicate a passing or failing grade.

Standards of comparison have been developed for different levels of education and experience. College freshmen must be compared to college freshmen, college seniors to college seniors, junior accountants to junior accountants, senior accountants to senior accountants, etc. Care must be exercised to be sure that the appropriate standard of comparison is selected.

Significance of Orientation Test. The Orientation Test can provide various indications of an individual's potential for public accounting. The total score gives an indication of his intellectual capacity and it is a clue to his potential, as limited by his intelligence.

There is a significant correlation between scores on the Orientation Test and grades earned in college accounting courses. To the extent that grades indicate work habits developed in college and to the extent such habits are carried over, a comparison of the test score and accounting grades may be indicative of how the individual will apply his efforts to the job.

Evaluation of the test results can have predictive value in relation to assignments made to a junior staff man and expectations as to his development for different levels in the firm. A high verbal score implies a potential for filling a position where the attribute of communication is important. Also, a high verbal score ordinarily indicates ability to understand instructions easily and perhaps handle a larger variety of assignments. The ability to write is tested only indirectly by this examination.

Score interpretation. A low score in the verbal phase of the test can be indicative of problems that might develop, such as the inability of the junior to express his audit examination findings adequately. The senior or in-charge accountant might have to spend considerable time in explaining the work and in instructing the junior. Verbal abilities can be increased; however, there may be a problem of encouraging and aiding the junior in this development.

A low verbal score should not necessarily preclude an individual's entering the public accounting field. Consideration must be given to the position being filled and the possibility of higher-level positions becoming available in the firm. An individual with a low verbal score but with adequate quantitative abilities may make satisfactory progress in positions up to and including the senior level of a firm.

A high quantitative score implies that the junior should be capable of handling detailed auditing assignments reasonably well, provided he possesses an adequate background in accounting and receives an introduction to the procedures involved. A high quantitative score seems to indicate the probability of success through the senior level of a firm although the evidence to date is not conclusive.

The success of an individual as he rises above the senior level is more and more dependent upon his abilities to communicate both orally and in writing, even for a person with a high quantitative score. Thus, success in reaching top-level positions is dependent on both verbal and quantitative abilities.

In evaluating a low quantitative result, which is indicative of a relative lack of facility with numerical data, one should use care in making judgments about the desirability of hiring or keeping an employee. A person may have fair potential for success in public accounting even though he has limited ability in handling quantitative data; however, he is unlikely to succeed if he is also very weak in linguistic ability. A combination of low scores on both aspects of the test, and thus a low total score, would be indicative of low potential to succeed in public accounting.

Certain attributes and characteristics which the Orientation Test does not measure are considered necessary in public accounting. The practitioner must exercise caution to be sure he does not draw conclusions which the test does not support. The test results should not be interpreted as a measure of whether the individual's personality is compatible with the requirements of successful practice, nor as indicative of personal interests and ambitions. Although the test can measure intellectual capacity and ability to learn accounting, the practitioner must not interpret the results of the Orientation Test as indicating that the person already possesses a knowledge of accounting principles and procedures.

The total score is a combination of scores reporting two different aspects of ability. Widely divergent verbal and quantitative scores could be offset in the total score. The practitioner must give consideration to both the verbal score and the quantitative score in his analysis and relate the evaluation of each score to the requirements of the position he is seeking to fill.

Intellectual capacity is just one of the essential characteristics necessary for success in public accounting. Therefore, a high score on the Orientation Test, by itself, does not predict success in the field, but the results help evaluate one significant aspect of a person's potential for public accounting.

The Achievement Test. The Achievement Test is designed to measure knowledge of accounting principles and procedures. Tests have been constructed for two different levels. Level I is designed especially for testing those who have had the equivalent of one year of college accounting study. Level II is designed to test individuals with the equivalent of at least fifteen semester hours of college accounting including cost accounting. The following comments pertain primarily to the Level II test; however, the comments would be equally applicable to evaluating the Level I results if the individual's state of development is recognized.

Forms of the Achievement Test are available which require either two or four hours of examination time. The two-hour form is the one used most often. For all practical purposes, the two-hour test is as reliable as a predictive device as the four-hour form.

The method of reporting Achievement Test results must be considered in interpreting and evaluating the scores. The objective of the test is to compare an individual's mastery of accounting principles and procedures with that of other individuals who have reasonably comparable backgrounds in education and/or experience. The individual's achievement is reported as a percentile rank, as previously discussed. Standards of comparison have been established on the two-hour form for each level of employment in public accounting as well as for college seniors. The practitioner must select the standard of comparison which is appropriate for the individual.

The results of the Achievement Test can be used in selecting, counseling, and assigning personnel. In the selection of personnel, the test results provide an invaluable supplement to other appraisal procedures; however, they are only a supplement. Probably one of the most significant features of the tests is the fact that they provide a uniform and standardized basis for comparing accounting knowledge of all job applicants regardless of the college attended and the grades reported. The Achievement Test can be used as a scientific measure to indicate the relative accounting knowledge found in a potential employee. It must be remembered that the scores are reported in relation to the acquired knowledge of others with a similar amount of education and/or experience.

Score interpretation. A low achievement score may indicate that the individual should be advised to engage in a program of additional study in accounting to correct his deficiencies, provided he has the essential mental abilities. A low score could be caused by many factors, such as low intelligence, poor application to studies, incomplete course of study, poorly conceived or ineffectively taught courses, or others. The test results do not point out specific areas of accounting knowledge in which the individual is deficient. Weaknesses in specific areas must be identified by means other than this test.

A low achievement score could indicate that problems will be encountered when work is assigned. The junior might have limited flexibility and adaptability, which could restrict the variety of his work assignments. Great care might have to be exercised in making work assignments to insure that they are within the junior's capabilities. The junior should be assigned to a supervisor who would understand the problem and properly use and develop the junior's abilities. Slower progress should be expected. Closer supervision during the initial period of employment probably would be necessary.

Conversely, an individual who ranks high in achievement should be expected to understand and carry out work assignments faster than normal. It might be desirable to select special work assignments for such a person which would rapidly move him through the procedures planned for new juniors.

The achievement score should be considered in assigning the junior to staff training programs. A high score would signify that he could be expected to handle and benefit from advanced programs, and he might be encouraged at an early date to develop his knowledge in a specialized area.

One word of caution is essential. A high achievement score is not necessarily an indication of the best prospect for employment or advancement. While there is very little chance that test results will overrate an individual, it is possible that he could be extremely well trained in accounting and actually be close to his maximum potential. Certainly he would be a good risk to handle assignments in the lower levels of public accounting, but he might not possess the intellectual capacity for top-level positions. Whether or not he could develop into a person capable of filling a top-level position could be answered, in part, by his results on the Orientation Test. It is important not to depend upon a single test; rather, the entire group of tests should be used, including the interest test described below and, even then, one must recognize that using the tests supplements other personnel evaluation procedures.

Technical knowledge and mastery of accounting concepts are learned, and the amount of knowledge and mastery can be increased if the individual has the appropriate intellectual capacity. The results are indicative of comparable achievement in accounting in an over-all sense. As mentioned before, they do not indicate or pinpoint specific areas of strength or weakness in accounting. The practitioner should bear in mind that the individuals taking the tests are generally a select group. Most of them are college graduates educated in accounting. Many of the weaker individuals have been weeded out in the education process.

The Achievement Test does not measure personal characteristics and only indirectly can the results be interpreted as indicating intellectual ability. The test scores do not invariably predict success in public accounting, but they can help identify the better risks for the first year or so and some of the problems in the development of an employee.

The Strong Vocational Interest Blank. The Strong Vocational Interest Blank is used to rate and compare interests of an individual with the interests of successful CPAs. It is an interest inventory designed to show the variety and distribution of a person's interests in different occupations. It may have some value to the person who takes the test. It is generally agreed that members of certain occupations usually have personal interests that fall into identifiable patterns. To the extent an individual's pattern of interests corresponds to the pattern characteristic of members of the occupation, there is greater likelihood of satisfaction with the work.

The interest inventory test is untimed, but it usually requires about thirty or forty minutes for completion. The report of the results shows the pattern of the individual's personal interests in twenty-seven different occupations. It also provides a comparison of the interests of the person examined with a pattern established for CPAs. The pattern was established by a testing program participated in by thousands of persons in various occupations and subsequently rechecked by testing 1,000 successful CPA practitioners.

Among the twenty-seven different occupations included, the classes of accountant, CPA, and closely allied occupations are obviously most significant to consider when advising individuals whether or not to enter or to remain in public accounting. Ratings that are widely divergent from the normal pattern for CPAs may be indicative of potential dissatisfaction with public accounting work. However, it should be remembered that many people have very wide patterns of interests while others have very narrow patterns.

The Strong blank is a valuable aid in understanding an individual and gaining an insight into one aspect of his personal characteristics. The practitioner, however, should not interpret test results as a measure of personality, ambition, or personal desires. It should be emphasized that an individual can be successful in public accounting even though his interests are not comparable to the established pattern. Personal desires and ambition can be so strong that they offset a seemingly incompatible pattern of interests. The practitioner should also bear in mind that interest patterns are subject to change, especially until an individual reaches the age of twenty-five, and therefore, compatible interests can be acquired or developed.

Administration of the tests. The testing program is widely used. A college program makes the test available to students in the fall, winter, and spring. A professional program is also in operation through which appropriate tests can be given to prospective or employed staff members at any time. If an individual took the tests in the college program, an employer, with the permission of the individual, can obtain a report of the test results from the AICPA office.

The tests and supplies are controlled by the AICPA. An employer can arrange to administer the tests to applicants and employees through the professional program. The procedure for administering the tests is relatively simple. A member of the firm is designated by the AICPA as an authorized examiner. The proctoring involves being sure the individual taking the tests understands the instructions and that he is told when to start and stop each examination, as timing is an essential element in the determination of scores.

The Orientation and Achievement Tests can be graded immediately by someone in the firm. They are objective-type tests and can be scored quickly and easily by clerical personnel. Grading in the firm has the advantage of making the results available immediately, which is convenient when interviewing a job applicant. If the user does not wish to do the scoring, the AICPA's grading service may be used. Even when tests are graded within the firm, used copies should always be returned to the AICPA office, where the scores determined in the firm are confirmed by the AICPA.

If the employer believes that the number of times the tests would be used does not warrant making arrangements to administer the tests in his office, he can arrange for the service at one of the testing centers that are located throughout the country.

Making use of the tests. Some employers establish minimum test scores as a condition of eligibility for employment. Of course some people who have scores below the desirable minimum for the firm may be employed if other personal attributes seem to compensate for them.

If test results are to be used in establishing minimum qualifications for selection and retention of employees, consideration should be given to many additional factors. The minimum acceptable percentile rank should be established only after the firm has had considerable experience in using the tests. Caution should be exercised to guard against setting a percentile cutoff which might be too high. Moreover, it should be recognized that small differences in percentile ranks are not significant. In addition, the establishment of employment standards should be reconsidered over a period of time after the tests have been given to all applicants. It is also important to establish minimum employment standards in light of the current staff's qualifications and abilities. Other factors to be considered in establishing the minimum acceptable qualifications are the size and location of the firm, the current requirements of the position which it is seeking to fill, the future potential in the firm from the point of view of both the applicant and the firm, and the supply of applicants upon which the firm can draw.

When the tests are used, it is desirable to inform the junior or applicant of the results in a personal interview. Test results should be kept confidential and the person tested should be so informed. The report should be in terms of percentile ranks, and such ranking should be explained and interpreted for the individual. If firm policy does not permit revealing exact results, the individual should be counseled by using general terms. The scores of other individuals in the firm should not be disclosed to a junior and his results should not be compared with other individuals in the firm during the interview.

The employer can use test results when investigating why an individual's actual performance varies from expectations resulting from interview and other impressions. The test results may indicate factors not apparent from other personnel procedures. It is also unwise to base judgments solely on test results where actual experience with a junior indicates better abilities. The tests may be an inaccurate measure if the individual has been ill or distracted when taking the tests. In addition, tests do not measure personal factors which may offset or overcome poor test results. If the results are out of line, some consideration should be given to retesting with another form of the test.

Use of the entire group of tests offered in the program is recommended if at all feasible. Each test is designed to indicate different aspects of personnel evaluation. If all tests cannot be used, consider the particular situation of the applicant. If he is a graduate of a recognized institution with high grades in accounting, the interest test may well be the most important. If there is any question of the soundness of his education in accounting, the achievement test may be more important. In general, it may be advisable to give first priority to the Orientation Test; second, to the Achievement Test; and third, to the Strong Vocational Interest Blank. The Orientation Test should be given most weight, particularly when evaluating personnel for potential advancement.

The testing program supplements the practitioner's personnel evaluation procedures by providing quick appraisal of an individual's attributes and abilities which often could otherwise be identified only after an extended period of observation and evaluation of job performance. Thus, use of the program should effect savings through possible reduction in employee turnover and increased efficiency of operations through maximum utilization of staff resources. If test results are not available for use in the selection process, the tests should be administered to all new employees at the earliest possible date to provide a basis for counseling and evaluating the new man. The tests are particularly helpful in identifying the especially gifted individuals for guidance into the profession of public accounting, in predicting their rapid development and success, and for culling applicants who would be really poor risks.

Validity of the tests. While the samples were relatively limited, there have been a number of studies made to determine the correlation between scores attained on the AICPA Personnel Tests and grades on accounting courses in college, as well as scoring on CPA examinations. It was found that there is positive correlation in both instances.

Internship

■ IN ADDITION to recruiting graduating seniors, an increasing number of firms of all sizes participate in internship programs.

This arrangement—which varies widely in detail even among the few colleges which use it—permits upperclassmen to gain practical experience by working for a firm during a part of the school year, usually from December through February.

Internship enables a firm to develop a relationship with promising students before their graduation. Moreover, the interns often become good-will ambassadors at college for the firm or profession which employed them.

A few firms are finding good men by co-operating with the small number of colleges which offer combined work-study programs to their students. One firm fills most of its openings by employing students who work in the firm for four or five months each year for three years. It is still too early to evaluate its program, but so far over 50 per cent of the students have stayed with the firm after graduation.

These programs give students an introduction to actual public accounting experience and an opportunity to blend practical experience with classroom study. They also give accounting firms an opportunity to preview the individual candidate.

Internship programs have been found most readily adaptable to colleges operating on the "quarter" system but a number of schools operating on a semester basis have made arrangements whereby their students are permitted to take part in such programs. Most public accounting firms experience a peak season, and the quarter system, on which a few colleges operate, best allows the internship program to operate in this busy season. Under that system the students may be available following the fall quarter, which ends before Christmas, and are engaged for full-time work for the entire winter quarter until late March or early April when the spring quarter begins.

From a long-range point of view, the recruiting of students for the permanent staff by hiring them in the winter quarter under the internship program may not always provide the best training that might be given. If the accounting firm is extremely busy and does not make a conscious effort to provide varied and selected experience for the interns, the students may receive very little attention and may be used almost entirely on clerical and routine work. On the other hand, if students attending college on a semester basis are hired for a semester under an internship program, it is easier to give more attention to training them, and their capabilities and progress can then be appraised more adequately. Also, the period of training can be much longer under the semester-internship plan as it may be started about July 1 and extend until early February.

In some cases a summer-internship program, in which only the three summer months are used for the training, has been followed. This is usually the most convenient for the students but it requires that the co-operating firms have sufficient summer work to give the trainees valuable experience. Obviously, the internship program must fit the needs of the accounting firm and some firms will be able to contribute more to the student's training at one time than at another. Whereas some accounting firms may be able to offer a very satisfactory period of internship in the summer months, in other firms there may not be enough work at that time to keep the permanent staff occupied.

Accounting firms situated favorably in the vicinity of colleges where accounting students are trained often find that they can obtain some students during the entire year, or a portion thereof, on a part-time basis. Although this may be beneficial to both parties, at least temporarily, it can hardly be considered a substitute for an internship program on a full-time basis. Usually, the part-time employee is not available for many of the larger or out-of-town engagements and he may be used best in office work or on small engagements, often of a bookkeeping type.

ONE SCHOOL'S EXPERIENCE

The following excerpts are from a report of the internship-program experiences of a large Midwestern college:

> It is interesting to observe that many firms do not ask the student to take an auditing course before he interns. . .
> Credit granted is three or six quarter-hours. It is considered desirable that the college maintain some control over the student while he interns.

Grades are based upon performance and evaluation, exactly as in other courses and appear to supply a significant incentive. . .

Practical experience obtained by an intern who works ten weeks in auditing may equal or exceed the benefit obtained from one or two formal accounting or auditing courses. . .

The minimum period of service required is ten weeks, to conform to the ten-week academic quarter. . .

A weekly report is initiated by the student and submitted by him to the college after it has been reviewed and signed by his supervisor. Mimeographed forms for this report are supplied by the college. It includes a designation of the type of business (not the client's name) and the type of audit or other work performed during each day of the week and total hours worked daily and weekly. This information enables the course supervisor to determine whether the student is actually on the job for the requisite number of weeks and whether he is being rotated on various junior duties such as cash, inventories, receivables, property, and test of transactions. The course supervisor would advise the firm if rotation of the intern's duties seemed insufficient.

The course supervisor also sends a report form for each intern to the firm near the end of the quarter. This form requests the firm to make an appraisal (A, excellent; B, superior; C, average; D, inferior) of the intern, comparing him with other first-year employees who have approximately the same academic training and limited experience, on each of the following twelve points: auditing aptitude and imagination; knowledge of accounting; analytical ability; ability to grasp instructions; ability to complete assignments; present competence (for new employee); accuracy regarding facts and figures; attitude (co-operation, reliability, interest in work); ability to develop the good will and respect of others; improvement in general performance; prospect of advancement; and prospect of becoming a CPA.

In the course of a ten-week period, the intern will normally have worked for several senior accountants. One of the office partners or personnel supervisors reviews the intern's performance and conduct with the senior accountants and uses their comments and conclusions as a basis for completing the appraisal. The appraisal form is the fundamental basis for determining the intern's course grade. Persistent late submission of weekly reports may lower the grade normally determined from the appraisal. The course supervisor does not show the firm's appraisal to the student, but he usually discusses with him any significant deficiencies reported.

Neither the offices nor the college attempt to extend the program beyond the winter quarter. Firms have indicated that the experience obtained by an intern during any other period would be neither intensive nor extensive and hence not representative. Also, the offices feel that generally they could not economically use an intern any other time.

After the middle of November, each student selected for an internship is called in by the course supervisor and given the name and address of the firm to which he has been assigned. Soon after that, the firm contacts the student to indicate the rate of pay and date he will be expected to appear for work; a copy of this correspondence goes to the course supervisor. The student then sends a confirming letter to the firm. . .

When an accounting firm takes an intern for the first time, a definite understanding is reached by the college course supervisor and the firm's personnel supervisor or partner with respect to each of the following items. In most respects, the intern is to be treated as a regular beginning junior accountant. The length of service is to be at least ten weeks. Service beyond ten weeks between these dates may be worked out between the student and the office. Matters of overtime, travel, and pay for the intern are to be determined by the office. His duties are to be rotated among assigned junior duties on several engagements. In general, these duties should include, among others, cash, inventories, receivables, property, and test of transactions. The intern has no obligation to take permanent employment with the office, and the office has no obligation to offer him permanent employment upon his graduation.

The course supervisor knows fairly early in November the approximate number of students who will be available for assignment. On the basis of this information, he notifies the interested firms and informs each that he anticipates being able to supply one or two interns for the winter. The personnel men or firm partners indicate in their reply the number of interns desired. . .

It may appear that the personnel supervisors or partners of the offices should be permitted to come to the college and interview all of the students who have indicated an intention to go out on the internship. Actually, however, this procedure would not ensure all of the offices equitable treatment. For example, the representative of the first office who came to interview might, in selecting all of the interns he wanted, cull the best from the entire group. . .

The matter of remuneration is the province of the firm, and the college makes no attempt to exercise any control over it. The intern is notified as to his monthly salary, overtime, and other financial arrangements. . . Since the college selects and assigns the interns to the office, the supervisor of the course feels that it is best if he does not know the monthly salary rate initially. After the intern has been assigned and has heard from the office, however, he usually informs the course supervisor of his monthly salary.

The trial employment period of at least ten weeks enables the intern to get the feel of public accounting. If he likes it, well and good; on the other hand, if he does not like it and does not desire to enter the profession, there is no questionable entry on his permanent employment record. For its part, the firm is able to observe the intern and his performance without incurring any obligation. While free to offer him a regular staff position, it is not bound to do so. Many offices have found that their participation in the program has provided them with a significant number of better-than-average staff men.

The student's remaining formal courses in accounting are made much more meaningful. He has seen a disbursement voucher, including the purchase requisition, bid-and-quotation sheet, purchase order, vendor's invoice, and receiving report. It means something to him when the professor talks about examining disbursement vouchers. The former intern's experiences considerably enrich the class discussion. In many instances, if the internship relationship has been satisfactory, the intern is offered regular staff employment to begin after his graduation. Therefore, the student, sure of a position when he graduates, is able to devote his last quarter of residence at the college entirely to his studies without time out to look for a job. Moreover, the internship has been a genuine learning experience for the student, and the public accounting firm has been able to obtain reasonably competent help during their busy season.

The fact that an internship program is in existence and that students go out on the program to a public accounting firm seems to impress upon intern and nonintern alike that each is training for a profession rather than merely taking a group of accounting courses in order to get some kind of a job.

The question might be raised whether there are drawbacks to a public accounting internship program. In point of fact, none has appeared, with the possible exception that the college does not now have and never has had a sufficient number of interns to fill the demands of the public accounting firms.

STATEMENT OF STANDARDS AND RESPONSIBILITIES UNDER PUBLIC ACCOUNTING INTERNSHIP PROGRAMS[1]

The conviction that a period of full-time employment in public accounting is a desirable part of an accounting curriculum dates back a number of years. Several factors may account for this need having been recognized early in the development of programs of collegiate training for public accounting. One of these was that many of the men who were closely connected with collegiate education were, or had been, practitioners. Probably they recognized that some of the qualities—some of the special techniques and special skills, as well as judgment—were not readily developed in classrooms by usual instructional methods. It is likely that they found, as many teachers find today, that subjects such as auditing cannot be taught effectively unless the student is able to visualize the scope of business operation and especially the variety, types, and kinds of business records with which the auditor works.

Whatever the cause, we find that almost from the beginning of collegiate instruction in accounting, some schools have operated programs under which a student obtains full-time employment with a public accounting firm for a period of several weeks or months during either his junior or senior years. These programs have generally been referred to as *internship programs*. At present, over forty schools are operating internship plans of one type or another. Fundamentally they are all attempting to meet the same need, but the details of the plans vary considerably.

In a number of schools which are on the quarter system, the student may work for an entire winter quarter. Schools which are on the semester system may provide for students' taking examinations early at the end of the first semester and registering late for the second semester. This time, together with the holidays normally falling within the period, permits six to eight weeks of full-time employment. There are also variations of these basic plans which aid in increasing the usefulness and effectiveness of internship programs.

There is considerable variation also as to granting credit. A number of schools grant credit for internship work and grade students on performance. They consider the student as fully enrolled during the internship period. Other schools do not grant credit, even though some of them may strongly

---

[1]Prepared by the Committee on Accounting Personnel of the AICPA (Samuel J. Broad, Chairman) and the Committee on Internships of the American Accounting Association (Frank S. Kaulback, Jr., Chairman). As it appeared in *The Journal of Accountancy*, April 1955, pp. 74 ff.

recommend internship to their accounting majors. Schools also vary in their requirements for students completing their course of study without delay because of the intervening internship programs. Some schools recommend that the student attend a summer session the year before interning, whereas others recommend that the student plan his last two years of work so as to be able to carry a somewhat reduced load in the year during which he is an intern. Generally, schools have been able to solve the problem of avoiding delayed graduation without too much difficulty.

This statement presents those principles which seem to be basic to the operation of an accounting internship program in a manner which enables it to contribute most to the total accounting education of participating students.

Purposes of internship. Internship programs have as their general objective the development of better-qualified accountants with a resulting benefit to accounting firms, to students, and to schools. The particular contribution to be made by internship programs must be sought in those values that the student can find in public accounting practice which are not ordinarily available in the school. If this training which he can receive in public accounting is helpful to him in either private or public accounting after graduation, it represents a significant contribution to his total educational experience.

The following objectives are an integral part of an effective internship program:

To enable the student to take up learning with more purpose and value upon returning to school. This is one of the most important purposes of an internship program. By reason of a period of experience, even though brief, a student has a much better grasp of what accounting is about. Greater awareness of the practical aspects of accounting enables the student to select his remaining courses more wisely and strengthens his desire to master the subject material. Afterwards he can make a better selection of courses. He will probably realize the importance of some areas about which he was doubtful before (English, effective speaking, etc.). For full benefit, it is important that the timing of the internship be carefully considered. If it comes too early, the student is likely to have an inadequate background of accounting. It is generally believed that students should have completed several courses in accounting before interning. These should include Elementary and Intermediate Accounting, Cost Accounting, and Elementary Auditing. Internships should be especially valuable to students who take postgraduate work, and some schools in their programs for a Master's degree in accounting require field work as a prerequisite.

To give maturity and confidence to the student. No matter how much theoretical education a man has, he cannot help but feel a little strange the first time he is confronted with the complexities of a business office. The internship period rubs off some of the "green." Placement departments of schools have reported that men who have had internship work fared much better in employment interviews.

To help the school place graduates. The last several years have seen the demand for men for public accounting work grow to such magnitude that the schools have not had to be much concerned about placement of graduates. This may not always be the case. A school with a good internship program will in the long run have the advantage in placing its graduates.

To provide a desirable trial period, to the advantage of both the student and the employer. If the internship is during January, February, and March, which include the usual peak period of work in most practices, the student experiences typical work in public accounting. Also he has the opportunity to observe different kinds of accounting work in private industry. As a result the student can make a sounder decision as to his job selection upon graduation.

Not only is this a desirable trial period for the student, but it benefits the employer. It provides some temporary help during a peak period. It also enables the employer to observe a prospective permanent employee without making a commitment for permanent employment.

To improve the school's curriculum. Students return to school from internship work with specific ideas of what they need to learn. They also return better qualified to judge the quality of the courses and teaching offered them. The employers learn about what is being taught. The employers and the schools get to know each other better. All of this should add up to improved curricula. Also, experience has shown that students who have interned make a definite contribution to the training of other students through discussions in classes, in organizations, and by general contact with other students.

Unless the employer, the school and the student realize and accept their responsibilities, one or more of the above purposes will not be accomplished. What are these responsibilities?

Responsibilities of the employer. *To inform school and student about salary, expenses, etc.* The employer should make entirely clear to the school and to the intern the salary he will pay, including his program for overtime, his dinner-money allowance, his travel-expense rules, and whether or not he will pay the student's fare from school to his office and return.

To pay a fair salary. The employer has an obligation to pay the student a fair salary for the work he does. This will generally be somewhat less than the regular starting salary for junior accountants.

To see that the student gets a clear understanding of work rules and standards of professional conduct. Not knowing what is expected of him creates frustrations which may well render a person practically incapable of doing good work. Employers should not fail to realize that the many questions regarding hours, travel, dress, etc., which are so obvious to the experienced man are unknown to the beginner. These matters, as well as rules of professional conduct, should be carefully explained to interns and a procedure for indoctrination of new men set up within the employer's firm.

To provide student with varied assignments. For an internship experience to contribute the most to the educational process, it must be carefully planned. A special effort should be made to vary the student's assignments so that he gets a broad view of public accounting. If at all practicable he should work for two or more seniors so that (1) he gets the experience of working under different personalities, and (2) there can be more than one source of appraisal of his work.

To give students adequate supervision. It is the employer's major responsibility to supervise the work of the intern in a manner which gives learning value to his experience. This involves detailed instruction as to each operation assigned, over-all general instruction regarding the engagement, and careful review and criticism of the work. The in-charge senior must be advised of the purpose of internships and should understand that "on-the-job training" is an important feature.

To evaluate the student's work and to discuss results with him. The intern has a right to know from the employer what the employer liked and didn't like about him and whether the employer has a definite view as to whether he should continue in public accounting. This is not a problem when the employer likes the student, can use him, and offers him a permanent job. In other cases the employee may not know whether his performance was acceptable or not. It should be standard practice for the employer to have a terminal conference with the student to discuss his work.

To furnish a report to the school. At the conclusion of the internship period the employer should report to the school. This report should be on the form provided by the school, if the school provides one, or otherwise in some other useful form. In every instance a report should be made. It should indicate the student's ability, aptitude, attitude, etc. It should describe the nature of the work the student did and perhaps even grade the student in various respects. Also the school should be informed as to whether the student was or will be offered employment.

Responsibilities of the school. Schools which organize and participate in internship programs do so in the belief that the programs contribute to the development of well-qualified accountants. Proper supervision and operation of an internship program, with the necessary follow-up, cannot be perfunctory. It requires time and effort on the part of someone who is directly responsible, as well as the co-operation of other members of the faculty of the school of business and perhaps other colleges within the university. Within the accounting department, one of the basic responsibilities is to arrange and plan the student's work in such a manner that he will benefit the most from the internship period without suffering a serious loss in value of other course work. Schools generally find it desirable to arrange to have the student take several accounting courses following the internship period so that he may benefit from the experience obtained on the job during his subsequent study of accounting. Probably under ideal conditions the internship should be in the junior year for students who do not expect to go beyond the undergraduate program, or in the senior year for those who expect to take graduate work. However, in many instances, this is not feasible because the arrangement of courses does not qualify the student technically for internship as early as his junior year.

Certain specific responsibilities of the school in relation to the operation of the internship program are as follows:

To provide qualified students. The major responsibility of the school is to approve for internship work only those students properly qualified. Qualifications might include academic background, mental and technical ability, maturity, personality, and vocational interest. Among other criteria of selection, many schools use the AICPA's Orientation and Achievement Tests and establish high scoring standards for eligibility in the program.

It is important that students selected to participate in an internship program be able to benefit from the experience without loss in their academic work.

To act as channel of communication between student and employer. The school should recognize that it has a responsibility to the student and the employer as a channel of information, recommendation, and complaint. The school should report to the employer the reaction of interns and make recommendations for improvements in the employer's program. All complaints, whether from the student or the employer, should be handled promptly.

To brief the student on standards for the junior accountant. Students should be briefed on what will be expected of them—professional ethics, conduct, appearance, actions, talk, travel, and so forth.

To require student reports. It is desirable that the school require reports from a student based on the work he did. These can be part of the basis for academic credit, where such credit is allowed for the program. Care must be taken that the students understand their reports must not violate professional confidences.

Student responsibilities. The major responsibility of the student is that he recognize the seriousness with which a man must face his job. He should seek out and comply with all of the rules of the employer, demonstrating a co-operative attitude and an interest in putting in a good day's work. He should behave as a business worker, not as a student. He should dress for business, not for the campus.

To treat clients' affairs as confidential. An important responsibility of the student is to recognize the extreme confidence in which the professional accountant holds the affairs of his client. His work reports should permit no close guesses as to where he was working. Under no circumstances should a client's affairs be discussed with persons not on the employer's staff, and then only with such staff members as have a legitimate concern with the particular engagement.

To accept the opportunity to learn. A student should recognize that the internship is a part of his educational experience and be alert to benefit from it. Fullest benefit is received only when the student maintains an attitude of receptiveness to the ideas, techniques, and objectives that he encounters.

It is hoped that this statement of goals of the internship programs, of responsibilities of each of the participants, and of standards which should be observed will aid in making internship programs more effective educational devices. The committees will welcome comments and suggestions on this subject.

Selecting Staff Members

■ ONE CPA DESCRIBED his firm's views as follows:

What are the guideposts in the selection of personnel? Admittedly, there are no tailor-made tools for use in selecting a prospect. All of us have had disappointing experiences with some of our brightest selectees and at least a few amazing examples of progress from men who appeared to be only fair or medium prospects at the outset of their employment.

Many of these mistakes in selection have stemmed from two factors: an acute shortage in personnel for the last decade, and the inexcusable egotism on the part of some of us who feel we can pick a prospective partner after a three-minute interview. Fortunately, certain guideposts enable us to minimize the chance of error.

In the first place, we should consider the type of individual we want. It has often been said that not everyone can be or wishes to be a partner, that every successful practitioner must keep a complement of run-of-the-mill juniors or seniors who are satisfied to do detailed work. Such an attitude should not be adopted by any progressive accountant. From the economic standpoint alone, it is unsound. All of us have seen our costs on a job leap entirely out of proportion because of the time it takes to correct errors. As far as possible, all new staff men should be viewed as prospective partners.

Perhaps because of the shortage of good men, few firms go beyond the personal interview in deciding whether to hire a candidate:

1. Aptitude, vocational interest, and achievement tests are rarely used, although if an applicant had already taken AICPA (or other) tests, the results are given consideration.

2. In many cases references are not checked.

3. There is little apparent recognition of the fact that grades from different colleges are not necessarily comparable—for example, a student in the top quarter at one institution may be inferior to a student in the second quarter at another school with higher standards.

4. In many cases college grades are not checked.

5. Despite heavy reliance on the interview as a selection factor, there has been little effort to analyze results and improve interviewing methods, or to judge applicants in terms of what the firm has learned from both good and bad experiences with employees hired in the past.

Here are some typical comments on selection techniques by some of the interviewed firms:

Personality and the impression the candidate might make upon a client is probably the most important factor. Grades rate next, although as long as they are above average, they are not the major factor. Some consideration is given to previous experience in private accounting, but not much weight to previous public accounting experience, since the firm prefers to train its own staff. Usually, all the partners see a promising candidate, but the two senior partners do most of the hiring.

Initial impression is very important. If he doesn't impress me, he probably won't impress clients. He has to have done pretty well in college. Some men have excellent grades, but they are poor practical accountants.

The client has an image of the way a professional should act. We like to maintain this image; we want a man who gives an impression of a professional man, who can handle himself well, has a good appearance, and can express himself.

Because of the importance of the interview, the campus interview is always followed by a visit to the office where three additional people talk with him; in addition, the boy goes out to lunch with some of the staff members and we get their opinion too.

We have a credit-report agency make careful investigations of references of all people employed.

The two most important things in selecting juniors are grades (we require at least a "B" average) and impression during interview. The latter is particularly important.

FACTORS IN THE SELECTION OF PERSONNEL

In selecting employees, most firms emphasize a candidate's college grades and the impression he makes during an interview. There is, however, wide variance in the relative importance given these two basic factors.

Appearance and manner. Of primary concern are the applicant's appearance and manner. This is quite understandable because of the nature of the assignments. Almost from the outset the men must work in the field, in the offices of the firm's clients. As juniors they work in groups with a senior accountant who has full responsibility for the work and who has the contacts with the management in the client organization. Consequently, the client has little or no direct contact with any of the juniors. They are *seen* but not *known*. Under such circumstances, the client's only basis for forming an impression of the junior is his appearance and manner as judged from casual observation and superficial contacts. No matter how competent and intelligent the man may be, if his appearance is unusual or his manner is lacking in warmth or appeal, he is very likely to forfeit the client's acceptance. Since the client's attitude is not subject to appeal, regardless of its fairness or merit, the astute accounting firm seeks juniors whose superficial characteristics will insure their acceptance by their clients.

In addition, the junior must also be accepted by another group in the organization in which he works. Since he is in no sense an executive, the majority of the persons with whom he must work are those in the lower grades in the client company. Many of these will be fearful that the outside accountants will find something that will reflect adversely on them. Others will resent public accountants solely because they are outsiders, "foreigners," so to speak. On the other hand, the good will of these company employees is often helpful; certainly, their ill will will make the junior's work more difficult. Hence, the ability to gain their friendship is important, even if the grounds are the superficial ones of appearance and manner. Since many of these subordinates in company bookkeeping departments are women, a good appearance and charm of manner are often very worthwhile assets in a junior accountant.

The danger here is the tendency for the recruiter to place disproportionate emphasis on appearance and manner. Granting that these attributes are highly desirable, they are not sufficient in and of themselves to guarantee a junior's success. Their place in the determination of the junior's success may be compared to his knowledge of elementary arithmetic: without it, he cannot succeed; with it he may or may not be successful. In consequence, appearance and manner may be thought of as preliminary or screening criteria. In other words, if the candidate is obviously unsuited in these respects, he should not be considered further. The fact that he has these qualifications means only that he has the first requisites for the work, not that he is ready to be hired.

Education and school grades. What is the minimum educational background considered necessary for public accounting? The majority of firms employ only those having college degrees. Many of them set up as a minimum educational requirement not only the college degree but also a major or specialization in accounting. Some firms have indicated that they will consider only applicants who have graduated with high scholastic rank. Admittedly, the possession of a college degree does not necessarily indicate that the holder is a well-educated person. Some people without college degrees have far more education than some with degrees have. However, statistics on successful candidates at CPA examinations indicate that a far larger percentage of the candidates who have college degrees pass the examination than those without, such percentages being determined in relation to the entire respective class taking the examination.

While applicants should be college-trained men, this is not intended as a rebuff to the many outstanding accountants who have not had the benefit of college training—nor is it meant to exclude the bright young men who cannot afford college, and who might prove better eventually than some of the college trainees. With respect to the former, they have had the equivalent of a college education through experience; but, generally, young men without college education will not be able to stand the competitive pace set by university graduates. They will not comprehend technical requirements demanded of beginning juniors until long after the college men have advanced to semi-seniors or even seniors. All this adds up to pretty expensive trainees and, indeed, questionable ones.

The school marks of the prospects are the most important guideposts in proper personnel selection. The accounting profession has no place in it for men of only average intelligence. The sooner all of us stop experimenting with prospects who do not have the mental qualifications to succeed, the sooner we shall improve our public relations, which suffer every time we are forced to admit to one of our veteran employees that we made a mistake when we hired him.

"C" students should not be barred from consideration if they are otherwise qualified. However, they ought to be requested to take the AICPA's tests designed to measure accounting aptitude. If they fail on the tests, they should be advised to look for employment in another field.

School marks, of course, are not all-inclusive in determining potentials, nor do they have the same meaning in every school. They must be judged in the light of the standards of the school and its reputation in comparison with similar institutions.

Some firms do not consider a prospect unless he ranks in the top 25 per cent of his class scholastically. But most seem to feel that so long as grades are above average they are secondary to the ability to get along with people. There is also an increasing interest in "well-rounded" men. A few firms entertain the possibility of hiring liberal-arts majors who would study accounting at night; but this plan is handicapped in some states by the legal requirements for the CPA certificate. Candidates who have concentrated almost entirely on accounting courses may be unable also to write clear English. There is growing concern over this block to effective communication between accountant and client.

General intelligence. The role of intelligence in success as a junior accountant is somewhat analogous to that of appearance and manner: an average or better intelligence is a prerequisite to success. On the other hand, this, by itself, does not necessarily insure success. Unfortunately, a high level of intelligence does not necessarily insure an equally high degree of judgment or common sense. There is no necessary correlation between the two qualities. A man may be outstandingly brilliant, but have the judgment of a small child. Consequently, while a candidate for accounting work must have average or better intelligence (otherwise he will have difficulty in mastering the techniques or dealing with the abstractions involved in the work), the mere fact that he is intelligent cannot be taken as a guarantee that he will do even a competent technical job. His judgment must be appraised on the basis of factors other than intelligence alone.

Fortunately, in public accounting work a better than average level of intelligence is never a liability. The public accountant's duties and work should offer such a continuing challenge that even the most brilliant mind should rarely find it dull or monotonous. Furthermore, a good man should always be able to see and chart his future which in itself should provide an intellectual challenge. Hence, while a high level of intelligence does not guarantee success, its presence in a candidate should never give cause for concern as might be the case in less challenging activities.

Experience. In the past some accounting firms recruited junior accountants from private industry after they had had some bookkeeping or other clerical experience. Currently there is a tendency among a majority of the firms to take candidates directly from college without any experience in accounting. While many firms have no minimum experience requirement, others require a specified period in their own office with duties other than those of junior accountant such as checking reports, filing, comparing, and other checking. Some small firms require bookkeeping experience for a year or more as a minimum experience requirement.

SEVEN DESIRABLE TRAITS OF THE JUNIOR ACCOUNTANT

What are the desirable traits of junior accountants, i.e., what traits ought they to have, and how do you determine them?

1. Occupationally stable. It is important that men be hired who will stay with the firm long enough to bring a return to the firm for the money invested, and more than that, advance to senior, supervisory, and perhaps major executive positions.

But some college men have strong though transient enthusiasms for different fields. One good student tried engineering for one year, business law another year, a third year economics, and finally finished up a major in accounting. Here, because of strong business background, he was chosen by a recruiter for an accounting firm.

However, his basic instability soon made itself felt in passing enthusiasms for different aspects of his job. Tasks energetically begun fell by the wayside, unfinished or barely finished to the senior accountant's satisfaction. The junior would overlook important instructions or forget to relay vital information to the senior. His interests ran off into all directions because he was basically unsettled, always seeking to try something else, and always only momentarily enthusiastic. There was no occupational stability here, no habit of staying at one activity for an extended period of time.

2. Uncomfortable when idle. Every man, when asked directly if he is industrious, energetic, and desirous of achievement, will promptly reply in the affirmative. No other answer is possible. Yet, as everyday evidence indicates, not every young man will labor steadily, conscientiously, and productively on his assigned tasks and duties for his employer.

The intelligent student who finds school work too easy, who has never had to earn any of his spending money, who has had his way through school paid by others, who has idled his summers away at resorts or in purely pleasurable activities, may never have developed the habit of working hard.

Naturally, in most public accounting firms, the juniors are either on an assignment, in which case they are perforce busy, or they are not assigned.

In this latter event, they may be idle, at least as far as billable time is concerned. But this does not mean that they need spend this time doing crossword puzzles or interfere with the work of others who are assigned by gossiping with them. Nor does it mean that they need to make a grandstand play of seeking work by charging into their supervisors' offices obviously demanding an assignment. The genuinely industrious man always, and usually quietly, finds himself something to do. It may be a matter of cleaning up odds and ends from previous jobs. It may even be office-boy work. The important thing is that he is forbearing and patient and, at the same time, constructively engaged. He has a strong desire to achieve.

3. The habit of thoroughness. The ability to persist in an activity despite difficulties and obstacles, and to finish what he has started, is characteristic of good young men. Many people are superficial in their habits. When confronted with complicated procedures involved in checking inventories, in verifying bank accounts, in vouching fixed assets, etc., they become careless. They do not get all of the facts. The interest of some men dwindles as complications develop; they will only half-heartedly follow a problem through to its ultimate completion. They have not formed the habit of meticulous thoroughness and attention to detail.

This sort of person is usually the product of a home in which he was rarely reprimanded for failure to do his best, or even scolded for not coming up to standard. While it is granted that a failure to get all of the facts is also indicative of plain stupidity, it is probable that in many cases it also grows out of carelessness.

4. Is he a good team member? Almost every business demands that its employees put the company's interest before their own and, if necessary, requires that the employees, on occasion, go beyond the ordinary requirements of their jobs and put in a few extra licks of work for the firm.

A man with ability to project his ambitions and unite those with company welfare and company goals is more apt to be successful in an organization than where the reverse is true. But that requires a particular type of personality.

Young men who have had sheltered lives either as only children, youngest children or sickly children, etc., who have been protected by overzealous parents, very often become demanding adults and continue to expect others to do for them. They have no drive towards doing for or contributing to others. Company or team loyalty is a wider concept than these individuals are capable of grasping; their usual goals are self-centered, and they approach all problems from the point of view of looking out for themselves first.

This type often has little regard either for a firm's good will or funds, sneers at other juniors who persist in staying overtime in order to finish some assigned task, and often takes short cuts on firm policy and procedure. It is this type of man who almost invariably resents anyone else's promotion and generally speaks critically of the top executives and company plans. He is the "lone wolf" in the organization who, regardless of his technical competence, is usually more of a liability than an asset because his inability to play as a member of the team causes him to become a disruptive force in every group with which he has contact.

5. Can he fend for himself? In every job there is a degree of self-reliance involved. The ability to make decisions is a part of self-reliance. Junior men are always called upon to make minor decisions. This may occur either when their seniors are out of town, home ill, or otherwise not available. They must also, as part of their own work, make some decisions, and gradually, if they are going to succeed, acquire the habit and ease of making more decisions involving matters of increasingly greater complexity and affecting more people.

However, some men never learn to make decisions because they are basically afraid of responsibility. They will avoid decisions whenever possible, ask seniors for opinions on what to do in the most obvious situations, etc.

6. He must get along with others. As already pointed out, the ability of any man to make and hold friends, to maintain good working relationships with others, and to obtain good personal acceptance by others, is extremely important in jobs which require direct, face-to-face contacts.

The ability to get along with other people is only in part an ability to be friendly with others. In good part, it is also the ability to accept criticism, to accept differences of opinion, to accept the fact that associates may be rivals without rivalry.

Occasionally, a junior accountant may turn out to be a sharply competitive, uncomfortably critical person, who regards all his associates and seniors as rivals, and who unnecessarily criticizes their conduct and work. At the same time, such an individual is fiercely resentful of any criticism which may be directed at him.

While such individuals may have excellent intelligence and good judgment involving materials, their conduct invariably is keyed to forcing others to co-operate with them rather than meeting colleagues or seniors halfway. Where their (unconscious) aggressive tactics arouse reactions, they endeavor to label all others as unco-operative. Should their work not be praised and lauded, they will sulk, pout, and criticize their superiors. The inevitable result of such prolonged behavior is an accounting firm broken up into cliques, with men pulling against each other.

7. Discipline, imagination, good judgment. Trainees who come in at the bottom of the accounting ladder are not expected to start out in positions of leadership. Nonetheless, a junior who does not possess certain basic traits will not develop into a senior, nor will he inspire confidence in juniors or clients even after years of experience.

Public accounting work is peculiar in that while leadership qualities are desirable, the prime requisite of a good junior is the ability to submit himself to discipline. At the outset he must be able to accept instructions and follow directions implicitly. He must first learn to do the detail work before he can begin to move up to where he can lead and instruct others. Only as he becomes skilled in the work does he begin to interpret, to use his judgment, and interpolate. The capacity to accept discipline is as important in a junior as is technical knowledge.

Because of this, most skilled recruiters want the man who is technically competent, who does his work well and conscientiously, and who follows instructions to the letter. Yet, they do not want the blind follower of instructions; they want a junior who can see the picture as a whole and know when to deviate from his instructions. In short, he must have perspective, imagination, and good judgment. These are rare qualities and their determination in an applicant is difficult.

In looking at these seven character traits, it may be interesting to notice that they are really part of a deeper and wider personality structure. In essence, anyone who has these desirable qualities is basically a mature person. Absence of these traits, or any one of them, indicates emotional immaturity; i.e., the failure of an individual to grow up emotionally. It is the emotionally immature who characteristically and invariably use bad judgment.

Compensation and Fringe Benefits

INCENTIVE AND MORALE

■ EMPLOYMENT TODAY is a two-way street. Not many years ago it was the applicant's responsibility to prove himself worthy of hire; the employer had merely to pick and choose. The practicalities of supply and demand have changed this. Moreover social and economic changes, plus a better understanding of human motivation, have made business and professional men aware that they have a responsibility toward the employee.

Certain provisions for personnel which were once referred to as voluntary "benefits" have come more and more to be considered basically as "compensation." To a great degree this is due to a change in social viewpoint. Once these were incidental benefits conferred, principally out of the generosity of the employer. Now they are looked upon as earned and as related directly to basic compensation and, in the case of organized labor, are negotiated with wage rates. Vacation time, sick leave, and similar items fall into this class.

A further reason for the change is attributable to the development of a broader outlook with respect to lifetime security for employees. Until recently the interest of employers as to security of personnel related primarily to security during their employment by the employer. Provision for the future was the individual problem of each employee and under economic conditions prevailing, the employees were supposed to provide personally for future security out of their basic compensation. Conditions have changed. The individual's preoccupation with lifetime security is much greater now and is influenced appreciably by the increasing difficulty of making individual provision for the future due to various causes, including the greater burden and prevalence of taxation and the tendency of industry to reduce the period of years of productive employment.

Personnel morale is not maintained merely by paying adequate or even better than run-of-the-mill compensation. Practically no one wants to be simply just as well off as he would be elsewhere. He wants—and it is a perfectly reasonable desire—to be better off than he would be elsewhere. It is therefore essential that in addition to all of the forms of compensation, direct and indirect, already discussed, there be some special incentive provided by the employment held which makes the position more desirable than one available elsewhere.

Such incentive may assume various forms. Examples are: a pleasant place in which to work; agreeable employer-employee relations; increases in compensation and advancement in position at reasonable, periodic intervals and in line with length of service, demonstrated efficiency, and capacity for growth; clearly defined and expressed personnel policies made known to staff; training programs; and so on.

For every employee there is more to a salaried position than simply earning a living at the moment. Both the beginner and the experienced worker think of the future. The older worker thinks of the future more in terms of continued security upon retirement. The beginner and the younger worker are interested more in getting a decent foothold and going up from there as far as opportunity and ability will take them. They also visualize security on retirement, but have more ambitious plans. There also is a natural desire to do work one likes or is most fitted for or which offers the greatest possibilities for progress.

Every employer who has his own ends to further and his own aspirations must consider these factors in selecting, training, compensating, and utilizing personnel. Where welfare programs provide realistically for the progress and betterment of each employee meriting recognition they provide equally for the welfare of the organization as a whole and create an *esprit de corps* which inspires each individual staff member to feel he is an integral, valuable, and valued part of the organization.

All firms cannot provide similar or equal incentives. Yet small firms are not necessarily at a disadvantage. Large bodies move slowly in more than one sense. In a small firm pay may not be as good initially or even later. Still advancement may be more rapid, breadth of experience may be acquired more quickly, there is certainly more intimate contact with the firm's general activities, and the path from, say, junior to partner may be more direct, shorter, and less impeded by competition.

In the accounting profession there is no obstacle, generally, to steady advancement from the lowest salaried position to a senior partnership other than purely personal limitations. This forms, probably, the highest incentive any employee can have. It is based primarily upon the realization that the more efficient a staff member becomes, the more desirable it is that he be utilized in the broadest possible area of activity. Such broadening of scope, responsibility, and performance carries with it inevitably commensurate advance in position, financial return, and prestige. An accounting firm proceeding along different lines is hardly functioning effectively.

It is probably because of adequate recognition by the profession generally of the principles and practices underlying maintenance of morale that there have been no moves toward unionization of staff personnel.

COMPENSATION PLANS IN GENERAL

The range of such plans is very great. At one end is the simple payment of a fixed salary to each employee. At the other extreme is payment of a fixed salary, with bonuses based on various production or profit schedules, numerous fringe benefits involving health, life and accident insurance, pensions, vacations graduated according to length of service, and so on. There may even be a percentage-of-net-profit basis in lieu of any salary, and in addition to all other compensation features there may be commissions to staff personnel for business brought to the firm. On all features other than straight salary, numerous variations are employed. For example, a percentage-of-profit basis may involve a share in all the profits from all business or merely a share of the profits on such engagements as the specific staff member covers in his assignments.

How much a staff member is paid depends upon a number of factors. The most important is, naturally, the nature and value of the service he renders. Positions are usually classified but within classification there can be a rather wide minimum-maximum range of pay. Training and experience have a decided bearing, as well as length of service. But there also are two additional factors that cannot be ignored. One is that compensation is sometimes based on what a firm must pay; the other that it is sometimes what the firm can afford to pay.

The compensation that a firm must pay is the minimum comparable rate for the specific classification in its area. If it will not pay that, it cannot secure personnel. If it cannot pay that, it is not established on a sound economic basis. Its income must be sufficient to pay at least the irreducible minimum set by competition within and without the profession. When its net income exceeds both minimum compensation needs and a normal profit for the principals, the answer to the question of how much the firm can afford to pay is governed solely by the attitudes of the principals. From the usual accounting standpoint, no part of straight salary actually involves profit sharing. Nevertheless it is clearly evident that a firm that pays appreciably more than current rates for stated classifications is sharing its prosperity with its staff and presumably in consideration of staff contributions to the firm's prosperity. The same would be true of fringe benefits except to the extent that certain of such benefits are in the course of time becoming general practice and therefore a normal cost.

The fixed relation between fees and staff compensation shows up unmistakably in the practice many firms have of figuring fees to clients at two-and-one-half (or some other ratio) times staff compensation or per day at one per cent of the annual compensation for each staff member. Reversing the formula, it is evident that where a staff member's productive time results in fees of $15,000 for the firm, his annual compensation, using the two-and-one-half-to-one ratio, would be about $6,000.

STARTING SALARIES

The firms most successful in hiring competent men have made at least some attempt to be reasonably competitive in terms of salaries and fringe benefits—both material and psychological.

A significant difference in thinking on starting salaries seems to exist among practitioners. One group usually sets a salary level and seeks men who will work for it. Other firms are more prepared to pay what may be necessary to hire the men they want.

Few firms start all college graduates at the identical rate. The spread within smaller firms generally does not exceed $25 a month. But in some of the multi-office firms starting salaries may vary as much as $100 a month. Few firms pay a specific premium for a graduate degree. The consensus seems to be that any superior ability reflected in the advanced degree will not show up until the man has acquired some practical experience, at which time a salary adjustment will be made. Variation in salaries based solely on geographical location or size of the firm is not as great as might be expected.

An informal survey of CPA firms, college placement officers, accounting faculties, and state societies, made by *The Journal of Accountancy* in the spring of 1961, showed that, as has been the trend for several years, offers to comparable-quality candidates tended to be at least $25 a month higher than the previous year.

Offers by the larger firms to job-hunting accounting majors who earned a Bachelor's degree in June 1961 ranged from $450 to $575 a month. Offers made to graduates with Master's degrees were generally $25 to $50 higher. The national firms tended to be fairly uniform in offers to applicants with comparable qualifications. Starting salaries in local firms appeared to be somewhat lower in some parts of the country.

The firms responding said that their top offers were being made only to a relatively few top-ranking graduates. Regional variations ran about $60 a month from the lowest average to the highest, except that the range was even greater in New York City. The apparent aptitude of the applicant, his academic standing, and the reputation of his school account in large part for the wide range in offers.

A salary survey made by The College Placement Council tended to support the data gathered by *The Journal of Accountancy*. On the basis of information collected from sixty-one participating colleges and universities up to March 17, 1961, the Council reported offers (summarized in Table 1) made by public accounting firms to seniors receiving Bachelor's degrees in 1961.

Table 1*

Area	Number of offers	Average	High	Low
East	58	$481	$525	$300
Midwest	37	479	525	425
Southeast	19	460	525	325
Southwest	46	450	500	350
West	78	472	525	360
National	238	$470	$525	$300

*Data from Salary Survey 1961 Recruiting Year, Report No. 2, April 1961, The College Placement Council, Inc., Bethlehem, Pa.

In the New York City area salaries offered to June 1961 graduates were also higher than those of the preceding year and ranged as follows:

Table 2*

	Public accounting	Private accounting
Monthly salary offers		
Male		
High	$530	$500
Low	315	333
Average	428	440
Female		
High	—	390
Low	—	303
Average	—	345

*Data from "Survey of Salary Offers to 1961 Bachelor Degree Graduates in the New York Area," Report of June 1, 1961, Metropolitan New York College Placement Officers Association, New York University.

SALARY INCREASES

The problem of skyrocketing starting salaries has created new nightmares and headaches for partners and individual practitioners. Not only is there an increasing inability to make the newcomer pay for himself, but to complicate matters further, salaries of older employees are being forced up by higher rewards offered recruits from college campuses.

A few firms have adopted the simplest (and most expensive) route and have granted blanket raises to all employees. From the viewpoints of morale and ease of administration, pay raises all along the line might be beneficial. It is doubtful, however, if many firms can bear the payroll increase of 15 or 20 per cent necessary to maintain existing wage relationships among employees.

The second and probably most effective answer is to give no general or blanket increases, but award merit raises to selected employees. Theoretically, the more valuable men will be retained and any dissatisfaction will be among less essential personnel. This plan may also embrace the development of wide salary ranges or brackets for personnel within a classification, accompanied by an attempt to discourage discussion of salaries among employees.

The system of wide pay variations for staff members within a bracket should tend to dampen jealousies and resentments if wages are not publicized. Any set rule against revelation by employees of salaries, however, may seriously impair morale and *esprit de corps*.

The wage structure may include a provision for periodic salary increases and cost-of-living adjustments which can be used to help solve the problem. Some firms report that periodic increases for new personnel will be reduced to offset in part their higher starting salaries.

Most firms declare that salary increases are based strictly on merit. Yet raises of some amount tend to be automatic for the first few years for these reasons:

1. The wish to maintain a differential between experienced men and the rising starting salaries of new men
2. The need to compete with the offers made by private industry
3. The desire to provide newer men with tangible evidence of their progress

In general, the staff man makes fairly steady progress for the first five or six years, at which point salaries tend to start leveling off. During this period, many firms give semiannual increases until a man has three or four years' experience or reaches a certain salary level. Further increases generally are made on an annual basis, the amount varying widely with the individual.

Salaries range widely at the fifth-year level of experience. An interesting point is that, in a number of cases, men who started at a lower-than-average salary will equal or surpass, at the five-year stage, colleagues who began at higher rates in other firms. For example, in one firm which pays a relatively low starting salary, its five-year men are earning salaries comparable to those reported by some national firms. Some smaller firms which may be unwilling (or unable) to subsidize the beginner can and do bring young men along rapidly once they have started to earn their own way.

PER-DIEM AND TEMPORARY EMPLOYEES

Some organizations employ some full-time staff employees on an hourly or per-diem basis of compensation. While exact details of such employment are not available, two possibilities seem logical. One is that small firms, where the volume of work is not adequate to provide for a regular basis of compensation, engage one or more permanent employees who work regularly for them over yearly periods but not for a regular number of hours a day or a regular number of days a week. Their workday or workweek is regulated by the work available and they are likely to fill in the remainder of their time with outside activities.

Small firms can, by paying staff men only for productive hours, reduce the risks inherent in irregular activities and thus be certain of profitable results from the fixed ratios of difference between income earned and salaries paid.

The other possibility is that, to some extent, payment on a per-diem basis constitutes profit sharing, since the daily rate paid is usually higher in equivalent than the going monthly rate and the employee who is willing to speculate on the extent of activity is in a position to earn more when he is fully occupied.

Where, in both types of cases, adequate volume or stability is attained, it usually is the practice to switch staff personnel to full-time employment on a weekly or other regular periodic compensation basis.

The general hiring of temporary staff personnel during busy seasons represents a different situation. Such employment constitutes a supplement to permanent personnel, but indicated improvement in stabilization of the workload has made the engagement of temporary employees less of a necessity. Normally it is advantageous for a firm to rehire the same temporary employees if their previous services proved satisfactory and they are available.

OVERTIME COMPENSATION

Such payments fall into two classes: those paid pursuant to Federal-Wage-and-Hour legislation and those paid at the discretion of the employer.

Many firms pay overtime rates at time and a half to the extent required by Wage-and-Hour regulations. Some simply pay the hourly rate for each hour in excess of the regular number of hours worked per week.

The treatment of overtime varies so widely that no pattern is evident. Overtime pay—speaking exclusively, of course, of those employees who by job definition are exempt from the provisions of the Federal Wage and Hour Law—ranges from none through straight time to time and a half and compensatory time off. Some firms informally consider overtime as a factor in computing annual bonuses.

Overtime policy at the senior level varies greatly. National firms pay at least straight-time rates to most of their staff members.

A particular point regarding payment for overtime under Federal Wage-and-Hour regulations deserves mention. This is that most firms make no attempt to base such payments upon whether the work performed by the firm or the employee comes within the ruling definition of interstate commerce. Obvious possible reasons for this attitude are: (1) the firm voluntarily extends the prescribed rate to all employees receiving pay within the federally fixed limits even though they are not engaged in interstate commerce, (2) the inability to come to any reasonably safe conclusion that a particular engagement or service does or does not involve employment in interstate commerce, (3) it is less expensive to make payment without regard to interstate-commerce relation than to keep detailed records to segregate hours affected from those exempt, and (4) it is inequitable as well as bad for employer-employee relations to base payment or nonpayment of overtime on so arbitrary and artificial a distinction.

Federal Wage-and-Hour-Law provisions for payment of overtime relate fundamentally to time in excess of a basic workweek of forty hours. However, many firms have variable basic workweeks or rates of pay which require averaging or other adjustment to establish a workable and equitable method of paying overtime acceptable under the law. There are several approved methods for such averaging or adjustment known as the irregular workweek, the Belo-type, and the long workweek plans.

The irregular workweek. This is known also as the fluctuating or variable workweek. Dividing the employee's weekly straight-time pay by the hours actually worked in that workweek will give his regular rate. This rate will, of course, vary if the number of hours worked varies. The excess over forty hours is the time for which the employee must be paid overtime in a single workweek consisting of seven consecutive days.

The Belo-type plan. This is a method in which there is (1) a regular hourly rate for the first forty hours, (2) another rate of 1½ times the regular rate for hours beyond forty and (3) a guaranty of a minimum weekly salary regardless of hours.

In this type of overtime pay computation, the regular rate is usually set low so that regular time plus overtime does not exceed the guaranteed minimum. If the regular rate is set at 1/60th of the weekly minimum, 53 1/3 hours (40 at regular rate and 13 1/3 at time-and-a-half) will produce a wage equal to the guaranteed minimum.

The long workweek plan. This makes it possible to comply with overtime provisions without increasing costs in the case of employees working *regular* workweeks in excess of forty hours. Such employees are placed on a regular workweek of more than forty hours (say forty-eight hours) at a stipulated salary (say $65) that includes overtime. The regular rate of pay is computed by dividing the salary ($65) by the total hours (48) plus half the number of hours in excess of forty. The regular rate is therefore $1.25 per hour, and the total pay is $50 for forty hours plus $15 (at time-and-a-half) for eight hours.

To make this arrangement effective, each such employee must understand clearly that his stated salary includes overtime for the hours in excess of forty, and also that if he works more or less than the stipulated normal long workweek on any occasion his pay will be increased or decreased in relation to overtime covered by his regular salary for the usual period.

Some firms that do not give financial compensation for overtime (other than to those earning within the federally prescribed salary limitation) provide added compensation in other ways. Two methods are equally favored: (1) offsetting the accumulated overtime by a proportionate increase in vacation time; (2) offsetting the overtime against unassigned slack-period time. In the latter case the employer gives the employee days or parts of days off whenever work schedules permit.

Supper money. Closely related to the matter of overtime is the subject of supper money. There seems to be some doubt as to when a special allowance for this should be made and whether such allowance, if made, is in addition to overtime.

In the absence of evidence of a definite rule on the subject, it is considered that certain general considerations should govern. To justify payment of a supper allowance, it would seem reasonable to expect that the period of overtime being worked should be long enough (1) to cause the employee to miss having his supper at home or elsewhere according to his usual routine or (2) to require a break in the overtime period so that the employee will have supper at a reasonable or his usual hour. Where a supper-money allowance is made, it is not considered that overtime should also be paid for the suppertime period. What the regular supper allowance should be would depend on individual firm decision and is usually the same amount for all classifications.

BONUS PLANS

Many firms have in effect a form of bonus or profit-sharing plan. Bonus arrangements can vary widely. They can mean occasional payments of appropriate amounts to individuals as a reward for unusually effective service in connection with a specific assignment or over a considerable period of time on general work. In such informal instances no other regulatory conditions are stipulated or considered. However, in some cases they may in effect be in lieu of an increase in salary where the performance of the staff member is so outstanding as to merit suitable recognition yet the economic stability of the firm or its future foreseeable income are not so certain as to permit an increase in staff remuneration which will constitute a permanent addition to the salary cost.

A rather peculiar argument is sometimes advanced in favor of an occasional bonus payment in lieu of a salary increase. This is that where a salary increase is granted the recipient improves his standard of living and is, in the sense of security or saving, no better off. It continues that if he receives a bonus as a lump sum he can use it for some such special purpose as a payment on mortgage principal or as savings, whereas he would not apply a moderate salary increase in like manner. It is then asserted as a conclusion that a bonus, under such conditions, is of greater benefit than a salary increase.

Where formal bonus payments are made at stated intervals various conditions may apply. All staff employees may be covered or only certain of them. The amount may be a stated percentage of base pay for each person or it may be a different percentage for each classification of personnel. Where there is modification as to coverage, it may be with respect to classifications or according to length of service. A minimum requirement may be established as to length of service and percentages varied accordingly.

Where periodic bonuses are in effect they represent actually a fixed increase in basic pay, and payroll costs are therefore higher proportionately than bare salary totals. Such bonuses may be as advantageous to employees as regular increases, yet to the employee they have the disadvantage of remaining optional as to actual payment or as to amount and therefore cannot be counted upon with certainty. The very nature of this disadvantage to the employee constitutes, of course, a distinct advantage to the employer.

In setting aside a specific total sum for bonus payments, all firms are, of course, governed by income results. This influence can be indirect or direct. In the indirect type, where the income received or foreseeable makes a bonus payment possible, the firm sets aside an arbitrary amount for allocation to individuals or classifications. In the direct type, the amount set aside periodically is not an amount set arbitrarily on each occasion but an actual percentage of net profits. In such event, while the resultant payments to personnel may be called bonuses they represent a sharing of profits. One important difference between receiving bonuses and sharing in profits is, of course, that the employees tend to view the latter as somewhat of a vested interest in the firm's earnings and the former as discretionary and uncertain. Yet, realistically, it cannot be ignored that employees consider all forms of compensation—whether straight salary, bonuses, profit sharing, cost-of-living index supplements, or others—as a permanent increment and any diminution in money amount of any one of them as a decrease in pay.

Most firms give some part of their staff some direct compensation in addition to base salaries. In many cases they grant a Christmas gift of one or two weeks' salary, usually having some relationship to seniority, but tending to be automatic. Sometimes a discretionary bonus—usually averaging 10 per cent of base pay—is given to staff members.

Although it seems fairly common for newer men to receive at least a token bonus, in several firms men do not participate until they become seniors. (This sometimes coincides with the discontinuance of overtime pay.)

PROFIT-SHARING PLANS

A formal profit-sharing fund or allocation may involve either a participation in all profits of the firm or in a specified portion or proportion. All employees may share in the participation, or only certain classes, or certain individuals. Determination of the personnel participating or of the extent of shares assigned may depend upon grade of classification, length of service, or specific assignments worked on, or they may reflect highly special arrangements with specific individuals. For instance, some firms have in effect profit-sharing agreements which provide that the employees share only in profits from engagements in which they take part. This custom is more prevalent among small firms.

The participation by a specific staff member in the return from business he brings in to his firm (as distinguished from participation in profits on engagements to which he is assigned) is more in the nature of a commission representing a sharing of the fee than profit sharing. There are, however, many instances of firms making a special allowance in figuring an employee's bonus for new business resulting from his efforts in lieu of paying him a specific commission based on actual fees.

Not all firms compute in the same way the "profits" (or bonus fund) to be divided among staff personnel. The following is a list of the principal items deductible from net billings:

General office expense
Occupancy cost
Report-preparation cost
Staff base salaries
Travel expense
Unproductive time allowance
Partners' time billed

Profit sharing does not always mean a present division or payment of funds. It can mean a plan with retirement provisions whereby a proportion of profits is set aside regularly to establish an income-earning fund which will furnish retirement benefits ultimately. It may be used to good advantage either to provide such benefits where the definite responsibility of fixed payments under a formal pension plan cannot be assumed or to supplement the retirement benefits already provided for under a formal pension plan.

A survey of CPA firms in California conducted in 1956 revealed that there was a definite correlation between the size of the practice and the existence of profit-sharing plans. None of the practitioners whose gross fees were less than $30,000 had any type of plan. Only five per cent of the nonnational partnerships had any plan. Less than half of the large nonnational firms (gross fees of from $100,000 to $500,000) had some type of profit-sharing plan. Plans involving participation of employees below the rank of senior were a rarity.

VACATION PROVISIONS

The generally accepted provision is for a regular vacation of two weeks for every employee who has been employed for a minimum period of one year. For permanent personnel employed less than one year, two methods are favored. One is to grant one week's vacation after six month's employment. The other grants one day of vacation for every month of employment.

It is customary to grant one additional week after either five, ten, or some other fixed period of years of service; sometimes a fourth week is made available to those having many years of service with the firm.

Leave of absence with pay may supplement regular vacation periods on occasion. This is more likely to be true for higher grades of personnel where services rendered are measured more by quality than by time and where such extra leave with pay is granted in recognition of the possible need for a longer recreational or recuperative period. This is likely to occur when a senior or supervisor long with the firm has put in an exceptional period of extra hours without added compensation.

The chief difficulty experienced by accounting firms with respect to vacations is scheduling them. The usual vacation season begins just as the mid-year busy period starts. Under these conditions, the common solution is usually to schedule vacations in line with the periods selected by personnel but subject to rearrangement should pressure of work make it imperative. There must be, of course, a definite understanding that such a possibility is a natural occupational hazard of the profession.

Some firms attempt to meet the problem by requiring personnel to take one week prior to the busy season and one after it. The disadvantages of this to the personnel are obvious, although some employees occasionally have a preference for such an arrangement. Another attempt at solution calls for one week of vacation in summer and the other in fall or winter. This also has an appeal for some staff members. It is, however, more readily applicable to those having three weeks' vacation who are willing to take two of them in fall or winter. The growing appreciation of fall months for vacations is helpful, but the end of a busy season often finds almost everyone anxious to get away promptly and feeling a real need to do so.

The problem of vacations for principals or partners has added complications. A sole proprietor often finds it impossible to get away either because there is work he must do or because he has no assistant capable of handling matters satisfactorily during any prolonged absence. As for partners, this difficulty would not seem to exist. Yet it does appear that there is reluctance on the part of many partners to go on vacation, and that where they fail to do so resultant impairment of their efficiency and productivity is inevitable. Some firms consider it so essential that partners take a vacation that they make it compulsory and even include this provision in their partnership agreements.

Generally there is no set schedule for partners' vacations. Firms seem to leave it to the determination of each individual as to when and how long vacations shall be. Most firms reporting on this particular point comment significantly that the time for a partner's vacation is "when he can get away." Junior partners, of course, are not usually allowed similar leeway and are governed by the decisions of senior partners.

SICK LEAVE

Sick leave applies normally to definitely limited periods of illness. Beyond the stipulated periods, if there is any further arrangement it is under a formal plan covering physical disability resulting from illness, frequently with insurance protection.

Most firms provide sick leave at full salary for limited periods. The period limitation generally is one day a month or two weeks a year. However, there is good reason to believe that firms have such limitations in order to have a definite indication of policy but do not enforce them rigidly. Exceptions are indicated to be so general as to reveal that the special considerations in each case govern. A good deal depends upon the length of service of the employee, his value to the firm, his degree of loyalty, his record, and the firm's ability to extend as much assistance as the particular circumstances seem to warrant.

Where the illness continues beyond the period stipulated for payment of full salary and it is not possible or desirable to continue full salary payment, some firms grant further sick leave on part pay for another stipulated period.

In certain industries and more particularly in the service of the Federal government, sick leave may be cumulative. This means that an employee is entitled to a specific number of days of sick leave yearly and if any part of this is not used during the year the unused portion is carried over and added to the newly accrued period. In effect, a vested right to such leave develops and as an inevitable result the leave may be used without any actual illness being considered a prerequisite. No such practice appears to have developed in the public accounting field.

PENSIONS AND RETIREMENT PLANS

For many accounting firms, and particularly small ones which have not yet achieved a degree of economic stability permitting a long-range forecast of approximate income, the adoption of a pension plan with more than nominal benefits for employees is rarely feasible. A formal pension plan calls for annual payment by the employer of a fixed sum regardless of the amount of business receipts or profits. However, for many firms it is possible to set aside annually from profits some portion of earnings to create a fund for the establishment of retirement benefits.

While few firms make planned provision for retirement, some make informal arrangements to take care of individuals as required. Others feel no need for a retirement program since their staffs are relatively young. They expect their better men to become partners in due course and are not interested in developing career staff members.

GROUP INSURANCE

The types of group insurance a firm may have in effect are life insurance, hospital insurance, accident insurance, and sickness insurance. While such plans are more prevalent in the larger firms, they are not unknown in the small ones. Some firms have their own plan and arrangements with insuring companies. Group insurance requires that there be an adequate minimum number in a group; few small firms can meet this requirement within their own organization even if all employees are willing to participate. For such organizations the possibility of their participating personnel forming part of a larger group which can fulfill minimum requirements is of great value. An outstanding example of this for the accounting profession is the widespread participation in the AICPA Insurance Trust.

Health and accident insurance is rarely provided. On the other hand hospitalization coverage is available in the majority of the firms on a voluntary basis; staff members pay their own premiums. A number of firms, however, pay the premium on "major medical" policies.

PROFESSIONAL EXPENSES

Another significant welfare activity is defraying expenses of staff members in attending meetings of professional societies, or assisting personnel in connection with study courses. In order to encourage staff men to become members of professional societies, many firms pay part or all of their dues.

There appears to be an increasing tendency for firms to pay some of these expenses. A few firms, however, feel professional participation is a personal obligation of the men and expect them to pay their own dues.

LIBRARY FACILITIES

The library of an accounting firm is of utmost benefit to its staff personnel when personal use is permitted and encouraged. One manifest form of encouragement is to bring certain appropriate books, magazines, and articles to the attention of staff members and, so far as it will not interfere with use of the library for firm purposes, to make the contents available for home reading under proper regulations as to issuance and return. Another practical way of making helpful professional literature available to staff members is to subscribe to certain publications on their behalf. In such cases, due regard is had, of course, to selecting periodicals for the grades and capacities of the individual staff members.

SALARY ADVANCES AND LOANS

Practically every firm must consider this matter on occasion. It is possible to formulate a policy but enforcement depends greatly upon the circumstances of each case. Broadly speaking, the making of advances and loans is not a desirable practice. When there is general provision for it, it is apt to be abused. Further, when staff members frequently have occasion to seek advances or loans a serious doubt exists that such personnel possess economic and temperamental stability.

Understandable emergencies may occur, however, where assistance of this sort may well be a wise procedure. This would occur, for instance, in the case of a competent and valued staff member with long service and a known record of stability who through an unforeseen circumstance beyond reasonable anticipation is faced with a need to make a large expenditure he cannot readily meet out of his own capital or earnings. Probably the best course for any firm is to have a definite rule against advances or loans with an unwritten reservation that in such highly unusual cases exception may be made on consideration of all the circumstances and on appropriate terms.

MEDICAL SERVICE

One feature sometimes found in welfare programs is free periodic medical examination of personnel. However, firms providing insurance plans which require a preliminary physical examination consider this sufficient. It has been suggested that permanent personnel should be examined at least once every two years at the expense of the firm. The value of this from the standpoints of both employer and employee seems quite evident.

POLICIES OF SELECTED FIRMS

Here are some pertinent quotations on the subject of employee compensation and fringe benefits:

. . . No payment for overtime, but unlike other firms we put the new man immediately on a bonus basis; at the end of the year, even if he has been with us only six months, he participates in a small share of the bonus pool which is based on profits distributed on a discretionary basis.

His overtime hours are credited throughout the year. The firm may require him to take up to two weeks of this as additional vacation, and he himself can take more if he so wishes. The remainder is paid out at Christmas time at his then rate of pay.

The rate of hiring varies with the man's background and his immediate needs. . . We feel that the starting rate is not too important since the individual's earnings, starting with his first year on the job, are based on a drawing account, which is guaranteed, plus a share in the earnings directly resulting from his own personal efforts. The dollar value of his own personal production is figured and from this is deducted $2,000 for occupancy charges and 25 per cent of the total, if he isn't a CPA, or 20 per cent for a CPA, which goes into the firm pool. The net total earnings thus arrived at may be adjusted upward or downward, based on a review of the individual's performance during the past year.

Salary is based on merit, but the individual's salary is reviewed at least once a year, and his progress reviewed with him.

We explain the relationship between salary and billing rate and then suggest that a new man set his own salary. He must recognize that he is going to have to make the grade and pull his own weight with clients. If he starts at too high a rate, a senior accountant will not ask to use him on many jobs unless his ability is so pronounced that he justifies the higher rate. However, this is a way of seeing how much confidence the man has in himself and illustrates the way we use the merit system.

We expect a man normally to justify a merit increase within the first six months.

We pay what we have to for juniors. We give raises semiannually. There aren't many five-year men on our staff now. At this stage they tend to go out on their own (not to other firms). Some go with private industry. We lost one man to industry who had been with us for six years: he was offered a forty-seven per cent increase in salary.

From the very start of the office . . . all staff men (except a few employed temporarily) have been on a percentage-of-net-profit basis rather than a salary. . . . On each payroll day the staff man receives cash in such a sum as is estimated to approximate one-quarter of his final credit for that month; at the month end, when the outcome for the month is known . . . credit is passed to his ledger account for his percentage of the net profit for the month, and his account charged with all cash furnished him during the month. Each man is also charged in the same account with any cash advanced for travel expenses, and credited with any bills turned in for the same. The use of the percentage basis rather than straight salary has as a whole worked out well with us. It ties the financial compensation to each man directly into the net income of the office, gives him his share directly during the heartbreaking grind of the winter months, and obviates all computations of overtime, etc. In one or two cases, where the men had been on straight salary for years with their previous employers, a little trouble was encountered in getting them to understand our basis and have faith that it would work out satisfactorily for them in the long run. In fact, we lost two otherwise good men during the slack period of one summer largely from this lack of ability to see the picture on a long-term basis.

The AICPA Group Life coverage is paid for by the firm; we have an additional $5,000 group life toward which a staff member contributes. The firm pays for hospitalization insurance; we do not have a retirement program. We pay expenses for membership in any and all professional societies; expenses incurred as a result of membership in civic and service groups; expenses incurred in attendance at professional meetings; the CPA examination fee; practically anything that may be considered a contribution to the man's professional development.

Since the job involves a great deal of travel, we cover each man with accident insurance in order to protect his family, but the man does not know about this.

When he is away on a job, we expect him to stay at the better hotels and otherwise live as befits a professional man.

We don't have much in the way of usual benefits, but we try to operate an informal, relaxed office where a man has an opportunity to make something of himself. Our experienced men are pretty much their own bosses.

Staff Training

■ THE CAREFUL SELECTION of personnel must be recognized as only the first step in developing a competent staff. A young accounting graduate and also a seasoned accountant recruited from private industry will need training in the fundamental phases of public accounting practice. In fact, they are only embarking upon a period of further study of accounting, auditing, and business problems when they enter public accounting. Ultimately, their studies may lead them into the most difficult of auditing problems, or into specialized fields such as tax accounting, cost analysis work, and the installation of accounting systems. The successful practitioner must plan for and assist his staff in the attainment of the best training possible.

A complete program will include four types of staff training. These are: (1) staff-training programs, (2) on-the-job training, (3) professional-development programs, and (4) individual study. Each will now be considered, with the exception of professional development (see Section 4, page 376).

THE AICPA PROGRAMS

Earlier in the history of the accounting profession, on-the-job training was the principal method of bridging the gap between the university classroom and public accounting practice.

In recent years, more and more public accounting firms have turned to staff-training programs to introduce the beginning accountant to the public accounting profession.

In 1960, the AICPA developed and presented a staff-training program for beginning accountants. The program, now presented annually at various sites throughout the country, permits every public accounting firm to provide formal intensive training in the techniques and procedures required in a staff accountant's first three years of practice.

In the short space of two weeks, the participants (1) attend lectures delivered by outstanding authorities on topics such as Audit Reports, Programs, and Working Papers; Internal Control; Cash; Receivables; Inventories; Plant, Property, and Equipment; Liabilities; and Accountant's Legal Responsibility; (2) participate in the section discussion of cases on Cash, Receivables, Inventories, Revenues, and Professional Ethics; (3) work on laboratory audit case-type situations on the subjects of Internal Control-Evaluation and Recommendation; Cash; Receivables; Securities; Inventories; Plant, Property, and Equipment; Liabilities; Payroll; Individual Income Tax; and Non-Certificate Examination; and (4) participate in discussion of findings, working paper procedures and opinion exceptions of each audit case situation.

The group is divided into smaller sections for discussion and case problem work. In each section there is "balance" of participation in terms of the size of sponsoring CPA firms and geographic representation. In working with the laboratory audit case-type materials, the members of each section form teams of four or five persons working as if they were members of the staff of a CPA firm.

The team members elect, for each session, a "senior" who is responsible for supervising his team's work. The primary reason for such teaming of individuals is to permit the detailed checking to be accomplished in minimum time so that maximum time can be devoted to discussion and gaining an understanding of the reasons for and the types of errors the various procedures are intended to detect.

Each section leader specifies that no "team" should be permanent; new teams have to be formed for each new audit case. For the second week the participants are reassigned to different sections. The objectives of the reassignment are to permit all or nearly all participants to work with each other, and allow the discussion leaders to work on a personal basis with a greater number of accountants (and vice versa).

The audit case materials are realistic: representative checks, vouchers, receiving reports, income-tax forms, *Moody's Dividend Record, Wall Street Journals,* and such, are included where necessary. The materials closely parallel actual data in many respects; some are inadequate in signatures, approvals, etc. The errors and breaches include nearly all possible situations a junior accountant could be expected to encounter in audit engagements.

Evening toastmaster sessions are held at which each participant speaks impromptu on any subject during the first week and on assigned but previously unannounced subjects during the second week. After the toastmaster sessions, the participants are expected to return to their rooms or to a reading room and prepare, by necessary reading or problem completion or both, for the next day's sessions. A well-stocked library is available for those who deem it necessary to review.

The results of examinations and separate comments presented to the AICPA by the instructional staff serve as the basis for AICPA reports to the individual CPA firms about their participants.

The advantages of the staff-training program as the first stage in training for a career in public accounting are manifold:

1. The staff member returns from such a program with sufficient technical knowledge to permit him to carry out his assignments effectively with a minimum of supervision.

2. Early in his professional career, the staff accountant is introduced to the need for continuous study and education.

3. The staff member is given an early opportunity to become acquainted with his profession and his professional associates.

4. Subsequent routine audit work is made more meaningful and palatable after the staff member is acquainted with the objectives and importance of these procedures . . . an important aspect of the staff-training program.

5. The responsibility for the difficult and costly initial training of staff accountants is transferred from the firm to a specially trained staff of practitioners.

Sponsorship of newly hired staff accountants for participation at a formal staff-training program should be supplemented in the public accounting firm with on-the-job training.

ON-THE-JOB TRAINING

Theoretically, on-the-job training offers the best opportunity for training juniors, particularly in the basic phases of auditing practice. For the beginner, working on an actual job under the instruction and supervision of a competent superior who makes a real effort to teach (or preferably to assist his pupil to learn) all that can be learned from the job offers an ideal relationship. One might even visualize this as a class with one student or an example of the tutorial system of instruction installed in the practice of public accounting. Actually, this ideal is not often achieved. Too often the seniors, managing supervisors, and partners are too intent upon accomplishing the work to the best of their own ability, and within the least possible time, and lose sight of their obligation to give training to the juniors on the job. In fact, it is difficult for a senior on a rush job to spread his efforts so as to give the junior all the training and help which he might give him if they were working on a less hurried type of engagement. Then, too, many able accountants may feel that they have little ability or aptitude for teaching, even as tutors rather than as lecturers, and that it is not reasonable to expect them to do much instructing while concentrating on turning out the job.

Reviewing the work papers. On-the-job training is required to train the staff accountant in the procedures peculiar to the public accounting firm and to broaden the training begun at the staff-training program.

Such training takes various forms in different firms. One method which has been adopted by some firms is to have the senior sit down with the junior staff assistant or assistants before beginning an engagement and review the working papers of the previous year together with the audit program proposed for the current year. This gives the assistants a picture of the entire engagement and affords them an opportunity to anticipate problems peculiar to the audit. To expedite this review, it is helpful if each assistant has the opportunity to look through the papers before meeting with the senior in charge for the discussion of the engagement. Obviously, the effectiveness of this procedure of previewing the job will depend upon the co-operation and skill of the in-charge accountant and upon his ability to give his assistants a worth-while participation in the work. If skillfully handled, such a review in advance of the actual work in the client's office will stimulate interest and enthusiasm in the staff men. Furthermore, the time spent should be more than offset by time saved later in the engagement. Also, without this required program of review, the senior himself often may neglect to study adequately the papers and the audit program from the prior year, and may enter upon the job without sufficiently planning the work.

There are other ways in which the man in charge of an audit can assist in training the men under him much as a matter of course and as a regular procedure. One is to let the assistant learn by doing rather than by memorizing what he is told to do. Unfortunately some people seem to think that teaching involves a lot of talking and explaining and itemizing of every step to be taken. The best teaching is done by giving juniors problems which are almost beyond their grasp and at the same time instilling in them the interest needed to work the problems through to successful solutions. When a senior has a difficult problem, or even problems that are not very difficult for him but which require care and attention, he may well pass them on to his assistants. This can be done on the job or informally at lunch or while traveling to or from the job. Sometimes a better answer or a new approach may result, either because the senior has clarified his problem in explaining it or because the junior has found a new approach to a solution.

Preparation for the assignment. If a file could be prepared on the larger clients describing in some detail the client's operation and accounting system for the junior to study with the prior years' audit papers, he could better prepare himself for an audit of that client. The file, which would be an addition to the permanent file, could contain a description of the accounts (more information than just a chart of accounts), a sample of the client's accounting forms if necessary, flow charts, and whatever other information might be useful. The explanation of the more unfamiliar accounts such as suspense, clearing, reserve, or unrealized gain or loss accounts could include the purpose for which they were created, the transactions that cause entries in and out of the account, and the position of the account in the client's financial statements.

A list and description of the source and support material for the original entries into the books, including their location in the client's office and the name of the persons or departments originating them, would be helpful. Also, a list of the more permanent office employees and their duties would assist the junior accountant in finding answers to any problems encountered in the audit. The file could be reviewed each year by the senior accountant on the audit and could be kept current with the internal-control questionnaire.

While the new accountant will and should learn the client's system and office procedure as the job progresses and while he can always ask the senior, he could better prepare himself for the job and enter his first audits with more knowledge and confidence by studying this file. The senior is not always available to answer, and a confused junior who has to question a client's employee may not get an adequate reply. With the file to study and use during the audit, the junior could ask with confidence and authority. Uncertainty displayed by a junior to the client and his employees is very detrimental to good client relationships. The more knowledge of the client's accounting system a junior can display, the more confident the client will be that the audit is worth the fee.

Explaining the assignment. Even in making assignments to junior assistants, a certain amount of training technique is essential. Merely to assign a detailed list of things to be done on one part of the engagement without giving any indication of why they are to be done is to invite inefficiency in the accomplishment of the tasks. A list or detailed schedule of work accompanied by suggestions as to why the work is being done usually will accomplish better results. Staff men cannot be taught to think if they are given little opportunity and encouragement to think out the purposes of their work assignments. By giving them a few reasons why the procedures are useful they will be encouraged to make their work more effective.

Criticizing the junior's work. After the completion of his first job or jobs, the junior should be counseled by the senior on the job about the quality of his work and the techniques he is using. The junior could be shown where his weaknesses lie and how to correct them. He could be encouraged to ask questions or make his own comments on the audit field work. If these conferences are held in an informal, helpful atmosphere, the junior will not feel belittled for he is usually anxious to know how he is progressing and how he can improve his work habits. And the fact that these problems and questions are discussed soon after the audit and are not left to a later date, perhaps even the yearly staff sessions, is most important.

Five training watchwords for seniors. The senior or in-charge accountant is responsible for training the juniors working under his supervision so well that they will develop rapidly into senior accountants competent enough to be in charge of engagements of their own.

The following five training watchwords are directed to seniors as a reminder of their training responsibilities:

Explain the purpose of each audit procedure being performed by juniors under your supervision. It is not enough to give your assistants last year's working papers, the program of examination, and just a cursory "Let me know if you need help." There is a natural reluctance on the part of most people to ask for help; everyone wishes to appear to best advantage in the eyes of his superiors. By volunteering explanatory comments rather than waiting for questions, you will remove any thoughts in the minds of your assistants that you expected them to know all the answers.

Test the judgment of those working under your supervision by asking for tentative conclusions for each of the technical problems they present to you. By informing your assistants of the strong and weak points in their analyses of technical areas and explaining your reasons for coming to the conclusions that are reached, you will help them get ready for greater responsibility in the future—in effect, to grow into the job that you are now performing. Keep in mind that you will progress to greater responsibility faster if you are able to develop people under your supervision.

Give your assistants the whole picture. It is easy for you to assign a number of different tasks to an assistant without relating how the work he is doing fits into the audit as a whole. Assistants who have a better understanding of how the work they are doing relates to the entire audit will tend to do a more meaningful and thoughtful job. A better audit will result.

Encourage your assistants to think. In any audit there are a number of audit procedures which by their nature are somewhat repetitive and monotonous. However, a mechanical performance of these procedures without thought of their implications is of little purpose. While discovery of fraud or irregularity is not the primary purpose of an opinion engagement, many clients expect an auditor to discover any major areas of weakness that may be present. Since it is during the more repetitive routine phases of an audit that misdoing is most apt to be discovered, alertness at such times is of utmost importance. Stimulate the imagination of your assistants regarding possible improvements in the client's accounting system or internal control procedures, possible modifications in the program of examination, or suggestions on how to better administer the audit. Ideas on these topics will pay dividends in many ways.

Review the working papers prepared by each assistant before the completion of the job. After an assistant has been reassigned to other work, it is very often impractical to find the time necessary to point out errors, omissions, or improvements which could have been made in an individual's job performance. While rating forms and personnel evaluations fulfill an important need, they cannot substitute for an individual review of job performance. The review should be made immediately upon conclusion of the job, while it is still fresh in the minds of both the senior and the assistant.

To summarize briefly, we may say that effective but practical on-the-job training can be obtained in all accounting offices if the accountant in charge of the job will give some attention to sharing the engagements with his assistants. Even a little sharing of the planning, the programming, the problems, and the peculiar questions that arise not only will give valuable training but will result in better work. Regardless of the size of the accounting office, on-the-job training by sharing the engagement is an available method of staff training.

INTRAFIRM PROGRAMS

Many medium-sized and large firms also develop their own staff-training program in recognition of the need for self-improvement and for the development of new methods and techniques.

The proper time for classes. Training classes may be held during office hours, on Saturday mornings, or in the evenings, but some firms prefer a short intensive period lasting from a few days to a few weeks. Small firms probably will have difficulty in devoting a period of weeks to an extensive program, although some might be able to pick a time of the year when a few days could be given over completely to the training of beginners or to classes in specialized fields. As an initial step, it may be well to adopt a modest program designed entirely for juniors and semi-seniors, with the classes held once a week for a period of two hours over perhaps eight or ten weeks. For this type of class, the time might be set for four to six o'clock, which is suggested principally to enable staff men to come in from jobs and yet not be delayed too long in getting home after the class. Some may prefer to start the class an hour earlier so that the entire class period is during office hours. Others may find it preferable to hold the class at the beginning of the day.

If this type of training program is set up, it is essential that a regular schedule be fixed in advance and adhered to throughout the period. If that is not done, the program is almost certain to fail of its purpose since it is impossible to fit in such a program in such a way as to be convenient at all times to all employees and not to require some readjustment of assignments. Firms that wait until there is a "good" time to hold such training sessions never start them.

Content of the course. *What should be excluded.* One approach to a decision as to the content of staff-training programs is to decide what not to include. Surely, it is not desirable to attempt to compete with college courses in principles of accounting, auditing, income taxes, and other subjects if these courses are available in classroom form or by correspondence. Such classes might be undertaken if it seemed advisable to stimulate the interest and effort of the staff members in self-education or perhaps in a correspondence course in which they have enrolled. A class of this type should be supplementary only and would differ materially from the usual classroom instruction. Review courses to prepare candidates for the CPA examination also should be excluded ordinarily, although this does not mean that the employer should fail to encourage and even to assist the staff members to prepare for the examination. These suggestions are made upon the premise that the best results from CPA review and other collegiate courses can be obtained by specialists whose chief occupation is in the field of preparing and teaching such courses.

Too often, when it is found that several of the beginning staff members are deficient in accounting principles or auditing theory, it is decided to include coverage of rather primary matters in the staff training class. In such cases it would appear preferable to have the laggard staff members catch up with the others by individual study or by taking specific college or correspondence courses, rather than to retard the speed of class instruction to the level of the lowest beginner.

A suggested class program. The AICPA has available *A Study Guide for Beginning Accountants,* which can be used as the basis for an intrafirm staff-training program. The following suggested class program can be integrated with the material in the study guide.

Conduct and standards. A staff manual may have been prepared covering thoroughly such matters as behavior and appearance; instructions for conduct in the staff office, in clients' offices, and when off duty; relationships with clients; secrecy regarding the firm's business and clients' affairs; and the necessary details of timesheets, vacations, sick leave, overtime pay, expense sheets, etc. Nevertheless, the new staff members should have these matters impressed upon them in a class meeting with an opportunity for discussion and for questions as to just what is expected.

Discussion might well include the attributes considered important in evaluating the personality of candidates to be selected for the staff. An additional subject closely affiliated with staff manual material is that of auditing standards. A short discussion of the general or personal standards, the standards of field work and those of reporting will provide an excellent introduction to auditing. All class members should read carefully *Generally Accepted Auditing Standards—Their Significance and Scope,* AICPA, 1954. One class meeting may be adequate for the subjects included in this part of the program.

Audit working papers. In this part of the course, the general plan of preparing working papers, their indexing, the organization of certain papers for the permanent file, the control of papers while on the job, and the general nature of the material to be included in a set of working papers should be discussed. Questions as to what is to be included in the permanent file papers rather than in the current-year set of papers should be considered. Also, the methods prescribed by the firm for filing tax return working papers and audit program papers should be explained. Particular attention should be given to the indexing system used by the firm and to listing on the working paper schedules exactly the work done in each part of the audit.

The subject matter for this part of the course should be available in the filed working papers within the office of the accounting firm. It is less confusing for the beginners if not more than two or three sets of papers are used for study. Often a thorough study of one set of papers will accomplish more than references to many sets. The papers chosen for study should evidence thoroughness and be representative of what is expected in form and content. These papers should be examined by all class members before the class meets, and the instructor must be well acquainted with the model papers. Otherwise, the questions which the beginners will bring to class may not be answered readily or sufficiently.

In this discussion it is assumed that the firm uses a "standard index" system wherein the same letter refers to the same asset or other account in all sets of papers. Also, each firm should teach its own method of filing the summary and control schedules, the rough draft of the audit report and statements, the adjusting journal entries and trial balances, and the detailed papers evidencing the confirmation of accounts receivable and those for details of the physical inventories. Perhaps some help in developing the best arrangement and details of papers can be obtained from textbooks or from published model sets, but for staff instruction purposes it is suggested that the study be confined almost entirely to the methods used by the particular firm conducting the class.

One or two meetings should be assigned to this subject of general instructions for preparing working papers.

Audit procedures. A few firms have developed what may be called an Audit Procedure Manual or an Auditing Instruction Book in which the usual procedures and techniques to be employed in each part of the auditing work are listed. Such a book, together with the set or sets of working papers previously studied (including the related audit programs for the respective engagements), will provide the basic material for this portion of the course. It is probable that most small and many medium-sized firms will not have prepared a formal auditing instruction book or manual, although it is advisable to do so. For these firms the working papers and audit programs will need to be the basic materials until such a manual has been developed. There should be reference books available. Comparisons should be made particularly with *Case Studies in Auditing Procedure, Codification of Statements on Auditing Procedure,* subsequent AICPA statements on auditing procedure, and material in recent editions of textbooks such as *Montgomery's Auditing.*[2]

It may be that an entire meeting, or more, will be needed for the subject of auditing the cash accounts. The starting point should be the most usual

[2]Lenhart and Defliese, *Montgomery's Auditing,* 8th ed., The Ronald Press Company, New York, 1957.

or standard method of the firm, and the student should see how the audit program and the working papers record the procedures followed and what evidences of the verification work are accumulated. In other words, it is suggested that the class be shown just what has been done on a job as the first step in their study. It is important that they be encouraged to think out the reasons why the different steps have been taken and to develop an understanding of the objectives of the entire procedure and of each part. Next, the class should be given variations in the cash audit procedures which are sometimes used. The reasons for variations and the adequacy of the methods should be discussed. As a final step, the members of the class should compare the methods followed by the firm with those in *Case Studies in Auditing Procedure,* particularly for similar types of engagements, and with the general methods specified in *Montgomery's Auditing.*

It may be well to emphasize that the most important part of the training in audit procedures is the development of reasons for the procedures.

Many persons can memorize a list of things to be done but, unless they understand why they are doing these things, their work may be deficient. Only when there is an understanding of the significance of each step and of the over-all procedure will the auditors be likely to recognize errors and deficiencies in the accounts. Furthermore, this realization of the "why" of each step is necessary in determining the extent to which each verification procedure is to be carried.

Many helpful suggestions may be made to the beginner in connection with the Instruction Manual, Audit Manual, or other list of procedures for verifying cash. For example, how to sort checks rapidly, what to scrutinize on each check, how to count and stack coins, bills, rolls, etc., and many other details may be discussed profitably. An interesting general discussion might be developed on the subject: "What and what not to tick."

The verification procedures and techniques for each of the major portions of the audit should then be studied according to the same type of plan as has been described for cash. Thus, one entire meeting might be required for the consideration of the usual procedures in verifying accounts and notes receivable. The actual practices of the firm, illustrated by the particular audit working papers used for illustrative purposes, would be the starting point. This would be followed by variations in the practice of the firm and by comparisons with the practices of others as indicated in the sources suggested above.

Considerable time may be needed in studying the inventory verification methods, particularly if many types of problems have been encountered by the firm and if the class is given an opportunity to consider various manufacturing processes with the accompanying problems of costing the goods in process and the finished jobs. If the auditing firm does not have many engagements involving manufacturing inventories it may be well to limit this part of the course to inventories of only one manufacturer in addition to those of one retailer or wholesaler.

It is not suggested that the study of audit programs be treated as a separate subject. The beginner needs to concentrate on the *usual* procedures and only the audit programs of the particular jobs which serve as basic material need be considered for illustrative purposes. The related parts of the programs should be taken up while the audit procedures are being studied for each of the major phases of the audit.

The auditing procedure portion of the staff-training course can be expanded easily to require many meetings. It is probable that four or five meetings may be very successful the first time the course is planned and given. This may not allow for a program in which the students actually do many of the procedures. That type of class is possible only when much more time is allotted to the training course than is contemplated in this suggested minimum. In the intensive and extended training courses, sets of books and records obtained from defunct corporations occasionally may be used to give the students actual work in the procedures.

Even in the shortened course here contemplated, some materials may be collected for illustrative purposes, such as checks, certificates of common and preferred stock, bonds, a trust indenture covering a bond issue, capital-stock certificate books, documents evidencing loans and the security pledged for the loans (such as the notes, mortgages, trust deeds, insurance policies, title insurance policies, or abstracts-of-title papers).

Preparation of financial statements and reports. Although the beginner will not be faced immediately with the problems of preparing financial statements and writing audit reports, he should be instructed in the practices of his employer early in his accounting experience. Preferably, the matters to be covered should be formalized in a *Standard Statement Presentation Manual.* This manual should state the usual classifications of items and the terminology to be used in financial statements and should give a standard wording for unqualified opinions, for qualified opinions, and for denials of opinions on financial statements.

If an accounting firm has not formalized all of its policies relative to the preparation of financial statements and the phraseology for opinions and denials of opinions thereon, it may be that staff bulletins or memoranda have been issued from time to time explaining and setting forth some of these policies. In the absence of written instructions on these matters, the instructor will find it necessary to review typical audit reports and summarize for the class the policies and procedures evidenced therein. Even better than this, assignments to members of the class to ascertain the standard practices of the firm will stimulate their interest and thinking. A few of the matters to be investigated are: standard titles for the usual financial statements, titles used for main headings of assets and of liabilities, order of arrangement of assets and liabilities, extent to which details are presented in various sections of the balance sheet, wording of so-called "reserve" accounts (such as allowance for depreciation, allowance for doubtful accounts, or estimated depreciation to date, estimated bad accounts, etc.), extent of the description of the capital stock accounts, use of "retained earnings" instead of earned surplus, details ordinarily included in the statements, use of footnotes to the balance sheet, a determination of the matters most commonly requiring footnote comments, and the ascertaining of standard phraseology for the opinions for short-form reports.

Some attention can be given profitably to the long-form report, because a knowledge of the subject matter usually covered helps in explaining the reasons for collecting certain data and for making certain investigations during the audit examination. The instructor may summarize the standard policies of the firm relative to long-form reports or, preferably, he may assign to the class members the task of ascertaining these policies from typical reports. For example, he may have the members of the class determine the main divisions of the usual report, the usual wording and coverage of the introductory paragraphs, the manner of listing or indexing the exhibits, and the type of material covered, together with the manner of presenting it in each section of the report. Some attention should be given to the style of the report, including the length of sentences, the extent to which introductory phrases or sentences are used, methods of varying the words and phrases in making comparisons of the data for two or more periods, and methods of avoiding hackneyed expressions or phrases. If staff members are used for the comparing and proving of typed reports, they will have had the opportunity to observe the customary physical setup of the reports of their employer. If a separate comparing and proving department is maintained, this opportunity may not have been given to the staff members. In that event, some consideration of the physical setup of reports is particularly needed so that, when members of the class are given opportunities to assist in preparing statements and other portions of the long-form report, they will be able to conform to the proper physical setups for the data.

One or two class meetings may be assigned to this final part of the class training. It is suggested that an intensive study of financial reports and statements will be more beneficial to semi-seniors and seniors than to beginning juniors and, therefore, an extended consideration of report-writing may be undertaken for advanced personnel. Reference material to be used, especially in an advanced course of study, would include published reports of companies and the latest edition of *Accounting Trends and Techniques,* published by the AICPA and based upon a thorough study of the annual corporate reports of six hundred companies.

The program for training beginners which has been outlined herein does not include a concentrated study of questionnaires on internal control. It is believed that this subject may be omitted from the class for junior accountants, except as specific parts of a questionnaire are to be considered in studying auditing procedures. Questionnaires relating to internal control are best understood after the auditor has had a wide experience in auditing work because there is a wide variance in the accounting systems and in the requirements of different enterprises. Generally, juniors lacking in experience do not grasp easily the significance of many of the questions. Then, too, they are discouraged to find that there are far too many questions to permit memorizing.

Teaching methods. The subject matter, the size of the class, and the abilities of the instructor must be considered in choosing the teaching methods. For example, some teachers who are excellent in small classes are not at all effective in handling large groups. The "discussion" method of teaching can be used very effectively in small groups, provided the group is not too small, but this method requires a great deal of skill in directing the discussion if it is used in large groups of forty or more people. Some subjects require the "exposition" (lecture) method of teaching, at least in part, in order to establish a starting point for a discussion period or for the use of illustrations and practice problems.

The discussion method. The discussion method should be used in preference to the exposition method whenever possible. Care must be taken, however, to avoid lengthy and inappropriate discussions. The key to a good discussion group lies in the selection of an imaginative leader who will devote time prior to the meeting to developing techniques for guiding the discussion. Not every person who lectures ably has the temperament or ability required of one who must tactfully turn aside an unprofitable line of thought and immediately stimulate a more profitable one.

The leader must direct the discussion by inserting questions and observations which develop the best thinking and which interest the students in seeking and arriving at the best solutions. For this purpose, a class of about ten persons usually is best. It is desirable that the class be limited to a maximum of twenty.

Illustrative material. Ideally, the discussion method should be supplemented by the use of illustrative material and of practice problems. Usually, practice problems comprise an important part of an intensive course; whereas, in a short course, meeting one afternoon or evening in a week for six, eight, or ten weeks, the problem material necessarily is restricted to very few, if any, problems. Instead, a great deal of illustrative material will be used in the form of working papers, audit programs, questionnaires on internal control, and audit reports. In all cases the object should be to have the students find out the answers (with assistance) in as many cases as possible, rather than to "stuff" them with many answers, conclusions, procedures, and other expository material without allowing them the opportunity to analyze questions and to formulate conclusions themselves.

The final examination. Sometimes it is necessary to plan for an examination in writing at the end of the course. A short course calls for a short examination only and a one-hour period may be found to be adequate. There are both advantages and disadvantages in having an examination. Students usually apply themselves more diligently to the course when they know they must sit for an examination. On the other hand, the thought of the examination may cause them to spend too much of the class hours in writing down bits of knowledge and in memorizing specific procedures in order to make a good grade on the examination. Consequently, the class discussion may suffer because of too much writing and too little thinking, and because of a detached point of view rather than an intensive interest in exploring an interesting subject. It may be advisable to abolish examinations in a staff-training course in order to emphasize and train the students to do some intensive and original thinking.

Some beliefs are held that tests and examinations indicate the effectiveness of the training program. In opposition to this, it may be observed that a truly successful program will be evident by the extent of the discussion and the intensity of the arguments stimulated in the classes.

A course in writing effective reports. The successful training program is one that will explain the principles and techniques of effective writing, show how they are applied in actual writing practice, and give continued critical supervision of the writer's product. Whatever his rank, the in-charge accountant is the logical man to write the report and letters concerning the engagement, because he is the one who possesses all the facts and knows all the ramifications of the job. The training program should be leveled at this man and the course of study designed for his benefit.

Who should teach the course? The classes of instruction should be conducted jointly at the training center by two teachers. One of these should be a partner or top-level staff accountant with a high degree of competence in writing. The other instructor should be a professional teacher of writing and English at a high school, college, or business school.

Instruction on a collaborative basis is preferable to instruction by either an accountant or a professional writing teacher working alone. The accountant is best qualified to guide the trainee in the analysis of accounting facts; in the organization and clarification of his thinking on accounting subjects; and in the determination of the scope, content, and reader adaptability of the accounting report or letter to be written. On the other hand, the professional writing teacher is best qualified to guide the trainee in such matters as physical structure and mechanics of writing, preciseness and simplicity of diction, and correct grammatical usage.

The subject matter of the course. The subject matter of the proposed course of study includes the writing of letters, special reports, and internal memoranda. These three media of communication comprise the bulk of the original writing demanded of the public accountant.

In presenting the three types of writing to staff accountants in class, the instructor should emphasize the principles affecting each type and point out essential differences. For example, the instructor might show that a letter written to a client in the same style as an internal memorandum to a staff associate or a partner violates the principle of reader adaptation. The staff accountant should be shown that letters are frequently conversational, informal; the writer must adapt his words, his style, to the needs of the reader and to his ability to comprehend. Letters to laymen on accounting subjects must contain simple, everyday words so that the reader can grasp the message quickly and easily. Factors of practical psychology involved in the writing of letters should be explained.

Instructors should stress the following factors as those which will result in clarity, as well as general effectiveness:

1. Use of simple, understandable words
2. Avoidance of professional jargon and word repetition
3. Use of short, simple sentences
4. Avoidance of pompous, pretentious diction
5. Avoidance of excessive use of the passive voice
6. Choice of words that precisely express the writer's thoughts
7. Use of a logical, clear organizational pattern and use of outlines

8. Development of smooth transitional phrases between main ideas and paragraphs

9. Attention to length of lines, layout, captioning, paragraphing, and other evidences of careful attention to physical structure and mechanics

10. Recognition of the needs, desires, and capabilities of the reader and adaptation of the writing to meet them

During the course, the trainee should be required to write letters, special reports, and internal memoranda. Lecturing is best kept to a basic minimum. Writing assignments should be criticized by the instructors and returned to the trainee for rewriting and resubmission. Original drafts might be used for the purpose of class discussion and criticism.

INDIVIDUAL STUDY

When an accountant stops learning he should be retired immediately. Throughout his professional career the accountant must ever be continuing his education. He may do this by engaging in professional activities in accounting organizations, by attending technical meetings, by taking college courses in residence or by correspondence, and by reading accounting literature. Thus a staff-training course for beginners is just a start in obtaining a practical accounting education. Juniors, seniors, managers, and partners all must keep up to date in their profession.

Each staff member, when eligible, should be encouraged to join the state and local societies of CPAs and the national societies such as the AICPA, the National Association of Accountants, and the American Accounting Association. Some firms pay the dues of their staff members and most allow a reasonable amount of time for engaging in committee work and executive activities in such societies. Some firms also pay the costs of monthly dinners, and the registration fees and convention expenses for any members of the staff who will attend these meetings. Other accountants feel that all or a part of these expenses, particularly the payment of dues, should be undertaken by the member himself so that he may take more pride and more interest in his affiliation.

In addition to the technical meetings provided through accounting societies, the individual accounting firm may hold very profitable meetings. The success of such meetings will depend upon the manner in which they are planned and conducted. Unless the meetings are made to cover interesting and worthwhile subjects in a profitable manner, they will soon become a duty rather than a privilege.

Technical meetings of the staff may best be held either during office hours or in connection with dinner meetings. Some firms of fifteen to forty employees have found that a dinner meeting followed by one or two technical papers prepared by staff members is very successful. The papers presented should be the result of extensive research on the part of the staff member. Very fine papers have been written by semi-senior and even junior staff members. Discussions should be encouraged and the writers of the papers may be the best persons to conduct the discussion period. Some firms have regular staff meetings for this purpose once each month during most of the year. It is important to have a suitable room for such meetings. The cost of the dinner should be paid by the accounting firm.

In most large cities and in many smaller places, evening and summer courses in accounting subjects are available in colleges or other schools. Some firms pay all or a part of the tuition for such courses for all members of the staff who enroll and complete the course. In the field of income taxes, in particular, it is worth while to encourage staff members to take and to retake scheduled courses, particularly after major changes have occurred in the tax laws. There are cases of staff accountants who take a tax course (the same course) regularly every year for many years.

In many states, a graduate-study conference, annual clinic, or similar event is scheduled each year by the local society of CPAs. The number allowed to enroll for the two- or three-day meeting necessarily may be restricted, but each firm should arrange to send as many of its staff as can be accommodated. These conferences have been very beneficial to those attending.

Every accounting office, no matter how small, should have a library even if it is no larger than one bookshelf. Books should be selected with care and should be available to staff members to read in the office or to borrow upon signing a properly controlled receipt.

Periodicals and books received by the accounting firm on special subjects should be routed to the staff member or members who are particularly interested or who are working in the field covered by the book or periodical. For example, publications relating to the oil industry should be routed regularly to all assistants, including juniors as well as seniors, who are engaged on, or who have been engaged on, jobs involving problems of oil accounting. Also, a memorandum note to members of the staff who should be interested can be written by the partner or principal when he observes articles in accounting magazines that should be of particular interest to the staff members.

ROTATION OF ASSIGNMENTS

Staff training should include a reasonable amount of rotation of employees in assignments to engagements. Junior assistants should be assigned to different superiors rather than working always under the same senior. They also should receive assignments on varied types of engagements. As to senior assistants, repeated assignments to the same jobs year after year will "make Jack a dull boy." Both the job and the man will benefit in many cases by having an occasional change in the in-charge accountant as well as in the assistants under him. When assistants are again assigned to a large job, some changes in their duties and responsibilities may be effected.

If the staff manager keeps the rotation of employees in mind and if he makes definite and obvious efforts to accomplish intelligent changes in assignments, the staff itself will be increasingly aware of the need for training.

Often a senior accountant will expect too much of beginners, particularly if he himself has worked on the same engagement for so many years that he has forgotten the unusual features that once troubled him.

New assignments with new problems may make the senior more tolerant of his assistants. Furthermore, if the staff manager will take a few moments to describe to the senior the previous training of the beginner and if he will mention any particular fields in which the junior is lacking, the senior (and the beginner) can profit accordingly. This may even encourage the senior to be increasingly tolerant, because he has been coached in the training and deficiencies of the particular man.

DEVELOPMENT OF SPECIALISTS

Many accounting firms believe there are important advantages of specialization in accounting work. One of the most important advantages is considered to be the opportunity to increase one's general practice because of the reputation and achievement attained in a special field. Next in importance is considered the opportunity to do what the practitioner prefers to do. Then too, the opportunity to command higher fees often is considered important, particularly if the special practice is developed in a relatively untouched or undeveloped field.

On the contrary, many feel that specialization may cause an accountant to lose touch with the field of general practice and his clients may tend to refer to him only those engagements which fall within the special field or fields for which he is best known. There also may be too great a dependence upon the continued development or success of the industries or the activities which are related to the specialized skills. Usually there is some danger in restricting the sources of fees to a specialty, and yet a somewhat complex organization may be needed to combine the specialty with general practice.

Most frequently specialization is found in the fields of income tax and management services. Among the large accounting firms it is common for a separate department to be set up for tax work and sometimes for management services. Also, departments may be maintained for that portion of the staff which is engaged in municipal and other governmental audits, for staff members engaged entirely in college and university audits, etc.

The needs of the individual firms may vary but in general specialization by staff members should not be encouraged until a broad training has been obtained. Certainly, at least two years of general training, and preferably as much as five years, should be obtained before embarking upon a specialized practice. Also, specialization by establishing separate departments should not be overdone to the extent that general staff members are excluded from such fields as tax work and system work. Tax problems are fundamental in nearly all of the public accountant's work, and no auditor can readily avoid problems of modernizing and improving accounting systems. In fact, almost every audit affords opportunities for suggestions in this area and a complete knowledge of the system in use must be obtained.

DEVELOPMENT OF STAFF MORALE

Staff morale may be described as the confidence, pride, and enthusiasm which members of the staff have in the firm with which they are associated. Needless to say, the maintenance of high ethical and technical performance by the firm is essential in obtaining this pride and confidence. If a firm is to be regarded highly by its employees, they must have reason to believe fervently that the best of work is being performed and that their employers are highly regarded in the profession.

Continued technical training of staff personnel through programs of training and by informal methods are important factors in developing this morale. The accounting firm that performs the best work must have workers who are trained in the best of techniques and standards. This is basic for good morale.

Nevertheless, something more is needed. An inherent and continuing enthusiasm for his job and for the success of his firm must be felt by each person who is a part of the organization. Such an enthusiasm, to the extent that it permeates the entire staff, helps to knit the organization together and to make a loyal working team. And it is reasonable to expect a staff to develop this loyalty and enthusiasm for the organization of which each member is a part. Certainly, staff members have a common interest in furthering the reputation and success of the firm. Whether they remain permanently with the employer or ultimately leave to enter private employment or to open up their own accounting practice, they will always want to believe that they have been working for the best firm in the profession.

CREATION OF STAFF LOYALTY

This satisfaction in one's job and in one's employer which, when sufficiently developed, may be described as "loyalty" can and must be encouraged by intelligent methods. For instance, when a job is well done is a word of praise ever given? Is bad work likely to receive a reprimand in public? Are juniors ever made to feel that they have a little recognition for their part in an assignment?

Loyalty is not a one-way street. Employers must evidence interest in their employees if they are to expect loyalty from them. In some firms the partners and principals make no attempt to know even the names of the men. This indicates a lack of interest in the welfare or even the existence of staff members whom they do not recognize as belonging to the staff. Whether the staff is large or small, each member will appreciate the feeling that he belongs which is given by friendly greetings from higher-ups who recognize him and call him by name. In small firms, particularly, if a real interest in the employees exists, it will be evidenced frequently by a friendly concern for the personal welfare of the employees and their families.

Under conditions of keen competition among staff members for advancement and for heavy assignments, disappointments are certain to occur. While these cannot be avoided, they may be kept at a minimum if appropriate explanations are made. It is better to acquaint the party who has failed to advance as fast as he has expected, or who has not received a coveted assignment, of the reasons for such treatment rather than to have his disappointment affect his loyalty and his work. Too often, postponement of a simple but satisfactory explanation causes not only a heartache but also a disgruntled employee.

Of course, adequate compensation must be paid if the firm wants loyal employees. If salaries are not up to the rates prevalent in the profession, enthusiasm for the job and the firm will be rare unless there are compensating factors, which is unlikely. A junior accountant may recognize that he is learning a profession, but if other juniors are paid more while enjoying equal opportunities for learning, explanations are in order or the junior will be lost.

Keeping staff members busy is very important for morale. Long periods of idle time are particularly difficult. On the other hand, busy periods in which considerable overtime may be necessary and the occasion of a rush job usually give a boost to morale. Unless so overdone as to injure health, or otherwise imposed unreasonably, the busy season experienced by many accountants usually gives a sense of accomplishment to the entire organization which makes them respect themselves, their jobs, and their employers. Likewise, the assignment of a difficult task may revive the enthusiasm of a senior who is stagnating. During slack seasons, special efforts should be made to utilize the time with training classes, professional reading, research, and the improvement of the auditing procedures of the firm.

STAFF MEETINGS AND SOCIAL ACTIVITIES

In accounting firms, staff meetings constitute an excellent medium for development of good staff morale. While they are held primarily to outline and discuss technical subjects and to improve performance of assignments and the proficiency of the staff, they are most effective when definite stress is laid upon the importance of the role of each individual as an essential factor in the functioning of the organization as a cohesive unit.

Many firms hold staff meetings at regular intervals. Some hold their meetings every other month, and others as often as once a week. The average for all firms is about ten a year with the average for small firms tending to be slightly higher. For the most part such meetings are held during regular office hours.

Unless technical meetings of the staff are made interesting as well as helpful they will discourage rather than improve the loyalty of workers. If the meetings become dull it is better to discontinue them temporarily and concentrate on obtaining better, although fewer, meetings.

Some firms have been quite successful in having their staff meetings combined with a dinner each month during most of the year. Usually the partners or managers will try to keep out of the discussion, at least in the early stages. Such meetings obviously require a suitable private dining room where a good meal can be had—at the expense of the firm. In some cases other staff meetings are held after working hours; sometimes they are before office hours; most often they are likely to be during the scheduled workday, either at the beginning or late in the day. Meetings of this sort may deal with special instructions to the staff, a discussion of actual audit cases or circumstances that have been encountered, consideration of the extension of certain audit procedures, discussion of special questions on internal control, and the study of income-tax laws, etc.

A survey of small-staff CPA offices would probably reveal that most of them never hold a staff meeting, and that the others hold them only rarely. Undoubtedly the psychological reason behind this omission is the feeling that communication between employer and employees is more or less automatic anyhow, so why bother with such pomp and ceremony? Such practitioners may wish to try a Monday morning staff meeting for the combined purpose of (1) lining up the entire week's work, (2) disseminating information of general interest, and (3) clearing up pressing problems encountered on pending engagements. This idea can be put into effect at any time. It is practical and will improve morale.

Somehow, either systematically or haphazardly, the week's work must be assigned. If the work is not preplanned and assigned, staff men may run out of work while the principal is tied up and be forced to waste several hours waiting to see him. When this happens, additional time is usually lost through numerous back-and-forth interruptions at odd intervals throughout the week, usually at times when uninterrupted production should be paramount. The prime purpose of the Monday morning preplanning session is to eliminate this waste time and to assure a smooth flow for the week ahead.

Discussion of new and nearly completed work and unexpected speed or slowness on pending jobs can all be integrated into a new work plan on Monday morning—the time when all hands are fresh and ready for action. It is a good idea to keep a record of the assignments given each person in vertical columns of a simple form so that, from week to week, progress on previous assignments can be noted, and expected progress on current assignments can be estimated.

The reason for getting the staff together bright and early Monday morning is essentially to assign the week's workload. The other benefits are spontaneous. Minor changes in internal policy can be explained. Meetings in the community during the coming week can be mentioned and, in some instances, accompanied with requests that certain staff members attend them. Each person present can probably contribute some interesting local business news or some recent professional development affecting the practice. It is a wise practice to invite each one present to volunteer anything on his mind. Someone may wish to report briefly on a book or article he has just read, to raise a question about some part of the previous week's engagement, and so on.

These meetings will usually last only fifteen minutes, never over an hour. They do not substitute for periodic instruction meetings on taxes, auditing, and other subjects. But they do accomplish for the small accounting organization the co-ordination of assignments, communication of plans and policies, and help on immediate problems, which large firms must accomplish through bulletins, and by having one partner devote all or most of his time to herding the staff, and co-ordinating and dispatching assignments.

Social meetings for the entire organization are useful in developing loyalty if they are properly planned and conducted. These occasions should be shared by all; sometimes—as at a picnic or beach party—the spouses and families may be included. Even though they are not held more often than once or twice a year (at Christmas and perhaps in early or late summer), they will bring better acquaintance and more friendliness to the staff.

A STAFF-TRAINING GUIDE

The following material has been taken from the *Guide to a Practical Staff Training Program* which was prepared and published by the Committee on Professional Education of the Michigan Association of Certified Public Accountants.[3]

This guide has been developed in an effort to assist in the establishment of a coherent, systematic staff-training program for practitioners not already having such a program.

The establishing of such a program will help to perform the following:

1. Pass on to the younger members of the profession the accumulated experience of the older members, which is the duty of all professional men.

2. Add to the stature of the profession, since the knowledge and skill of a profession can only be measured as the sum total of the knowledge and skill of the individual members.

3. Assure the practitioner's clients of better work.

4. Assure the public of a well-trained profession.

5. Act as an aid to recruitment, since the knowledge that the profession is willing to take the time, trouble, and expense to adequately train recruits may help to attract capable people to the profession.

There are many facets to a well-rounded training program and many ways in which adequate training of men can be accomplished. The major categories of staff-training can be classified as:

1. Indoctrination of the new junior into the firm and the profession

2. On-the-job training, that which the staff member receives in his daily work

3. Staff-training meetings conducted by more experienced men

4. Knowledge acquired by contact with members of the profession outside the office, i.e., membership in professional or allied organizations, attendance at meetings, etc.

Each of the above categories will be covered in more detail in the following sections of this guide.

It is understood of course that there are many methods of training staff and many things which the practitioner may find desirable to teach his men which are not covered in this guide. It is hoped, however, that some of the ideas contained may be of value to the practitioner in arriving at the desired result.

Basic indoctrination for new staff members. It should never be taken for

[3]*The Journal of Accountancy,* December 1956, pp. 71-75.

granted that a new staff member has obtained a sufficient understanding of the profession, or of its standards, rules of conduct, and opportunities. Frequently, it is a lack of understanding that causes promising men to leave the profession. Accordingly, the first basic instructions given to a new employee, during his indoctrination into the firm and the profession, should be designed to stimulate his interest in and develop his appreciation for the profession and his work, and to make clear the future which is available to him.

It is assumed that each employee will be informed of the rules of his employer's office. In addition, it is considered essential to provide him with the following information and instructions as soon as it is possible to do so:

1. Advise him as to the manner in which he is expected to conduct himself in a client's office, and explain the confidential nature of his work.

2. Request that he familiarize himself with the applicable section of *Duties of Junior and Senior Accountants*.

3. Provide him with copies of the *Code of Professional Ethics* of his state and of the American Institute of Certified Public Accountants, and a copy of the state accountancy law.

4. Make it clear to him that his employer is interested in helping him to prepare for the CPA examination, and for his future in the profession of accounting.

5. Show him the office library and advise him that it is provided for his use and benefit. If the office does not have a library, furnish him with a suggested list of books and reference material.

6. Direct his attention to the state society magazine and *The CPA* and make copies available to him monthly.

7. Suggest that he subscribe to *The Journal of Accountancy* and to other accounting publications.

It is important that the practitioner follow up at intervals to ascertain that the staff member has studied and understands the material given him. Invite his questions and comments, ask a few questions at opportune moments, and, if practical, give the trainees a written examination on selected sections of the materials which are listed above.

Training assistants on the job. Staff members receive the most effective training while working on actual assignments; this applies not only to new assistants, but to accountants at all levels of responsibility. It is important, therefore, that the practitioner stimulate thinking about on-the-job training practices among the more experienced accountants on his staff and also acquaint new members of the staff with the training they may expect to receive on the job.

The suggested training practices outlined hereafter, all of which have been used successfully, generally apply to all levels of men in their dealings with those whom they are supervising. It is not anticipated that all these practices will apply with equal force to each practitioner or can be put into effect on all assignments, but it is hoped that these suggestions will help the practitioner put into effect those practices which are applicable to his firm and to particular assignments.

Introduction to the job. 1. Notify the assistant of his assignment as far in advance as possible, so that he will have an opportunity to study the prior year's working papers and reports (which he should be encouraged to do).

2. Urge the assistant to do independent research in order to learn as

much as possible about the client's industry. Make specific suggestions as to reading material.

3. Explain the nature of the client's business and its position in the industry, including such matters as products, types of properties, operating methods, business policies, quality of personnel, etc.

4. Arrange for a tour of the client's facilities soon after the start of the engagement and encourage assistants to visit operating and service departments in carrying out assignments.

5. Explain generally the client's financial statements and accounts, accounting records, methods and procedures, system of internal control, and any unusual accounting problems expected to be encountered.

6. Introduce the assistant to the client's officials and employees with whom he is expected to come in contact.

Instructions for specific work assignments. 1. Review each step to be performed with the assistant, making use of the previous year's working papers for purposes of illustration.

2. Explain the meaning and purpose of the work to be undertaken, so that the assistant understands not only how the work should be done, *but why it is being done.*

3. Explain the relationship between the specific task being assigned and the job as a whole.

4. Show the assistant the records with which he will work, paying particular attention to any unusual aspects of the client's procedures relating thereto.

5. Ascertain that the assistant thoroughly understands the instructions before he proceeds with the work.

Review of work done. 1. While the work is in progress, keep sufficiently close contact with the assistant to ascertain that he is proceeding satisfactorily.

2. Review the work as promptly as possible after it is completed, preferably on the job and in the presence of the assistant.

3. Review the work thoroughly and critically.

4. Discuss the results of the review with the assistant, explaining how any errors were noted in the review, how or why they occurred, and how to avoid them in the future.

5. Require the assistant to correct his own errors and to complete any tasks which remain to be done.

6. Discuss with the assistant any deficiencies in his work, suggesting methods by which he might correct them.

7. Give consideration to questions and points raised by the assistant, allow him to participate in the follow-up and disposition thereof, and explain to him the reasons for whatever action is taken.

8. During the course of the review, question the assistant sufficiently to ascertain that he understands and is satisfied with the purpose, method, and results of the work.

Widening comprehension of the job. 1. Arrange for the assistant to perform at least a portion of the work on as many phases of the job as possible.

2. Encourage discussion of professional problems at lunch or dinner in such a way that all assistants participate. In discussions in public places, always bear in mind the confidential nature of the work.

3. Retain as many assistants as possible to the end of the job, so that they may observe what is required to complete an assignment. Utilize such assist-

ants to the fullest extent possible in preparing the draft report, exhibits, and memoranda.

Furthering progress and development of assistants. 1. Encourage the assistant to ask questions.

2. Urge the assistant to view his work critically and to make suggestions for improvement in programs, audit techniques, working papers, and planning of the work.

3. Encourage the assistant to develop a questioning attitude in carrying out his work, pointing out the importance of bringing to light any irregularities or errors in the accounts, deviations from prescribed accounting procedures, or weaknesses in internal control.

4. Do everything possible to imbue the assistant with the service concept. Give him frequent reminders that the client looks to the CPA for constructive suggestions.

5. Arrange for the assistant to obtain as broad and diversified experience as possible. Make an effort to assign him to different industries, and to different seniors or managers.

6. Assign work which will tax the assistant's capabilities and which carries responsibility somewhat beyond his immediate experience. Encourage him to acquire the habit of delegating work.

7. Permit the assistant to take as complete charge of his assignment as his capabilities permit. Encourage him to make decisions and take actions within the scope of his responsibility on the job, but caution him to inform the in-charge man of such decisions and actions.

8. Have frequent discussions with the assistant regarding his work performance. Praise work well done, and counsel him on means of overcoming any deficiencies.

9. Study the personal characteristics of the assistant, and work with him in his efforts to overcome any traits which may tend to retard his progress.

Developing writing ability. Good writing can be achieved only through constant practice and careful editing. Every opportunity should be taken to give assistants writing assignments, such as memoranda on unusual transactions or accounting points encountered in their work, memoranda dealing with procedures and internal control, sections of long-form reports, and letters or memoranda for the client. In some instances, it may be practicable for the assistant to prepare a brief memorandum on each phase of the work to which he was assigned; the memorandum could describe the work done and conclusions reached, together with recommendations regarding the clients' accounting procedures and internal control and audit procedures.

With regard to editing, deficiencies in spelling, punctuation, grammar, phrasing, and sentence structure should always be called to the attention of the assistant, whether they occur in informal notes, letters, memoranda, or reports. Generally, revisions of wording and corrections should be worked out with the assistant, and the reasons for the changes should be explained. However, it should be borne in mind that phrasing is often a matter of personal preference, and therefore changes in an assistant's draft should not be made if they do not result in definite improvements.

Training your staff as a group. A variety of methods may be employed in holding staff-training meetings within a firm, depending upon the size and composition of the staff, type of clientele and background of the staff members.

Some of the more important factors to be taken into consideration in planning a staff-training meeting program are as follows:

1. The type of meetings to be held, i.e., holding classes with a teacher or teachers and students or using the discussion-group approach with members of the group acting as discussion leaders.

The advisability of either approach to the subject is dependent primarily upon the maturity and experience of the group members. If the group is to be composed largely of young, inexperienced men (to be referred to as an *A* group), a class approach with a principal of the firm or one of the more experienced staff members, one whose authority and knowledge of the subject will be readily acknowledged by the group members, as a teacher is preferable. The primary objective of classes such as these would be to instill in the assistants a knowledge of the basic fundamentals of the profession and to help bridge the gap from academic theory to the practical aspects of the work of the public accountant. If the group comprises more experienced men (to be referred to as a *B* group) already well trained in the fundamentals of the profession, then discussion groups would probably be better adapted to their continued training. In discussion groups, all would have a chance to air their views and each would learn from the others. The discussion leaders would be members of the group on a rotating basis and each member of the group should have an opportunity to act as a discussion leader, if at all feasible.

If there is a mixed group, the type of meeting would be dictated by the predominance of one or the other of the above. If the experienced men are in the majority, the younger men, though it is true they will be less inclined to state their views, will learn much from the discussions. If the less experienced men make up the bulk of the group then a class would be justified from the standpoint of "the greater good for the greater number."

It is much the better policy, however, to keep the two levels of men in separate groups, even though it may result in a group or groups of only a few members. Some of the larger firms, where it is admittedly more feasible, segregate the men into three groups; roughly, juniors, semi-seniors, and seniors. Meeting with a group of men of equal caliber gives the staff member a chance to hear others' thoughts on problems common to all and also relieves him from any fear of airing his views due to the presence of these older, more experienced men. There may be times when the class is preferable to the discussion meeting, even for more experienced men; for example, the discussion of new tax laws or regulations, in which case the man discussing the topic (perhaps the tax man in the office) may be the only one of the group who has any real knowledge of the subject.

2. The type of topics to be used as material for each group.

The type of topic to be discussed will vary, depending upon the composition of the group, the type of work done by the firm and the background and previous training of the group members.

For an *A* group with little or no previous training, topics dealing with such matters as firm policies, methods used in performing assignments, detailed audit techniques, and discussion of accounting and auditing bulletins, AICPA and firm preferences as to preparation of work papers would probably be most valuable.

For a *B* group, such matters as planning and administration of assignments, internal control, and correlation with examination procedures, changes in tax laws or regulations, new accounting or auditing bulletins, on-the-job training, and review of working papers would be appropriate subjects for discussion.

It is not intended here to furnish a list of topics, as another section of this guide contains a comprehensive list of subjects suggested as material for a staff-training program.

The important thing is to bear in mind the experience and caliber of the members of the group and keep the topics at a level which will be of interest, but not so advanced that the cart is being put before the horse. The selection of topics should include not only those which may render the assistant more proficient in and give him a wider knowledge of the type of work performed by the firm, but should also include matters which will broaden his knowledge in other aspects of public accounting. This is as helpful to the firm as to the employee, as it generally seems to be true that if a firm has a staff capable of doing the work, even though it may not at present have such engagements, the engagements will be forthcoming. Therefore, the more rounded training the staff members have, the more possible it is that engagements will follow. The topics should be selected in conjunction with the staff members, so that matters of interest to them will be included. They should be scheduled and an agenda issued to each member of the group well in advance of the first meeting.

3. Period or periods during the year when it is most advisable to hold meetings of this nature.

The period during which it is most advantageous to hold staff-training meetings will depend most likely upon the amount of time available for such activities. Generally, it would not be advisable to hold such sessions during the heavy winter season, nor is the summer vacation period a particularly appropriate time. Most firms find that they have the maximum amount of time to devote to staff-training during the months of April and May and during the fall, perhaps October and November. These periods have another advantage from the standpoint of the noncertified staff member, in that they are immediately prior to the CPA examination and the information he will acquire in these classes or meetings may be of value in writing the examination.

However, it cannot be said with any degree of certainty that the above months are necessarily those which would be the best for all firms. Each firm undertaking a staff-training program should review its own activities and determine during what period of the year the time could be best used for such a purpose. It may be found in some cases that there is no one time during the year that is better than any other time, in which case the meetings could be scheduled through the year in such a fashion as will not put too great a burden on any one period. However, experience seems to have proven that, in order to have some sort of continuity, meetings should not be too far apart, especially if they deal with the same or related topics. What could be done then is to schedule groups of meetings on related topics at various times of the year, which would achieve a certain degree of continuity insofar as related subjects are concerned and still spread the meetings throughout the year.

In addition to these scheduled meetings it is usually wise to figure on perhaps two or three special meetings a year which cannot be scheduled in advance. These would be held to discuss some important event occurring during the year, such as a new tax law, a substantial change in an already existing tax law, an important change in firm policy, or some other timely development.

4. Whether meetings should be held during working hours or during off-duty hours.

The question of on whose time should the staff-training meetings be held is one which has been debated for some time within those firms which have established staff-training programs. It can be said that if a staff member wishes to improve himself and the firm is offering him the opportunity, he should be happy to avail himself of the chance for improvement without expecting to be paid for the time spent doing so. In other words, the staff member derives the greatest benefit from the training; therefore, he should be glad to do it on his own time.

On the other hand the arguments have been advanced that:

a. The firm derives as much benefit from his increased knowledge as the staff member does.

b. It is implicit in any profession (law, engineering, etc.) that when new men are employed, the employer shall continue their education and training. It is generally acknowledged that a profession cannot be wholly taught in colleges and universities, but that the fledgling professional man must continue his education after he enters his chosen field. That being the case, it is also implied that part of the compensation of a staff member is this training he is to receive. Therefore, it seems reasonable that the staff member should be trained during the normal working hours, whether it be on-the-job training or formal class training.

c. There will no doubt be work to be done outside the classroom which the staff member will be doing on his own time. Therefore, by using the firm's time for classroom work, the burden is divided more evenly.

d. As a practical consideration, if the classes are held outside the normal working hours, the question of overtime pay may be raised.

e. By holding the meetings on the firm's time, the firm can schedule the classes as it thinks best with reasonable assurance that all staff members will attend.

There are no doubt many arguments both for and against each of the above alternatives, other than those listed above. The trend, however, seems to be in the direction of a combination, i.e., holding some meetings during working hours and some at other times.

5. Size of groups.

The size of the groups is, of course, contingent upon the size of the staff. In larger firms the problem is to keep the groups from being too large, in smaller firms from being too small. In either a class or a discussion meeting, if the group is too large it is difficult to have everyone take part in discussion and there tend to be more distractions than in a smaller group. On the other hand, if the group is too small, there are not enough viewpoints expressed on the various topics. Based on past experience, it would seem advisable to limit the size of the groups to not more than fifteen or twenty and to try to keep each group not smaller than six to eight members. In any event, of course, the group cannot be larger than the staff. However, even though the staff is smaller than the above minimum, classes of this nature can still be a successful method of training, depending upon the willingness of the principal to devote the time and effort required.

For each level of staff to have its own group would encourage a freer exchange of views, allow a selection of topics of interest to each group and give the members of each group a chance to exchange thoughts on common problems.

6. Frequency and length of meetings.

Meetings should not be held too frequently as class members should have ample time to prepare for each meeting. On the other hand, they should not be spaced too far apart as that would destroy the continuity which may be of value in discussing related subjects.

A week between each scheduled meeting would possibly be a reasonable time as this would allow sufficient time for preparation and yet not be so long as to cause the members to lose the trend of thought from the previous meeting. The duration of the meetings should not exceed two and one-half to three hours as an attempt to assimilate a great deal of information in a short space of time usually leads to remembering very little or nothing. It is preferable to increase the number of meetings in order to cover the subjects rather than to increase the length of the meetings.

7. *Who should conduct meetings.*

Meetings of an *A* group would probably be of greater value if they were conducted by a more experienced member of the staff or perhaps by a principal of the firm. Inasmuch as group members are quite inexperienced, they are in need of someone to answer their questions, clarify their thinking, and guide them to the proper conclusions in the discussions.

Meetings of a *B* group, on the other hand, could be pretty well conducted by the members of the group chosen to act as discussion leaders on a rotating basis. However, even in a group of this type, it would be advantageous for a principal to be present at the meetings, not so much as an active participant, but as an adviser to settle, when called upon, any matter regarding which the members cannot reach a conclusion.

Staff-training meetings are supplemental to on-the-job training and, if at all possible, should be co-ordinated therewith. This can be effected by using some of the following:

a. Men in charge of assignments should be given an opportunity to participate in staff-training meetings so they will be acquainted with the matters discussed and will then be in a position to test the assistant on the job as to things learned in class, if it is practicable to do so.

b. Men in charge of assignments should note the weakness of staff members and discuss such matters in staff-training meetings, as well as correct the assistant immediately on the job.

c. Men in charge of assignments should have meetings devoted to teaching them how to best carry out on-the-job training.

In addition to the technical proficiency accruing to any firm from a well-trained staff, there are other factors of value which may not be as readily apparent, but which are nevertheless very real. For instance, in recruiting new staff members, quite often the question of what sort of training program the interviewing firm has to offer is raised. The firm that has no or only a haphazard program will find itself at a considerable disadvantage when attempting to attract desirable men in competition with firms which have complete, well-planned training programs.

This thought may be expanded to include the entire profession. We are always competing for the best available men with other professions and with private industry. In order to attract these desirable men into the profession, we have to offer many things, among them a training program comparable to or more comprehensive than that offered by our competitors of the other professions and private industry.

Another intangible benefit accruing to a firm from a program of staff-training classes is the feeling on the part of the staff members of belonging, of being part of the group, which is important from the standpoint of staff morale and the building up of the *esprit de corps* which every successful organization must have.

Encouraging participation in professional activities. A real effort should be made by the practitioner to encourage his staff to participate in professional activities and keep abreast of professional affairs. This effort should begin at the time a new man is first employed. In addition to calling to his attention the reading material issued by the various professional organizations, he should be encouraged to join those that are open to him. In many instances the meetings of the professional organizations, such as those of the state society of CPAs and its various chapters, are open and can be attended by nonmembers as well as members.

He should be encouraged to join the state society and the AICPA as soon as he is eligible and should be expected to take an active part in their affairs. By taking part in these professional activities he not only aids the growth of the profession but also accelerates his own growth as a professional man.

There are other organizations in allied fields, such as various business groups, which he should be encouraged to join. The staff member should be impressed with his civic responsibilities and encouraged to take part in civic and charitable activities. By so doing he will widen his horizons and achieve a rounded background which will make him more valuable to his employer and to his profession, which in turn will reflect itself in more rapid advancement and growth for the staff member himself.

It should be impressed upon the staff member that joining an organization without actively participating in its affairs serves little or no purpose. He should be expected to serve on committees and hold office if selected to do so. He should also be led to understand that accepting appointment to a committee or to an office without performing, to the best of his ability, the function of the office to which he has accepted appointment, is unfair to the organization and to himself. Every professional man must be willing to devote a reasonable amount of time to work which advances the profession as a whole, for only by the activities of such men does a profession achieve its status as such.

In order that the public accounting profession have its share of such men it is incumbent upon the practitioner to teach his staff members not only the techniques of public accounting but also imbue them with the spirit of service to the public and to the profession which the true professional man must have.

Suggested topics for staff-training meetings
1. *Auditing*
    a. Bulletins issued by the auditing procedures committee of the AICPA
    b. Auditing procedures followed by the firm
    c. Statement of Auditing Standards
    d. Audit working papers
    e. Internal control
    f. Audit planning and administration
2. *Duties and responsibilities of each class of assistants*
    a. Duties of a junior accountant
    b. Duties of a senior accountant
    c. Training men on the job
3. *Report-writing*
4. *Accounting*
    a. Bulletins issued by the accounting procedure committee of the AICPA
    b. Cost accounting

    č. Accounting for specific industries (those industries in which the firm has clients)
5. *Legal liability of the public accountant to his client and to the public*
6. *The Securities and Exchange Commission*
    a. Accounting releases
    b. Relation to the public accountant
7. *Reviewing working papers*
8. *Taxes*
    a. Federal income taxes
    b. State and local taxes
9. *Background and history of the public accounting profession and the firm*
10. *Review for the CPA examination*
11. *Ethics of the public accounting profession*
12. *Assisting the client with management advisory services*
13. *Lifo inventories*

CURRENT PRACTICES OF FIRMS

Despite the evident need for more and better accountants, staff-training appears to be largely a hit-or-miss proposition. Little attempt has been made in many firms to guide the development of the junior, or to set standards by which progress can be measured. Some firms are apt to look upon training as merely a series of courses. They contend (with some justification) that the organization of special courses is beyond their resources.

The responsibility for training is seldom centralized. Senior staff accountants undertake the day-to-day training of the men under them; but over-all responsibility is rarely assigned to a specific individual. Only a few firms designate a partner or a top man in each office as staff-training director.

The practices of firms are widely disparate. Some of them hold full-fledged schools; others simply show the library to a new man and suggest that he do some reading in his spare time. Orientation periods range from a few hours to a few days. Staff manuals, if they exist at all, are not always up to date or used. It is not unusual for firms to pass along policies and practices merely by word of mouth.

As might be expected, some of the larger firms offer this type of program:

1. A new man is given—and is expected to study—facts about the firm, a manual of audit procedures, AICPA publications, and periodicals such as *The Journal of Accountancy*. With greater experience, he is referred to more technical material.

2. Month-long training sessions are held for new men. They cover firm policies and procedures, working papers, audit programs, and report-writing.

3. Current developments in accounting are discussed at periodic staff meetings. These are usually held during working hours, although evening sessions are not unusual. One firm reports that men average twenty-five hours a year at such meetings.

4. Men are encouraged to take CPA review courses, either within the firm or at a local college.

5. Selected staff members attend meetings that cover special topics: taxes, management counsel, operations research.

While many of these devices are adaptable by all firms, they are used only sporadically. A few conduct the Michigan auditing course;[4] some have had success with a tax course given by means of phonograph records. Staff men are seldom sent to outside classes, and staff meetings seem to be planless and irregularly held in many firms.

Although there is agreement that practical experience is vital in staff training, many smaller firms tend to discount the value of off-the-job training. Because few of them have made sustained efforts to develop an effective approach to this area of training, they are apt to be disappointed in the results.

All firms subscribe to the doctrine of learning by doing. The how of this is a different matter. Although a new man is assigned to an engagement as soon as feasible, both for the sake of his experience and productive contribution to the firm, there is little agreement on method. Some firms tend to keep a new man on elementary work. Others expose him early to progressively complex assignments.

Primary responsibility for on-the-job training falls on in-charge accountants. Three major approaches are used.

Some rotate new men among their seniors. If the seniors can offer a variety of work, this has its advantages. Rotation may, however, mean merely doing the same thing for a different client under a new supervisor. Its basic disadvantage is the diffusion of effort and responsibility in developing the new man.

Other firms assign a new man to a specific senior as part of his crew for an indefinite period. The senior has a strong incentive to bring the man along as fast as possible—to get as much help as possible for the crew. But the new man sometimes gains experience only in a limited area for a limited variety of clients.

Some firms combine these approaches by assigning a junior to a specific supervisor for a given period of basic training. Then he is made available as needed.

Few firms have done much to train their seniors in the technique of training others. An in-charge accountant may have technical skill, but not be adept at imparting it to others.

Experienced staff members seem to receive little, if any, directed continuing training. One firm has a one-week annual meeting for new in-charge accountants; a few hold special staff sessions for experienced men. Men are occasionally sent to outside courses (electronic data processing, tax institutes).

Some senior accountants are, however, active in professional affairs. Building a close working relationship between seniors and partners serves, in some firms, as a foundation for informal training on an individualized basis.

When a new man is assigned to a client he is instructed to review the files

[4]Charles Lawrence, *A Study Guide for Beginning Accountants,* AICPA, 1957. See also "A Staff-Training Guide" in this volume, p. 174.

on that client and look over the previous reports. Before going out on the job, the senior will sit down with him for a number of hours and go over the previous working papers and discuss any problems involved in the engagement.

We make juniors stick to junior work for about two years, when he may be given a very small, simple jobber account with a lot of inside work. We use this as a test of how he is coming along. We are sometimes criticized for not giving our men more responsibility, but this practice is our responsibility and liability and we can't afford to take any chances.

After three days of indoctrination within the firm, he is assigned to a crew. These people practically live together on the job, get to know each other well, and training just naturally happens.

We expect the man to use his time between assignments to develop himself, but we don't try to police the way he does it. It is up to his own initiative.

We do not try to plan the kinds of assignments the assistant gets in his on-the-job training. However, the way our business has been expanding, and the way he works with a small team of usually not more than three men means that he is forced to assume more and more responsibility.

It is highly desirable to make sure that the young trained college graduate actually gets a taste of challenging work as soon as possible. We try to plan this.

We have staff meetings one night per week starting in September and running until December and starting again after peak is over in April (in addition to special meetings when necessary); all partners attend these meetings.

After our new men have been with us a year, we send them to a three-week staff school. We have found these schools useful in the development of the younger men and, although some firms advocate staff schools at the outset of employment, we have found that more can be derived from them after the men have wrestled with actual field problems for a year.

We hold periodic interviews on a frank basis and tell the men their shortcomings and what they must do to overcome them. If they are not measuring up, we tell them so, and help them to find employment outside of public practice. We also ask the men to be just as candid in measuring our organizational defects and to suggest possible improvements in the training program which will help them do a better job. We try to get them to grade the men for whom they have worked and, although we are not always successful in bringing out the weaknesses of our seniors, it is quite surprising at times the points which are made by your younger men about the deficiencies of their superiors.

Staff-training in a large firm. The staff-training director of a national accounting firm outlines below the program worked out by his organization to supply opportunities for its personnel to reach professional maturity.

Here are some of the specific things we do in our four-week course. We use a practice case, developed by us, in which the new man, through the learn-by-doing approach, is led through audit procedures which simulate an actual job. He reconciles bank balances, inspects cash vouchers, carries out procedures in the confirmation and checking of accounts receivable, audits accounts-payable records, and so on. He thus receives intensive training in the kind of work that he will be exposed to in the first year of his job experience.

The course is interspersed with talks by partners and managers on office routine, history of the organization, personnel matters, services which we are able to offer our clients, audit procedures in specific phases of an examination, techniques in the preparation of working papers, internal-accounting control, etc.

At the conclusion of the course we feel that we have done these things: (1) made the transition from the classroom to the job easier for the new man by giving him a feeling of confidence and assurance, (2) given him a good foundation in audit procedure, (3) acquainted him with the history of the firm, its policies, and practices and (4) made him a more useful and efficient man at the very outset of his job experience.

I would like to mention what we have done in our organization to meet this need for continuous training. I will limit my comments to our program for staff members from the junior through senior level. Our efforts are focused on two broad fronts—discussion group meetings and on-the-job training. First, a few words about our discussion group meetings.

Discussion group meetings. Let us look in on a typical discussion meeting. We schedule these discussion-group meetings at each office for spring or fall of the year at a time when there will be the least interference from pressure of work or vacations. So far as possible we try to place men of similar experience levels in the same group. This allows us to tailor our material, it makes for smaller, more homogeneous groups, and it helps to increase informality and freedom of discussion.

The discussion leader is one of the more experienced staff members. If one of the group acts as discussion leader, a more experienced man is in attendance to help out if necessary. The discussion leader is given free rein to conduct the meeting as he sees fit. He has been warned to avoid a lecture approach because the objective of the meeting is to stimulate the exchange of ideas among the members of the staff.

Who selects the subject? The staff-training director in charge of staff training at each office, except that each year there may be one or two subjects which we believe should receive the consideration of all offices. On subjects of continuing general interest we furnish discussion leaders with outlines and practice material to help them develop the topic.

In one particular meeting, the subject under discussion is cost accounting, one on which an outline has been prepared. The discussion leader had studied the outline in advance and selected the particular phases to be covered.

The participants also must do some advance preparation. An agenda had been circulated a week before which showed that standard cost systems and process cost systems were to be discussed, together with audit procedures applicable to inventory pricing where these systems were in effect. A member of the group had been assigned to give a brief explanation of standard costs and another had been given a similar assignment on process costs. Two others were to outline briefly the audit procedures. Reading references and a few questions were appended to the agenda. With this advance preparation the members of the group now carry on a lively discussion of the topic.

Advance preparation is of major importance. On occasion, participants even suggest topics for discussion. Sometimes each participant is asked to submit in writing, several days before the meeting, at least one question regarding an item on the agenda, with the understanding that he will take part in the ensuing discussion.

The subjects are endless. Here are just a few, selected from some of our meetings: audit planning and administration, duties and responsibilities of each class of assistant, on-the-job staff training, internal control, review of working papers, letter and report-writing, SEC matters, accounting research bulletins, efficiency in audit procedures, fraud, electronic data processing, observation of physical inventories, income taxes, outstanding articles in recent accounting literature. An inexhaustible source of ready-made case material exists in files of working papers and reports.

For junior accountants with not more than two years' experience we have found that a program leaning heavily toward auditing is of most immediate usefulness. We distribute a set of audit case studies in advance, and at the meetings they discuss the problems and possible solutions.

One of the most interesting elements of these meetings is the store of unusual and pertinent experiences elicited from the participants who may tell of a unique job or a particular occurrence during an audit. Capitalizing on this fact, certain assistants are asked to document an experience for discussion. A brief statement of facts and of the nature of the problem (audit procedures to be followed, treatment or disclosure in financial statements, reference in opinion, accounting procedures to be recommended, etc.) is prepared and distributed to participants for study in advance of the meeting. At the meeting each assistant acts as leader in the discussion of his own case study, the problem and possible solutions are thoroughly aired, followed by a presentation of the actual solution, illustrated by working papers, financial statements, opinions and reports.

We have another device that may be classed under group discussion—the panel discussion. Questions submitted by staff members several weeks in advance are classified as auditing, accounting, taxes, reporting, office procedures, etc. Then a panel is formed, composed of a partner, a manager, a tax specialist, and the office manager. The discussion from the floor at this type of meeting is usually at a lively level.

Apart from our regularly scheduled meetings, we also hold certain special meetings from time to time to discuss new developments, perhaps a new tax law or an important release by the SEC.

On-the-job training. What we have done in the area of on-the-job training is to put down in memorandum form what we consider to be tested and proven practices. Each member of our staff has a copy of this memorandum and it serves as a reminder to each in-charge assistant of the type of on-the-job training that he is required to give those placed under his supervision.

The memorandum has five main captions:

1. Introduction to the job
2. Instructions for specific work assignments
3. Review of work done
4. Furthering the assistants' progress and development
5. Developing writing ability

Are the points in the memorandum revolutionary? No. If I were to enumerate them, you would recognize them as good, solid, down-to-earth training practices. And the problem is—not whether they are effective, because we know they are—but whether they are being properly applied. And so we try to set up methods of ascertaining that our on-the-job training is really being carried out. Partners and managers who are in close touch with the jobs are in the best position to observe whether or not in-charge assistants are doing all that they should do in this direction. We use two stimulants. One is group discussion of the subject to maintain an awareness of its importance.

Filling out checklist. Another is the filling out of a checklist which enumerates each point in the memorandum. Each in-charge assistant is occasionally required to use the checklist on at least one of his jobs. The procedure is simple. He indicates by a check mark those points which are applicable to the particular job. At this stage the checklist is reviewed jointly by the in-charge assistant and the manager assigned to the job. They first agree on the applicability of the points. When the job is finished, the in-charge assistant completes the checklist indicating, again by a mark, which of the agreed points were fully performed, partially performed or not performed at all. The list is again jointly reviewed by the in-charge assistant and the manager. Here sometimes appropriate explanations must be made.

The checklist is a device to stimulate thinking about on-the-job staff training with the thought that the application of the principles to specific jobs will carry over to all other jobs.

Another plan which has been successfully used in some of our offices is an occasional informal study group. This may appeal to some because much of the material used may be of the ready-made variety. The men can proceed at their own pace and a great deal of supervision is not required. Certain features of this plan may be carried out on an individual basis to fill in time between assignments. There are a great many things that can be done in informal study groups and the ones illustrated will undoubtedly suggest others. Let's look for a minute at some typical informal sessions. . . .

This group is studying sets of working papers taken from the files. Two of the men are preparing from these the long-form report and opinion, memorandum to client on suggestions for improvement of internal control or accounting procedures, tax returns, and Form 10-K. They will then compare their efforts with documents actually issued to the clients. Several of the others meanwhile are rewriting reports and memorandums for training in different methods of presentation.

In another group, the men are making a critical review of the working papers, programs, and audit procedures. We have found that many worthwhile suggestions have developed from reviews of this kind.

Informal study groups may be used for other purposes, such as study of AICPA bulletins and case studies, discussion of articles in *The Journal of Accountancy,* NAA Bulletins and other publications, working out CPA problems, and comparing results with solutions.

From time to time the entire group holds informal discussions to exchange experiences gained during the course of their study.

Staff training in a small firm. Is it economically and practically possible for a local accounting firm of moderate size to develop and maintain an adequate program of staff training? A specific development program which has been successfully used in one such firm is outlined as follows:

Accomplishment of the staff-training goal of bridging the gap between classroom and practice, which includes indoctrination into the firm and the profession, can best be attained through use of a formal program, supplemented by on-the-job training. To meet this responsibility my firm has adopted as a basis for our formal staff-training program *A Study Guide for Beginning Accountants,* which was prepared for the Michigan Association of Certified Public Accountants and distributed by the AICPA.

The course is broken down into eight major sections, as follows:

1. The profession of public accounting: general background and personal challenge
2. The services performed by a public accountant
3. The audit: planning
4. The audit: working papers
5. Application of audit theory and practice to the examination of assets
6. Application of audit theory and practice to the examination of liabilities
7. Application of audit theory and practice to the ownership section of the financial statement
8. Application of audit theory and practice to the examination of income and expenses

The course requires the use of supplemental reading material which could very well be reviewed periodically by each of us, whether or not we use it specifically for staff training. A partial list of this supplemental material includes:

1. *Accountant's Legal Responsibility* by Saul Levy
2. *Audits of Savings and Loan Associations*
3. *Case Studies in Auditing Procedure, Internal Control,* and *Extent of Audit Samples*
4. *Generally Accepted Auditing Standards, Their Significance and Scope*
5. *Statements on Auditing Procedure*
6. *Accounting Research Bulletins*
7. *Duties of Junior and Senior Accountants*

In getting the program under way we were faced with two major problems: The first was that of timing and second was the question of who would be assigned the task of actually conducting the sessions. At the outset it did not appear to be economically sound, particularly since this program was being conducted on an experimental basis, to invest a great deal of time and money by holding the sessions during regular working hours. For this reason it was decided to hold a two-hour session each week for approximately forty-eight weeks. Each session commenced ten minutes after normal working hours and ended promptly two hours later. The decision to hold weekly meetings contributed largely to the related decision to spread the actual conduct of the course among four partners and four senior staff men with each weekly meeting being conducted jointly by one partner and one senior. Thus, each team of discussion leaders was faced with the task of additional preparation only once every four weeks.

Cost of conducting courses. From the standpoint of minimizing costs, this method of presentation accomplished two things. First, the meetings themselves were held after working hours. Second, with seven days between sessions, ample time was available for adequate preparation outside of office hours without the complete absorption of a man's free time. This utilization of outside time for preparation was expected not only of the juniors but also of the partners and seniors in preparing for leading the discussion. Thus, the cost of conducting the course was limited to actual cost of the material, which in our case averaged approximately $29 per student, plus the cost of meals following each session. It is worth noting that approximately half of those attending the sessions went home to eat after adjournment of the meeting in lieu of taking the additional time to eat out at firm expense. This would seem to indicate that the free meal had little or no significance as an incentive for attendance at the voluntary meetings.

Maintaining interest. Our next major area of concern was to keep each session as interesting as possible in order to instill in the staff an attitude of eager rather than dutiful attendance and participation. A complete set of audit working papers was selected from the case files to be used as an example of the firm's practice and methods as related to the various auditing techniques covered in the course. In addition, each discussion leader was instructed to inject the firm's views on specific points wherever possible, to explain the why of such views and to relate actual experiences where applicable—the object being to keep the sessions on a very realistic and practical basis and to avoid as much as possible any resemblance to the theoretical, classroom-type approach. The leaders were instructed to ask questions of the juniors as an inducement to get them to take an active part in the discussion. Communication requires both expression and impression and *effective* communication occurs only when the expression *equals* the impression. Thus, the more discussion, the greater the chance that proper understanding by the juniors is being attained. Here is where the decision to have *two* experienced men prepared to lead each session played an important role. During periods in which there was an apparent slowing down of interest, the two leaders engaged in a discussion between themselves. This invariably served as a stimulant and interest was quickly restored.

Interest seemed to fall to its lowest ebb at times when for one reason or another reference to firm experience was not practical or possible. These situations, however, were in the minority and a comparatively high rate of interest prevailed throughout the entire forty-eight weeks.

In addition to the formal program which I have just described we also conduct some other short formal courses which are pertinent to our type of practice. Since we feel that each man should have a working knowledge of income taxes, we hold periodic short sessions on how to use the firm's tax library. These are conducted by the partner in charge of our tax department, and are designed to instruct the new man in the tools available for doing a basic job of research. We find that these sessions are always accepted with a great deal of enthusiasm.

We have also conducted special courses on timely subjects whenever the occasion demands. For example, after enactment of the 1954 Internal Revenue Code we conducted a series of weekly meetings over several months during which the entire code was studied.

On-the-job training. All of these special sessions have also been held outside of normal working hours, with very little if any ill feeling from the staff. The secret in holding off-duty sessions seems to be to hold them close enough together to insure continuity but far enough apart so they do not become burdensome. The new man is eager for an opportunity to learn and he is willing to contribute, within reason, from his own time to take advantage of the opportunity.

Closely allied with the formal programs which I have just outlined is on-the-job training. Depending on the size of the staff, each senior has assigned to him one or more juniors. In accordance with the firm's *Guide to Training of New Personnel*, the more experienced man is expected to give the junior individual attention in these major respects:

1. Initiate him into the firm by introducing him to other members of the staff, by explaining the firm's policies, standards, etc.

2. Instill in him at an early date a sense of belonging both to the firm and to the profession.

3. Review with him completely the work programs of the engagements on which he will be employed.

4. Supervise his work carefully to make sure that work on the engagement is found for him that suits his individual developing ability, and that his time is used wisely.

5. Review his work fully, not only to prove its accuracy, but also to see that he gets all of the benefits that can come to him from on-the-job training.

6. Suggest appropriate supplemental reading material with particular emphasis on areas where he appears to be weak.

To make this a workable arrangement, every effort is made on the firm's part to assign seniors to engagements in company with the new man attached to them for training. In practice, of course, this is not always feasible, but we feel that in conscientiously striving for this end we come as close to complete achievement as is possible.

The most important element in this phase of training is the follow-up. This is necessary not only to insure performance but also to evaluate both the progress of the junior as a student *and* the ability and progress of the senior as an instructor. I make this last reference to evaluation of the senior because, although on-the-job training is generally considered to be for the benefit of the new man, it is also one of the first steps in the more advanced stages of the professional development of the senior. Here is one of his first opportunities to develop qualities of leadership by acquiring the art of conveying his thoughts to others in an articulate manner, by gaining confidence, and by the realization that he is making a contribution to the profession by assisting someone less experienced than he.

Measuring progress. The device which we have found to be most successful is the requirement that each senior make a separate report each quarter on each man assigned to him. The information required in the report deals generally with the new man's progress, what specific steps are being taken for improving him, such as suggested outside reading, and what means of follow-up are being employed to insure that the suggestions are carried out. In addition to the quarterly report, each senior is required to submit semi-annual rating reports for each man assigned to him. This report is designed to rate each individual on the basis of average progress and competence of other men at his level of experience. Also required in this report is an expression by the senior as to the junior's present and potential value to the firm.

These reports are assembled by the partner in charge of personnel and reviewed at least twice each year. During the time that these reviews are made, each individual is called in by the partner for the purpose of discussing his progress. We find that this practice is an excellent morale builder because it lets the relatively new man know that the partners in his firm are vitally interested in *his* individual progress. This also provides the partner with an opportunity to form his own opinion as to a particular individual's traits and characteristics which he can use as a basis for judging the rating ability of the senior.

Guidance and professional development. The area of staff training which I feel is most generally neglected is guidance for continuing professional development after advancement to senior and supervisory levels. After the initial training is completed, further development is generally left entirely to individual initiative. I do not mean to imply that the staff man should be completely relieved of any responsibility for his own progress. Any man entering a profession has the obligation to keep abreast of new developments and to strive continually to improve his skill and competence. We all know that one gets out of life no more than he is willing to put into it.

Nevertheless, we as professional men do have a definite responsibility for the continued education and development of our less experienced associates. This responsibility, in my opinion, is one of guiding rather than teaching. This phase of training in our firm consists of the following:

1. To insist on subscription to the literature of the profession
2. To encourage participation in professional activities, acceptance of speaking engagements and writing for publication
3. To provide each man with a plan of study which is tailored to his own individual needs and interests

RETAINING YOUNG PEOPLE IN THE PROFESSION

Here are the views of an experienced and successful CPA:

If long-range recruiting plans are to be effective, the profession of public accounting must be made attractive during the formative years.

The element of this approach receiving the greatest attention is, not surprisingly, beginning salaries. The profession will certainly have to keep relatively competitive in this respect. Most promising graduates, however, are smart enough to look beyond the starting salary in assessing career opportunities. The soundest advice a college adviser can give to the promising graduate who asks what to look for in his first job after graduation is to tell him to examine each job opportunity with one question in mind: "How much can I learn and develop in this position in the next five years?" No one right out of college is worth much to his employer. A person with five years of good solid experience who has had an opportunity to exercise initiative and responsibility is, however, in a good position no matter in what particular blind spot he may find himself at the moment. If he is not in a position to advance his present status (and in the majority of cases he will be) he is prepared and qualified to move out into other positions of responsibility and commensurate compensation.

The public accounting profession has a lot to sell to a person who accepts that advice. It offers first, and perhaps foremost in the minds of graduates, the opportunity to qualify for a CPA certificate. The CPA certificate is an attractive challenge. But if that is all the profession offers it will lose many of its good men at the end of the apprenticeship period.

We hear a lot of talk about security these days. But any employee worth his salt knows that the man with the most security is the man who can walk out the door at any time and find a number of attractive offers waiting. And that's exactly the kind of man firms should not want to lose. The employee who is easy to keep and to satisfy is likely to be the kind of person who is most expendable. In most topnotch accounting firms you will find someone doing a lot of planning and thinking about how to hold onto their best men and to make their positions attractive to them.

This involves putting yourself in the collective shoes of young staff men and asking yourself: what does the promising young man just getting his feet wet in professional life want? There are at least three answers to this question that may furnish food for thought to senior firm members.

First, the young professional man wants to feel important. Perhaps this is one of the strongest drives any of us have—to feel that we are doing something that is worth while and significant. Necessarily, the young accountant will be assigned at first to the more routine aspects of public accounting services. He may have little opportunity for contact with clients where he can see the over-all results of his work. His job will be made more attractive, however, if at every opportunity he is given a chance to take part in activities outside of the detailed checking and verification. Let him sit in on the conference in which plans for inventory taking are developed, and he will take a new interest in his part of the testing. See that he is introduced to the top personnel of the company whenever possible, so that he gets the feeling of being an important part of the engagement. He wants to feel that he is part of a professional team, not just an employee representing so many hours of billable time. Give him the opportunity to undertake smaller audits with a minimum of supervision as soon as he appears ready for the added responsibility. Invite him to attend professional meetings, and see that he is introduced as a firm member. If senior staff members consciously watch for opportunities to allow a promising junior to step into the limelight occasionally and take part in something outside his normal routine they will be surprised at how many such occasions develop where this can be done without serious inconvenience or loss of billable time. It will pay dividends in building not only professional pride but also firm loyalty.

The neophyte in public accounting wants to feel that he is learning and progressing in his profession. The average college graduate goes through three stages in his first professional experience. On graduation he goes out into the world convinced that he knows everything now and that it is only necessary to apply this vast store of knowledge to the sweeping solution of any and all problems he may encounter. In the middle of his first engagement he flounders in the unfamiliar and soon reaches the disillusive conclusion that he knows nothing and is hopelessly unprepared. Gradually he gains confidence in himself and begins to see that, although his background will stand him in good stead, he has a lot yet to learn. He may eventually reach the sage conclusion that for the conscientious professional man this learning process continues throughout his lifetime. At any rate it becomes evident that the best way to learn and develop is by doing new things and taking on new responsibilities.

One of the best opportunities to develop in the early stages of experience is afforded by working with senior accountants who take a conscious interest in explaining what is going on, and who take the trouble and effort to discuss the interesting and troublesome problems that arise in an engagement and the basis on which they are resolved.

Sometimes the easiest way to give young accountants an opportunity to develop a broader experience is for the senior to allow his assistants to take over a job he would normally do. Even if this involves a trade in which the senior does some of the work normally assigned to a junior accountant, it is an idea that should not be rejected. It is an odd fact that the routine assignments given younger staff men often encompass some of the more important aspects of an engagement.

Shifting staff men among assignments is another means of broadening the scope of their experience. There are many reasons why it is to a firm's advantage to keep staff men working on the same engagement over a number of years. Familiarity with the client's business and problems gained through repeated association often enables the accountant to render a better service as well as to cut the time on the engagement. Nothing is more likely to make a staff man feel that he is getting in a rut, however, than to be assigned to the same engagements year after year. What this calls for is not a complete reshuffling of jobs each year; obviously such a process would be chaotic. A conscious effort to discover a staff member's preferences and to switch engagements whenever it can be accomplished without serious inconveniences, however, will bring swift benefits in staff morale. The staff man will then have some assurance when he draws what he considers an undesirable assignment that it is not going to be his forever. As a matter of fact the engagements to which the greatest attention should be paid are (1) those which everyone on the staff considers particularly desirable, and (2) those which no one wants.

An accounting firm that tried the idea of an annual meeting, first on the senior and then on the junior level, at which time engagements and assignments were frankly discussed, reported surprising results. Assignments that were distasteful to one staff member ranked as highly desirable from another's viewpoint. One staff man favored the prospect of a local engagement in order to reduce travel time, while its present assignee was delighted to relinquish the job. There were of course engagements no one particularly relished and likewise some that were felt to be attractive by all. Arrangements were made to rotate personnel in these areas to some extent. The reaction of staff men to the idea was overwhelmingly favorable.

One of the recurring complaints of professional employers about college graduates is that they cannot write well. Wherever the fault lies, accounting firms may find a part of the solution in their own offices. Writing is an art that can be developed only through constant practice. Yet in the first years of his experience the average junior accountant has an opportunity to write practically nothing but working paper notes and perhaps letters home. Wherever possible young staff men should be given the opportunity to write. Let the promising young junior write the first draft of several sections of a long-form audit report, go over it with him, criticize it; then let him see the final draft and compare it with his efforts. Assign him the job of writing a report on some current topic during idle staff time. The time spent will pay dividends when he reaches the stage where writing is an important part of his responsibilities.

The third answer to the question, "What does the young staff man want?" is that he wants to know how he is doing. He expects to make mistakes and to be called on the carpet for them. Profiting from mistakes is an integral part of the learning process. He also expects to get credit and praise for good work when he deserves it. This requires more effort on the part of senior firm members than to sit back and wait for good performance to come to their attention; they should know from their own experience that the information that filters to the top is not always reliable and almost certainly not complete. The effort spent in making it a point to know who is responsible for all work and to distinguish the exceptional performance from the routine is distinctly worth while.

A firm partner once stated in a casual conversation that he had not seen some of his staff men for months, except when they came in to pick up their pay check. The inference apparently intended to be conveyed was that business was very good and that idle time was at a minimum. One wonders whether, aside from the fine results on the billing summary, such a situation is not cause for concern rather than pride. Every firm desires to build firm loyalty among its staff members, but in order to do so the firm must be more than a place to pick up a pay check. One of the things that prompts a person to enter into a professional career is the desire to be something more than a cog in a machine. Constant contact with senior firm members and the knowledge that they are aware of what he is doing and how he is doing cannot help but foster professional spirit in an accounting staff member, and the effect on his performance can be nothing but desirable.

To some accountants who remember the days when there were more competent people attempting to gain entrance into public accounting than could be absorbed, all this may appear to be a program for coddling young professional aspirants. The ultimate proof of benefit to any given firm and to the profession as a whole lies in the results.

Good young people are attracted to a choice of careers by the promise of material reward. It should not be forgotten—and it is not idle bombast to point out—that they are also attracted to the rigors of professional life by the challenge of individual responsibility, the desire to feel they are doing something important and worth while, and the aspiration to be a member of a group whose primary product is its brains, foresight, and ability.

If every senior firm member would consciously exert some extra effort along these lines, the word will get around. A firm's best salesmen are its satisfied clients. The profession's best publicity agents in attracting good talent are a group of satisfied young firm members who have the earmarks of success in the field.

Experiences in retaining staff members. Most firms are not satisfied with their ability to hold high-caliber men in their organizations. Those that meet competitive starting salaries fill their openings, but feel that public accounting is not attracting its share of the better graduates, partly because of the routine repetitive work given new men and partly because of the over-all level of staff compensation.

Many firms feel they cannot compete with the salaries offered experienced men by industry. They suffer a high turnover rate among men with four to seven years of experience. One major firm reports an annual loss of almost 100 senior accountants, mostly to industry. Travel, excessive overtime, type of work being performed, and lack of opportunity to advance are other factors cited as causes of turnover. (Transfers to other accounting firms represent only a small percentage of turnover.)

Some comments on this problem of keeping good men follow:

We lose some of our best men to our own clients—perhaps one every year. You know, you can't refuse a client who wants one of your own men.

We have lost a couple of juniors to other accounting firms. We think that when this happens it is usually for such reasons as: opportunity for broader experience in auditing bigger businesses with a larger firm; more money; more jobs with supervisory status.

In general, our attitude is:
1. Give the man a drawing account large enough to maintain standard of living and self-respect.
2. We try to do whatever should be done in keeping with the needs of human dignity.
3. We're all dedicated people—we hope it's contagious.
4. We get together and agree on how to solve our problems—we are a partnership, a team.
5. We do anything we can do to help a young man's professional development.

We believe one of our responsibilities is to come through with commitments which we make to the young person; it is important for the accounting profession to behave like a profession and not just talk about it.

Perhaps we are too commercial in our approach to our work; and if a staff man cannot feel he is in fact a professional man, who can blame him for going with another "business" where he can get more money?

One of the biggest problems is the lack of prestige, in large part due to the fact that many CPAs are not doing a really professional type of work.

Staff Utilization

■ UTILIZATION OF STAFF, from the procedural standpoint, is aimed at the basic objective of attaining the best results, measured in terms of both quantity and quality. It involves primarily, therefore, the adoption and application of methods found most effective for the purpose.

EFFICIENCY AND WORKING HOURS

In the formulation of the most productive working schedules, several factors require careful consideration. How long in consecutive hours the average individual can work effectively is governed by (1) the nature of the work, which may be physical or mental, easy or difficult, disagreeable or interesting, (2) the length and nature of respite dividing the daily and weekly work periods, (3) the training and experience of the worker, (4) the physical and mental condition of the employee, (5) the working conditions, (6) the individual purpose for which the worker is engaged in employment, and so on. In essence, work involves the output of energy which is limited and must be constantly renewed. The energy cannot be fully dissipated before renewal. Renewal must occur before diminution becomes harmful. Also efficiency decreases at an accelerating rate as energy is lost. Proper utilization therefore demands working schedules regulated by such considerations, with temporary deviations from regular hours made only in times of pressure and with full recognition of the declining curve of efficiency. There is a point at which excessive expenditure of energy may result in temporary or even permanent depreciation of the basic store of human energy represented by personnel. All this is, in effect, the background of the gradual evolution of current methods of utilization of personnel. Variables are manifestly introduced by the specific circumstances in each industry, field or profession, and in the case of each single individual.

In the accounting profession, firms generally have a seven- or an eight-hour day. This is exclusive of overtime. In general, the firms with a longer workday have a somewhat shorter regular workweek. A firm with a seven-hour day may have a thirty-five-hour week if it follows a five-day-week schedule. Where the workday is eight hours the regular workweek is clearly a forty-hour, five-day week.

Certain special factors tend to affect the public accountant's regular work hours and workdays. One is the obvious fact that staff members on engagements requiring their working on the premises of clients must frequently conform to the clients' working hours and days in order to have access to records and personnel. Another is that with the prevalence of the five-day week in the business world, accounting firms have to adjust their workweek accordingly or be sure their staff can be occupied productively in their own offices on Saturday mornings. The use of the five-day week by accounting firms is, therefore, quite likely to increase. A further probable influence is that in some geographical areas, and particularly in the larger cities, shorter hours are the rule.

WORKING OVERTIME

Overtime may be necessary in a public accounting office at almost any time of the year. When the need occurs outside of the year-end and midyear busy seasons, it applies usually to a specific engagement and even then perhaps only to some staff members. In such cases certain practices are sometimes considered advantageous. Some firms rotate overtime assignments among the staff and a few specifically give preference on overtime to those who request it. Of course, these procedures are subject necessarily to other considerations such as appropriate assignment of personnel to the engagement and to the effectiveness of over-all scheduling of all personnel on all engagements.

During the two customary rush periods of the year, overtime is general and involves increased hours for most staff members. A majority of firms increase the number of hours in their workweek during the peak season. Not all do it in the same way. Many of them use Saturday, others do overtime at night, and some use more consecutive hours in the day (a longer workday).

One point appears to explain why adding to consecutive hours in a day is least favored. Saturday, the preferred period for extra work, is presumably the time when most additional hours are available. It is also the best time to use to avoid excessive accumulation of hours during a single day or series of days, and therefore apt to produce a higher and more effective return per hour of overtime. For the same reason, though to a lesser degree, night work is preferable to working longer consecutive hours during the day because there is a helpful recuperative period intervening between the regular workday hours and the night overtime period. There are some firms that, where possible, like to break up the cumulative effect of overtime by permitting night work on alternate days only. There appears to be a strong feeling against Sunday work. It seems to be used only when there is no other alternative.

One method of averaging time over the year is to reduce the workweek during slack periods to less in days or hours than the regular workweek. The amount of reduction is governed, of course, not by the excess time worked during the busy periods but to the extent suggested by the extent of the slack. In other words, the reduction may be necessary but it is neither desirable nor welcome.

UTILIZING THE STAFF DURING SLACK PERIODS

Many firms find it expedient to reduce their workweek to less than forty hours during slack periods. Even so, there may still be occasions when there is not sufficient work to keep all staff members busy. Two major problems arise in this connection. Should personnel be required to report regularly to the office regardless? What can be done to keep the staff occupied even though not productively?

When staff members are idle for an appreciable length of time in an office, the mere visibility of their idleness creates a bad impression. Further, the idleness quickly impairs collective and individual morale.

Most firms require all staff members to report regularly to the office even when there is not sufficient work for them. This suggests strongly that some form of useful, if not directly productive, activity is carried on.

Actually, with the exercise of a little ingenuity there is no real lack of measures to keep staff members busy with matters that will be beneficial in the long run. Staff-training classes, technical reading, and improvement of report-writing are only a few of the activities that can serve the useful exploitation of any available spare time.

One of the greatest opportunities to use the staff effectively during slack periods is furnished by engagements which accountants accept usually more to take a useful part in community life than to engage in a remunerative activity. Institutional and other work of this sort, such as audits of hospitals, colleges, schools, clubs, and so on can generally be performed during slack periods. One firm doing an appreciable amount of such work is known to accept these engagements only for the period between May 1 and December 1 and to have thereby over a period of years balanced its time so efficiently that it hires no extra personnel in the peak seasons and loses a very small amount of unassigned productive time in the slack seasons.

Most firms have one or more accounts of a semicharitable nature, such as church, community chest, and similar audits. There is rarely any difficulty in securing consent to having this work done in the slack season, particularly if the consideration extended such clients as to fees is directly related to the possibility of doing the work at a time most convenient to the accountant.

RESPONSIBILITY FOR ASSIGNMENTS

One of the most important tasks in staff utilization is assignment of personnel. This requires considerably more than knowing what personnel is available and the abilities of the personnel. It requires a broad and comprehensive knowledge of accounting and of the special requirements of each engagement scheduled. Also requisite is the administrative ability to get the best results from the staff members available and to use them in such a way as to use the special abilities of each to the best advantage. This involves not only such use within a specific assignment but also in shifting personnel from one assignment to another. It may call for moving one or more men from one engagement to another before the first is finished. The doing of all these things follows certain well-defined patterns. In most firms assignments of field engagements to in-charge accountants are made usually by a principal of the firm. In other cases the assignments are made by managers or supervisors.

FACTORS IN ASSIGNING STAFF MEMBERS

The factors that must be considered in assigning a supervisor are: (1) familiarity with the specific engagement, (2) special qualifications, (3) size and scope of engagement, (4) availability, and (5) general professional ability.

The assignment of staff members to an engagement is affected also by certain factors, and these represent appreciably different methods of approach. The most important factor is the special requirements of the engagement. Another factor is the past performance of the assigned personnel as a team. The preferences of the supervisor or in-charge accountant as to their assisting personnel must be considered along with availability. Some try to get as many staff members as possible acquainted with each engagement. This makes individuals highly interchangeable, broadens staff experience, and lessens the loss felt when any staff member leaves the firm. While some firms restrict the duties of individual staff members principally to duties previously performed by them, most make an effort to give them different or more advanced duties. Many even require that the in-charge accountant use staff assistants so as to make them more competent generally in all phases of auditing.

While classification of personnel is, in general, an indication of the grade of work to which members of each classification are usually assigned, the relation of classification to actual assignment is not rigidly applied and the degree of application varies significantly according to the size of accounting firms.

In a majority of medium-sized firms the classifications of staff members according to assignment vary from one engagement to another. In the large firms this happens only infrequently since they have a big enough staff with sufficient personnel in each classification to assign duties more regularly in line with grades. The small firms, and particularly those with only two or three staff members, must inevitably often have personnel of higher grades performing duties falling within the scope of lower classifications, and also may sometimes assign some staff members to duties of the next highest grade as a matter of necessity.

In essence, the formal functional division of staff personnel into classifications does not bar a degree of fluidity of use both within classifications and upward and downward. Such fluidity or flexibility, as indicated, is greater in small firms but is also present in the large organizations to some extent.

There is, of course, another reason for this, beside the adapting of the staff to the work at hand. This is that as personnel in each grade becomes capable of handling the duties normally performed by members in the next higher classification, their ability to do so must be tested cautiously under careful supervision by assignment to work related to the higher classification. Size or complexity of an engagement also may play a part. Some engagements can only be handled by a fully experienced senior with past competent service as an in-charge accountant. Others, however, may permit use of a semi-senior as the in-charge accountant who, on a larger engagement, would be competent only to act as an assistant to the in-charge accountant.

The most obvious instance of duties performed outside the actual classification is that of the sole practitioner who has a new and small practice and no staff personnel. He performs the duties of all grades until such time as he acquires an assistant and then has to cope with assigning the latter to duties within the assistant's gradually increasing competence.

SCHEDULING WORK FOR COMPLETION

A factory production line cannot turn out goods as planned unless every related activity is scheduled and made to adhere to schedule. It is exactly the same in the systematic operation of a public accounting office.

The scheduling must be as accurate as possible, yet it cannot be too rigid. It must be sufficiently flexible to allow reasonably for contingencies and possible deviations, yet its goal must be to utilize to the utmost possible extent the staff available for the work definitely in hand over the scheduled period.

Most firms maintain a schedule of future engagements. Small firms are naturally less apt to have either volume and complexity of work or the size and classification of staff to make the careful scheduling and regulating of work practically imperative. The work schedule usually covers four weeks ahead. There are, however, many instances of longer periods ranging from sixty days to six months.

Among the important details carried on work schedules are the expected date of completion, the men assigned, the date each staff member will be available for another assignment, and the number and grade of man-hours estimated for each engagement.

TRANSFER OF STAFF PERSONNEL TO OTHER ENGAGEMENTS

Normally it is desirable to keep staff members on engagements until their specific assignments have been completed. In practice, however, it sometimes becomes necessary to transfer an individual from one assignment to another before completion of the first.

Transfers from assignments before their completion by the persons originally assigned may occur for any one of several reasons. These reasons are not necessarily given the same degree of importance or consideration by all firms. Transfers may be made to meet a deadline on another job, at a client's request, at the request of the in-charge accountant, for incompetence to perform the duties assigned, to make productive use of staff, at the request of the staff member concerned, and to provide the widest possible rotation of duties among staff members.

The indicated reasons for possible transfers from assignments prior to their completion point up informatively some of the essential qualifications a staff member should have to be most valuable to his firm and, in consequence, to himself. He must be adaptable to change and this adaptability should have a wide range for he must be equally able temperamentally to pursue an assignment unremittingly to its conclusion no matter how long, difficult, or even monotonous it may be, or to stop in the middle of such an assignment and take up another at any point without this affecting his interest, efficiency, or mood.

The staff man, too, must be able to get along diplomatically with clients and their personnel under all circumstances, and to make every in-charge accountant for whom he performs assignments consider him highly competent and as a man he wants on future engagements. His competence must extend also as widely as possible in the general field of accounting so that his firm may be able to use him advantageously in many ways and so that there will be little likelihood of his being given an assignment which he will not be able to handle well. And, clearly, it should never happen to him that a client requests his firm to take him off an assignment.

A staff member with all these qualities is clearly a paragon. But to the extent to which he approaches such an ideal, to that extent is he qualified to progress in his profession. There will be a very definite relation between the degree to which he possesses these qualities and the rapidity and nature of his advancement.

DELAYS IN THE WORK SCHEDULE

In adhering to working schedules, possible delays must be anticipated and avoided. Such delays may come in any phase of an engagement but the basic effect of all is to delay the report, with numerous vital consequences affecting both the client and the auditing firm.

There are various reasons why planned working schedules might not be met. Examples are: failure to write the basic substance of the report as work is performed in the field; failure to adjust the audit program to developments during the course of the audit; failure to discuss the report with the client before final typing; failure to prepare an adequate audit program; failure to obtain sufficient data from the client as to scope of the audit; failure to inform the in-charge accountant as to the nature of audit and report desired; the transferring of men to other engagements; and missing data because of lack of thoroughness due, possibly, to the inexperience of staff men promoted too fast.

Lamentably too often, the really fundamental cause of delay is lack of thorough preparation of working papers. Field work may be completed according to schedule but on review questions are asked which cannot be answered by reference to the working papers and they are found not to contain all data essential for the final report. Here, of course, it is not review or report preparation which is the direct cause of delay and loss of time but the inadequacy of field work which ostensibly has been completed according to and on schedule.

THE USE OF AUDIT PROGRAMS

The inadequacy of working papers is clearly related to the question of audit programs. Where there is a satisfactory and comprehensive audit program and it is carried out conscientiously, there is very little likelihood of inadequate working papers. Audit programs are considered here only from the standpoint of utilization of personnel. Most firms consider an audit program essential for every engagement, while others consider an audit program essential for some engagements; the decision would depend upon size and complexity of the audit. It is also likely that many who do not use a formal program nevertheless use notes or outlines which amount to an informal program.

There are various ways in which the use of audit programs contributes to the effective utilization of personnel. Such programs save time in giving instructions to staff; they eliminate any need to go back to take care of omissions, and they eliminate lost motion by some staff members who might not otherwise know how to proceed. They also prevent duplication of effort by personnel and are essential to secure maximum efficiency. On the other hand, possible disadvantages of audit programs are that, if too detailed, they may eliminate initiative. They also present the danger of getting stereotyped unless kept current, and so the program should be viewed as a guide only, subject to modification and simplification.

THE USE OF TIME ESTIMATES

In the preparation of effective working schedules, accurate estimation of required time is indispensable. Where the size and nature of an engagement require it, a time budget is the formal outcome of the estimating. In preparing such budgets one must consider certain major points in estimating time requirements for audits. These are: (1) nature and scope of audit, (2) prior experience on the same audit, (3) prior experience on similar audits, (4) general competence of personnel assigned, (5) estimates of the supervisor or in-charge accountant, (6) pressure of time in meeting the report date, and (7) the time of year at which audit occurs (peak or slack season).

A time estimate is not necessarily made an integral part of an audit program but there can be good reasons for making it so. However, firms that do not make time estimates a physical part of audit programs often make them comparable in detail by relating time subdivisions to the specific subdivisions of the working programs.

The ways in which firms consider a time budget particularly helpful in staff utilization are (1) it gives a basis for estimating when staff members on one engagement can be expected to be ready for another, (2) it gives staff members a time standard to go by, (3) it provides one basis for judging the performance of individuals, and (4) it tends to prevent improper allocation of time to different phases of an audit. Such a time budget helps to insure completion of engagements within a reasonable time and thus helps avoid having to explain excessive time and making fee adjustments.

A time budget, like anything else, can be used unwisely. In this respect these possibilities are to be guarded against: (1) a tendency on the part of staff members to spend automatically the allocated time (no more and no less) for each phase of an audit, (2) a tendency to repeat in preparing time budgets the time allocations for the same audit on prior occasions even if proved unsatisfactory, and (3) a likelihood of too much reliance on time budgets in estimating when personnel can be scheduled for another assignment.

Measuring and Rewarding Progress

■ NO FIRM CAN function effectively unless the partners know the abilities, potential, and limitations of their staff, and are in a position to measure the results accomplished. This requires rating standards—both for the individuals *per se,* and in comparison with other staff members in the firm.

Yet few firms seem to have established performance standards. Even a partner in a small firm, who may work closely with inexperienced men, is seldom completely familiar with the work of all his staff. Thus the responsibility for appraising performance often rests with the senior accountants. Do they know how to appraise the performance and progress of their crews? Are they able or willing to be frank and objective?

RATING AND REPORTING UPON PERFORMANCE

Most firms check and evaluate the progress of each staff member periodically. Usually this is done when promotions are being considered. However, it should be done more often than at promotion time, both for the benefit of the party or parties who make the staff assignments and to assist the employees.

In a small firm, it may be possible to watch the progress of each employee without written reports. For example, in one small firm, meetings of the four partners are held once each week, at lunch, and a frequent topic of discussion is the progress and performance of the staff members on their jobs.

Where the ratio of partners to staff is one to three or one to four (or even somewhat lower), this method may be adequate.

In large firms and where there are relatively many staff members in proportion to the number of partners or principals, a formal report on each assistant may be filed with the personnel director by the accountant in charge of each engagement at the close of the engagement. A very useful form for this, with the instructions for rating, can be found on pages 791, 792. It should be noted that definite grades are required as to several items evidencing auditing ability, as well as to professional qualifications, self-expression qualifications, and personal qualifications, respectively. A careful study of the factors listed in the instructions for consideration in making the ratings should be very helpful in checking the progress of any practitioner's staff members. Another useful form for grading junior accountants appears on page 793.

How does the client react to the staff members assigned to the job? Usually any comments obtained will be casual or spontaneous. They cannot very well be solicited. Not much criticism can be expected from this source unless the assistant is poor—or very good. But it should be recorded on the man's progress sheet with adequate explanation of the circumstances.

INTERPRETING THE RATINGS

Changes in remuneration usually are dependent on the progress indicated by the ratings given each employee. If there have been many individual ratings, a tabulation of the progress made on each item rated on successive assignments will be needed. But care must be exercised in comparing the ratings given by different persons. To make the grading comparable, an index of the severity of the grader may be needed. Thus, the graders may be rated as "very severe," "severe," "average," "lenient," and "very lenient." Letters may be used for this rating of graders and these can be affixed to the grades given by them to the other employees. A tabulation of successive grades received by an employee from various graders will give a better indication of the progress, or lack of it, when the severity of the grading is measured with the grades.

If there are many employees, a "ladder" showing the positions and particularly the salaries may be used. First, a ladder, which is a chart of the possible salaries for all employees, is made. Then the employees are all listed on the ladder and their relative positions and progress studied. The result in each instance can then be compared with previously adopted standards for retention, increase in compensation, and promotion.

DISCUSSIONS OF PROGRESS WITH STAFF MEMBERS

Reports on staff members afford an excellent opportunity for staff training. Interviews should be held with each employee periodically to discuss his weak as well as his good points. Specific references to reports on engagements should be made in a frank and friendly manner for his personal benefit. The suggestions given by such an interview may be more useful than many hours of class training.

ADVANCEMENT

Advancement in employment, aside from intangible forms, means an increase in compensation, promotion to a higher position, or a happy combination and coincidence of both. The employee finds it pleasant to be surprised by such occurrences. Where possible, it is useful as an incentive if the firm formally systemizes increases in compensation and promotions so as to provide for periodic advancement according to seniority and demonstrated ability. Exceptional cases, of course, should continue to be governed by the relevant special circumstances.

Basic policy and authority for advancement. In creation of basic policy, the formulation of certain standards to classify and evaluate personnel for advancement is desirable. This need is greater when the firm is large and its organizational structure complex. Many firms classify staff members for promotion according to certain professional characteristics and such characteristics are assigned varying weights for the different classifications. But these firms differ greatly in the listing of characteristics and assess them according to highly individualistic patterns. While greater standardization is doubtless desirable, both the listing of characteristics and the weight assigned to each will presumably still be governed basically by the special needs of each firm.

As to where final decision as to promotion rests, the responsibility in every instance is executive. In single proprietorships the owner of the practice is the authority. In partnerships the designation of authority will vary according to the number of partners, the executive duties assigned each, and the size and complexity of the organization. Most firms conduct periodic reviews of the records of staff members for promotion and compensation increases.

Timing of advancement. Timing as to promotions and salary increases is very important. Recognition of service of an employee should follow closely upon the heels of a reasonable period of demonstration of valuable service or of increased proficiency or ability. If it does not occur then, there is almost certain to ensue dissatisfaction on the part of the staff member, and definite impairment of his initiative, productivity, and even loyalty.

A rather obvious time for such matters is right after prolonged periods of greatest pressure of work. For practically all accounting firms one most auspicious occasion is after the rush of the year-end period with its particularly heavy tax-work burden. It is probably around May 1 that most firms reach the moment when the entire organization feels a sense of relief and usually great satisfaction at having come successfully through another period of high achievement and can appraise what has been done and what lies ahead.

Uneven progress. On occasion there may be instances where staff members who have had good records of performance and progress in the past have not done as well as usual during the recent period or as well as their known ability would warrant. Arbitrary adverse action in such cases is rarely justified. There is generally a definite cause for such a result and there should be no decisive judgment until a real effort has been made to ascertain and eliminate the undesirable unknown factor. The best results in this direction are most likely to be obtained by a friendly and frank discussion of the circumstances with the staff member by that partner having direct responsibility for him. Such discussion may reveal the existence of a cause that the firm can do something about. Even if it does not, the concern displayed by the firm may be helpful in improving the morale of the staff member by making him realize that there is a very real interest in his personal well-being and that he is considered to be a vital part of the organization and not viewed impersonally as a mere cog in a machine.

Obtaining the CPA certificate. Closely related to the subject of advancement is what a firm does when a staff member obtains his CPA certificate. Some grant a special increase in salary; others, where a certificate is a requisite for promotion to a stated classification, put through the promotion and the related increase. A few also place the certificate holders in a group as potentially eligible for partnership. Among firms where there is no such definite action, some sort of official firm acknowledgment is made through some ceremony. Generally this takes the form of a dinner in honor of the recipient of the certificate.

Allowing staff members to deal with clients. At a meeting of practitioners, the following question was asked: To what extent do you insist on handling all contact work with clients and to what extent do you allow this work to be done by other members of the staff who are not partners?

Most of the practitioners present were quite willing to give nonpartner staff members as much authority and freedom in handling clients as they were capable of assuming. The general opinion seemed to be that it is the profession's responsibility to develop younger men, and they cannot obtain professional status unless they learn how to deal with clients directly.

While no one reported any unfavorable experience in carrying out this policy, several indicated fear that if the staff members were allowed too much freedom, they might leave and take the clients with them. A number of those present thought that if any trouble did develop it was the practitioner's fault for not watching his staff men more closely and keeping in touch with what they were doing and saying.

Achieving partner status. Almost all firms claim that partnership opportunities are available in their organizations. Actually, these opportunities, in some cases, seem to be limited or long-deferred, although there is a growing willingness to admit a capable man to partnership when he is still in his early thirties.

Traditionally, the status of partner represents the goal of the ambitious young staff man and is the mark of arrival in the profession. He now assumes personal responsibility in the eyes of the public for his actions and those of his firm. Nonetheless, the term "partner" is sometimes applied to a man with such a modest interest in the firm—or with such a highly restricted scope—that he may be little more than a staff man who shares in a small way in its earnings. When a man achieves partnership status, therefore, it does not mean that the firm need no longer be concerned with his personal requirements.

WHEN PROGRESS LEVELS OFF

Generally, good men advance rapidly during their first few years. It is when a man becomes a senior accountant that he may reach a career plateau. Leveling off occurs in almost every field of endeavor. But one of the major problems in public accounting seems to be that leveling off is apt to start at an earlier age than in other occupations—sometimes when a man is still in his twenties. This flattening of the progress curve, before the advance to partnership, seems to be a primary reason why the accounting profession loses so many men at the five- or six-year experience level.

To bridge the gap, the more successful firms do several things: (1) they give the man increasing responsibility on more complicated jobs; (2) they place him in charge of accountants working on several jobs, and allow him closer contact and authority in dealing with a client; (3) they use titles such as *supervisor, manager, principal,* or *associate;* (4) they may give him a bonus, based on the over-all earnings of the practice.

In many instances seniors are placed with clients who are looking for capable people with the background these men offer. This ties the accounting firm closer to the client since one of its alumni is in a key position.

In other cases, firms have made very good use of seniors by making them specialists in systems, estate planning, budgeting, cost analysis, or management problems. While they are preparing to specialize, they may be used as audit supervisors. All their unassigned time during this period is devoted to the study of the particular specialty that they have chosen or have been assigned to.

When the men become specialists, naturally the firm can charge more for their services because they are worth more to the client. Because of these higher fees, the men can be paid more than they could earn as staff seniors.

CURRENT PRACTICES

Here is what some firms have to say about advancement opportunities in their organizations:

A new man is told that he can qualify for partnership as soon as he demonstrates that he can carry and develop clients on his own; we have no limit to the number of partners.

We never employ from the outside except for juniors—we always promote from within (one of our strongest talking points). We hope the new man will become a semi-senior in one and one-half to two years and a senior in three to four years if he's really top flight . . .

We have a firm policy (which we tell the people with whom we are discussing prospects) against career staff men. We expect a man to progress to the point where he becomes supervisor or manager within seven years. We think this is a strong recruiting argument for the outstanding people whom we want. On the average, the man becomes a manager at age thirty and a partner at somewhere between thirty-five and forty.

We expect a qualified man to become an in-charge accountant in five, six, or seven years.

We can tell the applicant that there is no ceiling to his earnings . . . and that since World War II we have never had to hold a man back for lack of opportunity.

Three of our seven partners were admitted at various times during the last ten years. They were between thirty-five and forty when they were admitted.

There are no present plans to add to the partnership. We feel a large number of partners results in a number of individual practices. The top seniors can make good money, since their income is actually a percentage of the fees they produce. But we will probably lose them in time.

Our partners get together once a year to discuss salaries. Since all but one of us do field work, we have a pretty good idea about how the men have been doing. If we don't know too much about a man, we might call in one of the seniors who has worked with him and ask his opinion about the man.

We tell the new man that he will be rated every three or four weeks by the man for whom he works, and that this rating of the senior will also be reviewed by the manager. This helps tell him no one person can impede his progress.

Each senior accountant grades all of his people on six or eight factors on each assignment. The senior does not talk to the man about his rating but he will, of course, discuss things he is doing badly, and we hope he gives him a kind word or two on things that are going well.

We don't try to formally appraise the individual's progress—at the right time, Mr. —— makes up what he thinks is an appropriate salary recommendation and then checks this with two or three of the partners who ought to be familiar with the man—they may check with some of the seniors who have supervised the junior.

The new man does not really hear anything from anybody about how well he is doing until I talk to him. I review all people every six months until they're earning $—— and annually after that. Before doing so, I have the ratings of all the seniors who have supervised the junior.

Sometimes when Mr. —— assigns him to a new job, this gives him a chance to pass the time of day with him, to ask him how things are coming along, etc.

In our organization the staff personnel are rotated among the supervisors and this gives us an opportunity to get an evaluation from each of the supervisors with respect to each member of the staff. The composite evaluation is made available to the staff member.

The staff personnel evaluation instructions used by the above firm are reproduced in part as follows:

In completing the evaluation sheet for each staff member, it should be borne in mind that the making of this rating sheet has several purposes:

1. It is to help the partners in selecting logical persons for promotion and in administering a sound salary policy.

2. By adding all the evaluation sheets together on a given staff member, the partners will have a basis for a frank discussion with the individual staff member so rated, to keep him posted with respect to his progress.

3. By evaluating the staff members each six months, progress of the person can be determined.

4. The evaluation sheets can be used as a basis to learn what the supervisors can do to help the staff member become a well-adjusted member of the staff.

5. The most important purpose is to develop and retain *capable* staff members.

In rating a person, be sure you do *not* compare the record of a junior with that of a senior.

The supervisor will keep in mind that the identification of the individual doing the rating should be kept anonymous at all times. The composite rating of all supervisors will be used in discussions with the staff member.

After you have completed your evaluation sheet on a staff member, lay it aside for a day or two. Go over it again—ask yourself—Have I been fair? Have I given the proper percentage to each element in the rating sheet? Have I considered each element in the rating sheet separately? Do my comments really support my checking? Would I be willing to sit down with the staff member and conscientiously and constructively discuss the rating sheet with the person? (This, of course, will not be asked of you.) Did I give proper consideration to specific instances and proper weight to all instances? Am I grading the man only on one job or on a composite of all jobs?

The rating sheet used by this firm appears in the Appendix, page 794.

General Personnel Policies

CONTRACTS OF EMPLOYMENT

■ IN EMPLOYING STAFF members one of the first questions which arise concerns whether or not written agreements covering the terms of employment are advisable. Such written contracts are not usually made with staff assistants who are in the lower grades of staff classification. Sometimes an exchange of letters, or the signature of acceptance on the employer's letter, is used. If a formal contract is adopted, its provisions will be similar to those for employees of higher rank except as to compensation, particularly for overtime work. (See the Appendix, pages 796-799, for two kinds of contracts.)

An employee with the rank of manager or principal, however, should always be covered by a contract of employment which sets forth his authority, duties, basis of compensation, profit-sharing plan, if any, and the period of the contract. Where contracts are used, it is customary to specify that the employee is to give his full time and attention to his employment and is not to engage in competitive practice during the period of the contract. Also, the provision may be made that for a period of two (or more) years after termination of employment he will not do work for any of the firm's clients, either on his own account or as an employee of another, and that he will not solicit such work from the clients. A clause also may be used to specify that the employee will not offer employment to any other employee of the firm during a period of perhaps two years after termination of employment.

In hiring juniors or seniors an accounting organization ordinarily is taking persons on trial and, therefore, the period of service may be terminated upon giving notice. Nevertheless, usually the best results will be obtained if the staff members understand that, while employment continues, their full time and attention is to be devoted to the employer's work so that conflicts of interest do not arise. The employing firm always should make its policy as to outside employment clearly known to the staff members so that a mutual understanding exists.

STAFF MANUALS

Staff manuals may be of two types. One is an administrative manual explaining the firm's personnel practices and policies. This type of manual is not for general distribution to members of the staff but is distributed to part-

211

ners and supervisors who have responsibility for personnel policies and practices of various offices.

The second type of manual is prepared for distribution to all staff members. This type of manual covers not only firm practices and procedures but may deal with such matters as appearance and behavior of staff men. An example of such a manual is included in the Appendix, page 800. In other cases written rules may not have been prepared and too little attention may have been given to such instruction. Lack of attention to the proper conduct of staff members is likely to affect adversely the appearance and actions, and therefore the self-respect, of these employees. Some of the most important instructions which affect staff morale are given below.

APPEARANCE AND GENERAL CONDUCT

Even a master's degree from a college does not insure that the recipient has learned the importance of neatness and propriety of dress, cleanliness in the care of his person, and a reasonable amount of dignity and decorum in his behavior. Some beginners need these matters called to their attention several times. Others have difficulty in learning that the importance of appearance and behavior is not limited to the working hours of the firm.

Although the employer cannot entirely prescribe the employee's conduct while away from work, the reflection upon the firm of inappropriate behavior and poor appearance, particularly in public places, can be suggested. Also, the importance of his general conduct to his own career and to the accounting profession should be pointed out. He should be encouraged to participate in worthy community and professional activities.

RELATIONS BETWEEN STAFF MEMBERS AND CLIENTS

Junior assistants should be informed that they are not to discuss their findings with, or direct their questions to, the client. The accountant in charge of the engagement will take up with the client all matters relating to the engagement, or will have a partner do so. Discussions by junior assistants with the client's employees regarding irregularities and loose methods are to be avoided. Courteous and friendly relations are to be maintained with these employees but only on a professional basis; the attitude should be one of dignified friendliness. The client's records should not be removed from his office except with his permission and a dated receipt must be given in such instances when removal is necessary. All assistants (and principals as well) must maintain independence in their mental attitude and must avoid relationships which might create an assumption of lack of independence. No staff member should have any financial interest in any of the firm's clients. Personal checks and salary checks should not be cashed in the client's offices and any rules of the client as to smoking during working hours should be observed. Fraternizing with employees of a client should be taboo.

SECRECY REGARDING THE FIRM'S BUSINESS

The affairs of the firm and of its clients are confidential matters. The accountant's work is undertaken in strict confidence and with an understanding of privacy. Therefore, the utmost care must be taken not to discuss or mention any of the affairs or even the name of a client outside of the office of the firm or that of the client. If the assistant needs to be reached by telephone from his home, the office of the firm should be called; the operator will then call the assistant and have him call his home.

BEHAVIOR OF A JUNIOR IN THE CLIENT'S OFFICE

The fundamentals of desirable behavior are based on common courtesy and common sense. However, each client may present some special problems. The seniors and partners who will be with the junior on an engagement should inform him of any special problem he may encounter. The supervisor will usually volunteer this information before the junior goes out to a client's office. If special information is not given, the junior should be sure to ask if there are any special problems which quite likely will be encountered.

Listed below are some common behavior patterns that should be observed by all juniors. The list is not complete but serves as a general guide.

1. When you are assigned work, listen intently, and aim for complete comprehension of what is expected. If in doubt, ask!

2. Do the work the way the firm prefers that it be done. Don't try to improve on the firm's techniques.

3. Ascertain from the senior the time allowed on the various phases of the work assigned. Attempt to work as carefully as possible within those time limits.

4. If the work should involve contact with the client's personnel, see that it is as brief, courteous, and discreet as possible.

5. When questions arise in connection with the work and the senior is busy or momentarily absent, make notes of any questions, findings, suggestions, etc., then work around the difficulties.

6. Don't roam around the premises of the client.

7. Make comments and suggestions concerning the client's record system to the senior, not to the client's personnel.

8. Don't intrude on conversations between employees of the client.

9. In conversations between the senior or partner and the client at which the junior is present, the junior should be only an observer.

10. Don't cash a paycheck at a client's office.

11. Don't seek informal friendships with the client's employees of the opposite sex.

12. Refrain from all acts and all comments reflecting adversely on one's personal or professional stature.

OUTSIDE EMPLOYMENT OFFERS TO STAFF MEMBERS

When a staff member receives an outside offer, an inducement in the form of a raise or a promotion is sometimes offered to retain him. Presumably what this implies is that consideration of the employee's value is accelerated ahead of the fixed time for periodic review.

Realistically, certain obvious factors would seem to be applicable to each case separately. Each employee represents an investment by the firm based upon his training and the nature of the experience afforded him. From that standpoint he has a definite future value based on expectation of further utilization. Another consideration is whether he can be replaced readily from within the organization, or, if necessary, from without. An examination of all these points will give an adequate basis for a decision as to whether there is an impelling reason to retain the staff member's services and, if there is, the nature and extent of the inducement to be considered.

A sincere interest in the personal welfare of the staff member also requires attention to other points. An important consideration is whether the outside offer is one which it would be to the undoubted advantage of the employee to accept from the standpoint of broader opportunity for the future even though at the moment the current employer can match or surpass the immediate return available in the position offered. Another possible consideration relates to the goodwill factor inherent for the firm in having former staff members holding responsible positions in the private accounting field. Particularly among the large firms there is a very decided appreciation of the definite advantages of having their "alumni" spread widely and strategically in the business world.

One of the most appreciative gestures a client of an accounting firm can make is applying for permission to hire a staff member of the firm. Often this points up clearly the effectiveness of past recommendations or reports to the client and a taking of appropriate measures in consequence which go so far as to secure qualified personnel from the accountant making the recommendation or report. By far the most frequent call is for seniors. The reaction to such requests in some cases, no matter what the grade, is unfavorable. One reason for this may be that personnel cannot then be spared because of the difficulty or impossibility of immediate replacement. Another may be that a specified individual cannot be spared although another of the same grade can be. A third may be that the accounting firm does not consider the person asked for or the grade to which the request relates to be appropriate for the opening.

REHIRING FORMER PERSONNEL

It happens sometimes that a competent staff member who has left an accounting firm becomes available again to the same firm. Whether, as a rule, such an employee should be rehired if there is an opening merits consideration. A staff member who has resigned to go elsewhere and presents himself later for rehiring does so probably because there is no other immediate possibility for him, at the same time knowing that his previous departure may be held against him or will, as it should, affect his relative seniority. The firm to which he applies for rehiring may well consider that such misgivings on his part will militate against the probability of completely satisfactory results. Where the former staff member is one who was released because someone had to be released and he was considered least qualified for retention, the desirability of rehiring such an individual when other more qualified candidates are available is definitely more than doubtful.

FILLING VACANCIES FROM WITHIN OR WITHOUT

Nothing is likely to impair staff morale more than filling a position from the outside when in lower classifications there is personnel qualified to fill it. Three inevitable results can be expected. The staff members who might reasonably have expected promotion are made to feel that they are not considered competent or eligible for higher positions. The entire staff is made to feel that the first choice for a higher position does not belong to them as a matter of right and therefore that there is no actual certainty of opportunity for advancement as broad as the firm's normal development should permit. The new staff member is apt to find all other employees unco-operative, particularly those who feel they have suffered by his hiring. Both he and the firm suffer accordingly. For such reasons, it is a well-recognized and almost invariably honored procedure throughout the business world to fill vacancies from present personnel unless the vacancy is a new one involving requirements which are not met by current personnel and are outside the usual organizational structure. Accounting firms generally conform.

Such a wise policy has one distressing aspect. While it increases the likelihood of long years of employment with appropriate advancement, it operates to bar the hiring in higher classifications of qualified individuals seeking employment. In effect, it insures that an older employee of higher grade has greater security for the future as long as he remains employed and little prospect of any if he finds himself unemployed.

DISCHARGING A STAFF MEMBER

The discharge of a staff member is a matter of great seriousness to the person involved. Humane considerations as well as the interests of the employer demand that such an action, even if for cause, be carried out in a manner that will not crush the individual's self-respect, nor make him feel that he is totally unqualified.

It is always an unenviable job to lay off an employee, particularly one who may have been on the staff for several years, at a time when jobs may be scarce, and if the individual involved has family responsibilities. The unpleasantness of this task can be reduced considerably if it is handled in a sympathetic manner, the reasons for the action reasonably explained, and some advice given to the individual as to what he might do about helping himself. In most cases, such an employee will leave without rancor and his regard for the firm may even be raised.

Employees who leave with a feeling of bitterness may spread malicious tales about their former employer among fellow accountants and, possibly, among clients. This is a situation that should be avoided. Staff morale can be adversely affected by stories of cold discharges.

Even in a large organization a staff member should not be released by merely giving him a discharge slip. He should be given the courtesy, as a professional man and employee, of a personal notice and explanation. If a man can be given advance notice, that is usually appreciated. Where a firm, as a matter of policy, does not like to keep men who know they have to leave, it would be fair to give them some extra severance pay in lieu of notice. The amount of severance pay is a matter for the conscience of the accountant and is controlled by a number of factors.

There undoubtedly are many cases where a release from a position (the word "release," for psychological reasons, is preferable to the term "discharge") for cause was the turning point in a man's career. It either spurred him on to greater effort or made him realize that his aptitudes were in another field. Some of these men later became very successful. A helping hand to the released staff man may keep him from making a serious mistake in charting his future course.

PLACING RELEASED PERSONNEL

Most firms make a determined effort to secure new positions for released personnel. Quite naturally, self-interest influences greatly the choice of fields in which the greatest effort is made. In a broad sense, there are three major fields available. These are: (1) other public accounting firms, (2) clients of the firm, and (3) other concerns.

Two further points are worthy of comment regarding placing of public accounting personnel in other fields. One is that while there are men with a seemingly adequate educational background who do not develop well as public accountants, such men, if completely satisfactory in all other essentials, may still be very valuable elsewhere. Such persons, having been educated intentionally for public accounting, will have therefore a more thorough and broader accounting background than would the average individual available for top clerical or supervisory positions or those involving an appreciable knowledge of general accounting. In such cases there is an opportunity to render both a client and a staff member a very great service.

The other point relates to the care to be exercised so as to avoid placing unqualified personnel or incompetent "castoffs" with clients or others for positions relating to accounting matters they cannot handle. The responsibility of the accounting firm making any placement of released personnel elsewhere is measured by the fact that the new employer is fully justified in assuming that the accounting firm is in fact giving an implied warranty of fitness.

TRAVEL EXPENSE AND ARRANGEMENTS

The practice of a flat traveling per-diem allowance plus transportation is gradually disappearing in favor of allowing actual reasonable expenditures. The preponderance of firms allow breakfast, lunch, and dinner, but some do not include lunch on the ground that this is not an added burden when away from home. Normal gratuities are considered to be reimbursable. Most firms give a mileage allowance to those using their own cars, regardless of the number of passengers. A few make small extra allowances for the first and second extra persons going on firm business.

Some firms permit those conducting protracted out-of-town engagements to come home for weekends provided the distance is not too great, transportation schedules are reasonable as to time consumption and cost, and the client's interest is not unduly affected. The custom of charging the client with traveling time within the normal workday is prevalent. Ordinarily, all traveling expense is charged at cost to clients on whose behalf disbursement is made.

Although overtime and travel are decreasing, they remain excessive in some firms. The attitude of the wife of a staff man is increasingly important. Formerly, most young employees were single. Now that many recent college graduates are married there is a growing reluctance to travel or put in overtime for extended periods.

The amount of out-of-town travel varies considerably among firms, and also among personnel within firms. While some feel it is no longer a problem, others cite it as a factor which prompts some young men to leave the profession. One firm eases the travel burden in this manner:

> When a man is out of town on a long trip, we put him on a per-diem basis, which enables him to take his wife at our expense. Some men make a tour out of some out-of-town engagements and they and their wives actually look forward to it.

FAIR EMPLOYMENT PRACTICES

Accounting firms are not subject to many of the restrictions upon hiring imposed by Federal or state laws. Problems arising from union membership, closed shops, and use of child labor should never arise in hiring professional employees. But all employers, including accounting firms, should plan their employment and personnel policies to avoid charges of discrimination because of race, creed, or color.

State antidiscrimination laws specify that it is unlawful for the employer to refuse to hire, or to discriminate in hiring, any individual because of his race, creed, color or national origin. In some states the law forbids an employer to ask questions that express, either directly or indirectly, any discrimination as to these characteristics. Under such conditions the employer should be careful in wording employment application blanks to avoid reference to such items as place of birth of the applicant and of his parents, nativity, lineage or ancestry, maiden name of wife or mother, and religion. Even in states not having discriminatory laws, the interviewer should exercise care to avoid any suggestion of discrimination. Careless remarks which indicate prejudice may be interpreted as evidencing policies of discrimination.

In employing people for public accounting, the employer must consider the personal attributes of the applicant, including his appearance, behavior, cleanliness, tact, aggressiveness, dignity, culture, and compatibility. The record of the rejections of applicants, showing the disposal of every application, should be clear as to the reasons for rejection so as to provide defense against charges of discrimination.

A number of states have laws that specify the maximum hours for which it is permissible for women to work. Usually, certain exceptions are specified or may be granted. For example, some laws do not apply to women in executive, administrative, or professional capacities or to those in creative, managerial, or intellectual work earning a stated minimum per month.

Relations with Others

Public Relations

■ THE REPUTATION of a professional accountant has always been one of his foremost concerns. Like any professional man in public practice, he has known that success depends upon what others think of him and that his practice grows and gains quality through satisfied clients. He has known that, as in the case of other professions, success is also related to the collective reputation of the profession as a whole.

The importance of reputation to CPAs may be even greater than it is for the other professions. The CPA's reputation for independence has frequently been called the most important value he has to offer clients. It is natural, therefore, that he should be intensely curious about what others think of him. Yet evaluating themselves poses a particularly difficult problem to CPAs. It is hard enough for anyone to see himself as others see him. The CPA, by the very nature of his work, is removed from the objective appraisal of "outsiders." He is called upon to keep his own counsel, and the requirement of independence has insulated him from outside opinion.

This heavy dependence on reputation has always stimulated in CPAs an interest in public relations, though they did not give it that label until after World War II. The difficulty which the individual encountered in coping with his personal public relations, and his growing awareness that accounting is little understood by its users, to say nothing of the general public, led the AICPA in 1947 to expand its public relations program.

Looking back and taking stock of what has been accomplished leads to three major conclusions: (1) important changes have occurred in what people think of accounting; (2) the changes have been wrought primarily by advances in accounting itself, by new accounting services offered to clients, and by changes in the attitudes of CPAs toward themselves, their profession, their daily tasks, and their clients; (3) public relations helped to bring about all these changes, but the information programs of the professional organizations could have accomplished little without the achievements of CPAs themselves.

Applying these lessons to the future, we may expect problems to grow out of the needs for accounting services and the way the profession meets them. Public relations can anticipate the problems and advise on how to solve them, but their solution will depend much more on the performance of CPAs.

AN EARLY ANALYSIS

The years immediately after World War II were years of especially searching self-examination for the profession. Three reliable opinion surveys were completed and published within twelve months, beginning early in 1947, on the attitudes of influential people toward CPAs and the work they do. Ten years later, a group of less comprehensive soundings was taken. These recent opinion tests, while unfortunately not directly comparable with the earlier surveys, nevertheless yield important clues.

Certain findings of the early postwar surveys stand out above the others. They show that CPAs were on the threshold of professional recognition but that they had not yet quite arrived there in the public's thinking, and their own preoccupation with professional status in those years reveals doubts within the profession itself. Recent tests show much progress, both in public attitudes and in the broader interests of the accountants. Certified Public Accountants have learned to take their professional status more in stride.

In 1947, high executives ranked teachers, dentists, lawyers, physicians, and apparently engineers above CPAs in professional status. As a general, unsolicited reaction, the executives would not think of CPAs when asked what groups they considered professional.

It is interesting to search the surveys for causes of this attitude. By 1947 accounting had already acquired many of the attributes of a profession, and these were well regarded. The legal and organizational controls exercised over the profession were widely admired. Less well accepted, however, were the completeness, impartiality, and accuracy of certified financial statements, though they were thought more dependable than those not certified. Perhaps lack of full confidence in the CPA's services helped to block recognition of him as a professional man.

THE NEED FOR PUBLIC RELATIONS

Of financial reporting in general a substantial portion of the public was distrustful. Half of the people in the country believed that most companies were making more than they were reporting, despite all the safeguards imposed by certified audits, Federal and state laws, and by the regulations of the SEC and the exchanges. A survey made by Elmo Roper was especially convincing on this point by virtue of its method and thoroughness. Of particular interest to the accounting profession was the attitude toward financial statements held by bankers and financial analysts, their most sophisticated consumers. This group was not inclined to take annual report figures at face value. In the words of Roper's 1948 report: "They feel that many annual reports try to paint company progress and prospects in the best light possible for the benefit of stockholders and that different, although equally legitimate, accounting procedures might have led to somewhat less optimistic conclusions. For them, the annual report is a document that presents a particular point of view toward the company's financial operations, and one that must be checked as a routine matter, by reference to other sources of information like tax returns and SEC reports."

Largely as a result of such disheartening findings, the profession determined on corrective measures. "Public relations" became the watchword, though it is probable that many members were not sure what it would do. Some may even have expected that by employing carefully phrased literature and certain other techniques, the profession's public relations problems could be made to go away. Not misled by any such false hopes, the AICPA set out methodically to build a public relations department, and many state and other national accounting societies retained professional staffs with a background in public relations.

YEARS OF ACCOMPLISHMENT

In the years that followed, a balanced public relations program has slowly taken form, and a working relationship between the AICPA and the state societies has spread a public relations network across the nation. This program has never been expensive, as public relations programs go. Even during the crisis in relations with the organized Bar, when the best outside public relations counsel in the country was retained, the course prescribed was one of moderation, composure, and dignity. The program has centered squarely on revealing the accomplishments of the accounting profession as demonstrated in the work of the AICPA and state societies and in the activities of individual members. From the beginning, it has stressed the role of the CPA himself as an ambassador for his profession, pointing out that the public's attitude toward accounting is a composite of the opinions held by many people of the CPAs they have seen, or whose work they have known, in actual experience. This emphasis on individual performance has increased over the years, with the help of the state societies and chapters. Yet one of the shortcomings of the program is still its failure, largely for shortage of funds, to carry the profession's public relations counseling to the member himself.

AN OBJECTIVE PARTIALLY ACHIEVED

All of the evidence available seems to indicate that accountancy, as practiced by *most* CPAs, is now considered a profession.

There is no single litmus test that shows this. People are not accustomed to drawing up standards and applying them to one vocation or another to see whether it is "professional." The various established professions are so different, one from another, that comparison between them is generally suspect as a means of according professional status. Also, no one contends that all CPAs fully meet professional standards, any more than all doctors or lawyers measure up. Yet it is safe to say that by the end of the 1950's enough of them did so for certified public accountants generally to have earned recognition as a profession.

This is, indeed, a major accomplishment. It represents the achievement of the central public relations objective of the decade. Yet it is easy to mistake it for something it is not—a propaganda victory. Repeated assertions of professionalism have never been an important part of the public relations program. They would have been tiresome and not very convincing. The fact is, as the surveys show, that nobody outside the profession cares very much whether the accountants should be considered "professional" or not. People don't spend much time contemplating these definitions. *What concerns them is whether or not they are getting the services they expect and need from CPAs.*

The overwhelming evidence is that they are. Two quite unrelated recent surveys show that businessmen generally rank the CPA at the top of the list of outside specialists in terms of value to the company—ahead of lawyers, insurance advisers, advertising agencies, labor relations consultants, management engineers and the rest. They consider the profession an indispensable adjunct of modern business life, a necessity to the nation's economic well-being. Progressive executives look first to the CPA to offer management services, and they would rather he provide them if he can, than seek these services elsewhere. "Progressiveness" is very much on people's minds as far as accountants are concerned. The cost of accounting services to clients is not at this time a major public relations problem—though it could become one in the future.

It might almost be said that professional recognition has come in by the back door. While CPAs have been diligently providing the services their clients needed and then applying public relations techniques to reveal them, the public has quietly bestowed the coveted mantle of professional recognition on them.

These changes in the image of the profession represent a marked improvement. They provide an excellent foundation on which the profession can build solidly for the future. Yet it could be unwise to gaze too fondly on this record. Times change, and new demands are pressed upon accounting.

As lawyers and doctors know, professionalism, like freedom, is never wholly won. Preserving it in a changing society takes work. It is well not to lose sight of how it was achieved—by providing services essential to the prosperity and welfare of our society. As these needs grow with the increasing complexity of business and government, accounting must keep pace or lose its hard-won esteem.

THE PROBLEM OF TAX PRACTICE

A still not completely solved problem may be the reputation of CPAs as tax advisers. The problem has two parts. One has to do with the CPA's reputation for independence. This quality, which he and others prize so highly, and which he struggles mightily to preserve, is the characteristic which most people think of first when "CPA" comes to mind. Yet they know him also as a tax adviser, and many people assume that when he wears this other hat, he must be showing his client how to report his profits in the most favorable light possible for tax purposes. When they think through this question at all (and not many people do), they frequently wonder whether this intensely independent professional man arrives at different figures when he reports for third parties than he does when he argues in his client's behalf before the Internal Revenue Service. The independence of the CPA as an auditor, contrasted with his position in tax practice, creates a confused picture in the public's mind. Explanation does not help much and seldom is given an opportunity anyway. The AICPA's committee on the ethics of tax practice is currently seeking solutions to the problem, but until they are found, it is unlikely that public relations techniques can do much to clarify the confusion that now exists.

The second part of the tax-practice problem involves lawyers and other tax advisers as well as CPAs and is potentially more hazardous. Stated simply, it is the underlying suspicion of the unsophisticated public that tax advice is slightly shady business. To many CPAs this possibility will seem incredible. Their own experience and observation tell them differently, and their own clients know it to be untrue. Nevertheless, the warning signals are plain to see, and it is unwise to ignore them. A rash of popular novels, short stories, plays and films, of which *Cash McCall* and *The Enemy Camp* are typical, suggests that conflicts in tax morality are endemic in an affluent society. Widely publicized Congressional inquiries have uncovered tax evasion so ingenious as to imply dishonest tax advice if not actually to discover it. It takes little imagination on the part of every taxpayer who wrestles with his own conscience to speculate on the integrity of other taxpayers confronted with even larger temptations than his own and in a position to afford expert assistance. It is unnecessary here to enlarge on the results of any decline in taxpayer morality. The concern of CPAs can be assumed. It is enough to identify the danger.

Specific steps should be taken by the profession now to protect itself before the problem becomes unmanageable. The most effective among them is to erase any impression that the CPA's role in tax practice is limited to technical areas and to reveal his understanding of the economic and social consequences of taxes. By its very nature, tax practice does not easily lend itself to broad public inspection. At the same time, people tend to distrust and misunderstand what they cannot see. The best means they have of satisfying themselves of the integrity of tax advisers is through repeated demonstrations that tax advisers are sensitive to the public welfare. CPAs have come a long way in the last decade, according to all the available evidence, in identifying themselves with public service by accepting leadership in their communities. Yet some of the old criticisms of them for withdrawal and reticence still persist. The profession's reputation in tax practice can best be protected by speaking out on tax policy in the broadest sense. That reputation will also be safeguarded by whatever each practitioner can do to reveal his concern for the welfare of his community and society generally.

DISTINGUISHING THE CPA

Another public relations problem for the years immediately ahead is the familiar one of establishing the distinction of the CPAs from all the other accountants and bookkeepers performing services of an accounting nature. Sometimes, particularly when dealing with Federal and state governments, it becomes necessary in the public interest for CPAs to draw precise comparisons between themselves and noncertified accountants. Such comparisons must be presented with great care, so that noncertified accountants and the work they do are not downgraded. Care must also be exercised that such comparisons do not appear invidious, for outsiders then suspect them. There is now some evidence of a growing public understanding of the distinctions between certified and noncertified accountants. These indications are far from substantiated, and more reliable surveys are needed to support or disprove them. Undoubtedly the understanding is still far from complete in many parts of the country.

A related problem seems to be the inability of some people, even those who recognize this distinction, to tell whether accountants they know are certified or not. Despite the clear benefits to be gained from being known as a CPA, many CPAs do not so identify themselves as often as they could. This is notably true of some of the larger firms, which are prevented by law in some states from designating themselves as "certified public accountants." Because of the inconvenience of using different designations in different states, they sometimes fail to call themselves CPAs in states where it is permissible. Important public relations opportunities for all concerned are wasted when this happens. Firms and practitioners who do not identify themselves as CPAs are losing the advantage of this mark of distinction, which is properly theirs. When large firms with fine reputations are prevented by law from establishing offices or using their rightful professional designation, all practitioners lose the benefits which great traditions could bring to the profession. But the most important loss of all is suffered by the public, as so often happens. Certification is designed by law to assure the public of the accounting standards it may expect. This assurance does not operate when the designation is not used. Finally, the surest way for the public to learn to distinguish the CPA and to appreciate what he stands for is by what people see when they look at CPAs around them. This recognition is retarded if they can't tell a CPA when they see one.

Client Relations

■ A YOUNG CPA, as the steward of an accounting firm that he hopes will be even greater in the future, should ask himself some questions:

How long has it been since I initiated a contact with a client to help him explore a problem even before he realized he had one? Do my clients automatically think of talking with me about their business problems on which I might have special knowledge? In short, are my clients aware that *my* business is to serve *their* business?

Unfortunately, there is some evidence to suggest that not all businessmen have that concept of CPAs today. Although they hold their accounting firms in high regard, many of these executives have a narrow view of the activities which they feel their CPAs are qualified to perform. If that is so, the situation can be improved only if the accountant considers himself—and reveals himself—as more than a skilled technician. The process of revelation begins, of course, with the clients already being served.

ROOM FOR IMPROVEMENT

Certain basic questions are always present in the minds of clients, even though they may seldom be spoken:

Is this professional firm really necessary to me? Does it have my needs and opportunities always in mind? Is it directed to the future—progressive, alert, a little ahead perhaps of my own people? Am I making the most of its services?

The one common characteristic of all professions is service to others. This single word *service* takes precedence over every other aspect of professional life. Indeed, the professions have not established strict educational and character requirements because they want to be exclusive. They do it to assure an accepted quality of service. However, the standards of acceptability do not remain constant. They must evolve to take advantage of technological improvements and to meet the changing demands of the people served. The accounting profession must therefore examine itself from time to time to see if it is doing all that it can to provide maximum service to its clients.

The recent spectacular growth of the profession has been largely in response to client needs for additional auditing and tax work—needs which arise from the increasing size and complexity of business and the requirements of banks, government regulatory agencies and the like. But the existence of these relatively fixed needs could impose an artificial limitation on the CPA's capacity to serve and on the client's awareness of the full range of the CPA's potential service. Under these circumstances, both the accountant and his client could drift from the concept of *dis*interested service to that of *un*interested service; to a kind of antiseptic detachment that pushes the CPA out of the main line of business development, which rests on creative insight and constructive imagination.

If an accountant is content to have it this way, it is likely that his clients will come to think of him as a necessary evil rather than as an essential adviser.

The reason for this is clear. Businesses do not exist for the purpose of publishing annual statements or paying taxes. They exist for the purpose of making profits. In pursuit of that objective in the complex world of today, management knows that it cannot master all that it needs to know to shape its business future wisely. Consequently, it relies on a great variety of outsiders to provide the special knowledge and skills required for profitable operations. What elements make these outside experts more valuable than other experts who could simply be added to the management staff?

One of them is comparative judgment. Management benefits not just from the expertness of the CPA, for example, but from the range of application of his expert knowledge—how similar problems were treated or similar situations handled in other companies or other industries.

Another element is objectivity. A fresh approach can lead to a beneficial change in perspective. The recommendations of well-informed outsiders are frequently accepted more readily than those originating within the company, for they are less likely to be motivated by personal ambitions or similar considerations. It is difficult to overestimate the value of objectivity—particularly to a small businessman who often has few people with sufficient understanding to consult about his problems.

Thirdly, the daily work pressures on internal management often preclude a creatively critical look by its own executives at its over-all operations. Time is the basic commodity in short supply in management circles. Needed changes are frequently deferred because no one has the time to determine what should or can be done. It takes all the running that many managements can do simply to stay in the same place. All this means that the outside professions which serve management have virtually *carte blanche* to keep their eyes open on behalf of their clients.

Right here lies the basic difference between the competent technician and the professional man. It may well be that some accounting firms prefer to provide only such technical services as are specifically requested of them. But modern machines can perform technical services—and quite intricate ones, too. Yet machines become obsolete. Professions do not—or should not.

Professions grow, in usefulness and influence, almost in geometric proportion to the broadening of their own concept of service. For then the concept of their usefulness and influence is also broadened in the minds of their clients.

PERFORMING EFFICIENTLY FOR THE CLIENT

Professional service is more than the key to sound client relations. It is also the objective of those relations. It is not merely a means to an end; it is also the end itself. An accounting engagement does not become a truly professional service until these elements are present:

1. Professional skills efficiently applied to specific needs
2. Effective communication of results so that the client is fully aware of the work accomplished
3. Constructive action taken or useful purpose served as a result of the CPA's conclusions or recommendations

It virtually goes without saying that there is no substitute for quality work. But to be truly professional, a practitioner must use his technical skills *creatively,* combining them with judgment and imagination in the light of existing circumstances. He must be constantly alert for ways to use his special knowledge for the benefit of his client. In many instances he must become aware of certain client needs before the client himself has recognized them and be prepared to take action to fulfill those needs. In order to do this, the accountant must not only know his client's business but must be familiar with the problems of the industry as a whole. For the CPA must not merely produce facts and figures. He must interpret them; he must give them meaning.

By adopting this approach, the CPA makes it easier for the client to relate his accounting services to the profitability of his business. As with any other aspect of his business, a client is apt to look upon the services of his professional advisers in terms of investment and yield. In his own mind, the concept of excess value plays an important part; for the value of the services is usually judged in relation to their cost. This may not be immediately reflected in terms of dollars saved or earned; but it is always present. This does not mean that the CPA should underprice his service. It does mean that he should strive to achieve the maximum benefit for the client in relation to the cost of his services.

Some measures which can be taken during an auditing engagement to satisfy a client's needs have been set forth by one experienced practitioner. He suggests:

1. Pointing out to clients, in advance of performance of services, specific and significant deficiencies in the scope of services stipulated by them in relation to the objectives of the services.
2. Explaining to clients receiving non-opinion reports the fundamentals involved, whereby an engagement restricted in scope makes it impossible for

the accountant to formulate or express an unqualified or qualified opinion.

3. Making specific recommendations to clients in reports on engagements as to remedial measures shown essential or desirable by the outcome of the engagement.

4. Indicating to clients during the course of the engagements any steps or procedures with respect to operations, internal control, accounting methods, which will be demonstrably advantageous.

It may occasionally be necessary to persuade a client to accept new or different accounting procedures for his own benefit. Even if the client objects to certain tests or other activities deemed necessary by the CPA for the proper conduct of the engagement, the accountant must stand firm. Naturally he will employ to the fullest his tact and persuasiveness in convincing the client without antagonizing him. If the CPA has won the client's respect, it is seldom necessary to explore the problem in detail. As John L. Carey describes it: "The very nature of the relationship puts the professional practitioner in the position of a fiduciary, in the sense of a position of trust and confidence. The standard of behavior of a fiduciary is commonly assumed to be that he shall exercise no less care in dealing with the affairs of those to whom he is responsible than he would in dealing with his own."[1]

The client has a right to assume that the accounting work is being performed efficiently and thus at a reasonable cost. Proper planning of the work, the use of competent men in grade, and adequate supervision are to be expected. If costs are incurred solely because of the accountant's inefficiency, the client should not have to pay them. One client has expressed it this way:

> We like to feel that auditors are practicing *for* us and not *on* us. Now that doesn't mean that we don't expect them to increase in knowledge and skill through experience gained on our work. But we do expect that the work be assigned to men capable of executing the engagement without undue loss of time because of lack of understanding of what should be done, poor knowledge of auditing techniques, or other substantial deficiencies in professional skill. If the auditor feels he isn't equipped to handle an engagement properly, he should tell us so when we offer it to him. That will increase our respect for him and confidence in his work.

On the other hand, poor record-keeping or inadequate operations on the client's part may make extended procedures necessary. In such cases, the CPA should try to correct the shortcomings. By thus helping to lower the cost of his services, he will be increasing their value.

COMMUNICATING RESULTS TO THE CLIENT

No matter how much work is done, or how well, results have a limited value unless they are clearly presented. Frequently a client (especially a smaller one) is not well versed in accounting, and needs assistance in extracting significant items from the maze of figures. The businessman expects his

[1]John L. Carey, *Professional Ethics of Certified Public Accountants*, AICPA, 1956, p. 161.

accountant to alert him to matters which require management decisions so that he will not be obliged to wade through pages of supporting data to get to the heart of the matter .

Much has been written about the inability of some accountants to express themselves concisely and simply. Most large firms devote a considerable part of their training schedule to report-writing. And for the last few years, the AICPA has had such a course in its professional development program. In many firms, however, this problem still receives inadequate attention.

One practitioner, who feels strongly about the value of a clear report, has this to say:

> The report is the only tangible result of all your efforts that the client can see. Have you changed your audit report form in the last three or four years? Have you added new comments that clarify the client's statement to him? Have you used the same language in all your reports? Have you tried to make the statements more readable for the client or his Board of Directors? . . .
>
> Your relationship with your client will be enhanced considerably if you change your reports every once in a while to include new data and new forms that explain his affairs more easily.
>
> In our firm we are constantly on the alert to present new ideas and new types of statements to our clients. Whenever we find a form being used by a national firm in published reports, or by contact with other accountants, we adopt those ideas that we find will be of most value to our clients.
>
> The client begins to realize that his accountant is giving thought and consideration to his business. This can be shown by the following example.
>
> We performed the audit for a quasi-public organization. As was our usual custom, we prepared the audit report and sent it to the client company. Because of the law under which they were regulated, they had to publish the statement in the newspapers. One of my friends read the published report and asked me to interpret some of the sections of the report for him. He was joking, I thought, but after reading the report myself, I realized that many of the terms we take for granted are "gobbledygook" words to many people. I immediately rewrote the statement in everyday language and presented it to the Board of Directors for their review. I suggested that we present two reports in the future—one in the usual accounting terminology and form, and the other in everyday language that the newspaper reader can understand. Why shouldn't we do the same for some of our clients who would better understand our statements if we wrote them more clearly in layman's language?

A good long-form report is, of course, only one way of communicating the results of an engagement. A number of firms find a separate "management memorandum," which outlines the significant features of the report, particularly effective. It is frequently used to make recommendations which might not have a place in the audit report, or which might be overlooked there.

Many accountants make it a practice to deliver the report to the client in person so that important aspects of it may be discussed with him at the time. Some clients will prefer that the report be delivered to them and they be allowed time to look it over and formulate questions to be discussed with the accountant at a later date.

When a report is completed, the CPA has an excellent opportunity to summarize orally its salient features and clarify recommendations. (A written digest of the results of these discussions is recommended by many firms, otherwise the client may overlook some of the points raised.) Unfortunately, many firms do not get together with a client after he has had an opportunity to look over a report. They tell the client that they will be available; but they do nothing more—apparently feeling that the client will make the overtures if clarification or discussion is desired. Yet a single telephone call by the CPA can often prevent a misunderstanding or aid a client in making effective use of the report.

Better still is a personal call or a luncheon date. The accountant should have in mind some major points he feels should be discussed. But even if the conference is not immediately productive, the accountant can establish the fact that he has a genuine interest in the client's welfare.

Work, of course, is worthless unless it serves a purpose. But unless an accounting engagement results in some action, either by the client or by others on his behalf, it may appear to be valueless. The action need not be spectacular. It may simply be the filing of a tax return or a necessary report with government regulatory agencies. But if these routine requirements are not properly met, the client will be penalized. Even in performing some of these tasks, substantial savings can often be made for the client by proper planning— for example, in tax work.

One practitioner suggests that a tax-planning checklist ought to be used to ensure that tax-saving advice is delivered to the client. The items on such a checklist might include:

1. The most economical form of business organization under the circumstances
2. Payment of maximum compensation and minimum dividends by a closed corporation
3. Making the most of the capital gains provisions of the code
4. Use of affiliates and subsidiaries
5. Sale and leaseback of property
6. Business ownership and operation of automobiles
7. Depreciation of new assets by one of the authorized accelerated methods[2]

The direct value of the CPA's more complex services is largely determined by the extent to which the client is willing to accept his expert knowledge. This willingness is based on the client's confidence in the skill and judgment of his CPA. Frequently, however, the client takes a narrow view of his CPA's ability to serve, thinking of him largely in terms of auditing and tax engagements. Yet, in the client's own interest, he ought to be made aware of the full range of services which his accountant is competent to perform. The CPA himself must assume responsibility for tactfully encouraging the client to act on his recommendations.

[2]C. S. Rockey, "Accountant's Relations with His Client," *Illinois CPA,* Spring 1957, pp. 41-54.

CREATING THE PROFESSIONAL IMAGE

Although corporations seem massive and impersonal, it is essential for the accountant to bear in mind that he is serving a corporate entity through the people who manage it. In short, he is dealing with people, not boxes on an organizational chart. A relationship founded on confidence between client and professional man can sometimes be as personal as that between doctor and patient. Admittedly, no set of rules can guarantee results in terms of satisfied clients. Human relations, fortunately, cannot be reduced to a formula. But the observance of certain fundamentals in client relations will enable the CPA to provide a truly professional service. The most important of these fundamentals is the accountant's professional image.

Industry spends billions of dollars each year on public relations. In harmony with industry's profit-making objectives, a business firm undertakes a public relations program to create a favorable impression upon its customers and the public. Similarly, a professional man must also be concerned with developing a favorable impression of himself within his community and among his clients in keeping with his objective of service.

Factors contributing to the professional image. Accountancy, as a relatively new profession, lacks the traditions of law and medicine. It has developed tremendously in the last fifty years; but the public's appreciation of its scope has lagged far behind. The individual CPA, therefore, must constantly exhibit the elements which create a professional image and contribute to client confidence: dedication, competence, and integrity.

This image, which forms the basis of his reputation, is a composite of many small impressions, each reflecting the manner in which the practice is conducted. For example:

The CPA's concept of his own value to his clients and his community significantly affects his prestige. If he regards himself merely as a temporary hired hand employed to perform narrowly prescribed tasks, he cannot hope to develop professional status in the eyes of his clients. The independence and integrity with which professional skills must be applied are to some extent jeopardized by an "employee" attitude. The professional man must act on the basis of what is right in his professional judgment without being influenced by expediency or external pressures.

Unless the CPA identifies himself with the production of profits for the client, he cannot expect the client to recognize that his services contribute to this goal. A physician treats a simple cut not because the healing of the cut is an end in itself, but because of its possible effect on the health of his patient. The accountant, too, must approach each of his duties with an eye to its contribution to his client's economic well-being.

Client interest, rather than self-interest, must be the dominant motivating force behind the professional image. If the CPA considers himself primarily a businessman, he will be inclined to base his services on profit potential. On the other hand, if he considers himself a professional, he will base his services on concern for the client's welfare. This in turn implies a constant willingness to increase competence, to keep up with new developments, to acquire more knowledge to better fulfill client needs.

Maintaining continuing year-round contact with the client is one of the most obvious means of demonstrating this willingness to serve. The professional image is not likely to be created if a CPA merely performs an audit, submits a report, and quickly disappears from view. Granted, a firm has many clients who urgently need attention, but from the client's point of view, *he* is the CPA's *only* client. There are many things a CPA can do to provide continuous year-round service to his client. (See "The Value of Continual Service," page 258.)

Unless the existing professional skills and attitudes are evident in day-to-day activities, the CPA's professional image cannot be fully developed in the minds of others. If, for example, he continually performs routine engagements involving a subprofessional level of skill, he cannot expect a client to regard him as professionally competent—for professional competence has never been demonstrated to the client. Or if the CPA performs an engagement strictly in accordance with the client's instructions, without any effort to advance constructive suggestions in keeping with his abilities, he has failed to reveal any special interest in the welfare of his client.

In all of these areas of development of the professional image, enthusiasm is essential. It should be encouraged in even the most routine-appearing engagements. For only in this way can a creative approach be taken to each problem. The attitude of a firm's personnel toward the work is also quickly apparent to the client. If staff men regard their assignments as dull and perform them in a lackluster manner, the client is bound to feel he is not receiving their best efforts.

Virtually all aspects of a CPA's life—professional, social, and personal—play a part in building the esteem in which he is held. Most firms agree on several important elements in the development of the proper professional image.

Personal characteristics and behavior. The CPA must not undervalue the impact of the first impression he makes on a prospective client. His professional bearing and poise, founded upon a genuine confidence in his ability to help, will go far in shaping the patron's conviction that he is a competent professional adviser.

Some clients apparently still think of the accountant as a rather cold, humorless, and somewhat negative person. This stereotype arose from the client's original concept of a CPA as someone who was engaged to investigate the work of others to see if they had committed errors, or worse.

These duties have long since been superseded by much broader ones. But the image of a personality in keeping with them often remains. It is even fostered by those accounting firms which, in an effort to avoid any possible stigma on their independence, forbid their staff members to have any contact with the client's personnel other than the minimum necessary to complete the engagement. The partners, in turn, remain aloof from the management.

This extreme approach is hardly conducive to sound personal relations between CPA and client. Of course, the accountant should not be overly friendly with people whose work is being audited for another party—that is, client's staff for client's management, client's management for the stockholders, and so on. But a middle ground between aloofness and intimacy seems appropriate in all cases. This might be described as dignified friendliness, with all it implications of interest, consideration, courtesy, pleasantness, absence of condescension, and respect for the other person.

It is also customary for a professional man to take a more active interest in community affairs than the average citizen. As a community leader, he is expected to be conservative in the sense that his family and social life reflect adherence to the important values of his society. He may deviate from these values and still be successful; but he probably achieves success in spite of his deviations rather than because of them.

To expect a client to reveal his most private affairs and to follow advice, the accountant must have earned the respect of his client. The client must know that money-making is not the prime interest of the accountant; if this were true, the client would hesitate to reveal the innermost secrets of his business and personal affairs in fear that the accountant would take advantage of such knowledge in pursuing his course of money-making.

A man's standard of living, his home and his car, the schools attended by his children—all of these are, rightly or wrongly, generally regarded as indications of his success. In the case of a professional man, however, an excessive display of wealth can lead to suspicion of his motives. If, for example, he is obviously far wealthier than his clients, he may run the risk of appearing to be more interested in his own income than in their welfare. The senior partner of a local firm in a medium-sized city became wealthy through some outside business investments. He began to live up to his newly acquired income and purchased one of the finest homes in town. For the first time, some of his clients began to question his fees and to wonder whether he was "getting too big" for them. He later moved to a less pretentious home; and even though he continued to live well, he was less blatant about it. As a result, his relations with his clients improved.

Office location and appearance. An office itself can make a significant impression on the client. Its location should be largely determined by the convenience of the clients it serves. Other than being situated usually in one of the better business districts, wide variations may exist due to differences in clientele. In some cases the central downtown area is best; in others such things as the adequacy of parking facilities may more than offset a central location. A client's first impression of a firm is quite often affected by the condition of its office. Yet many firms have not given the subject adequate attention. It is axiomatic that an office should be neat and comfortable; but some firms, in an effort to reflect an aura of dignity, actually create a depressing effect. Banks have found that dark interiors and heavy grilles, originally used to engender confidence, actually made them appear forbidding to their customers. Many of today's newer banks are proving that it is possible to appear solid without being stolid. And, of course, a modern, well-designed office not only creates a favorable impression, it also contributes to efficiency.

An attractive office aids in securing better personnel. It raises the practitioner in the esteem of his clients and the public generally. Such an office induces the clients to hold conferences at the accountant's office, rather than his own—a timesaver for the accountant.

Administration of the CPA's office. The degree of efficiency with which a CPA manages his own office may well be taken as a reliable indication of his professional attainments. The manner in which an office organizes, schedules, and controls its work therefore is not strictly an internal affair. For an efficient practice contributes to the financial success of a firm as it simultaneously increases its capacity to serve a client.

Commitments made and broken, needless interruption of a client's operations, dragging out an engagement because of inadequate work planning (or because not enough staff is available), offensive billing practices, delays in submitting reports—all these evidences of inefficient operation diminish a client's confidence in an accountant's ability to serve him effectively. Clearly advisers to business should operate in a businesslike fashion themselves.

Conduct of employees. The over-all impression a firm makes also depends on the day-to-day conduct of its employees. The conduct of the personnel on the job must always be such that it will reflect the professional dignity so essential to the accountant. The work must be performed in a dignified and businesslike manner. The accountant should always *look* and *be* efficient. His work must be performed in the client's office in such a way as to least interfere with the client and his employees. It must be done in a thorough manner so as to preclude the necessity for returning to the job to secure additional data to prepare the report, tax returns, etc.

The staff accountant, as a professional man, should naturally exemplify all the desirable characteristics of professionalism. He is often in closer contact with the client, or client's employees, than a partner. However, the staff accountant is likely to be a younger man on the threshold of his professional career. The partners and senior staff members, therefore, have a responsibility to develop not only his technical skills, but his other professional attributes.

Some firms feel that the professional attitude develops automatically with increasing technical skill. Others find that some staff members need instruction even on rudimentary aspects of manners, dress, and appearance. This should be unnecessary. Firms which include specific items on these matters in their written instructions, or which dwell overlong on examples of basic courtesy, may well detract from the professional attitude rather than contribute to it. The junior staff member may feel that his superiors do not regard him highly if their instructions belabor the obvious.

However, every firm, either implicitly or explicitly, verbally or in writing, should make clear to each staff member the standards of performance and conduct which will be expected of him, and follow up to see that those standards are met. (An example of a staff manual appears in the Appendix, page 800.)

Sometimes firms overlook the fact that general office personnel are as much representatives of the firm as the professional staff. Receptionists, telephone operators, bookkeepers, and secretaries often come into direct contact with clients and color their impressions of the firm as a whole. Here again the elements of courtesy and the impression of service have a significant effect. The manner adopted by receptionists and telephone operators in greeting visitors and handling calls, the way a secretary rises to the occasion when her superior is not available, are important to the development of sound client relations.

Much client contact with office employees is by telephone. Telephone courtesy is basically a matter of common sense; but almost everyone can profit by occasional suggestions for improvement. The local telephone company representative can work with a firm's operator to develop maximum efficiency and courtesy. The telephone business office has several pamphlets available which offer constructive suggestions on telephone usage.

All personnel who have any direct contact with the client should be familiar with the entire organization of the firm. If they are unable to answer a question, they should at least be able to refer it promptly to the proper source.

CLIENTS AND FEES

When do problems arise? Problems in this area generally arise with clients who have had little or no direct experience with the accounting firm or with established clients when special work is undertaken outside the scope of past engagements. However, some of the most ticklish problems arise where the purpose of the engagement remains the same, but changes within a client's organization complicate procedures or otherwise add to costs.

This seems to be true especially where the client has grown appreciably, or where a breakdown in internal record-keeping or control has occurred. Although these added costs may be significant, the CPA often feels he is firmly entrenched in the client's confidence and is sometimes tempted to go ahead without calling them to the client's attention in the early stages. To confront the client with an explanation after the job is completed, accompanied by a sizeable and unexpected increase in the fee, may well cause complications.

Clearing the air in advance. Here are several suggestions that help to prevent misunderstandings:

Pre-engagement conference. Many firms consider this the most important single preventive technique. This is the easiest time to sit down with the client and come to a clear understanding of what the client needs, what he will accept, and the approach the accountant will take. All matters which might represent sources of friction should be discussed. It is important to outline to the client, especially if he is unfamiliar with accounting technique, the methods which will be used. Care should be taken to point out that although it is impossible to predict accurately *all* problems which may arise, any significant variation from the client's concept of what is being done will be brought to his attention.

Any misunderstanding about the fee can best be resolved at this stage. The accountant should not make it appear that the fee is his primary concern. But a frank discussion of the fee is definitely in order if it is clear that the client has little idea of what is involved. If the client does not bring up the subject himself, but is evidently concerned about it, the accountant should introduce it into the discussion. An exact figure can rarely be given, but the client should have a general idea of what may be involved.

Preliminary surveys. These are particularly effective with a new client. They are frequently used as a basis for the pre-engagement conference, and although they may involve a few hours or days of work, they are invaluable in providing a basis for intelligent discussion.

Should a client or prospective client be charged for such a survey? The general practice of the firms queried is to include the costs of a survey in the overall fee, without itemizing it. When an engagement does not result, the cost is usually absorbed by the accounting firm. However, arrangements are sometimes made with a client to charge him for a written report on his needs regardless of whether or not the accountant is later engaged to undertake the work. This is especially true for special jobs, such as systems installation.

Written confirmation of engagement. This is considered to be highly desirable with new clients, and where significant changes are contemplated in the work for established clients. Although most of the interviewed firms did this occasionally, only a few followed a consistent policy. A written contractual type of agreement is seldom used; but an increasing number of firms have adopted the practice of sending a letter to the client outlining the results of the pre-engagement conference.

Comments from accountants. Here are some typical comments from accountants on the value of these three techniques:

> The primary purpose of the engagement should first be discussed with the client, followed by an outline of the services and form of report the accountant proposes to render. If the engagement calls for the certification of basic financial statements, it is desirable for the accountant to outline to the client, the *Auditing Procedures* and *Generally Accepted Auditing Standards* of the AICPA.

> Misunderstandings concerning the scope of an engagement can be minimized by writing a letter to the client, setting forth the terms of the engagement in clear, unequivocal language.

> Decisions made at a conference between accountant and client should be put on paper. Accountants forget what they are to do, clients remember wrongly, and trouble develops when there is no verification. A written record should be used by the accountant as a checklist during the engagement.

> We haven't been verifying our engagements in writing. We have considered this to be too formal and too rigid. However, we have had a little difficulty lately and I think that I shall insist on it for future clients.

> We usually submit a memorandum to the client clearly outlining the limits of what we will be doing. The client initials a copy and returns it to us.

> In the past we have made the mistake many times of allowing our first

interview with a prospective client to terminate without having discussed fees. Even though we knew the subject was in his mind, and, of course, in ours too, we would not bring it up. There were times when we would then proceed to do work resulting in a sizeable fee which we were afraid the client might question.

We have learned from experience that it is far better to discuss the fee situation with the client in the first interview even though we cannot tell him what the work will cost.

There are, of course, situations where we can approximate the cost, but even when we cannot, we should discuss the fee anyhow. If it is impossible to estimate what the cost will be, admit it.

In order to avoid misunderstandings concerning the fee, the following letter was sent by a practitioner to his client:

Dear Mr. ———

We are prepared to perform the annual audit of [your company] for the fiscal year ending ——— in accordance with generally accepted auditing standards with a view to submitting an unrestricted auditor's certificate thereon. Our fee shall be based on the following per diem schedule:

| Partner | $——— |
| Juniors | ——— |

Judging from our experience last year, we are of the belief that an unrestricted audit can be performed within a fee of $———. We commit ourselves not to exceed this figure without your permission, provided that we have the complementary privilege of concluding our assignment with a restricted certificate. If we are unable to submit an unrestricted certificate within a fee limit of $———, we shall seek your permission for a higher limit and upon your approval, shall proceed. If you do not grant your approval for a higher fee limit, then we shall conclude our work with a disclaimer similar to that used last year. Our fee last year was $——— and our certificate was restricted.

Client contact during the engagement. Many firms emphasized the need to inform the client of significant problems as soon as they develop, without waiting until the final report is submitted. In some cases, changes in the program can be made immediately. At the very least, the client is aware of what the CPA is doing. Some firms point out that a client's awareness of such a situation is increased if all the work possible is done in the client's office. A few firms even insist that the report drafts be prepared on the client's premises. Others feel that possible disruption of the client's routine and the inefficient conditions under which staff men must frequently work in a client's office, make it desirable to do no more work there than is necessary. Some comments:

We take up minor problems with the client's accounting department. But if it is important, we want top management to know and we go directly to them. This is one of the best ways to minimize fee complaints.

On our longer examinations we have made it a practice to have interim conferences with our clients. We review our progress to date and they become aware of any difficulties very shortly after we uncover them.

Keeping the staff members informed. Unless the senior accountant on a job is kept informed of decisions reached between the partners and client, problems may arise. Proper communication between partner and staff helps avoid unnecessary work, duplication of effort, or proposals made to solve problems which have already been settled.

We feel that the senior who works on a particular engagement should be present at all the pre-audit conferences. This is good not only from the standpoint of keeping the senior informed, but it also builds the client's confidence in the senior.

Explaining the fee. The technique of explaining the size of the fee or the scope of the engagement to the client will necessarily vary with the circumstances. The personality and business experience of the client, the magnitude of the accounting problems involved, and how well the accountant knows his client, all have a bearing on the approach taken.

In any case, explaining a fee involves a certain amount of selling technique, as this practitioner indicates:

No one of us enjoys discussing fees with his clients. Yet it is a necessary element of any successful practice. The nature of any professional occupation is such that the client is seldom able to appraise the value of the service rendered or the cost of rendering it. Professional people, then, must take the time to explain these matters to their clients. They must conduct their practices in such a way as to create as a by-product the mental attitudes in clients which will cause them to appraise the services fairly and pay a fair price willingly.

The techniques by which these mental attitudes are created may best be described by the term salesmanship. Though normally considered a non-professional term, salesmanship is the ingredient that accounts for substantial fee differences where all other factors are equal. Salesmanship is composed of such intangibles as self-confidence, strong nerves, ability to impress and convince a prospect, alertness to opportunities to bring out values and achievements, personal impressiveness, demonstrable competence, intuitive ability to recognize the proper approach, and the like. An accountant who is possessed of excessive humility or who is basically insecure may not negotiate the best fee arrangements.

This practitioner believes that in many instances the air can best be cleared and the problem solved by taking the time to talk plainly (but tactfully) to fee-allergic clients. He thinks that, when the occasion is suitable, the accountant's position might be presented somewhat in this vein:

As a successful businessman, you have developed the practice of weighing your costs against results obtained. As your adviser, your accountant encourages and assists you in this.

But when the question of the cost of your accountant's services is before you, a certain coyness is prone to come into play. Perhaps you shrink from suggesting that which you feel may offend a man whom you value and respect. So this little dissertation is offered to disclose to you that your accountant has some problems too. And with your fair-minded realization of his problems, you can see better how to use his abilities and facilities in approaching your own problems.

You want, and your accountant desires that you receive, the greatest relative value in results obtained for every dollar you spend for audit and tax service. Still, you would rather pay $2 and get $10 in value than to pay $1 and get only $3 in value. But to be able to give you that $10 in value, your accountant must meet and solve his own problems.

The demand for competent accounting services throughout the country is now far outrunning the supply. The supply has been lagging for the simple reason that for several years capable young men have been attracted to other fields by the better salaries offered. The salaries for young men in the field of public accounting have been held down in relation to other fields by the lack of understanding of the basic relation between accountants' fees and the salaries paid.

The fact has been well established by studies of costs in many accounting offices, both in this country and in England, that where any use of independent judgment and power of discrimination in accounting matters is required in the service rendered, there is a definite relation between the equivalent annual salary of the accountant and the minimum per-hour fee that must be charged. As an illustration, if his salary is $4,500 per year, his work of this character must yield $6.25 per hour in fees.

If you have a sharp pencil you will compute that $6.25 per hour on a full-time basis amounts in a year's time to somewhat more than $4,500. Many factors contribute to this spread and we will suggest here only a few.

The first is the cost of stand-by. You are not asked to pay for all of the time of the men needed to handle your accounting and tax service. Nor can any accounting organization, with the best possible management, make full use all year of all the time of all of the men it has available to serve its clients. So one part of your accountant's overhead is necessarily "unassigned time."

The next factor is the accountant's office overhead, including rent, supplies, equipment, technical library, and all of the other facilities that help you to get the greatest possible value out of the hours put in directly on your work. If you employed the accountants directly on a salary basis, these costs would be borne by you over and above the salary.

You are a businessman. You know the many elements in unavoidable overhead. But even beyond this there are two other "invisibles" that make the costs of the accountant still higher.

One of these arises in myriads of complex specific situations. Under our tax law the tax returns of many individuals and all partnership, corporation, and fiduciary returns are definitely complicated. On-the-spot research is usually required before any otherwise capable accountant can handle one. That costs money. And the fee must be correspondingly higher.

A second common instance is found in those cases whose complications require specialized knowledge. These can be successfully handled only by dint of extra training or intensive study. Such knowledge may be called into play on only relatively few occasions. Estate and inheritance tax returns and special-purpose investigations are in this class.

And finally, just a word about the accountant's attitude toward competition. As in all other business matters, competition must play a big part in your selection of an accountant. But good judgment on your part will lead you to discriminate on the basis of relative *real* results rather than the lowest immediate dollar cost. As a good businessman, you can do no less than just that.

Supporting the fee. It is not a new idea that people are more willing to pay for that which they can see. For the CPA, too, it is well to present tangible evidence of services performed.

One man expresses it this way:

> If an adequate fee is expected, write a report. In the past the majority of accountants collected their fees based upon some type of report presented to the client, most often either an audit report, a prepared tax return, tax protest, or something of a tangible nature. As the services of CPAs widen and embrace other aspects of the client's problems, all too frequently the accountant forgets the value of submitting a report.
>
> Estate-planning is a good example in point. A well-rounded estate-planning team consists of a trust officer, an attorney, a life underwriter, and a CPA. Often the full plan is evolved by the CPA. The underwriter looks to the future insurance premiums to compensate him, the trust officer will receive his compensation through future fees of the trust department, the attorney prepares a will, a trust agreement, or some other legal document and is compensated therefor. All too frequently the CPA, who masterminded the whole situation, submits no formal written report and as a result finds the collection of an adequate fee for his services a bit of a delicate problem. If, in the same situation, he had put to use his knowledge of report-writing and prepared and submitted to the client an over-all report of the whole plan, he probably would have received a very satisfactory fee. This is only one example, but in nearly all cases where a service is rendered, a formal report of some nature should be submitted if adequate compensation is expected.

"Don't give oral advice!" warns another accountant. If it is followed and is successful, the accountant has no proof that the suggestion was his. Often he receives no recognition. If it is not followed, he still may be blamed for bad reactions. Either way it is dangerous because no one knows (1) the factual basis of the oral opinion, (2) who furnished the alleged facts, (3) what advice actually was given, or (4) what specific step-by-step course of action was prescribed for the client. And, of course, these matters have a way of slipping from a client's mind at billing time.

Client reactions to the CPA's fees. The majority of businessmen feel that the fees charged by their CPA firms seem to be in keeping with the value of the services rendered by them.

The following illustrative quotes range all the way from "fair" to "exorbitant," and include remarks by a few executives who either believe the CPA does not charge enough for his services or would willingly pay more for additional services:

> That's a hard question. Well, of course, everything has its value. You judge the cost of advice on how much it's helpful in solving the problem —and how important it was to find a solution. If the CPA's counsel results in savings, he's entitled to a bigger fee. I don't mean tax gimmicks. They're seldom a saving in the long run. I mean more efficient methods of operating which lead to lower costs and higher profits. Though maybe we have a right to expect that from our CPA as a regular part of his service. Certainly, we have never quarreled about his charges. They've al-

ways been keyed to the usefulness of his service. I guess you could say that a CPA is worth what his services are worth to the client. And that's a good deal.

We are quite satisfied with his fees. They're not at all exorbitant.

They work hard and we don't mind paying them. Sometimes they will go overboard.

Yes, the fees are all right. The consensus around here is that they are too high, though.

Yes, they are commensurate with his services. Sometimes they are too little but not in my case. They should get more income to establish themselves as a proper profession.

Yes, I do; but there is a limit to everything. We have high labor costs and cannot afford too much in the line of CPA services.

Yes, there again they know the circumstances of each individual firm. I think they scale to the requirements of the firm. In the long run it's fair.

I guess so. We haven't shopped around to see what other guys charge. We feel that the fee is good considering what type of service we get. How do you know how much a doctor or a lawyer should charge? If you're sick, you pay whatever is required. It is hard to estimate professional fees. If you are dying, a million dollars isn't too much to pay the doctor.

Yes, I guess they are (commensurate with the service) but I feel it is hard to pin them down to a standard fee. Judgment is paid for and it's difficult to measure at a certain rate per hour. They do not give estimates for work to be done and sometimes it is hard to see the relationship between the fee and the service.

I would be willing to pay more if they would spend more time. Actually it is a cheap service when you consider how much you get.

Yes, they are in line. In fact, I would like to get the accountant involved more in the business and pay more for his services.

The money they might save you over a period of years is worth the charge which in itself is high.

Within reason. If I dealt with a corporation, I'd probably pay much more. It's cheaper in the long run than trying to do it yourself.

Too high, in general. The first audit is a rough one, and the fee is too high. You did want my real feeling, didn't you?

Pretty high. Can't complain too much. They're really pretty good. Yes, everything is high these days, and you have to expect that the CPA will be too.

Everybody's fees are too large. Oh, I guess they treat us very justly. Yes and no. As original customer he may favor us; but when he works extra, we pay more than we could get elsewhere due to the mutuality of the relationship, that is, we favor him.

All special fees are high. The CPA fees are fair in terms of their training and competence. The CPA should be a partnership and not a single individual for the certification of audits.

Exorbitant. Their fees are much too large. Much of this rises from the fact that we use a large out-of-state firm.

Unprofitable work. There will be occasions in every accounting practice when it will be found that the work being done for a client is not adequately profitable, because the fee is not sufficient to compensate for the salaries and the overhead costs incurred and leave a reasonable margin. This condition can arise either in cases of fixed-fee arrangements, when the work done exceeds the fixed fee, or in the case of work handled on a per-diem basis, when the client resists paying for the full time at regular rates of charge.

In every such case in which the work is thus found to be unprofitable or insufficiently profitable for the accountant, his first step, of course, is to determine whether or not the persons handling the assignment did so with reasonable dispatch and efficiency. If a new man was assigned to the work for the first time, or if there was inadequate supervision, poor planning, unnecessary attention to detail, or other similar conditions, it would not be fair to ask the client to pay more than a fair fee. The experience in such case should be turned into an object lesson so that future work for the client (and, in fact, future work for all other clients) does not suffer from a repetition.

In many cases, however, the solution is not that simple. The accountant may have conducted the work efficiently and well. The fixed fee may have been set too low in the first place or unexpected circumstances may have caused the work to exceed that originally contemplated. In such cases, the only practical thing to do is to explain the situation to the client and try to secure an adjustment for the finished work, if possible, and if that is not possible, for future assignments.

If a client is not willing to adjust a fixed-fee arrangement or to recognize the accrued charges on a per-diem basis when the work has been done efficiently, the accountant's first impulse may be to tell the client to seek accounting services elsewhere. Although some cases may justify this action, it is not always the sensible course.

It is entirely conceivable that the client may have a proper idea of the maximum amount that he can afford to pay for accounting services. If this is true and the client is reasonable, it is frequently possible to revise the arrangements to keep the client's fee in line and still make the work profitable for the accountant. A discussion with the client about the problem may develop a number of ways of accomplishing this. For example, the client may be receiving a "certified" report twice a year when once a year would be adequate. He may be receiving a certified report when he has no need for it, and a limited examination of the accounts by the auditor and the preparation of financial statements without a formal opinion would be sufficient. The client may not be aware of the amount of work done by the auditor that could be done by people within his own organization at a substantial saving in auditing time. A review of the work program may disclose changing circumstances, such as a substantial reduction in inventory or an improvement in internal control, justifying a reduction in the time scheduled for the assignment.

If the client is reasonable, a working plan can usually be developed on a basis satisfactory to both parties. There are cases in which a client under financial stress should receive special consideration, either in amount of fee or in time of payment. It is perfectly ethical and proper for an accountant to take into account the financial condition of his client. If the client is unreasonable, these possibilities will offer no solution and the accountant would be better off to terminate the relationship.

CONVINCING THE CLIENT THAT ACCOUNTING SERVICES INCREASE PROFITS

Many accounting firms feel that recognition of the accountant's contribution to the profit picture of his client stems from virtually all the elements comprising "professional service." But because of the narrow view of accounting held by some clients, these firms also think the accountant needs to educate his clients through constructive, well-handled engagements, and through a willingness to apply his expert knowledge to *all* areas of the client's affairs in which he is competent. Indeed, some firms suspect that their traditional function of auditing is deprecated by many management executives as merely the detection of bookkeeping errors or the verification of facts already known.

"But," as Mr. Carey[3] points out, "an audit is, or can be, a creative service. It can be in itself an analytical survey for management; an aid to communication with stockholders, employees, creditors; a buttress to good credit standing. It can also point up specific management problems—the need to strengthen internal control, to analyze costs, to prepare budgets, to revise insurance coverage, and so on.

"An audit can be as creative as the people who conduct it, and a creative audit can easily be identified with production of profits. Perhaps this is not widely recognized because independent audits, unlike the physician's examinations, have not been commonly followed by diagnosis and prescription.

"No professional man in his right mind will jeopardize client relations by venturing beyond the limits of his competence. But any CPA can raise significant questions and, if he cannot answer them himself, he can tell the client where expert professional advice can be found. This too is management counseling—and it identifies the CPA with the client's main goal: the production of profits."

Specific suggestions for contributing to profitability. Of course, the more a CPA can increase his competence to assist management in areas related to accounting, the more directly is his contribution recognized. There are certain things that virtually all practitioners can do to demonstrate their importance to the welfare of a client company. Here are some suggestions made by accounting firms:

Personal visits to the client's office during non-engagement periods can be

[3]John L. Carey, "From the Executive Director's Desk," The *CPA,* March 1956.

helpful in creating client good will. They create a feeling that the accountant is interested in the client's affairs beyond the strict limits of his engagement. The client takes these intangibles into account in evaluating the services of the accountant and is less likely to question the fee.

The accountant has a good opportunity while he is working with his client on an audit or tax engagement to stimulate a discussion of related matters not necessarily applicable to the work he is doing at the time. A competent and intelligent accountant can impress his client to the point where he will not make any important business move without consulting his accountant.

Recognition is based on communication. I think the following media all can strengthen the client's realization of the correlation between business profits and accounting:

1. Good *long-form reports,* with plenty of space devoted to operating ratios and operating aspects generally. Very few CPAs do justice to profit analyses in their reports; most still give more emphasis and space to the static (balance-sheet) phase as opposed to the dynamic or moving (profit statement) phase.

2. Good letters to the management on managerial matters after the completion of the engagement. These *management letters* will contain specific recommendations which usually would not be appropriate in the standard accountant's report.

3. Introducing and setting up *charts* on such matters as turnover, sales margins, volume (by product, by territory, etc.), labor cost and overhead costs. The client's own personnel should be encouraged to keep up these operating charts.

4. Timely *clippings* from business magazines, government publications, and professional and trade magazines concerning subjects bearing upon the client's profits.

The accountant has an excellent opportunity to indicate how his services can increase profits if he will keep himself up to date on the current tax laws and acquaint the client with savings that can be effected. In my opinion, the most important service today which directly profits the client is in the field of taxes.

There is still a huge untapped field for public accounting services. What will make potential clients decide to engage the services of an independent professional accountant? The answer is so obvious that it is all too often forgotten. A businessman takes the step because another businessman tells him that an accountant has saved money for him or helped him to make bigger profits.

The moral is simple. Every time an accountant helps a client to make or save money, *and makes the client aware of the fact,* he increases the potential market for his services and the services of his professional colleagues.

All too often businessmen cannot recall specific instances of the aid rendered by their CPAs. The CPA's position might be enhanced if his advice on management problems was rendered in a way that created a durable impression upon his client. In other words, the counsel might be more widely appreciated if it was generally communicated in a highly visible manner, such as a well-written memo, rather than delivered in casual conversation or buried in the context of a long-form audit report.

Management's view of the CPA's value. A substantial number of executives feel that the CPA is now important to the profitable management of their business.

"We couldn't live without him," says the treasurer of a lumber company. "If we didn't have him, we would have to hire some accountants for our staff, and it wouldn't be half as beneficial." Another man, the president of a laundry, rather wistfully says, "He's invaluable. I only wish we could lean on him for more pricing advice and so forth."

But there is a catch in all this praise. Most companies agree that CPAs are important to profitable operations *only because of their tax services*. Those who are interested in securing some additional help regard their own receptivity as simply a matter of common sense. "Anything profitable, we'd accept," says the president of a wholesale food distributor. "Our CPA might point out areas for cost-reduction studies. The accountant who regularly audits a business ought to become involved in it, ought to get interested in it. If he does, he should be invaluable to management."

Why is this attitude not shared by the majority? Some of the nay-sayers are concerned about accounting expenses. "We just couldn't afford too much of their services," observes the vice-president of a company which builds industrial furnaces. "Those boys get a lot of money." Another executive, the controller of a bottling plant, adds, "There is always more room for more value from the services of the accountant, but the practical limits of being a small firm require that cost analyses and other interpretations of the audit must be made by the company's officers rather than purchased from the CPA."

A number of clients are also skeptical about the abilities of their accountants. "They don't have a broad enough outlook," says the controller of a newspaper. An officer of a cement-manufacturing firm is even more blunt: "On many of these things, I do not and will not take my CPA's advice. He has a certain place in the scheme of things, a certain job to do. He does it well. But he and most of his colleagues don't really know business principles, just financial ones." The manager of a jewelry manufacturer has another criticism: "Outside of keeping his eye on overhead, he can't make the business more profitable. We live in the future in this business; all the CPA has is a record of the past."

Despite this negative attitude, some firms which have received suggestions on ways of increasing profits are grateful for the assistance. "He tells us how to run our business," says the president of a metal-working plant. "He tells us how much to spend for advertising, how much to pay for building, and so forth. In fact, his most important function is to provide us with counsel on how to operate this plant."

But some suggest that the advice offered by CPAs may be given too casually, and thus is too often quickly forgotten. "We frequently discuss business problems," says the vice-president of a dye factory, "but there has been nothing concrete. He just gives general advice." A vice-president-treasurer of a sporting-goods manufacturer says this: "He's given us good advice on quite a few occasions. He's a good man to discuss things with and to uncover problems before they get out of hand. Offhand, I can't think of any specific suggestion. But I'm sure there have been some from time to time."

Educating the client. Recalling the oft-expressed concern of clients to avoid commitments to pay for more time, CPAs suggesting additional services ought to strive to make clear their relation to profits. A number of company executives, for example, rate their advertising agency higher than their CPAs on the scale of usefulness because the former "contributed to sales." Yet CPAs perform such functions as controlling costs and inventories, improving office methods, and advising on credit policies. It would be natural to assume that anyone would know that these services have a significant relation to profits, but the fact remains that many clients fail to see the connection. This suggests that the additional services not only have to be positive forces in advancing the profitability of the client, they must also be recognized as such by the client. This understanding, moreover, ought not to be left to chance. It should be firmly established before any further work is undertaken (and any additional costs are incurred).

It seems obvious that an educational effort of this kind is desperately needed among many of these clients. Despite the apparently intimate relationship between clients and CPAs, it is evident that many CPAs have not yet completed the task of informing their clients about the wide range of useful services which accounting firms are willing and able to render. In fact, the CPA ought to consider whether or not he is now extracting enough information of value to management from the work already being performed and whether or not he is presenting it in a readily understandable and usable form.

INFORMING THE CLIENT ABOUT THE CPA FIRM AND THE SERVICES IT PERFORMS

The fact that so many CPAs do not maintain frequent contact with their clients may explain why so few clients have an accurate idea of the size of their accounting firms. How, in these circumstances, can the client be aware of the wide range of skills available to him? How can he be expected to appreciate fully the cost of conducting an accounting practice if he has no conception of the quality and size of the staff? As measures of enlightened self-interest, the CPA ought to consider adopting a number of time-tested methods of acquainting clients with the scope and character of the accounting talent within his firm. Perhaps this can be done by simply sitting down with the client for a few minutes and telling him about the firm. This could be supplemented by visits of the client to the firm's own office where he would have a chance to learn of its continuing need for first-rate quarters, equipment, and personnel. The client, too, should be notified of the admission of new partners in an announcement designed to create the right impression: that another man of high caliber has assumed greater responsibilities within the firm.

A CPA cannot hope to provide maximum service unless a client is fully aware of the services available and has confidence in the firm's ability to perform them. CPAs, like other professional men, are naturally reluctant to proclaim their own talents. But by failing to sell themselves effectively they reduce their ability to serve.

The more subtly a firm can make known its capabilities, the less probable it is that a client will feel "pressured." Direct methods have their place, not to pressure a client into accepting unneeded services, but to develop a client's awareness of a firm's status and ability. Many opportunities arise during the course of an engagement which can be used to good advantage to demonstrate a firm's capabilities.

Methods of informing clients. A number of specific methods for informing a client of a firm's ability must be earned and cannot be merely adopted.

Newspaper stories. A CPA who is active in his community will find that he is making news. This news is of general interest because people are naturally interested in those who are working for a better community. Kept within the bounds of professional propriety, such newspaper publicity for a CPA or a firm gives a client the feeling that he has a talented organization assisting him.

Government work. Handling engagements for state agencies, counties, school districts, municipalities, and the like, can be helpful in many instances. Not only does this result in justifiable publicity, but the client is likely to conclude that since such work must require considerable know-how, he might as well utilize it, too.

Using specialists. Many firms, even the smallest, encourage partners and staff to become especially adept in certain matters by taking courses, advanced reading and study, and through extensive experience. In smaller firms, these men often handle general assignments as well. Bringing in colleagues when special skills are helpful is an effective way of giving the client additional evidence of the firm's resources. The cost of handling similar special engagements is reduced, better and faster service is possible, and the prestige of the firm is enhanced. Similarly, interfirm referrals are advantageous to all concerned. As in medicine, the general practitioner gains rather than loses when he calls in a specialist, for if the client's needs are more fully met, the entire profession gains stature.

Client visits to the office. A client should be encouraged to come to a CPA's office from time to time. Although much of the work is done in the field, it is often helpful to have conferences with a client in the office. Seeing a firm's library and absorbing the professional atmosphere tend to make a client wonder if he has availed himself of all the talent a firm may have to offer.

Writing for publication. Although most articles and books by CPAs are for consumption within the profession, they frequently come to the attention of the client. Naturally he will assume that a man must be highly qualified if his colleagues are interested in what he has to say.

Firm brochures. Some large firms distribute material to their clients, primarily to aid in recruiting staff assistants. These documents usually contain a brief history of the firm, an outline of the types of services performed, and some discussion of the firm's personnel and their background. A number of smaller firms, too, have prepared such summaries for the use of their clients. Other firms feel that the ultimate distribution of such printed matter is difficult to control. They believe that this information is more effective if presented in a personal letter to the client. Also, it lessens the chance of the client forwarding the material to a non-client.

Sending material to the client. Cards announcing the admission of a new partner are sent to clients by a great many firms. In addition to bringing the name of the new partner to the client's attention, the card indicates the firm is a successful, growing one. Some firms mail news clippings on tax changes or other matters of interest to a client. These serve to indicate the CPA's interest in the affairs of the client. But if overdone, this material can lose its effectiveness. A few firms distribute periodic bulletins on specific subjects, generally dealing with certain aspects of taxes or management services. Their reception varies with helpfulness and manner of presentation. Here again, indiscriminate distribution must be avoided by the practitioner. Some comments:

> We suggest services that are needed, such as systems work, budgeting, tax planning, and opinion audits. However, I feel that care should be exercised to suggest services only when they are needed. I think harm may be done to the firm and the profession by overselling.

> Our bank, in connection with its public-relations program, invited the top personnel of certain depositors to a luncheon. The bank people tell us about the bank and the visitors are asked to tell about themselves. I was able to give a thumbnail sketch about the firm and the partners. This seems to have been very well received. Other bankers have since asked us about our firm and in order to give them a brief story we have developed a brief history of the firm and biographies of its personnel. This form is used only in reply to an inquiry.

> We do a lot of "internal referral" in our office. All of us freely admit to a client that a particular problem may be out of our own line but "so-and-so" of our firm has done some successful work in that area so perhaps he can help. Thus we gradually introduce our various partners and staff to our clients, and they soon find out that as a firm we have various talents upon which to draw. Recently, one client had a troublesome cost problem which he mentioned to our partner in charge of his audit; after another partner had analyzed his problem and visited with him with some suggestions, he said: "Where have you been keeping that fellow closeted? He did more for us in two days than we could have done for ourselves in two years!"

> The editor of a client's house organ asked us for material for a feature story to be called "Here Come Our Auditors." Working with one of our men he wrote a story which cleared up a lot of misconceptions about the nature of our work. It also had vignettes about the key staff members, including some of their nonprofessional achievements. For instance, one of the men was a halfback at the state university. This article served to "humanize" us in the minds of the employees. We passed the article on to other clients when they asked about us. As a result, similar articles appeared in other client house organs, *at their request.*

Some common misconceptions of clients. *Services rendered by CPAs.* There are apparently widespread misconceptions about the nature of audit reports.

Despite obvious restrictions placed upon the scope of audits, many clients are not inclined to make any distinctions about the degree of professional responsibility accepted by their CPAs. They seem much more impressed by the quality of the report's binding and by the presence of the CPA's signature. If this ignorance of the true nature of auditing is prevalent, then it constitutes a genuine peril which might one day prove to be extremely expensive. Certainly, every CPA would be well advised to determine whether or not his clients have a reasonably clear understanding of the situation. If they do not, then an educational campaign is urgently needed.

It also merits attention that, while audited statements are often used in seeking credit, businessmen rarely ask their CPAs to represent the company or to accompany a member of the management team in negotiations for a loan. This fact may merely establish the effectiveness of a CPA report in facilitating credit requests. But it may also suggest that clients have too narrow a concept of the CPA's role in financial management. If so, the CPA has another educational task to perform.

Despite the general feeling that a CPA's greatest usefulness lies in his assistance on tax problems, a surprising number of clients do not consult him in advance about company actions which might have serious tax consequences. Under these circumstances, tax strategy consists largely in avoiding past mistakes. It seems reasonable to suggest that the CPA cannot expect the client to recognize a tax problem when one occurs. He will fulfill his professional obligations and earn the client's gratitude only if he trains the businessman to consult him *before* an important decision is taken.

The CPA's role in uncovering fraud and errors. In spite of years of effort by the accounting profession to dispel the mistaken idea that the CPA's purpose is to uncover fraud and errors, some clients still misunderstand the objectives of the audit. The truth of the matter is clearly stated in the AICPA booklet:[4]

> The opinion of a CPA is not comparable to the certificate of a weighmaster who certifies as to the weight of a load of goods. As explained, financial data often cannot be gauged by precise standards. The CPA is not an insurer. He cannot guarantee that the figures presented in financial statements are literally correct.
>
> The objectives of an audit, in modern practice, are much broader in scope than the discovery of mathematical errors or the detection of defalcations or fraud.
>
> Moreover, while the usual audit which is undertaken to enable the CPA to express an opinion on the financial statements may not be relied upon to disclose minor defalcation or fraud, it is incumbent upon the CPA to be alert to the possibilities of irregularities and to inform the management about weaknesses in internal control which come to his attention and which conceivably could permit such irregularities to remain undisclosed.

The client should be acquainted with the fact that the cost of such guarantees against fraud and errors would be prohibitive, and that an effective system of controls and honesty insurance is the economical way to minimize

4*Audits by Certified Public Accountants: Their Nature and Significance,* AICPA, 1950, pp. 16 and 21.

the dangers. Moreover, it is this latter area, namely the establishment of adequate controls, that is well within the scope of the CPA's services.

Bookkeeping and the CPA. The comments of some executives indicate that the CPA's role in the bookkeeping function is not always clear even to management. The president of a cigar company observes that his CPA is not involved in the bookkeeping. Then he adds: "He has improved it and he looks it over regularly. We keep our books in good order so he doesn't do much." Another executive in the furniture business says that his CPA neither installed nor supervised the bookkeeping system and concludes with these words: "He makes suggestions, but our head accountant is skilled enough."

While bookkeeping services are unavoidably performed by some practitioners, it is well to avoid creating the impression that CPAs are merely expert bookkeepers. To this end, a good rule for the practicing accountant to observe is never to do for a client anything that the client's own staff and personnel can do. Frequently CPAs are called upon to render services for clients that are of a clerical rather than professional nature. In the long run, clients cannot pay professional fees for clerical service and the CPA who permits or encourages his client to use accountants for clerical duties will find that it will result either in dissatisfaction on the part of the client or in a fee reduction to the clerical level.

WORKING WITH THE CLIENT'S STAFF

Direct relations with the client's staff embraces three areas: avoiding inconvenience to the client, appraising the quality and efficiency of the employees, and utilizing their services in connection with the carrying out of the engagement.

Avoiding disruption in the client's office. Basically, the problem of office disruption is one of simple consideration and courtesy. For example, it is generally agreed that the client's convenience comes first. Engagements should be scheduled far enough in advance so that a client can have adequate notice of when the work will start. Peak periods of activity in the client's office should be avoided. Sufficient men, including at least one who is completely familiar with the client's operations, should be assigned for the sake of efficiency. Dragging an engagement out by working only one or two days a week should be avoided. Interim work can often be fitted in when a client's staff is not too busy. More flexibility can thus be developed, and proper scheduling of interim work can be mutually beneficial.

Some ways of achieving the co-operation of the client's staff are implicit in the instructions spelled out in a staff manual (see Appendix, page 800). Others are suggested by these complaints most frequently heard about accountants:

1. Insufficient desk space sometimes displaces a client's employees. It is the client's duty to see that there is enough working space, but if he doesn't mention it in preliminary discussions, the accountant should tell him the

number of auditors the client can expect. Once this number is decided, the accountant should not send an additional man at the last minute just because he is available.

2. Office machines may be regularly in use at specified times during the day. Staff men should be told not to request machines at those times. (Naturally, no client equipment should be used without the permission of the department head and of the employee who uses it.) A number of CPA firms have found it more convenient to supply their men with their own office machines. Some, especially those with small clients with limited space, bring portable folding aluminum tables which can be set up almost anywhere. It is not uncommon for a staff man to be supplied with his own ten-key adding machine.

3. The client's papers should be treated with respect. The staff should not mark or mishandle them.

4. Employees complain of frequent interruptions of their own work by accountants' questions. One satisfactory arrangement is to set aside a question-and-answer period each day. The accountant should also be aware of the employees' daily routines. When a request is made of an employee (especially if it may take some time), the accountant should bear in mind the schedules and daily routines of both of them. And the accountant should plan ahead so the employee will not be rushed at the last minute. Said one CPA: "It is surprising how quickly one can obtain a group of vouchers simply by telling the employee to pull them 'when you have the time.'"

5. The assignment of a completely new crew to an engagement every year or two can arouse the ire of the client's employees who must "break in" the new men to their accounting system. Rotation should take place, but there should be a minimum disruption of the client's offices. Many firms always send at least one of the same men to form an experienced nucleus. Others, in cases of one-man jobs or where the men are not available, brief the assigned personnel thoroughly and make a point of explaining to the client some of the advantages of rotation: a fresh outlook and the quicker service which results when a number of men become familiar with the client's affairs.

6. Some clients think auditors make too detailed an analysis and too many transcripts of the client's records, and therefore take too much time on the job.

7. Some accountants overemphasize a minor error by an employee; they may ridicule him in front of the staff and his own supervisor. When an error is found, it is better to ask the employee his method of arriving at his figure. The chances are he will find the error himself.

8. Some accountants do not observe the client's office rules about such things as smoking and coffee breaks.

Here are some comments by accountants themselves:

I have found it helpful to prepare, in advance of starting an engagement, an outline of the client's system of accounting, the work flow, and the names and duties of the key personnel. The accountant is able to lay out an examination program least likely to disrupt the work of the client's staff. The list of the names and duties of the key personnel eliminates unnecessary contacts.

A congenial staff is essential to getting co-operation from the client's employees. When it is gotten, it can mean a lot. A few years ago one of our men uncovered a $150,000 inventory loss, acting on a tip from an employee. It was a pretty tricky setup and if the employee hadn't told us, we might still be looking for it.

A simple telephone call will eliminate many disagreeable occasions. For example, if the client's staff is engaged in the preparation of a payroll on a Thursday, the accountant certainly should avoid commencing an engagement on that date.

We feel there should be prior arrangements for working space and equipment, especially in a new engagement. The firm should provide the equipment so staff men don't have to borrow from the client's employees. If we have their machine when they need it, it is most disruptive.

Intelligent handling of records can promote cooperation. We try to work on those not being used at the moment by the client. We replace records promptly. Sometimes we ask the client to assign a man to take out and replace all records and files for us, to save time and avoid misfilings.

Appraising the client's personnel. The quality of the client's personnel greatly affects the work which the accountant must do. The practitioner should take every opportunity to encourage the client to hire good bookkeepers, accounting clerks, and so on. If the basic daily work is not done well, it is difficult for higher-priced professional assistance to make it good. It should be made clear to the client that the adequacy of his records has a direct bearing on the fee.

The accountant should bring to the client's attention, preferably verbally, any serious shortcomings of members of the client's accounting staff. However, he should not be a "tattletale"; minor errors can usually be taken care of directly with the person involved in a helpful way, without condescension. Equal care should be taken to give credit where credit is due.

Utilizing the client's staff. In many engagements, if not most, the principal device for conservation of the auditor's time is his utilization of the client's staff. Normally, there is a vast amount of pre-audit work which can be performed by the staff of the client before the auditor makes his visit.

The auditor's duty is to check, prove, and verify, and he can perform this duty just as well by using schedules prepared by the client as he can by using those which he has written himself. An accounting schedule serves two purposes: (1) it provides information supporting items in statements and reports, and (2) it indicates the nature and extent of any verification work which is done. It is always possible to make notes of verification on such schedules as these or to prepare supplementary schedules.

Many times schedules furnished by the client will be carbon copies of statements prepared for some internal purpose. Lists of accounts receivable, accounts payable, trial balances of a subsidiary or a cost ledger, summaries of inventories, and lists of investments are examples of the types of schedules prepared for the client's own purpose, a copy of which could be utilized as a part of the working papers of the auditor. In other cases the client's staff will prepare schedules especially for the auditors, in which cases only the verification work need be completed by the audit staff.

It may be felt by some that such assistance by the client's staff is possible only in larger companies which have well-organized offices and smoothly functioning accounting systems. This is not necessarily true. With proper tactful handling of the request, it is surprising how much assistance can be secured in the smallest offices with the most limited personnel.

Further, the smaller client, in many instances, will especially welcome the request of the auditor for assistance from his staff because it will enable him to receive his report more promptly while helping to keep his auditing costs down.

The following material is intended to serve as a guide indicating the kind of schedules and data that clients may prepare at the request of the auditor.

Preparing work outlines beforehand. The auditor should prepare an outline of schedules for the client's employees to prepare. This outline should contain, in addition to the names of the accounts to be scheduled, the column headings and other pertinent information which would enable the auditor to incorporate each schedule in his audit working papers. The auditor must, of course, verify the accuracy of schedules prepared by the client's staff and must complete ordinary audit procedures.

This outline of schedules should be written or typed and should be in the hands of the client well in advance of the audit date. If the auditor does interim work, it is very easy to leave the outline and review it with the office manager at that time. Generally, oral instructions are not satisfactory because some pertinent information is usually missing, the schedules are incomplete, or because the schedules are prepared in such a way as to leave insufficient room in which to insert figures and make comments during the course of the audit. There is no time saved if the schedules have to be rewritten.

The resulting schedules prepared by the client's staff are most helpful because they save the auditor time which he would spend ordinarily in writing them. There is an additional benefit in that the office manager usually tries to have the schedule he prepares agree with the general ledger, thus almost forcing him to locate differences he might otherwise overlook. One office manager who has used this outline for many years always requests his annual check-off sheet to help him expedite the audit.

In cases where the general outline of schedules does not cover an unusual situation, the auditor can head up the columns on his working papers and leave them with the office manager to fill in the details. Regardless of the method used, the auditor should have the clients' staff prepare as many of the schedules as possible. Following are specific suggestions as to work the client's employees could do prior to the arrival of the auditor. These suggestions would be included in the outline the auditor sends to the client.

Cash on hand and in bank: Prepare a list of the petty-cash funds with the custodians' names and the amount for each fund. If possible, reimburse them as of the close of business on the balance-sheet date. If the auditor is unable to count the funds at the balance-sheet date, have some one count them and keep the details of each fund for his examination.

Make copies of all bank-account reconciliations as of the close of the year showing outstanding checks by number, date, and amount.

Government securities: Detail the government securities owned, giving type, date purchased, serial number, face value, cost, interest rate, interest accrued, and the market value at the balance-sheet date, and indicate the source of the market quotations.

Accounts receivable: Prepare an extra copy of the accounts-receivable trial balance and aging. Here a few suggestions from the auditor as to his requirements for segregating credit balances, nontrade accounts, and officers' and employees' accounts, can save time and can often make this schedule more useful to the client all during the year as well as to himself at the audit date. In addition, if the comments and notations usually made by the persons responsible for collecting the accounts can be inserted on the auditor's copy, it will help him in determining the adequacy of the provision for possible losses.

If the accounts receivable are to be negatively confirmed at the balance-sheet date, the auditor can have the client's personnel stamp the monthly statements with his request that the recipient examine the statement and notify the auditor directly if he disagrees in any particular. These statements can then be turned over to the auditor to be checked by him to the accounts-receivable ledgers for verification of amounts and addresses and to determine that statements were prepared for all accounts. The auditor can then eliminate statements on any accounts that are not to be confirmed and mail the rest in envelopes bearing his return address. If positive confirmations of the accounts are needed, the client's staff can be instructed to prepare the statements in triplicate: two copies can be sent to the debtor, one to be signed and returned, the third to be retained in the auditor's working-paper file.

Make an analysis of the provision for doubtful accounts with a correlated analysis of the bad-debt expense account. This analysis should contain the names of the accounts written off with appropriate comments as to why, the date bad debts were recovered, and the year in which the recovered account was written off.

Inventories: It is well to have the client's employees prepare an extra set of inventory instructions including the method of pricing. Many times it is possible to have the client prepare complete copies of the inventory with the prices and extensions included thereon. If that is not practicable, the summaries can be prepared in duplicate with one copy for the auditor's working papers. Any information and identification of inventories pledged should be noted.

Insurance: Prepare a list of the insurance policies in force at the balance-sheet date showing policy number, type of coverage, amount, period of the policy, total premium, and unexpired premium for each policy. Maintain the policies in the same order as the list to facilitate checking by the auditor. Many companies have their insurance broker prepare this schedule. Others have arranged to have their policies expire at the end of their fiscal years.

Investments: The schedule prepared for the investments would be similar to the one for government bonds. If the investment were in a subsidiary company, copies of the most recent balance-sheet and income statement should be available for the auditor.

Fixed assets: Maintain invoices and vouchers pertaining to changes in the fixed-asset accounts in a separate folder or folders. Prepare analyses of general ledger accounts for these assets. If the office manager maintains an equipment ledger, the reconciliation between depreciation expense and the related allowance accounts can be very helpful.

Payables: The notes payable should be detailed showing payee, date, due date, security, principal amount owing, and any interest prepaid or accrued.

Make an extra copy of the trial balance of accounts payable for the auditor and segregate the debit balances. If the payables are not on a current basis, then an age analysis should be prepared. Any efforts to pay the accounts prior to the balance-sheet date would reduce the size of the list and would reduce the time necessary to review and verify them.

List the names, amounts, and the period applicable to the accrued wages, salaries, and bonuses.

Profit and loss: Prepare analyses of various income and expense accounts such as taxes, interest paid, interest received, and miscellaneous income and expense. If the contributions are in a separate account, this account should be detailed. If they are included with dues and subscriptions, that account should be analyzed. Where there are numerous personal property tax bills, the tax analysis should contain information on the assessed value, the date, the amount, and sometimes to whom paid.

Other items: When possible the preparation of confirmation letters and forms should be done by the client's staff. These confirmations would be of the type usually sent to the company's attorney, large trade creditors, government agencies, public warehouses, and consignees by the auditor.

An extra copy of the year-end statements prepared by the client's staff can be useful to the auditor, particularly if it contains data pertaining to units manufactured, units sold, sales by territories, and other information not included in the general ledger accounts. This knowledge will assist the auditor in making comparisons. If the minutes are typed, an extra copy should be typed for the auditor's permanent file. These suggestions are not all-inclusive. They can, and should be, altered to fit the particular client.

The caliber of the bookkeeper or office manager and the availability of client's employees to prepare these schedules would be factors that the auditor would consider in the preparation of his outline for that client. The client's employees can assist during the audit by being available to answer questions and to prepare analyses of accounts not included in the outline. For example, if the auditor feels that the charges to repairs and maintenance might contain items that should be capitalized, he could ask the office manager to assemble the invoices substantiating charges to this account for his examination and then, if the auditor deemed it necessary, he could have him prepare an analysis of this account for the audit working papers.

Criticisms of the system. One of the criticisms of having the client's employees prepare these schedules is that the employees soon get to know too much about the general areas covered by the audit and possibly the methods used by the auditor. The employees also learn the functions that they perform and, if they are inclined to embezzle, it is only natural to assume that they will take advantage of this knowledge.

On the other hand, the client's employees know that the auditor will always reconcile the bank accounts at the balance-sheet date, but they cannot very well know for what period he will make a lapping test; or what he will foot of the month's cash receipts and disbursements; or whether or not he will prepare another bank reconciliation later in the audit.

Knowledge by client's personnel of accounting techniques need not destroy the effectiveness of the audit. Most of the larger corporations have CPAs on their internal auditing staff who are thoroughly familiar with auditing techniques. These firms are audited by independent accountants and no criticism is made that the internal audit staff knows the methods used by the independent auditor.

The other criticism is that the auditor accepts too many of the schedules as they are prepared and does not do enough detail verification. The preparation of these schedules by the office manager is purely a mechanical function performed by him to save the auditor's time. It in no way relieves the auditor of the responsibility of verifying the details shown on the schedules. The auditor does, however, have to exercise his professional judgment to determine the extent to which he needs to examine the supporting evidence to verify the client's statements in order to comply with generally accepted auditing standards. This will depend on the amount of internal control, the type of office manager, and various other factors with which the auditor is familiar.

A serious word of caution must be injected in conclusion. Only such work should be done by the client's staff as is consistent with the complete maintenance of the auditor's independent status and attitude. The assistance of the client's staff should be limited, therefore, to purely clerical work which requires no exercise of judgment or professional skill. Schedules and analyses prepared by the client's staff must be carefully reviewed and compared with the source records by the auditor.

Practitioners' experiences. Every effort should be made to point out to a client the savings which can be achieved if his employees are properly prepared for the engagement. But there are practical limits to what can be expected. Advance preparation is dependent on the size and knowledgeability of the client and the nature of his organization. One practitioner, in discussing this problem, complained: "Some of my clients just dump everything into a box and turn it over to me." To which a second practitioner replied: "How do you manage it? Mine don't even use a box."

No client is so small, no staff so hard pressed by work, that they both cannot greatly benefit from a well-organized, well-maintained system. Part of the CPA's obligation to his client is to demonstrate the necessity of adequate controls and record-keeping. It should be made clear to the client that it is more expensive for him if the CPA must handle this type of work.

As a professional man, the CPA seeks to provide maximum service at minimum cost, in keeping with the reasonable fee which he has a right to expect. Therefore he should strive to make the maximum practical use of the client's staff in keeping with the benefits which the client can receive. Some comments follow:

> My own experience has been to keep the clients fully informed of our wish to minimize our fee; to point out that the work done by the client and

his staff does reflect in the bill; to work with the client's staff to show them what work they can do.

The matter of getting the client's staff to do preparatory work is a touchy thing, especially in a smaller practitioner's clientele. I have heard criticism, "We do all their work and they get a flat fee for looking it over." On some smaller jobs it is easier for us to do the preparatory work from scratch. In the larger offices we expect the client's personnel to have everything "ready for the auditors."

In a study conducted some years ago, it was shown that by arranging for the client's staff to do much of the work, the savings in audit time ranged from approximately 15 to 36 per cent of the estimated time consumption had the staff not participated. The greater savings were accomplished by clients who were larger and who had more internal accounting personnel enjoying a higher level of talent.

OVERCOMING THE RELUCTANCE OF THE CLIENT TO CONSULT

A CPA may impress a client with his abilities, but he may still find that the client rarely seeks his advice and counsel. To overcome this, most firms feel there should be a continuous but subtle effort to convey to the client the concept that consulting time is his biggest professional bargain and that it can usually save him more trouble or yield greater profit than any other type of CPA service. Much of service is preventive: the planning ahead to meet expected events. If the CPA is merely presented with an accomplished fact, he is limited in the service he can perform.

The CPA's attitude toward fees will strongly affect the client's willingness to consult him. This doesn't mean an accountant shouldn't expect a fair fee for consultation. But if a client feels the meter is ticking every time he picks up the telephone or asks a question, he is inclined to avoid such calls.

The way consultation billing is handled has a major effect on the client. If each conference or telephone call is itemized, the client will try to evaluate the results in each instance and think of each in terms of a separate fee. Most firms surveyed incorporate many consultation charges in the over-all bill for the engagement, but do not identify them as such. When there are many conferences and calls or if they are not connected with the main purpose of the engagement, they are frequently lumped together into a separate item on the bill. The usual form seems to be "Consultations in re . . ." the general area concerned.

Creating opportunities which make it natural for a client to seek advice is another sound approach. Some examples are: going over the pencil draft of the report together; encouraging the client to get in touch with the accountant any time; taking the client out to lunch occasionally; dropping in to see him between engagements. A partner in one firm sets aside a certain amount of his time for these interim contacts. He keeps a tickler file of clients and makes a point of dropping in, lunching with, or telephoning each client at least once a quarter. He records each contact on the file card, including any significant items that might have come up.

Another CPA stresses the confidential relationship between the accountant and the client. He feels that when a client knows that what passes between them goes no further, the client tends to use his accountant as a sounding board for ideas. Thus the accountant is in a position to assist his client with plans in their earliest formative stages. Some firms describe their experience as follows:

We have found it is helpful to have "specialists" even though they may be partners or staff members who spend only part of their time in the particular area of their specialty. For example, one of my partners for several years has been studying and practicing system installation and revising. Although he handles several large audit jobs (and small ones as well) and does his share of tax work, he has found time to take systems courses and to investigate new accounting machines and methods. When streamlining is needed by a client or new machines are under consideration, the in-charge accountant will consult our partner-specialist and then offer some general suggestions to the client. But he will also say: "We have a pretty good man in this field who has done a lot of this sort of thing. I believe it may be helpful to have him make a brief survey and offer some suggestions." The result is that the partner enters the picture as an experienced specialist, whereas the in-charge accountant (even though he may be a partner and equally competent for the engagement) may only be an auditor in the mind of the client.

It's basically an educational matter based on our ability to produce. If our work shows our client we can help him, he is bound to make the most of it.

We do not notice a reluctance to consult us because of added costs, although this may exist without our knowledge. We overcome this, we think, because we do not render monthly bills; we bill at the conclusion of a major effort, sometimes only once a year. Therefore, a client does not get a bill each time he comes in or calls up, although a record is made of every professional contact with a client. At the billing time, a number of conferences will be included under the total charge as "miscellaneous conferences, etc." We think this is better than to bill separately for every single conference or phone conversation and it seems to work out because our people seem to feel free to call us about almost anything any time.

I am not sure the accountant should do anything to overcome a client's reluctance. I think the accountant should let the client know what services are available. Only when the client really feels a need for the services to the extent that he will seek them out, will the accountant have a good client.

THE VALUE OF CONTINUAL SERVICE

There is general agreement that the rendering of continual service to clients, apart from the performance of periodic engagements at relatively distant intervals, has a very tangible goodwill value from the standpoint of retaining the client and creating opportunities for more extensive service. There are numerous ways to keep in frequent contact with clients. Some of the more important methods are:

1. Consulting with client on costs

2. Consulting with client on business matters
3. Consulting with client on office procedures
4. Consulting with client on accounting procedures
5. Assisting with the financial planning
6. Assisting client with personal financial matters
7. Informing the client of tax and other changes affecting him
8. Appearing at board meetings
9. Encouraging phone calls from client's bookkeepers for information and advice
10. Discussing with the client his monthly statements, when possible
11. Assisting in office efficiency surveys
12. Making comparisons of the client's figures with national or other averages secured through trade associations
13. Discussing economic trends and government actions
14. Assisting, where practical, in real-estate matters

Clients who have the highest opinion of their CPAs and of their services are also the ones who see them frequently. Despite this fact, many CPAs visit their clients only twice a year or even less. The CPA, moreover, only rarely volunteers his services; management is ordinarily obliged to call upon him for aid. Of course, in some ways, this might be regarded as a happy situation. But it could be argued that laymen have a right to expect professional men to promote recognition of the full usefulness of their art *before,* rather than after the need for it becomes apparent to everyone.

The unavailability of the CPA can cause considerable resentment. Some typical comments reflecting that attitude follow:

Our CPA makes two audits per year. He comes in once a year for an inventory. I don't talk with him too often by phone. He's hard to get hold of. I'm pretty fed up with this.

I have heard of accountants who were hard to see. They just weren't available when you needed them—and you get someone else if that goes on too long. I must say that our CPA is always easy to see.

We tried to get our CPA to improve our office methods, but he never had the time so we hired this management firm. We paid it $125 a day. Our CPA blew his top. But it was his own fault. We now get a lot more services from him—and, naturally, we pay him a lot more than we did before.

The dangers of failing to provide continual services are forcibly brought home by the following practitioner:

Are you the "undertaker" type of accountant? Do you wait until the client's year is over and then review the statements and embalm them? You can spot problems in your clients' affairs long before he can. He is too close to his business to realize the pitfalls he is headed for. If you wait until the year is over, how much good can you do for him? Recognition of the problem is almost equivalent to solution.

You can point out danger spots to correct at once, but most surely you can have them corrected for the coming period. There are many areas that can be discussed and corrected. For example: low profit margins, high fixed expenses, high payroll, inadequate return on investment, improper and inadequate financing, and so forth.

HANDLING THE SIMULTANEOUS DEMANDS OF CLIENTS

The problem of availability is common to all firms, large or small. It cannot really be solved. Try as he will, the practitioner cannot be in two places at the same time. However, several suggestions are offered for minimizing possible harmful effects.

Most obvious is to do everything possible to cut down the frequency with which conflicts may occur. In accepting a new client, for example, the CPA should consider the effect of the extra workload on his ability to serve existing clients. If it crowds his schedule too much, he may have to add personnel, refuse the new client, give up one or more of his less desirable clients, or risk lowering the level of his service in general.

A number of firms strive to attain a "balanced" clientele, where closing dates are distributed throughout the year. This not only increases their capacity to serve, it also contributes to their efficiency. But in making up a work program a firm must allow a certain margin for emergencies. Some firms feel that many CPAs try to handle too many clients. They indicate that both firm and clients would be better off if these CPAs served fewer clients at a deeper level of penetration.

Difficulties arise, some say, when a client becomes too attached to a particular member of a firm and wants no one else to handle his work. Although *personal* service is necessary, the client should be encouraged to feel he is a *client of the firm,* not of a particular individual, and to accept the aid of any qualified member of the firm. Even when a client "belongs" to an individual partner, at least one other partner should keep fully informed of his affairs. The second partner's relationship with the client should be close enough so that he can step in, if the in-charge partner is unavailable, without creating in the client a feeling that he is receiving second-best treatment.

There are times when an individual is faced with inevitably conflicting demands on his time. A prompt and courteous acknowledgment of the request should be made with a tactful and frank personal explanation. This should not be left to someone else unless the man is out of town. A CPA can often get a good idea of the problem during this conversation. He may be able to offer interim suggestions which can be helpful. He should try to let the client know when he will be available. If the problem requires immediate action, the CPA may have to temporarily drop what he is doing. He has to weigh the relative merits of each case. The emergency nature of a new problem should be made clear to the original client. The client is apt to accept the situation, if it is tactfully explained, without objection, for the implication is that he can expect the same treatment if he is faced with an urgent matter. Some comments follow:

> Our partnership is organized on a functional basis (auditing, taxes, etc.) rather than by clients. Therefore, all three partners are considered responsi-

ble for each client. We have a standing rule that one of us will always be available to see a client within twenty-four hours of his request. We haven't failed yet.

As an individual practitioner, I am out of the office a good deal of the time, but I call in twice a day. If a client has telephoned, I try to call him back the same day.

My clients are my friends. I try to get them to understand my problems, just as I try to understand theirs.

When two or more clients want me at the same time, I try to talk to both or all of them explaining my situation, and I try to work out a program which minimizes dissatisfaction. Obviously, the things to be avoided are failure to respond at all and abrupt, discourteous refusal.

MANAGEMENT SERVICES AND INDEPENDENCE

The question is sometimes raised, in connection with the field of management services, whether it is possible for the CPA to become a "professional controller" or "accounting engineer" without losing his status as an *independent* professional accountant. He can, but the possibility under some circumstances of having his independence questioned is not one to be taken lightly.

It has been said that independence is fundamentally a state of mind, a subjective matter of which the accountant himself is the best judge, and which does not lend itself to determination by a set of objective criteria. At the same time the accountant must avoid putting himself into a situation where prima-facie evidence might create doubt as to his independence.

An accountant cannot be presumed to be independent if he allows himself to be put into an employee relationship with his client. His relations to management must be kept at the advisory level as distinct from the operating or decision-making level. To present a client's position in a controversy does not involve loss of independence if the matter is conducted with the highest degree of integrity and intellectual honesty. To give investment advice in connection with the purchase of a business, where the experience and knowledge of the accountant are pertinent to the facts of the case, involves no loss of independent professional status for a CPA, whereas setting himself up as a general investment counselor would obviously be improper.

This matter, then, like many other problems in human relations, boils down to the exercise of common sense and good judgment. There is no reason why the CPA should fear that he is stepping out of line if he expands his activities into areas where he is eminently qualified to offer valuable service to the business public.

KEEPING THE CLIENT'S CONFIDENCE

It hardly needs repeating that a positive confidential relationship between the accountant and client is essential, and that it involves considerably more than keeping knowledge of a client's affairs from coming through the accountant, directly or indirectly, to the attention of outsiders. In the case of an individual client, the confidential relationship is solely between the accountant and the client. The information obtained in such relationship is not to be divulged to any employee of the client, or to any relative of the client, including a wife or husband, without express and preferably written request by the client directed to the accountant.

In the case of a corporate client, the confidential relationship is between the accountant and corporation. The information covered by such relationship is not to be divulged to any corporate officer, executive, or any other individual (except those specified by the corporate authority making the engagement) without further express authorization, preferably in writing, by the same corporate authority. In the case of a partnership client, the confidential relationship is between the accountant and the partners; and the information covered by such relationship is not to be divulged to any other than a partner without express and preferably written request by the partner authorizing the engagement. Where information is desired by a partner other than the one authorizing the engagement, it is desirable to seek express authority for this from the partner authorizing the engagement.

The relationship between the practicing CPA and his client is governed by the same underlying principles whether he has a large practice or a small one. The small practitioner, however, is more likely to be a close personal friend and financial adviser to a small client and therefore the association is a much closer one.

The accountant must always conduct himself so that his clients, as well as other businessmen who may become his clients, will have confidence in his competence and trustworthiness. Rule 1.03 of the AICPA's *Code of Professional Ethics* has as its purpose to guide the accountant in his conduct as well as to assure those who engage his services that the relationship will be a confidential one.

RESPONSIBILITY OF CPA TO ALL PARTNERS OF THE CLIENT

The following case is illustrative of situations where one partner withholds information from other partners.

The client of the CPA is a partnership. The managing partner of the client has consistently drawn more than his pro-rata share of the earnings until such excess amounts to over $225,000. The CPA prepares the income-tax return and gives it to the managing partner who removes the schedule indicating the drawings and capital balances of each partner before passing the tax return along to the other partners. The CPA also prepares a financial report which only indicates total earnings and drawings, no separate schedule being included which shows detailed drawings and capital balances of each partner.

From the facts stated it may be assumed that the partnership being examined is a true partnership. In such a case, there is a community of interests among the partners, and each partner is an agent of the others. Accordingly, it seems that the mere fact that all of the arrangements for the engagement are handled by the managing partner would not be any reason why the CPA should treat him, rather than the partnership, as the client.

It follows that the CPA has as much responsibility for full disclosure of significant facts to one partner as to another. Accordingly, the CPA should insist that a schedule, showing the detailed drawings and capital balances of each partner, be made available to each of the partners, since the information contained in the report would be incomplete, so far as the partners themselves are concerned, unless such information is made available to them.

The CPA should discuss this matter with the managing partner and suggest that either the partners be brought together and the information presented to them or that the auditor be authorized to transmit the information to them individually. If the managing partner refuses to permit the auditor to make this information known to the other partners, he should advise the managing partner that, in the circumstances, he has no alternative but to withdraw from the engagement, and that if he does so, he will consider it necessary to notify all partners of the fact and his reason for the withdrawal.

If the managing partner still refuses to permit the disclosure of the information to the other partners, the CPA should then withdraw from the case and should notify all of the partners of the fact of his withdrawal and state clearly that he has done so because he has been prevented from furnishing them with information regarding the drawings and capital accounts of the partners which he considers to be essential to a reasonable understanding of the financial statements from the standpoint of the partners.

There are some businesses which are ostensibly partnerships but which, in fact, are not. It is not unheard of for an individual to give some of his employees nominal partnership status so as to increase their prestige in dealing with outsiders while, under the terms of the agreement, the business is run as an individual proprietorship.

In such situations, if there is any partnership agreement at all, the managing partner is usually authorized to run the business and to make such distributions of profits as he sees fit. The rest of the so-called partners are, in effect, only employees, having signed away any rights to be furnished with the information which a partner would normally be entitled to have. The nature of the agreement is a fact to be determined by the auditor and in such a situation, if the managing partner withholds information, there is no reason for the auditor to take steps to notify the other partners.

MAINTAINING THE PERSONAL TOUCH WITH THE CLIENT

Getting the feel of the client's affairs. How can the accountant with a growing practice best maintain a working knowledge of the financial affairs of an ever-increasing number of clients? There is one superior way, simple yet capable of being overlooked along the way. It is for the principal personally to perform the first services for each new major client.

Any old-time practitioner, when asked about any of his clients of long standing, will display an amazing comprehension of the essentials. Why? Because he knows the whole evolution of the enterprise. He remembers the founders, the first plant, the early products. The facts are easy for him to remember since they form a connected, unbroken story. Once a principal described in detail the financial structure of a ranching enterprise whose accounts one of his staff men had worked on for *twenty years*—but he had set up the accounts when the ranch had been purchased *forty* years before.

The grasp is never quite the same when the accountant enters the scene after the show is on the road. A business, after all, is an adventure as well as a venture. It is a personal, psychological, and historical unit as well as an economic and accounting unit. In short, a business, like a rock, an animal, or a word, can seldom be fully appreciated or rightly understood without a sure knowledge of its origin. With such knowledge, delegation is possible without fear of losing that main thread, the permanent feel of various clients' affairs.

Keeping up with the client's affairs. One CPA put it this way:

How can one grow, increase his staff, service more clients, and still give each client the same personal attention that he did as a sole practitioner? This problem plagues every practitioner as his firm grows. The problem is more acute as the firm starts increasing with more partners and staff men. One practitioner found a solution in his own firm:

Among the myriad activities required of practitioners in the day-by-day management of a practice (particularly those serving "small-to-medium" clients) one of the most important is that of acquiring, maintaining, and cultivating a firsthand familiarity with each client, his methods of operation, habits, policies, and objectives.

No audit program, control questionnaire, budget, financial statement, or other report currently in use, regardless of its comprehensiveness, furnishes all of the needed information. An examination of some recent requests from your own clients will bear out the necessity of having a *basic* familiarity with their affairs.

It seems that mere knowledge of purely financial results is no longer adequate to serve the client properly or to keep him contented. In many cases we have scheduled conferences with clients for the purpose of reviewing historical financial statements or budgetary forecasts only to discover that they prefer to discuss other matters and actually avoid participation in the discussion, unless they can sway the meeting toward their goal.

What are some of these subjects the client wants to discuss and with which he expects the accountant to have a firsthand knowledge? Perhaps he wants to discuss his prospective competitor who is negotiating to obtain a sales location across the street, and the effect the successful efforts of the intruder might have on his business, prices, and profits; or the fact that his landlord recently died and his building can now be purchased at a sacrifice price.

In the smaller practice, where the partner or practitioner performs the audit or finds himself in the position of supervisor in the field, this goal does not present much of a problem. He usually contacts the client directly many times in the course of an audit and through seeing virtually every detail in the books and records, as well as all underlying documents, and through living with the job, he usually develops a marked affinity with the client.

However, as long as the day has only twenty-four hours, everyone will agree that it is virtually impossible to take the time required for this exposure to details and simultaneously maintain a healthy record of progress and growth. Aside from this, most of us have the bad habit of wanting some time for reading, recreation, leisure, and other pursuits. The choice seems to be either (1) furnish your client with a personal-type service and restrict your growth or (2) advance your own progress, resulting in a cold, impersonal type of service to your clients.

We have attempted in our partnership to have our cake and eat it, too, through utilizing a series of procedures enabling us and our clients to enjoy the desired personal relationship while delegating to our staff the duty of gathering the required data.

The system as designed is not foolproof but in essence it does accomplish its purpose. The solution to this knotty problem appears somewhat as follows: First, we require every staff accountant on the job to prepare a brief audit note or comment regarding anything of significance noticed while conducting the audit. This comment which is directed to our supervisors to become part of our working-paper file might have nothing directly to do with the technical phases of the examination. Typical comments might be: "Client seems very unhappy with new bookkeeper's work—small wonder since he is overloading her with typing and filing chores"; "Heard client and attorney on phone—seems he is changing will as re: securities and real estate"; "Chatting with office manager—says he'll leave if pension plan is not adopted soon —probably be rough replacing him"; "That pending lawsuit will probably come to a head within thirty days"; "Client toying with idea to bring brother-in-law into business—he's that bad character who was involved in the county scandal"; "Look for a load of income during the next six months—they're running a promotion on product X"; "Books in a mess this month"; etc.

These audit notes supply us to some degree with the atmosphere prevailing at the client's place of business. In addition, they furnish the supervisors with certain data which they require periodically to complete a questionnaire entitled a "Reviewer's Report," which is directed to the partner-in-charge. This report, together with financial statements, audit report, tax returns and working-paper file serves as:

1. A partial guide for a client-accountant conference.

2. An evaluation list as to whether constructive thinking, curiosity, and initiative were exercised by our supervisors and staff.

3. A reminder of potential pitfalls (tax and otherwise) to be avoided by the client (pursuant to the accountant's advice).

4. A training tool encouraging the staff to develop analytical techniques which in turn enable them to assume more responsibilities and advance more rapidly.

The reviewer's report encompasses areas including tax, management, and audit. It is not intended to produce a complete survey of the client, nor to replace any existing reports, but rather to stimulate thinking which would in turn lead to significant decisions. It is prepared for small write-up-type clients about once a year and more frequently for the larger clients. In certain cases it is completed piecemeal throughout the year to prevent too heavy a workload at one time since the research required to complete the report properly is rather extensive and time-consuming. At present the report contains 114 separate items and is continually being edited and expanded to prevent obsolescence and improve its effectiveness. A few samples of the items contained in the report follow:

Question	*Typical Supervisor's Answer*
1. Comment re: adequacy of petty cash fund.	1. Inadequate — requires reimbursement about every three days—client feels insecure about increasing from $50 to $300.
2. Is the best banking institution being used?	2. Probably not—believe bank *C* might be more understanding of the problems in this business—bank *A* has been giving him a hard time on the $50,000 line.
3. How can we reduce bank service charges?	3. Bank *A* less expensive—see comparative analysis based on one month's operation.
4. Is client carrying too much cash for the business? Should excess funds be invested? What type of investment?	4. Yes, average need $3,000—carrying $15,000. How about that liquid five per cent deal we discussed?

The audit notes are prepared currently regardless of the frequency of the over-all report, and action might be taken on the audit notes on a current basis without waiting for the completion of a formal reviewer's report. While we find these procedures not only desirable but almost indispensable in our practice (consisting of approximately twenty-five people), we are certain they can be used to advantage in any size firm where the principals find it necessary to withdraw from the field work, and yet would like to service their clients with the efficiency of a larger firm and personal aspect of the smaller one.

Keeping the client informed. You read many newspapers, business and technical papers and benefit from the knowledge you gain. You can do your clients a service at the same time by following these suggestions:

When you come across an article or piece of news that makes you say to yourself, "I think client Jones would like to learn about this," cut the item out of the publication and send it to him. This little personal touch will add considerably to your client-relations program. The clients who receive these small items will remember this little service much longer than the number of pages of your audit report.

The tax services you read can also serve a purpose other than the obvious one. Often as you read cases and reports you can associate them directly with a particular client. Have a copy made of the page and send it to your client with a personal note. You might explain how his situation is similar to the one in the example.

Send out greeting cards on special occasions. A sympathy card or flowers at a time of bereavement will be much appreciated. Birthday and wedding anniversary cards are annual reminders that you think of your client at times other than when work is to be done. When one is ill send a get-well card.

Preserving the advantages of the fresh reaction. Most clients continue to engage the same accountant or accounting firm year after year, with scarcely a thought of changing. Others believe it wise, as a matter of basic policy, to change every five or six years in order to assure the advantages of both new insight and a fresh analytical approach. No one minds being the new appointee, but the accountants being replaced can hardly be blamed for lack of enthusiasm.

In the larger communities, as a general rule, the spur to keep alert and to hold the client is ever present because other accountants are astonishingly ready, able, and willing to take over. This automatic encouragement is frequently not present or is not so strong in thousands of smaller communities where perhaps only one or two CPAs are in public practice. There monopoly can encourage lackadaisical service, which in time can affect the good name of the profession itself. Can such a tendency be overcome?

This provokes the further question: what are the natural causes of slipshoddiness? Surely one of the causes is the practitioner's gradually, almost unconsciously, becoming overtolerant of substandard practices. This can happen easily through the hypnotic effect of monotonous repetition of the same procedures on successive engagements, whether they be monthly write-ups or annual audits.

That first good look at the client's affairs, that initial reaction, is the one which is likely to be the truest. Abnormalities, unorthodoxies of all descriptions, then make sharp impressions on one's mind. Those first impressions should be set down on paper immediately. The accountant who waits rapidly begins to accommodate himself to the unsound procedures; then to live with them; and finally, it becomes almost second nature for him to pride himself on his ability to thread his way through the maze of special peculiarities characterizing the client's affairs and procedures.

If this diagnosis is correct, the prescription for serving a client year after year, yet preserving as far as possible the advantages of the initial reaction, is occasionally to *rotate personnel* and, without exception, to plan succeeding engagements so that the *angle of approach* and the *relative emphasis* will be different each time.

PERSONAL RELATIONS WITH CLIENTS

The cultivation of friendly and personal relations with clients is definitely helpful to any practice whether just beginning or of long standing, but the practitioner should recognize the inherent dangers in the cultivation of such relations. There is an obvious point beyond which such relations should not go. It is the point beyond which friendship would tend to interfere with or hamper the accountant in the maintenance of his requisite attitude of professional independence. In other words, the relation of client and accountant should never be subordinate to the ties of personal friendship. The initiative in the development of friendly relations may come either from the client or from the accountant, but preferably from the former. However, the circumstances in each individual case should be decisive.

ADVICE FOR SMALL CORPORATION CLIENTS

What should the CPA say to the shareowners of a prospective small corporation when they first meet in his office? He might speak to them in this way:

1. This new corporation you are forming is an entity entirely separate from you gentlemen who own the controlling shares of its capital stock. To reap the full advantage of this modern economic invention you must act differently, usually more formally, than was the case when the business was a sole proprietorship or partnership. Do not treat it like the same old business under a different name.

2. Simple dealing and common sense, not fancy maneuvering, should prevail in the investment of capital, the establishment of executive compensation, and the distribution of earnings or assets. Wherever feasible, these should be clean-cut cash transactions, not accrual-journal entries.

3. Debtor-creditor relationships between a corporation and its controlling shareowners, whether in substantial or petty amounts, should normally be avoided in the interest of a clean financial structure and precise determination of corporate financial status. However, if needed loans cannot be obtained from nonshareowners, then the terms, the security, and the performance should, if anything, be more stern than if the transactions were with independent debtors or creditors. This is so because a quasi-fiduciary relationship has been created.

4. Summing up, the corporate entity is an instrument which permits marvelous business flexibility, expansion, efficiency, perpetuation, and protection. Maximize these benefits by pursuing the ABCs just mentioned. Surprisingly few small corporations do. As for the XYZs, consult your lawyer and your accountant at the first sign of trouble or misunderstanding. In the corporate realm, as everywhere, remember that an ounce of prevention is worth a pound of cure.

ROTATION OF AUDITORS

Arguments for rotation. Arguments in favor of rotation are summarized as follows:

1. A fresh viewpoint is desirable at more or less frequent intervals.

2. New blood ensures greater alertness.

3. Long-established familiarity between the auditor's representatives and the client's employees may lead to collusion.

4. Mistakes of the previous auditors may be detected and corrected.

5. A better distribution of audit engagements over a greater number of practitioners should be encouraged.

6. Competitive bidding between accounting firms would be stimulated, thus reducing audit costs.

7. (In direct contradiction.) Competitive bidding would be discouraged.

It will be observed that with the exception of the last three points the contentions affect predominantly the interests of clients rather than independent accountants. It should be stressed, however, that if the policy of rotation were adopted generally the probable effect would be the exact opposite of a wider distribution of audit engagements, for the reason that the larger firms naturally have more influential connections than the smaller. Accordingly, if a change were required, the tendency would be to select better-known practitioners. Conflicting contentions with respect to competitive bidding may be dismissed briefly—in professional activities it has been demonstrated time and again that the cheapest is the worst for all concerned.

Brief reference should be made to certain types of organizations wherein other practical considerations influence the choice of auditors. While large in number, these institutions are relatively unimportant in the economy as a whole. They embrace clubs and fraternal orders, religious and charitable organizations, service groups such as community chests, and small political subdivisions. Here the accounts may be so free from complexities that any experienced practitioner can conduct an initial audit as capably and almost as economically as his predecessor. In such instances political or social expediency may influence governing bodies to alternate or rotate audit engagements between deserving members or supporters, usually at no additional cost to the auditee. Although the change may have an upsetting effect upon the accounting department the damage is temporary.

Detection of collusion. Two of the arguments in favor of rotation appear to have little validity.

The first relates to the possibility of collusion between representatives of the practitioner and company employees. Fraudulent relationships between the two are at a minimum because (1) extreme care is exercised by all reputable firms in the selection of staff members of fitting professional and moral character, and (2) the improved methods of internal control of financial transactions now in effect in all well-managed institutions make collusion of this nature extremely difficult.

The next contention is that a change of auditors may lead to the discovery and correction of errors for which the predecessor firm is responsible. Of course, if the client has lost confidence in his auditors for any good reason, common sense dictates the engagement of another firm. But the reason should be far from trivial. On the other hand, to change auditors solely on the theory that they may have made undisclosed mistakes is as naive as dismissing a family doctor or lawyer without cause. Moreover, such an approach implies lack of confidence by management in its own internal-accounting organization where the mistakes, if any, may have originated.

Fresh viewpoint and new blood. The remaining contention is that a fresh viewpoint is obtained if a new firm is engaged to review the accounting procedures and to reanalyze financial problems. As a corollary proposition it is urged that the injection of new blood ensures greater alertness on the part of the individuals assigned to the examination. Unquestionably these claims have a degree of merit. But the practical question is whether the performance is worth the price of admission. In the succeeding analysis it is proper to assume that the current auditors and their potential successors possess equal professional competence and that both firms are staffed adequately to perform the engagement.

Internal rotation. It is the policy of practically all established firms to change staff assignments every few years. Usually these replacements occur more frequently at lower staff levels, so that individuals in the supervisory or partner groups may serve the same client for a considerably longer period. The *modus operandi* is explained by Carman Blough as follows:

> Most firms of auditors attempt to supply this same fresh viewpoint by having the supervisors who handle the job changed every few years, and occasionally by changing the partners in charge. It is almost universally true among accounting firms that there is an exchange of ideas and viewpoints among the members of the same firm, so that there is no great likelihood, if the firm is one which is competent and alert, that there will be any deterioration as a result of the same firm handling the matter. It is also common knowledge that policy-making partners of accounting firms are continually exchanging viewpoints with those of other firms, both privately and in public meetings, so that there is a pretty wide dissemination of varying views regarding problems of major importance.

By no means, however, is the policy of internal rotation universal in the case of large or medium-sized firms because many clients object strongly to the dislodgment of satisfactory personnel. They believe that the familiarity of the auditors' representatives with the problems, records, and history of the concern permits them to make a better examination. This reasoning is especially cogent where the auditors have performed such services as SEC work, tax advice, system studies, or management analyses.

In general, the same considerations influence management in cases where small firms or individual practitioners are the regular auditors. Although the limited size of the auditor's staff may preclude effective internal rotation, the intimate knowledge of the client's affairs, obtained perhaps over a long period, is deemed to outweigh the limited advantage found in the new-look approach.

The expense factor. The next objection to frequent changes of auditors is its undesirability from the standpoint of expense. In testimony before the SEC in the *McKesson & Robbins* case, Norman Lenhart stated that in many instances it costs twice as much to make the first audit as it does succeeding audits. In the same case Samuel Broad testified that it might take the new auditor two or three years to acquire close familiarity with all the accounting phases of the client.

It is true that in general not all of the change-over costs are met by the client in the first year of replacement. The business public should realize, however, that losses of this nature experienced by auditors must be offset if the accounting profession is to preserve sufficient financial health to maintain existing standards of service. Accordingly, the absolute and inevitable result of widespread adoption of the principle of rotation could lead to nothing but increased audit costs to all.

Another consideration is the upsetting effect of a transfer upon the accounting department of the auditee from the controller down. The assembly of historical data, location and identification of records, and other essential indoctrination are necessarily laborious processes. Furthermore, in the large number of cases in which the relationships between key individuals in the accounting department and representatives of the supplanted firm have been based on mutual respect, there is likely to be encountered a human tendency to withhold complete co-operation with the new auditors. In fact, many instances can be cited in which friction has been evident for an appreciable period.

Interval of rotation. Little needs to be said of the logical intervals between rotation. A change every year is the most costly and disturbing, every two years is almost as undesirable, but if the auditor has survived this critical period, enlightened management may well decide that there was no compelling reason for adopting the policy in the first place.

Very few practitioners have escaped a notification from a client that the policy of rotation has been adopted in order to obtain a new viewpoint. More often than not the spokesman for the client is guilty of faulty semantics. Perhaps outside influences have been too strong to overcome, even though the auditor's services are quite satisfactory. What the spokesman is really talking about is permanent replacement—rotation requires more than one spin.

WHEN CLIENT AND CPA PART COMPANY

In every practice there is a certain amount of client turnover. Some practices outgrow certain clients just as certain clients can outgrow the resources of an accounting firm. Sometimes conditions reach the point where a CPA cannot work in harmony with a client. Then it is time to end the relationship. But whatever the reason for the termination, whether initiated by the CPA or the client, the final expression of good client relations lies in the ability of the CPA to withdraw gracefully. One practitioner expresses it this way:

> We are very particular to "leave" a client as a friend. In those inevitable situations where a client ceases to use us, we do everything possible to co-operate with him and our successors (without concern as to whether we get paid for it) to make the transition as smooth as possible. This has paid off,

because several clients who have left us over the years for one reason or another have either returned to us or have recommended us to others. Usually, if they return, they are better clients than before.

RELATIONS WITH BANKERS

How CPAs rate with bankers. The material which follows is intended to aid CPAs in improving their relations with bankers—an objective that merits serious attention because both CPAs and bankers are concerned with promoting the economic health of the business community. Because of their common aim, they ought to understand each other. That understanding is important not only in terms of the welfare of their mutual clients; it is also important in advancing the self-interest of each group.

Much has been accomplished in recent years to generate better understanding. An increasing number of joint CPA-banker meetings have been held under the auspices of professional accounting societies and banker associations, notably the Robert Morris Associates. This is encouraging. But, in the final analysis, it is the interaction of individual CPAs and bankers in their day-to-day working activities which provides a true test of CPA-banker relations.

The CPA is well regarded by a great majority of commercial loan executives, both as an individual and as a member of a highly respected profession. He is considered helpful by nearly all bankers, and essential by a goodly number, in the banks' lending operations.

Bankers have their reasons for these attitudes. They regard the CPA's reports, particularly if unqualified, as vital documents. They feel that he has become more social and less introverted in recent years and recognize that he occupies an increasingly prominent position in his community. They applaud his technical standards and respect his ethical values. They attach great importance to his role as financial counselor, though they suspect that his clients do not fully share their high opinion of him. They attribute a wide range of skills to him in the area of finance and control, sometimes assuming that he is endowed with talents that the CPA himself is not prepared to claim. These compliments are gratifying. But the critical observations provide the basis for better understanding—and there are enough of them to justify the profession's concern.

The criticisms reveal areas in which CPAs might improve their services and indicate that some bankers need to acquire a better understanding of the environment in which the CPA works and the responsibilities that he can be normally expected to assume. This job of education belongs to the CPA, and the bankers would be delighted if he undertook it. Many of them bemoan the lack of personal contact with practicing accountants and recognize that this leads to insufficient knowledge and misconceptions of their individual capabilities. Many bankers qualify their critical remarks by saying that their words apply to only a few CPAs. Nonetheless, the adverse comments are worth remembering:

1. The CPA has too narrow a view of his own function.

2. He forgets the needs of a bank for credit information and fails to supply sufficient detail, particularly in terms of comparative data for prior years.

3. He is often too preoccupied to offer a creative service to his clients, thus confirming a widely held belief that he is merely a necessary evil imposed on a business by interested outsiders.

4. He is not insistent enough in convincing his clients of the value of a complete audit which would justify an unqualified opinion.

5. He is sometimes inclined to sacrifice his objectivity to the wishes of his clients.

These are obviously serious charges. If any CPA is guilty of them, he ought to reform, but if he feels, as many CPAs have a right to feel, that the charges are too severe, then he has an equal obligation to enlighten the banking executives in his community. In the following pages, relations between bankers and CPAs will be highlighted through candid opinions of accountants and their reports.

Policies on audit requests. Most commercial loan executives regularly request an independent audit before granting a loan or establishing a line of credit. To many the examinations are a matter of bank policy and exceptions are rarely permitted. Typical of these emphatic comments are the following:

> We request audits on all loans except those which involve only a nominal amount.

> Almost without exception we require audits covering three to five fiscal years.

> We try to get an audit from all prospective borrowers, especially new ones.

Despite the fairly rigid audit policy of some banks, many of those which regularly request audits indicate that their importance is contingent upon a number of factors. For example, enforcement of the audit requirement may depend largely on the size of the loan. The cost of an audit would be disproportionately high in the case of small or short-term loans and would not be justified in the light of the relatively small risk assumed by the bank. Other factors are the size of the customer's company, the reputation and over-all financial position of the borrower, their familiarity with the individual borrowers, and whether or not the account is a new one.

In many cases audits are not usually required from established customers who have had accounts with the banks for a number of years, unless they are seeking an increase in their line of credit. Bankers are largely concerned about obtaining as much information as possible on new borrowers. Other qualifications include the quality of the company's management and whether or not the loan will be secured.

Some banks require audits from their customers only on large loans or in special situations individually determined by the banker. Customarily in these cases, if the available balance sheets and profit-and-loss statements show a favorable position over a period of several years, these banks do not usually request an audit. Many bankers would often abandon the audit request if it aroused strong resistance on the part of the customer. However, there is definite evidence to suggest that the use of audits by banks is on the increase.

Representative comments. Here are some representative comments on bankers' audit requirements:

> We always ask for an independent audit, particularly if a loan is unsecured.

> Our insistence upon an audit depends on the size and type of loan requested and our opinion of the management.

> It is customary for us to require an audit for all term loans, but we try to get them on all companies if possible. However, we must make exceptions at times.

> Where credit exposure is great and it appears that the present statement of condition might not be too accurate, we insist upon an audit. This is relatively rare, however.

> We insist on it in the case of term loans and are trying to encourage our customers to accept an audit under other circumstances. We try to point out that an audit is of great value to the customer as well as to us.

> We prefer audits on all commercial accounts, but we get only a few percentage-wise.

> In many instances, one of the bank's executives who is a CPA will conduct the necessary audit himself. Although this is not an actual audit, he looks over the books thoroughly.

> Because of competition, our bank does not request an audit of a prospective customer. After the customer is sold, an audit is then requested if the bank feels that it is necessary.

> Each case is considered separately on its own merits. There are no set rules in this bank as to whether or not an audit is required.

Size of loans requiring audits. As already indicated, the size of the credit or loan request is often a determining factor in the bank's decision on whether or not to seek an independent audit. Many loan executives cite certain maximum amounts above which a loan normally would not be granted without an audit.

Size is an important factor with many banks. Many bankers merely say that audits are usually required on larger loans. However, a number of others indicate that these limits vary according to prior experience with losses on unaudited companies and the factors previously indicated as governing audit policy. The larger banks, as might be expected, have somewhat higher limits on the size of loans which will be granted without an audit. However, there are exceptions to this. For example, several of the largest and smallest banks require audits for all loans, while a number of large banks are represented among those citing low loan limits. About half the banks that grant loans up to $100,000 without audit are in the smaller category. Some of these banks are located in the smaller cities, and their familiarity with prospective borrowers often makes it unnecessary to require an audit. However, it seems generally true that smaller banks are less stringent in their audit requirements, either because they do not appreciate the value of an audit or because they are reluctant to insist upon an audit at the risk of losing a prospective borrower.

Representative comments. Typical quotations on loan limits follow:

> Size of the loan is of importance as well as the good reputation of the borrower. However, we have a maximum amount of $5,000 that can be loaned without an audit being made.

> We have no set limits but probably would not grant a loan over $50,000 without a complete audit.

> The size of the loan will depend on circumstances and the relationship of the customer to our bank. For example, an established concern with an excellent balance and good tax records could obtain a large loan without an audit.

> Our full legal limit of $350,000 has been extended in the past without audit. It depends on the over-all financial position of the borrower, the current management, and the schedule for repayment.

> We don't have a definite policy, but all loans over $1,000 are reviewed by our directors monthly and they usually require an audited statement.

> It depends on whether loans are being granted on the basis of security or signature. Loans under $10,000 are normally secured; those of larger amounts are frequently granted on the basis of financial strength indicated by the audit. Therefore, our maximum loan without an audit would be $10,000.

> Ordinarily $50,000 is our limit for an unsecured or unendorsed note. But, the company must have an excellent record in order to borrow as much as this without audit.

> We prefer audits in all cases. However, circumstances of the financial standing, size of loan, and the cost of the audit to the borrower frequently make this impractical.

> We have no policies as to the amount that is loaned without audit. However, we usually make the request on borderline cases where large amounts are involved.

In summary, the size of a loan emerges as the most significant element in the audit policy of the banks, with $25,000 representing the average limit above which audits are usually requested. These requirements are sometimes modified by considerations of past experience with the prospective borrower, the secured status of the loan, the nature of the company's business, and the reputation of its management.

The importance of opinions. Most loan executives maintain that they either look for or require an opinion on a report from an accountant. "If there is no opinion," one executive says, "we ask for it. We consider it to be of prime importance in judging the reliability of the statements." Some bankers, however, modify their comments with statements indicating that the opinion is not of too great importance in cases where the balance sheet indicates the company to be in an excellent position. In these cases they are apt to accept statements prepared by the customer.

A number of loan executives state that an opinion is not always received even when requested. "I receive audits all the time which are not even signed by a certain CPA, and I can't seem to get him to give an opinion," said one banker. A number of them feel that the cost is such a significant factor, especially with small business, that they are often not inclined to press for unqualified opinions except on larger loans. Some concede that their desire for such reports has to be subordinated to the practicalities of competition.

Representative comments. Although most loan executives appear to have a fairly clear understanding of the differences between unqualified opinions, qualified opinions, and disclaimers, some of them are obviously not familiar with the degree of responsibility assumed by the accountant. Typical of such comments are:

> Certainly we look for an opinion. If you don't get it, what do you have? We have to put responsibility for the figures somewhere.

> The opinion is not too important, because the accountant's signature should speak for itself.

> An unqualified opinion means that you know you can rely on the figures without reservation.

Although there is a heavy preference for unqualified opinions, qualified reports are usually acceptable, depending on the nature of the qualifications. On the other hand, disclaimed reports are generally approached with caution. Many banks consider that these reports have no more value than a company-prepared statement, and a number of bankers refuse to accept them from their customers. One loan executive in a medium-sized bank in the Southwest commented at length on this matter:

> An unqualified opinion of a reputable accountant is highly regarded. We feel we can rely heavily upon him. If an accountant "qualified" his opinion, the figures may or may not be depreciated, depending on the importance of its qualified item. For example, if the inventory account for a large share of the current assets has yet to be verified, it completely negates the value of the statement to us. We never accept disclaimed balance sheets.

Some bankers state that qualified or disclaimed reports mean more research for the bank. Although their final credit decisions are often based on factors other than the accountant's opinion, they place considerable emphasis on the unqualified report and usually study other reports with great care. Thus, the acceptance of a statement by many banks is largely dependent on the type of opinion rendered. Some typical views:

> We always shoot for an unqualified opinion. Usually a qualified opinion leaves a lot to be desired and might require further appraisal.

> We try to get an unqualified opinion in every case and make liberal allowances for those that are qualified. We will not accept a disclaimed report.

> We accept an unqualified report at face value. A qualified report puts more responsibility on the bank. In the case of a disclaimer the bank has to do much more investigation on its own.

> We expect the accountant to support his reputation by his opinion. There-

fore, the greater the reputation of the CPA, the more apt we are to accept his report at face value. We would not accept audits of all CPAs.

The unqualified opinion is most important to us. We don't have to worry if it's from a good accounting firm. If it is qualified we would probably have to check to satisfy ourselves.

The type of opinion is carefully examined, because it shows the scope of the CPA's engagement and how much confidence we can place in the figures.

The selection of accountants. Virtually all banks have recommended accountants to prospective or established customers. Some have recommended a particular firm under certain circumstances, especially when a specialist seemed to be needed. Most banks, however, ordinarily avoid recommending a single firm because of the risks of being accused of partiality and of assuming some responsibility for unsatisfactory reports.

The most common practice is to give the borrower a list of several accounting firms that the bank feels to be qualified. Although emphasizing their need to be impartial, the bankers acknowledge that they recommend CPAs who are familiar to them. As one executive explains it, "We can't afford to take chances on somebody we don't know." Some banks decline to recommend specific firms by name as a matter of policy. They either refer the customer to the classified telephone directory or otherwise leave the selection completely up to him.

Although they hesitate to participate in the initial selection of an accountant, many loan executives feel obligated to advise a customer or prospective borrower to change his accountant when, in the bank's view, such a change would be beneficial. This advice is actually offered only rarely, and more often in larger cities than in the smaller communities. The most frequently cited reasons for suggesting a change in accountants are:

1. Inadequate or incomplete reports
2. Present accountant is not certified
3. Failure to improve internal control, systems, and budgeting
4. Misleading or incorrect figures submitted
5. Specific weaknesses or need for a specialist
6. Incompetent to meet client's needs
7. Lack of confidence in accountant
8. Availability of larger firm for growing customer or large scale operations
9. Other accountants are more familiar with the customer's industry
10. Failure of accountant to co-operate with the bank
11. Local firm can provide better service than out-of-town accountants

Only very few bankers have ever urged a change in accountants because they felt their customer was being charged too much for the services rendered. However, many lending officers recognize differences in quality, ability, competence, and so on, among individual CPAs and firms. Generally, these differences are a matter of degree and often bear some relation to the specific needs of the banks' customers.

In evaluating the abilities of CPAs to satisfy their customers' needs, most bankers attach little importance to the size of the firm, providing it is equipped to furnish prompt and thorough service. They base their judgment on the reputation of the firm and on their experience with its personnel.

Representative comments. A majority of bankers express no preference between large and small firms as a group. Typical comments are:

> We are primarily interested in the caliber of men serving the particular account and we find excellent ones in firms of all sizes.

> We judge on the basis of the quality of the accounting work as it applies to our business.

Those who do have a preference usually qualify their statements by indicating that the preference applies only to certain situations. The advantages cited in favor of either group are often similar, suggesting that different bankers have had different experiences with both large and small firms. The remarks which seem to favor smaller local firms usually include a reference to their accessibility and close personal relations with the client; those which indicate a preference for larger firms most usually relate to the availability of specialists and the ease in handling multi-office clients.

Bankers generally consider membership in a state society and/or the AICPA to have some bearing on their evaluation of a CPA. Those in the Far West run opposite to the popular opinion, with only a minority in this region feeling that a CPA's local or national professional affiliations are of importance to them. The general feeling seems to be that the professional groups contribute to the development of their members and enforce high standards of performance. Some simply assume that most CPAs belong. "This bank has rarely found a CPA," one of them said, "who isn't a member of the AICPA."

The interest of bankers in professional membership was revealed in the following remarks:

> The possibility that a CPA has been barred from an association might be very important to us.

> We believe such membership serves as a recommendation.

> Associations help to broaden the CPA's knowledge. We feel that if he doesn't have enough interest to keep up with these organizations, he will let himself fall behind in ways which will directly affect his work.

> The only CPA we ever had trouble with was not a member of the Institute.

> Those who are members of the state or national associations are accepted as completely reputable. We would do additional checking on those who were not, before we accepted their work.

Determining the CPA's qualifications. After the opinion, the most important item in an audit report is the name of the accountant or firm signing the opinion. There are differences in accountants, just as there are differences in bankers, doctors, and lawyers. Accountants will be the first to admit that all elements of the profession are not yet up to the high level of quality to be found in the majority. This makes it incumbent upon the banker to know or to find out something about the professional standing of the accounting firm which prepared the report before he can rely unreservedly on the opinion expressed. An unqualified opinion in a short-form certificate over the signature of a known firm of high professional competence and integrity is far more reassuring than fifteen pages of detailed comment on the auditing procedures followed by an unknown firm of unknown, and hence questionable, standing in the profession.

Few banks take no precautions to determine the competence and reliability of a prospective borrower's accountant. Most of them initiate certain checks, keep certain records, or claim to know adequately the work of local accountants. Here are some of the different approaches adopted by the banks, many of them, of course, using more than one procedure.

1. Information is sought from other banks
2. Personal acquaintance with local accountants
3. Refer to card files, records, and directories
4. Accept CPA certificate as prima-facie evidence of competence
5. Prior experience with the bank is evaluated
6. Checks are made with other accountants
7. Check with accountants' associations
8. Credit services are investigated
9. Checks are made with other clients

In explaining the procedures of his bank, one loan executive said: "We keep files on all our customers' CPAs—this is more or less a character-reference file. If any accountant has caused us any burdensome trouble by his methods of preparation, or has advised his client not to submit certain information, or if he is involved in any questionable business operation that is under scrutiny, this information is put into the files. In addition, we also talk with other banks about accountants unknown to us and consider it a favorable factor if he is a member in good standing of the AICPA." Another executive in a large Midwestern city said: "Our bank requires that the accountant be a CPA. We keep an up-to-date index of all CPAs and note if they are satisfactory based upon our or other banks' past experience with them."

Clearly most banks are not only concerned with, but are often aware of the abilities and records of the accountants in their locale. If the accountant is unknown, the typical bank goes to some length to check on his reputation, frequently obtaining the needed information from another bank.

Role of the CPA in credit negotiations. Most bankers usually discuss with the borrower or with his accountant the type of financial report wanted. These discussions are primarily with the borrower; the accountant is consulted only in a minority of the cases. If an accountant is included, it is usually because the bank feels that special circumstances require his presence or because the customer has insisted upon his attendance. A good deal of hesitation is shown by many bankers in dealing directly with the accountant. The policy of most banks requires the loan executive to obtain a customer's permission in advance. Some bankers obviously fear that such a request might antagonize the borrower. However, it is also evident that most bankers feel that CPAs are usually not needed at the loan discussions. An officer of a medium-size Middle Eastern bank sums up this attitude in these words:

> The borrower is instructed clearly on what kind of financial report is required. The accountant is rarely approached, for he can get his instructions from our customer. However, if for some reason it is apparent that the borrower does not clearly understand what the bank wants, permission is requested to contact the auditor. When large amounts are involved and you are dealing with top-caliber management, it is seldom necessary to seek out the accountant.

In those cases where conference with the customers' accountants does take place, these loan executives believe that such joint meetings eliminate confusion and save time.

Although bankers are likely to talk to the borrower rather than to the accountant during preliminary discussions, many sometimes find it necessary, once the financial report is received, to discuss the data with the accountant. This ordinarily results from the bank's desire to verify certain items or procedures or to acquire additional information. It might be added that the need for such conferences would be appreciably reduced, if the borrower was encouraged to include his CPA in the preliminary discussions. Some of the reasons for consulting accountants after the statement is submitted are:

1. Clarification of data
2. Additional information required
3. Inadequacy of the statement
4. Accountant is best informed
5. Breakdown of receivables required

One loan executive cites several reasons why he found it profitable to hold frequent conferences with accountants. "It is often necessary to call on the accountant," he said, "for an analysis of receivables, the methods used in determining inventory values, and depreciation charges. Sometimes we have to specifically ask for a profit-and-loss statement or we find that balance-sheet items need verification." Another says: "Sometimes the bank requires more information on such things as stock ownerships and schedules for retiring long-term debt."

In the main, it appears that the accountant plays an important role in aiding banks to evaluate a prospective borrower's financial position. This assistance, however, is usually requested by the bank only after financial statements have been submitted.

"We could not extend credit without the CPAs." The statement characterizes the comments made by a number of bank executives who rate the work of the CPA as essential in their lending activities. Other executives appraise his services as very helpful, while a few find his work only somewhat helpful. Some typically favorable comments are the following:

> On large loans we must rely on the CPA's findings.

> They lend confidence to the figures submitted and reduce our research to a minimum.

In most cases we would not make a loan without a CPA's report.

The tendency to rate a CPA's services as essential increases with both the amount of the bank's deposits and the amount of loans for commercial purposes. Smaller banks in smaller cities tend to feel that their personal knowledge of local businesses reduces the significance of the CPA's opinion.

Bankers' opinions of CPA reports. In terms of dependability, thoroughness, and clarity, the CPA's reports are regarded with widespread favor. Bankers show a relatively high degree of satisfaction with the work of CPAs. But there are those who rate the CPA's work as only satisfactory or poor, or who think that it leaves much to be desired. General lack of explanation, nonadherence to generally accepted standards and, in particular, insufficient detail are held up as shortcomings. One banker's chief complaint is the CPA's tendency to submit fewer long-form reports:

> I am familiar with that very excellent procedure adopted by the AICPA which, I believe, is known as Bulletin 23. I am sure it is lived up to by the conscientious members of the respected accounting profession. But who, oh who, started on the short form of certificates? I recognize that it serves a useful function on the statements of large publicly owned corporations. Our primary concern here, however, is not with these but with the vast majority of our clients who are not in this category. For my part I am old-fashioned enough to like to know from the text in the report just what procedures were followed with respect to outside verification of assets and liabilities, examination of expense items, and additions to capital accounts and depreciation. I do not think I am wrong when I say that this type of report puts us in a better position to work with our other two partners in getting the kind of an audit that is most helpful all the way around.
>
> We certainly have an obligation to read all of the text in an audited report, not only the certificate and the figures. Where we do not do so, in my judgment we are making a mistake. Where there is no text to read, only the so-called short-form certificate, I for one feel that we are being deprived of information which we should have not only for our own benefit but for the good of all concerned.

In the following case, the accountant had submitted a long-form report, but the banker complained about the use of certain valuation procedures:

> I had lunch with Mr. — to discuss with the accountant what appeared to my lay mind to be somewhat irregular accounting procedure. Specifically this referred to (1) valuation of finished inventory at selling price rather than lower of cost or market, and (2) the write-up of fixed assets in the amount of $39,000 to conform with what the president of the company (not an independent appraiser) considered to be the current replacement cost of the shop equipment. In the words of the treasurer of the company, this write-up "had the effect of increasing net worth by $39,000 and thereby would make it easier for the firm to obtain trade credit."
>
> I should mention that the accountants' long-form report contained voluminous notes which fully explained all of the above transactions, and there was never any criticism of lack of disclosure by the accountant.
>
> The accountant acknowledged that the valuation of finished inventory and write-up of fixed assets was not particularly good practice, but that since

some of the various accounting manuals or authorities quoted precedent for such accounting treatment, he was therefore absolved as long as he disclosed the facts in his comments. Technically, I suppose the accountant is correct. However, I still maintain that it is desirable for a balance sheet to be so drawn that it will, insofar as possible, stand on its own feet without the necessity of wading through voluminous comments in order to interpret it. I also believe that there are numerous instances involving a small company with limited financial management ability when the accountant has a moral, if not legal, obligation to argue forcefully in favor of sound accounting practice, regardless of what the manuals may quote in the way of precedent. It goes without saying that the banker should back the accountant up in such an argument, and in the case at hand, we did back him up.

Bankers' suggestions for improving CPA reports. What might the CPA do to serve better the special needs of bankers? Again, a plea for more detail is generally heard:

The aging of receivables is not consistently done. Furthermore, reports should always identify stockholders and officers and give stock-ownership breakdowns if possible.

Contingent liabilities should be given in detail. Also the reconciliation of the surplus is a must.

We need more on the aging of receivables and the balances of inventory. Surplus reconciliation and stock ownership of closed corporations is also lacking.

The report should show if the tax returns have been audited by the government. We would benefit from age data on receivables and payables. We feel that the statement should be signed by the men who made the audit, not just the firm name.

Some audits do not break down inventories. We also need a better classification of assets.

We need more specific breakdown as to current and deferred assets and liabilities.

We would like to get the statement prepared for management which includes complete schedules.

Another banker offers a comprehensive explanation of how a CPA's report should be designed and what it should contain:

On new borrowers we want the latest fiscal-year-end financial statement plus comparable statements for the previous two years. Statements are to include the complete unqualified opinion of the auditor, with letter of transmittal. Financial data are to consist of: the balance sheet, profit-and-loss statement, aging of accounts receivable, bank loans (if any in existence), detailed breakdown of inventory as to raw materials, work in process, finished goods, reconciliation of the net working capital, reconciliation of the surplus account, reserves for doubtful accounts receivable, writeoff of bad debts on accounts receivable, auditor's notes on the company's tax status (covering the last year examined by the federal tax examiners), reserves set up for taxes, comments on any unusual items that need explaining such as "investment," long-term debt when created and how it is amortized, any restrictions relating to working capital, payment of dividends or other restrictions in effect as a result of long-term debt, dividends paid during the year, dividends declared, complete explanation of any contingent liability, sales commitments, purchase commitments, changes in treasury stock account if any, breakdown of bank lines in existence, a list of the stockholders if a closed corporation, management survey containing opinion as to capability of management, changes that have recently occurred or are contemplated in the company's basic policies, production, items produced, diversification, complete breakdown in the profit-and-loss statement of cost of goods sold and, of course, the accountant's signature. This represents my ideal of what we should get. What we do get is another story.

Most loan executives would welcome a great deal more data from the CPA. By way of summary, the items which are most in demand include:

1. Aging of receivables
2. Breakdown in schedules
3. Inventory breakdown
4. Reconciliation of surplus and net worth
5. More notes of explanation
6. More information on customers' tax status
7. More long-form reports
8. More uniform presentations

Bank customers' opinions of the CPA's services. Most loan executives believe that businessmen are generally satisfied with the services performed by their CPA. Some businessmen feel that the fees are too high. A number of loan officers regret the fact that accounting costs preclude more assistance to small business. A few bankers claim that their customers want more interpretive reports and constructive advice. Other criticisms include the businessman's lack of knowledge of what CPA services are available and their value to him, slowness of service, a need for more complete reports, and the nonuniformity of accounting procedures. Here are some typical suggestions:

Many businessmen feel CPAs don't offer enough constructive criticism and they have to pump them for comment or advice.

Some businessmen feel that fees charged by CPAs are too high. However, in most cases in this category the businessman does not realize the value and work involved in the job that a CPA does.

More long-form reports should be prepared. They would come as a natural result of a better selling job by the CPA.

CPAs should supply more complete information on the various phases of their clients' businesses.

The principal area for improvement lies in analyzing the financial conditions and offering suggestions for improving internal control, cost analysis, and accounting systems.

More uniform compliance with accounting procedures.

Speed of service can be improved. CPAs should be in a better position to suggest tax savings by being better informed on the subject.

CPAs should explain the amount of work involved in preparing a financial statement to prepare the customer for his bill.

They should provide service to the small business at a lower cost—perhaps on a clinic-type basis.

Many businessmen would like more attention to improvements in their methods of business management.

They should train client's bookkeepers better to follow the suggested system.

CPAs should demonstrate that their services are not only for tax purposes and to discourage dishonesty, they should show that their services provide other benefits such as helping business in securing credit, supplying statistical data, etc.

Bankers' views on the CPA's importance. While some bankers believe that a CPA's value to his client is equal to that of other professional men and consultants, such as lawyers, insurance counselors, advertising agencies, labor-relations consultants, and management engineers, others place the value of a CPA at an even higher level:

The CPA is of greater importance—the frequency of need puts the accountant in the vital category.

The CPA should rank first. He is one of the greatest assistants to business, and he is needed constantly.

Each has his own value, but, in my opinion, the CPA should be rated tops.

Some feel that the CPA's importance is contingent upon the size of his client. For example, one fairly large bank says: "The CPA would probably rank first in small and medium-sized businesses—probably lower in large businesses where labor relations and patent problems may make these specialists more important. Besides, these companies frequently have one or more CPAs on their own payrolls." A few executives fail to rank CPAs equally with other consultants and specialists. One reason for this, it is felt, is that individual CPAs have failed to measure up to their opportunities.

There are bankers who suspect that their own opinions might be higher than those of the CPA's clients. "The CPAs are of equal or greater value in our opinion," one of them said, "but probably not in the eyes of their clients who tend to look upon them as a necessary evil. CPAs need to do a better selling job on the value of their services." It seems reasonable to conclude that CPAs are valued advisers in the eyes of commercial-loan executives.

CPAs as a source of bank business. Most bankers recognize that the CPA himself can be a source of new business. It is common practice for CPAs to refer clients to their bank for a loan. Some bankers comment as follows:

Close relations have been mutually beneficial.

Some accountants refer their clients because they are familiar with our procedures and requirements through long association.

Yes, this is quite common. The CPA is an important source of business.

It is fairly common to get financial assistance for the client. It is more frequent with the smaller companies.

Desirability of frequent contact. An overwhelming majority of bank executives feel that frequent contact with CPAs is desirable in order to exchange views on common problems. "Frequent meetings would be beneficial to all," says one, "but the CPAs are too busy." The following indicate the pattern of bankers' comments:

Very little contact except when a loan is being considered for a client of theirs; there are now no casual visits.

They very seldom drop in to see us except in connection with the affairs of a particular client. However, the local Robert Morris Associates chapter and the local CPA association have joint meetings frequently at the committee level. This is very helpful but I would prefer more individual contact.

Very little contact. I feel that bankers and CPAs should be better acquainted and accountants should stop by the bank more often to discuss common clients, especially when an unusual problem exists.

Most of the CPAs we have dealings with drop in, discuss their work, and get the bankers' point of view. We feel that such contact is highly desirable.

The views of a small minority are reflected in such statements as these:

Personal contact has only occurred at this bank twice in the last two years. Wouldn't say not desirable, but serves little purpose. Such contacts should be confined to the joint interviews when borrowers bring their CPAs in when arranging for a loan.

We very rarely see a CPA. Don't think such type of contact is particularly worth while.

Occasional joint meetings are fine but individual contact is not desirable. If every accountant approached us, we'd have no time for our work and neither would they.

Bankers' general criticisms of CPAs. Some loan executives' observations may throw some additional light on CPA-banker relations.

They should speed up their services.

Unfortunately they don't all live up to the high standards set by their title.

It would be helpful if uniform methods were used by CPAs for treating the profit-and-loss statement and the financial balance sheet of contractors, builders, etc. They should be the same whether for taxes or other purposes.

Some CPAs are too concerned with holding the client and sometimes tread too close to the ethical line.

Most CPAs accept work which does not allow them, because of price, to do an acceptable job.

The CPA should not replace the management in negotiating for credit, and he should not accept more work than his staff can handle.

We feel that the businessman would benefit materially by enlarging the scope of his accountant's engagement. Many an accountant is hampered in the completeness of his work by money limitations placed by his client.

Steps the CPA can take. What can the CPA do to improve his personal relations with the local banker? Here is what some firms are doing:

1. Club, church, and civic activities provide an opportunity to get together with the banker outside the normal working situation.

2. Occasional luncheons appear to be effective. Some bank officers invite CPAs to lunch with their credit men to discuss generally their respective problems. There is no reason why the CPA could not take the initiative in this respect.

3. CPAs should make a continuing effort to get permission from their clients to discuss their affairs with the clients' bankers. Similarly they should encourage the bankers to impress upon their customers the need for closer CPA-banker contact.

4. Some firms make a point of telephoning the banker when a client's statement is to be used for credit purposes to offer further assistance if any explanations are desired.

5. Many banks have periodic meetings of their credit men and some CPAs have had the opportunity to attend or participate in them. More frequent invitations might result if the CPA would make himself available.

6. When specialists have been developed within a firm, the bankers should be made aware of their particular talents.

7. Occasional visits by the CPA with the local banker to discuss how well his reports have met the bank's needs and to explore other common problems are favored by many bankers.

8. Some CPAs take the initiative in bringing their clients and bankers together. One practice is to select several clients for individual meetings with their bankers during the slack season to discuss the client's specific financing problems and plans.

Other action which the CPA can take includes the following:

1. The maintenance of high standards of performance, including proper supervision of the staff to insure that the firm will be proud to have its name associated with all of its work. Bankers feel that good long-form reports are an important manifestation of the quality of the work. Therefore, these reports should be well written and consideration given to including a statement of source and application of funds and other special schedules when the reports are to be used for credit purposes.

2. By familiarizing himself with bank operations and requirements, as well as with general business conditions and economics, the CPA is in a bet-

ter position to represent the profession of business to both banker and client.

3. Many bankers evidently feel that CPAs are not aggressive enough in selling needed services to their client. This suggests that CPAs should be less reticent in encouraging their clients to make use of such services.

4. Active memberships in local, state, and national organizations, in addition to their other benefits, impress the banker with the willingness of the CPA to keep up to date and broaden his professional qualifications.

Since the CPA is, in a sense, the middleman between client and credit grantor, he cannot expect the banker to make all the overtures. More group meetings of CPAs and bankers appear in order. However, there is a limit to the value of group-exchanged ideas. These ought to be supplemented by exchanges between individuals, and CPAs would be well advised to make a greater effort to cultivate bankers. It cannot help but benefit all concerned.

THE SECURITY ANALYST AND FINANCIAL STATEMENTS

The following material was written by a security analyst.

The importance of financial statements. To an analyst, financial statements represent the most important tool in appraising whether or not a given security represents a good or poor value, and without adequate financial statements there could be no intelligent investment made. When any company comes to a prospective underwriter to discuss the sale of an issue of stocks or bonds, the first request is for a complete set of financial statements covering recent years' operations. To a very considerable degree the final decision of the underwriter, not only as to how the issue should be priced, but whether he is willing to do the business at all, is based on what is shown by the financial statements. But this is not all. While the underwriter may be willing to examine the company's own reported figures, before he proceeds he will insist that the statements receive a stamp of approval by means of a certificate from an independent CPA.

The first step involved in the underwriting of a new security issue is the establishment of contact between an interested company and prospective underwriters. When the company decides whom it would like to have as an underwriter, that underwriter will first of all want to know the financial history of the corporation. He probably will wish to see at least a five-year record of detailed balance sheets and income statements and, while company prepared figures may be perfectly acceptable in a preliminary way, he will want a review by an independent CPA before he signs up.

Selection of the accounting firm. Unfortunately, there is some tendency on the part of some underwriters to feel that this audit or review must be made by one of the national accounting firms. The principal reason for this is that a portion of a new offering of any size is usually sold outside the home territory, and if the statements are certified by a local firm which is not well known elsewhere, the thought is that there will not be as much confidence in the figures as would otherwise be the case. In other words, it is felt that the use of a well-known name adds prestige. On the other hand, some feel that any competent CPA, so long as he is independent, should be perfectly satisfactory.

Registration statement requirements. Once an agreement has been reached between the issuer and the underwriter, the preparation of a registration statement begins. There must be a certified balance sheet as of a date within one year unless the fiscal year has ended within ninety days prior to the date of the registration filing, in which case it may be as of the end of the preceding fiscal year. There must also be a balance sheet as of a date ninety days prior to the filing, but this need not be certified. Profit-and-loss statements for each of the past three fiscal years preceding the date of the latest certified balance sheet, as well as an interim income statement up to the date of the unaudited balance sheet, must also be supplied.

In addition, there must be similar consolidated statements filed if any subsidiaries exist and statements must be given for any significant nonconsolidated subsidiaries or affiliates. Appropriate information must also be given on various items of financial history, such as revaluation of property, restatements of capital, discounts and expense on previous issues of securities written off, and changes in surplus. All of this falls into the realm of the auditor. Once the registration has been filed, the SEC is free to come back for additional information or explanation and until the Commission is satisfied on all points, the registration cannot become effective to allow the offering to be made.

It is also customary for an underwriter to include in his agreement with the issuer a provision that for a period of years the company will supply the underwriter with certain interim figures, although ordinarily company figures are satisfactory so that no full audit is required. These are not necessarily published, although an analyst likes to see quarterly figures made generally available. It goes without saying that the more up-to-date the figures, the more intelligent his interpretation and conclusions can be.

Accounting practices. The trend of expanding the information given in footnotes to financial statements is well thought of by analysts. Frequently these footnotes will reveal facts which are of major importance to the security analyst in his examination of the figures themselves and in his appraisal of the security. He deals in financial information and the more of it he can obtain the better he can do our job.

One problem which is sometimes encountered is that in comparing results of two or more companies, it is found that their accounts are not always kept in exactly the same manner. This is particularly true with the oil companies, but it does occur in other industries as well.

The accountant's opinion usually includes a phrase to the effect that the financial statements have been prepared "in accordance with generally accepted accounting principles." However, recent writings by some of the leaders of the accounting profession have stressed the fact that two different methods of accounting which lead to significantly different results may both be described as following "generally accepted accounting principles." Obviously any qualified security analyst recognizes these factors and weighs them in his conclusions. The uninitiated public, however, many times is not aware of such differences. Therefore much importance is attached to complete and explanatory footnotes in the certified financial statements.

Recommendations by the security analyst. For some years the National Federation of Financial Analysts Societies has had an active national committee on corporate information, one of whose principal functions deals with the matter of improved reporting by managements and financial public relations in general. A few years ago this committee worked with a committee from the AICPA on the preparation of certain accounting research bulletins. The committee also has done considerable work with the SEC with respect to the material contained in the 9-K reports and some time ago the form of this report was changed to incorporate the changes suggested by our group. This has led to the availability of a great deal more interim income information·

Much of the activity of this general committee has been related to studies which have been made through subcommittees on annual reports of a considerable number of industries. These have concluded with general recommendations for improvement in the reports themselves and in some cases companies have adopted them. While these recommendations relate to the annual report itself and not just to the financial section, the latter does receive some comment. The suggestions pertaining to some of the industries may be of interest.

Merchandising companies

1. Report roughly the product mix between hard goods, soft goods, and home furnishings, with definitions (department store and mail-order houses only).
2. Report the square feet of space employed, and the number of units. Discuss location and the degree of modernization.
3. Report the gross margin (or cost of goods sold).
4. Report salaries and wages and fringe benefits, and the average number of employees.
5. Report real-estate costs with adequate definition. Also report rent and a summary of lease terms, including as a minimum the amount of fixed rent.
6. Report the square feet of space added in expansion, and the cost in terms of investment or rent obligation.
7. In the message portion of the report, place emphasis on the reasons for changes that have occurred, on current trends, and on the outlook for sales, prices, and major expense items.

Agricultural equipment industry

1. Report sales breakdown by divisions or some similar classification.
2. Capital expenditures in past periods and planned for the future deserve more attention, and changes in property accounts and related reserves should be detailed.
3. Foreign business and the methods by which it is handled and included

in operating results demand more detailed information.

4. Receivables and the method of financing them and the accounting methods employed are not handled in a uniform or generally satisfactory manner.

5. Detailed information regarding labor contracts and their expiration dates, pension funds, employee benefits, etc., is desirable.

6. The expenditures for research and its importance in terms of new products should be reported.

7. The management's report on operations should emphasize the reasons for the year's results, the current prospects, and the future outlook.

Installment finance industry

1. Present income accounts by the divisions engaged in finance, insurance, etc., should provide separate balance sheets, at least for finance company and insurance company operations.

2. Discuss financial requirements and dividend policy.

3. In automotive installment financing, add to breakdown of receivables purchased by type of paper, the proportion of retail automobile volume represented by new and used cars, the average maturity and average size of notes, the percentage with recourse, and Canadian purchases.

4. Provide a breakdown of maturities of outstanding receivables by semi-annual periods.

5. Provide information as to amount of bank loans available, amount of such loans in use, and other short-term commercial paper outstanding, as well as annual aggregate cost of such current borrowing in dollars and in per cent.

6. Disclose loss reserves and loss experience in terms of applicable receivables and in terms of historical experience. Comment upon the trend of repossessions and delinquencies.

7. Discuss accounting practice with respect to deferred income.

Other similar studies have been made on the casualty and fire insurance industry, the drug industry, aircrafts, nonferrous metals, railroads and office equipment.

Recommendations for greater uniformity. Bringing about greater uniformity of reports is not easy. Different tax problems, earnings and dividend requirements will result in varied corporate policies. CPAs' efforts over the years clearly indicate that they as well as the analysts want to see more complete corporate reports. Corporate reporting can be made more consistent if even these items are included in annual statements:

1. Figures for cash flow, particularly by petroleum companies

2. An explanation of why taxes paid vary from normal rates

3. Normal depreciation separated from accelerated amortization

4. Insurance companies' explanations of their equity in unearned premiums

5. More information on methods of valuing inventories, giving the base period for Lifo and the cushion or variation between market and book value

6. Finally, the problem of price-level depreciation. Managements which have made no provisions for replacements which are expected to be far in

excess of depreciation reserves should alert their stockholders to the problems that may lie ahead.

From the security analyst's point of view inclusions of these items would go far toward improving the quality of annual reports as well as stockholder relations.

Emphasis so far has been primarily from the point of view of stocks, because that is the type of security which is of most interest to individuals. The same general factors, however, apply equally to bonds.

Analysis of bonds. Since a bondholder is nothing more than a creditor of the corporation, analysis of bonds by the analyst must be similar to that which a commercial banker or other lender would make. Obviously, what they are both interested in is the ability of the corporation to pay interest when due and principal at maturity. The chief difference probably lies in the fact that bond credits generally extend for a longer period of time than is normally of interest to the banks or finance companies. The attractiveness of any given bond issue or any given credit depends of course on the rate of interest and the soundness of the loan, and here the old law of risk versus return applies. The credit man and the security analyst therefore really have an identical problem, that of determining how secure the company's finances and business prospects are in terms of the amount of the loan, and they must also use their judgment as to what the proper interest rate should be, considering the quality of the loan. There can be no precise formula laid down to determine what this should be, since security analysis is not an exact science and relies to a considerable extent on the experience and judgment of the individual analyst. Nevertheless, the basis for determining a company's credit standing and the true value of its outstanding bonds, both essentially depend on investment analysis.

The accounting profession and security analysts have a great deal in common. Dealing with security issues, both new and existing, requires the analysts to depend on financial statements and the men who prepare them for much of the material on which their judgments and analysis are based. There are of course other factors which must be considered, but it is the accountant's product which is the real essential to the analyst and his clientele in determining what security issues are most desirable for use in investing clients' funds.

CO-OPERATION WITH SURETY COMPANIES

The importance of financial statements. Suretyship is not insurance. There are three parties to a surety bond: the principal who is primarily liable, the surety which guarantees the principal will perform his duty or obligation, and the obligee in whose favor the obligation is issued. In insurance, the insurance company assumes the full risk and is liable to pay any resulting loss. The premium received is presumed to be commensurate with and sufficient to cover the hazard involved. However, in suretyship, the surety company, in theory at least, assumes little risk, since the principal, supported where necessary by supplementary safeguards such as cash collateral, joint control of securities or accounts, additional third party indemnity, and so on, stands between the surety and loss. The premium is in effect a service charge to compensate for the credit extended and the service rendered by the surety.

This element of credit, which is generally present in all lines of suretyship, makes it necessary that an important factor, if not the most important factor, in determining the acceptability of a risk by the surety, is the financial standing of the applicant as reflected by a current financial statement. Here the paths of the accountant and the surety come together, in that a financial statement of the applicant prepared by a CPA is essential to a proper evaluation of and prompt action upon the case in hand. Another factor is assurance that the business and accounting methods of the applicant are modern and efficient. Here, too, knowledge by the surety that the services of a CPA are a part of the system is helpful to the case.

Representatives of the AICPA and representatives of the surety industry have worked together on specific common problems. A review of the results may well be of interest.

The CPA and defalcations. Some years ago the AICPA expressed concern over the then increasing frequency of suits asserted by surety companies against accountants to recover losses sustained under fidelity bonds covering employees whose defalcations were not discovered by the CPA in auditing the accounts. The surety-claim man, in handling an employee dishonesty loss, is ever alert to the possibility of salvage from any proper source, such as from the defaulter himself, his family, or, through subrogation rights, from any concern which may have been involved to the extent of becoming legally liable to the insured and thus likewise liable to the surety. In the case of a loss committed over a considerable period of time, with one or more outside audits during such period, the surety occasionally concluded the accountant was negligent in the performance of his work and thus instituted suit for the amount involved. Such actions were in most part due to a misunderstanding of the responsibilities of the accountant to his client.

Agreements with the AICPA. Representatives of the AICPA, in submitting the problem to the surety industry, argued that audits, particularly those leading to the certification of financial statements, are not generally undertaken or designed for the purpose of discovering employee defalcation. It was also pointed out that it was to the mutual interest of accountants and sureties to avoid legal proceedings unless affirmative wrongdoing was involved. A committee of the AICPA and a committee of surety company executives considered the problem and proposed that certain procedures be followed in the handling of such cases in the future. These proposals were acceptable to a majority of the surety companies and the agreement entered into ten years ago is still in force and effect. Briefly, the agreement provides that no claim shall be asserted against a member of the AICPA unless in the opinion of an impartial panel gross negligence is involved. It further provides that if the surety pays a loss under a fidelity bond it shall submit all the facts to a committee of three persons appointed jointly by the AICPA and the Surety Association. Should the committee conclude that gross negligence is involved, the surety may then assert its claim.

The plan has eliminated much litigation which might otherwise have occurred, and has contributed to the strengthening of understanding and good relations between accountants and surety executives.

Co-operation in the fidelity field. A fertile area for mutual co-operation between accountants and sureties is in the so-called fidelity field. In the underwriting of fidelity risks the surety must have confidence that the insured conducts its operations in a businesslike manner, and that its method of operation and internal control is reasonable, supplemented as far as possible with periodic audit by an outside CPA. As a matter of good business, it is advisable for surety companies to recommend to their clients the advantages of the services of a CPA. Similarly, it would seem prudent for accountants, in dealing with a client, not only to point out any weaknesses observed in the system of internal control and to make suggestions for improvements to the end that the danger of employee dishonesty may be minimized, but also to recommend the advantages of fidelity-bond protection, explaining that while internal controls and CPA audits are a necessary part of good business management, such procedures should be supplemented by appropriate fidelity-bond coverage.

A further and more recent example of co-operation between the AICPA and the surety industry is represented by a booklet published under the title *Safeguards Against Employee Dishonesty in Business,* prepared jointly by the AICPA and the Surety Association of America. This booklet is designed to provide business management with a basic guide to sound internal control against embezzlement, together with an outline of the protection afforded by fidelity insurance. The booklet has had a wide distribution. It has proved and will continue to prove beneficial to the accountants and corporate sureties.

CPA's role in proving the loss. Still another area for co-operation is the period immediately following discovery of an employee dishonesty loss. An accountant is often engaged to assist the employer in proving the loss under a fidelity bond. In such matters, the security of the interests of the insured, the accountant, and the surety can be improved through mutual co-operation. The character of the factual proof required to substantiate the loss will depend upon the kind of fidelity coverage in force, the amount or amounts thereof, and the period or periods of time during which the defalcation was committed.

Many times a company has received in respect to claims filed under fidelity bonds, reports of CPAs engaged by the insured. Generally speaking, these reports are prepared with great care and diligence and, from the viewpoint of the insured and the accountant, serve their purpose. Frequently, however, such reports do not contain sufficient information to enable the surety to pass upon the question of its liability. It is suggested that the first important step for the accountants, when engaged to investigate a defalcation, is to examine and study the form of bond and, with the consent of the insured, to consult with the surety so that all pertinent facts regarding the coverage may be available to him. From the surety standpoint, it is important to determine who caused the loss and the amount thereof. When the loss occurred should be made the subject of special study. The date on which each item of loss occurred is likewise important. Defaulters frequently kite their stealings, robbing Peter to pay Paul. It is the date of the original default which establishes the date of liability. If a claim is presented and the dates and items of loss are missing, it may be necessary for the surety to make a re-audit, thereby causing an undue delay of adjustment.

In this connection, it should be mentioned that there is a trend toward the writing of fidelity bonds, especially in the bank field, on a discovery rather than a loss-sustained basis. Briefly this means that the protection applies in the amount of coverage carried at the time the loss is discovered rather than the amount in force at the time the dishonest act or acts were committed. Thus, where the discovery plan is operative, the factual information necessary to support the proof of loss is reduced considerably.

Under an approach with full co-operation between accountant, insured, and surety, the insured will benefit through prompt recovery from the surety. The accountant will benefit in that he may proceed directly with the job and may avoid work which has no bearing on the claim. The surety will benefit in that the claim may be disposed of as quickly as possible and to the satisfaction of the insured.

Claims against public officials. The public official field, comprising state, county, town, village, and other municipalities where surety bonds covering the honesty and the faithful performance of duties of municipal officers and employees are required, presents another area for co-operation between accountants and surety companies.

The surety, in determining the acceptability of a public official risk, is, of course, interested in the extent of the official's duties, his responsibility for the acts of deputies and subordinates, the business methods of his office, how he safeguards funds for which he is responsible, how he may relieve himself of depository liability, and the character and frequency of audits. While the auditing of the accounts of public officers is rather generally conducted by regular employees of the municipality, the surety at times can insist, as an underwriting condition, upon periodic audits by an outside CPA.

Of course, should an accountant be called upon to assist a public body in preparation of proof of loss under a bond covering a public officer, the mutual benefits of co-operation previously mentioned in regard to fidelity bonds apply with equal force to such cases. If the claim is made up entirely, or consists partly, of items of loss caused by the principal's failure in faithfully performing his duties as distinguished from acts of dishonesty, naturally additional particulars should be developed. Also, it should be borne in mind that the surety under an official bond is often liable for the acts of deputies and subordinates, even though the principal himself be entirely honest.

An article in a New Jersey newspaper some years ago mentioned the fact that a CPA, in making a city audit, discovered that a substantial amount of treasury certificates held by the city were in the form of bearer notes. The accountant promptly arranged to have the certificates converted to the name of the city, thus improving the position of the city and indirectly that of the surety which carried the bonds on the city officials.

Surety companies can and do benefit from the services of CPAs in the field of fiduciary suretyship. In estate matters fiduciaries of large and complicated estates are encouraged to have their accounts prepared by CPAs. Periodic audited reports prepared by CPAs, in some cases, are accepted by the surety in lieu of pressing for court-approved certified accounts.

Bonds for special situations. Another class of bond in which the services of an accountant are important to the surety underwriter is that of miscellaneous indemnity bonds. Usually these bonds cover special situations and are tailored to fit a great variety of business transactions. In most cases the extension of credit is involved. Therefore, the prime factor in determining the acceptability of the risk is the financial standing of the principal as reflected by his financial statement. Particular weight is given to statements prepared by CPAs in the evaluation of and prompt action on any given case. The accountant may be able to perform a valuable service for his client by suggesting the use of surety bonds to cover some particular situation in which his client either requires protection or may wish to offer protection to another against some business contingency.

Bonds guaranteeing the faithful performance of contracts for construction work, such as the erection of various public and private buildings, construction of roads, bridges, and dams, are an important class of corporate suretyship. This field offers accountants and surety executives another opportunity for co-operative action.

Contracts for the construction of public works are usually open to competitive bidding. Each bidder is required to furnish a bid bond and, if his proposal is accepted, a bond guaranteeing the faithful performance of the contract and a bond guaranteeing the payment of labor and material bills.

The underwriting of these bonds depends largely upon the character, capacity, and capital of the contractor. The surety endorses the obligation assumed by the contractor. In effect the surety lends its name to the contractor to enable him to secure the contract, whereas the banker lends money to the contractor to enable him to carry out the contract.

An important factor in the underwriting of this class of bond is to determine that the contractor has sufficient working capital to finance the contracts under way and the new contract he proposes to bid. Therefore, the underwriter's analysis of the financial statement submitted by a contractor has an important bearing on his decision. Comparatively few contractors engage CPAs to set up proper accounting and cost records and to audit their books. Accounting systems used by contractors range from the pure cash-receipts-and-disbursements basis to the accrual method either on a completed-contract basis or on a percentage-of-completion basis. Some contractors use a combination of cash and accrual method of bookkeeping, and still others keep books on one basis for tax purposes and report on a different basis for credit purposes. All of this has caused confusion in the minds of bankers, surety underwriters, and credit men.

By reason of the lack of uniformity in the treatment of current assets and current liabilities in the balance sheet, it is difficult to determine accurately the working-capital position of the contractor. At times the accounting method used in the preparation of the statement is not clear; nor for that matter, because of the varied terminology, is the nature of certain items appearing clear in the statement.

An attempt has here been made to cover the more important fields wherein co-operative effort is in the interest of the accounting profession and the surety industry. As a greater number of accountants and surety executives acquire more knowledge of each others' responsibilities and objectives, these and other areas will be developed to their mutual benefit.

THE ACCOUNTANT'S PART IN LABOR-MANAGEMENT RELATIONS

The accountant has emerged as a major figure in wage controversies. The briefs and arguments of unions and managements are crammed with accounting data, interpretation, and controversy. Both sides use the best accounting talent at their command. Both have been using, increasingly, accounting arguments in presenting their case and whatever one's attitude toward this development it may be helpful to be acquainted with the facts and their implications. Accountants' services will probably be more frequently called upon in the future in connection with the following three major aspects of labor-management relations: (1) preparation for negotiations, (2) actual negotiations, and (3) efforts to obtain public support. In addition, accountants render other services to labor-management relations such as payroll and social-security accounting, setting up and administering incentive systems and credit unions, preparation of union financial statements, etc.

Preparation for wage negotiations. Companies calculate the effect of wage changes on their financial position in terms of cash balance, working capital, budget, perhaps breakeven point, and probable profits at different wage concessions. Unions may use company financial data to estimate the ability of the firm to pay. There is, however, an important difference in the procedures: the company usually estimates *future* ability to pay; the union, limited in the available data, tends to figure in terms of *past* ability to pay.

Actual wage negotiations. During wage negotiations both employers and unions may use financial data to prove inability or ability to pay, respectively. The principle of ability to pay is at times applied by arbitrators.

Public support. Financial data are being used to get support from union members, employees, and the public for a position taken in bargaining negotiations. Examination of many union and company documents show that appeal for public sympathy is the major purpose of financial documentation and analysis. In the increasingly fierce and close battle to enlist vital press and radio support for one's cause, financial data are used.

It should be noted that when a company finds it necessary to reduce wages or to refuse a wage increase, the union leaders' position with their membership will be made less difficult and there may be a general gain of employee understanding of the company's position if a demonstration and explanation of inability to pay can be given.

Finally, there is a tendency for the size of the bargain to affect increasingly larger units, to cause more serious economic chain reactions with the issues more bitterly fought. Collective bargaining is becoming less private and more public in its impact. Hence there has been increasing governmental intervention in the form of fact-finding boards, some of which, particularly in steel and on the railroads, have taken account of the financial position of the companies involved.

Deciding what information to give. In the quest for financial enlightenment in labor-management relationships certain criteria will help management decide what information is called for. The accountant should analyze the nature of the request for financial data, i.e., whether it appears to be reasonable, unreasonable, or a misconception. He should advise management on the propriety and fairness of furnishing these data. He should particularly advise management on the probable inferences which may be drawn from any piece of information furnished. Likewise, he should particularly advise management as to the probable effect of furnishing fragments of information, out of context, in response to specific requests. The dangers of using such fragments are obvious, yet in its efforts to present a fair picture management and its accountants may be accused of failure to co-operate if they decline to furnish isolated bits of information without relation to the whole financial picture. The criteria for furnishing financial data are in general related to the reasonableness of the requests for information. Among the requests usually considered to be reasonable or necessary are those involving information which:

(1) Can be obtained anyway in the company's annual report, SEC and proxy statements, investment houses

(2) Aid in advancing the mutual objectives of labor and management or help in reducing or reconciling a difference of objectives

(3) Support the company's desire for an appreciation of its problem or aid labor in the proper exercise of its functions.

The interpretation of reasonable might be varied with the degree to which good faith exists between the two parties, the extent to which actual or potential disagreements arising out of financial information can be settled, and the expense involved in furnishing the data. Disclosure becomes mandatory when the NLRB holds that the information requested of the company was needed by the union. Reasonable requests for information would include explanation of accounting and financial terms and their interrelationships. Labor demands for information which may damage the company's executive position should not be complied with.

Misconceptions of accounting data. One of the most important functions of accountants in labor-management relationships relates to their assistance in clearing up misconceptions. Such errors tend to be particularly frequent in union comments on depreciation, profit calculation and representation, surplus, inventory appraisals, and reserves.

Some unions seem to consider depreciation as an accumulated sum of money available for the financing of wage increases. The amount contained in the surplus has also come under close scrutiny in union comments. Surplus and reserves are frequently believed to represent funds consisting of cash hoarded up by the company. Some people assume that the company does not know what to do with the surplus, and ask that this fund be disbursed as dividends, wages, and taxes.

A part of these difficulties appears to be semantics. Popular usage of such words as surplus and reserves is different from technical accounting usage. This problem may be overcome in time if the AICPA recommendations to abandon use of these words are more widely followed.

The real opportunity for accountants. The use of accounting and financial data in labor-management relations is an established fact. It is likely to spread. It raises a number of serious problems, such as the competence of those handling accounting data, the validity of accounting concepts, and the methods of presenting financial information. Specifically, if accounting is to be more useful in labor-management relations, there may need to be improvements in adapting accounting knowledge to the ability to comprehend by those concerned with it.

All this points to the need for co-operation of accounting, economics, and statistics to improve the measurement of revenue, the contributions of the different factors of production, and the sharing of gains on the basis of mutually agreed fairness. The field of industrial relations would benefit particularly from the competence which the accountant could bring to it.

THE CPA IN COMMUNITY SERVICE

The accounting profession can be permitted some satisfaction in the degree of participation by CPAs in community affairs. The almost legendary belief that accountants do not assume the public service obligations of professional men because they are a breed apart has been effectively refuted.

A survey conducted a few years ago by the AICPA's public relations department with the help of outside analysts showed that at least three-quarters of the members of the AICPA were engaged in *some* community service activity and that roughly 50 per cent of the membership were affiliated with *three or more* community service organizations. These figures seem to indicate either that the modern auditor never developed the protective shell described by Elbert Hubbard as cold, passive, noncommittal, and unresponsive or else he has had it stripped from him by the demands of mid-century American life.

Traditionalists need not fear that CPAs have suddenly blossomed en masse into community busybodies. The survey revealed that a great deal of public-service work has been done by CPAs for many years, even while the profession sometimes berated itself and talked wistfully of the benefits that *would* be derived if accountants *could* accept some community responsibility. Too, it showed that CPAs do not discharge the professional obligation of service to the community just with the scratch of a pen on a membership application. They actively served as officers or committeemen in more than half of the religious, civic, fraternal, educational, and charitable organizations to which they belonged.

In what capacity do CPAs serve? In church groups, for example, where it is not unusual to find a high proportion of membership to the number of people who participate in administrative affairs, over 60 per cent of the respondents said that they not only belonged to a church but sat on its governing body. The same was true of civic, business, and youth organizations. CPAs served more frequently as committeemen than as officers in these groups, but again the percentage of those elected or appointed to a position of leadership was well over the half mark.

"It is refreshing to see that CPAs are being asked to serve not merely because they do a good job keeping records, but also because their mature judgment is valued," was the way one CPA put it. But accountants in general would not agree with this observation. The consensus seemed to be that "no matter what organization I belong to, it is only a matter of time before I am serving as treasurer." And to some degree this is a valid statement. Community organizations receive a staggering amount of free professional accounting service, as accountants gravitate naturally to financial positions.

On the other hand, some of the respondents maintained that they render *no* accounting service to any of the organizations in which they are active, and some of these CPAs belonged to as many as seven or eight groups. The familiar cry that "most public service organizations put CPAs on the finance committee and then expect them to handle all the bookkeeping" does not stand up under the evidence of the survey. Only a few of the respondents doing community accounting work performed a bookkeeping service, with the bulk of what was done performed by young CPAs for their church group.

Apparently, accountants do not uniformly like being assigned or elected to the office of treasurer. Some seem to feel that this is a secondary assignment, one which is won by default and not by recognition of competence or personal popularity. But should professional accountants lament serving their communities in a capacity for which they are unchallenged in ability? Some CPAs think not. "I believe I can make my greatest contribution by doing what I do well—giving financial advice," said a respondent who was treasurer of no less than five organizations, "and I have discovered that the confidence in a public-service group is almost automatically strengthened when the members know that a CPA is handling the finances."

Desire to serve. Accountants who participate in community affairs have a tendency to picture themselves as exhausted pioneers. The comment "I don't know how much longer I can go on like this" is typical. It is an example of the feeling held by many accountants that they were carrying an inordinate share of the public-service load in their communities.

This plainly is not the case. Some accountants avoid community-service work because they still believe that it will force them into needless controversies ("I do not intend to get into an argument with a client's wife over the school budget"), and a few frankly admit that they have neither the desire nor the inclination to participate ("I have an aversion to public appearances"); but the survey proved that the community-service responsibility had been surprisingly well distributed among the members of the profession.

For example, the younger accountants, saddled with the problems of starting a career and family, still contributed a considerable amount of time, but they were not as active as the older members of the profession. One young CPA, who himself did not have time for outside activities, managed to fulfill his community obligations by proxy. "My wife is quite active," he explained, "and every time she joins a new organization, I know it won't be long before she brings the books home for me to give what she calls 'a quick audit.'" Another staff accountant summed up the general feeling of the younger group toward public-service work with this comment: "Much is lost by individuals who, in trying to make good with the firm, do not participate in community activities."

As might be expected, AICPA members between the ages of thirty to forty-five were the greatest givers of public service time. The slightly smaller contribution of time by those over forty-five is well complemented by the larger responsibilities they assume in community affairs. The senior age group is inclined to be more active in charitable and civic organizations (possibly because these are positions for which one is selected on the basis of experience and proven leadership), while accountants in the middle-age bracket are slightly more active in church, educational, and youth groups (organizations to which a good family man might belong). The young CPAs top their older colleagues in participation in the activities of fraternal organizations and businessmen's clubs (perhaps because these are groups to which one may apply for membership).

The survey provides an insight into the changes in interest which take place during a man's career. For example, as a CPA grows older, his degree of participation increases in church, charitable, and civic organizations; decreases in fraternal organizations; remains the same in businessmen's organizations; and increases in, then decreases in youth and educational organizations.

Regardless of size, accounting firms in all parts of the country indicate a desire to encourage employees and partners alike to devote a reasonable amount of on-the-job time to community-service work. The problem, of course, is to determine what is reasonable, particularly as far as employees are concerned. When a firm does not define its policy, the younger CPAs tend to limit even their off-hour activities, accepting the lack of encouragement as a sign that the firm frowns on too much outside activity. This, it seems, can cause an unexpected employee morale problem: "The firm where I was previously employed did not encourage participation in community affairs, which resulted in [a staff member] thinking of himself as just another hired hand," said one staff accountant.

Each year accountants spend thousands of man-hours installing accounting systems, drawing up budgets, auditing records, and preparing financial statements for community-service organizations ranging in size from the Ford Foundation to the East Pulaski Little Leaguers. Both of these organizations happen to retain a CPA on a fee basis, but a surprising number of the other groups in this category, especially the smaller ones, do not pay for the professional accounting service they receive.

It is impossible to determine from the survey's tabulated results whether CPAs have pushed or been pushed into the role of civic leadership; but the statistical fact remains that at least one-third of the respondents held what would have to be called prestige positions in their communities. Taking random samples, the record shows that CPAs serve as: trustees of hospitals, universities, libraries, and art museums; presidents of community theatrical clubs, symphony groups, and opera companies; and directors of the local United Fund, Red Cross, and Boy Scout organizations. Several CPAs serve as mayors, many act as city councilmen, and many more head important civic planning commissions.

Many survey respondents expressed concern over the lack of publicity CPAs receive for their community activities. "The local press always notes the occupation of several lawyers who serve on a civic committee with me, but invariably omits the CPA title after my name," said one AICPA member. If reporters, community-service groups, and the general public were occasionally reminded in a dignified, modest way that a person is a professional accountant—*a certified public accountant*—there would be fewer complaints that "CPAs as a group do not get sufficient recognition for their public service activities." One respondent wrote: "Of course, I enjoy seeing my name in the paper now and then, but I also am proud of the letters 'CPA' after my name. Where possible, I have always insisted the title be used, and in this way I feel I am doing my share to see that the profession receives credit for my small contributions."

In summary, it is tempting to try to draw a profile of the typical member who participates in community-service affairs:

1. He is in his early forties, married and the father of two or three teen-age children.

2. He lives in a city with a population of 100,000 or more, and travels each day to an office in which he and two or three partners earn comfortable livings.

3. He belongs to a church, attends services regularly, and has convinced the church clerk that his way of keeping the books has some merit.

4. He seldom misses the Wednesday meetings of his luncheon club, but frequently skips lodge night.

5. He audits the books for his church once a year, acts as treasurer for his luncheon club, and serves as chairman of the auditing committee for the local United Fund.

6. He thinks he'd like to cut down on his community activities "next year," but does not yet realize that he has been nominated by the school board to draft the financial presentation which will convince the taxpayers that Bexley High needs that new gymnasium.

CO-OPERATION AMONG ACCOUNTANTS

CPAs have demonstrated professional co-operation through the activities of the AICPA and the state CPA societies, which appoint committees, discuss the issues, and disseminate information; but true co-operation will result only from the efforts of individual accountants. The profession can never accomplish the desirable goals, unless everyone realizes that there is a shortage of qualified accountants and that the only ones who will be displaced are those who perform incompetent and inefficient work.

National and international accounting firms have grown to meet the need of performing audits and other special work for large corporations. At the same time, small accounting firms are equally important in the accounting profession and in our economic system. The large firms are sometimes engaged by clients of small firms to certify financial statements in registration statements for sales of securities. The quality of work of the small firm may not be questioned, but the underwriters may insist that a well-known firm be engaged for practical business reasons. In a few of these instances, both firms have continued satisfactorily to serve the same client in different capacities.

Referrals. The referral of specialized work from one CPA or firm to another is presently a rare occurrence. The medical profession is sometimes cited as an example of general practitioners and specialists working in co-operation with each other. The medical specialist, however, usually does not perform the services of a general practitioner, whereas the larger accounting firms offer not only specialized services but also audit and tax services of a general nature. One of the principal obstacles to referrals has been the feeling of many accountants that they might eventually lose a client completely by referring him to another accountant. Nevertheless, numerous cases can be cited where specialized work relating to management services or taxes has been done by other accountants without disturbing the original accountant-client relationship. The solution can come only through the actual demonstration by CPAs and firms of a spirit of co-operation and courtesy in these situations as they actually occur and the realization that the benefits of such an approach may be mutually advantageous.

Consultations. In a few instances, individual practitioners or small firms have engaged larger firms to consult with them in a confidential manner on special tax questions and other problems. This arrangement appears desirable from the standpoint of everyone concerned. Arrangements could also be made for consultation between accountants on a continuous basis whereby questions could be asked by letter, telephone, or in person, and fees for this service could be billed periodically. No valid reason appears to exist why more of this could not be done, and the net effect undoubtedly would be an improvement in performance for the profession.

How consultation services can be offered on an organized basis is demonstrated by the continuing education program of the Michigan Association of Certified Public Accountants. This postaudit review program is implemented on an individual basis rather than on a group basis. Bearing some operational resemblance to the AICPA's CPA consultation service, it is original in that it has initiated in Michigan a more or less formalized procedure aimed at one continuous objective: the gradual upgrading of CPA reports.

With the full knowledge and approval of the clients involved, the operation of the review service is as quoted below from a Michigan Association release (quoted with the Association's permission):

A member of the Association may, upon his request, have his report and working papers reviewed after the report has been submitted to his client. This program is based on the premise that a realistic contribution can be made to a CPA in his professional development if reports and working papers are reviewed objectively and criticized constructively by a reviewer who is not a member of the examining firm.

A review panel composed of members of the Association has been selected and each review will be made by a member of this panel. If a practitioner desires a review, he will submit his request to the office of the Association either by letter or telephone, and the request will be referred to a subcommittee of the Committee on Professional Education which is responsible for the administration of this program. A member of the subcommittee will then arrange an appointment between the practitioner and the reviewer. After the appointment has been arranged, only the practitioner and the reviewer will participate in the conduct of the review.

Each review under this program will be informal. No written report will be made by the reviewer but the practitioner may, if he desires, make notes for his own files regarding suggestions that the reviewer may have. Any discussion between the practitioner and the reviewer will be absolutely confidential, and the reviewer will not communicate his findings to anyone other than the practitioner. The reviewer will not receive any fee for his services, but the practitioner will be expected to reimburse the reviewer for any travel expenses incurred in conducting a review.

In our preliminary announcement of this program in the January 1961 issue of *The Michigan CPA*, we stated that we did not know of another similar program in use in any of the fifty states. Although the new program is basically a review program, it can be distinguished from any other review program now known to be in existence in the following two respects:

1. It is entirely *voluntary*. Reports and working papers will be reviewed under the postaudit review program only upon the request of a practitioner.

2. The sole function of the program is *education*. The findings of the reviewers will not be published or be used for disciplinary purposes, *under any circumstances*.

Developing a Practice

Starting a Practice

■ MANY NEW ACCOUNTING practices are being established successfully to serve clients other than large national corporations. Many of these new practices are in communities once considered too small to support a public accountant. Unfortunately, there has been a rather high mortality rate as well, since all too many practices have been started without sufficient planning and foresight.

Because the decision to open a public accounting office is one of the most important which the CPA will make during his professional career, he should know as much as possible of the experiences of those who have been successful and of those who have failed.

The accountant who plans to start his own practice may be an employee of another firm, a teacher who has been doing some accounting work as a sideline, an accounting employee of a corporation who has had an opportunity to observe the procedures of public accountants, or a governmental-agency representative employed on accounting or income-tax matters. Whatever may motivate him to consider developing his own accounting practice, he should make a careful study at the outset of those factors the possession of which are likely to mean success and the absence of which may mean failure. How much training is needed? How much previous experience is necessary? How much money will be required? What type of practice is anticipated? Which community should be selected? At what time of year should an office be opened?

These and many other questions should be considered well before the new practice is undertaken. If they can be answered satisfactorily, and if the accountant is willing to apply the high standards of conduct and professional skill established by the profession, his new venture can provide a successful and satisfying future.

DECISION TO TAKE THE STEP

Before considering the many factors involved in starting an accounting practice, the CPA who is contemplating taking this important step must first ask himself the most important question of all. Does he have the character and temperament required to practice a profession *on his own*? There will be no employer to make decisions; all decisions will henceforth be his. He must be willing to use his own judgment and accept full responsibility. He should bear in mind the high rate of failure of new businesses in general. There is always this risk and he must be willing to take it. There will no doubt be sacrifices required in time, effort, and perhaps even in his standard of living. But if a CPA is aware of these challenges and is still willing to accept them, he will find that the development of a successful accounting practice can be a most rewarding experience.

GETTING AN EARLY START

The time for a CPA to plan his independent practice is not when he has the CPA certificate in his hand, but rather when he first decides to become an accountant. This cannot be overemphasized.

The young accountant's most important advertisement is his personality, which at his early stage of development, may be all he can offer. But this is not to be scoffed at. People must have confidence in a person before they will entrust him with their business affairs. If this confidence is built up through years of acquaintance, possibly beginning in undergraduate years or while a member of a social club, and extended through the years, the young accountant will find that he is actually getting clients from people he has groomed himself and not merely strangers who question his ability or at least have not had enough contact with him to develop confidence in his abilities.

DESIRE TO SERVE

The profession of accountancy owes its remarkable growth in no small part to the fact that so many of its members have had as one of their foremost ideals that of service, to the business community as well as to the profession. This ideal has been so outstanding a quality of so many CPAs as to mark it as one of the primary qualifications for success in the profession. The young man who contemplates the establishment of his own office should first take inventory of his qualifications of character, temperament, aims, and interests. He should resolve to conduct his practice in a way that will lend dignity and respect to his profession. His new venture should be approached, not with the idea that it is a springboard to immediate financial success, but rather a profession which can provide a good and satisfying future in work well done and in friends acquired—a profession in which he can acquire the respect of his community.

However, there are many other things to consider. Except in rare instances, financial returns will seem discouragingly slow in the early years, as is the case with most professions. The accountant will have to prove himself in the beginning, and this in itself is a slow process. Those clients who will first come to the new office may want only bookkeeping jobs which may not test the full qualifications of the accountant. This type of job must be anticipated and the accountant should endeavor to keep it from dulling the vision of his original aims and ideals.

A practice of one's own provides an opportunity for the independence that accompanies self-employment and for the exercise of leadership. But it also provides its burdens. It will require self-reliance, self-discipline, and the ability to struggle through many discouragements. It requires the courage to exchange a regular monthly pay check with sick leave, vacation pay, bonuses, and social security benefits, for an uncertain future. It means exchanging supervised employment where difficult decisions can be passed to higher authority for the acceptance of personal responsibility. If the accountant has the qualifications, the courage, and the will to serve, the establishment of his practice has an excellent chance of success.

EDUCATIONAL REQUIREMENTS

The accountant's possibilities for success are enhanced greatly if he has received a CPA certificate and can practice as a CPA. There is general agreement also that a four-year college course with a major in accounting and study in related fields is extremely important. Many accountants without a college degree have established practices, just as many lawyers still practicing obtained their training by "reading law" as apprentices with a law firm. However, with the problems confronting the accountant becoming increasingly more complex, it is becoming more difficult for him to render competent service without a sound basic education.

Accounting concepts and procedures have shown continuous development over a period of years, thus increasing the need for continuing education for the accountant. Many young accountants have supplemented their basic education by taking night school courses or correspondence courses. Since tax laws and interpretations change constantly and since much of the early business of the new practice will grow out of income-tax return preparation, as much time as possible should be devoted to the continuing study of income-tax regulations. In a sense, the accountant who would progress never finishes his education.

PREVIOUS EXPERIENCE

One of the chief causes of failure of new accounting practices has been the lack of sufficient experience. The problems confronting the management of a small business can frequently be as difficult to solve as those of a large enterprise. Small businesses as a rule do not have the ablest of internal accountants, budget directors, financial advisors, and tax specialists. The management of a small business frequently has little or no knowledge of the importance of records or the value of financial reports. When problems related to these matters confront these businessmen, their best source of help is the CPA. It is essential, therefore, that the accountant obtain as much background experience as possible if he is to perform a proper service.

Previous practical experience in the field of public accounting is an absolute requisite for anyone planning to start a practice, either in his own behalf or as a partner. While the amount and extent of experience needed is somewhat difficult to define and can be established only within rather broad limits, some of the essentials of adequate experience can be described. The most important factors in this respect are: (1) quality of experience, (2) diversification of experience, and (3) length of experience.

With regard to experience the most important factor is quality. This attribute will be determined in considerable measure by the type of office in which the experience was obtained, qualifications of the supervisors, and character and ability of the accountant himself. The accountant should have the quality of experience that would result in promotion to the position of senior accountant at the least. The quality of experience can be gauged to a considerable extent by the type and extent of assignments which the employer has been willing to entrust to the accountant, the responsibilities which the accountant has been required to assume, and the decisions he has been compelled to make. A good measure of the quality of experience is whether or not the accountant has had complete charge of numerous reasonably important engagements.

A second important factor in experience is diversification. Unless the accountant plans to devote his time to a specialized field, he soon will find that he will be dealing with widely varying kinds of businesses. Therefore, it is obvious that he should have as general and comprehensive a participation as possible in the providing of accounting service for many types of business. Ideally, the accountant should try to determine the kind of community in which he hopes to establish his practice and then endeavor to gain his experience in an accounting office in that type of a community.

The minimum length of time required to obtain sufficient experience is generally considered to be three years. The time factor is affected by the training and ability of the accountant himself, the quality of services performed in the office in which he is employed, and the rate at which greater responsibilities are passed on to employees. The time required to obtain sufficient experience can be held to the minimum if the accountant has had the supervision and guidance of an experienced CPA.

FINANCIAL REQUIREMENTS

It is important for the accountant who hopes to establish his practice to determine as accurately as possible his financial requirements for the early period of the practice. Financial requirements will include provision for living expenses, office fixtures and equipment, office rent, operating supplies and expenses, salaries, and contingencies. These requirements will vary with different communities in different sections of the country.

Of course, any attempt to estimate one's financial requirements must give effect to such factors as the number of clients immediately available and the income that may be anticipated therefrom, the keenness of competition, the individual's capacity for making sound contacts, and the good fortune to obtain new work in the early months.

The amount of time required for a new practice to become self-supporting will vary with the circumstances, but this word of caution has been offered:

> Plan on at least five years. You might accomplish your goal in less time but you should certainly not count on it. If you plan to have a net income of say $7,500 after five years in practice, you can quickly figure out how much you will need to carry out this plan, assuming that the growth of your practice is steady.

> Marshal all the resources on which you can depend to fill the gap. These might include borrowing power, a rich uncle, a working wife, a part-time job which would not interfere with your public work, or a substantial savings account. Whatever the source, you can determine the sacrifices that you will have to make.

> In forecasting your budget, do not count on more than 1,400 hours per year of chargeable time. At first you will undoubtedly get in more, but you will be unable to keep this up indefinitely and, in the long run, you will find that even 1,400 hours is exhausting. You will also find that, as your staff grows, you will put in fewer productive hours yourself because nonproductive administrative and executive duties will consume some of your time.

While it should not be inferred that this is a typical case, the story of one practitioner's early struggle is presented to show how it is possible to make the most out of the least. This CPA started with no more capital than his last regular pay check.

1. He was fortunate in having a wife who could type. He and his wife therefore arranged to devote some of the space in their home to an office and she agreed to be the secretary-typist and answer the telephone.

2. He was able to obtain a part-time position to supplement his income. While the position did not match his professional attainments, it was only a temporary arrangement and served to subsidize his income until his practice became self-supporting.

3. He arranged to spend little or nothing the first year on equipment and tax services. He did buy one used typewriter and rented other equipment as necessary. For an adding machine he used his head. He was fortunate in having a friend with a tax library which he was able to consult whenever necessary.

4. He and his wife worked out a personal budget and stuck to it. They made a special point of avoiding any fixed overhead expenses, such as installment purchases, while they were getting the practice going.

As further proof of his success he submits his first profit-and-loss statement for the period from April 1 to March 30 of the succeeding year. He comments that he would not advise others to start on the first of April, but despite this, he did not make out too badly.

Fees collected		$3,523
Stationery and postage	$246	
Rental of equipment	27	
Professional dues and permits	53	
Tax service (first quarterly payment of subscription beginning in January)	42	
Purchase of used typewriter	81	
Total expenditures		449
Excess of collections over expenditures		$3,074
Income from part-time position		2,489
Available for personal expenses and expansion of practice		$5,563
Personal expenses incurred according to budget		4,800
Available for expansion of practice		$ 763

At the end of the first year he felt that his practice would support an office together with some modest investments in equipment.

In closing he said he certainly did not want to give the impression that starting a practice was easy. It was rough going and he and his wife had to make considerable sacrifices. But after five years he felt that it had all been worth while and not so bad as he had been led to believe by the literature on the subject.

APPRAISING THE COMMUNITY

In past years young accountants setting out on their own frequently opened their practices in the town in which they were employed, in the community where they were reared, or in their wife's home town. This choice has the advantage of providing a wide acquaintanceship at the outset, but this is offset frequently by many disadvantages. The community so chosen might not otherwise offer the best prospects for a public accountant. Frequently it is difficult to compel a healthy respect for professional ability among lifelong friends. Also, it is extremely difficult to maintain a fee scale on a professional level with friends of many years' standing.

If the possibility of some compelling reason for selecting one particular community is excluded, then the individual should select several communities in the general locality in which he would like to live, and the potentialities of each should be determined by as thorough a survey as possible. Such a survey should include such questions as:

1. What is the population of the community and the subordinate areas?
2. What is the trend of growth of the community as compared with other communities of comparable size?

3. What are the potentialities of the community for growth, and what is its attitude toward growth?

4. What is the degree of prosperity of the community in comparison with others surveyed?

5. What is the relationship of prosperity of the community to that of the state and nation?

6. What is the ratio of business to the population in the community and the subordinate area?

7. How diversified is business and industry? Does it consist of a few large or numerous small businesses?

8. What is the trend of growth of business and industry—has there been steady growth through the years, a downward trend, or erratic development?

9. Is the general nature of business and industry such that it will expand, slowly decline, or perhaps eventually move to a more suitable locality?

10. Is there general full-time employment, seasonal employment, or is employment relatively unpredictable?

11. Are there any businesses of the type in which the accountant is especially interested or in which he may have specialized knowledge?

12. To what extent do business and industry lack local accounting service yet require it to some definable degree?

13. What would such required service, if performed, conservatively yield?

14. How many individuals and firms are engaged in the practice of public accounting in the community, and what is their ratio to the volume of business and industry?

Some of this information might at first glance seem difficult to obtain, but diligent effort with the telephone and city directories, together with friendly conversations with bankers, lawyers, the directors of the credit bureau, the director of the Board of Trade or of the Chamber of Commerce, and secretaries of trade and professional associations, should yield a reasonably complete appraisal of the potentialities of the community.

Small community versus large city. There is a considerable variance of opinion as to the number of businesses required to support an accounting office. From observation and experience of many individual practitioners and small firms, it is thought that a progressive community with fifty businesses, counting even the smallest, can support a small accounting office. The successful establishment of accounting practices in such small communities is the best proof that it can be done.

In general, however, the smaller the community, the less the opportunity for growth. In a large city, one could expect that one's practice might some day be as large as one's abilities permitted. In a small community there is always the possibility that one might some day find oneself limited in one's growth by the size of the community. The small community, with its slower tempo of life and lower cost of living, has a great appeal, particularly to those who have small children or who were themselves raised in a small community. Much depends on what kind of life one wants to lead.

When trying to decide between a larger city and a small community, the

CPA must consider the type of work he wishes to do. If, for example, he is interested only in auditing, then he must be cautious about a small community. While a successful practice is often started by accepting bookkeeping and monthly write-ups, it might be a long time before the CPA gets enough auditing in a small community to support a practice. Of course he can hire bookkeepers once he is established, but some accountants fail to do this. Once they have adapted themselves to doing write-up work, they can no longer bring themselves to give it up; consequently they do not develop professionally.

Formula for a survey. Having completed an appraisal of the community, the final problem is to determine just how well, if at all, the community can support the new practice. There are many towns of 5,000 population that could support an individual accountant with one or two employees, depending on how intensively the accounting service potential is developed.

As far as surveys in general are concerned, those made by experts can be very wrong. There are many examples of this. First, a location should be selected where the CPA would like to live and then its potential investigated.

Every angle should be examined to the fullest possible extent. However, two points must be kept in mind. First, people in smaller communities will probably not have too clear an idea of what a CPA is. Second, if he is an outsider, they will tend to be loyal to the local men, even the incompetents. The value of their opinions is consequently limited.

One CPA who investigated a small community obtained a negative reaction from the lawyers, who were rounding out their incomes by doing some bookkeeping on the side and so looked upon him as competition.

Beware of promises of engagements. Occasionally someone will encourage the CPA by promising to use his influence to get him clients if he sets up practice. Somehow this help seldom materializes.

As a rough guide to a possible survey approach, this CPA suggests that the following formula be applied to a small community:

1. Estimate the total annual fee potential of the area in which you are interested by first determining the population of the area and then multiplying by $2. Larger communities will tend towards a higher figure.

2. Estimate the annual fees now being collected in the area. To do this, first determine the number of people engaged in the practice of public accounting, including public bookkeeping, in the area. Consider only those who maintain established offices or devote substantial time to their work. Include in your count all persons on the staff, including bookkeepers, typists, etc. Multiply this total by $6,000. The larger communities will again tend towards a higher figure.

3. Deduct the figure determined in (2) from (1). The result will be an indication of the potential yet to be developed. Remember that this represents close to the maximum potential. Even if you plan to practice in a community with no competition, you will do well if you get half the potential eventually.

These figures are based upon a very limited and crude personal survey.

They will undoubtedly be challenged by many practicing CPAs. However, they may prove useful until some more accurate formula becomes available.

Being the first CPA in the community. Would growth be more rapid if one went to a community where no CPA was yet practicing? The thought is that the cities might offer less opportunity because of the competition from established practitioners and firms. It would seem, however, that opportunities are better in a city where established CPAs already practice. In such communities it is not necessary to do any "missionary work." Even though they might not retain a CPA themselves, businessmen usually know who the CPA is and what he does.

Bankers in the larger cities usually require independently audited statements from those who are requesting credit. In the smaller communities, most bankers still accept financial statements prepared by the businessman himself, even with estimated figures and round numbers. While bankers prefer to get professionally prepared financial statements, they will not insist on them for fear that the prospective borrower will be resentful and seek his loan elsewhere.

In the smaller communities having no previous practicing CPA, he may be identified with the public bookkeepers. Hardly a community exists which does not have at least one bookkeeper holding himself out as a public accountant. The public has no way of distinguishing between the CPA and these public bookkeepers, who are usually referred to as CPAs even though they are not, and, as a result, he will suffer by comparison. It will take a long time to build up the proper image of a CPA in the eyes of the small-town businessman. This prospect might not discourage a younger accountant who can afford to invest some years in missionary work, but the wisdom of such a move for an older accountant is questionable.

OBTAINING OFFICE SPACE

The individual establishing a new practice should be interested in a number of factors with regard to office location which can be more important than the rental charged. Assuming that the maximum rental which can be paid has been fixed, the accountant can consider these other factors. A locality should be selected which is as consistent with the dignity of the profession as circumstances will permit. Preference should be given to a well-kept business area of good repute, most likely to furnish clients, and in reasonable proximity to any actual clients. The building selected should be appropriate to the practice of accounting.

It has been well said that "business comes where business is." While the young man with limited capital may have to conserve in all possible ways, he should not be too niggardly in the acquisition of office space. If at all possible, at least two rooms should be obtained since once the business begins to grow, the services of a stenographer will be required. Privacy for consultations is extremely important and provision should be made, if possible, at the outset for growing room.

If the accountant has made a complete analysis of his available capital and has determined that circumstances are such that he cannot afford to rent an office at the outset, there are other alternatives available. Some practices have been started successfully in the accountant's home. While this procedure will eliminate office rent, it also has such disadvantages as not being accessible readily to prospective clients, the possibility of numerous interruptions to handle personal matters, and the failure to establish what appears to be a professional entity. A more satisfactory alternative is obtaining desk room in an office where the nature of the work is not incompatible with the practice of public accounting. Perhaps the best location is in a law office, since it may provide an opportunity to obtain engagements from the attorney's clients who may be referred to the accountant. Another acceptable alternative would be desk room in the office of another CPA of good repute. This alternative provides at least three distinct advantages: (1) the possibility of performing work for the firm from which he leases desk room, (2) the opportunity to discuss accounting with others, and (3) the very helpful guidance to be obtained from an experienced CPA who has himself faced the many problems of establishing a practice.

This by no means limits the opportunities of desk space to law or public accounting offices. It might be obtained in dignified real estate offices, insurance offices, engineers' offices, and so on, if suitable privacy is assured. The important thing for the individual to remember when obtaining desk space is that he should limit himself to a choice of offices engaging in activities compatible with the activities, standards, and ethics of the accounting profession.

With respect to the nature of the CPA's office space, this advice has been offered:

> Whether or not you open an office immediately will of course depend upon your financial resources, but it is best to do so. The next best thing is to share an office with another professional man, such as an attorney. Bear in mind, however, that if you do this, you will probably not get referrals from other attorneys.
>
> Possibly you will have a home which will lend itself to an office arrangement. This will very substantially reduce your starting costs, but it too has its disadvantages. Many businessmen will expect you to accept their engagements at lower rates simply because you are working at home and perhaps have a part-time job or a working wife. Having your own well-equipped office independently will give the appearance of stability and contribute toward the support of a sound fee structure.

INVESTMENT IN EQUIPMENT

As the years pass, it becomes increasingly difficult for the small accountant to practice his profession by using only traditional tools and equipment. The printing calculator is replacing the straight adding machine. Duplicated audit reports are outmoding typed reports with one original and multiple carbon copies. The complexities of the income-tax laws and the increasing demand for professional services in this field are forcing many CPAs to buy expensive copying equipment. Those who are engaged in monthly write-up work are finding it necessary to purchase expensive bookkeeping machines. More recently, the punched tape machine has also commanded attention. Many small practitioners have thus built up a surprising capital investment in equipment.

In this respect, those who start their practice in larger cities have an advantage over those in the smaller communities, since there are companies in the cities which will lease most of the above-mentioned equipment. There are also companies or service bureaus which will do typing, copying, and duplicating for the practitioner. Such opportunities to conserve initial capital are not so universally available to the practitioner in the small community.

While the price itself is of course an influencing factor, one should beware of buying secondhand equipment. Secondhand furnishings sometimes advertise themselves and may create a poor impression. Secondhand machines must be obtained from a reputable organization which will back them with a service contract.

TIME OF YEAR TO BEGIN

The time of year in which the new office is opened is particularly important to the accountant who starts with few or no clients. Generally, more new clients are obtained in a small office between January 1 and April 15 than in any like period, since many accounting engagements will stem from tax-return preparation. It is at this period that management must give special attention to its records, not only because the banker or other creditors may want financial statements but because of the requirement for filing income-tax and other tax returns. This is the time when management is most likely to think of calling on the CPA for assistance. The office should be opened sufficiently ahead of time to gain the advantage offered by the heavy amount of tax work.

The consensus among small firms is that the office should be opened in September. This will provide a period of three months in which to get the office organized and make many personal contacts. These contacts should result in some employment for tax-return preparation. On his initial engagements, the alert accountant will find many opportunities for analyzing the clients' needs and perhaps for obtaining engagements that can be performed in the slower months to follow, thereby substantially shortening the period required to get the practice on a self-supporting basis.

ANNOUNCEMENTS

Once the preliminaries of getting the office opened are completed, the accountant should be prepared to send out his formal announcements. The announcement should be a dignified, engraved card stating the accountant's name, his intention to practice public accounting, and his location. Many

CPAs believe that the individual should begin to send out his formal announcements about two weeks before he commences to practice. The announcement should omit the date on which the practice will actually begin so that for some months to come it can still be sent to additional persons without appearance of delay, oversight, or afterthought. They should be addressed by hand so as to make it more likely that the announcement will receive personal attention. They should be sent only to persons with whom the accountant is personally acquainted. Publication of cards in newspapers or magazines is no longer permitted.

The new practitioner should be very careful to avoid sending announcements to clients of other public accountants, particularly officers and executives whom he has come to know in the course of his employment by other accountants. Of course, there is no objection to his making known to such persons that he is practicing in his own behalf, if the opportunity arises in the course of conversation. The accountant should never take the initiative in such situations. Announcements should not be prepared and mailed until the accountant is thoroughly familiar with the AICPA's *Code of Professional Ethics*.

The following are samples of typical announcements.

JOHN A. JONES, CPA
Member of the American Institute of Certified Public Accountants

Announces
the Opening of an Office
for the Practice of Public Accounting

in

New Martinsville, West Virginia
210 Main Street

JOHN A. JONES
Certified Public Accountant

Announces
the Opening of an Office
for the Practice of Accountancy

with Offices at

410 Main Street
Clarksville, Ohio

In addition to the formal announcement, the accountant establishing a new practice may make personal calls upon all his friends and acquaintances to bring his new activities to their attention. He should not call upon those served by other public accountants. Personal calls may begin even before the sending of the formal announcement, and the practice may continue for a considerable period thereafter. Care should be taken that nothing done or said will detract from the accountant's prestige or that of the profession.

STARTING WITH ASSOCIATES OR PARTNERS

The young man considering the opening of an office should consider well the advantages of associating himself with one or more other accountants, either as an association or a partnership. The greatest handicap to practice as an individual is the lack of opportunity to discuss with other accountants the many problems that arise. This difficulty has been alleviated partially by the efforts of the AICPA and state societies of CPAs in making available the skilled advice of highly trained men at many regional and local accounting conferences and meetings. This has been of invaluable assistance to many individuals, but it can solve the problem only partially. An association or partnership with others of comparable skill provides a community of professional interests and skills so that accounting in all its aspects can be freely and readily discussed. Another important advantage of this is that it provides an opportunity to give and secure mutual aid within limits that are appropriate to the agreed nature and extent of the association. In addition, this kind of arrangement, making possible as it does the sharing of expenses, reduces substantially the financial burden on each individual in the early months of the new practice.

Quite frequently, a partnership or association appears to the public to be a professional entity of more responsible and enduring nature than a one-man enterprise. This is particularly true of the businessman who, when selecting an accountant, is looking forward to a continuity of service which, in his estimation, can be obtained better from a partnership or association.

The appearance and arrangement of the office has some effect on prospective new clients at the beginning of the professional relationship. An association or partnership makes possible a larger, better arranged, and more impressive office.

An association provides also an opportunity for intensive development of professional and personal relations with accountants who may prove eventually to be excellent partnership material. There is also the possibility of retention of the practice of an associate who may become incapacitated, or of ready sale of a practice to an associate following any event which necessitates termination of activities.

Many firms believe that the accountant would do well to form a partnership rather than association at the very outset, pointing out such factors as:

1. It is easier to work with others from the start than to shift from a single practice later.

2. Opportunity is provided to pool limited resources in capital, equipment, technical skill, and clients.

3. A greater operating efficiency is provided when, as partners, the accountants can combine or specialize their efforts to fit a case.

4. There is the advantage of a community of professional skill and a greater opportunity for professional development.

5. A partnership creates an operating entity of an impressive and substantial nature which can survive the death or withdrawal of an individual member.

6. Individual expense is reduced substantially.

7. The partnership makes possible the obtaining of greater value for the financial investment.

8. It can provide greater service to clients in bringing to bear on their problems the advantage of more than one point of view on complicated and debatable matters.

9. The contacts of a partnership are combined and broadened.

ENGAGING IN ADDITIONAL OCCUPATIONS

Part-time bookkeeping. There are numerous other activities in which an accountant creating and developing his own practice can engage which will be particularly helpful, not only in providing additional income at the beginning of the practice, but also in leading to new acquaintances and to obtaining additional clients.

Possibly the most important sideline occupation from a financial standpoint is that of part-time bookkeeping. It is possible for the accountant to handle several bookkeeping assignments which do not involve too much detail.

Many successful practitioners, especially in small communities, will argue that some bookkeeping is an essential part of their practice from which they can never quite escape and, therefore, such work should not be treated as a sideline activity. The partial validity of their argument must be recognized. However, the degree of professionalism of the accountant is to a considerable extent a matter not only of skill but also of mental outlook. Certainly a well-trained and experienced accountant is qualified to deal with audits, systems, tax work, management counseling, and other types of service pertaining to his profession. Bookkeeping, while an important service, requires much less skill and is not a service which only a CPA can perform. For this reason, part-time bookkeeping always should be considered a sideline activity. When entering upon such work, the individual should be alert to the possibility of expanding and developing it to the point at which the bookkeeping can be turned over to a part- or full-time bookkeeper, and the accountant can then be free to perform those services for which he is especially equipped.

The individual accepting such engagements should be aware of the disadvantages inherent in such work. First, it may establish him in the minds of businessmen as merely a public bookkeeper, thereby limiting his professional prestige. Second, it may involve him in detail work to such a degree that he will not have time for the types of engagements for which he is peculiarly qualified. Third, it is apt to engross the individual to such an extent that he will lose the perspective and vision required to handle major accounting problems. Fourth, it may lead to the delegation of all such work to subordinates or clerks, thereby causing the principal to lose that intimate touch with the basic problems of his clients which is so important in the development and retention of a clientele. Fifth, and of great importance, is that bookkeeping may occupy so much of the individual's time that he cannot keep up on his reading of current accounting literature, professional articles, tax rulings, and other matters, and he may have little or no time to devote to his professional organizations.

Per-diem work. Another supplemental occupation in which the accountant can engage is per-diem work for other accountants. This work should be recognized for what it is—a source of money and experience, and should be entered into with the full understanding that it is not a source of clients.

Undoubtedly, there are instances where per-diem arrangements have worked out so well that they have blossomed into most satisfactory partnerships. But since these cases are probably in the minority, it is important for the beginning practitioner to avoid tying himself up excessively with such commitments. Sufficient time must be reserved for the all-important job of developing one's own practice.

Other occupations. Another supplement to income is part-time employment with former employers in businesses other than public accounting. The same disadvantages are inherent here as in public bookkeeping. The accountant should use care in obtaining such types of employment, so that nothing he does will be incompatible with the ethics of the profession of accountancy. The individual may in some cases supplement his income, and in all cases he can increase his acquaintanceship, by serving as treasurer, auditor, or some other officer, of clubs and other organizations.

When engaging in sideline activities, the accountant should keep in mind that the *Code of Professional Ethics* of the AICPA require that "a member shall not engage in any business or occupation conjointly with that of a public accountant, which is incompatible or inconsistent therewith."

Many accountants have found that part-time teaching provides an important supplement to their income. It also has provided an opportunity to meet and deal with business and professional men who are seeking young graduates for their businesses. An activity in which the accountant can profitably engage, although no immediate financial returns may be apparent, is that of occupying his free time with continued study and reading.

CONCENTRATING ON VOLUME

There are those who believe that the beginner should build up his practice at first on the principle of as many clients as possible, even if this involves a direct economic loss. This means trying not to turn down any work simply because the fee is modest so long as it gives one the opportunity to prove one's competence. One should not hesitate to refuse a per-diem engagement for someone else who might pay $35 in order to earn a $30 fee for oneself. The object at this early point in the beginner's career is to *increase the base of old clients* and through them to meet other people with whom they buy, sell, consult, and compete. It is these old clients, however humble, who are the nucleus and source of recommendations to others.

Consonant with this same principle of increasing the base of clients at almost any cost except that of reducing the quality of service, a beginner might be encouraged to grasp any legitimate opportunity to purchase a small practice or individual account. It will represent only a small investment compared with that which he has already made in education and time.

DEVELOPING ONE'S REPUTATION

Many practitioners believe that, along with technical skill, the accountant who succeeds most rapidly must also have the qualities of a competent salesman. This type of salesmanship is vastly different from that of a person engaged in the selling of merchandise or tangible property. The accountant must sell personal service and to do that he must find ethical ways of bringing his name before the largest number of prospective clients in a manner that will establish professional prestige. There are numerous activities in which the accountant can engage which will prove extremely helpful in developing a new practice:

1. The development and maintenance of pleasant and helpful relations with lawyers. The practices of law and of accountancy are very closely related, particularly in tax matters, and the lawyer is frequently in a position to refer accounting matters to the accountant whom he knows and in whom he has confidence.

2. The development and maintenance of helpful relationships with bankers and other credit executives. The accountant should use every opportunity to discuss with them financial statements, bulletins published by the AICPA, and articles concerning financial statements contained in bankers' journals. No opportunity should be missed wherein the accountant can point up the value of an independent examination of financial statements to the credit grantor.

3. Joining and taking an active interest in the affairs of a civic club. In most communities many of the business and professional men belong to a civic club such as Rotary, Kiwanis, Lions, Exchange, or one of several others. One purpose of such clubs is to help members become acquainted with each other. This factor enables the accountant to become acquainted quickly with a substantial segment of the business community.

4. Joining professional and trade associations and taking an active interest in the problems of those groups. In many communities there are chapters of tax associations, accounting groups, credit associations and other organizations made up of men whose daily problems are closely allied with accounting and tax practice. Here again the accountant is provided with an opportunity to build his acquaintanceship rapidly.

5. Engaging in definitely useful and recognized community service, such as participating in fund-raising campaigns. Many practitioners have said that the accountant should not attempt to solicit funds but rather should devote his energies along the lines for which he is best equipped, such as auditing receipts, preparing financial statements, and preparing budgets. If the accountant has school-age children, he can sometimes make sound business acquaintanceships through active participation in parent-teacher associations.

6. Joining at least one reputable social club or organization and working as effectively as possible on any job that may be assigned.

7. Serving enthusiastically and effectively on committees formed for the purpose of carrying out worth-while community projects.

8. Keeping in constant and purposeful touch with all friends and acquaintances along lines of mutual interest. The accountant should endeavor to keep them informed, within the limits of courtesy and good taste, of his professional progress and achievements. He should display an equally sincere interest in their business successes.

9. If the accountant has the ability, he should accept speaking engagements before local groups. He need not be a polished orator, but he should develop ability to present points in a pleasing and concise manner. Considerable assistance can be obtained from the Public Relations Department of the AICPA in speech preparation. That department has prepared a number of pattern speeches suitable for presentation before various groups. With the use of a little imagination, these speeches can be adapted to local interests.

10. If the accountant has some writing skill, he should devote some time to professional writing. Articles not only tend to bring the accountant's name before the business public but increase his professional qualifications because of the research involved.

11. The accountant should strive to remember his personal contacts with business and professional men and to remember circumstances of interest and significance in connection with his relationship with prospective clients.

Some believe that it would be definitely helpful to keep a written record of personal contacts with individuals. In this record the accountant should note dates and circumstances of the original contact and use the record tactfully in the development of his business and personal relationships. In smaller communities where contacts are usually rather frequent and more personal, a written record of acquaintanceships would probably be of little use. By the same implication, it would appear that the larger the city the more it becomes important to keep some sort of written record of business acquaintances who are seen infrequently.

It is not enough to *join* a social club or civic group. The accountant will probably find other CPAs already members. What *is* important is that he attract others. People must like him before they will engage him. It is not necessary for him to develop what is known as "a selling personality." But if he displays sound judgment, maturity, emotional stability, poise, tact, diplomacy, and a sense of humor and humanity; if he is a leader without engendering enmity or resentment, he can gain the respect and affection that elicits the comment: "I wouldn't dream of having anyone else but ——————— as my accountant."

The ability to convince, explain, instruct, or clarify by oral communication is the mark of the seasoned professional. Speaking before a group places him before many people at one time and on a plane of esteem which creates reputation. The spoken word may be the common language of sales, but the written word is often the pedestal on which reputation rests. The power of the written word is remarkable: many an "expert" has been created because he happened to write the first words about a particular subject.

ONE CPA'S SUCCESS STORY

In the beginning, I made a point of mixing with people whenever possible; I joined civic organizations, attended various social functions, and went where other people would be. When I had no work to do in the office, I did not stay there. However, in talking with people and in making new acquaintances, I did not actively solicit practice and tried not to give the impression that I was not busy—in fact, I attempted to appear as prosperous as my circumstances would permit. It is my definite impression that the old adage "success breeds success" is particularly true for the professional man. In this respect the self-employed professional man has an important advantage over the salaried employee: the public does not know the extent of his practice. (This is particularly true in a large city.)

I found among these acquaintances that the active business and professional men—bankers, attorneys, investment brokers, salesmen—were the most helpful in securing new clients. These men are themselves in contact with many people, many of whom are in a position to engage public accountants.

Knowing other CPAs is a great help. There is much to be learned by the novice from older and wiser heads meeting similar problems. It is well to be active in accounting organizations since it benefits everybody, including the public, when CPAs co-operate with one another. Securing practice from other CPAs is possible only in a limited sense; the employed accountant cannot hope for any permanent relationship with the client. However, it is possible under such circumstances to obtain valuable experience and knowledge of new forms of procedure perhaps not otherwise obtainable.

Another source of new contacts is teaching. When I first started in public practice, I approached a local university and offered my services as a part-time teacher of accounting. My application was accepted, and I have been so engaged at least one evening a week ever since. Although I had previously avoided occasions where I might be called upon to speak in public, my uneasiness soon wore off. I have gained personally from having to prepare lectures and keep ahead of the inquiring minds of my students, and on several occasions former students have recommended me to others for accounting and income-tax services.

I have avoided bookkeeping work for several reasons. The work is time-consuming, even if done by others under my supervision. The fees to be expected are rarely attractive; and, if a CPA spends a large part of his time keeping books, his prestige as a professional man is certainly not enhanced.

On the subject of fees, young CPAs may be faced with many bitter experiences. It is, I think, a natural tendency for beginning practitioners to under-charge for professional services. Probably this is due to a lack of confidence; however, it is a fault that must be overcome if one is to develop a desirable clientele and maintain the standards of the profession. Of course, sometimes it is difficult to evaluate intelligently the amount of time likely to be involved. In such cases I either quote fees based on a per-diem rate or state a maximum over-all fee which will not be exceeded. Often a new client will inquire at the outset the cost of work he needs done, and I think this is good and proper.

I should like to add one word of caution to all young accountants engrossed in the effort to accumulate a practice: never forget the element of courtesy in receiving favors. I always send a personal note of thanks to anyone who has made an effort on my behalf by recommending my services.

Obtaining Clients

■   THE ACCOUNTANT JUST starting his practice will find that in his community there will be many sources from which to attract potential users of his service. In addition to the sources described below, it must be mentioned, for the sake of completeness, that other accountants may be a source of clients. It is not an infrequent occurrence for a CPA to purchase the practice of or merge with another practitioner. Arrangements are often made with retiring accountants or with the estates of deceased practitioners.

NEWLY FORMED BUSINESSES

A particularly satisfactory source consists of individuals and firms starting a new business. In these instances, the accountant is able from the start to point out the necessity and usefulness of proper records. Quite frequently, in such situations the accountant recognizes the client's needs much more clearly than does the client himself. This recognition offers the opportunity for an intensive development of all the client's potential requirements. The accountant should be alert to the establishment of new businesses by those whom he has come to know through outside activities.

BUSINESSES WITH GROWING PAINS

Businesses which are reaching a stage where the management begins to recognize the need for some accounting service provide a second important source of clients. Many businesses of comparatively substantial size, particularly in smaller communities, have relied exclusively on their bookkeepers for financial statements, statistical information, tax-return preparation, completion of various forms required by the government, and other services. Eventually, problems will arise which untrained personnel cannot handle, and at this point the accountant is called in. On this engagement, no matter how simple, the accountant must be prepared to demonstrate not only his ability but also his capacity to provide many services of especial value to the management.

BUSINESSES WITH SPECIAL PROBLEMS

A third source of clients includes those individuals or firms who are seeking help in connection with tax disputes with governmental agencies. This is a very common source of more permanent engagements. To utilize it the accountant must have a thorough knowledge of tax regulations and should have a Treasury Department card. Generally, this type of work provides an opportunity for the accountant to acquire a thorough knowledge of the client's records and their shortcomings. Frequently, he can acquire an audit engagement by discussing these matters with the client.

There are many other sources of new clients available, all of them providing many opportunities for development over and beyond the original engagement. More and more there are those who find that the preparation of their own tax returns is becoming increasingly difficult. Lawyers, credit agencies, and others will sometimes wish to consult the accountant in some specific case which may lead to an engagement to perform more extensive accounting service. Those who have become dissatisfied with their present accountants constitute another source of clients. This type of client, however, is frequently undesirable because, generally, a client dissatisfied with one competent accountant is likely to be dissatisfied with others.

REFERRALS

Regardless of the sources available, many accountants say that most clients will result from recommendation. Some of the sources of such recommendations are:

1. Satisfied clients
2. Lawyers
3. Banks and other credit agencies
4. Business acquaintances
5. Personal friends
6. Clubs and other organizations of which the accountant is a member
7. Former associates
8. Real estate and insurance agencies
9. Secretaries of trade and professional associations

Of course, it is helpful to the new practice if the accountant has specific understandings with attorneys whereby, within the ethical standards of both professions, the attorneys would refer clients to the accountant on accounting problems and the accountant would refer clients to the lawyers on legal problems.

In connection with any new referral, the CPA should drop whatever he is doing and follow up the lead immediately, even if it means finishing the other work at night. This is one aspect of merchandising that accountants are allowed to do.

EXTENSION OF SERVICE TO PRESENT CLIENTS

It has been well said that "we often fail to see the opportunities in our own back yard." It is important to engage in intensive development of clients already being served. Indeed, this method of increasing a practice is the very life blood of the small office. Frequently, the first engagement for a client may be little more than a bookkeeping job. The importance of such an engagement is not the immediate financial return but the opportunity it provides for additional needed service.

Such additional services might encompass systems work, budgeting, cost accounting, estate planning, and various other special projects. In a normal practice the positive merchandising of such services might increase present fee income by 15 to 20 per cent.

It is generally agreed among sole practitioners that most of their clients should have additional accounting services. In many instances there is an appreciable difference between services actually performed for clients at their request and the extent of the services which they actually need. This is due chiefly to the fact that small businessmen in many cases have not been fully informed of the actual service which can be performed for them through an audit, nor of the nature and benefits of such work. This is an excellent field for extension of service.

The accountant should take definite ethical steps to provide the services that the client should reasonably require. Some of the steps which the accountant may take are:

1. Pointing out to clients, in advance of performance, specific and significant deficiencies in the scope of services stipulated by them in relation to the objectives of the services.

2. Explaining to clients receiving nonopinion reports the fundamentals involved whereby an engagement restricted in scope makes it impossible for the accountant to formulate or express an unqualified or qualified opinion.

3. Making specific recommendations to clients in reports on engagements as to remedial measures shown essential or desirable by the outcome of the engagement.

4. Indicating to clients during the course of engagements, any steps or procedures with respect to operations, internal control, accounting methods, etc., which will be demonstrably advantageous.

CHARITY WORK

Another potential source of new business is referrals or recognition received from the so-called charity jobs. Most CPAs handle work for charitable institutions, and do so not only as a civic duty, but also because it may lead to recognition of their name as a result of the widespread distribution of the reports. While charity work may not be a major source of new business, the possibility of referrals as well as the pride derived from doing their duty make the handling of such work a must for all firms.

Helping a Practice Grow

IMPORTANCE OF QUALITY SERVICE

■ SINCE A GREAT portion of new business comes from referrals from existing satisfied clients, the importance of satisfied clients cannot be overemphasized, not only from the standpoint of continuing relations with those clients, but also from the standpoint of work which they might refer to their accountant. At any cost, the CPA must do a thorough, complete, and prompt job on any assignment regardless of how small, not only because that is what the client is paying him for, but also because in many cases new work comes from small assignments which were never expected to result in new referrals.

If a client "who can't afford more" is accepted at a cheap fee, the quality of performance should not be reduced down to the price; instead, the client should be given more than he bargained for. If the work lacks quality, sooner or later it will cause dissatisfaction. The client quickly forgets that he bargained for something cheap. He expects the same kind of service he would buy at a premium price, and when this service is not forthcoming he will let others know about it.

J. C. Aspley, in *How to Sell Quality* (Dartnell Corporation, Chicago, 1952), has phrased it this way:

> Quality means repeat orders. It means trade that stays with you year in and year out. It means that you will be able to hold what you have and add to it. In short, it means enduring success, and not success built upon the quicksands of here-today-gone-tomorrow customers.

Once a client is convinced of the real value of his CPA's services, he will realize that he cannot afford to be without him at any price.

USE OF FREE TIME

The performance of services to clients in the most efficient and useful way is, of course, essential to the healthy growth of a CPA's practice. But a practitioner must be more than a good accountant; he must be an administrator, a promoter, even a salesman. He cannot spend all of his time performing services. Time must be devoted to many other activities in order to nurture the budding practice. The big question is how to use available time most effectively.

Here are some budgetary rules for time consumption. The primary purpose of this time budget is the elimination of waste time. Putting it in written form may point up the desirability of wiser consumption, and will also tend to direct the expenditure into those channels which have the highest overall value.

Taking the calendar week as a complete cycle, and the hour as the unit of measure, the total time available for all purposes is 168 hours. The accountant estimates that sleep, eating, and other essentials account for eleven hours of his day or seventy-seven hours per week. His week is subject to great variation, but dealing with the larger portion of the year he estimates approximately forty-two hours a week are consumed on the job. For the remaining forty-nine hours, he has a certain freedom of choice. Given these forty-nine hours, he should next segregate and define certain areas as follows:

1. Professional advancement
2. Increase of income
3. Recreation
4. Individual advancement
5. Public service and charity
6. Home and family

Professional advancement. Duties to his clientele and to himself call for the devotion of at least six hours per week to this area. Under this heading he should include professional reading, professional writing, teaching, attendance at accounting lectures and courses, and time and service devoted to professional organizations. For the professional man who has completed his formal schooling, informal but carefully directed conversation with his fellow practitioners is probably the easiest and most pleasant method of increasing the scope of his knowledge. Contact with other professionals is often recommended as one of the virtues of becoming a CPA.

Reading is a much faster method of learning, since the conscientious author has weighed his words carefully, but it requires more patience and concentration. *The Journal of Accountancy* and a regular tax bulletin are suggested as minimum reading requirements. And although it might seem unattainable to some, the absolute minimum requirement for time devoted to professional advancement should be set at six hours a week.

Increase of income. Present clients are the best source of additional income. But every person with whom the practitioner is acquainted has potential value in this area. Continual and frequent contact with as large a body of personal associates as possible is the best hope for an increase in an accountant's income. Ten hours of this budget should be devoted to strengthening relationships with clients and friends on the social level.

Recreation. The tempo of the times and of public accounting being what it is, six hours per week should be set aside for recreation. Physical sport is the most important form of avocation for the accountant. The time devoted to sport or some other form of recreation, such as music or painting, should certainly be substantial.

Individual advancement. The most expert accountant will fail to impress either the layman or his fellows if he does not have a sound acquaintance with the world around him. One CPA spends four hours a week with *The New York Times* and feels that at least four more hours of every week should be devoted to such things as books, plays, museums, and music. Adult education courses are a means of scheduling a minimum time in this area and an excellent way to grow as a human being.

Public service and charity. This area needs little discussion. Whether one's preference be in the field of public or charitable action, there can be little quarrel with the appropriation of six hours per week in this area.

Home and family. Saved for last is probably the most important avocational area. The essence of many a man's intrinsic success, his success as a human being, seems to depend largely on maintaining the strongest possible ties to his family. The budget allocates to it the thirteen hours remaining, and the wise man would also set aside all legal holidays and whatever vacation time he can command to be devoted to his wife and children.

The essence of utilizing this budget is in reviewing activities to see that the required minimum time is being spent in each area. A budget, of course, is valueless if not followed. Certainly any time allocation is impossible of exact fulfillment by human beings subject to human frailties. But if the practitioner can schedule as much time as possible in each area, such as professional lectures, adult education, tennis or handball, and concert series, he will have taken a step in the right direction. And more important, an occasional review of the past few weeks will give an indication of possible shortcomings and possible future improvement.

ACQUIRING SPECIALTIES

As the scope of services performed by CPAs has been expanded to meet the needs of our competitive economic system, a natural development has been for accountants to give special attention to the areas in which they have an interest and aptitude.

The subject of specialization within the accounting profession is frequently distorted to appear as a conflict between large firms on the one hand and small firms or individual practitioners on the other hand, under the erroneous assumption that only large firms can specialize and, therefore, unfair competition results. This misconception, to any extent that it may exist, can be overcome by a better understanding of the factors involved, since they do not relate to the size of firms.

Public accounting firms of various sizes have specialized along industry lines for many years. Several small and medium-size firms have attained reputations in particular industries that have extended far beyond the localities in which they have offices. Unusually good opportunities for firms such as these exist today, because clients are giving much greater attention than ever before to the experience and qualifications of the firms they engage.

Reputation as a specialist must, of course, be based on solid knowledge of the subject, but it can be enhanced by speaking and writing about it. When a new type of business is found among one's accounts, one should study and analyze it, write about it in the trade journals, speak before trade-association gatherings, and write manuals (if only a recommended code of accounts) concerning the administrative side of the industry or its special cost-accounting or budgeting problems. One's name will fast become a byword. And the specialist's fee is always higher than the general practitioner's.

The breadth and complexity of the field appear to have become such that no individual CPA can now hope to become an expert in all areas. If such a person remains in individual practice, the probability grows that occasions will arise when he must either deny his expertness in one or more of the more specialized areas and refer his client to others, or be found wanting by the client. (Instances of the former are beginning to appear with greater frequency; for example, a small practitioner refers SEC registration or management-advisory service work to another firm with the required specialists, while he carries out the examinations for which he is well equipped.)

An alternative to referrals in meeting the problem is for CPAs to associate themselves with others in a joint practice, thereby permitting each to concentrate on, and maintain the requisite expertness in, only a portion of the whole area. This goes, without doubt, partly to explain why multipartner firms show the greater rate of expansion.

MAINTAINING ETHICAL STANDARDS

Every professional man is subjected to subtle and sometimes not-to-subtle pressures. Almost every CPA encounters the problem of the client's request for an unqualified opinion, although all the required auditing procedures have not been performed, or when he has discovered income not reported on the client's books or tax return. We all understand one universal language: self-advantage. A future practice must not be jeopardized for an immediate, short-term material gain.

IMPORTANCE OF DELEGATING

During the early days of a practice, the CPA most often finds himself doing practically all the work, whether it be junior, senior, or even clerical, for there is generally no one else to do it.

As his staff grows, however, his habits must change if his practice is to flourish. This advice is offered by a successful practitioner:

> *Don't do yourself what others can do.* Delegate and then seek new ways to delegate even more. Concentrate only on checking the work of others; work papers, tax returns, reports, etc. Spend time on educating the staff and providing the "objective look," getting off at a distance and appraising the client, his business, and his problems. Analyze clients for new services you can render them.

The education of clients to the fact that an engagement need not be handled entirely in person by a principal is a *sine qua non* to a successful practice. After all, if your income is limited (like that of most doctors and dentists) to your own billable time, you can only push back your economic horizon by increasing your hourly fee rate. Also, your total income will be affected by sickness, vacations, and sometimes even by your inability to be in two places at one time. Worst of all, perhaps you will be so preoccupied by detailing the trees that you may not adequately examine the forest.

NEED FOR ASSOCIATES OR PARTNERS

The sooner young men who are in practice on their own account realize that future demands on the practicing CPA will be greater than the talents and capabilities that one man can offer, the better off they will be. One lone individual cannot by himself render to his clients all of the services that business is coming to expect from the accounting profession. The public is rapidly beginning to recognize this, and it will be increasingly difficult for the lone wolf to hold his clients, particularly if they are growing businesses. A plural name will do much to protect the practice, since the public does not realize whether the firm of Jones & Smith is composed merely of Mr. Jones and Mr. Smith or whether it represents a large organization of talented, capable practitioners.

In the beginning, the need for a partner is not always obvious to the new practitioner. Work continues to come in and the staff grows accordingly. The first addition to the staff is usually a full-time secretary. This is followed by the addition of one or more bookkeepers and typists and usually a succession of men, most of whom are disappointing. They all start with the high resolve to be CPAs but their ardor is often short-lived. Eventually they leave for a bookkeeping position with the excuse that they could not stand the pressure.

As time passes, it becomes increasingly apparent to the new practitioner that further growth is not likely without capable help at the partnership level. Most accountants hope that at least one of the men employed will develop into partnership material, but too often they come to the realization that this is not going to happen. It then becomes necessary to try to find the right type of man on the open market. It is usually quite a shock to the sole practitioner to learn that the salary expected by the caliber of man he has in mind is uncomfortably close to his own earnings. To hire such a man, he would obviously have to take much less for himself for some time, a sacrifice he is usually in no position to make, even though he realizes that it will result in more income in the long run.

As his practice and income grow, so do his financial requirements and he has no reserves to underwrite the salary. He might borrow some money, but this is a move which he is reluctant to make. He might, by working even longer hours, take on enough new accounts so that a new man would start earning his salary in a shorter period. The trouble is, suppose he does this and cannot find the right man. And if he could find such a man, would he be able to trust him, or would he leave in a few years, either taking some clients with him or leaving behind a burden of work which once again is too big for one man to handle?

Perhaps he should keep his practice as it is and not try to grow. But there are a number of objections to this solution. There is the danger, if he decides not to expand his staff, that he might someday be offered an engagement he could not handle. If he turns down such an opportunity, word would get around and he might not get another. He also fears that one of his present clients might grow to the point where he could not handle the work and would have to admit his inadequacy. He might increase his income somewhat by culling his practice, dropping those clients who are less profitable, leaving himself time to handle a few more profitable accounts. But this move does not appeal to him. He might increase his fees, but he is afraid that if he did so to any significant extent he would price himself out of the market.

Since he has always believed that if "you don't progress you slide backwards," the plan to maintain the *status quo* does not sound like a good solution.

Another plan to increase his income would be to get into some business on the side. He has had opportunities in the past to buy into a business, but has hesitated because of the risk involved and the time it might take away from his practice. His limited capital might compel him to borrow for such a venture, a move he rejected when he was considering how to finance a new man. He knows that other accountants have joined outside ventures and that some of them have succeeded so well that they gave up their practices entirely. This idea does not appeal to him, as he likes the work and does not want to divide his time and attention.

Another solution which he rejected at first keeps returning to his mind:

merge with another accountant. This, of course, would mean a partnership and would undoubtedly bring a host of new problems. The idea is a bit frightening, but it does have some obvious and appealing advantages.

First of all, there would be someone to talk to, someone with whom to share experiences and plans for the future, someone to help make tough decisions. There would be someone to fall back on in case of illness. Together, they could build a stronger and better organization than either could build separately. It would help to stabilize their incomes. Together they could better afford to get the kind of help they want, and would be able to handle larger and more important engagements. A merger would help to protect the value of his practice.

A partner would also allow for some degree of specialization, and he would no longer feel he has to be all things to all men. A further advantage would be that no great financial sacrifices would be necessary. In fact, financial benefits should be apparent fairly soon.

The need for an "alter ego" was forcibly brought home to this practitioner:

> One day in the third year of my new practice, just at the outset of the tax season, I fell ill. During the whole time I fretted in the sure knowledge that my practice (left in the hands of a secretary and a junior) was falling apart. Nothing of the sort happened. My clients developed the habit of not requiring my personal attention and appeared satisfied with the service rendered by the staff.
>
> From this I learned two lessons: Never be without a partner or strong senior staff man who has a vested interest in the business (the next sickness might last eight months, not eight days) and educate clients to expect that staff other than the principals will handle the bulk of the engagement.
>
> The right partner will supplement the fund of knowledge and skill available to clients, provide a ready listener to your individual problems, make available one more judgment for fee-setting discussions and staff-personnel headaches, and even provide, at times, the father confessor and encouragement we need in moments of pessimism.

DANGER OF POOR ADMINISTRATION

No matter how successful one has been in building a practice, poor administration is the way to lose it. Ordinarily, administration is thought of as unproductive, something that can be used to fill in between client engagements. Experience in retaining a clientele after it has been built, however, fortifies the opposite view: administration is what cleans, overhauls, and lubricates the productive machinery. If sound organization and administration are not given priority, or at least equal status, the whole production schedule or the quality of the professional product breaks down. Running one's own office efficiently is always the most productive engagement on the list.

As this CPA suggests, a change in attitude toward the operation of one's own business is essential:

> *Treat your own business as if it were a client of yours.* Be punctilious about the administrative details of your practice. Keep adequate records.

Maintain timecards for everyone, including principals. Construct a cost system by clients. Maintain tax controls and, while you are about it, be certain that your own firm meets all its obligations when due.

PROBLEM OF WRITE-UPS

In seeking to enlarge a CPA practice, there are two alternatives: doing more and more work for each client by going down to lower and lower levels of skill, or doing less and less work for each client by going up to higher and higher levels of proficiency. The first policy leads to wholesale bookkeeping. The second leads to a truly professional practice eventually ministered to a much larger clientele.

A young CPA probably must rely on write-up work as a means of starting his own practice. Even established CPA firms may make initial contracts with new clients by responding to requests for write-up service. Write-up engagements often lead to other professional accounting service.

But write-up work alone usually cannot command fees as high as auditing, tax, and management services. It is true that write-up work can be lucrative if organized and administered efficiently, with appropriate staff, or if combined with professional advice and assistance of various kinds. However, the sole practitioner who relies too heavily on manual write-up work, especially one who does all the work himself, may find that the only way to derive a satisfactory income is to work longer and longer hours. This makes it harder to improve his professional competence or to build an organization. He may become "too busy" to read or study, to attend professional meetings or courses, or to recruit and train a good staff assistant. His professional development may be impaired.

Now the situation is being complicated by the advent of the computer and the service centers. Basic data often can be converted into financial statements and statistical analyses at much less cost by machines than by manual write-up procedures. Some service centers advertise and solicit this type of work—in at least one instance through the medium of a bank. CPAs have been invited to collaborate with such service centers. This raises ethical questions. (For further discussion of machine write-ups, see page 336.)

How can a CPA carry the prestige of his title and professional qualifications into the area of write-up work, where he is competing with noncertified accountants, public bookkeepers, bookkeeping service companies, and some data processing service centers?

The answer is not for CPAs to abandon write-up work as unworthy of them. It is a useful service, often the first one needed by a new client. It can be organized, particularly now that data processing equipment is available, so that the work can be done economically without consuming too much of the CPA's time.

A sound answer to the question might be the following: If a CPA organizes his write-up engagements so that most of the work can be done by others— his own staff or client's employees—and then devotes his own efforts to services which increase the *profitability* of the client's business, he won't have to worry about nonprofessional competition. His superior education and training will show in the management-service area. But if all a CPA does is write-up work, no matter how good an accountant he is, there may be good bookkeepers who can do it just as well as he can—and may be willing to do it cheaper.

Approaching write-up work as a steppingstone to professional services requiring greater skills—auditing, tax planning, management services—may help solve a problem that seems to be troubling many practitioners. This approach seems particularly advisable when mechanization of write-up work is proceeding apace.

To sum up, write-up work is legitimate for a CPA if it is properly organized and is not all he tries to do; but if he does nothing else, and does all the work himself, can he escape nonprofessional competition or maintain his own professional prestige?

What are write-ups? While not all of the following services are performed with the same frequency by CPAs, they can all be included in the broad area of write-ups:

1. Posting all books and records including the books of original entry
2. Posting only general ledger accounts or similar controls
3. Monthly reviewing, adjusting books, and preparing financial statements without audit
4. Recording income and expenses as a basis for preparation of income-tax returns
5. Preparing sales tax reports, quarterly and annual payroll tax reports, and other county, state, or federal information reports
6. Performing all duties inherent in the work of a bookkeeper, e.g.,
    a. Preparing payrolls
    b. Keeping accounts receivable records
    c. Mailing monthly statements
    d. Preparing bank reconciliations
7. Performing certain work of a cost accounting nature, e.g.,
    a. Keeping perpetual inventory records
    b. Analyzing monthly production costs

How extensively are write-ups performed? A survey by the AICPA showed that a majority of firms of all sizes perform some kind of write-up services for clients. The first two services in the foregoing list are apparently offered most frequently. The third and fourth services are commonly offered, and somewhat more prevalently in the smaller firm.

In situations where write-ups are involved, the majority of firms do not go on to render an opinion on such clients' statements.

In all but a few small firms, experience has shown that the ratio of time devoted to write-ups to total chargeable time is greater than the ratio of fees derived from write-ups to the firm's total fees. The spread seems to be greater in the small firms. Moreover, most firms find this work less profitable than other work.

While there is no way of predicting the future of write-up work, it appears that the majority of firms of all sizes do not plan future expansion of these services.

Some practitioners' comments. The following comments indicate that CPAs' opinions vary widely as to the usefulness and desirability of performing write-up services for clients.

I have worked out this problem in my own practice by insisting that my smaller clients obtain part-time bookkeepers. I find that I need to relate to the job selection and training process fairly extensively and that turnover is distressingly high. However, I persist in my approach since I can demonstrate that my time is then released for a higher level of relationship, including such things as inventory control, budgeting, cash projections, and other management advisory work. . .

Write-up work, if properly organized, can be an area where the CPA performs a highly regarded and necessary service for small businesses at a very substantial profit. If the details of write-up work are performed by girls or even juniors with a CPA reviewing the work and acting as a part-time controller for the client, the service rendered can be more beneficial to small businesses than certified audits.

We only do write-up work for clients who are willing to pay a reasonable fee per hour. Usually they are willing to pay because they feel more secure in their income-tax position.

Write-up work, service work, monthly work, or whatever you want to call it, is the economic foundation of the small accounting firm, until such time as there is sufficient audit billing so that this type of work can be gradually eliminated.

Write-up work permits this office to retain good assistants on a permanent basis. It is also considered good training for the men, particularly in system installations and revisions.

It's needed by many a small business! By small I mean the one- and two-person office not the 100-250 employee classification! It's not professional except to the extent that it's a social contribution and appreciated by many a small businessman.

Write-up work in several instances has provided me with a more intimate knowledge of the client's operations and also has resulted in the audit engagement when the particular clients became successful enough to hire their own office personnel. This intimate knowledge has enabled me to assist the clients more fully in instances requiring more than simply a knowledge of the resultant figures recorded, such as in budgeting, division of management responsibilities, etc.

I have followed with much interest the numerous comments and articles in the publications of the AICPA regarding write-up work and firmly believe it does not degrade the professional status of a CPA if it is constantly foremost in his mind that he must not let it become the master. It will provide him with a starting point in his intended career and offer him unlimited possibilities, but it must certainly be controlled as to quantity and resultant time required.

Write-up work does lead to other types of engagements. It is very difficult, however, to overcome the client's thought that you are his bookkeeper and not a professional accountant.

After many years, many of the largest businesses in Taos, New Mexico, that had our write-up service in the beginning, now only employ us for professional work. We have a cordial relationship with two public bookkeepers in the area and often transfer write-up work to them after the initial phase. They in turn tend to send us corporation and estate-tax work.

With the use of data processing, we have been able to offer sales and cost analysis to our clients. This has met with enthusiasm at very little additional cost. We have attracted other accountants to use our equipment. Some have commanded a rate of $20 per hour from their clients. We feel that data processing is unquestionably the answer to write-up work.

Until approximately one year ago, we discouraged write-up work clients. We limited write-up work to only one or two more lucrative accounts. Since the advent of the punched-tape machines, we have begun to encourage and seek clients requesting write-up services.

It has always been our opinion that engaging in the less-qualified services had a tendency to classify us in such a group, severely limiting our potential for services and income in the larger and more difficult fields, where we were competent to serve.

Very valuable. More profitable than audits when done by machine. (Billings, 30 per cent; chargeable time, 15 per cent.)

This type of work permits us to maintain a normal staff consisting of five throughout the year. Were it not for write-up work, small firms such as ours would have the problem of trying to employ qualified men during the peak season only. It also provides an uninterrupted career for staff men.

A guide to write-up work. An individual practitioner offers his method of handling write-up work:

I would not hesitate in the least to supply whatever help is needed to bring the records up to date on books of original entry and install the general ledger accounts, but at this point there are two conditions that must be met:

1. The client must maintain the recording of receivables.
2. The business must have a good chance of success and growth, and the client must agree to hire a bookkeeper as soon as the need arises. I do not wish to be indefinitely committed to write-up work.

If these two requirements are met then I can consider accepting a further assignment if the client will agree to the following:

1. The client must maintain a daily record of sales, deposit the receipts in total, and discharge all expenses and liabilities, including payroll, by check, the check stubs indicating the nature of the charge.
2. Within the first ten to twelve days following the end of the month, the bank statement and canceled checks must be delivered to my office, together

with the daily record of sales, and the work must be called for when completed. It is necessary in most such cases to maintain payroll records and prepare
the quarterly and annual returns, as well as the employee W-2 forms.

3. The client must maintain a separate checking account for personal
expenses. The fee can be lowered considerably if only business transactions
are included in the write-up work.

4. The client should be available to answer questions on the telephone
about unusual transactions on the day the work is being done. The monthly
job of write-up work, including posting of the general ledger accounts, should
be completed in one day. This may take two persons, but if it takes longer
than twelve to fifteen man-hours each month, a bookkeeper should be hired.

5. The CPA must not hold on to a write-up job past the point where a
bookkeeper can be used more efficiently. Quite frequently the CPA will have
to train such an employee and perhaps post the general ledger for some time.
He will then be available for management services and audit of the accounts.

6. The write-up work is billed and settled monthly on a per-diem rate for
a junior. The installation of accounts, tax work, and financial statements are
billed separately at regular rates. Financial statements for these accounts are
prepared at the end of each year and as frequently as they are needed.

All write-up work assignments should be completed prior to the 15th of
the following month. This will deter the CPA from overloading his practice
with them.

Methods used in performing write-ups. At the present time, the vast majority
of accounting firms do write-up work by hand methods. A significant number,
however, make use of bookkeeping machines, punched tape, and punched
cards. A detailed discussion of the use of punched cards and tapes in
preparing clients' records appears in Section 7, pages 729-746.

SALESMANSHIP

The fact that present clients are a potential source of additional services
has already been discussed (refer back to "Extension of Services to Present Clients," page 325). One of the most valuable services the CPA can
offer to his present clients is management services. How do accountants get
management service assignments?

The question is propounded by practitioners who are competent, diligent,
and in every way capable of rendering valuable management services to
their clients, yet who are puzzled as to how to get beyond the audit and
tax-return engagements. Their training has been inadequate in only one
respect. The neglected ingredient has been salesmanship. Through the years
the practitioner has concentrated on developing his technical skills, absorbing a huge fund of knowledge, and acquiring a broad store of valuable
experience. Starting early in his training and uppermost in his mind during
practice is the canon that the ethical practitioner does not solicit accounts
nor does he advertise. Therefore, insufficient attention is devoted to the
techniques of salesmanship, public relations, and promotion.

The idea of developing a sales personality in a CPA by published articles often generates a negative reaction from many practitioners. The objection seems to be that if such articles are published, business people will learn to recognize the techniques and resent them; sales techniques should be a trade secret. But anyone who has made any study of the subject would recognize the complete fallacy of the argument. Newsstands, bookstores, correspondence schools, trade journals, and academic facilities provide a huge store of training material on the subject. These facilities are available to and are studied by business managers, not just salesmen.

As a result, businessmen have learned to expect certain characteristics of a salesman. The absence of any of these characteristics brands the salesman as inferior and he loses sales not because his product is inferior but because he is a poor salesman. The following characteristics are often ascribed to the accountant:

1. He is an introvert (happiest when immersed in books).
2. He is technically competent but unimaginative.
3. He is unconvincing—frequently suggesting new methods without proving the need (suspected of trying to build up a fee).

Perhaps an open discussion of the subject of professional salesmanship will promote a general attitude that other things will be expected of a CPA, such as:

1. He has an inquiring mind—primarily concerned about client's problems, present and future—interested in statistical history chiefly to the extent that it affords a basis for future planning.
2. He is technically competent—imaginative and ingenious in ferreting out problems, anticipating difficulties, and developing preventive measures and cures for them.
3. He makes logical and concise suggestions, convincingly presented and competently conceived, which go to the heart of the problem without burdening the client with a mass of detail.

Of course, being introverted is not the nasty thing that people have come to believe; there is a need and place for introverts. But every accounting firm needs salesmanship if it is going to survive, and that takes a different kind of talent.

Who is to do this sales job? The usual reaction is that the AICPA and the state societies must do the public-relations work. This is partly true, but neither the Institute nor your state society can call on your client and sell *you* or your abilities. Your client is not going to read reams of literature about the profession. His only contact with the profession is through you. You will have to do the sales job or it will remain undone.

The ability to communicate effectively. The sales problem cannot be reduced to a formula. A stock "sales pitch" can be detected at a hundred paces. However, there are certain stock techniques which should be expected of the practitioner. They include the ability to speak and write smoothly, logically, and convincingly, and also consideration of the client's knowledge of the subject, his temperament, and his personality. As a successful engineer stated it, "When a blueprint comes back from the shop for an explanation, the blueprint is wrong. There should be no need for further questions if the print is properly executed." The same should be true of accountants' reports, correspondence, and oral utterances. Without these qualities, sales effort may be doomed to failure.

Many accountants are technically competent to the point of brilliance. Their analytical skills scintillate and they have powers of penetration that are comparable to radar. When they sit down to put their findings into a written report their powers leave them. Their writings are often dull, stodgy, clumsy, and reveal no evidence of command of the English language, if holding reader interest is a criterion. When called upon to discuss a report orally or give a speech, they stumble, hesitate, speak in a monotone, and drone on to the end of a prepared piece. Numerous accounting undergraduates are prone to say, "Why should I study English composition, logic, and public speaking? After all, I'm going to be working with figures."

The ability to write or speak well is not a gift. Sales ability is not a gift. They are talents that are developed from hard work (1 per cent inspiration—99 per cent perspiration). One very successful salesman spent long hours before a mirror practicing speaking and studying his own mannerisms. He felt he had to sell the man in the mirror before he could sell a stranger. Successful writers say that "easy reading" means "hard writing." Easily read prose does not flow from the end of a pencil. It must be carefully planned, rewritten, reworded, and edited. It is successful only when it captures and holds the reader's attention and gets a point across.

Accountants occasionally express concern about the fact that management consultants are frequently called upon to perform work which is within the scope of the accountant's ability. Who is at fault? The blame rests with the individual accountant. True, he cannot solicit business, while a professional consultant can. But remember, the accountant is on the inside with a full knowledge of the client's problems. He is in the happy position of being able to anticipate problems. The consultant is on the outside with the serious handicap of having no detailed knowledge of the client's affairs and is a total stranger. The consultant must do a tremendous sales job to overcome these handicaps.

An obvious difference in attitude is apparent. Management consultants are sold on the services they render. They are sold on the organization they represent and its ability to do a job. They exude confidence in themselves, their careers, and the need for their services. They spread their gospel by telling people about what they do, and the better ones do not advertise. Many accountants seem to feel that if they act in the same way they are unprofessional. If CPAs have pride in their profession, confidence in their ability, and are convinced that they can render valuable services in today's economy, why should they be secretive about it?

Sales techniques. The practitioner must recognize that the knowledge and skills he has acquired are useful for only one purpose—application to client problems for better management of his affairs. In short, the skills which he professes to hold have one purpose—service to management. This would seem to minimize the need of special management service training if he takes full advantage of the talents already available to him.

In the second place, the practitioner must understand that this is a "sales job" within the framework of his own clientele. Traditionally, sales promotion is supposedly not a talent within the repertoire of the professional accountant; hence, for obvious reasons, selling of services should be confined to one's own clientele. Selling the attainments of the profession as a whole to the general public is essentially, but not entirely, a matter for our professional societies.

As a starting point, the practitioner should list from the table of contents of any comprehensive accounting reference the skills which he has and the services he feels competent to perform, setting the list up on a work sheet and ticking off the clients who need these services. He may be appalled to find how few services he is rendering many of his clients.

The next step is to plan a regular schedule of calls to discuss these needs. He may find that after several months or even a year he has sold nothing. But he will have developed sales techniques, started a few clients thinking, and convinced a few that he is interested in their problems. Eventually, he will be surprised to find that as much as two or three years later the effects of the sales effort will be felt. The client cannot be expected to presume the existence of unrevealed abilities. A CPA should not be surprised when a client calls in an expert to do a job that he could have done if he has not taken the time to tell him of his own ability to do the job and his need for it.

The next problem is a matter of presentation. One should not be a low-pressure salesman. "You don't want a budget, do you?" Businessmen want to be convinced. The fee consideration is important only in relation to the benefits to be derived. A project will not and should not be undertaken unless some potential benefit can be anticipated. If the accountant cannot convince the client of the ultimate value, the accountant is wrong or he is a poor salesman.

A problem of psychology. The matter of proper presentation is essentially a problem of psychology. Each individual will have to be approached with a presentation suited to his temperament, frequently at a time when it can be anticipated that he will be receptive. Nobody can tell how or when; it is a matter of individual judgment which, with experience, becomes increasingly accurate. Many times it is necessary to use several approaches at intervals with the same client. The object is to convince, not just to meet sales quotas.

A "back-door" approach is most apt to be successful in dealing with busy people. Endeavor to satisfy a client's wants by first presenting the conclusion, then explaining the techniques necessary to achieve that conclusion. In a recent case one client was continuously unhappy because of late and unreliable reports from his accounting department. A discussion of systems, methods, reorganization, and other improvements seemed to get nowhere. Starting at the beginning of the problem seemed to do nothing but start a mental cash register clicking. All he could visualize were added costs, expenses, and complexities. The requirements were submitted to several office-machine companies. One came up with a proposal that seemed to cover all the problems and ended up with machine-produced operating statements comparative by month and year-to-date. It was beautifully presented in a brochure.

The CPA suggested that the brochure be torn apart and reassembled, putting the financial statements first, daily cash-position report second, aging of receivables and payables report third, with the other features of the system to follow. When the brochure was presented the client was first shown the financial statements with the observation, "The system we are proposing will enable you to have financial statements like this no later than the tenth of each month." The ensuing conversation went something like this:

"That's wonderful! I want this system."

"Remember, it will cost about $7,000 for the machine and related equipment and supplies and several thousand for installation costs."

"Will it reduce personnel?"

"Probably not. Your present personnel can provide more data, faster and more accurately. The system is designed to solve your problems. Expense reduction did not enter into our thinking."

"It doesn't matter. I want this system."

The decision was made on the basis of the end result. Later he was pleased to learn from pages two and three that there were by-product reports that would be available. He never was particularly interested in the mechanics of the system which followed page three of the brochure.

Practically any competent salesman will tell you this is a common sales approach. However, some accountants attempt to sell the need of a program and fail miserably because they become so absorbed with technicalities that the client is bored to death long before the conclusion is reached. In this case, even the machine company with extensive sales experience prepared a brochure designed to sell accountants rather than management.

Consider another case. The accountants were retained by a new client of substantial proportions. He owned or controlled several companies. He had never had an audit leading to an unqualified opinion. He had retained them because he had seen some of their reports and made the statement, "Even though the reports were submitted without opinion, when I finished reading them I had no further questions to ask."

The accountants had been warned about three characteristics of this client:

1. He believed that opinion audits were an unnecessary expense.
2. He would have no part of cost systems; they were too expensive.
3. The word "budget" was anathema to him.

How would you induce such a client to change his thinking on all three points at once when your predecessor had been unable to do so in fifteen years? The solution was the back-door approach.

The conversation went something like this:

Accountant: "What are your prospects for the coming year?"

Client: "We expect to net before taxes $500,000."

Accountant: "That is not enough. After taxes, allowing for a reasonable increase in receivables and essential capital acquisitions, you will not have enough to meet your fixed commitments on debt retirement."

Client: "How much do we have to sell to meet these commitments?"

Accountant: "It is not a question of 'how much' but 'what.' We can't answer your question without some sort of product profit analysis to arrive at some conclusion as to profit margin by product. Increased sales of the wrong products obviously can reduce profit. In the absence of such an analysis we can only suggest expense control. Ideally, there should be a combination of the two with the objective of achieving a profit goal rather than just a sales goal."

The ensuing questions and answers revealed that the CPAs could not help him adequately at that point because the scope of their review had been limited. He could not help himself because he had insufficient data. Obviously, "product profit analysis" was a term used to describe better the phrase "cost system"; "expense control" was a term used to clarify the term "budgets"; the opinion audit was a logical development that would tend to assure him of complete control. So now all three phases are part of his operations. And the accountants still use the terms profit control, expense control, and annual review; never budget, cost system, or audit.

Now, what will be this client's reaction if he sees this in print? About two years after these procedures were instituted he observed, "You did a real selling job on me. You were the first ones to convince me of our need and we are sorry that we didn't see you many years sooner." He did not resent being "sold." Few business people do. Being sold merely means first being convinced and then having your convictions proved by subsequent events.

This type of approach is submitted as an example, not as an infallible business getter. It serves to illustrate only one point. A busy man is prepared to listen to you when he finds you are going to discuss something of interest to him. Let him know that much when you start to talk. Translate this into the composition of a written report. Do you like to wade through a thick report to find the conclusion? Neither does anyone else! State the conclusion first and let what follows be merely a statement of reasons and proof of the conclusion. If the report is composed with the conclusion at the end, the discussion often gets so bogged down with details that sometimes the conclusion is never reached and a lot of time has been consumed unproductively. When someone suggests "getting to the point" it is a sharp warning that all conversation prior to that moment has been wasted.

Another client may be of a different mind. He is desirous of being assured that each problem along the way is going to be solved. When he is satisfied in this respect he feels that he has arrived at the conclusion independently. The "conclusion first" technique is unsatisfactory to him. No inference can be drawn as to the respective merits of one type over another. The presentation will have to be made in the manner that suits the clients, and an understanding of the individual client is the only key to the proper approach.

In either case, the purpose must be clear before an initial interest can be kindled. Test yourself on this theory: Do you read the introductory remarks that head every article in *The Journal of Accountancy*? How many articles do you read or not read because these remarks indicate that the article may or may not be of interest to you?

Returning to the idea of a regular sales program, remember: do not hold out rosy hope for immediate results. Sometimes clients are in a receptive mood at the time of your call and you leave with an assignment that has very happily filled gaps in an otherwise slow season; sometimes they are not. But what is suggested is a basic doctrine known to every sales manager: *the salesman must make regular calls on customers.*

This, then, is the substance of that essential ingredient in developing a practice.

1. Know your product (the skill available in the profession).
2. Know your client—his needs, his temperament, his personnel.
3. Call on your clients regularly and show them how their needs can be satisfied by your skill (or product).
4. Ask for the order.

These elements are the basis of daily sales effort throughout the nation. Our profession has spent years developing its skills and techniques. Our job is to tell the consumer about it, or we will let the work go to others.

A LONG-RANGE PLAN FOR GROWTH

Quality service, high ethical standards, proper administration, and each of the other factors will all contribute to the growth of an accounting practice. But they should not be effected haphazardly. There should be a conscious, deliberate effort to co-ordinate all of the contributing factors into a master plan. Planning, then, is essential to efficient growth.

Few CPAs will find fault with that statement. But Mark Twain's old observation about the weather can be applied to planning: everyone talks about it, but no one—well, hardly anyone—does anything about it. Nonetheless, it is generally agreed in business circles that sound expansion of an enterprise should be planned in keeping with anticipated needs on the basis of a thorough knowledge of the business, its requirements, and its social and economic environment.

However, the plan must include the adoption of policies and procedures which will insure its effective operation. It must be reviewed and revised in the light of changing circumstances. It must, in other words, be managed. These are not new ideas. Much of the advice given by CPAs to their clients is in keeping with these principles. Yet, many firms apparently have no over-all plan to aid them in developing their own practices. The task of management is frequently postponed to another day—a day which never dawns.

A practitioner may seek to justify his neglect on the grounds that he is operating a professional practice, not a business, and that the growth of his firm is contingent upon the growth of his present clients. He argues that, as additional work is required, he will simply add to his staff, admit a new partner, or open a branch office. But, unless these needs are anticipated, the firm may be unprepared to take full advantage of its opportunities. Moreover, this passive approach is based on the false premise that the future is completely molded by outside forces. In addition, some practitioners regard planning as a luxury which only the larger firms can afford. It is true, of course, that the larger firm must formalize its procedures to a high degree as a means of encouraging compliance with its standards throughout the organization; but it is equally true that proper planning is equally important to the smaller firm. In fact, it is of paramount importance to the small marginal operators—marginal in terms of services rendered, not in terms of financial solvency. The CPA who provides just a minimum service to his clients can add volume only by working longer hours, but this approach is almost certain to impede the healthy growth of his firm. He will be obliged to make hasty decisions on the basis of inadequate knowledge and his mistakes will have a far greater adverse effect on his firm than on a larger organization. An error, for example, in hiring a junior accountant who proves to be unsatisfactory and must be discharged is more serious in a firm with three staff members than it is in one with fifteen or twenty where the work can be more easily absorbed by the remaining staff. Planning can also show much greater proportionate results in the small firm. It is not unlikely that a small practice can double in size within a few years, while a larger one would probably show a much smaller percentage increase.

There is, of course, no law that requires a CPA to expand his practice. He may prefer to derive a modest income from his own personal services without undue pressure, rather than attempt to build his firm or enlarge its clientele. Who can say that he is wrong? Yet, it must also be recognized that, in making this decision to restrict his practice, he may well have foreclosed any possibility of realizing his full potential. Without some assistance, he will usually be compelled to perform a number of duties which might better be handled by people with fewer qualifications.

There is still another course open to the practitioner: he can specialize. As a consultant, he can work alone and may be able to command impressive fees for his extraordinary knowledge and ability. Usually, however, he can accomplish this only after he has had extensive experience in such fields as taxes or management services and has established a substantial reputation in his community.

The plan to be outlined is not concerned with these unusual situations. It is addressed to the well-qualified local practitioner who is presently rendering the usual basic accounting services—auditing, tax work, bookkeeping, and write-up work—to a clientele of local businessmen. He aspires to develop a well-rounded professional practice, with a wide range of services, which will command adequate fees and contribute significantly to the financial health of his clients. He has access to a modest amount of capital, that is, he has either saved some money or can borrow it from a bank if necessary. He works fifty hours or more a week throughout the year in order to produce an annual income of about $10,000. He feels that in ten years he should be earning around $25,000 a year. But he finds himself on a plateau. The only way to increase his income seems to be to devote even more hours to his practice. "Where," he begins to wonder, "do I go from here?" The following material is designed to help him answer that question.

The practice as an economic enterprise. Before planning can be initiated, recognition must again be given to a simple concept: a professional practice, regardless of its nature, is an economic enterprise which has many of the elements of a business.

This is not to say that public accounting, any more than law or medicine, *is* a business. Nor does it means that a CPA must *act* like a businessman: that is, advertise, solicit, engage in competitive bidding, and focus upon profit as his primary goal. On the contrary, he can build a professional practice only by adhering strictly to the highest ethical standards.

But there is nothing inconsistent with this philosophy in recognizing that an accounting practice must be profitable if it is to render the best service. The practitioner must accumulate enough capital to enable him to improve his services. If the practice is to be successful and expand, it must be managed efficiently. If it is to be managed efficiently, the practitioner must not be so preoccupied with serving clients that he has little or no time to plan and execute his basic management functions.

In other words, while a professional practice may grow naturally, it will not build itself efficiently. The man who obtains his CPA certificate, hangs out his shingle, accepts whatever work comes along, and neglects the business aspects of his practice can hardly expect the best results. He may be able to make a living this way or even expand his volume, but he cannot *build* his practice to its full potential. Some CPAs may be born managers who execute their managerial functions intuitively. Most CPAs, however, will agree that effective management is the product of conscious effort.

The management function. All of the many definitions of "management" involve three basic functions: planning, execution, and evaluation. A good manager must determine sound objectives and develop policies which will best implement them: he must be a thinker. He must establish procedures to carry out policies and see that they are followed: he must be a doer. And he must measure the results in terms of the objectives: he must be an analyst.

These functions must be applied to a number of different activity areas within an enterprise. These might be called the elements of business, but they are as much a part of an accounting practice as they are of a manufacturing concern. They include:

1. *Research and development*: The creation and design of products or services.

2. *Production*: Making the product or service by the most economical means, in keeping with the standards of the organization.

3. *Personnel*: Recruiting, organizing, and directing the people who do the work, and providing adequate opportunities for advancement and job satisfaction.

4. *Marketing*: Directing and encouraging the flow of goods or services from producer to consumer.

5. *Finance and control*: Planning, directing, and controlling monetary operations in terms of costs and profitability.

6. *External relations*: Establishing satisfactory relations with customers or clients, the general public, and outside organizations which may be of assistance to the enterprise.

Obviously each of these elements is present in an accounting practice, although the techniques employed may vary between a business concern and a professional practice, for example, in marketing. It is in relation to these activities that plans for building a practice will be discussed.

Characteristics of the plan. As a practitioner undertakes to develop a program for building his practice, he should keep in mind the following features of a good plan:

1. *It should be written.* By forcing himself to put his plan on paper, the CPA can clarify his own thinking and relate it more logically to the various aspects of the practice.

2. *It should include a statement of the objectives of the firm.* These are the bench marks against which future progress can be measured.

3. *It should include the steps necessary to attain the objectives*, together with a rough timetable indicating when each step should be taken.

4. *It should be flexible.* A plan is not a strait jacket. It should permit modification as circumstances change, without elimination of those elements which have continuing validity.

In general terms, the plan consists of answers to these questions: Where do I want this practice to be five, ten, and fifteen years from now? What steps will it take to get there? The very act of planning is likely to reveal opportunities and needs which might otherwise be overlooked. In a sense, a plan tears down the fences of habit formed by preoccupation with daily routines.

As he begins to formulate his plan for growth, the practitioner must recognize the necessity of investing time and money in the future of his practice. He must be willing to sacrifice immediate income for future growth. Since time and money are largely interchangeable in accounting practice, the CPA can make his investments in either form. He may use his own income to provide working capital or he may borrow money from the bank to be repaid out of future earnings. He may take the time necessary for planning and execution of management functions either out of the chargeable time now allocated to clients, or out of his own time normally devoted to recreation or his family. The latter is at best a temporary expedient and, in the long run, some reorganization of his work schedule must be undertaken. In one way or another, however, he must assign sufficient hours and sufficient cash to the development and execution of his expansion plan.

Investment of either time or money demands courage. It requires confidence in one's ability to make the investment pay handsome dividends. But the risk can be easily justified: unless it is taken, opportunities for growth and increased income will be severely restricted.

Responsibility for executing the plan. Needless to say, the individual practitioner will have no problem in determining who should be responsible for developing and carrying out a plan. He is accountable only to himself for its success or failure. But he has another baffling problem: he must discipline himself to insure that he pays adequate attention to all the phases of his practice. Although he may delegate certain administrative or supervisory duties to a senior staff member, the ultimate responsibility for all of the firm's activities rests on him. But, presumably, the plans will often call for the eventual formation of a partnership. Then his situation will be similar to that of established partnerships which are planning their growth.

Some partnerships function, in effect, as an association of individual practices. The activities of this type of firm need to be co-ordinated and controlled if it is to attain the common goals of its members. Frequently partnerships may try to reach operating decisions through partner meetings. Many of these group decisions would be unnecessary if agreement had been reached on a plan which included the methods to be pursued. Although there may be some advantages to this kind of approach, it is a cumbersome way to make day-to-day decisions, especially when the time element is important.

Several major corporations a few years ago tried to apply the theory of "managing by committee." They found that two heads, while often better than one, could also collide with painful consequences. The committee decisions on planning and over-all policy proved to be effective, but the long-term results were often lamentable unless someone was clearly designated as being responsible and accountable for the execution of committee decisions. The same is true of accounting partnerships. All partners ought to have a voice in establishing the firm's plans and policies, but the failure to assign specified responsibilities for administering them can cause duplication of effort, dissension, and confusion.

How this should be handled depends both on the type and size of the firm. A managing partner may assume most of the responsibility for decision-making in many of the administrative areas. However, the managing partner in a large firm must delegate certain executive functions because the size of the operation precludes his personal supervision of all its elements. In the small firm the partners may be reluctant to surrender complete executive control to a single man unless he is clearly the dominant member of the firm. They may feel that they would be abrogating functions inherent in partner status. Besides, one man may not be best suited for all areas. It is often better to divide the various responsibilities among different partners in keeping with their abilities and interests. One partner, for example, may be charged with the task of establishing and maintaining the firm's technical standards; another may be concerned with recruiting, selecting, and over-all training of staff assistants; a third may handle internal administration, and so on. The main point is that *someone* must assume responsibility for each major activity and be held accountable for it.

Elements of the plan. *The services to be offered.* The development of any sound plans turns upon the type of services that a firm intends to offer its clients. As an initial step in planning, the present services must be analyzed to determine which ones should be expanded or curtailed, and decide whether new ones should be added to enable the firm both to serve its clients better and to utilize to the full the talents of its members. The firm, in other words, should have a good "product mix."

Bookkeeping and write-up work may be an essential part of the present practice. To what extent does the CPA wish to increase his volume of this work? Should he restrict it to a few clients who might develop into full-scale audit accounts or should he try to establish it on a basis which will make a major contribution to the firm's income? To what extent should he become personally involved or delegate work to his staff members, clients' employees, or others?

If the CPA is presently preparing a large volume of tax returns, he must answer some other questions. To what extent does he wish to increase the preparation of personal returns for officers of corporate clients or for outsiders? To what extent does he wish to encourage clients to enlist his aid in tax planning, the preventive medicine of taxes, with a view to the legitimate minimization of taxes? To what extent does he wish to enter the field of estate planning in collaboration with lawyers, trust officers, and insurance underwriters?

Does the practitioner wish to encourage clients to have opinion audits for the benefit of stockholders, banks, or commercial creditors? If so, should he accept as new clients only those who appear to be prospects for such audits? Or, in the case of small or closely held clients, should he make a concerted effort to undertake limited examinations leading to analytical reports for internal management guidance, rather than confine his work to drawing up profit-and-loss and related statements?

How far does he wish to extend his activities in the field of management services of an accounting nature, such as budgeting, cost control, systems installation, or assistance in financing? Is it desirable to get into areas less directly related to traditional accounting functions, for example, office methods and procedures, studies of work flow, and review of warehousing practices as relating to inventory turnover?

The answer to each of these questions involves consideration of how and by whom the service is to be rendered. The mere fact that the practitioner has a CPA certificate does not mean that he is competent in each of these areas. No one can master rapidly changing techniques in all of them. As each service is added to the proposed product line, the CPA must acquire competence through study or continuing-education courses or attract other people into his organization who can specialize in the field.

The addition of services will naturally stimulate the growth of the practice. As it grows, research and experimentation can be undertaken to decide what supplementary services might be added, or what subdivisions of the basic services can be identified and refined as additions to the over-all plan. For example, the tax service might be extended to estate planning, the budgeting service might be broadened to include aid in securing needed financing, and the service in controlling costs might lead to the installation of a standard cost system.

Performing the services. The production aspects of an accounting practice are, of course, directly related to the decisions on services to be performed. Nothing can be produced until those decisions have been made. But since the objective is to provide a quality service by the most economical means, production techniques may well determine in part the desirability of a particular service. Bookkeeping and write-up work can be cited to illustrate alternative approaches. On the one hand, if a firm must use experienced accountants on this work, it would probably be undesirable to undertake the engagement. On the other hand, if the work can be handled in the firm's office by a separate department equipped with bookkeeping machines and staffed by trained operators, the potential volume of this service might make it desirable for a particular firm.

Most of the business-management functions in the area of production are analogous to those found in accounting practice. However, the two most important are production planning and quality control.

1. The utilization of manpower and facilities: In planning for production, management must be concerned with co-ordinating the required manpower and facilities in such a manner as to attain its production objectives with the maximum efficiency. The manufacturer must anticipate his needs in order to schedule his production and the CPA must forecast the nature and volume of his work, so that it will be performed efficiently. While the manufacturer must relate his needs to men, materials, and machines, the CPA's primary consideration is manpower.

Many firms find that a monthly schedule of assignments is essential to the effective utilization of manpower. But, effective planning requires long-range forecasting. How far ahead should the firm attempt to plot its specific manpower needs? It is naturally easier to achieve a high degree of accuracy for longer periods of time if the amount of predictable repeat work in relation to the total practice is substantial. Yet, regardless of the amount of repetitive work, it can be used as a starting point for anticipating the time available for expanding services to existing or new clients.

Total manpower requirements must in turn be related to the nature of the work. To what extent should specialists be developed in relation to the present work and proposed objectives? Although specialization increases competence, it can also reduce a firm's flexibility. At what stage in the firm's program should specialization begin? It is evident that a firm must attain a certain amount of growth before the addition of many specialists becomes practical. Traditionally, specialization has followed functional lines: a firm may have auditors, tax specialists, perhaps a systems man, and it may even include, as in recent years, an expert in other phases of management services. Perhaps the firm should consider, depending on its objectives, industry specialists in addition to, or instead of, functional specialists. Would the firm's goals be served better by men who are familiar with the special accounting, auditing, and tax problems of specific industries such as oil development, retailing, and banking?

Provisions must be made for adequate facilities. How much office space is needed, both now and in the foreseeable future? How can it best be utilized? Should more space be leased than is immediately needed? Should part of it be sublet to facilitate proposed expansion when the need arises? How about mechanization? Can reproducing equipment and other office machines facilitate the flow of work? Can comptometer operators be used effectively to relieve staff accountants of some of their more routine duties and make them available for higher-grade work?

Operating procedures must be established. Management must determine the procedures to be adopted and issue clear instructions about them. Should audit guides, manuals, and similar written aids be developed? How much personal supervision should be employed to promote compliance? How satisfactory are present supervisory techniques?

2. *Controlling the quality of the service*: Volume production means nothing unless the end product adequately fills the need for which it is designed. Thus, standards must be developed to insure that the product or service is adequate. It is in this area of quality control that the analogy between a professional practice and a manufacturing enterprise diverges. Once a manufactured product meets maximum allowable tolerances, quality control has served its basic purpose. Even though closer tolerances may enable the product to perform better, there is often a rapid diminishing return in relation to the time and effort needed to improve it. The quality of accounting services is more open-ended. Once the minimum standards of the profession are met, improved quality and additional efforts to improve the quality of the service may well yield better than proportionate returns. Therefore, in establishing its standards and measuring the results against them, an accounting firm has to decide what it really wants. Is an audit engagement conducted in conformity with generally accepted accounting principles and auditing standards to be considered entirely satisfactory? Or should it be the bare minimum? What additional standards should the firm adopt to supplement or fill the gaps in generally accepted principles and procedures? Should the firm require that a conscious effort be made to detect and bring to the client's attention areas for improvement in his operations during the normal course of an audit?

In other work as well, there can be a world of difference between acceptable and creative service. Controls must be established to see that the work measures up to the firm's standards. Thus, a firm should organize a system of review, inspection, and in-process supervision of all its work, including correspondence, which will insure the quality of its service. Here, the audit review procedure can play a key part, but the entire system should be designed to answer this question: Are we satisfied to have this piece of work associated with our firm? Although control is generally regarded as an internal matter, the effectiveness of a firm's performance can often be gauged by the reactions of the client to the quality of the work performed.

Providing the manpower. As a practitioner or a firm develop their plans for growth, it is apparent that an organization is necessary. Since the capacity of any individual is limited, there must at some point be a division of labor and some degree of specialization. This means hiring, training, and supervising people. A young CPA may choose to build from the bottom—

first hiring staff and then admitting them to partnership while other staff men fill the lower ranks. Other CPAs may find it more desirable to merge with other practitioners. Personnel requirements should be projected ahead. Staff assistants should be employed before they are actually needed, to allow time for training before the anticipated demand for their services materializes.

Many assignment schedules have been wrecked because they were too tight: management did no foresee the client demand for services. If a practice is growing, new or special work always comes along. It cannot be performed successfully unless trained staff have been provided in advance. Therefore, a growing practice must invest in staff payroll without immediately knowing specifically where the service will be utilized. In a small organization, some practitioners feel, an overestimate of staff by 20 per cent is not excessive and if the staff is competent it will usually sell itself. This again involves risk: a willingness to sacrifice immediate income for potential growth.

Moreover, the practitioner should make every effort to keep staff members the year around. This policy will provide an incentive to develop engagements to keep the staff busy during normally slack periods. However, part of this time should be used for staff training. Many practitioners no longer use temporary staff, except in emergencies, for they feel that temporary men cannot become acquainted with all the firm's standards and procedures. Also, it is virtually impossible to build a cumulatively expanding capacity if there is no trained staff able to provide these services.

In personnel planning, various aspects must be considered: recruiting, selecting, testing, training, and so on. For a detailed discussion of these and other related areas, see Section 2, Staff Personnel, page 85.

The market for the services. Marketing encompasses the varied activities connected with directing and encouraging the flow of goods or services to the consumer or user. This might sound like a fancy way of saying advertising, soliciting, and selling. Marketing is these things, but it is more. It also includes market research, pricing, packaging, and physical distribution. Next to personnel administration, it is generally agreed that the marketing functions in an accounting practice are the most neglected. Part of this may be due to the inhibiting effect of the rules of professional conduct, especially the prohibitions against advertising and soliciting. Ethics are important. A profession cannot exist without them. But since certain *techniques* are prohibited, with good reason, many firms tend to ignore the *functions* which can and should be performed within the framework of a professional practice.

Some businessmen feel that their CPAs are technically competent but afflicted with "tunnel vision." In the view of these executives, CPAs lack imagination and aggressiveness. By aggressiveness, they do not mean the foot-in-the-door variety of salesmanship but an alertness to take advantage of opportunities to serve to the limit of their capacities. This alertness, combined with conscious planning, is essential to successful professional marketing. Here are some of the things the progressive firm should consider within each of the subelements of marketing.

1. Client surveys: How can the CPA serve best unless he is aware of and can analyze the market for his services? He must know his clients, his community, and the general business climate.

Some firms use "client survey" forms which contain basic information about their officers or owners, banker, insurance agent, and attempt to isolate and evaluate the elements of operations in which the CPA might effectively serve. Such a guide not only spotlights areas of potential service, but also can help measure the extent to which the needs of the client are being met. (An example of some of the questions which might be included appears on Appendix page 817.) Other firms, on a less formal basis, but with similar conscientiousness, look for weaknesses in the client's operations. Examination of audit working papers, for example, especially the review of internal control, can yield many opportunities for service.

But this is not enough. The CPA should become familiar with the client's industry, subscribe to trade journals, review industry statistics, in other words, get to know the client's market and his position in it. Beyond that is the element of economic awareness. As a sophisticated citizen, the CPA should keep up with and understand general business trends. Where is the economy going and why? How does it affect his clients? All this knowledge is not particularly helpful, unless it can be put to use: it must be sold.

2. *Selling the service*: The market having been uncovered, the next step is to sell the services to present clients and cultivate the many sources of potential clients. (See "Salesmanship" and "Obtaining Clients," pages 337 and 323, respectively.)

3. *The final product—the report*: Another neglected aspect of the marketing function is what is known in industry as packaging. In a professional accounting practice, this has to do with the form and style of reports and oral and written communications to the client. The physical appearance of reports is important, but not as important as their readability and content. They should be designed to tell the client what he most wants to know with the least effort on his part.

4. *The fee for the service*: A most important part of marketing activities is the matter of putting a fair price tag on the products or services. Within the context of an accounting practice this is the matter of fees. An inadequate fee scale can do more than any other single factor to restrict the growth of a practice. It can result in the "squirrel cage" of long hours at low rates which prevent the practitioner from improving his competence to perform high-level work in keeping with his potential. On the other hand, since overpricing can drive clients away, it is incumbent on the CPA to be worth what he charges and see that his client is aware of his value.

Fees must be sufficient to allow the principal or partners time to discharge the management functions efficiently, that is, sufficient to cover administrative as well as production costs. Fees must permit time for professional development through staff-training, continuing education, participation in professional affairs, community service, and the like. Perhaps this is another way of saying that fees must be sufficient to provide capital to be reinvested for expansion of the practice. Fees must also rise steadily to offset the eroding effects of inflation. Naturally, fees must be acceptable to the client if they are to be collected, which is another way of saying that services must be worth their cost to the client. Rarely will a client object to fees for services which he can relate directly to his profits.

Thus, fee policies become an integral part of a firm's over-all planning. They should not be developed on a haphazard basis. They should be carefully planned in keeping with the types of service to be offered, the future needs of the firm, and the objective of producing the income which the practitioner believes he is entitled to derive from his practice. In order to plan his fee structure efficiently, however, the CPA must know his costs and financial requirements. This brings up another major activity area of management, that of finance and control.

Finance and control. The subject of finance and control is perhaps the area of management most familiar to CPAs. It may be somewhat superfluous to introduce it here, for it embraces a number of services which CPAs customarily render to their clients. However, there is some evidence to suggest that CPAs do not always practice what they preach and fail to apply this knowledge to their own professional affairs.

Finance and control can be defined as planning, directing, and measuring the results of the firm's monetary operations. This includes, among other things, the forecasting of capital requirements. The CPA planning for the growth of his practice should engage in financial forecasting and recommend it to clients.

CPAs, by the very nature of their work, are inclined to be conservative. But does this mean that they should restrict their financial plans to the limits of their earned reserves? A healthy, growing enterprise is frequently short of cash. Perhaps, in terms of long-range growth, it might be better for a firm to make use of more capital than is presently available from earnings. A bank loan or the capital contribution of a new partner might be considered. In any case, the firm should not necessarily restrict its plans to its present cash situation. If it does, it may find that it is missing some inviting opportunities. In addition to developing internal or external sources of needed funds, the financial activity includes planning for taxes, developing policies on credit and collection (including billing procedures), and providing the necessary insurance coverage.

Under the heading of control come the usual accounting records, expense data, standards, and cost analyses. Before any plan can be properly executed, a firm must know how much and on what it spends its money. Consequently, effective time controls are indispensable to efficient operation. These controls should serve three purposes:

1. To see that staff working time is used as productively as possible
2. To make sure that work is properly charged to the client for whom it was performed
3. To enable the firm to review the adequacy of its fee structure

Then comes budgeting. How many accounting firms have budgets? All available evidence indicates that few of them do, which in turn suggests two questions: Is there any reason why a professional firm should not project its revenues, expenses, and profits as a means of measuring results against predetermined standards and analyzing the variances? How else can it effectively plan its future?

Within the accounting office, also, there is room for systems and procedures. Someone has to design various forms, records, and reports; someone should study clerical work flow and methods, possible utilization of accounting and office machines, reproducing equipment, and so on. These may be relatively minor functions in the early stages, but provision must be made to pay sufficient attention to them as the practice grows.

External relations. Although this catchall category contains elements closely intertwined with other activities, its importance should not be overlooked. Accounting firms need legal advice on such matters as partnership agreements, letters of arrangement with clients intended to limit legal liability, and compliance with general laws like the Fair Labor Standards Act and with statutory requirements involved in certain types of work done for government agencies. The CPA should also be aware of state laws regulating the accounting profession and the codes of ethics promulgated in accordance with them, in addition to general laws governing certain types of occupations, requiring filings in the names of partners, and so on.

Too much emphasis cannot be placed on the firm's reputation in its community. Is it regarded as a good citizen? Does it participate in community activities, contribute to worthy causes, enjoy good relations with banks, law firms, government agencies, and others with whom it comes in contact? In other words, is it taking the necessary steps to establish the image of a highly qualified group of men, dedicated to the principles of professional service?

The foregoing are the elements of an effective plan. They have been assembled here solely to place them in perspective as they relate to the over-all, long-range program. Since they are, in effect, the elements of the efficient administration of a CPA's practice, they have been treated only briefly here. Detailed developments of these areas will be found elsewhere in this volume.

Acquiring a Practice

■ AN INCREASINGLY PREVALENT method of enlarging practices is that of merging already existing practices. This procedure brings to the business advantages such as more economical operation, combination of skills, and broadening of contacts. Generally, the same considerations and cautions are applicable as in the case of an original partnership.

THE RETIRING PRINCIPAL

One method of development of a practice that appears to be growing in frequency is that of acquiring an interest in the accounting firm in which the accountant is employed. Many young men graduating from accounting schools now are seeking employment in practices owned by elderly principals with the idea of acquiring those practices eventually when the principal retires. In such cases the young accountant often becomes a partner without having to purchase an interest. Acquisition in this manner depends on the accountant's skill and his ability to develop sufficiently to make himself indispensable both to the principal and to the clients. An accountant who has obtained a part interest is obviously in a much better position to acquire the remaining interest in the event of death of the principal.

PURCHASE OF A PRACTICE

One important method of starting a practice and obtaining a nucleus of clients is to acquire by purchase an already existing practice. This method is likely to become more prevalent in future years. Such practices, with their goodwill as the main ingredient of the sales, have been sold with increasing frequency in recent years.

The purchase price. Generally, the method used to determine the goodwill of a practice has been based on a proportion of gross fees for a period of past years. For example, the method employed in the sale of a partial interest in a public accounting practice illustrates one approach, based upon past fees, to the problem of establishing a value for such an interest. The principal, a sole practitioner, sold a 25 per cent interest to each of two employees. The parties listed all of the practitioner's regular clients together with the average annual fees received from them, exclusive of fees from nonrecurring or special engagements. A value was then obtained for each of the regular clients by applying to the average annual fees the following percentages: 100 per cent for clients served for over four years; 75 per cent for clients served for from three to four years; 50 per cent for clients served for from two to three years; 25 per cent for clients served for from one to two years. No value was assigned to clients who were deemed to have no further value to the firm because of circumstances such as death of the client, dissolution, or transfer to another accountant.

Twenty-five per cent of all special fees received during the preceding four years was added to the value obtained for regular clients, as the principal believed that he had made enough contacts to insure continuance of the special fees. To this sum was added the book value of equipment and furniture to arrive at a total which, when divided by four, was considered to be the value of a 25 per cent interest in the practice. The computations involved in this approach are illustrated in Table 1:

Table I

Regular clients	Average annual fee	Years served	Applicable %	Value	Remarks
xxxx	$ 400	4	100	$ 400	
xxxx	700	1	25	175	
xxxx	300	2	50	150	
xxxx	1,000	4	100	1,000	
xxxx	400	3	75	300	
xxxx	50	4	...	...	Deceased
xxxx	100	3	...	...	Dissolved
—	...	...	...	...	

Total value of regular clients' accounts	$44,000
Average of four years' special fees ($4,000 @ 25%)	1,000
Equipment and furniture at book value	5,200
	$50,200
Valuation of 25% interest	$12,550

The client's position. In the available discussions of valuation on the basis of a proportion of past gross fees, not enough consideration has been given to what is perhaps the most important factor. How many of the clients whose accounts are included in the practice sold will remain with the purchaser and to what extent will their value to him vary from their previous value to the accountant who is selling? This point is stated eloquently by the unnamed author of "On Buying an Audit" in *The Accountant's Journal*:[1]

> The most a buyer can expect to get when purchasing an audit is an assurance that the concern audited will allow the buyer to do in the future the work which the retiring auditor has been doing in the past. Until such assurance is given, any proposed purchase is a gamble.

As to the possibility of determining with reasonable precision what specific

[1]*The Accountant's Journal* (New Zealand), June 1949, p. 288.

clients will remain with the purchaser of a practice, a ruling of the AICPA's committee on professional ethics is of significance:[2]

> . . . a member selling an accounting practice may not transfer confidential papers of a client without first obtaining his permission.

An obvious result of that ruling is that an accountant selling a practice must either (1) acquire the consent of his clients to the transfer of the working papers before he makes the sale or (2) make the sale subject to acquiring such consent from each client affected. In either event, it is possible, once the consents or refusals of clients have been received, to determine within reasonable limits which accounts will remain with the buyer and which are likely to go elsewhere. In any case, the consents should be received before the terms of sale are fixed.

This procedure will not foretell the annual future billings for accounts that can be counted on to stay with the purchaser. As was pointed out significantly by R. Sproull of England, further analysis of past gross fees is required.[3]

The character of the fees. Mr. Sproull indicates that the essence of valuation is to arrive first at the worth of a sound, even-going practice of the type for sale. Then there is added to or deducted from the worth appropriate values for whatever enhances or detracts to make it correspond to the actual practice being considered. Drawing on experiences of accountants in many scores of sales and purchases, Mr. Sproull makes many significant points. One is that gross fees are meaningless as generally applicable to a practice or in the comparison of several practices. Having no common-sense or scientific basis, the term should be dropped from use and a more accurate phrase used, such as "trimmed total fees." Thus the list of past fees should be adjusted to reduce them to a uniform basis over a period of years by the examination of nonrecurring fees, special fees, and fees from accounts with a discernible short life, for example, those in liquidation and those whose owner has died.

However, if an average of gross fees or, preferably, trimmed total fees is to be used as a basis for determining goodwill, this value should not be made a completely arbitrary determinant, as the amount of payment can be related to the actual future yield of the accounts. Where the accounts yield less than the average set as a standard, the seller, by appropriate provision in the sales agreement, can be made to rebate in proportion. If payments for the practice are to be made in installments, such adjustments can be deducted from installments due.

A good illustration of an American case in point is the sale of a practice which became the subject matter of the significant Richard S. Wyler tax case.[4] Wyler, selling his practice for $50,000, consulted his clients in advance,

[2]John L. Carey, *Professional Ethics of Certified Public Accountants,* AICPA, 1956, p. 168.

[3]R. Sproull, *Accountant's Fees and Profits,* Professional and Trade Books, Ltd., London, 1951, chap. 29, pp. 214-237.

[4]*Wyler vs. Commissioner,* 14 T.C. 1251 (1950).

secured their approval to the transaction, and transferred the working papers to the buyers. The contract of sale indicated his billings for the past three years (average about $60,000) and provided that if billings to these clients by the purchasers for the next three years did not total $180,000, Wyler would rebate a proportionate part of the $50,000 sale price.

The net-profit approach. Another basis for the evaluation of goodwill of a practice in the United States is to use the net profits of three to five past years. The use of this method requires the same analysis of gross fees as discussed previously. In addition, a careful study must be made of costs to determine as nearly as possible how the purchaser's costs will compare with those of the seller. One method having received considerable support is to value purchasable goodwill at 167 per cent of the amount of the average annual net profits. Other known formulas are three or five times the average annual earnings. (The foregoing formulas are offered as illustrations only and are not necessarily indicative of the current sale price of a practice.)

Other considerations. Mr. Sproull makes numerous points to which a buyer should give serious attention. Some of these are: the location of the practice, date of establishment, number and types of clients, the last year's total fees, and the last year's profits. Other useful information would be average rates charged for principal (and perhaps staff), relative chargeable days, and any special features of the practice. All of this information should be accumulated by the seller as a preliminary to entering into negotiations for the sale.

In addition, the buyer must inquire into the past ebb and flow of clients and attempt to estimate its range for future years. It seems to be higher in urban practices. Too many new clients in recent years can spell greater losses of clients ahead. Clients having less than three annual bills from the vendor are often worth less than other clients, and the shorter the term of connection with the accountant, the poorer can be the client's value in relation to fee. The buyer should determine the seller's reasons for selling.

Mr. Sproull suggests also that to assist a vendor to survey the value of his clientele or to enable a prospective buyer to collate information furnished him regarding a practice, it is sometimes desirable to make a schedule listing essential data concerning each client. Some of its features are: date of acquisition of client, services performed, dates and places of performance of services, fiscal year, time and fees of the last three years, time and fees of this year, time and fees estimated for next year, dates of billings and payments, other accountants possibly considered, financial status of client, possibility of future discontinuance or expansion, and reasons for loss of client, if applicable.

Prices paid for practices in England have varied widely. The variations depend on such factors as whether the practice is recently or long established; whether it is dynamic, static, or declining; whether it has fixed or variable fees, whether it has audit engagements which are very secure and easy to transfer, and so on. With a higher prospect of retention of clientele, the English seem to consider it adequate to guard against overpayment for a practice by withholding a percentage of the purchase price so as to guarantee a refund for any excess valuation over actual fees earned by the practice for the new buyer over a stipulated period. In the United States, however, where retention of substantially all clients is somewhat less certain, there is a growing tendency to base the purchase price of practices on a percentage of future fees earned over a specified period.

Basing the price on future profits. The buyer's efforts alone create income after the purchase, no other foundation having been laid by the former owner except introduction to his successor and the good word spoken for him. It has been said that, since the services rendered to clients by the buyer have far greater value than the good word spoken by the former owner, the amount attributable to the good offices of the seller should be an agreed small percentage of the profits earned by the buyer on the clients taken over by him and effective for a stated term of years. A fair price has been suggested to be 25 per cent of the profits earned from the former owner's clients in each of four years, plus an agreed price for furniture, equipment and so on; and, of course, the buyer would not be expected to give the seller any share of the profits from new clients acquired after the purchase.

Transfers of practices in the United States have been known to be based on a percentage of future fees for a specified period. Some valuations used were (1) 25 per cent of fees for the next four years, (2) 20 per cent of fees for the next five years, (3) 40 per cent, 30 per cent, 10 per cent, 5 per cent, 5 per cent and 5 per cent respectively of fees in the next six years, (4) 15 per cent of fees for the next five years, and (5) 15 per cent of fees for the next five years with 5 per cent per year for an additional period of five years.

The underlying reasons for basing such sales on a percentage of future fees are in essence as follows. Any speculation as to delivery of a clientele to a buyer should be at the seller's risk. If he has served his clients well and if he selects a responsible and competent buyer, he should be able to deliver a very substantial part of his clientele. If he does not have the best and closest possible ties with his clients and so cannot be certain that they will follow his recommendations as to his successor, he should get paid only on what he controls and can actually deliver. At the outset the seller should know more about the buyer than the clients do and, therefore, if he selects a poorly qualified buyer, he should assume the risk of client dissatisfaction occurring subsequent to the transfer.

Of course, sometimes a seller cannot deliver even to the most acceptable buyer some of his best clients with whom he is on excellent terms. In a relatively small community, for example, a client may be a close personal friend of one or more accountants. Therefore, this client probably would want to transfer his account to one of his friends rather than to have it go to a comparative stranger. Such an incident is known to have occurred in a city of approximately 35,000 with an additional 50,000 in surrounding areas. The seller transferred his practice to two competent employees who had been with him for four years. Although the young men were able to acquire a substantial nucleus of clients, a number of important clients transferred their accounts to other accountants whom they knew.

Making the transition. Mr. Sproull, in his discussion of transfers of practices in England, indicates that the transfer should be quick and clean and that the vendor should act only to the minimum extent of making introductions and insuring the buyer's familiarity with clients and details. He indicates further that the buyer is introduced generally by the vendor's letter, and that it is best that there be no personal attendance by the vendor in the majority of cases. This appears to be at variance with American opinion. Some practitioners believe strongly that, in the interests of continuity, it is best for the vendor to remain with the business for as long as six months and only withdraw gradually from the practice. As a final consideration, both the buyer and the vendor should be aware of the tax consequences of the sale of practices and of interests in them.

Mergers of Accounting Firms

■ SINCE WORLD WAR II, business concerns have been rushing to diversify their products or services by acquiring other companies with "know-how" and manpower in other business lines. Simultaneously, there has been a strong tendency to expand into new geographic areas.

One result of this tidal wave of diversification and dispersal of business has been a great upsurge in the number of nationwide and world-wide audits. As a corollary, the large accounting firms that have been serving these expanding companies have been obliged to enlarge their organizations and to follow their clients into new territories.

At the same time, another new development is having a decided effect on the practices of nearly all public accounting firms. For the last ten or more years a continuously increasing emphasis is being given to the role of the CPA in furnishing management services.

While a large audit practice has a tendency to develop specialists in different types of business, the field of management services demands even more in the way of specialization. One partner in a large firm states that the needs of a substantial clientele are so diversified today, particularly in the field of management services, that the fully staffed organization will require, if not a hundred specialists, at least men with experience and qualifications in a hundred specialties.

The large accounting firms have had to expand rapidly and open offices in many new locations to keep pace with the demands of their growing and moving clients. A substantial portion of that expansion has come about through mergers with local firms of CPAs.

Many other local practitioners have condemned these mergers as possibly detrimental to the profession. Some of the critics contend that the large firms may become so impersonal that they will cease to be professional organizations. Others regret the loss of the stronger and older local firms, for which the local business community, the professional accounting societies, and the profession generally have a real need. Many express the fear that the medium-sized local firm will shortly disappear and that all of the accounting services will eventually be furnished by large nationwide firms or by very small local organizations with staffs of perhaps less than ten people.

In one survey, questions were asked of the managing partners of the eight largest accounting firms, other national or multi-office firms, and former partners of local firms that have merged with national organizations. Though there continue to be many mergers of two or more small local firms, this study was confined to mergers of local or sectional firms with larger national firms. It is the latter which have generated most of the discussion at informal meetings of CPAs at the local level.

NUMBER OF MERGERS

How many mergers have there been in the last fifteen years? Those responding report a total of 163, ranging from more than 20 for some firms to none at the other end of the scale. That the trend is accelerating is evidenced by the fact that only 50 are reported for the ten years 1946-1955, compared with 113 during the last five years.

One firm reported that approximately 20 to 25 per cent of its present staff is traceable to mergers, but the average seems to be about 15 per cent.

WHY DO MERGERS OCCUR?

The viewpoint of the national firm. The first and most compelling reason, though it does not account for the majority of the mergers, is the desire or need for an office in a new area. Moving partners and staff into an area to start a new office usually leaves them with a great deal of idle time for the first few years, with accompanying frustration and stagnation. It is also considered by many to be much less costly to merge with an existing practice. In some cases, legislative impediments to opening new offices in some states have been a factor leading to merger.

Such factors as the following may influence the decision to open a new office.

1. Expanding clients needs service in the new area. If the work is not complex or voluminous, the accounting firm frequently arranges for local accountants to perform it on a referral basis. It is understandable that business concerns often want to look to one firm only for all accounting services. Clients, therefore, often pressure the large accounting firm into opening a new office, even though it will be a losing venture for several years. When the work is complicated or includes specialized management services, the large accounting firms feel there is no choice but to do the work with their own personnel.

2. The potential reduction or elimination of travel expenses into the area will benefit the client.

3. The reduction of travel for the staff will improve employee relations. Several managing partners point out that staff members feel much less willing today to travel on assignments than they did a generation ago.

4. The firm may feel impelled to maintain its competitive position in rapidly growing areas which may be under consideration by existing clients as expansion points.

The second reason for mergers, probably accounting for the majority of them, is the opportunity to strengthen or enlarge an existing office. In many cases the requirements of existing clients for services has expanded faster than the number of partners and other supervisory personnel assigned to the local office—a situation that can be corrected by bringing in the partners of a local firm. Many of the large firms feel that each office should be large enough to support either two partners or a partner and a principal, in order to provide continuity in event of death, disability, or retirement. That would probably mean a minimum staff of around thirty-five. If an office is smaller than that, a merger would probably be welcomed to enlarge the practice and increase the staff.

Other reasons given for mergers, sometimes as compelling and sometimes as collateral, include the following:

1. To bring into the organization as partners a group considered to have outstanding ability or an individual with superior knowledge in a specialized field such as banking and finance, insurance, transportation, and the like.

2. To increase personnel to a sufficient number to support full-time staff-training specialists, recruiters, and so forth. With professional trainers, better training procedures can be formulated and followed. The larger staff provides new employees with greater opportunities for choice of specialty or geographical location, thus tending to attract better men. The larger staff in multiple offices tends also to reduce travel time, thus improving staff morale.

3. To provide the volume and variety of high-level work to support more partners and to generate more income as an attraction to the more able men. A strong partnership organization provides more protection for its members in event of retirement, illness, disability, or death. A substantial number of partners also provides a source of capital to pay for the interests of retired or deceased partners. While a number of mergers were sought by local firms to retain clients who would otherwise have been lost, no national firm partner has stated that any were carried out primarily to obtain the local firm's clients. Increased staff was mentioned a number of times, from which increased revenues would normally follow, but the national firms seem to feel that their clientele and opportunities for service increase satisfactorily from year to year without recourse to mergers.

The viewpoint of the local firm. An answer to the question, "Why do local firms seek a merger with a national firm?" first requires a review of the general characteristics of the local firms which have merged with national firms.

In general, the local firms that enter into mergers with the large national firms have been established for more than thirty years, have more than twenty-five accountants on the staff, and have at least one partner, and perhaps more, approaching or past sixty-five years of age. It is of interest that a substantial number, if not a majority, of the merger negotiations are instigated by the local practitioners, not by the national firm partners.

The most compelling reason, offered more than half the time, is to protect or retain clients. The clients have grown and perhaps expanded into distant areas, to the extent that they now require services beyond the abilities of the local firm. This could be due to geographical dispersion, or to the need for highly specialized management services that the local firm cannot furnish. Or the client may have grown to the point that he must seek financial assistance either through large city banks or security underwriters, both of whom often insist on financial statements bearing national firm signatures.

The second reason in importance, and the primary one in perhaps a third of the cases, is financial. The older partners feel that the organization may lack the stability to guarantee them an acceptable retirement income and adequate payment for their interests in the firm on retirement or death. At the same time, the younger partners may be attracted by the idea of being a part of a much larger organization which underwrites such retirement benefits, either for their older partners or for themselves later on. Many people have expressed some satisfaction with the prospect of a life retirement income, apparently ranging with most firms in the neighborhood of $10,000 to $20,000 a year, based on the contractual obligation of a large multi-office firm with perhaps a hundred or more partners.

In third place among primary reasons is the possibility of enlarged professional opportunities for the younger practitioners. Many of them welcome the chance to escape from the administrative work involved in running a practice and would much prefer to concentrate on special areas of practice or on a special industry.

In a few cases, usually associated with becoming the local office of a national firm, the local practitioner is motivated by the possibility of using his abilities to better advantage on more important and more interesting work, and with the probability of increased income.

Another, though perhaps secondary, reason for mergers has been the unsatisfactory experience of some local firms in recruiting personnel, finding the time to interview students at many educational institutions, preparing employment brochures, and trying to compete with the larger firms which can promise applicants continuing education, specialization of their choice, and the working location they may desire.

REASONS FOR NOT MERGING

One large firm reports that it has entered into no domestic mergers during the last fifteen years. A number of reasons are offered, none of which is an objection to mergers as such. The principal objection seems to be the difficulty of retraining staff personnel who have not had the benefit of the firm's training program during all of their years in practice.

The older nonmerging local firms cite a number of reasons for their having resisted the merger trend. First, there is the belief that some of the partners would be too young and inexperienced to be granted partnership status by the national firm within a reasonable period of time and that, therefore, these men might have better opportunities for professional development and satisfactory income by retaining the local organization. The possibility of forced transfers to distant cities also seems to bother the local partners. The third most frequently heard reason has to do with possible imposition of controls from the national headquarters office which would limit the local partners' freedom of decision. Some of the older practitioners also do not like the thought of compulsory retirement and loss of their name identity in the local community.

RESULTS OF THE MERGERS

Effect on the partners. Generally speaking, all of the local firm partners are accepted immediately as partners in the national firm. One exception is the overage or retiring local partner for whom special contractual arrangements are usually made. Another is the younger local partner with insufficient experience to meet the national firm's requirements for partnership, who may be made a principal or manager but who nearly always seems to achieve partnership status within a few years.

No ex-local partner reports a decrease in income as a result of merger. On the contrary, almost all report an increase in income, some mentioning 15 per cent—though possible increases in income were almost never cited as a reason for merging. In a substantial number of mergers, possibly in a majority, the national firm apparently guarantees that the local partners will suffer no decrease in income for the next three years below their average for the previous three years. Some of the national firm partners, however, have suffered a small decrease in income for two or three years after a merger due to increased costs incurred while consolidating and co-ordinating the new practice with the whole firm.

There can be no uniformity, of course, in the incomes of partners in different firms, or possibly even among the partners in one large firm. No income survey was made in connection with these mergers but, taking into account different firm policies, a general pattern seems to appear that would apply to several firms.

The youngest and newest partners start with an annual income of not less than $20,000, probably more nearly $25,000. Within two or three years they will probably have progressed to the $30,000 to $35,000 bracket. Further progress depends on the man, his performance, and the size of his office. The average over-all for all partners is probably in the $40,000 to $60,000 range with higher figures in the $90,000 to $100,000 bracket applying to those with greater responsibilities in the larger offices. Still larger incomes may be realized by a few partners with over-all top responsibilities in such areas as accounting principles, SEC reporting, internal firm management, and the like.

It appears that the mergers have had little effect on the workload and responsibilities of the partners, either national or local. The local partners have continued with just about the same working hours. One or two have commented, however, on more liberal vacation policies than they enjoyed before. In some cases it has been necessary for the national firms to increase the workload on some of their partners during the first few years after a merger because of an intensive training and indoctrination program for the new additions. Many of the local partners report that their work has become more specialized and that they have been relieved of a substantial amount of burdensome administrative work in connection with office management and the recruiting and training of personnel.

Many partners in local firms have avoided mergers because they did not wish to sacrifice their freedom of action or move to some distant office. Virtually all of the partners of local firms that have merged report that they feel they have not lost any of their independence as a result of the merger. The large firms have certain policies with respect to audit procedures, report presentation, and the like, but within that framework the partners are apparently permitted great independence of thought and action. Although a number of the former local firm partners have moved to other locations, they also report that the transfers have given them greatly enlarged opportunities and they are happy about them.

The national firms have compulsory retirement programs at various ages from sixty to sixty-five. Some of the older partners in merged local firms have reported that they did not wish to retire that early, but they now find that it is a desirable program and are heartily in favor of it.

Without exception the local firm partners report that they have been welcomed into the large national organizations, treated entirely as equals, and made to feel that they are really part of the "family." There apparently has been no indication of a condescending attitude on the part of the national firm partners toward the new additions to their number.

Effect on the staffs of the local firms. Essentially all of the staffs of the merged local firms have continued with the organizations after the mergers. Any subsequent turnover has been no more than the normal amount under ordinary conditions.

In some instances the general compensation level in the local firm was approximately the same as in the national organization. In the majority of cases, however, it was lower and was soon raised to fit the national pattern. Subsequent salary increases have been in accordance with the over-all policies of the various national firms.

With respect to professional development of staff personnel, it has been reported in all but one or two cases that staff-training has been improved after the merger and there has been a tendency toward more specialization. Everyone has also reported that it has been much easier to recruit outstanding students for the national firm than for the local firm prior to the merger.

The local partners were asked whether their staff men appeared to be better trained and better equipped after the merger to advance within the firm or to start their own practices. The answers to this question have been inconclusive. One must conclude that there is but little difference either way.

In a few instances the national firm partners have felt that the local firm staffs were equal to their own and no training period was required. They have usually found it necessary, however, to concentrate on a fairly heavy training program for the local staffs extending over a period of about two years. At the end of that time they seem to feel that the newly acquired staff is equal in every way to the staff having its experience only with the national organization.

Effect on the clients of the local firm. It is of interest that more than 99 per cent of the local firm clients stay with the merged firm. A 2 per cent loss was reported in one merger but that was due to a conflict of interests.

The local firm partners were asked if the quality of services to their clients was improved after the merger. They feel that the quality of the audit services remained about the same. The quality of the tax services was about the same except in the more involved cases where a Washington office has often been helpful. Almost without exception the reports indicate material increases in the quality and extent of the management services rendered to the local firm clients.

With respect to fees, it appears that billing rates to clients applicable to all types of work have generally been increased after the mergers. It has been pointed out, however, that in some cases this did not result in over-all increases in fees because efficiencies instituted by the national firm enabled equivalent work to be completed in less time. It is admitted, however, that in many cases fees for the small local audits have been increased due to uniform and more rigid procedural requirements.

It appears that when a merger is announced the local firm's clients usually express concern about their work, desiring to be served by the same partner year after year. Upon being promised no change in contacting partners they seem satisfied. In general, the local partners of the merged firms feel that even after many years the small local client receives as much personal attention from the national firm as from a local firm except that a substantial part of that attention may come from a principal or a manager rather than from a partner.

The trend, then, is for a merged practice gradually to acquire more of the characteristics of a national firm practice, with emphasis on the larger clients. Smaller and smaller percentages of the gross revenues will come from engagements performed for small clients as the small clients expand or depart and new ones are not sought or secured as replacements.

Effect on the practice. Several of the local partners report that the office filing has been improved. Although a few think that the office bookkeeping methods have been improved, most of them feel that the billing and collecting methods were about equally well handled before and after the merger.

With respect to audit practices, virtually all local partners feel there has been a great improvement in the planning and budgeting of audit time. Not many feel that there has been any material change or improvement in audit procedures, but most of them are convinced that a decided improvement has occurred in the supervision of the audits and in reviewing the work. There has apparently been little change in efficiency of staff utilization or in maintaining productive hours.

Nearly all local partners comment on the substantial increase since the merger in conferences and seminars on technical subjects for both partners and staff. Professional development seems to receive much more attention in the national firm offices.

An effort has been made to learn more about the new clients that are attracted to the firm after the merger. Generally speaking, the national firm office does not want or get write-up work. It appears that such offices also do not attract small local audits or simple system installations and other minor management work for very small businesses. Some of that type of work comes to them, but not as high a proportion as flows normally to the local firms. Some express the opinion that the small clients receive services that are adequate and more satisfactory to them from the local firms where a partner often does the work or is in daily contact with it. With respect to tax engagements, the trend in the national office seems about the same as the trend in the local office. All of the local partners report that after the merger it has been much easier to attract and secure the larger local audits (say in the $2,500 to $5,000 annual fee range) and still easier to attract large audit engagements stemming from local contacts with fees in excess of $5,000.

Effect on the public. The local partner feels that the merger has increased his stature in the eyes of local bankers and other members of the business community. There was a time when local business people tended to resent the arrival of a national accounting firm in the community. That attitude seems to have changed, probably for two reasons. The public is now becoming more accustomed to bigness in business, perhaps as a result of the tendency toward business mergers. Probably more important are the public relations efforts of the national accounting firms in recent years. Their partners and other key personnel seem to make it a point to take a prominent part in local business and neighborhood activities of all kinds, indicative of a definite program designed to identify them with the local scene.

THE MERGER PATTERN

It seems that there is something approaching a merger pattern. As its clients expand and diversify, the local firm grows and prospers. After a period of some thirty years, many of the firm's clients have become fairly large and have either spread out geographically or have developed problems that require a range of management services which may be beyond the competence of the local accounting firm. Occasionally, one or two clients may grow so large that servicing their far-flung operations becomes a serious problem. At the same time, one or two of the partners are approaching retirement age. They question whether or not the firm will be able to continue without them and remain sufficiently profitable to provide retirement income for them and payment for their interests in the firm.

When this situation is coupled with the desire of a national accounting firm to keep abreast of its expanding and diversifying clientele, a favorable merger climate has been established.

THE FUTURE OF THE LOCAL FIRM

One might reach the conclusion that merger with a large national organization lies at the next turn of the road for every local firm of CPAs. That, however, does not appear to be a logical conclusion to draw from the information that has been developed.

In the first place, there are many accounting firms with sizable staffs located in smaller communities where "big business" and the large national accounting firms are not likely to appear. The well-organized local firms will continue to provide satisfactory service to the small- and medium-sized businesses in those communities.

It has been argued that because of mergers the strong local accounting firms in the larger cities are disappearing from the business scene. No one, however, has come forth with proof. The statistics show that the number of practitioners in the United States, both partnerships and sole proprietors, increases steadily year after year. For example, during the ten years from 1950 to 1960 the number of partnerships represented in the membership of the AICPA increased from 2,100 to 4,900 while, in the same period, sole practitioners increased from 3,200 to 6,500.

It is a fair assumption, therefore, that for every local accounting firm that disappears through mergers two or more take its place. Perhaps they, too, thirty years hence will be merged with some large organization but for the next few years they will be growing, expanding, and improving the character and quality of their services. In the meantime, they are taking the place in the business world and in the accounting profession so recently vacated by the older local firm which has disappeared as a separate entity by virtue of a merger.

A statement made by Andrew Barr, chief accountant for the Securities and Exchange Commission, at the annual meeting of the California Society of CPAs in June, 1961, would lend support to the belief that not all local firms are forced to merge to prevent the loss of clients who have grown to "big business" size. He reported that 363 separate accounting firms were named as principal accountant in 1,357 filings with the SEC during the calendar year 1960. The eight largest national accounting firms certified 851 of the statements; seven others served in from six to twenty filings; fifteen, in three to five; fifty-one, in two each; and 282 firms each in a single filing. That is evidence of important audit work being handled by local accounting firms.

Many local firms continue to serve clients with branch or subsidiary operations at distant points and the clients must be satisfied and well served, else the arrangements would not be continued. The distant work for such clients may be performed by staff members traveling to the various locations, or by other accountants to whom certain phases of the work may have been referred, or by a combination of the two.

SOLUTIONS OTHER THAN MERGER

The problems of local practitioners are sometimes solved by the formation of a partnership or merger of two or more small firms rather than by merger of a small practice with a large one. Another solution is increased co-operation within the accounting profession. There are cases in which a small firm enlists the services of another small or large firm to handle some phases of the engagement, without any fear of losing the client. This is most likely to happen when a correspondent is needed, when specialized management services are involved, or when additional accounting personnel or experience is necessary to handle an engagement such as a bank audit, SEC registration, or a specialized governmental examination.

In other professions, calling in consultants or specialists is becoming routine. In medicine, for example, there is renewed recognition of the importance of the general practitioner, but fewer and fewer patients would rely on a general practitioner unless they trusted him to call in a surgeon or specialist when particular technical knowledge was required.

Extent of referrals. Much has been said and written on the subject of referrals and a great deal of work is, no doubt, being referred at present, principally from New York and Chicago and other industrial and financial centers to accountants in smaller or less industrialized cities. Obviously, referrals are not wholly meeting the needs of the accounting profession or of the business community because some mergers have been arranged to eliminate referrals. Under the proper circumstances however, referrals have accomplished the desired result, and no one has denied that under those circumstances the use of referrals will continue without forcing the referring accounting firm into a merger situation.

The referrals are generally of audit work, usually inventory observation, and occasionally of audits of branch offices or of subsidiary or affiliated companies. Occasionally, work involving SEC registration is referred by local practitioners to national firms. On the other hand, referrals of management services among accounting firms have been extremely limited. The partners of merged local firms report, practically without exception, that the mergers have made greatly improved management services available to their clients. In view of the increasing emphasis on the role of the CPA in this field, it is evident that arrangements must be worked out through referrals, or specialist firms, or otherwise, to bring such improved and high level management services to the clients of the local accountants. The alternative can only be to advance management services to one of the prime reasons for mergers.

Transferring a Practice

BENEFITS OF A PLAN

■ IN RESPONSE TO recommendations of the advisory committee of local practitioners of the AICPA regarding orderly transfer of the practices of deceased or disabled practitioners, a number of state societies and local chapters have set up orderly professional emergency assistance plans which are being used with real benefits to the three important parties affected:

The deceased practitioner's estate. There is many a practitioner who, until recently, entertained little hope for salvaging anything substantial from his practice as the time arrived when he could no longer carry it on. The dismal thought was that the clients would have to transplant themselves to others' hands as best they could, while his estate's main efforts would be to try to collect the accounts receivable. To such a practitioner, the new possibility of being able to realize as much as one year's additional gross fees comes as a complete (and completely pleasant) surprise. Without question, the greatest and most direct benefits of a preplanned transfer of a practice go to the family of the deceased or disabled practitioner.

The client. The transferring of his account to another office is likely to be an annoying, unpleasant, and inconvenient task for the average client. The onus is largely removed, however, when he can rest assured that such transfer can and will be smoothly made to another practitioner of his own choice through the good offices of a special committee of the nearest chapter of the state society. The fact that this machinery is being provided for his service and benefit, as well as for the estate involved, cannot fail to impress him anew with the high public aims and sincere service standards of the accounting profession.

The purchasing practitioner. The office taking over the new account benefits because the transfer is effected in a timely, considerate, dignified, and mutually confident manner. His pecuniary benefits from the arrangement are, it is true, largely deferred to the future. (Usually he realizes something because the payout is generally made over a period of several years, e.g., one third of fees each year.) Nevertheless, he has the satisfaction of knowing that he is helping his erstwhile colleague and at the same time cementing good will between his profession and his community. Moreover, he can note with satisfaction that he is forging one more link in a permanent chain that may some day inure to the substantial direct benefit of his own family.

ILLUSTRATIVE PLANS

The Bridgeport Plan. A well-known plan which accomplishes these objectives was developed by the Bridgeport, Conn., chapter of the Connecticut Society of CPAs. It is known as the Bridgeport Plan. This was the first detailed plan and it served as a model for later ones. It utilizes a "disaster committee" of local accountants who dispose of a practice when disaster strikes. The committee compiles a list of CPAs interested in buying additional accounts. When a death occurs, the committee helps clients to choose another CPA from the list before the client's affairs deteriorate. Each CPA taking over a client agrees to pay the widow or estate 33 1/3 per cent of the fees he receives for his services to the client over a period of three years. (Other arrangements can be and have been made.)

The individual practitioner may find that his state society or local chapter has adopted such a plan. He should contact the appropriate committee and begin to put his own practice in transferable condition by assembling the necessary data concerning his clientele. These data include:

1. Date of acquisition of client
2. Type of service performed
3. Dates and places of performing services
4. Fiscal year
5. Time and fees last three years
6. Time and fees this year
7. Time and fees estimated for next year
8. Dates of billings and payments
9. Financial status of client (in general terms)

The Illinois Plan. The Illinois Society of CPAs has presented an ideally workable plan.

This plan is administered by a committee of the society known as the Emergency Assistance Committee which consists of nine members to be appointed according to the bylaws of the society.

The members of the society receive a copy of the plan and the committee secures from such members who are sole practitioners and who desire to participate in the plan, a signed statement in a suggested form provided.

On the form suggested, the participant is requested to list the names of not less than two nor more than six members of the society who, in his opinion, could best serve the interests of his clients. The participant has the privilege of adding or removing names at any time within the limits of two and six mentioned above.

The plan provides for assistance to disabled participants or to the estate of a deceased participant. A participant is a member of the state society who has agreed in advance in a written statement filed with the society to participate in the emergency assistance plan.

Upon the death of a participant, the Emergency Assistance Committee meets with the representative of the estate. If they agree that the committee may assist in the disposal of the practice, the committee secures the written approval on a suggested form. The committee is then furnished with a list of the decedent's clients.

Then a letter is sent from the decedent's representative to each of the decedent's clients to advise that the Emergency Assistance Committee has been requested to assist the representative of the decedent and is submitting a list of the names and addresses of the possible successors as previously named by the decedent, and to invite the client to select a successor and notify the committee. Such notification (on another suggested form) authorizes the representative to distribute any books and records of the client to the successor designated by the client, for which a form of receipt is recommended. The committee may assist disabled eligible members by following a similar procedure.

The basis of compensation is most interesting. The successor shall pay the representative 25 per cent of the fees earned from the client for the successor's services to the client during a period of forty-eight months after the decedent's death. The total amount paid, however, is not to exceed the fees earned by the decedent during the twelve months preceding his death.

The plan further suggests that invoicing may be made by the representative for the work in process and work unbilled at the time of the decedent's death. However, if requested by the representative, it may be invoiced by the successor and remitted in full to the representative.

As in all facets of the administration of our practices, it is well to have a formal plan adopted in advance to meet any emergencies that may arise.

SUGGESTED PLANS FOR RETIREMENT OF A PRACTITIONER

Sale of the practice. The objectives of the retiring practitioner are threefold:

1. Adequate income for himself and his dependents
2. Continuing high-caliber service for his clients
3. Suitable outlets for his energy and interests

Most practitioners seek these objectives through sale of their entire interest. The market is excellent: in certain areas, prices range up to 150 per cent of gross annual fees.

Let us assume that what must be considered a favorable deal is made. A $50,000 practice is sold for $50,000, payable 30 per cent down and the balance in three annual installments of 25, 25, and 20 per cent. To the extent that the price includes payment for unrealized receivables, it is taxable as ordinary income [IRC, sec. 751(a)] after setting aside 25 per cent capital-gains tax from each payment, as this plan qualifies for the installment treatment [IRC, sec. 453(b)(2)(A)]. The balance is to be invested to yield say, 6 per cent. Seeking a higher permanent return would probably move the capital outside the area of safety. The seller can look forward to the following income:

First year	$ 675
Second year	1,237
Third year	1,800
Fourth year and thereafter	2,250
Twenty-year total (including principal of $37,500)	$79,462

Such a return may prove attractive to one with substantial independent earnings, but the practitioner not so blessed will find himself faced with the choice of risking his capital to produce a higher yield, making the strenuous effort needed to launch a completely new enterprise, eating into his principal sum, or skimping along on an income insufficient to permit him to enjoy his retirement. And what provisions can he make for his family? The security of a trust usually means a modest rate of return, while an attempt to earn more without trust protection exposes the principal to dangers of mismanagement and aimless dissipation by his beneficiaries.

How can the seller be certain that his clients, now absorbed by a larger practice, will find the same personal attention to which they are accustomed and entitled? He cannot, unless he is familiar with the operations of the purchaser. He can justifiably assume that his successor has both ability and good faith, but not a schedule so flexible as to preclude the possibility that some of his former clients may be shunted into the background.

When the practitioner has actually retired, how will he spend his time? Perhaps he will be occupied with managing his substantial accumulated investments. Perhaps he is eagerly waiting to begin some new activity or study, something which has always fascinated him, but which his busy professional life has forced him to disregard. Perhaps his prime wish is to spend the rest of his days in tranquil relaxation. Perhaps physical infirmity will force him to make the psychological adjustment necessary to accept a sedentary existence. If none of these factors is present to a significant degree, he will unhappily long for those days of frantic telephone calls, report deadlines, and crucial conferences.

Development of younger partner. Is there another avenue to successful retirement less fraught with pitfalls than the sale of one's entire accounting practice? Let us consider once again a practice which grosses $50,000, assuming a net income of $20,000 for the sole principal. The firm operates with a three-man staff, including a capable young CPA of partnership caliber earning $7,500 per annum. This man is the key to the problem, for he is to eventually acquire full control.

The essence of the plan is the gradual withdrawal of the principal from active duty. Assuming that it becomes necessary to engage an additional staff man at $5,000 and that the new partner is to continue receiving his salary of $7,500, the annual partnership net profit is reduced to $15,000. Profits are to be divided as shown in Table 2 on the following page.

This agreement contemplates that at the end of twenty years, or upon the death of the retiring partner, whichever is later, the new partner is to become sole owner of the practice. Other suggested features of the arrangement are as follows:

1. Upon the death of the retiring partner, his estate shall succeed to all his retirement rights under the agreement.

2. Action is to be gradual, over a period of years; the retiring partner's prime responsibility is to build client confidence in his successor.

3. The withdrawing partner should remain a member of the firm until termination of his interest. He should continue to serve in a consultative capacity, spending such time as is mutually desirable.

4. Fees paid by new clients obtained by the retiring partner are to be subject to the profit-sharing provisions set forth above. He is not to share in fees paid by clients which the new partner or staff members may acquire.

Table 2

| Year | New partner | | | | Retiring partner | |
| | Profits | | | | Profits | |
	%	Amount	Salary	Total	%	Amount
1st	25	$ 3,750	$7,500	$ 11,250	75	$ 11,250
2nd	33 1/3	5,000	7,500	12,500	66 2/3	10,000
3rd	40	6,000	7,500	13,500	60	9,000
4th	50	7,500	7,500	15,000	50	7,500
5th-10th	60	9,000	7,500	16,500	40	6,000
11th-20th	75	11,250	7,500	18,750	25	3,750
				$338,750		$111,250

Despite the fact that the retiring partner is to share in the profits up to twenty years after he terminates full-time duty, the average certified staff man would jump at the chance of participating in such a plan. He is to acquire a substantial immediate interest with no capital investment. Although his salary is to remain constant, his total earnings are to rise from $7,500 to a minimum average of almost $17,000 over the twenty-year period. This can be augmented by the addition of new clients or the expansion of services to existing ones. The retiring partner should share in any increased billings resulting from his own efforts, as suggested above.

It must be stressed that the proposed arrangement is merely a suggestion, subject to such revisions as may be necessary to effect maximum fairness to both participants. This will depend largely upon the time which the older partner plans to devote to the practice after he ends his full-time schedule.

Tax consequences. 1. All payments made by the partnership to the retiring partner to the extent of the tax basis of his interest in partnership property (excluding unrealized receivables) constitute a nontaxable return of capital. The difference between this tax basis and the fair market value of such property is taxable as capital gain. Everything in excess of the fair market value is taxable as ordinary income [IRC, sec. 736, reg. 1.736-1(b)(5)].

2. The partners can agree upon any method of allocating the annual payments so long as the total amount allocated to the partner's interest in partnership property does not exceed the fair market value at the date of his retirement [reg. 1.736-1(b)(5)(iii)].

3. Capital gain treatment could be accomplished by an outright sale of interest by the old partner to the new [IRC, sec. 741]. If a sale is not desired, it could be obtained to the extent that the partnership agreement specifies that distributions by the partnership to the retiring partner in exchange for his interest are to include payment for goodwill [IRC, sec. 736(b)].

4. In any event, amounts received attributable to unrealized receivables are taxable as ordinary income [IRC, sec. 751(a)].

5. While beneficial to the retiring partner, capital-gain treatment would increase the tax burden of the new partner, which would generally be contrary to the intentions of the parties. If the retiring partner were in a high tax bracket, a plan could conceivably be worked out under which he would accept a smaller percentage of the profits in exchange for capital-gain treatment, the net effect of which would be a higher after-tax income for both parties.

6. Ordinary income would cause the withdrawing partner to forfeit any social-security benefits to which he would otherwise become entitled from age sixty-five to seventy-two. After age seventy-two, there would be no loss of benefits.

Over-all effects of plan. How effective will this plan be in attaining the announced objectives of the retiring practitioner? Incomewise, it returns about $111,000 over a twenty-year period as opposed to about $80,000 yielded by the sale of the entire practice. The latter figure includes both principal and income; both figures are before deducting income tax for the year in which received. While this $31,000 difference may be reduced by the possible loss of social-security benefits for seven years (between ages 65 and 72), a fair comparison must give weight to the following factors:

1. Under an outright sale, the net proceeds will be subject to reduction by (a) the extent to which unrealized receivables result in taxation as ordinary income, (b) loss of clientele in the first year. Most purchasers will insist on a guarantee covering this period.

2. An inactive partner can still increase his income through the acquisition of new clients, but an ex-practitioner cannot.

3. Many practices grossing $50,000 net substantially more than the $20,000 used in our illustration.

4. The amount of salary paid to the partner and the new staff man will vary with the nature of the practice, its location, and so forth.

Merger with established firm. Is there still another method available, perhaps superior to the two already discussed? Under certain conditions, the answer is "yes." We must first recognize that the retiring practitioner could not expect the same profit-sharing percentage from an established firm that he could from a younger partner. Nevertheless, it is possible that the resulting savings in overhead would so increase the net profit available for distribution that, notwithstanding his reduced percentage, he would receive a higher return from a merger. There also may be specialized talent available in the new entity to help solve particular client problems. However, he would probably find that joining forces in this fashion would give him a much smaller measure of managerial freedom. If inactivity is what the retiring practitioner wants, this would prove to be an advantage.

The beauty of this arrangement is its flexibility. The profit-sharing provisions can be tailored to fit the time which the retiring partner is to devote to the firm. This will be determined by his willingness, his capacity, and the needs of the practice.

Professional Development

A PLANNED PROGRAM

■ PROFESSIONAL DEVELOPMENT means first the responsibility that the members of the accounting profession assume for the training and development of the men who are presently getting started in this field.

Technical staff-training is completely different from professional training and development. It is a basic assumption that each firm must undertake a sustained program of technical staff-training. Only through such training can the profession maintain proper work standards and at the same time advance in accounting theory and practice and tax accounting. The following material, however, is limited to the professional development of the individual.

True professional development is a planned program that will offer a man the training and guidance in the necessary management skills, the encouragement to take time to participate in professional and community activities, and the desire to contribute to his profession, all of which are requisite to recognition and identification as a true professional man in the opinion of the public.

The requirements for professional development can be broken down into five component parts:

1. Personal identity and recognition are of utmost importance if a man is to attain stature and be respected as professional.

2. A man must have internal executive and management training which will qualify him for future use as a manager or partner in a public accounting office, or qualify him to operate his own firm.

3. A man must be encouraged by his firm to take the necessary time

to do his part in civic, state, and national activities affecting his profession, his community, his church, and his fellow man.

4. A man must be encouraged by financial support from his firm to participate fully in professional activities and other projects, including the development of outside contacts.

5. A man must be instilled with a desire to contribute to the profession through service, published articles, speeches, or research: the first requirement of a profession.

Identity and recognition. The first factor is concerned with the identity and recognition of the man, not only on the job but in everyday life. The junior of today is the senior of tomorrow, and the senior of today is the principal, partner, or executive of tomorrow. Time passes quickly, and professional development is something that cannot be put off without jeopardizing the very core of professional existence.

A staff man, or even a junior accountant, on occasion should be brought into conferences with the client so that his identity and association with the job are established. In this manner, it is very easy to give recognition and credit to the man for his work, his suggestions or new ideas, which will help to increase his stature in the client's eyes.

The more rapidly the personal identity of a staff man is established, the sooner his superior finds a larger quantity of his own time available for supervision of an increased volume of work. Why? Because after a period of time the client calls the staff man instead of his superior on certain of his problems.

We are not in the position of a painting contractor who obtains a job and sends three men over to complete the work and then renders a bill for paint and X hours of labor at X dollars per hour. The client does not even care who the painters are by name or identity because he assumes that they are able to complete the required work properly.

With the accounting profession, however, when three men are sent over to a job it is vitally important that they become known individually for their separate skills and identified as individuals in the eyes of all departments of the client's company. A professional accounting firm is not a chain store which sells its products under a firm label. Business is attracted and retained on the basis of the identity of each individual who represents the firm.

Management training. The second factor in the definition of professional development is internal executive and management training. This area includes full and complete disclosure in an accounting office, whereby all phases of operations are explained to staff men. Only in this way will they learn how to manage and operate a public accounting office and become familiar with all the problems that must be solved at the management level.

A staff man should have a thorough understanding of the billing rates charged to clients so that he will realize the basis on which charges are computed. This training will help him to have a proper respect for the evaluation of his chargeable time. The relationship of billing rates to his compensation must be explained so that he fully understands when an hour of his work is charged to a particular client that he is affected directly as an individual. He must be informed that as his accounting billing rate can be increased, his compensation will be favorably affected as well. Too often this important detail of billing rates and compensation is classified information and treated as top secret.

A staff man should be brought in when accounts are billed so that he will understand the procedure and problems that go with a timely presentation of a statement for services rendered. He will then understand the problems concerned with adjustments that are often required in billing rates to allow for factors that result in the raising or lowering of the final fee in relation to the actual time record. He should be trained to understand the internal office workings involved in the assignments of work, the flow of work, and the control of jobs. He should be encouraged to work up new ideas, suggest new forms and methods, and make recommendations for the improvement of the internal system of his office.

Some years ago, the General Electric Company made a three-year study of the subject, "How Managers Are Made and How You Can Grow Your Own Executives." Certain excerpts from the study were published in *Nation's Business* (March-April 1956). The following condensed comments are taken directly from the General Electric study:

> Management development is self-development and no company or industry can afford to let new managers just happen.
>
> You cannot count upon a man to get ahead in a business just because he has talent, and experience alone does not insure his capability on the job.
>
> Management is a distinct skill; the practice of management is far ahead of its translation into actual rules or procedures that can be tabulated.
>
> The leaders, managers, and executives of today are going to be judged more and more by their ability to develop their own people, which requires encouragement and assistance in self-improvement at every level.
>
> You cannot buy that state of mind with high pay scales; you have to build it by adding up a lot of the little things in life.

Here is the summary comment by Ralph J. Cordiner, Chairman, which forcefully brings home the whole point: "Not customers, not products, not plants, not money, but managers and executives may be the limit of General Electric's growth." If the General Electric Company is so concerned with the training of managers and executives, it surely must be time for the accounting profession to examine itself in light of these comments and to adopt management-development programs that will insure its growth and continuity.

Professional activities. The third factor in the definition of professional development is the encouragement by management of participation in all activities that affect the profession. Time should be allowed for the state society, the AICPA, and other projects and activities affecting a man's community, state, church, and fellow man.

An effective way for a man to gain confidence and recognition as a professional is to work on committees, speakers' bureaus, fund solicitations, and similar projects that require time and assistance from people in every community. We all have an obligation to contribute in these areas.

A high-priority item under this program is a requirement that a man complete some formal speech training, perhaps in a Toastmasters Club, so as to learn to express himself clearly and intelligently. Of course, this type of training will have a double advantage, as the man will also be able to discuss business affairs more adequately with clients when the occasion arises.

Apparently, everyone does not believe this training so necessary. Partners of some accounting firms express the thought that they will take care of the contacts, new business, and civic activity for their firm and that they have no desire to develop a core of "eager-beaver" speakers on civic affairs among their men. It is obviously quite impossible to reconcile that type of thinking with the basic requirements of a profession.

After having been given the opportunity to take a good speaking course, a man should be ready to accept assignments with the speakers' bureau for the United Fund agencies, the Red Cross, the symphony association, the cancer drive, the polio fund or any of the many such projects that are a part of our community life. He will be ready for a committee assignment in the state society by which he can develop and become better known among his fellow workers.

A profession is judged every day by its participation in community activities. If our men are encouraged to participate in civic and professional affairs and to take the necessary time, it will help them to develop confidence and raise the stature of the CPA in the eyes of community leaders.

Financial assistance. The fourth factor in the definition of professional development is financial support so that staff members can participate in the many projects and activities that require expenditures which may seem substantial to a man on a staff salary. Particular reference is made to the firm's underwriting of costs in the following areas:

1. Additional training courses for specialized subjects, such as the AICPA continuing education courses and tax institutes

2. Costs of membership in the state society and AICPA

3. Costs of attendance at state society and AICPA and special committee meetings when possible

4. Costs of membership in various service clubs such as Rotary, City Club, and Kiwanis

5. Costs of membership in Toastmasters clubs

6. Costs of attendance at regional graduate-study conferences and conventions

7. The payment of dues and out-of-pocket costs at social and athletic clubs which would include entertainment expense for clients and other appropriate contacts

These are the principal items where encouragement by financial support would mean much to a staff man who is having trouble enough getting by at a salary level which surely could not cover very many of these items.

Many practitioners may say, "Why pay all these costs and increase the firm's expense? A man will not develop an appreciation for such activities if they don't cost him anything." Some may also say, "Nobody paid these costs for me when I was a young man, so why should our firm pay them for the men of today?"

In the first place, if a man is not really interested in his professional development, he is not the type of man that you should engage to help build your firm's future. But the newer man in the profession knows very little about the various opportunities for professional development. After a few months of association with a firm, he begins to develop a feeling of the firm policy on this subject and how it directly affects him. If there is a warm and receptive feeling to progressive ideas on the professional level, he will respond and will rapidly become an active moving force in the activities in which he participates.

If a man is encouraged to meet people and broaden his areas of contact, it can only make him a happier man, a better staff man, and more of a credit to the firm he serves. Moreover, valuable contact work can be done at the secondary level with clients, that is, contacts with company comptrollers, bookkeepers, office accountants, secretaries, payroll departments, production employees, sales force, and other departments of clients that judge our operations as CPAs. A man should be encouraged by his firm to spend some time with these people in the client's office and on occasion take them to lunch and feel comfortable in so doing because he knows that he is part of his firm team.

There is no expense referred to here that is not truly professional expense. The failure of many firms to underwrite these costs is probably not so much the amount involved, but more often an archaic policy handed down over a period of years. Many firms are steeped in tradition and are still following certain practices adopted many years ago by the founders. Obviously, such practices must be reviewed and modernized if accountancy is to maintain a high place as a profession. No doubt most proprietors and partners treat such expenses as company expense. It does not take much further thinking to adopt this program completely and pass it down the line to practically every man on the staff.

The results of a planned program that encourages a man by this type of financial support can make a staff man feel he is part of the team. He develops a feeling of belonging to an organization and becomes aware of his potential in the ultimate development of contacts leading to new business. Many firms are already underwriting costs of this kind to varying degrees.

Contributions to the profession. The fifth factor in the definition of professional development is the requirement that there must be instilled in each man a desire to make his contribution to the profession through committee service, writing articles, delivering speeches, or the technical research that is a minimum requisite in any profession.

There are many fine, outstanding CPAs who contribute much time and effort to research, publishing, and other areas. However, some men have not been trained from the start to feel that a moral obligation exists for them to put something back for those who follow so that the profession will improve.

One of the most satisfying ways of feeling that you have put something back in the profession is to help a younger man set up his own office. Too often a man leaves an accounting firm with a feeling of animosity, which prevents his receiving any farewell blessing at the time of his departure. The usual man opening an office has to find out the facts of life for himself because his former firm has usually contributed only to his technical training and has not trained him to be an executive in the operation of his own business. There is no way to measure the good will and satisfaction developed by assisting in this situation, and it really is an obligation of people in the profession to make it a little easier for a man to get started and survive the first few years.

Here are some of the results to be expected from fulfillment of the firm's obligations in the area of professional development.

1. There will be less costly turnover in CPA firms, and avoidance of problems with clients who cannot understand the failure to retain a good man.

2. If a man is retained and accepted as a true member of a profession, there will be very few individual problems with him. The charging of his time at a top rate will be easy and the payment of adequate compensation through salary, bonus, and profit participation will be a pleasure because he is instrumental in producing more profits for the firm.

3. The firm will achieve continuity, which is the hope of everyone operating a business or professional firm today.

If a man feels that he is part of the team on a long-range basis, he will develop a professional attitude and a feeling of being in business for himself in his daily work. He will not desire to leave your firm because he knows that as the firm grows, he grows. This is the only way to build up a mutual trust that is stronger than any written contract. If a man can feel that he is eventually building his future and providing for his retirement, if he can experience the thrill of developing a new account and watching the firm profit from such a relationship, he is the greatest asset that can ever be had in the accounting profession.

The only asset that the accounting profession has in any firm, whether local, national, or international, is the man who has been properly trained in every facet of his work, who has found his niche in his chosen field. To paraphrase Mr. Cordiner: "Not clients, not firm goodwill, not machines, not money, but men who have not been developed professionally may be the limit of the growth of accounting as a profession."

Continuing education. *The need to keep up to date.* The continuing effect of inflation on the practice of the CPA requires a progressive increase from year to year in the fees he receives for his services. The practitioner's services must be worth the fee. A continuing education program is designed to aid just that, to increase the CPA's competence in ever-expanding areas of service.

Professional competence is not attained by passing the CPA examination alone. That is only a beginning. The briefest review of the accounting literature of twenty-five or even ten years ago tells us that accounting theories and concepts are constantly changing, horizons constantly expanding. Generally recognized principles of accounting are being expanded. Standards of auditing procedure and reporting are being modified. New ideas in audit sampling methods and other audit techniques are being advanced. The income-tax laws are changing from year to year, bringing new problems in tax accounting practice. New opportunities for services by CPAs, such as management advisory service, are being explored. Governmental accounting and auditing, both local and larger, is becoming a common field. New or enlarged outlets for the CPA's services are being opened up in many other areas, such as insurance companies, banks, savings and loan associations, and pension and welfare funds. There are others, and there will be more.

In order to achieve and maintain his competence, the CPA must study. He studied to pass the CPA examination and that, together with the early years of his experience, brought him to a certain level of competence. Continued reading of professional periodicals and other technical literature may keep him abreast of some of the developments in the profession. Such haphazard and inefficient methods cannot, however, bring him professional competence in the new and dynamic fields just mentioned or keep him abreast of all the things that are happening in our rapidly growing profession. Growing complexity and specialization in all of the professions have created a need for more or less formal postgraduate training.

Dr. Earl J. McGrath, former U. S. Commissioner of Education, spoke at length on this subject of continuing education for professional people at the 1957 annual meeting of the AICPA in New Orleans. On the basis of his studies of the educational needs of all the professions and their efforts to meet them, he felt obliged to say that "accounting is far behind the others." The indictment seems fully justified by recent studies conducted by the AICPA staff. These studies reveal that a number of organizations serving lawyers, doctors, engineers, insurance men, bankers, credit executives, and business managers have established elaborate programs of education for their members. They offer a wide variety of choices to their members for instruction by correspondence, seminars, and lectures, ranging from a day to several weeks in length. Almost all of these activities are self-supporting. The American Management Association, for example, with 28,000 members, held 1,037 meetings, events, or courses, during the fiscal year ended June 1958, with a total meeting attendance of 75,000. The American Bar Association, jointly with the American Law Institute, has a comprehensive program which provides material for educational courses given by the various state and local bar associations. In 1957 alone there were 13,676 enrollments by California lawyers in continuing education courses and over $200,000 was paid in tuition for them. In one year (1957) more than 1,000 postgraduate courses were presented by the medical profession with more than 35,000 physicians enrolled in formal courses, and 65,000 taking some form of postgraduate education. Incidentally, the American Academy of General Practice has a firm policy of expelling any member who fails to devote at least one hour a week to organized professional study and has, in fact, dropped over a thousand members in the last ten years for neglecting to comply with this requirement.

The AICPA continuing education program. The AICPA is now doing something about this situation. An ambitious new and enlarged program of continuing education was authorized by its governing body in 1958, with an initial appropriation of $50,000. The program was barely launched, however, before it became obvious that it would have to go far beyond vocational training and embrace all the aspects of a professional life. Consequently, a more descriptive title, *professional development,* was adopted to clarify the nature and indicate the broad scope of the program.

At the AICPA 1958 meeting in Detroit, a board of managers was elected as the first step in implementing the program. Shortly after its election, the board employed a staff director to head the new division of the AICPA, the Division of Professional Development. It also adopted an organization plan for the division and, in doing so, stated the long-range objectives as follows:

I. The objective of the Division of Professional Development of the AICPA is to increase the competence and the stature of CPAs by making available to them and their staff assistants a well-rounded program of continuing education. Although it is possible that this program may, when completely developed, relieve the universities of some of the vocational training that they have had to incorporate in their curriculums, it is intended that the courses will supplement and complement the university's role. The courses offered and to be offered by the Division of Professional Development are not intended to replace or duplicate any training belonging in a college curriculum.

   A. A variety of courses will be offered to meet the principal needs of the majority of the members of the AICPA.
      1. Courses on technical and related subjects will be developed at various levels, from junior accountants to partners.
      2. Courses on the administrative aspects of an accounting practice will be offered to all practitioners: individuals, small firms, medium-size firms, and large firms.
      3. Courses intended to broaden the scope of the CPA's knowledge and to extend it to various fields will be offered.

   B. Courses will be adapted to various methods of presentation so as to serve, with most economy and efficiency, members in metropolitan areas as well as those in less-populated areas. If, for example, sixteen hours of class time are needed, the materials will permit presentation (a) in two full days, (b) in four half-day sessions, (c) in eight two-hour sessions, or (d) any other combination appropriate to individual situations.

II. It is intended that the division will be operated on a self-sustaining basis.

III. The problem of obtaining instructional staffs of persons who are both technically qualified practitioners and effective leaders may have to be solved by providing practitioners with instruction in effective teaching methods.

Professional development courses. A variety of professional development courses is being developed by the AICPA and presented locally by state societies and chapters throughout the country. These courses permit every public accounting firm to provide specialized instruction and training for members of its senior staff. (For further description of the staff-training program, see Section 2, page 155.)

The following list is representative of the kind and variety of courses available:

1. Administration of an Accounting Practice Series

    a. Accountants' Fees: Their Determination and Collection. A one-day seminar on the setting of per-diem rates, time accumulation, and billing procedures.

    b. Management of a Tax Practice. A one-day seminar on the administration of a tax practice: office organization, staff problems, and processing returns.

    c. Building an Accounting Practice. A two-day clinic on expanding an accounting practice, which covers management services, attracting new clients, attracting competent personnel, and planning for growth.

    d. How to Manage Yourself, Your Staff, and Your Practice. A two-day clinic on getting the most out of available time.

    e. Minimizing the CPA's Legal Liability. A one-day seminar on the responsibilities of CPAs under common, judicial, and statutory law.

2. Tax-Planning Series

    a. Problems of Closely Held Corporations. A one-day seminar on tax problems peculiar to the owner of the small corporation.

    b. Purchase, Sale, or Liquidation of a Corporate Business. A one-day seminar on how to effect tax savings when purchasing or selling the assets or stock of a corporate business.

    c. Pension and Profit-Sharing Plans. A one-day seminar on selected executive compensation plans intended to minimize the impact of taxes.

    d. The CPA's Role in Estate Planning. A four-day workshop seminar on estate-planning with special emphasis on specific client groups.

3. Auditing

    a. Writing Auditing Reports. A two-day seminar on the scope and content of long-form reports and the wording of qualifications and disclaimers in short-form reports.

    b. Generally Accepted Auditing Standards. Three individual one-day seminars—one each in general standards, standards of field work, and standards of reporting—which discuss specific criteria for the application of generally accepted auditing standards.

4. Management Services

    a. Budgeting for Profits in Small Business. A three-day workshop seminar on budgeting techniques and their application. The course includes the development of a comprehensive budget for small manufacturers.

PROFESSIONAL ORGANIZATIONS

The accounting profession came into being because people needed its services. Changing circumstances have altered the needs and broadened the scope and form of the services required, but the profession has kept pace with the increasing demands made upon it and has expanded rapidly. Greater numerical strength has not been the only characteristic of its phenomenal growth, however. A natural complement to this physical expansion has been the development of its professional organizations and literature, for it is only through organization that a profession's needs for self-regulation can be met, and it is only through its literature that the techniques and rules which have been developed for the guidance of its members can be communicated to them.

American Institute of Certified Public Accountants. During the years which have elapsed since its emergence as the single national association of CPAs, the AICPA has grown from a small organization, concentrating on a few basic activities, to a large one, concerning itself with any and all problems affecting the professional practice of CPAs. The broad scope of the AICPA's interests is evidenced by the varied activities in which it engages. Its objectives, as recited in the bylaws, are the following:

1. To unite the accountancy profession in the United States as constituted by the certified public accountants of the several states, territories, possessions, and the District of Columbia
2. To promote and maintain high professional and moral standards within the accountancy profession
3. To assist in the maintenance of high standards for the certified public accountant certificate
4. To develop and maintain standards for the examination of candidates for admission
5. To safeguard the interests of certified public accountants
6. To advance accounting research
7. To develop and improve accountancy education
8. To encourage cordial relations among certified public accountants practicing in the United States of America and accountants of similar status in the other countries of the world

In addition, the following were adopted by the Council upon recommendation by the committee on long-range objectives:

It is an objective of the Institute to serve as the national organization of certified public accountants in and out of public practice, and to develop and maintain the form of organization best adapted to the needs of all its members.

It is an objective of the Institute to encourage co-operation and consultation among national organizations of accountants to the end that the entire accounting function may make its greatest contribution to the public welfare.

Pending the time when public practitioners within the accounting function are either CPAs or those with a clearly differentiating title, there will be a group of non-CPAs who are presently permitted to practice as "public accountants" and whose right to continue to do so during their lifetime must be respected. It is an objective of the Institute that CPAs and their professional societies should develop and maintain friendly co-operative relations with this transitional group with the purpose of improving educational, technical, and ethical standards, and providing aid in fulfilling the requirements for the CPA certificate.

It is an objective of the Institute that by voluntary agreement the plans, programs, procedures and activities of the state societies and the Institute be co-ordinated to the fullest extent possible, and their respective areas of responsibility be clearly delineated; and in particular that the state societies and the Institute adopt a uniform code of ethics and enforcement procedures.

The work of the AICPA, all of which is directed toward the achievement of these objectives, benefits each of its members in a different manner, depending upon the special problems connected with his practice. However, a general consideration of its activities, grouped according to the objectives at which they are aimed, will help to point out the many valuable ways in which the AICPA serves its membership as a whole.

Unity of the profession. It is significant that the purpose which is stated first in the AICPA's bylaws is "to unite the accountancy profession"; for unless the support of all eligible accountants is enlisted, none of the other objectives can be fully realized. It is particularly important for CPAs to join together for mutual advancement and protection. As members of a young and rapidly growing profession, they need a greater public understanding of their functions than they have yet attained and wider recognition of the importance of high standards for the CPA certificate. The AICPA's influence in dealing with legislators, other professions, and the general public depends upon the extent to which it can claim to speak for the whole profession. Its rapid growth in recent years furnishes convincing evidence that the individual accountant realizes the value which he derives from his membership. However, the continued expansion of the AICPA depends upon the active co-operation of all eligible CPAs. Membership is open to holders of CPA certificates who have had two years of public accounting experience or its equivalent and who are in work related to accounting.

The AICPA is achieving its objective of uniting the accounting profession not only by uniting the efforts of its individual members but also by co-ordinating the work of the state societies. Although the AICPA exercises no authority of any kind over the policies or activities of the state societies, the existence of both state organizations and the national society makes for a type of unity which could not otherwise be achieved. The state societies are the sources of information and advice which, collected and interpreted in the AICPA, accurately reflect a cross section of professional opinion throughout the nation and permit the profession as a whole to work with maximum effectiveness.

The AICPA also works closely with other organizations in the accounting field. It maintains active co-operative relations with the American Accounting Association, the Controllers Institute of America, the National Association of Accountants, and The Institute of Internal Auditors.

Professional standards. Early in its history the AICPA began actively to develop standards of professional conduct, recognizing that self-discipline is a necessary foundation for public confidence. All members of the AICPA subscribe to its *Code of Professional Ethics*—rules which they themselves have developed and which they may amend from time to time as changing conditions require. These rules emphasize independence, standards of practice, and ethical conduct. They appear on pages 821-824 of the Appendix, along with the "Numbered Opinions of the Committee on Professional Ethics."

High standards for the CPA certificate. Since its founding, the AICPA has worked for the establishment of uniform standards for accounting examinations throughout the country, for it recognizes that the prestige of the profession in one state is not independent of its standing in another and that its nationwide prestige depends on the maintenance of high standards in every state. Today these examinations, which are prepared by the Board of Examiners of the AICPA, are used by all of the states, the District of Columbia, Puerto Rico, and the Virgin Islands. All but one of the states avail themselves of the AICPA's advisory grading service performed under the direction of the Board of Examiners. In all cases, however, it is the individual state board which makes the final evaluation of a candidate's ability as demonstrated by the examination.

Safeguarding the interests of CPAs. Because public opinion may effectively determine the extent of the profession's growth and development, the AICPA has for many years carried on programs to inform the public about CPAs and their work. The rapid increase in the number of CPAs and their dispersion into smaller communities where no CPA has practiced before have added to the need for these activities. Therefore, the AICPA has developed a long-range, national public relations program which designates the audiences the accounting profession desires to reach and gives a detailed analysis of the central ideas and facts it wants them to know. An organized effort has been undertaken to inform small businessmen of what the CPA is, what his standards are, and what he can do for them. As a part of this program, the AICPA provides pamphlets and reprints which can be distributed by state societies, colleges, or individual members. It has articles published in scores of trade magazines and engages in co-operative activity with trade associations. The AICPA furnishes speakers for meetings of many nonaccounting organizations. It presents network radio and television programs and also prepares transcriptions for presentation on local stations. As a result of all these AICPA activities, many small businessmen are learning about the accounting profession and the advantages of good accounting service.

An important part of the AICPA's work of safeguarding the interests of CPAs is accomplished through its co-operation with outside groups. In the governmental field, it maintains close relations with Federal agencies in order to preserve the standing of CPAs before these agencies, and it represents the profession in opposing any Federal legislation which would tend to limit its opportunities. The committee on relations with the Securities and Exchange Commission confers from time to time with the Commission's accounting staff and presents the profession's views on problems of current interest as well as on any proposed changes in the rules or regulations under the Acts administered by the Commission.

Among the national business and professional groups with which the AICPA works are lawyers and bankers. Through long and patient negotiation between members of the AICPA and members of the American Bar Association, a statement relating to practice in the field of Federal income taxation was prepared and approved by the governing bodies of both organizations. This statement serves as a guide in resolving such questions of jurisdiction as may arise between the two professions. The combined efforts of the committee on auditing procedure, the research department, and the public relations department have helped to develop among bankers and other credit men a better understanding of the CPA's work. In order to obtain the co-operation of credit grantors in the maintenance of high standards, the AICPA arranges joint meetings of accountants and bankers at the community level and prepares articles on the CPA's responsibilities which are published in periodicals directed to bankers. In all of these ways it helps to increase the acceptance by bankers of audited financial statements.

As a means of improving its service to the growing number of smaller firms and individual practitioners represented in its membership, the AICPA has in recent years formed an advisory committee of individual practitioners which is made up of members from every part of the nation. The purpose of this committee is to review all of the activities of the AICPA, with the object of recommending to Council such measures as will make the AICPA more useful to its members, particularly in the smaller communities.

Advancing accounting research. In 1939 the work of several of the AICPA's technical committees was consolidated in the hands of an enlarged committee on accounting procedure, and a research department was created to work under the direction of this committee. The AICPA had two basic objectives in mind when it organized the research department—to contribute to the advance of accounting and auditing knowledge, and to develop information which would help the individual CPA. The statements and case studies of the committee on auditing procedure are designed to improve the standards and techniques of public accounting. The Accounting Research Bulletins, issued by the former committee on accounting procedure, were published in final form in 1961. They are recognized as authoritative statements of generally accepted accounting procedure.

In 1960 a new structure was created. The AICPA's Accounting Research Division was given authority to publish studies of current problems. The Accounting Principles Board was created to consider the studies published by the Accounting Research Director, and on the basis of these studies to issue highly authoritative pronouncements.

Technical information service. In 1950 a technical information service was organized in the research department of the AICPA. Its purpose is to enable individual practitioners and members of smaller firms, whose opportunities for consultation with other informed practitioners are limited, to obtain an outside, competent opinion on problems which arise in their daily work. All written questions received are promptly answered through the co-operative effort of the research department and the technical committees. This service is available to any AICPA member.

Developing and improving accountancy education. The AICPA has always maintained a keen interest in the development of accounting education at the university level. Its committee on education holds joint meetings with a corresponding committee of the American Accounting Association, a large part of whose membership is composed of teachers of accounting. Special committees also confer from time to time with representatives of colleges and universities regarding their accounting curricula. The AICPA sponsors graduate study conferences which are held at various schools throughout the country and are attended by both practicing accountants and educators.

An important development in accountancy education in recent years has resulted from the work of the AICPA committee on selection of personnel. Under the auspices of the AICPA, a College Accounting Testing Program was developed. The scores made by the students taking these tests are evaluated on the basis of nationwide norms and now are being used by many employers as an important factor in careful personnel selection and by colleges as a guidance aid.

Library facilities. One of the important functions of a professional organization is to provide library facilities for its members. The AICPA library houses over 45,000 books and pamphlets, many of foreign origin, covering accounting, taxes, and related business subjects. Materials may be borrowed in person or by mail by all members, and, under certain conditions, by nonmembers.

In a recent year, the library was used by 13,000 visitors, and 31,000 reference questions were handled at the library and by telephone.

In addition to their usual functions, the AICPA's library staff compiles, by subject and author, a comprehensive index of all accounting and related literature published in the English language. Published biennially, the *Accountants' Index* is a most useful inclusion in the practitioner's library.

Cordial relations among accountants. Through its annual meeting and the regional meetings which it sponsors, the AICPA seeks to foster a widening acquaintance among CPAs of different states and different sections of the country. In addition, field trips by the officers and staff of the AICPA bring members in all parts of the country into personal contact with representatives of their national organization.

The AICPA participates actively in the Inter-American Conference on Accounting and the International Congress on Accounting. In these ways it endeavors to develop and maintain friendly relations with accountants of similar status in other countries so that full co-operation among members of the profession will be possible throughout the world.

All the activities in which the AICPA engages, regardless of the fact that they may be directed at different objectives, have one important characteristic in common—they are all a means of strengthening public confidence in the accounting profession as a whole. Each CPA must have public understanding if he is to enjoy the fullest opportunity to maintain professional standards and to render maximum public service. Therefore, the work of the AICPA cannot fail to be of real, though perhaps indirect, benefit to each of its members, regardless of the size of his practice.

State societies. The AICPA can act as the listening post and keep the profession informed of current developments; it can help in the formulation of policies on the national level; but the state societies must act on the information and bring about application of the policies in each part of the country.

The objectives of these societies, though applied over different areas, are parallel to those of the AICPA, and the work of the national and local organizations is complementary. All of the state societies have as their basic aims the maintenance of high professional and ethical standards, the development of educational and technical services which will assist the members in their day-to-day work, and the protection of the interests of the public and of the members. Most societies have a strict code of ethics which is rigidly enforced.

Although the activities of the various state societies differ to some extent, the following are illustrative of the services which the societies provide. All of the societies' programs of membership services are geared to give members a maximum of practical aid in their work. During the year most of the societies schedule several tax lectures and technical meetings for their chapters. These meetings stimulate the interchange of ideas among members and provide for the discussion of problems of a local nature. The societies' technical committees are continually engaged in research in general as well as in specialized fields. The work of these committees culminates in papers which are read at the meetings, in articles in the societies' official publications, or in special reports. In these ways the benefits of their research are passed on to the entire membership. The technical committees are also available to answer the inquiries of members and to give them advice when needed. In addition to the regularly scheduled local meetings of the state societies, several regional conferences are held each year under the auspices of groups of state societies and with the co-operation of the AICPA.

The national public relations program developed by the AICPA has already been mentioned. Because the most important part of public relations work is personal and local, the AICPA distributed to the state societies copies of a handbook which outlines the national program and describes the methods to be used in organizing and carrying out state and local programs. One of the important objectives of these programs is the development of ways of improving the practice and status of small firms and individual practitioners. The AICPA has designed a program of public relations clinics, sponsored by state societies and chapters, which provide systematic surveys, discussion, and planning to identify and solve the problems of local firms and to help them take advantage of public relations opportunities. The societies' efforts to inform bankers and credit grantors of the types of service rendered by accountants have met with much success. Some of the societies which provide bankers and credit men with copies of their yearbooks, containing the roster of membership and the code of ethics, report that on several occasions they have received requests for more detailed information about certain of the members listed. Small firms and individual practitioners benefit from this distribution of the societies' yearbooks because often, in the past, only the larger accounting firms were considered for engagements in the absence of information as to the names and qualifications of others in practice.

Although the objectives of the state societies are parallel to those of the AICPA, certain functions can be performed by one group more effectively than by the other. State legislation, for example, is a subject that must be dealt with by state societies and members of the profession in the states in which there is legislative activity. The type of accounting legislation that will effectively serve the profession and the public interest is best determined by those who are fully aware of local problems. However, standards must be national in scope. Uniform legislation and interstate reciprocity are in the interests of the entire profession, and it is through the AICPA that the views and experiences of different state societies can be brought together and uniform accountancy laws recommended.

There are two basic divisions to the task which the state societies must perform in connection with state legislation. First, they must make certain that no bill of interest to accountants escapes the societies' notice, and second, they must present the profession's views on every important bill to all those who may influence the bill's course. Whenever bills affecting accountancy are introduced, the societies must promptly take steps to get their views before the right people. This is a problem primarily of personal contact. To present the profession's position effectively requires direct lines of communication to committees, key legislators, and interested government officials. The state societies have done extensive work in establishing favorable contacts with members of these groups. In order to alert the societies to pending legislation which will affect the profession, the AICPA endeavors to provide them with all available information concerning bills which will be acted on at current sessions of the legislatures before the sessions convene. The AICPA distributes to the societies legislative kits which contain suggestions and material for handling legislative problems. In addition, the AICPA has on several occasions actively assisted various state societies in opposing undesirable legislation and in encouraging the successful passage of desirable measures.

Like the activities of the AICPA, those of the state societies are a means of increasing the prestige of the accounting profession in the eyes of the public. While all members benefit greatly from the programs of the state societies, individual practitioners and those who practice in small communities derive particular advantage from their membership because of the societies' efforts to explain the status of the CPA and the value of his services to local businessmen who are in need of these services.

Other accounting organizations. The AICPA on the national level and the state societies of CPAs on the local level are the only organizations composed solely of CPAs. However, there are several professional organizations whose members work in closely allied fields and have many interests and problems in common with the practicing CPA. The activities of four of these associations will be described briefly at this point. Such descriptions are not intended to be exhaustive, but are given merely to review for the reader the scope of activity of these organizations and their contributions to the field of accounting.

American Accounting Association. The objectives of the American Accounting Association, as stated in its bylaws, are:

1. To encourage and sponsor research in accounting, and to publish or aid in the publication of the results of research
2. To develop accounting principles and standards, and to seek their endorsement or adoption by business enterprises, public and private accountants, and governmental bodies
3. To promote studies of accounting as an agency of control of business enterprise and of economic affairs in general
4. To improve methods of instruction, and to demonstrate the social benefits of a more widespread knowledge of accounting

Members of the American Accounting Association derive considerable benefit from the Association's activities in sponsoring accounting research. The work of its committee on accounting concepts and standards is concerned with the determination and expression of desirable accounting objectives and principles. The committee's findings are published in the Association's quarterly journal and, from time to time, special studies and research monographs also are issued. In addition, close contacts are maintained with all research projects in the field of accounting and allied subjects.

The American Accounting Association co-operates closely with other professional accounting organizations. Its committees on CPA examinations, internship programs, and selection of personnel, work continually with the corresponding committees of the AICPA. The American Accounting Association has formed committees on co-operation with the Controllers Institute and with The Institute of Internal Auditors. One objective of the Association's closer affiliation with these latter groups is the development of internship opportunities in the industrial field.

Membership is open to accounting teachers, public and private accountants, governmental accountants, and other persons interested in the advancement of accounting. The teachers of accounting have had a large part in building the professional literature which has served to articulate the basic concepts of accounting as a framework for practice. There exists, therefore, a natural community of interest between teachers and practitioners. Anything which leads to a better acquaintance between the two groups, to mutual understanding, and to full and frank discussion of their common problems is of value to the profession. The work of the American Accounting Association assists in accomplishing all of these desirable objectives. Accordingly, membership in the Association and participation in its activities benefit the individual CPA as well as the profession as a whole.

National Association of Accountants. The National Association of Accountants is an organization devoted to the study of the problems of industrial accounting. Local chapters have been organized in many principal cities of the United States. In addition, many industrial accountants in numerous foreign countries are members. Membership in the Association is open to anyone who is interested in its objectives which are:

1. To develop a better understanding of the true nature and value of accounting, especially cost accounting, in industry
2. To study and improve technical methods and to establish sound general principles
3. To study the relation of the accounting department to the other departments of industry and business and to develop the most effective means of supplying usable information to these departments
4. To supply to its members information on the most up-to-date methods and to assist them in solving their individual problems

Each of the Association's chapters has its own funds and conducts its own affairs under general rules of operation established by the National Association in order to insure uniformity. Monthly meetings are held by each chapter at which industrial accounting problems are discussed by members as well as by outstanding speakers from many fields throughout the country. It has always been the practice of the Association to restrict the subjects for all its meetings and discussions to practical problems. Case studies dealing with the accounting methods of specific industries or with accounting procedures in a particular area are presented frequently at chapter meetings. In addition to the regular monthly meetings, many chapters hold one or two special meetings each year to discuss industrial accounting matters of particular current importance. Every year, each chapter also presents one or more series of discussion forum meetings consisting of several sessions on some important phase of industrial accounting. These forums provide an intensive coverage of the subject and stimulate the interchange of experience and viewpoints.

The National Association conducts an International Cost Conference each year. The technical sessions at these conferences have gained a widespread reputation for the high standard of the material presented and the ability and experience of the men who enter into the discussions. One of the distinguishing characteristics of these sessions is the emphasis which is placed upon actual practice. The Association also sponsors regional conferences in which sectional groups of chapters participate. These conferences are designed to bridge a gap between chapter meetings and the International Conference by providing a means for exchange of ideas among members located in a particular section of the country.

The Association maintains a research staff which studies industrial cost-accounting problems and methods under the supervision of a committee on research. This committee of more than thirty members includes leading industrial executives, professional accountants, and educators. The results of the studies made by the research staff are distributed to the members from time to time.

A technical service department, devoted exclusively to the service of members, is maintained at national headquarters. Its files include several hundred uniform cost systems developed by various trade associations. There also is an extensive library of books on industrial accounting. Members of the Association may submit questions to the technical service department which furnishes them with answers prepared by other members who have had experience with the problem involved.

The concepts and practices of cost accounting are undergoing continual change as more complex needs and applications arise. Through its efforts to establish sound general principles and to develop improved technical methods to meet the changing requirements of industry, the National Association of Accountants renders a service to the entire accounting profession.

Controllers Institute of America. The Controllers Institute of America is an organization in which active membership is limited exclusively to executives who perform the duties of a controller as defined by the Institute and who serve companies of sufficient size to qualify. It was established in 1931, and its members are financial and accounting officers of the leading business concerns. In addition to the class of active members, there is a class of associate members which is open only by invitation of the Board of Directors to educators, writers, and others in the field of controllership and in related fields. Local chapters of the Controllers Institute have been established in more than forty cities of the United States as well as in Canada and Puerto Rico. The Institute's principal objectives are to develop a progressive concept of controllership, adequate to meet the requirements of modern business, to educate business management and the public in understanding this concept, and to assist the controller in giving it full expression in his own organization.

The Controllers Institute provides its members with a medium through which they may receive and exchange ideas in the field of business management. Each local chapter or "control" holds regularly scheduled monthly meetings. In addition to these individual chapter meetings, there are four regional spring conferences and an annual meeting of the entire organization. An important feature of this annual meeting is the period set aside for industry conferences which enable members to have separate discussion meetings on problems peculiar to their own industries.

The research work of the Controllers Institute is carried on by the Controllership Foundation. Institute members and others send the Foundation suggestions for research, educational, and other projects. After a thorough search of other work in the field concerned and of current projects of other research organizations in order to prevent possible duplication, several suggested subjects are submitted to the Institute membership for vote. The final decision as to which projects will be undertaken, however, is made by the Board of Trustees of the Foundation which then allocates the necessary funds. Each research project is guided by a specially chosen advisory panel of members of the Controllers Institute and, when completed, the results of the study are published.

Although active membership in Controllers Institute of America is not open to practicing CPAs, the Institute's work is of service to them because of the contribution which it makes to the development of sound techniques in the dynamic field of business management.

Institute of Internal Auditors. The Institute of Internal Auditors is today the recognized professional organization in the field of internal auditing. It was organized in 1941 by a group of twenty-four men who felt that an organization was needed to develop the true professional status of internal auditing and to provide a medium for the interchange of ideas and information among those engaged in its practice. Growth in membership in the Institute has been steady, and today it includes representatives of every field of private and governmental enterprise. From the beginning, membership has been restricted to those who are directly concerned with internal auditing, in the belief that such a limitation is necessary if the organization's activities are to continue to be focused on its original objectives. However, the community of interest between internal auditors and CPAs has been recognized by the Institute since its formation, and it has made provision for the admission, as associate members, of CPAs as well as eligible educators and others engaged in fields related to internal auditing.

The maximum value of Institute membership comes with participation in the activities of a local chapter group. The first chapter was organized in New York, a little more than a year after the formation of the national body. At the close of the Institute's tenth year there were forty chapters, including four in Canada, two in the Philippine Islands, and two in Europe. Most of the chapters hold monthly meetings, and a number of the larger ones have separate meetings of technical study groups. In addition, there are three regional conferences and a conference of the entire organization each year.

Since its foundation the Institute has been active in the field of research. Much work was done in the early years on various surveys and projects relating to audit techniques in specific industries, and in 1947 the research committee issued a statement defining the responsibilities of the internal auditor.

The importance of maintaining a close relationship between a company's internal-audit department and its public accountants, to the mutual advantage of both the company and the outside auditors, has become increasingly evident in recent years. In the "Tentative Statement of Auditing Standards," published in 1947 by the committee on auditing procedure of the AICPA, it is stated that "Where an internal auditing department exists the independent auditor very properly accords that fact appropriate weight in selecting and applying his auditing procedures. The advantages of strong internal auditing departments are becoming better recognized by many concerns of sufficient size to warrant maintaining such an organization." Because the work of a functioning internal-audit department is helpful to the public accountant, all the activities of the Institute of Internal Auditors which are aimed at improving methods and winning wider acceptance by management are of benefit to him.

Student organizations. There are some organizations composed of students of accounting in the colleges and business schools. Some, in the form of college professional fraternities such as Beta Alpha Psi, are national in scope; most school accounting clubs or societies are local. Some state societies of CPAs have established student affiliates or junior memberships. Since such organizations are potentially effective media for developing an informed interest in the profession, members of the profession would do well to encourage and aid in their sound development.

Partnerships

The partnership often has been cited as the ideal form of organization for the practice of public accounting. Properly set up, it can combine the range of facilities usually available in a corporate structure with the personal service and liability characteristics of the sole proprietorship. At the same time it avoids the drawbacks of both: The corporate form is unsuited to a professional practice primarily because it lacks personal liability; the proprietorship, because it is often limited in the scope and depth of its services.

Advantages and Disadvantages of Partnerships

■ MANY ACCOUNTANTS who prefer to practice in a partnership give these reasons for doing so:

1. The size of the practice may require top-level supervision by several people.
2. A partnership makes available a wider range of talents than can be

supplied by one man. An individual accountant can specialize without restricting the services available to his firm's clients.

3. It provides broader opportunities to discuss and solve problems of practice with others of similar capacity and interest.

4. A firm with greater physical capacity, properly supervised, may be able to handle larger engagements more adequately and expeditiously.

5. Exceptional staff accountants are provided with greater incentives. The goal of partnership helps to attract and keep good staff men.

6. More time is usually available to a partner than an individual practitioner for his own professional development.

7. The practice has greater stability and continuity, which is reassuring to both the client and the members of the firm. Disruptions are minimized during illness or vacation. Retirement plans and automatic death benefits are more easily available in a partnership organization.

8. Because of the broader base of operations, a partner often may be able to achieve a higher net income than he could by practicing alone.

Despite the advantages of partnership, there are cases where a sole proprietorship may be wiser. An individual's temperament may preclude the intimate association and teamwork necessary among partners. A firm's client potential may be so small that the practice cannot adequately support additional principals. Or occasionally, a man qualified to assume partner status may not be available. Yet some sole practitioners with an established and growing practice still hesitate to take in partners for reasons which are either economic or which reflect a lack of confidence in others. Some practitioners may feel, for example, that:

1. A new partner may win over the clients, then leave and take much of the practice with him.

2. A new partner may become overbearing or may attempt to overshadow the original practitioner.

3. A new partner may not contribute as much as was originally expected to the welfare of the firm.

4. It would be unwise or impossible for the practitioner to give up any part of his present income, although a partnership might benefit him in the long run.

5. It is necessary that a prospective partner make a substantial cash payment for goodwill. The practitioners may feel that they have built up the practice and established a valuable intangible asset that should not be given away.

Prerequisites for a Partnership

■ THERE ARE ENOUGH elements of truth in these various reasons to indicate that an effective partnership cannot be entered into lightly. Clearly if it is to succeed, it must be based on respect for each other's abilities and on mutual confidence.

The preamble to the agreement of one firm expresses it this way:

> The partnership is among the most rewarding, but most fragile, of human relationships. Through it the individual may project and realize himself to a degree not otherwise attainable. The satisfactions are to be measured not alone in money but in limitless spiritual and intellectual values. Some men, and some women, are incapable of such an association. Care should be taken to choose partners with a view toward a continuing harmony within the group, but one element of which is the individual's capacity for assuming a full share of the technical burden.
>
> There is little likelihood of successful outcome where partners are admitted from outside the organization—this for want of the long wearing-in process of one individual on another, which is perhaps the only trustworthy basis for judgment. Partnership is essentially an arrangement among friends. Efforts should never be relaxed toward preserving the uniform friendship of each member for all others. This effort is often most fruitful when directed by the individual toward himself to excise feelings of jealousy and examples of bad manners. Do not expect that anyone's opinion of you, not even your warmest friends', will ever quite match your own.

Any time two or more people combine their talents and energies to achieve a common end, problems may arise. These problems vary with the characteristics of the individuals concerned, the circumstances under which they join together, and the goals to be achieved. Solutions can be proposed in advance to take care of important foreseeable problems. Machinery can be set up to handle the unforeseeable ones. But in the final analysis good faith, mutual understanding, and tolerance are necessary to achieve the greatest results.

Partnership problems arise in a variety of areas—the terms of the agreement; income-tax considerations; operation of the practice and distribution of duties; basis of compensation; withdrawal, retirement, dissolution, and many others. Arrangements vary widely, and rightly so. When individuals propose to pool their talents and energies under a number of different circumstances, uniform provisions cannot apply to all cases. However, a presentation of the methods used by established firms can serve to point out certain underlying principles, and to demonstrate certain successful techniques which can be adapted to similar situations.

Types of Organization

■ IN GENERAL, partnerships can be classified in two ways:

1. Loose association versus integrated organization
2. Single-class versus multiclass partnerships

LOOSE ASSOCIATION VERSUS INTEGRATED ORGANIZATION

At one end of the scale is the type of firm that is very closely knit; the members collaborate fully; clients belong to the firm and not to an individual; income is shared according to a predetermined, fixed plan; and, within reason, it constitutes an "all-for-the-firm" combination.

At the other end is the loose confederation of individual practitioners. In this instance the firm provides essentially a means for the sharing of office facilities plus the advantage each partner may derive from the representation that he is a member of a firm. Clients belong to the individual members; staff members belong to specific partners; the co-operation of partners is limited to matters of office administration mainly, with some friendly discussion of accounting and tax problems; income is shared in accordance with fees attributable to each participant less a proportionate share of the office expense. This type of firm constitutes an "each-for-himself" arrangement in which the members are associates rather than partners.

Although several variations of these two forms exist, the basic difference between them is whether the income of each partner is predominantly based on fees from his "personal" clients or on the firm's over-all gross. One variation is to have "branch-office" or "special" partners who share only in the income produced by the offices with which they are connected. Some firms operate on the "loose-association" principle only during the early years of practice, and consider this a temporary measure for a trial period, after which new and more closely integrated arrangements are made.

There appears to be a number of small accounting firms which represent a *combination* of individual practices (in which each partner handles his "origin" as his clients) rather than a *merger* of several practices in which the clients all belong to the firm. This situation has the appearance of a hedge against the day when the firm may fall apart and each partner can conveniently "pick up *his* marbles and go home." The major fault of this system is that it does not make for a closely welded organization in which clients can take growing pride or place increasing confidence. The better practice for operating purposes is to treat all clients as clients of the firm, even though, for statistical and profit-sharing purposes, the clients may belong to the individual partners.

Most firms find it impossible to eradicate this tendency toward personalized practice. Except in fringe circumstances where the practice is more of an association than a firm, the attachment of important clients to an individual rather than to the firm should be discouraged. Many firms follow a definite program of rotating assignments every two or three years, both as to partners and staff. However, it is inescapable, in a personal-service profession, and more particularly in tax practice, that personalized relationships will exist.

SINGLE-CLASS VERSUS MULTICLASS PARTNERS

A most common arrangement is to have one class of partners. Although their interest in earnings may be appreciably different, all the partners in these firms share in the over-all earnings. Nor are any rights or duties reserved to a particular group of partners. In single-office firms with a second class of partner, the junior partners generally participate in over-all earnings but do not have a proprietary interest in the firm. In these cases, certain decisions are made exclusively by the senior partners, although the juniors are consulted.

Sources of Partners

■ FORMING A PARTNERSHIP for a young accountant is an extremely serious step. Before going into business as a partner with another person, a great deal of time should be spent in ascertaining whether the person in question is of the personality, temperament, ability, and vision that can make for a happy association for the rest of a business life. When two men who were trained by the same firm embark on the practice of public accounting, their chances of establishing a lasting organization are far greater than when two or more men from different firms attempt to form such an association. This is not only because they have shared the same type of training, but also because they have had the opportunity of knowing a great deal about each other.

The most satisfactory way for a practitioner to obtain partners is to train and develop them himself. As the individual practitioner's workload increases, it is the natural thing to employ an assistant. The assistants selected should be young men who are potential future partner material. No matter how carefully men are screened and selected, a certain percentage of them turn out to be disappointments. Why then ever start with a man who it is thought cannot develop?

In general, firms prefer to draw new partners from their staffs. There appear to be three basic advantages to this policy:

1. The existing partners have ample opportunity to observe the capabilities of the individual: his technical competence, ambition, initiative, and supervisory skills, as well as his ability to get along with the staff, the clients, and the partners. A new partner must "fit in," and it is only through continued surveillance that the partners can assess a prospective partner's strong and weak points.

2. In his capacity as a staff man, the candidate has become familiar with the policies and procedures of the firm. Having worked closely with many of the clients, he has an intimate knowledge of their problems.

3. The logical ambition of a staff accountant is to become a partner in his firm. Unless the capable man can realistically look forward to that opportunity, the firm will find it difficult to maintain a topnotch staff. Its best men will go elsewhere.

One firm, with twelve partners, outlined its over-all policy as follows:

We do not bring in trained or experienced men from the outside. Every one starts with us as a junior accountant. We employ only college graduates and our present maximum age is twenty-six. Our general plan is this: a man coming with us at age twenty-four should be a CPA by the time he is twenty-seven years of age. By the time he is thirty we should know whether he is partner material, or whether he would be happier and better adapted in private accounting.

If the man is judged to be partner material, he is encouraged to put quite a bit of effort into civic and community work. For example, the Junior Chamber of Commerce, college alumni associations, church work. At about the same time he is encouraged to join some proper club, a country club, or one of the town clubs. The firm pays his dues. He is expected to select a specialization such as budgeting, a particular area of taxation, systems and electronic accounting, profit-sharing, or some other specialized field. We expect everyone to be a good all-around accountant and tax man, but he must also develop into an expert in some particular aspect of our service.

Circumstances may be such that there is no qualified staff man available at the time an additional partner is needed. A specialist may be required to round out the facilities. Or rapid growth may make it difficult to supervise work properly. On these occasions staff members or partners of other firms have proven to be logical candidates, subject of course to ethical negotiations. Too, some accountants in industry, teaching, or government seek opportunities to return to practice and have developed skills of great value to a firm.

When it is necessary to go outside the firm for partnership material, it is generally deemed inadvisable to admit the new man to the partnership immediately. Many firms find it practical for the man to join the staff, perhaps in a special position and even on a participating basis, for a trial period of a couple of years. In this way both the prospective partner and the present members of the firm can get to know each other in the working situation. Then if they find the relationship unsatisfactory other arrangements can be made without disrupting the partnership.

Mergers of existing firms are still another source of partner material. Under these circumstances a short-term partnership agreement of the "association" type frequently serves as the trial period, whether the action represents a consolidation of practice between firms of almost equal size or an assimilation of a smaller practice by a larger one. Of course, the more thorough the investigation and the more intimately the partners are acquainted beforehand, the greater the possibilities of a fruitful long-term relationship.

PLANNING FOR NEW PARTNERS

Some firms have provisions in their partnership agreement calling for the admission of new partners at stated intervals. Although it is perhaps unusual to reduce this to writing, a number of firms have established policies to promote younger men. Ten-year intervals between different partner "groups" is considered ideal, with the youngest partners being in their middle thirties. Many smaller firms, which may have some difficulty in planning by specific age groups, are taking steps to insure that retiring partners will be replaced by experienced, mature men who, in turn, are backed up by bright young men in training.

Factors in Selecting New Partners

■ WHAT BASIC QUALITIES does a firm look for in a new partner? While it is difficult to rank specific characteristics, all agree that a man of partnership caliber must be more than an expert accountant. Technical ability is a primary consideration, yet many firms feel that personality traits and dedication are of equal importance.

As one practitioner phrased it: "Extreme ability without the necessary drive will not do the job, nor will a good personality without something to back it up. However, I believe that what I would call 'desire to serve' might be the most important characteristic." He feels that it is the combination of these three factors which determines a CPA's ability to serve present clients and attract new ones.

TECHNICAL ABILITY

A prospective partner's technical achievements are measured in terms of his intelligence, skills, and experience, and by the manner in which he applies these attributes. He must be able to plan, program, and see that assignments are carried out properly. Closely allied with this, in the thinking of many, is a combination of creative ability, initiative, imagination, perseverance in solving problems, and an analytical aptitude considered necessary to the proper application of technical skills. There is a tendency, especially among the larger firms, to expect a new partner to have developed a specialty. However, some firms are more interested in exceptional all-around men.

PERSONALITY AND TEMPERAMENT

Of great importance is a prospective partner's social characteristics—his ability to work well with other people; his capacity to command the confidence and respect of clients, partners, and staff. He should, it is felt, also be a competent supervisor, able to work effectively under pressure. He should be willing and able to train and encourage staff members. He should be a leader, but not a "climber," and give evidence of ability to continue to study and grow. His conduct at social engagements and his interest in civic affairs are weighed by a number of firms. An important consideration to some firms is the personality traits of a prospective partner's wife. Does she get along well with people? Does she aid and support her husband's ambition and his desire to serve? Or is she likely to impede his development? It is naturally assumed that any partner would have to be a man of unquestionable integrity.

DEDICATION

A man's willingness to place the interests of his firm above his own—and those of the client above both—is considered heavily by many firms. They want a partner who is deeply devoted to his chosen field. They expect him to further develop his professional abilities. They expect him to have a sense of responsibility toward his work, his firm, and the profession as a whole.

Of course, a man's ability to attract new clients is an important factor in his selection. However, many firms, without deprecating it, feel that this ability is an adjunct to a number of qualities which contribute to the long-term growth of the firm.

Backgrounds of New Partners

AGE

■ IN SELECTING a new partner, one of the first things that has to be considered is age. In the past few years there have been an alarming number of fine accounting practices sold out—merged, if we are to use the more genteel expression. Possibly these firms had let their partners get "bunched" as to age, found themselves getting old together, and had few if any younger men of sufficient strength to perform the job of carrying on. They had to merge. This problem of age is an individual matter for each accounting office, since it must fit into the pattern of the ages of the persons already associated with the firm.

In practice, new partners have been known to be as young as twenty-five years, with the most common age being in the middle thirties. In some cases admission is deferred until a man has obtained his CPA certificate.

EXPERIENCE AND EDUCATION

Men have become partners with as little as four years' public accounting experience, but nine years is more typical. Since most partners come from a firm's staff, most of their experience has been with that firm. The vast majority of new partners have a baccalaureate degree; a small minority hold a Master's degree.

Admission of New Partners

PROCEDURE FOR SELECTING NEW PARTNERS

■ GENERALLY A PROSPECTIVE partner has been under observation for some time by the existing partners before he is formally proposed. In firms with a single class of partners, usually any partner may propose a candidate. There appears to be an increasing tendency among smaller firms to place a likely candidate in training before final consideration is given. The partners, during the course of perhaps two or more years, increase his responsibilities to prepare him for partner duties and gauge his ability to assume them. Sometimes a new position is created, such as "executive senior," "supervisor," or "associate," in keeping with the prospect's expanding duties. Often he participates in the profits on a bonus basis.

Although a formal vote is not taken in many instances, firms having only "general" partners usually require the unanimous consent of all partners to admit new men. In actuality, younger partners with a smaller interest tend to defer to the wishes of the older partners. But in many firms the qualifications of a prospective partner are thoroughly discussed among all partners, and complete approval from all concerned is necessary. In one case, the older partners tend to defer to their *younger* associates on new admissions. They reason that younger men should have the predominant voice since they will be working with the new partner longer than the older partners will.

Some single-class partnerships base admissions on a simple majority vote (regardless of the amount of financial interest of the individual partners). Others use the majority interest in the firm as the yardstick. One firm of six partners requires the approval of the managing partner and enough other votes to represent the majority interest in the firm. An eight-partner firm specifies that the executive committee (consisting of the three oldest partners) may admit a new partner upon the written approval of at least three-quarters of all partners, representing a minimum of 65 per cent interest in the firm.

Of the firms with multiclass partners, many require the unanimous consent of the "capital" partners, the "non-capital" partners having no vote. In some cases, non-capital partners are consulted in a practical effort to reach general agreement among all partners, while others require unanimous approval of all partners whether they have a capital interest or not.

One multi-office organization has the following requirements: The unanimous approval of the resident partners in the operating office involved and a numerical majority of the firm's management committee. Another multi-office firm elects "participating" (non-capital) partners upon the recommendation of the managing partner with majority approval of the executive committee members. Prospective general partners are recommended by the managing partner from among the participating partners, but to become effective this requires the consent of three-quarters of the general partners, representing at least 75 per cent of the general partners' interest in the firm.

CAPITAL REQUIREMENTS FOR NEW PARTNERS

Amount of the investment. In discussing capital, Lorin A. Torrey observes:[1]

> Ordinarily, the capital requirements of a professional partnership are the working capital needed to carry on business until fees are collected plus any amounts needed for office equipment. . .
>
> In a professional firm it seems to me that the capital should be furnished by the partners in ratio to their participation in the firm. In other words, capital accounts should be in proportion to their profit arrangements. Capital is not an important factor in producing income, so there is little need for inactive participants to furnish capital to the firm. Exceptions may be desirable or necessary in case of new partners or retiring or deceased partners. If it is agreed that the capital accounts should be in proportion to the partners' profit participations, interest should be charged on a partner's deficiency in capital. As an inducement to eliminate deficiencies in capital as soon as possible, the interest charged may be slightly higher than the interest a bank would charge on a loan to the partnership. Conversely, partners should be compensated when they furnish more than their required share of the capital. Sometimes, interest on overages in capital is slightly lower than the rate of interest charged on deficiencies.
>
> In order to avoid misunderstandings, I usually suggest that the partners' capital accounts should be stated at fixed or agreed amounts. Deficiencies in capital then appear as advances to partners and overages appear as loans from partners.

Firms appear to be in general agreement with many of these statements, except that they do not generally charge interest on deficiencies in the capital accounts of new partners.

It is a widespread practice for both national and local firms to require a capital investment to be made by a newly admitted partner. Wide variety exists, however, in the methods employed in the determination of amount and timing of payment of the capital investment. In general, the capital contribution is designed to represent the incoming partner's share of the working capital required for operation of the firm. The total amount of working capital is a stipulated fixed amount in some cases and, in others, the actual working capital employed at the date of admission is used to calculate the capital investment. Some firms require an amount to be invested which is equal to the new partner's profit-and-loss sharing per-

---

[1]"Value of Partnership Interests and Changes in Partnership," California Society of CPAs, Sixth Annual Tax Accounting Conference, 1955, pp. 121-128.

centage multplied by the total capital investment of all partners.

A procedure which appears to be growing in use is that of dividing the total capital interest in the firm into *units*. An incoming partner is assigned a certain number of units, the number being determined by the same persons who are responsible for new partner selection. The required capital investment is the number of units assigned to the new partner multiplied by the per-unit working capital of the firm. As indicated above, this may be a fixed amount or it may be based on the actual working capital on the date of admission.

Evaluating goodwill. Only a minority of firms attempt to compute goodwill when making a capital interest available to a prospective or existing partner. Most firms, in determining the amount to be paid, base it either upon book value of the firm or upon the amounts of existing capital. Firms which evaluate goodwill financially vary widely in size, so this factor in itself does not appear to influence attitudes toward this practice.

No general pattern is evident in the techniques employed to compute goodwill. The most commonly used formula is 100 per cent of the average annual gross fees for the last three years. One firm uses 100 per cent of the preceding year's gross. Another firm, which has calculated goodwill at 100 per cent of one year's net income, will use the latest annual gross fees in the future. Some firms employ a formula of 50 per cent of the preceding year's gross fees. (In one of these cases—an individual practitioner forming a partnership with a staff member—the selling price of the practice was estimated as the equivalent of one year's gross fees. A 50 per cent discount was then placed on this amount in consideration of the employee's past contributions to the development of the firm.)

Other percentages used by single firms, based on a three-year average gross, are 50 per cent, 66⅔ per cent, and 75 per cent. One firm, which computes capital in terms of "units" figures the selling price per "unit" as prorated book value plus one-and-a-half times the three-year average net earnings per share.

Goodwill consists of a number of different elements. Many are intangible. The variety of bases used to determine goodwill may indicate a lack of general acceptance of its components or of how they should be measured. This is perhaps the basic reason why many firms do not even attempt to place a dollar value on this factor.

Terms of payment. The timing of the payment by a newly admitted partner of his capital investment varies from payment in full on admission to no immediate payment, with a variety of situations between. One national firm requires full payment on admission, with the firm being prepared to assist the new partner, if necessary, in borrowing the amount required. Another national firm will lend the new partner the required amount, charging the same rate of interest as is paid on firm borrowing. The typical procedure, however, seems to be to permit the newly admitted partner to make his capital contribution by means of withholding from his share of income over a relatively short period, three to five years being most common. One local firm uses an interesting compromise procedure. The portion of the required investment representing the new partner's share of cash, supplies, and furniture and fixtures is payable in full on admission. The remainder of the required investment representing the proportionate share of accounts receivable and work in process (at cost) is payable from earnings over a three-year period. In some cases in which capital is invested over a period of years, early payment is encouraged by the payment of interest on paid-in capital or the charging of interest on any unpaid balance of the required capital investment.

Firms which have a single class of partners generally require that a capital account be built up. A few provide for minimum down payments. In most cases the new partner has some flexibility in the way he builds his account. But some firms specify one of two methods. The more common practice is for the new partner to leave in the firm most of his income outside of his salary or "draw" and an amount sufficient to cover the income tax on the balance until his account is paid up. The other method is similar but makes no provision for paying the income tax on the amount left in the firm.

In a few cases interest is charged on unpaid balances (at 5 per cent); but many firms pay interest on capital accounts. The usual annual rate is 5 per cent or 6 per cent, with the latter predominating. However, some pay up to 10 per cent. These interest payments are made out of firm income before profit sharing. Partners who are deficient in their accounts are thereby penalized.

In most single-class partnerships, the capital investment of each partner is proportionate to his interest in the earnings. Generally, the capital contribution of the new partners is made directly into the firm, and the other partners do not withdraw a corresponding amount from their accounts. In firms where the capital contribution is not directly related to profit sharing, the working capital is usually established at a relatively fixed amount based on their operational experience; and since most of these firms pay interest on the capital accounts the existing partners are willing to accept a nominal initial contribution from the newly admitted partners.

In firms with more than one category of partners, the junior level is generally on a profit-sharing basis but has no proprietary interest. One such firm does require a capital contribution. This firm consists of two general partners and eleven special partners. In effect, both partner groups are general partners with certain rights reserved for the two founding partners, such as selection of new partners, permanent membership on the five-man management committee (the other memberships rotate annually), and veto power over any vote. Each new partner in this firm is expected to build up a capital account of $12,000 over a period of years, which is equal to that of the other partners and has no direct relation to earnings. Another multi-office firm, with "resident" partners participating only in the earnings of the operating office to which they are assigned, permits a designated amount of capital to be paid into that particular office. The offices of this firm are, in effect, separate partnerships. Since 10 per cent annual interest is paid on this capital, most new partners take advantage of the opportunity.

NEW PARTNER DUTIES AND RESPONSIBILITIES

When a staff man is first admitted to a partnership his duties do not ordinarily change drastically. They usually represent some expansion of his previous duties; and he gradually assumes additional responsibilities as he demonstrates capacity to handle them. He will generally have been supervising engagements, and frequently may now become partner-in-charge for a number of them. He may review and bill the accounts under his supervision subject, in the early stages, to final review by an older partner. In some cases he will handle his assigned clients completely on his own, but consult the older partners when he encounters rough spots.

There are firms that assign some administrative duties to a new partner immediately upon his admission. Even in departmentalized firms, where the new partners have specialties prior to admission, these responsibilities are assigned early. For example, in one firm of nine partners, each of the three partners who have been admitted during the last three years is the final authority in one of these areas:

1. Personnel changes and staff assignments
2. Final review of audit reports and changes in technical procedures for report-writing or audit-programming
3. Recommendations to clients concerning the use of office machines

In general, firms desire that younger partners be full-fledged members of the partnership team and have a voice in over-all management. In firms with non-capital or special partners, the junior partners do not officially participate in policy-making, but it is general practice to discuss changes with them in advance. Certain rights which are reserved to the capital partners in multiclass firms are also reserved to the older partners or the executive committee in a few single-class firms. Among the rights mentioned are:

1. Change in the name of the partnership
2. Admission of new partners (multiclass firms)
3. Division of profits
4. Opening or closing offices
5. Internal accounting method
6. Admitting a junior partner to senior status (multiclass firms)

Regardless of specifically assigned duties, once a man becomes a partner he must assume or continue to maintain certain general responsibilities which become especially incumbent upon him as the personification of his firm and his profession. These include the maintenance of high technical, ethical, and moral standards in relationship to his clients, his firm, the staff, and the community.

PROVISIONS IN THE PARTNERSHIP AGREEMENT

It is not necessary to deal with admission of partners extensively in an agreement. One can anticipate neither the firm's status at the time of a prospective admission nor the standing of the candidate. For this reason many agreements are silent on the subject, but some deal with it very briefly, touching on one or more of the following aspects:

1. The minimum percentage or number of partners' votes required for affirmative action
2. Class of partners which may vote on admissions
3. Whether or not a capital investment is required
4. Whether or not a payment is to be made for goodwill
5. Effect of admission on participation percentages of retired partners and interests of estates

Questions such as the profit share, salary if any, and other pertinent conditions for the new partner can be considered only when the occasion arises.

Examples of how admissions are dealt with in agreements are contained in the following excerpts:

Additional partners may be admitted on such terms and conditions as are agreeable to all active partners, but the admission of additional partner or partners shall be on such a basis that it will not reduce the share of a withdrawing partner or the estate of a deceased partner.

Eighty per cent in interest of the partners shall have the right to admit additional general partners.

In the event that the number of administrative partners shall at any time be reduced to less than five by the death, retirement, or withdrawal of an administrative partner or otherwise, then within six months thereafter a new administrative partner or partners shall be chosen by a majority in interest of the remaining administrative partners, it being the intention that the number of administrative partners shall never be less than five for any period of longer than six months.

The withdrawal or death of one or more partners, or the admission of one or more new partners, shall not terminate this agreement. . . Any additional partners admitted shall be required to become parties to this agreement as a condition to admission to the firm and shall sign the original of this agreement as evidence thereof at that time.

Division of the Profits

■ IN PRINCIPLE, the objective in the profit-allocation process is to give recognition to three factors: capital invested, personal services contributed, and reward for the entrepreneurial function. These considerations would seem to indicate a scheme of profit sharing which would include in the computations of each partner's share of earnings the allowance of interest on capital investment and a salary allowance, with any remaining income allocated on the basis of each partner's agreed percentage interest or number of units.

It appears, however, that profit-sharing arrangements with this degree of complexity are not typical in the profession. The most prevalent plans for division of profits are (1) salary-plus-profit share and (2) straight profit share. Other plans are based on the recorded contribution of fees by a partner, time devoted to the firm's business, or a combination of both. Some firms add an incentive element to a profit-share or salary-plus-profit-share plan. The incentive is in the form of a percentage of the gross fee, for a stated period, of new clients secured by a partner. (The treatment of outside income as that of the partnership is discussed on page 486.)

The amount of each partner's salary allowance appears to be determined by agreement of all partners in local firms (although sometimes this function is performed individually by the senior partner). An executive or management committee generally establishes salary allowances in national firms.

SALARY-PLUS-PROFIT-SHARE METHOD

This method provides that partners get an annual salary and that such salaries be treated as expenses. It is intended that the salary reflect the time devoted to the firm, variations in productivity, and differences in the services performed. As to the sharing of the income remaining after such salary payments, that is based on capital proportions as a rule, or merely on an established schedule of percentages. Thus, as some partners increase their activities or as others decrease their activities, salary adjustments can be made. The profit share is looked upon virtually as a property right.

This plan is of a type that perhaps should not be used by a newly formed firm of young members. It is likely that their talents have not been definitely established or become fully known to each other. Moreover, there will probably be no variations in time devoted to the business. In the absence of these factors the salary provision may be premature.

Personal factors to be considered. The formulas or methods of establishing a basic salary vary. Those most commonly used are productive time, percentage-interest brackets, seniority, and experience. Productive time has some strong adherents, but obviously this method becomes less valid as administrative and managerial duties increase with growth. The majority simply establish an arbitrary salary scale to meet minimum personal requirements, and distribute the remainder under profit-sharing formulas.

What basis is used to evaluate the salary and profit percentage for new partners? Ages and abilities differ considerably: some partners may demonstrate ability to secure new engagements, while others may become specialists in taxation, systems work, or some field of industry which has resulted in enhancing the reputation of the firm and influencing the recommendation of many clients to the firm.

On the subject of evaluating a partner, weight should be given to many factors such as:

1. Number of years a staff member and number of years a partner
2. Hours charged to clients at the firm's per-hour or per-diem rates
3. Total billings by the partner for office and staff other than his own time and whether such billings are usual rates or considerably in excess of usual rates
4. Source of services rendered by a partner, whether it was firm work originally turned over to him, clients he secured from his own friends, or clients developed through firm work
5. Technical ability
6. Ability to develop unusual interest of client
7. Ability as a specialist in costs and systems, taxes, brokerage, hotels and clubs, and so on
8. Co-operation in the administrative problems of the firm
9. Activity in community affairs
10. Activity in accounting societies
11. Health and vitality
12. Growth in clientele
13. Losses in clientele due to errors of omission or commission

STRAIGHT PROFIT-SHARE METHOD

This is the simplest method to establish and to administer. Yet, it is not necessarily the most equitable plan. It is suitable for a new firm of young partners and for any firm that prefers a simple formula for the division of income. Drawings against profits are usually allowed on a weekly, semi-monthly, or monthly schedule. The drawings are usually less than the anticipated annual income, thereby permitting the "splitting of a melon" once or twice a year, perhaps leaving a little to be added to the "rainy-day" reserve.

FEES-PRODUCED AND/OR TIME-WORKED METHODS

Some firms divide income according to each partner's proportion of the gross fees by which it is produced. In relatively few cases, time worked is added to the formula. The latter method appears to be relatively uncommon and the former is not as popular as either of the foregoing profit-share plans.

The fees-produced method is sometimes used where two individuals merge their practice and cannot find a simple profit-share basis on which they can agree. This is a more materialistic approach and one which is not conducive to the fullest measure of co-operation. Gross fees do not necessarily yield proportionate net-income results. Some jobs are more profitable than others. Therefore, the fees-produced method more equitably should be a net-fees method, that is where each partner retains his own billings less estimated office expense and overhead. This, it is believed, could work only under limited and special circumstances.

Assignment to a specific partner of a part of the gross or net fees from new clients obtained by that partner also appears to involve unnecessary or even undesirable complexity. Presumably new client contacts are a normal part of the contribution of all partners to the success of the firm. If one or more partners make conspicuously significant contributions in this area, the salary allowance procedure would seem preferable to achieve interpartner equity in the allocation of earnings.

Time devoted to the business is not truly a measure of a partner's contribution to the firm's welfare. One may contribute much in the way of clients and service in little time, and another contribute less in more time.

Incentives for new clients may at first thought appear to be a practical, business-like arrangement. This, however, loses some of its force upon careful consideration. The obtaining of new clients may so often be due to the contributions of more than one partner that the attempt to make an allocation may be disruptive. Some partners are in the nature of "catalytic agents": they are not expected to produce business themselves but their very membership in the firm is capitalized on by others. In this connection the comments of Ira N. Frisbee on the subject of accountants' partnership agreements are cited because of their pointedness:

> Some agreements provide for extra shares of a portion of the profits to partners obtaining new clients and charge them similarly for the loss of clients. Some specify the number of hours for a base share of profits, with an additional share for excess hours. These and similar charges and credits would appear to be unjustified in the usual partnership. The obtaining of clients and the number of hours of chargeable or of total time do not necessarily indicate the value of a partner. To make special provisions for profit sharings on such bases is likely to increase jealousies and misunderstandings when more important contributions or services by other partners are not recognized.[2]

There are a few agreements which provide that the distribution of profits is to be determined by the partners at periodic intervals. In some instances

[2]Ira N. Frisbee, "Organizing and Perpetuating an Accounting Partnership," *New Responsibilities of the Accounting Profession,* AICPA, 1948, p. 40.

the senior partners have that exclusive privilege. This arrangement, while intended to distribute earnings equitably in accordance with production, nevertheless creates the problem of frequent review of income production, time devoted to the firm, and consideration of unusual achievements. The criteria can be so vague and the accomplishments so indefinable that the harmonious relations of the partners may be disrupted if disagreements are numerous and sharp. Except in unusual circumstances, as in the case of an exceptional "windfall," a review should not be made more frequently than every five years.

Some firms use share or unit devices to establish capital interests and profit-sharing ratios. In such cases there is no unusual problem in division because the income is divided among the total shares or units according to the contract terms and the amount allocable to each partner is thereby determined. This arrangement is utilized mainly by large firms.

SHARING OF LOSSES

With respect to the sharing of losses it is observed that they are shared commonly in the same proportions as profits. This rule is applicable where no specific reference is made to losses. However, there are cases where by arrangement some partner or partners assume all losses. This situation prevails mainly where there are junior partners. The motivation for such exemptions is that the junior partner may not be able to absorb a loss, or that it might not be good for morale. To protect the exempt partners against loss, in the event of suit or other contingency, an indemnity provision is included in the agreement. Some contracts provide that a loss due to wilful neglect or conduct of a partner is chargeable in full to him.

TREATMENT IN THE PARTNERSHIP AGREEMENT

In fixing partners' salaries or profit shares the problem is more one of relationships than of the amount allotted to any one partner. In other words, it does not matter (within financial bounds) what partner A's salary is fixed at so long as, by comparison, that of partner B is fair and reasonable. The same applies to profit-share percentages. Obviously the aggregate salaries should be within the firm's predictable income limits. By the same token, profit-share advances should be less than realized earnings.

Revisions in the arrangement. An important consideration is to provide in the partnership agreement for change in the profit-allocation formula. Changes in the value of a partner's services may occur rapidly and it is vitally important for the preservation of good relations between partners to have an agreed procedure for prompt reflection of these changes in the division of earnings.

A technical feature of the profit-share provision that is worthy of note is that it may be expedient to place the profit-share percentages, salaries, and also the capital interests on a schedule which is annexed to the agreement and initialed by all or a specified majority of partners. This facilitates revision of the schedule in the event of a change in partners or any of the subject points without requiring a rewriting of the agreement itself, if the agreement provides for such a separate schedule and its periodic revision.

Determination of income. Two important provisions in the partnership agreement which are closely related to allocation of income are the method of accounting employed in the determination of income and the frequency of the determination and resulting allocation to individual partners. There appears to be essentially unanimous employment of the cash basis of income determination for regular recurring purposes. Adjustment to the accrual basis is occasionally stipulated for special purposes such as the determination of the interest of a withdrawing or deceased partner. The frequency of income determination and allocation is not nearly so uniform. Some firms do so quarterly, others semiannually or annually.

Drawings. A related matter which should be covered by a specific provision in the agreement is the amount which a partner is entitled to withdraw from the firm. When salary allowances are employed these amounts usually represent the limit on drawings pending periodic allocation of earnings. One local firm's agreement provided for the withdrawal of salary and up to 75 per cent of the estimated share of income after salaries. The important point is that this matter should be covered in the agreement rather than the specific form of coverage.

In summary, the partnership contract should contain a clear-cut formula for the allocation of partnership income which recognizes, as accurately as possible, the contribution of the several partners to the success of the firm. Of particular importance is the provision for change in any particular procedure, in order that prompt recognition may be given to altered circumstances involving the value of partners' services.

Examples of variations. Profit-share arrangements present more diversity than any other provision in partnership agreements. Evidence of this situation is found in the following excerpts from agreements comprising common situations as well as some oddities.

The partners shall equally share in all profits and losses.

It is further understood and agreed that the partners will share in the earnings and profits of the partnership as follows, to wit:
The parties of the first part (three persons) shall each receive as salaries $——— per week. The parties of the second part (three persons) shall each receive as salaries $——— per week. The partnership profits, after the deduction of the aforesaid interest and partners' salaries, shall then be divided as follows, to wit: Parties of the first part —% (divided among names and respective percentages varying), and parties of the second part —% (divided equally amongst named persons).

... the salaries of the members of the firm shall be as follows: (names and varying amounts). However, the foregoing is subject to adjustment by the mutual consent of the partners, but shall continue as aforesaid if the partners are unable to agree on any other adjustment, and the salaries as herein stipulated shall continue until the partners mutually agree on a change.

Profits and losses shall be borne ratably in proportion to the respective interests of all partners in the net income. The distributive share of profit or loss of each partner shall be determined by dividing the total shares of interests in income of both capital and non-capital partners, into the amount of net profit or loss after the deduction of interest on capital ... and by multiplying the amount so obtained by the number of such interests in income held by each partner.

When, as a result of withdrawal, retirement, death, or other cause, the percentage participation of a partner or his estate in partnership net profits is terminated, such percentage shall be absorbed by increasing the percentage participations of the remaining partners in the net profits of the partnership in the proportions that their respective required shares of partnership capital bear to the total required shares of all the remaining partners.

The profits of the partnership shall be divided annually on such basis as shall be mutually agreed to by the partners.

Profits will be computed no less frequently than once a year. Partners' drawings and distributions of profits will be effected as agreed upon by the partners from time to time.

Salaries of partners shall be computed at the end of each month, and each partners' account credited with his salary, to be computed on the following basis:

1. —% of the net fees credited to the fees account of each partner, plus . . .

2. $———— for each hour devoted to office, gratis, or other nonproductive business time

The following amounts shall be minimum yearly salaries, and if the respective salaries as computed under paragraphs (above) amount to less than the following minimums, there shall be credited at the close of each fiscal year to the respective salary accounts such amounts as are necessary to make up such minimum salaries: (names and amounts).

Interest shall be computed on monthly balances in salary or drawing accounts of partners at the rate of —% per annum, interest to be charged or credited at the close of each year and added or deducted in determining net earnings or losses available for division.

Net profits or losses resulting after deducting . . . partners' salaries, and plus or minus interest on partners' drawing accounts (monthly balances at —% per annum) shall be divided among the partners, in the proportions specified . . . except that if a partner fails to earn in any year the minimum salary provided in paragraph — then for the purpose only of computing the division of profits for such year, the fractions specified in paragraph — as representing such partners' interest, shall be reduced by a percentage equal to one-half that obtained by dividing such deficiency by the minimum salary provided.

The factors so reduced shall be combined with the remaining factors and a substitute ratio ascertained by which profits for the year will be divided.

For the purpose of this agreement all determinations of net income or loss shall be on the accrual basis of accounting, notwithstanding the partnership reports on a cash basis for income-tax purposes.

In lieu of salaries the partners shall be entitled to monthly drawing accounts based upon the following annual rates (names and amounts).

Net income sufficient to pay such drawing accounts must be earned first, and thereafter any remaining net income shall be distributed upon the following basis:

1. Fifteen per cent shall be set aside for employee bonuses: One-third of such amount to be distributed to the individual employees on a merit basis, and the remaining two-thirds according to the following formula: three units for each full year of service; one unit for each dollar of monthly salary. Employees with less than one year of service shall not participate in the formula distribution.

2. Eighty-five per cent as additional distribution to partners divided in the following manner (names and percentages).

Should the net income be insufficient to pay drawing accounts in full such deficiency shall be charged to the accounts of the partners according to the percentages just listed.

Any partner shall have the right to withdraw the full amount of his distributable share of net income immediately upon final determination following the close of each fiscal year. Monthly withdrawals against the distributable earnings of the current fiscal year in excess of drawing account allowances may be made by any partner, provided such withdrawals shall not exceed 50 per cent of such excess. The provision with respect to withdrawings against current interim earnings may be modified as to any partner, with the consent of all other partners, when otherwise a hardship may result to a partner due to circumstances beyond his control.

Whenever drawings in excess of the proper proportion of the annual salaries stated in paragraph — shall be taken by any partner, the partners' accounts may be adjusted and disbursements made to the other partners from the funds of the partnership so that the undrawn earnings of no partner shall equal a greater proportion of the total undrawn earnings than that set forth in paragraph — above.

The senior partner shall be entitled to draw a salary of $——— per year, and each of the junior partners shall be entitled to draw salary as follows: (names and amounts).

All salaries paid to each of the partners as above provided shall be charged to the expense account of the partnership.

The senior partner shall determine, from time to time, the amount of the net profits of the partnership to be distributed and the junior partners shall be entitled to share only in the net profits accruing and/or distributed within the term of the partnership in accordance with such determination by the senior partner. The division of net profits shall be as follows:

1. To the senior partner —% thereof
2. To each of the junior partners —% thereof

Net losses, if any, sustained by the partnership shall be borne by the partners in the same proportion.

The profits from said business shall be distributed in the following proportions:

1. The parties hereto shall be entitled to receive monthly drawing accounts as follows:

$$A \ \$\rule{2cm}{0.4pt} \qquad B \ \$\rule{2cm}{0.4pt} \qquad C \ \$\rule{2cm}{0.4pt}$$

Such amounts received pursuant to such drawings shall be charged respectively against the share of profits of each of the partners, but the share of the profits including drawing accounts of the partner (name) shall be at least $———— over the full term of this agreement.

2. In the event that the said profits from said business shall be more than $————, then all such profits over $———— shall be distributed in the proportions of

$$A: \ 25\%, \ B: \ 25\%, \ C: \ 50\%$$

The losses of said partnership shall be borne in the following proportions:

$$A: \ 1/3, \ B: \ 1/3, \ C: \ 1/3$$

Participation Schedule: Attached hereto and made a part hereof is a schedule designated "Participation Schedule No. 1 — Effective ————," in which are set forth the names of the several partners, the partners designated as administrative partners, the annual salary of each partner, the ratios and units of participation in the distributable profits and stated capital and the amount of the stated capital of each partner, all as of the time of the taking effect of this agreement.

After the payment of all partnership expenses, the net profits shall be divided as follows:

(names and percentages)

Irrespective of the amounts produced by the foregoing percentages and irrespective of the amount, presence, or absence of net profits, the parties hereto do hereby jointly and severally guarantee to ———— the following minimum amounts free from any firm liabilities of any nature whatsoever:

(names and amounts)

Any deficiency required to be met pursuant to the aforesaid guarantee shall be paid to ———— in or prior to three months following the close of the fiscal period . . . (and) be met by the guaranteeing parties as among themselves in the same proportions as . . . firm losses.

The net losses shall be borne as follows:

(names and percentages)

Losses sustained by the partnership shall be made up by the partners enumerated . . . in cash at the end of the year and in the proportions set opposite their respective names.

For the purposes of determining profits and losses as well as for the purposes of the minimum guaranteed . . . each fiscal year shall be considered separately and profits earned in one fiscal year shall not be offset against losses sustained in any prior or subsequent fiscal year.

The profits shall be distributed as and when convenient. . . If any partner shall not withdraw the whole or any of his share in the net profits, he shall not be entitled to receive interest (thereon) nor shall he be entitled by reason thereof to an increase in his share of the profits of the partnership. The partners shall not receive salaries.

A partner shall be entitled to —% of the first two years' fees received . . . from any new client . . . obtained by said partner. Said per cent shall be charged as an expense of the partnership. For the purpose of this subdivision, the first two years shall be deemed the period of two years from the date on which the new client retains the firm. ————'s decision as to whether any client is a new client and as to whether such client was obtained by a particular partner shall be final and binding on all the parties hereto.

The partnership profits will be divided as follows: Jones (full time partner) will receive the first $————— profits for the year and the excess will be divided equally. In the event that the profits do not equal $—————, Jones will be entitled to receive full amount thereof.

The division of the profits as set forth above, contemplates that each partner will contribute to the partnership, in business and value of services, substantially the same contribution as was made in (year). At the end of each year, the partners will review their contributions in the light of this stipulation and if it appears that such contributions are materially different from those in (year) the partners will mutually agree upon a variation in share or the profits (over $—————) to which each shall be entitled for the preceding year.

The first ————— thousand dollars of net income as hereinbefore defined is designated "the first division of net income" and shall be divided equally among the three partners. The next amount divided designated as "first excess of net income" over the above sum shall be divided —————% to A, —————% to B and —————% to C, and the "second excess of net income" being the (balance) shall be divided equally. In the first fiscal year of the partnership under this agreement the "first excess of net income" shall be $—————, and in each succeeding year it shall be reduced by $—————. The first excess amount shall not be cumulative if net income earned in any year should fall short of the amount designated.

The losses of the business, if any there be, shall be borne as follows: The losses . . . up to a maximum of the total of the partners' salaries shall be borne by the partners in the same proportion as the salary of each partner bears to the total partners' salaries; losses, if any there be, in excess of the total partners' salaries in any fiscal year shall be borne in the same proportion as profits are shared.

In addition to salaries as hereinbefore provided, each of the partners and all staff accountants employed by the partnership shall be entitled to participate in a bonus to be calculated at the end of each fiscal year of the partnership in the following manner:

Each net fee for partnership services shall be allocated proportionately among such of the partners and staff accountants as shall have performed services in or in connection with the particular work resulting in such fee. Said allocation shall be based both on the number of hours of service performed by such partner or staff accountant on the particular work and the rate per hour as fixed from time to time by the partners as the hourly rate chargeable to clients for such partner's or staff accountant's services. The amounts thus allocated to a partner or staff accountant shall be accumulated to the end of each fiscal year of the partnership and 50% of the total amount thus allocated shall be such partner's or staff accountant's total compensation for such fiscal year, and the amount by which such total compensation shall exceed the fixed salary previously drawn by said partner or staff accountant shall be paid or credited to him. If the amount of the fixed salary previously drawn by such partner or staff accountant shall be in excess of his total compensation computed as aforesaid, no bonus will be earned or paid.

Various agreements also contain relevant provisions which are summarized as follows:

1. On the determination of net income, salaries are determined by the Management Board and are treated as operating expenses. Also there is a

provision that "as to any fiscal year when the net income . . . shall exceed
$——————, an amount not exceeding one half of such excess may be appor-
tioned by the Management Board to one or more partners . . . for the purpose
of effecting additional compensation for individual service of special benefit
to the partnership. . ."

2. Partners are to be paid 50 per cent of their earnings plus 10 per cent
of the total fee from clients introduced by them plus a proportion of the net
earnings after partners' compensation as above based on the ratio of the
partners' individually introduced business to the total business of the firm.

3. The distribution of profits of the partnership is on a unit basis, which
unit basis is increased as additional partners are admitted and decreased as
partners retire.

4. Profits are divided according to the percentage interests of the various
partners in the firm. Losses are shared by the senior partners proportionately
to their interests but junior partners bear no share of any loss.

Junior partners receive a stipulated salary plus a small percentage of interest
in the business, and the total earnings are subject to a minimum quantity.
However, in arriving at the percentage share of junior partners in the profits,
nominal salary amounts for the senior partners are first deducted.

The amount of cash drawings which each partner may make during the year
is stipulated.

5. Each partner has a basic percentage of income (after allowance of interest on capital) specified in the partnership agreement. The agreement also
contains a schedule expressing the actual hours devoted by a partner to partnership activities in a year as a percentage of 2,000 hours. The basic
profit-sharing percentage is multiplied by the approximate per cent to determine a weighted percentage. For example, if Partner A's basic percentage
was 40 per cent and during a given year he worked 2,200 hours (as defined),
his adjusted percentage would be 44 (110 per cent times 40). His share
of income for this year (after deduction of interest on capital) would be
the fraction which 44 represents of the total adjusted percentages of all
partners. In essence, this scheme appears to be a rather complex method
of securing the same results which might be obtained by a flexible salary
allowance procedure. Among the complexities is the necessity for defining
in detail in the agreement what constitutes hours devoted to the affairs of
the partnership, including such activities as professional society participation
and reading periodical and other literature. Each partner must then maintain
a detailed record of his hours in order to carry out the prescribed procedure.

CURRENT PRACTICES—NEW PARTNERS

While some firms determine new partners' total compensation on the basis
of a percentage of the net earnings, most use salary plus a percentage of
the remaining earnings. Usually, the same method is applied to all partners.
In a few cases, junior partners are on a salary-plus-percentage basis, while
the older partners have a "draw" against their percentage interest.

Straight percentage of net earnings. The use of a straight percentage appears to be more predominant in smaller firms with a single class of partners. These firms generally establish the percentage of initial participation on a basis which would yield an amount equivalent to the new partner's previous earnings as a staff man plus an amount which would be regarded as a substantial raise. Once a man enters into a partnership with these firms, he is usually liable for any losses in proportion to his interest and is generally given no minimum guarantee. However, one firm of four equal partners, grossing about $230,000 a year, made this provision for two additional partners who were admitted: Each new partner received an interest equal to one-half that of the older partners (10 per cent over-all interest). In the event that the younger partners should earn less than $6,500, they would also receive 60 per cent of the older partners' share in excess of $10,000.

Here are some examples of other straight-percentage arrangements initially made with new partners:

A twenty-eight-year-old specialist in management services was given an interest in a firm which had four partners. His share amounted to $12,000 and was increased in his second year as a partner.

A thirty-year-old staff man with five years' experience was given a 20 per cent interest by the two existing partners. Gross fees were about $80,000 and the net income of the firm was about $50,000.

The newest partner in a fifteen-partner firm grossing well over $750,000 received a 3 per cent interest which yielded about $11,000 during his first year. He was thirty-two years old, held an MBA, and had about eight years' experience with the firm.

Two staff men each received a 12 per cent interest, representing almost one-half of the average interest held by the other three partners. Gross fees were in the $100,000 to $200,000 bracket.

In this five-partner firm with a net income of about $100,000, the managing partner recommends profit distribution, subject to majority approval. The newest partner, admitted two years ago, earned about $10,000.

A $750-a-month drawing account is charged against the 10 per cent interest given to a staff man in his late thirties. He had about ten years' experience in this six-partner firm with annual billings of about $450,000.

Salary plus profit share. This arrangement, salary plus a share of the profits, seems to be favored by the majority, with salaries established for each partner considered as an expense. The income remaining after payment of these salaries is distributed according to agreed-upon percentages which most commonly are in direct proportion to the capital interest. In firms which have some non-capital partners, the profit share of these partners is generally deducted before distribution is made on the capital-interest basis. However, some firms have established the participating percentages independently of the amount of the individual partners' capital contribution. Frequently, interest is paid on capital in these cases, although this practice is by no means limited to these situations. There seems to be a trend toward salary-plus arrangements with interest being paid on the capital investment.

Determining salaries. Some firms establish nominal salaries to cover current living expenses on an almost equal basis among the partners. But a more common practice seems to establish variations which will give partial recognition to such factors as time spent, productivity, and administrative responsibilities. Even under the former situation the salary represents only a minimum guarantee for new partners. One firm in this category uses salaries to reflect variations in partner hours. Their salaries are based on $3.20 per hour for each chargeable or nonchargeable hour worked.

The salaries of newly admitted partners in these firms represent the great bulk of their income during the earlier years, since their initial interest is usually quite small. Salary increases for younger partners also provide a means by which some firms can compensate younger partners as their value increases, without having older partners relinquish a substantial portion of their capital interest before they are ready to reduce control. Salary paid a new partner usually represents some increase over the salary paid him as a staff man.

Determining profit share. Firms which pay salaries to their partners generally make available a small profit-sharing percentage under the initial arrangement with a former staff man. In firms with a single class of partners, this percentage is usually based on over-all earnings. Multi-office firms with junior partners generally limit participation to the earnings of the office where the new partner is assigned. Where non-capital partners are members of a single-office firm (and in some multi-office firms), the profit share is based on over-all earnings. Generally no fees from any of the clients are exempted from these calculations, but a few firms make special provisions for new client development. The amount of the profit-sharing interest to be made available is generally arrived at through discussion among all the existing (or general) partners. An increase of roughly 10 per cent in total compensation during the first year is the figure most often given for new partners.

Some initial salary-plus-profit-sharing arrangements are:

Salary was $1,200 more than total compensation as a staff man plus 3 per cent interest in the profits of this four-partner firm grossing about $200,000 a year. Age at admission, under thirty.

This thirty-three-year-old former IRS agent, with three years' experience in the firm, received a $7,500 salary and a 10 per cent interest in all the firm net income exceeding 90 per cent of the amount realized by the firm during the year preceding his admission. He earned about $9,300 during his first year as one of five partners in this firm, which employs six full-time staff accountants and grosses about $165,000.

This thirty-one-year-old staff member remained at his existing salary of $7,800 and received a 1½ per cent interest, which yielded an additional $2,167 during his first year. This is a firm with nine general partners, which netted about $145,000 in addition to $95,000 in partner salaries, on a gross of about $650,000.

A junior partner, age twenty-five, received a 2½ per cent interest in this eight-partner firm (gross annual fees of $250,000) in addition to a salary equal to that of all the other partners.

An eight-partner firm with an annual volume of approximately $600,000 compensated its newest partner with a salary of $9,600 and made available four units of capital interest at $1,500 each which resulted in an additional $4,000 during his first year.

This eight-man organization, including five partners, proposes to offer a 2 per cent interest (worth about $1,500 a year) to a staff member in his late twenties, in addition to a salary of $7,500.

In his middle thirties, a new partner in an eight-partner firm in the $250,000 to $500,000 category received a salary of $11,500 and a small percentage which raised his total income to about $15,000.

With some increase over his staff salary and a 3 per cent interest, a new partner in this six-partner firm earns about $15,000.

Additional benefits for partners. The incomes of new partners are usually based exclusively on a combination of profit-sharing interest on capital and salary. However, some firms have specific provisions for additional compensation to partners who are directly responsible for the acquisition of new clients.

Although all new clients are regarded as belonging to the firm, extra compensation is paid in cases where the new business is clearly derived from specific partners. One firm pays 15 per cent of the gross fee for the first year and 10 per cent of the second-year's fee to the partner involved. Another pays 25 per cent for the first year only. A third firm grants 25 per cent of the annual fee during each of the first three years to the partner. In the first two cases, the arrangement was made with the younger partners only, while the third applied to all partners.

In most firms fringe benefits do not differ from those available to the staff. Life insurance usually varies in amount, with partners having an opportunity for increased coverage. A more liberal vacation is permitted partners in some cases. Dues and expenses of partners for professional, civic, and certain social organizations and meetings are frequently paid by the firm. But these usually are also paid (though on a more limited basis) for staff members of these firms. A retirement benefit available to partners is not available to the staff in a few firms.

Increasing the share of younger partners. Although some firms make specific commitments to increase the participation of a new partner at the time he is admitted, most confine themselves to telling the new partner that his progress depends on his performance. It is generally assumed that the older partners will provide further participation rights as the younger men develop. Firms usually review their distribution every few years in order to recognize any changes in the contributions of the partners to the general welfare of the firm. In a number of cases this is done annually.

Some firms agree on the participation arrangements at the beginning of each fiscal year, to be effective during the coming year. Others determine it on the basis of the year just ending. Changes are usually made by common consent of the general partners. But in firms having "executive" or "management" committees, changes in distribution are frequently decided by these groups. In some cases the determination is made by the managing partner, who generally consults the older partners. In such firms, the managing partner is usually a surviving founding partner and has a controlling interest in the firm.

In practice, the changes made in the distribution of profits rarely decrease the dollar income of any partner, but provide increased compensation to those partners who are contributing the most to the continuing growth of the firm. An exception occurs where older partners withdraw gradually over a period of years. In a number of firms a retiring or withdrawing partner's interest is made available in proportion to the existing interest of the other partners. However, most prefer that this be decided among the remaining partners or by the executive committee.

Among the firms which make commitments to provide an increasing interest to new partners, the following plans are typical:

In some firms, upon the admission of new partners, the older partners agree to make their interest available in specified amounts over a period of years. This is basically a gradual retirement procedure. For example, one-eighth of the older partner's interest each year for eight years; in another case, the arrangement is one-tenth for each of ten years. One firm has a guaranteed succession in which the entire interest of the first senior partner to withdraw or retire is made available to the oldest junior partner. That partner's prior interest then reverts to the junior partner "pool."

In a third case a minimum additional interest is made available at the rate of 1 per cent each year, for five years. Here the firm operates on a salary-plus basis, with the initial interest of the new partner established at 5 per cent.

In their original arrangements with new partners, some firms provide that the younger partners have more participation in the firm's future growth than in its existing business. This is done by establishing two or more brackets of net income. Within each bracket a percentage participation is determined. In the upper brackets, profit sharing is on an almost equal basis for all partners. Salaries of varying amounts are paid by these firms prior to profit distribution. In one case the highest salary is about 175 per cent of the lowest. In one four-partner firm, the newest partner receives a salary of $10,000 and a 15 per cent interest in the earnings, net of salaries up to a point which exceeds the current net income by about 25 per cent. He has a 25 per cent interest in the profits above that level. Another uses four brackets, the first of which is somewhat below the present earnings of the firm. These firms feel that this system gives the younger partner a greater stake in the growth of the organization, much of which will result from their efforts. Generally however, the initial arrangement is not considered rigid and adjustments are made from time to time.

The Partnership Agreement

GENERAL CONSIDERATIONS

■ THERE ARE MANY small and medium-sized accounting firms, and perhaps some large ones too, that have been functioning for years on the basis of an oral understanding or with a very limited and inadequate written partnership agreement. This condition prevails for understandable, human reasons, and many such cases have probably developed in the following manner:

1. Two young men, embarking on their first partnership venture, feel that the need for any agreement, and particularly an extensive written agreement, for their personal-service enterprise appears to be remote. At least, the matter can be postponed.

2. As the firm functions satisfactorily for years with no agreement, or a very sketchy written agreement, the absence of a more comprehensive understanding is hardly noticed. True, there is an awareness of the need for a sound, written partnership agreement, particularly since the members of the firm themselves so advise others, but the matter is postponed for later consideration.

3. Finally, when the partners hear of a firm that has dissolved or of a partner who died, or if they are thinking of having wills prepared, then the desire for a full-fledged agreement becomes strong. But how can a personal-service professional practice be dealt with in an agreement? What should be done about a deceased partner? How can a partnership be disentangled? These questions can seem so overwhelming that the preparation of an agreement is delayed unreasonably in some cases, and perhaps never carried out in others.

It is not recommended that accountants prepare their own agreements. On the contrary, an attorney should be utilized, but the accountants might first determine the provisions they desire, then review them with an attorney and have him prepare a formal agreement. In this connection, it is essential to bear in mind that only a lawyer can decide whether any contractual provision quoted or otherwise set forth therein actually possesses legal validity, that any such provision, though presumably valid in the jurisdiction where originally used, may not be so in another, and that the best judgment as to the use of any specific content or wording is that of the lawyer preparing the agreement.

The agreement must take into account the provisions of the state partnership laws as well as the laws governing the practice of CPAs within the state. Where it is contemplated to have an out-of-state branch, or otherwise practice in other states, consideration must be given to the laws of the foreign states.

One of the most forceful reasons for the preparation of an agreement at the earliest possible moment is that at the outset of a new venture the "will to agree" is at its greatest height. On the other hand, if a formula for dissolution must be developed when partners are separating and have perhaps become unfriendly, the consequences are apt to be unpleasant and costly.

Another aspect which is worthy of consideration is that a partnership agreement reflects the status of the members as of the time the agreement is formed. Men who are embarking on their first venture and are under the spell of their hopes and aspirations, who look upon their effort as a friendly as well as a business tie, and who feel that they are all "starting from scratch," will enter into an agreement that may vary considerably from that between two or more veteran individual practitioners who desire to join forces. However, the status of partners within a firm is bound to change in time. One partner may do substantially better than another in obtaining new clients, or one may develop outstanding capabilities which are more helpful to the firm's reputation. For this reason an agreement should not be considered an unchangeable instrument, but, like a will, one which should be intelligently revised as conditions warrant.

The subject of human relations is not included here though it may well be one of the most important aspects. One cannot write good human relations into an agreement except, in a limited sense, where provision is made for the arbitration of controversies. Every partner must realize that each one of the firm is a distinctive individual, possessing peculiar personality traits, strong points, and weaknesses. All partners cannot act and think alike. If these distinctions are frankly discussed in advance, there may be less disappointment and misunderstanding thereafter.

It is not possible to get into an agreement a provision to cover every conceivable contingency. First, all possibilities just cannot be visualized, and second, the drafting of such an instrument might never be completed. Some areas of agreement must be left for discussion and a meeting of the minds when, as, and if unanticipated developments arise.

An example of a typical partnership agreement appears on page 830.

LEGAL AND PROFESSIONAL STATUS OF PARTNERSHIP

An accounting partnership must not only be organized within the framework of the state in which it will be domiciled, it must also conform to the requirements of the state's professional laws, if any, governing the public practice of accountancy. The former requirements can be attended to by an attorney, the latter should be known to the accountants even prior to any affiliation. When the firm extends its operations outside the state new problems may arise.

The use of the title Certified Public Accountants is subject to statutory conditions in many states. Firms whose partners are members of the AICPA and of the state CPA societies must conform to their rules as to representations of membership, etc.

Where the estates of deceased partners have an interest in the income or assets of an accounting firm, related legal and professional questions should be checked and reviewed. Similarly, where a wholly or partly inactive partner retains a profit-sharing interest, the firm's position in the light of such agreement should be ascertained.

When a staff member is given a profit-sharing interest, a question may develop as to whether or not he has become a partner, depending on other aspects of his working arrangement. This subject should receive attention from a legal standpoint when the problem arises.

A final point to consider is whether the partnership is of a continuing type; that is, whether under the applicable state law the firm must liquidate and terminate upon the death of a partner, or if by agreement it may continue without interruption.

WRITTEN VERSUS ORAL AGREEMENTS

There are many oral contracts in existence. Quite a few small firms and even some good-sized ones have them. This is probably so because the agreements cover only a few basic conditions. All unspecified points are to be dealt with, when, as, and if they arise. It is this aspect, obviously, which can be troublesome when an understanding cannot be reached on a new issue.

The simplicity of an oral agreement is the major reason for its use. Issues that appear to be improbable or lie in the distant future need not be dealt with. Besides, it is very easy to agree to draw up a comprehensive written agreement as soon as time permits, if ever. Written agreements are obviously more difficult to prepare because greater care must be given to them. The very fact that they are written means that everything pertinent should be included, and that the language must be weighed and considered carefully. An oral understanding is based upon discussion, which is usually informal and friendly, and, so long as the intent is presumably clear, no problem of drafting and weighing of words is involved. But intent is not always established easily when proof is required, and the matters left for future agreement may not later be settled as easily as when discussed without the pressure of the event, and when the will to agree was at its best.

The written agreement has one psychological advantage, namely, that it forces action on subjects that might otherwise be ignored because the provision cannot be worked out easily. For example, the termination of a partnership is a matter that is not simple to work out and is often omitted even from written agreements. Yet that is one of the problems that can be most troublesome when a partnership is dissolved, for any reason, unless some reasonable procedure has been specified, definitely and clearly, in advance. Should ill will have been engendered among the partners, the dissolution might well lead to acrimonious incidents and litigation.

The following actual comments stress the importance of the written agreement:

From my experience my (major) contribution to your subject would be (to emphasize) the absolute necessity of having a complete written and legal partnership agreement whenever any man is brought into a firm. . . . It is only when you have had the unfortunate experience I have had that you realize the necessity for a comprehensive and written agreement.

Our agreement and profit-sharing formula is the result of hundreds of hours of study, negotiation, and of course, bitter and expensive experience.

No matter what the terms may be, they are of less importance than the necessity to put them in writing. It is at the beginning of a partnership association that the enthusiasm and good will lend themselves to an amicable and fair arrangement; and not when a later conflict is magnified by the lack of a written understanding.

Limitations of Partners' Outside Activities

■ AS A RULE, partners in any business or profession are expected to devote all of their time and best efforts in their firm's behalf. This is the situation in the accounting field, too. There are some exceptions, but in such instances the departures are specified or require the consent of the partnership. The compensation plans may make some allowance for the reduction in time devoted to the firm's business, but not in all cases.

Illustrative of the complete ban against outside activities are the following provisions:

At all times during the continuance of these articles each partner shall give his full time and attention, and use his best endeavor, and to the utmost of his skill and power exert himself for the joint interest and profit of all.

Each partner shall devote his entire working time and energy to the business of the partnership. No partner shall engage in any other business or become an officer or director of a corporation organized for profit without the consent of his partners.

Certain types of outside activities are permissible in some agreements. Exclusions cover public writing, speeches, lectures, acting as director, officer, fiduciary (if it does not impair the firm's independence), and various other efforts. The earnings from these sources are in some instances retained by the partners and in others are turned over to the firm. Instances of such provisions are the following:

Each of the partners shall at all times devote his entire time and attention to the business of the partnership, except that this provision shall not be deemed to prohibit the writing of books, pamphlets, and other printed articles, regardless of how distributed; the delivering of lectures, speeches, and other addresses . . . The fees, earnings, and other emoluments therefrom shall . . . belong exclusively to the partner or partners so engaged . . . It is understood and agreed, however, that in the event that the services of any of the partnership employees are used in the preparation for profit of such books, pamphlets . . . the partner using the same shall reimburse and pay . . . the actual costs of the services so used.

Any earnings of the individual partners from work which others might wish done by the partner as an individual and not as a firm—such as acting as temporary treasurer or comptroller, and so forth—shall be accounted for to the firm and be considered as earnings of the partnership, and not as earnings of the individual.

It is understood and agreed that each partner shall devote his whole time to the business of this partnership, and shall during its continuance engage in no other business, nor accept any office or trust that may interfere with his attendance at its place of business; except that it is hereby expressly agreed that this does not preclude (partner) from continuing as a partner of (firm) and devoting such of his time as may be required of him as such partner . . .

Some partnership agreements contain limitations or restrictions on outside investments by the partners. One such agreement provides that no partner may acquire any investments in a business or property when the opportunity arises from a client contact or association, without offering to all partners the right to participate in proportion to their interests in the partnership. A restriction on outside investments, either jointly with clients or arising out of client connections, may be included in agreements because of the possible effect of such investments on the accountant's independence.

Other types of limitations on partners' activities and obligations assumed are indicated in the following clauses:

Each of the partners shall at all times . . . pay and satisfy his own personal debts.

. . . each of the junior partners hereby agrees that he shall not engage directly or indirectly in any form of business or professional activity of any nature without the written approval of the senior partner first had and obtained. (Note:—No reference is made as to senior partner's activities.)

None of the junior partners shall engage in any dealings or transactions with, or represent, act for, or serve any person, partnership, firm, association, or corporation without the consent of the senior partner, or whom or which any of the partners shall previously, in writing have requested him not to trust, deal with, transact business with, or serve.

Each of the partners who shall own or operate an automobile shall, at all times, maintain policies of insurance against liability for damages to property and against liability for personal injuries, the latter policy to be in the amount of at least $———— for injuries to one person, and $———— to more than one person, resulting from the ownership or operation of such automobile.

Each partner agrees that if he prepares for publication articles pertaining to professional work such as that done by the firm, the periodicals to which they are to be submitted and the general tenor and character of the articles are to be approved by the firm. Among other things it shall be at the discretion of the firm whether the firm name appears in any way in connection with the articles, and the firm is to have the privilege, if it so desires, of copyrighting and reprinting any such articles.

Partners must notify each other of outside activities. Each may not . . . buy stocks or bonds on margin.

Without the consent of his copartners no partner shall engage directly or indirectly in any business whatsoever in competition with or incompatible with the business of the partnership.

Each partner shall devote his entire working time and energy to the business of the partnership. No partner shall engage in any other business or become an officer or director of a corporation organized for profit without the consent of his partners. No partner shall, during the continuance of the partnership, sell, assign, transfer, pledge, or otherwise dispose of his interest in the partnership business or assets, except with the written consent of all of the other partners.

No partner shall sign or endorse a note or any obligation as an accommodation to anyone other than a partner or the partnership, or become surety on any bond or undertaking, or make any guarantee of payment or performance without the consent of his partners.

One agreement is so worded as to provide in effect that younger partners must devote full time to business, and partners over sixty-five years of age only such time and effort as they find convenient.

Some agreements provide that a specified partner serve the firm only as called upon. This situation covers partners who render only consultation and advisory services. In other cases a partner agrees to devote only as much time as he reasonably can. These situations usually involve a partner who controls the firm or is valuable to the firm because of his prestige or client contacts. Partners who are close to retirement may also operate on this basis. The following is an example of such clauses:

That the first party and the second party shall devote all of their time and attention to the business of the partnership, and shall not, during the term of the partnership, either directly or indirectly, engage in any other business.

That the party of the third part shall devote as much of his time and attention to the business of the partnership as may reasonably be requested for consultations with the other partners.

Some agreements contain a specific provision limiting the amount of expenses that may be incurred by any partner for nonrecoverable expenses charged to the firm—such as for entertainment, local traveling, and similar items. A clause of this kind sometimes avoids disagreements among partners as to the extent to which such activities should be undertaken.

Standards to Be Maintained

■ SOME AGREEMENTS contain clauses requiring certain standards to be observed:

Each partner obligates himself to maintain a high standard of professional work and conduct . . .
Each partner shall make every effort to build up the business as a firm and not for the individual members thereof.

Each of the partners agrees to conduct himself in manner befitting a professional man and in strict accordance with the ethics of the accounting profession and the rules and regulations of the State Society of Certified Public Accountants and they shall become members of said society and retain such membership during the period of this partnership agreement.

Each partner must be a state-licensed CPA. Each partner must be a member of the AICPA and a state society of CPAs.

One agreement states in substance that any partner who commits an act involving moral turpitude may be required to withdraw.

Capital Contributions

■ THE NEED FOR CAPITAL is a relatively minor matter in a small accounting partnership, as is the case with other personal service organizations. Capital is needed at the outset to equip an office. Funds are required to finance payrolls and office expenses. In time, earnings retained in the firm replace the original capital investment. For this reason some firms do not have capital accounts on their records. Instead, they use titles such as personal accounts and profit distribution account. Where payrolls are very large, as in the case of audits of large national corporations, and a number of engagements are under way at one time, substantial capital is required. Bank loans are sometimes resorted to in such instances to relieve the financial strain.

Capital is not always paid in with cash. There are firms whose initial capital consisted partially of contributions of office equipment and books. Clients turned over to a firm have, in cases, also been valued and considered as capital investment.

Some very large firms, and perhaps a few small ones, use shares or units to represent partners' capital interests. These shares or units are transferable under prescribed conditions. Apart from representing capital they usually carry rights to shares of profit and participation in management. The rank of partners is determined by the number of shares owned. Its advantage is in the ease of transfer of interests, but consideration must be given to the possibility of the partnership being held to be an association taxable as a corporation.

The large majority of agreements provide that capital be invested and retained in the firm in an amount proportionate to the profit-share arrangement. There are agreements which call for the payment of interest on capital investments, others which also call for the collection of interest on capital deficiencies. Many agreements make no reference to interest on capital or deficiencies.

TREATMENT IN THE PARTNERSHIP AGREEMENT

The following are excerpts from actual agreements illustrative of the types of understandings that are in effect:

The capital of the partnership shall be $————, and shall be contributed in the following proportions . . . Any depletion of capital shall be made good through assessments against all the partners in the above proportions. The partners shall contribute in the same proportion any additional capital which they may consider necessary or desirable in the operation of the partnership business.

The parties agree that the firm shall commence business with a cash capital of $———— which shall be separate from their investments in the form of furniture and equipment, and for that purpose the parties agree to make cash deposits in the firm bank account upon the signing of this agreement as follows: (names and amounts).

No interest shall be allowed or paid on partners' capital accounts.

Capital: A and B agree to and hereby contribute to the capital of said partnership $———— each in cash; all of the office equipment, furniture, books, supplies, papers, and other equipment valued at $———— which are used by them in their current practice of public accounting; purchased goodwill in the amount of $————, and $———— in cash for the office cash fund of said partnership.

C agrees to and hereby contributes to the capital of said partnership $———— in cash.

The partners further agree that the capital of said partnership shall also consist of such sum, or sums of money, as from time to time shall be required, and shall be contributed in such portions as shall from time to time be agreed upon between them.

For the purpose of this agreement the partners shall be considered as having made equal contributions to the capital of said partnership.

The amount of the aggregate capital to be contributed in the above proportions shall be determined from time to time and shall approximate the amount required to furnish such office furniture, fixtures, and equipment as may be necessary or desirable for the efficient operation of the business, plus the minimum amount of accounts receivable (consisting principally of uncollected fees) at the end of any month in the preceding year.

For the purpose of providing funds to finance the business of the copartnership the profits of the several copartners which have not been drawn out by them and appearing to their credit on the books of the copartnership are treated for the purpose of this agreement as the capital of the copartnership. Each copartner shall be credited on the books of the firm with the profits thus left in the business by him from time to time. This paragraph shall not apply to the estate of a deceased partner.

It is understood and agreed that each partner will be paid interest at the rate of ———% per annum on his average monthly investment in the partnership capital, this interest to be considered as an expense in determining the partnership profits.

The following accounts shall be provided for each of the capital partners:

1. Capital account, in which shall be exhibited the amount of his original capital contribution, and the adjustments which have resulted from additional investment or contribution of capital, or of permanent drawings or retirements of capital. This account will also be adjusted to reflect the fluctuation in the valuation of the goodwill of the partnership . . .

2. Personal account, in which shall be recorded the respective share of the profits and losses allocable to each capital partner and his current drawings . . . This account will also be credited with an amount equal to 6 per cent per annum upon the amount of capital standing to the credit of the particular capital partner at the beginning of each fiscal year.

In addition, the following three summaries of actual provisions may be of interest:

1. The respective investment of each partner is the same proportion of the total investment as his profit-share proportion, and is represented by his capital account on the books of the copartnership, plus his proportionate interest in any surplus or undivided earnings.

Capital fixed at $——— and contributed and maintained by A, B, C, and D in the following percentages ———, ———, ———, ———. Any deficiency bears interest at 6 per cent per annum payable to other partners according to their percentage participations, but this interest provision may be waived as to any partner if all consent. Interest is paid at 6 per cent per annum on average balance of each partner's capital account, but, unless A determines otherwise, no such interest shall be paid on any amount in excess of a partner's required capital contribution. Such interest payments shall be charged as a firm expense and paid whether or not there are sufficient net earnings.

2. Capital contributions are required to be made in cash with the added provision that the required amount may be provided by the application of 60 per cent of the withdrawable net income of the partnership.

3. The amounts contributed by each partner are based upon the percentages of profits or losses of each partner. Interest shall be credited to partners on their capital accounts and charged or credited as the case may be on

June 30 and December 31 of each year on the monthly balances in the current accounts provided, however, that no interest shall be charged for money drawn by way of salary, but in so far as salary drawings may have been deferred and credited to current accounts of the partners, interest shall be credited.

NON-CAPITAL PARTNERS

Not all partners are required to make an investment in the firm. This applies to junior partners in certain instances, and to "working" partners. The prevalence of such exceptions is not known. Opportunities may nevertheless be provided for such partners to acquire capital interests in the firm as their status in the firm advances. The ownership of a financial interest is advantageous as an evidence of good faith and a more binding tie to the firm. It may be facilitated by providing that a percentage of the partner's profit share be retained in the firm until his capital account has been built up to an agreed amount.

Administration of the Practice

■ PARTNERSHIP AGREEMENTS, written and oral, may indicate which partners are charged with the responsibility for policies and other administrative measures, but do not describe or fix the program for managing the practice. This, of course, is a practical approach because administration should be left to the daily considerations of those in charge, who, as a rule, are the members having a preponderant interest in the firm, as well as the required experience and ability.

Management consists of two major functions. The first deals with policies: standards for audits, reports, staff, new engagements, fees, and so on. The second deals with the supervision of the practice and observance that set standards are complied with. In some instances the functions are combined, in others they are segregated. However, a clear-cut distinction may not be possible with respect to all administrative matters. Generally administration is linked to control and dictated by a majority of the partners in interest except as to matters where unanimous or other specified agreement is required.

The selection of the person who is generally in charge of administration is dependent on the constitution of the firm. In an organization consisting of a senior and one or more junior partners, the senior partner may reserve for himself full authority. In large firms, commonly, the senior partners (sometimes referred to as capital, goodwill, or founder partners, or as members) constitute the administrative partners. Some of them designate one partner as the managing partner and in some instances he is compensated for such services. The administration of a small firm may be shared by the partners in an individualistic manner. As it grows, and administration becomes more important, one partner will somehow emerge as the executive and the partners as a group may deal only with policy questions. Particular phases of administration are divided among partners, in many firms, but general policies are fixed by the partners as a whole.

TREATMENT IN THE PARTNERSHIP AGREEMENT

Many agreements contain no references to administration. Where they do appear it is usually because the responsibility is definitely placed in the hands of a specified partner or group of partners. A few selected illustrations of such provisions are here submitted:

> The partners agree that the general conduct of the partnership business in respect to relations with clients, employees, and others, and the general control of the partnership funds shall be supervised by —————.

> Each partner shall have power on behalf of the firm to sign checks, endorse checks for deposit, and sign drafts in the regular course of the business; to incur the firm liability on notes for loans for the conduct of the regular business; to enter into contracts with clients to do accounting work, subject to the provisions of paragraph —— (which paragraph permits the managing partner to reject any proposed work when in his opinion such work would not be to the best interest of the firm), and to engage upon such work; to engage assistants for cases and for the office; to render reports to clients; to render bills to clients; to purchase supplies or equipment; in general, to enter into any obligations and exercise any functions which any partner would be called upon to enter into or exercise in the proper and legitimate carrying on of the business were he the sole proprietor instead of a partner, except that the managing partner shall normally, when available, exercise the above functions unless one or more of such functions shall be by him specifically delegated to one of the junior partners.

> The management and control of all business of the partnership shall be under the direction of the goodwill partners sitting as a managing board. . . . One of the goodwill partners shall be chosen by the board as a business manager who shall be . . . subject to the orders of the managing board.

> The business and affairs of the partnership shall be managed and controlled by the administrative partners and all matters involving the general policy of the firm and its administration shall be decided by the administrative partners. Except as in this agreement otherwise specifically provided, in the event of any difference of opinion among the administrative partners, any matter or question shall be decided by a majority in interest of the administrative partners.

> The financial affairs and business of the firm shall be under the management of the senior partner who shall have sole control of its cash funds and final determination with respect to any and all matters pertaining to the conduct of the firm's practice. The junior partners agree to abide by the decision of the

senior partner with respect to all of the activities of the partnership . . .

Mr. ——————— shall be the managing partner of the partnership, and, except to the extent otherwise provided in this agreement, his decision shall control with respect to the management and conduct of the partnership business. Where the provisions of this agreement provide for or require the consent or agreement of the partners with respect to any matter, a decision of a majority of the partners shall control unless otherwise provided.

All matters of policy, procedure, participations, and general administration shall be determined by agreement of the partners. In the event of inability to agree upon any matter except those matters (dealing with withdrawal) requiring unanimous action by certain partners, the decision of the surviving active partners in the order that the signatures are affixed to this instrument shall be final and binding on all parties.

The charge or charges for any and all services rendered by the partnership or any member thereof to any person, firm, association, or corporation, shall be fixed by the senior partner, or, in his absence, by the manager and administrative assistant.

The matter of voting rights is a subject which should get consideration and attention particularly when the partners are not all on an equal footing. The administrative matters which may require partners' approval or disapproval fall into two major categories. First is that group of subjects which involves the partners themselves and matters of similar importance. Included herein are matters such as admission of partners, fixing of profit shares and salaries, retirement and death benefits, and so on. Second is the group of subjects which deals with operations, such as hiring of staff, staff salaries, operating policies, and the like.

The first group of subjects is ordinarily the province of the senior partners; the second is open to all partners. Thus, the admission of a new partner might require 75 or 100 per cent approval of the senior partners whereas the question of bonuses to be granted the staff might require a majority vote of all partners.

Even where all partners are of equal rank, voting rules might be set up. Some matters may properly be settled by a majority vote: for example, hiring an extra senior. But the subject of complete dissolution of the firm and matters of similar importance should perhaps have more than a simple majority approval.

Usually each partner entitled to vote has one vote, but sometimes voting representation is given a different basis. This takes the form of giving each partner voting rights in relation to his share of capital interest. On this capital apportionment basis, a partner having a one-third capital interest would have one-third of the authorized voting power.

LIMITATIONS ON PARTNERS' POWERS

Reference has already been made to restrictive clauses governing the activities of partners outside of the firm's scope. Some contracts, in addition, contain provisions dealing with limitations on the activities of partners within the orbit of the practice. These restrictions pertain essentially to administrative matters. Illustrations of the latter provisions are here submitted:

Each partner, with the exception of the managing partner, shall consult at least one other partner, obtaining his consent before doing any of the following: Engaging assistants with direct or implied promise of permanency; incurring special expense in traveling or otherwise for the purpose of securing business; purchasing fixed equipment; engaging offices and signing leases; incurring firm obligations for loans; and, generally, when new outlay, beyond the ordinary outlay for prosecuting the work in hand, is contemplated.

No partner may make reports to clients without placing copies of such reports in the firm files.

Whenever practicable, all reports prepared shall be submitted to the managing partner, or in his absence, to one of the other partners before being sent out, in order that uniformity of style and method may be adopted, and in order that the work may have the benefit of the consideration of more than one partner.

No notes or any evidence of indebtedness shall be executed in the name of the partnership without the signatures or written consent of the majority of the partners who shall represent at least 75 per cent of the partnership capital.

No partner shall undertake any firm business, the desirability of which may be questionable under general firm policies, without first submitting the engagement for approval by the management committee.

Without the consent of his copartners no partner shall . . . hire or discharge any employee; compromise or release debts owing to the partnership; make any contract in the partnership name involving more than $250; sign or endorse any negotiable paper so as to create a liability contingent or otherwise on the firm's part; use the partnership name, credit, or property for other than partnership purposes . . .

All differences as to policies shall be decided by a majority in interest of the partners, and no partner shall knowingly do any act in relation thereto contrary to the decision of the majority.

Also applicable is the rather unusual clause that no partner shall perform work which can be done just as well by a staff member.

Absence on Military Service

■ LEAVE-OF-ABSENCE provisions are not common in agreements, yet one type of leave—military service—can arise in almost any firm and involve young as well as older partners. Other leaves of absence may be taken for reasons such as the acceptance of a teaching or research assignment, to write a book, or to take a position with a government agency, or for other meritorious purposes. It is reasonable to assume that such contingencies can be dealt with satisfactorily as they arise. Nevertheless some forethought, and perhaps even a provision therefor, may avoid subsequent misunderstanding, acrimony, or even an impasse.

The following are illustrations of provisions that have been adopted:

Vacations and voluntary leaves of absence, including voluntary enlistments as distinguished from enlistment when a draft call is anticipated, shall be taken as mutually agreed upon. Financial arrangements as to the sharing of profits and losses, salaries to the remaining partners used in determining said profits and losses, capital investment, etc., shall be as mutually agreed upon at the time of such absences.

In the event that a partner involuntarily, including enlistment when a draft call is anticipated, becomes a member of the military services . . . salaries to the remaining partners shall be credited at the rate of 150 per cent of the highest current monthly basic salary paid to accountants employed by the firm, plus bonus (when such bonus is measured by salary), for the period of such absence, excluding the first thirty days. Consideration shall be given to vacations not taken previously or during the current year in determining the end of the waiting period. [It is presumed that the partner on leave continues to draw his usual allowance during all of his absence from the firm.]

In the event that either of the parties hereto shall be inducted into the armed services of the United States Government, and actually called for active service, or in the event of the illness of (specified partners) which may prevent either from personally attending to the business of the partnership and in the opinion of the remaining partners it becomes necessary to retain the services of an outside accountant, then and in those events the salary paid to such employee up to the sum of one-half of the monthly drawings shall be a charge against the drawing account of either who may be absent on account of such induction or of such illness, but whatever sum is paid to such employee over and above one-half of the monthly drawings shall be considered a partnership expense and charged to the partnership business, during the term of the partnership.

Junior Partners

■ MOST FIRMS do not officially designate any particular type of partner as a junior member. The term is generally and loosely used to identify the most recent additions to partnership status. There are many employees on a profit-sharing-only arrangement, who are referred to erroneously as junior partners; and there are other agreements where younger men are in fact taken into the partnership under the terms of an agreement, sharing in profits but without a so-called right to a capital interest. They may or may not have a right to later succession to the status of general partner. This is probably the only circumstance where the term is correctly applied.

The creation of junior partners becomes increasingly important as a firm grows, and as partners become overburdened or reach an advanced age. Another factor of considerable influence is the desirability of retaining, permanently if practical, staff men of unusual talent and capacity. It appears that the purported complexities of the junior partner problem are probably overrated. Anxieties as to the difficulties that may develop from the addition of a junior partner to the firm are often found to be unwarranted in actual experience.

If a firm is to be perpetuated, new partners must be added. As senior partners disappear from the picture, junior partners should be able to step into their places. Likewise, the ranks of the junior partners can be filled from the staff, which is one of the opportunities that can be held out to the rank and file.

Small firms are not necessarily barred from having one or even two junior partners. It is reasonable to expect that a junior partner will contribute more to a firm than a staff man. The pride of position and a new sense of responsibility will inevitably reflect themselves in a greater interest in client relations, profitableness of the operations, and securing of new clients. Moreover, the increased compensation, if any, may soon be offset by the benefits that will accrue from the increased enthusiasm and effort.

The duties of many junior partners vary little from their duties as senior accountants, supervisors, or office managers. They do, however, participate in partners' meetings but they are not privileged to vote on every issue. Certain issues, as reviewed elsewhere, and representing matters such as admission of a partner, adjustment of partners' salaries and profit shares, and retirements are reserved for senior partners. In time, they may be assigned, or assume with implied approval, new or more important functions. This is a matter of natural development. Junior partners should be trained to assume greater responsibilities as conditions warrant.

Eventually, in the course of years, the junior partner or partners assume increasing responsibilities and the senior partner or partners reduce their activities. In this process the distinction between junior and senior partners gradually diminishes. The stage is then reached where the only difference between them may be in capital shares, profit shares, or salaries, and finally, many junior partners become senior partners.

RELATIONS BETWEEN JUNIOR AND SENIOR PARTNERS

Illustrative of the most frequent type of arrangements governing relations between junior and senior partners are the following excerpts from two agreements:

> A majority in interest of the partners shall have the right to introduce as non-capital partners such members of the staff or other individuals as they may see fit under separate agreement as to salary and other remuneration, with or without interest in profits, and with an agreement to indemnify them against liability for losses or debts of the firm; no such agreement, however, shall entitle such persons to a voice in the management or to any additional (death, involuntary retirement . . .) benefits but any interest in profits so granted to such non-capital partners shall be treated as an expense and be deducted before determining the (earnings . . .) of the partnership.

> The senior partner shall have the right to require the withdrawal and resignation from the partnership of any junior partner by reason of conduct deemed by the senior partner to be injurious or detrimental to the partnership. In the event that such right be exercised, or in the event of the voluntary withdrawal or resignation of a junior partner . . . there shall be paid to the withdrawing partner in full for all of his right, title, and interest in and to the partnership, a sum equivalent to the amount payable to him as salary for a period of ——— months together with the amount of his credit balance upon the books of account of the partnership. There shall also be paid to him, within ——— days subsequent to his withdrawal or resignation, a sum equivalent to his share of the net profits of the partnership accrued to the close of the second month after which such withdrawal or resignation shall occur.

> Such retiring or withdrawing partner shall, upon request, make, execute, or deliver such instruments and perform such acts as the continuing partners may require in order to more effectually vest in them all of his right, title, and interest in the partnership.

> Such retiring partner shall not at any time solicit or perform the work of any clients of the partnership and shall not at any time disclose to any person, firm or corporation the name of any client or clients of the partnership, or any of its transactions, and such retiring partner shall not at any time use the firm name, nor, either in conjunction with his own name or otherwise, use the words "formerly of" or "late of" or any other combination of words containing the firm name.

FINANCIAL ARRANGEMENTS

With respect to the subject of financial arrangements, there is considerable latitude, and accordingly marked variations are found to prevail. The dominant pattern is a salary plus percentage of profits, yet some junior partners do not receive a profit share. Instead they get bonuses. The bonus plan, while not as definite as a profit-share plan, obviates the need for opening the firm's records to the junior partner and of making explanations of abnormal items. Moreover, in many instances the profit-share plan is not such in reality because junior partners are not required to share loss and are even assured a minimum annual remuneration. Any fair and reasonable financial arrangement will usually be found satisfactory to the prospective junior partner, particularly where there is no doubt as to the integrity of the other parties. There is no doubt that the title "partner" has tremendous appeal and a reasonable arrangement can readily be worked out in this atmosphere.

The course followed in each instance reflects to an important extent the character traits of the individuals. Men who are trusting, generous, and of an understanding nature will make arrangements that are more liberal than those made by men who are not similarly constituted. In addition, firms that have a highly profitable practice can afford to be more liberal.

Likewise, the personality of the junior partner, as reflected in evidences of his loyalty, appreciation, trust, and understanding, will influence the partners in the formulation of the arrangements. The staff man who creates the impression that he is interested mainly in monetary rewards, or that he is of an overly suspicious nature, will be dealt with in a more controlled and rigid manner than one otherwise constituted.

In the consideration of the salary to be paid there is no need for any immediate material adjustment as a result of the admission to partnership. The gain can come from the profit share, enlarged expense allowances, life insurance protection paid for by the firm, and other incidental benefits. Thus the fixed overhead need not necessarily be increased. Profit-share percentages start at rates varying from 1 to 5 per cent commonly, depending on the amount of the senior partners' salaries and whether they are treated as expenses for profit-share purposes.

Some firms provide that junior partners share in earnings over an annual minimum. This minimum may be the average earnings of the past five years. In such instances the salary should be as adequate as possible and the profit share higher than would otherwise be allowed. It must always be borne in mind that the junior partner should be able to maintain a standard of living consistent with his position. Moreover, care must be taken not to create a situation whereby a new partner is disillusioned by failure to earn any profit share because of an abnormal minimum.

The advancement of a junior partner should be more frequently by salary adjustment than by percentage of profit. Changes in profit shares are a more delicate subject than changes in salaries. In the latter respect, the problem of junior partners is not entirely dissimilar from that of senior partners.

There are firms that do make their books and financial statements available to junior partners from the outset. Others do not start on this basis but change to it in time, whereas still others never do, though a profit-share arrangement exists. If there is complete trust, a serious question may never arise but in the event of a withdrawal full disclosure may then be demanded. Mention should again be made at this point that some agreements contain limitation periods after which no claim may be raised by a partner for an accounting.

As to limitations on the activities of junior partners within and outside the firm, they are subject, of course, to all of the limitations placed on all partners by the terms of the agreement. In addition they are also subject to certain subordination to the senior partners with respect to administrative and policy matters, and the initiation of new engagements.

Capital contributions are not usually expected from junior partners. However, in time they may be encouraged to permit part of their profit shares to accumulate in the firm and to earn interest if interest is paid to other partners. Some firms may make a capital contribution a condition for admittance and there are instances where an interest in the firm is actually purchased from the partners. These are unusual, however, and are apt to involve men who have not been taken in from the ranks.

SEPARATION OR WITHDRAWAL FROM THE FIRM

The provision dealing with the broad subject of separation from the firm require careful attention for junior partners as well as for senior partners. Retirement benefits may be available to a junior partner (usually a remote situation) after a specified number of years service, in amounts proportionate to the senior partners' benefits. This presumes that such benefits are available to senior partners. Death benefits are more frequently available to junior partners, through life insurance or by payments from the firm to the estate. The benefit payments by the firm should be based on years of service, annual earnings, and finally, should be in reasonable proportion to the payments to senior partners. In the two foregoing respects the consideration should be similar, at least, to that which would be accorded an old, faithful executive. Social-security benefits may, of course, be taken into account, if any will be received.

Where withdrawal is involved by involuntary action of the junior partner or by a demand for his resignation, certain protective provisions should be considered. These provisions may be in the partnership agreement or in a separate agreement with the junior partner. They provide, as a rule, that the junior partner upon separation from the firm will not communicate this fact to clients, will not solicit them, will not advertise his former association, or in any other way take advantage of his former connection. There are some agreements which provide some security against violations by this method: a part of the junior partners' earnings is retained by the firm; only part is paid to him upon his withdrawal and the balance is paid to him in two or three years if he has lived up to the conditions of his contract.

Whatever amounts are due a junior partner on account of balances in his capital or personal account are paid out on the same terms as, or shorter terms than similar distributions to senior partners.

Matters of illness and incapacity of junior partners are dealt with, in the few instances observed, on a scale considerably below that affecting senior partners. It is likely that, despite the absence of such a provision in an agreement, upon the occurrence of serious illness or incapacity the firm will take some steps to provide aid.

With respect to military service, little specific reference thereto appears to exist. In some instances the agreement provides that a junior partner is to be restored to his position on his return and some minimum benefits paid to him during his absence. Nevertheless, though many agreements are silent on this point, it may in any event be the intention and the practice of some of the firms to act similarly.

COMPENSATION FOR NEW CLIENTS

Some provision should be made for clients obtained by junior partners. Whether there should be extra compensation therefor, and how much, are not questions that can easily be settled satisfactorily. Unfortunately, like many other situations, it depends upon the circumstances in each case. Good support can be found for either side of the issue. It may be argued as follows: Where the profit share and salary, if any, are generous, and the junior partner is closely integrated with the senior partners, and his continued progress is reasonably assured, then obtaining clients for the firm may call for no extra reward unless such payments are, as a matter of policy, made to all partners.

Where, on the other hand, the junior partner's annual earnings are not on a very satisfactory basis, then some reward, in the form of an annual percentage of gross fees, will serve to raise his earnings and provide incentive for trying to develop more new clients. Others may argue that, regardless of compensation status, all partners have the obligation to do everything in their power to advance the firm's interests, and developing new clients is just one phase of the fulfillment of this obligation. Some junior partners may be satisfied to receive no extra remuneration in the belief that they may thereby assure or expedite their further advancement in the firm.

It is of interest to note that titles other than that of junior partner are in use, to wit: non-goodwill partner, non-capital partner, nonadministrative partner, and the term associate. However, the last term is also used for semi-independent staff men who have some clients of their own and yet continue to serve the firm, their names appearing on the firm's letterhead. Some firms avoid classifying partners. Since their profit-sharing arrangements are such as to call for divisions of income according to value to the firm, and salaries are fixed according to capacity and experience, and administration of the firm's affairs is naturally centered in experienced hands, they find it unnecessary to make any formal distinctions.

Providing for Death, Withdrawal, Incapacity

■ IT HAS FREQUENTLY been stated that it is easier to get into a partnership than out of it. (This is borne out, to some degree, by the fact that the major portion of many agreements is devoted to withdrawal, death, retirement, and related provisions.) This is particularly so in the case of smaller firms where initial agreement is likely to be restricted to only immediate needs, and broad and detailed revision is left for later.

The subjects of retirement, withdrawal, and death of a partner alone warrant a written agreement. In these instances, more than any other, advance understandings are desirable. This is so for several reasons. Because no two people can be expected to reach identical conclusions years later, as to how to deal with one of these problems, there is a great likelihood of disappointments and misconceptions. Regardless of how well-intentioned the parties may be, the valuation yardstick used by each of them will vary and consequently there are bound to be differences. It does not follow, patently, that differences cannot be compromised and all concerned be satisfied. But it does not always work out that way. Moreover, changing conditions may even affect the personalities and attitudes of some persons. The addition of new partners, also, might create difficulties at a later date.

In one case, two members of a firm were forced to seek outside advice in reaching an agreement on what should be done for one of them who desired to retire because of age. In this instance, the two had been pleasantly associated for many years and had previously given no thought to retirement. Despite best intentions and sincerity, the valuation yardsticks used by each varied considerably. It was obvious that the differences, though reconcilable, must have been disturbing and that some disappointment had thereby been engendered. There is no doubt that the windup of years of association could have been far more wholesome and gratifying had there been no need to work out a retirement agreement at that late date.

An advance accord, modified as necessary to reflect changed conditions, is essential for those who recognize the need for estate or other long-term planning. It is perhaps more in order for young people to engage in long-term planning than for older ones. At present, it takes much longer to build up a retirement fund and income than ever before.

The ease of mind created by an agreement covering at least the essentials will prove to be an important factor in the cohesiveness of the partners.

Separations occur in the case of death, retirement, withdrawal, dissolution, and leave of absence. In the case of retirement, it may be:

1. After reaching a specified age or having completed a stated number of years of service
2. Because of a permanent disability

Withdrawal from a firm may be for any of the following reasons:

1. To go into business, practice alone, or with another firm (or to some other field)
2. Expulsion from the firm

Leave of absence from the firm may be due to military service, other temporary engagements, or illness.

DEATH OF A PARTNER

The need for a plan to liquidate the interest of a deceased partner is one of the most impelling motives for a partnership agreement. It is a "progressive" provision requiring change as the firm grows to insure that the terms are realistic and consistent with the changed position. After a certain stage has been reached, revision may be required only at long intervals, if at all.

Certain of the death provisions are of an invariable nature. These provide for paying out of a partner's capital and other credits due him. But, as a firm grows in age and affluence it may add new elements such as payments of death benefits to the widow or estate, and payments for goodwill where such is recognized. Moreover, it may increase such benefits as improvement in its position warrants.

As to the liquidation of capital and other credits due a partner, this procedure is described later.

Varying partnership organizations call for correspondingly different methods of acquiring a deceased partner's interest. To illustrate, a firm consisting of one senior partner and several junior partners has a different problem from one having two equal partners. A firm having many partners generally has less difficulty financially than one with few partners. But where the partners are all approximately of the same age, several deaths may occur within the course of only a few years. This possibility should not be disregarded.

Effective date of termination. The date of terminating the interest of the deceased is important. Some agreements provide for a special closing as of the date of death, but it can, and should be fixed as of the close of the partnership fiscal year unless there are compelling reasons for some other termination date. Whether or not the partner's estate is to receive a share of the income between the date of death and the end of the year is a matter for agreement. Frequently, the partner's profit share is continued to the end of the year.

Interests of the estate and survivors. As to the form of the disposition of the interest, relatively few agreements refer to it as a purchase of the deceased partner's share in the firm. Most contracts refer to it as the liquidation of his interest or the reversion of the interest to the surviving partners or to the firm. The different tax connotations and tax benefits to the estate and surviving partners may well exercise the decisive influence in the choice of a plan.

In some instances estates or widows are continued as if they were partners in that they share in the profits (not losses, in some cases) for a specified period of years. The validity of such arrangements for a professional firm must be carefully checked with state statutes and rules of ethics or professional conduct of the national and state accounting societies.

In one instance the following provision was made for a partner's widow:

> Beginning with the first day of the following fiscal year, the widow of the deceased partner shall share in the partnership profits so long as she remains unmarried or is charged with the support of minor children of the deceased, or for a period of ten years from the first day following the close of the current fiscal year in which the said partner shall have died, whichever is longer; with the share to such widow computed as follows . . .

The agreement goes beyond the widow, providing in addition as follows:

> If wife does not survive partner having minor children, or minor children survive wife after death of partner, profit sharing above shall be made instead to the legal guardian of the child or children for use in their support until the youngest becomes of age, at which time profit sharing ceases.

An instance of the continuance of the estate as a member of the firm is illustrated in this clause:

> The estate of a deceased partner shall continue as a member of the partnership for a period of three years as hereinafter provided, and shall participate in the net earnings but not the net losses of the partnership, but such estate shall have no voice in the administration of the affairs of the partnership.

The *Code of Professional Ethics* of the AICPA does not preclude the inactive affiliations of a retired partner or of an estate of a deceased partner for the sole purpose of sharing income for a specified period.[3] However, it would not be proper to make an executor a partner with all of the rights and privileges of one, unless that person was a CPA and not otherwise unqualified.

Illustrations of provisions. The purchase of a deceased partner's share is illustrated in the following excerpts:

> In the case of the death, incapacity, or retirement of a partner the remaining senior partners have the right to buy such partner's interest in accordance with their relative interests in the business prior to such purchase.

> No partner shall have any right, title, or interest in any of the specific assets of the partnership, such as files, records, papers, equipment, and so forth, but his proportionate interest therein shall be expressed only in the dollar amount

[3]See Opinion No. 6, "Numbered Opinions of the Committee on Professional Ethics," *CPA,* January 1958. (Reprinted in the Appendix of this volume, p. 826.)

of his capital account as set forth above. In the event of the death of any partner (or voluntary withdrawal, as specified in another clause) each for himself binds his heirs, executors, administrators, and representatives to accept the amount of his capital account in full settlement of all his interest in the partnership assets; and the surviving and continuing partners agree to purchase, on that basis, the net interest of any decedent (or retiring partner) in the assets of the partnership and assume and agree to pay all partnership liabilities.

Other known death-benefit plans are summarized very briefly to disclose further the variety of patterns:

A comprehensive agreement covering senior and junior partners provides the following payments in addition to capital, loans, etc.

Estate of deceased senior partner receives:

1. A specified dollar amount for relinquishing its right or interest in the firm name, payable over a five-year period.

2. A stated percentage of net profit, before partners' salaries, for five years, but not to exceed a stated maximum.

Estate of junior partner receives only the benefits in item (2) above but in a lower percentage and lower maximum.

The partners covenant, each with each, that in the event of the death or retirement of a partner: (1) The sum of his capital account and of his personal account (including all credits which would be due him . . . were he an active member up to the end of the month of his death or retirement) shall be paid in cash, without interest, in four semiannual installments. . . (2) Each partner conveys to the surviving or remaining partners all his interest in the goodwill and the partnership name and a majority of the surviving or remaining partners, if they so elect, may continue to use the partnership name.

A suggested clause might provide the following:

The beneficiary of a deceased eligible but unretired partner shall be paid one-half his then salary for a normal week during a period of four years after death; the period for a deceased partner who was ineligible for retirement shall be fixed by majority vote.

Typical of many agreements are the following clauses:

Upon the death of any partner, the firm shall not be dissolved thereby but shall continue on the same basis of profit sharing agreed to for the current year until the close of the then current fiscal year.

Upon the death, retirement, or withdrawal of any of the partners during the term of the partnership the interest of the deceased, retiring or withdrawing partner in the firm assets and business shall be and become vested in and transferred to the surviving or continuing partners in proportion of their participations in the stated capital and distributable profits . . .

The legal representatives of the deceased partner shall be deemed to have assigned, transferred and set over to the continuing partners all of the deceased partner's right, title and interest in and to the assets of the partnership, without any further act on the part of said legal representatives and said legal representatives of the deceased partner shall, upon request, execute, acknowledge and deliver such instruments and perform such acts as the continuing partners may require in order more effectively to vest in them all of the deceased partner's right, title, and interest in and to the said assets.

The following is a condensation of certain interesting requirements of a comprehensive agreement:

1. The estate of a deceased partner is to receive for five years a stated percentage of the net profit of the firm. These percentages, however, are lower than the percentages effective when the partner was alive. The reduced percentage is justified on the ground that estates do not share losses.

2. A bank trustee is appointed to determine (a) that the agreement is faithfully performed insofar as an estate is involved and (b) that the interest of a deceased partner's estate is not impaired. The bank is given the right to move for a dissolution of the firm to protect the interest of an estate or estates. In the event of dissolution, balances due estates are given a priority over payments of capital to surviving partners.

Agreements generally make it a point to exclude estates and widows from any voice in management. In the above case a similar provision exists but the bank is injected as soon as a death occurs to receive copies of monthly balance sheets and income statements so as to be able to observe the financial soundness of the firm and to act to prevent loss to the estate.

Protection of an estate is accomplished by other means in other agreements. One agreement provides that the partners are jointly and severally liable for the indebtedness to an estate.

In another instance provision is made as follows for the eventuality of an inadequacy of a firm's income to make fixed goodwill payments to an estate, possibly due to a dissolution of the firm. Payment of goodwill is required to be made from the gross income of the firm or, interestingly, from fees:

> For any public accounting work engaged in by the surviving or remaining partners, or any of them, including sums received from and employment by any corporation, partnership, or individual engaged in the public accounting business—provided that no surviving or remaining partner shall be liable hereunder for any part of the collections made by any other party to this agreement who does not remain in partnership with him.

Another plan provides that fixed amounts are payable, for five years after death, from net profit if earned. Net profits of the partnership for the purpose of this paragraph are to be computed without deduction of partners' salaries as an expense and the payments to the deceased partner's estate are deemed an expense payable prior to any compensation to partners by way of salary, profit share, or otherwise.

One unusually farsighted provision covers the simultaneous death of two or more partners, or a mass retirement in this manner:

> In the event that all the senior partners with the exception of one shall simultaneously die, become incapacitated, or decide to retire, payments to them or their estates shall be subordinated to a fixed salary allowance to the sole surviving partner.

RETIREMENT FOR AGE

A retirement compensation plan is one of the long-range provisions in a partnership agreement. Young accountants may be inclined to ignore it because the prospect is distant. This may not be an entirely impractical view except for certain psychological benefits that might otherwise be obtained. However, on the grounds that an agreement should be reached when the will to agree is greatest and the disturbing effect of the event not imminent, this provision should perhaps be considered by young men. It could have a perpetuating effect on a partnership and increase the incentive for the development of a firm that will be able to pension its partners. Social-security benefits, where or when applicable to partners, may never be a substitute for a partners' retirement plan, since at best they will probably merely supplement it.

The need for a plan. A retirement plan is of advantage to the firm as well as to the partner who desires to retire. Should there be no such arrangement, a partner who is not financially independent might resist retirement for as long as possible, even beyond a proper limit, to the detriment of the firm. Moreover, a partner whose capacity for accomplishment has been materially reduced by age or disability should make place for a more vigorous partner.

On the other hand, it might be harsh to turn out a partner who has devoted many years of his life to helping build up and maintain a firm's practice, with only his capital-account balance to carry on. Capital-account balances often are relatively small sums. The consequences of such action might well be that the retired partner would have to supplement his independent income by engaging in a competitive practice.

The retirement benefits contemplated herein do not include any element of goodwill, but deal with consideration for years of service to the firm and advisory or other services to be rendered after retirement. If it is desired to give recognition to goodwill in lieu of retirement benefits, a clear-cut distinction should be made. The grounds for each type of benefit must be soundly established and the tax aspects determined as conclusively as possible. An unfavorable change in the income-tax status may materially reduce the benefits to the beneficiary or increase the cost to the firm.

For the very reason that it is a long-range plan, requiring some visualization of the future both as to general economic conditions and as to what the firm's position may be when the retirements become operative, this subject requires careful consideration. In those instances where all the partners are of about the same age a dilemma might well develop in the event of mass retirements or other incidents. The simple solution, however, and one that is practical for other reasons, is to bring "new blood" into a firm at reasonable intervals so as to permit older partners to reduce their activity and eventually retire.

Where a retiring partner has earned unusually large special fees for the firm, and it does not appear likely that the remaining partners will be able to continue such earnings, it may be necessary to adjust the retirement allowance so as to avoid undue hardship on the firm. This would not be an injustice if that partner had been compensated adequately for his unusual contributions to the firm.

The time for retirement. The provision in the agreement setting a specific age for compulsory retirement should serve to avoid unpleasant controversy over the retirement of a partner whose effectiveness is diminishing to the possible detriment of the firm. The most common age is sixty-five, although examples of compulsory retirement both below and above this age can be found. In the case of national firms in particular, provisions for gradual retirement often beginning at age sixty are rather frequent. Retirement may be mandatory at a stated age, or optional with the retiring partner, or at the will of a majority of the partners.

Some large firms effect retirement on a two-step basis: First the partners become advisory partners and are considered to be available for consultation when needed. This, in effect, is nothing more than their continuance as part-time partners. No reference is necessarily made as to the time that must be expended in the firm's behalf. It is sufficient that they be available for consultation on problems of clients they had supervised in the past or on matters in which they are specialists. The second and final step is total retirement.

Smaller firms may find this procedure useful inasmuch as it will permit a gradual transition of a partner, in stages, from active to partly active to inactive. An arrangement of this nature should be helpful to the firm in the retention of clients supervised by the retiring partner. Even an inactive partner may desire some mild form of activity, unless he is physically unable to render any service. Provision for post-retirement services need not be made in the agreement but can be dealt with as an administrative matter.

The use of a limited partnership has developed in instances where it was desired to continue a partly or fully retired partner in the firm either for advisory services, for the use of his name, or for profit sharing in accordance with the retirement plan. These arrangements are not necessarily of the legal limited-partnership type where the public is informed by advertising that certain partners have only limited liabilities, which arrangements some accountants hold to be unprofessional. Where the limitation is from within, and the active partners agree to hold the limited partners free from loss, there seems to be no ground for objection.

The problems involved. The major problems of retirement provisions are the following:

1. Amount of the annual payments
2. Period of years in which payments will be made
3. When retirement becomes effective

Firms operating with oral agreements generally have no benefit provisions for retirement for age and disability. That does not necessarily mean that such payments will not be made. What may be intended is that the problem will be dealt with when it arises, according to the means of the firm and the consciences of the partners. Even firms with written agreements often do not provide for retirement benefits for age or disability; probably these also intend to deal with the problem when it arises.

In addition to the retirement compensation, the partner obviously is entitled to receive payment of his capital, loans to the firm, if any, and his participation in uncollected fees and work in progress if such are not included in the capital account.

Amount of retirement provision. Partnership agreement provisions for retirement benefits payable to partners retiring as a result of age are characterized by their diversity. In one local firm no provision for retirement income payments is included in the agreement on the grounds that providing for retirement income is a personal responsibility of a professional man and should not involve the partnership of which he is a partner. This appears to represent a definitely minority position, however, some sort of provision for retirement income payments being typical. In general, most firms indicate that a partner retiring as a result of age will receive a substantially reduced participation in firm earnings for a specified period of years or for life. In most cases, the amount payable each year is a function of the earnings of the partnership for that year. As a result, the receipt of retirement benefits and the amount thereof are contingent on the continued profitability of the firm. However, one national firm does provide minimum and maximum amounts which may be received, thus reducing the element of uncertainty.

The amount of reduction in participation varies between firms. One national firm provides that the retiring partner will receive one-fifth of his retirement date percentage of income. A local firm's agreement provides that the retired partner will receive one-half of his regular share of income for five years and then one-third for life, the amounts being determined by the income of the year of payment. In this firm an additional amount is payable to the retired partner for any new clients which he obtains for the partnership.

The retirement-allowance provisions of two agreements are here described in the belief that the details submitted may adequately disclose the major factors that must be contemplated in a retirement plan. Accountants should be able to use these data in the formulation or revision of their own plans, making such adaptations and innovations as they may require.

Illustrative plan I. This is applicable to partners of a large accounting firm reaching the age of sixty-five. It provides substantially the following benefits:

Apart from the repayment of his capital and other credits, the retiring partner is paid six annual retirement benefits. These payments start at the end of one year after the retirement (not necessarily the firm's fiscal year-end date) and are made annually. Other payment arrangements are possible if approved by the stated partners. The total allowance is determined as follows, and is payable out of distributable profits:

1. An amount determined by a decision of the majority in interest of the administrative partners, but in no event less than the smaller of the following:
   a. An amount equal to three times the annual average of the total salary and profit share earned by the retiring partner within the ten years next preceding the year of retirement, or
   b. An amount equal to the sum of the total salary and profit share which he would have earned within the succeeding three years, including the year of retirement as the first (and with his ratio of participation in profits unaltered). In the calculation of profits, salaries paid to new partners and interest on their capital are treated as expenses.

The effect of clause 1b is to provide a margin of safety for the firm if earnings decline in the years following the retirement. The firm retains the right, by decision of a majority of the administrative partners within one year from the date of retirement, to fix the retirement allowance at an amount not below that computed under clause 1a and to pay it in full immediately. This decision is binding on the retiring and surviving partners. It is further provided that, if annual installments are paid, the first three are to be of an amount no less than equivalent to 50 per cent of the annual salary of the retired partner as of the date of retirement, or no less than a specified amount.

The mechanics of the payments involve the calculation first of a tentative amount, as soon as practicable after the retirement, on the basis of prior earnings, or a larger amount if fixed by the partners. However, should the safety clause 1b become operative, then it is provided that future payments be reduced by the excess paid unless otherwise decided by the administrative partners. In no event are payments made prior to the redetermination recoverable from the partner out of payments still due.

Illustrative plan II. Under this plan a partner may retire after either (a) twenty-five years of service as a partner; or (b) he has reached the age of sixty-five, whichever occurs earlier. The retirement allowance is paid for life, out of firm profits, in accordance with a "years-of-service" scale which starts at 15 per cent for twenty-five years of service and graduates upward at $1\frac{1}{2}$ per cent annually until a maximum of 30 per cent is reached for thirty-five or more years of service. The percentage is applied against the lower of two amounts, to determine the annual benefit. These amounts are the following:

1. The annual income, profit share plus salary, to which he would have been entitled had he not retired.

2. An amount of income equal to his average annual earnings, profit share plus salary, during either the five-year period, or two-year period immediately preceding the year in which the retirement becomes effective, whichever is lower.

The agreement provides further that a partner desiring to retire may nevertheless be required to serve on a half-time basis for a period of from three to six years, dependent on the will of the remaining partners. The intent is to cushion the effect of the withdrawal of an important partner. In such event the partner would be paid one-half or other proportion, dependent on time actually devoted to the firm, of his active scale of salary and profit share. Such time is included in determining the applicable "years-served" percentage.

Protection of retirement allowances is provided for by a provision that the active partners agree not to dissolve, divide, sell, or in any other way dispose of the practice without the approval of the retired partners. If this rule is violated, the obligations become personal liabilities to the active partners. A retired partner is encouraged to obtain business for the firm by the allowance of an annual share of $12\frac{1}{2}$ per cent of fees therefrom. However, a distinction is made between fully and partially retired partners, the former getting the allowance on all new business, the latter only on clients not stemming from prior clients of the firm. A noncompetition clause exists which calls for a cancellation of the retirement benefits in the event of violation.

Other illustrative plans. Another simple method of compensation contemplates the payment to a retired partner over a period of five years of an annual amount equivalent to 15 per cent of his annual billings. Detail is lacking as to how the annual billings are determined in this particular instance, but it is likely that it represents either the partner's billings in the year preceding that of retirement or the average of the two or three preceding years.

The following has been offered as a suggested retirement plan:

> A partner who has reached the age of sixty and has had at least ten years of service is eligible for retirement. If he retires (but need not), he is entitled to receive one-half his current salary for a normal week during a period of four years after retirement.

Other points that may be covered in retirement plans are the following:

1. The interest of the retired partner may be divided among the continuing partners in proportion to their capital or profit-share interest. To carry out his withdrawal properly, the retiring partner agrees to do whatever is necessary to vest effectually in the remaining partners all of his right, title, and interest in the partnership.

2. There are instances where the retiring partners or estates of deceased partners are given the right to make an examination of the firm's books until their retirement payments (or death benefits) are completed. In one instance retired partners are entitled to receive copies of the firm's annual statements.

3. Retirement provisions involving fixed amount payments should be reviewed at least every five years to insure that the plan is representative of the firm's position and ability to pay. A plan which uses a percentage of profits as a basis or a "ceiling" will avoid the difficulties of the fixed payment plan. In any event, changes in benefits should not be made except when a drastic change, and one of apparently indefinite duration, has occurred in a firm's position.

Notice of intention to retire. Many agreements do not include a specific provision for the period of notice of intention to retire (or withdraw) or for the method of communicating such notice. This is a surprising situation because it is of little consequence as a drafting problem yet a great advantage in the preparation for the event.

Notice periods may range from thirty days to one year, with two months being common. Notice of intention to retire is required by registered mail, as a rule, addressed to one of the following: (a) all of the partners, (b) administrative partner or partners, (c) the firm. The office, or main office address, is specified as the location to which the notice is to be mailed. Some agreements contain specific dollar penalty provisions for failure to give the required notice, such penalty, however, being subject to modification by the other partners. This is an indication of the seriousness attached to the requirement of notice.

Limitations on retirements. Where there are a number of partners of similar age in a firm it is conceivable that a mass retirement could occur. To avoid such an incident one agreement provides that, except for reasons of disability, only one retirement may take place in a two-year period.

VOLUNTARY WITHDRAWAL

Reasons for withdrawal. The term withdrawal applies to any of a number of reasons for resignation from membership in the firm. Common grounds for a voluntary separation are the following:

1. Disagreement or other discontent with partners
2. Desire to practice alone
3. Desire to join another accounting firm
4. Desire to go into private accounting work
5. Desire to enter another field or the teaching profession
6. Other personal motivations, such as moving to another section of the country

The first three causes may involve an unpleasant situation whereas the last three situations need not necessarily engender any ill will. In any event, a withdrawal for any reason creates a serious problem for the firm, and may possibly require a physical dissolution, change in firm name, division of clientele and staff, or other difficult arrangements. Hence a withdrawal should not be an impetuous action and the provisions relating thereto are, usually and deservedly, not as liberal as for retirement for age or in the event of death.

Where the withdrawal, by agreement or by law, will bring about a dissolution of the firm, the references thereto may be confined to notice and the mechanics of the dissolution, but where there shall not be a dissolution, specific terms for the withdrawal are necessary.

Provision to negotiate. All oral agreements, actually or by implication, intend that when a partner desires to withdraw from the firm, he will negotiate the terms of his withdrawal. Some written agreements, perhaps in the realization of the difficulty of advance understanding on this issue, merely provide for negotiation without a definite formula or with a reference to the pattern to be followed. The following clause illustrates the latter viewpoint:

> Should any partner wish to voluntarily withdraw from the firm to retire or to engage in any other activity not in conflict with the business of the firm, such partner may negotiate a settlement with the continuing partners relative to any intangible values in excess of balances in capital and drawing accounts, determined in accordance with the provisions of paragraph — (pertains to participation in profits after death.)

In the following summary of a partnership agreement appears this significant illustration of the distinction between retirement and withdrawal terms:

> If he retires, he gets both his interest in tangible and intangible capital; if he withdraws he receives only his interest in the tangible capital.

Type of organization. The provisions covering withdrawal of a partner vary widely but nevertheless they generally reflect the nature of the association itself. For example, where a partnership in effect has been little more than an association of two individual practitioners who operated independently to a large extent, the resignation is carried out relatively easily because there is not much to untangle. In such a case there is a dissolution of the firm.

However, where partnerships have developed in size and form over a period of years, and some partners have come in from the ranks of the staff, and the method of operation has been on a "firm" basis rather than on the "individual partner" basis, a resignation is not a simple matter and it may involve some sacrifices by the withdrawing partner. In such cases a partnership dissolution does not necessarily accompany a withdrawal.

Factors to be considered. Most partnership agreements, oral and written, make provision for conditions such as these in providing for withdrawal: Notice of intention is required for periods suitable in the individual case and differing in extent from one to six months, two months being common. (See "Notice of intention to retire," page 454.) In such instances the effective date is not necessarily the fiscal-year-end date as is sometimes the case in other forms of withdrawal. Reference also is made to whether or not such action requires a dissolution, in which event all of the dissolution provisions (if any) become effective. The right to use of the established firm name, or retention of the name of the withdrawing partner, are other conditions which are dealt with.

Goodwill and the withdrawal of clients. Important in all resignations is the question of withdrawal of clients and competition with the continuing partners. Some partnership agreements are drastic in this respect, and include provisions to the effect that upon withdrawal a partner agrees not to solicit, directly or indirectly, or even handle clients of the firm. Moreover, he may even be barred from using the firm name and exploiting his former association. One large firm agreement contains a stated penalty for the violation of the noncompetition clause.

Goodwill payments are more likely to be found in local than in national firms. Some agreements provide that a resigning partner is not entitled to any consideration for goodwill, where it may be otherwise considered; nor may he "withdraw" the clients contributed or supervised by him nor receive any profit-share distribution beyond the date of his inactivity, though such privilege is available under other circumstances.

An illustration of a provision calling for a division of clients is the following:

> In the event that the withdrawing partner shall elect to take a share of the business of the partnership in lieu of cash as herein provided, the partners shall divide the business of the partnership, in so far as it is possible, so that the withdrawing partner shall retain the clients with whom, and with whose work he is most familiar . . . shall continue to be served by him.

Where a withdrawing partner is entitled to a share in the firm's goodwill there is usually a companion noncompetition clause. This view is exemplified in the following clause:

> It is agreed, however, that any partner who voluntarily withdraws from the partnership may elect not to accept payment for his interest in the goodwill of the partnership, in which event the prohibitions against engaging in public accounting work as set out in paragraph — shall not be effective.

But there also are noncompetition clauses in contracts where the existence of goodwill values is disavowed.

On the other hand, some agreements do provide, and properly so, for the withdrawal of specified clients and even the acceptance of engagements from clients of the former partnership if offered. The following is an illustration of a compromise provision:

> Should the withdrawing partner intend to engage in the practice of public accounting immediately upon withdrawal, he shall not be entitled to take any partnership business with him, but shall not be prevented from accepting an engagement from a client of the former partnership.

The severity or liberality of the withdrawal conditions, as previously indicated, depends largely on the nature of the association, its origin, and its development. No general rule therefore can be evolved that will be universally acceptable. But this much is definite: the withdrawal of a partner can most equitably be negotiated when the imminence of the matter and the accompanying emotional reactions are not aggravating conditions.

Some agreements contain a reference to withdrawal by junior partners. In such cases the provisions are slightly more stringent as to competition, since most such partners are selected from the staff. The junior partner is usually entitled to his accumulated capital, profit share to date of withdrawal, and any similar credits due him.

Where a partner withdraws to enter a noncompetitive field he may expect better consideration than otherwise. This may not represent a considerable advantage but it permits negotiation on a friendly basis, where there is no withdrawal provision or where it is inadequate.

Illustrations of provisions. Several additional illustrations of withdrawal provisions are submitted herewith:

> After a voluntary dissolution of said partnership, if the withdrawing partner elects to take cash for his interest in said partnership, as herein provided, he agrees not to perform any accounting service for any client served by the partnership within a period of twelve months immediately preceding the date of dissolution for a period of two years immediately following the date of dissolution of said partnership. (The partnership interest in this case includes goodwill).

> A partner may withdraw from the partnership at the end of any month by giving not less than sixty days prior written notice thereof to the other partners. The withdrawal of a partner shall have no effect upon the continuance of the partnership business. . .

> Voluntary retirement may take place by mutual consent, or by the giving of two months' notice in writing to the others by the one wishing to retire. In the event of voluntary retirement of any partner, the purchase of goodwill must necessarily be upon such terms as shall be mutually agreed upon. It is, however, agreed that in the event of voluntary retirement or dissolution by expiration of the partnership, and lacking any other agreement, there shall be made such a division of the business and goodwill as shall appear equitable, taking into consideration the source of the business, namely, the business of a part-

ner prior to his entry into the partnership, or business secured through such former clients, or a partner's personal connections. Such a division having been made, each partner shall refrain from soliciting in any way, directly or indirectly, the business allocated to the others.

In the event that one partner gives notice to the other partners of his desire to retire from the partnership or to dissolve the same . . . the partnership shall be dissolved and the business of the partnership shall be terminated in the manner provided for termination of the partnership by death or "permanent incapacity" . . . *except* that after the partnership has been in existence for a period of one year, the withdrawing partner may elect to take in lieu of the cash payment, as provided in paragraph — a share of the business of said partnership to be determined as follows:

1. The partners shall determine the total gross business done by the firm, including that done by an accountant, or accountants, employed by the partnership for a period of twelve months immediately preceding the date of termination, excluding any amounts billed as "expense" as distinguished from "service." Provided, however, that the last fiscal year of the partnership shall be used, if date of termination is not more than three months after the close of said fiscal year.

2. The profits of the partnership shall next be determined for said twelve-month period to which shall be added the total compensation paid or payable to any full-time accountant or accountants employed by the partnership, (either as salary, wages, or bonus) during said period. This total shall be designated for the purpose of this agreement as "the total net accounting fees" of the partnership.

3. The share of the retiring partner, (including his "base salary" and percentage paid, or payable) in "the total net accounting fees" shall next be computed.

4. The share of the business which the retiring partner may take in lieu of cash, shall be equal to the proportion of the total gross business of the firm for said twelve-month period represented by the ratio which his share of the total net accounting fees bears to the total net accounting fees for said period. In determining said share, the total billing to each client chosen for services during the preceding fiscal year, or the twelve months preceding the date of termination, whichever period is used to determine total gross business, shall be the measure of said business. The physical assets of the partnership, (furniture, fixtures, office equipment, books, supplies, and so forth) together with any lease of premises, shall belong to the remaining partners and shall not enter into the share of the business to be taken by the retiring partner.

5. In the event that the withdrawing partner shall elect to take a share of the business of the partnership in lieu of cash as herein provided, the partners shall divide the business of the partnership, in so far as it is possible, so that the withdrawing partner shall retain the clients with whom, and with whose problems he is most familiar, and that the clients served by any accountant, hired by the partnership, shall continue to be served by him.

The final aspect of a withdrawal is the payment of the partner's capital, his share of undistributed profits, and all other liabilities to him. In some instances it is specified that a partner may withdraw items contributed by him such as furniture, files, books, and other property.

Specific illustrations of provisions dealing with withdrawals, payment of capital, and other pertinent subjects are included below under other captions.

INCAPACITY AND SICK LEAVE

In one national firm each case of sickness is handled on the merits of the specific case. On the other hand, there would be some merit in more formal coverage of this point, including a definition of partial or complete disability and the stipulation of a maximum period of absence at the end of which a change in the partner's financial relationship with the firm occurs. One local firm provides in its agreement that after three months' absence the partner's participation in income is reduced 50 per cent and one year's absence shall constitute full voluntary withdrawal.

Sickness and disability may be progressive developments and there is no clear-cut line of demarcation. For that reason the understandings usually contain arbitrary criteria. Sickness in itself is not a serious problem when of short duration. Only when it becomes extensive or indefinite, and indicative of a permanent disability, does a difficult question develop.

Incapacity. Provisions in the partnership agreement reflect, for obvious reasons, the personal relationships of the partners. Where two brothers are involved, or a father and son, or even two friends with great attachment for each other, sickness or disability payments may have no limitation other than ability to pay. However, in the average business association, provisions such as those which follow are the rule.

The involuntary retirement of a partner may take place by the continued illness or disability of a partner preventing his regular attention to business for a period of twelve consecutive months in the case of a junior partner, and twenty-four consecutive months in the case of the managing partner—at the end of which time the other partners are hereby empowered to retire him from the firm, and his goodwill, if the retiring partner consents thereto and so desires, shall become subject to purchase under the conditions enumerated below. The remaining partners severally and collectively obligate themselves to purchase the goodwill in such case if the retiring partner is willing to sell. If the retiring partner is unwilling to sell his goodwill the remaining partners will give consideration to accommodation management of business for his connections (clients). After the expiration of the first six consecutive months of disability in the case of a junior partner the "first division of net income" to which he is entitled . . . shall be reduced by 50 per cent for the remainder of all or any part of the succeeding six months' period of disability; after the expiration of the first twelve consecutive months of disability in the case of the managing partner the "first division of net income" to which he is entitled . . . shall be reduced by 50 per cent for the remainder of all or any part of the succeeding twelve months' period of disability. *This agreement provides elsewhere for the dissolution of the firm due to such involuntary retirement and the liquidation of the partners' interests.*

Should a partner become incapacitated, his interest in the business may be acquired by the remaining senior partners and paid for as indicated under the withdrawal section. Incapacity is deemed to mean the inability of a partner to attend to the partnership business for a period of at least one year.

For purpose of this agreement "permanent incapacity" shall be defined either as: (a) loss of certified public accountant's certificate for a period of longer than one year by action of the State Board of Accounting of (State), or any court of competent jurisdiction or (b) inability to actively participate in the business of the partnership on account of the physical or mental condition of said partner for a period longer than forty-two consecutive weeks, exclusive of the provisions made herein for vacations and sick leave.

Should sickness or accident temporarily incapacitate any partner, his drawing account allowance shall continue in full for a period of six months commencing with the month following that in which such sickness or accident occurred. For the next succeeding six months the drawing account allowance shall be reduced to 50 per cent, and for the next succeeding twelve months it shall be reduced to 25 per cent. Any partner so affected shall continue to participate to the full extent in any net income or loss distribution, as hereinbefore defined, for the period during which drawing accounts continue, or in other words, for two full years commencing with the month following that in which sickness or accident occurred.

In the event that any partner becomes incapacitated, the active partners shall determine upon a fair and reasonable course for the mutual protection of the firm and the incapacitated partner; the unanimous conclusion of the active partners, communicated in writing, shall be accepted as binding on all parties, and their personal representatives.

One firm sums up its special arrangement as follows:

Incapacity means any total disability which prevents a partner from practicing or engaging in the profession during a continuous six-month period upon the expiration of which the remaining partners may claim incapacity and if such incapacity does not cease or the incapacitated partner does not return and resume practice within thirty days, incapacity shall be deemed complete and settlement will be made with the partner in the same way as if he had died.

The provision as to incapacity of another agreement gives the following details:

Any goodwill partner shall be entitled to withdraw from the partnership on the ground of incapacity, which is defined to include only the following causes, to wit: insanity, either judicially determined or found by the managing board of partners to exist, a condition of health that shall preclude active participation in all business affairs, or after five years' active participation in the affairs of the partnership as a goodwill partner, including the business heretofore conducted by —————, such condition of health as shall reasonably require an abandonment of active practice as necessary to prolong life. The incapacity of any goodwill partner having been brought to the attention of the managing board, the interest of such goodwill partner in the capital, profits, and goodwill of the partnership shall be ascertained upon request made by the interested party or his guardian, which interest shall be determined and made payable in the same amounts and in the same manner as hereinbefore provided for in the event of the death of a goodwill partner. The managing board shall be entitled, in the first instance, to determine whether the condition of health of such goodwill partner be such as to warrant or require his retirement on the ground of incapacity but a certificate of a reputable physician shall be a prima-facie evidence of the condition of health of the partner desiring to retire.

Options to rejoin the firm. Options to rejoin the firm are not common, presumably because this is a difficult situation, fraught with possible unpleasantness, and one that might have too many "ifs" for advance understanding.

One agreement, in summary, provides merely the following, apparently leaving some aspects to the consideration of the remaining partners when the issue must be met:

> The senior partner may elect to rejoin the firm within two years after retirement for incapacity. If the option is not exercised within the two-year period he must dispose of his interest in the firm. A junior partner has one year in which to act.

The physical or mental ability of a partner to rejoin should not be settled on a unilateral basis, as there must be an accord between both sides.

Sick leave. Sick leave, apart from disability, is referred to in some agreements. In one instance a six-week vacation period is fixed, together with a four-week sick-leave period, with pay. After a total absence of ten weeks from active practice the subject partner goes off the payroll but receives his full share of the profits for the calendar year. If the illness continues for a year, incapacity is deemed to have developed. This is the type of provision that may be left for disposition as the situation arises.

EXPULSION OF A PARTNER

Provisions for the forced retirement of a partner for cause are found in the agreements of some firms. In a firm having two partners a dissolution is readily possible if the conduct of one partner has become intolerable to the other. The same procedure can be followed in a larger firm but the complaining partners may sometimes organize a new firm and thereby continue their association. However, in a very large firm dissolution is not a matter that is lightly contemplated; therefore in such cases there are provisions for the forced retirement of partners, for cause, generally upon the unanimous action of the administrative partners or as otherwise agreed.

In cases where a firm consists of one senior partner and the other partners are junior partners it is usually found that the senior partner reserves the right to remove a junior partner from the firm for cause. The penalty, apart from any stigma resulting from the forced dissociation, and the necessity to seek a new association, is usually the loss of benefits payable to a partner retiring voluntarily. Such benefits may be a share of goodwill, compensation for noncompetition agreement, or an actual pension allowance. Capital and undistributed profit shares are, however, payable in full.

Cause is defined to include various actions, and the following are specified in the data reviewed: Encumbrance or assignment of partnership interest for debt, bankruptcy, loss of CPA certificate, wilful misconduct, bad faith, misconduct resulting in loss of money or prestige to the firm, moral turpitude, continued inattention to business (except in case of illness), or merely the best interests of the firm.

The following excerpts from agreements indicate how the matter is dealt with in some instances:

In the event that any partner's association or affiliation with this firm shall become detrimental or harmful to its best interest, and this fact shall be determined unanimously by the other partners after fair consideration, a partner may be asked to withdraw. In this case, however, no limitations are imposed by this agreement as to competitive practice.

The senior partner shall have the right to require the withdrawal and resignation from the partnership of any junior partner by reason of conduct deemed by the senior partner to be injurious or detrimental to the partnership. In the event that such right be exercised, or in the event of the voluntary withdrawal or resignation of a junior partner . . . there shall be paid to the withdrawing partner in full for all of his right, title, and interest in and to the partnership, a sum equivalent to the amount payable to him as salary for a period of . . . months together with the amount of his credit balance upon the books of account of the partnership. There shall also be paid to him, within ————— days subsequent to the date of his withdrawal or resignation, a sum equivalent to his share of the net profits of the partnership accrued to the close of the second month (following the month) during which such withdrawal or resignation shall occur.

Upon the withdrawal of any junior partner the partnership shall be continued by the remaining partners and the share of the withdrawing partner, after the payments above set forth have been made to him, shall be divided among the remaining partners in proportion to their respective interests in the net profits of the partnership.

Such retiring or withdrawing partner shall, upon request, make, execute or deliver such instruments and perform such acts as the continuing partners may require in order more effectually to vest in them all of his right, title, and interest in the partnership.

Such retiring partner shall not at any time solicit or perform the work of any clients of the partnership and shall not at any time disclose to any person, firm or corporation the name of any client or clients of the partnership, or any of its transactions, and such retiring partner shall not at any time use the firm name, nor, either in conjunction with his own name or otherwise, use the words "formerly" or "late of" or any other combination of words containing the firm name.

If any partner, not voluntarily withdrawing, shall be deprived of his interest by the vote of the other partners under the provisions of the agreement, he shall accept in full payment and satisfaction of his interest one-fifth of the amount his estate would have received (for goodwill) in the case of his death, plus his proportionate share of the undistributed net earnings, if any, which have accumulated to the date of his withdrawal and which stand to his credit on the books.

DISSOLUTION OF A PARTNERSHIP

In some agreements it is provided that a dissolution is mandatory in the event of any of the following occurrences:

1. Death of a partner

2. Withdrawal by a partner
3. Bankruptcy of a partner
4. Expiration of the contract term, without a renewal
5. General agreement
6. Decision of the sole senior partner or of the senior partners

Other agreements, generally of larger firms, specifically provide for dissolution only upon agreement of a majority of all or certain stipulated partners. Other events call for only a change in the membership but not for dissolution. Both of the foregoing positions may be warranted and necessary in individual cases.

To illustrate: if one partner of a two-man firm dies or withdraws there is no alternative but to dissolve. However, there are two possibilities: first, that one member may acquire the interest of the other; second, that the assets, tangible and intangible, must be divided. Thus, in one instance there is a legal but not a physical dissolution; in the second, both phases must be dealt with.

A well-established firm consisting of three or more partners may, for very good reasons, resist physical liquidation except by general agreement of the partners. This position is understandable when the difficulties and costs of the division of a large firm are comprehended. So long as a partner may be detached without a breakup of the continuity of a firm this procedure is most desirable.

The subjects requiring consideration in any dissolution are, generally, the following:

1. Tangible Capital Division and Related Problems
   a. Division of net assets among partners
   b. Disposition of equipment and library
   c. Completion of work in progress
   d. Collection of outstanding accounts
   e. Settlements with retired partners and estates to whom there are liabilities
2. Intangible Capital Division and Related Problems
   a. Division of clients and files
   b. Distribution of staff
   c. Disposition of firm name
   d. Continuity of service to clients
   e. Disposition of office lease and other contracts

Upon recognition of the complexity of the problems involved there is little wonder why, in many agreements which make some reference to dissolution, the mechanics are left to be determined when the need has arisen. This is undoubtedly the understanding where oral agreements are in effect. This may, in some cases, work out satisfactorily. But there surely are instances where, because of a strained atmosphere prevailing at the time of the dissolution, the problems are aggravated by the lack of advance agreement, and litigation is required to settle disagreements.

Although it may be questionable whether such mechanics need be written out in advance, when the dissolution is decided upon, the mechanics should be planned carefully and the procedures and agreements reached might well be written up as a supplementary contract.

Nature of the organization. The seriousness of the problem of dissolution has a direct relation to the cohesiveness and position of the partnership. Where a firm is, in reality, a loose association of independent practitioners, each dealing exclusively with his clients, and the firm as such has been largely one in name only, a dissolution should not be too difficult because the disposition of intangible assets should not be troublesome. To the contrary, if a firm has developed a reputation, is well integrated, has taken in partners from the ranks, has obtained clients because of its standing, and there has been a measure of collaboration among the partners, the problems of dissolution are obviously such as to make it complex and costly. It is worthy of reiteration that problems of dissolution should not all be left for a time when the heat of aroused emotions will render the solution extra difficult. The best time to lay down fundamental rules is when the prospect is remote and when the will to reach a reasonable understanding about an unpleasant situation is most favorable.

Tangible capital division. The so-called "tangible" capital division presents no challenge because it is largely a simple accounting problem. Some difficulty may be encountered in the disposition of work in progress, but the other aspects are elementary. However, in the illustrative provisions which appear on page 467 will be found instances of the mechanics in use.

To the extent possible, all work in progress at date of dissolution should be completed by the firm. If this is not possible, each engagement should be completed by the partner to whom the client will be allocated in the dissolution. The value of work completed should be treated as a firm asset for capital determination and charged to the partner to whom distributed. It is conceivable that some matters, because of their contingent nature, cannot be evaluated. These matters can only be left in suspense until completed and an agreement reached as to the allocation of the fees between the firm and the one who will complete them. This too is a business arrangement which accountants are well qualified to determine. The intangibles provide the difficult problems. In this sphere, particularly, advance agreement is desirable.

Division of clientele. How should clients be divided? One answer to the question is that clients should be allocated first according to partners who brought them into the firm; second, to partners supervising them. Where clients originated with one partner and have been supervised for a long period by another, the one engaged in the supervision should, except in unusual circumstances, take over the clients on the ground that he is most likely to retain them.

However, the foregoing suggestion is an oversimplification of the problem. If a client is considered to be an asset of the firm, though intangible, why should it not be valued, added to the firm's capital, and be taken into account in the distribution of capital? This second method is actually specified in a few instances. Should it develop, in this event, that a partner has received, in clients, more than his capital interest, he should reimburse the firm for the excess realized. For this purpose, all clients might be valued, for instance, at one year's average gross fees, based on the last five years or less. Nevertheless, even the second method may be inequitable in so far as it affects clients who were brought into the firm at its initiation or by the partner upon his admission. Such clients should properly be excluded from being treated as firm assets unless the partner received some credit for them. This type of arrangement also is in effect.

In one instance there is an understanding that clients who cannot be allocated because of disagreement are to be sold and the proceeds added to the tangible capital.

After the allocation is provided for, some agreements add a noncompetition clause to insure the definiteness of the arrangement. Nothing, patently, will make a client continue with one partner when he prefers another. Thus, such allocations should be on as realistic a basis as possible and it may even be desirable to cautiously obtain an advance reaction from clients.

The question may be raised as to whether clients should be consulted about the distribution of their accounts prior to any allocation. It should not be answered hastily because of the possible risk that some clients might use this opportunity to make an entirely new arrangement. Obviously, clients should be transferred intelligently and with the prospect of continuation. The matter of consultation, however, should be settled by consideration of the status of the individual clients, the nature and strength of their ties to any individual partner, their satisfaction with the firm as a whole, the ability of the senior in charge to help the transition, and any other considerations relevant in each case.

Files and working papers should follow the client. Assurances may be requested, if expedient, to insure that papers pertaining to prior years will be available in the event of need for reference in a matter involving the firm.

Distribution of staff. To the extent that it is practical and expedient, staff men should be requested to affiliate themselves with those partners to whose clients they can give most continuity of service. The outcome is not predictable for obvious reasons. To avoid undue hardships, some arrangement should be made as soon as a dissolution is decided upon to assure continuity of service to clients and in that connection a friendly agreement should be reached on the desired allocation of staff.

Continuity of service to clients. Nothing should be permitted to interrupt service to clients. The old structure should be dismantled with such intelligence that the occupants are transferred with no undue annoyance or harmful effects. This type of co-operation needs more than a written provision; it requires an understanding on the part of all concerned that it is to their individual welfares and for the good of their profession, that everything necessary to carry on an orderly and equitable dissolution be done in the right spirit.

Disposition of office lease and other contracts. All contractual obligations must be listed, and their liquidation, or assumption by certain partners, should be fixed in the supplementary agreement covering the dissolution. Apart from the lease, there may be tax service subscriptions, insurance, and other minor contracts which must be disposed of. In times of office space shortages and rent controls the office lease may have considerable value. It might be fair to turn it over to the majority of the partners who continue their association.

Disposition of firm name. Only where the firm name has acquired considerable value is there any problem as to its disposition. In the large majority of cases each new segment of a former firm will use a title indicative of its actual members. But there are cases where the firm name is worthy of perpetuation and then questions arise. Who should be entitled to use it? May the name of a noncontinuing partner be retained in the title? These questions are not easily answered.

It appears that the preponderance of custom, where a firm name is to be perpetuated, is that the name be used by any group that constitutes a majority of the former partners. However, it seems that specific agreement is essential to make such use legally effective. Some agreements provide that a noncontinuing partner's name shall not be used, others contain definite conditions for the transfer of the name. Consideration should be given to state laws and professional society rules of ethics regarding the relation between firm names and the names of the constituent members.

In the case of well-established firms, the firm name may be the most important intangible asset. Partners of all firms are concerned to keep it free from blemish and to enhance its standing within the profession and in business circles. So valuable is the firm name that its ownership and use are jealously guarded. In many instances the firm name and goodwill are closely linked.

Agreements usually fix the firm name. Title to the name in the event of death or retirement of a partner, or a dissolution of the firm, is fixed in many agreements. In some, the firm name belongs to one partner (usually a "one-senior-partner" firm), in some it belongs to all partners. There are agreements which prohibit the use of a retired or deceased partner's name whereas others, to the contrary, specifically permit it.

Illustrations of provisions dealing with "one-man" title to a firm name are the following:

> No partner, other than ———, shall use the firm name either alone or in conjunction with his own name or use any other combination of words containing the firm name.

> It is hereby understood and agreed that the firm name "X & Company" is the exclusive property of the managing partner, and that upon dissolution of the partnership by expiration; upon voluntary retirement of any of the partners; . . . upon dissolution by death . . .; or any other change or dissolution, the firm name "X & Company" shall be the exclusive property of . . . "X" and shall be subject to transfer with his goodwill only in the event of his death or in the event of his voluntary sale thereof.

> In case of the dissolution or termination of the partnership "A" shall have

the sole and exclusive right to partnership name and to the use thereof, and "B" shall not either directly or indirectly use the same.

The following provisions pertain to situations arising from the death or retirement of a partner:

Each partner agrees, however, that the firm may continue to use his name in its business after his death without compensation, if the surviving partners shall so elect.

The firm name ———— shall belong to and may be used by the partnership and shall not be sold or disposed of so long as the partnership shall continue in existence. Upon the dissolution of the partnership or the termination thereof as provided in article — hereof, the firm name shall become the property of the then surviving administrative partners and may be disposed of in such manner and upon such terms as a majority in interest of the administrative partners shall determine. In the event of the death, retirement, or withdrawal of any of the partners during the term of the partnership, the deceased, retiring, or withdrawing partner shall have no interest in the firm name and shall have no right to receive any payment therefor.

The continuing partners and their successors, if any, shall have the right to use the name of the retired partner in the style or title of the firm name.

Therefore, mutually understood and agreed that upon the death of any or all of the partners of the first part, the surviving partners will pay to the estate of the deceased partner $———— for the relinquishment of any rights he or his estate may have in the firm name of ————, this payment to be made in five equal instalments, beginning within one year from date of death.

If, at the time of death or retirement of a partner, his name is used in the firm name of the partnership, the partners of the continuing or successor firm shall have the right, but shall not be required, to continue such use.

The managing board may at any time, by unanimous consent of the goodwill partners, change the partnership name, otherwise the name shall not be changed on account of the decease or retirement of any partner whose name appears as part of the firm name. If, however, the partnership shall at any time become insolvent, which shall be held to include not only an excess of liability over assets but also inability to pay or extend partnership obligations, then any partner who shall have retired from the firm shall have the right to require his name to be dropped from the firm name.

Illustration of provisions. Various provisions on dissolution are here submitted:

Upon any dissolution of the partnership, all working papers, correspondence, audit reports, tax returns, and so forth, contributed by the respective partners . . . together with all subsequent working papers, correspondence, audit reports, tax returns, and so forth, added to the partnership plant shall be divided between the parties in such manner that each partner receives all such working papers, correspondence, audit reports, tax returns . . . as relate to the respective clients which heretofore have been or hereafter may be secured directly or indirectly by each such respective party.

The partnership may be terminated by —% in interest of partners giving notice to other partners at least thirty days prior to effective date.

It is, however, agreed that in the event of voluntary retirement or dissolution by expiration of the partnership, and lacking any other agreement, there shall be made such a division of the business and goodwill as shall appear equitable; taking into consideration the source of the business, namely, the business of a partner prior to his entry into the partnership, or business secured through such former clients, or a partner's personal connections. Such a division having been made, each partner shall refrain from soliciting in any way, directly or indirectly, the business allocated to the others.

It is hereby understood and agreed that the accounts of the business as of date (of agreement), and all new business or accounts arising from such accounts and all new business or accounts brought into the business through the efforts of "A" shall be known as "A accounts," and all new business or accounts brought in to the business by "B" shall be known as "B accounts," and upon the discontinuance of the partnership business or in the case of its dissolution by agreement or death of one of the partners, said "A accounts" and working papers and tax files shall be distributed to "A" and such "B accounts" and working papers and tax files shall be distributed to "B."

Upon the termination of the partnership by reason of its expiration or for any other cause, an account shall be taken and rendered of its affairs and business and, after the payment of its obligations, division of such of its assets as are not the exclusive property of the senior partner, as hereinabove provided, shall be made to all of the partners in the proportions herein agreed upon with respect to the division of the net profits. In taking such account, however, the goodwill and firm name shall not be valued as a partnership asset, but shall belong to the senior partner exclusively, except as hereinabove provided in case of the death of the senior partner.

In the event of dissolution of the said firm, either by withdrawal or death of one of the parties, "A" or his heirs, executors, administrators or legal representatives shall be entitled to retain all clients or accounts of said partnership, except those clients or accounts as have heretofore been designated in writing by the said "A" to belong to either "B" or "C"; all net profits up to time of said dissolution shall be shared, and losses if any, up to the time of said dissolution shall be borne between them upon the terms hereinabove set forth, but neither "B" nor "C" shall be entitled to share in any of the present capital investment of said partnership, nor in any goodwill, nor in any furniture, furnishings or equipment of the partnership offices.

That if any disagreement shall arise between the parties, in respect of . . . its dissolution . . . the same shall be decided and determined by arbitrators; and each of the parties shall select one of such arbitrators, and the decision of two of such arbitrators, when made in writing, shall be conclusive upon the parties hereto.

Upon the termination of this agreement either voluntarily by either party, or by the death of either party, the clients whose names now appear on the attached initialed list or whose names may later be added thereto . . . shall be regarded as clients of Richard Roe, while all other clients shall be regarded as clients of John Smith and both parties to this agreement hereby agree to refrain for a period of three years from the rendering of any accounting service to the client of the other except as hereinafter provided.

Upon dissolution of the firm (excepting dissolution by the death of any partner) the first parties and the second party shall each withdraw the furniture and equipment contributed by them, at the appraised value as hereinabove provided, less depreciation of 20 per cent per annum, the said valuation to be charged to their respective capital accounts. Thereafter distribution in liquidation shall be made as the interests of the parties may appear.

Upon dissolution of the firm an accounting shall be prepared showing work in progress. The fees to be received from such work after the dissolution shall be divided among the parties on a basis to be agreed upon at dissolution, the intent being that the proportion of interest in the partnership be maintained in such division.

Avoidance of dissolution. Though state laws may hold that the withdrawal of a partner automatically dissolves the firm, it does not follow that a liquidation is always necessary. In this respect, particularly, the advice of counsel will be helpful.

Some firms, particularly large ones, provide specifically that the withdrawal of a partner does not require a dissolution of the firm. This position is wise because there is no reason why the practice cannot be continued without interruption despite the withdrawal of a partner. Some arrangements will obviously be necessary to fill the vacuum but these matters can be dealt with without business interruption. A legal dissolution could be a costly, time-consuming, and annoying matter and, if practical, it should be avoided.

It is with these thoughts in mind that some partnership agreements contain provisions such as the following:

The death, retirement or withdrawal of any partner shall not dissolve the partnership between the other partners.

In case of retirement by any partner, said partner agrees that he shall not insist upon a complete liquidation but shall withdraw upon receiving his share of capital.

If any of the partners shall die during the existence of the partnership neither the partnership nor the interest therein of the deceased partner shall terminate but shall continue subject to the terms and conditions hereinafter set forth . . .

There are cases, nevertheless, where a formal dissolution is unavoidable, as in the case of a withdrawal from a two-man firm or where the partners decide to dissolve the partnership. The termination of a partnership as of the date of a withdrawal of a member may cause a pyramiding of the income of more than one partnership taxable year into one taxable year of the retiring or deceased partners. In periods of high tax rates this occurrence could be very costly. As a practical matter, the possible tax consequences alone make it important to give this subject adequate consideration in advance.

NONCOMPETITION CLAUSE

A restriction against competition by a retiring or withdrawing partner is a prevalent practice. The periods involved vary and so do area limitations.

An illustration of one such provision is the following:

> The withdrawn partner shall not engage directly or indirectly in the practice of accounting in or within five miles of the cities of —————— and —————————, for a period of five years from the date of his withdrawal, and if, at the time of his withdrawal, his name is used in the firm name of the partnership, the partners of the continuing or successor firm shall have the right (but shall not be required) to continue such use during said five-year period.

Other noncompetition provisions that prevail are the following:

1. Not to contact, directly or indirectly, for the purpose of securing business, any of the known clients of the firm
2. Not to accept, without the firm's written consent, any business from any of the firm's clients
3. Not to disclose any information as to the firm's clients or the affairs of said clients
4. Not to refer to himself for business purposes as "formerly of" or "lately of" the firm

One firm imposes a penalty on a partner who violates a noncompetition clause, wilfully or unintentionally (at request of client), of an amount equal to 125 per cent of one year's gross fee. Where a penalty is not fixed by mutual agreement, which is the common situation, the damages, if any, must be settled by legal action or arbitration.

Where a partner retires without receiving any retirement benefits but nevertheless is subjected to a restrictive clause, some agreements provide that he is to receive either a payment for goodwill interest or for the noncompetition agreement.

A noncompetition clause must not be too severe or it will run the risk of being invalid because it is against public policy. This violation was found to exist in an agreement and it resulted in a much publicized law suit.[4] This case involved the withdrawal of a partner from a firm with numerous offices situated over a wide area of the country. The remaining partners sought to hold him to a covenant not to practice accountancy within a hundred miles of any office of the firm. The withdrawn partner was subsequently unable to make any new association that would not violate this restrictive covenant. Since there was no payment for goodwill nor any continuing participation in the partnership, the court found, on appeal, that the terms of the agreement were too harsh. In part, the court expressed this opinion:

> In determining the validity or invalidity of a restrictive clause such as the one here in question, each case must be decided on its own particular facts. On the state of facts here disclosed, we hold that the restrictive clause is, as against this plaintiff, unreasonably broad in its scope, resulting in undue hardship to plaintiff wholly disproportionate to any proper need for defendants' protection, and is against public policy, and invalid and void for lack of mutuality and consideration.

[4]For a more detailed discussion of the issues of this case, see the text of the opinion of the New York State Supreme Court, Appellate Division, Lynch vs. Bailey, *The Journal of Accountancy,* May 1950, pp. 431-435.

FINANCIAL STATEMENTS TO FIX VALUES OF PARTNERS' INTERESTS

Agreements should contain provision for the preparation of financial statements to determine the value of the interest of a partner. The thought aroused in the drafting of this provision will cause more adequate consideration of all of the balance-sheet items, some of which might otherwise be viewed with indifference or ignored and yet later turn out to be important.

The provision should state the basis on which the balance sheet is to be prepared—either cash or accrual. If the records are on a cash basis but the statement is to be on an accrual basis, careful references must be made as to how some accruals are to be computed, particularly work in process, bad-debt allowances, and valuations of equipment and library. Intangibles, if any, should be dealt with definitely, either to be included or excluded, and if included then the valuation basis should be fixed.

It would be helpful to provide that the statement on which a valuation will be based be submitted to a partner who desires to retire or to the estate of a deceased partner, and that if no objections are raised within a specified period of time it become fixed, final, and free from later contention. Some agreements permit an examination of the records in this connection. Differences of opinion must be given recognition and a plan for their settlement established. One agreement covers this contingency in the following manner:

> If withdrawing partner does not accept and approve the statement within thirty days after it is furnished, the remaining partners may employ a CPA to audit the books and report on the interests of the retiring partner. His decision shall be binding and the partners agree not to institute proceedings against the remaining partners for any other accounting, except in the event of failure to pay the sum certified.

Somewhat similar provisions appear in other agreements. In one instance it is provided that the signatures of the remaining partners on the statement make the financial statement final and beyond appeal, except as to subsequent review by the partners if a question of fact is raised. Other agreements have general arbitration clauses which would cover disputes as to financial statements.

Some agreements provide that financial statements be furnished to payees during the period in which payments are being made to retired partners or estates. The right to check such statements would require agreement of the partners, if desired. It may suffice, for all practical purposes, to have the opinion as to the statements include a reference to the fact that the distributive shares for the year, paid or to be paid, are calculated in accordance with the agreement.

VALUATION OF WORK IN PROCESS

Work in process is an item which may materially affect the valuation of an interest in an accounting partnership. Inasmuch as there may be sincere differences of opinion as to the method to be employed, advance agreement on this subject is desirable.

Two principles of valuation exist—one using cost and the second using billable amounts. The cost method is probably most prevalent. The other policy prevails where there is an intent to be liberal in the valuation. Where an accrual-basis accounting system is used, and costs are charged to job cost accounts, the records will disclose the work in process and the costs accrued. In some firms, though on a cash basis, client time and cost records are nevertheless employed. Here too there may be no difficulty. Where no running record of job costs exists, it becomes necessary to draw up a list of unfinished matters and costs incurred. Here there may be questions as to cost determination. Care must be taken to include matters which have been completed but which, for some reason, have not been billed.

Even the term "cost" may require some definition. Shall it include only staff salaries or shall administrative salaries be included? Shall office overhead be allocated to each job? Most agreements shed no light on these questions.

Questions and answers on the valuation of work in process[5] are reproduced herewith:

Question: In case of death of a partner, how should work in process be valued in case of: (a) regularly recurring audits; (b) single engagements, undertaken on a flat-fee basis or at per-diem rates; and (c) retainers on tax cases?

Answer: There should be provision in the partnership agreement calling for valuation of work in process in the event of death of a partner. It might provide that all work in process should be handled by the surviving partners and charged upon the basis of the cost of the actual time expended in the completion of the work . . .

A member: . . . I recently terminated a partnership and although our agreement was a good one, we were left to decide what should be done with the work in process. We decided, after much discussion, that the following should be done: In each case the work would be completed by the partner who would take over the service of the client; the fees would be held in trust, as a partnership asset; at the time that the work was completed, an accounting would be had. Only the actual costs would be charged to the expenses of a particular job, that is, the labor costs of the senior or junior; the excess of the amount of the fee over these costs would be divided among the partners in their profit-sharing ratio, irrespective of whether it was a per-diem engagement, a tax engagement, or any other type of engagement. In other words, we "let it ride" as long as we possibly could, until we could determine the actual net cash value of that particular job . . .

Another committee member: I feel that the question of valuation of work in process might have been handled a bit differently, because there are accounting firms which keep their records on an accrual basis. They have cost records for individual engagements and post current costs to these cost records. It should not be too much of a problem, therefore, at the close of any period, to make some valuation of work in process based upon accumulated costs. Of course, as with any inventory of work in process, you might go beyond the recorded accumulated costs and perhaps give consideration to other factors. There are partnership agreements that provide specifically for some basis of valuing work in process . . .

[5]This was the subject of a committee meeting reported in the *New York Certified Public Accountant*, February 1946.

There are differences of opinion as to the proper basis for valuation. It may be provided that, following the death of a partner, the estate will receive the partner's share of the entire profit realized upon completion of each job in process. A more equitable arrangement, however, will provide that the estate shall receive a proportion of the final profit on each job which is to be determined by finding the ratio of the standard billing price for the work in process at death to the entire standard billing price of the completed job.

Where routine audit engagements are involved, the problem of valuation may be simple, as time and billing rates can be applied easily to work performed. However, where special matters are in process, the fees for which may have little relation to time and where the final date of completion is not determinable, a problem exists. Such matters may be disposed of in this manner, which is not a cost basis:

1. List the special matters in process.
2. Have the supervising partners indicate the stage of completion.
3. Provide that the portion of the fee earned as of the settlement date is to be fixed by the partner supervising the engagement, when it is completed.
4. Agree that the retired or deceased partner's share is to be paid upon collection of the fee.

In one agreement there appears this instance of a valuation formula not on a cost basis:

> The value of the then work in process shall be increased to an amount which shall be twice the cost thereof as then stated on the copartnership ledger.

It is conceivable that work in process costs may not be collected in full or in part. A similar risk attaches to uncollected billed accounts. This contingency may be met by making an allowance for doubtful items or by paying the pro-rata share to a partner when collected.

GOODWILL AND VALUATION

The existence of goodwill. Many accountants and attorneys contend that goodwill which can be evaluated and transferred cannot exist in a personal-service partnership. This view is well expressed as follows:

> Professional goodwill clings to its creator, can be dissociated from him only to a limited extent, and at best is a fragile thing in other hands. There is a vast difference between furnishing an opportunity and delivering goodwill.

Those who share that feeling back it up by definite statements in their partnership agreements to the effect that goodwill is to be considered nonexistent or that no value is to be placed thereon. The latter position does not necessarily constitute a denial of its existence and may be only a mutual understanding that it is not to be valued. In many partnership agreements no reference to goodwill appears. This may mean one of the following four possibilities: (1) that goodwill had not yet been recognized at the date of the agreement; (2) that the matter was just overlooked; (3) that goodwill was not considered to have any value; or (4) that it was intended that no value be placed on it in any event.

It has been said as to goodwill in an accounting partnership that the elements that produce true partnership results are too intangible and too indefinable to be measured even approximately. There are however many contrary viewpoints, as evidenced by the fact that a goodly number of partnership agreements do specifically acknowledge the existence of goodwill and provide for its valuation and purchase from the estate of a deceased partner or from a retiring partner. There probably are instances where, because of a material improvement in the status of a firm, a former denial or disregard of goodwill value has been replaced by an acknowledgment. The mere fact that individual clients and clientele have been sold demonstrates that tangible value can be placed upon such intangibles and the clientele may therefore be considered to have a goodwill value.

Inasmuch as agreements do not set forth the reasons for the expressed views as to goodwill, pro or con, or their reasons for making no reference to goodwill, the grounds can be surmised only by a process of rationalization. Where it is contended that goodwill does not exist, that position may have been taken for any of these reasons:

1. The firm is relatively new or small and the existence of goodwill as a firm asset just is not visualized.

2. Clients of a deceased or retired partner may not be retained very long after the separation date.

3. The valuation of goodwill presents such complexities as to warrant its total disregard.

4. The firm represents a loose aggregation of individual practitioners and changes in membership are easily possible.

5. The firm does not have an outstanding reputation in its community and does not receive recommendations of new matters from banks, credit grantors, attorneys, and so forth.

6. The death or withdrawal of the one partner responsible for the company's growth and position will surely result in a diminution of its practice and prestige.

At this point the views of an accountant who strongly dissents from the position that goodwill exists in an accounting firm deserve consideration as supplementing the foregoing points.

> I am one of those who believe that goodwill in the commercial sense cannot exist in a professional personal-service partnership. I recognize that there are some who do accept goodwill as such, but I am convinced that what they attempt to value as goodwill is in reality a combination of intangibles inherent in a going concern consisting of a cohesive group of professional persons who combine their talents to serve their clients. I believe in a retirement plan, but by the time that partial retirement is completed, the partner should have effectively transferred his clients' responsibilities and control to his associates so that there remains no goodwill to be purchased from him. I consider a payment or series of payments to a deceased partner to be in lieu of retirement rather than a purchase of his clients under the name of "goodwill." Perhaps

the two-partner type of firm has a different and more difficult problem of evaluating the amount to be paid by the survivor to the deceased partner's estate. But, in my opinion, such a payment is merely a fair recognition of the future earnings which he helped create and which are realized after his death, and not a purchase of goodwill.

Those who do make provision for goodwill may have done so for any of these reasons:

1. The firm enjoys an outstanding reputation and receives recommendations of new matters from banks and other sources because of its record of good work and service, and the firm's status does not depend on any one partner.

2. The firm's policy is such as to have more than one partner acquainted with each client and the loss of one partner would not likely result in the loss of clients on a large scale.

3. The relations between the firm and many of its clients have extended over a long term, have been satisfactory, and have resulted in an accumulation of such intimate knowledge of clients' affairs, that, barring any deterioration in future services, the relations should continue indefinitely, regardless of changes in one principal or executive on either side. The loss of a few clients due to the withdrawal of a partner may not necessarily be serious and does not negate the possibility of the existence of goodwill.

4. Other accountants would gladly pay some amount, small or large, for goodwill to become a partner in, or to acquire the clientele of, certain accounting firms.

Illustration of provisions. *Goodwill recognized.* The following illustrations of goodwill clauses will be helpful as guides:

It is agreed between the parties hereto that the goodwill of the partnership has at any date a value equal to 25 per cent of the collectible charges (fees) whether billed, accrued, or work in process, for services rendered (the gross value of such services) during the two years immediately succeeding such date . . .

This account (partner's capital account) will also be adjusted to reflect the fluctuation in the valuation of the goodwill of the partnership, which shall be determined as of the last day of each fiscal year of the partnership as follows: By computing the average of the annual profits of the partnership and including if necessary those of the preceding partnership or partnerships, which have accrued to the capital interests during the three years next preceding the end of such fiscal year, and multiplying the amount of such average profits by one and two-thirds.

Goodwill arises only in the event of the death of an active partner in which case a 10 per cent commission on business classified as his is paid to his survivors for a period of three years.

Policies of term insurance are to be taken out . . . for the term of the aforementioned partnership . . . and upon the death of either (partner) the amount paid thereunder shall represent the deceased person's interest in the accounts and goodwill of the partnership . . .

475

Upon the dissolution of the firm by the death of a party there shall be added to the regular assets of the firm a sum for the value of the firm's goodwill, which shall be credited among the partners (surviving and deceased) according to the profit-share ratio as above provided. The sum to be added to the assets as goodwill shall be equal to one-third of the total of the gross yearly charges of the firm for services for the fiscal year then last past. If the period be less than one year the amount charged in such period shall be increased as the proportion of the period covered bears to a full year.

Goodwill not recognized. Illustrations of the disavowal or nominal value of goodwill are the following:

There shall be no increase in the book value of furniture, equipment, library or tax services; nor shall any value be placed on goodwill, the evanescent nature of which is recognized.

Because of the personal nature of the business of accounting, the parties hereto realize that the value of the goodwill of the partnership, if any, is nominal. No partner, withdrawn or retired partner, or estate of a deceased partner shall have any individual or separate interest in the goodwill of the partnership, if any . . .

There shall be no value placed on the goodwill of the partnership name at any time in computing the capital invested either for original investment or for the liquidation of the partnership.

All rights which any partner may have enjoyed in the firm name, established business, and so forth shall pass immediately upon death to the surviving partners, in consideration of the terms and conditions set forth in this paragraph . . . [*The consideration referred to is the participation by the estate in the firm's earnings for a limited period.*]

Amounts to be paid to the estate of a deceased partner or to an involuntarily retiring partner for its or his interest in the business shall include no sum of money for goodwill in the partnership, which shall be deemed to have no value, but there shall be paid to the estate of a deceased partner or to an involuntarily retiring partner in accordance with the terms hereof, additional sums . . . [*The additional sums vary amongst partners and, briefly, constitute a year's salary plus an excess over the amount of such salary determined from a computation of the partners' average earnings.*]

Upon dissolution the right to use firm name and goodwill shall pass to any firm designated by —— per cent in interest of the partners, but not otherwise, it being expressly understood that each partner and associate waives all claims for compensation for goodwill or use of firm name in event of withdrawal, or death, or dissolution, and use of name by firm in which he is not included.

Should goodwill be recognized? To insure a mutual understanding of the term goodwill, the following definition and pertinent comments are offered:

The term goodwill is used in this discussion as encompassing certain intangibles which may acquire value by virtue of their apparent permanence or because they may be salable. Included therein are factors such as (1) firm prestige, (2) profitableness of the practice, (3) better-than-average organization of partners and staff, (4) the ability to retain clients despite changes in principals in the accountant's or client's organization, and (5) the possibility of transferring clients for a consideration.

Intangibles, for the most part, develop and grow at a moderate pace. For that reason, and because of their very nature, the creation of these values may just not be given any unusual consideration. Nothing can deteriorate so quickly as confidence and goodwill. This is one of the major reasons for the long-held views that goodwill does not have a tangible value in a personal-service, professional organization. Despite that hazard, there are quite a few old and illustrious firm names in the accounting field and many small firms that are soundly entrenched in their communities.

Here are additional factors which should be considered before a decision is reached to adopt a goodwill basis or a retirement and death-benefit basis.

1. A fair retirement plan is more suitable, in the case of medium and large firms, than compensation for an interest in a firm's goodwill. A pension is a gratifying and honorable reward for past services by a partner, no different than for a stockholder-officer of a corporation. For small firms a retirement plan may not be feasible. If a partner dies before retirement, payments may be made to his estate in partial payment for retirement allowances he might otherwise eventually have received. But in the absence of a retirement plan, some other recognition should be given to the intangible values inherent in the firm.

2. The presence of a goodwill value in a practice may be disregarded even where, in fact, it may actually exist. This is a voluntary arrangement and undoubtedly binding upon the partners. However, this position should not be taken merely because of the complexity of the valuation, as is sometimes the case, unless the amount involved is not material. Where, however, goodwill is disavowed and yet payments are provided for, which are not clearly distinguishable, the substance may overcome the form.

3. Regardless of the possibility that goodwill may exist, and even if no consideration therefor is fixed (which is the privilege of the contracting parties), payments may be made to an estate of a deceased partner for past services of the partner and any assistance that the estate may furnish in retaining the clients supervised by the deceased partner. Payments may be made annually to retired partners for being available for advisory or consultation services, for services in helping retain the clients whom they used to contact, and for agreeing to refrain from entering into any competitive practice. Such payments should not be considered alternatives of goodwill for, in fact, some of them might well be made in addition to goodwill payments, if so desired.

4. Since the specific payment of goodwill is not tax deductible, it would be well to consider the use of life insurance to help finance the burden and assure partners of compliance with such provision.

5. Where there is no insurance cushion, goodwill payments might be made over a period up to three years, perhaps providing some security for the payment of this obligation.

Evaluating goodwill. The valuation of goodwill, where recognized, may be based on one of the three common methods in use. These are:

1. Capitalization of earnings
2. Capitalization of fees
3. Fixed amount, settled by insurance proceeds or otherwise

Though these valuation methods may in some respects resemble those used in calculating retirement allowances, the similarity in itself should not result in a conclusion that a retirement plan necessarily encompasses goodwill. As to the earnings method, at least one year's earnings averaged over the past three to five years is a fair minimum. If more than one year's earnings are to be used as a base, then the average should be spread over at least the past five to ten years. Five years' earnings is probably the maximum goodwill valuation base, as a practical matter, and a factor of two to three times average earnings may be adequate in a majority of cases.

The goodwill valuation may be made for the partnership as a whole, and the subject partner's capital percentage share thereof determined, or the subject partner's individual earnings used as the base. It is not possible to determine in advance which of these two methods is preferable but the former one appears to be more common.

Another factor requiring consideration is the definition of earnings. Is it the amount before or after partners' salaries, if any? Where such salaries are to be consolidated with earnings, the "times earnings" factor obviously cannot be as large as where such salaries are excluded from earnings.

With respect to the fees basis for valuation, one firm uses 30 per cent of a year's billings. Other methods use equivalents of 33 1/3 per cent and 50 per cent. The amounts used are the billings of the past one or two years. These percentages appear somewhat inconsistent with the fact that the price placed on a clientele where a sale is involved may range from two-thirds to one year's gross billings and is seemingly low in relation to the net profit bases, assuming that partners' salaries (if any) are not treated as an expense.

There are several references to valuation placed on clienteles.[6] Some of these references relate to the following quotations which are noteworthy because valuation of clientele may, for all practical purposes, be synonymous with valuation of goodwill:

> An arrangement which has been found satisfactory is to give the seller payment for tangibles and agree to give him, say 100 per cent of the earnings for each of the two years following the date of the sale and 50 per cent of the earnings of the third and fourth years.

> The better plan for a purchaser would, I think, be to establish some relationship under which he would give a commission to the vendor based on the actual fees received out of a certain designated list of clients, such commission being restricted to, say, from 15 to 20 per cent of gross fees, at the outside, and for a limited period only, say three years.

> I am inclined to suggest that the fairest method, both to the buyer and the seller, would be for the buyer to undertake to pay to the seller a percentage

[6]See "Valuation of Goodwill in an Accounting Practice," *New York Certified Public Accountant,* June 1946, p. 295.

478

upon each gross fee for each of a period of years. . . . The percentage might range anywhere from 10 to 20 per cent upon each fee, and the period of time over which these payments would be payable might range from five to ten years. Naturally, if the percentage agreed upon should approach the higher limit just mentioned, the period of years would tend to be reduced.

A method which is growing in favor . . . is . . . that business should be transferred from one practitioner to another . . . on one year's purchase of the gross fees, payment being spread over three years on the understanding that no payment will be made in respect of work which is not renewed to the purchaser. In respect of any appointments which are not renewed in the second or third year the purchaser is entitled to reduce the payment due for goodwill in that year by a proportionate amount.[7]

Where recognized, one year's billings from accounts secured or supervised actively by the partner, is a fair basis for goodwill valuation in a well-knit, homogeneous firm, where the likelihood of retention of clients is considered to be good. This is in line, it is felt, with the previous suggestion that on an earnings basis goodwill may in many cases be valued at two or three times earnings.

As to the use of a predetermined, fixed amount for the goodwill valuation, its sole merit is simplicity: no formula to be fixed and no calculations to be made thereafter. However, arriving at the amount is no simple matter in itself and it may well be based on one of the formulas here reviewed. But as the firm's position changes, an inequity may develop unless the amount is revised.

Under the condition of a gradual retirement of a living partner for whom a salary is provided after retirement, the need for goodwill valuation is not acute. In such a situation, during the period of the partial retirement, a successor partner or partners are to be developed to carry on the business and to increase the goodwill. But for a retirement that is to occur entirely at a definite date, a valuation formula should be set forth in the partnership agreement, particularly if the retiring partner is a founder of the business. A common basis is to take as the goodwill value from one to two years' profits, computed by finding the average annual net income for the past three or more years. Such an amount may be varied according to the number of years the partner has been in the firm, or for other reasons, and often it includes his share of the entire income, including so-called partners' salaries and interest on investment, rather than the excess of profits over salary and interest.

A rather interesting and seemingly fair method of paying for goodwill is on the basis of a reducing percentage of the gross fees in subsequent period. Thus, as high as 8 per cent of the entire gross income might be paid the first year after retirement or death and 1 per cent less in each succeeding year, such as 7 per cent the second, and 6 per cent the third, until eight years have elapsed when no more payments are to be made. Although the payments are based upon gross income they do not qualify as an expense of the continuing partnership but are to be treated as a purchase of goodwill. From the standpoint of the retiring partner or his estate the plan may have considerable appeal because a larger total payment will be expected under such an extended

[7]W. G. Rodger, "Professional Goodwill," *The Accountant's Journal* (New Zealand), September 30, 1945, p. 53.

plan than would be received if settlement were in a lump sum. The burden of payment by the remaining partners should be lighter because of the deferral over several years and also because the amount depends upon the volume of work obtained.

The lump-sum settlement, based upon a valuation formula that depends upon past profits, appears to be quite common and it has the advantage that there is a definite determinable goodwill value for estate-tax purposes. Leniency in the provision for payment can be provided by permitting several semiannual, or even annual, payments.[8]

The continuance of one or more partners creates a condition in which a higher proportionate value should be placed on the retiring partner's interest. In effect, there is an appreciable difference in value dependent upon the "going-concern" or "sell-out" aspects of the transfer.

PLANS FOR PAYMENT OF CAPITAL AND OTHER BALANCES

In addition to providing for the determination of the amount to be paid to a withdrawing partner, it is essential that the agreement stipulate when payments will be made. In a small firm in particular, the necessity for making a substantial lump-sum payment may create severe working capital problems, which may be avoided by appropriate provisions of the partnership contract.

The plan for the liquidation of a partner's interest should be carefully considered and drawn up. It should provide for full or installment payments; fix the dates thereof; state whether or not interest is payable; cover defaults; fix security, if any is to be furnished; and such other clauses as the parties deem advisable. Here, as in other instances, there is variety in the plans in use.

Where the amount to be paid out is relatively small, the payment may be in full within thirty days after determination of the total due. Should the amount involved be substantial, the payments might extend over a period of several years. If payments are to be made over an extended term, security provisions might be considered.

Some agreements vary the terms of payment depending on the reasons for the separation. One agreement provides that capital be paid out in equal quarterly installments, without interest, over a period of one year in the event of retirement. In the event of death, however, the payments are extended over a three-year period. Another agreement calls for payments of capital balances to an estate in twelve equal monthly installments, but in ninety days to a retiring partner. Withdrawing partners apparently are paid in shorter periods than estates, presumably on the ground that they may desire to use the funds as soon as obtainable.

The question of what is to be done about payments in the event a partner dies while receiving retirement pay is not referred to except in very few agreements. One contract states that unpaid balances are to be paid to the partner's estate. Where the agreement is silent can it be assumed that the balance will be paid to the estate? Because of such a possibility, it is important

[8]Ira N. Frisbee, "Organizing and Perpetuating an Accounting Partnership," *New Responsibilities of the Accounting Profession,* AICPA, 1948, p. 40.

that, where it is so desired, payments to a retired or withdrawn partner definitely constitute a liability.

Illustration of provisions. Some of the methods in use are disclosed by the following representative arrangements:

In the absence of any agreement to the contrary the total amount due a withdrawing partner because of balances in capital and drawing accounts shall be paid in cash within a period of ninety days from the effective date of this withdrawal.

However, if such purchase settlement exceeds $5,000, the surviving and continuing partners may, if they elect, limit their payments to $5,000 per year by giving notes bearing 5 per cent interest evidencing the unpaid balance.

Balance due the estate to be paid within twenty-four months.

The capital interest of a deceased partner shall be determined and settled as soon as possible but in not more than five years from date of death payable in equal quarterly installments without interest.

Each of the following represents a summarization of provisions appearing in partnership agreements:

1. The partner's stated capital shall be paid in six equal semiannual installments, commencing six months after separation.
2. The share of the distributable profits, to date of separation, shall be paid in the ensuing fiscal year as the majority of the administrative partners may determine.
3. Other indebtedness to the partner, if any, are payable at the separation date.
4. Remaining partners agree to reduce their participation in profits by 10 per cent until all payments to estate of senior partner are completed. Also, to take out enough life insurance in favor of estate to guarantee their pro-rata share of payments.

1. *Tangible capital*: Estimated one-half within six months, and the balance within one year from date of death or retirement, or within one month after realization (of assets constituting capital) if not realized within a one-year period.
2. *Intangible capital (Goodwill)*: First payment: eighteen months after retirement or death, and balance semiannually until balance is paid.

1. A stipulated sum for the goodwill share payable over a period of five years.
2. The balance in his capital account payable within six months after death.
3. The deceased partner's share of the net profits on an accrual basis to the last day of the month immediately preceding the date of the death and payable within sixty days after death.

His capital shall be paid in quarterly installments during the fiscal year following the date of termination of the partnership.

1. Undrawn earnings (capital and profit share on a cash basis): payable within thirty days after end of fiscal year in which death occurs.

2. Share of uncollected fees: included as part of profit share payable to estate from income of next three years.

3. Fees unpaid after three years: estimated amount realizable to be paid with profit share for third year.

1. Cash-basis capital: due immediately.

2. Pro-rata share of collections of accounts receivable: payable on tenth day after month of collection.

1. *Rights in firm name*: Payable in five equal installments beginning within one year from date of death.

2. *Tangible capital*: Payable in three annual installments beginning within one year from date of death.

1. *Tangible capital*: As soon as practical, but in any event within sixty days after withdrawal or death.

2. *Goodwill*: Monthly payments until paid off out of collections from fees in accordance with formula therefor.

The above provisions as to tangible capital and goodwill are modified for new partners as follows:

It is further agreed that the provisions . . . in respect to death or voluntary withdrawal . . . shall not apply to the "new partners" if death or withdrawal . . . occur within a period of four years from the date of this agreement. In such event (they) shall be paid . . . the amount of cash that he or they paid for the interest acquired . . . and this amount shall be the purchase price of his or their interest in the partnership instead of the amounts set forth in paragraphs —. It is further agreed that in such event the prohibitions set forth in paragraph — on engaging in public practice shall not apply.

The payment of capital and profit share to a partner forced to retire from a firm is specified in one agreement as follows:

His interest in the capital shall be paid to him by the remaining partners, without any interest thereon, in four equal quarterly installments commencing three months after the date of his expulsion, and the balance of his share of the profits shall be paid to him when ascertained after the end of the fiscal year. . .

In another agreement, provisions for payment of tangible capital are set up somewhat as follows:

Tangible capital:
1. Twenty-five per cent of the estimated amount payable at the end of three months after retirement or death.

2. Fifteen per cent of the estimated amount at the end of the next four three-month periods.

3. The balance, which will then have been determined, is payable at expiration of eighteen months.

4. Unpaid balances bear interest at 5 per cent.
Goodwill: Payable in forty-eight consecutive monthly installments.

Security for payments. The question of securing the payment of retirement (or death) benefits, though apparently rarely considered, nevertheless is deserving of some thought prior to a decision to provide for it or disregard it. There are several methods of providing for security, each having its own peculiar appeal:

1. An agreement that retirement allowances are to be treated as an expense prior to partners' salaries and profit shares. This provision can be varied as to the amount or percentage of preference.

2. An agreement to invest a percentage of the firm's annual profits in a fund to guarantee the payment of the benefits. The fund could be started before any benefits are payable, to help build it up to a specified maximum as quickly as possible. A suggestion as to a satisfactory level is the following: An amount sufficient to pay the largest potential benefit claim (retirement or death) of an active partner with additions for the unpaid claims of retired and deceased partners. Obviously the funds should be invested to earn an increment and provision must therefore by made for the form of investment, custody, and accounting. The contributions to the fund made by retired or deceased partners during their active periods are to be refunded because they are equivalent to capital account investments.

3. A one-premium annuity contract purchased at the date of retirement, to transfer the responsibility for payments from the firm to an insurance company.

4. The acceptance of the retirement payment by the remaining partners as personal liabilities in the event of subsequent disposal of part or all of the firm, merger, dissolution, and other changes.

5. A provision that a default in the plan calls for a liquidation of the firm unless remedied within a short stated period.

In one agreement there is a provision that in the event a firm should split up after the senior partner's death and before payment is completed in full for the assets and practice, the estate should decide whether (1) to accept from each remaining partner a sum representing his share of the total due the estate or (2) to sell the assets and the practice on the open market to the highest bidder. It continues:

In the event option (2) is elected by the estate, the remaining partners agree hereby (not) to induce any of the accounts of the firm to accept them as their accountant, in place of the firm. In the event a client of the firm, of his own volition, should elect to retain one of the partners, said partner agrees, in order to maintain the corpus of the senior partner's estate and avoid any legal action, to pay the estate a sum equal to 125 per cent of the fees rceived from said client over the twelve months preceding separation or death of senior partner, such sum to be paid quarterly in equal payments over a period of two years.

In one agreement the estate of a deceased partner leases to the survivor its interest in "goodwill, files, correspondence, and clientele owned by (deceased partner)." The monthly rental is 20 per cent of all amounts earned by the survivor while using the firm name (which he is required to do for five years) for a period of five years. In addition, the survivor has an option to buy the leased items, at the end of the term, for $100. In another agreement, in the event of default in the terms or failure to exercise the option "the representative of said estate shall have the right to sell the goodwill herein mentioned to others, retaining as liquidated damages any and all amounts that may have been paid under this paragraph by the party of the second part."

Another security provision worthy of note requires that, during the period during which there is a liability to a retired partner or to the estate of a deceased partner, all remaining partners are to reduce their profit shares by 10 per cent to preserve cash and assure the payments, and take out enough life insurance in favor of the estate to guarantee their pro-rata share of payments.

Life insurance. The use of life insurance as a means of assuring the availability of funds for the liquidation of the interest of a deceased partner is fairly widespread. However, certain accounting factors must be considered in agreeing on the settlements, to avoid unforeseen inequities. These factors involve the accounting treatment of the premiums paid and their offset against the insurance proceeds.

There are instances where the life insurance proceeds constitute full payment for the deceased partner's interest in the firm and, in some cases, in the goodwill. This may be a dangerous situation if there is laxity in revising the insurance in conformity with changes in the firm's position. It would be more reasonable to apply the proceeds as a minimum payment on account of the value placed on the partner's share. In some instances the insurance is paid to the firm, in others directly to the surviving partners. Legal security probably should be the guiding consideration in selecting the beneficiary.

The treatment of payment of the premiums and proceeds varies, as indicated in the following illustrations:

> The cost for the premiums of said policies shall be considered a business expense and charged to the partnership business.

> Whereas, the annual premiums on said policies are paid out of the profits and proceeds of the partnership business . . . it is agreed . . . the proceeds of insurance on his death paid to the surviving partners shall be used to pay the estate of the deceased partner the amount of (his) undrawn earnings (capital) in the partnership. In the event that the proceeds of life insurance exceed the undrawn earnings the excess shall be paid into the partnership funds . . . the surviving partners shall participate in the proceeds of life insurance in the ratio of the division of partnership earnings. . .

> Whereas the partnership has taken out a policy of group life insurance, which includes insurance on the lives of the partners, which insurance is payable, as to the partners, to beneficiaries named by them, and not to the partnership, it is agreed that insurance payments made to such beneficiaries shall be construed in effect to belong to the partnership as it was constituted prior to the decease of the partner involved to the extent hereinafter set forth, and the current account of such partner shall be charged with the amount of such payment up to the amount of his current account balance, and any remaining part to his capital or other accounts, with the same force and effect as if the partnership had paid such sum to or for the account of the partner involved, except as hereinafter next provided. If the sum paid by the insurance company shall exceed the aggregate of all sums found to be due by the partnership to the estate of the deceased partner (after his current account has been credited with his share of the amount of the insurance money), such excess shall not be required to be repaid to the partnership.

Insurance-premiums expense, in one case, is charged to partners other than the insured except that the amount in excess of the term rate is charged to the account of the insured. Obviously, the insurability of partners is a condition precedent to an insurance plan. Where only one of several partners is not insurable, it may nevertheless be desirable to utilize insurance to the extent possible. Summaries of provisions in two agreements state:

1. Insurance premiums are paid by the firm but charged to the beneficiaries of the policies.

2. In ultimate effect, insurance premiums are paid by all of the partners other than the partner upon whose life the insurance is carried. The premiums are paid by the partnership for account of such partners. That part of the premium which represents the (increase in the) cash-surrender value of policies is carried continuously as an account receivable against the interested partners. . .

DIVISION OF WITHDRAWN PARTNERS' INTEREST AMONG REMAINING PARTNERS

In the event of death of a partner, or withdrawal for any reason, it is generally provided that his interest is to be apportioned among the continuing partners in accordance with their respective profit-sharing interests. A companion provision calls for compliance by the estate or retired partner, in making legally and otherwise effective the transfer of the interest to the remaining partners. The following are representative provisions:

The retiring partner, upon receipt of the payments mentioned in subdivision — of paragraph —, shall be deemed to have assigned, transferred, and set over to the continuing partners, all of his right, title, and interest in and to the assets of the partnership, without any further act on the part of such retiring partner. Such retiring partner shall, upon request, execute, acknowledge and deliver such instruments and perform such acts as the continuing partners may require in order to more effectively vest in them all the retiring partner's said right, title, and interest in and to said assets.

The percentage of profits to which any retiring partner is entitled shall, following his retirement, be added to the percentages of the remaining partners in the proportion that the percentage of each remaining partner as set forth in subdivision — of paragraph — bears to the total percentage of all the remaining partners as set forth in said subdivision —. Similar adjustment shall be made with respect to percentage of losses, the percentages in subdivision — of paragraph — being used for such purpose.

Some agreements refer to the acquisition of an interest in the form of a "buy-sell" provision whereby the firm acquires the partner's share for a stated consideration. This is usually done where goodwill is valued in determining capital, but it also may be applicable where rights to a firm name and other intangibles are involved. As a matter of caution, one agreement holds that the transfer of the interest takes place only after the stipulated payments have been made in full.

ARBITRATION

A significant number of agreements provide that disagreements which cannot be settled by the partners are to be submitted for arbitration. In some instances the American Arbitration Association is specified as the agency for this purpose. The following is a provision appearing in one agreement:

> That if any disagreement shall arise between the parties, in respect of the conduct of the partnership business, or of its dissolution, or in respect of any other matter, cause, or thing, whatsoever, not herein otherwise provided for, the same shall be decided and determined by arbitrators; and each of the parties shall select one of the arbitrators, and the decision of two of such arbitrators, when made in writing, shall be conclusive upon the parties hereto.

As a rule, such provisions provide that the two designated arbitrators select a third and that a decision of two of the three is conclusive. A typical, blanket provision is the following:

> Any controversy or claim arising out of or relating to this contract or the breach thereof, shall be settled by arbitration, in accordance with the rules, then obtaining, of the American Arbitration Association, and judgment upon the award rendered may be entered in the highest court of the forum, state or federal, having jurisdiction.

The Pooling of Outside Income

■ IT IS NOT UNCOMMON for partners to be faced with a situation where it is advantageous to the partnership for one or more of the partners at the same time to render services outside the partnership to others as an employee. An example of this might be where such members serve on the faculty of a local university. Under these circumstances, there can be an agreement providing that any salaries or other compensation received by a partner in his individual name shall, notwithstanding, be treated as a part of the gross income of the partnership. For federal income tax purposes the compensation earned by an individual in his own name may not be included in the gross income of a partnership of which he is a member.

This situation poses the business problem of how to allow, in arranging the division of partnership profits, for the fact that the salaried partner devotes less time to the partnership than he could if he did not have to spend part of his time earning the salary; while at the same time his partner may devote full time to the partnership.

One solution to this problem would be to adjust the profit-sharing percentages to give the salaried partner a lesser participation, allowing him to retain the salary as his own. But there are many practical objections to this solution; because it is difficult to compare the productivity of various activities in terms of hours or dollars, the time and attention taken by the salaried work may not be fixed, and all the factors which would be considered in compensating for the salaried work are subject to change. Thus at best this solution is an awkward one, and at worst it may create friction among the partners.

The solution often adopted, therefore, is that the partners agree that their entire working time shall be for the benefit of the partnership, and that any salaries or other compensation which may be received by a partner in his individual name shall be treated as a part of the gross income of the partnership.

RECONCILING BOOK INCOME WITH TAX INCOME

The purpose here is to show the methods whereby a partnership may keep its books so as to obtain the business advantages of pooling partners' salary income, and at the same time readily reconcile the book income to a partnership income without salaries which will meet the federal requirements.

Two steps are involved. First, distribute the income, including pooled salary, on the books in accordance with the partnership agreement. Second, arrive at partnership income and its distribution for federal purposes by subtracting the amount of pooled salary from the distributive share of the partner or partners who earned the pooled salary. In the tax-return capital reconciliation, the pooled salary then is treated as a capital contribution from the partner who earned it.

One further theoretical point needs to be settled before examples can be given to demonstrate the practical results of pooling salaries for business reasons combined with de-pooling to satisfy the tax collector. A salary these days is a net amount of money received after deductions have been made from a gross salary for income and social-security taxes. Partners could agree to pool either the net salary or the gross salary, but it seems preferable to pool the gross salary, and, in the absence of specification in their agreement, to interpret it to apply to the gross salary. This treatment is consonant with the business reason for pooling salary in the first place, since the gross salary is the pure distillation of the partner's effort, unadulterated by the amount of tax deductions, which will vary according to the entirely unrelated consideration of the number of exemptions for withholding to which the individual may be entitled, and since the salaried partner ultimately will personally enjoy the benefits of the deducted taxes.

ILLUSTRATION

As an example of the working out of this recommended accounting, let us take a situation where two accountants decide to form a partnership for public practice. One of them has an opportunity for part-time salaried work teaching accounting, and since they expect at first to have more time than clients, they agree that one shall take the teaching position, and to compensate for the time which this will require him to take away from the public practice, he agrees to contribute his salary as a part of the gross income of the partnership. The partners further agree to share profits and losses (including the pooled salary) equally and to keep their capital accounts equal. Each contributes $1,000 for furniture and working capital. They start their partnership on January 1, 1958 and partner A's salaried teaching commences on the same day. Partner A's teaching salary is assumed to be received as shown in Table 1.

Each salary check is deposited in the partnership bank account, and the total for a year as it affects the partnership accounts is summarized in Table 2.

Assuming net income from accounting practice as indicated for the first three years, accounting in accordance with the partnership agreement will lead to the results per books shown in Table 3.

Table I

Gross salary per year		$3,600
Deductions*		
Federal income tax	$412	
F.I.C.A.	108	520
Net amount received		$3,080

*For convenience, the F.I.C.A. tax is computed at a fixed three per cent per year, disregarding the statutory rates for the years involved; and income tax is taken at an approximate amount assuming two exemptions.

Table 2

Dr. Cash in bank	$3,080	
Dr. Drawing account, Partner A	520	
Cr. Income—Salaries		$3,600

Table 3

	1958	1959	1960
Net income from independent accounting practice	$(1,000)	$3,000	$6,000
Salary contributed by Partner A	3,600	3,600	3,600
Net income per books	$ 2,600	$6,600	$9,600
Net income credited to partners' capital accounts on the books:			
Partner A	$ 1,300	$3,300	$4,800
Partner B	1,300	3,300	4,800

To prepare the federal partnership income return we subtract the salary income from the book net income and from the share thereof of the partner who held the salaried position. Since we cannot escape the fact that the salary went into the partnership bank account and was used to pay its expenses or was divided between the partners, we then have to treat it as a contribution of capital from the salaried partner. The foregoing book position thus works out on a partnership income return as shown in Table 4.

The reconciliation between book and tax treatment is made in the capital accounts analysis schedule of Form 1065. (See Table 5.)

Since Partner *A* reports both his salary and his share of income or loss from the partnership, the net effect on his individual return is the same as his total profit share per the firm's books. This is as it should be, since the pooling of salary in a partnership is done purely for business reasons, and is not a tax-avoidance technique.

Table 4

	1958	1959	1960
Ordinary net income or (loss)	$(1,000)	$3,000	$6,000
Partners' shares of ordinary net income or (loss):			
A	$(2,300)	$ (300)	$1,200
B	1,300	3,300	4,800

Table 5

	Partner A	Partner B	Total
Beginning capital contributed	$ 1,000	$1,000	$ 2,000
Ordinary net income or (loss), 1958	(2,300)	1,300	(1,000)
Additional capital contribution (gross salary)	3,600		3,600
Subtotal	2,300	2,300	4,600
Drawings:			
A's automatic draw of the deductions from his salary	520		520
Draw B would have to make to keep their capital accounts even		520	520
Assumed drawn toward living expenses	600	600	1,200
Total drawings	1,120	1,120	2,240
Capital accounts, December 31, 1958	1,180	1,180	2,360
Ordinary net income, 1959	(300)	3,300	3,000
Additional capital contribution	3,600		3,600
Subtotal	4,480	4,480	8,960
Drawings (including $100 per month each for living expenses)	1,720	1,720	3,440
Capital accounts, December 31, 1959	2,760	2,760	5,520
Ordinary net income, 1960	1,200	4,800	6,000
Additional capital contribution	3,600		3,600
Subtotal	7,560	7,560	15,120
Drawings (including $200 per month each for living expenses)	2,920	2,920	5,840
Capital accounts, December 31, 1960	$ 4,640	$4,640	$ 9,280

DIFFERENT TAX YEARS

On the other hand, if the partners showed good business reasons to effect a fiscal year for the firm while remaining on a calendar year themselves, the reporting of income on their individual returns and on the partnership return would not coincide.

For example, assume that all other facts remain unchanged except that the firm begins its year on July 1, 1958, and Partner A begins teaching at the same time. In his 1958 return, A would report $1,800 of salary, but neither partner would report his share of the first year's tax loss until he filed his 1959 return.

Because of this difference in the timing of their taxable income between the partners, there could have been a difference in the amount of tax, had tax rates changed during the periods illustrated. A would have been at a disadvantage with a rate reduction and B with a rate increase.

OTHER TAX CONSIDERATIONS

The self-employment income will be the same as the ordinary net income—$2,300 loss for A and $1,300 income for B in 1958. For federal purposes A's salary is excluded from the partnership, so the income or loss which remains must be the fruits of the partnership's trade or business, even though the capital which is the source of B's income had its origin as salary subjected to F.I.C.A. tax. Revenue Ruling 54-223, IRB 1954-24,9, can be interpreted as not in conflict with the foregoing.

The ruling holds: "No part of such wages paid over to the other partners in accordance with the partnership agreement may be considered as 'gross income derived . . . from any trade or business' carried on by such other partners . . . for purposes of computing their 'net earnings from self-employment.'" As these partnerships are viewed, the wages of the salaried partner are never paid over as such to the other partner, and the nonsalaried partner takes his distributive share for his services in the trade or business of the partnership. It would be immaterial that the capital supplying the non-salaried partner's credit had its source in someone else's wages.

The tax-accounting principles applied in handling this partnership problem would not be affected by the limitation in sec. 704(d), since the salaried partner's partnership loss is more than covered by the capital contribution of his salary. (The section referred to limits a partner's deduction for his share of the firm's loss to the basis of his interest.)

Selected Tax Problems
of Accounting Partnerships

■ TAXES AND THEIR possible effects are an important part of every CPA's practice. But the CPA is not only a tax practitioner, he is also a taxpayer. This material is addressed to the CPA in his latter capacity. It is limited to a review of some of the federal tax problems to be encountered by a partnership engaged in the professional practice of accountancy.

In all discussions of tax planning, it is necessary to remember that nontax aspects are important. Sound business and economic planning may not be the same thing as tax saving. It is important to keep in mind the economic implications of a partnership plan and to avoid saddling the partnership with excessive long-term commitments in an effort to procure a tax saving.

There are situations where the federal income-tax consequences of events will differ from those under state law. This is not only with respect to taxes but also to general laws governing partnerships. For example, the federal income-tax rules as to termination and continuation of a partnership differ considerably from state laws. Because of the many possible variations in these differences, no attempt will be made here to discuss state or local tax implications of the problems. However, this should not be taken to mean that such matters are of minor importance. The effect of state law must be considered as part of any business planning by the CPA.

This material is subject to the frailty so common to all publications in the tax field. Answers to tax questions are continually changing. The tremendous volume of official releases from Congress, the Treasury Department, and the courts requires the alert practitioner to be ever watchful. One can never be too sure of what the future will bring.

DOES A PARTNERSHIP EXIST?

Before any discussion of particular partnership tax problems, it is advisable to understand what form of organization will be considered a partnership under federal income-tax law. The existence or nonexistence of a partnership from a tax viewpoint is important for several reasons. If it is held that a partnership does not exist, income of the organization may be taxed to one member or to a different entity. Thus, the partnership may be considered no more than an employment arrangement. It may be so organized that it will be considered an association to be taxed as a corporation. (See Reference 1, page 526.)

A partnership, although it pays no tax, files a return for its own accounting period and determines income under its own accounting method. If a partnership is considered to be nonexistent for federal income-tax purposes, income reported by the participants might be determined for different years and under different accounting methods. This may result in differing amounts of income and, in one year, may cause a substantial bunching of income.

If there is a sale of a partnership interest, gain will be from the sale of a capital asset, subject to exceptions discussed on page 508; sale of a proprietorship is fragmented completely.

Numerous elections may be made by a partnership. If the partnership does not exist for income-tax purposes, the elections will be invalid with possible unfortunate consequences for the would-be partners. Thus, it is important to determine whether or not a partnership exists. The most common definition of a partnership is: ". . . an association of two or more persons to carry on as co-owners of a business for profit." (Ref. 2, page 526.) The Internal Revenue Code has a broader definition: "The term 'partnership' includes a syndicate, group, pool, joint venture, or other unincorporated organization, through or by means of which any business, financial operation, or venture is carried on. . . ." (Ref. 3, page 526.) Recognition of a partnership under state law is not controlling for federal income-tax purposes. The surrounding circumstances decide whether or not a partnership has been formed.

For example, a group of CPAs rent office space and share all expenses including audit and office personnel, but practice as individuals. This is a convenient and not uncommon arrangement. The individual participants are unable to afford full office accommodations and this type of agreement is of great help in getting started. Is there a partnership? In all probability, a simple expense-sharing arrangement is not a partnership but this would not be so if, in addition to sharing expenses, the CPAs joined in the rendering of services to clients.

A question may arise when a practice is sold and the seller is to receive payment over a period of several years. Assume that an individual practitioner purchases a practice from another individual and agrees to make payments for a period of time equal to 40 per cent of the net income from the practice. Would the seller under such circumstances be considered a temporary partner? It is doubtful that this arrangement would be considered a partnership in the absence of an agreement expressing the intent to form a partnership. (Ref. 4, page 526.) The buyer probably would prefer that there be a partnership as the 40 per cent of income would not be taxed to him but to the seller as a distributive share. The seller, on the other hand, probably would prefer to consider his payments for the sale of goodwill, thereby obtaining capital gain. Presumably such conflicts can be resolved by careful drafting of the sales agreement and possibly by an adjustment in purchase price to compensate the party who would not get the tax result he sought.

A fairly common arrangement for compensating valuable employees is to provide for a bonus based on a percentage of profits. A mere compensation device does not result in the creation of a junior partner. (Ref. 5, page 526.) Other circumstances demonstrating an intent to form a partnership would have to be present, such as participation in management decisions, articles of partnership, and holding out to the public of the partnership.

Family partnership. Frequently, partnerships are established with members of the family. For example, many a CPA looks forward to the day when he can form an accounting partnership with his son. In deciding whether the family partnership so formed is acceptable for income-tax purposes, it is necessary to keep in mind the basic income-tax rule that income is taxed to the person who earns it through his own labor and skill and the use of his capital. (Ref. 6, page 526.) The income attributable to capital interests must be proportionate to such interests and proper allowance must be made for services. (Ref. 7, page 526.) Although a CPA firm requires in many instances a substantial amount of working capital to meet expenses and to maintain an office, it is the view of the Internal Revenue Service that capital is not a material income-producing factor since income is derived principally from the personal services performed by the members of the firm. (Ref. 8, page 526.) Since capital is not considered a material income-producing factor in a professional partnership, it would seem that an important test of validity of the family partnership practicing accountancy would be the allowance for services.

In providing an allowance for services, consideration must be given to all facts and circumstances. One partner may have greater managerial ability than another; one may have greater technical ability. The amount which would be paid a person who is not a partner for comparable services is important. (Ref. 9, page 526.) Thus, if a son is not capable of assuming full charge of a job, it would be difficult to justify an allowance for services equal to his father's. Even where the son could take full charge, other factors, such as the relationship between clients and the father, may suggest that his services are worth less.

THE AGREEMENT

A partnership by its nature must have some form of agreement, which may be oral or written, sketchy or detailed. For tax purposes, it can be extremely important, for the answers to several tax questions may be found in the partnership agreement. It can set forth the distributive shares of income or loss and the capital interest of each partner. There are a number of tax problems which may arise depending upon the interest in profits and capital of partners. Thus, a partnership may not adopt or change to a taxable year different from that of a principal partner. A principal partner for this purpose has an interest of at least five per cent in profits or capital. (Ref. 10, page 526.)

Whether or not a partnership continues in existence or terminates for federal income-tax purposes depends in many instances on the profits or capital interests of certain partners. (Ref. 11, page 526.) This is important in deciding whether new elections must be made, whether a fiscal year can be retained, and so on.

The agreement is a valuable tool in planning for the retirement or death of partners. If desired, provision can be made to permit a retiring or a deceased partner's estate to treat as capital gain part of the payment received for the interest. (Ref. 12, page 526.) The agreement may be worded to permit or prevent the bunching of income in a deceased partner's final return. (Ref. 13, page 526.) The agreement may reduce controversy over estate-tax values by providing for the purchase of a deceased partner's interest. (Ref. 14, page 526.)

These comments are intended only to make clear the importance of the partnership agreement in helping resolve certain tax problems. The problems described briefly above will be explained in greater detail below.

Amending the agreement. For tax purposes a partnership has considerable flexibility as to the effective date of amendments to the agreement. The agreement includes any modifications adopted by the partners in accordance with it up to the date for filing the partnership tax return. Extensions are not counted. (Ref. 15, page 526.) Thus, in preparing a tax return for the calendar year 1960, a partnership would give effect to any amendments made to its agreement up to April 15, 1961. It is permissible, however, for an amendment to provide by its terms that it is not retroactive in effect.

It is not clear how far the partnership may go in amending its agreement. It would seem that the principles used in examining the validity of the basic agreement also would apply in determining the validity of an amendment. An amendment which has a business purpose and is not a sham or tax-avoidance scheme should be permitted. (Ref. 16, page 526.) Thus, a change in the allocation of income among the partners to recognize the exceptional contribution of a partner would seem reasonable and should be recognized. On the other hand, a change made to permit partners to shift tax liabilities probably would not be acceptable.

INCOME OF PARTNERSHIPS AND PARTNERS

Although a partnership as such does not pay federal income tax, it is required to file an income-tax return and compute its taxable income. The return is for information purposes and, among other things, supplies the necessary data for partners to prepare their individual returns. The Internal Revenue Code requires that the partnership return provide information as to the partnership's gross income and allowable deductions, names and addresses of the partners entitled to share in the distribution of taxable income, and their distributive shares.

Distributive shares. Information as to distributive shares is analyzed to permit the individual partners to prepare their personal returns and give effect to special provisions of the Code which apply to their shares of partnership income and deductions. Thus, a partnership's taxable income is computed separately from such other partnership items as capital gains and losses, sec. 1231 gains and losses, dividend income, charitable contributions, foreign taxes which may be claimed as credit against U. S. tax, partially exempt interest, and a number of other items such as bad-debt recoveries, gain or loss recognized as a result of certain partnership distributions, etc. (Ref. 17, page 526.) In preparing their individual returns, the partners report their distributive share of each such separately stated item for the partnership year which ends with or within the partner's taxable year. (Ref. 18, page 526.) Any such items are reported on a partner's return as though realized or incurred directly by the partner. (Ref. 19, page 526.) Thus, the partner adds to his own charitable contributions, his share of the partnership's contributions before applying the limitation on such deduction. If the partner's interest is subject to community property laws, his share of income and deductions will be reported by the partner and his spouse in equal portions. (Ref. 20, page 526.)

Gross income of a partner. If it is necessary to compute a partner's gross income, although each partner in preparing his return shows only his share of partnership taxable income, the distributive share of gross income of the partnership is taken into account. (Ref. 21, page 526.) The partner's distributive share of gross income is in proportion to his distributive share of partnership income, loss, etc. (Ref. 22, page 526.) Thus, if a partner reports one-fourth of taxable income, one-fourth of gross income was reported. [An example of the application of this principle is the assessment of taxes, etc., beyond the three-year period as provided in sec. 6501(e)(1).]

Guaranteed payments. A partner's income from a partnership may include more than his distributive share of income. Frequently, a partnership agreement will provide for partners' salaries or interest on invested capital. Such amounts, determined without regard to partnership income, are termed "guaranteed payments." For accounting purposes, such payments are usually considered as a distribution of profits rather than an expense, but in the event such payments exceed income or there is a loss prior to the allowance of salaries or interest on capital (unless the agreement provides otherwise), the full allowances should be deducted from income or added to the loss, and the resulting figure allocated to partners in the loss ratio. (Ref. 23, page 526.) For tax purposes, the IRC is clear that such payments are to be treated as an expense for the purpose of determining the partnership's taxable income, and as income to the partner regardless of whether or not the partnership has taxable income. (Ref. 24, page 526.) Under earlier law, the payments were treated as a distribution of profits and when profits were insufficient much confusion resulted. Now, if guaranteed payments exceed the income of the partnership before deducting payments, the partners, in effect, net their guaranteed payments and the loss after the payments.

The partner reports these amounts as ordinary income for his taxable year in which, or with which, the partnership year of deduction ends. (Ref. 25, page 526.) Thus, if the partnership is on a January 31 year, guaranteed payments received during the period from February 1, 1960 to December 31, 1960 would be reported on the partner's 1961 tax return.

Guaranteed payments are treated in this manner, namely, as though made to one who is not a partner, only for purposes of computing the taxable income of the partnership and recipient partner. Salary payments to partners are not subject to withholding taxes. Social security taxes are not paid on salaries but all guaranteed payments are includible for purposes of the tax paid by the partners on self-employment income. Partners receiving salaries are not considered employees for purposes of deducting payments for group insurance plans, pension, profit sharing, and other deferred compensation plans, sick-pay exclusion, and the like.

Guaranteed payments are not considered a distribution of profits for purposes of determining a partner's interest in profits. Therefore, such payments are not taken into account in deciding whether a partner is a principal partner, whether gain or losses in transactions with partnership are specially treated, and whether or not a partnership has terminated. However, in determining a partner's interest in profits, a salary dependent upon profits must be taken into account. Suppose an agreement provided that a partner shall receive as salary 30 per cent of partnership profits and that, after deducting that salary, the balance is to be divided equally among him and his two partners. The agreement would seem to indicate that the salaried partner's share of profits was 33 1/3 per cent. However, he is entitled to 30 per cent of the profits as salary and 23 1/3 per cent (one-third of the remaining 70 per cent) of the profits as a distributed share. Therefore, his interest in profits is 53 1/3 per cent.

Expense allowances. Partners, although not employees, may be subject to rules, with respect to expense allowances, similar to those generally applicable to employees. If the partner is required to account to the partnership for the expense allowance, and the expenses are equal to the allowance, the expenses and the allowance need not be reported. If the allowance exceeds the expenses, the excess would appear to be akin to a guaranteed payment and should be reported as income. If the expenses exceed the allowance, a deduction may be claimed for the excess if the partnership agreement provides that partners are expected to incur expenses. (Ref. 26, page 526.)

The partnership return now requests information as to expense-account allowances paid to partners whose total distributive share of income, salary, and expense allowances exceeds $10,000. This information is required for all partners, except that if a firm has more than twenty-five partners, it is required only for the twenty-five with the highest individual totals.

An expense-account allowance includes amounts other than compensation received as an advance or reimbursement and amounts paid by the partnership on behalf of a partner. However, this does not include fringe benefits, such as hospitalization. Expenses which will be billed to clients are counted, but there should be sufficient records to justify the business purpose of the expenditure. (Ref. 27, page 526.)

Deductibility of losses. A partnership may have a net loss from operations. If so, the agreement should provide in what manner the loss is to be distributed to the partners. Those partners who, in accordance with the agreement bear the losses, are entitled to a deduction. The deduction may not exceed the partner's basis for his interest determined as of the end of the partnership's taxable year in which the loss was incurred. To the extent the available loss exceeds the partner's basis, he can hold in abeyance the deduction for such excess until his basis has increased. (Ref. 28, page 526.)

There are several ways to reduce the amount of losses which may not be deducted immediately. If a loss is anticipated, a partner can increase his basis by a contribution to capital before the end of the year. If this is done, the money or property contributed should not be withdrawn at the beginning of the following year as it would give the transaction the appearance of sham.

As an alternative, the partnership could borrow money. Increases in partnership liabilities increase the basis of partners for their interests. (Ref. 29, page 526.) Such loans should be bona fide and perhaps for a purpose other than merely to furnish an additional basis for the partners to support their loss deduction. The partnership agreement may provide that a liability arise from the partners to each other or to the partnership to repay any deficiencies in capital. Since this is not an increase in the partnership's liabilities, it does not affect a partner's basis for his interest and is not taken into account in determining the loss which may be deducted.

As noted earlier, there are a number of items of income and deductions which are computed separately. If the total of the separately computed deductions exceeds the partner's basis, the deductions are allowed proportionately in the year incurred. (Ref. 30, page 526.) Thus, there may be held in abeyance separate losses arising out of capital-asset transactions, sales of sec. 1231 assets, accounting practice, and so on. Actually, this will be of limited importance to an accounting partnership since there are few occasions where such separate losses arise for the accounting firm. An interesting exception to this rule appears to exist with respect to charitable contributions. The Regulations for limitation of deductible losses from a partnership omit mention of charitable contributions. Presumably, the partner's share of contributions is deductible by him without regard to his basis for his interest and subject only to the percentage limitations applicable to the deduction for charitable contribution.

BASIS OF A PARTNER'S INTEREST

There are several occasions when it is necessary to ascertain the basis of a partner's interest in a partnership in order to determine the tax liability of the partner. As described above, a partner's basis for his interest sets a limit on the amount of loss which the partner may deduct. In ascertaining a basis for this purpose the necessary computations are made as of the end of the taxable year of the partnership. This is so even though the partnership and partner are on different taxable years. Under other circumstances, it may be necessary to determine the basis as of some date during the partnership year. Thus, in order to compute gain or loss upon the sale, exchange, or liquidation of a partnership interest, the basis is determined as of the date of such sale, exchange, or liquidation. (Ref. 31, page 526.)

General rule. The starting point for the determination of a partner's basis for his interest is the amount of money he contributed to the partnership plus any property he contributed, the latter taken at the adjusted basis to the partner at the time of contribution. If the interest was acquired in a manner other than by contribution, the appropriate rule for basis of property could be applicable (for example, cost, fair market value at date of death, and so on).

However, a partner's cost for his interest, whether acquired by purchase or contribution, is only a starting point. Any additional contributions to capital or purchases of additional interests are included. Adjustments are necessary to give effect to the partnership's activities since the partner acquired his interest. The partner's basis for his interest is increased by his distributive share of the partnership's taxable income. Two other "plus" adjustments are required but they would not apply to most accounting partnerships—the basis is increased by the distributive share of tax-exempt income and by the distributive share of depletion deductions in excess of the basis of depletable property. (Ref. 32, page 526.) Since the adjustment is for a share of exempt income, nonrecognized gain would not be taken into account. Thus, if as a result of an involuntary conversion, a partnership had a gain and this gain was not recognized in whole or in part under sec. 1033, the portion of gain *not* recognized would not enter into the computation of a partner's basis for his interest.

After making all plus adjustments, the basis is reduced (but not below zero) by any distributions to a partner of money or property. In the case of a money distribution, the amount of reduction is the amount of the distribution. In the case of property, the reduction in basis is equal to the basis of such property to the partner. (Ref. 33, page 526.) As a rule, if the partner's interest is not being liquidated, the basis to him of distributed property is the same as its adjusted basis to the partnership, but this amount may not exceed the partner's basis for his interest after adjustment for any money received in the distribution. (Ref. 34, page 526.) Reductions are made for the distributive shares of partnership losses and nondeductible expenditures which are not capital in nature. (Ref. 35, page 526.)

Alternative rule. As can be seen, the computation of basis can be a difficult chore where the partnership has existed for a long period of time. An alternative method of computing basis is permitted where it is not practicable to compute basis as described above, or where it seems reasonable to assume that the alternative computation will not produce a result substantially different. Under the alternative rule, a partner's basis for his interest is his share of the adjusted basis of partnership property which would be distributable to him in the event the partnership terminates. (Ref. 36, page 526.)

Even where the alternative computation is made, further adjustments may be required under the Regulations. An adjustment may be required to eliminate a discrepancy which may arise out of a transfer of an interest. For example, suppose D buys for $12,500 a one-third interest in an accounting partnership whose assets have a basis of $22,500, but are worth $37,500. D's basis for his interest is his cost $12,500. However, his share of the partnership's basis is only $7,500. The Regulations provide that for purposes of the alternative rule, he has an adjustment of $5,000, which may be taken into account at the time D's basis is determined under the alternative rule. (Ref. 37, page 526.)

Liabilities as part of basis. It is important to realize that the Internal Revenue Code treats changes in certain liabilities of partners or the partnership as though partners contributed money to the partnership, or as though the partnership made a distribution of money. (Ref. 38, page 526.) If a partner should assume liabilities of the partnership, his assumption will be considered as a contribution of money and will increase the basis for his interest. On the other hand, if the partnership should assume liabilities of an individual partner, the assumption will be considered a distribution of money to the partner. As a partnership's liabilities increase, each partner who shares in the liabilities has an increase in his basis. As the partnership's liabilities decrease, the partners have a decrease in basis.

In general, a partner is considered to share in the liabilities in the same proportion as he shares in partnership losses. (Ref. 39, page 526.) Although for this purposes "liabilities" are not defined by the Code or Regulations, it is likely that the term includes all debts, whether or not the underlying expenditure is deductible and regardless of the partnership's method of accounting. The simplest way to determine whether there has been an increase or decrease in a partner's share of liabilities would be to compare liabilities as of the time the interest was acquired and as of the time it is necessary to ascertain the basis for the partner's interest.

OPTIONAL-BASIS ADJUSTMENTS

Other problems may arise with respect to basis. A partner who acquires an interest by purchase may find that the basis for his interest is high in contrast to his share of the partnership's basis for property. Thus, if depreciable property is owned, the new partner may be deprived of the benefit of deductions for the appreciation realized by his purchase. As the result of a distribution of partnership property, the partnership may find that a high-basis property distributed to a partner has a lower basis in the partner's hands, but the lost basis is not available to anyone. Adjustments are permitted to obtain use of this otherwise lost basis. The partnership may elect to adjust basis in a fashion similar to that described for the alternative rule of determining the basis of an interest.

If the partnership so elects, the basis of property remaining in the partnership after a distribution is adjusted upward by the amount of gain recognized to the distributee partner and by the amount of any decrease in the basis of property distributed as contrasted with the basis of that property to the partnership. A downward adjustment is required if the distributee has a recognized loss or if the basis of any distributed property is increased. (Ref. 40, page 526.) Although certain distributions are treated as sales or exchanges and result in gains or losses and changes in the basis of property, no adjustment is permitted for such distributions. (Ref. 41, page 526.)

The partnership makes the election and the same election applies not only to adjustments arising out of a distribution but also to those arising out of the transfer of an interest. However, the adjustment in this latter instance is only for the benefit of the partner who acquired the interest. An upward adjustment in basis of partnership property is made where the partner's basis for his interest exceeds his proportionate share of the basis of partnership assets. A downward adjustment is made where the basis of the assets exceeds the basis for his interest. (Ref. 42, page 526.)

The Regulations permit a partnership to revoke an election for good business reasons but not to avoid making an undesired adjustment. (Ref. 43, page 526.) Thus, an election made at a time when upward adjustments to basis would be permitted may require downward adjustments at a later date. The double effect of an election requires that one consider very carefully the significance of the benefit sought in the light of possible future effects.

Where an adjustment is available, it must be applied to eliminate differences between the fair market value and the basis of partnership assets, including goodwill. (Ref. 44, page 526.) Thus, if an upward adjustment is permitted, it is allocated only to assets whose values exceed their basis. If a downward adjustment is to be made, it is allocated only to assets whose values are less than basis, but, in this case, an adjustment may not reduce basis below zero. Permission can be obtained from the district director to make both upward and downward adjustments, which as a net equal the adjustment permitted upon a satisfactory showing of the values used in setting a price for transfer of an interest, or valuation for estate tax, or the distribution. (Ref. 45, page 526.) It is possible that such permission would not be given in advance. However, the adjustments could be made as considered appropriate and approval obtained at the time the question is raised upon an examination of the return.

The adjustment must be allocated to assets similar in character to those which give rise to the adjustment. If there are no such assets (as might happen in the event of a distribution), or where a downward adjustment would decrease the basis below zero, the unusable part of the adjustment is held in abeyance until additional property of appropriate character is acquired. (Ref. 46, page 526.)

CONTRIBUTIONS TO A PARTNERSHIP

Every partnership requires capital in order to carry on operations. In the case of an accounting partnership, the capital may be represented originally by furniture, fixtures, and funds needed to pay operating expenses. The source of capital would be contributions from the individual partners. Money and property are the most likely contributions to capital. Thus, one partner may contribute a furnished office and library in exchange for his capital interest. Another will contribute cash.

Where the contribution is in the form of money, which is usually the case, there are no tax problems. The partner's capital account can be credited with his contribution and the partner's basis for his interest is the amount of money which he contributed.

Contribution of property. A contribution of property may present problems where the contributed property is appreciated or depreciated. In a service organization, such as an accounting partnership, the problems are not serious since the relative lack of importance of property makes the partners less inclined to take advantage of special provisions in the law relating to allocation of gain, loss, or other deductions attributable to the contributed property. (Ref. 47, page 526.) However, it may be considered desirable to provide for an allocation of partnership income which will tend to eliminate variations between the basis and value of contributed property. For example, Mr. *A* contributes for his one-fourth interest in the partnership a furnished office, his library, and his present practice. His basis for the contributed property is $2,000 but his capital account is credited with $16,000, the value of the property he contributed. The library was valued at $1,000, the goodwill attributable to the contributed practice at $12,000, and the office at $3,000.

A's basis for the contributed property will be the basis for his interest and his basis for the contributed property is carried over by the partnership. (Ref. 48, page 526.) More than likely, the entire basis will be attributable to the office furnishings. The cost of the library was probably charged to expense as incurred and the library would have a zero basis. As for the practice, unless some of it was acquired by purchase, it would have a zero basis. If the partners wish, they may provide in their agreement that the depreciation deductions will be allocated to offset the effect of the difference between value and basis of the office furniture. Thus, Mr. *A* has acquired a one-fourth interest. His partners have, in effect, a three-fourths interest in the property contributed by *A*, including the depreciable property valued at $3,000. Assuming a remaining estimated useful life of five years, this would entitle Mr. *A*'s partners to the benefit of depreciation deductions in the total amount of $450 (omitting salvage from our discussion for purposes of simplicity). However, the basis of the property is only $2,000 and only $400 in depreciation would be allowable each year. Therefore, the entire $400 in depreciation is allocated to *A*'s partners.

Similar provision may be made in the agreement as to the treatment of gain or loss which may arise with respect to contributed property. The special allocations provided would be for the purpose of eliminating the difference between basis and value.

For most professional accounting partnerships, this question of contributed property is not important. If the partners prefer, they may omit all mention of such special allocation in the agreement, and the allocation of deductions or gains attributable to contributed property will be in the same manner as though the property had been purchased.

Alternatives to contributing property. Before contributing property to a partnership, it may be advisable to consider possible alternatives. For example, instead of contributing property, such as office equipment, perhaps it can be sold to the partnership. If the property has appreciated in value, the selling partner would have a taxable gain, possibly a long-term capital gain. (Ref. 49, page 526.) If he contributes the proceeds, even if only the net proceeds, he may have a higher basis for his partnership interest. In addition, the partnership would have a higher basis for the property and would obtain increased depreciation deductions.

For example, if Mr. A referred to above had sold the property to the partnership for $3,000, he would have a gain of $1,000. After contributing the net proceeds to the partnership, the basis for his interest would be $2,750 (assuming the alternative tax applied), as contrasted with $2,000 if he contributed the property. The partnership would be entitled to $600 in annual depreciation and each partner would be entitled to $150 in depreciation as contrasted with the result under a contribution of the property—no deduction for Mr. A and $133 for each of the other partners.

The contributing partner could lease the office equipment to the partnership. If this is done, the partnership would deduct the rentals paid. The partner who owned the property would offset his rental income with depreciation deductions and his share of the rental expense of the partnership. For example, if Mr. A leased his office equipment with a basis of $2,000 instead of contributing it to the partnership, and rent of $600 per year were agreed upon, Mr. A's income would be increased $50. (Rent income of $600 less annual depreciation of $400, based on a five-year life, and less A's $150 share of partnership rent expense.) However, the other partners get a total rent deduction which is equal to the depreciation they would be entitled to on the value of the rented property.

Obviously, the decision to sell, lease, or contribute cannot be made unilaterally by Mr. A. The wishes of his associates must be considered, particularly since the alternatives to contribution involve cash outlays. Also, it may be necessary to consider the effect of provisions governing the treatment of sales or exchanges between persons and partnerships. (See page 504.)

ACCOUNTING PERIOD

Partnerships are limited in the selection of an accounting period. A partnership may not change to or adopt a taxable year, which differs from that of all its principal partners unless it can establish a business reason for so doing. A principal partner is one who has an interest of at least 5 per cent in the profits or capital of a partnership. Under this definition there will not be many accounting partnerships where the diversification of ownership is so great that the limitations will not apply because no partner owns at least 5 per cent of profits or capital. Similar restrictions are applied to a principal partner. Unless permission is received, he may not change to a taxable year other than that of a partnership in which he is a principal partner. (Ref. 50, page 526.)

In most instances, the effect of these provisions is that a newly formed partnership must adopt the calendar year as the taxable year. However, most accounting firms (if not all) operate at a peak level during the period from

December to April completing audits, preparing various reports including tax returns, and reviewing results of operations with clients. The activity during this period makes it quite difficult for partners in an accounting firm to devote adequate attention to their own problems as a partnership. A year ending some time between May and November is more practical for most accounting firms. The particular circumstances of a firm's practice will be of considerable importance in selecting an appropriate taxable year.

Adopting an accounting period. There are several alternatives open to a newly formed accounting partnership. The partnership may adopt without permission a taxable year which is the same as the year of its principal partners. Thus, if all partners have been filing individual returns on a calendar-year basis, the partnership would adopt the calendar year. If the partners had been filing individual returns on the same fiscal year, the partnership would adopt the fiscal year. If the partners are reporting on different years, the partnership may adopt the calendar year. (Ref. 51, page 526.)

At the time the partnership is formed, the principal partners could obtain permission to change their individual accounting periods to a particular fiscal year. The partnership can then adopt without permission the same period as that to which the partners are changing. (Ref. 52, page 526.) The prospective partners would submit their request for permission to change their individual accounting periods by filing Form 1128 with the Commissioner of Internal Revenue on or before the last day of the month following the close of the short period for which a return would be required to effect the new accounting period. (Ref. 53, page 526.) For example, if the prospective partners have been filing returns on a calendar year and would like the partnership to adopt for convenience a fiscal year ending June 30, the partners should file Form 1128 not later than July 31.

The partners-to-be must present a substantial business purpose for the change. It would seem that the desire of the partnership to use a more convenient reporting period would be a substantial business purpose. The partners' spouses should file requests for permission to change. If this is not done, a partner and his spouse would have different taxable years and would lose the advantage of income-splitting by filing joint returns.

A factor to be considered is the cost to the partners of changing their individual accounting periods. Where a taxpayer changes his accounting period, it is necessary to file a return and pay tax on his annualized income for the period beginning with the day after the close of the old taxable year and ending with the day before the start of the new year. If the early months of the partners' old taxable years have been very profitable, the tax cost of the change might be substantial in contrast to the benefits to be derived from the partnership's ability to use a fiscal year.

The partnership may adopt a different taxable year than its principal partners if a substantial business purpose can be shown. The Regulations offer as a specific example of sufficient business purpose the desire to change to a natural business year. (Ref. 54, page 526.) For this purpose, the IRS has held that the taxable year should end at, or soon after, the close of the peak period of business. (Ref. 55, page 526.)

In the case of most accounting partnerships, the calendar year is an unnatural business year. Under the circumstances, perhaps the accounting partnership could request permission to adopt a taxable year different from that of its principal partners. However, if all the partners are able to make a concurrent change, the IRS probably will prefer that this change be made if possible.

It is possible that the partners may not be able to change to the proposed fiscal year. Some of the partners may have an interest in other partnerships already reporting on a different fiscal year. For example, *A, B, C,* and *D* are forming a partnership to engage in the practice of public accounting. All have been filing individual returns on a calendar year. *A* is a principal partner with members of his family in the ownership and operation of several office buildings, and that partnership has been using a fiscal year ending August 31. *B* is a principal partner of a partnership which offers a CPA coaching course and reports its income on a year ending May 31. The *ABCD* partnership would like to use a June 30 year. It would be difficult for *A* and *B* to obtain permission to change to a June 30 year because they are partners in other partnerships reporting on a year other than June 30. Under the circumstances, it would seem that permission could be received for the partnership to adopt a June 30 year, even though the partners will report on a calendar year.

Change of accounting period. The problems encountered in a change of accounting period are similar to those in adoption of an accounting period. If the partners are willing to change their accounting periods, then the partnership may do likewise. (Ref. 56, page 526.) Under appropriate circumstances this may not be required if impractical. But even where the year sought is a natural business year, it appears that unless other conditions are present (such as interests in other partnerships), the IRS prefers that the partners make conforming changes. It is interesting to note that this will not affect future partners. Thus, *A, B,* and *C* may change their reporting period to permit the *ABC* partnership to adopt or change to a June 30 year. Sometime later when *D* becomes a member of the partnership, it does not seem that he will be required to change his accounting period.

WHEN A PARTNER IS NOT A PARTNER

Gains and losses in transactions between partners and partnerships. It was suggested earlier that a partner might prefer to sell rather than contribute property to a partnership. In general, such transactions are viewed as taking place between the partnership and an outsider, that is, one who is not a partner. This general rule is subject to a few exceptions. If the transaction takes place between the partnership and a partner who owns directly or indirectly more than a 50 per cent interest in capital or profits, any loss which may be realized will not be recognized. This is also true if the transaction is between two partnerships in which the same persons own directly or indirectly more than a 50 per cent interest in the capital or profits. (Ref. 57, page 526.)

In determining the percentage of ownership, an individual is considered to own constructively interests owned by his brothers, sisters, wife, ancestors, and lineal descendants. (Ref. 58, page 527.) For example, assume that three brothers, *A, B,* and *C,* form an accounting partnership with equal interests. *A* wishes to sell to the partnership, at a loss, an office building which he owns. The partnership expects to use the building as its offices. Regardless of the fairness of the price, *A*'s loss will not be recognized. Although he actually owns only a one-third interest in the partnership, he constructively owns 100 per cent of the partnership. However, if the partnership subsequently sells the building at a gain, the amount of gain to be recognized is reduced by the disallowed loss. (Ref. 59, page 527.)

If the transaction is between a partnership and a partner who owns directly or indirectly more than 80 per cent in capital or profits, or between two partnerships in which the same persons own directly or indirectly more than an 80 per cent interest in capital or profits, and the property transferred is not in the hands of the transferee a capital asset, any gain realized will be ordinary income. (Ref. 60, page 527.) Assume that the building in the above example is sold to the partnership at a gain. It had been used by *A* in his accounting practice and, although the land and building would not be capital assets, *A*'s gain could be treated as gain from the sale or exchange of a capital asset. (Ref. 61, page 527.) However, the land and building will not be capital assets of the partnership. The seller constructively owns more than an 80 per cent interest in capital or profits of the partnership and the gain is ordinary income.

Other aspects of constructive ownership. Rules of constructive ownership may attribute ownership of an interest to one who is not a partner, for example, a spouse. The provisions for nonrecognition of loss and ordinary income treatment gains are applicable only to transactions between a partnership and a partner. By definition, a partner must be a member of the partnership. (Ref. 62, page 527.) Therefore, if a transaction is between a partnership and an individual who has no direct interest, these special provisions would not apply. Thus, if Mrs. *A* owned the building in the above example, there would be no problem with respect to reporting a gain as capital gain. As to a loss, a portion thereof would be disallowed as incurred in a transaction between husband and wife. (Ref. 63, page 527.)

The rules can make a partner constructive owner of an interest attributed to an outsider. However, such reattribution applies only where the interest is owned constructively by a corporation, partnership, estate, or trust. Reattribution in the case of family relationships is not permitted. (Ref. 64, page 527.) Thus, if *A* and *B* are equal partners and *A*'s wife is *B*'s sister, neither *A* nor *B* would be held to own constructively the other's interest by virtue of the interests attributed to Mrs. *A.* But, if *A* should die and the partnership agreement provided for the estate to continue as a partner, *A*'s interest would be attributed to Mrs. *A* by virtue of her interest in the estate. That interest in turn would be attributed to her brother *B,* giving him a 100 per cent interest for purposes of these rules.

TERMINATIONS, CONTINUATIONS, MERGERS, DIVISIONS

Under the Uniform Partnership Act, a partnership may be in dissolution for any of a number of reasons: the partnership may be for a specified term and the term has ended; an event may occur which makes it illegal to carry on as a partnership; and so on. For purposes of the Act, a partnership in dissolution has not terminated until its affairs are wound up, that is, until obligations of the partnership are discharged and the remaining assets are distributed. (Ref. 65, page 527.)

Effects of terminations. The Internal Revenue Code makes no distinction as to dissolution or termination and whether or not a partnership has terminated for federal income-tax purposes is not governed by state or local law. (Ref. 66, page 527.) When a partnership terminates for federal income-tax purposes, a return will be required for the taxable year ending on the date of termination. It is presumed that assets were distributed to the partners as of the date of termination, subject to liabilities. Thus, in addition to distributive shares of income or loss for the period ending on the termination date, the individual partners may have recognizable gain or loss on the distribution. (Ref. 67, page 527.) Any successor partnership will be considered a new partnership. If the terminated partnership was on a fiscal year, a successor partnership would have to obtain permission to use the same accounting period. If such permission is not obtained, the close of the taxable year by virtue of a termination would result in the bunching into one year of the partners' shares of income for the fiscal year plus shares from the partnership for that portion of the calendar year the successor was in existence. In addition, the successor partnership will have to make new elections with regard to such matters as depreciation and accounting methods.

Termination under the Internal Revenue Code. As long as the partnership continues business activities as a partnership, it will be considered as continuing in existence. (Ref. 68, page 527.) There is one exception to this general rule, which is discussed below, but death, retirement, or expulsion of a partner, and admission of new partners will not as a rule terminate an existing partnership. When one member of a two-man partnership retires or dies, there is no longer a partnership, but the Regulations provide that the partnership will be presumed to continue as long as payments are made to the retiring partner, estate, or successor in interest of a deceased partner. (Ref. 69, page 527.) When a partnership terminates because of this general rule, the date of termination is postponed until the partnership affairs are wound up. (Ref. 70, page 527.) Presumably, this would be decided under local law.

Sales or exchanges during a twelve-month period. The exception to the general rule is that the partnership is terminated for income-tax purposes if during any twelve-month period there are sales or exchanges of 50 per cent or more of the total interests in capital and 50 per cent or more of the total interests in profits. (Ref. 71, page 527.) Note that the total sales or exchanges must be of both capital and profit interests. Sales or exchanges among the partners are included. Assume that A and B have been partners and A owns 80 per cent of capital and profits. Three valuable employees, D, E, and F are to be made partners, and it is agreed that this will be accomplished by A selling to each a 15 per cent interest. In addition, A sells to B a 5 per cent interest. The total interests sold are 50 per cent and the partnership is terminated.

Gifts of a partnership interest are not counted for this purpose. Liquidation of an interest is not a sale or exchange. The contribution of property to a partnership in exchange for an interest does not constitute a sale or exchange of an interest even though the interest as acquired results in a reduction of other partners' interests. (Ref. 72, page 527.) Thus, if A and B are equal partners and during a twelve-month period C and D acquire by contribution total interests of 50 per cent in capital and profits with a reduction of the interests of A and B, the partnership does not terminate.

Suppose that immediately after C's contribution, A received a distribution approximately equal to the money or property contributed. This could be considered a step transaction. The intermediate contribution and distribution would be ignored and the transaction treated as a sale or exchange. (Ref. 73, page 527.) This could be so even if the distribution is in complete liquidation of a partner's interest. How long should A wait to avoid this result? This is not clear. The Regulations look at distributions before and after the contribution of property. If possible, care should be taken to avoid any situation which could raise a question because of the proximity in time of the contribution and subsequent distribution.

Successive sales of the same interest or part of the same interest are not counted more than once. Thus, if A sells a 30 per cent interest to D, and D subsequently (within the twelve months) sells his interests to E, the partnership does not terminate since only a 30 per cent interest was sold. (Ref. 74, page 527.)

The twelve-month period is not the partnership's taxable year, but rather any period of twelve consecutive months. The period can begin on any day of the month, and it is necessary to add sales made at different times during the year. Thus, a sale by A of a 30 per cent interest to D on May 12, 1959, and a sale by B of a 30 per cent interest to E on March 27, 1960, results in a termination of the partnership on March 27.

When a partnership terminates because of sales or exchanges, the termination is as of the date of the last sale or exchange which resulted in the transfer of 50 per cent or more in capital and profits interests. (Ref. 75, page 527.) As of that date, it is presumed that all assets of the partnership were distributed to the partners and immediately thereafter the assets were contributed to a new successor partnership. (Ref. 76, page 527.)

It is possible that a partnership will terminate inadvertently as a result of transfer of interests, resulting in possible bunching of income and loss of a fiscal year. On the other hand, termination may be advantageous. Termination would require that the new partnership adopt an accounting method and could thus facilitate a change in accounting method. It is possible that the bunching of income upon termination will be desirable since the partners may have unusually large nonbusiness deductions. In any event, the possibility of termination and its consequences should not be overlooked at any time that the partners contemplate sale or exchange of all or part of their interests.

Mergers and divisions. A fairly common occurrence is the merger of accounting partnerships to form a larger partnership or the division of a partnership into two or more smaller partnerships. In planning such mergers or divisions, possible tax consequences should be considered.

In the event of a merger of two or more partnerships, the resulting partnership is a continuation of the component firm whose partners own interests of more than 50 per cent in the capital and profits of the resulting partnership. The other partnerships are terminated. If no partnership qualifies, then all the merging partnerships are terminated. Termination in this case is as of the date of consolidation. The terminated partnerships file returns for the taxable year ending on the date of consolidation. The continuing partnership files its returns for the year of the continued partnership, showing therein that it is the result of a merger as of a particular date. (Ref. 77, page 527.)

When a partnership divides into more than one partnership, any resulting partnership whose members owned more than 50 per cent of capital and profits of the original partnership, is a continuation of that partnership. If none of the resulting partnerships qualify, the original partnership is terminated. Those partners who become members of a new partnership are considered to have received a liquidating distribution of their interests as of the day of the division and to have contributed the proceeds to the new partnership. The new partnership must adopt a taxable year, an accounting method, and make any other elections necessary. The continuing partnership, if any, will file for the taxable year of the original partnership, indicating therein that it is a continuation of a former partnership. (Ref. 78, page 527.)

These rules for federal income-tax purposes do not affect in any way the privileges and duties of a partnership and its partners under state or local law. Thus, a partnership which is continued for federal income-tax purposes may have terminated for state-tax purposes and other requirements such as registration with state-accounting boards. Care should be taken that unnecessary penalties are not incurred under state and local law for failure to recognize that a partnership which has continued under the Internal Revenue Code has terminated under state law. (Ref. 79, page 527.)

SALE OF INTEREST

Generally, an interest in a partnership is considered a capital asset. Gain or loss arising from the sale or exchange of an interest or part of an interest will be recognized as capital gain or loss. This general rule is subject to an exception of great importance to accounting partnerships using the cash receipts and disbursements method for reporting income. Without regard to whether or not there is an over-all gain on the transfer of the interest, if there is gain attributable to unrealized receivables,[9] that gain is considered ordinary income. (Ref. 80, page 527.)

Gain attributable to unrealized receivables. Unrealized receivables are, among other things, rights to payment for services rendered or to be rendered where the amounts have not been includible in income because of the method of accounting. (Ref. 81, page 527.) In a partnership reporting income on the cash basis, all uncollected fees, whether or not billed, would be unrealized receivables. Work in process would also be considered unrealized receivables.

When a partner sells all or part of his partnership interests, he computes gain or loss attributable to the unrealized receivables separately from that attributable to the rest of his interest. The sale price, as allocated by the parties in an arm's-length transaction, will be regarded as correct. (Ref. 82, page 527.) The basis for the partner's share of unrealized receivables is ascertained as though his share had been distributed to him before the sale. As a rule, this will be the same as the basis of the receivables to the partnership. (Ref. 83, page 527.)

If the partnership is on the cash basis, the basis of its accounts receivables is usually zero. However, this need not be the case. For example, if a portion of the partnership's unrealized receivables had been acquired by purchase, a partner selling his interest would have some basis for his share of unrealized receivables. If the selling partner had acquired his interest in the partnership by purchase and the election for optional basis adjustment is in effect (see page 499), the selling partner would have a basis adjustment for his interest in accounts receivables. Even if the election is not in effect, under certain conditions the adjustment is permitted. (Ref. 84, page 527.)

Thus, the sale or exchange of a partnership interest is split into two transactions: one for the sale of an interest in unrealized receivables and one for the sale of an interest in other assets. If there are unrealized receivables, the selling partner will have ordinary income in virtually all instances. As to the other part of the transaction, he may have no gain or loss; he may have capital gain; he may even have capital loss. Under no circumstances will the results of the two transactions be offset against each other. Thus, a partner may have a net loss on the sale but have to report ordinary income and a capital loss.

Information required on the return. The selling partner must set forth in his return certain information with respect to the unrealized receivables. The sale of the interest is shown in its two parts: a sale of unrealized receivables and a sale of the balance of his interest. If any special basis adjustment is claimed, the computation of the adjustment and the method of allocation should be explained. (Ref. 85, page 527.)

Goodwill. Payments for goodwill represent a capital expenditure and are not deductible. Under the circumstances, it is doubtful whether many taxpayers

---

[9]Certain items of inventory may be held by a partnership which would require separate computation of gain as ordinary income. Since this is not applicable to an accounting partnership, this discussion does not include that aspect of the problem.

would want to pay for goodwill when acquiring an accounting practice or an interest in an accounting partnership. The seller, of course, prefers to sell goodwill as the gain thereon is capital gain.

The Tax Court has held in *Horton* and *Myler* (Refs. 86 and 87, page 527) that there is transferable goodwill in an accounting practice. These cases arose from the sale of individual practices, as distinguished from the sale of a partnership interest. In *Horton* the taxpayer transferred rights to the exclusive use of the firm name and the agreement of sale included a covenant not to compete. The government sought to tax as ordinary income amounts reported as paid for goodwill on the ground that the payment was for the covenant. The Tax Court held that the sale of goodwill and the covenant were separable. The court noted that the contract of sale provided specifically for the sale of goodwill as an asset of the seller and concluded that both parties to the agreement recognized the existence of goodwill as an asset.

In *Wyler*, the contract provided for a transfer of the taxpayer's practice, sale of his business assets, the entry of the taxpayer as a partner in the buying partnership, and a payment of $50,000 for goodwill. The contract provided for the manner of compensating the taxpayer for his services as partner. The taxpayer agreed not to solicit or perform accounting services for the clients of the buyer for three years after the agreement terminated. One clause of the agreement stated that the contract was for personal services. The taxpayer reported the $50,000 as gain from the sale of a capital asset. The IRS sought to treat the payment as ordinary income, alleging that it was for personal services. Based on oral testimony and written memoranda of discussions prior to the contract, the Tax Court found that there was a sale of goodwill. The court found that although the contract was for personal services, the compensation for such services was set forth in other provisions. The IRS argued that the goodwill of a professional man is not salable. The court disagreed, citing, among others, *Horton*.

In determining whether goodwill is to be considered an asset of a partnership, *Estate of Masquelette* (Ref. 88, page 527) is of interest. In that case, the taxpayer and his partner sold their interests in a branch office partnership to the resident partners of the latter firm. The contract of sale provided for a covenant against competition from the taxpayer and specifically prohibited the buyers from using the firm name. The taxpayer reported the amounts received over and above his equity as capital gain from the sale of intangible assets including goodwill. The IRS took the position that the covenant against competition was separable from the rest of the sale and sought to allocate part of the price to the covenant as ordinary income. Although the contract did not provide expressly for the sale of goodwill, the court found that this was not necessary since the agreement was to sell all assets of the branch office. The prohibition against use of the firm name was considered reasonable and intended only to protect the taxpayer from possible embarrassment. Although the price might have been higher if the use of the name were included, the failure to transfer such right did not prevent the transfer of goodwill. In any event, the seller was limited in use of the firm name in the area because of the covenant against competition. The court found that the covenant was a nonseverable part of the conveyance of goodwill and, accordingly, upheld the taxpayer.

The IRS has announced that it will follow the decision in *Masquelette,* but "only to the extent that it stands for the proposition that the existence of transferable goodwill may be recognized in connection with the sale of a business or a profession, the success of which is *not* dependent solely upon the personal qualifications of the owner, even though such a sale does not involve the assignment of the right to the exclusive use of the firm name." (Ref. 89, page 527.)

This statement with respect to *Masquelette* was issued as a clarification of the goodwill question as discussed in Rev. Rul. 57-480 (Ref. 90, page 527), which held that a following based on acquaintanceship does not constitute goodwill and that there is no transferable goodwill in the case of a sale of the business of a professional man where the success of the business depends solely upon the professional skill, ability, integrity, and other personal characteristics of the owner, and there is no valid assignment of the exclusive right to the firm name. Thus, it would seem that the IRS would not be impressed by an allocation of the purchase price to goodwill, represented by the selling partner.

If a partnership interest is sold, it would seem that there could be some goodwill. However, if the selling partner's name was part of the firm name and is to be removed from the firm name after the sale, it is possible that the existence of goodwill would be challenged since the IRS takes the view that if the success of the firm is attributable to the professional skill of its owner, no goodwill is sold unless the sale includes a right to the exclusive use of the firm name.

What if only part of an interest is sold? According to Rev. Rul. 57-480, if the sale "purports to assign a right to use the firm name," nothing will be realized from the sale of goodwill if the seller's name is in the firm name and he continues as a member of the firm.

If it is found that there was no goodwill, that part of the price allocated to goodwill will be assigned to other assets sold. If assigned to unrealized receivables, there may be a substantial effect. If assigned to other assets of the partnership, the gain on the sale will not be affected since the interest sold is treated as a unit, except for the fragmentation attributable to unrealized receivables. If the agreement provides for a covenant not to compete, it is likely that the amounts paid for so-called goodwill will be added to the payment for the covenant and taxed as ordinary income.

CLOSING THE TAXABLE YEAR—SALES, EXCHANGES, LIQUIDATIONS

Under certain circumstances, the taxable year of a partnership may close prior to the normal year-end date. For example, the termination of a partnership results in a closing of the partnership year and requires that a partnership return be filed. This is a closing of the year as to all partners. It is possible for the partnership year to close only to one of the partners. When a partner sells his interest or his interest is liquidated (and the partnership is not terminated because of such transactions), the taxable year of the partnership closes as to him. (Ref. 91, page 527.) The partnership does not file a return but the partner includes in taxable income for the year in which his membership ended (and as a result of which the partnership year closed as to him) his distributive share of the items of partnership income for the period which ended with the sale, exchange, or liquidation of his interest.

Bunching of income. If a selling partner files his tax returns on a different taxable year from the partnership, and the sale is at any time other than the end of the partnership year, there may be a bunching of income in the partner's return. For example, assume that the *EFG* partnership determines its income on a taxable year ending June 30. *E,* who files his return on a calendar year, sells his interest in the partnership as of December 31, 1959. *E*'s return for 1959 will include his distributive share of partnership income for the year ended June 30, 1959, and his distributive share of income for the period July 1 to December 31, 1959, or a total of eighteen months' income. By changes in the dates, the total income to be reported may vary from thirteen to twenty-three months.

The Regulations make it clear that it is not necessary to have an interim closing of the partnership's books in order to determine his distributive share for the period ending with the termination of his interest. (Ref. 92, page 527.) (This is quite helpful but if an accounting firm has a large practice and a substantial amount of work in process, an interim closing may be preferred.) By agreement among the partners, there may be allocated to the former partner a pro-rata portion of the partnership's income for the full partnership year. Any reasonable method of proration is permitted. It may be based on the period of time before and after the termination of the partner's interest, or it may be more equitable to apportion the income on the basis of chargeable time before and after the partner terminated his interest.

Assume the *ABCD* partnership is engaged in the practice of public accounting. The firm uses the calendar year as its taxable year. The busiest time is from January 1 to June 30, and the chargeable time during that period averages two-thirds of the total hours during the year. *D* sells his one-fourth interest to the other partners as of June 30, 1960. The partners could agree that two-thirds of the partnership's income for 1960 was earned during the first six months. *D* would report as income from the *ABCD* partnership one-sixth (one-fourth of two-thirds) of the partnership income for 1960. On the other hand, the partners could agree that regardless of the distribution of chargeable hours, the year's income is earned in equal amounts each month because expenses of the slower period are required if the firm is to offer the increased service in the earlier months, and that such expenses should not be charged to the slow period only. If so, *D* would report for 1960 one-eighth (one-fourth of one-half) of the partnership's income for 1960.

Distributive shares in the year of sale. Since an interim closing of partnership books is not required, information required by a selling partner to prepare his personal return for the year of sale may not be available until some time after the return is due. For example, assume that on December 31, 1960 an interest is sold in a partnership filing its returns on a June 30 year. The selling partner has been reporting on a calendar year.

In his 1960 return, due on April 15, 1961, the partner is required to report a distributive share of income for the partnership period July 1 to December 31, 1960. His share for that period also is taken into account in determining the basis for his interest and the possible gain or loss arising out of the sale, exchange, or liquidation. (Ref. 93, page 527.) However, information as to his distributive share may not be available until October 15, 1961 when the partnership return is due. If the partnership has obtained an extension of time for filing its return, the information will be available at an even later date.

The Regulations offer no solution to this problem. The partner could estimate his distributive share but this would require the filing of an amended return when correct figures are available. It may be preferable for him to request an extension of time for filing this return. Another alternative, and possibly the simplest, would be for the partners to agree upon an arbitrary determination of the partner's distributive share for the period ended December 31, 1960. In view of the flexibility allowed in amending the partnership agreement, this should be acceptable.

The above discussion does not apply to a sale, exchange, or liquidation of less than the entire interest. Under such circumstances, the partnership year does not close, but appropriate adjustments are reflected in the distributive shares of partners who disposed of less than their entire interest. For example, assume that A, B, and C are partners owning interests of 20, 20, and 60 per cent, respectively. C sells one-third of his interest to D at a time of the year at which the partners agree that one-half of the partnership's income for the current year has been earned. C's distributive share for the year would be 50 per cent (60 per cent for one-half year or 30 per cent, plus 40 per cent for one-half year or 20 per cent). D would report 10 per cent (20 per cent for one-half year).

CLOSING THE TAXABLE YEAR—DEATH OF A PARTNER

When a partner's interest is terminated as a result of death and if the partnership does not terminate, the taxable year of the partnership continues as to all partners, including the deceased partner until the end of the partnership's taxable year. The final return of the decedent partner will include only his distributive share for the partnership year ending with his death. In this manner, the bunching problem is avoided. The distributive share for the later period is reported by the estate or other successor in interest. (Ref. 94, page 527.) If the decedent's interest is sold, exchanged, or liquidated by the estate, the taxable year of the partnership would close as to the estate with the same consequences as described on pages 508 and 511. (Ref. 95, page 527.)

The Regulations provide an exception to the general rule that death of a partner will not close the taxable year of the partnership as to the deceased partner. If under the terms of an agreement existing at the date of death, a sale or exchange of the decedent partner's interest takes place as of the date of death, then the partnership year closes as to the decedent as of the date of death. This does not occur if the transfer as of the date of death is by virtue of inheritance or some other testamentary disposition. (Ref. 96, page 527.) Thus, if the partnership agreement provided that as of the date of death, any partner's interest would be considered sold to the remaining partners as of that date, the partnership year would close as to the decedent on the date of death. His final return would include his distributive share for the period of the partnership ending on the date of death as well as his distributive share for any other partnership year which ended in his final taxable year.

Without an agreement as described above, a deceased partner's final return will not include any distributive share of partnership income for the period ending with the date of death. If the partner and partnership are on the same taxable year, no distributive shares will be reported on the final return. Although at first glance this may appear desirable, there are situations when this results in a greater tax. This also may be true when the partner and partnership use different years, and the final return, except for this provision, would include twenty-three months of income. For example, if the income were reported on the decedent's final return, the income tax might be less because of income-splitting than would be paid if the distributive share were included in the first return of the estate. Another possibility is that the decedent may have incurred substantial deductions prior to death which would offset the distributive income for the period ending with death.

Increasing the income in the final return can be accomplished by an agreement as described above that the deceased partner's interest will be considered sold as of the day of death. This would close the taxable year with respect to such partner, but this approach presents some disadvantages. There must be an existing agreement at the date of death to sell or exchange the interest, but it cannot be known in advance whether it will be advantageous to close the partnership year. It would seem that the agreement should be with the surviving partners, since any payments from the partnership would be in liquidation of an interest and would close the taxable year as to the estate. Thus the partners would have to provide for the funds necessary to acquire each other's interests.

As an alternative, the partnership agreement can provide that partners may designate a successor in interest in the event of death. If a partner in accordance with this agreement designates his wife, no income is reported by the estate and, under the Regulations, the distributive share of income for the partnership year ending with or within her year may be included in a joint return with the deceased partner. (Ref. 97, page 527.) On the other hand, the final return, if filed separately, would include no distributive share. Another advantage is the possibility that the spouse may qualify as a "surviving spouse" and be permitted income-splitting benefits for two more years. The designation of a spouse as a successor may not be practicable in a CPA partnership. If the spouse is not a CPA, designation as a partner would present ethical or legal problems of continuing activities as a partnership of CPAs.

Steps may be taken in the administration of the estate to reduce the income-tax effect of the nonbunching of partnership income in the final return. If the estate has income, an election should be considered to deduct administrative expenses for income-tax purposes rather than for estate-tax purposes. (Ref. 98, page 527.) If the executor is authorized to make distributions, such distributions when made are allowable as deductions on the estate's income-tax return. A distribution to the spouse will transfer income from the estate to the spouse and, in fact, can permit considerable flexibility depending upon the amount of the distribution. The spouse would report distribution for the estate's year ending in or with her year. (Ref. 99, page 527). Care should be taken to insure that a taxable year is selected for the estate which will permit inclusion of any earlier distributions in the spouse's return for the year of death. If a joint return is filed with the estate, this will permit use of any otherwise unusable deductions of the decedent.

In making such distributions, it should be remembered that even distributions of principal are distributions of income unless the distribution is in satisfaction of a gift, a bequest of a specific sum or of specific property, and paid in not more than three installments. (Ref. 100, page 527.) Thus, the transfer of a home to the surviving spouse could result in the transfer of income.

PLANNING FOR RETIREMENT OR DEATH

The partnership form of business operation is at a distinct disadvantage in planning for retirement or death of partners as contrasted with the corporate form of organization. The lower income-tax rates generally applicable to a corporation permit a more rapid build-up of an estate. The corporation can adopt a greater range of fringe benefits for all its employees, including officer-stockholders, and deduct the cost. Medical insurance, stock options, group life insurance, and other benefits may be the subject of plans the cost of which is deductible. The partnership can adopt similar plans, but cannot deduct any portion of the cost attributable to benefits for its partners since they are not employees.

Legal and ethical requirements make it impossible to practice public accounting in a corporation (Ref. 101, page 527), but even if the partnership is less attractive as a planning vehicle than the corporation, there are a number of advantages to the partnership as contrasted with the individual proprietor. With a partnership, it is possible to agree on the criteria to be employed later in setting a price for an interest in the event of death or retirement. Partnership agreements can and frequently do provide for an orderly method of paying for the interest of a retired or deceased partner. Surviving partners provide a possible market for each partner's interest. The individual practitioner often cannot make arrangements as conveniently until the time for retirement and his executor can act only after death.

These are nontax factors. In addition, the Internal Revenue Code permits substantial flexibility in planning the tax effect of payments to be made by a partnership to retiring partners or the estate of a deceased partner. Depending upon the partners' planning, payments over and above a partners' capital interest may be deductible by the partners and ordinary income to the recipient, or nondeductible by the partners and capital gain to the recipient. Alternatively, the partners may provide for the sale of an interest to the remaining or surviving partners (see page 508). In the case of a deceased partner (see page 513), it is possible to keep open or close the partnership year as to the deceased partner, thereby preventing or permitting bunching in the partner's final return.

Valuation of an interest. A partnership interest is a valuable asset. The partnership agreement should provide a method for the valuation of an interest to be used as a basis in making payments to a retired partner or partner's estate in the event of death. Typically, an agreement could provide that a partner's interest consists of a number of things, each of which contributes to the value of the interest. The partner's capital account or the book value of his interest would be a starting point. If the partnership owns substantial tangible assets or has investments, it may be desirable to adjust book values to reflect appreciation or depreciation. In most instances of accounting partnerships, this will not be necessary since the typical accounting partnership, relatively speaking, does not have substantial amounts of tangible assets or investments.

Any determination of value should take into account undistributed earnings. The accounting records will reflect any undistributed earnings as of the end of the last fiscal period. However, it is necessary to determine whether there are any earnings since the date at which the retiring or deceased partner did not withdraw. This need not be a problem in the case of a retiring partner. The date of retirement is selected by the partners and can be set as of the close of a fiscal year, rather than at an interim date. When a partner dies, it is usually simpler to compute earnings as of the end of the prior or current month, rather than as at the date of death. It is not necessary to provide for a closing of the books. As noted earlier, in the event of a sale (see page 508) it is possible to provide for a portion of the current earnings to be allocated to the deceased partner. By taking into account a partner's drawings for the current fiscal period, his undistributed earnings would be determined. If the partner is overdrawn, the amount could be considered as a partial payment of the partner's capital account.

Payments may be made for any uncollected fees. This would be an important factor if the accounting partnership used the cash method. Under the accrual method, uncollected fees would be reflected in the undistributed earnings. Under the cash method, however, income is recorded when the fee is collected. Accordingly, completed work which has been billed but no payment received as of the date of death or retirement, represents a right to income earned prior to the termination of the partner's interest but not reflected in the accounts.

Similarly, work in process should be taken into account. This will be a factor for both cash and accrual-basis taxpayers. To the extent that work for any client is in process, there is potential income earned as of the valuation date. The partners could consider as work in process any services performed for clients for which a bill has not been submitted.

Although it does not seem common, partners may want to provide for goodwill. Problems may exist where it is sought to allocate to goodwill part of the selling price of an interest. In the case of a retiring or deceased partner however, it is possible for the agreement to provide for goodwill payments. If so, this allocation will be acceptable for income-tax purposes.

Other questions require consideration. Should there be a difference in the amount of payments made to a retiring partner as contrasted with a deceased partner? Should retired partners be available for consultation with or without additional compensation? Should lump-sum payments be made or should payments be over a period of time, thus providing a form of pension plan? The answers to these and similar questions will depend on each partnership.

Planning payments. In planning payments, it is desirable to keep in mind the social-security benefits which may be available. Partners in a CPA firm would be covered and can depend upon a nontaxable monthly benefit which would form a good base for retirement income.

Obviously, it is necessary in setting a price to consider the effect on the partners who will make the payments. Allowance can be made for the fact that the income of the remaining partners would be increased ultimately by virtue of there being one less distributive share. On the other hand, in some instances the retirement or death of a partner may have a harmful effect on the partnership and actually result in a decrease in income.

It may be simpler to provide for a single amount based on prior or future earnings in lieu of separate payments for each item, such as capital accounts, undistributed earnings, etc. Thus an agreement might provide for the payment of 200 per cent of a partner's average distributive share for the five years prior to death or retirement. Alternatively, it could be provided that the partner's distributive share or a fixed percentage thereof, would continue to be paid to him for, say, three years on retirement or, in the event of death, to his estate or a designated successor.

Income-tax treatment of payments. Regardless of whether the amount of payments is determined by reference to earnings or a totaling of the values of partnership assets, it is necessary to understand what is represented by the partnership interest. This is what will determine the income-tax treatment of the former partner and the remaining partners.

Section 736 is the important income-tax provision for payments made by a partnership to retiring partners, estate, or other successor in interest of a deceased partner. It applies only to payments made in complete liquidation of a partner's interest and is not applicable to any transaction between partners. (Ref. 102, page 527.) A sale by partner A to partner B of his entire interest in partnership ABC would not come under sec. 736. However, amounts paid by partnership ABC to A to liquidate his entire interest would be subject to it.

If the payments made qualify under sec. 736, the retired partner or his successor will be treated as a partner until the interest is liquidated. This is only for federal income-tax purposes and will not affect treatment of the partner or successor under local law. If a member of a two-man partnership dies and payments are made to his estate in accordance with sec. 736, for federal income-tax purposes the partnership continues until the entire interest is liquidated (see page 505). (Ref. 103, page 527.) This may seem to present an ethical problem for an accounting firm because of the prohibition against sharing fees with the laity. However, since the partnership exists only for tax purposes, it would seem that there is no sharing of fees in the legal sense.

Some of the items which can make up a partner's interest were described above: capital account, appreciation of assets, undistributed earnings, and the like. Sec. 736 requires that the payments made to the retiring or deceased partner's successor in interest be analyzed and broken down into payments for the partnership interest (that is, the interest in partnership assets), goodwill, unrealized receivables, and other payments. (Ref. 104, page 527.) This analysis is necessary regardless of the manner in which the payments are determined. There is no difference if payments are based on income of the partnership during the period payments are made, if payments are based on past earnings, or if a flat sum is paid.

Payment for an interest in partnership property. Amounts paid for the partner's interest in partnership property are treated as a distribution. Generally, this may not include payments for goodwill or unrealized receivables. The valuation placed by the partners on a partner's interest in an arm's-length transaction usually will be acceptable. (Ref. 105, page 527.) If payments are treated as a distribution, the partnership and remaining partners are permitted no deduction. (Ref. 106, page 527.) Generally, the recipient will recognize no gain unless the amount of money received (including reduction in the partner's share of liabilities) exceeds the basis for the interest. Loss will not be recognized unless only money or an interest in unrealized receivables is received, and the sum of money and basis of the unrealized receivables is less than the basis of the interest. (Ref. 107, page 527.) Any gain or loss recognized as a result of the liquidating distribution will be a capital gain or loss (Ref. 108, page 527) and is taken into account for the partner's taxable year in which payment is received. (Ref. 109, page 527.)

Payments for an interest in unrealized receivables are not considered as paid for an interest in property. These amounts will be treated as a guaranteed payment or as a distributive share of income. (Ref. 110, page 527.) The effect of this usually is to cause the payments to be treated as ordinary income. This would be so even if the distribution were only in money and interest on unrealized receivables. As noted above, this permits the recognition of a capital loss where realized. However, to the extent that the payment is for an interest in unrealized receivables, there would be ordinary income.

Payments for goodwill. Any payments made to the partner or his estate by the partnership for an interest in goodwill over and above the basis which the firm has for goodwill, are a distributive share of partnership income or a guaranteed payment. In most cases such payments from an accounting partnership represent ordinary income. Whether the payment is a distributive share or a guaranteed payment, the effect on the remaining partners is a reduction of their income. However, if the partnership agreement provides for a reasonable payment with respect to goodwill, such amounts are included with the payments for the partner's interest in property and treated as a distribution. (Ref. 111, page 527.) Thus, depending on the partnership agreement, amounts paid for goodwill may be capital gain for the recipient (where the agreement provides for goodwill) or ordinary income to the recipient (where there is no provision). As with the partner's interest, the valuation of goodwill (where provided for) will be acceptable to the IRS if arrived at in an arm's-length transaction. (Ref. 112, page 527.)

Other payments. All other amounts paid on account of a partner's death or retirement are a distributive share of income or a guaranteed payment. The classification of any payments (including goodwill, if not provided for) as a distributive share or guaranteed payment depends on the timing and method of determining the payment. If the payments are determined with reference to current partnership income (e.g., 20 per cent of partnership income for three years), they are a distributive share. If determined without reference to current earnings (e.g., an amount equal to 20 per cent of the prior five years' earnings to be paid in three annual installments), they are guaranteed payments. (Ref. 113, page 527.) Any payments treated as guaranteed payments or distributive shares are reported by the partnership and partner as of the last day of the partnership year for which the amounts are a deduction or a distributive share. (Ref. 114, page 527.)

In most accounting partnerships, there is little difference whether the payments are distributive shares or guaranteed payments. If an accounting firm has capital gain in one year, the effect may be different since a portion of the payment would then be capital gain if the payments are a distributive share. As a rule, however, for the accounting partnership the distinction is more likely to be a nuisance than anything else.

Fixed payments over a period of years. If payments are made over a period of more than one year and are fixed in amount, the recipient determines by proportion the amount of each year's payments attributable to his interest in the partnership property (and treated as a distribution) and other payments. The proportion is based on the agreed payments. The amount treated as a distribution will bear to the total agreed payments during the year the same ratio that the total agreed payments for the partner's interest in property bear to the total agreed payments. (Ref. 115, page 527.)

For example, the partners agree that A's interest in property is worth $30,000 and that for his interest in property and for other items A will be paid ten annual installments of $5,000. No provision is made for goodwill. On this basis, $3,000 of each year's payments is for the interest in partnership property and, accordingly, will be treated as a distribution. The balance will be a guaranteed payment deductible by the remaining partners and ordinary income to the recipient.

If in any year A receives less than $3,000, the entire amount received is a distribution and the shortage can be carried forward. Thus, if under the agreement A received in 1959 only $2,000, that amount would be a distribution. If in 1960 he received $8,000, $4,000 would be a distribution and the balance a guaranteed payment. The partner or his estate have a choice with respect to reporting recognizable gain or loss on the portion of payments treated as a distribution. The recipient can wait until the payments exceed the basis before reporting any gain, or defer the recognition of loss until the liquidation of the interest has terminated. On the other hand, the recipient may elect, in the return for the first year in which payments are received, to report the gain or loss proportionately over the years as payments are received. (Ref. 116, page 527.)

Varying payments over a period of years. If the payments are determined by reference to the income of the partnership, any payments received are, unless the partners agree otherwise, presumed to be for the interest in partnership property (exclusive of goodwill unless provided for and unrealized receivables), until the value of that interest has been received. Such payments would be a distribution. When the value of the interest has been received, all payments thereafter would be a distributive share of partnership income, presumably ordinary income to the recipient and a reduction of the income reported by the remaining partners. (Ref. 117, page 527.)

Thus, assume in our earlier example that instead of a fixed amount each year, A was to receive 15 per cent of the partnership's profits for ten years. Any payments received up to a cumulative total of $30,000 would be a distribution in liquidation of A's interest. Thereafter, any payments received would be a guaranteed payment. It is possible that when the payout is based on the firm's future profits, there will be no payments over the value of the partner's interest in property.

Whether payments are fixed in amount or will vary with partnership income, the payments can be broken down in some other manner if the partners desire. Any arrangement will be acceptable, provided it does not allocate to the interest in property (exclusive of goodwill not provided for and unrealized receivables) an amount greater than its fair value at the date of death or retirement. (Ref. 118, page 527.)

Partial liquidation. Section 736 applies only to a complete liquidation of a partner's interest. If an interest is partially liquidated, all payments received are treated as a distribution. (Ref. 119, page 527.) But, if a partner receives a disproportionately greater distribution of assets other than unrealized receivables and a disproportionately smaller distribution of unrealized receivables,[10] the excess over his proportionate share of other assets will be treated as a sale or exchange of the portion of unrealized receivables not received. (Ref. 120, page 527.) If the distribution pattern is reversed, that is if a proportionately greater amount of unrealized receivables is received, then the distribution is a sale or exchange of the portion of other assets not received.

[10]As with the sale of an interest, certain inventories may be held by a partnership which would cause a similar result. Since such property is not likely to be held by an accounting partnership, discussion is limited to unrealized receivables.

For example, *A* has a 30 per cent interest in an accounting partnership with:

	Basis	Value
Cash	$25,000	$25,000
Unrealized receivables	—	20,000
Furniture, library, etc.	3,000	5,000
	$28,000	$50,000
Liabilities	10,000	
A capital	5,400	
B capital	5,400	
C capital	7,200	
	$28,000	

It is agreed that *A* will receive a distribution in cash of $4,000 and his interest in the partnership will be reduced to 20 per cent. This will cause a reduction of $1,000 in his share of the partnership's liabilities and, therefore, the total distribution is $5,000. (Ref. 121, page 527.) However, *A*'s share of cash and other assets (except unrealized receivables) attributable to the 10 per cent reduction is only $3,000 (10 per cent of $25,000 and $5,000). The excess of $2,000 is a sale by *A* to the partnership of a portion of his interest in the unrealized receivables. These receivables have, in his hands, a zero basis (Ref. 122, page 527) and his gain on the sale to the partnership is $2,000, taxed as ordinary income.

Payments to an estate. When a partner dies, the basis for his interest to the estate is the fair market value of such interest. Thus, payments received for the interest in property would be received by the estate without realization of gain or loss. On the other hand, payments for unrealized receivables, goodwill (if not provided in the agreement), and the like, are items of income in respect of a decedent and, although valued for estate-tax purposes, are reported by the recipient in the same manner as if received by the decedent. (Ref. 123, page 527.) Thus, such amounts will be ordinary income. If an estate tax is paid, the recipient of the payments may deduct that portion of the estate tax attributable to the income reported. (Ref. 124, page 527.)

For example, assume that the *ABC* partnership agrees to pay *A*'s estate or heirs $8,000 a year for five years in complete liquidation of *A*'s interest. It is agreed that $25,000 of these payments are for *A*'s interest in partnership property and the balance of $15,000 for his interest in unrealized receivables and goodwill (which was not provided for in the partnership agreement). Thus, of each year's payments, $3,000 will be taxed as ordinary income to the estate or heir. Although the value of such payment was included in *A*'s estate, the payments have no basis to the estate. Assume further that the difference in estate tax between including and excluding the value of these payments ($15,000) in the gross estate, is $2,900. If the payments are made as agreed, the recipient would report each year $3,000 as a guaranteed payment (ordinary income) from the partnership, and would be permitted a deduction (assuming the standard deduction is not claimed) of $580 ($3,000/15,000 of $2,900). As to the payments for the interest in property, the value for estate-tax purposes of the partnership interest will be the basis in the hands of the estate and, therefore, the payments to the estate for the interest in partnership property will result in no tax.

Sale to a partner. As noted earlier sec. 736 applies only to payments from the partnership. Instead of providing that payments will be made by the partnership, the agreement may be that the partners will undertake to purchase one another's interests in the event of death or retirement. Any payments so received will be a sale or exchange of the interest. In the event of retirement, payments attributable to unrealized receivables will be ordinary income. However, if a sale is made by the estate or the deceased partner's successor, the payments for unrealized receivables do not appear to be income in respect to the decedent. As such they will have a basis to the estate equal to fair market value. Thus, the sale by the estate to another partner would realize no income. This distinction in treatment has been criticized. (Ref. 125, page 527.)

Estate-tax considerations. In addition to the value of interest in the partnership, the right to receive payments over and above that value is includible in the gross estate. This has been settled for a number of years. An early case held that such payments if based on future earnings were not includible (Ref. 126, page 527), but the case is no longer followed and is readily distinguished by the courts. (Ref. 127, page 527.)

Valuation of the rights to receive future payments is not easy. Will the firm be able to make the payments if it survives as a partnership? Will the partnership earn enough income to meet this obligation? How are future earnings to be estimated for purposes of valuing payments based on future earnings? In some situations, the payments may be so uncertain that a very low estate-tax value would be supportable, but it is doubtful that a zero value would be acceptable to the IRS. In other situations, only a small discount in value would be permitted. And this would be only to take into account the period of time over which payments will be made.

It has been suggested that estate tax with respect to these payments may be eliminated by a separate contract with the partner's spouse. (Ref. 128, page 528.) The support for this approach is a Supreme Court decision (Ref. 129, page 528) involving concurrent purchases of an annuity and life insurance contract. The taxpayer had been required to purchase the annuity in order to obtain the life insurance. The taxpayer kept the annuity contract and made a gift of the life insurance. The court rejected the argument of the IRS that the two contracts should be merged into one to permit an estate tax based upon a transfer with life income retained.

Similarly, the argument has been made, a partnership agreement could provide for compensation to the partners and for retirement payments. A separate contract could be made (with the spouse directly or with the partner who would then assign the contract to the spouse) for death benefits. Assuming sufficient contingencies to make such payments (for example, continued membership in the partnership) the contract would have little or no value for gift-tax purposes. Since the contract is with the spouse, its value would be excluded from the estate.

However, this approach to planning has not been tested. The partnership arrangement is not at arm's length, and the possibility of the court finding one contract would seem greater than with the insurance contract described above. In addition, it is not clear whether the payments made under the separate retirement contract would be deductible by the partnership.

INCOME ATTRIBUTABLE TO SEVERAL TAXABLE YEARS

On occasion, income earned over a period of time may be received or accrued in one taxable year. Because of the graduated income-tax rates this bunching of income in one year subjects it to a higher tax than would be applicable if the income could have been reported ratably over the period of time it was earned. There are a number of provisions in the Internal Revenue Code which provide an averaging technique for the computation of tax in the year income is received or accrued. Section 1301, compensation from an employment covering a period of at least thirty-six months, is of greatest interest to the CPA partnership.

Section 1301 applies to an individual or partnership and relates to compensation for an employment or arrangement to accomplish a particular result. If the arrangement is for the performance of general services, sec. 1301 is not applicable. (Ref. 130, page 528.) For example, an agreement to perform auditing, accounting, and tax services for a client would be for the performance of general services. In the course of rendering such services, it is quite likely that a number of separate and unrelated projects may arise, but since the arrangement is not for the accomplishment of a particular result, the arrangement would not qualify. On the other hand, assume that special problems arise with respect to the tax return for one year. The client and the accounting firm agree that these problems are outside the arrangement and that compensation should be separate. This would be a separate employment and, if other conditions are met, sec. 1301 would apply.

The employment must extend over a period of at least thirty-six months. The individual or partnership must have received or accrued at least 80 per cent of the total compensation for the employment in the taxable year for which relief is sought. If these conditions are met, the tax for the year of receipt or accrual which is attributable to the compensation for employment shall not be greater than the aggregate of taxes which would have been paid had the amount been received or accrued ratably over the period of employment preceding the date of accrual or receipt. (Ref. 131, page 528.)

For example, assume that on September 30, 1960, $40,000 is received as the entire compensation from an engagement in which services were rendered over a forty-month period ending on September 30, 1960. In determining the tax attributable to this compensation, $1,000 would be allocated to each month. Thus $7,000 is allocable to 1957, $12,000 to 1958, $12,000 to 1959, and $9,000 to 1960. If the compensation had been received on February 1, 1960 but the employment had actually ended on September 30, 1960, the compensation would be spread over only the thirty-two months preceding the receipt of the compensation. Thus $8,750 is allocated to 1957, $15,000 to 1958, $15,000 to 1959, and $1,250 to 1960. (Ref. 132, page 528.)

The Regulations outline the steps to be taken in the computation of tax where the compensation received or accrued qualifies under sec. 1301. (Ref. 133, page 528.) The principles are the same regardless of whether the services were performed by an individual or a partnership. In the case of a partnership, as explained below, not all partners may qualify, but those who do would compute tax for the year of receipt or accrual in the following manner:

1. Compute the tax for the year of receipt or accrual, including in gross income the total compensation that was received or accrued.

2. Compute the tax for the year without such inclusion.

3. Compute the tax attributable to the compensation allocable to each taxable year. This would be the difference between the tax for each year including the allocable compensation and the tax without such compensation. It may be necessary to recompute the medical-expense deduction or to reconsider the standard deduction. A greater amount of charitable contributions may be deductible. It may be necessary to recompute the tax of years to which no part of the compensation was attributable in order to take into account the effect of an allocation to a year in which there was a net operating loss. The computation of tax for any of these years is not affected by the statute of limitations. The sole purpose of the computation is to set a ceiling on the tax for the year of receipt or accrual.

4. The tax for the year of receipt or accrual is the lesser of the tax computed under (1) or the total of the taxes computed under (2) and (3).

Which partners are eligible. If the services have been rendered by a partnership, the partners may benefit from the provision of sec. 1301. It is immaterial whether or not a particular partner performed any services in connection with the employment. Any member of the partnership shall be entitled to the benefits of sec. 1301 if he has been a member of the partnership continuously for a period of thirty-six months preceding the date of receipt or accrual, or for the period of employment preceding the receipt or accrual. If the partner was not a member of the firm for the entire period of the employment, the allocation of his share shall be only over the period he was a member of the firm prior to the date of receipt or accrual. A member of a partnership may include as a period of membership any period immediately prior to becoming a partner during which he was an employee and the partnership was engaged in the employment. (Ref. 134, page 528.)

For example, assume that on June 1, 1954, A became an employee of a CPA firm and a partner on June 1, 1958. On June 1, 1956, the firm was engaged to perform accounting services for an estate. The engagement was completed on June 1, 1960, and fees of $20,000 were received, which met the requirements of sec. 1301. A's share of this fee is $2,400, and he can allocate his share ratably to the period from June 1, 1956 to May 31, 1960.

However, if *A* had left the employ of the firm on June 1, 1957, and returned on June 1, 1958, as a partner, he would not be eligible for the benefits of sec. 1301. He was not a member of the partnership *continuously* for thirty-six months prior to the receipt of the compensation, nor was he a member *continuously* for the period of employment prior to the receipt.

Effect of termination of a partnership. The termination of a partnership has no effect on an employment under sec. 1301 and any partners who continue in the employment either as individuals or in another partnership will be eligible for the benefits of sec. 1301. (Ref. 135, page 528.) For example, partnership *AB* begins an employment on January 1, 1956. On January 1, 1958 the partnership terminates and *A* continues in the employment which is completed on January 31, 1960, at which time *A* receives the entire compensation. *A* would be entitled to the benefits of sec. 1301.

Suppose that on January 1, 1958 the partnership *AB* had terminated as a result of *B*'s sale of his interest to *C,* and partnership *AC* continued the employment. Only *A* would be eligible under sec. 1301 since he had a continuous interest in the employment for more than thirty-six months. *C* was not a member of the partnership for at least thirty-six months prior to the receipt, and he was not a member of the partnership for the period of the employment prior to the receipt.

Retiring partners. A partner who has retired under local law will continue to be a partner until his interest in such compensation has terminated. This is consistent with the provisions of sec. 736, governing the treatment of payments to a retired partner. However, sec. 1301 relief will be available only if on the date of retirement (according to local law) the partner would have qualified for relief. The allocation is permitted only for the period preceding the date of retirement. (Ref. 136, page 528.)

Although the Regulations do not cover this point, it would seem that the same would be true in the case of a deceased partner. Thus, the successor in interest of a deceased partner is treated as a partner while the interest is being liquidated. If, at the date of death, the partner would have been eligible for sec. 1301 benefits had compensation been received, his estate or other successor in interest would be eligible for sec. 1301 relief.

If an individual begins an employment and continues with others in a partnership, the entire arrangement shall be treated as a single employment covering the period during which work was done by an individual and the period during which the partnership did the work. When the compensation is received, the other members of the partnership can only take into consideration the period during which services were performed by the partnership. (Ref. 137, page 528.) Thus the other partners will not be eligible for sec. 1301 benefits if the partnership as such was not engaged in the employment for at least thirty-six months. Assuming eligibility under sec. 1301, the other partners may not go back prior to the date the partnership began work on the employment.

A partnership presumably will have some flexibility in ascertaining the share of the sec. 1301 compensation to be allocated to each partner. The only limitation would be that the allocation must have economic significance and not be an attempt to avoid tax.

REFERENCES TO SELECTED TAX PROBLEMS OF ACCOUNTING PARTNERSHIPS

Unless otherwise stated, all references are to the Internal Revenue Code of 1954 and Regulations thereunder.

1. See reg. sec. 301.7701-2
2. Uniform Partnership Act, sec. 6(1)
3. Sec. 7701(a)(2)
4. *Herzberg,* DC dd, 6/19/59
5. *Ottolander,* 5 BTA 651(1926), acq. C.B. VI-1, 5
6. Reg. sec. 1.704-1(e)(1)(i)
7. Sec. 704(e); reg. sec. 1.704-1(e)(3)
8. Reg. sec. 1.704-1(e)(1)(iv); reg. sec. 1.1361-2(e)(2)
9. Reg. sec. 1.704-1(e)(3)(c)
10. Sec. 706(b)
11. Sec. 708(b)(1)(B), 708(b)(2); see page 506.
12. Sec. 736(b)(2)(B); see page 515.
13. Reg. sec. 1.706-1(c)(3)(iv); see page 513.
14. *Angela Fiorito,* 33 TC No. 51 (1959), acq. IRB 1960-20, 7
15. Sec. 761(c)
16. Reg. sec. 1.704-1(b)(2)
17. Sec. 702(a); Reg. sec. 1.702-1(a)
18. Sec. 706(a)
19. Sec. 702(b)
20. Reg. sec. 1.702-1(d)
21. Sec. 702(c)
22. Reg. sec. 1.702-1(c)(2)
23. Finney and Miller, *Advanced Accounting,* 5th ed., 1960, pp. 9, 11
24. Sec. 707(c)
25. Reg. sec. 1.707-1(c)
26. *Robert J. Wallendal* 31 TC 1249 (1959)
27. TIR 221, and attachment thereto, 4/4/60
28. Sec. 704(d); reg. sec. 1.704-1(d)(1)
29. Sec. 752(a); reg. sec. 1.752-1(a)(1)
30. Sec. 1.704-1(d)(2)
31. Reg. sec. 1.705-1(a)(1)
32. Sec. 1.705(a)(1)
33. Sec. 705(a)(2)
34. Sec. 732(a)
35. Sec. 705(a)(2)
36. Sec. 705(b)
37. Reg. sec. 1.705-1(b)
38. Sec. 752(a)
39. Reg. sec. 1.752-1(e)
40. Secs. 734, 754
41. Reg. sec. 1.734-2(b)(2)
42. Sec. 743
43. Reg. sec. 1.754-1(c)
44. Reg. sec. 1.755-1(a)(1)
45. Reg. sec. 1.755-1(a)(2)
46. Sec. 755(b); reg. sec. 1.755-1(b)(4)
47. Sec. 704(c)
48. Secs. 722, 723
49. Sec. 1231(a)
50. Sec. 706(b)
51. Reg. sec. 1.706-1(b)(1)(ii)
52. Reg. sec. 1.706-1(b)(1)(ii)
53. Reg. sec. 1.442-1(b)(1)
54. Reg. sec. 1.706-1(b)(4)(iii)
55. Rev. rul. 60-182, IRB 1960-19, 18
56. Reg. sec. 1.706-1(b)(1)(iii)
57. Sec. 707(b)(1)

58. Sec. 707(b)(3)
59. Secs. 707(b)(1), 267(d)
60. Sec. 707(b)(2)
61. Sec. 1231(a)
62. Sec. 761(b);
    reg. sec. 1.707-1(b)(3)
63. Reg. sec. 1.707-1(b)(3);
    reg. sec. 1.267(b)(1)(b)
64. Secs. 707(b)(3); 267(c)(5)
65. Uniform Partnership Act,
    secs. 30-32
66. Reg. sec. 1.706-1(c)(1)
67. Sec. 731
68. Sec. 708(b)(1)
69. Reg. sec. 1.736-1(a)(6);
    reg. sec. 1.708-1(b)(1)(i)
70. Reg. sec. 1.708-1(b)(1)(iii)(a)
71. Sec. 708(b)(1)(B)
72. Reg. sec. 1.708-1(b)(1)(ii)
73. Reg. sec. 1.731-1(c)(3)
74. Reg. sec. 1.708-1(b)(1)(ii)
75. Reg. sec. 1.708-1(b)(1)(iii)(b)
76. Reg. sec. 1.708-1(b)(1)(iv)
77. Sec. 708(b)(2)(A);
    reg. sec. 1.708-1(b)(2)(i)
78. Sec. 708(b)(2)(B);
    reg. sec. 1.708-1(b)(2)(ii)
79. For a detailed discussion of differences between state and federal laws relating to partnerships, see Sullivan, "Conflicts Between State Partnership Laws and the Internal Revenue Code," 15 *Tax Law Review,* pp. 105, 229
80. Sec. 751(a)
81. Sec. 751(c)
82. Reg. sec. 1.751-1(a)(2)
83. Ibid.; Sec. 732(a)
84. Sec. 732(d)
85. Reg. sec. 1.751-1(a)(3)
86. 13 TC 143 (1949)
87. 14 TC 1251 (1950) (The IRS has acquiesced only in the results of *Horton* and *Wyler,* CB 1959-2, 5, 7.)
88. 239 F2d 322 (1957)
89. Rev. rul. 60-301, IRB 60-38, 7
90. CB 1957-2, 47
91. Sec. 706(c)(2)
92. Reg. sec. 1.706-1(c)(2)(ii)
93. Reg. sec. 1.705-1(a)(1);
    reg. sec. 1.706-1(c)(2)(ii), Ex.

94. Sec. 706(c)(1);
    reg. sec. 1.706-1(c)(3)(ii)
95. Reg. sec. 1.706-1(c)(3)(i)
96. Reg. sec. 1.706-1(c)(3)(iv)
97. Reg. sec. 1.706-1(c)(3)(iii)
98. Sec. 642(g)
99. Secs. 661, 662
100. Sec. 663
101. AICPA *Rules of Professional Conduct,* Rule 11; Treasury Department Circular 230, Sec. 10.29. As to legal requirements, see generally *Accountancy Law Reporter,* Commerce Clearing House.
102. Reg. sec. 1.736-1(a)(1)(i)
103. Reg. sec. 1.736-1(a)(1)(ii);
     reg. sec. 1.736-1(a)(6)
104. Reg. sec. 1.736-1(a)(2)
105. Sec. 736(b);
     reg. sec. 1.736-1(b)(1)
106. Reg. sec. 1.736-1(a)(2)
107. Sec. 731(a)
108. Sec. 741
109. Reg. sec. 1.736-1(a)(5)
110. Sec. 736(b)(2)(A)
111. Sec. 736(b)(2)(B)
112. Reg. sec. 1.736-1(b)(3)
113. Sec. 736(a)
114. Reg. sec. 1.736-1(a)(5)
115. Reg. sec. 1.736-1(b)(5)(i)
116. Reg. sec. 1.736-1(b)(6)
117. Reg. sec. 1.736-1(b)(5)(ii)
118. Reg. sec. 1.736-1(b)(5)(iii)
119. Reg. sec. 1.761-1(d)
120. Sec. 751(b); reg. sec. 1.751-1(b)
121. Sec. 752(b)
122. Reg. sec. 1.751-1(b)(2)(iii)
123. Sec. 753
124. Sec. 691(c)
125. Willis, *Handbook of Partnership Taxation,* p. 391; MacKay, "How the Professional Firm Should Plan for the Retirement or Death of Partners," *Journal of Taxation,* July 1959, p. 55; Report of Advisory Group on Subchapter K (Dec. 31, 1957), p. 44
126. *Bull. vs. U.S.,* 295 US 247 (1935)
127. *McLennen vs. Comm'r,* 131 F2d 165 (1st Cir. 1942); *Estate of Riegelman vs. Comm'r,* 253 F2d 315 (CA-2 1958) for Congres-

sional comment, see Sen. Rep. 1622 (83rd Cong. 2d Sess.), p. 405

128. MacKay, "How the Professional Firm Should Plan for the Retirement or Death of Partners," *Journal of Taxation,* July 1959, p. 55

129. *Fidelity-Philadelphia Trust Co. vs. Smith,* 356 US 274 (1958)

130. Reg. sec. 1.1301-2(b)

131. Sec. 1301(a)

132. Reg. sec. 1.1301-2(c)

133. Reg. sec. 1.1301-2(d)

134. Sec. 1301(c); reg. sec. 1.1301-2(e)(1); reg. sec. 1.1301-2(e)(4)

135. Reg. sec. 1.1301-2(e)(5)

136. Reg. sec. 1.1301-2(e)(2)(iv)

137. Reg. sec. 1.1301-2(e)(3)

SECTION
SIX

Office Management

Responsibility for Office Management

ONLY A MINORITY of small firms designate office managers in charge of office organization and control. However, most medium-sized and large firms have such an administrator.

In small firms, the office manager is generally a partner, but in the larger firms this is true to a much lesser degree. When the office manager is not a partner, he is usually an accountant and his administrative duties tend to be limited in scope in definite relation to his knowledge and experience.

Where there is no designated office manager, office organization and control are usually handled by a partner or all partners acting collectively as to all matters, or individually as to specific phases. It is not uncommon for tax departments to have as their managers partners who are attorneys as well as CPAs, although of course they do not practice as attorneys. Very often, they are former Internal Revenue Service employees.

DUTIES OF OFFICE MANAGER

The duty assigned most frequently to the office manager is that of engaging and discharging nonaccounting personnel. Other duties often assigned are the administration of all nonaccounting phases of operation, engagement and discharge of temporary staff personnel, engagement and discharge of juniors, billing of clients, handling of staff pay records, engagement and discharge of seniors, collection of accounts, and assignment of juniors and seniors to work responsibilities.

With less frequency the following duties also are assigned: direction of staff training programs, review of untyped reports, handling of firm's correspondence, review of working papers, review of final typed and corrected reports, assignment of supervisors, supervision of proofreading and proof of computations, reviewing of tax returns, reception of clients and visitors, and employment of supervisors. Added duties sometimes include purchasing of supplies, keeping of firm's books, control of stationery, preparation of office procedures and systems, and preparation of weekly staff location reports.

The Partner as a Manager

THE NEW PARTNER

■ MOST NEW PARTNERS are men who have held positions as seniors. Some left their jobs to organize new firms; others were promoted to partnership in their old organizations. But for all there has been a period of adjustment, more or less painful.

This twilight zone in which the new partner finds himself as he struggles to get accustomed to his new duties is a difficult one for him and for the senior partners of his firm. Well-disciplined staff men find the change-over less difficult and are more amenable to continued coaching by the older partners. They are also less inclined to attempt to supervise their assignments from the pinnacle of their new desks, but instead will get out into the field where they can get the feel of the work as it progresses.

Dividing the work. Experience proves that the best procedure is to assign certain clients to each new partner as his particular responsibility, regardless of origin, subject only to consultation with older partners and to a review of the completed work by an older partner before the final typing of the reports. Once assigned, supervision of the clients' problems becomes a current thing, since all calls and correspondence will be routed to the particular partner-in-charge.

The workload of the firm must be divided as fairly as possible among the partners, with the understanding always that the allocation must be flexible because of future changes in the firm's clientele, hopefully through the addition of bigger and better clients.

Here the twilight zone earlier referred to will evidence itself when it becomes apparent that some new partners will readily adapt themselves to having a number of engagements simultaneously in progress under their supervision, while others will find it hard to spread their efforts efficiently. Unless the latter type of partner has a definitely limited capacity, patient coaching by older partners will help overcome his handicap.

The technician versus the manager. There is, of course, a considerable difference between supervision as a supervising senior and supervision as a partner-in-charge. The difference lies not so much in degree of technical skill as in the level at which the partner deals with the clients' personnel and that of his own staff. He is no longer a senior, to take over where a partner left off after a preliminary survey. Neither can he turn back the papers to a partner when the field work is finished. He is that partner! He must assume partner's responsibility. And he must conduct himself accordingly with client and staff personnel. One of his earliest impressions will be that his firm lost a good senior in making him a partner, with the resultant dearth of good senior material to help him in his hour of need.

The new partner will find that supervision of accounting engagements at the partner's level must be tailored to the technical demands of each engagement and the capabilities, experience, and competence of the assigned staff personnel.

For purposes of this discussion, it is presumed that a preliminary conference, including a survey of the records, has been had with the client. It also presupposes that the partner-in-charge has either had previous experience in the client's field or that he has done sufficient research to acquire a working knowledge of its problems and peculiarities, as well as its major statistics.

Too many accounting engagements are completed on the telephone; too many sets of working papers lack essential data when the field work is terminated; too many principals and supervising seniors think less of each other after too many engagements. Why? Because of inadequate supervision at the principal, or partner, level.

The average-sized staff usually has a couple of capable supervising seniors, but from there on the trend is likely to be downward. Some seniors have ability but no imagination; some have both qualities; some have less of the first quality than they believe. Some seniors perform capably if given very good assistants; some do well with very ordinary assistants.

ORGANIZING THE FIELD WORK

When the principal briefs his supervising senior (in some instances he may brief the whole crew), he should be in a position to impart the purpose and scope of the engagement and the special elements and personalities involved. At this point the principal should also indicate to the senior the type of report required, general program, over-all budget, and sometimes the allocation of work among the assistants.

The field work gets off to a better start if the principal accompanies the crew to the client's place of business to make the necessary introductions at the proper levels. Establishing the prestige of the senior is very important, so that he may be assured of complete co-operation. He should be introduced at the highest possible level commensurate with the size of the client's organization and the capabilities of the senior. It should be apparent from this that any shortcomings in crew personnel caused by having assigned a less than first-rate senior or adequate assistants will have to be filled in by the principal.

KEEPING IN TOUCH WITH THE CLIENT

The principal thereafter should maintain contact with the field work, timing his visits with the advancement of the work in its progressive stages, and dividing his time between the client's executive personnel—at as high a level as possible—and the staff senior.

The principal should endeavor to cultivate sufficiently cordial relations with the top executives to have them welcome him to informal discussions of the client's problems and to provide the necessary liaison between top management and the possible needs of the senior in charge. Probably more time should be spent visiting with the client's personnel than with the senior staff man, for experience proves that many things of interest will be disclosed in the course of such contacts. The time budget should be reviewed on each visit in the field.

THE TIME BUDGET

Time is of paramount importance. The new partner must develop a firm hand in controlling it. He may have to get hard-boiled. Assignments generally require more, rather than less, time than has been scheduled. Many hours can be lost if a busily occupied senior fails to note that an assistant is wasting time on nonessentials. Or a senior may lose control by failing to see that the program is constantly kept checked off as to completed work. Or he may delay unduly the preparation of that important schedule, "Unfinished Work," which presages the completion of the field work. In the old days, night work frequently covered up these lapses. Nowadays, the client's office objects to keeping the office open nights to accommodate the staff, and the wages-and-hours law makes it expensive. The new partner will find that he does a favor to all if he keeps a tight rein to insure holding to the scheduled pace. No engagement can be said to be managed properly if time is not controlled and kept within desired bounds.

WINDING UP THE ENGAGEMENT

As the engagement progresses to an end, the questions raised by the crew should be reduced gradually to major points, and arrangements should be made for a closing conference. This conference should be scheduled well in advance so that it can be held in an orderly manner with all necessary personnel present, including the principal and the client's top executive.

Following the closing conference, the form of the report should again be discussed with the senior who will then proceed to set up the schedules (some of which may be prepared by the assistants) and the rough draft. If at all practicable, definite dates should be set for the completion of the report. The rough draft and the working papers should then be reviewed by the principal and passed along for checking and final review. The new partner will find that one of his most critical duties is editing reports written by his staff. Good reports will do much for his reputation.

If the procedures outlined are followed with reasonable sagacity, it should be possible to evolve a satisfactory report from the working papers without a telephone finish and without a loss of mutual respect between the senior and the principal. Why? Because the principal tailored his supervision to the technical requirements of the engagement and the capabilities of the assigned staff personnel, and then followed through with close co-operation all the way. An engagement cannot be properly supervised by remote control.

The new partner's mettle, it can thus be seen, is tried early in his new position, and the strain increases as engagements under his supervision multiply and grow in size. He learns that if he is to retain his health and good humor he must avoid, except in emergencies, being drawn into direct work on engagements as he maintains proper contact with them, even though the capabilities of the senior staff members have apparently deteriorated since the new partner left their ranks. With some partners, it's a gift; with others it comes the hard way—few men are born with the ability properly to supervise accounting engagements.

Preparation of Reports

THE FORM MANUAL

■   FOR THE GUIDANCE of the typists (and the staff man), it is helpful to maintain a book or folder containing model forms of letters, reports, financial statements, and schedules. This may be done by saving copies of good letters and reports, or by mounting model report paragraphs on sheets or cards by topic. A few illustrations are contained in the Style Manual (Appendix, page 834). These can be supplemented by others selected from current work from time to time.

Thus if a staff man is called upon to write an opinion, a qualified opinion, a balance-sheet footnote, detailed report comments, or a balance sheet for a client in a specialized industry, he can find a guide which will save his time and which will result in more uniform reports emanating from the accounting firm. The "model" manual is also an easy method of training new typists to conform to the established margins, indentations, capitalizations, and other practices preferred by the firm.

Report-form kit. Over a period of several years, a firm of accountants undertook to develop a manual called the "Standard Report-form Kit." Its purpose is to standardize report and statement presentation. This is the way it works:

1. They did not want to spend the time or incur the expense of setting up a complete report manual of "XYZ Companies" as the national firms do, so they decided to use copies of existing reports and limit the use of these kits to the office premises.

2. They set up a loose-leaf binder for each partner, senior staff member, and one for the typing department. This amounted to seven binders.

3. They selected as the first model a long-form audit report for a client whose fiscal year ended on September 30. The purpose of this selection was twofold—first, because it was a large and complex report; and second, because this would serve as a model for December 31 closings coming up.

4. All partners and senior staff members were called upon to suggest changes and improvements in audit reports. When the draft of the report of this client was prepared the suggestions were incorporated in it.

5. When the report was typed, an extra seven copies were made and inserted in the loose-leaf binder marked "Standard Report-form Kit." These were distributed to those mentioned above with a memo calling attention to improvements and changes made.

6. With this as a nucleus, the kit was launched and subsequent reports began to conform. The reviewer was instructed to be on the lookout for other representative or special reports and to mark them for inclusion in the kit by preparing an extra seven copies. He was required to write a memo with each one calling attention to the special problems.

7. It is the firm's policy to review and replace these forms as additional changes are made.

8. The typing department copy is marked with notations covering spacing, indentation, centering, underlining, etc., which have speeded up this process and improved the quality at the same time. This makes it easier to train new typists, too.

9. There is much less discussion of report-writing problems among the staff since they now have a definitive source of information which reflects the firm policy and procedure.

After three years of operation, the kit contained four sections with various types of reports as follows:

1. Long-form audit reports: (a) corporation, (b) corporation with two

wholly owned subsidiaries, (c) limited partnership, (d) nonprofit corporation.

2. Interim reports: Samples of monthly, quarterly, and semiannual reports.

3. Special reports: Reports on reorganizations, specific industries, etc.

4. Certificate forms: Examples of short-form reports with various exceptions, qualified opinions, etc.

Since adoption of the "Standard Report-form Kit," the job of report preparation and review in this firm has been considerably lightened, and clients, bankers, and even fellow accountants constantly remark on the high standards and consistent high quality of the reports.

Standard paragraphs. One firm has pretyped models of standard report paragraphs, prenumbered, to which the senior refers when writing his pencil comments. For example, under Accounts Receivable he may instruct the typist to "copy paragraphs 1, 6, and 8, after which type the following. . ." He then inserts the appropriate additional material. Another applies similar treatment to writing semiannual reports of audit of homestead associations, of which he has many as clients, since the audit requirements are largely standardized by the Federal and state examining authorities. In the opinion of his firm the pretyped material is easily woven into the pencil draft.

WHOLE-DOLLAR ACCOUNTING

Whole-dollar accounting has been defined as "a technique applied to general accounting procedures through which the last two digits of dollar-and-cent amounts are eliminated and amounts are recorded in whole dollars." It has also been known as centless, pennyless bookkeeping, or cents elimination. The major advantages of whole-dollar accounting are as follows:

1. The average figure consists of five figures. It is easy to see that eliminating the last two penny digits will cut all work dealing with these figures by 40 per cent.

2. Errors occur most frequently in pennies when posting, tabulating, typing, or checking. By eliminating pennies, errors are easier to locate and figures easier to handle.

3. An important saving is made in report space. A multicolumn schedule becomes less crowded and, in some cases, smaller-sized paper can be used.

4. Easier reading of reports is obtained by eliminating pennies.

An application of whole-dollar accounting is being made by some firms in connection with monthly and interim financial statements. A number of smaller clients, for whom these accountants do work on a monthly or quarterly basis, receive condensed operating data on forms which are purchased from a national system-form company. Through the application of whole-dollar accounting, the time saved in the preparation, typing, and checking of these reports makes it possible to service these accounts profitably. The client in turn is highly pleased with an operating statement that he can easily read, interpret, and compare with prior periods.

REPORTING TO MANAGEMENT ON INTERNAL CONTROL

The inexperienced man may do more harm than good in his reports on internal control tests. By emphasizing the unimportant along with the important, he may negate the effect of the recommendations made. Any report to management should include three basic parts: the deficiencies found, the possibilities of fraud or error, and corrective measures recommended.

In considering methods of reporting to management on internal control, care must be taken to pick the one most apt to meet with management response and the one most suited for the type of shortcoming to be discussed. Reports may be oral in the case of minor divergences from the required system. For the most part, however, reports should be in written form so that management will have a permanent record of the discrepancies, and so that the CPA will be on record as having called the discrepancies to the attention of management.

The reporting should be concise, accurate, and, above all, the remedy suggested should be practicable both from the standpoint of operation and of additional cost in relation to the risk involved. The pointing out of a discrepancy between the system in operation and the system as prescribed carries little weight with management unless at the same time the risks inherent in such discrepancy are disclosed and a suitable remedy is recommended. Reporting should always have a positive approach: what is wrong, what are the possible results, how can the wrong be righted. Following is an example of how *not* to submit a letter on internal control to management:

"During the course of our examination, the following matters which came to our attention are, we believe, worthy of your consideration:

1. Petty cash fund ($25 in amount) left unattended during lunch period.
2. Receipts from gum machine are not removed in the presence of a second person.
3. The cashier maintains the accounts receivable ledger and the sales journal.
4. Receiving reports are not prepared when material is received and payment of invoices is made without any check as to the actual receipt of merchandise covered by the invoice.
5. The stamp fund was short $2 at the time of our cash count.
6. In our review of payroll and personnel records it was noted that the cashier had not taken a vacation in seven years."

It can readily be seen that this letter is the work of an "eager beaver." This is an excellent example of trying to cover too much ground. Items 1, 2, and 5 could well have been omitted from this letter. By their presence they tend to belittle the serious defects in the system as outlined in items 3, 4, and 6. While the letter points out certain discrepancies, its approach is definitely a negative one. No explanation is given of the possible risks involved in items 3 and 6, and the risk involved in item 4 is shown only by inference. It would be no surprise if management failed to act on a letter of this type. An explanation of the risk involved in each item and a recommendation as to its correction would strengthen the letter.

Processing Reports

■ IT IS IMPORTANT that the accountant's office carry out uniform and consistent procedures in processing the financial statements and reports from the time of completion by the accountant in charge.

For an office which handles numerous special and nonrecurring engagements, it has been found helpful to use a form which accompanies the report draft through checking, typing, and final delivery. This form indicates the client's name and address, the number of copies to be typed, the name and address of each person who is to receive a copy of the report, and how many copies he is to receive. The form also provides spaces for the name or initials of the persons who prepared the report, reviewed it, typed it, checked it, and sent it out, together with the date each of these operations was performed. Some firms whose practices consist primarily of monthly or recurring audits provide a rubber stamp at the upper right-hand corner of the first report pencil sheet, for the name of the preparer and checker. A card file is maintained in the typing room, indicating, for each client, the name and address of those who are to receive copies, the number of copies to be typed, and other pertinent data.

GENERAL PROCEDURE FOR HANDLING REPORTS

The usual sequence of events in connection with report-writing and review is outlined in the following:

1. Preparation of the pencil draft of the financial statements, including footnotes and comments, by the accountant in charge or partner, usually at the client's premises

2. Review of the pencil draft and audit workpapers, and comparison with the prior report, if any, by a partner or supervisor either at the client's premises or at the accountant's office

3. Discussion of salient points or of whole report with client

4. Editing or amplification of the report

5. Typing (Other reproduction methods are discussed on page 584.)

6. Checking of pencil report to typed sheets; proving footings and extensions

7. Checking cross references and schedules within the report

8. Correcting indicated typographical errors by the typist

9. Review of corrected copy by manager or partner

10. Binding of report and addressing of envelopes for delivery or mailing

11. Affixing signature by partner (some firms do this step before the report is bound; it is easier to sign unbound sheets)

12. Delivery to client

Some firms feel that as much as possible in connection with the report should be done at the client's office, so that the client can see how much time is spent on his engagement.

There is considerable difference in practice in timing the review of the report with the client (step 3 in the foregoing list). Some accountants review the statements and report in detail with the client while the material is in pencil form, and this is the more common practice. Others review merely the adjusting entries with the client before the report is typed and then review the report itself after typing, when it is more readable and presents a better impression. Usually this choice varies with the wishes of the client or the time schedules of the accountant, but it is generally believed that a review of the report with the client at one stage or another is highly desirable.

Before the report is reviewed with the client, it should be reviewed with the partner responsible for the engagement, unless it is much the same as previous reports for that client. (See page 557 for a full discussion of report-reviewing.)

CONTROLLING THE WORK

A simple schedule can be maintained to control the flow of work from the date an audit engagement is commenced to the date when the report is finally mailed to the client. This schedule would comprise the following items arranged in columnar form:

1. Client's name
2. Audit date
3. Senior in charge
4. Usual audit time
5. Date audit commenced
6. Date audit completed
7. Date report turned in for review
8. Date review completed
9. Date put into typing department
10. Date put into checking department
11. Date sent out to client
12. Special comments, such as "rush," "date promised client," and "hold for confirmation"

The schedule would be kept by the office manager or other person in charge of staff assignments, who would fill in the information required for the foregoing items 1 through 9. Once a day the information could be completed as to items 10 and 11 by the person in charge of the typing or checking department. Examination of the information by the office manager would focus attention on an unusual amount of time required to complete an engagement, or to type a report, and would permit a follow-up through any stage of office procedure. Examples of different types of work-control records will be found in Section 7, pages 752-774.

Some firms maintain a record in the typing department, either instead of or as a supplement to the foregoing record, accounting for each report from the time it is placed for typing to the time it is mailed or delivered to the client. Such a record may contain items 1, 2, 9, 10, and 11 of the foregoing list, plus such information as the name of typist, number of copies typed, whether "mailed" or "delivered" to client, and number of typing department hours spent on the report.

If the record indicates any wide disparity between the date reports enter the typing room and the date typing is actually started, the matter should be looked into—it may indicate either an abnormal backlog of work or some fault in the way the work is being handled.

A file should be maintained indicating on a card for each client, the client's name and address, the person to whom reports are addressed, the number of copies to be typed, the number of office or extra copies, and whether reports are to be mailed or delivered. By referring to the card before a report is typed, errors in number of copies or distribution may be avoided.

TYPING

Report style. It is desirable that financial statements and reports be uniformly typed. The following matters should be standardized: Spacing, indentation, capitalization, underscoring, punctuation, dollar signs, and double or single spacing. A typing manual helps to keep reports uniform over the years, and also assures uniformity where there is more than one office. An illustrative typing style manual entitled "Style Manual for Report Writers, Typists and Stenographers of a Public Accounting Office" is presented in the Appendix, pages 834-893. While certain features of this manual may not appeal to some accountants, it is representative of the content of a typical manual and is readily adaptable for use in an accounting practice.

Suggestions for the typist. In an office of medium size, with several girls, reports can be divided so that each girl types a few sheets, so as to cut down the time that would be involved if only one girl were to do a large report by herself.

It should be borne in mind that, since the appearance of a report is important, the ribbons on each typewriter should have had about the same amount of usage. This is not as difficult as it sounds. It takes only a minute or two to change a ribbon if necessary and it does not mean that the ribbon taken off the machine must be thrown away. It should be saved and used for correspondence, reports which do not have to be matched, corrections, office matters, and similar work. A few ribbon spools should be saved. Having a number of spools on hand makes it easy to change a ribbon.

Reaching the bottom of a sheet while only two or three lines remain to be typed is one of the hazards of statistical typing. With experience, a typist will have an idea of just how much she can put on one sheet without crowding. With a sample of a previous report before her, she can tell whether any items have been added or eliminated. If there is no sample obtainable, by counting the number of lines on the pencil copy, allowing for the handwriting, and comparing this with the writing space on the paper she plans to use, she should have an idea as to whether she can get the statement on one sheet or be forced to break it and continue on another. If she must break it, a good breaking point should be chosen, not one that will leave figures dangling without a total or one that carries over just one or two lines. If footnotes relate to a single statement and are intended to be portrayed with it, every effort should be made to put them on the same sheet as the items which they explain.

A pencil mark placed on the left-hand side of the sheet before typing, about an inch and one-half from the bottom, serves as a warning mark to the typist that she is nearing the end of a sheet. If a statement is being typed, she is able to judge if it can be completed or must be carried forward, and find a convenient line to break it.

If a pencil mark is also placed on the left-hand side of a sheet about one-quarter of an inch from the bottom, it will serve to indicate where the page number is to be placed so that all are uniform.

A spread balance sheet, one with assets on the left side and liabilities on the right side, will usually fit on an 11 by 17 sheet and make a better appearance than if the assets are listed on one sheet and the liabilities on another, since it allows for ready comparison and analysis. Placing assets on one page and liabilities on another is undesirable. On a spread balance sheet, an attempt should be made to space the current assets opposite the current liabilities; the totals of the two sides should likewise appear on the same bottom line, in order to give a neatly finished appearance to the statement.

In cases when there are not too many items, a balance sheet may be typed on a single 8½ by 11 sheet, by placing the assets at the top and the liabilities below the center, providing the figures do not require more than two columns. Crowding on a sheet makes it difficult to read and gives a jumbled appearance; on the other hand, too much space between columns gives a disjointed appearance and wastes the time of the reader attempting to make comparisons.

There should be a rigid rule for indentations. There may be a three-space indentation for the first line and two spaces for the balance or an even two spaces for each indentation. The Style Manual in the Appendix, pages 890-91, uses indentation to the 3rd, 5th, 7th, and so on.

Comparative profit-and-loss statements should be arranged with the figures for the current year in the first column reading from left to right, since the client is most interested in what happened this year and only for comparison purposes requires the figures for previous years.

Sometimes an "increase and decrease" column is used on comparative statements. At one time it was fairly common practice to put the "decrease" figures in red, despite the fact that this required fitting the typewriter with a two-color ribbon and using red carbon paper, specially inserted, on the copies whenever a red figure appeared. This practice is becoming obsolete. Decrease figures are designated by placing an asterisk after the amount (with appropriate footnoting that "asterisks designate decreases") or by the use of parentheses enclosing the decreases.

Comment pages should not be crowded. They should be double-spaced and each sheet should be started on the same line, whether it be four, five, or six lines down from the top. The writing should not extend any farther down the sheet than about eight lines from the bottom, to allow for page numbering below the last line. Tabulations which appear in comments should not be broken, if possible. This may be difficult at times but if the comments are scanned before the typist starts, she can usually determine about where a tabulation should start and end.

Erasures on reports. The simplest way to avoid strike-overs in reports or correspondence is not to permit them at all. Strike-overs are unsightly and are evidence of careless typing. Corrections can be simplified by using high-grade paper, erasers, and shields. It is not necessary to "scrub" when an erasure is made, since many light applications of the eraser will save the paper and assist in giving the appearance of a perfect report. Sometimes when erasing an original which is deeply imprinted, a little paper cement may be applied over the wording to be erased, then rubbed off with the finger; the dark smudge will come off with the cement and reduce the amount of erasing required.

Corrections on carbon copies should be made in carbon. Typing corrections should be as nearly invisible as possible. Sometimes if a typist is careful in the way she arranges her carbon initially, she can put all her sheets in at one time with a carbon between each sheet and make her correction that way. However, in most instances, each sheet has to be corrected separately, and if, when the typist places her sheet in the typewriter, she arranges it exactly where she wants her keys to strike, and then places over the correction area a small piece of carbon and as many thicknesses of the same paper as are required, the fact that it is a correction will not be visible on the final copy. By thicknesses of paper is meant that for the first carbon copy she needs only one thickness, for the second, two thicknesses and so on. She can make her job easier by preparing some "correcting carbon" in her spare time. A small piece of carbon under one, two, or as many thicknesses of paper as are desired may be stapled together and used as the occasion arises. If the office practice is to show red figures in reports, it is necessary to use typewriter ribbons with a combination of red and black. When red figures are being inserted the typist should endeavor to put in as many red figures at one time as is convenient by placing pieces of red carbon under her black carbon in the area where the red figures are to appear. As she types, the figures will appear in red on all the copies.

An error, if caught while typing, can be corrected while the papers are still in the machine by erasing on all copies, after placing sheets of blank paper under the carbons to avoid smudging while erasing, and typing in the correction.

COPIES OF REPORTS

It is necessary that at least one typed copy of each report be retained in the office, and desirable that where there are several typed runs of a report, one office copy of each be retained and marked to identify the set to which it belongs. Some firms make an additional copy to be used as the working copy for next year's report, or to avoid retyping in case a need develops during the year for an extra copy for a bank or credit grantor. Firms which have branch offices usually require each branch office to prepare an extra copy of every report for scrutiny or post-review by the head office.

PROOFREADING

Before the pencil copy of the report or financial statements is typed, it is important that it be reviewed either by a principal or by a trained person assigned to this work. The person reviewing the work should initial it for typing and typists should not accept any work not so initialed.

Once a firm employs more than two or three staff men, it is desirable that reports be proofread by someone other than the typist. In the larger firms specific personnel do this work on a full-time basis. The smaller firm may utilize the early morning or late afternoon hours of its juniors or assistants. Some firms employ college students (accounting majors) on a part-time basis.

Proofreading may be done in several ways. It may be done by having one person alone compare the pencil copy line by line with the typed report. This is often the only method possible in the small office and in time one individual can acquire remarkable proficiency and speed. Some accountants consider that this is the best way. But it is more common, when personnel are available, to have two persons proofread. Where two persons are used, one may read the typed report aloud while the other checks the reading with the original draft, or one may read the original draft aloud while the other checks the typed report. This last method is preferred by most firms using two persons in proofreading.

After comparing, the typed sheets should be footed and final totals cross-footed. Where red figures are put in by separate carbons, each copy should be scanned to see that the red came through.

Corrections should be marked on the office or file copy and made by the typist after all checking and referencing is completed. A designated person other than the typist who did the correcting should then review to see that all copies have been properly corrected. The office or proving copy should be a clear copy on which all figures and words are easily read.

The office copy of each typewritten page may be rubber-stamped in the upper right- or left-hand corner as follows and initialed in order to establish responsibility for the respective work done:

```
┌─────────────────────────────────────────────┐
│                                             │
│   Date typed _____        │
│   Typed by _____          │
│   Proofread by _____      │
│   Footed by _____         │
│   Cross-referenced by _____        │
│                                             │
│        _____              │
│                                             │
└─────────────────────────────────────────────┘
```

FINAL REVIEW AND DELIVERY

After the report has been reviewed, typed, proofread, and corrected it is usually submitted to the principal for signature and final scanning.

Some firms do not bind the report until after it is signed, as this saves unbinding in case the signing partner orders any revisions. In offices where the reports have been sufficiently and systematically reviewed and referenced before or after typing, they are usually submitted to the principal for signature in final bound form. This saves time and additional handling.

The transmittal letters and addressed envelopes should be submitted to the principal with the reports. This gives him an opportunity to consider the mailing directions, so that reports are not likely to reach the wrong persons in the client's office.

Usually audit reports are considered by clients to be confidential documents. For this reason care is required to see that they are addressed to a responsible person, usually the treasurer or principal executive, in an envelope clearly marked "confidential" so that it is not opened in the usual mail-handling. Where, in the case of a corporation, there is some question as to the person or persons to whom the report should be delivered, it is desirable to address it to the specific source of corporate authority authorizing the report.

In a majority of cases, especially for recurring engagements, the reports are mailed. However, some firms make it a practice to have a principal deliver the report personally and discuss it with the client. Many of the larger firms deliver "rush" reports to nearby clients by messenger. Some firms send special or year-end reports by registered mail.

A large number of firms send a separate letter of transmittal with their reports (although this is usually an unnecessary duplication of effort). It appears advisable, however, to write a letter, accompanying all reports to be printed for security holders or others, requesting that a printer's proof be submitted to the accounting firm for review, before any printed reports are released by the client to stockholders or the public.

ONE FIRM'S APPROACH TO REPORT-PROCESSING

The following material represents excerpts taken from a practitioner's comments concerning report-processing in his firm.

Computations for the previous year are not recomputed; they are referenced to the last year's report unless there were some changes made in between. Working capital ratio, book value per share of common stock outstanding, and all other statistics in the context are recomputed.

When the referencer receives the report, he gives it an over-all glance to see if all footings, computations, and the like, have been completed. The name of the client is confirmed, and the fact established that the business is operating as a corporation, partnership, or sole proprietorship. This is the first step in referencing because of the continued usage throughout the report and the varied terminology applied to each.

The index and listing of exhibits are checked next. The wording in the index, of course, should agree exactly with that on each exhibit.

The history section of the report is read carefully with special attention given to the chronology and completeness. It is best to compare it with the history in the previous audit report and verify only transactions of the current period.

All figures are then checked. Supporting exhibits are checked first because any errors there would ultimately affect the principal exhibits as well as the text, thereby causing unnecessary work. If the report is on a comparative basis, the prior year's figures are checked to the preceding report. If any differences are found due to reclassification, they are reconciled. The beginning inventory is closely checked, not only to the comparative income statement, but also to the closing inventory as shown on the prior year's balance sheet. Beginning cost and accumulated depreciation of fixed assets are checked to the preceding year.

The complete text is then read. The referencer must always be alert in checking spelling, punctuation, construction of sentences, and consistency in names and terminology.

When an exhibit or schedule is too large to be typed on the standard (9⅜" by 11⅜") paper used for audit reports, it may be typed on a fourteen-pitch typewriter, which types fourteen spaces to the inch horizontally and eight spaces vertically. (The ordinary elite machine allows only twelve and six spaces respectively.)

Exhibits or schedules which are too large for either machine have to be reduced photographically. The typist must prepare a sheet large enough to type the exhibit, but the width and length of the sheet must be in proportion to the size of the regular audit paper. A line is ruled around the sheet leaving a margin on all sides to match the margin on the other sheets of the report. The exhibit is then typed on a regular machine. After the usual footing, reading, referencing, and checking, it is sent to a company which produces a negative of the page, reducing it to the size of the report paper. A plate is burned from the negative.

While the report is being proofread, the mats are ruled. Because a typewriter prints jagged lines, they should be drawn in by hand with ruling ink and an ordinary ruling pen.

After the report has been typed, proofread, and corrected, a final referencer —one who has not worked on the report before—checks it for meaning, continuity, sentence structure, spelling, and setup. He also makes sure that the figures in the comments agree with those in the statements themselves. Any errors are corrected, the corrections are checked, and the report is ready for the operator.

The operator is trained to expect perfect copies from his duplicating machine. Some of the problems are: getting uniform inking on all sheets, correcting imperfections in typing (such as fuzziness caused by splattering of carbon ribbon), and adjusting the ink low enough to avoid leaving fine black specks on the background of the finished copy. If the typewriter embosses the mat, the operator tries various methods of correcting this imperfection.

As soon as he achieves a perfect copy, the operator runs off the necessary number of copies for the client plus two for the office. One copy is also run off on work paper to be used as a guide for the next year's report.

Review Procedures

REVIEW OF THE FIELD WORK

■ **Responsibilities of the firm.** The need for supervision and review of work is imposed by a requirement far more vital and demanding than a purely contractual obligation to perform an agreed assignment satisfactorily. This higher requirement stems directly from the fact that CPAs are engaged by clients to perform personal service of a professional character. A responsibility devolves therefore upon the accountants to insure that the service rendered is actually personal and that it is performed according to the explicit standards of the profession. Performance of various phases of an engagement may be delegated to subordinates, but responsibility for its competent performance as a whole cannot be. It remains primary and indefeasible as to the principal and can only be met, where tasks are delegated, by comprehensive internal supervision and review that give the service rendered its requisite personal and professional character.

A condition associated with the practice of public accountancy, which in many respects is singular to that work, is represented by the interest maintained in the examination and in the report thereon by persons other than the accountant and the client. These persons are generally referred to as third parties and they comprise investors, bankers, security dealers, and others who are concerned with the financial affairs of the company. While it is true that a confidential relationship exists between the accountant and his client, the client will not hesitate to submit the report to third parties without seeking the consent of the accountant. A test often employed is for the accountant to ask himself what information he would want the report to contain if he were a third-party user. Reports for special purposes require special presentation to meet the desired ends.

The need for review. There are different purposes for which a review of the work and the report is made. One is to make sure that the information contained in the working papers is correctly brought into the financial statements and that the exact facts developed during the examination are completely disclosed. This attaches importance to the use of certain formal and standard review procedures.

On the other hand, review should take place not only after the field work is performed but also throughout the entire period of control of the engagement, and, logically, should begin as early as acceptance of the client. Thus there is also preview and supervision as well as review, and it is felt that the extent and nature of such comprehensive scrutiny inevitably vary with each engagement. This leads to the conviction that the particular procedures and methods to be used cannot be reduced to a common denominator applicable to every case and on the contrary are a matter for the personal judgment, responsibility, and decision of the principal or firm.

To hold to a hard and fast set of rules to govern review procedures of all accountants is to advocate methods that either could not or would not be applied. The reason for this is obvious. Accounting firms are not all the same size; they range from the individual practitioner to the large firms having hundreds of accountants of varying degrees of special knowledge and ability. A firm of accountants comprising but a few men is in no position to establish the classification of accountants that exists among the large firms. Partners of small firms may be doing the most routine auditing tasks in the morning and deciding policy questions in the afternoon—indeed they are often interrupted in one to do the other.

It is a difficult matter to require that an accountant who personally does the work and signs the statements must apply to himself the same close check and scrutiny of the work done that he would apply to the work of another accountant. And yet there is scarcely any accountant worthy of the name who has not at some time looked at his own working papers during a subsequent examination and wondered how he could have handled an item as he originally handled it.

That there is need to review the work on the engagement, no rational accountant can deny. Review is necessary because the responsibility for the accurate and thorough performance of the engagement rests upon the individual practitioner or the accounting firm issuing the report. Great as may be the confidence reposed in the accountant writing the report, he should not be permitted to speak for a firm unless a review has been made of his work, because of the obligation for accuracy and completeness of work resting upon the firm. Review is necessary also to make certain that the performance of duties delegated to subordinates has been accurate and thorough; to make certain that the engagement has been completed in accordance with the terms governing it; and to recognize and handle developments which have an unforeseen bearing on the scope, purpose, and ultimate value of the engagement.

Errors. If the reasons already advanced are not sufficient to establish the necessity for a review of the work and report, there remains as another reason the need to guard against that ever-present enemy—errors. Errors of principle, errors of judgment, and plain old errors of mathematical exactness. Accountants are not phenomenal men. They are subject to all the chances for error that are present in life and guarding against error is always uppermost in their minds. Substantially all accountants welcome a review of their work because they are so conscious of their own frailties; nevertheless, staff seniors should be indoctrinated with the idea that no report should be submitted for review unless it is believed to be letter and figure correct, and no report should be turned in when its writer knows that changes will have to be made therein before it can be typed.

There should be no great arguments on behalf of the necessity of review. It is an axiom of accounting practice that the work and reports are to be reviewed in the best manner that the circumstances of the engagement will permit.

General scope of the review. Basically, to be adequately comprehensive, review must ultimately have covered the nature and extent of the work done, the inspection and check of the working papers assembled, and the careful editing of the completed report and statements. This will not have been done unless the following fundamental questions can be answered with completely satisfactory certainty:

1. Were the audit and extent of verification, including independent confirmation, sufficiently comprehensive?
2. Are the assets properly valued and clearly stated?
3. Has adequate provision been made for all liabilities, direct and contingent?
4. Are income charges and credits properly classified?
5. Have correct accounting principles been applied and has their application been consistent?
6. Do the working papers contain all analyses, schedules, and explanations necessary to support the statements and opinion?
7. Does the report present correctly, intelligently, and adequately the results of the examination?

Minimum review for the small firm. Larger offices can afford the functional classification of a report-review department that can delve in detail into the reports before typing with reference to work papers and checking a myriad of potential trouble spots that can and do appear in reports. Small offices and individual practitioners cannot afford the functional division of duties but at the same time they cannot afford to evade or avoid the function of some form of final scanning or review of reports just before typing. In the performance of this function, even though it be merely a scanning operation, the following five points appear to cover the bare essentials in broad areas that must be reviewed regardless of office size:

1. *Adequacy of scope.* First of all, have you stated a scope? If you have, is it an adequate statement of your range of responsibility?
2. *Propriety of opinion.* First of all, have you stated an opinion or a disclaimer, if one is required? Is it within the limits of the responsibility you should be taking? Does it state the responsibility you wish to assume?

3. *Consistency of style within report.* Does the report style maintain a uniform manner of format, capitalization, headings, and appearance in general within itself?

4. *Conformity of style with office policy.* Do the report style and appearance conform appropriately with the standards you have established for all reports issuing from your office?

5. *Compatibility with AICPA standards.* Does the report in general keep within the bounds of general professional pronouncements of auditing and reporting standards to qualify as prudent and adequate professional work?

Levels of responsibility. The use of the term principal is an all-embracing one. In small firms the principal often is the individual practitioner or one of the partners. Large firms have a ladder of authority extending through an organization from juniors to semi-seniors, to seniors, to in-charge accountants, to principals, and to partners.

Responsibility for the adequacy of accounting work exists in tiers. To say that the accountant controlling the engagement must satisfy himself that every adding-machine tape has been correctly listed or that every posting has been correctly checked is too absurd to admit of argument. Competency and integrity of subordinate employees are not qualities to be reinvestigated with each engagement. These qualities may be looked into during the first few engagements of a new member of the staff, but as a rule accountants soon learn the degree of reliance that can be placed on the different staff members.

The practice throughout the country with respect to partners' responsibilities is not uniform. Some firms have one partner review all reports issued from the office, but in such cases this partner, generally known as the report editor, rarely attends at the scene of the engagement. Other firms hold each partner responsible for certain engagements and this responsibility, depending upon the size of the firm, extends from attendance at the scene of the engagement to reviewing the reports and signing the statements.

Some accountants rely entirely upon the reviewer to detect their errors of commission or of omission. However, the proper attitude for the staff man is to try to execute correct work and apply thereto the best judgment of which he is capable, often scrutinizing his finished work as if he were to be its final reviewer.

The basic responsibility rests upon the man who does the work; his responsibility extends to the accountant in charge of the engagement. Both parties are responsible to the partners. A partner takes upon his firm the responsibility which follows the approving of an engagement and the signing of the report. This does not mean that every partner must review the work and statements and give his consent to the signing. Few engagements would ever be finished if this concept were rigorously applied. Disputed and doubtful points and policy questions continuously engage the attention of more than one partner, but routine engagements are entrusted to the decision of one partner and he makes the decisions even though they may be binding on all partners.

The field review. *The time for review.* Proper review should occur not only after the field work has been finished but also throughout the entire period of the engagement. This involves preview before starting, supervision during, and review at the completion of the field work. The extent and nature of each review necessarily vary with each engagement because of differing conditions; they cannot be reduced to a standardized or rigid process because they are matters of the principal or partner's personal judgment.

Much of review is preview and most of it is supervision. Consideration of the procedures employed by the field auditor would seem to be inseparable from consideration of the data to which the procedures are being applied, and the review itself, to be genuinely effective, appears to be inseparable from continuous supervision of all the examination's phases from the earliest stages of planning to the final editing of the auditor's report. This being the case, it becomes obvious that all of the functions of review except final editing of the report may best be performed in the field.

Field review of the work of staff men on an engagement is conducted by (1) the in-charge accountant or (2) a principal, partner, supervisor, or specially qualified staff member. The second practice is somewhat more prevalent. Basically it depends on such factors as the size and nature of the engagement, the qualifications and experience of the in-charge accountant, and any relevant special circumstances. Where the first method is used, it also is generally considered desirable to have at least one field visit made by someone having higher responsibility for the engagement than the in-charge accountant.

Many advantages result from field visits under the second method. Some of the more obvious and important are these: Major problems encountered by the accountant in charge as the engagement progresses can be disposed of promptly. It becomes possible to give immediate consideration to and take action on changes in the original scope as their need develops. There can be immediate discussion with the client of controversial questions and of proposed adjustments. The engagement can be examined critically as a whole more effectively from the standpoint of procedures in use than by a less intimate and more remote office review after completion of the engagement. The last statement has obvious special application to (1) out-of-town engagements, particularly when the report is required for a set date, and (2) the fact that most auditing engagements are carried out during the busy year-end season.

The frequency of field visits to an engagement during its progress depends upon the size, scope, and complexity of the engagement, whether or not it is an initial engagement, the rapidity with which it must be completed, a knowledge of the industry in general and the client in particular, as well as the presence of special problems.

Degree of internal control. The initial act of a field review may be directed toward an evaluation of the work done to establish the effectiveness of the system of internal control. While great developments have been made during the past decade in establishing and installing methods of internal check and control, the fact remains that the smaller accountant rarely encounters a well-maintained internal control system and consequently he enlarges the scope of his examination to meet the conditions he finds. Internal control as a system may or may not exist in small businesses, but the fact remains that the active head of a small business has far greater knowledge of the activities than is readily conceded and the accountant making the examination recognizes this.

Closing the audit. Many firms use the plan of having a capable senior accountant, assisted by one or more juniors, stay at the scene of the engagement until the field work is finished and then have a partner or principal arrive to "close" the audit. This feature of the work is far more than a series of perfunctory questions as to the performance of the audit. To a listener the questions may sound indifferent or mechanical, but each question has a definite meaning and purpose and, if the questions are not satisfactorily answered, additional investigation is ordered forthwith.

Most firms have devoted much time and thought to the development of techniques for this purpose. It has been found impossible to solve the problem by rigid rules of procedure. A method adopted in one instance might be wholly inappropriate in another. The infinite variety of circumstances and the infinite shades of difference in personal attributes of the individuals working together as principals and staff assistants preclude widespread application of a uniform pattern of procedure. It is generally believed that a principal well acquainted with the assistant who submits a draft report may by skillful questioning determine whether or not he may safely accept the assistant's representations.

Reliance on the staff. To approach the question of a review of field work with a view that no reliance at all can be placed on the men doing or supervising the work would lead to the principal or partner redoing all the work. This would be impossible as well as completely unsatisfactory to the accounting firm, client, and staff assistants who are quick to resent an implication that they have not properly done their work or that their principal reposes no confidence in them.

Closely connected with the question of field supervision and review is the matter of standard minimum qualifications for an in-charge accountant. Here again there must be reasonable variation related to the basic demands of each engagement. A reasonably definite specification is that he must have the ability and experience adequate for the specific engagement of which he is given field charge. Many firms add to this the even more far-reaching requirement that he must have been with the principal or firm long enough and under such appropriate conditions as to have been fully tested as to competence and character.

A further essential is careful consideration as to the selection of all staff members, not only with respect to their specific assignments on individual engagements but also as to their general employment. Regarding the broader scope, a minimum requirement is that staff members have such character and education as to indicate definitely the possession of essential moral and professional integrity. Practically all firms consider this merely a preliminary requisite. They supplement it rigorously by requiring that every new staff member work for a reasonable period under such restrictive conditions that those not possessing the requisite moral and professional standards are certain to be eliminated.

The audit program. Another important factor from the standpoint of supervision and review is the audit program. Its value in this respect begins with its initial preparation for it serves to guide the in-charge accountant and is thereafter useful in checking his conduct of the engagement. Usually it is prepared by a principal, partner, or supervisor with the accountant in charge. It is prepared preferably in the client's office, where there is close contact with actual conditions. More often than not, however, it is necessary to prepare it in advance, and then the in-charge accountant is given leeway to develop any special line of inquiry which may seem desirable to him. Such a possibility is, of course, another which has obvious relevance to the degree to which field visits to the engagement may be necessary.

Reviewing the working papers. Field review, starting with the trial balance and the program, undertakes to determine whether the agreed-upon scope of the examination has been at least equaled. The next step is to see that the trial balance work sheet is clearly and legibly prepared and properly completed. With this as a basis, the reviewer can then begin the examination of supporting schedules: first, by comparing balances thereon with the trial balance, and second, by seeing that the items on the schedules are properly part of the account to which they have been charged.

At this point it is realized anew that rules, regulations, and standardization, no matter how helpful when used judiciously, must always remain subordinate to the vigilant exercise of intelligence, knowledge, experience, and judgment as dictated by varying circumstances. No one has summed up this inescapable reality more incisively than Colonel Robert H. Montgomery in his epigrammatic "The Curse of Balancing," (*The Journal of Accountancy,* August 1950). How can standardized procedures be applied effectively to the many problems that arise which in themselves are absolutely different from any other which has arisen or been reported upon? Recourse must be had, he asserts, to two basic and fundamental principles—truth and disclosure: "Tell the story and let the chips fall where they may!"

During the course of the item-by-item review of the trial balance and examination of supporting schedules, inquiry may be made into various details of the work performed. For instance, the replies to confirmation requests may be examined. Thereafter the senior accountant will make known to his principal the special problems encountered during the engagement, so that together they can then be resolved by discussion with the client or by proper adjustment.

After reviewing the main points of the auditing procedure the principal can undertake a broad view of the year's activities. This will often bring to light the answer to whether or not the senior accountant has applied to the examination:[1]

> That degree of vigilance, inquisitiveness and analysis of the evidence available that is necessary in professional undertaking and is recommended in all well-known and authoritative works on auditing.

Questions directed toward this end often include: Are the earnings more or less than last year? What is the main reason for the increase or decrease? Are the accounts receivable good and collectible? Are they really accounts receivable? Are there any large credit balances? Is the allowance for possible losses, if one is carried, too much or too little? Was confirmation satisfactory?

[1]SEC "Accounting Series Release No. 64."

Are inventories comparable to last year? Are inventory records good? Is any large round amount taken from the total? Is gross profit margin in line with preceding year? Have additions to fixed properties been approved? Have corporate minutes been read and expression given to all liabilities mentioned therein? Are all known contingent liabilities developed?

These questions and many more that will occur to the reviewer may be asked for two purposes: To decide whether or not certain matters need more review, analysis, or work, and to test the thoroughness of the senior's work and supervision.

The audit report. All field reviews of work done and papers accumulated must be conducted with the end in mind of writing the report which will contain the finished financial statements, together with their related comments, be these either explanatory or amplifying. It is in the final review that the decision is made as to the content of statements and schedules that are to appear in the report, and ever-present care should be taken to see that the working papers contain supporting information for the leading exhibits in the report.

In cases where the tax returns are to be made, the working papers must contain all the information necessary to complete the various schedules that are a part of the returns. This includes such expense accounts as taxes, officers' salaries, contributions, and data regarding the disposals of capital assets.

While most authorities agree that the client's office is the proper place to make the exhibits and schedules that are to go into the report, this is not always possible. The pressure of other matters, the required review at other points, the starting of a new engagement, as well as the ever-present desire to get back home, cause accountants to write their reports at places other than the client's offices and in many cases long after the audit has been completed.

Ideally each examination should be completely finished and its report written before the next engagement is started. Acountants are simply not able to meet this ideal condition and the finishing work is more often than not, especially during the peak season, done at nights with the pressures and anxieties which accompany the conducting of two or three assignments at the same time.

The "afterthought" audit. After the field work has been finished, all points of the field review thoroughly covered, and the report written, the report must have an office review, and this is often a face-reddening experience for both the principal and the senior who have worked on the examination.

The mere realization that there is to be such an office review should by itself make what may well be termed an "afterthought" audit an extremely rare phenomenon, and yet this occurs with deplorable frequency. A review may develop that some item of essential information has been overlooked. This omission is remedied by calling again at the client's office, by telephoning for it, or, in the case of out-of-town engagements, writing for it. The omission is thus remedied but should not have occurred and leaves an unfavorable impression upon the client, the accountant, and the staff. It would not have occurred had the in-charge accountant asked himself and acted on one last question in the field, namely, "Has every required item of information been obtained that is needed to complete this engagement?" Where an audit program is used, each item can be checked off as finished and care taken that all are checked. Where no such program is used, a less formal checklist can be prepared on which are recorded all items that are temporarily unfinished as the engagement progresses and which receives a final checking at the end of the engagement.

The office review. Whether or not there is an adequate field review, there should always be an office review before the report is released, its extent and scope depending in large part upon the scope of the field review. The records examined in an office review are the working papers and the report. Where there is a formal audit program, this is studied first and the working papers and the report related to it. Such a review is conducted in accordance with definite principles of reviewing stated hereafter.

Review of the working papers is fundamental to supply reliable evidence that there is a solid foundation for the report. There are times after the submission of a report when the in-charge accountant is no longer available to answer questions that may have arisen. It is particularly on such occasions that thorough, well-arranged, and properly indexed and reviewed working papers are invaluable.

Who does the reviewing? The office review is not conducted by the same process in all offices. Some firms have an employee who is designated as the chief-of-staff whose normal duties consist in part of assigning the accountants to the engagements and reviewing the working papers and the report after the audit is finished. Smaller firms having more than one partner decide which partner is to control the engagement all the way through to its completion, and each partner has a series of clients for whose audits he is responsible.

There are advantages to both systems and some firms use a part of each, but usually the office review is the duty of a partner. Quite frequently this is a partner who has had no contact with the engagement or with the men doing the work as it progressed. At first this may appear to be a disadvantage, but far more frequently it is an advantage because it brings to the work an entirely new mind which has to be convinced of the thoroughness of the work and the correctness of the statements, as well as one in a better position to judge how the finished report appears from the viewpoint of the client, the firm, and third parties.

The reviewer's approach. There are four major points which the reviewer must keep constantly in mind: (1) he must have confidence, based on his observation, in the accountant's integrity and ability; (2) he must have adequate supporting data in orderly arrangement; (3) he must have special knowledge of the particular subject or have available for conferences associates who are familiar with the business under review; and (4) he must approach his task with a view to developing the utmost possibilities of the engagement. All these points are essential and interdependent and on them, to the extent that they are observed, depends the effectiveness of the reviewer's work.

If the review of the audit program, working papers, and finished report, is done at one time, the reviewer has an opportunity to contribute greatly to the development of staff members and improvement of their work.

A general discussion of sufficiency of office review of working papers would be incomplete without specific reference to the views expressed by the Securities and Exchange Commission in the Interstate Hosiery Mills case in 1939.[2] The SEC felt that adequate review to insure integration of the original work papers with the financial statements should serve not only to disclose intentional or accidental misstatements but also be a method of internal check and control on the work of the firm's subordinates. Such review, though not necessarily done by a partner, should at least be done by one well versed in the firm's procedures and in the general principles and terminology of auditing and accounting; and where not done by a partner, it should be made by a person independent of those actually performing or supervising the audit work, as well as of those preparing the draft of the financial statements. Such review must be more than a series of perfunctory questions as to performance of particular items in an audit program; and explanation of unusual items should not be accepted without support in detail from the working papers.

Following the field review. The degree of intensity with which the field or office review is conducted is affected by the relevant factors applying to the engagement. When the field review has been conducted by a competent supervisor, a thorough and complete check in the office thereof results only in a duplication of work. Often the papers, by their very appearance, will denote the nature and extent of the review required. When the working papers are neat, orderly, and properly indexed to their accompanying schedules, confirmation forms are complete, and there are no doubtful or troublesome points, the review in the office can be completed in a relatively short time.

In such cases, after an inspection of the working papers, the office review will prove to be of more value if it is mainly concerned with satisfactory answers to such basic questions as:

1. Has a thorough job been done?
2. Has it been found necessary to do any more work not called for originally by the audit program?
3. Are the working papers sufficiently explanatory?
4. Are there items involving possible differences of opinion as to proper accounting treatments?
5. Have consistent accounting practices been employed by the client?
6. Have the final statements been reviewed and discussed with the client before the office review?
7. What should be explained in footnotes?
8. What items are new this time and have they been properly handled?
9. What in the audit and report is different this time and why?

The smaller firms usually settle all of their debatable points during the progress of the engagement by consultation of the accountant in charge either with the partner who reviews the papers or with someone else in authority.

It has been claimed that one criterion to apply to working papers is that they may be introduced as evidence in court proceedings and must be sufficiently clear to be understood, without explanation, should it be impossible to have in support of them the testimony of the accountant who

[2]SEC Official Release No. 2048, March 18, 1949.

prepared them. While this unmistakably would make for clear and revealing working papers, actually only a very small percentage of audit engagements result in litigation. By far the most prevalent test of the completeness of working papers is their ability to supply the answers to questions which often occur to clients after the final report has been typed and delivered.

In the absence of a field review. In cases where it has been found impossible to have a comprehensive field review of the engagement made by a supervisor or partner, the necessity for a more searching office review of the working papers becomes apparent. The office reviewer then serves in the place of the field reviewer and extends his review to cover all points considered to be necessary or desirable. These extended points include:

1. Review of the items on the trial balance and related work sheets
2. Check of auditor's journal entries for propriety and inclusion
3. Review of the work sheets to see that they support the figures in the financial statements
4. Review of bank reconciliations and inspection of confirmations
5. Review of confirmations to see that there are no liabilities, real or contingent, developed by the replies
6. Inspection of content of petty cash count
7. Review of inventory testing to see whether efficient checking of extensions and additions has been made; also checking to see whether client's inventory certificate has been signed
8. Check of gross profit margin
9. Check of papers to see whether they contain information in support of items added to fixed assets; inspection of depreciation schedules
10. Check of insurance schedules and comparison with asset values
11. Check to see whether capital stock has been proved and whether a complete analysis of retained earnings, contributed surplus, and reserves are in the papers
12. Review of copies of contracts and legal documents, or excerpts therefrom, to determine that they have been given effect to by the client

This list could be prolonged considerably, and almost every firm has certain special items to which it considers that the reviewer of working papers should give definite attention. Illustrations are the possible overadequacy of the allowance for doubtful accounts, criteria used by client in fixing depreciation rates (whether definite appraisal, considered opinion of engineers, guesswork, etc.), and scrutiny of insurance coverage to ascertain whether there are assets belonging wholly or in part to others.

Invariably the review of working papers calls for consultation with the in-charge accountant by the reviewer. Sometimes this is done while the working papers are being examined, but it is done just as frequently after their examination. More often than not the reviewer makes a written record of the questions and comments to be discussed, but only infrequently is the in-charge accountant required to put his own answers and comments in writing. On occasion, however, the reviewer will record them himself.

Flexibility of approach. The basic process of becoming satisfied as to the sufficiency of the work of staff personnel does not lend itself to inflexible standardization. Despite the seeming informality of the procedure of questioning assistants, each query is certain to have definite meaning and purpose, and unless all are answered to the entire satisfaction of the reviewer, a most significant conclusion is reached. It is that the engagement is still to be completed.

There are many other reasons why review of working papers cannot be effectively reduced to unyielding uniformity. Clearly any rigidly fixed standard of review of working papers cannot be applied reasonably when such modifying factors as the following are to be considered: (1) the engagement reviewed is a monthly audit, instead of a quarterly, semiannual, or annual one; (2) there is skilled over-all field supervision and review of the engagement as it progresses by some competent person in addition to the in-charge accountant; (3) the working papers and reports for several previous audit periods were previously reviewed in detail; (4) no major changes have been made in the audit procedure since the previous audit; and (5) no major changes have occurred in the client's financial condition since the previous audit.

To a large extent, review is an item-by-item and question-by-question matter. As one account after another is reviewed, in the sequence of the statement items or the working-paper arrangement, questions suggest themselves to the reviewer, each question being directed at the thoroughness of the analysis, the sufficiency of verification, or the adequacy of the presentation. In the final analysis, under such a procedure (whether or not aided by checklists or other partly standardized approaches), the effectiveness of the review depends primarily upon the inquisitorial skill of the reviewer.

Review of statements and adjustments with client. It has been found to be an excellent practice to have a discussion with the client regarding the financial statements after they have been completed. This is usually done by a principal or partner, but sometimes by the accountant in charge. While it is now generally understood that financial statements are the representations of management, nevertheless the fact remains that more often than not the balance sheet and income statement as prepared by the accountant are the first and only ones seen by the small client during the year. It is a rarity for the average small practitioner to have finished financial statements submitted to him for examination and approval. However, the factual representations contained in the statements, no matter who prepares the actual formal statements are, and of necessity must be, those of the client. The client cannot be excused for presenting statements which are known to be false any more than can the CPA, and the content of the statements should be seriously considered by the client in all cases.

During the discussions of the financial statements, the accountant is able to explain to the client the significance of the changes and developments that are being made in accounting procedure, auditing standards, and statement presentation. It is at this time that the adjustments and corrections found to be necessary are explained to the client, and here too the client is afforded an opportunity to obtain certain salient information which he may want to know.

Some accountants prefer to have this talk with the client after the report has been typed and delivered. Others take the untyped statements into the conference. Either way is satisfactory, but there is nothing that can bring an accountant and his client into closer mutual understanding than conversations of this nature and, if at all possible, they should always be held. As a matter of fact, in many cases the discussion turns into a joint review of the statements and report, stimulated by questions of the client as to the composition of items or the significance of comparisons and other relationships. Such review has in many cases brought new information to light.

Correction of errors. During the course of the examination, the average accountant will locate errors either of principle, entry, or mechanics that will require correction. The simplest and easiest method of assembling these errors is to make a list of entries for inclusion in the working papers. As a rule the errors are shown to the bookkeeper as they are found and the correcting entry made in the working papers at that time.

When the audit is finished, all of the correcting entries are entered in the general journal for posting to the proper accounts. Some firms refuse to let their accountants make entries on any of the clients' books. Others are not so particular, but the small practitioner will have to use his best judgment as to the proper means of achieving the desired result. There is no good purpose to be served in refusing, as a matter of principle, to render the necessary, proper, and helpful assistance which the client wants the bookkeeper to have. The accountant must adapt himself to the conditions and circumstances surrounding his engagement if he is to render the service expected of him by his client. The reviewer will include consideration of these entries in his review and discussion of the engagement as a whole.

REVIEW OF THE REPORT

Distinguished from and additional to the field review and the office review is the final review of the report itself. The generally accepted term, at least among the smaller firms, for this feature of the work is report-editing. The term is not entirely representative of the work done, because the review of the report extends beyond the scope of what is usually considered manuscript-editing and includes some reconsideration of the audit work as well as a review of the report itself.

Clerical review. The first part of the report review is accomplished by clerical procedures of proofreading, footing, recomputing, referencing, and inter-checking, following the typing. These may disclose, in addition to any mechanical errors in typing, many types of errors in the statements and report that would not necessarily be evident in the field or office reviews.

These clerical phases, which may precede or follow the final analytical review of the report in its finished form, are therefore highly important.

Who reviews the report? Basically, final report reviews are divided into two phases. The first is a subjective analytical examination of the various steps taken and the procedure followed in the engagement. The second is an objective over-all study of the engagement as a whole to develop fully its significance, value, and application. In smaller engagements both phases are apt to be covered simultaneously and by the same reviewer.

Report reviews are made almost invariably by a principal or a partner. This is particularly true of the objective phase where only very rarely is a supervisor or some eminently qualified staff member given such an assignment. However, no matter what the official status of the reviewer is, one requirement is always enforced. He must be so qualified by knowledge of accounting principles, familiarity with the special accounting practices and procedures of the particular industry, and acquaintance with the major problems of the client that searching inquiry by him of the in-charge accountant and his examination of the significant items in the report and related papers will produce formulation of an independent and reliable judgment as to the adequacy of the work done and the clarity and basic soundness of the financial statements.

Objective review. Generally, the basic steps of the objective part of the report review are these: (1) the report and the statements are read and studied carefully; (2) the audit program is considered in relation to the report; (3) the preceding report for the client, if any, is examined and compared with the current one to make certain that all essential data and pertinent qualifications have been covered; (4) notes are made during the examination of the report of items requiring explanation or further investigation; (5) questions and comments as to the report are discussed with the in-charge accountant and with any previous reviewer of any phase of the engagement; (6) the report reviewer makes definitely certain that the certificate prepared is adequate; and (7) changes in the report, other than typographical or grammatical, are made but only after conference with the in-charge accountant and others who have supervised or reviewed specific phases of the engagement.

A very important part of the report review is that pertaining to the textual or comment part of the report. Above all the comments should be accurate. Acrimonious or poorly founded statements about the financial condition of the business or of its records can result only in stirring up strife and discord. The comments should be entirely factual and the accountant should be sure of the facts. Hopeful predictions and congratulatory statements, while they make nice reading for the client, have no place in a report and should be deleted by the reviewer.

The long-form report. Most reports rendered by the small and moderate-sized accounting firms have come to be termed "long-form reports." These consist of a textual or comment section, balance sheet, income statement, and surplus statements, with schedules supporting certain items when necessary or desirable. While there is no standard order of arrangement, each firm has or should have a uniform method of report construction.

558

Clients who desire a long-form report for management and special uses may also request the accountant to prepare a short-form report to be used in connection with their published report to stockholders. Where both forms of report are prepared, based upon the same audit, the reports should be reviewed in close comparison with each other to safeguard against the possibility of inconsistencies and to guard against the possibility of a later claim that the condensed report suppressed material information or that it should have been qualified by some of the details disclosed in the long-form report.

Subjective review. Occasionally there will be found in the comment section of a report a statement that certain work required under generally accepted auditing standards has not been done, with no reasons furnished for this omission, which often is material. The accountant has little control over the desires of the client to have, or not to have, complete work done, but he does have sole and entire control over his own certificate or opinion. It is incumbent upon the accountant to bear in mind the requirements of Rule 2.03 of the AICPA's *Code of Professional Ethics* (see Appendix, page 821), as they affect the significance of his examination and the fairness of the financial statements.

It is in this field that the reviewer is called upon to make difficult decisions, to the extent either of overruling the field supervisor or going contrary to the wishes of the client. Also in the field of difficult decisions are those relating to disclosure. Full, fair, and straightforward disclosure of all facts necessary to make the statements informative and not misleading are not only required, but also are a "must" of good report-writing and reviewing.

From the standpoints of the client and interested third parties, the reviewer in the final analysis should have these queries in mind:

1. Exactly what does the report tell them?
2. Have their specific needs and problems been taken fully into account?
3. Precisely what can they determine from the report?
4. Does it give them sufficient factual evidence for effective decision and action?

And from the standpoint of the accounting principal or firm, the following points call for the reviewer's determination:

1. Has the engagement been completed with professional accuracy and competence in full compliance with all its terms?
2. Do all comments in the report convey exactly what is intended?
3. Have all exceptions and qualifications been set forth clearly?

Only when these questions have been satisfactorily answered is the report ready for release.

THE REVIEW QUESTIONNAIRE

Some firms have adopted a formalized approach to review procedures, as a guide or aid to the reviewers. Where there is such a formalized procedure for over-all review of working papers and reports, some firms have embodied this in a written questionnaire. Others follow the same general pattern without actually using a written questionnaire.

Generally the review questionnaire, written or oral, has four main subdivisions. The first covers basic data, the second representations by client, the third working papers and report, and the fourth release of the report.

Basic data. Under basic data, some of the initial points covered are the actual nature of the engagement, the agreement concerning it, its exact scope, the specific purpose of the report, nature and extent of any special arrangements, and so on. Later some other elements taken up are discussion with the client of the statements as finally prepared, discussion with the client of any required adjustment entries, and whether a separate letter should go to the client regarding recommendations, exceptions, and other matters not normally included in reports.

Representations by the client. During the course of an examination many representations regarding assets, liabilities, or revenue items are made to the accountant by the client or by his representatives. Usually these are made orally, in which event the accountant makes appropriate record of them in the working papers. However, written representations by the client are usually required when they relate to the more material items, such as accounts receivable, inventories, liabilities, and contingencies, but the practice as to this is not uniform.

There are variations among accounting firms in what is covered in writing and in the method of expressing the representations. Probably the two most important governing factors are materiality of the representation and the importance of avoiding any future misunderstanding regarding it. Generally only the larger firms have preprinted standard forms for written representations as moderate-sized and smaller firms have relatively much less use for them. This subject is fully treated in the Codification of Statements on Auditing Procedures.[3]

Many times when a form is used it must be extended to cover other items, if, in the judgment of the accountant in charge of the engagement or of the reviewer, the inclusion of such items is necessary or desirable. Hence where a report questionnaire is used, it makes certain with respect to representations by clients that all significant and material ones have been put in acceptable written form and that all those as to accounts receivable, inventories, and liabilities (including contingent) are adequate.

Audit working papers and reports. This subdivision of the review questionnaire is certain to be the most extensive. Its length will vary, naturally, according to the importance of the engagement, but the following items will give a representative idea of its contents.

1. Has receipt of needed confirmations been reviewed and approved as to

[3]Codification of Statements on Auditing Procedures, AICPA, 1951, pp. 48-57.

(a) accounts receivable, (b) accounts payable, (c) cash, (d) inventories, and (e) assets held by others?

2. Where the client's representations as to physical inventories were subjected to physical tests by the accountants, have the adequacy and findings of such physical tests been reviewed and approved?

3. Have the elements and the total of current assets been reviewed and approved?

4. Have the elements and the total of current liabilities been reviewed and approved?

5. Have all significant and material exceptions, problems or weaknesses in the system of internal control been set forth in a summary statement or schedule in the working papers by the in-charge accountant?

6. Have all said exceptions, and so forth, in (5) above been reviewed, commented upon, or disposed of?

7. Has audit procedure used in lieu of confirmations been reviewed and deemed adequate as to accounts receivable and accounts payable?

8. Has appropriate disclosure been made of the valuation and depreciation basis underlying the fixed assets?

Report release. Before the report is ready for signing and release, the following final questions provided by the questionnaire must be answered:

1. Are the report and the scope of the work performed in accordance with the customary or agreed-upon terms of the engagement?

2. Has a sufficient and reasonable review of the working papers been made?

3. Are the form, content, and terminology of the report satisfactory?

4. Has the need for footnotes or amplifying comments been carefully considered, and has appropriate disclosure been made?

5. Have the statements in the report been prepared according to appropriate standards for disclosure?

6. Are any qualifications or exceptions such as to raise a question as to the appropriateness of giving an opinion?

A precaution often taken with respect to review questionnaires is to frame the questions in such a way that affirmative answers are normally necessary in order to insure that satisfactory action has been taken on the points involved. A further safeguard enforced is that all negative answers must be supplemented by a satisfactory explanatory statement.

Clearly, where review questionnaires are used, each firm will have special questions of its own in the light of the general nature of its engagements, its policies, and its particular practices and procedures. And it will also presume that any relevant queries will be made that occur to the reviewer when such a questionnaire is applied to the review of each engagement. The following response from a firm, asked what it added on each occasion, is revealing: "Just many little things. The report is our finished product. Nothing is left undone that comes to mind at the time."

ILLUSTRATIONS OF REVIEW PRACTICES

As illustrations of review practices, the Appendix includes the following combination of material actually used by accounting firms:

1. An illustrative in-charge accountant's review questionnaire (page 894)
2. An illustrative office review questionnaire (page 896)
3. An illustrative checklist for report review (page 899)

The first is designed for use by the accountant in charge of the engagement and, when completed, is turned in with the working papers and draft of the report. It is intended to be a checklist of responsibilities and work in addition to that provided automatically by the trial balance and working papers themselves.

The second is usable as a questionnaire or checklist for the office or field review of the working papers by the principal or partner. This, too, is supplementary to questions normally arising from the review of the working papers and statements themselves.

The third illustration deals with the review of the report as distinguished from the working papers. It contains both a statement of policy for report review and a checklist. It assumes that if all of this material is recognized in the review of the report before typing, the mechanical procedures of interchecking and proofing by the clerical staff will accomplish substantially all of the additional safeguards required, and the final issuance of the report will then involve merely the reading and signing by a partner or principal.

REVIEW PROCEDURES FOR OTHER WORK

The following is a discussion of the review problems involved in assignments other than the usual audit reports. Review of tax returns is omitted here, but is covered on page 567.

System installation. The installation of a system of accounts does not readily yield itself to an office review. System work is done best when the installation is undertaken by one who is skilled at such work. The work requires the services of one who possesses imagination and ability to see the end from the beginning. Every business has some methods that cause variations to appear in the accounts and these must be recognized and provided for.

The customary installation of accounting systems by smaller accounting firms must be what their clients term a simple system. This involves a general ledger, cashbooks, journals, and such auxiliary records as are necessary. Often the accountant has to buy from the stationer's store the blank books required, insert the required headings, and perhaps make the opening entries, after which there ensues a series of instructions to some person who is to function as bookkeeper.

Such work is not adaptable to review in the accountant's office by accountants superior to the one making the installation. A memorandum of the nature and extent of the work done is made for the files, and this consists of a written record of all pertinent information, such as the chart of accounts, instructions left with the bookkeeper, and a brief narrative of the conditions surrounding the engagement. This, however, is mostly historical and it is impracticable to conduct an adequate office review of the work done. This omission is not serious, because if there are faults in the system they will soon be developed in the execution of the entries covering the daily work, and the necessary adjustments or alterations are made at the client's office.

Special investigations. A distinctive feature of the special investigations which accountants are retained to make is that their clients have an exact object in view. In some cases special investigations include the normal examinations of the financial position of a company and its operating results for a given period, but many are separate and distinct therefrom. Usually this class of work is undertaken with a purpose far different than is required for the annual accounting work, and wherever possible a capable accountant with specialized knowledge of the work required to be done is selected.

Accountants are versatile men and if the special investigation has accounting or auditing as its basis, the average skilled accountant may undertake the work. The various peculiar conditions of the client's operations are studied and learned by the accountant in charge as he progresses with the work to such an extent that, upon its completion, he possesses a special knowledge of the work so complete that subsequent review of his work by his office superior is most difficult, if not impossible.

The review of a report to be rendered to the client as a result of a special investigation does not differ from that given to the report of a regular examination. Each report differs according to the information desired and results obtained. Some reports are entirely narrative, with but few, if any, accompanying financial schedules or exhibits. Other reports are replete with financial statements of various kinds and forms, in which cases there is usually a more or less detailed recital of the salient points contained in the statements.

The working papers for a special investigation, while not necessarily arranged in the form used for a regular examination, should be complete and their contents easily followed into the finished report. Source information and reasons supporting new, unusual, or extraordinary conditions should appear in the working papers.

The review of reports on special investigations should be made with special attention to the purpose of the engagement and the clearness of the presentation of the subject matter. It happens sometimes that an accountant conducting a special investigation gets to know his subject so well that he falsely assumes that the client has knowledge equal to his and that complete or detailed exposition is not necessary. When this occurs the primary purpose of the investigation is defeated; the reviewer should use as a test the clearness of the report to him, and where it is ambiguous or the facts are not completely presented he should have it rewritten.

In smaller firms the practice of frequent consultations with the reviewing authority regarding points in the work is the custom. It is a salutary one, often resulting in the development of ideas helpful to all parties.

Other work. Closely connected with the regular examinations made by accountants are the engagements which require the preparation of financial statements and their supporting schedules in the form required by governmental commissions, agencies, or bureaus. The most outstanding of these are the statements to be submitted either to the Securities and Exchange Commission or the Federal Power Commission.

Other work which accountants are called upon to perform includes the preparation of accounts for estates, trusts, or guardianships, which must meet the requirements of courts or of commissioners appointed by the courts. Statements rendered for receivers or referees, or trustees in bankruptcy or receivership, also demand a presentation of facts in a specified manner. Budget preparation and projection of present financial results into the future also may occupy the attention of the practicing accountant.

Miscellaneous work, whatever may be its nature or purpose, requires the selection of accountants best equipped to complete the work. The review of specialized work is not easy and frequently it requires consultation with the accountant in charge of the engagement, but the main principles of reviewing exist for special engagements as well as for routine or regular examination. Often a reviewer's professed lack of knowledge of a particular operation proves to be an advantage, for in seeking enlightenment on certain items, he develops a need for a different presentation which results in an improvement to the report.

INFORMING THE STAFF MAN OF THE RESULTS OF THE REVIEW

While it is essential that all the necessary corrections be made after review, it is wise to see to it that the same mistakes are not committed again. To this end, one firm employs the following procedure:

In order to keep staff accountants currently informed of the appraisal of their work, a review form for audit work papers, report and tax returns is prepared in duplicate for all jobs on which an audit report is rendered. After the work is reviewed and the form is filled in by the reviewer, the original is filed in a loose-leaf notebook under a tab showing the name of the staff man who prepared the report. The copy is given to the staff man with the expectation that he will endeavor not to make the same mistake(s) that he previously made. The original and duplicate of the form, which is on three-ring notebook paper, are prepared by the man who writes the audit report, with the following information filled in.

> Name of client . . . .
> Engagement . . . .
> Date of engagement . . . .
> Supervisor . . . .
> Accountant in charge . . . .
> Report written by . . . .

There is a short space on the form to indicate in the affirmative or negative if the following matters have been properly handled.

Work papers
Audit program (completed in order)
PWP (permanent work papers, completed in order)
Confirmations (received on all appropriate accounts; some men have tendency to turn in for review before all are received)
Questionnaires filled in (relates to tax, management services, etc.)
All sheets attached (in the work papers; some men fail to attach all sheets, particularly confirmation forms, in the work-paper binder)
Logical arrangement (arrangement of analyses, with related ones on the same page)
Properly indexed
Neatness
Management letter
Time budget next year

Report manuscript
Logical arrangement
Proper separation of unaudited data
Auditors' report (proper form, wording of exceptions and qualifications, etc.)
Neatness
Dates
Dollar signs ⎫ We follow the practice that the typist has a right to type
Capitalization ⎬ what she sees.

Remarks. (Lines taking up about two-thirds of the page for comments on items marked "no")

Tax returns. (Several lines for remarks on preparation of the tax returns)

The above captions tend to serve as a checklist for the staff man to see that he has the job complete, including work papers, report and tax returns.

Originally, the form was prepared with one or two lines after each caption for comments. However, we found that usually one or two topics were commented on and the rest were all right. For the subjects on which the reviewer had comment, there was not enough room for his remarks. Therefore, the form was rearranged with a small amount of space after each subject for the insertion of "yes" or "no." When "no" is entered after one of the subjects, then a comment is made below as to why.

When the report, tax return, and work papers are prepared by one staff accountant and turned over to a senior staff member who is not a partner for detailed checking and review, the review sheet is prepared in blue or black ink or pencil. Subsequently, when a partner gives the report a cursory review, his comments are made in red, using red carbon to print on the copy.

For the semiannual or annual review of a staff man's progress, the remarks from the review sheets prepared since the last personnel review are summarized and used in connection with the appraisal of his work. This procedure keeps the staff man currently informed as to the status of his work and the areas for improvement.

Handling Tax Returns

GENERAL POLICIES

■ **Who should prepare the return?** All modern accountants possess a working knowledge of federal and state income tax laws and regulations. Not all accountants have or pretend to have adequate knowledge and experience to handle protested cases. As a rule there is in every firm one person, usually a partner, who makes a sincere effort to keep abreast of the continual changes in the law, the regulations, and the decisions of the courts as they affect income taxes. This in itself is a full-time work, difficult and often troublesome, but it does equip one person not only to handle most of the tax matters of his firm but also to review the tax work of others in the firm.

It is desirable as far as the organization will permit to have only men skilled in tax knowledge prepare the original returns, on the assumption that staff men who are engaged principally in auditing work are not "tax-minded." It is impracticable, however, in smaller firms to have tax men prepare all of the returns that now are required to be filed. This extends not only to income-tax returns but to the many other returns, such as property returns, declarations, and so on.

The practice generally employed is to have the accountant who is in charge of the engagement prepare the return and submit it for review by the men who constitute the tax department or by the one person most skilled in tax knowledge. The preparation of the return should be undertaken with the idea that it must be easy to review. Submitting a tax return with the idea that the reviewing authority will correct its deficiencies is poor workmanship and should under no circumstances be done.

While income-tax returns are usually prepared by the principal or accountant who is familiar with the client's accounting and tax problems, in some firms, the required tax information is assembled in the working papers and the returns are then prepared by a person or persons in the firm's tax department.

It is desirable that the federal income-tax return be either prepared or reviewed by a person familiar with the client's affairs. The pencil copy should then be reviewed by a principal or by a trained member of the tax staff, for accuracy of computation, for completeness, and with a view towards suggestions for present or future tax savings.

Having the accountant in charge of the engagement prepare the returns has in general proved to be satisfactory and it is the only method available to the smaller firms. Doubtful points arising in the consideration of items as they are developed are discussed with the tax department or the principal tax authority in the firm before the return is made, so that these items may receive the correct handling. An important and often neglected feature of this work is to have the accountant who is to prepare the return be told just why a specific item is includable as income or not deductible as an expense. In most cases it is the accountant preparing the return who must tell the taxpayer of the decision regarding the doubtful item, and unless he can give the taxpayer the reasons governing the decision, he is at a disadvantage.

Control of the work. In the tax departments of some firms, a list is maintained of all returns prepared by the firm, chronologically arranged by the date due at the various government offices. Persons responsible for their preparation are advised by the tax department several weeks before the due date as a reminder and so that extensions may be obtained in ample time, if necessary. This is important because of penalties and interest which may be incurred by the client if returns are filed late.

For a detailed description of work-control procedures, see "Tickler Files and Follow-up Files," pages 669-674, as well as "Notched Card System," page 578, and "Another Firm's Use of Cards," page 581.

Reviewing the return. The returns as submitted for review should consist of a pencil copy of the completed returns and all schedules completely filled in. The tax should be computed and all doubtful points resolved. It is desirable that a copy at least of the preceding year's return accompany the current return when it is submitted for review. When both federal and state income-tax returns are prepared at the same time, any difference in taxable income appearing on the two returns should be reconciled and the reconciliation sent with the returns to the reviewer. This can be further improved by showing a complete reconciliation with the book income. Some states require these reconciliations to accompany the return; others do not.

In reviewing the return, the totals of all schedules are checked to their places on the return and the schedules are inspected to see that all items therein are taxable income or proper deductions, as the case may be. In reviewing returns of individuals, the reviewer does not have an opportunity to make a complete check because the absence of a balance sheet and analysis of surplus limits him to an examination of the schedules submitted and a recomputation of the tax liability. Several firms publish a booklet of detailed tables affording a handy check on tax computations.

Corporation returns afford an opportunity for the reviewer to make a more satisfactory check because such returns are complete as to the statement of income, balance sheet, and surplus statement. In their review, the items on the income statement are determined to have their proper places in the tax return and the surplus statement is scrutinized to see whether or not the items appearing therein are properly excludable from the face of the return. The reviewer independently recomputes the tax liability.

If it should happen that the accountant preparing the return has not had an opportunity of discussing a doubtful item with the tax department prior to submitting the return for review, he should attach a memorandum to the return explaining the item and how it was handled, thereby not relying on the reviewer to discover the item.

Many firms have a form containing instructions and other pertinent data to accompany the return when it is submitted for review. The following is a good example:

Figure I

Date promised

Client
....

Period | Fed. income
....

No. of Copies: Returns   Schedules | State income
....

Prepared by   Approved by | State intangible
....

Information   ☐ Secured from audit | Fed. declaration
 ☐ Taken from books without audit
 ☐ Furnished by taxpayer | State franchise

Charge to
....

Remarks
....

....

....

Typed by
....   Verified by

Read   To
....   Corrected by

Assembled by
....   Approved by

Date mailed
....

Corrections
....

(The form provides ten additional lines below for noting corrections)

In a smaller firm, a simple but effective procedure is the use of a rubber stamp in the upper corner of the pencil copy of the return, as follows:

568

```
┌─────────────────────────────────────────┐
│                                         │
│   Prepared by . . . . . . . . . . . . . . . . .  │
│   Date . . . . . . . . . . . . . . . . . . . . .  │
│   Approved by . . . . . . . . . . . . . . . .  │
│   Date . . . . . . . . . . . . . . . . . . . . .  │
│   Typed by . . . . . . . . . . . . . . . . . . . │
│   Typing checked by . . . . . . . . . . . .  │
│                                         │
└─────────────────────────────────────────┘
```

Processing the return. After the returns are completed they are either processed through the firm's reproducing machines (see page 582 for a detailed description of the several varieties) or typed in duplicate so that the taxpayer may be furnished with a copy. In the latter case, the returns and their accompanying schedules must pass through a process of verification, proofreading, and assembling of schedules in every way similar to that required for an audit report. After this the finished returns are inspected again by the reviewing authority for signature, wherever signature of the person preparing the return is required. It then gets a final scrutiny at his hands, is signed, and is ready for delivery to the taxpayer.

The number of copies. Some firms type an original and one copy of each return, one for the government and one for the client's files. The pencil copy is thus the accounting firm's only retained copy. It is well to consider the advisability of typing an original and two copies. It is no more work and results in a typed copy for the firm's files of each return which is sent out. In case of subsequent dispute as to just what was sent out or if the client's copy goes astray, an exact copy will be helpful.

Completion and delivery. Some firms bind the client's copy of the tax return in a regular report cover. This facilitates filing and handling by the client and in general offers a neater and more effective appearance.

It is an excellent practice in transmitting returns to the taxpayer to have a covering letter accompany them, stating how and by whom it is to be signed, where it is to be filed, and the amount of taxes to be paid at the time of filing. It is important that a copy of it be retained in the accountant's office with the date of transmission shown thereon. This is an important document to have in a case where the taxpayer overlooks filing the return within the required period of time.

Most firms send either a printed or typewritten letter of transmittal with each return, indicating the amount of tax due, date due, place of filing, and other information. It is usually unnecessary to type a special letter for each return. The use of forms can save much typing time, since only the name and address, amount of tax, date, and place of filing need to be filled in.

In order to avoid clients' misplacing or not filing returns mailed to them, some accounting firms have the client sign the return and mail it back to the accountant with the check to the tax collector. The accountant delivers the returns to the tax collector and obtains a receipt therefor. This is not wholly desirable as it places an added and unnecessary burden of follow-up on the accounting firm. Other accounting firms request the client to sign a copy of the letter of transmittal which accompanies the returns and to mail the letter back to the accountant's office at the time the tax return is filed.

SPEEDING UP THE PROCEDURE

Avoiding typing. It cannot be denied that the typing stage of the tax-return process is relatively unproductive. Typing does give extra copies, sure legibility, a degree of neatness (only as great as the typist's competence), and possibly a certain professional dignity, but are these attractions worth the cost of labor and supplies and the time needed to check each copy?

Many accountants have decided that, if copies can be obtained some other way, the advantages of typing are not worth the cost. Several methods are being used to eliminate the typing bottleneck and increase profits. You can choose the one best suited to your practice.

Fundamentally all these methods are alike. The tax return is prepared in pencil and duplicate copies are made by one process or another. Obviously, any such process must meet these tests:

1. The copies must be acceptable to federal and state governments.
2. The copies must be acceptable to the client.
3. The requirements of the process must not significantly increase the accountant's preparation time.
4. The cost must be lower than typing.

The obvious objection that clients will not accept handwritten copies has been rather easily overcome in actual practice. A number of large national accounting firms are now handwriting returns and they report two tested ways to overcome this objection:

1. Use printed supplemental schedules to reduce the actual amount of writing to a minimum.
2. If your writing is absolutely illegible, learn to print. Your child does it in the first grade. Surely you can do as well.

The Internal Revenue Service and state governments have no objection to handwritten returns. Neither will your clients, if they receive a faster job at lower cost.

For the few meticulous clients, use handwritten supplemental schedules for everything possible so that the amount of typing on the official form is at a minimum. Then type the official form and bind in the handwritten schedules. For a detailed description of the various types of reproducing equipment, see page 582.

Supplemental schedules. An integral part of every method that avoids typing

returns is a good assortment of printed supplemental schedules for depreciation, rental income and expenses, profit and loss from business and profession,
gains and losses, itemized deductions, and for many other common items which
would otherwise be drawn up on columnar paper for each individual return.

Generally, a schedule drawn up in pencil on blank paper is not acceptable
to the client; but, if a printed form is used and only figures and a very small
amount of writing are inserted, the finished schedule looks neat and professional in spite of the pencil-writing. Several publishing companies now sell a
variety of supplemental schedules. These stock items should meet most of
your needs for schedules. Incidentally, they also save preparation time, because you do not have to head up columns and, on some forms, federal and
state totals are reconciled.

Larger firms also print some of their own schedules, based on frequency
studies of prior returns. For instance, a schedule may be made up of "other
deductions" for Form 1120 with fifteen or twenty expense headings printed in.

While many accountants prefer to submit separate schedules rather than
complete those appearing on the return, this may not be the method preferred
by the taxing authorities. With the increased use of automatic data processing,
for example, the IRS's initial processing of returns is not facilitated by the
excessive use of separate schedules.

Pencil carbon copies. In the past, most accountants have found pencil carbon
copies unsatisfactory for two reasons:

1. It is impractical to make pencil carbons of the government-issued
official forms because they are printed on both sides. With the carbon inter-
leaved, you cannot flip from one page to another as is so often required.

2. Riders and additional schedules drawn up on blank paper in pencil are
not acceptable to clients.

Both of these problems have been solved: the last one by the use of printed
supplemental schedules as outlined above; the first by the use of official forms
that are printed on one side of the paper only. Several publishing companies
now print official U.S. and some state forms on thin paper on one side of
the sheet only. These forms are printed by a photographic process, so they are
exact duplicates of the official form and are approved for filing by the respective governments.

Using these pads of single pages, your office girl can insert carbon paper
between the top three or four sheets and tear them off ready for your use in
preparing the return. The glue used in padding holds the sheets in register
even after they are torn off the pad. Your printed supplemental schedules
should be likewise prepared by her. You can then write on any page of the
official forms or any supplemental schedule without shifting carbon paper.

It is important that you use pencil carbon paper—not typewriter carbon.
The latter requires too hard an impression. Before you buy, test the carbon
paper for erasing qualities, and ask about non-smear coated paper which
considerably reduces soiling of the hands.

Accountants using the pencil-carbon method say that if you remember that what you are writing will be used as the final product, you will find yourself turning out legible copy.

ILLUSTRATIVE PROCEDURES

Firms keeping a written record, by client, of tax work performed, generally include the following information:

1. Nature of tax return (that is, income franchise, etc.)
2. Kind of tax (federal, state, or local)
3. Calendar of dates when returns are due
4. Who performed the work
5. Tax returns audited by the IRS
6. Delivery dates and other pertinent data on returns delivered to clients
7. Special information of a confidential nature on clients' tax matters

Tax calendar. One small practitioner uses a "tax calendar" (Figure 3), for businesses and individuals. He sends the client a copy with the return. On the first of every month he sends a tax reminder form to his clients. It is called a "Reminder on taxes and reports—other than income taxes," and it lists the various returns to be filed.

In sending clients their returns, he also includes a memo of instructions and a prestamped envelope addressed to the District Director of Internal Revenue or the state collector of revenue (Figure 2). He has a rubber stamp for the name and address of each collector of taxes, which saves stenographic time in addressing. The envelope return name and address are his own. If delivery is not made, the envelope is returned to him which places him on notice.

Figure 2. Memo of Instructions

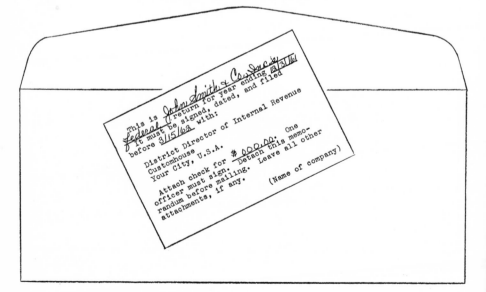

Figure 3. Income Tax Calendar for Individuals

Memo from:

        (Name of Accounting Firm)

        1961 INCOME TAX CALENDAR

      Mr. & Mrs. _____

		Amount to Pay		
Deadline	Thing to Do	Husband	Wife	Joint
4/15/61	File 1960 Federal Return	$	$	$
4/15/61	File 1961 Federal Estimate, Pay 1/4			
5/15/61	File 1960 State Return, Pay 1/3			
6/15/61	Pay 2nd and 1/4 Federal Estimate			
8/15/61	Pay 2nd 1/3 State Tax			
9/15/61	Pay 3rd 1/4 Federal Estimate			
11/15/61	Pay 3rd 1/3 State Tax			
1/15/62	Pay 4th 1/4 Federal Estimate			

                        was

Note: Your 1961 Estimate   based on 1960 earn-
                   was not
    ings. If not, it must be amended by 1/15/62
    to equal at least 70% of the actual tax;
    otherwise it requires no amendment.

    Make all Federal checks
      payable to: Director of
                    Internal Revenue

    Make all State of
    _____ checks payable
    to: Collector of Revenue,
                    State of _____

Notifying the client in advance. *A simple postcard.* One year, after their annual tax return season frenzy was over, the partners of one firm wondered why some people had not called for an annual visit. They were surprised to discover that even people who are willing to pay a reasonable fee for service seemed to have a feeling that they were imposing on a CPA when seeking his advice and assistance.

As an experiment, the firm sent out postcards one year to everyone for whom they had prepared a return the prior year, suggesting a date and time when they would be pleased to assist with tax returns. They were completely dumbfounded when people appeared at the appointed hour exhibiting their postcards and explaining to the secretary that they had appointments.

Clients' reactions. The experiment was so successful that the following year the firm sent individually typed letters with even better results. Clients were much more impressed by the personal letter and showed them with some pride to their friends, which resulted in additional referrals. They seemed to take great delight in being able to say, "*My* accountant automatically sets up an appointment each year and reminds me of it."

A sample letter. A sample letter follows. It is designed to cover several things. First, this firm feels the client should be aware that his patronage is remembered and appreciated. Any notion that he is imposing should be dispelled; he should be impressed that the firm values his account. (Of course, the letters are sent *only* to those clients served by the firm the previous year.)

October 7, 1961

Mr. John Doe
2156 Montreal St.
Toledo, Ohio

Dear Mr. Doe:

In reviewing our work for the forthcoming federal income tax filing season, we are endeavoring to plan our work schedule so that we can serve our clients in the most efficient manner possible. In order to give your tax returns proper attention without undue time pressure, we have taken the liberty of blocking out some time to confer with you.

We appreciated the opportunity to serve you last year and sincerely hope that we may do so again this year. To serve you if you are planning to call on us, we have set aside conference time for you on (date). We would suggest about (time) if this is convenient.

If either the date or the time is inconvenient, please call our secretary who will be pleased to suggest alternate times.

If you have had problems this year which are materially different from those of last year it might be well to call us so that we can outline the data that will be required to complete your return.

We are looking forward to the pleasure of serving you again.

Very truly yours,
Thomas Smith and Co.
By . . . .

A second point which is important is the suggestion that if the client's affairs are materially different from the prior year it might be well to call for instructions as to what data will be needed. This proved a timesaver because invariably the client will get out his last year's return and refresh his mind as to what he should bring in. If something is different, he will call and the groundwork can be laid to avoid last-minute scurrying.

The client's appointment. It is important to suggest to the client that he may call and set an alternate time if he wishes. A secretary maintains a list of open time and is prepared to shift the schedule as needed. Surprisingly, there are comparatively few changes since the partners give some thought to the known habits of each client and attempt to set times which will be convenient to him. Also, they attempt to allow sufficient time to consider his case when he arrives.

In actual practice the partners block out Saturdays and times during the week when they will be available. The clients' files are out when they arrive and usually a staff man is available to confer with the client and assemble the essential data. When a partner finally sits down with the client most of the detail work is done, and the return can be discussed in a short period of time.

The firm installed a copying machine as an experiment. When a client asked when his return would be ready, he was told that it could be ready in a few minutes if he would accept photocopies. If he preferred it typed, it might take several days. Every single client asked for photocopies, expressing appreciation for our efficiency in the use of the copy machine and in the reminder letters. The relief from typing and proofreading was tremendous.

Often the question is debated as to whether or not a CPA can afford to take on a great amount of individual tax return preparation. Probably there is no conclusive answer to this question. The partners in this firm feel that they cannot refuse to do it with impunity. They are convinced that it can be handled efficiently and profitably, in a manner which brings goodwill and highly desirable referrals. Finally, the staff puts in less night work.

Individual questionnaire. "The best memory is a pencil and paper." How many times have CPAs had to do a tax return over again because the client forgot to give complete information? The questionnaire shown in Figure 4 (page 576) is a good reminder for the client and a handy checklist for the accountant. It is sent in advance to the client, and reminds him of data he needs for his tax return. In going over the return, the accountant need take only a few minutes to check over the questionnaire; he is quickly reminded of items which may have been overlooked. When every number is checked, he is sure everything is accounted for. Although much of the information is basic, the questionnaire is a timesaver during a period when forgetfulness can waste time—and time is a valuable commodity.

Carbonized tax forms. There are many accountants who use copying and duplicating machines in the preparation of tax returns. There are still many others who do not use any kind of duplicating equipment. Yet through careful planning a great deal of overtime can be saved by accounting and typing staffs.

One CPA's procedures, which have resulted in considerable saving of time during the rush period, involve the use of carbonized income-tax returns and schedules. Returns and schedules, both official and unofficial, are regularly

Figure 4. Individual Income Tax Questionnaire

1. Does client qualify as "head of household"
2. Does client qualify for retirement income credit
3. Has either spouse died during the past two years
4. Has wife separate income, if so:
   a. From wages
   b. Are W-2s submitted
   c. Occupation
   d. Other sources—specify
5. Has client filed an estimated declaration
   a. Do we have record of payments
   b. Are there any credit carry-overs
   c. Has original estimate been amended
   d. Has full amount of declaration been paid
6. Has client income from wages
   a. Are W-2s submitted
7. Has client any excludable "sick pay"
8. Business income
9. Farm income
10. Income from dividends
    a. Domestic
    b. Foreign
    c. Insurance companies
11. Are stocks listed in name of husband and wife
12. Interest income
13. Capital gains and losses
14. Gains or losses from sale of other than capital assets
15. Pensions
16. Annuities
17. Income from rental property
18. Income from royalties
19. Partnership income
20. Income from estates and/or trusts
21. Director's fees
22. Commissions received—without W-2 reporting
23. Has client sold his home during the year
24. Have any insurance policies matured or been cancelled
25. Building and loan maturities
26. Have U.S. bonds been redeemed or cashed
27. Were any personal assets sold (auto, etc.)
28. Contributions
29. Interest paid
30. Has a single premium annuity been bought
31. Tax paid
    a. Federal income
    b. State income
    c. Real estate
    d. Social security
    e. Auto
    f. State liquor
    g. Gasoline
    h. Excise
    i. State sales
32. Medical expenses and dental expenses
33. Casualty losses
34. Losses on guaranty of loans
35. Accounting and tax fees paid
36. Investment advisory services costs
37. Travel expenses
    a. Local
    b. Away from home
38. Automobile expenses
39. Business entertainment
40. Association or business dues
41. Bad debts
42. Convention expenses
43. Alimony or maintenance payments
44. Should separate state returns be filed
45. Is a return necessary for any dependent
46. Discuss next year's declaration

used for 1040 1040ES, Schedules *C* and *D,* 1065 and 1120, as well as schedules for depreciation, travel, rentals, and so forth.

Filling in information in advance. The use of carbonized tax forms is no innovation: they have been available for some time. However, over a period of years this firm has developed a technique of typing in advance as much information as possible on the unofficial schedules and official tax returns. A supply of unofficial forms and schedules is kept on hand at all times, and pretyping on these schedules may be done at any time during the year. The official tax forms usually are available some time in November and the pretyping on these forms may be begun as soon as they are received.

Advantages of pretyping. The pretyping procedure follows this pattern. As soon as practicable after each filing season, each partner reviews the returns prepared during the filing season. From past association with and knowledge of each client, they are able to determine which information may be typed in advance. This information is checked with a red pencil. The office secretary may, at any time during the year, know which forms should be placed in the client's files and what information may be pretyped.

This means that by the beginning of the filing season, much of the work has been done. The method has the following advantages:

1. Although the total work is not decreased, the period during which the work is actually done is greatly extended.

2. It can serve as a training program for the typist. Even though she may not have been employed during the previous tax season, she will become thoroughly familiar with the forms and schedules prior to the tax season.

3. The time of the typist is more fully utilized.

4. When the typist is doing part of her own typing in advance, she is reducing a portion of the accountants' "writing." The firm uses the last copy of each return or schedule which has been pretyped as an office copy. The office copies need to be completed in pencil when the final information is available during the tax season. The typist knows that only the pencil information, which has been added since she pretyped the forms, has to be added to the returns and schedules.

Information that can be pretyped. It may be well to consider some of the information which may be typed in advance. On Form 1040, as an example, the client's name, address, names of dependents, and employer may be typed in advance. If there is a possibility that any of this information may change, it should be omitted. On Form 1040, Schedule *C,* as another example, in many cases all information except the amount of the current year's earnings may be pretyped. This includes the maximum amount subject to self-employment tax and the amount of the self-employment tax, in many instances.

With reference to depreciation schedules, many of the firm's clients have no detailed record of fixed assets owned other than the schedule which accompanies their tax return. For this reason, it has been necessary to prepare detailed depreciation schedules. In many cases, the complete schedules may be pretyped. The firm has experimented with typing in the current year's depreciation. This means that if there are no changes, the schedule is complete prior to the tax season. If there are additions and/or disposals, adjustment can be made following the subtotals which have been typed on the schedule.

On the average, as much as 50 per cent of the information may be typed in advance. This means that this much work will not have to be written by the accountants, typed, or checked during the tax season. It may make the difference between hiring additional personnel for a short period or accomplishing the work with regular, well-trained personnel. It goes a long way toward minimizing overtime.

Tax return transmittal form. Many clients waste valuable office time by calling and asking obvious questions concerning the amount of tax or installment due. They ask to whom the check should be drawn and where the return and checks should be mailed. Sometimes they also want to know how many persons must sign the return and where they should sign.

The form shown in Figure 5, devised by a small practitioner, provides a quick way to handle client queries on most tax returns. Some firms attach a different instruction sheet and form to each type of return, such as federal 1040, 1040*ES,* 1120, state individual return, and so on. A form can be specially designed for every other type of return, for refunds due, and for refunds applied against the next year's estimate.

These preprinted instruction forms may be used by accountants to serve their clients better and to save their own valuable time during the filing period. The forms save time for typists assembling returns. They merely have to insert the figures in the proper blank spaces.

As an additional service to their clients, many firms include with the tax forms envelopes addressed to the taxing authorities. Some firms include an envelope for clients' use in keeping their copies. Other firms provide manila folders in which the tax returns are stapled and ready for filing.

Notched card system. Following is a detailed description of one firm's use of a notched card system for controlling tax work.

We set up a card system to avoid overlooking returns due for clients and to aid in providing a means of control throughout the processing of returns. With the growth of the firm and the increase in the number of clients, we felt that the card system would provide a more versatile method than the loose-leaf book which had been used. The basic information in the book, type of return, when processed, final disposition, and staff designation, was carried to the cards. Time is saved with the cards since a new book does not have to be typed up each year and cards for new clients can be inserted in alphabetical order.

Other uses of the cards. In addition to the control feature, we have found that the cards are useful as a convenient source of addresses and phone numbers, and as a ready reference to the staff member responsible for a client. The cards also accumulate information over a period of years, since one line in most cases will suffice for one year's work, in so far as income-tax returns are concerned. As the time for income-tax season approaches, it becomes necessary to determine the approximate number of forms that will be needed for the year. Since cards are notched for the federal and state income-tax forms and printed schedules are most commonly used, they can be sorted and counted easily.

We have provided space for the name, address, and phone number of each client. A space is also provided for remarks. We have principally used this space to note such data as the fiscal year, employer's identification number, etc. A small section which is marked "staff" is used for the initials of the staff member responsible for the client whose name appears on the card. Each staff member has been assigned a number which he keeps as long as he is with the firm. The section of the card for notching marked "staff" is then notched in accordance with the number assigned to the staff member.

Figure 5. Tax Return Transmittal Form Letter

P. R. STEWART & CO.

26 Sycamore St.
Wallingford, Conn.

. . . .

. . . .

. . . .

. . . .

These instructions apply to the enclosed tax return. Please comply with them.

Draw check to
( ) Internal Revenue Service
( ) Tax Commissioner
( ) Administrator Unemployment
Compensation
( ) . . . .

Mail to address checked
( ) Director of Internal Revenue
( ) Administrator Unemployment
Comp., Hartford
( ) State Tax Commissioner,
Hartford
( ) Secretary of State, Hartford
( ) . . . .

Amount of check
( ) Full amount of tax
( ) Installment of $. . . . .
( ) . . . .

To be signed on page . . . .
( ) by taxpayer
( ) by any officer or partner
( ) by two officers
( ) . . . .

Notary's signature
( ) required
( ) not required
( ) notary's seal required
( ) . . . .

File return by . . . .

P. R. Stewart, CPA
By . . . .

Form of the cards. The main body of the card carries three divisions. Each of these divisions is broken down into a section marked "checked," a column with a *T*, and a section marked "mailed." In use, we head each division with the appropriate return, such as "Federal individual," "State individual," and "Estimate." The columns within each division are used in the following sequence: First, when a return has been prepared by a staff member and given to the typing department, a notation is made in the checked column showing the year of the return. Second, after the return has been checked mathematically and for correct handling of the material, the checker's initials and the date checked are entered in a column headed "checked." After the return has been typed and proofread, the date is entered in a column headed "T." A column marked "mailed" is reserved for the final disposition of the return. We date with a rubber stamp when we mail the signed return directly to the office of filing. If the client is to be responsible for the filing of the return, we note that fact by writing "client" and the date the return was turned over to the client.

Related forms. In order to provide information for the setting up of cards for new clients or new work a "new account" sheet is filled out by the staff member responsible for the account. This form carries all information needed for the preparation of new cards.

In conjunction with the cards, we use an information or instruction sheet with each return. White sheets are used for work to be done in a routine manner and pink sheets for rush work. The instruction sheets are used for all work, whether recorded on cards or not. This instruction sheet is filled out by the staff member and contains information as to the type of return or returns prepared, the client's name, the date needed, and instructions as to its disposition.

Since many clients take their returns home for examination or to obtain a signature, we found that we needed some control other than the card in order to know the status of the return at all times. The bottom portion of the instruction sheet has a section designed to provide information as to whether the client is to mail his own return, or bring the return back to our office for mailing. The instruction sheets which indicate that the client is to bring the return back to our office are filed alphabetically until such time as the client actually brings the forms to the office.

Filing the cards. We have four file drawers to accommodate our cards. The first of these is marked "Work to be done," and the cards are filed alphabetically in groups according to the due date. As soon as a staff member has prepared a return, the card is transferred to the "Work in process" drawer. When the return has been completed for the current year, and final disposition is made of it, the card is transferred to the drawer marked "Completed work." The bulk of the cards falls due in April, since this is the principal due date of all calendar-year federal and state income-tax returns. We carry separate cards for monthly and quarterly reports, such as wage reports, excise tax returns, sales tax returns, etc., and these are filed in our fourth file drawer, apart from income-tax work.

We have adopted the use of colored cards as follows:

Buff for yearly requirements
Blue for quarterly requirements
Salmon for monthly requirements
White for claims for refund

Further coding could be done by combining card colors with different colors of ink. We are expanding the use of our cards to include financial statements and audit reports.

Preparing for the coming season. In the late fall of each year we prepare a list of clients for the coming year for each staff member. Since the cards are notched for the staff members, it is very simple to sort the cards which belong to each staff member and type the list from the cards. Throughout the year, as each filing deadline approaches, the cards remaining in the "Work to be done" file drawer for the particular filing period can be easily sorted and reminder lists prepared for the staff members.

From actual practice we find that the final date of any major deadline, such as the April 15, should be left open for the clearing of returns which have already been typed. Therefore we believe that the preparation of returns on the last day should be eliminated, or at least kept to a minimum. This will allow ample time on the last day to check the cards which remain in the "Work to be done" file, and to check out the returns which are called for by the cards in the "Work in process" file, and which show no final disposition.

580

Typing control. As a further aid to the smooth flow of work after material is ready for typing, we have prepared a schedule to be used in listing each job for typing. For each job the sheet lists the staff, client, date due or needed, date put out for typing and date completed by the typing department. All rush work is entered in red and thus stands out as needing to be taken care of first. The use of the schedule makes it possible to see that work flows through as it should, in the order in which it is put out for typing, with the urgent material being handled ahead of routine.

Another firm's use of cards. Here are a few comments taken from another practitioner's description of his firm's use of the card system for controlling tax returns:

The basis of the system is the edge-sort edge-punched card. One of these cards is prepared on each tax return, whether federal, state, or local. Consequently, a client doing business in many states might require more than fifty individual cards. The cards are rotated through three files—the inactive file, the pending file, and the typing file.

Once a month, the office manager sorts out of the inactive file the cards for all clients whose fiscal year ends in that month. These cards are then sorted into groups by the accountant who has the responsibility for preparation of the return. A list is prepared for each accountant of all his clients closing their books in that month, the tax returns which must be prepared for that client within the next twelve months, and the due date on each. Each accountant uses this as a checklist throughout the year. The cards themselves are re-sorted by due date and filed in the pending file which has twelve tabs, one for each month.

Shortly before the first of every month, the office manager pulls from the pending file all cards for returns due in the following month but not yet received for typing. These cards are sorted by the responsible accountant. A follow-up list is prepared showing the client, the return, the date due, and the responsible accountant. Copies of the list are made for all accountants involved and for the partners. After this list is prepared, the cards are returned to the pending file.

Of course, there are exceptions which require specialized handling. However, these have been few and not particularly complex.

Pretyping W-2 forms. Here is a procedure that one man uses to save time for his typists.

In his practice he prepares many payroll returns and W-2 forms at the year's end. In order to save time, it has been his practice to pretype these forms during the year, with the employer's number, name, and address and the employee's social security number, name, and address. This leaves only the amount earned, withholding tax taken, and social security tax paid to be filled in after the first quarter is completed. Many hours have thus been saved during the tax season, when time is valuable.

Duplicating and Copying Equipment[4]

■ AUDIT REPORTS, tax returns and many other products of a public practitioner's labor must be prepared in multiple copies. An attempt will be made to evaluate the several duplicating and copying methods but it is recognized that it is very difficult to choose a particular piece of equipment as the best for a particular task.

KINDS OF DUPLICATING AND COPYING MACHINES

The field of duplicating and copying can be classified as follows: (Charts giving pertinent data on the equipment employing the processes described will be found in the Appendix, pages 902-903.)

1. Photocopy methods
2. Diazo method
3. Dye-transfer method
4. Heat-transfer method
5. Spirit-duplicating method
6. Stencil-duplicating method
7. Offset methods (Office lithography)
8. Electrostatic method

Photocopy methods. As the name implies, photocopy utilizes the principles of photography in its process of duplicating. However, a camera is not used. The copy to be duplicated is brought into contact with sensitized paper and exposed to light. After exposure, the sensitized paper is sent through a developer solution. The result is an exact copy of the document exposed to the sensitive paper. Some manufacturers build machines that accomplish this operation in a one-step operation; that is, when the sensitive paper is "developed" it is the positive copy. Other machines require a two-step operation: the sensitive paper is a negative copy, necessitating a positive print to be made in a second step.

Diazo method. This copying method utilizes a chemical reaction in which diazonium salt and a second chemical, known as a coupler, react to form a dye. The process works in the following way. Special paper containing the diazo, the coupler, and a stabilizing chemical which prevents the

[4]Report of the committee on accounting and office equipment, AICPA, 1960-61.

582

diazo and the coupler from reacting, is brought into contact with the copy to be duplicated. An ultraviolet light is beamed through the copy and renders impotent the diazo on the special paper, except where the copy would not permit the light to penetrate. A chemical, such as ammonia, removes or neutralizes the stabilizer enabling the diazo and the coupler to react to form a dye on the special paper which is, in effect, a duplicate of the copy to be reproduced. The only special requirement for this process is that the copy to be reproduced must be on translucent paper.

Dye-transfer method. This process is a hybrid process combining certain phases of a photocopy method and a chemical-reaction method such as diazo. As in photocopy, a sheet of sensitized paper is brought into contact with the copy and exposed to light. Where light strikes the sensitive paper it is desensitized. After exposure, the sensitive paper is passed through a liquid which reacts to form a dye. Since the only active area is the area shielded from light, an exact duplicate is produced of the copy brought into contact with the special paper.

Heat-transfer method. This method is based on the principle that dark objects absorb more light than light objects and thereby generate more heat. Special paper sensitive to heat is brought into contact with the copy to be reproduced and is exposed to infrared light. As the dark-ink copy absorbs the light it generates enough heat to affect the special paper. The copy is literally burned into the special paper. This method also has an important requirement for success. The copy must be prepared by using some heat-absorbing material. Carbon-based ink and pencil are best. Not all inks will reproduce satisfactorily.

Spirit-duplicating method. In this method a special master must be prepared utilizing a special aniline dye carbon which is placed face up under the master. After the material to be copied is placed on the master with a typewriter or other writing aid, the carbon paper is removed and the master is placed on the revolving drum of a machine which permits special paper, moistened slightly with an alcohol solution, to be brought into contact with the carbon on the underside of the master, and a carbon or dye transfer is made.

Stencil-duplicating method. This particular method is so named because the master which must be prepared is called a stencil. This master can be made of paper, plastic, or other material, as long as the stencil base is porous. The porous base is then coated with a waxy substance. The master is prepared on a typewriter or with the aid of a stylus by cutting the wax coating on the stencil, so that ink may pass through the stencil in the patterns cut. The stencil is then placed on the drum of a special machine which contains a dye or ink. The drum is rotated and brought into contact with blank copy paper. The ink passes through the cuts in the stencil so that a reproduction of the copy on the stencil is made on the blank copy paper.

Offset methods. This process is commonly called office printing because it is a simpler version of photo-offset lithography, which is a process used in the commercial printing industry. The offset process utilizes the principle that oil and water are immiscible. The first step is to prepare a master much as in the spirit method or in the stencil method. The copy must be placed on the master with some oil- or grease-based substance. This master is placed on a drum of a special machine. The master is first passed through a set of rollers where it is moistened. The next phase is to ink the master by drawing it through inking rollers. The ink is repelled from the moistened area but attracted to the copy prepared with a grease base. The inked master is then passed over a rubber drum or mat depositing the inked copy on the mat. The mat is then brought into contact with the copy paper creating a nearly perfect image. The product of this method is probably closer to commercial printing than any other office duplicating or copying method.

Electrostatic method. Utilizing a fundamental electrical principle that opposites attract and like electrical charges repel each other, manufacturers have produced a copying method. The copy to be reproduced is projected onto a plate bearing a positive electrical charge. The light used in projection cancels the electrically charged plate everywhere except where the copy did not permit the light to pass through. A finely ground negatively charged powder is brought into contact with the plate and is attracted to the lines and letters of the copy. A sheet of positively charged paper is placed on the plate. The powder adheres to the paper and when the paper is exposed to heat a fusion takes place causing the powder to permanently adhere to the paper in the exact image of the original copy. Offset masters can easily be prepared in this way as well as spirit masters or translucent copies for use in diazo equipment.

DUPLICATING MACHINES FOR AUDIT REPORTS

Duplicating and copying machines were first introduced in accounting offices as an aid in the preparation of tax returns. Today duplicating equipment is used extensively in the preparation of audit and other reports to clients. Where carbon paper is used in typing additional copies of audit reports, time is required to assemble sheets for typing, make individual corrections on such sheets, and worry about proper alignment: finally, the end product is not uniform. Usually the first few copies are quite acceptable, but after that they become progressively less legible. Consequently, any typing of more than five reports would normally require a second typing of the same material.

With duplicating equipment, a large number of copies may be made from a single typed sheet. The typist's problems are greatly reduced and the final copy is as good as the reproduction method and the paper upon which it is reproduced.

Offset. The offset machine has probably gained the widest acceptance among duplicating machines for the reproduction of audit and other reports in the medium-sized and larger offices. Its greatest advantage is that it produces a large number of copies in a very short period of time; however, most accountants use the machine because of the simplicity of typing and correcting and the appearance of the final copies. The offset machine is used with one carbon copy to facilitate proofreading, checking, and making corrections. The masters used with these machines vary in quality, depending on the number of copies that have to be reproduced. There are short-run masters for less than ten copies, medium-run masters for between fifty and one hundred copies, and long-run masters for more than that. Masters can be corrected with no special effort other than the use of a soft eraser and the normal amount of care. Another advantage is the fact that reproductions are of a very high quality, regardless of the type of paper used. Moreover, there is no limitation as to the grade, weight, or color of paper used, and the machine will reproduce charts, graphs, and the like which cannot be prepared on a typewriter. There are certain disadvantages in the use of the offset machine. Usually this type of equipment requires space set off from the general office because of size, noise factor, and the like. In addition, this equipment usually requires a special operator. There are limitations as to the size of the schedules that may be run; however, there are offset machines on the market which will run double pages. Double pages can also be run on smaller machines through the use of a folded page run through twice. Finally, there is the time involved in setup and preparation.

Diazo. The diazo method of reproduction is used quite extensively in accounting offices for audit and other reports. It seems to have wider acceptance in the smaller office. This method has advantages for short runs of audit reports. The typing is on translucent paper and the corrections can be made simply by literally cutting out words or paragraphs of the report and replacing them with the proper information. The fact that changes were made is not noticeable on the final report. The end product is acceptable though not of the quality of offset. The problem in the use of this machine is the time required to prepare long runs and the fact that standard paper cannot be used for the final product. In the past the paper used in this process had a tendency to darken and yellow. However, manufacturers are currently improving the paper. This drawback may eventually be overcome by improvements in the paper used for reproduction.

Electrostatic method. Electrostatic equipment is being introduced into the report department of a number of offices. It can serve as an all-purpose machine. It combines speed of operation with good permanent reproduction. No special type of paper is required for the end product, thus permitting use of good quality paper for reports. The machine will copy from any type of material. It has the advantage of being quiet and its operation is simple enough not to require a specially trained operator. It also eliminates the start-up factor.

The disadvantage of electrostatic equipment is that until recently it was available from only one source on a rental basis. Now, however, other companies are entering the field and other machines will be available, in different sizes, to be purchased outright.

DUPLICATING TAX RETURNS

The basic advantages sought by the use of duplicating equipment in the preparation of copies of reports are much the same as those desired in the duplication of tax returns. There are, however, substantial differences in the points of emphasis and the problems involved in the performance of these tasks.

Very few accounting firms have solved completely the problem of the excessive workload that they are confronted with in the tax season. This imbalance seems to vary in inverse proportion to the size of the firm. Perhaps this can be explained by the fact that smaller firms seem to have a greater proportion of individual income-tax returns, which creates for them an unusual volume of work during the tax season. The problem of easing the workload is universal and is present in practices of almost any size.

The problems involved. In the processing of tax returns, the results most sought after from the use of duplicating equipment are acceptability by the taxing agency, economy of time and cost, and presentability, usually in that order.

Today the Federal government and most state taxing agencies permit use of duplicating equipment in the preparation of tax returns. The latest requirements pertaining to duplication of Federal returns are found in Revenue Procedure 61-31, I.R.B. 1961-44,19, which appears in the Appendix, page 904. Most of the states having laws where taxes are based upon net income give some recognition to the use of reproduced returns. Most of these states have specific requirements which reproduction must meet. In all cases inquiry should be made as to the specific requirements of the states where filings are to be made. In selecting duplicating equipment it is necessary to consider the capabilities of the equipment as they pertain to the standards required by the taxing agencies. Some of the more common requirements are:

1. An acceptable copy
2. Reproductions on paper of the same color as that of the original forms
3. Weight and quality of paper must meet prescribed standards

Some states have additional requirements such as that duplicated returns must be reproduced on both sides of a single sheet where the official form is so constructed. Since many duplicating processes require special sensitized paper, this gives rise to the question of whether paper of the proper color will always be available, particularly if the official colors are changed from year to year.

Both Federal government and the various states reserve the right to reject any return which does not meet their particular requirements as to quality of stock used, size, and legibility.

Diazo. The diazo process is frequently used in duplicating tax returns. It has the following advantages. It is relatively inexpensive; it is fast; and it is a single-step process. The end product is acceptable to most taxing authorities. It has many advantages in common with most duplicating processes: it relieves the typing department of an almost impossible burden during the tax season. It also eliminates the necessity of a second check of the finished product since the finished product is a reproduction of the return after it has been prepared and reviewed in its final form. The diazo process will reproduce pencil copies, thus eliminating all typing on the returns. Some firms who employ this process will type in the names and addresses of the taxpayers.

The diazo method also has some disadvantages, however: the original must be prepared on a translucent form which is light in weight and printed on only one side; there is some lack of uniformity in appearance due to the varying degree of legibility of the handwriting of the personnel preparing the returns; the copies tend to discolor with age; and lastly there is the problem of storing quantities of the paper for any period of time.

Offset. Tax returns may also be prepared by the offset process. The mechanics of preparing a tax return in this manner are as follows. The tax-form information is preprinted on offset masters which can be written on with a special reproducing pencil in the same way as would be done on the translucent forms used in the previously discussed methods. The masters thus prepared can be checked with a nonreproducing pencil before they are actually run on the machine. Three copies will generally be run on the machine: one to be filed, one for the taxpayer, and one for the accountant. The master which has been checked loses its check marks in the process and, of course, cannot be retained in any case for the accountant's files because of size and drying-out and cracking problems.

The advantages of the offset operation are, as in the other previously discussed duplicating methods, that typing and rechecking the return can be avoided. A further advantage over the duplicating machines is the generally clearer reproduction and the fact that the returns are prepared on standard paper. The latter factor becomes important where the returns are handled frequently in connection with subsequent revenue agent's examinations.

There are no special problems in writing up the master preprinted with the tax-return form other than the requirement that the special reproducing pencil be used. However, the use of offset masters does require special care in making erasures and rewriting figures. A soft eraser is needed to avoid removing some of the coating of the master, which would cause a smear to appear on the final copy.

The time required to run the copies of the tax return is primarily taken up in placing the master on the machine, preparing it with a chemical solution, and cleaning up fingerprints and smudges. The average time needed to put a master on the machine and run it might be a minute or two. The major problem in the use of the offset machine would appear to be the complication of running a relatively expensive machine and training a competent operator.

It should also be mentioned in connection with the preparation of tax returns that the offset machine can be used for standard letters of transmittal to the taxpayers and Internal Revenue Service.

Electrostatic method. Electrostatic equipment may also be used for the reproduction of tax returns. The advantages in using this type of equipment stem from the fact that the reproduction can be made from a pen or pencil copy prepared directly on forms furnished by the IRS and various state taxing agencies. This eliminates translucent forms as well as any type of master copy. The reproduction time is good. The disadvantages at present are the cost and the limitation on equipment available.

The other three methods of copy and reproduction—photocopy, heat-transfer, and dye transfer—are being used in the preparation of copies of tax returns and schedules but they do not seem to be as generally accepted as the processes described above.

OTHER APPLICATIONS OF DUPLICATING EQUIPMENT

It was pointed out above that the two principal areas of duplication needs in a practitioner's office are audit and other reports and tax returns. A few of the peripheral uses of duplicating and copying methods will now be investigated.

Staff training. Few offices can afford to ignore the continuing educational needs of all members of the staff from the managing partner to the greenest junior. There is a need to disseminate announcements of new developments in the area of accounting and office equipment, new audit techniques, new techniques to be used in the client-accountant meeting when audit reports are delivered, and pronouncements of the AICPA.

Duplicating and copying equipment plays an important role in this area. Thermographic methods permit transparencies to be prepared for use with projection equipment. For group meetings, staff classes, and the like, this kind of equipment is a very effective visual-aid device. It can also be used to communicate certain key conclusions to client personnel after a management advisory service commission or audit has been completed.

Various photocopy methods have been used in the staff-training area to reproduce official releases of the AICPA, the SEC and the IRS. All of the other methods of duplication have been used effectively to reproduce staff manuals and other firm-wide communications which are disseminated regularly.

Work-paper duplications. It is often necessary to leave with the client certain schedules, analyses, adjusting journal entries, and the like, which are part of the audit work papers. Depreciation and fixed asset schedules, tax basis computations involving return of capital dividends, and stock right allocations are only a few examples. In most cases the schedules, analyses, and journal entries which must be given to the client have been reconciled several times during the course of work-paper preparation and review. If exact duplicates of these portions of the work papers could be made without the need to review for transcription errors, much time and effort could be saved. Photocopy, chemical, thermographic, and electrostatic methods are commonly used to remove the probability of transcription error and the need to proof typed schedules, adjusting entries, and so on. All of these methods provide for exact duplication without need for the preparation of a special master.

Inter- and intra-office communication. According to the criteria established above, any of the discussed duplicating and copying methods could be used in the area of inter- and intra-office communication. Quality of product and cost of reproduction of the copies are essential considerations in the type of equipment used. The offset process yields copy of the finest quality, but at the highest cost, and it requires preparation of a master. Most often, where exact copying is required, where master preparation is not wanted or possible, and where relatively few prints are needed, photocopy or heat transfer are used. Diazo and an electrostatic method could be used but cost is a factor.

Where newsletters, firm bulletins, or policy need to be disseminated, dye-transfer methods are often used. If the firm desires a higher degree of quality, the diazo and electrostatic methods can be used as well as offset. What kind of equipment to use in these areas can usually be easily determined after four questions have been considered:

1. What kind of duplication equipment is justified by the two principal areas of reports and tax returns?
2. Do these areas take up all the use time of the equipment used?
3. To what extent will duplication equipment be utilized in peripheral areas?
4. Can the duplication equipment utilized in the report and tax-return areas be used in the peripheral areas?

It seems apparent that if the duplication equipment used to reproduce tax returns and reports can be used for staff training or other peripheral purpose, and if machine saturation has not been reached, only one kind of equipment is necessary. On the other hand, if question (2) is answered affirmatively and/or question (4) negatively, a need is present for additional duplication equipment which will best service the peripheral areas. For example, if offset is the only duplication method used, it would not be utilized economically in short-run situations such as the dissemination to five partners of the essential points of a letter from the IRS concerning some controversial ruling.

EXPERIENCES OF PRACTITIONERS

How one firm utilized reproducing equipment. We found the use of preprinted masters of great value. Here is how it works. Any copy can be printed on the master in advance, in quantity. This can be done to order from your own copy. Then, the information for a specific client can be typewritten or written in pencil on this preprinted master, put in the machine, and printed copies will contain that material which was preprinted as well as the later information written in. This, for example, gives us as many copies as we want, with no typing, no proofreading, and no errors.

Tax return preparation. One of the best uses to which we have put the offset machine as a timesaver is during the tax season in the preparation of certain tax returns.

We have eliminated a great deal of the writing of certain schedules such as (1) income from business or profession, (2) the depreciation schedule, (3) rental property schedules, (4) dividend and interest income, (5) deductions for tax return.

On the preprinted master the business schedule is combined with the depreciation schedule on one form and usually covers most taxpayers.

We have designed a form which has been preprinted on paper masters. We use this form on all returns where a business or professional schedule is needed. Since this master is preprinted we save the necessity of writing the various headings on this form, such as income, cost of goods sold, and expenses of all kinds. The bottom part of this form is similar in design to the depreciation schedule in the tax returns. We then fill in with a special pencil only the name of the taxpayer, address, year of the return, and the figures. This form is then checked and run off (with others that have accumulated during the day) on the offset machine. This procedure saves typing of the schedule and rechecking after typing. The girls have run off as many as fourteen schedules in one half-hour. The normal typing and checking time saved we estimate at about four to five hours. The time saved in writing out the schedules is almost as much.

A client's reaction. We also found great use for the machine in preparing form letters and instructions which we attach to all returns. An example of what our clients think about these forms is shown by the following letter we received from an attorney whose return we prepared.

> While I cannot be too happy over the fact that I am required to pay as much as you indicate it is necessary for me to pay, I want to take this opportunity to express my appreciation of the concise and efficient manner in which the enclosures were delivered to me, together with the precise and comprehensive instructions. Frankly, it was a pleasure to observe the manner in which your firm handled the matter. The slips attached to each of the returns with the specific instructions left no room for doubt as to what was to be done by the busy taxpayer who places confidence and reliance upon you.

Monthly jobs. Those practitioners who do a large number of monthly jobs know that writing out the trial balance, profit-and-loss statement, balance sheets, and other schedules is one of the most time-consuming parts of the work each month. We have saved a great deal of time along this line by running off a twelve- to fifteen-month supply of pro formas of these forms. The masters are kept and next year we run off another year's supply; if corrections are needed all we do is erase the wrong caption and type in the new one. The time saved resulted in one of two things: (1) Where we were spending more time than we were being paid for, as is the case of many monthly jobs, we saved ourselves money; (2) where we were getting a sufficient fee we used the saved time in extending our audit procedures or in some other useful manner.

Some of our clients get statements on a special form. We have run these forms through the machine and made enough copies so that the auditor could then also use these as work sheets, just filling in the figures. The typist also saves time because all she does is type in the figures. The account captions are already printed.

Other forms that we have run off may not necessarily save time but they now are uniformly filled out by our staff members. Some of these forms are: bank reconciliation form, petty cash count work sheet, dividends received, interest received, and depreciation schedule and work sheet.

Whenever we have a special audit and a special kind of confirmation form is needed we type the master and run off as many as we need. Since we have a preprinted letterhead form, all we do is type out the complete confirmation form, even filling in the date and the name of the client. In some cases the person who has to sign the confirmation can sign his name at the same time. This saves us much time that normally would be spent stamping in date and company name and saves the time of the person who has to sign confirmations granting permission for desired information.

Other functions. One of the worst bottlenecks in an office occurs when many reports are needed and the typists have to retype the report several times in order to get the required number of copies. One of our audits is a hospital that requires twenty-six copies of our report, one for each director. All we do now is type the report once on the paper masters and run off as many copies as we need. Last year our typists spent eighteen and one-half hours typing this report. This year the total time of typing and running off the necessary copies only took four hours, a considerable saving.

Because the machine is available we find that we run off forms that we normally would not use because they would be too expensive to print. We have also saved a great deal of money in the cost of paper. We now purchase paper directly from a paper manufacturer in quantities that are most economical.

Because of the machine's availability we have also been able to institute certain practices which have enhanced client good will and given us a certain amount of professional protection. To illustrate, two particular instances may be cited among many. Relative to the good-will factor we send to all clients a monthly newsletter, the contents of which are prepared by firm members. This is a one-page affair, set up on a preprinted letterhead master, which gives in capsule form current tidbits of general interest, such as: principal changes in tax laws; tax saving methods; IRS and revenue agents' present practices; what items agents are giving most attention to in examinations; what taxes and returns will be required in the following months; rulings and regulations of various administrative agencies which are general and affect most businesses; new business methods and practices; hints on how to save postage, express charges, and stationery; office routines and procedures; and any data which we think will interest the client. These newsletters have brought us many compliments not only because of the contents but also because of the brevity of each item and the simplicity of language avoiding technical phraseology.

Relative to the matter of protection we use the machine to a great extent in facilitating our procedures. Several times during the year it is necessary to advise various groups of clients about certain items. Copies of these letters, all of which appear personalized when they come off the machine, are retained in each client's file as our evidence of notification to them. In June or September we notify all clients whose current declarations of estimated tax are less than the prior year's and advise them of the necessity of filing amended estimates to avoid penalties, if their income is as much as or greater than the previous year's.

Strip accounting. A further use of the diazo-process machine is described by the following practitioner:

There are few practitioners who have bought a copying machine for preparation of tax returns who do not feel that this device is the greatest invention since the wheel. It seems poor economics to let such equipment stay idle eight months of the year. A very fine use of copying machines is the preparation of financial statements in strip accounting form, which not only cuts down typing time but also makes the statements easy to prepare and above all gives the client a much deeper insight into his business.

What are strip statements? Conventional statements come in impressively bound covers. They usually show the balance sheet at the last date of the period and operating figures year to date and for the last period. Such figures alone are usually meaningless. What interests the client or the accountant who advises him more than anything else is the trend. This trend only becomes apparent if one lays a number of statements previously rendered side by side to trace a particular item.

By contrast, strip accounting statements show all pertinent figures for an entire year side by side. When setting up the statement form for a year, side captions are typed on a piece of thirteen-column translucent work paper and each column is headed for one accounting period. Each month one set of figures is typed in one column and then a copy is run off. Since the report for the month of February also contains the figures for the month of January, there is no need to retain the statement mailed for January and the client is advised to destroy it, just as we discard superseded pages of the loose-leaf tax service.

Form of the statements. Since we want to show at least twelve sets of figures on one page it is not possible to use more than one column a month. For this reason we generally show balance sheets by the subtraction method starting with cash and ending with stockholders equity.

This type of statement shows among other things at one glance the net working capital, by far the most important figure for day-to-day management purposes.

Operating statements are also shown with one column used per month. This of course makes it difficult to present detailed figures on one page and so one report may consist of quite a few pages. For instance a typical operating statement may consist of: Schedule of operations, schedule of expenses, and schedule of departmental operations. Each one of these operating schedules is prepared in two sets, one showing the cumulative figures (year to year) and one showing the figures for each month or other accounting period.

To help control so many sheets of paper we furnish our clients with ring binders bearing our name. The ring binders have tabs showing the location of each statement. However, it has been our experience that statements are only inserted in these binders if an employee of the client is given the job to keep the binder up to date.

How it is done. For our purposes we use translucent paper with fifty-four lines on an 11 by 17 sheet, with thirteen columns and item space. The vertical spacing of the horizontal lines is set up for a standard typewriter so that a sheet once inserted in the typewriter requires no adjustment as the lines are selected by the carriage return. The lines are printed green on the translucent paper which gives faint reproduction on the copy. This reproduction is just sufficient to guide the reader across the sheet but not so heavy as to interfere with the typed text or figures. The copy is run on yellow paper, the color used for Partnership Returns Form 1065, a color which we also use when reproducing pro forma statements and journal entries because this paper is easier on the eyes than white paper.

Preparation of financial statements is easy because only figures have to be inserted and not side captions. Subtracting out of figures for the current period goes very fast because the year-to-date figures for this period and the immediately preceding period show up next to each other. The pencil copy set is kept on cardboard backers and one set contains all statements year to date while the other set contains the period figures. This makes it possible to subtract out the periodical figures without flipping pages.

When setting up the form for the year one has to leave plenty of space on the form so that additional side captions can be inserted. A year is a long time and many things not dreamt of at the beginning must be included as we progress.

One may ask, why should it be necessary to type statements instead of reproducing pencil copies? The reason is that one set of translucent sheets in pencil would not stand a year's handling in an active file. Also changes and erasures would show up and make a poor looking statement. Actually the typing job does not take long, especially since one can insert all vertical lines on a drafting board when the first statement is prepared. Also we omit cents which cuts down the typing job and at the same time makes the statements more readable for the client.

In view of the fact that the statement is given in loose-leaf form in which pages can be substituted, we type on each sheet the words "prepared from the books of account without audit," even if we do give the client certified financial statements, because we have no safeguards against fraudulent substitution.

Reaction to strip statements. At first we had to sell our clients on accepting these reports. Now, however, we could not reconvert them to the other form if we wanted to do so. Figures which are out of line stand out like a sore thumb and even clients with limited accounting knowledge can pick them out without trouble. While this is embarrassing, we can also say that many errors which previously crept into the beautifully bound reports were caught by our staff because the accountant could see at a glance that something was amiss.

Bankers and other credit grantors who know that we prepare these strip statements prefer them over conventional statements because they feel that any window dressing can be detected easily. A cynic may consider this a disadvantage.

At this writing we have no more clients to whom we render monthly or quarterly statements in conventional form. However, we do usually prepare a year-end statement in conventional form where the client does not want to disclose to outsiders too intimate a picture of his operations.

Paper-saving suggestion. The problem of special paper for some reproducing machines was solved in the following office.

We bought a household refrigerator for our office to store the paper we use on our diazo reproducing machine. We find that in the refrigerator this paper keeps indefinitely.

Not only does this permit us to buy paper in larger quantities but we are not constantly running out of paper as we did when we bought from hand to mouth in order to avoid having paper deteriorate while it was kept at room temperature.

USE OF COMMERCIAL REPRODUCTION SERVICE

Many accounting firms employ the services of an outside firm to reproduce some of their materials. Preponderantly, the work sent out is of a type requiring many copies. It includes confirmation letters, court report schedules, clients' bulletins, questionnaires, special letters, time reports and other forms, and special schedules to be submitted with audit reports, especially during rush periods. Some practitioners also send out audit reports, presumably with clients' permission or when the report is to be published. Other firms frown on this practice.

Other Office Equipment

■ INVESTMENT IN OFFICE machines and equipment can run high and wrong selections may prove costly. Before deciding on such purchases, the person charged with this responsibility should make thorough reference to catalogues, periodicals, and other literature on the subject. Available equipment is constantly improving. Therefore, keeping up with developments requires continual examination of the latest information on the subject. On the other hand, not all firms can or find it necessary to buy special items. Rental is their solution, particularly when the need is only temporary or occasional.

ELECTRIC TYPEWRITERS

Electric typewriters have found favor with more and more accountants. A majority of firms now use them. Wide-carriage machines predominate, of course.

Electric machines meet the requirements of quality of work, speed and ease of operation. They are less fatiguing. The appearance of the finished audit report is a credit to the firm issuing it. The original has the appearance of printing. Because of the carbon paper ribbon, there is a definite improvement in the sharpness and uniformity of type impressions on carbon copies. It is easier to adjust the pressure of keys for various numbers of carbon copies. Several typists may type different sections of the same long report without that well-known complaint that the ribbon variations spoil the effect. Variable unit spacing, which makes it possible to line up the right-hand margin, is available only on electric machines. The sharp copies produced are better for offset reproduction.

By means of a "justifier" on some models, it is possible to attain an even, vertical margin on the right side of the paper. One additional typing of the same material is required, however. This can be accomplished without the justifier but calls for extreme care on the part of the typist. The process is useful for writing papers and other documents where formality is a prerequisite, but the use of this feature is seldom, if ever, applied to standard audit reports. The greater attractiveness does not compensate for the added time and effort.

As to the disadvantages of electric typewriters, firms stress mainly their cost, frequent and higher maintenance charges, and the fact that failure of power puts them out of use. Beginners tend to shy away from them, but their dislike is soon dissipated, as they quickly learn to enjoy the lighter touch.

ADDING, CALCULATING, AND BOOKKEEPING EQUIPMENT

The profession uses almost every type of adding machine made. Electrically operated adding machines predominate. Many of them are portable and are used not only in the office but in the field. Adding machine stands seem to be disappearing, although some offices still use them.

Some firms use the combination rapid-calculating features of adding machines and do not invest in special calculating units. A few object to the rapid calculators on the ground that no tape is available. Some prefer the combination feature because they cannot easily transport two machines to field engagements. In some firms, comptometer operators, considered part of the audit staff, go into the field and foot books of original entry, inventory calculations, and other records. While not many CPA firms use bookkeeping machines for their general bookkeeping, some use them for payroll and time recording purposes.

POSTAGE AND SEALING MACHINES

Postage meter and envelope sealing machines are gaining in popularity. Other mail room units such as mail openers, precision scales, postage charts, stamp affixers, and all-electric multisealers are also available. Individual practitioners and small firms would probably find little use for, and would not profit by, postage meter machines with their high-speed automatic sealing and postage printing equipment, or the protective features afforded by metered mail machines. The larger offices can hardly do without this type of equipment, particularly when numerous confirmation circulars are mailed.

The detachable postage meter is taken to the post office periodically where it is opened (no outsider can possess a key) and, upon advance payment of postage, it is set to deliver the postage paid for. It automatically computes and imprints, whether the need is for a first-class letter or for a package. The outstanding protective feature is that the possibility of unauthorized use of stamps is eliminated.

MICROFILMING

Microfilming work papers and records of special significance which are to be destroyed now prevails in some of the larger firms. The equipment can also be used in the field.

EQUIPMENT FOR DICTATION

Many firms now have mechanical equipment for dictation. Such equipment, when available, is used by all partners. To a lesser extent, the use of such equipment is extended to supervisors and seniors.

One great advantage of dictating equipment is that the flow of work in the typing department can be leveled. The equipment can be utilized, of course, at nights, over week ends, and during rush periods.

A practitioner who finds it practical to dictate his reports on a portable dictating machine, can use it at the scene of an engagement and even take it out of town. Such machines weigh relatively little and fit within a special, larger-sized brief case. Since the recording medium is lightweight and flexible, it can be fitted in an envelope of normal size, and forwarded by mail.

Office Layout and Furnishings

■ THE SMALL PRACTITIONER has a relatively simple problem in this respect. His space and staff are limited and he is not overburdened with clients. What difficulties he faces in arrangement are not complicated. If he has only one small room, he uses it as best he can and concentrates on getting enough clients. They will furnish the best means of providing more extensive facilities.

When he expands, his organization and layout troubles really begin. He obtains more space but has to use it for more and increasingly varied purposes. There are perplexing alternatives imposed by gradual specialization and departmentalization.

GENERAL LAYOUT

The main objective in arrangement is to save steps and safeguard against lost motion. Small firms must adapt as much of the ideal as is possible for them under their special circumstances. With certain alternatives noted, an adequate office for medium-sized and larger organizations is predicated on reasonable compactness, with the various private offices, the library or conference room, and the working spaces of key men (such as supervisors and reviewers) flanking the main staff room, the tax and filing departments, and the stenographic room. Of course, circumstances would alter cases. It is usually considered preferable to have the tax department separate, though near the staff room. The head tax man, whether a partner or employed executive, should be located as close as possible to his assistants. The bookkeeper-cashier should be near the partner or office manager whose responsibility it is to manage the office. The waiting room should be sufficiently spacious to afford comfort to visitors. If the switchboard is located in this room, the operator may serve as receptionist. It is desirable to have halls leading to entrances of the various parts of the office in order to overcome confusion and provide for more satisfactory handling of visitors; this of course adds to the cost of space.

FURNISHINGS

The furniture throughout the office, including the reception room, should be attractive but dignified; in other words, of a nature consistent with a professional atmosphere. It should not be gaudy, extravagant, or ornate. Those preferring simplicity have plain furniture, well arranged, neat, and in good condition; they do not consider that unusually fine furnishings will affect clients or provide a satisfactory substitute for effective service. Of paramount importance, however, is the desirability of indicating to clients and prospects that the office is well equipped to take care of their needs.

Most practitioners do not hang their CPA certificates, certificates of membership in state societies and college fraternities, and similar certificates in the waiting room. But many do display them in their private offices. Most waiting rooms are decorated with a reasonable number of pictures or prints of a type consonant with the profession's nature. This should not be overdone. Some prefer not to display membership certificates and diplomas even in their own private offices. Some firms keep their walls free of adornment.

SEPARATE OFFICES

The majority of firms have private offices enclosed from outside view on four sides, but some of the private offices make extensive use of glass. The argument in favor of glass partitions is that it permits more effective maintenance and review of decorum, and communication with other members of the force without the necessity of telephoning. The argument against this transparency is that it frequently occasions discomfiture of clients or others who would prefer greater privacy.

Private secretaries should have their office locations near to the executives they serve. The ideal for the large establishments is a secretarial office or space immediately adjoining the principal with a direct-entrance door from one to the other. Or two secretaries may share an office located between the two private offices of the men they serve.

STAFF ROOMS

In lieu of desks to accommodate staff men, large tables are used frequently. The accountants are not assigned space but utilize such vacancies as they may select to do their work. Of course, there must be sufficient chairs. If a separate stationery room is not provided, the staff room may contain a cabinet for work paper, envelopes, and the stationery and supplies appropriate for staff use. The stenographic department should be similarly accommodated.

Some firms subdivide their staff rooms under a plan which separates specialists from the general staff. One large firm has segregated its accountants into two separate offices: one to accommodate those who are specialists in one or several services, the other to accommodate the general staff. Desks are assigned specifically only to four staff supervisors and certain other key men.

Practices vary widely as to space allotted to staff members. Some firms provide individual offices to partners, supervisors, and seniors, with large rooms for juniors. Others allow no more than two seniors to a room and no more than four or six juniors to a room. In the words of one firm, "a cubby-hole and desk for every junior has been found a good expenditure for increased productivity."

In the staff room should be placed one or several metal drawer cabinets in which the staff men can store their papers. It is inconsistent with the order and decorum that should pervade the professional accounting office that papers be strewn on desks, tables, and tops of file cabinets when not in use.

STORAGE SPACE

It is desirable that the firm's books and private records and valuable papers belonging to clients be safeguarded by means of a metal safe. The minimum protection is a fire-resistant, locked file drawer or cabinet of drawers.

Space for a coat and hat room or lockers is important. Duplicating and photostat machines, postage meters, and the like are best kept separately, although some firms place them in the file, staff, or stenographic rooms. If such equipment is noisy, it should be placed as far from office workers as is feasible.

The file room should preferably be assigned to two persons in order to provide relief. A lock should be supplied, and keys should be issued only to those two persons and perhaps one partner. Location of the file room near the staff room and tax department is desirable.

OFFICE SPACE REQUIREMENTS

Although up-to-date statistics are not available, a survey taken some years ago may be helpful in indicating the number of square feet of office space used by accounting firms. The figures shown in Table 1 were compiled by size of firm: "small" representing those with from one to fifteen partners and staff men; "medium," sixteen to thirty-five; and "large," over thirty-five.

Table I

| | Area in square feet | | |
	Average	Smallest	Largest
Small firms	1,270	220	2,700
Medium firms	3,970	2,640	6,600
Large firms	4,500	3,500	Unlimited

Most firms utilize almost all of the space they have. One firm of seven partners, each with his private office, reports with terse realism: "All seven partners seldom present." One reports spotty staff room utilization during the week and heaviest use during the weekend. It adds that its policy is to let the offices bulge until it needs more space. Another uses all its office space to an extent of "approximately 120 per cent." One small firm says, "Our offices were recently designed after years of putting up with 'must do.' We had an engineer work it out."

Six small firms with a staff of from one to five men report space occupancy averaging 525 square feet. Small firms with larger staffs report an average of 1,416 square feet.

Average occupancy by various firms is, of course, only partially significant. It would be much more helpful if information were available as to the square-foot area required per person in organizations of various sizes. Such information, however, cannot be too precise because of the many variable factors such as (1) preferences as to number and size of private offices; (2) compactness and arrangement of space available; and (3) extent of needs for furniture, files, reproducing equipment, and other items.

The approach used most frequently seems to be to figure the amount of space needed according to the basic requirements of each type of personnel and the essential equipment, and then to adjust this to the space available. An accountant or accounting firm, with no previous experience, could use as a rough rule of thumb a requirement of approximately 250 square feet for each partner and 50 square feet for each staff and clerical worker. This rough formula gives some consideration to the fact that staff men are not expected to be in the office for more than a small portion of their time and that their quarters should be interchangeable.

ALLOCATION OF SPACE

The largest portion of the space in the accountant's office is, of course, allocated to the staff and partners. Staff rooms and partners' offices may take up anywhere from 15 to 50 per cent of the total space. The clerical staff may utilize from 5 to 30 per cent of the space; storage, from 5 to 35 per cent; tax room, from 5 to 15 per cent; library, 1 to 15 per cent; conference rooms, 3 to 11 per cent; and reception office, 1 to 20 per cent. (These figures were taken from the same survey referred to above, under "Office Space Requirements." They are approximate and are offered only as a rough guide.)

The actual allocation in any specific case will be determined by the size of the office suite, the nature of the practice, the availability of warehouse storage space, and other factors. The same space may serve more than one function.

NUMBER AND KIND OF OFFICES

The majority of large firms have two or more staff rooms, but most small firms have only one. Partners of almost all firms are provided with separate offices. A minority offers separate offices for seniors. One firm uses a corner of its reception room as desk space for part-time assistants. An unusual form of facility arranged by one firm is a glass-enclosed section for revenue agents visiting the office.

Some practitioners place their top seniors in a room separate from their juniors and other seniors; others put them all together. A few assign two or more accountants to the same desk. Most of them assign desk space to each, even juniors.

Privacy and efficiency are the major advantages of numerous staff rooms. Some say that such provision makes employees happier and more secure, keeps idle or semi-idle accountants from disturbing busy ones, and causes less confusion. In addition, the ceiling of the room closest to noisy machines can be soundproofed, thus saving the cost of soundproofing the greater area of a large single staff room. Of course, supervision according to type of engagement is facilitated by proper arrangement.

The main disadvantages of numerous staff rooms are: added cost, inaccessibility of files and office machines, inconvenience in advising among staff members, less close contact between supervisors and staff, and lost motion. More telephone and buzzer extensions and more lighting fixtures are needed. Supervision over decorum is more difficult. The preponderant practice is away from the use of large staff rooms and in favor of smaller private working spaces.

Most small and medium-size firms appear to be equipped to accommodate all of their accounting staff in the office at one time. But with the big firms, the larger the staff, the smaller the amount of table space generally provided per person.

ONE PRACTITIONER'S OFFICE LAYOUT

As an example of what can be accomplished through careful planning, the following diagram of one firm's office layout is offered together with the practitioner's comments.

Figure 6. Office Layout

In general, we have found this office layout extremely workable. As you have probably noted, all offices occupy the perimeter, thereby enjoying some association with the outdoors through the full-length windows in each office. The center area is devoted to those facilities in which only occasional time is spent (file room, multilith room, and library).

All exterior walls are finished both inside and out with a beige brick. All partitions are plaster or wood paneling. All ceilings are covered with acoustical tile, into which are recessed the lighting fixtures. Since all windows are fixed, the air supply is constantly circulating through a central air-handling units, which filters the air and controls its temperature.

All of our files are kept in the open-shelf vertical files. We found this means of filing far superior to traditional drawer filing. Reference to file material becomes easier; furthermore, a great deal of filing space may be saved, in that files may extend from floor to ceiling. In the middle of our file room we now store two supply cabinets, four file cabinets, and a safe. As our filing needs grow, these cabinets will be replaced with additional vertical file units.

Our receptionist sits at a desk in the typing office. She faces an opening through which all those who enter or leave the office are visible. At her desk is the control equipment for our telephones, music controls, as well as a microphone which controls our paging system.

The conference room and library are separated by a folding wall as the partition. While this partition is normally closed, its presence adds considerable flexibility to this area. For large staff meetings, and the like, this folding partition is opened.

While our quarters may appear somewhat lavish, we feel that the added space and convenience pay for themselves many times over. Were we to divide our total annual rental by the gross hours worked by all members of our staff, the rental cost would approximate 30¢ per hour. The difference between these comfortable quarters and minimal accommodations might be 5 to 10¢ per hour worked. This slight premium seems to us an insignificant contribution to greater comfort and efficiency. Morale, too, is greatly benefited by giving each member of the staff his own desk in a private (or, at the very least, a semiprivate) office. Naturally, there are incalculable public relations benefits to be gained from a spacious, well-appointed office.

Maintaining the Files

PRESERVATION AND ACCESSIBILITY OF RECORDS

■ ONE OF THE problems of operating an accounting practice is that of preserving records. This has two aspects: the availability of current records and the retention of records no longer in current use but nevertheless too important to be destroyed.

Three years is the period applied most frequently as the time stamping a file as current. Some firms use two years as a guide, others ten or more. Of course, the period may be dependent upon whether the client is an active account.

Many firms keep their current and active records under lock, and some even protect their inactive records similarly. Most file their working papers, reports, and correspondence separately.

Firms of all sizes generally permit staff members ready access to reports, working papers, and correspondence. One large firm states that access to files by staff members is granted to seniors only. The majority does not require staff members to sign receipts when moving papers from any files. Most place especially confidential documents in a safe or vault.

SPACE FOR FILING

While all firms keep their current files within the office, some store inactive records at the home of a principal or partner and some use a vault or other room in a basement or on another floor in their building. Others use private rooms in public warehouses with the practitioner having the only keys to the store rooms.

METHOD OF STORAGE

Most firms store inactive records in steel cabinets, some in wooden boxes, with others using cardboard boxes stored in fireproof vaults or rooms. Those making packages of records are in the minority. Some stack their folders or packages on shelves in a filing room, within or away from the office.

Here are two suggestions concerning storage of files:

1. Acquire a roomy vault, file all matters on shelves continuously, prop-

erly card-indexed so that it will be unnecessary to go through all stacks to find, for instance, a six-year series of files for one client.

2. Strip files of all except the most important papers. Destroy accounts receivable confirmations and other bulky material after three or four years, especially where accounts are audited year after year. Separate files of tax returns and related papers should be kept even after examination by tax authorities.

FILE-ROOM PERSONNEL

In filing, knowing what is wanted is half the battle. Knowing how to do it is the other half. One accountant states that, regardless of the method of filing, a system will stand or fall depending on the person in charge. The mistake is too often made of entrusting files to too young and inexperienced a person. Perhaps the ideal is to have an active but mature former accountant, male or female, as chief of the filing department. This person's knowledge of accounting will be of definite advantage in supervising the arrangement or the checking of work papers as to proper filing position and dates.

It is not uncommon to find retired clerical employees of the Federal or municipal governments in charge of files of accounting firms. This is now more prevalent in larger firms. Resultant tangible advantages are constancy and good judgment. Some firms employ retired policemen or firemen to help deliver files and requisitions and to run errands. One large firm uses the services of a middle-aged woman as chief and other middle-aged women as helpers in the filing and mail rooms.

FILING METHODS

The majority of firms use an alphabetical arrangement for general filing. Those who file numerically may lose some time through indexing and placing numbers on the file jackets and folders, and must refer to index cards when a file is needed; but the numerical system may afford greater speed in locating desired material, as well as greater security against loss or misplacement. The person doing the actual filing has an added safeguard against error when the name of the client is tied in with that client's file number. Other advantages claimed by the number system adherents are (1) it is not necessary to retain as much space on shelves or in cabinets when it is known that the next file will carry the next number as when space must be provided for more jackets under the same letter; (2) the field men, most of whom seem to have the inclination to want to pick jackets of their "own" clients out of the files themselves instead of going through prescribed channels, do not find it as easy to violate the rules if they are not well acquainted with the file numbers of their clients.

The numbers are usually in locked index boxes. The index is usually recorded on 4 by 6 cards, or slightly larger. Sometimes the cards are of varied colors, a separate color being utilized, say, for (1) copies of audit reports;

(2) working papers; (3) copies of income-tax returns; (4) correspondence—general; (5) correspondence—private (confidential or special); and (6) interoffice communications.

A large proportion of the accountants who file alphabetically use no index. The only safeguard against loss of a jacket is usually found to be reference to the records kept by the partner, principal, or supervisor in the master tickler file. Some concerns file their intra-office communications within their private correspondence section of the file room and never permit them to leave the office.

Practice of the firms. A majority of all firms subdivide their general files into four classifications: correspondence, working papers, reports, and tax returns. Most of these firms keep each of the subdivisions in a separate file, which is arranged by names of clients and maintain separate sections for current and noncurrent, active and inactive.

The great majority of small firms arrange clients' files alphabetically rather than numerically. While most large and medium firms also use the alphabetic setup, there is a greater incidence of use of the numerical system in the larger firms. A formal index system is more prevalent in the larger firms. Many firms do not require a written memorandum to be placed in the file when material is removed.

Only a slight majority of accounting firms provide for periodic destruction of files; some even make microfilm copies of material to be destroyed. There are those who offer old working papers and reports to the client before destroying them. Some of the factors that influence record retention are availability of space, governmental regulations, and statute of limitations as to legal liability.

METHODS OF DESTRUCTION

There is a wide variation in methods of disposition of old working papers. Two devices to protect the confidential nature of contents, are (1) to mutilate papers before casting them into a wastebasket and (2) to afford firm supervision over destruction of records by warehouses. The important point to remember is the auditor's responsibility to his client never to run the hazard of the latter's private business getting into the possession of outsiders.

SUGGESTIONS FROM PRACTITIONERS

The following excerpts are taken from actual practice and suggestions of practicing accountants.

Retention and destruction. While one practitioner discovered useless papers in his own files, reference to old files is frequent enough so that he prefers not to use warehouse space, which is inconvenient and otherwise unsatisfactory. In order to keep twenty-five years of files with him and still reduce filing space, he adopted the following schedule of record retention:

Table 2

Present clients		Former clients	
Documents	*Keep*	*Documents*	*Keep*
1. Tax returns	Indefinitely	1. Working papers of	
2. Working papers	"	regular former cli-	
3. Audit report	"	ents with certified	
4. Correspondence file	"	reports	Ten years
5. Interim pencil		2. Working papers of	
reports	Last one only	regular former cli-	
6. Confirmations	One year	ents with noncerti-	
7. Copies of inventories	" "	fied reports	Five years
8. Typed interim		3. Tax returns	Indefinitely
reports	Two years	4. All other papers	Five years

The firm keeps a record of the papers destroyed and date of destruction in case a question should arise in the future. A partner must approve the list before the files are destroyed. Files normally are pruned every summer, although sometimes two or three years go by before it is done. But when someone remarks that more file cabinets are needed, the current files are attacked with renewed vigor before additional equipment is bought. The schedule is conservative, but it has been adequate. It removes the bulky papers without making it necessary to do a page-by-page analysis of each file.

Filing. There seem to be two schools of thought on the subject of filing and storage of accumulated papers. One holds that set rules can be laid down as to how long each type of document should be retained, the other maintains that it depends entirely on the peculiarities of each client's file.

Obviously, there is no universal answer. The only solution appears to be that each firm establish its own policies, based on careful reasoning and consideration of the firm's own experience. What is most needed in formulating such policies is a checklist or syllabus. A modest one appears below, intended purely to help each firm define its own filing and storage policies.

I. File classifications
    A. By entities concerned
        1. Nonclients (administrative files)
        2. Clients
            a. Corporations
            b. Partnerships, estates and trusts
            c. Individuals
    B. By usage or frequency of reference
        1. Active files (all active clients)
        2. Inactive files
            a. Nonclient and/or administrative matters

   b. Active clients
   c. Former clients
  3. Storage files
   a. Nonclient
   b. Active clients
   c. Former clients
 C. By nature of subject matter or form of documents
  1. Correspondence files (letters and memoranda)
  2. Report files
   a. Typed copies
   b. Rough draft (pencil) copies
  3. Work-paper files
   a. Current
   b. Permanent
  4. Tax files
   a. Current
   b. Permanent

II. Basic plan of arrangement or grouping of client files
 A. Alphabetically by clients, each set of client files being together and normally comprising the four classes shown in I*C* above.
 B. By type of documents, per I*C* above, arranged alphabetically by clients; that is, all correspondence files are in one drawer, arranged alphabetically by clients.

III. A few principles of filing
 A. Keeping track of the files
 B. Specific rules
 C. Separation of unlike files
 D. Cross-referencing
 E. Identification
  1. Alphabetical, or
  2. Numerical

The classification and basic arrangement of files (I and II) apply to practices of all sizes. A larger firm can and usually does expand the subdivisions. In point is the division of clients into corporations, partnerships, estates, and individuals. In a small firm this would represent excessive refinement and would tend to make particular files harder to find.

The grouping of files by like types of documents (II*B*) might at first seem to be a startling innovation, but it has advantages. Usually only one or two particular files of any client are needed on any one occasion; seldom are all the files needed at once. Because different kinds of files (I*C*) vary considerably in length, width, thickness, and format, they are much neater, more compact, and homogeneous if each class of material (correspondence, reports, work papers, tax returns) is filed together in separate cabinets or sections, arranged alphabetically by clients. This separation of unlike files puts a premium on cross-referencing, but it's worth the price.

Most people will agree that few things in life are more infuriating and embarrassing than being unable to find a file. At all times, files should be in one of three places: the file cabinet, the basket of the secretary or file clerk, in transit back to the file cabinet, or being used or worked on. Files not being worked on should never be put into desk drawers or briefcases. In the small firm not employing a file clerk, "out" cards are the *sine qua non,* but getting into the habit of using them is not easy. Strict rules are in order. Here is a fairly comprehensive specimen:

> Each and every file removed from any file drawer at any time of day or night, for any purpose whatsoever, and whether for a brief or a long period of time, must be replaced by an "out" card, on which is recorded the name of the file, the date taken, and the signature of the person removing the file. When finished with the file, return it to the top basket on the secretary's desk. She will replace the file, remove the "out" card, and cross off the recording thereon.

Storage and disposal plan. Table 3 shows a simplified plan for systematically storing and disposing of accounting office records. The policy indicated for each class of material and the reason for that policy are outlined in the next four paragraphs.

Correspondence. The table indicates that the hypothetical firm keeps its correspondence in the active files ten years, then has all the material (letters and memoranda) microfilmed. Reasoning: correspondence is not destroyed because it is felt that, more than any other material, it explains entire situations, peculiar circumstances, personal views, special interpretations, and between-the-lines background information not found in any other recorded medium.

Table 3

Period to be held (in years)

Class of material	Office	Storage	Reproduce	Destroy
Correspondence	10	No	Microfilm	Never
Typed reports............	Indef.	Former clients only, 10	Microfilm	Never
Rough draft reports........	2	2	No	Burn
Nonpermanent work papers.	2	2	No	Burn
Permanent work papers.....	Hold	No	Yes	Never
Nonpermanent tax files.....	3	3	No	Burn
Permanent tax files........	Hold	No	Yes	Never

Reports. The rough draft reports are treated the same as the nonpermanent work papers: held two years in the office, an additional two years in storage, then burned. The typed reports are never destroyed because they are gold mines of information and constitute the finished professional product. Relative to their great importance and constant usefulness, they take up little space. Accordingly, they are held in the office for an indefinitely long period, then are microfilmed. The only typed reports placed in storage are those of former clients. After ten years of storage they are microfilmed.

Work papers. Here is where sheer bulk becomes a serious problem. The key to the problem is a good set of permanent work papers, which are added to year by year from the cross-indexed annual work papers. The permanent work papers are always retained in the office, never transferred or destroyed. If this policy is carried out, wholesale destruction of material is feasible. Fortified by faith in the information contained in the correspondence file, the typed report file, and the permanent work paper file, the office illustrated holds the ordinary work papers in the office two years only, transfers them to storage for another two years, then has them cremated. (Note: Many small firms keep their rough draft reports in the same folder with the ordinary work papers, hence the storage-disposal policy for them is the same.)

Tax files. An innovation well worth considering is establishment of a permanent tax file to serve the same purpose as the permanent work-paper file. It should include all pertinent data on tax bases of assets and securities, prior tax "cases," recapitalizations and reorganizations, and the like. The way is then cleared for a much shorter retention period for the year-to-year tax files. Taking advantage of this, the policy indicated by the table is to hold nonpermanent tax files in the office until the three-year statute of limitations has run, then another three years in storage until the six-year period has expired. Justification for this policy rests on the fact that copies of tax returns are submitted to all clients, and that certified copies may be ordered from the Internal Revenue Service if required.

The cremation of all tax returns over six years old and all nonpermanent audit work papers over four years old really gets rid of bulk en masse. These are the steps assuring the success of the disposal part of the plan.

Plainly enough, the determination of the best storage and disposal policies involves a weighing of opposite risks. Be eventually smothered with paper or occasionally destroy a document you might later need.

Items that tend to accumulate. One practitioner has this to say:

The most effective incentive for a better utilization of office space is provided by a change of office location. Then the discarding of material which is no longer valuable enough for moving into new and costly space becomes mandatory.

An extensive storage reduction project falls roughly into three phases:

1. The return of unclaimed records to clients or former clients should be a continuing program. Ledgers, journals, bank statements, and other belongings of small clients seem to have an affinity for the offices of CPAs. Moving the records back home helps to keep the storage problem more normal.

2. Then there are those things that can move out by the wastebasket route without supervised destruction. Old printed matter from various government agencies can stay around too long. The *Wall Street Journal* tends to take up space in our office. We keep back numbers perhaps longer than necessary because of their detailed market coverage. An old number is very valuable when market values are needed for estate-tax returns or other reasons. Fifteen months is long enough to keep them for estate-tax valuations.

Loose-leaf tax services use up a large amount of space. Since most of the valuable features of the old volumes are brought over into the current year's service, the overage volumes can be systematically discarded. On request, publishers will give careful suggestions on what should be retained.

Magazines can take up a lot of room. If a technical magazine has a possible future value, we usually keep it. We never discard a copy of *The Journal of Accountancy*.

3. Confidential files of clients that require careful handling present the biggest problem. It is very easy to allow the files of a valuable client to become too bulky. The cost of a careful review of the file may be more expensive than the extra storage. In this area, however, certain types of situations may provide quick storage-reduction opportunities. Very old files of deceased clients can frequently be destroyed where basis established through estate-tax valuations will make any future reference to basis in the hands of the decedent unnecessary.

In offices with much tax practice, there is some turnover in clients. There are some transients; corporations liquidate; individuals die or move away. Tax files for such former clients should be kept until the returns are barred by the statute of limitations, often longer. The day comes, though, when the responsibility for keeping the file has been discharged. There is no obligation to provide perpetual storage for such old records. Modern office space is valuable and retention of records should be based on a consideration of their value.

Some records have a high potential value. Estate-tax returns that fix the basis of important properties should be kept for a very long time. Lengthy depreciation schedules and records that would be difficult to reconstruct should never be carelessly destroyed.

Supplies and Stationery

■ AN ACCOUNTANT should give careful thought to his policy in selecting supplies and stationery. Not only is this an important item of expense, but the right selection will aid in the handling of his practice.

WORKING PAPERS

There are numerous concerns supplying standardized audit working papers. Some of these concerns are operated or managed by CPAs. Sizes, colors, rulings, punching, binding edges, and so forth, conform to the preferences of members of the profession.

Instead of stereotyped preprinted work-sheet forms, one large firm uses models that it prepares in advance by the offset process. Its argument is that preferences of the principals are better met by this process than by forcing the use of forms which, in part, do not meet their tastes. Certain model sheets are produced in greater number than others. The forms are prepared on the firm's own stock of blank work paper. The senior going out on an engagement takes along the number of sheets which he estimates will be needed in each case, based upon reference to the previous year's file. Loose forms soil and spoil and this may be a slight offset to the saving in accountants' time, but not a material one.

Practices of firms. A majority of firms make some attempt to pretype periodic working papers and skeleton financial reports for use in filling in statements of clients. The principal items presented are headings for analysis sheets, working trial balances (account names), and the usual column headings for work sheets.

White work papers are not very popular. Yellow seems to be most prevalent; buff and green are also widely used.

LETTERS AND REPORTS

Letters and reports offer an opportunity to create a favorable impression of the firm in the minds of known and unknown readers. This public relations aspect, in addition to the usual reasons such as professional appearance and neatness, warrants that care be taken before sending out correspondence and reports.

Letterheads and envelopes. The original letterhead sheets should preferably be engraved on 16- or 20-pound rag paper. The 8½ by 11 size is most commonly used. The letterhead may be set up in one of the following ways:

JOHN J. JONES
Certified Public Accountant
611 West Broadway
New York 22, N. Y.
ORegon 5-9122

JOHN J. JONES
Certified Public Accountant

611 West Broadway
New York 22, N. Y.
ORegon 5-9122

JOHN J. JONES
Certified Public Accountant

Member, American Institute of
Certified Public Accountants

611 West Broadway
New York 22, N. Y.
ORegon 5-9122

It is not considered desirable to claim special proficiency or to specify classes of service on the letterhead; consequently, such wording as "income tax consultants," "systems experts," and similar descriptions should not be used. (See *Code of Professional Ethics,* Rule 4.01 and Opinion No. 5, Appendix pages 823, 826.) It is customary, however, for firms with more than one office to list the names of offices in an upper corner of the letterhead. Occasionally the names of partners of the firm are shown on the letterhead.

The special letterhead sheets used when extra copies of letters are sent out may be printed rather than engraved and may have the word "copy" printed in large, thin letters across the center of the sheet or at its head. These sheets may be 12-pound stock or may be the same weight as the letterhead sheet, with the lighter weight preferred and in more common use. Envelopes should preferably be of the same paper stock as the letterhead, with the return address in the upper left-hand corner. Some firms use United States Post Office prestamped envelopes, printed to order; this saves time affixing stamps and is especially useful when getting out a volume of mail.

It is practical to use window envelopes 6½ inches wide, or 9½ inches wide, with the firm name printed in the upper left corner, to save time when mailing confirmation requests. These envelopes are not considered satisfactory or of sufficient dignity for use with correspondence.

Billheads usually are the same stock as letterheads, using half-size sheets. If it is the policy of the firm to render billings in detail or with considerable description of the services, the regular letterhead is used.

Report paper. It is well for the new practitioner to make a complete study of sizes and weights of paper. Finished bond paper that is too heavy reduces the clarity of carbon copies. Some onion skin paper is too thin for use in audit reports. Paper that is too large will not fit in the files of bankers, attorneys, and the Internal Revenue Service.

Reports should be typewritten on rag-content bond paper of good quality, on which the accounting firm's name is suitably engraved, printed, or watermarked. The great majority of firms use 100 per cent rag paper, although some firms use 50 per cent or 75 per cent rag content. The majority apparently use 13-pound stock for report purposes, with many using 16-pound paper. Some firms employ 20-pound sheets for important correspondence but not for reports.

The sizes of paper used for financial statement- and report-typing vary greatly. Some firms use only three sizes while others use as many as ten sizes. The dimensions range from those based upon 8½ inches (such as 8½ by 14 and 8½ by 17) to those based upon 13 inches (such as 13 by 13½, 13 by 17, 13 by 18½, and 13 by 21), with many measurements in between these ranges. There is a trend toward the adoption of the 8½- by 11-inch report size, mainly because clients find that this fits more satisfactorily into the files.

In order that wide sheets of schedules or tabulations will readily fold to a uniform report size, and keeping in mind the desire of banks and creditors for reports which will fit into standard files, the following sizes should prove satisfactory: 8½ by 11, 11 by 13, 11 by 17, 11 by 19½, and 11 by 26. These are the best sizes for folding to 8½ by 11 reports.

Some firms never use a sheet larger than 8½ by 11 in the formal audit report. For exhibits such as balance sheets, two sheets are utilized with the assets appearing at the left of the binding edge and the liabilities at the right. The objection to this is that no typing appears on the reverse side of either the assets or liabilities sheets, and the reader may be surprised when first introduced to this procedure. In order to utilize to the fullest advantage this comparatively small-size paper, some firms omit the two penny columns and the decimal point that precedes them.

Each page following the letterhead sheet of the report should bear, in small type, the neatly printed or engraved firm name in the upper left-hand corner or at the bottom center of the sheet. Alternatively, some firms use paper watermarked in the center with the firm name. This increases the cost and also requires large stationery orders, usually a ton of paper at a time being the minimum quantity for a run, but larger firms consider it to be visually effective.

Paper of 16-pound stock is used for reports requiring not more than seven or eight copies. In order that twelve or even fourteen copies may be typewritten in one run, the same sizes are sometimes also purchased in onion skin paper.

If the accounting practice includes listed companies, it is necessary, in addition to the foregoing sizes of paper to carry an 8½- by 13-inch sheet and a 17 by 13 sheet which folds to 8½ by 13, for use in SEC registration statements or annual SEC *10K* reports.

It also will usually be desirable to stock the 8½ by 11 and 11 by 17 sizes in a plain, unwatermarked and unprinted paper for use in copying schedules to be attached to tax returns, or for statistical or financial data compiled for clients or others without audit.

CARBON PAPER

It is important to test various types and grades of carbon paper on the firm's typewriters and report stationery. The quality of the work turned out by different carbon papers varies greatly, especially where numerous copies must be typewritten at one run. Cheap carbon paper is undesirable, and it is usually more satisfactory to use the more expensive types manufactured especially for statistical typing purposes.

REPORT COVERS AND ENVELOPES

The report may be bound in a cover of good pliable kraft (heavy paper) stock; light grey, buff or light blue are popular colors. There seems to be a decided preference for cardboard covers with heavy paper as a second choice, and grey or brown are favored colors.

A cover of 9 by 11½ inches will fit the 8½ by 11 sheet size; for other report sizes a cover one-half inch larger in each dimension than the folded sheet is adequate. The cover should bear the firm's name, or name and address, followed by the title "Certified Public Accountants" (if proper), engraved or printed at the center bottom or bottom right.

The title of each report is shown either at the center top or in the center of the page. Some firms type the titles while others have them imprinted specially for each audit or special report. Each accounting firm should have a standard way of designating the title of a report. For audit reports a common form of title is as follows:

Auditors' Report

GREEN MANUFACTURING COMPANY

June 30, 1961

An alternative form sometimes used is this:

GREEN MANUFACTURING COMPANY

Report

as at June 30, 1961

Other styles may be used, but it is generally desirable to follow on the cover the order or format used in statement headings.

In the case of unaudited financial statements, on which no opinion is intended to be expressed by the accountant, care must be taken to see that the method of presentation is not such as to cause the reader to assume that the accountant intended to assume any responsibility. One way to do this is to use plain stationery and plain covers, without the name or watermark of the auditor appearing on them. A more common and preferable way, and the one stipulated by Rule 2.03 of the AICPA's *Code of Professional Ethics,* is to designate on the cover and on each statement the fact that the data are "prepared from the books without audit"; in such a case a cover style could be:

GREEN MANUFACTURING COMPANY

Financial Statements

(Prepared from the Books without Audit)

June 30, 1961

Any similar style which conveys this information is permissible in such cases.

Some accounting firms use a flysheet immediately following the cover, bearing the same title as appears on the cover. Other firms omit the flysheet, but present an index as the first sheet. The index usually indicates the pages of comments and lists each financial statement and schedule in numbered sequence.

Some firms bind lengthy survey or other special reports in cloth or leather covers. However, good quality engraved kraft or heavy paper covers will usually suffice, and the practice of using fancy covers is becoming uncommon.

The report will look best bound at the left-hand side, and reports are generally so bound, except that for monthly statements, tax protests, single sheets, short-form and informal reports, SEC matters, and the like, binding at the top is preferred. Most firms bind reports with eyelets and some use brass fasteners. Some draw ribbon through the eyelets, others use staples and a strip of gummed tape covering them. The plain eyelets or fasteners are most commonly used, and the ribbon type is considered to be somewhat old-fashioned and unnecessary.

The mailing envelopes for reports may be 10 by 12½ inches in size, white, tan, or light grey, and of a reasonably heavy weight since they must hold several copies of reports.

It has been found feasible when SEC work is done, or in case of accountings for decedents' estates or other work for courts or attorneys which is typed on legal size (8½ by 13) sheets, to use 10- by 15-inch envelopes for mailing these items.

CONTROL OVER SUPPLIES

Supplies and stationery cost is a substantial one in the accountant's expense statement. In most firms the physical handling is probably a bit loose. Rarely indeed are there practitioners using such refinements as perpetual inventories, printed or written requisitions, or even periodic physical inventory-taking—except at the close of the accounting year, and not even then in some firms. Although most firms place the responsibility for purchasing on one individual, there are many who permit the head stenographer to buy all the supplies needed for her department without clearing through a partner or office executive.

The size of the firm, naturally, governs the extent to which controls should be applied. It would be absurd for the beginner with perhaps one or two staff assistants and one secretary-typist who also does most of the bookkeeping, to employ requisitions and purchase orders and to maintain perpetual records of inventories on stationery and supplies. But larger firms are wise to at least keep control of their most expensive supply items.

An intelligent middle ground should be sought, especially by the small and medium-sized firms. The following constitutes minimum watchfulness:

1. Check frequently on high-cost, large-volume items, the stocks of which undergo almost daily withdrawals by staff members and others, especially if withdrawals are not cleared by some official employee in charge.

2. Check on items, regardless of cost, which are special to the firm, obtainable from perhaps one or few suppliers, and consequently not as easy to acquire as are the more standard, competitive products. These should be watched, not necessarily from the standpoint of cost only, but also in the light of the inconvenience their unexpected depletion would cause.

Among those usually coming within the two categories outlined above are ruled columnar work paper, preprinted work sheets, and special forms, such as confirmations bearing the firm name. This is, of course, only a partial list. Some other high-cost stationery need not have as close surveillance. Falling under that latter classification would be those items with which the head stenographer comes in daily contact, such as engraved letterheads, envelopes, report covers, and made-to-order report bond paper with particular rulings. Since these are usually in packs of a certain number each, and stacked in cabinets or shelves to which the stenographers, by virtue of their daily needs, frequently resort, it would be unlikely that they failed to observe the degree of diminution of the various packs and arrange for reorder.

Postage, especially in medium-sized and large firms, is worthy of consideration; but too much time should not be given to worrying about relatively low-cost units, such as carbon paper, typewriter ribbons, file folders, second sheets, and the like.

Practices of accounting firms. When an office manager or some other executive has charge of purchasing—a desirable control when feasible—the solution to the problem of waste is eased. He establishes maximum-minimum requirements. Even without a system of requisitions, purchase orders, and formal inventory cards or accounts, he can pursue a course similar to the one adopted by one medium-sized firm. This firm runs off inventory blanks which show, by classifications, all sizes and kinds of supplies used in the office. These blanks serve the following purposes:

1. A physical inventory of quantities only (ignoring broken packages) is taken in pencil at the close of each month.

2. Using the same type of sheets, listings are made in ink from vendors' invoices of the dates and numbers of packages of stationery and supplies received, continuing until the end of the semi-annual period. No inventories are recorded on this sheet.

3. At the close of the first and second half of each fiscal year, a complete physical inventory is taken, priced, and extended.

4. A summary is then prepared showing inventory at the first of the period, purchases, inventory at the end of the period, and amount used. By keeping past performance figures, a fair judgment can be formed regarding waste as well as future inventory requirements.

This firm purchases from one producer, at an agreed price fixed in advance, columnar work paper and certain confirmation forms not expected to change. The producer stocks two years' supply and the firm draws against this stock as needed, at which time the producer invoices the firm. The firm guarantees the purchase of the entire quantity, subject to the usual warranties of quality.

Another firm, a small one, saves considerable time by taking physical inventory of stationery and supplies as follows:

1. A sample sheet of the item about to be counted is lifted from one of the stacks or from a loose group of the forms.

2. After counting, the number of packages is written on the sample sheet.

3. The inventory quantities and descriptions are listed from the sample sheets.

Most firms place the responsibility for purchasing supplies on one individual. In some cases he is a partner, in others, the office manager. In the latter case, it is usual to have a partner at least supervise the activity.

Many large and medium firms do not attempt to maintain perpetual inventory records of supplies. Such records are rare in small firms. Even the few firms that make use of written requisitions do not attempt to make charges to specific departments. It is common practice merely to permit all staff members to take supplies as needed.

Furnishing office supplies to out-of-town clients. Many practitioners have problems with supplying certain stationery and office supplies to their clients. One practitioner has this to say:

> Since many of our clients are located in small towns or even out in the country where office supply stores are not nearby, we are often asked to get them necessary supplies, such as accounting paper, ledgers, journals, and sheets. In addition to this, they see the supplies which our staff uses and very frequently ask if they cannot buy some of our pads and work sheets.
>
> Over a period of years we donated a great many supplies to our clients, not because we are particularly generous, but because the amounts involved seemed at the time too small to mention; more often we just simply forgot to send them a bill. After we had opened our first two branch offices the situation became worse. These offices were carrying away supplies which were not being charged to their account.
>
> After some study of the situation we developed a requisition form and we now use it for both customers and branch offices. A supply of these forms is carried by each member of our staff who goes out in the field. We also have a supply at the desk in the main office. Whenever any supplies leave the office, it is the duty of the girl at the desk to see that a requisition form is filled out. If one of the men comes in from the field with a request for supplies from a client, he gives it to the desk girl to see that the material is sent. She then holds all of these requisitions in a file and at the end of the month they are turned over to the bookkeeping department.
>
> Clients are billed at 10 per cent above the cost shown on the requisition. The branch offices are charged at cost by journal entry.
>
> Once we began keeping track of these charges, we were surprised at the amount of supplies that for years had been going out of our office and for which we had never been paid.

Nonstaff Employees

SELECTION OF OFFICE PERSONNEL

■ WHEN ENGAGING general office help, great importance should be attached to the following points: (1) ability and willingness to do quantities of columnar typing and tabulation, (2) liking for work involving figures and detail, (3) adequate knowledge of English, (4) willingness to work overtime during peak seasons, and (5) ability and willingness to use special purpose (broad-carriage) typewriters. Knowledge of general office routine is not considered essential, and proficiency in using adding machines, calculators, etc., and a knowledge of bookkeeping are considered unimportant by many. The significant difference between important and unimportant is, obviously, that basic qualifications are important while others, no matter how helpful in a subordinate way, can be dispensed with if not available or can be ultimately imparted. To the small firm there seems to be an indication that what must be looked for particularly is willingness to learn and work, some basic knowledge, and a definite indication of potential capacities along required lines.

Often, reliable female office help is difficult to obtain. Whether or not this is the case, an enlightened employment policy will pay dividends. Office hours and vacation policy should conform to local practice.

In recent years it has become increasingly difficult to obtain employees if Saturday morning work is in the schedule. So in most places the typing department is closed on Saturdays, except for the first few months of the year.

A person not suited by inclination and qualification for the work assigned to him or her will always be a square peg in a round hole. The CPA's work is specialized work. Each employee's talents should be fitted to that part of the office work for which he is most suited. A typist who hates tabulating and columnar transcription is headed for dismal failure in a public accountant's office. The time to discover any such failings is when investigating the application. The employer must be resolute in making choices based on an intelligent hiring policy.

In a small office, the stenographer is frequently the only nonstaff employee. Under those circumstances, she is called upon to do bookkeeping work, but very seldom handles the general books of the firm. In some cases the stenographer enters receipts and disbursements in the cash book and posts time to the time ledger. It is not good practice to permit staff members to post time records.

Sometimes the duties of the one office assistant encompass several phases of activity. Besides receiving visitors and answering the telephone, she must file literature, pamphlets, and tax service reports for the library; file audit work papers, audit reports, tax returns, and letters; keep track of the stationery needs; maintain the accounts receivable and other ledgers, as well as cash records; and keep records on staff location. All this leaves little time for comparing and checking typed reports against original manuscripts, and taking care of personal matters for her employer, to say nothing of running errands.

In view of the variety of work required of an office assistant in a small organization, the importance of having an unusually competent person is increased. Care must be exercised in selection of such an assistant.

For a small office it is well to hire a girl who has had some experience with a larger accounting firm. However, in a small community this may not be feasible. In fact, a practitioner just starting his office may find a thoroughly experienced person somewhat beyond his means and he is more apt to lose trained personnel to larger firms than to secure competent workers from them. He is likely to find that he will have to select and train someone with simply potential ability and aptitudes, and perhaps, initially at least, use only part-time office help. He should therefore seek at the outset a married woman who has had previous experience in an accounting office in his town or in a larger center and who is receptive to income from part-time work.

For a larger firm, with one or two experienced girls, it is practical in hiring additional help to obtain young women with a small amount of typing experience and train them in the firm's procedures. The more experienced girls can then handle the more complicated work, permitting the less experienced ones to do the smaller reports and tax returns. If the size of the office does not justify a full-time clerk or telephone operator, the new girl can also assume some of these duties.

Most firms employ only female stenographers. Some of the large and medium firms have a preference for college-trained or partly college-trained stenographers and typists, especially those doing secretarial work. Smaller firms indicate preference for at least high school graduates, very few of them employing secretaries or even typists who have less than high school training.

Sources of personnel. The main sources for typists are private employment agencies, help-wanted advertisements in newspapers, business schools, situation-wanted advertisements, leads furnished by associates or employees, and records of previous applicants for employment. The sources to use depend on such factors as nature and urgency of the need, past experience in securing help, and the general or special customs followed in the community.

Responsibility for hiring. Some medium-sized and large firms place the responsibility of hiring and firing, regardless of type of employee, upon one personnel manager who may or may not be a partner. Other firms permit the staff supervisor to employ staff accountants, but that person has nothing to do with other applicants. Under those circumstances either the managing partner or office manager selects nonstaff employees.

Screening applicants. The natural starting point in the selection of employees is the filing by them of an application. Most application forms ask the same questions. (Examples are given in the Appendix, pages 787-789.)

It has been stated by some that too great confidence is not placed in letters of recommendation. One personnel official prides himself on his record of successful choices, and a factor to which he gives credit is his policy of *telephoning references,* long distance if necessary, instead of writing to them. He makes the point that people will be less candid in a letter than in conversation.

In larger cities, employment agencies and psychological organizations offer services intended to assist employers in selecting suitable employees. There is reason to believe that these organizations vary in quality.

A number of standardized tests are available for use as aids in employing clerical and office personnel. Examples are:

1. Minnesota Clerical Test (The Psychological Corporation, New York City)
2. Blackstone Stenographic Proficiency Test (Harcourt, Brace and World, Tarrytown, N. Y.)
3. Thurstone Examination in Typing (Harcourt, Brace and World)
4. Thurstone Test of Mental Alertness (Science Research Associates, Chicago)
5. Benge Clerical Test *D* (The Psychological Corporation)
6. DAT Clerical Speed and Accuracy Test (The Psychological Corporation)
7. Purdue Clerical Adaptability Test (distributed by University Book Store, Purdue University, Lafayette, Ind.)
8. SRA Tests of Clerical Aptitude (Science Research Associates)
9. Seashore-Bennett Stenographic Proficiency Test (The Psychological Corporation)
10. Otis Self-Administering Test of Mental Ability (Harcourt, Brace and World)

These tests vary as to time required and difficulty of administration and interpretation. Some, such as the Otis and Minnesota Tests, are relatively quick and easy to administer. However, all tests require experience to assure sound evaluation. Tests may be purchased from the publisher, and a wide range of tests (their own publications and those of certain other publishers) may be purchased from The Psychological Corporation, 304 East 45th Street, New York, N.Y. Tests and scoring services may be obtained from the Educational Records Bureau, 21 Audubon Avenue, New York, N.Y. The Educational Records Bureau does not sell tests to institutions planning to score their own tests unless these institutions hold membership in the Bureau.

One large firm operating many branches places great emphasis on the importance of a comprehensive application blank and a most thorough investigation of every detail of the applicant's general education, technical training, and experience. Applicants file triplicate application blanks, two of them remaining as carefully guarded parts of the firm's permanent records, one at the main office, the other at the branch at which the applicant applied. The third copy is utilized as a current document pending completion of investigation, and is placed in a general file if the applicant is employed; otherwise, it is destroyed. Using a type of large "scrapbook" for the purpose, both offices will keep a photograph of the employee and a narrative record of all pertinent information.

Some firms insist on at least two interviews with each applicant. The last conference is usually with one or sometimes two senior partners of the firm. This, however, applies particularly to key executives and staff accountants.

SUPPLYING PERSONNEL FOR CLIENTS

Accounting firms are frequently asked by their clients for assistance in locating personnel. One firm, through its staff-personnel manager, prepares a monthly report for all partners showing applications for positions as well as openings with clients as of the close of each month. These reports show (1) jobs available, (2) applicants available, and (3) jobs filled. A follow-up is maintained for the benefit of the applicants, as well as the clients. This procedure is reported to have developed the goodwill of clients.

CONTRACTS AND RECORDS

A common incident of employment is the signing by both parties of an "employment letter" or contract which covers matters relating to starting salary, annual vacation, notices of termination, and so forth. Some firms also require that a "deed of secrecy" be signed by the employee, who pledges to keep inviolate during and after his incumbency any and all knowledge of clients' affairs. Examples of employment contracts used by a large firm are reproduced in the Appendix, pages 796-799.

It seems desirable that a careful classification for filing of applications be maintained and that none be destroyed immediately, unless it is certain that the applicant cannot be used by the firm or by a client. The file should be kept current. After one year, all applications of unsuccessful applicants should be destroyed, unless there is a good reason for further retention. Application forms of personnel employed should be transferred to the employment files and retained permanently.

TRAINING OFFICE EMPLOYEES

It is tragic when the carelessness of office employees, say in the review department or in comparing and checking, destroys the confidence and goodwill of clients developed by good work in the field and by able services on the part of partners and key department heads. The sole safeguard against such a hazard is persistent and systematic control of office routine. Such control is much easier if the employees possess the capabilities to do the work properly and if they have been adequately trained in their jobs.

Where there are several office employees, higher employees must be trained to delegate reasonable authority to subordinates. A chief employee who does not utilize his or her assistants' time and services to the greatest possible advantage is clearly inefficient.

Some firms have a new employee work for about a month studying their typing manual, which has rules, examples, and explanations for setting up most types of statements, report comments, and the like. To relieve the monotony, the new girl is given simple work and tax returns to type.

In the review of working papers, reports, and tax returns, reviewers cannot delegate all authority or responsibiity. But they can train their aides in strict adherence to proper procedures and so pass on their own experience for the benefit of the firm and to the advantage of those instructed.

Instructions and manuals. As an aid in training employees, and as a means of maintaining employee morale and obtaining more uniform and consistent office work, a manual (or series of manuals) on procedure is desirable. While such manuals are difficult to prepare and require revision from time to time, they can be of great help in the operation of an accounting practice. As the size of the staff increases, the desirability of written manuals and office bulletins also increases. These might cover the following topics:

1. Personal conduct and professional ethics
2. Hours, compensation, time and expense diaries, and reports
3. General office instructions, equipment, telephone, correspondence, file room
4. Library (pamphlets, books, and tax services)
5. Audit manual
6. Preparation, processing, distributing, and filing of reports and tax returns. It is most desirable that members of the staff inform themselves quickly on the ways of the firm, its techniques, and grow into harmony with its ideals and traditions. The formal manuals and bulletins assist in this endeavor. Supplementing these from time to time can be written memoranda on special topics.

A checklist of indoctrination procedures for use with new employees is reproduced in the Appendix, page 907.

Extent of use of manuals. It would appear that the most widely used types of manuals are those covering general staff regulations and audit-procedure instructions. Less frequently used are instructions for statement forms, report preparations, and stenographic instructions. Some firms even prepare written instructions for filing, reviewing procedures, and preparation of tax returns.

The large firms naturally tend more toward special manuals for separate purposes rather than a general one for all. Also there is a tendency to use generalized manuals for staff regulations and review instructions, while the preference is definitely for specific manuals covering instructions on audit procedures and preparation of tax returns.

Most firms furnish a copy of relevant manuals to every employee, and those that do not make an office copy available to all. Manuals are usually compiled in loose-leaf form and are reviewed and revised periodically.

Form of manuals. Where a firm prepares a manual covering any area of its operations, it should make provision for revisions. By using the loose-leaf form, pages can be revised and a manual kept up to date without revising it completely. Some firms send out instructions to their personnel in the form of memoranda rather than manuals. These instructions may be revised readily by issuance of a new memorandum on the same matter.

Some firms use leather-bound books or other attractive bindings for their loose-leaf instruction sheets. Others use 8½-by-11 or legal-sized paper. One medium-sized organization uses binders, one for each partner and staff member, in which are filed pertinent office memoranda on audit procedures, taxes, government regulations as to prices, wages, renegotiation, and other subjects.

Contents of manuals. One large firm divides its tax-department manual into two sections. One section deals with the review of tax returns and the other with the handling of tax cases. The first section contains tax checklists on income and deductions, special rulings, and decisions. The second section covers generally accepted methods of preparing protests and conduct in dealing with internal revenue agents and conferees.

Some firms of medium and large size have office-procedure manuals or sections on office procedures in comprehensive manuals. They deal with such matters as office hours, salaries, overtime, night and week-end work, vacations, notice of termination of employment, and policy on sick leave and fringe compensation. An example of a staff personnel manual appears in the Appendix, pages 800-815.

One large firm's office manager no longer believes in formal staff and office manuals. His firm tries to be flexible even on office hours and vacations. Its policy is to issue brief informal regulations to employees with revisions as the occasion demands. They are mimeographed and delivered to each person.

OTHER FACTORS IN EMPLOYEE RELATIONS

No deductions should be made for time lost as a result of minor illnesses; the office environment should be pleasant; employee relations should be affable and courteous; salary increases should be made at least annually; bonuses should be paid at least annually for length of service, for excessive overtime, for extra duties assumed, and so on. Not all of the latter provisions can be put into effect immediately in a small, new practice. But they should be instituted as the practice grows and makes them possible, for they in turn contribute to the establishment of an enduring and expanding organization.

The employees should work steadily and should be willing to work a little longer when a rush assignment demands it. However, the day of the slave driver or the constantly rushing type of supervisor is past and those tactics will not produce consistent or accurate work or help retain employees.

In the training of a stenographer or typist, it should be brought to her attention with considerable emphasis that an accountant supplies nothing except professional service, and that the quality of his service is reflected in the nature of his advice and in the form of the report his client receives. Also that since the report is the only tangible thing the client sees, he may estimate the worth of the accountant by the appearance and content of his report.

Where there is an office staff of more than one person, it is usually advisable to have the stenographers (other than personal secretaries in the case of larger firms) and the typists work in one room. The stenographers answer a bell or buzzer connected to the rooms of the members of the firm or members of the staff who dictate. The dictation usually consists of answering the mail, writing memos to clients, interoffice memos, and other types of work which under ordinary circumstances would not have to be reviewed by some other person except perhaps for final approval.

Usually comments pertaining to a report are not dictated. The accountant writes the report in longhand in draft form, which is reviewed by his senior, the chief of staff, or a member of the firm. Proficient accountants, however, may dictate their reports, sometimes in draft, and this may save expensive time at the lesser cost of some added clerical time. This is a practice which deserves encouragement because it is valuable in saving time for the firm when skilled accountants are in short supply.

UTILIZATION OF PERSONNEL

At the inception of a CPA's practice, the office girl is usually a combination typist, stenographer, file clerk, and receptionist. As the firm grows and additional office help is required, departmentalization of operations may take place. One or more girls may take dictation and type correspondence and report comments, another girl or girls may type financial and statistical statements. Filing may be a full-time job for another employee.

The point in the firm's progress at which departmentalization becomes necessary must be decided separately by each firm. However, considering the problems of training office help and the salary costs involved, it is important that proper utilization be made of all available time.

For instance, many state tax returns require income or expense schedules or balance sheets, similar to those on the Federal income-tax return. In those cases, typing several extra copies at the time the client's Federal return is prepared may obviate later retyping for state tax purposes. During slow periods, typists might make pro-forma copies of financial statements and reports, omitting the current figures, which will be filled in at the conclusion of the audit. Giving the auditors these pro-forma copies will save time during the busy season. Also since these pro-formas are drawn up in the established form and are easy to read, it will also result in saving time when the girls finally type the report for the client.

Office Routine

THE RECEPTIONIST

■   THE USUAL PROCEDURE for receiving clients is to have the telephone operator stationed in the waiting room or outer office as a receptionist. She is the first to greet clients and other visitors. It is important that she be polite, intelligent, well-groomed, well-mannered, and well-spoken. Poise, patience, and a good telephone voice are imperative, as well as a maturity which insures the thoughtful handling of messages and a real awareness of their significance. A telephone call may be a firm's first contact with a prospective client. Unless the telephone operator is courteous, efficient, and understanding, it may be the last. For this reason, many firms have definite rules for proper handling of all telephone communications and for the reception of clients and other visitors.

Receptionists should be provided with pertinent information concerning clients, such as names of executives. They are usually given some additional duties to perform, such as answering the telephone, taking dictation, typing, filing, bookkeeping, handling monthly write-ups, mimeographing, mailing, and keeping records of daily staff attendance.

Most firms try to have a partner available at all times to talk with clients who visit their office. Others provide for the presence of a responsible staff member.

TELEPHONE PROCEDURES

The switchboard operator (or the person designated to answer the telephone) should be kept informed as to the exact location of staff members at all times.

A record should be kept of long distance calls in order to charge the amount to the right client or expense account. This record is built up by having the office operator ask the telephone-company toll operator to state the amount (including tax) after completion of each call. If the reports are prepared weekly, it is well to have a report prepared as to the last day of the month so that billings to clients are complete.

HANDLING OF INCOMING MAIL

An effort should be made to reply to correspondence the same day it is received, if its nature permits. This will prevent an accumulation of work and will also enhance the firm's reputation for efficiency and promptness.

Not many firms keep a record of each letter which comes in and requires a reply. But those that do find it useful where several persons answer mail, especially to follow up those men who have a tendency to accumulate papers on their desks. This record may be maintained by the person who opens the mail or by the office manager or partner who receives all mail.

A simple form of loose-leaf or bound copybook or blank book, ruled as follows, with a space or two between each day's entries, will suffice for this purpose:

INCOMING MAIL REPORT

Date————————

Name of sender	General subject of letter	Person to whom given for reply	Date reply is mailed

As all the items on a page are replied to, a red line can be drawn diagonally across the page. Open items should be followed up perhaps twice weekly.

In one firm, copies of the incoming mail report are routed to the partners for their information. Audit confirmations, all received in preaddressed envelopes, go directly to the filing department in this firm and do not pass through the regular incoming mail procedures. The filing department routes the contents to the seniors concerned.

In other firms the name of the man who is to reply is written in pencil on the upper right-hand corner of the incoming letter and it is placed on his desk or in his mail folder for reply. This system is quite casual and usually works well only when all mail is signed by one person who has a good memory.

A reading file or extra copies of letters and other documents for partners and key executives is normal procedure in many offices. One large firm places copies, latest on top, in a loose-leaf binder in the firm's library. The readers initial each as read, until all proper parties have read them. The last of the designated readers destroys the copy.

OUTGOING MAIL

The use of first-class mail. It is believed that most accounting firms favor the use of first-class over registered mail for sending reports and tax returns to clients. Generally, both returns and reports can be readily duplicated or replaced and, furthermore, registry can be a time-consuming procedure. However, if the mailing includes some of the client's materials which are being returned to him, then the added responsibility may call for the use of registered mail.

Signing letters. It does not seem advisable to allow too many persons to sign firm mail. The more signers, the more difficult it is to achieve uniformity of language or practice and the more difficult to fix responsibility. There is no harm in staff men dictating or writing letters, but signing should be the prescribed and exclusive duty of a partner or manager. Where this is done it is usually the custom to place on the office copy only the initials of the staff member who prepared the letter. In some cases, though less frequently, the initials are also placed on the original letter. In addition to restricting the signing of letters and reports to partners, some firms follow the practice of having the partners sign the firm name, and not as individuals.

The use of form letters. Much of the correspondence in an accountant's office can be reduced to form letters not requiring individual typing or signature. For instance, letters accompanying tax returns sent to clients for signature and filing, confirmation requests, form letters advising clients of pertinent changes in Federal or state income, franchise or payroll tax requirements, and similar matter, may be reproduced in quantity to save typing and signing time. This is common practice.

File copies. Not all firms file office copies of correspondence with clients in the same way. Some file them chronologically, some alphabetically by clients, some in a special correspondence folder for each client, and some in the client's audit file (where there is an auditing engagement).

Extra copies. As a firm expands it will be found practical to type, in addition to the file copy, one, two, or more copies of all correspondence dealing with client's problems, taxes, or fees. One copy could be placed in the front of the working-paper folder for the information of the staff man at the time he next visits the client's office. Some firms circulate an extra copy of all such letters, on distinctively colored paper, among partners or managers for perusal and initialing. Some firms route a colored copy to the staff man usually serving the client so that he is currently informed on all matters affecting that client.

In one firm of medium size, four copies of all correspondence and memoranda are prepared and distributed as follows:

1. Original to the party addressed
2. Duplicate white tissue to an alphabetical correspondence file, this being filed promptly
3. Triplicate pink tissue to the accountant in charge of the client, this being initialed by him and then sent to the working-paper files
4. Quadruplicate blue tissue, circulated among the partners for information and used as a follow-up copy for an indicated person and date when the subject requires it.

In this procedure, additional white tissue copies marked "copy" in large, thin, red letters are used when others are to be informed. Where several copies are made for different purposes, the use of different colored sheets aids the filing procedure.

Removal of correspondence from the file. Few firms are so small as to dispense with the requirement that when correspondence is removed from the files, a written and informative record be made of such removal. Usually this record identifies definitely the material taken, names the person removing it, and gives the date of removal. One firm requires that the record also show the purpose for which removal is made. The value of this addition lies in the fact that it is apt to suggest where the papers may be found if they are not readily located.

SECRETARIAL ASSISTANCE

Some firms have some secretaries assigned to specific partners and supervisors, and others have no definite assignments, but stenographers are made available to partners and staff members as the need arises. In practically all cases, whether they have specific assignments or not, secretaries, when not engaged in secretarial duties, are used for filing, miscellaneous, typing, proofreading, and other routine activities.

Some organizations find it desirable to supplement their other facilities by part-time or outside assistants. One firm is served by an extra stenographer-typist on a part-time basis. She is available for from three to five days per week during rush season and can be called on short notice during the entire year. Some firms have the advantage of acquaintance with someone upon whom they can call for special work. Others use public stenographers but discretion must be exercised in selecting persons to work on material of a confidential nature. Public stenographers should be used mainly for emergency work, and it is desirable to obtain the clients' permission for any confidential material.

OFFICE HOURS

As to office hours, accounting firms are generally changing their policies to conform to developments in industry and private business. The trend is definitely away from night work. The reasons are: (1) overwork impedes efficiency, is likely to dull keenness of perception, and places a severe physical strain upon staff members; (2) professions should abide by the changing times which call for a greater share of relaxation for employees; (3) a reasonable work schedule tends toward better employer-employee relationships. Those favoring the increasingly common practice of Saturdays off say most of their clients cannot be reached anyway. One firm goes so far as to keep the workweek down to forty hours; if night work becomes necessary, time off is given to maintain the forty-hour schedule.

On the average, smaller firms are much more flexible in their working hours than large firms, usually regulating the time of staff men to meet the varying workload. In the larger firms, an effort is made to adhere to a fixed workweek; most require permission of a supervisor or a partner before a staff man may work overtime.

Saturday work is on the decline, despite heavy volumes of work. Very few accountants work a full day on Saturday, and then at irregular intervals. Some firms require a half-day on Saturday during the busy times only. Practices are trending rapidly toward the elimination of all Saturday work.

Traveling time. Traveling time consumed during the working day is usually charged to the client and need not be done on the employees' time, but some firms recommend to their staffs that they do as much traveling as possible in "off hours," so as not to require billing to clients.

OFFICE CONDUCT OF EMPLOYEES

Naturally, rules prescribed as to the conduct of employees vary. Accountants are made aware of the professional nature of their services. Of paramount importance among the items of conduct is the need for the client's confidence that his private affairs will be kept with utmost secrecy. Nothing can affect that confidence more quickly than when a firm's employee makes statements or drops hints on confidential matters of others when speaking to a client. Some organizations even detail in their manuals suggestions to their employees regarding decorum, low-tone conversation at the office and over the telephone, and acceptable dress. One goes so far as to discuss manicured finger nails and shined shoes.

The majority of firms have rules in effect on the following:

1. Exact office hours
2. Personal conversations while in clients' offices
3. Use of idle time
4. Keeping staff desks and tables clear of papers and file folders when not in use

Others have rules on dress of employees and on use of telephones by staff members.

The Accountant's Library

ORGANIZATION AND SUPERVISION

■ THE OFFICE LIBRARY is usually handicapped at birth because its accumulation is apt to be begun in a rather haphazard manner. Books and other matter of genuine reference value may either be passed by unnoticed through the routine filing mill or, what is almost as bad, they may be left neglected in desks and odd corners. It is desirable to collect in the library all books and source material scattered through the organization and buried in private offices and bookcases. For all practical purposes, unless assembled, they are often not available and of no value to others in the firm. The physical handling, storing, and filing of books, pamphlets, periodicals, releases, and the like, may be safely delegated to a filing clerk or secretary, but a sufficiently well-educated member of the organization should assume supervisory responsibility and perform some of the duties of a librarian, regardless of whether or not he is officially designated as such. The formal title and position of librarian will, of course, only be used in those few instances when the book collection is very large and important enough to warrant it.

The superintendence of library reference material should, wherever possible, be entrusted to the colleague who is by education and temperament best suited to attack problems requiring such research. Such tasks often can be handled advantageously by a person well acquainted with current accounting literature. He need not have any great knowledge of library technique but he should be well read in the more studious aspects of accountancy and especially in those which infringe upon the active practice of the firm. He should know books, references, and sources of information, and he should be able to analyze facts and interpret accounting questions and problems presented to him. It is increasingly important that he be familiar with the procedure and pronouncements of the various official bodies and authorities and the publications in which their orders, opinions, and decisions appear. Taxation and its questions, however, have become such vast and intricate subjects that they must be left to the tax man, and the person in charge of the library cannot, as a general rule, be expected to engage in difficult tax-case research. To his younger associates he may well be a guide, helping them to find their way along paths to which their education has not accustomed them; for example, assisting them to find applicable SEC rules or regulations. As the experienced member of the firm, he should play the role of a scientific secretary; he should carefully keep them abreast of all news and professional data which are at all likely to have any bearing on their work. This will save them much valuable time.

FILLING THE NEEDS OF THE PARTICULAR PRACTICE

Ponderous tomes and texts, however valuable these may sometimes be, are not the real lifeblood of the practitioner's library. That is to be found in a constant stream of printed matter of vital, topical, up-to-the-minute interest. A great deal of this will probably flow into the office as the "automatic" accompaniment of the firm's business, but those who wish to command a really useful reference library will assiduously supplement it from many other sources. Numerous professional magazines are received by subscription. Separate issues should be preserved in the library and bound annually. Once the library is satisfactorily supplied with those journals and publications which are of common interest to the entire profession, emphasis should be directed to the collection of items which will be helpful in the firm's particular practice. To know his clients and their problems, the accountant nearly always has several separate and valuable sources of information:

1. Publications of business and finance of a general nature
2. Technical periodicals and trade papers, publications devoted to the news trends of particular types of business
3. Trade associations, which continually collect and publish statistical data and other information on the specific fields they service

As there is hardly any business which is not affected directly or indirectly by some form of government regulation, so there is often at least one state or federal authority whose regulations or decisions are of importance to the client's business. The Securities and Exchange Commission, the Interstate Commerce Commission, the Federal Power Commission, the Federal Communications Commission, and the Small Business Administration, to mention only a few federal agencies, all release announcements of varying interest to accountants. The various state public service commissions, for example, release material important to firms engaged in the audit of public utilities.

Some of these publications are available free of charge, some from a regional office, others from the central office only. Most federal publications can be obtained for a nominal charge from the Superintendent of Documents, Government Printing Office, Washington 25, D.C.

The application of practical accountancy to various problems may be further facilitated by gathering in the library matter of a somewhat different character. Printed corporate reports to stockholders, prospectuses issued in connection with the sale of securities, stock-listing applications, will all be found to offer a wealth of information on present-day thinking in the accounting profession. They invariably represent the finished product of practicing accountants and they frequently exhibit the attitudes taken towards new and difficult problems. The importance of these documents as a source of original accounting information can hardly be overestimated. In general they may be easily obtained from the corporation and investment banking or brokerage firms concerned. When received they should be circulated among those likely to be interested for notice of any remarkable and noteworthy accounting features. It is helpful to segregate these reports by classifying them as to industrials, utilities, banking, insurance, real estate, nonprofit organizations, and so on. A breakdown according to the type of industry will also prove to be of help.

Finally, in some firms, a policy might be established whereby important reports, research studies, abstracts from certain published articles, clippings, pamphlets, and the like, are kept in special files covering particular topics.

INDEXING

Having selected what his library requires, the accountant will be faced with the problem of convenient arrangement and cataloguing, if necessary. As long as the number of books is rather limited there is no great necessity for an elaborate system of indexing. However, an index by authors, titles, and topics will be especially useful when the person most familiar with the library is not readily available for consultation. It is good to remember that many magazines publish annual or semiannual indices, which should be carefully husbanded and kept readily accessible. (A simple system for the small firm's library is suggested on page 639.)

CONTROLLING WITHDRAWALS

Books and other materials should be rubber-stamped with the firm's name, given an inventory number, and a small paper pocket should be pasted inside on the back of the book or pamphlet. In that pocket a card should be inserted on which has been typed the title, author, and copy number of the book. Whenever an individual removes a book from the shelves, he should write his name and date of receipt on this card and drop it in a small box provided therefor. Should an item not be found on the shelves, a check of these cards will show who is holding the book. When books are returned, the card should be replaced in the pocket.

KEEPING THE STAFF UP TO DATE

Newly acquired books and periodicals should be circulated to interested members of the organization before being placed on the shelves. In that connection, many firms will find it useful to distribute to each accountant copies of new AICPA publications and new SEC Accounting Releases, and perhaps other material of particular importance. The auditor out of town a long time will surely appreciate being kept up to date in that manner.

OUTSIDE LIBRARIES

It will happen now and then that the problem to be tackled is beyond the scope and resources of the office library. The accountant who is in proper touch with his professional organization has the services of its library at his disposal. He should use them and he may also have a good public or university library near him. There are many special libraries all over the country, Federal Reserve bank libraries, stock exchange libraries, various state and federal libraries, and many others.

PRACTICES OF FIRMS

Most firms have libraries. Many keep up-to-date card indexes on their books. One accountant states that his firm's accounting books and pamphlets of lasting interest are indexed three ways: by author, title, and subject. Periodicals, except those of lasting interest, are retained for only a short time. Particularly interesting articles are cut out of the periodicals and placed in an indexed scrapbook. A master list of the books in the library is prepared at irregular intervals for distribution to the staff. As new books are added, a notice is placed on the bulletin board. This accountant suggests that every CPA obtain the Accountants' Index, issued by the AICPA.

PROFESSIONAL LITERATURE

While the needs of each accountant vary according to the types of business which he serves, there are certain sources of information with which all should be familiar. Some of them are periodicals or bulletins dealing with specific subjects and some are standard texts. Most textbooks, by their very nature, deal in a generalized manner with a description of principles or procedures rather than with the wide variety of differing situations encountered in actual practice. It is the current periodicals, releases, and bulletins of the AICPA, other accounting organizations, and regulatory bodies which keep the practitioner up to date on the methods of handling the varied problems which arise because of the complex structure of today's business. It is not feasible to present here a lengthy bibliography of the books and periodicals which comprise the literature of accounting. The average CPA is primarily interested in knowing which of the many available publications will be most useful to him in his practice. An attempt will be made to offer suggestions for worthwhile inclusions. All materials mentioned will not be useful to all practitioners; nor is the omission of a publication intended to indicate that it is not useful.

American Institute of CPAs. The official publication of the AICPA is *The Journal of Accountancy* which is published monthly. An editorial in the first issue, published by the predecessor organization in November 1905, stated:

The editors present the first issue of *The Journal of Accountancy* to the American accountants in the belief that this magazine marks the beginning of a movement which has for its object the establishment of accountancy in law and opinion as a learned profession.

That this movement has been successful has been adequately illustrated by the discussion of the AICPA's growth. The rise in circulation of *The Journal*, which today is distributed not only to all AICPA members, but to tens of thousands of other subscribers as well, is a further indication of this success. In addition to presenting timely comment by the editors and articles by leading accountants and other authorities in their particular fields, *The Journal* conducts several regular departments designed especially to be of use to the CPA in his practice.

The Journal is available in microfilm, through an agreement with University Microfilms, Ann Arbor, Michigan. The magazine's film copy is available only at the end of a volume year and contains the index of the preceding six months' published material. The film is on metal reels, labeled for easy reference. Sales are restricted to subscribers to the paper edition.

As an added means of keeping its members in touch with professional happenings, the AICPA publishes a monthly internal membership bulletin, the *CPA*. Through its wide news coverage members are informed of recent developments which affect their interests in any way.

From time to time, various committees of the AICPA have issued formal pronouncements recognized by the profession as the most authoritative statements on the subjects involved. The *Accounting Research and Terminology Bulletins* (Final Edition, 1961), for example, which deal with general accounting principles and their application to specific matters, summarize studies made by the old committee on accounting procedure. The pronouncements of the committee on auditing procedure were originally issued as Statements on Auditing Procedure. In 1951 a single pamphlet, replacing the twenty-four statements issued up to that time, was published. This booklet, entitled *Codification of Statements on Auditing Procedure,* consolidated the more valuable and useful features of the previous twenty-four pronouncements. Since then, numerous additional statements have been issued.

In 1954 the committee on auditing procedure issued a special report which was published under the title *Generally Accepted Auditing Standards—Their Significance and Scope.* It is important to note that this report is concerned primarily with auditing standards, as differentiated from auditing procedures. The committee believed that the most satisfactory method of presenting auditing procedures was by a series of case studies illustrating audit procedures adopted and applied in actual examinations. Case studies in auditing procedure have been issued, describing the audit procedures actually followed by practitioners in examinations of various types of business organizations. Plans are under way to issue industry audit guides instead of case studies in the future.

The committee on auditing procedure also has made a comprehensive study of internal control. The results of this study were published in 1949 under the title *Internal Control—Elements of a Co-ordinated System and Its Importance to Management and the Independent Public Accountant.* A series of case studies in internal control was then instituted.

In 1960 a new structure was created. The AICPA's Accounting Research Division was authorized to publish studies of current acounting problems and the Accounting Principles Board was created to consider the studies published by the Accounting Research Director and to issue authoritative pronouncements.

A comprehensive listing and discussion of the many phases of management services was published by the AICPA in 1956 under the title, *A Classification of Management Services by CPAs,* and in 1957 under the title, *Management Services by CPAs.* Prepared by the AICPA committee on management services, these publications deal with such areas as budgeting, financing, cost control, office management, and review of management controls.

In 1949 the research department of the AICPA, with the advice of the committee on auditing procedure, issued a pamphlet entitled *Audits by Certified Public Accountants—Their Nature and Significance.* This booklet, designed for the use of credit executives and others concerned with the work of the independent CPA, describes in general terms what the CPA does in order that he may express an opinion on financial statements. It was followed in 1956 by *Forty Questions and Answers about Audit Reports,* to answer in nontechnical language questions commonly asked by bankers about CPA audits, opinions, and reports.

In 1951 the public relations department of the AICPA prepared a pamphlet entitled *Your CPA's Responsibility* to explain Auditing Procedure Statement No. 23 (now Rule 19 of the Rules of Professional Conduct) to the clients of smaller CPA firms. Another public relations leaflet issued in 1951, *Why CPA Standards Are Important to You,* answers some of the questions most frequently asked about CPAs and their professional standards.

In 1940 the AICPA published a booklet outlining an audit program for savings-and-loan associations. This booklet was an important factor in raising the standards of independent audits of these associations. With the passage of time, new developments in their accounting practices took place which were not covered. A revised edition of the booklet, entitled *Audits of Savings and Loan Associations,* was therefore issued by the committee on auditing procedure in 1951. Another revision is scheduled for release in 1962.

In 1946 the Council of the AICPA initiated a long-range program for the analysis of corporate reports. Each year since then the research department, succeeded by the technical services division, has reviewed hundreds of these reports and has published a survey showing the manner in which various items are treated in the financial statements. This survey, which is entitled *Accounting Trends and Techniques,* points up, by means of numerous comparative tabulations, significant accounting trends during the period since the studies were started.

A pamphlet published by the AICPA under the title *Do You Close Your Books on New Year's Eve?* contains a chart to be used in determining a company's natural business year. A list of suggested fiscal closing dates for different types of business is published separately.

Each year the AICPA publishes the complete text of selected technical papers presented at the annual meeting. It also publishes from time to time various pamphlets, all of which are designed to promote a general recognition of the professional stature of CPAs.

American Accounting Association. The major publication of the American Accounting Association is the official quarterly journal, the *Accounting Review,* which was first issued in 1926. Articles in the *Review* cover practically the entire range of accounting subject matter. However, some attempt is made to feature articles on current developments in accounting theory, as contrasted with those of more specialized technical significance. Papers presented at the annual meetings of the Association also are included in the *Accounting Review.*

From time to time the American Accounting Association publishes research monographs, as well as special studies of various kinds. A research monograph entitled *An Introduction to Corporate Accounting Standards* by W. A. Paton and A. C. Littleton, which was originally published in 1940, was reprinted in 1951 and in 1955. In 1936 the executive committee of the Association issued *A Tentative Statement of Accounting Principles Affecting Corporate Reports.* The latest revision of this statement, published in 1957, is entitled *Accounting and Reporting Standards for Corporate Financial Statements and Preceding Statements and Supplements.*

National Association of Accountants. The official publication of the National Association of Accountants is the *NAA Bulletin* which is issued monthly. Each issue is devoted to technical information, news and information on the activities of the Association, and recent developments of interest to industrial accountants, as well as a review of books and articles in the field of current literature. The results of studies made by the research staff of the Association (a favorite area is cost accounting) are published from time to time in a special section of the *Bulletin.* Each year the Association publishes in the *Bulletin* its "Conference Proceedings," a complete report of all papers and discussions presented at the annual conference. These papers cover practical cost and accounting information on a variety of subjects.

Controllers Institute of America. The Controllers Institute of America publishes monthly *The Controller Magazine.* It also publishes pamphlets from time to time. While some of these deal solely with the functions and contributions of controllers, others, such as *Replacement Costs and Depreciation Policies* and *Tax Principles and Problems,* concern problems of more widespread interest.

Institute of Internal Auditors. The Institute of Internal Auditors publishes a quarterly periodical, *The Internal Auditor,* which was started in 1944. Prior to 1949 both technical papers and Institute news were contained in each issue. Since that time, however, a separate publication, the *Members News Bulletin,* has been devoted to news items. The Institute also has published several books on various phases of internal auditing, and each year it issues a volume containing the complete text of all papers presented at the annual meeting (*Conference Proceedings*).

GOVERNMENT PUBLICATIONS

Government publications cover a wide variety of subjects. Of those which are concerned with accounting matters, some are of interest to certain accountants and not to others, depending upon the types of business which they serve. For example, accountants with clients whose accounting methods are under the jurisdiction of regulatory authorities such as the FPC, the FCC, and the ICC, must use the current uniform systems of accounts prescribed by them. In addition, these accountants will be interested in the periodic releases and annual reports of the commissions. Regardless of the types of business represented in his practice, however, every accountant must keep abreast of the rules, regulations, and official releases of the SEC. The series of accounting releases, which are incorporated by reference in Regulation S-X, contain the opinions expressed from time to time by the chief accountant on controversial questions arising in connection with registration statements and annual reports filed with the SEC. Information on current developments in accounting and auditing also is included in the SEC's annual reports which outline its activities under the different statutes entrusted to it.

The Treasury Department issues many publications, such as the weekly *Internal Revenue Bulletin,* which supplement the Federal tax service.

The Department of Commerce publishes monthly *The Survey of Current Business* and *Business Cycle Developments,* as well as occasional specific business bulletins.

TAX AND FINANCIAL PUBLICATIONS

The following is a valuable, but by no means exhaustive, list of tax publications:

1. *U. S. Tax Week,* published weekly by Fallon Law Book Co., Inc., Albany, New York

2. *Taxes—The Tax Magazine,* published monthly by Commerce Clearing House, Inc., Chicago, Ill.

3. *The Journal of Taxation,* published monthly by William S. Papworth, New York City

4. *What's Happening in Taxation and Government Regulation,* published weekly by Prentice-Hall, Inc., Englewood Cliffs, N.J.

5. *The Tax Executive,* published quarterly by Tax Executives Institute, Inc., Washington, D.C.

6. *National Tax Journal,* published quarterly by The National Tax Association, Harrisburg, Pa.

7. "Tax Report" in the *Daily Report for Executives,* published daily by the Bureau of National Affairs, Washington, D.C.

8. *Tax Research Report,* published bimonthly by the Tax Research Institute, New York City.

9. *Business International,* published weekly by Business International Corporation, New York City

Every accountant, regardless of the size of his practice, needs to have dividend guides and stock and bond quotation records available for ready reference. Such records are published by Moody's Investors Service and by Standard & Poor's Corporation, among others. Moody's also publishes five yearly manuals which contain detailed historical financial information.

REFERENCE BOOKS

The accountant's library should include the standard reference works—an unabridged dictionary, an encyclopedia, almanacs, and directories of various types. The *Accountants' Handbook,* the *Accountant's Cost Handbook,* and the *Financial Handbook* furnish the accountant with a wealth of authoritative information. His library also should include the federal and state tax services and any other services which can assist him and his clients in complying with government regulations. Every accountant's library should include *The Accountant's Index,* published by the library staff of the AICPA. This index provides a key to all works on accounting published in the English language. Material published up to the year 1920 was indexed in the original volume, and the accounting literature published since then has been indexed in supplements which now are issued biennially.

SETTING UP AND MAINTAINING A SYSTEMS AND SERVICES FILE

A complete office should have some place to go to find the latest ideas on equipment, forms, systems, services, and the like. Much of this information comes through the mail in advertisements and is worth saving. Sometimes it seems easier to throw it away than to work out a system for filing it.

The very nature of the material precludes filing it with regular library material, but here is a system that can be used whether a firm has an indexed reference library or not.

Equipment needed

1. One file drawer
2. Twelve vertical file pockets with 3½-inch capacity

How to set up file

1. Number the file pockets from one to twelve in bold black numbers on the upper left corner of the exposed edge.
2. On the right corner paste typed labels as follows:
    a. Accounting and bookkeeping machines
    b. Duplicating machines and methods
    c. Files and filing systems
    d. Voice reproduction and mailing machines and ideas
    e. Reviews of books and other references
    f. Services to clients

g. Services to accountants

h. Adding and calculating machines

i. Standard bookkeeping forms

j. Ideas for CPA practices

k. Accounting aids (i.e., key sort, etc.)

l. Samples of annual reports

3. Take present pile of unsorted material, mark each with number corresponding to above list, and file. The number insures that the item will be returned to the same place.

How to maintain file

1. Incoming literature is read by partners. Anything of interest is marked "save" and placed in file box.

2. Filer collects, eliminates duplicates, codes material with proper number in upper right corner, and files accordingly.

3. The file must be culled periodically to eliminate duplications and out-of-date material.

LIBRARY CONTROL FOR THE SMALL ACCOUNTING OFFICE

One of the housekeeping items consistently relegated to the "should" or postponable category in many small offices is the task of setting up rudimentary controls for the firm's books and pamphlets.

The following steps toward library control will prove themselves and two people can install them in one or two days' time:

1. Count books. Purchase about three times as many small cards as there are books (two-thirds for immediate use, one-third for future supply). Also purchase a box for the cards.

2. Make a two-way card index for each book: An A-Z one by *author* and a decimal one by *subject*. The framework of the subject index might be:

        100 Accounting

        200 Cost Accounting

        300 Auditing

        400 Economics

        500 Management

        600 Texts on Specific Businesses

        700 Manuals, References, Directories

        800 Open

        900 Open

3. Assign a filing number for each book. Thus a book on fisheries would be 600-37 if it was the 37th book purchased in the "600" or business series.

4. Write the filing number inside the front cover of each book, and type or write the same number on each of the two cards.

The operation of the controls is easy. When a book is taken from the library, the person's name and date are written in pencil on the back of the corresponding decimal card. When the book is returned to the library, the name and date are crossed off the card and the book put back in its regular place.

SUGGESTIONS FOR A LIBRARY

There are many excellent texts in accounting, auditing, and related subjects, but naturally each practicing accountant will not find it necessary or feasible to include all of them in his library. All members of the AICPA may borrow, either by mail or in person, from the AICPA's library of over 45,000 books, periodicals, and pamphlets. The books suggested as suitable for inclusion in an accountant's library include representative texts dealing with the major topics of general interest to the accounting profession. Of course, the following list is not intended to be either definitive or exhaustive. In some instances, the books listed for a particular subject are the most recent ones published in that field, and for this reason they have been given preference over earlier texts which, however, may also be very useful. In order to furnish a guide to accountants who, because of the nature of their practice, require books on specialized accounting, some books of this type have been included in this list. Most of the available information on specialized types of accounting is published in periodicals, such as *The Journal of Accountancy,* the *NAA Bulletin,* and the publications of the state societies. An extensive bibliography of specialized accounting literature is contained in J. K. Lasser's *Handbook of Accounting Methods* (1954) and in his *Handbook of Cost Accounting Methods* (1949). In addition, information which has been published on any phase of specialized accounting can be located through *The Accountants' Index* referred to above.

A selected list of books suggested for an accountant's library by the AICPA library will be found in the Appendix, pages 908-913.

Insurance for Accountants

■ A WELL-PLANNED insurance program can be of critical importance to an accountant. It can mean the difference between the successful continuation of a practice, or its demise; it can mean the difference between financial protection and financial hardship for the dependents of a practitioner or his staff.

CPAs are closely concerned with their clients' insurance needs, yet frequently neglect their own programs. Nor is it enough to establish a program—and then ignore it. The decreasing value of the dollar, as well as the trend toward large awards for damages, may have destroyed much of its effectiveness.

In the vast majority of cases, insurance policies are drawn up in the firm name, although a few accounting firms follow the practice of naming the individual partners as the insured.

LIABILITY INSURANCE

Accountants' professional liability. Everyone in the profession has heard of suits against practitioners for negligence, fraud, or breach of contract. Court decisions against accountants have, in some cases, resulted in high judgments. Other suits, though not culminating in a verdict against the accountant, have been costly from the standpoint of defense alone. Some cases do not reach the litigation stage but are settled out of court without publicity.

CPAs have become increasingly aware of the need for professional liability insurance. Most practitioners carry such coverage, incidence, in general, increasing with the size of the staff. Loss limits in effect range from $25,000 for offices with less than six staff members to $1 million for firms with fifty or more staff members. Coverage of the national firms runs between $5 and $10 million.

Despite constant care in the application of the highest standards of professional skill, every accountant should minimize his exposure to financial loss in the practice of his profession by carrying adequate professional liability insurance. A valuable feature of this insurance is that it affords protection for claims made during the policy term, even though the work was performed prior to its acquisition. Also, for a moderate charge, the policy can be extended up to six years beyond its termination date, to cover work performed while the policy was in effect.

Limits of coverage. The possibility of suits and the amounts which may be claimed increase in direct proportion to the scope of the accounting firm's activities. Since it is impossible to estimate how large a verdict may be awarded in an accountant's liability suit, it is advisable to insure for the highest limit of coverage that can be afforded.

A suit may not only imperil the accounting firm's capital; it may also place each member's personal assets in jeopardy. This means that some or all of the partners in a firm could be forced into bankruptcy by a large adverse judgment if the firm had no insurance, or an inadequate amount of it.

Today most professional liability insurance covers liability under the Securities Act of 1933 and work performed under the Securities Exchange Act of 1934. Several companies charge extra for this coverage. (See description of the New York State Society plan in the Appendix, page 914.)

As with most other forms of liability insurance, the unit cost of limits in excess of the basic policy decreases as the limit increases. For example:

Table 4

Limits of coverage		Rate per thousand*		
Per claim	Aggregate	5 staff	10 staff	Increase over basic policy
$ 20,000	$ 40,000	$3.15	$4.20	—
30,000	60,000	2.72	3.63	30%
50,000	100,000	2.26	3.02	80%
100,000	200,000	1.58	2.10	150%
250,000	500,000	.82	1.09	225%

*Based on New York Society rates for a one-year policy. A three-year policy reduces premiums by 17%.

State society plans. During the last few years an increasing number of state societies have made professional liability insurance available to members at better than the standard rates charged by the American insurance companies. The recently revised plan of the New York State Society carries rates and features generally as favorable as those available from the underwriters at Lloyd's of London.

Thirty-three state societies[5] have now approved or sponsored plans and a number of others are giving this important subject active consideration.

It seems likely that the time will come when most of this insurance will be placed with state society plans. In addition to the lower initial cost (and the lower net cost if the plan allows a bonus for no claims), the advantages of a state society plan include: broad policy contracts,[6] careful selection of risks

[5]These states are: Alabama, Arizona, Arkansas, California, Colorado, Connecticut, Florida, Georgia, Illinois, Kansas, Kentucky, Louisiana, Maryland, Massachusetts, Michigan, Minnesota, Mississippi, Montana, New Jersey, New Mexico, New York, North Carolina, Ohio, Pennsylvania, Rhode Island, South Carolina, Tennessee, Texas, Utah, Virginia, Washington, Washington, D.C., West Virginia.

[6]Special policy contracts were drawn up by underwriters in collaboration with committees of the New York State Society of CPAs and the Pennsylvania Institute of CPAs. The New York Society's policy form has also been adapted by twenty-five of the states listed in footnote 5.

through collaboration with state society committees makes possible lower costs, and better claim service because of the greater value to the underwriting company of a large group of policies versus individual policies. The insurance company is also less inclined to challenge certain borderline situations because of the risk of alienating an influential group. However, it may be more advantageous for certain firms to carry individual policies in which their special problems can be covered.

General public liability. In these days when virtually every injury case involves second- or third-party liability, proper insurance to cover claims for bodily injuries or property damage due to the negligence of partners or employees inside or outside of the office is a basic necessity to an accounting firm.

Bodily injury limits of $50/100,000 and a property damage limit of $5,000 is minimal. It costs only about six per cent more to double these limits. The time saved by principals through reliance upon trained insurance company experts to handle negligence claims may alone be worth the entire premium cost. The policy provides full investigating and legal expense coverage in addition to the judgment or settlement limits per claim.

A New York firm had an experience recently which underscores the need for adequate liability insurance. It was faced with a suit for $100,000 by someone who had been seriously injured by tripping over the briefcase of one of its staff members in a public restaurant. Because it carried no insurance, the firm itself had all of the bother and expense of investigating and handling the claim. The partners considered themselves fortunate in being able to settle before suit for $4,000. A $100/250,000 general public liability insurance policy would have cost them about $42 a year.

Probably only about half of the firms carry insurance against claims alleging bodily injury or property damage due to negligent acts of the accounting firm's principals or its employees.

While such claims are infrequent, this coverage is comparable in some ways to the property damage feature of the standard automobile liability policy. Many of the firms carrying this feature are insured for the old basic limit of $5,000—an inadequate amount in these days of inflated values. The minimum should be $10,000 and it would be safer to carry $25,000. The five times greater protection costs only 16 per cent more than the $5,000 limit.

The policy should be written on the comprehensive form which covers all activities and hazards not specifically excluded by the policy. It includes new exposures and changes during the policy term without the necessity of notifying the insurance company. It prevents gaps in coverage by combining under one contract what used to require several to achieve proper protection. Any nonownership automobile liability insurance or coverage on firm-owned cars which is needed may be included in this policy. To cover certain borderline claims, the words "caused by accident" in the insuring clause should be revised to an "occurrence" basis.

It is also advisable to carry general liability insurance with the same company which insures workmen's compensation. This eliminates the chance of any controversy on whether an employee was injured in the course of his employment or was a member of the public at the time of accident.

Automobile liability. If a partner's or employee's automobile is likely to be used for business purposes, the firm may be named as a defendant in a suit for bodily injuries or property damage arising from an accident. All standard policies automatically include the interest of the firm if the firm has any legal responsibility for the use of the automobile, but it is important that bodily injury and property damage liability limits be adequate on all employee-owned cars used on firm business.

It is permissible to include the firm's name as an additional insured on the policies covering employee-owned automobiles. This, however, is not recommended. The firm may then become equally responsible as party to the contract for payment of premium, filing notice of loss, and so forth. The automatic protection furnished by the standard policy gives the firm all the necessary coverage without the additional responsibilities.

If no firm-owned cars are used in the practice, it is advisable to obtain, in the firm's name, a blanket nonownership automobile liability policy at nominal cost (less than $25 a year for $100/300,000 in many areas) to cover the firm's liability for all claims. This insurance covers such hidden risks as lapse of an employee's policy and inadequate coverage. It also provides excess protection over the employees' policy limits.

Automobile liability insurance is generally carried by accounting firms. The bodily injury limits range from $25/50,000 for the smaller offices up to $250/500,000 for the larger ones. Minimums of $100/200,000 are recommended for the smaller firms and practitioners, $250/500,000 for all others except the national firms. The latter should carry no less than $500/1,000,000. The extra costs are:

For	$100/300,000	vs.	$ 25/ 50,000—13%
For	250/500,000	vs.	100/300,000— 6%
For	500/1,000,000	vs.	250/500,000— 6%

The old $5,000 or even $10,000 property damage liability limits are too often carried. Such limits are not sufficient in view of rising repair costs and higher valued cars and trucks (many with costly cargoes) on the highways. Sometimes the owner of a car or truck damaged by the insured claims more for loss of its use during a prolonged repair period than for the direct repair cost. A $25,000 property damage limit should be the minimum. It costs only 20% more than $5,000 and 10% more than $10,000.

The insurance should be written on a comprehensive policy form in order to cover all cars owned, rented, or used on behalf of the firm even in the absence of any specific notification of changes to the insurance company during the policy year. It should, of course, provide protection on rented vehicles.

Workmen's compensation. If an accounting office has one or more employees in addition to the principal or partners, it is necessary (in New York State at least) to carry workmen's compensation insurance. The law in other states may not require public accounting firms to carry such insurance. Nonetheless, the protection is still advisable. The premium rates for traveling accountants and clerical staff are quite reasonable.

Under this insurance all employees (owner or partners are excluded) are paid weekly benefits, medical reimbursement, and other statutory coverage required under the state's workmen's compensation law if they become involved in accidents arising out of their occupation. The accidents may occur in or out of the employer's office and, if the policy has been properly endorsed, employees at branch offices will be covered for the benefits provided by the laws of states where the branch offices are located should those laws be broader than the laws of the headquarters state.

In addition to providing statutory medical and indemnity to injured employees, a separate section of the policy will pay any damages for which the firm may be legally obligated because of work-connected injuries which are not necessarily subject to the statutory benefits—for example, a permanent injury which does not prevent the employee from pursuing his normal work. Also, third parties who may have been held responsible for injuries to an employee can directly sue the employer by contending that he was negligent.

New York and some other states do not permit the insurance companies to limit this additional coverage to a fixed amount, although claims for certain occupational diseases are limited in New York to $50,000. There are many states, however, where the standard policy limit is $25,000 unless otherwise endorsed. A limit of $100,000 is recommended whenever the basic policy limit is less. The extra premium cost is small.

However, seven states (Arizona, Nevada, North Dakota, Ohio, Oregon, Washington, and Wyoming) have compulsory "monopolistic" state funds and supplementary private compensation plans are restricted. Practitioners located in these states should familiarize themselves with these restrictions or prohibitions.

Statutory disability benefits. The laws of New York, New Jersey, California, and Rhode Island require that nonoccupational accident and sickness insurance be provided for all employees. The New York law specifically states that the insurance must be provided if there are one or more employees besides the owner or partners.

Both the New York and California CPA societies sponsor group plans which enable firms, with at least one partner who is a member of the society, to obtain this insurance on a highly favorable cost basis. The starting rate in New York, for example, is $1.50 per employee per month, and the New York law permits deducting from the employee's salary up to $1.30 per month. Year-end refunds are paid when loss experience is favorable. This will be a growing opportunity for the state societies to serve their members as more states enact disability benefits laws.

PROPERTY INSURANCE

Fire, extended coverages, sprinkler leakage, burglary and theft. One of the first things an accountant checks in a client's insurance program is the fire and extended coverages on plant, machinery, and inventory to be sure that the amount is sufficient to cover a serious loss and equals or exceeds the percentage of any coinsurance clause in the policies. Yet many accountants do not insure their own office furniture, equipment, and supplies against fire loss. However, in cases where the value of these assets is relatively small, a number of firms prefer to self-insure; they feel that a maximum loss would not create a financial hardship. One national firm carries this insurance only on its home office.

Of those firms which have fire protection, some do not have the extended coverages available at small extra cost under the fire policy. Some of the national firms do not carry fire, extended coverages, or the special office contents policy described below. Offices in buildings equipped with automatic sprinklers should also carry low-cost sprinkler leakage insurance to cover water damage from an accidental leak. Sprinkler leakage insurance of 25 per cent of value should be sufficient since it is unlikely that a sprinkler system leak will damage any greater proportion of the office contents. However, a higher proportion of the furnishings in smaller offices is apt to be damaged by a single leak, so consideration might be given to higher coverage in these cases.

A coinsurance clause, which imposes a loss penalty when insurance does not equal or exceed the agreed-upon percentage (80 to 90 per cent or 100 per cent), is required in fire insurance policies covering most major cities throughout the country. In establishing the amount of insurance which should be carried on office contents, the present "insurable" value should be first determined. This is the present replacement cost less a reasonable allowance for physical depreciation. To this amount should be added the value of office supplies. Improvements to the building made by the tenant—such as painting, built-in paneling, shelves, and the like, which cannot be removed without defacing the premises (check terms of lease covering alterations or attachments made by tenant)—should be valued on an amortized basis and included in the insurance amount so that the tenant can collect under his policy in case of fire or other insured damage. In this connection it is important that the insuring clause of the policy include the words "improvements and betterments." In some cases it may be possible to insure major improvements jointly with the landlord, with the method of distributing the loss proceeds specified in the lease.

If the policy contains a coinsurance (or average) clause, it is advisable to carry insurance for the total amount as explained above, even if the 80 per cent or 90 per cent clause is used in the policy. This assures full coverage in case of a total loss and provides a 10 per cent leeway under the 90 per cent clause (or a 20 per cent leeway with 80 per cent clause) if a partial loss occurs toward the end of a three- or five-year policy during which additions may have been made (such as air conditioning) without a corresponding increase in the policy amount.

Office contents special form. The newest development in office contents insurance, particularly suitable for accounting firms, is the office contents special form policy. For a small rate loading (usually 15¢ per $100 on the first

$5,000 of coverage per location, with lower rates as limit is increased), the standard fire policy may be broadened to cover practically *all risks* of physical losses or damage except earthquake, flood, mysterious disappearance, and fraud. One of the important improvements over the usual office contents policy is that theft of office equipment is covered. The policy also covers office equipment off the premises up to 10 per cent of the policy limit. A valuable feature of this special policy is burglary and robbery coverage up to $250 on currency, money, and stamps. A $50 deductible applies to theft losses and water damage other than flood which is not covered. All fire, extended coverages, sprinkler leakage, burglary, and vandalism losses are paid in full.

The great majority of firms carry the old style specific perils insurance. Only a minority of both practitioners and partnerships carry this newer form. Every public accounting firm should carry the broader office contents special form of policy on its main office and branch offices, if any. If separate sprinkler leakage and burglary and theft insurance is being carried, it may be found that this better policy costs no more and often costs less than the specific perils type.

Valuable papers and records. This policy covers the cost of reproducing work sheets, clients' bookkeeping records, and other valuable data which are lost, destroyed, or damaged by any cause—subject to the usual exclusions of war, wear and tear, and any dishonest or criminal act by the insured. It not only covers such data in the accountant's office; it covers up to 10 per cent (maximum $5,000) of the policy limit while the documents are being used at or carried to and from a client's office or the locations of a photostater, printer, etc., excluding outside storage locations.

The moderate premium cost, slightly over $1 per $1,000 a year in a well-rated building, is based on the accountant's office fire insurance rate. There is no coinsurance feature to consider; but the policy amount should be sufficient to cover the maximum loss exposure.

Although this policy is advisable for all accounting firms, only a minority of firms appear to carry it. However, in insured offices with staffs of six or more, the limits range from $4,000 to $200,000.

Most firms carrying valuable-paper coverage insure their working papers, and many include reports. The problem of determining the value of papers is a difficult one, and many firms merely use an arbitrary lump sum. Others attempt to compute the approximate cost of reproducing the lost papers, for example, replacement time at regular billing rates.

Business interruption or extra expense. This form of insurance is seldom, if ever, needed by an accounting firm. If a fire, explosion, or windstorm rendered the office untenantable, other facilities could usually be acquired without much difficulty. The principal loss would be the extra cost of restoring files, records, and the like, which can be largely recovered through the valuable-records insurance previously described. Very few practitioners and firms carry this insurance.

DISHONESTY INSURANCE

Very few of those in the two- to fifty-employee group carry fidelity insurance. By contrast, most firms (other than national) with over fifty employees do carry it. As would be expected, practically all of the national firms carry fidelity coverage. However, a minority of these insured firms have the comprehensive policy described below.

Fidelity, burglary, robbery, forgery, and money or securities damage or destruction losses may be insured as needed under separate bonds or policies. However, the coverage is broader under a comprehensive dishonesty, destruction, and disappearance (or 3-D) policy, and sometimes is less expensive.

Fidelity. Dishonesty of employees is the feature of the comprehensive policy usually responsible for the greatest proportion of the premium cost. The insurance adviser should be furnished with a schedule of employees and an analysis of their duties so that he can advise whether the fidelity coverage should be on the blanket position or commercial form of policy. Full information will also aid him in negotiating the most favorable premium with the insurance company. To ascertain what loss limit should be carried, the formula developed jointly by the Surety Association of America and the AICPA should be used.[7] An adequate over-all loss limit and the commercial form will usually be cheaper and at the same time provide proper insurance.

Burglary, robbery, theft, damage and destruction. Burglary of safes, theft of money, securities, stamps, office machines, and the like, from the office premises, and damage to the premises and equipment are other features of the comprehensive policy. The premium is, of course, based on the loss limit needed to cover such possible losses. This part of the policy also provides *all risks*, coverage on money and securities. Money and securities destroyed or damaged in a fire are not covered under standard fire policies. Property belonging to others in the accountant's custody for which he is liable, may be included under this policy if it is properly endorsed.

Forgery. Losses sustained through the criminal alteration or forgery of the firm's checks may also be covered. This part of the premium may be cut in half if forgeries by employees are excluded. This saving can be justified if there is a sufficiently high fidelity limit because these losses caused by employees would be treated as infidelities. This insurance is relatively inexpensive and should be carried to protect all of the business and personal checking accounts. All checks are covered, including those not written on check-protector machines.

Safe-deposit boxes. The CPA's or client's property in safe-deposit boxes may be included under the comprehensive policy if desired. Rates are subject to value and types of property insured, banks' vault construction, and so forth.

[7]*How Much Dishonesty Insurance,* Surety Association of America, 60 John Street, New York 38, July 1956.

PRACTITIONER AND EMPLOYEE BENEFITS

Because so-called "fringe benefits" have become increasingly important in attracting and holding employees of high quality, the CPA should consider providing, or making available at low cost, various forms of employee insurance benefits.

Business and industry, with their liberal and varied insurance plans, have a considerable advantage over accounting firms in attracting new recruits. Fortunately, even the practitioner with only a few employees can provide life and the various medical expense insurance coverages explained below.

Group life. Group life insurance is basically annual renewable term insurance at wholesale rates. For groups of ten or more, there are usually no medical qualifications or restrictions because of age or sex. The rates are substantially lower than under individual policies largely because of savings in acquisition and administrative costs. Each group premium is based upon the amounts and ages at inception date and is recalculated each year. On groups over ten there may be year-end dividends for good loss experience.

Most recent policies provide, in case an employee becomes permanently and totally disabled before age sixty, for the continuance of the insurance without a premium charge as long as the employee remains totally disabled.

A valuable group life policy provision is the conversion feature under which an employee may convert all or part of his group life insurance to an individual policy within thirty-one days of termination of employment for any reason and without any medical qualification.

Accidental death and dismemberment insurance is usually written as a companion coverage to the group life insurance and provides specified lump-sum benefits for loss of life, limbs, or sight, arising out of an accident, either occupational or nonoccupational, anywhere in the world.

Most firms with two or more employees provide life insurance for their staffs. Many of these firms are under the AICPA group life plan. Usually the covered firm pays the full cost. Every practitioner desiring group life benefits for himself and his staff should investigate this plan.

The size and expanding scope of the AICPA plan means that the practitioner and small and medium-sized firms can obtain coverage at a remarkably low net cost. The rate is $1.17 per $1,000 per month for life insurance and an equal amount of accidental death and dismemberment insurance. However, the net rate for the year ended March 31, 1961 was only $.60 after a refund of 49.1 per cent.

Accident and sickness—Nonstatutory. A small, but increasing number of firms and practitioners located in states where there is no statutory nonoccupational accident and sickness insurance law now carry group accident and sickness insurance. In most cases the firm pays the entire cost. This coverage is not usually available on a group basis unless there are five or more lives insured.

If hospital, surgical, or other medical benefits coverage is provided or made available, the employer is justified in using the weekly benefits paid under the group policy to offset, in so far as possible, the salary which is continued during an employee's disability.

Some firms just insure the cost of prolonged illnesses, which can be substantial in the case of higher salaried staff members, on a one-, two-, or three-month deductible basis. This is relatively inexpensive insurance because of the large rate discounts for the waiting period prior to the payment of benefits. Such a policy could also pick up after the statutory disability benefits cease in such states as New York, New Jersey, and California.

Hospital, surgical, and major medical. *Hospitalization* insurance is made available by the majority of firms and practitioners with staff. All of the national firms and most firms with over six employees are insured. In some firms, the employees pay all of the hospitalization premium, while other firms pay the entire cost. A number of firms pay from 25 per cent to 50 per cent of the premium. The most prevalent coverage is through local Blue Cross Hospital Service Associations.

Surgical benefits are available in many firms. Most of the insurance is placed with local Blue Shield organizations and the balance with private insurance companies. Practices vary as to whether employer or employee bears the cost. As with the hospitalization premium, the sole practitioners generally assume the full cost of surgical coverage for their staffs.

The usual surgical plan, whether Blue Shield or insured, has a schedule of maximum benefits payable for each type of surgical procedure. The usual schedule has a maximum of $200—$250 for the most severe operations, with comparatively smaller allowances for less complicated surgery. However, in most areas, schedules with higher benefits are available at increased cost.

Most of the Blue Shield and insured plans also have an optional provision for reimbursement for medical services. A typical plan might allow $5 per day for doctors' visits in the hospital or home and $4 per day for visits in the doctor's office, limited to a specified number of visits for each period of disability or per year.

In some areas of the country there are nonprofit surgical-medical plans other than the Blue Shield. For example, in the metropolitan New York area there is the Health Insurance Plan of Greater New York (HIP) which provides comprehensive medical care including preventive care, regular health checkups, child care, eye tests, diagnostic checkups, as well as the usual surgical-medical services. Another nonprofit doctors' organization operating in the New York area is Group Health Insurance, Inc. (GHI) which features surgical, medical, diagnostic, and visiting nurse services.

As with Blue Shield, these are prepaid medical plans, designed particularly for the lower-paid employees, in which the participating doctors agree to accept the fee specified in the plan as full compensation for their services. Normally, the cost of such comprehensive plans is greater than the usual Blue Shield or insurance company surgical plans.

Major medical insurance, the newest and one of the most important employee benefits, is carried by comparatively few firms. However, most of the national firms and firms with over twenty-five in staff provide this important coverage. Many of these firms pay its entire cost. Major medical is also called catastrophe insurance because it pays 75 per cent to 85 per cent of all medical costs above a moderate deductible. It steps in after Blue Cross, Blue Shield, and other basic medical insurance benefits cease. It is not limited to hospital confinements and covers many of the special and usually costly expenses not taken care of by other policies.

Two basic forms of major medical policy are available. The usual one carries a calendar year deductible and the maximum loss limit ($5,000, $7,500, or $10,000) is on a lifetime basis. However, the full coverage may be reinstated, after benefits are received by filing evidence of full recovery and good heath. Total disability is not required under this type of policy. The other form, however, requires total disability before benefits are payable and the deductible must be exceeded for the particular disability. Under this form, the maximum limit only applies to each period of disability and there is no lifetime maximum.

New comprehensive medical. As the rates charged by Blue Cross continue to rise, the employer who pays all or a large part of the premium may find it necessary or desirable to look into the cost of plans provided by private insurance companies. If their employees are in better physical condition than the average of their community, the larger firms may lower their cost by earning the dividends or experience refunds allowed by insurance companies for better-than-average loss experience.

Firms considering medical benefits for their staffs should investigate the advantages of the new comprehensive medical benefits insurance policy before committing themselves to a local hospitalization and surgical plan and to an insurance company for major medical coverage. The new comprehensive policy combines under one contract, with one insurer, the coverage usually offered by Blue Cross and Blue Shield supplemented by excess major medical. With increasing Blue Cross rates, the cost for equal or better comprehensive coverage may be the same or less.

Disability of principals and partners. A CPA's most valuable asset is his time. Individual practitioners particularly need weekly indemnity to replace income lost or reduced during an illness.

Because partners and principals are excluded under workmen's compensation and disability laws, consideration should be given to individual disability policies covering loss of partners' time due to any accident or sickness. Such coverage is available up to $1,000 a month at reduced rates where there is a one-, three-, or six-month waiting period.

Most firms in such states as New York, New Jersey, Massachusetts, California, and Illinois where the state societies have sponsored accident and sickness insurance plans, subscribe for these insurance benefits on partners and principals. The firm often assumes all or part of the cost, sometimes with the understanding that the weekly disability benefits will be used to offset salary or regular drawings.

These state society plans provide broad coverage at lower than the cost of comparable individual policies. In addition to an accidental death and dismemberment benefit (usually $5,000), weekly indemnities from $25 to $150 are included. In case of a serious accident, these plans could pay up to $39,000 (260 weeks at $150) and in case of a prolonged sickness up to $15,600 (104 weeks at $150). With supplementary coverage, the 104-week limit on sickness benefits may be extended at additional cost.

Several state society plans now provide *high limit accidental death and dismemberment* protection either as a rider to the basic weekly indemnity and medical policies or through separate policies.

Benefits in amounts of $10,000 to $500,000 are available at rates of 90¢ to $1 per $1,000. Although the policies are principally to cover the CPA himself, some society plans will also insure the spouse and/or employees of the CPA.

Coverage is usually on the broad form, twenty-four-hour basis, but one state society plan offers the option of the more limited public conveyance protection at a rate of only 50¢ per $1,000. In addition to the basic principal sum, several plans include such features as medical reimbursement, disability income, and indemnity for permanent, total disability.

In addition to weekly indemnity and reimbursement of medical expenses, the individual practitioner should consider *business expense disability insurance*. This type of insurance reimburses the insured for such expenses as rent, employees' salaries, utilities, depreciation, contributions, dues, etc., incurred during a period of continuous total disability. Coverage is available in amounts from $100 to $1,000 a month for periods of one year. Although this insurance is of primary concern to practitioners with little or no income-producing staff, full benefits are paid regardless of the income generated by the office during the period of disability. Applicants must be between eighteen and sixty-four years of age; but the insurance can be renewed until age seventy with the insurance company's consent.

The rates approximate $25 a year per $100 of monthly indemnity for those between eighteen and fifty-four (the cost is lower under state society sponsored plans). This means that a practitioner could have $6,000 ($1,000 a month for six months) of his business expense reimbursed during a year in which he is disabled for six months at a cost of $250 a year. The cost of this insurance is a deductible expense according to sec. 162 of the Internal Revenue Code.

Payments are made from the first day of accident disability. Sickness disabilities under thirty days are excluded; but the benefits are paid in full retroactively if the sickness extends beyond thirty days. One of the companies offering this insurance requires a fourteen-day waiting period but pays for fifteen months.

State society plans. The basic coverage under most of the state society accident and sickness insurance plans provides or makes optionally available hospital, surgical, and major medical benefits. Several of them permit the inclusion of dependents. If a firm needs extra medical expense insurance for partners and other higher-salaried employees, it should consider this coverage for all who qualify by being state society members. With most of these plans new society members are accepted regardless of their medical history if application is made within forty-five days after joining the society.

Travel accident. Many accounting firms are saving the time of partners and seniors by encouraging air travel. The over-all record on air travel accidents is remarkably favorable, but when accidents do happen they are usually serious. For this reason it is advisable to take out accident insurance available at all airports, or to carry a blanket policy which automatically covers the insured for substantial amounts on all air trips taken during the year. This latter arrangement eliminates the chance of forgetting to take out the trip insurance. The cost of the blanket policy is somewhat higher; but there are other advantages over the trip-ticket airsurance. For about 10 per cent more than the 40 to 45¢ per $1,000 a year cost of blanket air travel coverage, it is possible to obtain accident coverage by all modes of public transportation (airlines, railroads, buses, taxis, and steamships). While only a minority of firms with a staff of twenty-six and over (including national firms) provide travel accident insurance, most of those which do carry such insurance have purchased the broad public conveyance form of policy.

Among smaller firms (those with staffs under twenty-five), this seems to be a neglected area of insurance. This is probably due to the fact that these firms undertake only limited travel. It can, however, be important to the practitioner and partners of firms whose family or professional associates should have the benefit of $25,000 to $100,000 in case of accidental death while traveling.

BUSINESS LIFE INSURANCE

Business life insurance should be considered if the untimely death of a partner would represent a serious financial loss to the firm. The insurance would not only cover the loss to the practice; it could be used to liquidate his interest in capital and goodwill. If such a provision is included in the partnership agreement, it can be used to cover salary continuation or other payments to the widow of the deceased or to his estate.

Even though annual or convertible term life insurance may require less premium outlay in the early years, ordinary whole life policies usually are better in the long run because cash value is built up.

Some firms, however, prefer the "protection only" feature of term insurance in combination with other provisions for liquidating a deceased partner's interest. Unless the cash is available this method usually involves a greater risk than insurance. Here is how one such firm describes its approach:

> About seven years ago we took out term insurance on the partners' lives, some for five years and some for ten years. Meanwhile, we have been investing a small percentage of the firm's gross receipts in listed securities. The amount so invested is greater than the difference between term insurance and ordinary life insurance premiums, but not a prohibitive amount. By the time the first five-year terms expired, the investment account was in a position to take care of the capital account of any partner who would have

died at that time, and by the end of ten years we hope that it will be sufficient to take care of the capital accounts of two partners, although we are uncertain that this will be the case. In any event, we have been able to build up sufficient investments so that insurance is no longer our sole line of defense.

One of the attractive things about a partnership building up an investment portfolio to take care of the possible death of a partner is that the fund is there for paying off the capital account of whichever partner dies first; unlike a life insurance policy which covers only specific partners. Naturally, we expect that if one partner dies before the investment account has built up sufficiently to take care of the death of two partners, we will re-examine the insurance picture with the view of taking out additional term insurance until the investment account has again been built back up.

Of course, we have also taken accidental death insurance on all partners, so that in the event of the death of more than one partner as the result of an accident, we will be protected.

If several partners are insured under business life policies, it is, of course, important that an agreement be drawn spelling out the ownership and beneficiary arrangements under each policy and that a provision be made for a partner leaving or retiring to take over all or part of the insurance on his own life.

Accounting firms arrange in numerous ways for the payments of premiums on the lives of partners. Premiums may be paid by partners on all of their lives according to their respective shares in the profits; they may be paid from a pool to which partners contribute on some other stipulated basis; or they may be paid by each partner on each of his partners' lives or his appropriate share of the total premiums on the insurance covering his partners. Some firms provide that each partner pay in the amount of the premium on his own policy.

DETERMINING THE PROPER INSURANCE

This discussion of various forms of insurance has emphasized the broad comprehensive policies as suitable for the typical needs of accounting firms. However, many firms and practitioners have special problems and varying abilities to withstand possible losses. Insurance, like any other personal service, should be tailored to fit the particular needs of the individual practitioner or firm. Unneeded features merely add to costs, without extending the desired protection. On the other hand, special conditions can dictate special coverage. For example, firms which arrange annual outings and similar events for their employees frequently find it desirable to secure special accident insurance coverage for the specific occasion. The cost is usually small and the policy protects against unusual accidents in athletic events and similar activities.

An adequate insurance program considers the possible severity of loss in relation to the cost for protection against it. Both the degree of exposure (the probability factor) and the financial condition of the firm play a part in this relationship, with the probability or experience being closely correlated with the cost. In addition to appraising these elements, the opinion of an insurance adviser who is familiar with the individual needs and the options best suited to meet them, should be sought before major changes in coverage are made.

How much insurance can a practitioner or firm afford? Certain forms of insurance (especially professional liability, where the experience has been good and the rates relatively low), are of paramount importance to every firm. Most practitioners will *probably* never suffer a loss, but they cannot afford the *possibility* of having a claim seriously impair their financial position. Therefore, they should, at a minimum, protect themselves against catastrophic loss. In this connection, consideration can be given to deductible features as a means of minimizing costs while still providing protection against major losses.

The median expenditure for firm protection insurance in the smaller offices is about one-half of 1 per cent of gross annual fees, with the larger offices allotting a slightly smaller percentage. However, the figures for the 75th percentile points for most office groups were double the median. (These data issue from a survey, some of the results of which appear on pages 918, 919.) In view of the fact that there are a number of areas of apparent neglect by many firms, the amounts represented by these figures are probably insufficient, especially for the smaller firms. The suggested programs on Appendix page 916, together with estimated rate ranges, include not only the essential elements of firm insurance, but desirable protection for the practitioner/ partner, employees, and their dependents. No attempt has been made to show the costs of such programs because of the extremely wide range in rates (for example, fire insurance can vary between 10¢ and $1.50 per $100), but realistic consideration has been given to value and cost. Some practitioners may disagree with certain suggested coverages—and indeed these amounts cannot be considered universally applicable. But these suggestions and other material are offered as guides in appraising individual programs.

Branch Office Management

WITH THE VERY large firms which operate branches in many cities of the United States and in foreign countries, the procedures are so standardized that little diversification is to be found regardless of location of the offices. Generally, less standardization becomes apparent as firm sizes get smaller, although there are exceptions. Since major policies, objectives, and attitudes usually spring from the main office, having been tested there and found desirable, it is important that sufficient control by the home office be maintained over the branches to insure adherence to these desired practices. A large measure of uniformity should prevail, even in routine matters. For example, audit reports issued by all branches should be standardized.

While branch office operations vary widely, the majority of firms pursue these policies:

1. Branch office management is in charge of a resident partner, who may or may not delegate the function.

2. Procedures are designed to minimize variations from home office practices.

3. Branch managers are brought in to the home office for conferences frequently.

4. Reports are written in the branches. In branches having resident partners, reports are signed by them; when in charge of a non-partner manager, reports are usually signed at the home office.

5. Many firms have their branches process and type reports. Most keep the permanent files of reports and working papers for branch office clients at the branch. In most instances, copies of typed reports and tax returns go to the main office.

6. When under a resident partner, the branch does its own billing and collecting; the opposite prevails when the manager is not a partner.

7. In many cases, the resident branch partners are not general partners of the firm, but participate in the affairs of their particular branch only.

THE NEED FOR FREQUENT MEETINGS

Nothing can take the place of personal contact in keeping the operations of branches running smoothly. Through one means or another, meetings between main and branch office personnel should be held frequently. The partners should get together with each other and with assistants. Specialists at the home office should confer with their colleagues at branches, particularly the tax men. Many round-table discussions should be held. Junior staff members should not be ignored. On the contrary, their participation in the deliberations will give them a feeling of recognition and is bound to lift morale. Besides, it is not at all unusual to learn matters of consequence from the lower ranks. If there are many branches, at least one meeting each year should be held with all the partners present.

BRANCH OFFICE REPORTS

Reports issued by a branch office are seldom referred to the main office in advance of issuance when the branch office is equipped to complete the report. There are some who think this should be done but the impracticability of such procedure will prevent general compliance. Partners or branch managers should sign the reports, and rarely, if ever, should anyone of lesser authority be permitted to sign for them. Accounting firms maintaining liability insurance coverage are sometimes required to furnish their insurance carriers with a list containing the names of those of the firm who are properly authorized to sign the reports.

Some firms with a number of offices permit each office to complete and deliver its own reports and then send a copy of each to the firm's principal office for post-review. The results are valuable in insuring standardization of reporting methods, in maintaining high quality of report-writing (especially footnote-writing) and generally establishing adherence to the firm's reporting standards.

Some firms believe that a policy of permitting no reports to be released by a branch before home-office review is the only safe course. The majority, however, not only permit the branch office to prepare its own reports, but also allow the branch manager to sign them. This is sometimes true even in cases where the manager is not a partner.

One medium-sized firm permits its single branch office to process and type its interim reports on monthly and quarterly as well as run-of-the-mill small engagements, but no annual reports are released without home-office reviews of them and their supporting working papers. Sometimes the review takes place after the branch has already typed the report. No trouble of significance has ensued from this practice.

INTERCHANGE OF FIELD WORKERS

The advantage of interchange of field workers is enjoyed by firms with branches, but only to a limited degree if the branches are few. A small firm with a nearby branch using three staff assistants sends men from the home office when requisitioned by the branch manager. A more-or-less regular schedule is maintained, however, thus minimizing sudden calls.

BRANCH OFFICE RECORDS AND FILES

Records similar to those at the home office are necessary at the branches, except that usually cash disbursements other than revolving fund payments are made by the main office. Branch records should include, but are not always limited to, accounts receivable collection lists (not ledgers, which are almost always kept by the home office), a simple general ledger with home office controlling account, a cash receipts record supported by deposit slips bearing payors' names, time reports and records, expense reports and records, and accountants' service records. Financial statements should be prepared by the branches at frequent and regular intervals. Permanent files of reports and working papers should also be kept at the branch.

INQUIRY INTO LOCAL LAWS

It is important to obtain legal advice from an attorney of the state where a new branch office is planned. The period of residence prior to opening, the matter of certification of partners, and other elements of partnership requirements should be inquired into before definite arrangements are made.

Helpful Suggestions from Practitioners

SETTING UP REPORTS AND WORK PAPERS IN ADVANCE

■ QUITE A FEW accountants use preprinted report and work-paper schedules. These are available commercially. Others prepare them in advance of the audits either on the typewriter or by hand.

One accountant uses a gelatine duplicating machine to provide the client with a copy of adjusting journal entries without the necessity of typing. All working sheet trial balances and other work sheets to be used monthly are prepared on the typewriter, many copies at a time. An extra copy of the audit report of the current period is prepared, omitting figures and dates as an aid in preparing the next report. The time saved is substantial. This CPA prepares the audit program for the next period before leaving the scene of the engagement.

One time-saving device calls for typing in advance copies of the skeleton statements and exhibits and some of the work papers for all regular clients. The pencil figures and changes can be inserted easily, if the pre-typed sheets are prepared intelligently.

In an article in *The New York Certified Public Accountant*[8] Chan pointed out that during the slow seasons it is helpful to prepare pro-forma outlines of the lengthier reports and schedules, inserting prior year's comparative figures and putting these outlines in the work-paper folders so that at the time of the next audit valuable time is saved. He also stated that a little busy-season time can be saved on corporate tax returns by filling in during slack times the names, addresses, prior-year balance sheet figures and answers to questions.

MANAGING AND IDENTIFYING WORK PAPERS

Following are some helpful hints offered by a practicing CPA who has carefully thought out the problems of preparation and use of work papers.

> The practice of binding audit working papers and notes in slide-clasp covers makes it difficult for more than one person to refer to the file in following through on a succeeding engagement. To eliminate this bottleneck, we devised a procedure which has proved satisfactory in our practice, and

[8]Stephen Chan, "Internal Control of the Accountant's Practice," *The New York Certified Public Accountant,* July 1949, p. 441.

which we recommend to anyone who might be interested in giving it a trial.

Since we use sidebound working papers which are 8½ by 11 inches, or fold to those dimensions, the only tool necessary is a three-ring notebook cover equipped with four divider sheets. The dividers are tabbed: (1) minutes and records, (2) balance sheet, (3) operating statement and (4) prior year.

As a preliminary to each recurring engagement, the secretary heads up as many of the standard working papers as possible, following the prior year's forms and any notations requiring changes. These are placed in the notebook in front of the first divider, together with notes or correspondence developed or occurring since completion of the previous examination. The prior year's working papers are inserted in the notebook behind the fourth divider, and since they are not fastened together they may be removed individually for reference. If space permits, the sheets comprising the pencil copy of the prior year's report are stapled together in the upper left-hand corner and inserted following the working papers.

As current working papers are completed, they are filed in the appropriate section of the notebook, and if a single paper includes both balance sheet and operating statement information (for example, prepaid insurance and insurance expense) it is filed in the balance sheet section. A code mark on the principal work sheets indicates completion of the supporting working paper pending final sorting, numbering, and indexing.

Another time saver used in connection with this procedure is a rubber stamp, made up in advance by the secretary from fonts of movable type. This lists the name of the client, the period covered by the audit, and provides a space for the number finally assigned to the sheet. The stamp is applied to each sheet, in the upper right-hand corner, as it is taken from supply, and immediately identifies it as a part of our file for that particular engagement. Schedules or notes to be left with the client are not stamped, although they frequently are exact copies of working papers.

Our audit "tool kit" also includes a stamp pad of the color currently in use as a part of our red-purple-blue three-year cycle. Thus, the color with which corresponding working papers are stamped identifies them at a glance as belonging in the current or prior year's file.

STANDARD FORM FOR AUDIT INFORMATION FROM ATTORNEYS

In order to standardize its request for information from clients' attorneys, a CPA firm has developed a form letter that serves the function:

We have designed a standard form of request to attorneys covering the audit search or confirmation concerning contingent liabilities in audits. This letter is made in triplicate, the original being addressed to the attorney, the copy designed as a response by the attorney, and the third copy representing our audit work sheet file copy showing the request was forwarded and to whom. The following is a quotation from a letter received from a firm of attorneys whom we regard rather highly:

"At long last someone has done something about the request for a statement of legal counsel in connection with an audit by a CPA. Your form is wonderful and we hope that it will become standard practice."

We have also received favorable comments from other attorneys. Apparently the legal profession welcomed such a short cut in this chore.

To: ....

In connection with our audit of the accounts of ....
.... as of ....
will you please inform us on the attached form, if you have knowledge of
any deferred or contingent liabilities which the company may have as of this
date. The following indicates some of the things we have in mind.

	Yes	None
1. Unsettled or pending lawsuits, judgments, or claims	......	......
2. Pending or prospective claims, whether or not in litigation, such as claims for damages, defective goods, patent infringements, or the like	......	......
3. Claims for additional payments, refunds, or penalties arising from alleged violations of laws or regulations relating to wages, trade, etc.	......	......
4. Commitments of the company to purchase any of its stock, the stock or assets of another, or any other securities or business	......	......
5. Any other major purchase commitments, other than those in the ordinary course of the conduct of their business, such as the purchase or construction of properties, or the like, representing substantial amounts	......	......
6. Subordination of debt agreements by stockholders, officers, or other creditors	......	......
7. Guarantees of debt of above by stockholders, officers, or others	......	......
8. Accommodation notes or acceptances, or similar endorsements or guarantees of obligations of others	......	......
9. Leases—renewals or new leases in process or in prospect	......	......
10. Any other matter representing a contingent liability	......	......
11. Any unbilled charges for services of your office	......	......

Your prompt response, using the enclosed self-addressed envelope, would
be appreciated.

Approved: JONES and JONES, CPAs

....   By ....

USE OF PHOTOCOPIES IN ACCOUNT CONFIRMATIONS

In the July 1959 issue of *The Mortgage Banker,* Mr. Dan W. Middleton,
vice president of Kirbo, Mills & McAlpin, Inc., described how his mortgage
company provides borrowers with the tax information they need and obtains
confirmation of their balances for audit purposes by sending photocopies of
the borrowers' accounts to them.

Mr. Middleton's company sends photocopies to all borrowers who request
statements and to all accounts selected for confirmation by their CPAs. He
said that the number of requests for further explanation of account balances
has dropped very substantially since this procedure has been adopted. Instead of having to write a lengthy letter of explanation when a borrower

questions his balance, the mortgage company notes its explanation on a photo-copy of the account and sends it to the borrower.

Accountants who frequently send confirmation requests to banks and mortgage companies might find it very useful to call attention to this procedure.

METHOD OF CIRCULARIZING ACCOUNTS RECEIVABLE

This practitioner has a method of circularizing accounts receivable which he describes as follows:

After the accounts have been balanced and checked in the normal manner and are ready to be circularized, we pull the statements on the accounts which are selected. Then, rather than make a circularization schedule, we make a small concealed tick mark on the statement, which is necessary to control the accounts which we have selected, and give the statements to the typist to prepare the confirmations. When she types the confirmations, she also makes a carbon copy on blank paper. This can be on the back of old forms or scrap paper. The duplicate shows the information normally listed on the circularization schedule, i.e., name, address, confirmation number, amount, and date. When second requests are necessary, a rubber stamp is used on the duplicates which tells the typist which confirmations to type.

The summary of the circularization is prepared on a separate schedule and all necessary additional work on the accounts not replying is noted on the duplicates. This practice saves a great amount of time in circularizing accounts since all of the listing procedure is eliminated.

SUGGESTIONS FOR ACCOUNTS RECEIVABLE

For those who are looking for further suggestions concerning confirmation procedures for accounts receivable or payable, these methods are offered by a practicing accountant:

1. *Mailing envelope* is unstamped, permitting use of a client's postage meter and relieving us of having higher reimbursable expenses to charge the client.

2. *Reply envelope* has back flap dated to correspond with the date on which confirmation was mailed so that we can separate replies from more than one mailing during a period. With several clients, we have the envelopes printed in different colors where the quantity confirmed is large. (Client A—blue, client B—pink, client C—gray, etc.)

3. *Confirmation form* is printed in duplicate and, as in 2 above, where mailing is large the two lines at the top and the signature are printed. The form fits the envelopes, and the yellow copy is kept by us as the "detail list" of accounts confirmed and matched with the white when returned. This way we can tabulate the quantity and dollar amount confirmed (and percentage) and the quantity and dollar amount replies received.

4. *Billing memo* is prepared at confirmation time where we are going to charge the client specifically for that cash outlay, not including staff time, etc.

5. We have a charge account at the post office for our postage dues.

USE OF MICROFILM

While this accountant uses a microfilm technique on the audit of a rather specialized client, this idea may also be used in other audits where receivables and payables are large in number:

Occasionally one phase of an audit requires a great many staff hours in a short period of time. This sometimes means that although his staff is otherwise quite adequate, if the small practitioner is unable to "borrow" personnel from other CPAs or to obtain temporary help in some other manner, he might have to decline an engagement.

Audits of finance companies or other businesses having a large number of customers' accounts involve this problem. For example, a not untypical consumer finance company might have two thousand open accounts with balances representing 90 per cent of the company's total assets. The importance of the audit of the receivables in such a case obviously cannot be overemphasized. As it is often impractical for the consumer finance client to prepare a schedule of receivables, the auditor must do considerable work with the receivables ledger (invariably ledger cards) before relinquishing physical control of it. This work would include running a tape for comparison with the control account, aging the accounts, or checking the client's aging schedule, preparing confirmation forms or scheduling accounts for confirmation, and perhaps preparing schedules for further audit work (footing, examining documents, etc.).

The staff time necessary at one "sitting" can be reduced drastically by the use of microfilm. If all ledger cards are turned over to the auditor and a tape is run to insure their presence, the cards can be microfilmed very rapidly (about fifty per minute) with a portable camera. All additional work can be done later, much of it in the accountant's office, from the processed microfilm with the aid of a viewer. The necessary microfilm equipment can, of course, be rented.

The client should appreciate the additional fire protection the CPA has furnished, because the latter's microfilm working papers could be converted quickly into a duplicate set of ledger cards.

THE VERSATILE ADDING MACHINE

According to this accountant, the simple adding machine has been highly underrated:

Most accountants use an adding machine at least occasionally, but when utilized to maximum advantage, it can do the work of almost another man on the staff, especially for the practice that contains a quantity of small accounts. First of all, the machine must be of the ten-key variety in contrast to the full keyboard. The practitioner must learn the simple touch system so that he can add a long column of figures without taking his eyes off the paper. It is easy to learn because there are so few keys, and the resulting speed is astonishing. It is also important that the machine be electric and portable with a carrying case, as one of the major benefits is using it at clients' places of business where the client does not have a machine.

Increased speed with the machine will be a time saver of all phases of accounting dealing with computations, including footing and crossfooting, preparation and checking of reports and tax returns, and figuring discounts, commissions, and percentages.

A novel use of the machine is for bank reconciliations. Start with the opening balance per books, add the deposit total, subtract the total of checks and take a subtotal which gives the ending balance. Then subtract the deposits in transit, add the outstanding checks, and total the machine to give the balance per bank statement. Thus, you have the whole reconciliation on one concise tape which may be stapled or scotch-taped into the cash journal to act as a permanent record.

Another handy use is with trial balances. Combine debits and credits on one tape and take a subtotal just after the equity section of the general ledger. You know immediately if the ledger is in balance, without making a single pencil entry on a work sheet. Once a balance is reached, the subtotal is the profit (or loss) figure before adjustments. And income, direct cost, and other expense groupings will stand out for quick reference. Often sufficient information may be obtained and discussed with the client to obviate the necessity for interim statements entirely.

Let me say that I have found the adding machine to be as important a tool as my pencil or working paper. The increased cost to the office of rolls of tape and new ribbons which are consumed in great quantity is repaid in time saved many times during each day of the year.

Accounting Reports, Records, and Procedures

The Need for an Adequate Accounting System

■ MOST ACCOUNTING PRACTICES go through a metamorphosis. An individual starting a practice normally makes considerable progress in volume of work in his first few years of business. In the first year of practice, normal or average progress in many areas appears to be that the individual will double his gross income. This may not represent a large amount of money, but it is a large percentage increase. Usually, many small jobs are represented in this increase, and progress is judged by the balance in the cash account.

While a professional practice may grow naturally, it will not build itself efficiently without conscious direction. The practitioner who neglects the business aspects of his practice can hardly expect the best results. It seems logical then that a beginning practitioner should provide a good accounting system which will prove to be the basis for evaluating results.

The practitioner's record-keeping problems become more acute when he starts considering the need for assistance. As people are added to his staff, the need for adequate internal financial records soon becomes apparent, and the lack of adequate reports of what has gone before leaves a void in the information that the practitioner needs in order to determine fee scales, the number of staff people required, and the salaries he can afford to pay.

When first obtaining assistance or personnel, the practitioner usually finds that he needs half a person. Sometimes by improvisation he gets suitable part-time help, but eventually a full-time person is hired. As more people are added, more records become necessary and an evaluation of individual staff members' profitability as well as over-all profitability becomes an important factor that must be watched continuously.

Most practices develop to a point where it is poor business to continue certain classes of work which, although originally quite important, are now unprofitable. Many practitioners for some sentimental reason carry this work at a loss, but good internal reporting usually leads to a proper evaluation in determining whether most, if not all of these, like a tadpole's tail during meta-morphosis, should be dropped. Often proper evaluation and discussions re-sulting from them turn these clients into profitable accounts.

Another record-keeping problem is encountered when partners are added. The problem is especially acute upon a merger of two or more practices, where each of the principals uses a different method of accounting, or where the records fail to disclose enough information to properly evaluate the new partnership interest.

Because of the many changes in the development of an individual practice into an established accounting firm, the use of a sound, even though elemen-tary, accounting and financial reporting system is fundamental. Only God and nature can make a frog out of a tadpole; accounting practices need the human hand for guidance.

Treatment in the Partnership Agreement

■ ACCOUNTANTS' PARTNERSHIP AGREEMENTS commonly make some refer-ence to the records to be kept, the accounting basis, and reports to be sub-mitted to partners. The records are not detailed but the basis, cash or accrual, is frequently stipulated.

A few agreement abstracts are submitted for illustrative purposes.

The fiscal year of the partnership shall be May 1 to April 30. Proper books of account shall be kept wherefrom the "realized gross income" and "net income" as herein defined, may be ascertained at any time. Such accounts when properly completed for any fiscal year, after giving effect to the provi-sions of this agreement (as evidenced by the filing of tax returns based there-on) shall be considered to be conclusive and binding upon the parties to this agreement.

A general account shall be taken of the affairs of the partnership at the close of business on the 30th day of June and the 31st day of December of each year. Such account shall be signed by all the partners, and after such signing, shall be binding on all and not reopened save for a manifest error discovered within ninety days thereafter.

Said books of account shall be maintained on the basis of a fiscal year ending . . . . and on the cash receipts and disbursements method of accounting. The books . . . shall at all times be kept . . . in the principal place of business of the partnership and each partner shall at all times have access to said records or any of them.

Accurate books of account of all the business transactions and affairs of said partnership shall be kept, and said books shall be audited by an independent auditor at least once a year. . .

Full and complete accounts shall be kept of the partnership business, and the profits or losses determined annually on the accrual basis. . .

The goodwill partners and the employees holding non-goodwill shares shall have the right at any reasonable time to examine the books of the partnership but such right shall be exercised by them personally and not by any agent or attorney. . .

One agreement provides in substance that so-called junior partners, as a practical fact, are not permitted to examine the firm's books except in the event of a disagreement requiring the application of the arbitration provision included in the agreement.

In some agreements there are special provisions for reports to retired partners and to the estates of deceased partners where they are receiving profit-share payments from the firm or where they are creditors.

What Does the Accounting System Comprise?

■ WHEN CONSIDERING an accounting system, one must envision an orderly plan wherein a multitude of forms, books, and procedures are integrated to produce the desired result. A list of clients' needs, a written instruction for the preparation of a bill, or a simple diary may be as vital as journals or ledgers.

For this reason the present section will include discussions of such areas as the tickler system, staff-location records, work forecasts, and certain statistics for managerial use. As contemplated here, the system of accounting embraces not only the recording of transactions, but also the control of work performed, the planning for staff requirements, the measurement of employee efficiency, and other areas.

Controlling the Work

PREPARING FOR A NEW CLIENT

■ THE MOMENT a new client is secured by an accounting firm, a responsibility is assumed. Tax returns must be filed on time and work scheduled to meet specific deadlines.

Many firms have a checklist called "New Client Data Sheet" which is filled in at the time of engagement by the client. This form serves many purposes. It details the various items that are vital to the proper scheduling of work. It also serves the purpose of setting up a routing slip for use within the accountant's office so that the proper internal records are prepared.

The person responsible for making the initial contact with the client usually prepares the form, which should be approved by a partner. On the form, indication is given as to the type of work to be done and whether it is to be monthly, quarterly, semiannual, or annual.

The form can then be utilized by the person in charge of scheduling, who makes up a regular schedule card for use in the preparation of engagement sheets, or in any other method used by an office for scheduling work.

A discussion of the specific applications of this "checklist" procedure appears under "Tickler Files and Follow-up Files" (page 669).

Where there was a previous accountant, it is always wise to have that accountant's name and the reasons for the change. This saves many embarrassing situations and gives the office a reference should work papers be necessary or should the previous accountant have to be consulted.

Some offices have an addressograph plate for each client so that news items and newsletters can be sent. The Christmas card list is an excellent idea so that the client is not forgotten at Christmas time, nor any of the persons in the organization who should receive Christmas cards. The tax file card is prepared and given to the person in charge of seeing that tax returns are properly scheduled and go out on time. The telephone index is given to the receptionist or to whoever is in charge of the master files for clients. The client's work schedule is prepared and if an engagement sheet is necessary for work to be done immediately, it is prepared then.

If there is more than one partner in the firm, it is always well to submit to those who are not familiar with the engagement the name of the client and any information that seems necessary. By this means all the partners are aware of new clients coming into the firm.

It has been the practice of one firm, whenever a client is secured, to try to determine who recommended them. They then take the time to send this person a note of thanks, and they feel that it is not only plain common courtesy, but good business. The person receiving it is quite appreciative of the note and is apt to refer other clients, if for no other reason than that the firm took time to say "thank you."

Most firms do not have signed contracts with clients. Many simply confirm understandings by letter. Some write the letters in duplicate summarizing the proposed scope and fee arrangement. In one case, the client is asked to sign the duplicate and return it to the accountant. Many firms of all sizes send out a letter giving a brief statement of the scope of the work to be done on all new assignments.

TICKLER FILES AND FOLLOW-UP FILES

It is found that tickler files and follow-up files generally are maintained under two main divisions: (1) those having to do with auditing and accounting engagements or special services to be performed by the accounting staff, and (2) those having to do with income-tax returns, advice, and tax controversies with revenue agents and conferees. In some instances, the same file records are used for engagements of the accounting staff and those of the tax staff. When separated, there is usually some cross-control. For a more complete description of the handling of tax returns see Section 6, page 566.

Generally, the routine follow-up is handled by the supervisor in charge of the staff. In the smaller firms this is usually one of the partners. In the larger firms it may be the office manager.

Most firms maintain some kind of tickler or follow-up files. Some use these files for correspondence, most use them for reports, but probably every firm having such a system uses it for tax return control. The following are typical of the data that might be included in a system of tickler or follow-up files:

1. Date for beginning a particular project (preparation of return, audit, etc.)
2. Names of staff members who are to do the work
3. Date when work must be turned over for typing (or other reproducing) and review
4. Date when work must be completed for delivery
5. Date when bills are to be sent out
6. Date when fees should be collected

Illustrative procedure. One large firm with no branch offices follows several steps as a matter of course when a new client is obtained. To assure the punctual application of these steps, a checklist printed in advance records the following:

1. New client's name, address, and phone number
2. Business organization (such as corporation or partnership)

3. Type of business, including products handled, wholesale or retail, price range
4. Date of end of fiscal year
5. Names of officers, bookkeepers, and other key persons
6. Affiliated companies
7. Frequency of audit (such as monthly and annual)
8. General remarks

Then follows a list of various federal, state, and city tax returns which the business must file, with space to check those returns that the accounting firm is to prepare. At the bottom of the sheet is a small tabulation headed "Date noted in office records." This is followed by spaces for entering the date on which the foregoing information was entered on the accounting firm's client phone list, staff assignment sheet, billing book, and other records. It also would seem to be desirable that each client's federal social security number and state unemployment insurance and sales tax registration numbers be entered on this form, so that these data are readily available if and when required.

One medium-sized firm enters its initial information on one of two printed forms, depending on whether or not the engagement is to be done monthly. (See Figures 35 and 36, pages 773 and 774.) In each case, the first page of the series (balance of series is a detailed program) is followed by internal control questionnaire sheet(s). The firm also fills in the notice of contract form which is filed in the office manager's office. No new form is made for succeeding work, as it is easy to record any minor changes on the original.

Everything pertaining to the client from that point on clears through the office personnel manager. He is the one who co-ordinates all office activities and is the central clearing point of office procedure on all matters relating to all clients. He is the first person through whom the notice of contract passes and as a final step, usually, all billings against clients pass through him.

The following examples are presented in order to demonstrate how work-control procedures can vary according to the firm's size and needs.

A large firm with many branch offices
1. Purpose of tickler or follow-up system:
To control the flow of audit, accounting, and tax engagements. To safeguard against errors of commission and omission in contacting proper persons, meeting deadlines, and keeping promises.
2. Party, or parties, having top responsibility:
Final responsibility rests with the staff manager. His background training on the firm's staff, his intimate knowledge of problems of the field and of report reviewing, and his thorough working knowledge of tax affairs, together with his long experience with the firm, fit him for the post. The partners have delegated to him full authority consonant with his responsibility. He shares responsibility for tax controls with the head of tax department. His many years of experience with the firm in the tax department has provided a deep-rooted recognition of the need for protection through an adequate follow-up system.
3. Initial step in opening of follow-up record:
New engagements are always closed by one of the partners who writes an

office memo and, as in the case of all outgoing correspondence, the pink copy goes to the personnel staff manager. The latter's secretary immediately prepares the following control cards:

    a. Client master card, in white, measuring 6 by 8 inches, reproduced on page 752 (Figure 16)

    b. Five operation cards of different colors, each measuring 4 by 6 inches

The card for controlling progress of auditing or other accounting engagements and one of the cards for controlling progress of tax returns are shown in Figures 17 and 18, page 753. The other three tax cards have the same wording as the one reproduced. On the tax control cards, returns due before the 15th of the month are flagged with red metal tabs in the upper right-hand corner.

    4. Follow-up procedure:

Tickler cards. The larger, *client master card* is immediately filed alphabetically in a cabinet in the private office of the staff manager. This arrangement provides an index of all clients, the type of work to be done, and the pertinent information necessary for each.

Only one white operations card, controlling the progress of auditing or other accounting engagements, is prepared. The others, all having to do with the preparation of income-tax returns, are made out in duplicate, one each for the staff manager, the others for the tax department. A blue card is for Form 1120, federal corporation income-tax returns. An orange color is for trusts, partnerships, and individuals. A yellow is for state income-tax returns. The duplicate tax cards are first examined by the staff manager, then sent to the tax department. The original white operations card is returned to his secretary for current filing.

The *card for audit control* is filed according to fiscal closing date of the client in a small cabinet. When work begins on the engagement, the name of the in-charge accountant is placed on line 2 "In charge" (Figure 17, page 753). The card is then sent by the secretary to the staff manager who retains it during the progress of the work. Line 3, "Preliminary started," is to cover the starting date of such advance work as inventory observation, surprise count of cash, mailing of accounts receivable confirmations, etc. The appropriate dates are entered on lines 4 through 8 as the work progresses. The card is then returned to the secretary after the total "Field hours" has been entered on line 9. The card is used only on one side, and has four columns to cover four separate accounting periods.

All cards for each particular month are placed on the staff manager's desk weekly, whether or not the job is started. He retains only those he wishes and sends back the others. By this method he is fully aware of the progress of each engagement. This follow-up system is used for audit clients and for every other type of accounting engagement.

The staff manager also watches the progress of tax return preparation, as a precaution against failure to have a client's return in his hands on time for filing.

The *tax control cards* (originals) are filed by the secretary according to the due date of each return. As shown in Figure 18, page 753, line 2 provides for the in-charge man's name, as soon as he has been assigned. The staff manager, with the card before him, makes a note of the assignment. Again, the appropriate dates are entered as each step is completed. After the return is mailed, the card is again filed alphabetically by due date in the secretary's special cabinet.

The duplicate cards in the tax department are entered by the secretary of the head tax man and are filed according to due dates of returns in the same manner as are the originals.

The staff manager receives monthly a form, termed master tax calendar, on all returns due for filing the following month. It has five columns, as follows:

    Taxpayer   Returns (No. of form)   Assigned   Due   Mailed

At the same time, each senior to whom the preparation of returns has been assigned receives a similar record covering his assignments.

The operations cards described above are also used to prepare work forecasts (see pages 689, 770, and 771).

A small individual practitioner. No later than twenty-four hours after an agreement is made, this practitioner transcribes from his own notes in ink onto a double insert card all pertinent data on a new engagement or a change in an old one.

Tickler cards. Into one side of the card "jacket" goes the permanent card, clipped to the jacket, one for each client. The information recorded on this card is given in Figure 19, page 754. Into the opposite side of the jacket is inserted without permanent fastening, but held in with sufficient strength, the same client's current requirements with later record as these are met. This is the visible index side.

When the file is closed, the following can be seen in the visible index:

1. Name, type of organization, street address, post office box number, and telephone number

2. Fiscal year close (red ink line drawn vertically immediately after month number—in this case 10, for October)

3. Scheduled date for starting next work—November 8th (in this case, 8th per stopping point of orange transparent-slide indicator; November, per 11 showing through small hole in blue indicator)

4. Two reports per year (as shown by number 2, printed on orange indicator at left)

5. Identification of in-charge accountant (as shown by number 4 printed on orange indicator at right)

The meaning of the three orange and the blue flag signals is easily identified by their relative positions. All signals are of transparent plastic material.

As noted in Figure 19, page 754, the removable, current requirement card shows the function to be performed next (the first listed one appearing without a check mark at left). When the time comes to perform that function, the card is taken out and placed in an active file to which the practitioner refers daily for a quick perusal of every job then in process. As soon as that duty is performed the card is checked off, the next function is written on it, and it is again placed in its proper insert, the signal flags being adjusted to suit. The permanent card is not removed except when changes in the data it carries are needed.

A sole practitioner with a branch. This small firm, a sole practitioner, has a main office and one small branch a short distance away. His simple record for follow-up of tax returns is illustrated in Figure 20, page 755. The sheets are filed alphabetically and by fiscal closings in a ring binder.

A small firm. To enable staff members to keep an effective running inventory of client work completed and still in process, a small firm devised a loose-leaf form which contains the vital data on each client, and provides a quick reference record enabling others in the office to know what any absent staff member does and has done on all regular engagements. (See Figure 21, page 756.) Note that the client's work request and the basis of the charges for the work are clearly established at the very outset.

A variation on the use of visible records. The following modification of a visible record file affords further control of tax returns.

A visible record for each client has been found to be extremely valuable to us during the tax season. During the month of December, as time is available, red tabs are placed at the left side on cards of all clients for whom tax services are to be rendered. This appears, on its face, to be a duplication since the client's card is already marked in crayon with a red mark in the month for which a tax return must be filed; however, the reason for the additional tab will soon become apparent.

As tax information is received from a client and the tax return is at least begun, the red tab is removed from that client's card and it is thereby readily determinable that information on that particular taxpayer is in the office and that the return is available to be worked on. When the return is completed and delivered to the client, a white tab is placed over the red mark in the month when the tax return is due, which means that on April 16th, for example, there will be no red tabs left on the left side of the card, nor will there be any red marks visible in the month of April.

Needle-sorted punch cards. The needle-sorted punch card is one excellent means of speeding the administration of the CPA's practice. Its requirements are simple: (1) the cards, (2) a manual notcher, (3) a sorting needle, and (4) a container.

One corner of the cards is cut diagonally so that they can be kept in proper position. Each hole is given a special meaning or significance. The card is then notched at the appropriate hole or combination of holes. Sorting the cards can be done very quickly. The sorting needle, which resembles a knitting needle, is thrust through the hole selected and holds as many as three hundred cards at one time. The cards which are unslotted are lifted away and the slotted or wanted cards drop off. This process is repeated until all of the required information is assembled. Figure 1 (page 674) shows such a card.

For sorting purposes various essential information is converted into the punched slots on the border. This conversion utilizes the letter code illustrated in Figure 2 (page 674). As indicated, the code number is made up by combinations of the digits 1, 2, 4, and 7. Furthermore, if the code number represents a letter in the latter half of the alphabet, the slot N-Z is punched.

Starting at the lower left-hand corner and proceeding clockwise, the card accommodates the information in this order: name of client; deadline months (regardless of what the deadlines may be); nonpayroll tax-return deadlines; payroll tax deadlines; fiscal year; declaration of estimated tax; space reserved; nature of the entity; and dates when client is to be billed.

While the cards are often very useful for getting quick information, the real payoff comes when the cards are sorted at the beginning of the month and the monthly engagement list is prepared.

Control of typing. A "Weekly Office Report" is used by a medium-sized firm as an additional summary of information from the typing department to the partners and office manager. It is a preprinted form with spaces for work completed, work in progress, and work on hand. The client's name, description of the item (return, report, etc.), and other pertinent data are listed in the proper section. This contributes to control of workload and follow-up.

Figure I

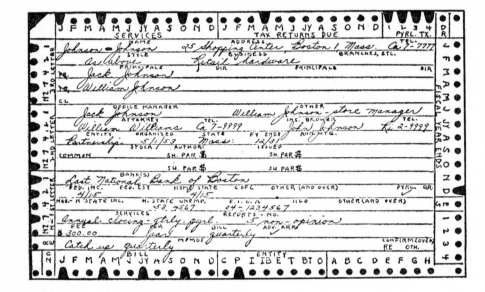

Figure 2. Letter Guide (slot first three letters of name)

Number	A-M		N-Z	1	2	4	7
1 is	A	or	N	X			
2 is	B	or	O		X		
3 is	C	or	P	X	X		
4 is	D	or	Q			X	
5 is	E	or	R	X		X	
6 is	F	or	S		X	X	
7 is	G	or	T				X
8 is	H	or	U	X			X
9 is	I	or	V		X		X
10 is	J	or	W	X	X		X
11 is	K	or	X			X	X
12 is	L	or	Y	X		X	X
13 is	M	or	Z		X	X	X

Records for
Control of Time and Costs

CONTROL OF TIME

■ THE FINANCIAL SUCCESS of an accounting practice is closely related to the efficient use of time. Most elements of a fee are dependent, to some extent, on time. As represented by salaries and other payroll expenses, time is usually the largest single cost of an engagement. Since it is one of the few objectively measurable factors in determining a fee, the flow of *all* costs, plus the financial return to the practitioner, are generally allocated to an engagement on the basis of the man-hours devoted to it.

Acceptability of a fee to a client generally assumes that the accountant will perform the work with reasonable efficiency without devoting an excessive amount of time to it. Therefore, to the extent that a firm can effectively control the use of time, it can control the significant relationship between its costs and the fees it receives for its services.

Certified public accountants are expert in allocating the income and expenses of their clients. No CPA, for example, would permit a client to dispose of a product without accounting for that disposition. Yet the same firm may well have no accurate or useful record of the disposition of its own chief asset—time.

Obviously, records themselves do not provide control. The most elaborate system can provide only information. Someone must interpret it, and apply it to decision-making. In the larger firms, where top management cannot be expected to be completely familiar with the day-to-day performance of each staff member, data culled from detailed records must be relied upon for information. A smaller practitioner, completely familiar with the activities of his clients and the work of his staff, can base many of his decisions on personal observation. Indeed, some smaller firms feel that it is a waste of time to maintain detailed time records. In some cases, there may be an element of truth in this. But fundamentally even the smallest practitioner cannot afford to rely solely on observation and memory. He must have some records by which to gauge the efficiency of his business operations, and to give him a basis for effective control over the productivity of his practice.

Clearly, there can be no single set of procedures ideal for all firms. There is too much variation in the type of client served and the kind of service rendered. And these variations have significant effects on the ways in which a firm utilizes the time of its staff.

Purpose of control. Controls on time in an accounting firm should serve three interrelated purposes:

1. To see that the working time of both staff and principals is used as productively as possible. This does not necessarily mean that each person must achieve the maximum possible number of chargeable hours. A certain amount of time should be devoted to staff training, special research projects, study of current developments in accounting, and professional and civic activities. Indeed, the proper planning of such "nonproductive" activities may, in the long run, increase a firm's productivity more than if every hour of every day were charged directly to a client.

2. To make sure that work is properly charged. Unless the person responsible for setting the fee can easily determine the type of work performed and the time invested by the various grades of accountants in each engagement, it will be difficult to fix a realistic fee.

3. The third purpose of time control is to enable a firm to review the adequacy of its fee structure by analyzing the average hourly return as it relates to operating costs. If a firm is not sure of its costs for each individual engagement, it cannot properly plan to recover, on an over-all basis, a return which will produce a necessary or desirable net income at year's end. If a firm must wait until the end of a year to see how much is left over for the partners after the bills are paid, it is obviously not in a position to do anything about an undesirable result for that year.

Standards for control. Before a firm can establish specific time-control procedures, it should develop a set of realistic standards by which day-to-day performance can be measured, such as tentative income and potential chargeable time.

Many firms do not make up formal budgets. But in order to operate effectively a firm must have some idea of what income it may expect and what its costs are apt to be during the coming year. Often these figures are merely rough projections from previous years, but they can serve as a guide in comparing the current year's performance. Sometimes the prior years' figures on a monthly income statement are sufficient.

These factors are largely determined by a realistic evaluation of the amount of chargeable time that can be expected from staff and partners, and the over-all average rate which can be expected from that time. Firms have different ideas on how much chargeable time is a realistic expectation. However, there seems to be general agreement that 1,600 chargeable hours a year is about all that can be expected from each staff man without the use of overtime.

With a minimum time standard established, and with a rate applied to it for each individual or classification of accountant—based on salary plus an allocation for overhead and partners' compensation—control becomes possible over most of the cost elements.

A word of caution might be offered at this point. Not only is it necessary to be realistic in estimating staff time unassigned, but an adequate amount of unassigned time is desirable for several reasons:

1. Time is available for nonrecurring work, for which fees are usually larger than the per-diem rates charged for regular recurring engagements. The firm is also in a better position to accept desirable new clients.

2. It is easier to maintain a high-quality staff. The tendency to keep poorly qualified men because of the pressure of work is minimized.

3. The firm can undertake special research, provide the opportunity for advanced study and training, and pay sufficient attention to the administrative aspects of the practice.

Records required. A firm's record system should ideally be a compromise between two extremes. On the one hand, it should be adequate to accomplish the three purposes of time control—optimum productivity, proper allocation to clients, and analysis of costs. On the other hand, it should be simple enough so that productive personnel do not spend excessive time on what are basically housekeeping chores. Time spent in maintaining records and assigning staff men does not contribute directly to the firm's income. Yet if operational flaws can be detected and changed before they snowball into significant items, this time can be worth a great deal more than a comparable period of chargeable time in its ultimate contribution to a firm's over-all productivity.

BASIC RECORDS AND FORMS

The following are some of the most commonly used records for time and billing controls:

1. *Time reports.* The basic productivity record is generally a periodic report submitted by each staff member accounting for all of his time, both chargeable and nonchargeable.

2. *Summary production record.* Individual time sheets are usually posted to a monthly and/or cumulative time record covering the entire staff. This breaks down total time into productive and various elements of nonproductive time.

3. *Client ledger.* A card (known by a variety of names) is normally kept for each client. Appearing on each client's ledger card or sheet is a record of all time and expenses charged to that client.

These basic records can yield a great deal of information about the functioning of a firm and the effectiveness of individual staff members. Among their values:

1. A productivity ratio can be developed for each accountant, and for the firm as a whole, relative both to time involved and to salary costs. This can be most useful in salary reviews. One approach is to compute the ratio of chargeable hours to normal working hours for the month.

2. When the total productive hours are compared to the total time available, management has a guide to the amount of additional work the firm can handle and to the periods of the year best suited for the extra workload.

3. The records indicate variations in the time required to do the same job for the same client over a long period. If a staff man is taking longer to do a certain job, he may not be as competent as his predecessor; on the other hand, the volume of work may have increased. In the one case, a personnel

problem may be indicated; in the other, a fee adjustment may be warranted.

4. Analysis of the basic time records will help to check out a client's fee performance, and to evaluate each client's relative contribution to a firm's total income.

5. Nonchargeable time can be analyzed, both to reduce it if it proves excessive, and to see that the staff spends enough time in the areas of research and professional development.

6. The records may yield clues to excessive overtime, if any. The pinpointing of particularly slack periods may provide a solution, such as greater use of interim work during the slow periods.

7. Downward adjustments from the standard rates can be reviewed and perhaps reduced.

8. If a client is concerned about the size of his bill, detailed time records enable a practitioner to support his fee.

Staff location records. Since most staff time in the majority of firms is spent outside of the firm's office, some record of location of personnel is considered essential.

Most practitioners maintain some daily location record on all men. Such records range from office blackboard entries made by the men themselves to a comprehensive location sheet prepared for the office manager each morning.

The personnel staff manager of one large firm maintains frequent contact with his field men. They do not always report personally to him, but they report to the switchboard-receptionist every morning as to their whereabouts. She keeps a revolving-type visible index file next to her switchboard containing a card for each field accountant, each one's name appearing at the bottom of his card. The size is 3 by 5 inches, divided in half by a line down the middle, each half for a separate week. Useable on both sides, one card will serve four weeks. A card covering two weeks for one employee is illustrated in Figure 3 (opposite).

Every morning at 9:00 A.M. the personnel staff manager makes it a matter of routine to check with the receptionist on personnel location. The same record is kept for the tax men as for the staff accountants. The firm believes it is good to telephone the field men occasionally to check on them. The surprise element is valuable.

A large firm uses a "staff secretary," a man whose office adjoins the office manager. The staff secretary is charged with the duty of ascertaining the location of all staff men and keeps a running record for himself and for the office manager. The accountants report to him by telephone each morning upon arrival at clients' premises. He collects time reports periodically and generally acts as assistant to the office manager.

In addition to listing basic information such as names of accountants, engagements to which assigned, and location of engagements, many firms add dates on which accountants will be available for other assignments. Often, particularly in medium and large firms, definite personnel reservations for future assignments are indicated.

Time reports. The time report is generally a simple form on which is entered

Figure 3

Client	Client
10/8 _Hardie_	10/15 _Hardie_
10/9 "	10/16 "
10/10 "	10/17 _In office_
10/11 "	10/18 "
10/12 "	10/19 "
10/13 "	10/20
10/14	10/21
Accountant's Name:	_Smith, Roger_

the man's name, the period covered, and the allocation of the total charge-able hours put in each day. This includes not only the name of the client involved but also a brief description of work performed. Nonchargeable time is usually shown separately, with an explanation for each major classification (e.g., unassigned, vacation, sick, administrative). Frequently each individual also compiles a summary showing the total time he has worked for each client during a given period.

All firms use some form of time reports. Other names applied are time sheet, report of services, and service report. Generally the time totaled daily, weekly, semimonthly, or monthly is posted formally to a summary sheet for the period as the basis for the charges to clients. Some practitioners await completion of the engagement, at which time they take adding machine tapes, or machine-add the time on the back of the office copies of invoices sent to clients. Another simple approach is to file with the working papers a memo of time spent.

An extremely useful variation of the time report shows the detail of the work performed: for example, accounts receivable inventory, etc. This can be further summarized by client. Such a summary is especially useful in deter-mining billing classification and planning repeat engagements. Examples of forms serving these functions appear on pages 776-777.

Illustrations of various time and expense reports appear at the end of this Section, pages 757-764 (Figures 22-27).

One firm files its time reports in a time control record book. The first sheet of the time control book (a post binder in this case) consists of an alpha-betical listing of each staff member down the left-hand side of the page. Op-posite the name, and running across the sheet, are spaces in which the weekly amounts of chargeable, nonchargeable, and total time are posted for each individual. These figures are taken from the summary on the time sheets.

This summary record serves a dual purpose: (1) it indicates which time sheets have been received; (2) it serves as a control of hours posted to clients' ledger sheet. Nonchargeable time is informally reviewed at stated intervals. Excessive nonchargeable time is investigated. Actually, staff men in this firm have little nonproductive time.

An interesting variation of time report procedures is described under "The Envelope System," on page 686.

Frequency of reports. The frequency with which time reports are submitted ranges from daily to monthly; weekly reports seem to predominate. Most firms feel the weekly basis gives them better control over the progress of in-process work and unassigned staff time. Another variation requires reports to be filed on the 10th, 20th, and last day of each month.

While most firms do not require daily time reports, one advantage of daily reporting is that unassigned time is more quickly noted, and corrective measures can thus be better assured.

Time units. The minimum units of time posted may vary among firms, but a quarter of an hour seems to be the most common. Some firms use half-hour units; a few record only full hours. Within a firm, as a practical matter, fractional hours have varying significance. Many staff members work full days and even weeks on a single assignment. Partners, on the other hand, are frequently involved with a number of clients during a relatively short period.

The unit of time used should be small enough to allocate accurately all of the time devoted to specific clients, and to minimize the short periods of time which are often absorbed by the firm. Some practitioners favor the use of "units" rather than fractional hours. They are easy to accumulate and can be assigned a billing value without translating an hourly rate into a fraction. (For example, one hour might be four units priced at $2 a unit rather than at $8 an hour.) A few firms find the decimal system effective, especially where the billing rate is not applied until the fee is computed.

The unit system illustrated. While most accounting offices keep track of their time in hours and fractions thereof, the fractions enormously complicate the time controls. Not only that, when half-hours are the lowest time spans recognized, there is the perpetual problem of whether or not to put down five-, ten-, or twenty-minute consultations. The adoption of units, with one unit representing a quarter-hour or, regardless of time, the smallest unit of service recognized by the practitioner, will definitely help on both counts, i.e., simplify the office timekeeping, and capture on paper elusive trickles of potential revenue.

Thus if an $8-per-hour man works 7½ hours on one client only for a day, he records thirty units (@ $2 = $60) rather than 7½ hours (@ $8 = $60). By the same token, if a principal gives the answer to an important technical question in a five-minute telephone conversation, he jots down on his time sheet the name of the client, the subject of the call, the one unit, and the charge. At the end of a busy 7½-hour day of consulting, the principal's time sheet thus might show thirty-two or thirty-six units instead of thirty, and the charges for the several units of service might vary, depending on the decision at the time.

It is axiomatic that the smaller the practice the wider the range in levels of skill required of any one man in a day's work. The only fair policy is to charge the client for *what* is done, not *who* does it. Incidentally, this policy of strict fairness rightly places a premium on efficient advance scheduling and sound organizational structure so that the higher the caliber of man the less junior-level work he will perform.

To illustrate the use of *units* in place of *hours* as well as the practice of using *variable rates* in accordance with the value of the various services, a specimen time sheet (Figure 4, page 682) of the principal of a small firm is reproduced. Note these features: (1) the ease of footing and cross-footing the whole units—there are no fractional hours to bother with; (2) the variations in rates; (3) the allotment of space between non-clients and clients; and (4) the extra space allowed for descriptive information as to the two clients for whom it was expected the most work would be done during that week.

This form lends itself to posting weekly totals only of units and dollars from the time sheets to the clients' individual accounts. In preparing the descriptions of the work done when billing, the time sheets are referred to directly, thereby saving a great deal of posting and general rehandling of the same information.

Code for charging time. In one firm a code is used to record the classes of services performed on each engagement. It simplifies each man's task of daily recording on his weekly time sheet the type of work he has performed. Then, at the conclusion of the engagement, it gives the partner who prepares the billings the kind of information he needs for a correct description and pricing of the services rendered.

All job assignment sheets carry a seven-digit number, i.e., 0000-000. The first four digits indicate the client permanent file number.

The last three digits indicate the period and class of services performed. The first digit indicates the year, i.e., 2 designates the year 1962. The second and third digits indicate the period or class of work, as shown on page 683.

The code's usage can be clarified by taking a concrete example. Assume that a client is on a monthly audit basis. The code starts off with the client's number, which may be 2345. Then the first of the code digit numbers represents the fiscal year in which the client's year ended. For example: 1 indicates that the client's fiscal year ended in 1961, 2 in 1962 and 3 in 1963. The second and third digits indicate the period or class of work done as follows: 01 represents a monthly audit for the month of January, 02 for the month of February, and so on through 12, which represents the month of December.

Where an audit is done once a year, the number 15 is used to show that it is an annual engagement. If semiannual audits are performed, the numbers 21 or 22 are used. The first 2 indicates that two audits are performed a year and the second 1 or 2 means that it is the first-half or second-half audit. Where quarterly engagements are performed, the 41, 42, 43, and 44 are similarly indicative.

Should any special work be done, in addition to the regular annual, semiannual, or quarterly engagement—such as preparing special cost analyses— the auditor shows the client's number 2345 and the code number 276 which shows that he performed special cost analysis work for the fiscal year to end in 1962 and that this was additional to his normal regular quarterly audit. The numbers 70 through 99 cover many of the typical "special" jobs.

Figure 4

Office Middletown Person Principal TIME REPORT, WEEK ENDED 10/8/58

NON-CLIENT WORK	EXPLANATION	Mon.	Tues.	Wed.	Thurs.	Fri.	Sat.	Sun.	Total
Personal		12	2						14
AICPA	Practitioners Forum Contribution		4						4
Alma Mater Club	Treasurer's Report			3					3
Travel	To Branch Office	16		3					19
Administration	Reviewing Timesheets, Billings	4	10	3	2	2			21
	Totals	32	14	11	2	2			61

CLIENT	DESCRIPTIVE DETAIL FOR BILLING PURPOSES	Mon. U $		Tues. U $		Wed. U $		Thurs. U $		Fri. U $		Sat. U $		Sun. U $		Total U $	
Big Company	Conference w/ official re Financial Statements	8	28	2	7												
	Conference re "Plant" valuation					6	21										
	Conference re duplication of records							6	21								
	Regular Financial Report									5	17						
																27	94
Estate Trust	Letter to attorney			4	12												
	Insurance analysis					4	20										
																8	32
Eastern Co.	Admn., phone conversation re finances	1	5	1	5											2	10
Tax Client #1	Phone conversation re gift tax			1	3											1	3
Tax Client #2	Phone conversation			1	3			1	3							2	6
Water Co.	Phone conversation	2	6			2	6									4	12
Land Co.	Phone conversation									1	NC					1	NC
Loan Co.	Conference with staff man			1	2	1	3	4	12	4	12					10	29
Cotton Gin	Conference with staff man re account			1	3	1	3	2	6							4	12
Profit-Sharing Plan	Conference re amt. of Prem./ Disc. Bonds; Chg. replace to Dep. on Reserve					2	6			1	3					3	9
Transportation Co.	Rate Case, conference with officials					2	6			10	30					12	36
Machinery Co.	Re audit of receivables			1	3											1	3
Tax Client	Interest on contract problem									2	6					2	6
Church	Conference re audits							4	8							4	8
	Totals	9	33	13	41	19	68	17	50	23	68					81	260

John Principal
Person Reporting

John Principal
Approval

682

01 January	62 Tax return—Year ending in 1962
02 February	70 Analysis or report—Special
03 March	71 Attorney consultation for client
04 April	72 Audits—Special
05 May	73 Board of directors meeting
06 June	74 Budget work
07 July	75 Casualty insurance consultation
08 August	76 Cost analysis work
09 September	77 Credit & collection work
10 October	78 Deliver & review report with clients
11 November	79 Embezzlements
12 December	80 Employee hiring & interviews for
15 Annual engagement	clients
16 Annual report to Secretary of State	81 Estate-planning
21 Semiannual engagement—1st six	82 Instructions to bookkeepers
months	83 General management conferences
22 Semiannual engagement—2nd six	84 Gift tax work
months	85 Life insurance consultations
25 Closing books	86 Loan arrangements
31 Payroll returns—First quarter	87 Promotional conferences
32 Payroll returns—Second quarter	88 Renegotiation of contracts
33 Payroll returns—Third quarter	89 Retyping of data—Client's fault
34 Payroll returns—Fourth quarter	90 Retyping of data—Firm's fault
41 1st-quarter engagement	91 Reworking of data—Client's fault
42 2nd-quarter engagement	92 Reworking of data—Firm's fault
43 3rd-quarter engagement	93 Systems work
44 4th-quarter engagement	94 Tax examinations
60 Tax return—Year ending in 1960	95 Tax research & consultation
61 Tax return—Year ending in 1961	96 Inventory supervision

99 Licenses

There will be situations in practices throughout the country not covered in the specimen code above. However, the essential idea can be used since the categories may be adjusted to each particular situation.

Summary production records. Many firms keep production records on their staff in order to evaluate their abilities and efficiency. Some base the compensation of their field men on the results shown. A case illustrating staff efficiency records is presented on pages 703-707. Another purpose for which work progress records are maintained by firms is to determine whether assignment schedules are being met, and if not, the reasons for such failure. These records also help to plan the anticipated work obligations to clients.

One accountant, in emphasizing the importance of cost records, suggests that "fees produced by each man, as well as the cost of each engagement, should be determined" and states that the first feature "calls for keeping a separate fee-income account for each productive member of the staff and, as bills are written up or down, making adjustments to these fee accounts." He states that records of this character are designed to make the principal, as well as the members of the staff, sensitive to the importance of improving fee production and efficiency and controlling the cost of separate assignments.

One small firm keeps a monthly record of production of each partner and staff accountant, as well as of each stenographer. This record balances with monthly (and annual) charges to accounts receivable (for fees) and credits to fees account.

A large firm uses an "Accountant's Service Record." These forms, one each for every month, are filled in for the main office and branch offices. The names of the various accountants are written one under the other and the fees produced by each during the specified periods are entered in the columns. The grand total of the fees entered on all forms is the basis of the debit to "unbilled services" and the credit to "revenue." A summary of these monthly forms is prepared so that annual statistics, controlled by the general ledger, are maintained.

A medium-sized firm prepares a weekly "Unassigned Time Summary" for each accountant, its purpose being to indicate to what extent the unassigned time is attributable to an oversized staff or any marked falling off of special assignments. This form lists the staff men who had unassigned time during the week and gives comparative totals for the same week last year.

A large firm supplements the usual follow-up data with a written engagement progress report on each job weekly, prepared by the senior in charge to cover his work, as well as that of his assistants, in terms of total time. An example of such a report follows:

Total hours to beginning of this week	104
Total hours during this week	70
To date	174
Original estimate of total hours to complete	210
Remaining hours	36
Estimated hours to complete	56
Variance	20

Instructions given at the bottom of the form are to the effect that the report must be submitted weekly by the accountant to his supervisor, attached to the weekly time report. Excess of actual time over total allotted time must be shown in red.

It is claimed that considerable time is saved through this means of making the men time-conscious. A conference is held with the in-charge accountant when the "variance" figure is large in the hope that the estimated remaining hours can be reduced. The firm is adamant in its demands that unassigned time be kept at the minimum consistent with performing thorough work, and uses this progress report to accomplish this purpose.

For illustrations of how production and efficiency data can be presented in statement form, see "Modified Statements for Managerial Use," pages 701-708.

Some firms enter and extend billing rates on this form (in some cases even for nonproductive time). This gives them at a glance a full picture of each man's theoretical contribution to the firm's total fee income and the potential loss due to his nonproductive time.

Some firms give incentive bonuses computed on the basis of individual production. Under such circumstances, more consideration is given to flat fees billing, particularly for tax work and special services. However, flat fees based on inadequate estimates produce less revenue than the amount which could have been earned on a per-day or per-hour basis. Staff morale is endangered when earnings of some accountants are affected favorably or adversely by reason of unwise administrative policy.

The rates used to "cost" the accumulated time charges are either those for individual employees, or for a general classification, such as junior, senior, tax specialist, and the like. When overtime pay is a factor, it seems to be prevalent to ignore it in costing, making no distinction as to regular and overtime rates. Some firms recognize the overtime factor by posting 1½ hours for overtime, extending all time at the same rates.

As to time charges for nonstaff employees, one practitioner has this to say:

"We have abandoned keeping time records on typing, proofreading, and machine time and have substituted standard rates per page based on cost studies. This means keeping a record of report pages, but that is much less work than entering time records for all the clerical activities."

The client ledger is often all that is needed to determine the fee to be charged if an adequate description of the work is included. When "standard" billing rates are posted to the card as well, the person doing the billing can quickly see the effect of any fee adjustments that might be contemplated. In some cases, too, these forms contain columns for the billing history, including adjustments from standard rates; thus they can also function as the accounts receivable ledger.

Client ledger. Other names used for this record are work-in-progress ledger, process ledger, time ledger, combined time ledger and accounts receivable, unbilled receivables, clients ledger, record of charges to client, individual client's record, and cost sheets.

From the individual time reports or summaries, the name of each man, the amount of time he has put in for the client during the period, and a brief description of the type of work are posted to the client ledger card. Usually the chargeable expenses and time of other employees, such as typists (if the firm charges the client directly for such services), are also entered. It seems to be fairly common practice to extend the time at billing rates, rather than at cost. When, however, time records are maintained at cost, they can be adjusted to selling price at the end of the accounting period, at the completion of an engagement, or at billing time.

Examples of client ledger sheets. Examples of time ledger sheets and of combination time and amount records used by several firms are reproduced in Figures 28 and 29, pages 765-767.

The form on page 765 is the ledger sheet (one for each client) of unbilled receivables as used by a large firm operating several branches. Both sides are the same. It forms the basis of a monthly charge (from the five columns indicated) to unbilled receivables with a credit to fees earned, accumulated and posted semimonthly from the time reports. Accumulations are at standard billing rates used by the firm. The "amount of expense" column receives its debits directly from the cash disbursements book. If the actual billing is for an amount in excess of accumulated charges, the actual amount is placed in "amount of bill" column, the difference in "adjustment" column (in black) signifying a credit to income. If adjustment represents a debit to income, the figure is entered in red. At the close of each month the black and red adjustment figures entered that month are added, and the net debit or credit is charged or credited to the "unbilled receivables—clients," control with the contra to billing adjustments.

This firm also uses a salmon colored sheet which is an exact duplicate as to printing and columnar arrangement on both sides. It is used as a reserve against the "unbilled receivables" carried on the preceding sheet whenever the accumulated dollar amounts are deemed to be partly unrealizable from the client.

All billings must be approved by the partner in charge of the client. Each month, lists in triplicate, classified by the partner in charge, are prepared including all "balance unbilled" amounts in the ledger. Each in-charge partner gets his particular list, the duplicates of all lists go to the managing partner, and the triplicates are retained by the business office. Each partner indicates on his copy the clients to be billed that month, and the business office then prepares drafts of bills for his approval. The firm does not use an accounts receivable ledger, utilizing copies of invoices instead.

In another firm, dollar cost summaries (cost here is exclusive of overhead) are computed monthly and after entry in separate columns provided at the bottom of the "cost sheet," these costs are accumulated in general ledger controlling accounts for (1) partners' time in process, (2) staff time in process, and (3) expenses in process. The cost is determined at the close of each month by applying the per-hour salary rate of each employee involved to the hours worked on each engagement and adding to this amount the expenses incurred. Credits to the individual (inventory) accounts and their controls arise from tabulating the cost of engagements completed and billed during the month.

The envelope system. Instead of using the more traditional form of employees' time record sheets, one firm (six partners, fifteen staff, and five clerical employees) uses individual time tickets prepared by each employee for each client for whom he works during a semimonthly pay period. Each partner and each staff member records work performance on colored time tickets: white for chargeable, buff for all nonchargeable classifications (office nonchargeable, holiday, vacation, sick and absent time). Staff accountants and clerical employees prepare their own time tickets immediately following the close of the semimonthly period. Thus they perform a portion of the record-keeping for clients' records rather than burden a clerical employee with far more posting time. Time tickets for partners and—during the busy times of the year—for other key employees, are prepared by a clerical employee from their appointment books. Figure 5B shows the chargeable time ticket for accountant Doe who worked on a systems survey for Ace, Inc., on June 23, 24, 25, and 30, for a total of 22½ hours. Figure 5C shows the dates when Doe had nonchargeable hours during the half-month ended June 30, 1958, together with explanations if indicated.

Each employee further prepares a covering envelope (Figure 5D) which serves in place of an ordinary timecard and lists the total hours worked by him in the various categories during the current pay period. He encloses in that envelope the time tickets totaling exactly the amount of hours shown on its face.

The first step in the pricing of these tickets is to extend the total hours shown on the outside of the envelope at the employee's billing rate to arrive at a total value of his chargeable, nonchargeable, vacation time, and so on. Then each of the white tickets contained in the envelope, representing the total work performed for any one client during the current half-month period, is extended at the same billing rate. This is done by reference to tables, and all cents are disregarded. The total of the extensions on the individual time tickets must equal the total of the extension on the outside of the envelope. Once the total charges contained in each employee's envelope have been balanced against the summary, these tickets may be sorted and totaled by client and posted to the client's receivable record. Thus only a single posting is made for all time chargeable to a client during a period.

Clients' records are also maintained via an envelope system (Figure 5E). The face of these envelopes is divided into two sections. The left section represents an accumulation of unbilled services; the right section represents the accounts receivable record of billed and unpaid services. The total amount of time, summarized by an adding machine tape stapled to that client's tickets for the current pay period, is posted to the unbilled services section of the envelope. Tickets for these charges are kept inside the envelope until all work represented by them has been billed to the client and the fee received. These tickets, as prepared by the employees themselves, yield a full description of the work performed. It is a relatively simple matter, at billing time, to review all time tickets comprising the accumulation of charges and to evaluate the importance of the work to the client.

The operation of this firm's time control system requires approximately one to three hours per month of each staff accountant. It takes about one-quarter of the office manager's time and about one-third of the time of the clerical employee working on the time tickets and the client's records. One of the partners spends from two to six hours a month on the general supervision of time control records.

Expense reports. Expense reports are sometimes combined with time reports on the same form. Most firms, however, use separate expense forms obtainable from printers' stocks, while others are designed to order. Some forms used by practitioners are included at the end of this section, on pages 757-760 and 764.

Bill draft. Since accumulated time charges are only one factor in determining the amount to be billed on an engagement, there must be some adjustment to the work in process. Some firms make provision for such adjustments on the client's ledger card. An example of this appears on page 765.

In order to further facilitate and standardize billing procedures, some firms use a form which might be described as a bill draft. Such a form used by one large firm is shown in Figure 30, page 768. At billing time, the wording is selected from the standard, preprinted paragraphs on billing in the consecu-

Figure 5. Time Reports and Billing Record

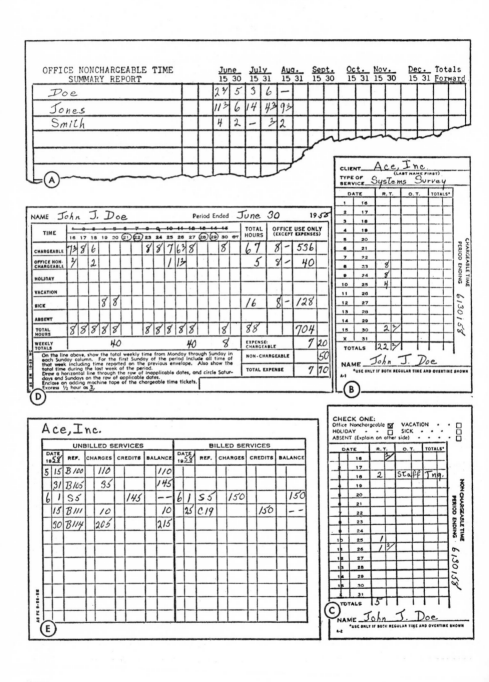

tively numbered bill draft, as checked; or, if none applies, special wording is inserted under (5). The bill draft thus represents the original and a permanent record of actual charges. The original bill is sent to the client; the duplicate is filed, with the latest data on top, in a binder as a current accounts receivable ledger. This procedure eliminates posting. Payment by the client of his bill in full causes removal of the duplicate from the current to a "paid invoices" binder. Payments on account are recorded on the related duplicates, the reduced amounts being shown. A triplicate invoice constitutes the billing register, and the monthly total is debited to "Accounts Receivable, Control" and credited to "Unbilled Receivables—Clients, Control." The bill draft is numbered with a numbering machine.

Work forecasts. The great majority of firms prepare forecasts or programs of work. Some do so only for short periods, such as for one month at a time; others will spread their predictions over three months to six months; while still others utilize both short-range and long-range programs.

Each month the staff manager of one large firm has two columnar sheets prepared for him. The first, "Estimated Inventory of Work on Closings as of . . . ., 19 . . .," is maintained in conjunction with the second sheet, which is the short-range forecast for the month during which most of the work appearing on the first sheet is to be done. Examples of these two sheets, with fictitious names for clients and accountants, appear in Figures 31 and 32, pages 769 and 770. Each estimated inventory sheet represents one month's closings only and is kept open until that month's work is completed, no matter when that may be. The sheet is prepared from the operations cards (shown in Figures 17 and 18, page 753 and explained under "Tickler Files and Follow-up Files," page 669) and includes the estimated time to prepare income-tax returns as well as to do other work.

Two forecasts are thereby used, one short-range and the other long-range. The short-range forecast will contain many of the same names that appear on the first inventory sheet, but not necessarily all of them. It will also contain names not appearing on the previous month's closing sheet, because of unfinished work coming from previous inventory sheets.

The long-range forecast is prepared by the staff manager's office. This firm prepares such a forecast for the period beginning October 1 and ending April 30 of the following year, to take in the rush season (see Figure 33, page 771). Two lines are utilized for each staff accountant. On the first line to the right of his name are listed in red pencil the names of the clients he served last year. The name is extended so as to include the actual time worked on that client the year before. The names of those to whom the accountant is assigned during the current period are entered in black pencil on the second line. These names are made to take up the time spaces based on estimated days required to finish each client's work. Those accountants still on the staff in the current year are listed first, and those who left during the year are entered next. The red entries covering last year assignments are listed opposite these former staff accountants' names. However, these are crossed out when the assignments for this year have been made to other accountants.

The tax men and the partners are not included in this firm's long-range forecast since all income-tax returns are first prepared by members of the audit staff. A master tax calendar is prepared by the 15th of each month for the tax returns due in the following month. This calendar is also prepared from the tax operations cards.

A most unusual program is maintained by a large practitioner who is always about six months ahead with his tack board and tack heads of several colors. On this board, the clients to be served within the period are listed horizontally at the top and the days of each month are listed vertically in the left margin. Each of the twenty or more men is represented by a colored tack head, well indexed. These tacks are moved to the cross spaces for clients and opening dates of engagements. One man, if expected to work in ten places during the period covered, would be symbolized on the board by ten buttons of the same color.

On large jobs, it is sometimes necessary to break down time forecasts into specific phases of the engagement. A form for this purpose appears in Figure 34, page 772. This system generally requires a staff time report showing a similar breakdown.

Here are the high points of the forecast system used by a firm consisting of six partners, about fifteen staff accountants, and five clerical employees.

Information on pending assignments comes from a check on tickler or work-control records, as well as from a weekly assignment schedule (Figure 6). This weekly schedule is turned in every Thursday by each staff member. It contains the following information: a listing for the days of the next week of all clients for whom he expects to perform work; a summary, at the bottom of the schedule, of assignments on which he expects to work during the two or three weeks following that week; and requests for any assistance needed during the engagements listed on the current schedule.

From this weekly record and the various tickler records, the office manager prepares the work forecast and makes staff assignments.

Figure 6. Weekly Assignment Schedule

TENTATIVE WORK SCHEDULE FOR WEEK BEGINNING *6-30-58*
(to be submitted before preceding Friday morning)

Monday	ACE, INC.
Tuesday	ACE, INC.
Wednesday	GAS PRODUCERS COUNCIL
Thursday	UNASSIGNED
Friday	HOLIDAY
Saturday	

Plans for following week--remarks:

UNASSIGNED

7/14 — 18 GAS PROD. COUNCIL -- WILL

NEED 1 SEMI-SR. ASSISTANT

Signed *J. J. DOE*

OTHER RECORDS

Records of meetings, conversations, and opinions. Not many firms maintain records of informal opinions given to clients, but the great majority do so in detail with respect to formal opinions. Many also make a record of all meetings and conversations with or on behalf of a client.

One firm requires dictation of memos of all conversations and meetings, which are then filed with the intra-office communications in a special private folder which never leaves the office. This requirement also is applicable to tax engagements. All opinions of importance are addressed in writing to the client, and a copy is retained in the appropriate file.

One medium-sized firm keeps "minutes," in a loose-leaf book arranged in chronological order, of all meetings with clients and discussions held by the partners on important matters.

The uses of the interoffice memo. The best memory is a pencil and paper. Everyone who takes the time can use memos to advantage.

As one firm grew, the problem of intra-office communication became more complex. The members discovered that the only way to make sure that memos were not lost or forgotten was to make three copies. One copy would be kept by the person who originated the memo. One copy would go to the person to whom the memo was written, and the third copy would go into the client's file. The person who originated the memo would keep his copy in a file for follow-up. The copy in the client's file served as protection in case both members of the staff should somehow fail to follow through. This three-way check practically eliminated the possibility of a memo getting lost.

The firm uses a triplicate snap-out form, 8 by 8½ inches, a standard size. They buy these forms unprinted and have a printer put on a heading similar to a letterhead, with a date line on the right side and two lines on the left side for the name of the party to whom the memo is addressed. Only the top copy is printed, and what appears on the second and third copies is just what comes through on the carbon paper.

After the form was in use for some time the firm discovered that it was performing a number of functions not contemplated when they originally designed it. The most common ones are:

Brief correspondence. It is a very simple matter to dash off a hasty note to a client without the formality of a letter. The firm keeps one copy, sending two to the client. He can reply on one of the copies.

Receipt. Occasionally clients insist on paying in cash. This form serves as a receipt, with the original going to the client and the two carbons into office files.

A simple invoice. There are a number of times, particularly during tax season, when the firm prepares a simple return and does not want to put the billing through the usual routine. They then use this form to make an invoice or statement by hand, giving the client one copy and using the two carbons in our filing procedure.

Work orders. Whenever anyone brings in work from the field which is to be done by the office staff, this form is frequently used as an instruction sheet or work order. The original and one carbon go with the work. The second carbon for follow-up remains with the person who originated the order. The person who does the work returns it with one carbon, keeping the original for his time record.

Summer work. During the busy season partners frequently see many things that can or should be done but do not need to be done immediately. They write a note as a reminder to look into the matter during the summer when work is slower. The third copy is kept for follow-up by the person originating the idea, the second copy goes into the client's file, and the first copy goes into a pool held by one of the partners. He collects all such work orders from the whole staff. During the summer season these are reviewed by the partners and assigned to a staff member.

A Uniform Chart of Accounts

■ THE USE BY PRACTITIONERS of a *uniform* chart of accounts can serve a dual and interrelated purpose. It can be used to improve the operation of their own practices, and also to establish a base for the collection of comparable statistics for the benefit of the entire profession.

Obviously an accounting system, chart of accounts, or financial reports suitable for use by a national or even a large local accounting firm will have little resemblance to those maintained or required by a sole practitioner or a small firm. The attempt here is to provide material as a starting point in an effort to improve the financial records and reports of those practices that have neglected them, and to provide a basic reporting tool for the exchange of information within the profession.

Use of the proposed uniform chart of accounts will provide maximum comparability and will facilitate the development of accurate statistics on the practice management aspects of the profession. This will benefit all practitioners individually. At the same time, it will provide a fuller understanding of the profession's economic status, and thus aid in the development of national, state, and local programs designed to advance the cause of the accounting profession.

The chart of accounts which follows has been specifically designed to meet the requirements of individual practitioners and firms. It is not detailed. Explanations are provided to indicate the items included in each account classification. Firms which presently have or wish to have more detailed information may easily add subaccount classifications under the main headings provided. All expenses of operating a practice may be fitted into the chart's twenty-one expense account classifications, each of which (with one exception, "other operating expense") is descriptive of a major type of expense.

The chart of accounts is recommended for adoption by the profession as a *uniform chart of accounts*. All newly organized firms and those planning internal accounting changes are urged to adopt it. It is believed that those with satisfactory accounting systems can make relatively minor changes which would permit the classifications appearing in their financial statements to fit the uniform chart so that comparative statistics developed from periodic future surveys will have more meaning and significance.

ACCOUNT CLASSIFICATION

ASSETS

100 **Cash**
   109 Petty cash
110 **Receivables**
   111 Notes receivable
   112 Accounts receivable
   113 Unbilled receivables
   114 Unbilled expenses

120 *Allowance for Doubtful Accounts*
130 **Partners' and Employees' Accounts**
140 **Deposits and Prepaid Expenses**
150 **Investments**
160 **Building**
170 **Leasehold Improvements**
180 **Furniture, Equipment and Autos**
   185 Library

190 *Accumulated Depreciation and Amortization*

LIABILITIES

200 **Payables**
   201 Notes and loans payable
   202 Accounts payable
210 **Unearned Income**
220 **Employee Withholdings**
230 **Accrued Expenses**
250 **Long-Term Liabilities**

CAPITAL

300 **Capital Accounts**
350 **Drawing Accounts**
390 **Profit and Loss**

INCOME

400 **Income from Professional Services**

401 Auditing
402 Taxes
403 Management and advisory services
404 Other accounting services

500 Salaries and Outside Services
501 Salaries—partners or proprietor
502 Salaries—accounting staff
503 Salaries—other
504 Outside services

600 Operating Expenses
601 Contributions
602 Equipment expense
603 Firm relations
604 Insurance
605 Occupancy and maintenance
606 Other operating expense
607 Postage and express
608 Professional development
609 Professional membership expense
610 Provision for doubtful accounts
611 Publications
612 Stationery, printing, and supplies
613 Taxes—other
614 Taxes—payroll
615 Telephone and telegraph
616 Travel and subsistence
617 Welfare and group benefits

NONOPERATING INCOME

700 Other Income

EXPLANATION OF ACCOUNT CLASSIFICATION

ASSETS

100 Cash in banks

109 Petty cash
   Include postage fund and other prepaid petty cash items

111 Notes receivable

112 Accounts receivable

113 Unbilled receivables
   Include unbilled services or work in process evaluated at standard
   billing rates or at an average billing rate

114 Unbilled expenses
   Include all out-of-pocket expenses made for clients
   Use as a "clearing account"

120 *Allowance for doubtful accounts*

130 Partners' and employees' accounts
   Include expense advances and loans

140 Deposits and prepaid expenses
   Include prepaid insurance, interest, and other prepayments and deposits

150 Investments
   Include investments in securities, club memberships, and other sundry investments

160 Building

170 Leasehold improvements

180 Furniture, equipment, and autos

185 Library

190 *Accumulated depreciation and amortization*

LIABILITIES

201 Notes and loans payable
   Include notes and loans payable to banks, partners, and others within one year

202 Accounts payable
   Include payables for operating expenses and outside services

210 Unearned income
   Include all fees received or billed in advance of performing services

220 Employee withholdings
   Include amounts withheld from employees for social security, federal and state taxes, bond deductions, group insurance, etc.

230 Accrued expenses
   Include all accrued items related to salaries and compensation (see note under the heading of Salaries and Outside Services); liability for federal and state payroll taxes and other sundry accruals

250 Long-term debt
   Include all debt maturing after one year

CAPITAL

300 Capital accounts (one for each partner)

350 Drawing accounts (one for each partner)

390 Profit and loss

401 Auditing
Include audits in which opinion is qualified or in which disclaimer is issued

402 Taxes
Include tax returns, tax examinations, tax assessment appeals, and estate planning

403 Management and advisory services
Include systems installations, investigations, cost analyses, and other consulting and management services

404 Other accounting services
Include preparation of nonaudited statements and write-ups

SALARIES AND OUTSIDE SERVICES

501 Salaries—partners or proprietor

502 Salaries—accounting staff

503 Salaries—other
Include stenographers, typists, and other indirect salaries

504 Outside services
Include consultation with other firms, work performed by others of both a professional and nonprofessional nature relating to engagements, professional referral fee costs, and cost of data processing

Note: Salaries, other than for partners or proprietor, include all salaries, wages, commissions, bonuses, profit sharing, overtime; in general, all items of direct compensation for services, including provisions for vacations, sick benefits, separation pay, military leave pay, holiday pay, etc.

OPERATING EXPENSES

601 Contributions
Include all donations or contributions to religious, welfare, charitable, educational, and similar institutions

602 Equipment expense
Include depreciation of furniture and equipment (see account 616 for auto expenses), rental of equipment, repairs and maintenance of equipment, and small items not capitalized

603 Firm relations
Include dues of social clubs, travel incident to new clients, and other business promotional expenses

604 Insurance
   Include casualty and liability insurance premiums, travel insurance, nonownership liability insurance for employees' automobiles, and workmen's compensation insurance

605 Occupancy and maintenance
   Include the cost of rent, heat, light, water, property taxes, depreciation of building, repairs to building, amortization of leasehold improvements, insurance on building, and janitorial

606 Other operating expense
   Include bank charges, interest expense, legal services for the firm (including notary and collection services), staff recruitment (including travel expenses in visiting schools, lunches, and travel expenses of prospective employees), fees paid to employment agencies, newspaper ads, medical examinations of new employees, and all other general or unclassified expenses

607 Postage and express

608 Professional development
   Include all expenses incurred in connection with staff-training and education, including cost of books and other literature obtained primarily for educational purposes; cost of luncheons, dinners, travel, and other expenses in connection with training programs

609 Professional membership expense
   Include professional dues, fees, meeting expenses and travel, and all related expenses incurred with respect to professional organizations, professional activities, and speeches

610 Provision for doubtful accounts
   Include provision for doubtful accounts or for actual bad debts written off

611 Publications
   Include depreciation of library and cost of all periodicals

612 Stationery, printing, and supplies
   Include the cost of stationery, office supplies, duplicating supplies, photostats, printing costs, etc.

613 Taxes—other
   Include business activity taxes and licenses (property and payroll taxes are included elsewhere)

614 Taxes—payroll
   Include social security, state unemployment compensation, and federal unemployment

615 Telephone and telegraph

616 Travel and subsistence
   Include depreciation of automobiles, auto repairs, licenses, gas, etc., for cars owned by the firm; cost of auto rentals, carfare, bus, and use of car reimbursements; meals, supper money, hotel, and other nonchargeable travel and subsistence expenses not connected with firm relations, professional development, or professional membership expenses

617 Welfare and group benefits
   Include premiums for group life insurance, Blue Cross, and accident and health plans; cost of social events for employees

NONOPERATING INCOME

700 Other income
   Include gains on sale of assets, investment income, and miscellaneous income

Accounting Statements and Statistics

COMPARATIVE STATEMENT OF INCOME

■ THE PRESENTATION of comparative financial statements brings out more clearly the nature and trends of current changes affecting the practice.

A comparative statement of income, illustrated in Figure 7, is presented for uniform reporting. It is in an annual reporting format, but can be adapted for interim internal reporting. Salaries are shown as a separate category. Operating expenses include a few accounts classified by function and for this reason no breakdown of fixed and variable expenses is made on the income statement. The classification of expenses in this manner has the merit of simplicity because it limits the number of accounts required and provides a uniform basis for reporting by the profession. Firms that wish to prepare breakeven point computations or charts, can determine fixed and variable expenses by account analysis.

It is strongly recommended that financial statements be prepared monthly on the accrual basis that includes unbilled receivables in income.

Figure 7. Comparative Statement of Income

	This Period		Last Period		Increase
Income from Professional Services	$	%	$	%	(decrease)
Auditing	126,332	59.41	106,451	57.44	19,881
Taxes	34,716	16.33	28,693	15.49	6,023
Management and advisory services	9,047	4.25	11,498	6.21	(2,451)
Other accounting services	42,555	20.01	38,673	20.86	3,882
Total	212,650	100.00	185,315	100.00	27,335
Salaries and Outside Services					
Salaries—partners or proprietor	50,400	23.70	48,000	25.90	2,400
Salaries—accounting staff	63,933	30.06	57,649	31.11	6,284
Salaries—other	9,200	4.33	8,800	4.75	400
Outside services	1,300	.61	1,142	.62	158
Total	124,833	58.70	115,591	62.38	9,242
Gross Profit	87,817	41.30	69,724	37.62	18,093
Operating Expenses					
Contributions	300	.14	300	.16	—
Equipment expense	4,239	1.99	3,710	2.00	529
Firm relations	1,406	.66	1,053	.57	353
Insurance	441	.21	354	.19	87
Occupancy and maintenance	7,058	3.32	6,601	3.56	457
Other operating expenses	595	.28	390	.21	205
Postage and express	881	.41	715	.39	166
Professional development	750	.35	559	.30	191
Professional membership expense	1,402	.66	638	.34	764
Provision for doubtful accounts .	225	.11	640	.35	(415)
Publications	1,506	.71	1,659	.90	(153)
Stationery, printing, and supplies	4,053	1.91	3,949	2.13	104
Taxes—other	537	.25	342	.18	195
Taxes—payroll	2,433	1.14	2,020	1.10	413
Telephone and telegraph	2,384	1.12	2,158	1.16	226
Travel and subsistence	2,861	1.35	2,710	1.46	151
Welfare and group benefits	1,926	.91	1,609	.87	317
Total	32,997	15.52	29,407	15.87	3,590
Operating Income	54,820	25.78	40,317	21.75	14,503
Other Income	55	.02	—	—	55
Net Income	54,875	25.80	40,317	21.75	14,558

Ordinarily the statement of income should be prepared in final form by the 10th of the month. Other informational reports (accounts receivable, fees billed summaries, etc.) should also be prepared within that time. One large firm with a number of branches prepares a "quickie" statement of income by the fifth working day after the close of the month in order to give the managing partner an estimate of the profitability of operations for that month to discuss at the monthly partners' meeting.

Some firms use the thirteen-month year and prepare statements at the end of each four-week period. One of the advantages of the four-week period is that the periodic statements are more readily comparable, since each period covers the same number of days and an equal number of Saturdays and Sundays. Even under this method, holidays and vacations within certain periods prevent the statements from being wholly comparable from period to period.

COMPARATIVE BALANCE SHEET

The comparative balance sheet, illustrated in Figure 8, is intended to indicate an appropriate order of arrangement and detail. It can easily be expanded to accommodate other required accounts and still remain a concise and clear presentation. No illustration is presented for changes in partners' capital accounts, although one would be prepared for internal use.

Figure 8. Comparative Balance Sheet

Assets

	Current date		Prior date	
Current Assets	$	%	$	%
Cash in bank and on hand	25,641	26.12	23,745	27.13
Notes receivable	2,000	2.04	—	—
Accounts receivable—current	32,800	33.42	29,100	33.25
Accounts receivable—over 90 days	823	.84	1,450	1.66
Unbilled receivables	20,000	20.38	17,200	19.65
Unbilled expenses	1,800	1.82	1,400	1.60
Total	57,423	58.50	49,150	56.16
Less estimated doubtful accounts	600	.61	1,040	1.19
Total	56,823	57.89	48,110	54.97
Partners' and employees' accounts	869	.89	1,050	1.20
Deposits and prepaid expenses	278	.28	308	.36
Total current assets	83,611	85.18	73,213	83.66
Investments	1,300	1.33	—	—
Fixed Assets				
Leasehold improvements	4,090	4.17	4,090	4.67
Furniture, equipment, and autos	26,592	27.08	24,632	28.15
Library	634	.65	634	.72
Total	31,316	31.90	29,356	33.54
Less accumulated depreciation and amortization	18,073	18.41	15,052	17.20
Total fixed assets	13,243	13.49	14,304	16.34
Total assets	98,154	100.00	87,517	100.00

Liabilities and Capital

	Current date		Prior date	
Current Liabilities				
Notes and loans payable	14,000	14.26	9,000	10.28
Accounts payable	980	1.00	1,250	1.43
Unearned income	4,271	4.35	3,000	3.43
Employee withholdings	748	.76	681	.78
Accrued expenses	605	.62	740	.84
Total current liabilities	20,604	20.99	14,671	16.76
Long-term Debt	—	—	7,500	8.57
Total liabilities	20,604	20.99	22,171	25.33
Capital				
Capital account(s)	77,550	79.01	65,346	74.67
Total liabilities and capital	98,154	100.00	87,517	100.00

MODIFIED STATEMENTS FOR MANAGERIAL USE

While the comparative statements described above are recommended for general use, there are numerous supplementary statistics which can be helpful in the administration of a practice. The following monthly statements are prepared by a six-partner firm with thirty staff men.

Balance sheet. In addition to the balance sheet proper, two tabulations—doubtful accounts receivable, and accounts receivable as a per cent of monthly fees—are inserted at the bottom of the page. The firm does not accrue fees of doubtful collectibility, but a separate ledger is kept on them. The monthly total represents the control on this ledger. By indicating accounts receivable as a per cent of fees, the managing partner can readily see the firm's over-all billing and collection performance. Efforts are made to keep this figure under 400 per cent of monthly fees.

Income statement (monthly and cumulative). Fees earned for the partner, staff, and stenographic groups are entered separately. (A separate sheet contains a breakdown of fees earned by each individual.) This record points out variations from the "desirable result" based on chargeable time. For the purpose of these statements, partner salaries are considered as an operating expense before arriving at net income. At the bottom of the page the following percentage relationships are shown: partners' and staff salaries to partners' and staff fees earned; stenographic salaries to stenographic fees earned; other operating expenses to total fees earned; and net income to total fees earned (see Figure 9).

Rate and time statistics (monthly and cumulative). The following averages or totals are posted vertically, first for partners as a group and then repeated for the staff as a group:

1. Average per diem earned, based on chargeable time and total time.
2. Total chargeable, unassigned, and personal time (including vacations, sick time, etc.) stated in hours. From the total of these three items is deducted the total "standard" time. (Standard time is eight hours per day, Monday through Friday, less holidays. This standard figure is computed each month.)
3. Excess time (overtime) is shown in hours, and also as a percentage of standard, total, chargeable, unassigned, and personal time.

The various components of total time contained in (2) and (3) are shown separately for each individual on supplementary sheets (see Figure 10).

Fees earned, by client. A sheet is maintained for each partner, with the clients assigned to him listed alphabetically down the left side of the page. Each month the fees (at standard rates) and the billing adjustments (differences between standard and actual) are entered as separate figures on the same line. The totals at the bottom of the page indicate the over-all per-diem fees, billing adjustments, and net fees for the month for each partner's clients. This statement, posted from the client ledger at the time the monthly entries are made,

Figure 9. Income Statement

INCOME STATEMENTS - CUMULATIVE 1958	1958 Budget	Prior Year	January	April
INCOME - FEES EARNED (at per diem rates)				
Partners	96 000 -	95 192 50	8 080 -	29 147 50
Staff	282 000 -	262 155 50	23 771 -	101 785 -
Stenos	12 000 -	11 454 -	706 -	3 425 -
Sub-Total	390 000 -	368 802 -	32 557 -	134 357 50
Prior Year's			28 811 50	121 021 50
Per diem adjustments		(12 389 71)		(1 935 68)
Doubtful items		(3 738 10)		2 350 93
Miscellaneous				
Total Income	390 000 -	352 674 19	32 557 -	134 772 75
Prior Year's			28 811 50	121 312 62
OPERATING EXPENSES				
Salaries - Partners	84 000 -	84 000 -	7 000 -	28 000 -
Staff	130 000 -	116 274 30	10 235 -	42 268 19
Stenos	25 000 -	24 427 04	2 065 07	8 185 07
Total Salaries	239 000 -	224 701 34	19 300 07	78 453 26
Office rent	16 800 -	15 099 15	1 391 10	5 564 40
Office supplies and repairs	8 000 -	7 995 13	97 80	2 087 36
Telephone, telegraph and postage	4 000 -	4 222 99	40 40	1 273 59
Dues and subscriptions	5 500 -	5 375 92	100 -	2 401 21
Travel and meals	2 800 -	2 710 -	75 45	664 38
Entertainment, gifts and flowers	2 200 -	2 130 33		815 70
Taxes	3 000 -	2 931 43	129 90	999 93
Insurance	1 000 -	1 093 63		1 281 55
Professional activities	8 000 -	13 984 29	1 543 75	3 362 83
Depreciation	4 000 -	3 802 41		
Miscellaneous	3 000 -	2 825 39	34 69	623 25
Contributions	700 -	615 50		581 -
Employees' bonuses	10 000 -	7 000 -		
Total Expenses Other Than Salaries	69 000 -	69 786 17	3 413 09	19 655 20
Total Operating Expenses	308 000 -	294 487 51	22 713 16	98 108 46
Prior Year's			20 355 36	87 389 45
NET INCOME - Current Year	82 000 -	58 186 68	9 843 84	36 664 29
Net Income - Prior Year			8 456 14	33 923 17
STATISTICAL - As a % of Fees Earned				
Partners' and staff salaries to partners' and staff fees earned			54 11	53 67
Steno salaries to steno fees earned			292 50	238 98
Other operating expenses			10 48	14 63
Net income			30 24	27 29

provides the managing partner with a good deal of information about the performance of each client and each partner. The source of excessive variations from the desirable fee are evident, and action can be taken to determine the reasons for the variations. Income analysis to determine the relative fee value of various clients can easily be undertaken.

As can be seen from the description of these records, there is some duplication of information. Other records could probably be combined on a single page. However, the managing partner finds it easier to deal with specific items if they are listed separately. Some of the material is not reviewed unless the summary indicates trouble areas, but the information is there when needed.

Figure 10. Accountants' Statistics

Figure 10. Accountants' Statistics

ACCOUNTANTS' STATISTICS - CUMULATIVE 1958	January		April		May	June
PARTNERS						
Average per diem earned by partners based on:						
Chargeable time	127	87	124	10		
Total time	56	85	55	90		
Stated in hours:						
Chargeable time	505	½	1 879			
Unassigned time	607	½	2 190	½		
Personal time	24		102			
Total Time	1 137		4 171	½		
Less - Standard time	1 104		4 101			
Excess Time*	33		70	½		
As a % of total time:						
Chargeable time	44	46	45	04		
Unassigned time	53	43	52	51		
Personal time	2	11	2	45		
Excess time as a % of standard time	2	99	1	72		
STAFF						
Average per diem earned by staff based on:						
Chargeable time	66	15	67	76		
Total time	49	67	55	82		
Stated in hours:						
Chargeable time	2 875		12 017	½		
Unassigned time	780	½	1 917			
Personal time	173		652	½		
Total Time	3 828	½	14 587			
Less - Standard time	3 738		14 049			
Excess Time	90	½	538			
As a % of total time:						
Chargeable time	75	09	82	39		
Unassigned time	20	39	13	14		
Personal time	4	52	4	47		
Excess time as a % of standard time	2	42	3	83		

*Overtime

SOME USEFUL STATISTICS

Another firm, consisting of two partners, ten to fourteen staff men, and two to three clerical employees, compiles some additional statistics for managerial use:

Engagement cost is the first function of our accounting system. It is nothing more than an individual job cost system.

For a staff accountant whose base annual salary is $6,000 per year, we expect his total annual duty hours will equal 2,132 hours or 41 hours per week. We simply use 120 per cent, which is $7,200 divided by 2,132 hours;

this gives $3.37 per hour, or in multiples of 20 cents, $3.40 per hour. It has been our experience that the 120 per cent factor is adequate to absorb the actual productive, chargeable time which we expect an employee to normally charge to engagements.

Everyone's time, including partners' time, is accounted for in this manner. If time is actually spent on an engagement but is not of a quality to warrant charging it to the client, such time becomes nonproductive engagement time and does not enter into our engagement time and cost records.

Experience has taught us that as staff members become more experienced, they can better utilize their total duty time; so we set standards for each class of staff member.

Class of service analysis. For each class of service rendered (auditing and accounting, income tax preparation, etc.) we prepare the following comparative analysis:

1. Percentage of gross profit to fees
2. Percentage of the total of gross fees
3. Percentage of the total of gross profit
4. Fees billed per engagement hour
5. Cost per engagement hour, based on standard cost
6. Gross profit per engagement hour, based on standard cost
7. Total engagement hours
8. Percentage of total engagement hours
9. Engagement hours per $1,000 of fees
10. Engagement hours per $1,000 of cost
11. Engagement hours per $1,000 of gross profit

Staff income and production data. We believe we should know who actually produces our fees. Consequently, we maintain what we term a Nonengagement Cost Account on each staff member. On this ledger sheet we also maintain statistical information relative to engagement hours, non-engagement hours, engagement hour cost and fee credits.

If a fee is written up or down solely because of the quality of work performed by a staff member, his fee income credits are either increased or reduced. If a write-up or write-down is made for any other reason, it is charged or credited to firm income.

When we compute gross profit produced by a staff member, we abandon the "Standard Cost" theory and compute his cost at actual annual total salary cost. We discuss quite freely and frankly with the staff member his production of fees and his profitability to the firm. Table 1 contains most of the information which is essential as a historical guide toward obtaining more and better quality engagement hours out of a staff member's total annual duty hours. Although the illustration shows only the data for two men, the actual tabulation covers the entire staff including partners.

As stated earlier, we set for each staff member a standard per-hour fee range. From the information contained in Table 1, we know by individual staff member and by class of staff how much, on the average, we actually billed our clients. In Table 2, the hourly fee rates which we hoped we could charge would appear in brackets beside the actual average rates billed.

Table I. Staff Income and Production Data

Fiscal Year Ended October 31, 1958

	1958-59 standard	Standard hr. fee rate	Actual hr. fee rate	Fees billed	Annual total salary cost	Gross profit
Adam Jones .	$8.75	$8.00	$7.96	16,000	9,000	7,000
Henry Smith .	8.25	7.50	7.68	14,000	8,000	6,000
Total—1958		$7.75	$7.82	30,000	17,000	13,000
Total—1957		$7.50	$7.13	42,000	25,000	17,000

	Profit percentage	Standard engagement hours	Actual engagement hours	Non-engagement hours	Total duty hours	Average work week
Adam Jones	43%	2,000 82%	1,970 83%	400 17%	2,370 100%	46 hr.
Henry Smith	43%	1,900 82%	1,890 81%	450 19%	2,340 100%	45 hr.
Total—1958	43%	3,900 82%	3,860 82%	850 18%	4,710 100%	
Total—1957	40%	6,200 82%	5,900 78%	1,650 22%	7,550 100%	

Table 2. Staff Income and Production Data

Fiscal Years Ended October 31, 1958 and 1957

Gross Fees	Hourly fee rate 1958		1957		Total fees billed 1958	1957	Increase (decrease)
Senior staff	(x.xx)	x.xx	(x.xx)	x.xx	xx,xxx.xx	xx,xxx.xx	(xx,xxx.xx)
Semi-senior staff ..	(x.xx)	x.xx	(x.xx)	x.xx	xx,xxx.xx	xx,xxx.xx	(xxx.xx)
Income tax staff (trainee)	(x.xx)	x.xx	(x.xx)	x.xx	x,xxx.xx	x,xxx.xx	xxx.xx
Junior staff	(x.xx)	x.xx	(x.xx)	x.xx	x,xxx.xx	xx,xxx.xx	(x,xxx.xx)
Accounting service staff	(x.xx)	x.xx	(x.xx)	x.xx	xx,xxx.xx	xx,xxx.xx	(xx,xxx.xx)
Terminated staff ..	(x.xx)	x.xx	(x.xx)	x.xx	x,xxx.xx	x,xxx.xx	x,xxx.xx
Stenographic staff .	(x.xx)	x.xx	(x.xx)	x.xx	x,xxx.xx	xx,xxx.xx	(x,xxx.xx)
Staff director	(x.xx)	x.xx	(x.xx)	x.xx	xx,xxx.xx	x,xxx.xx	x,xxx.xx
Total staff		x.xx		x.xx	xxx,xxx.xx	xxx,xxx.xx	(xx,xxx.xx)
Partners and firm .	(xx.xx)	xx.xx	(xx.xx)	xx.xx	xx,xxx.xx	xx,xxx.xx	x,xxx.xx
Total		x.xx		x.xx	xxx,xxx.xx	xxx,xxx.xx	(xx,xxx.xx)

Percentage of Gross Fees			
Senior staff	20%	24%	(4%)
Semi-senior staff	16	15	1
Income tax staff (trainee)	6	5	1
Junior staff	5	6	(1)
Accounting service staff	8	18	(10)
Terminated staff	6	2	4
Stenographic staff	6	8	(2)
Staff director	8	5	3
Total staff	75%	83%	(8%)
Partners and firm	25	17	8
Total	100%	100%	

Again using our basic information set forth before, we can determine by class of staff who produces the gross profit. Attention is again directed to the fact that staff cost in this instance is annual total salary cost whereas partners' cost is on a predetermined fixed fee per engagement hour. Our gross profit by class is set forth in a schedule showing the gross profit rate per engagement hour and total gross profit for the current and prior years. The percentage of gross profit contributed by each class of staff is also included on a comparative basis.

Other information such as the following may be obtained simply by recasting information heretofore set forth:

1. Engagement hours as a percentage of total hours by class of staff
2. Staff time in man years (2,132 hours based on 41 hours per week)
3. Percentage of staff engagement time to total duty time

Evaluating the data. Our standard costing procedures do not absorb the whole of our annual total salary costs into our engagement costs. We think this is proper inasmuch as we do not believe that an engagement should be charged for all of our costs of a staff member's idle time, vacation time, sick time, research time, coffee time, and other nonproductive time.

This unabsorbed salary cost (amounts are assumed) is analyzed as follows:

Annual total salary costs	$74,000	100%
Unabsorbed annual salary costs	16,000	21
Staff salary costs in standard engagement costs	58,000	79%
Partners' standard engagement costs	9,500	
Total standard engagement costs	$67,500	

Based on the over-all average, we had hoped that 73 per cent of all staff duty time would be chargeable to engagements. As it turned out, 70 per cent of all staff duty time was charged to engagements. This proves to us that our standard costing is reasonably accurate since we find that we did absorb into engagement costs 79 per cent of the annual total staff salary costs.

Perhaps a better analysis of this would be to eliminate the stenographic staff time from the total base. We can easily do that in the following manner:

	Staff account- ants	Steno- graphic	Total
Annual total salary costs	64,000	10,000	74,000
Unabsorbed annual salary costs	9,800	6,200	16,000
Staff salary costs in standard engagement costs	54,200	3,800	58,000
Percentage of total	84%	38%	78%

We had expected to have, on the average, 82 per cent of all staff accountants' time charged to engagement cost. We actually had 76 per cent of their time so charged. Dollarwise our system charged 84 per cent of their total salary costs into engagements. This again proves to us that our costing formula is within reasonable bounds of accuracy.

This also tells us that we have an overhead cost of $16,000 for unabsorbed staff time which is equal to 81¢ for each staff engagement hour or 72¢ per hour based on total engagement hours. When this is added to our other overhead costs, we then have $1.92 overhead rate for each engagement hour of work.

It also points up the fact that we render write-up work services solely for the convenience of the client. Our average hourly rate of gross profit for this type of service was $1.98, and our overhead cost was $1.92, leaving only 6¢ per hour of profit. For our own use we prepare an income statement in the form shown in Table 3.

No doubt there will be those who will initially say the system is too detailed, too complicated, too costly, and is not feasible or desirable. It is in fact quite simple and very inexpensive.

We believe we have a fair idea of what we are doing and how we are treating our clients relative to fees. This system has pointed out to us various deficiencies in our fee policies. It points up inefficiencies in the utilization of our own and staff time. It points up vividly the efficiency or inefficiency of certain staff members. It enables us to evaluate our personnel.

Table 3. Income Statement

	Staff	Partners and firm	1957-58 Total	1956-57 Total
Income				
Fees	XXX,XXX.XX	XX,XXX.XX	XXX,XXX.XX	XXX,XXX.XX
Direct Costs				
Annual total staff salary costs ..	XX,XXX.XX	X,XXX.XX	XX,XXX.XX	XXX,XXX.XX
Less: Unabsorbed salary costs .	XX,XXX.XX		XX,XXX.XX	XX,XXX.XX
	XX,XXX.XX	X,XXX.XX	XX,XXX.XX	XX,XXX.XX
Gross Profit	XX,XXX.XX	XX,XXX.XX	XX,XXX.XX	XX,XXX.XX
Expenses				
Unabsorbed salary costs			XX,XXX.XX	XX,XXX.XX
All other expenses			XX,XXX.XX	XX,XXX.XX
			XX,XXX.XX	XX,XXX.XX
Profit			XX,XXX.XX	XX,XXX.XX
Add: Partners' engagement			X,XXX.XX	X,XXX.XX
Time charges				
Partners' Profit			XX,XXX.XX	XX,XXX.XX

ANALYSIS OF VARIANCES

One practitioner incorporates in his firm's engagement sheets a time-cost budget which facilitates a monthly analysis of all substantial variances from standard.

One group of variances is considered to be attributable to either good or bad performance in planning or executing the work. This group includes:

1. Insufficient familiarity with the job

2. Too high-grade a man on the job
3. Too low-grade a man on the job
4. Time gained from unusual smoothness of the job
5. Time lost from errors or carelessness on the job
6. Time lost from physical or mental condition of the man given the assignment
7. Reviewer's time lost from changing or correcting the original accountant's work
8. Time lost in the typing department

A second group of variances is not chargeable to performance by the accounting organization but simply to unfortunate circumstances the results of which necessarily have to be absorbed and cannot be charged to the client. Among such circumstances are interference on the job; starting before the client is ready; poor working conditions; unforeseeable interruptions or delays; and others of this general character.

A third group of variances is imputed to the job itself. These are chargeable to the client. Typical of such variances are:

1. Budgetary estimate too high or too low
2. Extra work requested that was not allowed for in the budget
3. Combining more than one period's work
4. Unusually good bookkeeping by client's staff (hence a lower bill)
5. Unusually bad bookkeeping by client's staff (sometimes requiring part of the bookkeeping to be done by the accounting firm)

Methods of Accounting

CASH VERSUS ACCRUAL BASIS

■ THE BOOKS AND RECORDS maintained by an accounting firm do not differ materially from those of any other business organization. From a general accounting standpoint, it is of course preferable that the books be kept on the accrual basis. Distorted results can frequently be produced by the cash method because the fees billed and collected are not necessarily matched with related costs and expenses. It is quite possible that the expenses of an unusually large engagement may be incurred in a period of low cash receipts, and the fee for the engagement collected in a later period when offsetting deductions are abnormally low. The results produced by the accrual method furnish more reliable data on which to make accurate determinations and to base decisions.

If the tax effects, for one reason or another, pose an obstacle to changing from cash to accrual accounting, the firm's *internal financial reporting* statements and schedules should nevertheless be based on accrual accounting. The reasons for preparing financial statements on the accrual basis are exactly the same as those pointed out to clients in order to convince them of the wisdom of using the accrual method. The budgeting of income and expenses and other statistical internal reporting are predicated on accrual accounting.

As to the frequency of use of the cash and accrual bases, the results of a recent survey are shown on page 718.

Should unbilled services be included in fees? Some accountants exclude unbilled services from income, even when on the accrual basis, because they regard work in process as inventory. However, others believe with considerable logic that as services are performed they are in reality sold. In his *Accounting Concepts of Profit,* Stephen Gilman expresses this view when he draws the following analogy: "by . . . common consent the rendering of service is assumed to result in a contractual relationship somewhat similar to the delivery of goods." No one will deny that *services are the stock in trade of a practitioner.* It follows then that as services are performed they are in fact sold. For those firms on the accrual method that do not accrue income from services until billed, all costs incurred on unbilled jobs should be set up as a deferred charge if rational results are to be obtained.

Cash basis. Years ago most accountants kept their records on a cash basis. There were probably many considerations that led them to adopt this method. The two main reasons for using the cash method today, however, are its tax advantages and its apparent simplicity. Some accountants believe that these merits fully outweigh any substantial argument against its use. There is no doubt that the cash basis of accounting is used by many individual practitioners and firms because its use delays the date on which taxable income accrues. Nevertheless, many accountants feel that this reason is not sufficient to justify the maintenance of records that are deficient in material respects.

There is a tendency for new firms to use the cash method of accounting in preparing their financial statements. Basing financial statements on accrual accounting is especially important to new firms, because it provides them with a better management tool when they may need it the most.

Hybrid basis. Various combinations of cash and accrual accounting are found in practice. Hybrid accounting methods generally develop as the practice grows in order to relate certain income or costs to the period in which they are applicable. The likelihood is that many small- and medium-sized firms use some form of combination cash and accrual basis.

Accrual basis. The accrual method is almost a necessity with a large firm or with a firm having a large number of partners. It offers the maximum advantage from a management viewpoint of permitting quick and accurate determination of income and expense, the key to determining profitability. Further, the accrual method renders it possible to obtain statistical information necessary to manage the firm's activities. It is especially desirable in situations in which profit-sharing bonuses are computed.

In J. K. Lasser's *Standard Handbook for Accountants* (McGraw-Hill Book Co., New York, 1956) the advantages of recording charges on the accrual basis are listed as follows: (1) the progress of the engagement may be readily measured by comparison of charges with estimates prepared in advance; (2) comparison of fees earned from month to month and year to year, indicating trends in the progress of the practice, are available; (3) in seeking credit the accumulated value of unbilled receivables, a definite asset, appears in the records; and (4) no other method furnishes such accurate information regarding income and profits.

Two questions of treatment that would not occur under the cash basis of accounting arise with regard to the accrual method. The first concerns the treatment to be accorded income when an engagement is accepted on a fixed fee basis. In this circumstance it is advisable to accumulate income on the basis of the estimated percentage of completion. Where the percentage of completion is very difficult to estimate, however, it may be more practical to accumulate income (at standard rates, if they are employed) up to the amount of the fixed fee, and then to write off the excess as incurred.

The second question concerns the accounting for contingent fees resulting from tax engagements. Obviously, the accrual method is not adaptable in this circumstance. Probably the best method is to accumulate income in a separate account at per-diem rates.

Whether or not an allowance or a writeoff should be provided would depend on the circumstances; in any event sound judgment must be used.

Converting from cash to accrual basis. Methods presently used by practitioners to convert from cash to accrual basis include the following:

1. Journal entry
2. Supplementary ledger giving effect to accrual basis entries
3. Two entirely complete ledgers—one on the cash basis and the other on the accrual basis
4. Separate columns in the general ledger, one for cash basis, the other for accrual basis entries
5. Accrual accounts in the ledger which are disregarded for reporting on the cash basis (usually only unbilled services are accrued under this method)
6. Worksheet

As a cautionary note, it appears that the work sheet is the most satisfactory method of converting from the cash to the accrual basis for internal reporting. In a well-noted tax case (*J. C. Patchen*, 258 F. 2d, 544, Rev'g 27 TC 592), the Commissioner required a partnership that changed its bookkeeping method in 1948 from the cash to the accrual basis but continued to use the cash method for tax purposes, to change to the accrual method for tax purposes, under a provision of the law [1939 Code sec. 41, similar to 1954 Code sec. 446(a), (b)] that a taxpayer must report income in accordance with the accounting method *regularly employed* in keeping its books. The Tax Court agreed. The 5th Circuit, U.S. Court of Appeals, reversed the decision of the Tax Court and held that the Commissioner had no power to require computation of distributable partnership income on the accrual basis since the books accurately reflected the income on the cash basis after recognized accounting adjustments were made. However, the Commissioner has not acquiesced.

Formula for conversion of income. The following formula can be used to convert income from the cash to the accrual basis:

1. Collections. This is the starting figure.
2. Change in receivables. Subtract beginning accounts receivable and add ending accounts receivable.
3. Change in unbilled receivables (work in process). Subtract beginning unbilled receivables and add ending unbilled receivables.

Unbilled services should be evaluated at standard billing rates or at an average billing rate. For simplicity in making the computation, it is suggested that an over-all standard rate based on experience be used in determining unbilled services.

THE NATURAL BUSINESS YEAR

Selection of an annual accounting period other than the calendar year is strongly recommended for businesses that display evident seasonal fluctuations in activity, as does the public accounting profession. The Natural Business Year Council defines the natural business year as the annual period which ends when the business activities of the enterprise have reached the lowest point in their annual cycle. Accountants have been recommending the adoption of a natural business year by indicating, as an important advantage of such adoption, the probability of more complete and reliable financial statements, since at the close of the natural business year incomplete transactions would ordinarily be at a minimum.

A large percentage of practitioners and firms recommend fiscal years ending between June 30 and September 30. Of course, current federal and state requirements must be considered in establishing a fiscal year.

THE USE OF BUDGETS

It would appear that only a minority of accounting firms use money budgets. The reasons given for not using such a budget are: (1) conditions fluctuate too much to make ordinary budgeting practical, and (2) the benefits derived do not compensate for the time consumed in constructing the budget. Large, unexpected tax fees and special fees can distort revenue estimates. Also, it is difficult to predict staff salaries because the need for additional men cannot be predicted without a better long-term knowledge than is available as to how audit engagements will flow. Previous attempts at budgeting have left some firms unconvinced as to the value of so doing. One firm experienced a 45 per cent overestimate in net profits for one year. It is ironical that these same accountants who serve clients in preparing budgets claim that budgeting is more feasible and more beneficial to industrial business than to those engaged in professions. This is especially true with functional budgeting, where each department, even including some of the junior employees, assumes a proportionate responsibility for accuracy in estimating. They hold that, with practicing accountants, there are other ways to watch and control costs and efficiency, such as work forecasts (budgeting of personnel). They feel this is closer to the CPA's needs, gets to the core of his real planning problem, and can be adjusted easily if done at sufficiently frequent intervals. In actuality, according to this argument, personnel budgets are indirectly money budgets in their significant phases, and they take relatively little time to prepare.

One medium-sized firm, which makes quarterly work forecasts, also prepares a corresponding revenue budget of "repeat business," and measures those computations against the anticipated salaries related to this business. This encompasses the whole or any part of "repeat" annual or semiannual engagements falling within the quarter. It includes no part of known extra audit or tax fees, or related handling charges. Statistics are maintained and studied, the dual objective being to satisfy considerations of financing and economy and also to encourage, first, the conversion of as much business as possible to the "repeat" category, and second, the change-over of as many as possible of clients' closing periods from a calendar year to a natural fiscal year. The firm prepares and studies monthly financial and income statements, which show cumulative revenues and expenses. It deems that this, together with its "repeat business" budget, constitutes adequate surveillance.

"You cannot really control costs," says the managing partner of a six-partner firm with thirty staff men. He feels that the function of management in an accounting office is to control gross income so that it will cover costs.

Once the necessary staff is hired, this man holds, costs are fairly well established. The payroll must be met; rent and telephone bills must be paid. Although people can be laid off and office space reduced, there are certain continuing, fixed overhead expenses vital to the operation of the practice.

On the other hand, except for special work, gross income usually consists of rates for time, which must be extended, billed, and collected. The gross is therefore achieved by control of time and billing rates in order to make the available time as productive as possible. In addition, collectibility requires some machinery to prevent a client from being surprised by a bill.

This firm, unlike many in the profession, prepares an annual budget. It is based on an anticipated 1,400 productive hours for each individual (except the managing partner) at his established rate. In practice, some staff members put in more time; others, especially juniors and partners, may put in less. The more mature person usually has more productive time since he does not need as much instruction and supervision.

The per-diem billing rate used for each individual is one per cent of his annual salary, with his rate automatically increasing to the nearest dollar when his salary is increased. Although the rates of the partners are more arbitrary, they are based on one per cent of a presumed salary. These rates are predicated on the assumption that salary cost per productive hour should not exceed 50 per cent of gross fees. The per-diem billing rate of one per cent of annual salary results in salaries being 50 per cent of gross fees, based on an assigned 200 chargeable days per man per year. This rate goes into the books, which are kept on an accrual basis, as the basic amount which should be recovered from the client. Although this type of dollar-time budget may be considered a rough estimate (the operating results are actually within 10 per cent of the budget), this firm finds it helpful for these reasons:

1. It can determine whether the estimated income is satisfactory in relation to the estimated costs.

2. It guides the firm in scheduling or deferring special additional expenses.

3. It indicates whether the over-all fee structure is satisfactory in relation to costs, or whether adjustments are needed.

4. It permits the firm, by comparing available time for the current year to the time used in serving regular clients during the previous year, to estimate the amount of time left free for special work. The firm can also plan in advance a schedule for hiring and training new men so they will be ready when needed.

ALLOCATING COSTS

One practitioner provides a method of allocating costs to each job which is not necessarily tied into the firm's general books. He suggests the method of analysis and allocation, and sets up an expense budget and distribution. He recognizes the differences between departments (for example, audit and tax departments) and says that only by doing so can a cost system yield accurate information. These differences may take the form of differences in pay scales, hours chargeable to clients, working space, and other overhead costs. The following is a condensation of his recommendations:

Set up predetermined costs and rates annually, semiannually, quarterly, or monthly. Because the annual basis is more real than a shorter period and requires less work, he favors the annual basis.

The first step, then, is to estimate the expenses for the ensuing fiscal year (ignoring expenses chargeable to clients). The ultimate goal is to distribute total estimated expenses to each classification of direct workers, such as tax partner, juniors on audit staff, and stenographers, to determine the cost rate for each classification. This rate is then applied to hours recorded on each engagement for each classification of direct workers. This will yield costs of jobs.

At least two ways of estimating or budgeting expenses are possible. The first is based on past history. Using last year's expenses, a factor is applied to bring them to what is believed they will amount to during the current year. The second is based on the future and involves estimating the number of hours required in each direct worker classification (partners, seniors, and juniors) on each planned engagement. This, together with an estimate of new business, should be consolidated in a "production" budget expressed in terms of hours.

Charts should be set up and a summary made of the procedures to get cost rates and job costs. The charts help materially to understand the procedures quickly. The procedures are:

1. Estimate the expenses for the period.
2. Distribute the expenses to all departments, direct and indirect.
3. Distribute the expenses of the indirect departments to the direct departments.
4. Distribute the expenses of the direct departments to each direct worker classification within each department.
5. Estimate chargeable hours in each direct worker classification for the period.
6. Divide total expenses of each direct worker classification by estimated chargeable hours to get the cost rate.
7. Accumulate the hours in each direct worker classification on job sheets, multiply each total by the cost rate, and add the out-of-pocket expenses to get the costs of the various engagements.

The results expressed in the job sheet show whether the fee for the engagement was adequate. But the sheet should be put to further uses: first, as a means of control of costs; second, as a means of appraisal of individual efficiency; and third, perhaps as a means of profit-sharing arrangement.

Some bases used in prorating expenses may not be strictly logical, and may be chosen because the data are easier to obtain.

Using few bases rather than many facilitates the work of distributing the expenses to departments and direct worker classifications. Short cuts can be used provided the resulting error is small. The margin of this error should be determined and kept in mind.

Many firms believe that such refinements of internal accounting provide interesting exercises in costing principles but are unnecessary and not sufficiently beneficial to be worth while. However, simple but effective departmental statements can be prepared on a basis of charging salary costs directly to departments and allocating other expenses on the basis of productive mandays in each department.

For an illustration of the use of standard costs, see "Some Useful Statistics," pages 703-707.

Costing the proprietor's salary. Proprietors' or partners' salaries should be established in order to indicate a cost factor in producing income from services. Practitioners encountering the problem of stating salaries and evaluating the cost of their services to the firm should consider one of the following three suggested methods:

1. *Individual evaluation.* The practitioner or partners place an arbitrary value for services to the practice or firm. Examples of minimum salaries:
    (a) Practitioner starting a new practice: For the first year use salary received on prior job; thereafter, methods 2 or 3 following, but not less than first year's figure.
    (b) Established practitioner with staff: Use a minimum equal to the salary of the highest paid senior or manager.

2. *Billing rate*. Salary equal to one-third of the billing rate based on estimated total hours (chargeable and nonchargeable) for the year is
assigned.

> Example: A total of 2,100 hours is estimated for the year; billing
> rate, $20:
>
> > 2,100 hours × $20 .... $42,000
> > 1/3 × $42,000 .... $14,000

3. *Standard formula*. Multiply the billing rate by 2,000 hours and take
40% of the result.

> Example: The billing rate is $20:
>
> > 2,000 hours × $20 .... $40,000
> > 40% × $40,000 ...... $16,000

Chargeable time alone ordinarily cannot be a criterion on which to base a
minimum salary because it is misleading in that it may not indicate the value
of the services to the practice or firm. The standard formula provided in
method 3 should prove to be satisfactory in the majority of cases where
salaries have not been previously established.

A Survey of Accountants' Expenses

OBJECTIVES OF THE SURVEY

■ THE PURPOSE of the following presentation is to enable the practicing CPA
to compare his major expense items with those of other CPAs who are practicing under similar circumstances.

Every practitioner is aware that a fee for professional services must not
only recover the costs directly attributable to the engagement, but must also
cover a portion of the accounting firm's overhead expenses. Consequently, the
relationship between fees and costs is important in establishing the degree of
financial success which individual practitioners or partners can expect from
their practices. Moreover, since expenses form the basis for computing the
overhead factor in the hourly or per-diem rates, they affect the amount of
revenue derived from fees, as well as the net results.

No two accounting firms, of course, are exactly alike. Any analysis of an
accounting firm's total costs must recognize these inevitable differences. Accordingly, in designing the survey care was taken to isolate the variations in
accounting practices which might directly affect the results.

One point must be heavily underscored. This analysis is concerned solely
with out-of-pocket expenses. It does not cover the time devoted to various
aspects of a practice. The decision to exclude time costs was dictated in part

by the difficulty of measuring such costs and by the wide variations among firms in their methods of computing them. Nonetheless, if this omission is not kept in mind, the results may prove misleading. The financial investment in supplementary professional training, for example, may appear deplorably low—and, in fact, it may be far too low in comparison with the amount invested by other professions—but the dollars-and-cents contribution to this area of accounting practice is not a realistic measure of the costs of professional development. The major expense, of course, would have to be stated in terms of time.

The highlights uncovered in the survey, and variations which exist among different size offices in cities of varying population are briefly discussed in the following pages. The Appendix includes a table showing the median and middle 50% ranges for each expense (page 918).

No practitioner can expect that his expenses will be identical with the "typical" response of his group for every item of cost. Nor does the fact that the typical office within each group shows a certain distribution of expenses mean that this situation is ideal.

However, the practicing accountant can be guided by the pattern existing among offices of similar size. By comparing his net income percentage to his group, he has a gauge of the relative profitability of his office. Even if his net income compares favorably, he should examine his major expenses in the light of those of his colleagues. Some expenses may vary widely from the middle 50 per cent range, and still be satisfactory under the circumstances. But where this situation exists, the practitioner naturally should attempt to uncover the reasons for the differences. For example, an unusually low salary expense may indicate comparatively low staff compensation, or the firm may be employing lower quality personnel than is generally found in firms of comparable size.

By using these patterns of existing practice as a frame of reference, the initial steps in effective cost control can be undertaken by individual offices. This helps insure that fees are based on costs which are fair to the client and yet yield the return needed for the firm to maintain a sound financial position and provide adequate compensation to the partners and the staff.

METHOD OF SURVEY

Before summarizing the results, a word about the methods used: A questionnaire was mailed at the end of 1958 to a nationwide random sample of 3,300 offices of local and regional firms represented in the AICPA's membership. National firms were not included because the practice of these firms in centralizing some activities, in apportioning certain expenses among branch offices, and in using various methods to determine office income based on interoffice billings would have distorted the results.

The questionnaire sought information on the major or commonly used expense classifications within each of the four functional categories:

1. Staff compensation and other direct labor costs
2. Professional development

3. Client and public relations
4. Office and administrative expenses

Supplementary information on net income and fee production of partners, professional, and clerical staffs was also requested.

There were 1,046 usable replies. They include about 10 per cent of all the firms represented in the membership of the AICPA. As nearly as can be determined, the number of respondent firms within each major size classification was in rough proportion to their distribution within the membership.

In an effort to determine the significance of variations that might be traceable to geographic regions or other factors, preliminary analysis was made of basic groups within each of these classifications. No significant differences existed among the regional areas, other factors being similar. Wide fluctuations appeared among offices in the different gross-fee classifications. Gross fees are of course dependent on the number of personnel but variations appeared to be more closely correlated with office size than the actual amount of fees. The population of the community in which respondents are located appeared to have some significance in certain respects. Accordingly, the summary analyses were made on the basis of office and community size.

FINDINGS OF THE SURVEY

Cash versus accrual basis. Evidently the great majority of firms feel that the advantage of paying income taxes only on cash received outweighs the more accurate portrayal of the financial condition of the practice which results from the accrual basis of accounting, for 73 per cent of the offices keep their books on a cash basis. It is true that some firms maintain their records on both bases, but the extent of this practice was not determined. However, there is a greater tendency for the larger firms to employ the accrual method. Table 4 shows the distribution of the cash, accrual, and hybrid bases of accounting among offices of different sizes.

Fee production. *Partners and individual practitioners.* The percentage of gross fees attributable to the personal production of partners or practitioners varies widely according to composition of the organization, ratio of staff to principals, and total personnel in the office.

However, even in the largest offices, the chargeable time of partners is a significant part of gross income. The smallest percentage is found in offices with more than six partners in cities of over a half-million population. Here the median contribution to gross fees is about 20 per cent, with somewhat larger percentages occurring in those few offices of this size found in smaller cities.

At the other end of the scale is the individual practitioner without any full-time professional staff whose income is entirely, or almost entirely, derived from his personal fees. Individual practitioners with from one to four staff accountants personally contribute from 45 to 50 per cent of the fees and there appears to be no relation to the size of the community in this instance.

Table 4. Accounting Basis According to Size of Office

Size of office	Accounting basis		
	Cash	Accrual	Hybrid
Sole practitioner (no staff)	88.4%	9.1%	2.5%
Sole practitioner (1 to 4 staff)	79.7	17.5	2.8
Sole practitioner (5 or more staff)	79.5	20.5	—
Two/three partners (less than 5 staff)	72.6	23.0	4.4
Two/three partners (5 or more staff)	56.8	36.3	6.9
Four/six partners (less than 20 staff)	43.3	44.8	11.9
Four/six partners (20 or more staff)	33.3	53.4	13.3
Over six partners (less than 20 staff)	33.3	50.0	16.7
Over six partners (20 or more staff)	25.0	68.8	6.2
Total all offices	73.5%	22.2%	4.3%

Partners in two- or three-partner offices account for a median of 65 per cent of the fees where fewer than five staff men are employed and 35 per cent of the fees in offices with five or more accountant employees. The partners' contribution of the latter group generally runs slightly less than the median in the larger cities. However, this may be due more to variations in the size of staff than to community population.

In the four- to six-partner offices, those with less than twenty staff men have a median contribution to fees by partners of 54 per cent, with somewhat less than 30 per cent representing the median for such firms with larger staffs.

Staff accountants. Naturally the percentage fee production of staff accountants is roughly inversely proportional to the productivity of the partners. Perhaps the most significant feature here is the relationship between staff salaries and staff billings. Most firms feel that the billing rate for a staff accountant should be at least twice his direct salary cost, and many believe it should be higher. Yet, many of the respondents to this survey indicate that the fees produced by their staff accountants are less than double the salary costs (see Figure 12). Although there are a number of exceptions in all groups of offices, only the larger firms in the larger cities consistently were able to keep their staff salary costs at or below 50 per cent of staff fees produced. The general pattern seems to be for staff salary costs to run approximately 55 per cent of the fees for staff services.

This suggests that fees for staff members in general may be too low in relation to their salaries, that the staff may not be utilized to optimum advantage, or a combination of the two.

Office and clerical assistants. Although the nonprofessional staff of an accounting office usually is not a direct producer of substantial fees, there appears to be a continuing trend to bill clients directly for some of the services performed by these employees.

Until recent years, the salaries of general office employees were considered to be strictly an overhead item by many firms. However, studies conducted by several state societies have shown that somewhat over half the firms made some charge for certain nonprofessional work. This survey indicates that over three-quarters of the offices in most of the size classifications now have some such arrangement. Usually, these billings enable the firms to recover 60 per cent or more of all nonprofessional salary costs.

The fee contribution of clerical services, such as typing reports, handling

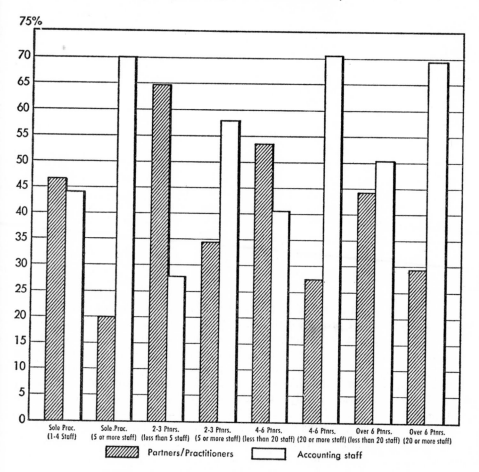

Figure II. Median Fees Billed for Principals and Accounting Staff
(as a percentage of total office fees)

Sole Proc. (1-4 Staff) — Sole Proc. (5 or more staff) — 2-3 Ptnrs. (less than 5 staff) — 2-3 Ptnrs. (5 or more staff) — 4-6 Ptnrs. (less than 20 staff) — 4-6 Ptnrs. (20 or more staff) — Over 6 Ptnrs. (less than 20 staff) — Over 6 Ptnrs. (20 or more staff)

Partners/Practitioners   Accounting staff

confirmations, and so on, generally accounts for about 5 per cent of gross fees, for most office-size groups. Exceptions are the individual practitioner without professional staff and the largest offices, where the medians are somewhat lower. The percentage fee production of these employees tends to decrease in the larger cities for office groups of comparable size.

General office salaries tend to remain a relatively constant percentage of fees, regardless of the size of the office. Except for sole practitioners with no staff accountants, who often have no more than part-time clerical assistance, these salaries usually range from 7½ to 8½ per cent of the gross fees.

Professional development. Three groups of expense items were included under this broad classification: professional dues and meetings, publications, and training.

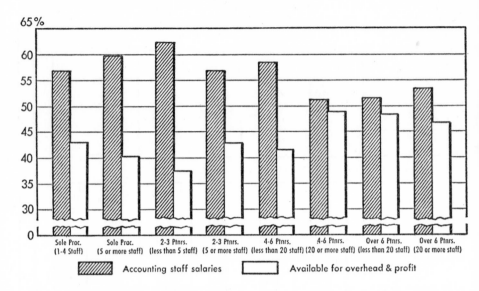

Figure 12
Median Breakdown of Staff Billings Between Salaries and Overhead Profit

Individual practitioners devote about 2-1/3 per cent of their incomes to the general area of professional development, the bulk of it representing the costs of tax services and other publications. Over-all professional development expenses in small and large partnerships are roughly 1½ per cent of gross fees, with professional dues and meeting expenses running somewhat higher than tax and other publications in the larger offices. However, practices of individual offices vary widely as evidenced by the ranges encountered in the middle 50 per cent of the offices (that is, the 25th and 75th percentiles). In some groups it varies as much as 300 per cent and in some categories the upper limit of the range is almost 100 per cent higher than the median.

These are the breakdowns within each of the sub-categories:

Professional dues and meetings. Medians for the various groups surveyed range from 0.2 to 1.9 per cent of gross fees. Except for individual practitioners with no accounting staff, who usually spend about 1 per cent of their incomes on professional dues and meetings, the typical office in most other classifications stated that about 0.5 per cent of their income goes for this purpose. This holds true, regardless of office size. The relative constancy of this figure may be due in part to the increasing tendency of many firms to pay the dues and expenses for their staff and partners. In the case of two small groups of medium-size firms (about fifty in all) who were recently asked this question, over two-thirds indicated that they pay professional dues for partners and staff.

Tax services, books and subscriptions. Probably because of the minimum requirements of all practicing CPAs for tax services and professional publications, the smallest offices devoted a larger proportion of their income than did the larger. Individual practitioners without staff reported that 1.6 per cent of their gross fees is spent for such publications; about 1 per cent was cited by other individual practitioners and two- or three-partner firms. Although the larger firms show a decline in the proportionate amount, this frequently represents a much greater dollar investment.

The fact that good reference libraries are more readily found in larger cities seems to have little effect on this expense. Variations appear to be almost wholly traceable to firm size.

Staff training and special study. The great majority of the firms with less than four to six partners and more than twenty staff accountants have virtually no direct expenses in the area of staff training, special study (partners and staff), and other professional developmental activity, outside of professional society meetings. In only 25 per cent of these smaller firms do such expenses exceed one-tenth of one per cent of the gross fees. This figure represents the median for the larger firms where the 75th percentile point is about half of one per cent. As emphasized earlier, these figures include only out-of-pocket expenses and do not reflect the time spent by partners and senior staff members in training the younger members of the staff. Time is, of course, the major investment in any such training program. However, the results indicate that most firms have relatively little money directly invested in special study for either partners or staff.

Client and public relations expenses. How much of an office's income is spent directly on client relations and efforts to become known favorably in the community?

Here again, much of this activity is not found in an expense statement, for the largest investment is in time, often on the partners' or employees' own time. However, the direct expenses associated with entertainment, dissemination of material to clients, costs of membership in nonprofessional organizations borne by the firm, and similar items give some indication of a firm's activity in this area.

Individual practitioners have the highest proportionate expenditure (2.3 per cent for those without staff and 1.9 per cent for those with one to four staff members), and the offices with more than six partners and twenty staff men have the least (1.1 per cent). Most of the other office groups fall about midway between these two extremes.

Respondent offices were also asked to indicate the percentage of gross fees which represented contributions. Policies regarding contributions in the name of the firm and those of individual partners varied so widely that the resulting figures had no significance. In some offices it is evidently the practice to make substantial contributions to certain organizations and charities, usually those of a civic nature, in the name of the firm, with the individual partners making other personal contributions. In others, all contributions are made personally by the partners.

Office and administrative expenses. The remaining costs fall within this category. They are primarily those which have to do with the accountant's "plant and equipment" and related expenses of maintaining a practice. However, automobile and other travel expenses are also included. Individual items are shown in the Appendix table (page 918). Only those which might be considered the most significant are discussed here.

Occupancy expense. Except for salaries, occupancy charges represent the largest group of expenses for an accounting practice. These charges are composed of different elements, depending on whether the quarters are leased or owned by the firm. Therefore, only a single figure, which would represent the entire cost of office space, was sought to facilitate comparisons. Respondent offices were asked to give the total charges for rent, leasehold improvements, and utilities; or depreciation, maintenance, taxes, interest, and insurance for offices owned by the firm.

The individual practitioner without accounting assistants pays proportionately more for occupancy costs—almost six per cent of his income—than do the other groups. He also shows the widest range between the 25th and 75th percentile points (from 3.8 to 8.4 per cent). However, there are smaller fluctuations in occupancy costs among all groups of offices than in any other expense except salaries.

As office size increases, this expense becomes a smaller percentage, but is by no means proportionate to the number of personnel. The spread within the middle 50 per cent tends to narrow until there is only 1 per cent difference in the over-six-partner office group. The median is 3.8 per cent and the 75th percentile is 4.2 per cent.

The occupancy charges, as a percentage of fees for each office size, are shown in Table 5.

Table 5. Occupancy Expense as a Percentage of Gross Fees

	Median	Middle 50% range From	To
Individual practitioner (no staff)	5.9%	3.8%	8.4%
Individual practitioner (with staff)	4.8	3.5	6.2
Two/three partners (less than 5 staff)	4.6	3.1	5.9
Two/three partners (5 or more staff)	4.1	3.2	5.5
Four/six partners (less than 20 staff)	4.5	3.1	5.5
Four/six partners (20 or more staff)	4.0	3.1	4.9
Over six partners	3.8	3.3	4.2

These figures indicate that more than three-quarters of the offices of all sizes find that a minimum of 3 per cent of gross fees must be devoted to office space, regardless of the amount of total income.

Size of community appears to have some limited bearing on occupancy expense. The small partnership offices and individual practitioners, which are the only groups consistently found in cities of all sizes, generally spend more of their income on occupancy in the larger cities than in the smaller. However, in cities of over a million population, this percentage tends to drop somewhat.

Perhaps the most significant fact is that the median occupancy expense for every office-size group is higher in cities of 500,000 to 1,000,000 than the median for these groups as a whole. Does this suggest that the costs of offices and utilities in these cities are generally higher than for comparable quarters in cities of other sizes? Or is there a greater concentration of accounting offices in the first-class office buildings of these cities than is true in other communities?

Office supplies and expense. The costs of office supplies generally remain a constant proportion of gross fees, regardless of the office size. This constancy is illustrated by the fact that the medians for each office size do not vary by more than a few tenths of a per cent, with most of them at 2 per cent. What differences were noted occur among the smaller individual practitioner and two- or three-partner offices with less than five staff members. Here, medians are slightly higher. Even these variations appear to result partly from differences in community size, for a larger proportion of the smaller firms are found in smaller cities. However, in comparing various office sizes within the same population areas, these smaller firms tended to run several tenths of a per cent higher.

Generally speaking, offices of all sizes in the smaller cities, especially those under 100,000, tend to run about 30 per cent higher than the over-all median. Offices in cities of over one million are usually appreciably less than the median—about 1.6 per cent for all groups. The smallest offices were an exception and 2 per cent is typical in these cases.

The replies to this question indicate normal distribution, with the middle 50 per cent range running from 1.5 to 3 per cent in most cases—except in cities of over one million where the range was several tenths less at both the upper and lower limits. The same is true for the largest firms, which are concentrated in cities of this size.

Telephone and telegraph. Percentage expenditures for these services vary inversely with the size of the offices. The medians ranged from a high of 1.8 per cent of the income of sole practitioners without staff down to 0.7 per cent for offices with over six partners and more than twenty staff members.

About 25 per cent of the individual practitioners spend more than 3 per cent of their incomes on these services; few of the largest firms are much above the medians for their groups.

Community size does not appear to have any significant effect on the expenses in this category.

Automobile expense. This is a major item only with smaller firms. In the case of individual practitioners without staff, automobile expenses (including depreciation) are equal to clerical salary and occupancy expenses. They amount to almost 6 per cent of their gross fees. This figure falls off rapidly in the larger office groups to a median of three-tenths of 1 per cent in offices with four to six partners and more than twenty staff. Few of the offices in the over-six-partner category indicate any expense of this item and the same is true for over 25 per cent of the two/three-partner groups with more than five staff and the four/six-partner offices.

Although it might be expected that automobile expenses would be lower in the large cities, because of the local concentration of clients and better public transportation, such was not the case. Community size bears little or no relationship to this expense item.

Depreciation. Except for the offices in the largest size group, where the median is about one-half of one per cent, the midpoint for the offices surveyed is about 1 per cent of their gross fees, regardless of their size. However, the median points for each group tend to get progressively lower, as city size increases. Frequently the medians for each office size in cities with over one million people are almost 50 per cent lower than for the office size group as a whole. Although the great majority of offices in most of the office size groups have some depreciation charges, more than 25 per cent of the smallest and largest offices in cities over a million population show no such charge.

Insurance. This category is confined to types of insurance carried for the protection of the firm such as comprehensive and accountant's liability, valuable papers, and other protection. It does not include the various forms of employee benefit insurance. These are included under staff compensation expenses.

Accounting offices generally spend about the same proportion of their income on insurance, irrespective of the number of personnel or the size of the city in which the practice is located. The median for each group is about four-tenths of one per cent. However, the smaller offices show a much wider range than the other firms. A number of them spend appreciably more than the general median, but there is a greater tendency among these smaller offices to carry no insurance of this type. More than 35 per cent of the sole practitioners without staff in cities over 25,000 have none.

Other expenses. About 1.5 per cent of the gross fee income of many offices is devoted to such expenses as equipment maintenance, travel (other than automobile), taxes (other than income or payroll), costs of outside services (including legal counsel), and items not specifically covered by the survey. These expenses tend to run somewhat lower for individual practitioners and a little higher for offices with more than six partners. Some of the findings on specific items are:

1. Equipment maintenance generally runs between two- and three-tenths of one per cent; less for practitioners without staff.
2. Travel expenses vary appreciably among the offices, without much relation to size of office or community, but they rarely exceed one per cent. The variations may be due to different practices in billing clients for these items and the fact that some offices carry this expense under the purpose for which it is incurred.
3. Taxes other than income or payroll are insignificant, but tend to maintain a one-tenth of one per cent proportion for all offices except the largest ones, where the median was double that of the other offices.
4. Legal and other outside services are rarely employed in the operation of an accounting practice. Only a small number of the offices indicate such an expense, and generally it is an insignificant item.

Net income. After the staff is compensated, the rent paid, and other creditors satisfied, the balance of the income reverts to the partners or practitioner. Excluding the matter of income taxes, what percentage of net income can various-size offices expect from their practices?

As would be expected, the ratio of partners to staff has the most significant bearing on this point, since the net includes partners' salaries or drawings. However, there is a fairly large spread within the middle 50 per cent range

Figure 13. Middle Ranges of Net Income (as percentages of gross fees)

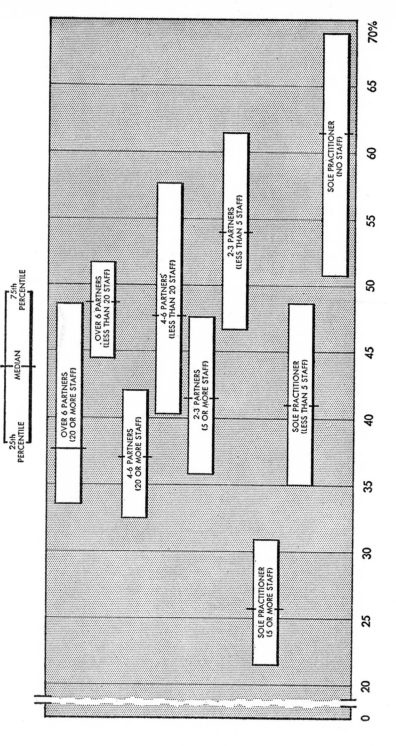

in most groups. This indicates that a number of firms are not only able to achieve a substantially higher yield than others of similar size, but they also show a better percentage result than some offices in other size groups where the ratio of partners to staff is lower (see Figure 13).

Some variations in net income percentage are found among similar offices in different-size communities. Most notably, the medians for sole practitioners were lowest in the smaller cities, especially those under 50,000, and highest in cities with populations over one million. On the other hand, firms with two to six partners generally have higher net income percentages in the small communities and less in cities of over one million population. This may be due to variations in the type of practices conducted by the offices in different-size communities.

Offices vary widely in their methods of distributing net income among the partners. Some apportion the entire amount on the basis of the profit-sharing interest of the partners, with each partner's drawings deducted from his share. Others pay nominal salaries after which profits are shared. A third group pays rather generous salaries, which bear some relation to the partner's contribution to the firm. Generally, the major portion of net income is paid out in salaries in these latter cases and the salary therefore represents a substantial portion of a partner's total compensation. About 68 per cent of the firms with four or more partners deduct salaries before applying profit-sharing percentages.

SOME GENERAL OBSERVATIONS

Many of the expense items discussed appear to fall into three basic categories, as they relate to the size of an accounting practice.

1. *Those expenses which vary directly with the size of office;* that is, the larger the office, the greater the proportion of income spent on the item. Only one type of expense—staff accountants' salaries and other direct labor costs —falls into this category. This is also the largest expense item for most offices. However, this expense has a closer correlation with the partner-staff ratio than it does with the sheer number of personnel in the office.

2. *Those expenses which vary inversely with the size of the office.* Many of these are expenses which usually require a minimum dollar expenditure for every practice, and, although the dollar amounts frequently increase in the larger firms, they decline in proportion to the larger fee income. These items include tax services and other publications, client and public relations expense, occupancy charges, telephone and telegraph, and automobile expense.

3. *Those expenses which remain in fairly constant proportion to gross fees,* regardless of office size. Within this group are: general office salaries, office supplies, depreciation (other than automobile), insurance, equipment maintenance, travel (other than automobile), and taxes (other than income and payroll). Professional dues and meetings generally fall in this category, although individual practitioners spend a higher portion of their income on these items.

Figure 14. Where the Fee Dollar Goes: Sole Practitioners

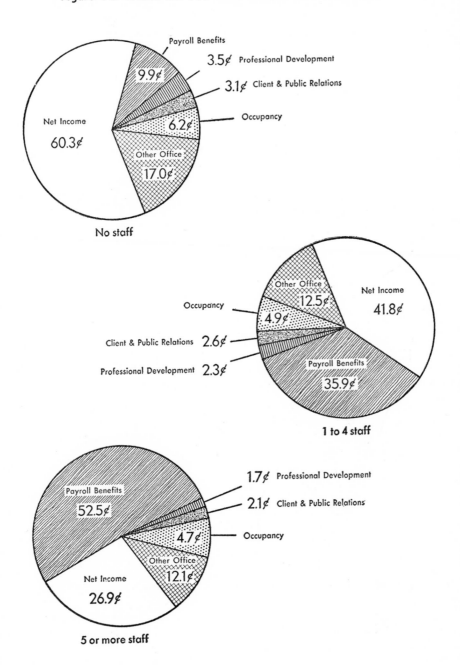

Payroll Benefits
9.9¢

3.5¢ Professional Development

3.1¢ Client & Public Relations

Occupancy
6.2¢

Net Income
60.3¢

Other Office
17.0¢

No staff

Other Office
12.5¢

Net Income
41.8¢

Occupancy
4.9¢

Client & Public Relations 2.6¢

Professional Development 2.3¢

Payroll Benefits
35.9¢

1 to 4 staff

Payroll Benefits
52.5¢

1.7¢ Professional Development

2.1¢ Client & Public Relations

Occupancy
4.7¢

Other Office
12.1¢

Net Income
26.9¢

5 or more staff

727

Figure 15. Where the Fee Dollar Goes: Partnership Offices

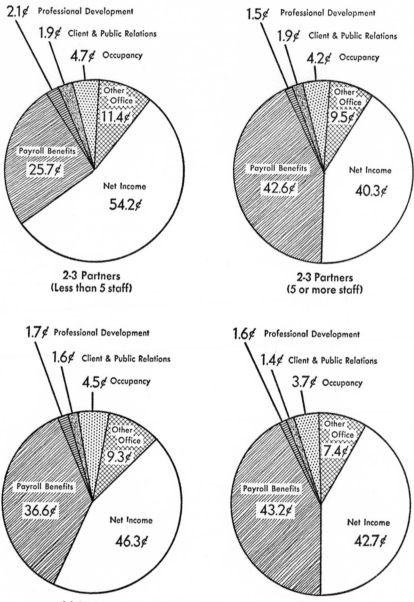

2.1¢ Professional Development
1.9¢ Client & Public Relations
4.7¢ Occupancy
Other Office 11.4¢
Payroll Benefits 25.7¢
Net Income 54.2¢

2-3 Partners
(Less than 5 staff)

1.5¢ Professional Development
1.9¢ Client & Public Relations
4.2¢ Occupancy
Other Office 9.5¢
Payroll Benefits 42.6¢
Net Income 40.3¢

2-3 Partners
(5 or more staff)

1.7¢ Professional Development
1.6¢ Client & Public Relations
4.5¢ Occupancy
Other Office 9.3¢
Payroll Benefits 36.6¢
Net Income 46.3¢

4-6 Partners

1.6¢ Professional Development
1.4¢ Client & Public Relations
3.7¢ Occupancy
Other Office 7.4¢
Payroll Benefits 43.2¢
Net Income 42.7¢

over 6 Partners

The population of the community evidently has an effect on all offices in just two cases. Offices in cities with 500,000 to 1,000,000 people tend to have a higher percentage of occupancy expense. Office supplies are generally proportionately higher in the small cities.

In reviewing the figures cited in this survey, it must be borne in mind that a smaller proportionate expenditure in a larger office rarely indicates a smaller dollar amount and in most cases is significantly higher. For example, a firm which grosses $250,000 a year of which half of one per cent goes for tax services and other publications is still spending more than twice as much as a firm grossing $50,000 and spending one per cent of its income on these services.

This was not intended to be an interpretative study. Although some of the facts are known, much information is lacking on the reasons why some expenses are incurred in certain proportions. Obviously, some are rather inflexible and depend on the expenditures for closely related items. Others are generally based on the size of the office or other factors, but vary widely among individual offices. Under these circumstances, interpretation could be little more than speculation.

This study merely shows the common relationships of various items of expense to total fee income. These relationships, which are brought out in the detailed Appendix table, page 918, are important. An office's net income percentage may appear to be satisfactory, but certain expenses may be disproportionately high, or low, when compared with similar practices. Although some of these variations from the "average" may be fully justified, the practitioner should be aware of their existence.

Punched-card
Accounting for Write-ups

■ ONE OF THE serious objections to write-up work is the excessive demands it can make on the CPA's time. One means of reducing such demands is to put the small client on punched-card accounting. It should be noted that processing centers which will punch and process punched cards are now operating in all large cities and in most smaller cities in the 25,000 to 75,000 population range.

Recent technical developments in the use of punched paper tape and small, relatively inexpensive computer equipment may well open new vistas to the CPA, from the standpoint of both (1) performance of write-up work and (2) ease of production of statistical reports for the guidance of client management.

STATISTICAL REPORTS FOR MANAGEMENT

Many CPAs are becoming increasingly aware of the fact that they can be of real help to client management by making more data available on which decisions can be based. If such reports can be prepared with relatively little extra time and cost by using punched-paper tape and processing equipment, the CPA can obviously improve his worth to his clients.

The areas in which analyses may be very worth while will of course vary with the nature of the client's business. A few areas of fairly universal applicability are analyses of (1) profits attributable to each salesman, (2) inventory turnover by specific item, (3) profitability by product by store, (4) sales and profits by customer, and (5) delivery costs by truck by product. This listing is only a sample of a few possible applications.

After two months' experience with punched tape, one CPA firm expects to be in a position to supply even its smallest client with the following data:

1. Comparative statements of profit or loss, this month and year-to-date with last year's month and year-to-date, both dollars and percentages
2. Over-and-under-budget schedules
3. Over-and-under-industry averages
4. Fifteen or twenty standard ratios, and which of these are out of line

PUNCHED-CARD PROCEDURES

Basically, the operations start with the preparation of punched paper tape, either specifically for one purpose or as a by-product of some other operation. This tape, which contains symbols identifying each specific item, as well as the amount of the item, is then fed into processing equipment which gathers like items together, accumulates totals, and prints out statements. In brief, the whole operation can be divided into two parts—preparation of input data and processing. A brief description of some of the variations used in each follows.

Preparation of input data. In the typical write-up job, input data is obtained by the use of an adding machine with an attachment which punches paper tape as it records on the adding-machine tape. The accountant records each transaction in this manner for the period under review, either in the client's office or in his own, using a predetermined chart of accounts for coding all transactions. Since tape-punching adding machines have all the sound effects of a small machine gun, there are some advantages for the client to having this done in the CPA's office.

Tape punching adding machines weigh thirty-five to fifty pounds; so they are portable if the porter is strong enough. However, it is generally agreed that it is far better to have documents brought to the machine, than vice versa.

Another possible way of obtaining paper-tape input which is useful in gathering statistics of the sort mentioned earlier under "Statistical Reports for Management" is the addition of a paper-tape punch to a conventional bookkeeping machine so that paper tape is produced automatically as other documents are produced. This adaptation is available from several firms in the bookkeeping machine field, and is particularly useful in recording statistics from inventory records, invoices, and the like.

One further possibility of preparing input which avoids the use of paper tape is mark-sense cards from which, by checking the appropriate box with a particular kind of pencil, a special machine can automatically prepare a punched card. In general, many people feel that mark-sensing is the least desirable method of input because of its limitation to twenty-seven characters per card and, unless the person using the pencil is meticulously accurate, mistakes and failure to register will occur.

Processing. At this point we assume that we have either punched cards or punched paper tape which reflects all transactions under review ready for processing. By and large, there are two broad possibilities for use in processing at an economic level. These are conventional punched-card equipment or a computer.

Conventional tabulating equipment leases for $1,000, or slightly higher, per month for the complement needed. In this case it is necessary to put the paper tapes through a converter which transfers the information to punched cards. The punched cards are then put through a sorting and collating routine and then run through a tabulating machine to print out totals.

There are a number of smaller computers now available at only slightly higher cost than conventional punched-card equipment. An advantage of the computers is that paper tape may be fed directly to them without going through the punched-card conversion. The specific needs must be closely studied in determining which equipment is best for any given purpose because of the relatively limited storage capacity in the smaller computer.

WHAT ARE THE ALTERNATIVES?

The CPA has a number of possible alternatives as to what he might do with regard to both input and processing.

Input. Three of the more obvious alternatives for input are set forth below:

1. The purchase of a tape-punching adding machine would cost somewhere between $1,800 and $2,500; or one might be leased for about $50 a month. *If the CPA owns the equipment,* he can certainly service his clients as he sees fit and might well conduct his audit concurrently with the punching of the details for statement preparation. If he or his employees control the use of the machine, the error margin is of course cut way down. In addition to write-up work, he can use it to prepare special tapes for items on which a statistical analysis is desired.

2. In considering write-up work, having the tape-punching adding machine or paper-tape attachment *owned and operated by the client* generally is less desirable. The chance for error is so great that it is unlikely that the tapes can be processed for statement production at any reasonable fee. On the other

hand, where a fair amount of statistical analysis is desirable and this statistical information can be automatically put on tapes as the product of a regular accounting-machine operation, a client installation may be most worth while.

3. The typical *service center* runs on a volume basis, and generally does unsatisfactory work when it does all the punching of the clients' information. The service center usually lacks sufficient knowledge of the clients' problems to punch the input data satisfactorily.

Processing. In the processing area there are also three major alternatives:

1. *The CPA may lease tabulating equipment.* At a monthly cost of between $1,000 and $1,500 for tabulating equipment, a CPA can be in a position to help his clients substantially by producing both statements and special studies. On the other hand, the economics of the situation should be closely investigated to ensure that there will be sufficient demand for profitable work so that the equipment can be kept busy a major portion of the time.

2. *Owning a computer* presents virtually the same problems associated with tabulating equipment. If the computer can be fully programed, with profitable work for clients, it can, despite its higher cost, produce much more work because of its greater speed. On the other hand, the amount of training time needed to make one's employees competent in the use of this sort of equipment can be very substantial.

3. *Using a service center* is another alternative. The quality of work and the dependability of time schedules provided by service centers vary greatly from operation to operation. If any given CPA can establish good relationships with a dependable service center, he will find that a lot of mechanical headaches will be taken off his hands. He might in some cases lose a small amount of profit, but it is a great help to know that someone else has the headache of getting a mechanical job done.

FACTORS TO BE CONSIDERED

Before deciding whether to convert to punched-card accounting, the CPA must consider many aspects of his particular situation: his own staff level, the competence and ability of the clients' employees, the nature of the client, and the type of service rendered. Specifically, here are a few factors that warrant consideration:

1. Number of clients and volume of transactions
2. Period of delay occasioned by outside processing
3. Cost of equipment (tape puncher, tabulator, computer), and cost of service-bureau processing
4. Availability of standard programs for processing information other than general ledger transactions
5. Incidence of errors and ease of corrections
6. Training of personnel
7. Servicing of equipment
8. Portability of equipment

9. Acceptability by the client
10. Modification of auditing and tax work procedures

The costs involved. While the following costs are only approximate and subject to change, they are offered to give some idea of the range of outlays that can be expected.

Equipment. The cost of a tape-punching adding machine ranges from $1,800 to $2,500, depending upon column capacity and extra features desired. It can be leased for $50 per month and up. A medium-sized computer leases for somewhere between $1,500 and $1,700 per month, plus taxes. Tabulating equipment runs somewhat lower: $1,000 to $1,500 per month, plus taxes.

Processing. The typical going rate charged by service bureaus for processing write-up work runs from 4 to 7¢ per transaction. There may be approximately three hundred transactions per month in the average job. For processing costs encountered in specific cases, see pages 741 and 743.

Client resistance. How will the client react to the absence of detailed, handwritten records and differences in form of statement presentation? This factor may require some selling, but it is not an insurmountable obstacle. Some have found that clients wholeheartedly accepted this changed method of preparing and maintaining their accounting records. If a client wishes to keep his records confidential, all of his documents may be identified solely by number while they are in the data processing center. Most clients will not object to the processing center using their name.

Selling the client. It has been suggested that a CPA might present the situation to his client in the following way:

> With costs and expenses constantly increasing, and particularly those for efficient office workers, the maintenance of effective accounting service at the present fee schedule has presented a continual problem, to which I've given a great deal of time and thought.
>
> In an effort to solve this problem to our mutual benefit, I have consulted representatives of a data processing center on the feasibility of using their services to perform routine bookkeeping processes in connection with my clients' accounts.
>
> The data processing center is equipped with punched-card equipment to process bookkeeping data, maintain all necessary journals, ledgers, and other records to comply with state and federal taxing requirements, and produce financial statements and data for reports and returns for taxing and other agencies. Your records will still be processed by our office, with the same type of running audit, and with monthly adjustments made, reports completed, and comments prepared on your progress, as in the past.
>
> The staff of the data processing center is fully conscious of the confidential relationship necessary in handling your records. In addition, your transactions can be handled by number identification only, if you so desire, at the data processing center.
>
> I am confident that, by utilizing this service, I will be able to give you the quality of accounting service you have been used to, without having to consider a possible fee increase in the near future. Should you be unwilling

to have your data processed mechanically, we will continue to handle all the work of your account in our office; however, the possibility of a fee revision in that case should be considered.

Time saved. Will a significant reduction in staff and stenographic time result from the introduction of data processing? The answer will depend in large measure on the frequency and complexity of reports rendered and the volume of transactions to be recorded. After almost a year of operation, one firm reported a reduction of from 30 to 70 per cent in staff time on write-up engagements. Stenographic time was practically eliminated on most of these engagements. Of added interest is the fact that several marginal and loss accounts became profitable after conversion to data processing methods.

If an eight-hour assignment is performed in six hours through the use of automation, there may be some question as to whether or not any real savings are attained when consideration is given to such factors as the time spent traveling to and from clients' offices and the ability of personnel to utilize productively any spare time which may become available. However, when time required on assignments is reduced by 50 per cent or more, and in those cases where fractional parts of working days on larger engagements are eliminated, a very real saving may be effected. The results are particularly significant where supervisory people are engulfed in a mass of detail work.

Selecting a service bureau. When selecting a service bureau, the CPA should try if possible to deal with a local bureau, since so many small problems do arise. A local bureau has a definite advantage when reworking, additional journal entries, or a rush job are needed.

The accountant should be within easy telephone distance of the data processing center: the center can make routine corrections of the client's source data, but corrections which require judgment will have to be referred by the center to the CPA for decision. A processing center requiring long distance calls or dependent upon mail will lack the flexibility necessary for the success of this system.

The accountant must also make sure that the bureau selected will give the utmost co-operation during a test-run period. One firm tested seven clients for three months, working the bugs out of the system. They then destroyed the entire test run (they had been doing the work using also their regular procedures during this period) so that their old-style general ledgers would have a clear transition to punched paper tape.

All aspects of the service bureau's rates should be checked. Some quote a low rate per card, but count the balance-forward cards as well as the current month's transactions in determining their card count. Some charge for paper and cards separately; some include them in the price.

Ethics. The AICPA and its committee on data processing centers have received reports from CPAs in various parts of the country to the effect that clients are being solicited by service centers offering to take over all bookkeeping and statement production, thus eliminating the need for the CPA. This sort of solicitation, added to the impact of articles which have painted an overly glowing picture of the ease of moving to punched tape, quite naturally push the CPA to reassess his method of doing business. A number of CPAs, seeing the potential drain of profitable clients, have queried the AICPA about organizing separate corporations for service center operations, and "fighting fire with fire" through solicitation by such a corporation. Opinion Number 7 of the AICPA's ethics committee, however, definitely states that such procedure would be in violation of Rule 4.05, *Code of Professional Ethics*. (See Appendix page 821 for the rules and opinions.)

Auditing and tax work. In connection with year-end audit and tax work, certain information required in schedules and analyses may not be as readily obtainable from records prepared on data processing equipment as it would be in manually kept records. In connection therewith, one CPA firm found it best to update its required schedules during each visit to the client's office. Specifically, it maintains at a minimum details as to fixed asset additions and retirements, charitable contributions, taxes (other than income taxes), and information with respect to any unusual or nonrecurring transactions.

One firm describes how the use of punched-card equipment has modified auditing procedures as follows:

> The entries recorded on the transaction listing are identified as to account, reference, and amount. Unless the mechanical equipment has failed, which is comparatively rare, the appropriate general ledger accounts have been correctly posted and the records are in balance. Therefore, in order to be satisfied as to the accuracy of the information recorded, it is only necessary to examine in the usual manner the documents which support entries on the transaction listings. Footing and cross-footing of books of original entry and tracing postings to general ledger accounts are practically eliminated because these have been automatic-machine processes. Should one desire to review and/or analyze the activities in a particular account for a period of one year, it would be necessary to refer to twelve trial balances and twelve transaction listings, if recording was done on a monthly basis and no detailed analyses were maintained. However, a situation of this type is not a serious problem if one anticipates one's needs in advance. At relatively moderate rates, the service organization will prepare detailed listings of transactions recorded in all accounts or in a few selected accounts.
>
> To summarize, the following information will be available to facilitate audit procedures:
>
> 1. Detailed trial balances
> 2. Detailed transaction listings
> 3. Detailed account analyses
>
> Some or all of these records may become part of the audit work papers. In addition, it is occasionally advantageous to record adjusting, reclassifying, and closing entries on punched paper tape to complete working trial balances and prepare report drafts of financial statements. Whether or not this medium is employed in the manner just described, the information must eventually be machine-recorded in order to provide the client with complete records as of the close of each fiscal year.

Another firm reports the following experience:

Our practice is made up predominantly of monthly noncertified reports, where the client's personnel have written up the books of original entry, and our function, aside from our normal accounting procedures, verification, and tying-in of various control accounts, consisted of the following semi-skilled functions:

1. Posting books of original entry to a general ledger
2. Taking off a trial balance
3. Preparing pencil copy of balance sheet and profit and loss statement monthly (with occasional percentage analyses)
4. Typing balance sheet and profit and loss statement monthly

Our approach was to continue to perform the same accounting procedures, verification, and tying-in that we did before, but to eliminate the necessity of our personnel doing any of the above four steps. The solution was to put our clients' totals of the books of original entry on punched tape.

Our first step was to make a detailed analysis of our practice and determine what percentage and how many of our clients lent themselves to punched tape.

We first eliminated the following categories of clients from being potential punched-tape clients.

1. Single-entry clients
2. Once-a-year clients
3. Dormant clients
4. Land development clients, builders, multiple corporations, and other overly complicated jobs (We might change our mind on some of these some day.)
5. Certified audits and situations where the general ledger is posted prior to our engagement (We might switch these also, but not now.)

We included in our list of punched-tape clients those few on which we write up the books of original entry. We next identified all punched-tape clients by client number, numbering from 100 to 999, leaving spaces so that our clients would always be in numerical, as well as approximate alphabetical sequence. On our clients with departments, branches, or with more than one location, we classified each location, etc., as a separate client number.

RECOMMENDATIONS OF THE AICPA COMMITTEE ON DATA PROCESSING CENTERS

No slate of recommendations can be set forth which will apply to every CPA, because of the varying needs and demands of his practice. It is suggested that each CPA consider the following recommendations in the light of his own problems and in the following order:

1. All CPAs should understand what kinds of equipment are available, what the needs of their own practices are, and be prepared to be of service to their clients as the circumstances dictate.

2. Punched paper tape is here to stay and can be effectively used by many clients.

3. CPAs doing a substantial amount of write-up work should consider the possibility of acquiring a tape-punching adding machine for use in their practices.

4. No CPA should consider adding a data processing unit (whether computer or conventional tabulating equipment) for use solely on write-up work.

5. CPAs should encourage clients to add paper tape attachments to existing accounting machines where economical and where by-product statistical reports may be of help to management.

6. CPAs may want to consider establishment of their own data processing centers when (1) local service centers either do not exist or are of poor quality, or (2) some other good reason exists for having such operations under their control, as long as they realize that "get-ready" costs may be sizeable before they attain a profitable basis.

7. In general, CPAs will be well advised to concentrate on giving advice and counsel to clients and to minimize clerical service except where no one else is available to perform satisfactorily.

THE SOURCE-DATA METHOD

The system of punched-card accounting described here does not use punched tape. Instead, the service center punches cards directly from original journals compiled mainly by the small client.

Designing the accounting records. After the client's permission is secured, the CPA, in conjunction with the processing center, should design the accounting records to be used under this system. The first of these, and of primary importance, is the chart of accounts. The system typically requires an expanded chart. There are two reasons for this. First, each type of transaction that may require analysis now or later should preferably have a separate account number and name. For example, instead of one employer's payroll tax account, it is suggested that a separate account be set up for state unemployment, federal unemployment, and so on. However, the accountant may also wish to consolidate some accounts. For example, firms that sell on credit should open a single control account for accounts receivable. Cards are punched for debits and credits to individual accounts and a supplementary schedule of accounts receivable is printed at intervals. Any consolidation will shorten the length of the financial statements, since the total cards used to print the general ledger are also used to print the balance sheet and income statement.

A second reason for the rather lengthy chart of accounts is that a separate account number must be used for each title line in the printed general ledger and financial statements. For example, an account number should be given to the general heading, current assets, and the like. This permits the tabulating equipment to automatically place in sequence each header line, subtitle, and subtotal. In addition, the accountant may wish to number the accounts in a manner that will allow each account number to be printed in alphabetical sequence for the financial statements. Basically then, the chart of accounts is similar to, but more detailed than, the chart of accounts necessary for hand-posting.

The processing center will make a card (including account name and number) for each account and will print several copies of the chart of accounts. The accountant will leave several copies with the client and keep a copy himself. The client refers to this chart of accounts as he makes the daily or weekly entries in the three basic journals that he maintains. These are the cash receipts, cash disbursements, and payroll journals. The CPA maintains the general journal.

Cash receipts journal. The cash receipts journal can be designed on single sheets of paper. The most successful method appears to be a journal either printed or dittoed on the face of a convenient size of envelope. Assume that a cash receipts journal is designed in the form of an envelope. The number of envelopes the client uses during the month will depend upon whether the client balances and enters his cash daily (approximately twenty envelopes), or weekly (approximately five or six envelopes). The face of the cash receipt journal will contain account numbers and names of the frequently used accounts plus space for miscellaneous entries. It is suggested that the following type of transactions be entered by the client on the front of this journal: sales (cash and on account), receipts from cash sales and on account, miscellaneous receipts, cash short and over, cash payouts, deposits, and so on. The client must balance his own cash registers and analyze his receipts and payouts in the categories shown above. All source documents pertaining to these transactions are placed in the envelope, including deposit slips, receipts for money received on account, cash register tapes, and the like.

Cash disbursements journal. The cash disbursements journal can be designed on a single sheet of paper, but it is recommended that the client secure voucher checks with one or two carbons attached. If voucher checks are used, the cash disbursements journal consists merely of a carbon of the checks written during the month, since the client will have been instructed to place the account number affected (e.g., purchases) on the lower half of the voucher. Petty cash should be kept on the imprest system with a voucher check written for reimbursement. It will be noted that no accounts-payable register need be kept. The accounts payable can be set up each month by the CPA when he makes the general journal adjustments.

Payroll journal. The third journal the client keeps is the payroll journal. It is recommended that this journal be set up on a single sheet of paper with information as to employee's name, social security number, payroll number, regular hours worked, overtime hours, gross salary, deductions, and net amount due the employees. The credit should be to accrued payroll. This allows a check on the accuracy of payments made to the employees. The processing center accumulates earnings and taxes by employees and prints an earnings register showing these accumulated amounts.

Review of the client's work. Shortly after the end of the month, the client forwards to the accountant the cash receipts, cash disbursements (which may include the suppliers' statements), and the payroll journal. A staff member will usually review the journals and enclosed documents for obvious errors and make the bank reconciliation. This review lasts an average of ninety minutes.

Preparing the punched cards. The three journals are then forwarded by the accountant to the processing center. The processing center will punch an individual card for each account listed on the face of the cash receipts journal, for each check listed on the cash disbursements journal, and for each line on the payroll journal. Multiple cards are punched if two or more accounts are affected by a single check. In punching these cards, it is important to remember that the processing center needs to know only three things about each transaction: (a) the account number, (b) whether a debit or credit, and (c) the amount. However, for cross-reference purposes, the processing center should add a source code. For example, Code 1 could be punched into all cards originating from the cash receipts journal, Code 2, for the cash disbursements journal, Code 3, for the payroll journal, and Code 4, for the general journal. Since this code is printed on the trial balance and general ledger, it provides a valuable means for quickly locating source data at a later time if necessary. The processing center takes, in addition, the date of the transaction from the client's source data while the name of each account has been punched on the cards when the chart of accounts was made up.

Preliminary trial balance and the payroll register. After the processing center punches a card for each transaction, a printing run is made. These cards, after the first month, are automatically added to the cards carrying the prior month's balances for each general ledger account. This run is the preliminary trial balance. A run of the payroll cards gives the earnings register. The processing center forwards the earnings register and trial balance to the accountant. In addition, the client's source data are returned.

Monthly adjustments. On receipt of the trial balance from the processing center, the CPA or a staff member prepares to make the monthly adjustments. It is suggested that these adjustments be made on regular four-column general journal paper. The reversing type of adjustments will include the inventory adjustment, the profit adjustment, accrued liabilities, the accounts payable adjustment, and so on. The information for the accounts payable adjustment is secured from the unpaid statements and invoices which the client forwards to the accountant as they come in from the suppliers a few days after the close of the month. The processing center can automatically reverse these accounts the following month and incorporate the reversals in next month's trial balance. The nonreversing adjustments would include depreciation expense, amortization, and the like.

The two-stage method of trial balance (with the general ledger as the second trial balance) has been found very desirable since it gives flexibility of review and adjustment prior to the final run. It is definitely not recommended that the final trial balance (general ledger) be attempted in one stage. The superiority of the two-stage method can be explained by the fact that it allows the accountant to make adjusting journal entries after preliminary figures have been accumulated in the first trial balance.

Reviewing the trial balance and setting up the adjustments can usually be handled by a staff member in approximately ninety minutes.

General ledger and statements. The general journal adjustments are next sent to the processing center where cards are punched for each entry. The general journal cards are then merged with the preliminary trial balance cards, and the general ledger is run by the processing center. It consists of the beginning balances in each account, a separate line for each transaction affecting that account, and the closing balance.

The processing center segregates the total and header cards and then prints the client's balance sheet and income statement. The income statement cards contain information to print both year to date and the last month's operations.

The processing center returns two copies (or more, if desired) of the general ledger and the financial statements to the accountant. The accountant reviews the financial statements and makes whatever analysis he deems necessary. This may include comparison of figures with those of prior months and years, ratio analysis, and so on. It is estimated that this takes the CPA approximately a half-hour. The source documents, one copy of the general ledger and earnings register, and as many copies as are necessary of the financial statements are now sent to the client. The accountant keeps the other copies of the accounting records for his file.

Cumulative earnings records. The processing center will run, at monthly, quarterly, or annual intervals, a supplementary run of the earnings register from the cards it has punched. This run automatically gives the cumulative earning record for each employee, cumulative payroll taxes, Form 941 schedules, and so forth. An automatic by-product of this run is the printing of the complete W-2 form for each employee at the end of the year.

Advantages of the source-data method. A summary of the possible advantages of this method of machine-accounting for small clients, as compared to the conventional write-up procedure, is as follows:

1. Only about a half-hour of the CPA's time and three hours of staff time per month are necessary to service a typical small client under this method. This frees the CPA's time for more remunerative employment.

2. By keeping a copy of the client's general ledger, payroll summary, and financial statements, the accountant has a complete and detailed set of the client's books.

3. The client has, in printed form, a general ledger and earnings register showing in detail each transaction that has occurred during the prior month.

4. Cumulative earnings records, W-2's, etc., are automatic by-products of this system.

5. No investment by the CPA in machine-accounting equipment of any type is necessary.

6. There is no noisy machinery operating in the accountant's office with the resulting possibility of employee irritation. In addition, there is no necessity to give special punched-card equipment training to employees.

7. The time schedule that this system allows has not been mentioned, but it offers one of its biggest advantages. The processing center can deliver the original trial balance within two or three days after submission of the client's source data, and the final trial balance (general ledger) and financial state-

ments within two or three days after the accountant submits the general journal. The result is that statements can be in the client's hands within one to two weeks after the receipt of source data from the client.

8. The service cost at the processing center of $5 to $20 a month per client (assuming the accountant has twenty clients or so), is believed to be quite representative. It should be noted that this payment to the processing center is not an additional cost to the CPA, since punched-card methods allow him to accomplish his regular volume of work with a reduced staff.

SOME PRACTITIONERS' EXPERIENCES

In order to provide the reader with further insight into the techniques involved in punched-card accounting, the experiences of a number of CPA firms are presented here. It will be seen that the specific approach varies according to the circumstances.

A small firm's use of punched tape. The following is an account of the transition to punched tape of a two-partner firm having eight staff men and two clerical employees.

Our firm is in its second month of processing tapes through a local service bureau. We feel that this is the opportune time to tell of our trials and tribulations—not a year from now, when all of our problems will probably seem smaller in retrospect.

The chart of accounts. My partner spent the better part of his free time for three months, designing our master chart of accounts. Our basic account numbering system was a five-digit code, wherein the first two digits designated the major category, such as current assets, and the last three indicated the specific account.

Detecting errors in coding. We added a sixth digit to our five-digit system, known as the redundant or check digit. This is an extra digit added to each account number. Its computation is based solely upon the other five digits and their sequence. The data processing equipment has the ability to instantly compute the redundant digit, so that if we, at the punching or any other step in our procedure, assign or punch a number with an improper redundant digit, we are called by our service bureau for correction. This catches transposition, as well as any other type of punching error, on account numbers. Our taped account numbers are matched against the master chart of accounts. We average about twenty error cards per month, all of which are caught by our service bureau through the use of the redundant digit. All of these errors are on account numbers. No balancing errors as to dollar amounts can leave our office, inasmuch as our totals of our clients' books of original entry must always be zero.

Summarizing the books of original entry. After the client's personnel have written up the books of original entry, we use what we have labeled "pick-off sheets" for recapping. These are multicolumn work sheets on which we enter the summary postings of the distributions of each of the books of original entry. The setup is such that the account names and code numbers appear on the left-hand side, while two columns are provided for each month across the remainder of the sheet. The function is to prove the debits and credits of the month's transactions. This also gives us a quick comparison with prior months' postings, while working in the client's office, as well as a simple guide for the tape-punching operator, inasmuch as account numbers and dollar figures are quickly visible merely by folding over our sixteen-column work sheets.

On a memo basis, we tie in various details to our controls through the use of our "tie-in sheets," which show, for selected key accounts, the opening balance, the month's transactions, and the closing balance. This provides such proofs as accounts receivable control balance, cash in bank for bank reconciliation purposes, and so on. This is merely the beginning of our program, which varies with the client, industry, complexity, internal control, etc.

We have a few clients for whom we have been doing the bookkeeping and the writing up of the books of original entry. On these few, we still do the same write-up; however, we do not post to the general ledger, take off trial balance, prepare statements, and the like. We put these clients on pick-off and tie-in sheets in order to standardize our practice. This is the basic difference between our procedures and the source-data method advocated by the service bureaus. We are trying to get away from writing up books of original entry, and the service bureaus have been pushing this phase.

Punched-tape procedures. We enter only once for each client our CPA number, the client number, and the month. This static information repeats on every card. We enter the code number for the journal at the time we punch the first item in this journal. The journal code repeats until we have a subtotal of zero. We then enter the code for our second journal, repeating the process until all our journals are entered, still subtotaling to zero. We then punch the total button. The total symbol tells the tape-to-card converter that we have completed the punching for the month for the client. This punching takes approximately ten minutes per client per month.

Service bureau operations. When we began operations with our local service bureau, we sent them a list of our clients by client number, indicating entity form, fiscal year-end, and if a partnership, profit-and-loss-sharing percentages for the individual partners. If a corporation, we indicated loss carry-forwards, and the like, or any information needed in setting up the proper corporate tax.

When our punched paper tapes arrive at the service bureau, they are in an envelope with an adding-machine tape and transmittal notes, indicating what we need in the particular month as far as number of copies of the balance sheet, profit-and-loss statement, year-to-date profit-and-loss statements, etc. The tapes are first put through the tape-to-card converter, and the cards are then sorted in numerical sequence and matched with our master chart of accounts.

They are then merged with the prior month's balance forward cards; and the general ledger is then run on the tabulating equipment with separate totals on balance sheet and profit or loss items, indicating at this step the profit or loss for the month and for the year to date. We find this useful at fiscal year-end, as we can then discuss year-end adjustments with our client prior to running the balance sheet and profit-or-loss statement. The service bureau then processes the current month's cards through the computer where the month and year-to-date percentages are punched for every income statement item, and the corporate income tax is computed monthly, if needed. Incidentally, the computer sets up no tax on sole proprietors, partnerships, or pseudos, but sets up the proper taxes on all our corporations, considering loss carry-overs, carry-backs, first-year's operations, nondeductible items, and so on. We have the closing-entry procedure wired into the program also, so that when each client's fiscal year-end comes up, the corporation tax payable-current year is closed to corporation tax payable-prior year, and all profit-or-loss statement items are closed to earned surplus. If we wish, we can rerun the twelve individual monthly general ledgers, creating one general ledger for the year, rather than twelve individual general ledgers. We feel that this will smooth over our conversion to data processing with the Internal Revenue agents. They might feel that twelve monthly general ledgers are more difficult to audit than one yearly general ledger. The rerunning of the general ledger is referred to as a "history list."

At fiscal year-end, we need extra reports made up with only year-to-date figures thereon. The tabulator operator merely has the tabulating machine hold back the monthly figures. We have found tremendous flexibility at the service bureau, and all our requests for added information have been honored.

Advantages of punched tape over source-data method. In the system just described, the original source data is not forwarded to the service bureau. Instead, only the punched tapes are sent there for processing. The advantages of this system are:

1. Precontrolled tapes. There are very few discrepancies when the general ledgers and reports are received from our service bureau.
2. Much cheaper than source-data method. Average cost, about $7 per client per month (including paper, cards, etc.). Source-data method runs about $15 per month per client.
3. This should lead to more professional type work. Other method might lead to less professional type work.
4. Local service bureau likes this program, as there are much fewer reruns than in the previous program, less grief, and more profit. This will probably create competition, and should drive the rates down.

What the change-over has accomplished. Our clients' opinion of our conversion is that they are receiving much more informative reports, faster. They also commend us for this progressive step. They have been taking similar steps in their own businesses.

Our opinion is that we will not save much money as against the manual method by our conversion to tape, *but* we will give our clients faster and better service. In most instances, we receive our completed reports back from the service bureau seventy-two hours after we leave the client's office. We will put in less overtime. We feel it will upgrade our practice, engaging us more and more into management service work as the natural outgrowth of providing our clients with additional information.

A CPA firm's experience with a computer

The firm first became interested in the possible advantages of electronic data processing for small and medium-size companies when a client installed a computer a few years ago. A survey of the client's operation had revealed the need for improved budgeting controls and the client selected the computer as the means of getting the timely information essential to any improvement. At the end of the first three months of the system's operation, the company's margin of profit had substantially increased. This, analysis indicated, was due to the various tight controls made possible, especially the ability to post and classify purchase orders against the budget daily.

Once they were convinced that electronic data processing offered substantial advantages even to small firms, the partners studied the possible ways in which these advantages could be extended to companies that could not justify the cost of available equipment. The CPA firm decided to use the facilities of an outside service bureau, supervising its work for the firm's regular clients. An outside consultant who had been advising the partners on the possible alternatives was asked to assist in preparing for the service bureau approach, and an accountant with extensive machine-accounting experience was hired on a full-time basis.

Upon hearing of the CPA firm's plan, a company which had a computer suggested that the CPAs take over the equipment and its staff. The medium-sized company had discovered that it only needed 20 per cent of the computer's time for its own work. The company became a general client of the CPA firm and, as such, employed them to carry on the electronic data processing the company needed.

The accountants, therefore, found themselves with a computer and a trained, experienced staff to operate it. The immediate availability of equipment and trained staff eliminated the two major objections that had previously caused the CPA firm to reject the idea of acquiring their own equipment.

The new service met with immediate acceptance by clients and the present use amply justifies the operating costs. It has proved possible to serve clients at a cost no higher than they would normally pay for manual clerical work and to get the results to them very much faster. For example, daily reports are available at the start of the next working day, and monthly reports are ready fifteen to twenty days sooner than would be possible under a manual system.

Why one firm discontinued the punched-tape method

After one year of experience in this field, we have decided to abandon punched-tape accounting temporarily. This decision does not imply that punched-tape accounting has no place in a CPA office, but it is our opinion that at the present time, the detriments outweigh the benefits for the following reasons:

1. *Delay in processing tapes.* The service center attempted to schedule work by individual CPAs and not by CPAs as a class. This resulted in a contract providing for two servicings per month with a setup charge for additional services. To provide the kind of service to which our clients had been accustomed, the costs appear to be prohibitive. We tried various combinations of bimonthly schedules and found that no matter what combination was devised, some clients during the month did not meet the deadlines. As much as three weeks elapsed from the time data was given our office until a finished report was delivered to the client. We also found that, with the utmost co-operation from the client, the fastest we could deliver a report via punched-tape machine accounting was a week to ten days. Our clients were most unhappy with the delay.

2. *Difficulties encountered in correcting mistakes.* We found that frequently two months were necessary to correct the mistakes made in accumulating data for processing. If a wrong code number was used by the client or by our staff, it was frequently discovered too late to correct in the next month's accounting run and the error had to be corrected in the second run following. This caused numerous memorandum-type adjustments in the intervening months and wasted a considerable amount of time on the jobs.

3. *Difficulty encountered at end-of-year closings.* Many of our clients do not provide inventories, accounts receivable, or accounts payable immediately upon close of the fiscal year. Frequently, inventories were taken at the

date of closing but priced and extended at later dates by the clients' employees, when it would least interfere with their regular work. It is not uncommon for a client to fall two or three months behind at the close of his year. If we attempted to catch up on a month-by-month basis through the punched-tape machine, we found it would take six months to catch up with a client who had fallen behind three months. The answer to this situation was to process transactions monthly without an opening balance sheet or to catch up with the work in one lump: either solution required spending extra time on the job.

4. *Employee fatigue.* The punched-tape attachment sounds like a machine gun operating in the office. This noise was partially eliminated by putting the machine and operator in a private office to which the door was closed, but the machine noise was responsible for an excessive amount of employee fatigue. We found that the efficiency of a person's work decreased sharply after the first hour of running the machine; after the second hour, efficiency decreased to a point where the work had to be almost entirely redone. It is our opinion that no employee should be scheduled for more than a sixty- to ninety-minute shift each morning or afternoon.

5. *Employee antagonism toward machine accounting.* We found that since the punched-tape machine was new, a natural antagonism and resentment arose among our employees. This, coupled with the difficulties of correcting errors, caused the employees to blame human errors on the accounting machine in conferences with a client. Such action resulted in certain clients demanding that their accounts be taken off the punched-tape machine, when their demands were not warranted.

6. *Clients not suited to punched-tape machine.* Only the work of some of our clients is adaptable to machine operation—the so-called "clean" accounts. It is very difficult to process information for clients whose records are not current, fairly accurate, and for which the coding has not been correctly maintained. With certain other clients, machine production was constantly delayed while the operator tried to obtain information from the client.

7. *Difficulty in analyzing certain accounts.* We had several occasions to analyze certain accounts for clients or Internal Revenue agents. We found that the records produced by punched-tape accounting showed disbursements or purchases by folio and amount thereof, but there was no ready identification of the folio. When working from handwritten records, the vendor or payee frequently discloses the information desired in analyzing the account in question, but with the punched-tape machine, it was necessary to look up the check or voucher to ascertain the needed information. By the time we attempted to analyze said accounts, this original posting information had been returned to the client's office and was sometimes not available or difficult to recover. Greater difficulty will probably be experienced in attempting to analyze records three to five years old.

8. We were advised that it would be extremely impractical to make one run of data and prepare subsidiary records therefrom. The processing center should be able to prepare accounts receivable, accounts payable, and/or cost records from a single run, depending upon the wishes of the client, without the necessity of an involved setup. The setup charges proposed when this was requested from our existing service facilities were prohibitive and discouraged several clients from having records processed in this manner.

The above defects are not insurmountable, but they present problems to which ready solutions have not yet been found. We feel that electronic computers are capable of producing better results than mechanical process-ing, but at the present time the rental cost of an electronic computer is too great for a small firm.

How one firm makes full use of a single tape-punching machine. The following practitioner is not in favor of transporting the tape-punching machine to the client's office:

> In connection with the recording process, I have often been asked whether or not our staff people transport the tape-punching machine to clients' offices. I know this is done by some individual practitioners, but I seriously question its practicability for any but the smallest of firms. In the first place, we are talking about a fairly substantial investment for a small accounting organization, one which cannot produce at the optimum level when its activity is so restricted. For a firm such as ours, with several offices, or for a firm with a staff of several accountants, the most practical approach would appear to be the acquisition of a single tape-punching machine operated by a clerical employee to duplicate tapes prepared by accountants on standard adding machines in clients' offices. Although there is some duplication of time involved, it is not material in view of the fact that an average operator in our office, using a ten-key machine, is able to attain a recording and checking speed of at least 400 transactions per hour.

Mechanizing the CPA's Accounting System

RECORDING STAFF TIME WITH A BOOKKEEPING MACHINE

■ MEDIUM- AND LARGER-SIZED firms which recommend machine bookkeep-ing to clients will find many uses for it within their own offices.

After conducting a study of the recording of staff time with a bookkeeping machine, a practitioner installed such a machine in his office. The machine bookkeeping system has:

1. Greatly reduced the work required to post time records
2. Simplified the job so that almost anyone in the office can be taught to do it
3. Given up-to-the-minute balances of unbilled time as soon as each week's posting is completed
4. Proved accuracy of posting immediately, with easy checking to find differences
5. Shown each staff member's nonchargeable time up to date, telling how effectively each staff member has been utilized

Several methods were investigated, considering the size of the firm and the number of entries to be made in the records. Finally a simple two-register bookkeeping machine was installed. Such a machine would provide speed, simplicity, and adaptability to other possible work.

Card-filing system. To supplement the machine, a ledger card file would give quick access to information. For this reason, the practitioner installed an inexpensive visible posting tray to house the machine-posted time record cards.

Cards are overlapped in wide rows in the file, with headings and right-hand (balance) columns visible. The visibility greatly speeds up finding cards for posting. Since each time sheet may list several clients, not necessarily alphabetically, speed in finding cards means that items can be posted in whatever sequence they appear on time sheets. All chargeable items on a time sheet are posted at one time, without rehandling sheets.

The visible balances make it easy to get information or to prepare summaries, since the cards need not be removed from the tray. Shading of the next column to the left signals that a card has been removed. This signal speeds up refiling after posting and helps to get the card back in the right place.

Time record cards. A separate time record card is used for each client, engagement, and staff class. If necessary, a separate card is used to accumulate time by staff class for each portion of the engagement, such as auditing, writing reports, preparing tax returns, and traveling. The use of separate cards makes possible any number of breakdowns of time without exceeding the totaling capacity of the bookkeeping machine. A separate card is also used for each staff member, to accumulate his nonchargeable time for the year.

The time record card has columns for week-ending date, staff member (code number posted), time worked (this week), old balance, and to date. The card makes no provision for dollar values of time spent. It is more economical to extend the balance-to-date whenever required, rather than to extend each entry before posting.

A different card color is used for each staff class. This speeds up finding cards for posting, since there is a color change between each client and the proper card color can be seen instantly. The card colors also help to show up mispostings. One digit of the staff member's code number is his staff class. A discrepancy between the number and the color is easily spotted when the card is handled.

Time sheets. The time record clerk takes three steps before machine-processing:

1. Arranges the sheets in groups by staff class
2. Checks off time sheets on a preprinted list of names to see that all sheets for the week have been received
3. Foots and crossfoots the sheets by eye

Weekly time summary. Before posting to the cards, the bookkeeping machine is used to make a listing (in duplicate on a blank proof sheet) of each group of time sheets by staff class. This listing, the weekly time summary, shows staff member number, total chargeable hours, and total nonchargeable hours. Totals of both chargeable and nonchargeable hours are printed after listing each group of time sheets by staff class.

The weekly time summary has several uses:

1. It serves as proof that the week's time has been posted correctly to the time record cards. The totals must agree with the totals from the posting run.

2. After proof, one copy goes to the office manager as his weekly report of hours worked.

3. Another copy goes to the payroll clerk as his overtime record.

Posting to time record cards. Each item on the time sheet is then posted to a time record card. Two runs are made for each group of sheets by staff class:

1. Chargeable hours are posted. The machine is cleared. The total is proved with total chargeable hours for the staff class on weekly time summary.

2. Nonchargeable hours are posted to the card for each staff member's nonchargeable time. The machine is cleared. The total is proved with total nonchargeable hours for the staff class on the weekly time summary.

A proof sheet behind the time record shows each posting, for checking back if necessary.

In addition to the proof of totals posted with the weekly time summary, there is also proof that the previous balance has been picked up correctly. The machine procedure provides for picking up the old balance twice, at the beginning and at the end of each posting. If the amounts picked up agree, the machine prints "00" on the proof sheet. If the amounts disagree, it prints the difference. The proof sheet is scanned after posting to see that "00" appears on each line. After proof, the time sheet is filed in a folder for each staff member, for use at the year-end. Weekly totals of chargeable time are posted to an unbilled time control card for each staff class.

Recording billing. When an engagement is billed, the relevant cards are removed from the unbilled file. Each is marked "billed" with the date, below the last line posted. The balances on all cards pulled are listed with an adding machine. The balance on each card is then posted to reduce the balance on the unbilled time control card for the staff class. The machine total of postings is proved with the adding-machine tape. The cards for the billed engagement are then used for costing and filed in a closed file.

Annual time summary. The remaining task for the time record system, to accumulate time worked for the year for each staff member, is done very easily with the machine.

The folder of time sheets for each staff member is used for an annual time summary. The machine prepares a listing on a blank proof sheet showing staff member, chargeable time, and nonchargeable time.

PUNCHED-CARD SYSTEM

The following is a presentation of some of the highlights of a system used by a two-partner firm with ten staff men and several clerical employees. Several years ago the details of their cost system were turned over to the local office of a punched-card service. Its sales representative, a CPA, helped devise a system that has not only cut bookkeeping expense, but also provides prompt information as to the time and "standard" cost and fees on every engagement.

When the bookkeeper receives the biweekly time sheets, she enters the client's code number from a visible index file and sends them to the business machine office. Included are the time sheets turned in by the stenographers, typists, bookkeeper, and multilith operator. (This firm charges clients for the direct time of clerical employees.) The punched-card service furnishes five reports. The first two cover the two-week period only.

Biweekly reports. The first report totals, by individual clients, the time charged to each client's account for the period. This report gives the firm an idea of the time currently charged to each engagement.

Client's name	Client's code no.	Total hours	Standard cost	Billable amount
Abrams Lumber Co. ...	103	11.25	64.60	74.93
Baldwin Press	703	7	54.60	63.00
Corcoran Co.	267	15	103.00	115.00
Sterling Drill	360	63.50	358.95	446.75
Totals		1,167	7,388.54	8,426.66

The second report details the time put in by personnel working on the current engagements. This checks with the clients' totals in the first report:

Client's name	Acc'ts. initials	Hours	Standard cost	Billable amount
Abrams Lumber Co.	RT	.50	5.40	6.00
	CC	7.75	49.60	58.13
	RV	2.25	7.20	8.10
	MD	.25	.80	.90
	FP	.50	1.60	1.80
Totals		11.25	64.60	74.93

Work-in-process ledger. The third report constitutes the work-in-process ledger at the end of the current period, as it cumulates all of the unbilled time to date. It enables the firm to check the total time put in against estimated fees that may have been submitted to clients and to approximate anticipated profit if bills are rendered at standard rates.

In effect, this report cumulates all costs on each engagement, because items are not deducted from the report until the final bill has been rendered. While an engagement is in process, the firm frequently mails an interim bill to the client covering the approximate charges to date. These bills become debits to the client's accounts, but they are credited to a deferred account, which is closed out of the fee account when the final billing has been made.

Client's name	Client's code no.	Hours	Standard cost	Billable amount
ABC Co.	127	95.75	679.49	785.87
Abrams Lumber ..	103	44.25	269.03	311.04
Adams Dept. Store	145	337.50	2,040.59	2,300.86
Yale Press Co. ...	842	181.50	1,121.71	1,258.81
Zero Ice Cream Co.	896	88.25	525.91	613.19
Totals		20,243	136,156.82	155,463.80

Cumulative time and expense summaries. The next report gives in detail the cumulated time spent by personnel on each client for the year to date. It supports the preceding summary:

Client	Accountant	Hours	Standard cost	Billable amount
Adams Dept. Store	AC	8.50	47.57	53.27
	MK	130.00	963.60	1,114.00
	CC	51.25	251.13	281.88
	SG	65.75	307.18	342.88
	TV	67.50	322.86	361.38
	MD	4.25	13.50	15.30
	RT	8.00	25.30	28.80
	FF	2.25	7.20	1.10
	Expense		102.25	102.25
Totals		337.50	2,040.59	2,300.86

This report is sent to the firm in duplicate, so that the carbon copy may be cut apart and details of in-process engagements distributed to the partner or senior accountant in charge. He uses this as a check against his estimated time and fees. If the engagement is complete, the carbon strip furnishes the information needed to fix the fee and suggests the description of services rendered to be put on the client's invoice.

When the partner in charge of a given client is ready to bill, he pastes the carbon strip on a preprinted 8½- by 11-inch sheet which contains space for a description of the engagement. Owing to his familiarity with the work done, the partner can usually fill this in without referring to other records. In another column, the partner enters the fee to be charged and the wording to be used on the bill.

The fifth report is a summary of the expense items shown on the reverse side of the accountant's time sheets. Direct chargeable expense is added to the cumulated costs on each client's account.

After clients' bills are prepared, the business machine office is advised of the accumulated hours, costs, and fees to be deducted from the cumulated totals to date. This constitutes the debit to cost of fees and the credit to work in process for control purposes in the general ledger. At the same time, the firm charges the client and credits fees with the actual amount billed. Any differences between tabulated fees and actual billings are reflected in a fee variance account.

Other available analyses. Current and historical information by client or accountant is always available on the punched cards. Therefore, periodic analyses can be made of the performance of individuals or clients for a variety of purposes. Among these are analyses of productive and nonproductive staff time, which can also be extended at the cost or basic billing rate in this firm. This can be of great help when staff bonuses are determined. Although the staff of this firm is on a salaried basis, this type of report would provide timely and accurate payroll information in cases where staff members are on a drawing account, receiving a certain portion of the fees they earn.

All these reports are reviewed by the senior partner as soon as they are available—usually within a day or two after the time records have been submitted to the business machine office. Any adjustments on the billing amounts are made directly on the reports. These are maintained chronologically and represent the current and historical record of the firm's operation.

Only the posting to the client's ledger from these reports is handled within the firm. Even so, only the cumulative totals of costs, charges, and adjustments are extended along with interim bills and payments made by the client.

Possible modifications. The reports used by this firm can easily be modified to provide quick and accurate information to large and small firms under a variety of circumstances.

For example, the type of work classifications which appear only on the accountant's time reports can be incorporated in the service reports to give the partner an idea of what has been done for the client. (This firm has not deemed this information necessary, since the partners are familiar with the work to be performed for all their clients and are basically interested in the amount of time involved.) Some firms might find that they would not need a separate listing for "standard cost" and basic "billing amount." If costs are accurately incorporated in a realistic billing rate, extension of this rate might be an adequate guide to determine the "resistance point" in setting the fee.

Advantages and disadvantages. The firm finds the following advantages to this mechanized system of recording time and costs:

1. Ledgers are always current. This enables billing to be accurate and prompt, and reduces the working capital tied up in client's accounts.
2. The firm is always currently informed on budgeted time for engagements while they are still in progress.
3. From the punched cards on each client and each employee, many supplementary reports may be obtained for analysis of services, bonus computations, and the like.
4. The tabulation of indirect time as coded on time sheets gives a good analysis of the nonchargeable payroll.
5. Mechanized time controls are more economical than a manual system and free the bookkeeper for other essential services.

There is one basic disadvantage to this system. Even when the work classification codes appear in the reports, it is difficult to note unusual aspects of an engagement or significant contributions which should be considered in setting the fee. It is necessary to refer to the original time reports or working papers to evaluate these elements. However, many manual methods are also inadequate in this respect. It seems that a mechanized system of recording time might be especially suited to a firm whose practice is largely devoted to recurrent services of similar nature to regular clients.

VARIOUS SPECIMEN FORMS

On this and the following pages (752-777) a variety of forms appear; all of them are referred to in the text of Section 7.

Figure 16. Client Master Card

[Name of Company]   CLIENT MASTER CARD

Client ———————————————————— | Corporation ——Partnership ———

Individual ———Fiduciary ———

Street ——————————— Tel. ——— | Order ————————————

State of incorporation ————

City ————————— Zone — State ——— | Date org. or incorp. ————

Principals ——————————————————————————————

———————————————————————Mail reports to ————————

Partner contact ————————————Referred by ————————

Related clients ——————————————————————

Attorney ——————————————————————

Type of business ——————————————————————

RECURRING OPERATIONS CARDS IN ACTIVE FILE		NONRECURRING OPERATIONS
——Annual Audit State tax returns & due dates		Cards in history file
——Annual statements ————————		Description Date mailed
——Monthly statements ————————		———— ————
——Quarterly statements ————————		———— ————
Ending ——————— Special tax matters ———		———— ————
Monthly work, no report ————— ————————		———— ————
Other ————————— ————————		———— ————
——————————————		———— ————
—————————— Special reports ———		———— ————
——1120——1065 ————————		———— ————
——1040——1040ES Cont'd. on reverse side —		———— ————
Other ————————		———— ————

Remarks

	1	2	3	4	5	6	7	8	9	10	11	12	YEAR ENDS

Figure 17. Operations Card—Audit

[Name of Company]   **OPERATIONS CARD**

Client _____

Assignment _____ As of _____

Mail to _____

Recurring _____ Nonrecurring _____ No. of copies _____ Due date _____

For Ended				
In Charge				
Preliminary—Started				
Preliminary—Finished				
Final—Started				
Final—Finished				
In Review				
Mailed				
Field Hours				

Remarks:

Figure 18. Operations Card—Tax Work

Client _____

Assignment _____ As of _____

Mail to _____

Recurring _____ Nonrecurring _____ No. of copies _____ Due date _____

For Ended			
In Charge			
Completed by Accountant			
Received—Review Department			
Received—Tax Department			
Review Completed			
Received—Comparing & Proving			
Mailed			
Field Hours			

Remarks:

Figure 19. Tickler Card (Front)

John Doe & Co.	PERMANENT CARD
President, John Doe, Sr.	
Vice President, John Doe, Jr.	
Secretary, Mrs. John Doe	
Treasurer, Mrs. John Doe, Jr.	
Directors: Officers + A.B. Smith, Comptroller	
Bookkeeper, Miss Mary Brown	
Attorney: B.C. Jones, c/o Jones, Jones, Jones, & Jones, 1452 XYZ Bldg,	RA 6369

Fiscal Year Ends Oct. 31   Chartered May 2, 1922.

Engagement: Semi-annual audit

                   Income Tax Returns

                   Corporation Franchise Tax Returns

Special Features: Occupational tax due August 1.

Figure 19. Tickler Card (Reverse)

✓ 1949-50 Audit Report and Returns mailed 1-3-51
✓ City Occupational Tax 2-1-51   Ok - ame.
✓ State   "   "   3-1-51   Ok - ame
✓ 5-1-51 Commence S/A Examination   Ok - ame
✓ 6-10-51 Delivered S/A Report to J.D. Jr.   ame   also handled
                                                                occupational
✓ Bring up 9 mo. 8-1-51   Completed 9-2-51   B.
✓ Pre-closing visit Oct.
   Commence audit about 11/8/51

Orange Indicator		Red Line	Blue Indicator	Orange Slide Indicator	Orange Indicator

Mr. Doe | Sr. | Private Phone LY 1429

| 1 | 2 | 3 | 4 | 5 | 6 | 7 | 8 | 9 | 10 | 11 | 12 | 1 - 3 - 5 - 7 | 9 - 11 - 13 - 15 - 17 - 19 - 21 - 23 - 25 - 27 - 29 | |

2 | John Doe & Co., Inc.   Corp.   432 James St. | N.O. 12   RA 6369 | 4

Figure 20. Follow-up on Tax Returns

FOLLOW-UP ON TAX RETURNS

John Doe Corporation

Year Ended _____

Sent To Office For Typing	Final Filing Date	Return Delivered To Client	
			FEDERAL TAX RETURNS
			STATE TAX RETURNS

Figure 21. Client Information Record

Name of Client: Fiscal year
Address: Title
Owners' names: Title
                                            Title

Regular fee or rate charged
Date of first engagement   Assigned to:
Comments

	Date work completed		
(X)*(O)†	1961	1962	1963

Annual audit
Bookkeeping
Income tax returns:
  State
  Federal
Intangible returns
FICA returns:
  1st qtr
  2nd qtr
  3rd qtr
  4th qtr
U.C. returns:
  1st qtr
  2nd qtr
  3rd qtr
  4th qtr
  Annual fed.
Domestic corp.
Corp. registration
Ad valorem
Sales tax
  J.
  F.
  M.
  A.
  M.
  J.
  J.
  A.
  S.
  O.
  N.
  D.
Other:

*"X" indicates that we are charged with the duty to perform this item.
†"O" indicates that we do not do it unless specifically asked to.

Figure 22. Time and Expense Report (Front)

NAME OF COMPANY – TIME REPORT

CLIENT'S NAME	NATURE OF ASSIGNMENT	ASSIGN. NO	DISTRIBUTION OF TIME BY DAYS															HRS	RATE	AMOUNT	TOTAL EXPENSE
			1 16	2 17	3 18	4 19	5 20	6 21	7 22	8 23	9 24	10 25	11 26	12 27	13 28	14 29	15 30	31			

TOTAL CLIENT'S HOURS

ADMINISTRATIVE

UNASSIGNED

TAX AND ACCOUNTING RESEARCH

NAME

TOTAL HOURS PRESENT

HOURS ABSENT: { ILLNESS

VACATIONS AND HOLIDAYS

OTHER TIME OFF

TOTAL HOURS RECORDED

HALF MONTH ENDED

Figure 22. Time and Expense Report (Reverse)

NAME OF COMPANY - EXPENSE REPORT

DESCRIPTION	1 / 16	2 / 17	3 / 18	4 / 19	5 / 20	6 / 21	7 / 22	8 / 23	9 / 24	10 / 25	11 / 26	12 / 27	13 / 28	14 / 29	15 / 30	31	Total
Transportation Type*																	
From To																	
From To																	
From To																	
Rooms																	
Meals																	
Taxi & Limousine																	
Tips																	
Laundry & Valet																	
Total																	

*Indicate Auto Mileage _____

Bal From Last Report

| Advances | Cash | |
| | Tickets | |

Total Advances

Total Expense This Report

| Returns | Cash | |
| | Tickets | |

Balance Due Firm

758

Figure 23. Expense Report

EXPENSE REPORT

NAME _____

OFFICE _____ WEEK ENDED _____, 19___

DAY	Monday	Tuesday	Wednesday	Thursday	Friday	Saturday	Sunday	TOTAL
I T I N E R A R Y								
MILEAGE CHARGEABLE								
TRANSPORTATION								
MILEAGE								
HOTEL								
MEALS								
TOTAL								

D I S T R I B U T I O N

	D E B I T S				C R E D I T S	
CLIENT	Order No.	Amount	Account No.	Amount	Account No.	Amount
TOTAL						

R E M A R K S

759

Figure 24. Expense Report

EXPENSE REPORT
(SEE INSTRUCTIONS ON REVERSE SIDE)

OFFICE _____

ASSISTANT'S NAME _____

PERIOD ENDING _____ 19 ____

DATE REC'D BY OFFICE _____

(PLEASE PRINT)

DATE	DETAILS OF EXPENSES CHARGEABLE TO CLIENTS (LIST CLIENTS NAMES ALPHABETICALLY)	DETAILS	TOTALS BY CLIENTS	POSTED

TOTALS (TO SUMMARY) _____

CHECKED BY _____   APPROVED BY _____   ASSISTANT'S SIGNATURE _____

DATE	DETAILS OF EXPENSES CHARGEABLE TO ORGANIZATION, ETC.	DETAILS	TOTAL	POSTED

TOTAL (TO SUMMARY)

SUMMARY

DATE	CASH ACCOUNT	RECEIPTS	PAYMENTS
	BALANCE FROM LAST REPORT		
	RECEIPTS (GIVE DATE AND OFFICE)		
	REFUNDS AND ADVANCES TO OTHER ASSISTANTS (GIVE DATE AND OFFICE)		
	TOTAL EXPENDITURES		
	CHARGEABLE TO CLIENTS		
	CHARGEABLE TO ORG., ETC.		
	BALANCE AT END OF PERIOD		

INSTRUCTIONS FOR PREPARATION OF EXPENSE REPORT

PER DIEM ALLOWANCES:

MEALS—SHOW NUMBER OF DAYS CHARGEABLE TO EACH CLIENT COMPUTED AT AUTHORIZED PER DIEM RATE. THE NUMBER OF DAYS CHARGED SHOULD BE THE NUMBER OF DAYS FOR TRIP ACTUALLY FALLING WITHIN THE PERIOD COVERED BY THE REPORT.

ROOM—SHOW NUMBER OF DAYS CHARGEABLE TO EACH CLIENT COMPUTED AT AUTHORIZED PER DIEM RATE, AS IN THE CASE OF MEALS. THE NUMBER OF DAYS CHARGED SHOULD BE THE NUMBER OF DAYS FOR THE TRIP ACTUALLY FALLING WITHIN THE PERIOD COVERED BY THE REPORT.

IF HOTEL BILL IS NOT PAID TO END OF PERIOD, ATTACH RECEIPTS FOR PREVIOUS CURRENT PAYMENTS AND STATE THAT RECEIPT FOR REMAINDER OF PERIOD WILL BE SUBMITTED AT A LATER DATE. CONSECUTIVE RECEIPTS FOR ALL HOTEL BILLS MUST BE SUBMITTED BEFORE SETTLEMENT OF EXPENSE BALANCE IS MADE.

SCHEDULES SHOWING AUTHORIZED PER DIEM RATES ARE ON FILE AT EACH OF THE FIRM'S OFFICES. IF THERE ARE NOT READILY AVAILABLE CONSULT STAFF MEMBER IN CHARGE OF WORK.

RAILROAD FARES:

POINTS OF DEPARTURE AND ARRIVAL SHOULD ALWAYS BE SHOWN. WHERE PULLMAN ACCOMMODATIONS ARE USED THE STUBS SHOULD BE ATTACHED TO EXPENSE REPORT. FARES SHOULD BE SHOWN AS FOLLOWS:

DATE 1949	DETAILS OF EXPENSES CHARGEABLE TO CLIENTS (LIST CLIENTS NAMES ALPHABETICALLY)	DETAILS	TOTALS BY CLIENTS	POSTED
June 5	Empire Manufacturing Co.			
	New York to Atlanta, Ga.			
	R.R. Fare	$28.44		
	Pullman (Lower)	7.55		
	Tax	5.40	$41.39	

OTHER EXPENSES:

THESE SHOULD BE ITEMIZED:—

EXPENSE REPORTS SHOULD BE APPROVED BY THE MANAGER OR SENIOR IN CHARGE OF THE WORK. IF HE IS NOT AVAILABLE MAKE A NOTATION TO THIS EFFECT ON THE FACE OF THE REPORT AND THE OFFICE TO WHICH YOU ARE REPORTING WILL SECURE THE NECESSARY APPROVAL.

EXPENSE REPORTS ARE ORDINARILY DUE ON THE FIRST AND SIXTEENTH OF EACH MONTH. HOWEVER, UPON COMPLETION OF TRIPS AND RETURN TO THE FIRM'S OFFICE AT OTHER TIMES DURING THE MONTH THE RELATIVE EXPENSE REPORT SHOULD BE SUBMITTED NOT LATER THAN THE DAY FOLLOWING SUCH RETURN. THE FINAL EXPENSE REPORT MUST BE ACCOMPANIED BY ANY CASH BALANCE DUE TO THE FIRM.

IT IS IMPORTANT THAT EXPENSE REPORTS BE SUBMITTED ON TIME FOR THE REASON THAT SALARY CHECK WILL BE WITHHELD UNTIL REPORT IS RECEIVED.

Figure 25. Weekly Time Report

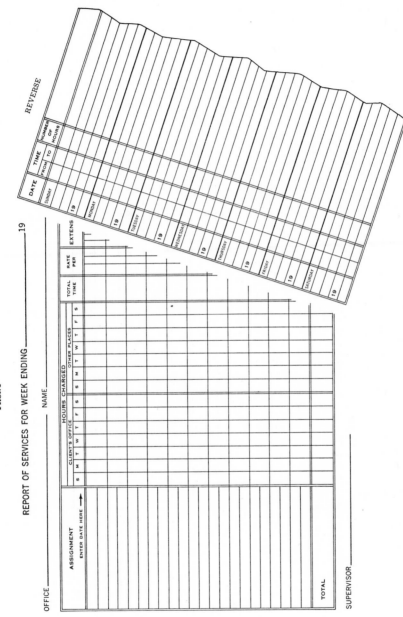

Figure 26. Daily Time Report

CLIENT		DATE		19
PLACE		REPORTED BY		
(STATE NAME IN FULL)				
(WHERE WORK WAS DONE)				

SERVICES: GIVE BRIEF EXPLANATION AS TO CHARACTER AND VOLUME OF WORK PERFORMED IN SUCH FORM AS TO INDICATE THE DAILY PROGRESS MADE.

EXAMINATION:		HOURS
As of or Period	AUDIT	
	SYSTEM	
	SPECIAL	

MAKE SEPARATE TIME REPORT FOR EACH CLIENT AND FOR UNASSIGNED OR LOST TIME.

REPORTS TO BE MADE OUT IN OWN HANDWRITING.

ALL REPORTS TO BE APPROVED BY SENIOR IN CHARGE,

Approved ———————

Entered ———————
Time Ledger

Figure 27. Weekly Time and Expense Report (Front)

WEEKLY TIME SHEET

Hotel (if out of town) _____ Week ended_____ , 19____
Residence
Street Address _____ Phone (Residence)_____ Name_____

Client	Nature of Engagement (Segregate Special Work)	Work Done (show only Std. WP No., if work is shown thereon)	Hours								✓
			S	M	T	W	T	F	S	Total	
Brought forward											
Total Direct											
Management											
New Business Development											
Office and General (explain):											
Vacations											
Unassigned											
Other Indirect (explain):											
Total											

Approved:_____
(Senior in Charge)   (Supervisor)

Figure 27. Weekly Time and Expense Report (Reverse)

WEEKLY EXPENSE REPORT

Week ended_____, 19_____

Name_____

	Sun.	Mon.	Tues.	Wed.	Thurs.	Fri.	Sat.	Total
Breakfast								
Lunch								
Dinner								
Total Meals – including tips								
Railroad Fare								
Station Porters								
Parlor Car								
" " Porters								
Sleeping Car								
" " Porters								
Hotel Room (attach bill)								
" " Porters								
Taxi – to Station								
" – from Station								
" – Other (explain)								
Parcel Room Charges								
Laundry and Pressing								
Auto Allowance								
Telephone – outside								
Telegram – "								
Postage – "								
Street Car Fare								
Other (explain)								
Total								

DISTRIBUTION

Client	Nature of Eng.	Sun.	Mon.	Tues.	Wed.	Thurs.	Fri.	Sat.	Total
Local Car Fare (total)									
Total									

SUMMARY OF ACCOUNT	Dr. (Di sbs.)	Cr. (Recd.)	
Bal. at beginning of week			
Total Disbursements, as above			
Received (detail):			
			Approved:_____
			(Senior in Charge)
Total			_____
Balance at end of week – Net			Supervisor

764

Figure 28. Client Ledger Sheet

UNBILLED RECEIVABLES—CLIENTS

LEDGER SHEET NUMBER ______

Client ____________________

Address ____________________

Attention: ____________________

Billings must be on basis indicated and must be approved by partner in charge.

Basis of Billing

Monthly ______; Quarterly ______

Annually ______; Assignment ______

Fixed monthly charge ______

Partner to review bill ______

Date	Accountant or Invoice No.	DESCRIPTION OF WORK PERFORMED, NATURE OF EXPENSE OR SUMMARY OF INVOICE	Hours Charged	AMOUNT OF CHARGED TIME BY CLASSIFICATION					Amount of Expense	BILLING		Balance Unbilled
				Partners	Tax Staff	Audit Staff	Office			Adjustment	Amount of Bill	
		Balances forwarded										

Figure 29. Client Ledger Sheet (Front)

ACCOUNTANT		EXPENSE	HOURS								BILLING		
			TOTAL	ABC	DEF	GHI			TYPING	TRAVEL TIME	DATE	AMOUNT	
CLIENT X Y Z MANUFACTURING COMPANY													
ENGAGEMENT 1961 AUDIT													
Nov. 1960	ABC	10.25	7	5						2			
	DEF	5.00	11½		9½					2			
	GHI	12.00	13			11				2			
	TYPIST		2						2				
Jan. 61	DEF		3		3								
Feb. 61	ABC		10	10									
	DEF		5		5								
TOTALS			51½	15	17½	11			2	6			

766

Figure 29. Client Ledger Sheet (Reverse)

			ANALYSIS FOR FINAL BILLING		
ACCOUNTANT	HOURLY RATE	TOTAL HOURS	IDEAL FEE	BILLED FEE	MEMO
ABC	10.00	15	150.00	153.81	
DEF	6.00	17 1/2	105.00	107.67	
GHI	4.00	11	44.00	45.12	
TYPIST	3.00	2	6.00	6.15	
TRAVEL	None	6			
TOTAL FOR ACCOUNTANTS		51 1/2	305.00	312.75	Ratio-of Billed Fee to Ideal Fee 102.54%
EXPENSE			37.25	37.25	
TOTAL			342.25	350.00	

767

Figure 30. Bill Draft

[Name of Company]
Bill Draft

CLIENT ———————————— BILL DRAFT NO. ———

ADDRESS ————————————

————————— ATTENTION ———————— DATE OF BILL ———

(please check)

——(1) Regular (Special) accounting and tax services rendered
during the month of ——— (period from ——— to
———) $———

——(2) Services rendered in connection with examination of accounts (preparation of financial statements from books
without audit) as at ——— and preparation of report
thereon; preparation of corporation income tax return
for the year ended ——— (fiscal year ended ———);
preparation of State of ——— income tax return
for the year ——— (fiscal year ended ———); and
preparation of partnership return of income for the year
ended ——— (fiscal year ended ———) $———

——(3) Special services rendered during the month of ———
in connection with review of installation of accounting
system and procedures $———

——(4) Services rendered in connection with preparation of Federal income tax return for the year ——— and preparation of declaration of estimated tax for the year
——— $———

——(5) Other services—detail text of bill

$———

Travel and hotel expenses $———

Total $———

LEDGER DATA AS OF ——— 19—

LEDGER SHEETS BALANCE AMOUNT BILLED   BILLING ADJUSTMENT BALANCE

SPECIAL ALLOCATIONS AND REMARKS

Prepared by ———————
Approved by: ———

———
Supervisor ———————
Typed by — Bill #———

Figure 31. Estimated Inventory of Work on Closings

Estimated Inventory of Work on Closings, As of June 30, 1961

(As Listed From Operations Cards – Excluding Monthly Accounts)

Client	Work Required	Estimated Time No. of Men	Estimated Time Days	Partner In Charge	Supervisor	In-Charge Accountant	Assistants	Estimated Starting Date	Field Work Date Begun	Field Work Date Completed	Field Work Days Consumed	Report Mailed	Remarks
Doe Motor Co.	A - Yr.	2	12	L.M.P.	Jones	D. Sewell	Smith	7/1	7/5	7/20		8/14	
Brothing, Inc.	A - Q	2	20	L.M.F.	J. White	C. Brown	B. Brown	7/3	7/3	7/18		8/10	
Acworwood, Ltd.	Spec. 149-50-51	1	35	M.S.	Jones	Gray	none	7/1	7/1				
La. Police Exchange	A - SA	3	27	L.M.F.	Jones	Writtle	Marks, Mizhado	7/8	7/10	7/10		7/27	
Jeromes Co. of Jamestown	A - Yr.	1	5	L.F.P.	Jones	Gore	none	7/3	7/3	7/02		8/12	
Murtagh Wheel Co.	A - SA	2	10	F.H.P.	Brune	Gore	Marks	7/15	7/18				
Alloy Mills	A - Q	1	6	M.S.	J. White	C. Brown	none	7/8	7/8				
Stafford, Inc.	A - SA	2	15	L.H.P.	Brune	Kaplan	Whitman	7/18	7/17	7/25			

Legend

A - Audit

SPEC - Special Service

Yr. - Year Annual

Q - Quarterly

770

Figure 32. Short-range Forecast and Staff Location Chart

(Name of Company)

Short-Range Forecast - Month of July, 1961

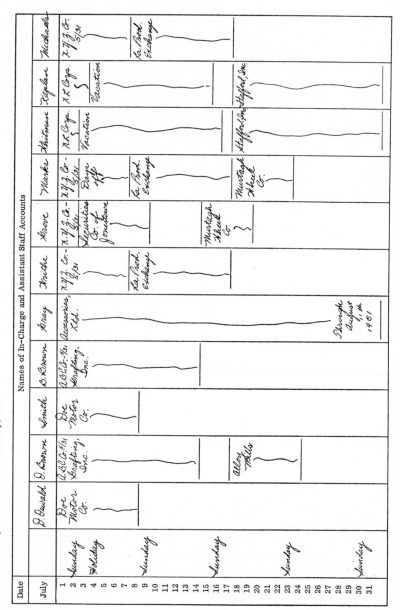

Figure 33. Long-range Work Forecast

(Name of Company)

Long-Range Forecast   October 1, 1961 to April 30, 1962

Names of Accountants (Excluding Partners and Tax Staff)	WEEKS ENDING											
	Oct. 7	Oct.14	Oct. 21	Oct. 28	Nov. 4	Nov. 11	Nov. 18	Nov. 25	Dec. 2	Dec. 9	Dec. 16	Dec. 23
D. Oswald	←First Nat'l Bank→ ←Marshall Equipment Co.→		←Marshall Equipment Co.→			←Johnsons-Busch Co.→		Johnsons-Busch Co.				

Note: Two Lines are used for each man. The first line (in red) shows actual time. Last year, the second (in black) shows estimated time this year.

Figure 34. Detailed Engagement Time Budget

TIME BUDGET

Examination

Client _____ Date _____

Approved   Supervisor _____ Date _____

Prepared by _____   Partner _____ Date _____

Preliminary Work: Final Work:

Start: _____ End _____   Start _____ End _____

Budget (in hours)

	May to Nov.	Dec. to Apr.
Cash		
Receivables:		
Confirmation of balances		
Checking ledgers, etc.		
Inventories:		
Observation of physical counts		
Price tests, etc.		
Investments		
Plant accounts		
Reserves for depreciation		
Deferred charges		
Notes and accounts payable		
Provision for taxes		
Other accrued liabilities		
Reserves		
Capital stock and surplus		
Income accounts		
Costs and expense accounts		
Current provision for taxes		
Other P and L accounts		
Minutes, agreements, etc.		
Conferences with client		
General supervision and planning		
Report and statement		
Survey of internal control		
Maintenance of permanent files		
Travel		
Other matters		
Total budgeted hours		
Total actual hours preceding engagement		

(Excludes tax and report departments' time)

Figure 35. Engagement Program—Other than Monthly

[Name of Company]

ENGAGEMENT PROGRAM
AUDITS OR ENGAGEMENTS OTHER THAN MONTHLY

Date ....

Approved by ....

A. CLIENT—OFFICIAL TITLE (Print) ....

....

B. LOCATION OF OFFICE ....

....

C. TO WHOM REPORT SHOULD BE ADDRESSED ....

....

D. PERIOD TO BE COVERED BY ENGAGEMENT ....

    1—From .... To close of business ....

    2—As of close of business ....

E. SPECIFIC NATURE OF SERVICE (Include special instructions as to scope of engagement, etc.) ....

....

....

....

F. REPORT—NUMBER OF COPIES (........); SHOULD INCLUDE:

    1. Comments.

        a. Comprehensive ....

        b. Special emphasis on:

            1. Internal control ....

            2. Operations ....

        c. Certificate ....

    2. Balance Sheet ....

    3. Statement of Surplus ....

    4. Statement of Profit and Loss ....

    5. Statement of Income and Expense ....

    6. Statement of Operations ....

    7. Special Schedules ....

....

....

G. WORK ON ENGAGEMENT COMMENCED .... COMPLETED ....

H. ACCOUNTANTS ....

I. TIME—Audit and Tax Returns ...... COMMENTS .... REVIEW ......

GENERAL INSTRUCTIONS

Complete the Internal Control questionnaire (Page 2) before adopting the engagement program, as the information from this source is most important in determining the scope and extent of examination necessary for proper verification. The engagement program is primarily a valuable guide for the accountant on an engagement as it suggests the most important operations to be covered in the audit procedure. The accountant in charge should confer with the supervising partner before deleting or curtailing the adopted program or increasing the scope; and the said partner should note in the program his approval of the change. The accountant in charge should study the program before commencing the actual work so that he will be able to organize the routine of the procedure.

Cash counts should be "surprise" counts and should be made simultaneously at all locations, and at the same time all investments and negotiable instruments should be placed under the control of the accountant until examined.

Inaccurate or incomplete programs will be returned for correction; hence before leaving client's office be certain that the program is complete or changes therein are approved and supported by good reasons.

An "X" should be placed at the left of the item in the program indicating that the item should be included in the procedure, and an "X" should be also placed over the numerals at the top of the columns indicating the months in the period in which the items of procedure are to be applied. The hours (to ¼ hr.) consumed in completing the procedure should be noted in the proper column and the initials of the accountant performing the item of procedure should be placed in the column headed "acct." as each operation is completed together with a " ✓ " in the "month" column indicating the completion thereof.

Figure 36. Engagement Program—Monthly

[Name of Company]

ENGAGEMENT PROGRAM

BOOKKEEPING AND SPECIAL MONTHLY EXAMINATION

ENGAGEMENT:

MONTHLY .... Approx. date of Visit ....   Date ....

QUARTERLY ....   Approved by ....

SEMI-ANNUALLY ....

ANNUAL CLOSING DATE ....

A—Client—Official Title (print) ....

Executive to contact ....

B—Location of Office .... Location of Records ....

Type of Business .... Type of Organization ....

C—Period to be covered by engagement:

1. From .... To close of business ....

....

D—Specific Nature of Service (include Special Instructions as to scope of engagement, etc.) ....

....

....

....

E—Report—Typed (......)—Pencil Copy (......).

Monthly ...., quarterly ...., semi-annually ...., annually ....

1. With Comments ....

2. Without Comments ....

3. Number of Copies ....

4. Address to (if other than client) ....

F—General:

Period	Time	DETAIL WORK Accountant		SUPERVISION AND REVIEW Time	Name	TOTAL TIME
1.	....	....		....	....	....
2.	....	....		....	....	....
3.	....	....		....	....	....
3.	....	....		....	....	....
4.	....	....		....	....	....
5.	....	....		....	....	....
6.	....	....		....	....	....
7.	....	....		....	....	....
8.	....	....		....	....	....
9.	....	....		....	....	....
10.	....	....		....	....	....
11.	....	....		....	....	....
12.	....	....		....	....	....
Total	....	....		....	....	....

SPECIAL INSTRUCTIONS

The accountant assigned to a Bookkeeping engagement should study the program carefully and familiarize himself as to the detail work called for. He should also study the operation of the business and be familiar with the actual system of handling transactions. He should ascertain the nature of the General Ledger accounts and should be certain that the workpapers contain a chart of the operating accounts. (This may not be necessary if a Trial Balance is included in workpapers.)

If possible, where a monthly Trial Balance is required, this should be taken on 16 column worksheet using one column for each month with Assets, Liabilities, Income and Expenses on separate sheets as provided for in the Procedure Manual. Continuing schedules of Property accounts and analyses of certain expenses can be carried in workpapers each month, adding the month's transactions on the monthly visit, thus eliminating the necessity for additional time for preparing such schedules at the time of the annual closing.

The Accountant actually performing the work of the engagement should note briefly in spaces provided any recommendations for changes in system that will improve the system of recording transactions and the system of internal control. These changes should be discussed with the Supervising partner and "cleared" by him by a notation of his action thereon. All recommendations should be dated and signed by the accountant.

Approval of the supervising partner should be obtained before any changes in the scope of this engagement are made.

Figure 37. Notice of Contract (Front)

NOTICE OF CONTRACT

Date ——————— 196 ——

Client ———————————————	NAMES OF PARTNERS
Street and No. —————————	————————————————
Town and State ———————	————————————————
Kind of Business ———————	————————————————
Corporation — Partnership —	————————————————
Single Proprietorship —	Name of Proprietor —————
Closing Period —————————	Name of Office Manager, Comptroller,
	Auditor or Head Bookkeeper
MANAGEMENT	————————————————
Name of Pres. —————————	When Ready to Start —————
Names of Principal Stockholders	Arranged by ——— With ———
	Kind of Service ———————

Figure 37. Notice of Contract (Reverse)

PER DIEM RATES AGREED TO

Partners ——————— $ ———
Seniors ——————— $ ———
Juniors ——————— $ ———
Typists ——————— $ ———
Are Expenses to be added? ———
Maximum Fee Agreed to $ ———
Flat Price Agreed to $ ———
Are Expenses to be added? ———
Are We to Prepare Franchise and Capital
  Stock Tax Returns? ———
Agreed Fee Therefor $ ———
Are We to Prepare Federal and State
  Income Tax Returns? ———
Agreed Fee Therefor $ ———

Figure 38. Daily Work Analysis Schedule

CLIENT ______________________________ REPORTED BY ______________________________

	TOTAL HOURS																																					
DATES	TODAY	TO DATE	CASH	RECEIVABLES-CONFIRMATIONS	RECEIVABLES-CHECKING, ETC.	INVENTORIES-QUANTITIES	INVENTORIES-PRICE TESTS, ETC.	INVESTMENTS	PLANT ACCOUNTS	RESERVES FOR DEPRECIATION	DEFERRED CHARGES			NOTES AND ACCOUNTS PAYABLE	FEDERAL AND STATE TAX ACCRUALS	OTHER ACCRUALS	RESERVES	CAPITAL STOCK AND SURPLUS			INCOME ACCOUNTS	COSTS AND EXPENSE ACCOUNTS	CURRENT YEAR'S PROV., FED. & STATE TAXES	OTHER P. & L. ACCOUNTS			MINUTES & CONTRACTS	CONFERENCES WITH CLIENT	GENERAL SUPERVISION	REPORT AND STATEMENTS			PREPARATION OF FEDERAL TAX RETURN	PREPARATION OF STATE TAX RETURNS	SPECIAL TAX WORK (EXPLAIN)			TRAVEL
15-DAY SUB-TOTALS																																						
MONTHLY TOTALS																																						

Figure 39. Summary Classification of Time

SUMMARY CLASSIFICATION OF TIME

CLIENTS_____

CLASSIFICATION OF WORK	19 PRELIMINARY	19 YEAR END	19 TOTAL	19 PRELIMINARY	19 YEAR END	19 TOTAL	19 PRELIMINARY	19 YEAR END	19 TOTAL	19 PRELIMINARY	19 YEAR END	19 TOTAL	19 PRELIMINARY	19 YEAR END	19 TOTAL
YEARS ENDED_____															
CASH															
RECEIVABLES:															
CONFIRMATION OF BALANCES															
CHECKING LEDGERS, ETC.															
INVENTORIES:															
OBSERVATION OF PHYSICAL COUNTS															
PRICE TESTS, ETC.															
INVESTMENTS															
PLANT ACCOUNTS															
RESERVES FOR DEPRECIATION															
DEFERRED CHARGES															
NOTES AND ACCOUNTS PAYABLE															
PROVISION FOR TAXES															
OTHER ACCRUED LIABILITIES															
RESERVES															
CAPITAL STOCK AND SURPLUS															
INCOME ACCOUNTS															
COSTS AND EXPENSE ACCOUNTS															
CURRENT PROVISION FOR TAXES															
OTHER P. & L. ACCOUNTS															
MINUTES, AGREEMENTS, ETC.															
CONFERENCES WITH CLIENT															
GENERAL SUPERVISION AND PLANNING															
REPORT AND STATEMENTS															
10-K															
PREPARATION OF TAX RETURNS:															
FEDERAL															
STATE															
SPECIAL TAX WORK															
SURVEY OF INTERNAL CONTROL															
MAINTENANCE OF PERMANENT FILES															
TRAVEL															
OTHER MATTERS (SPECIFY IF MATERIAL)															
TOTAL HOURS															

POSTED FROM DAILY
WORK ANALYSIS SCHEDULES

777

Appendix

Contents

Appendix to Section One (Fees)

STATEMENT ON COMPETITIVE BIDDING FOR AUDIT SERVICES

The following statement was issued jointly by the general committee on accounting of the Municipal Finance Officers Association of the United States and Canada and the committee on local governmental accounting of the AICPA. It is a revision of a joint statement issued in 1955. It was distributed by MFOA to associations of government officials and was made available by the Institute to state CPA societies for local distribution.

Competitive bidding can be an effective tool in government when properly used.

It enables a governmental agency to obtain commodities of the highest possible quality at the lowest possible price.

This is a useful method only if the items purchased can be measured by exact specifications. A request for bids on a commodity or item of equipment, for example, can specify quality, grade, and other recognized specifications for which acceptable standards have been formulated—and the delivered commodity or equipment can be tested to ensure compliance with these standards. Units of measurement and performance for construction projects can also be determined and specified.

Competitive bidding, however, is not an effective procedure in arranging for an independent audit.

It is not effective for the simple reason that an audit is not something which can be covered by rigid specifications. An audit is a professional service requiring professional independence, skill, and judgment. An independent auditor should have as much latitude as he may find necessary to be assured that the records are in order and that the system of accounts is functioning properly.

Yet many governmental agencies continue to call for competitive bids in obtaining the services of independent certified public accountants.

This confusion of principle, incidentally, is confined almost exclusively to independent auditing services. It is not common practice for government officials to advertise for bids in order to engage appraisers in condemnation actions, lawyers to represent them in court, or architects or engineers to prepare plans and supervise construction of a building or a highway.

It may be that public officials continue to use competitive bidding in the belief that it is legally required with respect to professional services. If this impression exists, legal opinion should be sought in order to settle the question.

If selected by a process of competitive bidding, the independent auditor will approach his work with an awareness that he has somewhat demeaned his profession in accepting an engagement on a bid basis. Moreover, he will generally be hampered by either overly detailed or inadequate specifications which he had no part in framing and therefore may be required to perform work which, in his professional judgment, need not be done, or precluded from doing work which he knows ought to be done.

Independent auditors should not be subject to arbitrary dictation in matters pertaining to their work, and auditing should not be placed on the lowest possible standard of performance which can be made acceptable.

This statement is not intended to challenge the right of governmental officials to obtain some estimate of their auditing expenses. Once a governmental agency has decided to engage an independent auditor, it ought to discuss the engagement with the auditor it believes to be best qualified to render the most satisfactory service. After the independent auditor has surveyed the fiscal records and identified the principal problems, it should be possible to develop an understanding on the scope of his audit and on the length of time which will be required for its completion. The independent auditor should then be in a position, if required, to give an estimate of the cost of the service which is not likely to be exceeded unless he encounters unforeseen problems.

This approach to the selection of an independent auditor, reflecting a legitimate concern for costs, is perfectly reasonable and acceptable. But no one gains—indeed, everyone is likely to lose—when auditors are selected by competitive bidding on the basis of the lowest possible price.

It would be in the best interest of all concerned for political subdivisions employing a certified public accountant or firm of certified public accountants to do so in the same way in which they would select an attorney, doctor, or other professional adviser—choose the one in whom they have confidence, discuss the work to be done, and agree on the basis for the fee.

Appendix to Section Two (Staff Personnel)

LETTER TO SELECTED STUDENTS*

Dear . . . . :

The firm of certified public accountants, Smith, Jones & Doe, hopes that you find this pamphlet helpful in making a constructive choice of career. The American Institute of Certified Public Accountants, which published it, is our national professional society; accordingly, you may be confident that its contents are significant and authoritative.

In addition, we would like to give you some information about our own firm.

Smith, Jones & Doe was founded in 1921 by John W. Smith and has grown steadily ever since. From its first decade, the firm has rendered significant accounting services in every important area of economic activity in and around Usonia City. Today, our client index includes over one hundred business classifications. In addition, we serve a variety of institutional and governmental clients.

The firm now has three partners and seven staff accountants. Mr. Robert C. Doe, the present senior partner, leads the firm in stimulating a strong interest in education. Mr. Doe has been professor of accounting at Usonia State College and is now professor emeritus. So it is not surprising that men employed by Smith, Jones & Doe have an unusually good opportunity to meet the experience requirement for attaining the CPA Certificate. Twenty-five staff men in the firm have passed the CPA Examination, ten during the past four years.

While the Certificate is a distinction that any professional accountant in public practice should attain, we believe it is only one of the opportunities open to those who work for our firm. In general, our staff accountants have a chance to grow and become the best kind of general accounting practitioners, capable of rendering expertly all major public accounting services.

Many of our clients are small and medium-size businesses, and a staff man who audits these businesses must examine every aspect of financial management without being submerged in any single part of the procedure. This work necessarily provides invaluable perspective on what makes business "tick." Also, a staff man soon acquires rounded experience in estate planning, tax services, and other management services. While acquiring all this experience, the staff man has the direct help of the firm's partners.

After a staff accountant has established his competence and capabilities, Smith, Jones & Doe rely upon him to deal directly with clients. The firm feels

*This letter, the "Student Information Blank" (p. 785), and the "Evaluation Sheet" (p. 786), were originally part of a kit produced by the advisory committee on personnel recruiting of the AICPA.

that it is in the interest of both staff man and firm to expand his activities. He is expected to advance rapidly in terms of responsibilities assumed and in terms of professional status. We can say with candid pride that the staff man is likely to find that the community has great respect for him because of his association with the firm.

The partners regard the certified public accountant as a member of an honored and learned profession. Consequently, staff men are encouraged to continue their studies. The firm provides for the use of study materials prepared by the American Institute of Certified Public Accountants and participation in its professional development program. Members of the firm regularly participate in the Usonia Regional Accounting Conference; and they serve as members of the committees of the Usonia State Society of Certified Public Accountants. The partners feel that this activity is beneficial both to the firm and to the profession as a whole.

Such, in broad summary, are the characteristics of Smith, Jones & Doe as they are likely to affect a staff accountant's professional advancement. Also, we would like to give you some information about those conditions that affect the personal lives of the men who work for the firm.

The concentration of the activities of Smith, Jones & Doe within a 200-mile radius from Usonia City makes it possible to restrict the amount of travel required of staff men. A man is rarely out of town more than ten nights a year.

Among the factors that affect the personal lives of the men in our firm is the happy circumstance that we work and live in Usonia City. The constant growth and increasing prosperity of both city and surrounding area augur well for the future of the whole business community, including Smith, Jones & Doe. Also, the location of the firm's offices in a relatively small and well-planned city reduces commutation time to a minimum, while the accessibility of lakes and countryside helps to keep us healthy and relaxed.

In sum, we believe that Smith, Jones & Doe provides an environment conducive to positive professional growth and happy personal adjustment.

This letter is merely a generalized statement of what our firm is and what it offers to the potential professional accountant. We like to regard it as an introduction of our firm to those students who we have reason to believe are likely to become first-class professional accountants. I would welcome your inquiries. However, if you don't call me within a few days, I shall call you.

Sincerely yours,

STUDENT INFORMATION BLANK

This form will furnish us with helpful information about you that we would otherwise need to obtain during the initial interview. We can thus devote maximum time to answering your questions. Please fill out in your own handwriting.

Name ....
First   Middle Initial   Last

College
address .... Telephone ....

Home
address .... Telephone ....

          Height ....   Married ......   No. of

Age ......   Weight ....   Single ....   dependents ....

High school .... Graduation date ....

College ....

Other college attended ....

Results of AICPA tests:

Number of accounting   Orientation test ...... Date taken ....

credits you will have   Level I .... Date taken ....

had by graduation ....   Level II .... Date taken ......

Quality point averages: (Indicate highest mark attainable, i.e., A, 4.0, etc.

........)   Over-all .... Accounting subjects ....

College activities (honors, societies, elective offices, athletics)
Non-college activities(hobbies, civic groups, etc.)
Military status (subject to draft, ROTC, etc.)

Employment record:

Employer and address	Nature of work	From - To	Hours per week approximately
....	....	....	....
....	....	....	....
....	....	....	....

Date ....   Signature ....

EVALUATION SHEET

1. Check the appropriate spots on the lines so as to roughly indicate an estimated percentile rating. Underscore the appropriate words.

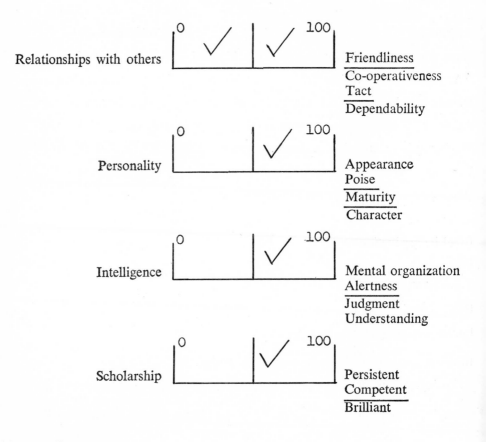

Average

Relationships with others 0 ✓ ✓ 100   Friendliness
Co-operativeness
Tact
Dependability

Personality 0 ✓ 100   Appearance
Poise
Maturity
Character

Intelligence 0 ✓ 100   Mental organization
Alertness
Judgment
Understanding

Scholarship 0 ✓ 100   Persistent
Competent
Brilliant

2. Comments:

STAFF AND NONSTAFF APPLICATION BLANK (Front)*

Complete in your
own handwriting
using ink

APPLICATION FOR EMPLOYMENT

Application for position as . . . . Date . . . .

NAME . . . .
      (Please print name)   (Last)   (First)   (Middle)

ADDRESS . . . . City . . . . Telephone Number . . . .

Have you ever applied to this firm for a position? . . . . . . Date . . . .

Who referred you to this firm? . . . .

Date of birth . . . . Place of birth . . . . U. S. Citizen . . . . . .

Age . . . . . . Height . . . . . . Weight . . . . . . Physical defects . . . .

Married ( )   Single ( )   Separated ( )   Divorced ( )   Widowed ( )

Full name of husband or wife . . . . Your sex . . . . . .

Dependents, names, ages, and relationships . . . .

. . . .

In case of accident notify . . . .

Date available . . . .

Time lost through illness during last two years . . . .

Draft Status . . . . Social Security No. . . . .

Father's occupation . . . .

References — other than relatives (name three)

     Name   Address   Occupation

. . . .

. . . .

. . . .

(over)

*Source: *CPA Handbook,* AICPA, 1952, Ch. 7, App. B, pp. 7-9. (One of a co-ordinated set of forms for a public accountant's office.)

STAFF APPLICATION BLANK (Reverse)

Education	Years	Name and Location of School	Course of Study	Degree
High School	. . . .			
College	. . . .			
Business	. . . .			
Other	. . . .			
	. . . .			

EXPERIENCE

Give complete record of all employment you have had. Record most recent position first and work back. May we write to your present employer? . . . .

Dates of Employment (Month & Year)	Name and Address of Employer	Annual Salary	Description
From . . . . To	Name . . . . Address . . . . Immediate Supervisor	Start . . . . . . Final	Duties . . . . Reason for leaving . . . .
From . . . . To	Name . . . . Address . . . . Immediate Supervisor	Start . . . . . . Final	Duties . . . . Reason for leaving . . . .
From . . . . To	Name . . . . Address . . . . Immediate Supervisor	Start . . . . . . Final	Duties . . . . Reason for leaving . . . .
From . . . . To	Name . . . . Address . . . . Immediate Supervisor	Start . . . . . . Final	Duties . . . . Reason for leaving . . . .

Do you have a C.P.A. certificate? . . . . . . Date obtained . . . . State in which taken . . . . . . Do you plan to take C.P.A. examination? . . . . .

I affirm that all of the information I have set forth in this application is true to the best of my knowledge and belief

. . . .

Signature in full

Remarks

. . . .

Education	Years	Name and Location of School	Course of Study	Degree
High School	. . . .			
College	. . . .			
Business	. . . .			
Other	. . . .			
	. . . .			

EXPERIENCE

Give complete record of all employment you have had. Record most recent position first and work back. May we write to your present employer? . . . .

Dates of Employment (Month & Year)	Name and Address of Employer	Annual Salary	Description
From . . . . To	Name . . . . Address . . . . Immediate Supervisor	Start . . . . . . Final	Duties . . . . Reason for leaving . . . .
From . . . . To	Name . . . . Address . . . . Immediate Supervisor	Start . . . . . . Final	Duties . . . . Reason for leaving . . . .
From . . . . To	Name . . . . Address . . . . Immediate Supervisor	Start . . . . . . Final	Duties . . . . Reason for leaving . . . .
From . . . . To	Name . . . . Address . . . . Immediate Supervisor	Start . . . . . . Final	Duties . . . . Reason for leaving . . . .

Check below the appliances and equipment that you know how to operate:

( ) Adding machine   ( ) Addressograph   ( ) Calculator   ( ) Comptometer
( ) Dictating equipment   ( ) Duplicating machine ( ) Electric typewriter   ( ) Graphotype
( ) Switchboard   ( ) Office offset   ( ) Typewriter   ( ) Stenotype
( ) Varityper

Typewriting speed (words per minute) . . . . . .
Stenographic speed (words per minute) . . . . . .
Transcribing speed (words per minute) . . . . . .

I affirm that all of the information I have set forth in this application is true to the best of my knowledge and belief

. . . .

Remarks   Signature in full

. . . .

. . . .

INTERVIEWER'S RECORD*

Name ——————————————————————————Age ————— Single —— Married——

Major Interest ————————————————————————————————

Hometown ——————————————————————(Wife's) ——————————————

Location Preference ——————————————Reason ——————————————

——

Father's Occupation Is (Was) ——————————————————————————————

Persons Who Are Well Acquainted with Applicant's Scholastic and General Ability:
           Name   Evaluation

1. ————————————   ————————————————————

2. ————————————   ————————————————————

3. ————————————   ————————————————————

Acctg. Courses ————————————————————————————————

AICPA Test Scores ——————————————————————————————

Co. Repr. Checks (✓) the Evaluation of Each Quality Listed	Unsat.	Quest.	Satisf.	Very Good	Superior	Remarks (use reverse side for additional space)
Appearance						
Mental Alertness						
Attitude						
Aggressiveness						
Cap. for Dev.						
Interest in Us						
Do You Recommend Employment?	State Work for Which Best Suited					Company - Location
What Commitments Were Made by Interviewer?						
Date	Name of Interviewer					Company

*Source: *CPA Handbook*, AICPA, 1952, Ch. 9, App. A, p. 11.

Name .... Date of Reports ....

(SEE REVERSE SIDE FOR INSTRUCTIONS)

	Assistant		*Light*	*Senior* Medium	*Heavy*	*Other* Designate
	Junior	*Semi-senior*				
What level of work did this employee perform as the basis for your rating?	—	—	—	—	—	——
1. Technical knowledge (its adequacy for level of work indicated)	60 . . . . Deficient in working knowledge of fundamentals	70 . . . . Needs more basic information to become productive		80 . . . . Has sufficient knowledge to do good work	90 . . . 100 Excellently prepared for duties	
2. On-the-job performance (see reverse side for definition)	60 . . . . Unsatisfactory	70 . . . . Occasionally satisfactory		80 . . . . Quite consistently satisfactory	90 . . . 100 High grade performance at all times	
3. Capacity for future growth (leadership)	60 . . . . Lacks qualifications to make headway	70 . . . . Ability limited to intermediate assignments		80 . . . . Is able to handle increasingly responsible assignments	90 . . . 100 Should progress to high level of responsibility	
4. Ability to write reports, notes to financial statements, etc. (if applicable)	60 . . . . Incapable of original reporting; careless with facts	70 . . . . Can follow previous routine reports. Original work not good		80 . . . . Fair, but requires editing	90 . . . 100 English and presentation good; facts carefully stated	
5. Development of assistants (if applicable)	60 . . . . Lacks ability to instruct less experienced men	70 . . . . Sometimes does not get assistants to understand what is expected of them		80 . . . . Generally successful in transmitting knowledge to assistants	90 . . . 100 Does excellent job of training assistants	

If you were discussing his rating with this employee, what would you consider the most constructive thing to tell him with respect to his performance and preparation for future responsibility? (BE SURE TO ANSWER THIS QUESTION)

....
....
....
....
....

Date .... Signed ....

*Source: *CPA Handbook*, AICPA, 1952, Ch. 9, App. A, p. 3.

When completing an Employee Progress Report for a given individual it should be borne in mind that the making of this rating has a twofold purpose. First, it is to help the management in selecting logical persons for promotion and in administering a sound salary policy. Second, a frank discussion with the employee so rated will keep him posted with respect to his progress and point out ways in which he might be able to improve his record.

In rating a person be sure you do not compare the record of a beginner with the performance you expect from a more experienced person. For instance, if you are rating a junior accountant on technical knowledge, be sure to evaluate this characteristic on the basis of what a junior accountant must know about auditing procedure and do not give him a low rating because he does not happen to know as much as the senior for whom he is working. Acquirement of further knowledge will come with additional training. Attached are specifications covering the responsibilities of junior, semi-senior, and senior accountants to serve as a guide in rating staff members.

If a rating is discussed by the management with an employee, the identification of the rater will be kept anonymous at all times. A rating would not be discussed with an employee, usually, unless there were two or three ratings by different individuals which could be consolidated into a composite rating, thus affording the individual a more valid rating and protecting the identity of the raters to an even greater extent.

On-the-job performance. This is a broad category and the rating should be made carefully. It should take into consideration the amount of work performed, the degree of accuracy and neatness, dependability as to attendance and industry, success in getting along with associates and with members of the client's organization, analytical ability in understanding assignments, and resourcefulness in planning and executing the work. It is an omnibus rating but by giving the man you consider best the highest rating and the man you consider poorest the lower rating, you will have a man-to-man comparison which will give an accurate picture of the relative abilities of the persons you rate. Cover any specific weaknesses by your answer to the question at the bottom of the report.

PROGRESS REPORT ON JUNIOR ACCOUNTANT*

On Mr. . . . .   Date:

By Mr. . . . .

Work done at: · · · · · · · · · · · · · · · · · ·

Dates: . . . .

	GOOD	FAIR	POOR
Ability to grasp a situation			
Ability to follow instructions			
Ability to work with others			
Ability to work without supervision . . .			
Ability to command respect			
Ability to direct others			
Accuracy and freedom from errors			
Adaptability			
Conduct in client's office			
Constructive thinking			
Liking for his work			
Legibility of writing			
Mathematical ability			
Neatness of work			
Neatness of appearance			
Originality in work			
Personality			
Punctuality			
Receptiveness to criticism			
Speed in covering assigned tasks			
Technical knowledge			

REMARKS: . . . .

. . . .

. . . .

. . . .

NOTE TO SENIOR: Try to answer all questions, but do not answer a question unless you have had an opportunity to form a fair opinion, taking into consideration the junior accountant's previous experience and technical training.

*Source: *CPA Handbook*, AICPA, 1952, Ch. 9, App. A, p. 5.

STAFF PERSONNEL RATING SHEET*

	Points
I. Working Papers & Tax Returns:	
Presentability of Work	
A. Completeness	40
B. Conciseness	20
C. Neatness	30
D. Clearness	30
E. Adequately cross-referenced	30
F. Properly indexed & dated	30
G. Sheets initialed	20
H. Accuracy of detailed work	100
I. Accuracy of final results	100
II. Technical Ability:	
A. Knowledge of accounting & auditing theory	40
B. Application of accounting & auditing theory on job	40
C. Inquiry into accounting systems, internal control, etc.	50
D. Ability to prepare financial statements & schedules	50
E. Knowledge of income tax laws	50
F. Application of income tax law in preparing tax returns	50
III. Application to Work:	
A. Completing assignments in allotted time	100
B. Attention to broad phases of assignment	50
C. Ability to organize work	50
D. Initiative on job	50
E. Attention to pertinent detail	50
F. Resourcefulness on job	40
IV. Sense of Responsibility:	
A. Loyalty to firm	30

	Points
1. Does he try at all times to sell firm?	
2. Does he have pride in the firm and in knowledge that he is an essential part of the organization?	
B. Carrying out instructions	20
1. When given specific instructions, does he follow through?	
C. Self-reliance on job	20
1. Does he try to find answer before asking?	
D. Dependability	30
1. Does he get to work on time?	
2. Does he look after jobs assigned to him?	
3. Ability to work without supervision	
4. Does he follow instructions?	
E. Co-operativeness	30
1. Willing to work overtime when necessary	
2. Willing to travel when necessary on workdays, evenings, or Sundays	
3. Does he co-operate on job with supervisor?	
4. Does he accept advice and decisions?	
5. Does he work with other staff members?	

*Source: Practitioners Forum, *The Journal of Accountancy,* November 1959, pp. 83-84.

V. Professional Qualifications:
    A. Effectiveness in meeting and dealing with clients   100
    B. Judgment in presenting problems to superiors   100
    C. Education or training for public accounting   30
    D. Accuracy of judgment or decisions   200
    E. Effectiveness in presenting ideas or facts to superiors   150
    F. Ability to adapt education and training to company policies and procedures   30
    G. Ability to write   30
    H. Ability to speak   20
    I. Professional interest (CPA associations, clubs, sports, etc.)   10

VI. Personal Qualifications:
    A. Personal appearance   50
    B. Physical fitness (sickness)   30
    C. Personality   50
    D. Initiative in self-improvement (study, CPA or tax cases and law)   50
        Total   2,000

These questions do not enter into the point rating. However, you should answer each one.

RATING SHEET

A. Based on the staff member's classification, do you think he is qualified to perform:
    1. Senior work   . . . .
    2. Semi-senior work   . . . .
    3. Junior work   . . . .
B. In each classification, would you grade the man:
    1. Heavy   . . . .
    2. Average   . . . .
    3. Light   . . . .
C. When the staff member has worked on your jobs, have you discussed with him:
    1. Good work he has done   . . . .
    2. Poor performance   . . . .
    3. Deficiencies which you think he can correct   . . . .
    4. Steps that can be taken to correct deficiencies on that or other jobs   . . . .
D. In "C" above, what was the staff member's reaction to your comments?
    1. Appreciative   . . . .
    2. Receptive   . . . .
    3. Indifferent   . . . .
    4. Antagonistic   . . . .
E. Are you *glad, satisfied,* or *unhappy* when this staff member is assigned to your jobs?
F. Would you prefer *NOT* to have the staff member assigned to your jobs?
G. What training do you feel is needed for development and advancement?
    . . . .
    . . . .
    . . . .
H. Does he have potential for advancement in our firm?   . . . .
I. Is he ready for advancement in rank and salary *now*?   . . . .
J. Give any general or specific comments regarding the staff member.
    . . . .
    . . . .
    . . . .
    . . . .

Dated . . . .
    By . . . .

EMPLOYMENT CONTRACT FOR EMPLOYEES
SUBJECT TO FEDERAL WAGE AND HOUR LAW*

This contract is made and agreed to this ...... day of ....
A.D. .... by and between (Name of Company), Certified Public Accountants, of ...., a copartnership, hereinafter called the
company, and ...., hereinafter called the employee.
In consideration of the mutual covenants herein set forth, the company hereby
employs the employee upon the following terms and conditions:

1. The company will pay the employee a salary of $ .... per month,
payable in equal semimonthly installments, it being understood that this salary
represents a regular rate of pay of .... per hour for each forty hours worked
in each workweek and a rate .... for all hours worked in excess of
forty but not to exceed .... hours in each workweek and that the company guarantees to the employee this pay for the above-named .... hours
in each workweek during which the employee actually renders services or
has time off in accordance with the provisions of paragraph (2), even if in any one
workweek the employee should work less than the said .... hours. In case
the employee should work, in any one workweek, in excess of .... hours,
any such excess will be paid to him at 1½ times his regular rate or ....
per hour, which excess will be paid simultaneously with his regular pay at the
end of the month following the rendition of services in excess of .... hours
per week.†

2. The employee agrees to work for the company in the classification of
.... and to render satisfactory services within the
customary meaning of that term, and further agrees to devote his full time to
such employment. Full time shall be defined to mean the established working
hours of the company, to the exclusion of other business activity, plus such
reasonable overtime as the requirements of the company and the servicing of its
clients dictate, consistent with the usual service standards of the accounting profession and of the company; provided, however, that during any calendar year
the employee shall not be required to devote more than 2,024 working hours,
less any allowable vacation time. In the event the employee is not employed by
the company during the entire calendar year, he shall not be required to devote
more than such number of working hours (on the basis of 2,024 per year less any
allowable vacation time) as corresponds pro rata to the portion of the calendar
year during which the employee was actually employed by the company. To
effect these provisions by which the employee is not required to devote more than
2,024 hours per year (or such applicable portion thereof) less any vacation time,
the company may give the employee time off at any time. For any time worked
by the employee in excess of the 2,024 hours (or applicable portion thereof) less
allowable vacation, and for which no time off is given, the employee will be paid
at least 1½ times his regular rate, and such amount will be paid within a reasonable time, not to exceed three months, following the end of the calendar year
during which such excess hours were worked.

3. The employee shall not undertake any work as tax consultant, accountant,

*Source: *CPA Handbook*, AICPA, 1952, Ch. 9, App. B, pp. 33-34.

†The language and provisions of this paragraph contemplate features of the Belo-type
plan of employee compensation. If, for the purpose of adapting the contract language
to provide for another type of compensatory plan, it is desired to study in greater
detail the several alternative compensation arrangements which are acceptable for non-
exempt personnel, see paragraph 25,520 ff. of CCH, Inc.'s *Labor Law Reporter—
Wages, Hours* (Vol. 2).

auditor, or bookkeeper, directly or indirectly, for any person, firm, or corporation as long as he is in the employ of the company, nor shall he maintain any office facilities other than those furnished to him by the company. He shall, however, refer to the company any work of said nature which may come to his attention or under his control, but the company shall have the right to accept or reject such work within its sole discretion.

4. It is understood and agreed that when and as the abilities demonstrated by the employee shall so warrant, in the judgment of the company, he shall be advanced in position and duties to a position bearing a higher rate of compensation, notwithstanding the provisions of paragraph (1) hereof. Any such change in classification or compensation shall not affect the other provisions and restrictions in this agreement.

5. The employee hereby agrees that for a period of three years after the termination of his employment by the company, either voluntary or involuntary, he will not on either his own account or as a member of a firm, or on behalf of another employer, or otherwise, directly or indirectly, work as a tax consultant, accountant, auditor, or bookkeeper for or solicit such business from, any client of the company.

6. Both parties hereby agree that this contract shall continue for one year from the date executed, and from year to year thereafter, it also being understood that the term of employment may be terminated by either party at the end of any month during the first or any succeeding year by giving to the other party adequate oral or written notice. Adequate notice shall be defined as notice of one calendar week during the first six months of the contract and two calendar weeks thereafter.

7. The employee further agrees that for a period of two years after the termination of his employment under the provisions of this contract he will not employ nor offer to employ nor solicit employment of any employee of the company.

8. In the event that the employee violates the terms of any part of this agreement, the company shall have the right to apply to any court or competent jurisdiction for an injunction restraining the employee from further violation. The employee further agrees that he will pay on demand to the company as liquidated damages for any violation of paragraph (5) of this agreement a sum equivalent to the fees charged by the company in the preceding twelve months to the client or clients for whom any work was done or solicited.

9. The employee agrees that his right of termination as set forth in paragraph (6) shall be effective only during the period April 1 to October 31, inclusive, of each calendar year.

WITNESSETH the hands and seals of the parties hereto the day and year above written.

(Name of Company)   (SEAL)

WITNESS:

. . . .

(Name)

. . . .

(Address)

. . . .

(Name)

. . . .

(Address)

By . . . . Partner

. . . . (SEAL)

(the Employee)

EMPLOYMENT CONTRACT FOR EMPLOYEES
NOT SUBJECT TO FEDERAL WAGE AND HOUR LAW*

This contract is made and agreed to this .... day of ....
A.D. .... by and between (Name of Company), Certified Public Accountants, of (city), (state), a copartnership, hereinafter called the company, and
........................., hereinafter called the employee. In consideration of the mutual covenants herein set forth, the company hereby employs the
employee upon the following terms and conditions:

1. The company will pay the employee a salary of $........ (........
..........) per month, payable in equal semimonthly installments during the
period of actual employment and only during that period in which services are
actually rendered.

2. The employee agrees to work for the company in the classification of a
.... and to render satisfactory services
within the customary meaning of that term, and further agrees to devote his full
time to such employment. Full time shall be defined to mean the regularly established working hours of the company, plus such reasonable overtime as the requirements of the company and the servicing of its clients dictate, consistent with the
usual service standards of the accounting profession and of the company.

3. The employee shall not undertake any work as tax consultant, accountant,
auditor, or bookkeeper, directly or indirectly, for any person, firm, or corporation
as long as he is in the employ of the company, nor shall he maintain any office
facilities other than those furnished to him by the company. He shall, however,
refer to the company any work of said nature which may come to his attention or
under his control, but the company shall have the right to accept or reject such
work within its sole discretion.

4. It is understood and agreed that when and as the abilities demonstrated by
the employee shall so warrant, in the judgment of the company, he shall be advanced in position and duties to a position bearing a higher rate of compensation,
notwithstanding the provisions of paragraph (1) hereof. Any such change in
classification or compensation shall not affect the other provisions and restrictions
in this agreement.

5. The employee hereby agrees that for a period of three years after the
termination of his employment by the company, either voluntary or involuntary,
he will not on either his own account or as a member of a firm, or on behalf of
another employer, or otherwise, directly or indirectly, work as a tax consultant,
accountant, auditor or bookkeeper for or solicit such business from, any client
of the company.

6. Both parties hereby agree that this contract shall continue for one year from
the date executed, and from year to year thereafter, it also being understood
that the term of employment may be terminated by either party at the end of any
month during the first or any succeeding year by giving to the other party adequate oral or written notice. Adequate notice shall be defined as notice of one
calendar week during the first six months of the contract and two calendar weeks
thereafter.

7. The employee further agrees that for a period of two years after the termination of his employment under the provisions of this contract he will not employ
nor offer to employ nor solicit employment of any employee of the company.

8. In the event that the employee violates the terms of any part of this agreement, the company shall have the right to apply to any court or competent juris-

*Source: *CPA Handbook,* AICPA, 1952, Ch. 9, App. B, pp. 31-32.

diction for an injunction restraining the employee from further violation. The employee further agrees that he will pay on demand to the company as liquidated damages for any violation of paragraph (5) of this agreement a sum equivalent to the fees charged by the company in the preceding twelve months to the client or clients for whom any work was done or solicited.

9. The employee agrees that his right of termination as set forth in paragraph (6) shall be effective only during the period April 1 to October 31, inclusive, of each calendar year.

WITNESSETH the hands and seals of the parties hereto the day and year above written.

(Name of Company)   (SEAL)

By . . . . Partner

. . . . (SEAL)
(the Employee)

WITNESS:

. . . .
(Name)

. . . .
(Address)

. . . .
(Name)

. . . .
(Address)

STAFF MANUAL

An example of a staff manual used for staff instructions and guidance

A major portion of the staff manual of a large, national firm of certified public accountants is reproduced on the following pages as a good example of such a manual given to staff employees. It should serve to suggest the nature of items which may be covered appropriately in such a publication and, with suitable modifications, may aid other firms in the preparation of their own manuals.

CONTENTS

The purpose of this manual is to provide staff members with standards of conduct and suggestions which the firm considers necessary or desirable that its representatives follow. These standards and suggestions are the result of many years of experience in dealing with situations encountered in the conduct of the firm's work. The firm recognizes that all possible circumstances cannot be foreseen, and the manual purposely is flexible and therefore adaptable to unusual circumstances. Constructive suggestions for its improvement are always welcomed.

This manual does not outline auditing procedures or accounting methods. It deals with office routines and like matters and is for the information and guidance of members of our staff.

The firm would like to have each staff member become imbued with the spirit and ideals of the firm so that he will approach his work with a keen sense of responsibility for the tasks entrusted to him.

A brief reference to the history of the firm is included at this point.

Staff members should read the *Code of Professional Ethics* promulgated by the AICPA and consider them the general expression of the firm in respect of all matters therein contained. (*These rules are reprinted on page 823.*)

Personal conduct. *Contact with clients.* Each member of the staff is a representative of the firm. It is important that his contacts with clients and business associates be such as will reflect credit on the firm. Many things, such as personal appearance, habits, behavior, attitude toward clients and employees, and so on, help to form the impression made upon clients and others. Care should be exercised to avoid anything which may create an unfavorable impression.

Any staff member who is related to a client or to an officer or employee having a responsible position in a client's organization must bring such fact to the attention of our personnel manager upon being advised of assignment to such a client.

It is desirable that staff members do not become intimate with clients and their employees. The attitude toward both should be one of dignified friendliness and relations should not be such as to be the cause of embarrassment.

Clients and their employees should not be antagonized. They should be accorded courteous, dignified treatment under all circumstances. Staff members should maintain their equanimity and dignity at all times. In the event of unpleasant developments or disagreements with a client, the incident should be reported immediately to the supervisor or partner in charge.

Confidential matters. Discussion by staff members of the details of an examination should not be held within hearing of the client or his employees. The business of the firm must not be discussed with outsiders nor in public places with other employees of the firm.

The work of the public accountant relates to the affairs of others. Therefore, all matters becoming known to a staff member through his work for clients must be held in strict confidence. A client's affairs must not be discussed with a client's employees except by instruction of the client. Any request on the part of a client for information as to the scope of the examination or with respect to the contents of our working papers should be referred to the supervisor or senior in charge. Staff members must not discuss their work or any feature of it with anyone except members of our organization. This rule prohibits such discussion with members of your family, close friends, or others. Discussion of a client's affairs with other staff members should be limited to those currently engaged upon the work.

Financial transactions with clients. Money or gratuities must not be accepted from clients and any such offers must be reported promptly to the firm. Personal checks must not be cashed at clients' offices. Money must not be borrowed from or other debts contracted with clients or their employees.

Personal investments. No member of our organization shall own or acquire any securities issued by, or have any financial interest in, a client whose balance sheet or affairs he examines while in our employ.

Relations of supervisors, seniors, and assistants. The supervisor in charge is responsible for the proper conduct of the examination and preparation of the report, and the senior in direct charge of the engagement is specifically responsible for the work done on the engagement. The senior will determine the work to be done by each assistant, giving due consideration to the accounting ability and capacity of the assistant. He must have knowledge of the capabilities of the assistants assigned to him. If he has had no previous experience with an assistant assigned to him, he should ascertain from the personnel department the assistant's qualifications. As much as possible of the detail work should be assigned to juniors. Every effort should be made to avoid using, on the routine and elementary phases of the work, men who are capable of more advanced work. All work of junior assistants must be reviewed carefully either by the senior in charge or by one of his senior assistants. Juniors should be questioned upon all phases of the work they performed immediately upon its completion.

If the personnel assigned to an engagement is not suitable for handling the work in a capable and economical manner, it is the duty of the supervisor or senior in charge to report the condition promptly to the personnel department. If such condition is not corrected promptly, the supervisor or senior should inform the partner in charge of the engagement.

Assistants should not undertake work which they do not thoroughly comprehend. If they do not understand the character and purpose of the work assigned to them, they should have the instructions clarified before proceeding with the work. It is expected that assistants will give loyal co-operation and support to supervisors and seniors and that supervisors and seniors will do everything practicable to aid assistants in increasing their knowledge and skill.

No outside work. Experience has shown that to render the most effective service to clients, staff members must give their exclusive attention to the work of the firm. Accordingly they are not permitted to solicit or to undertake any accounting work for their own account.

Use of personal automobile. The use of a staff member's car on business of the firm should be limited to occasions when it would be impracticable to use other means of transportation. (See "Automobile Transportation" concerning reimbursement for use of personal automobile.)

Smoking. Judgment should be exercised with reference to smoking in the office of any client. Rules of the client regarding smoking should be observed.

Criticism. The clientele, work, fees, or characteristics of other public accountants should not be commented upon, criticized, or discussed with clients or clients' employees.

Staff members should not criticize a client's accounting system or discuss it with the client or his employees unless authorized to do so by a partner or supervisor. Criticisms or suggestions of staff members concerning a client's accounting system should be reported to the senior in charge for his consideration.

Offer of employment. Staff members must not solicit clients for employment. If a staff member is approached by a client with an offer of employment, the matter should be discussed promptly with the firm. The firm is pleased when an opportunity for advancement comes to any member of its staff and will gladly discuss questions of this kind with the staff member, giving due consideration to his best interest. Staff members must not discuss with a client or a client's employees such matters as the length of time he has been with the firm or the amount of his compensation.

Articles written for publication. The firm encourages the writing of articles for publication in accounting and other periodicals. Such articles usually indicate the firm connection of the writer. Embarrassment to the firm or to the staff member may result from the publication of articles prepared by a staff member which express views or conclusions differing from those held by the firm.

The firm, therefore, requires that any article prepared for publication by a staff member on the subjects of taxes, auditing, or accounting be submitted to the firm for review and approval before submission to a publisher.

Professional work. *Quality of work.* The firm requires each staff member to safeguard the firm's interests and to perform in an intelligent and creditable manner all work assigned to him. No assignment should be considered unimportant or unworthy of his best efforts. Important discoveries are frequently the result of intelligent and painstaking attention to matters of seemingly minor importance. The responsibility of a staff member is not fulfilled simply by seeing that the results of his work are set forth in his oral and written reports. He is responsible for carrying on the work as expeditiously as possible so that the cost will be kept within reasonable limits. The supervisor or the senior in charge should not permit any conditions to continue which operate to prolong the work unduly or bring discredit upon the staff or the firm.

Audit programs. An audit program approved by a partner exists for each recurring engagement. Based upon our review of the system of internal control and accounting procedures, the supervisor should give consideration to the adequacy of the program in the light of existing conditions. Changes in programs should be made only after consultation with and approval by a partner.

In undertaking work upon a new engagement, the partner in charge, together with the supervisor, will determine the scope of the examination to be made. If the engagement is expected to recur, a permanent binder and audit program should be prepared. If it is of a special nature and not recurring, a schedule should be prepared indicating the scope of the engagement and the work done. The notation at the head of each audit program, relative to changes in programs as required by circumstances, should receive careful consideration. Suggestions as to the best procedure are invited and no work should be undertaken without understanding the instructions and the reasons for them. If, in the judgment of a staff member, it appears desirable to do more or less than specified in the audit program, the staff member should submit the question to his immediate superior. The partner in charge must be consulted regarding important features developed during the progress of the work.

Working papers. Every staff member should become thoroughly familiar with the contents of the latest firm bulletins concerning engagements, audit programs, working papers, and so forth.

Assistance from clients' employees. Clients should be urged to have employees assist us by locating and arranging documents, papers, etc., as requested and by preparing for our use those schedules which can be checked by us to determine their accuracy. Clients' employees should not have access to our working papers and should not be informed of the progress or extent of the examination.

If the client's employees delay our work by negligence or deliberate failure to provide required information, relief usually can be obtained by discussing the matter with officials of the client. In the event of delay or failure to secure desired information, we will be considered at fault if we have not sought remedy from the proper person in the client's organization.

Report progress of work. The supervisor in charge should be kept informed of the progress of the work. Work which ordinarily would be done by client's employees should not be undertaken by us without approval of the supervisor or partner in charge. The senior in charge of the engagement is required to report promptly to the supervisor in writing, any factors which affect the scope of the work or prolong the examination beyond the time anticipated. The following factors are listed as examples of matters which should be so reported:

Requests by the client for additional services (including current work)
Instructions to client's employees at client's request
Accounts not ready for examination
Checks, vouchers, or other required papers badly filed
Material delay in securing data

If satisfactory progress cannot be made because of lack of co-operation, inadequate records, or unsatisfactory working conditions, the firm should be advised promptly. Excuses for delay will not be accepted by the firm unless it has been advised previously of the existence of unsatisfactory conditions.

Prospective clients or additional work for clients. Staff members should not agree to proceed with work for a prospective client unless approval of a partner is first obtained, or to do work in addition to that for which arrangements were made with the firm unless approval of a supervisor is first obtained.

Excessive time. The supervisor should note carefully the amount of time estimated or required on past examinations, and if such time is likely to be exceeded in the current engagement, the partner in charge should be notified at once.

Reports ready for review. The supervisor and partner should be informed, in advance, when reports will be ready for review so that reviews may be made promptly.

Assignments. All matters relating to assignments must be taken up with the personnel department. Any assignments made by partners should be reported immediately by staff members to the personnel department.

Assignment data requests, indicating the number of assistants needed and the approximate period each assistant will be required, should be prepared by the supervisor and submitted to the personnel department at the time the engagement memorandum is prepared. If it later develops that the engagement will extend beyond the estimated period, the personnel department should be notified of such change without delay. This department also must be notified of the availability of a staff member not later than the day before releasing him from an engagement. This rule serves to facilitate assignment to other work. The senior in charge of the work is responsible for this notification, but it is the duty of the assistant to call the matter to the senior's attention.

In the event that a client's office is to be closed for any reason (except holidays observed by the firm) the personnel department should be informed as early as possible so that, if practicable, other work may be arranged for that day.

When staff members are unable to report at the office or at the client's office by reason of illness or other cause, they should notify the office by telephone or telegraph, so that the client may be notified. Should staff members be on out-of-town engagements, the client's office, as well as the personnel department, should be notified directly.

When staff members are to report to the office for reassignment on the next working day and have not received an assignment, they should not leave the client's office before the firm's regular closing hours without communicating with the personnel department. It is often necessary, at the very close of the working day, to communicate with staff members regarding their next assignment.

All staff members reported by a senior as available for a new assignment on a certain day should be released on schedule unless other arrangements are made previously with the personnel department. To enable us to start engagements promptly as scheduled, strict adherence to the above rule is necessary.

Keep in touch with office. Staff members must keep the office informed of their whereabouts during business hours. Upon leaving the office they should advise the telephone operator where they may be reached during their absence from the office. If working at a location more than one mail day away, notify the office by telegraph of any change in location.

Staff members assigned to out-of-town engagements should inform the office of the name of the hotel at which they plan to stop. If subsequently a change is made, the office should be informed immediately by telegraph.

Staff members should notify the office promptly of any change of home address or telephone number. In the absence of a telephone, the nearest pay station or private telephone from which he may be called should be furnished to the personnel department.

Receipt of clients' records. Books, checks, or other papers, the property of clients, should not be taken from clients' offices without their consent. Such papers should be kept in a separate envelope marked, "To be returned to Mr. . . . ." The file department must be advised immediately when a client's records are brought into our office and returned to the client so that appropriate notation of their receipt and return can be made. Such records, when returned, should be accompanied by a letter. A punctilious regard for the client's property will maintain his respect for our business methods. Keys or other articles borrowed from clients should be returned promptly when no longer required.

Care of clients' records. Books and papers of clients should not be disfigured in any way and, to this end, all check marks made on the books should be small and neat, but not obscure. Notations should not be made on the books.

Marking or stamping records. Do not mark or stamp over the figures or reading matter on checks, vouchers, and invoices. Particular care should be taken to keep vouchers and other papers in their regular order and to return them to their proper places in the files, etc.

Care of working papers. The senior in charge is responsible for the proper care of all working papers, and so on, during the course of the engagement. Working papers must be kept in possession of a staff member. They should be securely locked up whenever they are out of his possession. Brief cases, etc., containing working papers should be placed in the client's safe, vault, or other fireproof compartment each night and over week ends. In certain instances, it may be desirable that working papers be in the possession of the senior at all times and not kept in the client's safe overnight.

Work suspended. Occasionally, it becomes necessary to suspend work upon an engagement. In such instances, working papers should be suitably indexed or marked and placed in the custody of the file department or in the bag vault to facilitate continuing the work in the absence of the men originally assigned to the engagement. Working papers must not be left at a client's office if work is suspended for an indefinite period.

Arrangements for engagements. Supervisors are to make the arrangements for recurring engagements or bring to the attention of the partner in charge engagements for which arrangements should be made by the partner. The arrangements for each engagement should be confirmed by letter and an engagement memorandum prepared for review and approval of a partner.

One engagement memorandum covering the work to be performed for each client should be prepared by the supervisor at least once each year. Separate engagement memorandums must be prepared to cover special engagements and work in addition to that contemplated in the engagement memorandum on file.

If an engagement requires work by any of our other offices, arrangements should be made with such office as far as possible in advance of the starting date.

Interoffice engagements. Instructions to other offices covering work for clients should be sent in duplicate well in advance of the examination date. These instructions should state clearly and definitely the scope of the examination and work to be performed by the other offices. The preceding year's working papers retained in our file should be forwarded under separate cover.

All reports, either in manuscript or draft form, and working papers covering the work which our office does for other offices should be sent to the other office only after review by a supervisor and after the letter of transmittal has been signed by a partner of this office.

Office memorandums. An office memorandum must be prepared by staff members with respect to any important matters which should be called to the attention of a partner. Examples of such matters are:

1. Conferences with clients on significant accounting problems
2. Conferences with representatives of the Internal Revenue Service, with counsel, and with clients in regard to tax matters
3. Conditions materially affecting the progress of an examination

Frequently, telephone messages received in the office by a partner, supervisor, or senior must be passed along to other staff members on a particular assignment. If the other staff members cannot be communicated with promptly, it will generally be found desirable to record the telephone message in an office memorandum directed to the interested persons.

Reports. *Draft reports at clients' offices.* All work on an engagement should be completed, as far as possible, at the office of the client. A client may not be aware of the time spent on an engagement if a considerable amount of work is done away from his office. Furthermore, it is frequently necessary to refer to the client's records while drafting the report. This is more expeditiously done if the report is prepared at the client's office.

Explicit phraseology. Reports should be constructed to focus attention upon significant facts or conditions. Good English and clarity of expression are prime requisites. Worth-while opinions or suggestions are essential. Make reports concise and explicit, and have in mind that the recipient may not be familiar with technical accounting terms.

Accuracy. Drafts of reports should not be prepared carelessly, and the report department should not be relied upon to detect and correct errors of spelling, grammar, and arithmetic. An error in a subsidiary schedule has made necessary the retyping of many pages of a report and has caused expense and serious delay which could have been avoided.

Every staff member should become familiar with the latest firm bulletins relating to the preparation and typing of reports.

Approval for typing. The report department will accept for typing only manuscripts which have been approved by a partner or supervisor. After typing is completed and compared, but before final review by a partner, the supervisor in charge of the engagement must read carefully the complete report or statement and indicate that he has made such review by initialing the office copy.

Published statements. It is the policy of the firm to check the printer's proofs of all published statements bearing the firm name and to obtain copies of the reports published. The accountant in charge of each engagement in which the publication of statements is involved should refer to the latest firm bulletin concerning published reports.

Working hours. *The working day.* The office operates on a regular workweek of forty hours consisting of five days of 7¼ hours each and one day (Saturday) of 3¾ hours. Office hours are from 9 A.M. to 5 P.M. from Monday through Friday, with an allowance of forty-five minutes for luncheon, and on Saturdays from 9 A.M. to 12:45 P.M., without any time allowance for luncheon. It is important that staff members report punctually. When not assigned to work, attendance at the office is required unless definitely excused.

However, members of our organization are not required to report to the office on Saturdays or to work that day unless the circumstances of an engagement require it. Staff members who desire to work at the office on Saturday should obtain a key for this purpose from the personnel manager. Arrangements for the procurement of supplies or working papers from the file room should be made on Friday. Partners will make themselves available at any time when necessary.

When engaged on work for clients outside the office of the firm, staff members should observe, within reason, the hours of the offices in which they are working. Whenever the client's office hours prevent a full working day being devoted to the work, staff members should charge 7¼ hours and bring the matter to the attention of the partner in charge. However, the "time off" account, and not the client, should be charged for the time on Saturday mornings when no work is performed.

Traveling time. Days spent in traveling, except Saturdays (after 12:45 P.M.), Sundays, and holidays, should be charged to the client. In such cases, the time charged should be limited to the usual office hours. As much traveling as possible should be done at night, but no charge should be made to the client for night traveling.

Overtime. Circumstances at times require the extension of our regular working day by an overtime period. The firm appreciates that staff members accept such situations as unavoidable. During winter months, in particular, it is often necessary to work overtime, but every effort should be made to avoid unnecessary overtime work or keep it within reasonable limits. Overtime work may be undertaken only upon approval of the senior in charge. The firm recognizes that the attempt to maintain the highly concentrated attention demanded by our work over unduly prolonged periods is likely to dull keenness of perception and places a severe physical strain upon staff members; hence demands from clients for excessive overtime work should be discouraged and discussed with a partner.

Vacations. Members of the staff who have been in the service of the firm for a year or more are entitled to two weeks' vacation each year at a time when their duties will permit. A three weeks' vacation is granted to staff members with more than five years' service and a month's vacation is granted to those with more than twenty-five years' service. Leaves of absence for military service may be included in computing firm service time. Permanent staff members who have been with the firm for less than one year will be entitled to one day's vacation for each month of employment up to June 30. Additional vacation allowances will arise from overtime credits mentioned in "Pay for Overtime." Requests for preferred vacation periods should be made prior to May 1 of each year.

Time reports. *Importance of time reports.* Time reports and daily work analysis schedules constitute basic records upon which the firm in a variety of circumstances must depend. Both should be complete and clear so that reference to other sources for similar information will not be necessary. Where there are subsidiary or otherwise related companies or branches, state the hours devoted on work performed for each separate company or branch, giving the location.

Time recorded. Time should be charged in units of one-half hour except where one-quarter of an hour is necessary to complete charging a full 7¼ hours for each day. Time reports must be prepared to account for 7¼ hours for each working day (Saturday, 3¾ hours). If work is required on other than an official working day, time reports should be prepared only for the time actually worked.

Classifications of time. Staff members are required to comply strictly with the following time classifications:

1. Time on assignments for clients is to be charged to the client who is to be billed for services. Assistants should ascertain from the supervisor or the senior in charge of the engagement to whom the time should be charged. Our client is not always the company whose records or statements we examine.

2. Unassigned time. This classification is to be used when staff members are awaiting assignment. It will be charged for work of a miscellaneous nature which members of the staff may be asked to do during such waiting time and which is not to be charged to a client or to some other account. It will also be charged for time spent in reviewing accounting and auditing pronouncements and tax and court decisions and rulings if such time is not properly chargeable to clients or research.

3. Research. This account will be charged for time spent on research or statistical work when authorized by a partner and when such time is for the benefit of all offices of the firm. Such work will include the compilation of data from published reports and the review of tax laws, decisions, and rulings, when not made for the account of clients but for the preparation of bulletins which are distributed to all offices. This account should also be charged for time spent on research, etc., in connection with meetings or conventions of national professional societies. Time reports charged to research must be approved by the partner who made the assignment.

4. Publications. Time devoted to the various publications of the firm should

be charged to the separate account provided for each publication.

5. Administration. Members of the staff, except supervisors and members of the tax department, will rarely have occasion to use this account. Other members of the staff should charge time to this account only upon specific instructions of a partner or the personnel manager. This account also should be charged with time relating to participation in activities of chapters of local or state professional societies.

6. Vacation. This classification is to be used for absence from the office for the regular vacation period defined under the caption "Vacation" in this manual.

7. Holidays. This classification is to be used for absence from the office on such public holidays as are recognized by the office, notification of which is posted on the bulletin boards. Generally these are: New Year's Day, Lincoln's Birthday, Washington's Birthday, Memorial Day, Independence Day, Labor Day, Columbus Day, Thanksgiving Day, and Christmas Day.

8. Sick time. This classification is to be charged for absence from the office by reason of personal sickness.

9. Lost time. This classification will be charged for absence due to illness in the immediate family and other involuntary reasons such as jury duty.

10. Time off. This classification is to be charged for time taken off by members of the staff at the convenience of the firm.

11. Training school. Time spent by trainees while attending our training school will be charged to this account. Staff members will also charge this account for time devoted to the preparation of material and presentation of subjects at the training school.

Personnel reports. Written personnel reports are prepared by supervisors concerning the abilities of seniors working under their direction. Similarly, seniors prepare such reports relative to the abilities of their assistants. These reports form the basis for assigning more responsible work to staff members who have shown the capacity to accept greater responsibility. The reports should be carefully prepared and returned to the personnel manager promptly.

Compensation. *Salaries.* Salaries are paid on the first and sixteenth days of the month for semimonthly periods ending on the preceding days.

Salary checks. If so requested, salary checks will be deposited by us in employees' bank accounts. Arrangements have been made for cashing salary checks at a nearby bank. Salary checks must not be cashed at a client's office.

Pay for overtime. Overtime is paid only to those staff members who are subject to the provisions of the Fair Labor Standards Act. All time over forty hours per week, exclusive of "time off" and "lost time" (not "sick time") during that week, is credited at time and one-half. Such credit is reduced at straight time to the extent of "prepaid time," that is, the excess of "time off" in previous weeks over overtime credits. Any remaining net overtime is paid, on a regular pay date, to the end of the latest full week reported on the preceding semimonthly time report. Staff members who have more "time off" than overtime credits continue to receive full salary and no overtime is paid until the overtime credits exceed all past "time off."

Staff members exempt from the provisions of the Fair Labor Standards Act are not paid overtime unless specific arrangements to the contary are made at date of employment. However, for many years it has been the practice of the firm to grant time off based on overtime credits when staff members are not engaged on work for clients.

Salary deductions. Federal insurance contributions, Federal income tax withholdings, and state disability benefits law contributions are deducted from salaries in accordance with current laws.

Surety bond. All employees are required to be bonded by a company selected by the firm and at the firm's expense.

Notice on leaving. The notice required to be given, by either the firm or the employee, on the discontinuance of their relations will depend upon the arrangements mutually agreed upon, if any, when becoming employed.

Traveling expenses. *Out-of-town engagements.* It is the desire of the firm that staff members shall travel and live while on out-of-town engagements in a manner befitting their professional standing and that they be reimbursed for business expenses actually incurred. At the same time, it is necessary that the expenses be kept at a minimum. Staff members should live comfortably without being extravagant. The personnel department will arrange for transportation and hotel reservations in advance, whenever practicable.

Automobile transportation. The mileage allowance for authorized use of personal automobiles by staff members on firm business is at the rate of .... cents per mile. Within cities, public travel facilities generally offer the most rapid and convenient transportation, and staff members should use their cars on firm business only when these facilities are inadequate. If a staff member uses his car on firm business when other satisfactory means of transportation are available and a car is not required by the particular circumstances of an engagement, reimbursement will be limited to the amount of the rail or bus fare between the points involved.

Type of expenses. The following list indicates the character of expenses for which reimbursement will be made:
Traveling:
  Fare (except when provided by the firm or the client)
  Sleeping and chair cars (one berth or seat)
  Transfers (personal baggage)
  Gratuities (porters in Pullman cars, hotels, etc.)
  Mileage for personal automobile
Subsistence:
  Rooms and meals (including gratuities)
  Laundry, clothes pressing, carfares, and such things as are usual to include in expenses, depending on locality and conditions
Miscellaneous:
  Telegrams and telephone charges, relating to business matters
  Postage
  Other (to be itemized)
All traveling expenses are limited to reasonable amounts depending on locality and circumstances.

Rooms by the week. Consideration should be given to the probable length of time that will be required to complete an engagement. When feasible, secure hotel accommodations by the week at reduced weekly rates. Week-end trips home are authorized when the related travel expense would not exceed subsistence for the week end out of town.

Family allowance. In lieu of reimbursement for actual cost of room and meals, a flat allowance may be granted to a staff member assigned to a lengthy out-of-town engagement if accompanied by members of his family. Such arrangements should be made with and approved by the partner in charge of the engagement.

Expenses, government work. Staff members assigned to engagements involving expenses for the account of any division of the government should inform themselves of the government regulations regarding expense allowances and vouchers.

Expense reports. *Expenses out of town.* Prior to departure on out-of-town engagements, staff members are furnished a cash fund for expenses. Such funds should be accounted for by expense reports, supported by receipted hotel bills and such other vouchers as are obtainable. All out-of-town expenses must be reported on the regular form provided for that purpose and must be approved by the supervisor or senior in charge of the engagement, if present at the location. A report of all expenses must be made promptly at the close of each engagement and where the engagement is of more than two weeks' duration, a report should be made at least weekly. Settlement for funds advanced must be made at the termination of each assignment. Any unexpended balance should not be carried forward and used for another assignment.

Expenses in town. On all work in the city where the related expenses are of an incidental nature, application for reimbursement should be made on the petty cash expense form. Reimbursement for such expenses may be obtained from the cashier on presentation of a petty cash expense slip approved by the senior in charge of the engagement. An allowance of $.... will be made for supper expense when it is necessary to work in a client's office or in our office ten hours or more a day. In the event it is necessary to work five hours or more on a Saturday, an allowance of $.... will be granted for luncheon; on a Sunday or holiday such allowance will be $.....

Equipment and supplies. *Equipment and supplies provided.* Portfolios, folders, working paper, pencils, erasers, etc., are provided for the use of staff members and may be obtained from the file department.

Keys. Office keys and portfolio keys will be issued to staff members at the discretion of the firm. Care should be taken to guard against loss of keys and to see that they are returned to the personnel manager when a staff member leaves the employ of the firm.

Brief cases. Brief cases containing working papers and stationery supplies will be prepared in advance for each engagement and kept in the file room, tagged with the name of the client and the senior in charge. Staff members should give the file department instructions in advance regarding the make-up of brief cases. Requests for additional supplies should be transmitted to the file department.

Brief cases are charged out to the senior in charge of the engagement for which they are withdrawn. It is the responsibility of the senior to determine that brief cases are returned to the file department immediately upon completion of the engagements.

Transfer cases. When completion of an examination or report is postponed, all papers should be transferred from brief cases to red manila envelopes. Return the brief cases to the file room and place the envelopes in the bag vault.

Bag vault. The bag vault adjacent to the staff rooms is reserved for papers pertaining to uncompleted engagements. All brief cases, packages, and special envelopes should be clearly marked with the names of the clients and the seniors in charge. Working papers to be filed or clients' records to be returned should not be retained in the vault after the work is completed.

Wasting paper. Care should be taken not to waste paper. Do not use time reports, expense slips, or ruled paper for rough calculations which are not to be retained as part of the working papers. Stationery should not be left behind at clients' offices. Unused stationery should be returned to the file room on completion of an engagement.

Machines. Adding and calculating machines, slide rules, etc., are provided for the use of staff members.

Library. The library is provided for the use and information of the staff. Books may be withdrawn upon application to the librarians (floor receptionists) and upon signing the card to be found in the envelope attached to the back cover. Books withdrawn must be returned to the librarian within a period of three weeks or be renewed at the end of that time.

Required reading. The firm issues bulletins regarding audit procedure and tax matters to the staff from time to time. These bulletins must be read carefully and their instructions followed. Binders containing copies of bulletins previously issued are available in the library and in the file department.

Bulletins issued by the AICPA and the SEC also should be read.

The firm has compiled a cumulative index of all of the above bulletins which should be consulted as needed.

Mail and telegraphic communication. *Address mail to firm.* All communications pertaining to firm business should be addressed to the firm and not to individuals. In addressing mail to the firm, do not write on the envelope anything indicative of its contents, as such indication may provide pertinent information to anyone seeking to tamper with the mail.

Subject head. Correspondence with the firm concerning work in progress, etc., must contain the name of the client at the head of the letter.

Separate letter for each client. In writing to the firm in regard to the affairs of more than one client, write a separate letter relative to each client.

Incoming mail. To avoid delay due to absence of staff members, clients should be requested to address all correspondence pertaining to firm business to the firm and not to an individual. Mail bearing a client's name on the envelope or wrapper will be opened upon receipt, directed to a partner, and then sent to a supervisor.

Outgoing mail. All letters to clients, clients' employees, or to other offices of the firm relating to the business of the firm must be written in name of the firm.

All mail approved and signed by firm. No letters relating to the business of the firm may be sent out without first having been submitted to a partner for approval and signature.

Firm stationery. Firm stationery may not be used for any letter not relating to the business of the firm.

Telephone calls. Personal telephone calls should be kept at a minimum. Incoming calls other than in relation to the business of the firm should be discouraged. A client's telephone should never be used for personal calls except in an emergency. If it is necessary to make a long distance call from a client's office on matters not connected with our work for that client, the staff member must ascertain the cost of the call and pay for it at the time. The name, address, or telephone number of a client must not be disclosed to friends or others outside the office. Should it become necessary for relatives or friends to communicate with a member of the staff, the office of the firm is to be called, and not that of the client.

Mailing list. The report department maintains records for the proper addressing of correspondence to clients. This record is kept up to date principally through the data furnished by staff members on the "Mailing List" form. The form is furnished by the file department.

If significant changes in a client's personnel or changes in address, corporate name, etc., come to the attention of a staff member, he must prepare an "Amendment to Engagement Memorandum" or a revised "Mailing List" form immediately.

It is very important that the mailing list be revised currently and, to accomplish this objective, the full co-operation of the staff in reporting changes is required.

Files. *Correspondence.* The file department maintains files of the firm's correspondence with each client. The files, which may be obtained by staff members by calling at the file department, must be returned to that department at the close of each day and must never be removed from the office of the firm.

Reports and tax returns. "Blue" office copies of reports and office copies of tax returns may be obtained from the file department upon request. They must not be removed from the office of the firm except in special cases and then only when sanctioned by a partner.

"Yellow" office copies of reports or of schedules accompanying tax returns are also kept in the file department. They may be used or cut up to facilitate the preparation of reports and tax returns for the next engagement for the client.

Miscellaneous. The file department maintains files of working papers, claims for refund, Treasury Department documents, and briefs for each client. Only the working papers may be removed from the office.

Appendix to Section Four
(Developing a Practice)

REMINDER LIST FOR SPECIAL SERVICES*

The following reminder list is a composite of questions asked by several firms to uncover areas in which they might supplement their services to clients. It is by no means complete, and tax questions are in general omitted. But it may suggest topics which can be discussed with officers or key personnel of clients, when appropriate. Whenever they visit a client's office for audit, tax, or other services, accountants should seek to obtain an understanding of the general business problems (as well as accounting problems) of greatest concern to top management. If they apply their specialized training to those problems, they may be able to submit suggestions which will be of special service to their clients.

I.   General Matters

  A. Recapitalization desirable?
   1. More common stock?
   2. Preferred issue?
   3. Bonds or mortgage with deductible interest?
  B. Are present dividend policies satisfactory?
   1. Cash dividends excessive in relation to working capital?
   2. Appreciated assets which should be distributed?
  C. Public distribution of securities desirable?
   1. Management viewpoint?
   2. Stockholders viewpoint (particularly if closely held)?
  D. Spinoff or split-up desirable?
  E. Any advantageous merger prospects which should be explored?
  F. Separate corporations desirable?
   1. Real estate?
   2. Sales?
   3. Foreign?
   4. Other states?
  G. Company informed of its share of total industry?
   1. Results analyzed and compared with available industry statistics?
  H. Voting counts needed?
   1. Proxies?
   2. Shop elections?
  I. Company a "good citizen"?
   1. Senior executives participating in civic affairs?
   2. Junior executives encouraged to participate?
  J. Data required for labor union negotiations?
  K. New plant locations desirable?
   1. Improved distribution?
   2. Accessibility of labor and materials?
  L. Assistance needed in compiling economic statistics?
  M. Management using charts in dealing with department heads?

*Source: Economics of Accounting Practice Bulletin 13, *Planning a Practice for Growth,* AICPA, 1960, pp. 36-41.

II. Finance and Control
    A. Organization charts:
        1. In existence?
        2. Complete?
        3. Clear as to authority and responsibility?
    B. Budgets:
        1. Long term for capital requirements, plant expansion, sales?
        2. Cash flow projections?
        3. Income and operational budgets:
            a. Used effectively, three months, six months, year?
            b. Adjusted monthly on moving basis?
            c. Production schedules tied in?
        4. Differences investigated, explanations required?
    C. Difficulty in obtaining financing?
        1. Short-term funds?
        2. Intermediate- or long-term funds?
        3. Any unusual problems?
    D. Management reports:
        1. Daily or other period sensitive indicators furnished to top management (e.g., personnel census, cash, orders, shipments)?
        2. Weekly reports to department heads and foreman?
        3. Monthly reports:
            a. Received early enough?
            b. Cumulative and comparative?
            c. Tied into budgets?
        4. Too many reports?
        5. Copies to right people and being used effectively?
    E. Controller's duties:
        1. Report to president?
        2. Ever report to board of directors?
        3. Capable of fully analyzing results?
        4. Co-operating fully with management and operating personnel?
        5. Effective in cost reduction and expense control?
        6. Useful in "buy or make" decisions?
    F. Plant capital expenditures:
        1. Formal authorization plan in effect?
        2. Proposed additions studied for economic justification?
        3. Adequate follow-up and comparison of actual and estimated costs?
    G. Credit and collection policies clearly established?
        1. Sound in relation to competitors?
        2. Carried out as instructed?
    H. Market analysis and research being done?
        1. Used in budgeting?
    I. Surplus funds:
        1. Kept busy?
        2. Investments conservative?
        3. Rate of return normal?

III. Office Management
    A. Sufficient manuals and written instructions?
        1. Written clearly?
        2. Up to date?
    B. Internal auditing being done to inspect and enforce manual procedures?

C. Clerical workloads and planning:
   1. Standards established?
   2. Workloads and production measured?
   3. Excessive overtime?
D. Office layout physically efficient?
E. Filing problems?
F. Record retention and destruction program:
   1. Formally planned and approved?
   2. Actually being carried out?
G. Control over forms and reports?
   1. Duplications eliminated?

IV. General Accounting
A. Chart of accounts adequate?
   1. Numerical coding desirable?
B. Standard monthly journal entries in use?
C. Voucher checks used?
D. Replace accounts-payable ledger with voucher ledger or unpaid invoice file?
E. Replace accounts-receivable ledger with duplicate invoice file?
F. Petty cash under control?
   1. Imprest system used?
G. Sales records:
   1. Summarized efficiently?
   2. Classified adequately?
H. Monthly statements to customers unnecessarily detailed?
I. Duplications in gathering operating data?
J. Property, plant and equipment records:
   1. Plant ledger maintained?
   2. Up to date?
   3. Simplification possible?
   4. Location records reliable? Necessary?
   5. Physical inventory desirable?
   6. Book-basis or tax-basis depreciation studies desirable?
K. Prenumbered forms being used?
   1. Purchase orders?
   2. Receiving reports?
   3. Sales orders?
   4. Others?
L. Employee earnings record and checks prepared in one operation?
M. Inventory records:
   1. Perpetual inventories maintained for all classes of materials?
   2. Turnover studied?
   3. Obsolete items written off?
N. Possible uses of machine accounting:
   1. New uses for present equipment?
   2. Electronic equipment?
   3. Punched card equipment?
   4. Pegboards?

V. Cost Accounting
A. Tied to general ledger?
B. Any standards obsolete?
   1. Labor, material, overhead?

2. Production or operating ratios, e.g., **KWH** used by departments, machine speeds, pieces produced per hour or other physical ratios?
- C. More cost centers or departments, or fewer?
- D. Cost accounting approach fully developed?
  1. Engineering?
  2. Distribution?
  3. Administration?
- E. Plant capacity soundly determined?
- F. Indirect expenses reasonably distributed?
- G. Variances analyzed, explained, and used as tool to improve operations?
- H. All cost accounting necessary to be repeated monthly, or should some be discontinued and performed only at other intervals?
- I. Cost-volume relationships fully developed?
- J. Breakeven points known?
- K. Fringe benefit costs grouped with other labor costs in reports?
- L. Cost data considered when setting prices of product?
  1. Inflation factors included?
- M. Company getting its fair share of competitive bids?

VI. Estate Planning
- A. Situations studied and programs established for:
  1. Principal officers?
  2. Directors?
  3. Stockholders (if closely held)?
- B. All have wills?
- C. Taking advantage of gift tax exemptions?
- D. Providing liquid assets for estate taxes?
- E. Providing adequately for education of children?
- F. Charitable foundations desirable?

VII. Insurance
- A. All insurable risk areas covered:
  1. General liability and property damage?
  2. Products liability or other liabilities peculiar to business?
  3. Fire and extended coverages?
  4. Bonding of employees?
  5. Business interruption?
  6. Compensation and disability?
     a. Are employees so classified as to minimize premiums?
  7. Vehicles operated by employees?
  8. Life insurance on officers and key employees desirable?
- B. Are comprehensive policies used where appropriate?
- C. Insurance written by one or several agencies?
- D. Expiration dates of policies satisfactory?
- E. Fully qualified insurance counsel?
- F. Any claims to be prepared?
- G. Has a complete insurance study been made recently?

VIII. Personnel
- A. Accounting personnel qualified, competent, and effective?
- B. Openings for key finance or accounting personnel?
- C. Areas in which improved incentives could be offered to employees?
- D. Adequate provisions for replacement of key personnel?
- E. Improved plans for employee training needed?

F. Review of compensation plans desirable?
   1. Bonus or profit sharing?
   2. Pension plans?
   3. Stock-option plans?
   4. Savings funds?

CODE OF PROFESSIONAL ETHICS
American Institute of Certified Public Accountants
As Amended March 6, 1962

The reliance of the public and the business community on sound financial report-
ing and advice on business affairs imposes on the accounting profession an obliga-
tion to maintain high standards of technical competence, morality and integrity.
To this end, a member or associate of the American Institute of Certified Public
Accountants shall at all times maintain independence of thought and action, hold
the affairs of his clients in strict confidence, strive continuously to improve his
professional skills, observe generally accepted auditing standards, promote sound
and informative financial reporting, uphold the dignity and honor of the ac-
counting profession, and maintain high standards of personal conduct.

In further recognition of the public interest and his obligation to the profession,
a member or associate agrees to comply with the following rules of ethical con-
duct, the enumeration of which should not be construed as a denial of the existence
of other standards of conduct not specifically mentioned:

ARTICLE I—RELATIONS WITH CLIENTS AND PUBLIC

1.01. A member or associate shall not express his opinion on financial statements of any enterprise financed in whole or in part by public distribution of securities, if he owns or is committed to acquire a financial interest in the enterprise
which is substantial either in relation to its capital or to his own personal fortune, or
if a member of his immediate family owns or is committed to acquire a substantial
interest in the enterprise. A member or associate shall not express his opinion on
financial statements which are used as a basis of credit if he owns or is committed
to acquire a financial interest in the enterprise which is substantial either in relation to its capital or to his own personal fortune, or if a member of his immediate
family owns or is committed to acquire a substantial interest in the enterprise, unless
in his report he discloses such interest. [Old Rule 13.]*

---

*The new Rule 1.01, adopted by the membership March 6, 1962, will become
effective January 1, 1964. It reads as follows:

Neither a member or associate, nor a firm of which he is a partner, shall
express an opinion on financial statements of any enterprise unless he and his
firm are in fact independent with respect to such enterprise.

Independence is not susceptible of precise definition, but is an expression of
the professional integrity of the individual. A member or associate, before expressing his opinion on financial statements, has the responsibility of assessing
his relationships with an enterprise to determine whether, in the circumstances,
he might expect his opinion to be considered independent, objective and unbiased
by one who had knowledge of all the facts.

A member or associate will be considered not independent, for example, with
respect to any enterprise if he, or one of his partners, (a) during the period of
his professional engagement or at the time of expressing his opinion, had, or
was committed to acquire, any direct financial interest or material indirect finan-

1.02. A member or associate shall not commit an act discreditable to the profession. (See Institute's by-laws, Article V, Section 4*d*.)

1.03. A member or associate shall not violate the confidential relationship between himself and his client. [Old Rule 16.] (See Opinion No. 3, following.)

1.04. Professional service shall not be rendered or offered for a fee which shall be contingent upon the findings or results of such service. This rule does not apply to cases involving federal, state, or other taxes, in which the findings are those of the tax authorities and not those of the accountant. Fees to be fixed by courts or other public authorities, which are therefore of an indeterminate amount at the time when an engagement is undertaken, are not regarded as contingent fees within the meaning of this rule. [Old Rule 9.]

ARTICLE 2—TECHNICAL STANDARDS

2.01. A member or associate shall not sign a report purporting to express his opinion as the result of examination of financial statements unless they have been examined by him, a member or an employee of his firm, a member or associate of the Institute, a member of a similar association in a foreign country, or a certified public accountant of a state or territory of the United States or the District of Columbia. [Old Rule 6.]

2.02. In expressing an opinion on representations in financial statements which he has examined, a member or associate may be held guilty of an act discreditable to the profession if

(a) he fails to disclose a material fact known to him which is not disclosed in the financial statements but disclosure of which is necessary to make the financial statements not misleading; or

(b) he fails to report any material misstatement known to him to appear in the financial statement; or

(c) he is materially negligent in the conduct of his examination or in making his report thereon; or

(d) he fails to acquire sufficient information to warrant expression of an opinion, or his exceptions are sufficiently material to negative the expression of an opinion; or

(e) he fails to direct attention to any material departure from generally accepted accounting principles or to disclose any material omission of generally accepted auditing procedure applicable in the circumstances. [Old Rule 5.] (See Opinion No. 8, following.)

2.03. A member or associate shall not permit his name to be associated with

---

cial interest in the enterprise, or (b) during the period of his professional engagement, at the time of expressing his opinion or during the period covered by the financial statements, was connected with the enterprise as a promoter, underwriter, voting trustee, director, officer or key employee. In cases where a member or associate ceases to be the independent accountant for an enterprise and is subsequently called upon to re-express a previously expressed opinion on financial statements, the phrase "at the time of expressing his opinion" refers only to the time at which the member or associate first expressed his opinion on the financial statements in question. The word "director" is not intended to apply to a connection in such a capacity with a charitable, religious, civic or other similar type of nonprofit organization when the duties performed in such a capacity are such as to make it clear that the member or associate can express an independent opinion on the financial statements. The example cited in this paragraph, of circumstances under which a member or associate will be considered not independent, is not intended to be all-inclusive.

statements purporting to show financial position or results of operations in such a manner as to imply that he is acting as an independent public accountant unless he shall:

(a) express an unqualified opinion, or

(b) express a qualified opinion, or

(c) disclaim an opinion on the statements taken as a whole and indicate clearly his reasons therefor, or

(d) when unaudited financial statements are presented on his stationery without his comments, disclose prominently on each page of the financial statements that they were not audited. [Old Rule 19.] (See Opinion No. 8, following.)

2.04. A member or associate shall not permit his name to be used in conjunction with an estimate of earnings contingent upon future transactions in a manner which may lead to the belief that the member or associate vouches for the accuracy of the forecast. [Old Rule 12.] (See Opinion No. 10, following.)

ARTICLE 3—PROMOTIONAL PRACTICES

3.01. A member or associate shall not advertise his professional attainments or services.

Publication in a newspaper, magazine or similar medium of an announcement or what is technically known as a card is prohibited.

A listing in a directory is restricted to the name, title, address and telephone number of the person or firm, and it shall not appear in a box, or other form of display or in a type or style which differentiates it from other listings in the same directory. Listing of the same name in more than one place in a classified directory is prohibited. [Old Rule 10.] (See Opinions Nos. 1, 2, 4, and 9, following.)

3.02. A member or associate shall not directly or indirectly solicit clients by circulars or advertisements, nor by personal communication or interview, not warranted by existing personal relations. [First part of old Rule 7; see Rule 5.01 for second part.] (See Opinion No. 1, following.)

3.03. A member or associate shall not make a competitive bid for a professional engagement. Competitive bidding for public accounting services is not in the public interest, is a form of solicitation, and is unprofessional. [Old Rule 14, as revised.]

3.04. Commissions, brokerage, or other participation in the fees or profits of professional work shall not be allowed directly or indirectly to the laity by a member or associate.

Commissions, brokerage, or other participation in the fees, charges, or profits of work recommended or turned over to the laity as incident to services for clients shall not be accepted directly or indirectly by a member or associate. [Old Rule 3.] (See Opinion No. 6, following.)

ARTICLE 4—OPERATING PRACTICES

4.01. A firm or partnership, all the individual members of which are members of the Institute, may describe itself as "Members of the American Institute of Certified Public Accountants," but a firm or partnership, not all the individual members of which are members of the Institute, or an individual practicing under a style denoting a partnership when in fact there be no partner or partners, or a corporation, or an individual or individuals practicing under a style denoting a corporate organization shall not use the designation "Members of the American Institute of Certified Public Accountants." [Old Rule 1.]

4.02. A member or associate shall not allow any person to practice in his name who is not in partnership with him or in his employ. [Old Rule 2.]

4.03. A member or associate in his practice of public accounting shall not permit an employee to perform for the member's or associate's clients any services which the member or associate himself or his firm is not permitted to perform. [Old Rule 17.]

4.04. A member or associate shall not engage in any business or occupation conjointly with that of a public accountant, which is incompatible or inconsistent therewith. [Old Rule 4.]

4.05. A member or associate engaged in an occupation in which he renders services of a type performed by public accountants, or renders other professional services, must observe the by-laws and Code of Professional Ethics of the Institute in the conduct of that occupation. [Old Rule 15, as revised.] (See Opinion No. 7, following.)

4.06. A member or associate shall not be an officer, director, stockholder, representative, or agent of any corporation engaged in the practice of public accounting in any state or territory of the United States or the District of Columbia. [Old Rule 11.]

ARTICLE 5—RELATIONS WITH FELLOW MEMBERS

5.01. A member or associate shall not encroach upon the practice of another public accountant. A member or associate may furnish service to those who request it. [Second part of old Rule 7.] (See Opinion No. 1, following.)

5.02. A member or associate who receives an engagement for services by referral from another member or associate shall not extend his services beyond the specific engagement without consulting with the referring member or associate. [Old Rule 18.]

5.03. Direct or indirect offer of employment shall not be made by a member or associate to an employee of another public accountant without first informing such accountant. This rule shall not be construed so as to inhibit negotiations with anyone who of his own initiative or in response to public advertisement shall apply to a member or associate for employment. [Old Rule 8.]

NUMBERED OPINIONS OF THE AICPA COMMITTEE ON PROFESSIONAL ETHICS

Opinion No. I

Newsletters, Publications

Impropriety of member furnishing clients and others with tax and similar booklets prepared by others and imprinted with firm name of member

In the opinion of the committee, imprinting the name of the accountant on newsletters, tax booklets or other similar publications which are prepared by others and distributed by a member of the Institute does not add to the usefulness of the material to the reader. Use of the imprint, in the committee's opinion, is objectionable in that it tends to suggest (and has been interpreted by many as a means of) circumventing Rule 3.01 of the *Code of Professional Ethics,* which says that a member shall not advertise his services.

It is the conclusion of the committee that distribution of newsletters, tax booklets or similar publications, prepared by others, when imprinted with the name of the accountant furnishing the material, is not in the interest of the public or the profession.

The committee sees no grounds for objection to furnishing material of the type indicated to clients or others provided that such material does not carry the imprint described and provided that such distribution is limited in a manner consistent with Rules 3.02 and 5.01.

(Published in the *CPA,* December 1956)

Opinion No. 2

Responsibility of Member for Acts of
Third Parties on His Behalf

Member may not carry out, through others, acts
which he is prohibited from directly performing under
Institute by-laws and Code of Professional Ethics

A member should not cause others to carry out on his behalf either with or without compensation acts which, if carried out by a member, would place him in violation of the Institute's code or by-laws. To illustrate this principle, the committee has ruled that a member would be in violation of the Institute's Code of Professional Ethics if, with his approval:

1. A nonprofit organization in recognition of accounting services which had been rendered by a member placed without charge an advertisement of the firm in the organization's bulletin;

2. A bank announced to its depositors that a CPA would be at a desk on the main floor of the bank at certain hours and days during the tax season to assist customers in preparation of tax returns for a fee;

3. A trade association in its official publication announced that a certain certified public accountant, member of the Institute, who long had served the association as independent accountant, was especially well qualified and available to assist association members in dealing with accounting and tax problems peculiar to the industry.

(Published in the *CPA*, December 1956)

Opinion No. 3

Confidence of a Client

Seller of accounting practice should not give the
purchaser access to working papers, income tax re-
turns, and correspondence pertaining to accounts be-
ing sold without first obtaining permission of client

The seller of an accounting practice has a duty under Rule 1.03, pertaining to confidential relations, first to obtain permission of the client to make available to a purchaser working papers and other documents.

(Published in the *CPA*, January 1957)

Opinion No. 4

Authorship—Propriety of Showing Firm Affiliation of Author

Responsibility of author for publisher's promotion efforts

Many certified public accountants, members of the Institute, are especially well qualified to write authoritatively on accounting, taxes, auditing, management and related subjects, and, in the interests of the public and the profession, are encouraged to write under their names articles and books for publication. In the opinion of the committee, it is of value to the reader to know the author's background (degrees he holds, professional society affiliation, and the firm with which he is associated). It is held that publication of such information is not in violation of Rule 3.01.

It is the opinion of the committee that an author who is a member of the Institute has the responsibility to ascertain that the publisher or others promoting distribution of his work keep within the bounds of professional dignity and do not make claims concerning the author or his writing that are not factual or in good taste.

(Published in the *CPA,* February 1957)

Opinion No. 5
Prohibited Self-Designations—Use of Title "Tax Consultant," "Tax Specialist," or Similar Description Forbidden

The "Statement of Principles Relating to Practice in the Field of Federal Income Taxation, Promulgated in 1951 by the National Conference of Lawyers and Certified Public Accountants," was approved by the Institute's Council. Section 5 of this statement reads as follows:

> *5. Prohibited Self-Designations.* An accountant should not describe himself as a "tax consultant" or "tax expert" or use any similar phrase. Lawyers, similarly, are prohibited by the canons of ethics of the American Bar Association and the opinions relating thereto, from advertising a special branch of law practice.

Under Article V, Section 4, of the Institute's by-laws a member renders himself liable to expulsion or suspension by the trial board if he refuses to give effect to any decision of the Institute or the Council.

It is the opinion of the committee that a reasonable period of time has elapsed since the adoption of the Statement of Principles by Council within which the members could revise their stationery, directory and other listings so as to conform with the Statement.

(Published in the *CPA,* March 1957)

Opinion No. 6
Concept of "Laity" in Sharing of Fees

Concept of laity as used in Rule 3.04, interpreted to prohibit sharing of fees, profits, or commissions with others not in public practice; propriety of joint services

Rule 3.04 provides that: "Commissions, brokerage, or other participation in the fees or profits of professional work shall not be allowed directly or indirectly to the laity by a member or associate.

"Commissions, brokerage, or other participation in the fees, charges, or profits of work recommended or turned over to the laity as incident to services for clients shall not be accepted directly or indirectly by a member or associate."

There has been no precise definition of the word "laity" as used in Rule 3.04 and it is the belief of the committee that no useful purpose would be accomplished by attempting to establish a special definition for use solely within the accounting profession which would include certain nonaccounting professional groups and exclude other such groups. It is the view of the committee that Rule 3.04 should be interpreted as intending to prohibit a member in public practice from receiving or paying a commission or sharing a fee with *any individual or firm not engaged or employed in the practice of public accounting.*

Rule 3.04 is not intended to apply to payments to a retired partner of a public accounting firm or to the heirs of a deceased partner or of a deceased member. Also in view of the fact that the term "laity" has not been authoritatively defined, the committee feels it would be unreasonable to apply its present interpretation to arrangements made in good faith and already existing between certified public accountants and individuals not presently in the practice of public accounting. It is the hope of the committee that within a reasonable time Rule 3.04 may be amended so as to clarify the word "laity" by referring instead to any individual or firm not engaged or employed in the practice of public accounting. In the meantime an understanding of, and voluntary compliance with, the committee's views should facilitate the transition.

The committee believes there is nothing contrary to the public interest or in violation of the rules of conduct in a firm of certified public accountants coordinating its work with that of an engineering, legal or other professional firm on a specific project for a single client. In such cases care should be taken by the accounting firm not to extend its services beyond its particular field and that any reports or recommendations rendered make clear the limitation of responsibilities assumed and services rendered.

Neither Rule 3.04 nor any of the other Institute rules of ethical conduct at present prohibit a partnership by a member of the Institute in public practice with a person who is not a certified public accountant. The committee, however, looks forward to the day when such public accounting partnerships will be composed solely of certified public accountants.

(Published in the *CPA*, January 1958)

Opinion No. 7
Statistical Tabulating Services

The committee on professional ethics has, in recent years, responded to several inquiries in regard to the possible violation of the Institute's Code of Professional Ethics by members who operate statistical tabulating service bureaus.

In practically all cases the tabulating services include or contemplate the accumulation of data to be used for accounting purposes, the maintenance of accounts, and bookkeeping services. This type of service is similar to so-called "write-up work" or bookkeeping service rendered by many public accountants.

Some members have formed separate partnerships which perform statistical tabulating services. Some of these organizations were apparently formed under the erroneous impression that the Institute's rules of ethical conduct would not be applicable.

The committee finds it is proper for members to conduct statistical tabulating service bureaus. The committee holds, however, that any such separate organization in which a member has an interest should not be permitted to do things which the member in public practice is prohibited from doing as a member of the Institute, such as advertising, soliciting business, or practicing in corporate form.

It is the opinion of the committee that any member of the Institute who has any interest in an organization which renders statistical tabulating services is either directly or indirectly rendering "services of a type performed by public accountants" and, therefore, must observe the by-laws and Rule 4.05, which requires compliance with the Code of Professional Ethics of the Institute.

(Published in the *CPA*, December 1958)

Opinion No. 8
Denial of Opinion Does Not Discharge
Responsibility in All Cases

Where the CPA believes financial statements contain false or misleading information, mere denial of opinion held insufficient

Rule 2.02 deals with a member's responsibilities in expressing an opinion on representations in financial statements. The rule does not, however, specifically refer to situations where an opinion is denied, either by disclaimer or by reference to the statements as "prepared without audit." When an accountant denies an opinion on financial statements under Rule 2.03, which incorporates the provisions of Auditing Statement 23, he is in effect stating that he has insufficient grounds for an opinion as to whether or not the statements constitute a fair presentation. Rule 2.03 provides that, where an opinion is denied, the accountant must indicate clearly his reasons therefor.

In a circumstance where a member believes the financial statements are false or misleading as a whole or in any significant respect, it is the opinion of the committee that he should require adjustments of the accounts or adequate disclosure of the facts, as the case may be, and failing this the independent accountant should refuse to permit his name to be associated with the statements in any way.

(Published in the *CPA,* February 1959)

Opinion No. 9
Distribution of Literature

Though members may prepare printed material indicating services they are qualified to render, distribution of such material should be limited to clients

There has come to the attention of the committee with increasing frequency printed material bearing a member's name and address or that of his firm, which is devoted either to informing others of the services the member or his firm is prepared to render or dealing with a specialized subject in a manner that might suggest the firm's ability to serve in a specialized field or geographical area.

The committee feels that such material is entirely proper when its distribution is carefully restricted to clients, but that failure to control the circulation of such literature directly or through third parties may place the member whose name it bears in violation of Rule 3.01 of the Institute's Code of Professional Ethics prohibiting advertising.

The committee believes that a member who produces any literature or material which may be considered promotional in nature, must assume responsibility to guard and control its distribution. It is recognized by the committee that in isolated cases a client, not knowing the profession's restrictions on the distribution of such material, may pass on to the client of another member material he found of interest. Such an isolated instance would not necessarily be viewed as unethical practice. Where there is evidence that reasonable control has not been maintained to limit distribution of such material, it is the view of the committee that it must, in the interest of the profession, strictly enforce both the spirit and the letter of Rule 3.01, which provides "A member or associate shall not advertise his professional attainments or services. . ."

(Published in the *CPA,* May 1960)

Opinion No. 10
Responsibility of Members for Pro-forma Statements and Forecasts under Rule 2.04

In preparing for management any special purpose financial statement anticipating results of future operations, a member must disclose the source of the information used and the major assumptions made, and he must indicate that he does not vouch for the accuracy of the forecast

Rule 2.04 provides that "A member or associate shall not permit his name to be used in conjunction with an estimate of earnings contingent upon future transactions in a manner which may lead to the belief that the member or associate vouches for the accuracy of the forecast."

The ethics committee is well aware that pro-forma statements of financial position and results of operation, cost analyses, budgets and other similar special purpose financial data which set forth anticipated results of future operations are important tools of management and furnish valuable guides for determining the future conduct of business.

The committee is of the opinion that Rule 2.04 does not prohibit a member from preparing or from assisting a client in the preparation of such statements and analyses. However, when a member associates his name with such statements and analyses, or permits his name to be associated therewith, there shall be the presumption that such data may be used by parties other than the client. In such cases, full disclosure must be made of the source of the information used or the major assumptions made in the preparation of the statements and analyses, the character of the work performed by the member, and the degree of responsibility he is taking. Such disclosure should be made on each statement or in the member's letter or report attached to the statements. The letter or report of the member must also clearly indicate that the member does not vouch for the accuracy of the forecast. It is the opinion of the committee that full and adequate disclosure would put any reader of such statements on notice and restrict the statements to their intended use.

(Published in the *CPA,* November 1960)

Appendix to Section Five (Partnerships)

SPECIMEN FORM OF PARTNERSHIP AGREEMENT*

AGREEMENT made January 2, 1961, among Henry Ayers, of New York, N.Y., Richard Bolton, of Forest Hills, N.Y., Bruce Clark, of Rye, N.Y., James Davis, of New York, N.Y., and George Wilson, of New York, N.Y.

1. *Name and Business.* The parties do hereby form a partnership to engage in the practice of public accountancy under the name of Ayers, Bolton, and Clark, the principal office to be in New York, N.Y.

2. *Term.* The partnership shall begin on January 1, 1961, and shall continue until terminated as herein provided.

3. *Capital.* Whenever required in the business of the partnership, capital shall be contributed by the partners in the proportions in which they share in partnership profits and losses. This paragraph shall not apply to the estate of a deceased partner.

4. *Profit and Loss.* The net profits of the partnership shall be divided and the net losses of the partnership shall be borne in the following proportions, except that all losses resulting from the wrongful act or gross negligence of any partner shall be charged to him in full:

Henry Ayers	40%
Richard Bolton	30%
Bruce Clark	20%
James Davis	5%
George Wilson	5%

The senior partners shall have the right to adjust the bases of participation by junior partners in profits and losses without the consent of the junior partners.

5. *Salaries and Drawings.* Any partner, except the estate of a deceased partner, shall have the right to draw against anticipated earnings, in monthly installments, an amount not in excess of 85% of his earnings for the preceding year, but in no event shall a partner's withdrawals exceed his interest in the partnership business. Any amounts so withdrawn shall be charged against that partner's distributive share of the profits of the partnership business. Any partner shall have the right, at the end of any calendar year, to withdraw the balance of his share of the partnership profits for that year. The drawings of partners during the first year of the partnership shall be agreed upon among all the partners.

6. *Interest.* No interest shall be paid to partners on any contributions to capital.

7. *Management, Duties, and Restrictions.* The partnership shall be composed of senior partners and junior partners. Henry Ayers, Richard Bolton, and Bruce Clark shall be senior partners. The senior partners shall have the right to admit additional partners upon such terms as they may determine, but the participation percentage in net earnings of the estate of a deceased partner shall not be altered

*Reprinted from Rabkin and Johnson's *Current Legal Forms with Tax Analysis,* Matthew Bender & Company, Inc., Albany 1, New York, 1961, Vol. 1 of six, pp. 60-67. (Preceding explanatory comment omitted.)

nor the period of participation curtailed. All of the partners shall participate in the conduct of partnership affairs and each partner shall devote his entire time thereto. In matters relating to the general management of the partnership business, a decision by the majority of the partners shall be binding upon the partnership, but on questions of firm policy the decision of a majority of the senior partners shall prevail. The estate of a deceased partner shall continue as a member of the partnership as hereinafter provided, but such estate shall have no voice in the management of the partnership business.

8. *Banking.* All funds of the partnership are to be deposited in its name in such checking account or accounts as shall be designated by the partners. All withdrawals therefrom are to be made upon checks signed by any senior partner.

9. *Books.* The partnership books shall be maintained at the principal office of the partnership, and any partner shall at all times have access thereto. The books shall be kept on a cash basis and shall be closed and balanced at the end of each calendar year. An audit shall be made as of the closing date.

10. *Termination.* In the event of the retirement of any partner or the voluntary liquidation of the partnership, the following procedure shall be observed:

(a) *Retirement.* Any partner shall have the right to retire from the partnership at the end of any calendar year. Written notice of intention to retire shall be served upon the other partners at the office of the partnership at least three months before the end of the calendar year. The retirement of any partner shall have no effect upon the continuance of the partnership business. The partnership books shall be closed at the end of the calendar year in the regular way and the retiring partner shall be paid the amount of his capital account as then shown on the partnership books. Any partner who voluntarily withdraws from the partnership in accordance with the provisions of this paragraph shall not receive the benefits which accrue where withdrawal is caused by the death of a partner. The remaining partners, together with any new partners, shall have the right to continue the business under the same firm name, and if the business is so continued, the retiring partner shall not engage in the practice of public accountancy in the State of New York, except as an employee, for a period of two years from the date of retirement.

(b) *Liquidation.* In the event that all of the partners agree to terminate the partnership business, they shall share in any profits and losses of the business during the period of liquidation in the same proportions in which they shared the profits and losses prior to the termination of the partnership business. The proceeds of liquidation shall be distributed first in proportionate discharge of the undrawn earnings of the partners, then in such manner as to make the capital accounts of the partners proportionate to the capital accounts in the partnership as at the date of its organization, and the balance shall be distributed in proportionate discharge of the respective capital accounts of the partners. Notwithstanding the foregoing, if the surviving partners terminate the partnership before the expiration of the five-year period following the end of the month in which a partner dies, the capital interest of a deceased partner, his share in the work in process, and the post-death share of the earnings of the estate of a deceased partner, as hereinafter provided, shall be paid in full out of the liquidation proceeds of the partnership before any sums shall be paid to the surviving partners. For this purpose the earnings attributable to the estate of a deceased partner for the balance of the five-year period shall be computed on the basis of the average annual net earnings of the partnership for the two preceding calendar years.

11. *Death.* Upon the death of any partner the partnership business shall not terminate but shall be continued as a partnership among the surviving partners and the estate of a deceased partner. In such event the division of income and the payment of the deceased partner's capital shall be as follows:

(a) *Income.* The estate of a deceased partner shall participate in the net earnings and net losses of the partnership for a period of five years, from the first day of the month following the month of death of the partner, in the following proportions:

Henry Ayers	20%
Richard Bolton	15%
Bruce Clark	10%
James Davis	3%
George Wilson	3%

The share of profits to which the estate of a deceased partner is entitled shall be paid to the estate in quarterly installments based upon 85% of the participation of the deceased partner or of the estate in the net profits of the preceding year. Any necessary adjustments shall be made upon the closing of the books for each calendar year, and the final adjustment shall be made at the end of the five-year participation period. Payments to the estate under this paragraph shall be based on calendar year quarterly periods, the first payment to cover the calendar year quarter ending next after the death of the partner, and the final payment to be made at the end of the five-year period. To absorb the difference between the deceased partner's proportionate interest in the profits of the partnership and the participation percentage of his estate, the interests of the surviving partners in the partnership shall be increased in the proportions of their respective interests as stated in paragraph 4.

(b) *Capital.* The interest of a deceased partner in the capital of the partnership shall be determined as of the end of the month in which his death occurs, and shall be paid to his estate in equal quarterly installments, without interest, over a period of five years, the first payment to be made at the end of the calendar year quarter in which the death occurs. The deceased partner's capital interest shall equal his capital account as shown on the partnership books at the beginning of the calendar year in which his death occurred, increased by his share of partnership profits or decreased by his share of partnership losses for the period from the beginning of the calendar year in which his death occurred until the end of the month in which his death occurred, reduced by his drawings during such period.

(c) *Work in process.* The interest of a deceased partner in the work in process shall be paid to his estate in equal quarterly installments, without interest, over a period of two years, the first payment to be made at the end of the calendar quarter in which the death occurs. The interest of a deceased partner in the work in process at the time of death shall be determined by the surviving partners as of the end of the month in which his death occurs. The amount so payable with respect to work in process shall be capitalized on the partnership books. When the partnership shall receive payment on account of such work in process, the share attributable to the decedent shall be credited to that account, and shall be deducted in computing the amount otherwise payable to the estate under subdivision (a) of this paragraph.

12. *Termination of Deceased Partner's Interest.* When the estate of a deceased partner shall have received the payments provided in paragraphs 10 and 11, such estate shall have no further interest in the partnership or in the partnership assets and property.

13. *Use of Name of Deceased Partner.* The surviving partners shall have the right to continue to use the name of any deceased partner in the partnership name.

14. *Expulsion.* In the event that any partner shall violate any of these articles, or by misconduct or willful inattention to the business welfare of the partnership seriously injure the business of the partnership, any two of the senior partners shall have the right to elect that the delinquent partner shall retire, the election to be exercised by written notice to the delinquent partner. If such notice is given, the delinquent partner shall be deemed to have retired from the partnership on

the date fixed in such notice and shall not be entitled to participate in any future profits of the partnership. Any loss due to delinquency shall be charged against the capital account of the delinquent partner before he is entitled to withdraw his capital interest.

IN WITNESS WHEREOF the parties have signed and sealed this agreement.

. . . . (L.S.)
Henry Ayers

. . . . (L.S.)
Richard Bolton

. . . . (L.S.)
Bruce Clark

. . . . (L.S.)
James Davis

. . . . (L.S.)
George Wilson

Appendix to Section Six
(Office Management)

STYLE MANUAL for report writers, typists, and stenographers of a public accounting office*

COMPILED BY MAURICE H. STANS

This Style Manual has been compiled in instruction form so that any firm which wishes to do so may use it without change. Some firms may prefer to use it as a guide in drawing up a Style Manual of their own.

CONTENTS

*Reprinted from the *CPA Handbook*, AICPA, 1952, Ch. 8, App. A, p. 1.

This Manual is designed for the use of report writers, typists and stenographers to help them attain excellence in preparing the firm's correspondence and reports. Every writer, typist and stenographer should keep in mind that the letters and reports he or she writes become daily representatives from the firm to the clients, bringing to them, by their neatness and general appearance, a message of reliability and prestige. It should, therefore, be his or her constant endeavor to maintain high standards of performance.

It should always be the principal responsibility of the stenographer or typist to produce a neatly written letter or report, to observe the firm's rules for style, to adhere to the rules of grammatical correctness and to punctuate and spell properly.

The Manual is a compendium of the requirements of the office with reference to correspondence and report form, content and arrangement. The Manual presumes, naturally, a knowledge of the essentials of grammar, punctuation and spelling.

The Manual has been prepared as a practical reference book and, for convenience, is divided into the following sections:

I. Audit reports--general comments
II. Preparation of text of report
III. Tabulations, outlines, lists, quotations and other indented material
IV. Typing of statements and schedules
V. Correspondence
VI. Tax returns
VII. Proofreading
VIII. Illustrative list of stationery and supplies for an accounting firm
IX. Books recommended for reference

The instructions are not designed as an exhaustive treatise on style but are intended merely to cover basic practices in report and letter writing.

---

*Acknowledgment is made to International Accountants Society, Inc. for permission to use, in the preparation of this Manual, some of the material appearing in its"Style Manual for Text Writers and Typists."

For pertinent information not contained herein the
user is referred to any good current dictionary,
preferably unabridged.

This Manual has been devised with the
principal objective of presenting material as simply
as possible and, thereby, providing for the maximum
saving of time. It has eliminated, wherever possible,
unnecessary flourishes such as underlining, extensive
capitalization, and punctuation not required to
make the meaning clear.

I.   AUDIT REPORTS--GENERAL COMMENTS

A well-typed report is the result of careful
and thoughtful work on the part of the typist. It
should follow the form approved by the firm, but judgment should be exercised in planning the setup of the
report as a whole. Each page should be well balanced;
paragraphs should break in the right places; tables
should be centered and not broken, except when it is
necessary to break a table which is longer than a page;
page numbers should be in the exact center and a uniform
distance from the bottom of the sheet; type should be
clean and alignment even; and there should be no
"strike-overs" or visible erasures.

The typist should never be persuaded that
there is not sufficient time to do a perfect piece of
work. If a finished page is not up to standard, it
should be retyped immediately, not after it has gone
through the processes of proofreading, ruling and
checking. The report represents the firm, and there
should be no compromise with the standards which have
been established.

If changes are made and it is necessary to
erase after the report has been completed, each copy
should be matched by inserting a small piece of paper
and carbon between the ribbon and the typed sheet.
A word should never be erased, leaving a blank space.
A number of consecutive words or a whole line should
never be erased, and erased words should never be
replaced with a word more than one space longer or
shorter.

Before beginning to type a report,
instructions should be checked. These should be in
writing. Instructions for covers should be checked.
The entire draft should be reviewed and the spacing of
headings and tables planned. If the report of the

previous year is used as a guide, and a noticeable deviation is found in setup or in the spelling of proper names, the person in authority should be consulted. The names of persons, company names and subsidiaries and trade names should be checked and kept consistent throughout the report and the accompanying statements. Particular attention should be given to this when more than one person is working on the report.

Number of Copies

The number of copies designated should be typed together with an office copy, if that has not been included in the number requested. Good carbons should be used for every page of the report and for each statement; after use a few times these carbons should be saved for report drafts or correspondence. Every copy of the first page should be typed on report head sheets and all copies of the following pages on report second sheets.

II.   PREPARATION OF TEXT OF REPORT

Reports should be typed on one side of the paper only and should be double-spaced except in the case of inserted tables, statements, classifications of accounts, lists and similar material, which should be single-spaced.   Spacing should be regular at all times; that is, there should be no extra space above or below a center heading, side heading or tabular matter.

Headings within the text are of two types: (1) center headings and (2) side headings.

The center heading should be exactly centered on its line and typed in solid capitals.   The center heading need not be underlined.   Example:

SCOPE OF AUDIT

The side heading is a subordinate heading; it should be placed at the left-hand margin and solidly underlined.   The first letter of each major word should be capitalized.

A side heading should not follow immediately after a center heading; there should be at least one paragraph of comments or instructions between the two.

Page Numbering

Every page of the report, except page 1, should be consecutively numbered at the bottom in the center between left and right margins.

<u>Paragraphing</u>

Paragraph indentations should be uniform. This Manual uses paragraph indentations of ten blank spaces.

Indented material within the body of a letter or report is set in five blank spaces from the left-hand margin, ends five blank spaces short of the right-hand margin, and the block style is used. (See Section III of this Style Manual for detailed rules and illustrations of indented material.)

<u>Capitalization</u>

Capitalization should be avoided as far as possible. The names of accounts, statements and departments, the titles of officers and department heads, etc., should be in lower-case letters. One exception is "Board of Directors," which is capitalized. When saying "the directors," however, there is no capitalization. The expression "the board" should not be used.

Any body of men or any government act which has some specific name should be capitalized when the full name is given. Example:

The Robinson-Patman Act. (After having been mentioned once by name, it should be referred to as "the act.")

Personal titles written with personal names should be capitalized only when part of an address or of a listing. Example:

Howard Jones, President
Atlas Steel Company

In the body of written material no capitalization of the title is required. Example:

Howard Jones, president of Atlas Steel Company

A few general rules of capitalization are also applicable to accountants' writing, these being:

1. Capitalize all proper nouns and proper adjectives, including the days of the week, the months and specific holidays, but not the seasons.

2. Capitalize the names of points of the compass when used for sections of a country, but not for mere directions. Example:

He lives in the East.
He walked east on Madison Street.

3. Capitalize each important word in the title of a book, musical composition, magazine, etc. Prepositions, conjunc-

tions and articles are not capitalized
except at the beginning of the title.

Hyphens

Hyphens are a great aid to readability and
understanding, but they should be used sparingly and
with discretion. A hyphen is used between words when
the phrase will be more easily understood if so written.
For instance, a hyphen should be used with compound
adjectives and should always be used between a prefix
and a proper name, such as pro-British. The hyphen also
is used in joining an adjective with a noun used as an
adjective, in joining two nouns used as an adjective,
in expressing compound numerals, and in joining com-
pounds made up of nouns and prepositional phrases.
Examples:
> We speak of "capital stock," but of
> "capital-stock records."
> Fifty-four; one-half year; day-to-day
> transactions.

Consistency

The names of companies should be accurate and
should be kept uniform. If the legal name is "The Black
Company," for example, be sure that "The" is always
used and always capitalized and that "Company" is always
spelled out, not abbreviated. Always spell out "and"
in a company name unless an ampersand (&) is part of the
official name. If a statement has an item called
"selling and administrative expense" that item should
be called exactly that each time it appears.

Footnotes

Footnotes are soldom used in the text of
reports. When used, the footnote is designated by a
numeral (if there are more than two), or by asterisks
(if there are only one or two), not by the word "Note."
(See instructions on asterisks, page 863.)

Dashes

Dashes are not found on typewriter keyboards;
therefore, two hyphens should be substituted. Example:
> He does not know where he is going--or why.
> (Note that there is no space before or after
> the hyphens.)

The dash (two hyphens) is used in joining
compound names of accounts, such as "allowance for
depreciation--plant," and "allowance for deprecia-
tion--office." When names of such accounts appear in
the text, the sentence should be so worded that confu-

sion is avoided. This may be done in one of two ways:
(1) putting the exact name of the account in quotations,
or (2) setting off the name with commas. Examples:
You should then debit "fixed assets--plant"
and credit "notes payable."
You should then debit account 126, fixed
assets--plant, and credit account 211,
accounts payable.

Parentheses

When parenthetical material forms a part of
the sentence, the period should be placed outside (as,
for instance, here).

When the material within the parentheses is an
independent imperative or declarative sentence, the
period should be placed inside. Example:
He spent three years in France. (The exact
dates are uncertain.) Later he returned to
America.

A comma should not appear immediately preceding the parenthesis. If a comma is needed after a
phrase written in parentheses, it should be typed
outside. Example:
Here he gives a belated, though stilted (and
somewhat obscure), exposition of the subject.

Underlining

In the text of a report or letter, underlining is occasionally used for emphasis. In such
cases, each word should be underlined _separately_, not
underlined solidly as in side headings. Example:
The popular method of arranging business
figures is _according_ _to_ _date_.

Headings which appear in solid capitals
should not be underlined.

Numerals

Numerals should not be used at the beginning
of a sentence. Preferably, the sentence should be rearranged; and, if this is not possible, then the number
should be spelled. If two related numbers occur at the
beginning of a sentence, both should be spelled.

In any example or illustration the writing of
amounts should be governed by whether any amounts in
the illustration carry cents. Example:
If I buy something for $2.00 on which I
receive a 10% discount, my net bill is
$1.80. (The $1.80 governs the writing of
the $2.00, which otherwise would be
written "$2.")

In the writing of cents only, such as twenty-five cents, the form "25¢" should be used in the text and "$.25" in tabular matter. The only exception to the rule of using "25¢" in the text is in the case of a sentence which contains also an amount in both dollars and cents. Example:

... was priced at $1.02, and the next units are priced at $.95. (Here the $1.02 governs the style of writing the $.95.)

Numbers should not be split between lines. If only part of the number or amount can be put on one line, the entire amount should be carried to the next line. For example, this is improper:

Then we may calculate that the gross profit on sales for the current year is 33-1/3%, which is one-third of $105,-000, or $35,000.

It should be written as follows:

Then we may calculate that the gross profit on sales for the current year is 33-1/3%, which is one-third of $105,000, or $35,000.

In written material, numbers up to one hundred and round numbers over one hundred should be spelled out; figures should be used for numbers above one hundred, except the round numbers. However, if some numbers are under one hundred and some over one hundred in the same sentence, figures should be used for all of them. Examples:

There were 87 categories in the inventory; these included approximately 3,100 items. These are offered in groups of 60 and 120. The company has 7,499 employees.

To avoid confusion, adjoining numbers should not be written in the body of a letter; the number requiring fewer words should be spelled out and figures should be used for the other. Example:

Between 1930 and 1940, ten thousand men were employed. Of the original ten thousand, 943 are still with us.

Figures should be used in the following cases:

1. In numbers representing money ($1.19; $6,000.00)
2. Market quotations (the stock sells at 6-1/2)
3. Dimension (32" x 21")
4. Dates, street numbers, numbered objects, numbers containing decimals (89 Cedar Street; Room 4; Vol. 6; 9.17 yards)

The suffixes "th," "st," "nd," and "rd" are omitted from a date when the month precedes it. When the month is not named, or when the month follows the date,they should be added. Examples:

> May 1
> Your letter of the 1st
> 10th of the month
> 10th of May

Fractions

Regardless of the fact that there are typewriter keys for ¼, ½, etc., fractions should be typed as follows for clearness on carbon copies: 1/4, 1/2, etc. A whole number and a fraction are joined with a hyphen, thus: 21-1/2. Simple fractions appearing in written material should be written out, as in "Two-thirds of those present voted for the resolution."

Numerals connected by symbols, such as in equations, paper sizes, etc., should be separated from symbols by one space.

Example:

> 8-1/2" x 11"
> 2,534 x 7,723 = 19,570,082

Zero Amounts

In tabular matter where zero amounts are to be shown, the following rules apply:

1. In a column where the amounts consist of dollars only, <u>one hyphen</u> should be placed in the "tens" column.
2. In a column where the amounts consist of dollars and cents, <u>one hyphen</u> should be placed in the decimal column. Examples:

a.	Cardboard	$3,725
	Tissue	—
	Twine	2,842
b.	Cardboard	$3,725.22
	Tissue	—
	Twine	2,842.80

Dates

When mentioning dates in the text material, the names of months should be spelled out, not abbreviated, such as December 1, 1961 (not Dec. 1, 1961). The only place where such an abbreviation is permissible is in journal entries. When only the month and the year are given, the comma is usually omitted.

The only places where a completely numerical abbreviation is permissible, such as 12/1/61, are (1) in

"T" accounts, and (2) in columnar matter where one column of data consists entirely of dates, as in the example below:

Policy	Kind of insurance	Amount	Date	Term
212642	Building--fire	$25,000	7/7/61	1 year
345618	Building--fire	20,000	7/1/61	1 year

Percentages

The percentage sign (%), not the words "per cent," should be used in the text when preceded by a number.

The words "per cent" should be used in columnar headings of tables and lists and in the text when not preceded by a number.

Journal Entries

A journal entry is composed of three parts: (1) the account and the amount debited, (2) the account and the amount credited, and (3) the explanation of the entry.

When a journal entry appears as an inserted item in a report or other textual matter, it should be indented five spaces. In other words, the account(s) debited should start at the sixth space; the account(s) credited, five blank spaces to the right of the debits; and the explanation, flush with the debits. The spacing of these three parts of the journal is invariable. Each entry should be single-spaced, with double-spacing between the entry and the explanation, and triple-spacing between the entries. If the journal entries are numbered, the journal entry number is centered on the third line below the preceding entry and only double-spacing is therefore required between journal entries.

The dollar sign in each isolated journal entry, that is, one journal entry standing alone, should be placed directly in front of the amount. Example:

```
    Cash                                    $200
         Accounts receivable                    $200
    John Jones paid his account in full.
```

In a series of journal entries the spacing of the dollar sign for the entries is governed by the entry which carries the largest amount. Example:

```
Taxes                                    $  200
     Accrued real estate taxes                   $  200
Tax accrual for July

Accounts payable                         1,000
     Accounts receivable                         1,000
Transfer between contra
accounts of Hall Company.
```

The dollar signs should be shown only in the first
entry of a series. Account names in a journal entry
should not be followed by the word "account." (Use
"Cash," not "Cash account.")
     Occasionally a journal entry will contain an
account name which is so long that it will not fit into
the available space, and a second line must be used.
When this occurs, the second and succeeding lines of the
account name should be indented two spaces from the
first line. Example:

```
Factory expense                          $8,100
Selling and administrative
  expense                                1,000
Mortgage expense                           800
     Supplies                                    $   200
     Unexpired insurance                           1,200
     Patents                                       5,400
     Unamortized discount
       and expense on first
       mortgage note                                 800
     Accrued personal property
       taxes                                         900
     Accrued real estate taxes                     1,400
```

To charge supplies, insurance,
patent amortization, bond discount and expense, and taxes to
expense accounts.

     Although the second and succeeding lines of
an account name are indented two spaces, the second and
succeeding lines of the explanation section should be
carried flush with the first line of that section. The
right-hand margin of the explanation section should be
as uniform as possible.
     Sometimes the date and account number are

included with journal entries. This requires starting the material at the left margin with no indentation. If only the date is used, it is placed at the left margin preceding the first account debited. (See first example following.)

If both the date and the account number are given, two alternatives are available:

1. The date may be centered above the journal entry, with the account number placed at the left margin. (See second example.)
2. The date may be placed at the left and the account numbers shown in parentheses following the names of the accounts. (See third example.)

Examples:
1961

Dec. 31	Factory ledger balancing account	$1,200	
	Lost profit on returned sales	800	
	Accounts receivable		$2,000

First example, where only the date is given without giving the account numbers.

December 31, 1961

420	Factory ledger balancing account	$1,200	
703	Lost profit on returned sales	800	
403-01	Accounts receivable		$2,000

Second example, where both date and account numbers are given. Notice that the date is written out in full when it is centered above the entry.

1961

Dec. 31	Factory ledger balancing account (420)	$1,200	
	Lost profit on returned sales (703)	800	
	Accounts receivable (403-01)		$2,000

Third example, where the ledger folio number is shown in parentheses.

If the journal entries are numbered, the number should be centered on the line above the entry, or below the date, whichever is appropriate.

Rarely, a list or table of figures appears as part of the explanation section of a journal entry. When this occurs, the list should be centered on the page. Example:

1961

Dec. 31	Common stock subscribed	$81,000	
	Preferred stock subscribed	76,000	
	Common stock issued		$81,000
	Preferred stock issued		76,000

To record issuance of capital stock:

Issue to	Common	Preferred
V. Larson	$48,000	$30,000
M. Olson	32,000	20,000
W. Marine	1,000	26,000
	$81,000	$76,000

Illustrative Report Cover and Report Letter

Examples of a cover for an audit report and a letter showing the form of, and containing typing instructions for, the audit report letter follow:

THE BLANK CORPORATION

AUDITORS' REPORT

December 31, 1961

JOHN JONES & COMPANY
Certified Public Accountants
Cincinnati

BEVAN, BEMIS & COMPANY
1166 Edgewood Street
Dallas 4, Texas

February 8, 1962

The Blank Company
11 Chestnut Street
Ogden, Utah

Gentlemen:

This is a pattern for report typing, with some further instructions regarding spacing and setup. The report is double-spaced throughout. Lists of exhibits and tables are centered and single-spaced with a double space preceding and following, as illustrated below:

Exhibit I--Balance sheet, December 31, 1961

II--Statement of income and retained earnings for the year ended December 31, 1961

III--Statement of cost of goods sold for the year ended December 31, 1961

Columnar headings are typed with only the first letter of the first word capitalized. It is expected that judgment will be used in spacing when it is necessary to avoid breaking a table. Some preliminary drafting is often helpful. A table should appear as follows:

	Year ended December 31,		Percentage to net sales	
	1961	1960	1961	1960
Cost of goods sold	$1,111.11	$1,111.11	10.00	10.00
Depreciation	111.11	111.11	.00	.00
Totals	$1,222.22	$1,222.22	10.00	10.00

848

When a total of one column is carried to the next column, it appears on the same line as the last figure in the first column:

```
$111,111.11
 11,111.11
    111.11    $122,333.33
```

In all tables leave a minimum of two spaces between columns of figures. When calculating space for a column, always find the longest figure and be sure to include space for the dollar sign. Often it is necessary to base the calculation on the column heading if it is wider than the figures to be tabulated.

A new paragraph should not be started at the bottom of a page unless there is room for at least two lines, with two or more lines to carry over to the next page. Never break a word between pages. Try to keep the narrative introducing a table on the same page with the table.

THIS IS A SAMPLE OF A CENTER HEADING

The narrative begins two spaces below the heading with double-spacing throughout the report.

A Side Heading in a Report

Commence the paragraph two spaces below a side heading and continue with double-spacing; double-space before typing the next side heading.

An example of a two-line side heading follows:

Advertising Expense Including
  Cost of Catalogs

The heading begins at the left-hand margin and the continuation line is indented two blank spaces. The entire heading is single-spaced and underlined. No punctuation appears at the end of the heading.

An example of a side heading with subheadings follows:

<u>Selling Expenses</u>

<u>Salaries</u>
<u>Traveling Expense</u>
<u>Advertising</u>

The first subheading is dropped one line and indented five blank spaces. If text appears between the subheadings, double-spacing should be used throughout. If no text appears between the subheadings, they should be single-spaced with a double space between the last subheading and the text.

Try to keep side headings within half the width of the page. If possible arrange the spacing of a report so that an important main heading will come at the top of the page.

Very truly yours,

BEVAN, BEMIS & COMPANY
(signed manually)

III. TABULATIONS, OUTLINES, LISTS, QUOTATIONS AND OTHER INDENTED MATERIAL

Tabular material should always be single-spaced and should be centered on the page with equalized spacing between columns. Not less than two spaces should be left between any two columns of figures. Tabular material may, if necessary extend to the left-hand and right-hand margins.

For example, a short inserted tabulation in textual matter would appear as follows:

Accounts	Debits	Credits
Cash	$12,360	
Merchandise inventory	12,000	
Land	4,000	
Buildings	15,000	
Deferred charges	180	
Investment		$25,000
Surplus		12,900
Sales		23,000
Purchase	17,000	
Operating expense	360	
Totals	$60,900	$60,900

Except for tabulations, the following general rule can be applied to all indented material:

1. If there are forty spaces or less in the longest line, the indented material should be centered on the page.

2. If there are more than forty spaces in a line, the indented material should be indented five blank spaces from the left-hand margin and should extend to not less than five blank spaces from the right-hand margin.

Classifications of Accounts

Classifications of accounts should be tabulated with indentations as follows:

CLASSIFICATION OF GENERAL LEDGER ACCOUNTS
(Blocked-Number System)

10 Cash and receivables
    11 Cash in banks
    12 Cashier's imprest cash fund

100 Stores inventories
   101 Supplies
   102 Materials

200 Unapportioned expense

   Expense pools group
   201 Water expense
   202 Gas expense

   General factory expense group
   231 Factory administration department
   232 Purchasing department

Two spaces should be left between the number and the following word. Each succeeding group of numbers should be indented flush with the first word in the preceding line. The placement of lower numbers is governed by the highest number in any column of numbers; for instance number 11 is indented an additional space in order to leave room for number 101.

Outlines

In some places it is necessary to present material in simple outline form. Sections in such outlines should be identified in the following order:

Indentation	Identification	Example
5	Arabic numerals	9.
9	Lower-case letters	a.
13	Arabic numerals in parentheses	(9)
18	Lower-case letters in parentheses	(a)

The numbers of the first section of such an outline should start at the sixth space in from the left-hand margin.

The identification number or letter of each

successive section should be indented to a point exactly
under the first letter in the first word of the preceding section.

All items in the outline are single-spaced,
except that double-spacing should be used between the
items of the _first_ rank (Arabic numerals).

Example:

    9.   Accrued accounts
       a. Prepare a subsidiary schedule for
           each class of tax to show:
         (1) Amount accrued during year
              and charged to expense
           (a) Reconcile with total
                tax expense
           (b) Examine tax bills and
                supporting data

   10.   Debit balances
       a. Determine nature of such transac-
           tions and validity of the items
       b. If the amounts involved are
           material, confirm by direct
           correspondence

If an outline requires more than four sections, as listed above, the rules given here should be
ignored and the rules on the presentation of complex
outlines should be followed. (See below.)

Outlines (complex)

Some outlines, such as checklists, may be
more complex and may require a more elaborate structure. In these cases, two new identifications series
may be provided, these preceding the four given above,
as follows:

Section	Identification	Example
1.	Roman numerals	XIV.
2.	Capital letters	A.
3.	Arabic numerals	9.
4.	Lower-case letters	a.
5.	Arabic numerals in parentheses	(9)
6.	Lower-case letter in parentheses	(a)

When this method of identification is used,
the numbers of the first section of such a checklist

should start at the left-hand margin of the page. The longest number governs the placement of all others.

. The titles in the first section (Roman numerals) should be solidly underlined.

Double-spacing should be used between the first and second <u>sections</u> (that is, between items bearing Roman numerals and items bearing capital letters), and also between <u>items</u> of the second section (that is, between items bearing capital letters). Everything else in the checklist should be single-spaced. Example:

CHECKLIST OF AUDIT SUGGESTIONS

I. <u>General suggestions for beginning the audit</u>

    A. Assuming that books are in balance and that balances and footings have been inked in, compare trial balances at beginning and end of period, etc.

    B. Prepare working trial balance

XXIII. <u>General</u>

    A. With respect to every phase of the work, check for consistency and for compliance with..., etc.

    B. Audit by inspection
       1. Make comparisons of sales volume in relation to:
          a. Receivables (aged)
            (1) Current
            (2) Delinquent
          b. Sales commissions
            (1) Domestic
            (2) Foreign
          c. Returns and allowances
      12. Compare fixed overhead costs by years

<u>Lists</u>

The two rules previously given govern the placement of lists on the page, as follows:

    1. If a list consists of items no one of which is longer than forty spaces pica type (including the highest number),

the list should be exactly centered on page and single-spaced. (See Example 1 following.)

2. If a list consists of items longer than forty spaces pica type, the numbers should start at the paragraph indentation for inserted material and the items should extend to five spaces short of the right-hand margin. If any item consists of more than one line the second and succeeding lines should be carried flush with the first line; the items should be single-spaced with double-spacing between the items. (See Examples 2 and 3 following.)

The highest number in any list governs the placement of the lower numbers. For example, a list of 121 items requiring two lines each should be set up as follows:

1. This is indented to the eighth space because the highest number takes two more spaces.
12. This is indented to the seventh space because the highest number takes one more space.
121. This is the highest number in the list and therefore is indented to the sixth space (paragraph indentation for inserted material).

In any list two spaces, and only two, should be inserted between the number and the following word.

If any item in a list contains tabular matter, such tabular matter should start flush with the first word of the item. Count the spaces from the left margin of the page to the first word in the item. The tabular matter should end exactly that many spaces from the right margin regardless of the width of the item itself. This centers the tabulation on the page (Example 4). In rare instances it may be impossible to follow this rule, the tabular matter being too wide to fit into such space. Where this happens, the tabular matter should end exactly at the right-hand margin of the page (Example 5). Examples:

Example 1

1. Saving of daily time
2. Neat, legible records
3. Automatic date printing
4. Mechanical computation

Example 2

1. Each item may be transferred to a card.
2. Instead of cards, slips may be used.
3. When cards are prepared, copies may be made.

Example 3

1. Each item called for by a multiple form requisition may be transferred to a new slip or card.
2. Instead of preparing slips or cards for the requisition, individual tabulating cards may be prepared.
3. At the time the multiple requisition is prepared, carbon copies may be made.

Example 4

1. Additional provision for depreciation of fixed assets as follows:

Buildings	2% of cost
Furniture and fixtures	10% of cost
Delivery equipment	20% of cost

2. Accounts receivable amounting to $1,700 are known to be uncollectible and should be charged off.
3. Additional provision for doubtful items amounting to 1% of net sales should be recorded.

Example 5

1. An invoice for insurance premiums which should have been charged to prepaid expenses has been charged as follows:

Manufacturing expense	$1,500
Selling, general and administrative expense	500
Total	$2,000

2. The prepaid expenses expire at the rate of
   $300 per month. These items are chargeable
   as follows:

   Manufacturing expense   75%
   Selling, general and administrative
      expense   25%

Quotations

A short quotation should form part of a sentence of the text. Example:

He said that he "would favor the concept
without approving its adoption."

A long quotation should be single-spaced and set forth separately, starting at the paragraph indentation for inserted material (five blank spaces) and continuing to the same number of spaces from the right-hand margin. The first quotation mark in this instance should come at the fifth space, and the first word should start at the sixth space. The second and succeeding lines are flush with the first word of the first line. Two examples follow:

"These are measures and methods adopted
within the organization itself to safeguard
the cash and other assets of the company
as well as to check the clerical accuracy
of the bookkeeping."

"...measures and methods adopted within the
organization itself to safeguard the cash
and other assets of the company as well as
to check the clerical accuracy of the
bookkeeping."

If several paragraphs from one source are quoted, the quotation marks should appear at the beginning of each paragraph and at the end of the last paragraph only.

All quoted material should be *exactly* quoted. The only permissible changes in a quotation are (1) a spelling error, (2) alignment on the page, and (3) omission of parts, which should be indicated by a series of three periods as in the following example:

"These are measures adopted . . . to check the clerical accuracy of the bookkeeping."

Periods and commas always precede the quotation mark at the end of a quotation. All other punctuation marks are placed inside the quotation marks only when they belong to the quoted material; when they belong to the entire sentence, they are placed outside.

IV.   TYPING OF STATEMENTS AND SCHEDULES

Statements and schedules should be single-spaced and should always be centered on the page unless they are to be bound on the left-hand side, in which case they should be one-half inch off center to allow for binding.

Ordinarily, a statement or schedule should not be split between pages. However, occasionally a long statement, such as a trial balance or list of expenses, will extend beyond one page. In this case it should be carried forward without subtotals or other designation. The title of the second page should be the same as the first with the word "continued" added in parentheses.

Abbreviations should never be used in the body of a statement or report. For example, use "depreciation," not "depr."; use "inventory" not "inv."; etc. It is also preferable not to use abbreviations in headings, but sometimes it is unavoidable.

The word "account" is never used within a statement; for example, use "Cash in bank," not "Cash in bank account."

If the amounts in a statement are all dollar amounts, the zero cents should not be shown; for example, an amount would be typed $20,000, not $20,000.00.

In a series of columnar figures the "total" column should ordinarily appear as the last column to the right. However, in instances where the total is of much greater significance than the individual items, the total should appear in the first column from the left.

In presenting comparative statements in columnar form for two or more years, the latest year's figures should be shown in the first column from the left.

Oversized Statements

When it is necessary to use a sheet of paper larger than the standard report size, such sheet should be folded to the standard size after typing.

Headings

Ordinarily, the heading of a statement or schedule consists of three parts: (1) the name of the corporation or person (in capitals and lower case), (2) the title of the statement (in solid capitals), and (3) the date or period (in capitals and lower case). There should be double-spacing between each of these lines.

Columnar headings should be typed with only the first letter of the first word capitalized.

Spacing

Two or more spaces, depending on the size of the body of the statement, should be used between the last line of the heading and the first line of the body of the statement. In the case of the balance sheet, double-spacing is used between the centered word "ASSETS" and the side heading "CURRENT ASSETS."

Statements divided into sections should have double-spacing between the sections.

Indentation

Indentation on statements and schedules should be to the 3rd, 5th, 7th, 9th, 11th, 13th and 15th spaces progressively from left to right. (Paragraph indentations in this Manual are to the 11th space as are the "Total" designations after a column of figures.)

The second line of a descriptive passage in

the body of a statement or schedule should be indented
to the third space. Example:

    Common stock, authorized 500 shares
        of $10 par value; issued and out-
        standing, 456 shares $4,560

       Items listed under a group heading should be
indented to the third space under the preceding line.
No punctuation is used to indicate subitems. Examples:

                CURRENT ASSETS
                    Cash
                    Accounts receivable
                    Inventories
                        Raw materials
                        Work in progress
                        Finished goods

Capitalization

       The center caption and the main side captions
of the balance sheet and the main side captions of the
statement of income should be solidly capitalized with
no punctuation following. Otherwise, capitalization
should never be used in the body of the statement except
for the first word in the line or sentence or for proper
nouns. Example:

                        ASSETS

        CURRENT ASSETS
            Cash in bank
            Cash on hand
            Accounts receivable

Underlining

       Except for columnar headings and rulings for
subtotals and totals, underlining in statements should
not be used.

       In any statement or ruled table the figures
should be centered under each columnar heading, and
the heading underlined.

       If the heading is longer than any amount
beneath it, the entire heading should be underlined.

Example:

Accounts
<u>receivable</u>
$375.25
264.16

If the heading is shorter than the figures beneath it, the underlining should be typed the full length of the largest amount beneath it, including the dollar sign. Example:

<u>   Cash   </u>
$ 1,000.25
3,500,000.75

When statements contain reference numbers following the dollar amounts, the underlining of the heading should be extended over that reference number. Example:

<u>   Debits   </u>
$110,000 (12)

Headings over columns of <u>descriptive</u> material (not amounts) should be underlined only to the extent of their own length. Example:

<u>Items</u>
Cash
Accounts receivable
Inventories

Rulings within tabular matter, before and after totals, should not be carried over or under the dollar signs. Example:

$1,475,000
250
<u>67,000</u>
$<u>1,542,250</u>

In the body of financial statements and other schedules, single rulings are used only where necessary to indicate the point of subtraction or addition.

861

Double rulings are used at the end of a column or tabulation. For examples, see the illustrative financial
statements beginning on page 888 of this style manual.

When double rulings are required, the two
lines should be typed with sufficient spacing between
them so that there is no possibility of mistaking the two
as being one line. Example:

Not: $1,542,250   But: $1,542,250

Typewriters can be fitted with double
underscore keys.

Dollar Signs

In any list of money amounts the dollar sign
should be typed at the head of each column and repeated
only before and after a double ruling. Examples:

$2,300	
2,300	$ 4,600
2,400	
2,400	
2,400	7,200
	$11,800
	$ 9,000
	3,000
	5,500
	17,500
$3,000	
2,000	
1,500	6,500
	$11,000

Percentages

In statements and schedules the percentage
sign (%) should not be used alone as a columnar heading.
The words "per cent" should be used instead. When this
is done, no sign is typed after the figures in the
column. If a columnar heading should be "Increase" or
"Decrease" or some other designation, and the figures
under the heading are percentages, the sign is typed
after the first figure in the column and also before
and after a double ruling. Example:

Per cent	Increase
10	12.5%
25	7.1
5	10.0
40	29.6%
5	5.5%
1	1.0
6	5.6
12	12.1%

Asterisks

The asterisk indicating a loss, a deficit or a "red" figure follows the figure to which it refers. It should not be enclosed in parentheses. The column in which that figure appears may be headed:

Profit
or Loss*

The asterisk also is used sometimes as a footnote reference in statements (unless it already has been used to indicate a loss), but only when there are one or two footnotes on a page; if more than two, numerals are used. When the asterisk is used, it should be typed after the figure or word to which it refers and before the footnote itself. The footnote is placed at the close of the statement on a vertical line with the left-hand margin of the statement, thus:

*See statement showing correction of net profits.
**See analysis of earned surplus.

If a footnote is so long that it requires more than one line, the second and following lines should be indented two spaces.

Group Headings

A balance sheet may contain items of equal rank, but some of the items may represent group headings. This fact is distinguished by indenting the subsidiary group items two spaces, without punctuation.

Example:

Cash		$100.25
Receivables		
Accounts receivable	$50.00	
Notes receivable	<u>60.00</u>	110.00
Inventory		<u>80.00</u>
Total		$<u>290.25</u>

When <u>one</u> deduction appears on a statement with the word "less" preceding it, the word "less" should form part of the phrase and should not be followed by punctuation. Example:

Accounts receivable		$100
Less allowance for doubtful accounts		<u>10</u> $90

When a deduction consisting of <u>more than one</u> item is made, the word "less" should be followed by the items listed thereunder, indented two spaces. Example:

Total liabilities		$100,000
Less		
Notes payable, due 1950	$10,000	
Debentures, due 1956	<u>40,000</u>	<u>50,000</u>
Net amount		$<u>50,000</u>

Designation of Exhibits

The exhibits of tabular material in the next section are indexed according to page number rather than by designation as "Exhibit" or "Schedule." In certain instances, however, it may be desirable to designate the material according to exhibit number. Where this additional designation is made it should be shown in the upper right-hand corner of the statement or schedule as in the following example:

Exhibit I

The Filler Corporation
BALANCE SHEET
December 31, 1961

Syllabification

The general rules of syllabification in typing material are important and should be observed in accountants' reports and correspondence:

1. Divide only between syllables; words of one syllable should not be divided.

2. Prefixes and suffixes usually may be divided from the root. (ex-pand; con-clude; work-ing)

   > NOTE: Rules 3 and 4 take precedence over this rule.

3. A single consonant goes with the preceding or the following vowel, according to the pronunciation. (pro-duce; prod-uct; va-por; vap-id)

4. Two adjoining consonants are usually divided (dic-tion; col-lision; pater-nal; lan-tern; com-mis-sion). But two letters which make a single sound, such as "sh," "ck," "ph," or "th" are not divided. (preach-ing)

5. Suffixes such as "cial," "sion," and "tion" should not be divided. (cru-cial; commis-sion; composi-tion)

6. Do not divide names of persons or other proper nouns.

7. Do not divide initials preceding a name, or such combinations as 55 B.C., 2:20 a.m., Y.M.C.A., or Lieut. Col.

8. Do not divide a word at the end of a page.

9. Do not divide a word already hyphenated, such as "self-control."

10. Do not carry less than three letters to another line.

11. Do not separate figures at the end of a line: $1,425.35.

12. Do not divide words at the ends of more than two consecutive sentences.

Illustrative Statements

Financial statements using these rules are illustrated on pages 888-893, following.

V.   CORRESPONDENCE

The following material relates specifically to correspondence. The general rules regarding the form, paragraphing, capitalization, quotations, underlining, numerals, and other material appearing in the portions of this Manual dealing with report writing are equally applicable to correspondence.

There are two types of letters in an accounting firm's correspondence, these being:
1.   A formal letter
2.   An informal letter

Formal Letter

A formal letter is frequently used in the following circumstances and other situations where formality is deemed desirable:
1.   A letter pertaining to working arrangements, fees or other business matters.
2.   A letter of opinion on an accounting or tax matter.
3.   A letter covering transmittal of a report, a tax return or other documents.

Such a letter carries the singular person throughout when written by a sole practitioner and the plural person throughout when written by a firm.

Formal correspondence should always be addressed to or for the attention of an individual, in order that it may have confidential treatment at the receiving end. This is particularly true in the case of letters transmitting reports, tax returns, and other documents.

A formal letter may be addressed in either one of the following two fashions:

Mr. John A. Jones, President
Jones Manufacturing Company
321 West Erie Street
Chicago 6, Illinois

                 or

Jones Manufacturing Company
321 West Erie Street
Chicago 6, Illinois

          Attention: Mr. John A. Jones, President

The title of the addressee should be stated.

          Formal letters must always be signed by a
principal (partner or practitioner). The closing may
take either one of the following two forms:

                    Very truly yours,

          (manually) John Smith & Company

                         or

                    Very truly yours,

                    JOHN SMITH & COMPANY

                    By

                         John Smith
                         Partner

Informal Letter

          An informal letter is one addressed to an
individual and considered more or less in the nature
of a personal communication. It is signed by the writer
with his own name. All such letters written by anyone
but a principal (partner or practitioner) must be
cleared with a principal if they relate to the firm's
business in any way. An informal letter carries the
singular person throughout.

Names

          It is a good practice to have the name of the
writer typed beneath the written signature in order to
insure correct deciphering. The stenographer should do
this in all cases unless requested not to do so.

          As in the case of reports, names and addresses

should always be exact. The proper legal names of all organizations should be used. Abbreviations in names, addresses and other matter should be avoided.

Date Line

The date line should be typed three lines below the printed head of the letter, its position corresponding as nearly as possible to the right-hand margin of the letter.

Address

The address should be single-spaced. The title of the person addressed should appear on the same line as the name, if possible. If any part of the address is too long to look well on one line, a second line should be used. City and state should not be abbreviated.

The address should be at least two lines below the date line, the exact distance varying with the length of the letter. The block form should be used, with open punctuation (no commas at ends of the lines).

References

Certain communications may require reference to previous correspondence or to the subject matter. This may be done by a reference line immediately following the address, in this form:

        Re: Your file No. 1219

                or

        Re: Federal income tax return for 1961

In cases where both a "reference" line and "attention" line appear in the same letter, they should be placed in the folowing manner:

        Doe, Doe & Doe
        135 South LaSalle Street
        Chicago 2, Illinois

                Attention: Mr. William Doe
                        Re: Federal income tax return for 1961

Neither line should be underscored.

Salutation

The salutation should be typed two lines below the address or the last line of any inserted reference.

In a letter addressed to a firm or corporation, the salutation should be "Gentlemen:" even though the letter is marked for the attention of an individual. In informal correspondence, the salutation should be provided by the dictator.

Body of Letter

The letter should begin two lines below the salutation. All letters should be single-spaced regardless of number of lines. A letter should never have only one paragraph unless it contains only one sentence.

Double-spacing should be used between paragraphs. Paragraphs should be indented ten spaces from the left margin.

All lines should be as uniform as possible, without too many divisions of words.

A new paragraph should not be started at the bottom of a page unless there is room for at least two lines. Not less than two lines should ever be carried to another page.

Complimentary Close

For formal letters the complimentary close should be "Very truly yours." For informal letters it should be "Sincerely," unless some other expression is dictated. The complimentary close should be placed two lines below the last line of the letter and to the right of center.

Reference Initials

Each letter and memorandum should carry the initials of the dictator in the lower left-hand corner, followed by a colon and the stenographer's initials, thus: AVC:TE

Enclosures

When enclosures are transmitted, that fact

should be indicated in the lower left-hand corner,
appearing below the reference initials as, for
instance: Enclosures 4

Continuation Pages

Continuation pages of a letter should have
only the name of the addressee at the top of each page,
at the left-hand margin. The number of each continuation page should be inserted at the top of the page in
the center, and the date should be placed at the right.
Spacing should be equalized.

Number of Copies

In the case of all correspondence and memorandums, the number of copies required by firm practice
should be made. These should be handled and filed in
accordance with the established system of the office.
Copies for persons outside the firm should be made on
special "COPY" tissue sheets.

Envelopes

Envelopes should be addressed in block style,
without indentations.

Appearance

Accounting firms maintain high standards of
workmanship and appearance in reports and correspondence. Strike-overs are not acceptable, nor are crowded
words. Erasures must be neat without tearing the paper,
and they should be practically undetectable. The
material should be balanced attractively on the page,
with equal margins. Typewriters, ribbons and carbon
paper must be clean and in good condition.

Telegrams

In preparing Western Union blanks for transmission, the same number of copies should be made
as is required for letters and office memorandums.

In the proper spaces on the blank, the type
of service desired and the account to be charged should
be indicated on all copies.

The date, time and place from which sent

should be typed in the upper right-hand corner. The
address and signature should be shown in full. The
entire telegram should be typed in capitals with necessary punctuation, using numerals for dates and amounts.

The copies are distributed in the same manner
as copies of other correspondence.

Illustrative Letters and Memorandums

Specimen formal and informal letters and
specimen office memorandums follow this portion of the
Manual. These illustrate the form used in the date
line, the address, the salutation, the paragraphing,
the complimentary close, the signature and other
features.

Also included are completed examples of
Western Union telegram forms and of journal entries
as the latter would be transmitted to a client.

BEVAN, BEMIS & COMPANY
1166 Edgewood Street
Dallas 4, Texas

July 3, 1961

American Institute of CPAs
270 Madison Avenue
New York 16, New York

Re: Correspondence

Gentlemen:

This is a standard form to be used when typing a letter.

The address should begin at least two spaces below the date line and the margin should be set so that the letter will be well balanced on the page. The width of the margin is determined by the length of the letter.

Indent paragraphs ten spaces from the left-hand margin. The lines should be approximately uniform in length and a dictionary should be consulted when in doubt as to the proper division of a word. All letters are to be single-spaced with a double space between paragraphs. Follow each period with two spaces before commencing the next sentence.

Never release a letter with a visible erasure. If words are to be deleted or changes are made after a letter has been completed ALWAYS retype. A letter reflects the firm's standard and a letter with untidy erasures, uneven margins, fuzzy type or poorly balanced setup should not be released for signature.

The complimentary close should be written two spaces below the last line of the letter. Leave a margin of at least an inch at the bottom of the page.

Very truly yours,

BEVAN, BEMIS & COMPANY

REC:SD

By

Robert E. Carter
Partner

FORMAL LETTER

BEVAN, BEMIS & COMPANY
1166 Edgewood Street
Dallas 4, Texas

July 3, 1961

Mr. David A. Matthews, President
The Winslow National Bank
Winslow, Maine

Dear Mr. Matthews:

This is the form to be used in writing letters
of more than one page in length.

Before typing a letter be sure that the type
and platen are clean. Keep a reliable type cleaner at
hand and use it frequently. Watch the alignment of
type and have defective type bars repaired. Use a
lightly inked black ribbon in order to produce a clear,
sharp impression.

"When quotations are set out separately,
place the quotation marks four blank spaces
from the margin of the letter. Single-space
the lines irrespective of the spacing of the
letter proper. There should be a double
space preceding and following the quotation
and between quotation paragraphs.

"In an indented quotation place quotation
marks at the beginning of each paragraph of
the matter quoted and at the end of the
concluding paragraph.

"Errors associated with the use of quotation
marks generally arise in connection with
the position of other punctuation marks
which happen to be used with them. (See
pages 857, 858.)"

Registered mail or air mail should be clearly
marked in capitals at the upper right-hand corner of
the letter, also on all file copies and the envelope.
A notation should be made at the foot of the letter
when there are enclosures. This notation should clearly
indicate the number of enclosures.

873

Leave a margin of at least one inch at the bottom of the page. Never carry a single line of a paragraph to the second page. Try to break a paragraph so that there are two or more lines on the first page and as many on the second. If this is not feasible, carry the entire paragraph to the second page.

On the second and following pages the name of the addressee is to be typed from the upper left-hand margin, the number of the page in the center and the date in the upper right-hand corner. It is not necessary to repeat the entire address; if the letter is addressed to a company, write the company name on the second page but if it is addressed to an officer of the company, type only his name.

The spacing will be determined by the number of lines on the page but the margins must match those on the first page. If there are only a few lines to be carried over, the first paragraph should be dropped well below the date line but never to the middle of the page.

A letter second sheet should be used for all pages following the first, with the same number of copies throughout. Always check the number of copies after you have inserted the paper in the typewriter.

Very truly yours,

BEVAN, BEMIS & COMPANY

By

Robert E. Carter
Partner

REC:SD
Enclosures 5

FORMAL LETTER

BEVAN, BEMIS & COMPANY
1166 Edgewood Street
Dallas 4, Texas

July 3, 1961

American Institute of CPAs
270 Madison Avenue
New York 16, New York

    Attention: Mr. John L. Carey, Executive
        Director

Gentlemen:

   Letters consisting of two or more short paragraphs should follow the proportions laid down for the full-page letter, using wider margins to secure a harmonious appearance on the letterhead.

   The initials of the dictator and the stenographer appear at the lower left.

   Carbon paper which has been used for reports may be used again for the file copies of letters. However, if the letter is to be sent out in duplicate, be sure that carbon paper is in good condition.

        Very truly yours,

      (manually) Bevan, Bemis & Company

REK:SD

INFORMAL LETTER

December 29, 1961

Mr. Robert White
150 North Lake Avenue
Upstate, Illinois

Dear Bob:

Pursuant to our meeting yesterday, I enclose drafts of two office memorandums concerning The ABC Company. These were prepared as a result of our discussions of the problems involved. Will you please review them and let me have your comments so that I can forward them to Bill Jones, indicating that they are the result of our joint discussions?

I will also advise Bill that you and I are considering an alternative procedure. This will be the one suggested by you of transferring the buildings to a building corporation. In order to visualize the results, I will proceed to make some computations which will be submitted to you and we will then jointly inform Bill as to the result of our considerations.

Sincerely,

(Space for manual signature)

John Smith

JS:L
Enclosures 2

February 27, 1962

Mr. Louis R. Ajax, Controller
Ajax Printing Company
600 North Park Avenue
Chicago, Illinois

Dear Louis:

      I find that it will be convenient for me to
meet with you this coming Monday, March 5. However,
I suggest that you come to my office because the
papers will be more readily available for our use in
connection with the work we are planning to do.

      The forms have been received so we should
have no difficulty in getting started.

              Sincerely,

           (Space for manual signature)

              John Smith

JS:L

BEVAN, BEMIS & COMPANY
OFFICE MEMORANDUM

Date	July 14, 1961		
To	J. C. Adams	**From**	Fred Smith
Client	Jones Manufacturing Company		
Subject	Annual Audit		

      Fred Williams, the treasurer of this
client, phoned today and asked that we prepare eleven
copies of the annual audit report hereafter instead
of six.

      Please make appropriate notations on your
records.

FS:LMC

WESTERN UNION
TELEGRAM
W. P. MARSHALL, PRESIDENT

1206 (4-55)

NO. WDS.-CL. OF SVC.	PD. OR COLL.	CASH NO.	CHARGE TO THE ACCOUNT OF	TIME FILED
			BEVAN, BEMIS & COMPANY	

Send the following message, subject to the terms on back hereof, which are hereby agreed to

NEW YORK
AUGUST 8, 1961

BEVAN, BEMIS & COMPANY
1166 EDGEWOOD STREET
DALLAS 4, TEXAS

PUNCTUATION MAY BE USED IN TELEGRAMS. WHEN TYPING

DATES AND AMOUNTS USE NUMERALS. (THE BALANCE AT JANUARY 31,

1961 WAS $697,324.56) SIGN FULL NAME

BEVAN, BEMIS & COMPANY

WESTERN UNION
TELEGRAM
W. P. MARSHALL, PRESIDENT

1206 (4-55)

NO. WDS.-CL. OF SVC.	PD. OR COLL.	CASH NO.	CHARGE TO THE ACCOUNT OF	TIME FILED
			BEVAN, BEMIS & COMPANY	

Send the following message, subject to the terms on back hereof, which are hereby agreed to

(FILE COPY)   10:30 AM
                               NEW YORK
          FWL:TJM   AUGUST 8, 1961

BEVAN, BEMIS & COMPANY
1166 EDGEWOOD STREET
DALLAS 4, TEXAS

PUNCTUATION MAY BE USED IN TELEGRAMS. WHEN TYPING DATES

AND AMOUNTS USE NUMERALS. (THE BALANCE AT JANUARY 31, 1961 WAS

$697,324.56) SIGN FULL NAME

BEVAN, BEMIS & COMPANY

CHARGE - THE BLANK COMPANY

878

The Blank Corporation

JOURNAL ENTRIES

June 30, 1961

	Debit	Credit
Cash	$ 5,000	
Buildings	160,000	
Land	25,000	
Machinery and equipment	224,000	
Capital stock, 1,000 shares common		$100,000
Capital stock, 1,000 shares preferred		100,000
Paid-in surplus		214,000
	$414,000	$414,000

       To record acquisition of assets as
authorized by directors' minutes,
April 28, 1961

Accounts receivable	$ 1,639	
Accounts payable		$ 1,639

To transfer credit balances in accounts
receivable to accounts payable as follows:
Williams Ship Co. $1,039
Jones Steel Co.   600

Accrued interest receivable	2,630	
Interest income		2,630

To record interest on debit balances
for June 1961

Machinery and equipment	2,600	
Repairs		2,600

To remove from repairs account cost of
a new pump, erroneously charged

879

VI.   TAX RETURNS

Tax returns must be typed carefully.   To obtain the best results, a wide-carriage typewriter with elite type should be used.   Two-fold and three-fold tax forms should be opened, and carbon sheets wide enough to cover the entire typing surface should be used.   When the forms have been inserted into the typewriter, the copies should be checked to see that they are in perfect alignment.   This can be done by sticking a sharp pin through all of the forms.   If this "pin check" is made frequently and the tax forms are adjusted as the typing progresses, all of the copies will register perfectly.

Number of Copies

Three copies should be typed, unless more are requested.   The third copy should be stamped with the checking stamp and used as an office copy for the firm's files.   The first carbon copy should be the client's file copy.

Schedules

Tax schedules should be typed on regular weight paper and the totals should be double-underscored on the typewriter.   The headings should not be underscored.   A checking stamp should be placed on the third copy of every schedule.   Occasionally the instructions call for enough copies to be used with several tax returns.   In that case, the proper schedule numbers should be typed on the various copies, and an office copy should be retained for each set of returns.

Schedule Numbers

Schedule numbers should be written in the upper right-hand corner of the page and should conform to the numbers on the tax return.

Tax Forms

Since tax forms are printed on fairly heavy paper, two typings should be made if more than five copies are requested.   When there is more than one typing, only one office copy should be stamped, but there should be a checking stamp for each typing.

Proofreading

All tax work must be Comptometer-checked and proofread in the proofreading department. Corrections must be made neatly and checked carefully. Since it is difficult to make neat corrections on tax forms, any tax returns requiring major changes should be retyped.

Illustrative Tax Transmittal Letters

Examples of form letters for use in forwarding tax forms follow. These illustrations lack dates, addresses, salutations, etc., which should be filled in by the typist.

FORM LETTER FOR DECLARATION OF
ESTIMATED FEDERAL INCOME TAX
(Alternative items shown in parentheses)

We enclose, in duplicate, your (amended) 1962 declaration of estimated Federal income tax.

The original should be signed by you (and your wife), dated, and forwarded to the Director of Internal Revenue for your district in time to be received on or before April 15, 1962.

A check in the amount of $......, payable to the Internal Revenue Service, should accompany the declaration.

The duplicate copy of this declaration should be retained in your files.

(This declaration is based upon an estimated tax equal to or greater than that indicated on your final return for 1961. Accordingly, no amendment of this declaration will be required, regardless of any increase in your 1962 income. In the event your income decreases substantially, you should consider amending this declaration. In either case, a final return for 1962 will be due April 15, 1963.)

(This declaration is based upon an estimated taxable income of $......, which is less than the amount shown on your 1961 return. If it should become apparent during the year that your 1962 income will exceed the amount estimated, it may become necessary to file an amended declaration on the appropriate due date of installments. Penalties will be avoided if this is done or if a final 1962 income tax return is filed on or before January 31, 1963.)

FORM LETTER FOR INDIVIDUAL FEDERAL INCOME TAX RETURN
(Alternative items shown in parentheses)

We enclose, in duplicate, your 1961 Federal individual income tax return.

The original of this return should be properly signed by you (and your wife), dated, and forwarded to the Director of Internal Revenue for your district in time to be received on or before April 15, 1962. (The original of Form W-2 issued by your employer must accompany the signed return when filed.)

An overpayment of tax in the amount of $...... is indicated at Item 17 on the first page of the return, and the treatment to be accorded such overpayment is indicated at Item 18.

The duplicate copy of this return should be retained in your files.

FORM LETTER FOR INDIVIDUAL INCOME TAX RETURN
(Alternative items shown in parentheses)

We are enclosing, in duplicate, your 1961 Federal individual income tax return.

The original should be signed by you (and your wife), dated, and forwarded to the Director of Internal Revenue for your district in time to be received on or before April 15, 1962. (The original of Form W-2 issued by your employer must accompany the signed return when filed.)

A check for the tax due in the amount of $......, payable to the Internal Revenue Service, should accompany the return.

The duplicate copy of this return should be retained in your files.

FORM LETTER FOR FEDERAL PARTNERSHIP INCOME TAX RETURN

We enclose, in duplicate, your Federal partnership return of income for the year ended ....

The original should be signed and dated by a partner and forwarded to the Director of Internal Revenue for your district in time to be received on or before ....

No tax payment is due in connection with this return as each partner's share of the net income and credits of the partnership is reportable by him individually in his personal Federal income tax return.

The duplicate copy of this return should be retained in your files.

FORM LETTER FOR FEDERAL CORPORATION INCOME TAX RETURN

We enclose, in duplicate, your Federal corporation income tax return for the year ended ....

The original should be signed by an officer, dated, and forwarded to the Director of Internal Revenue for your district in time to be received on or before ....

The tax in the amount of $.... may be paid, by check to the Internal Revenue Service, either in full at the time of filing the return or in two installments as follows:

    1st installment due within return 50%
    2nd installment due three months
      from due date of return 50%

The duplicate copy of this return should be retained in your files.

VII. PROOFREADING

All accounting work must be compared by two persons, one who reads from the draft and one who holds the finished copy. Some work may require a second reading which may be done by a single proofreader.

Editing is the dictator's responsibility; and, while proofreaders should question grammatical construction, no changes should be made in the text unless approved by the dictator.

The proofreader must be trained to read clearly at a fairly rapid, but even, pace. She should read spacing, capitalization, and punctuation as well as text and should spell all proper names. She should stop immediately when the copyholder marks a correction, and should watch her place so that she may continue promptly.

The copyholder must learn to concentrate and should never allow her attention to wander or to be distracted. She must be alert and must follow the text letter by letter. She should watch for

        Errors in setup
        Typographical errors
        Transposed letters and figures
        Misspelled words
        Spelling of proper words
        Consistent spelling
        Capitalization
        Punctuation
        Proper division of words between lines
        Grammatical construction
        Bad erasures

Proofreaders should use a red pencil and should make all correction marks in the left-hand margin, placing a light mark under the word or letter to be corrected. Standard proofreader's symbols should be used. All typists and readers should familiarize themselves with these marks. (See Hints to Proofreaders, page 221, MANUAL OF STYLE, UNIVERSITY OF CHICAGO PRESS.)

VIII. ILLUSTRATIVE LIST OF STATIONERY AND SUPPLIES FOR AN ACCOUNTING FIRM

	Description	Use
Letters	Engraved bond letterheads, 8-1/2 x 11	All correspondence
	Second (continuing) sheets	All correspondence
	Tissue sheets printed "copy"	Copies to parties outside firm
	White tissue	Correspondence file
	Blue tissue	Review by partners; follow-up file
	Pink tissue	Supervising accountant; working papers
Billing	Engraved bond letterhead - 5 x 8-1/2	Bills to clients
Memorandums	4-part memorandum form (copies same colors as correspondence copies)	Interoffice and intraoffice correspondence and file memorandums
Envelopes	No. 6-3/4 size	Bills and one-page letters
	No. 10 size	Letters of more than one page
	No. 6-1/4 size (printed return envelope)	Return correspondence
	Large manila (8-1/2 x 11)	Unfolded long letters
	Large manila (10 x 15)	Mailing reports
Telegrams	Western Union telegram blanks (short and long sizes)	All telegrams
Reports	Report letterheads - 8-1/2 x 11 13-pound paper	First page of reports
	Report second sheets (name imprinted or watermarked) 13-pound paper	Continuing pages of reports
	Wide statement sheets - 11 x 14 and 11 x 17	Schedules and statements

	Office copy sheets (plain) 8-1/2 x 11, 11 x 14, and 11 x 17	Retained copies of reports
Plain Paper	Plain 13-pound sheets, 8-1/2 x 11 and 11 x 17	Tax schedules; tax protests; drafts of letters; memorandums and reports; financial statements without opinion
Legal Size Paper	Watermarked or engraved, 8-1/2 x 13 and 13 x 17	Estate accounts, SEC reports, and other special reports
Covers	Buff covers with firm's name	Opinion reports
	White covers, plain	Nonopinion reports
	Blue office copy covers	Office copies of reports
	White backing sheets	Tax protests, court papers
Binding Materials	Eyelets, washers and machine	Binding reports
Carbon Paper	Hard-finished black carbon paper, lightweight (sizes needed for all paper sizes)	All typing work
Supplies	Black typewriter ribbons, erasers, erasing shields, time reports, typewriter brushes and cleaning fluid, file folders and dividers, paper clips, pencils (black and red), scratch pads, and mimeograph and multilith paper	

IX. BOOKS RECOMMENDED FOR REFERENCE

The following books will prove helpful in supplementing and in applying the rules included in this Manual.

Webster's <u>New International Dictionary</u>, Unabridged, G. & C. Merriam Co.

<u>A Manual of Style</u>, The University of Chicago Press

<u>Complete Secretary's Handbook</u>, Davis and Miller, Prentice-Hall

<u>Standard Handbook for Secretaries,</u> Hutchinson, Whittlesey House

United States Government Printing Office <u>Style Manual</u>

The Filler Corporation

STATEMENT OF INCOME

Year ended December 31, 1961

SALES
  Gross sales, less returns, allow-
    ances and discounts $1,385,624.76

COST OF GOODS SOLD   1,056,614.22
        Gross profit   329,010.54

SELLING AND ADMINISTRATIVE EXPENSES
  Selling expenses $124,373.62
  Administrative expenses   131,817.10   256,190.72
        Operating profit   72,819.82

OTHER INCOME
  Interest and dividends   725.01
  Gain on sale of fixed assets   1,050.00   1,775.01
                                74,594.83

OTHER DEDUCTIONS
  Interest   6,700.00
  Amortization of discount and ex-
    pense on first mortgage note   983.42   7,683.42
        Net income (before income
          taxes)   66,911.41

INCOME TAXES
  Federal normal tax and surtax   22,316.48
        NET INCOME $ 44,594.93

The Filler Corporation
COMPARATIVE STATEMENT OF INCOME
Years ended December 31, 1961 and 1960

	Year ended December 31, 1961	Year ended December 31, 1960	Increase decrease*
SALES			
Gross sales, less returns, allowances and discounts	$1,385,624.76	$1,039,561.99	$346,062.77
COST OF GOODS SOLD	1,056,614.22	752,744.62	303,869.60
Gross profit	329,010.54	286,817.37	42,193.17
SELLING AND ADMINISTRATIVE EXPENSES			
Selling expenses	124,373.62	107,385.02	16,988.60
Administrative expenses	131,817.10	125,132.62	6,684.48
	256,190.72	232,517.64	23,673.08
Operating profit	72,819.82	54,299.73	18,520.09
OTHER INCOME			
Interest and dividends	725.01	793.00	67.99*
Gain on sale of fixed assets	1,050.00	–	1,050.00
	1,775.01	793.00	982.01
	74,594.83	55,092.73	19,502.10
OTHER DEDUCTIONS			
Interest	6,700.00	6,700.00	–
Amortization of discount and expense on first mortgage note	983.42	983.42	–
	7,683.42	7,683.42	–
Net income (before income taxes)	66,911.41	47,409.31	19,502.10
INCOME TAXES			
Federal normal tax and surtax	22,316.48	17,473.94	4,842.54
NET INCOME	$ 44,594.93	$ 29,935.37	$ 14,659.56

889

The Filler Corporation

BALANCE SHEET

March 31, 1961

ASSETS

CURRENT ASSETS
  Cash $ 5,269.92

  Accounts receivable
    Customers $25,673.63
    Officers and employees   3,816.49
                              29,490.12
  Less allowance for doubtful
    accounts   2,700.00   26,790.12
  Inventories--at the lower of
    cost (determined by the
    first-in-first-out method)
    or market
    Raw materials   21,642.79
    Work in process   10,749.62
    Finished goods   5,253.13   37,645.54
  Insurance premiums unexpired   837.15 $70,542.7

FIXED ASSETS
  Machinery and other equipment
    --at cost   26,895.92
  Less accumulated depreciation   4,956.18   21,939.7

                                             $92,482.4

(Continued)

LIABILITIES

CURRENT LIABILITIES
  Accounts payable--trade $41,482.69
  Income taxes for the year
    ended December 31, 1960--
    unpaid portion   2,348.16
  Accrued liabilities
    Income taxes for the three
      months ended March 31,
      1961--estimated $ 700.00
    Salaries and wages   693.00
    Taxes (other than income
      taxes)   277.24   1,670.24 $45,501.09

CAPITAL
  Capital stock--authorized,
    5,000 shares of $10.00 par
    value; issued and outstand-
    ing, 1,000 shares   10,000.00
  Retained earnings   36,981.38   46,981.38
                                   $92,482.47

ASSETS

CURRENT ASSETS

Cash		$ 20,296.29	
United States Government securities--at cost, plus accrued interest (principal amount, $25,000.00; quoted market price, $26,593.20)		25,692.47	
Accounts receivable			
Customers	$255,673.63		
Officers, employees and other	14,816.49		
	270,490.12		
Less allowance for doubtful accounts	9,500.00	260,990.12	
Inventories--at the lower of cost (determined by the first-in-first-out method) or market			
Raw materials and supplies	121,642.79		
Work in process	43,749.26		
Finished goods	17,356.30	182,748.35	
Prepaid expenses and sundry deposits		8,120.41	$497,847.64

INVESTMENTS

Investment in subsidiary 500 shares (100%) of the capital stock of Justin, Inc.--at cost	56,289.72		
Advances to Justin, Inc.	20,000.00	76,289.72	
Other securities--at cost		10,264.89	86,554.61

FIXED ASSETS

Land--at cost		20,000.00	
Buildings, machinery and equipment, furniture and fixtures--at cost	421,693.72		
Less accumulated depreciation	149,262.73	272,430.99	
Leasehold improvements--at cost, less $7,969.47 amortization		15,692.74	308,123.73

DEFERRED CHARGES AND OTHER ASSETS

Cash surrender value of life insurance		3,692.78	
Patents--at cost, less $5,269.72 amortization		6,169.72	
Unamortized discount and expense on first mortgage note		4,179.48	14,041.98
			$906,567,96

BALANCE SHEET
December 31, 1961

LIABILITIES

CURRENT LIABILITIES

Notes payable to bank (unsecured)		$ 25,000.00	
Current maturities of first mortgage note		20,000.00	
Accounts payable			
Trade	$148,069.73		
Employees and other	6,066.35	154,136.08	
Income taxes for the year ended December 31, 1961		22,316.48	
Accrued liabilities			
Salaries and wages	8,692.00		
Taxes (other than income taxes)	7,277.24	15,969.24	$237,421.80

FUNDED DEBT

First mortgage 4% note, payable in quarterly installments of $5,000	155,000.00	
Less current maturities	20,000.00	135,000.00

CAPITAL

Contributed capital			
6% cumulative preferred stock--authorized, 1,500 shares of $100 par value; issued and outstanding, 1,450 shares	145,000.00		
Common stock--authorized, 4,000 shares of $100 par value; issued and outstanding, 2,000 shares	200,000.00		
Capital contributed in excess of par value of common stock	50,000.00	395,000.00	
Retained earnings			
Appropriated for possible future decline in inventories	20,000.00		
Unappropriated	119,146.16	139,146.16	534,146.16
			$906,567.96

IN-CHARGE ACCOUNTANT'S REVIEW QUESTIONNAIRE*

This questionnaire (used by a national firm of accountants) is to be completed for each audit and signed by the accountant in charge before the working papers and report are submitted to a principal or partner for the firm's review. It is the sole responsibility of the accountant in charge of the assignment, and is intended to supplement his own review of all the papers and of their co-ordination with the trial balance and financial statements. It is expected that, for each item in the balance sheet (and the important items in the income statement), the working papers will show an analysis of the composition of the item, a description of the method of verification, any adjustments, and the amount verified by the in-charge accountant for inclusion in the statements. These questions are therefore intended to supplement the information customarily readily obtained from a review of the working papers.

If a question requires a more complete answer than space permits, or if any answer is in the negative, full details should be given on a separate sheet or in the working papers themselves, with a notation on the questionnaire as to where the answer will be found.

I. *Questions Concerned with the Adequacy of the Examination*

1. Has the system of internal control been surveyed and tested and the audit program completed on a basis consistent with the weaknesses and strengths disclosed? ——

2. Viewing the financial statements as a whole, are you satisfied as to their propriety, substantial accuracy, conformity with generally accepted accounting principles, and consistency with financial statements of prior periods? ——

3. Have you given adequate consideration to possible losses such as those from unfilled contract orders, purchase commitments for future delivery, and proposed dispositions of assets? ——

4. Have all unusual points or questions been summarized and properly disposed of? ——

5. Have all items on the audit program and work sheets been initialed by those doing the work? ——

6. Has the work of all assistants been thoroughly reviewed? ——

7. Has the permanent file been reviewed and have all pertinent items for the current period been inserted? ——

8. Have our correspondence files been reviewed for pertinent information or opinions? ——

9. Have the corporate minutes of current (and prior) years been reviewed and are all matters therein correctly reflected in the accounts? ——

10. Have trust indentures, loan agreements, major contracts, preferred stock provisions, and similar items been reviewed for compliance with all requirements? ——

11. Has insurance coverage been tested for adequacy against the client's estimates of actual values? ——

12. Have reasons been determined and noted for any major changes in assets, liabilities, or operations since the last audit? ——

*Reprinted from the CPA Handbook, AICPA, 1952, Ch. 11, App. A, p. 1.

II. Questions Related to the Report

1. If any assets are pledged or subject to lien or restriction, has disclosure been made? — —
2. Have all material contingencies such as litigations, dividends in arrears and other defaults, stock options, renegotiation, retained earnings restrictions, dated surplus and similar items been disclosed? — -
3. Have all intercompany profits in transactions with affiliated companies been eliminated? ——
4. Have all changes in accounting policies during the period been disclosed? ——
5. Has the basis of valuing each material asset been disclosed? — —
6. Has the treatment of profits and losses of subsidiary companies (if not consolidated) been disclosed? ——
7. Have you determined that no material changes occurred from the balance sheet date to the date of completion of the field work? ——
8. Is the report free of material deviations from firm policies or manuals? ——
9. Do you believe that we can give an unqualified certificate on the basis of our examination? ——

III. Questions Related to Pending Matters

1. If we prepare SEC reports, have all necessary data been secured? ——
2. Have suggestions for improvements in the system of internal control or in the accounting procedures and financial reports of the client been summarized for a letter of recommendation? ——
3. Have all necessary confirmations been received (including those relating to life insurance, assets in custody of others and liabilities, both fixed and contingent)? ——
4. Has the customary letter of representation by the client been received? ——
5. Do the corporate minutes record all actions which, in your opinion, should have been taken (salaries, dividends, major contracts, and similar actions)? ——
6. If we regularly prepare tax returns for the client, have the returns been completed? ——
7. Has our tax staff been consulted in respect to all tax problems needing attention? ——
8. If the books and statements are not in agreement with tax returns, have reconciling schedules been prepared? ——
9. Are there any other items of open business which will require attention? ——

IV. Questions Related to Client Relations

1. Was the work done without any limitations by the client? ——
2. Was the engagement conducted within the intended scope of the assignment (without a request by the client for extra services)? ——
3. Are you satisfied that the audit did not disclose any suspicions of irregularities in regard to cash or other assets or transactions? ——
4. Has the client reviewed and approved:
   a. All adjustments? ——
   b. Financial statements? ——
   c. The report letter? ——

5. Were our relations with the client as strong at the end of the engagement as at the beginning? ____

V. *Questions Related to Efficiency of Our Examination*
  1. Did we apply interim procedures to the maximum extent possible? ____
  2. Has our examination been conducted with a maximum of efficiency? ____
  3. Did you give on-the-job training to your assistants? ____

Prepared by ....Date...................
Reviewed by ....Date...............

OFFICE REVIEW QUESTIONNAIRE*

This questionnaire (used by a national firm of accountants) is for the guidance of the partner or principal making the detailed review of the working papers, either in the field or in the office, after the in-charge accountant or supervisor has completed his questionnaire (page 894). In the event that any or all items in this questionnaire are not answered in the field, it is expected that they will be completed upon review in the office. The review of the financial statements and report is considered a separate function and is based on another questionnaire or checklist. An illustration of report review policy and procedure, including a checklist (used by a different accounting firm) appears on page 899.

General
1. Have you reviewed the in-charge accountant's questionnaire and satisfied yourself that:
  a. The judgments of the in-charge accountant were sound? ____
  b. His representations as to facts and work done were supported by the papers? ____
  c. Matters requiring further attention will be taken care of at the appropriate time? ____
  d. There are no dangerous open disclaimers by the in-charge accountant prejudicial to the interests of the firm? ____
2. Have you satisfied yourself that:
  a. The papers contain an adequate review of the system of internal control? ____
  b. The audit was completed in a manner consistent with the strengths and weaknesses of the system of internal control? ____
  c. The in-charge accountant's suggestions for transmission to the client, if any, are consistent with the best interests of the client and the firm? ____
  d. Appropriate changes in the next examination, if any, have been provided for? ____
3. Do the papers show who was responsible for preparing each schedule and who reviewed each schedule? ____
4. Is the permanent file adequate and up to date? ____
5. Do the papers include complete explanations as to:
  a. Changes in accounting policies? ____
  b. All questions requiring decisions as to conformity with generally accepted accounting principles? ____

*Reprinted from the *CPA Handbook,* AICPA, 1952, Ch. 11, App. B, p. 1.

    c. All questions requiring decisions as to conformity with generally accepted auditing standards?   ——

    d. All matters requiring disclosure?   ——

6. Do the papers substantiate an unqualified certificate?   ——

Cash

1. Do the papers indicate a sufficient audit of cash and related transactions to give adequate assurance of:

    a. Accuracy of the cash balances stated?   ——

    b. Availability of cash and absence of liens?   ——

    c. Absence of fraud?   ——

Receivables

1. Do the papers show that we have satisfied the audit requirements with regard to confirmation of receivables?   ——

2. Are you satisfied that the receivables are fairly valued at the amounts stated, are the property of the client, and have not been pledged without disclosure? Do the papers establish that our representations are adequately supported?   ——

Securities

1. Do the papers establish the existence of the securities, that title is in the client, that they are free of undisclosed liens, and that they are fairly valued at the amounts stated?   ——

2. Do the papers demonstrate that the income expectable from these securities has been computed and accounted for?   ——

Inventories

1. Do the papers show that we have satisfied the audit requirements of the extensions of auditing procedure with regard to physical inspection of inventories?   ——

2. Do the papers establish:

    a. An adequate test of the book inventories and cost records?   ——

    b. An adequate plan governing the physical count?   ——

    c. Adequate supervision and testing by the in-charge accountant as to:

        (1) Quantities?   ——

        (2) Ownership?   ——

        (3) Ascertainment of cost?   ——

        (4) Clerical accuracy?   ——

        (5) Method of costing out into current operations?   ——

        (6) Ascertainment of the lower of cost or market?   ——

        (7) Obsolescence and other factors influencing value?   ——

    d. That the inventories are balanced?   ——

    e. Consistency?   ——

    f. General compliance with Accounting Research Bulletin #43, *Restatement and Revision,* Chapter 4?   ——

3. Do the papers establish the propriety of the relationship between sales and purchase and production costs charged to operations of the period? Was the cutoff procedure adequate?   ——

4. Do the papers include inventory confirmations, if appropriate, and an inventory representation?   ——

Prepaid Expenses, Deferred Charges, and Intangible Assets

1. Do the papers establish:
   a. Cost? ———
   b. Substantial accuracy, appropriateness, and consistency of amortization? ———
2. Are the details sufficient for proper classification and adequate disclosure? ———

Fixed Assets

1. Are the bases of valuation described adequately in the papers? ——
2. Do the papers adequately support the division of expenditures between assets and expenses? ——
3. Do the papers establish that the assets exist, and that they are owned by the client? ———
4. Are the assets still usable? Still in use? ———

Liabilities

1. Do the papers show an adequate search for unrecorded liabilities, both fixed and contingent? ———
2. Do the papers substantiate that value has been received in connection with all recorded liabilities? ———
3. Do the papers show that the recorded liabilities of material amount have been tested? ———
4. Do the papers include a liability representation and letters from attorneys? ———
5. Do the papers establish the adequacy of the computations of accruals? ——
6. Do the papers give adequate attention to contractual provisions, liens, and limitations? ———
7. Do the papers establish the proper liability for taxes and make provision for disclosure of tax contingencies? Have audit adjustments and revenue agent's reports been taken into account? ———

Contributed Capital and Retained Earnings

1. Do the papers establish to your satisfaction the quality of the examination of capital stock? ———
2. Do the papers contain an adequate analysis of capital paid in in excess of the recorded value of stock, and have transactions during the period been adequately vouched? ——
3. Do the papers contain an adequate analysis of retained earnings? Have transactions been adequately vouched and classified? ——

Income and Expense

1. Do the papers establish the adequacy of the matching of cost and revenue? ———
2. Do the papers establish the propriety of revenues reported for the period? ———
3. Do the papers reveal an adequate test for unreported income? ———
4. Do the papers reveal adequate testing of expenses by analysis, comparison, and relations with other accounts? ——
5. Is the determination of income consistent with last period? ———

ILLUSTRATIVE CHECKLIST FOR REPORT REVIEW*

This checklist is not intended to be all-inclusive or to establish minimum or maximum procedures that are to be followed by the report review department. It has been prepared solely as an indication of the types of items that could be considered.

Has the Engagement Been Adequately Planned?

1. Audit program:
   a. Is it sufficiently inclusive? (Separate program for branches, etc.?) —— —
   b. Is it "tailor-made" for the engagement? ———
   c. Has it been brought up to date? ———
   d. Has it been currently amplified or modified after consideration of results of check of internal control or to meet new situations? —— —
   e. Was it approved by a partner? —— —
2. Time budgets:
   a. Was a time budget prepared in advance? —— —
   b. Has actual time been compared with budget? ———

Audit Memorandums

1. Are suitable memorandums, where appropriate, on file or noted in the working papers from:
   a. Partner? ———
   b. Supervisor? ———
   c. Senior? ———
   d. Assistants? —— —
   e. Tax department? —— —
2. Extent of partner's participation in engagement as indicated by memorandums written or reviewed by him, working papers reviewed, letters written, conferences attended, etc.? ———
3. Are important phases of the engagement discussed adequately in the memorandums? —— —
   a. Internal control:
      (1) Is statement made regarding adequacy? ———
      (2) Is statement made regarding effectiveness with which internal control is being carried out? —— —
      (3) If weaknesses exist, has audit program or scope of examination been expanded to take care of the situation? —— —
   b. Confirmation of accounts receivable:
      (1) Is a comment made that the responses were satisfactory? ———
      (2) Is a comment made that differences were disposed of? ———
      (3) Is a comment made that adequate steps were taken with respect to important accounts not replying to positive requests? ———
   c. Allowance for doubtful accounts:
      (1) Does the memorandum fully discuss adequacy of allowance in the light of past experience, present conditions, and probable conditions in the foreseeable future, both in the industry and in business generally? ———
      (2) Does the memorandum show what reasoning was gone through to determine that allowance was adequate? —— —

*Reprinted from the *CPA Handbook*, AICPA, 1952, Ch. 11, App. C, p. 5.

    d. Inventories:
        (1) Does memorandum adequately discuss extent of our physical observation?   ——
        (2) Does memorandum adequately discuss extent of our clerical tests?   ——
        (3) Does memorandum adequately discuss extent of our pricing tests?   ——
        (4) Does memorandum treat fully with question of obsolete and unusable materials and parts?   ——
    c. What changes took place in property, plant, and equipment and depreciation policies?   ——
    f. Accounts payable statements:
        (1) Is there a comment that differences between books and statements were followed up?   ——
    g. Does memorandum cover the Federal and state tax situation?   ——
    h. Does memorandum cover contingent liabilities?   ——
    i. What are the dividend and other restrictions?   ——
4. Has every question raised in the memorandums been answered? (Are there any "open items"?)   ——
5. Does it appear that the decisions reached in the memorandums were influenced by the client's wishes? (If so, state to what extent.)   ——
6. Are any dangerous statements left unsatisfied, viz.: "reserve not adequate," "checking not satisfactory," "pricing erroneous," "no check made because point not covered by audit program," etc.?   . . . .
7. If accepted accounting principles have not been observed but no exceptions taken, is statement made of effect on net income for the year?   ——
8. Have any disclaimers been made which appear to protect staff members rather than the firm?   ——
9. Is indication given of review of post-balance sheet transactions to the date of our report; post-balance sheet examination of minutes; etc.?   ——

Working Papers

1. Can the work done be readily determined from the working papers?   ——
2. Are there any items requiring further action or consideration that were left unanswered, viz.: criticisms, suggestions, differences, unfinished work, question marks, etc.?   ——
3. Are any dangerous statements left unsatisfied?   ——
4. Are the papers dated and initialed or signed by the accountants who prepared them?   ——
5. Do the papers indicate that the senior has reviewed all the work of his assistants?   ——
6. Do the papers indicate that they have been reviewed by the supervisor or partner?   ——
7. Are the papers bound and arranged in an orderly fashion?   ——
8. Were negative confirmations requests used in respect of accounts receivable where no reply could be expected?   ——
9. Is there any indication of superfluous work, such as duplication of work or schedules, unnecessary analyses of accounts or transactions, etc.?   ——

Letter of Representations from Client

1. Has letter signed by appropriate officials been obtained?   ——

Permanent File
1. Is the outline of the system of internal control kept up to date? ——
2. Does the permanent file appear to be in good shape in other respects? ——

Letter re Weaknesses
1. Has such a letter been prepared? ——
2. What is its present status? ——
3. Where important weaknesses are indicated, has scope of examination been expanded to take care of the situation? ——

Accountants' Report
1. Does the report conform with the requirements of Rule 2.03 of the *Code of Professional Ethics* (page 822) and other applicable statements of the committee on auditing procedure of the AICPA? ——
2. Does the report conform to arrangements with the client as to form and scope? ——
3. Does the report conform to all practices and requirements of the firm? ——
4. Do the supplementary data include information that tends to qualify the information given in the short-form report? ——

COMPARISON OF OFFICE COPYING PROCESSES*

Process	Number of Copies Per Minute	Paper Cost (8½" x 11")		Copy Size		Will Copy Originals		Approximate Machine Prices			Characteristics
		First Copy	Additional Copies	Width	Length	In All Colors	Both Sides	8½" to 11" Width	12" to 18" Width	Over 18" Width	
Diazo	4 to 15	1 cent	Same	9 to 54 in.	Any	Yes	No	$300 to $675	$650 to $2,000	$1,100 to $12,000	Originals must be translucent and printed on one side only. Paper cost is cheap; fast, single-step process; uses chemicals.
Dye Transfer	5	9 cents	1 cent	8½ to 11 in.	11 to 17 in.	Yes	Yes	$100 to $425			Equipment is inexpensive. Extra copies (5-10) are cheap and easy to make; requires chemicals; wet process.
Electrostatic	7	1 cent plus monthly rental or 3½ to 5 cents	Same	8½ to 11 in.	14 in. to any	Yes	Yes	$500 to $1,500, or lease			Dry, one-step process; makes photographic copy of original.
Photocopy Photo Transfer (Silver Transfer)	2 to 6	8 to 9 cents	3½ to 9 cents	8½ to 24 in.	11 in. to any	Yes	Yes	$100 to $600	$150 to $600	$425 to $650	Wet process, either one- or two-step; uses chemicals; can copy any type original. Negatives may be used to make additional copies.
Heat Transfer	2 to 12	2 to 5 cents	Same	8½ to 14 in.	14 in. to any	No	Yes	$209 to $995			Fast, dry one-step process; easy to use. Cannot copy ink and many colors, and copies lack photographic sharpness.

*The prices and unit costs appearing in this chart are for comparative purposes only. They are approximate and subject to change.
Source: Report of the committee on accounting and office equipment, AICPA, 1960-61.

COMPARISON OF OFFICE DUPLICATING PROCESSES*

Process	Number of Copies with One Master	Copies per Minute	Sheet Size		Paper Cost		Price of Equipment	Characteristics
			Width	Length	Master	Copy		
Offset	Up to 40,000	90 to 150	3 to 20 inches	5 to 24 inches	2 cents and up	Depends on paper and run	$1,200 to $8,000	Copies are of high quality, adaptable for color work, requires operator training. Masters can also be prepared by photocopy, dye transfer, and other copying methods.
Spirit	150 to 300	100 to 120	8½ to 18 inches	14 to 18 inches	5 to 7 cents	¼ to 1/3 cent	$50 to $1,695	Copies become fainter as run continues, variety of colors possible but purple gives best results.
Stencil	5,000 to 20,000	40 to 200	8½ to 17¼ inches	14 to 18 inches	12 to 32 cents	1/5 cent up	$50 to $1,450	Quality of duplicating very good, low cost on high volume work, various colored inks can be used, masters can be prepared by electronic, photographic or direct methods.

*The prices and unit costs appearing in this chart are for comparative purposes only. They are approximate and subject to change.
Source: Report of the committee on accounting and office equipment, AICPA, 1960-61.

REVENUE PROCEDURE ON REPRODUCTIONS OF TAX RETURNS

26 CFR 601.602: Forms and instructions. Rev. Proc. 61-31
(Also Part I, Sections 6001, 6011, 6018,
6019; 1.6001-1, 1.6011-1, 20.6018-1,
25.6019-1.)

Reproduced copies of certain Federal tax return forms and schedules may be used for filing purposes in lieu of the applicable official forms, subject, however, to prescribed conditions.

Revenue Procedure 60-27, C.B. 1960-2, 1003, superseded.

Section 1. Purpose

The purpose of this Revenue Procedure is to restate the requirements of the Internal Revenue Service relating to the preparation of acceptable reproductions of Federal tax return forms and schedules for filing purposes in lieu of the official forms and schedules.

Section 2. Specifications

Subject to the conditions enumerated in sec. 3 following, the Service will accept, for filing purposes, reproduced copies of any of the following tax return forms and schedules:

Employee's Withholding Exemption Certificate, Form W-4
U.S. Estate Tax Return, Form 706
U.S. Gift Tax Return, Form 709
Life Insurance Statement, Form 712
Claim, Form 843
U.S. Exempt Cooperative Association Income Tax Return, Form 990-C
U.S. Return of Employees' Trust Described in Section 401(a) and Exempt
   Under Section 501(a) of the Internal Revenue Code of 1954, Form 990-P
U.S. Individual Income Tax Return, Form 1040
Supplemental Schedule of Income and Credits, Schedule B (Form 1040)
Profit (or Loss) From Business or Profession, Schedule C (Form 1040)
Gains and Losses from Sales or Exchanges of Property, Schedule D (Form
   1040)
U.S. Departing Alien Income Tax Return, Form 1040C
Declaration of Estimated Tax, Form 1040-ES
Schedule of Farm Income and Expenses, Schedule F (Form 1040)
U.S. Fiduciary Income Tax Return, Form 1041
Allocation of Accumulation Distribution, Schedule J (Form 1041)
U.S. Partnership Return of Income, Form 1065
Gains and Losses from Sales or Exchanges of Property, Schedule D (Form
   1065)
Statement in Support of Credit Claimed by Domestic Corporation for Taxes
   Paid or Accrued to a Foreign Country or a Possession of the United States,
   Form 1118
U.S. Corporation Income Tax Return, Form 1120
Schedule of Gains and Losses from Sales or Exchanges of Property, Sched-
   ule D (Form 1120)
U.S. Small Business Corporation Return of Income, Form 1120-S
Gains and Losses from Sales or Exchanges of Property, Schedule D (Form
   1120-S)

Return of Information and Authorization and Consent of Subsidiary Corporation Included in a United States Consolidated Income Tax Return, Form 1122

Statement for the Purpose of Extending Time for Payment of Taxes by Corporations Expecting Carrybacks, Form 1138

Application for Tentative Carryback Adjustment, Form 1139

Section 3. Conditions

.01 Reproductions must be facsimiles of the official form, produced by photo-offset, photoengraving, photocopying, or other similar reproduction process.

.02 Reproductions must be on paper of substantially the same weight and texture and of a quality at least as good as that used in the official form.

.03 Reproductions must substantially duplicate the colors of the paper and/or ink of the official form in order to be acceptable.

.04 Reproductions must have a high standard of legibility, both as to original form and as to filled-in matter. The Internal Revenue Service reserves the right to reject any reproductions with poor legibility, to withdraw the benefits of this Revenue Procedure from any firm or individual, and to reject any process which fails to meet these standards.

.05 Reproductions of Schedule C-3 and Schedule F-1, Form 1040, which contain Schedule SE, U.S. Report of Self-Employment Income, must be on properly perforated paper of substantially the same weight and texture as that used in the official form.

.06 Reproductions can be the same size as that of the official form. However, the standard commercial size of 8½ by 11 (as noted in columns 2 and 3 of table in sec. 5 following) will be accepted, but no tolerances will be permitted in the image size of printed material.

Section 4. Additional Instructions

.01 The Service ordinarily does not undertake to approve or disapprove the specific equipment or process used in reproducing official forms, but requires only that the reproduced forms and schedules satisfy the stated conditions.

.02 While it is preferred that both sides of the paper be used in making reproductions, resulting in the same page arrangement as that of the official form, the Service will not object if only one side of the paper is used or if the reproduction has a different fold than that provided on the official form.

.03 Reproductions of forms may be made after insertion of the six computations and other required information. However, all signatures on forms to be filed with the Service must be original signatures, affixed subsequent to the reproduction process.

.04 Reproductions of forms and schedules meeting the above conditions may be used without the prior approval of the Service. However, if specific approval of a reproduction of any such form or schedule is desired, or if the use of a reproduction of any form or schedule not listed herein or otherwise specifically authorized is desired, a sample of the proposed reproduction should be forwarded, by letter, to the Commissioner of Internal Revenue, Attention: D:S:P, Washington 25, D.C., for consideration.

Section 5. Physical Aspects

The conditions with respect to size, number of printed pages, and color of both paper and ink are as follows:

Form no.	Official IRS trim size[1]	Tolerances permitted in size[2]	Number of printed pages	Color of— Paper	Color of— Ink
(1)	(2)	(3)	(4)	(5)	(6)
W-4	7⅞ x 3⁷/₁₆	8 x 3½	2	White	Black
706	8⅜ x 11	8⅞ x 11	40	White	Black
709	8½ x 11	....	2	Buff	Black
712	8 x 10½	8½ x 11	1	White	Black
843	8 x 10½	8½ x 11	2	White	Black
990-C	8½ x 13⅞	8½ x 14	4	White	Black
990-P	8 x 10½	8½ x 11	3	White	Black
1040	8 x 11	8½ x 11	4	White	Black
Schedule B, 1040	8 x 11	8½ x 11	2	White	Black
Schedule C, 1040	7⅞ x 11	8½ x 11	4	White	Black
Schedule D, 1040	8 x 11	8½ x 11	2	White	Black
1040C	7⅞ x 11	8½ x 11	4	White	Black
1962 1040-ES	8 x 10½	8½ x 11	2	White	Black
Schedule F, 1040	7⅞ x 11	8½ x 11	4	White	Black
1041	7⅞ x 11	8½ x 11	4	Pink	Black
Schedule J, 1041	7⅞ x 11	8½ x 11	2	Pink	Black
1065	8 x 11	8½ x 11	4	Yellow	Black
Schedule D, 1065	8 x 11	8½ x 11	2	Yellow	Black
1118	11 x 8½	....	2	White	Black
1120	8 x 11	8½ x 11	4	Blue	Black
Schedule D, 1120	8 x 11	8½ x 11	4	Blue	Black
1120S	8½ x 11	....	4	Green	Black
Schedule D, 1120S	8½ x 11	....	2	Green	Black
1122	8 x 10½	8½ x 11	1	Blue	Black
1138	8½ x 10½	8½ x 11	2	White	Black
1139	8½ x 11	....	3	White	Black

[1] Sizes shown are for single forms furnished by Internal Revenue Service offices: forms supplied in Income Tax Packages are 8⅜″ by 11″.
[2] Forms cannot exceed sizes shown, nor be less than size of official forms.

INDOCTRINATION PROCEDURES*

Name _____

Date _____

Procedures to be followed with new staff members:

(The personnel assigned to instructing these persons are to initial to indicate that each of the following items has been taken care of):

Procure:
Withholding tax information (W-4)
Hospitalization Insurance Record
Group Insurance Record
Savings bond application

Introduce to:
Members of firm
Staff
Office personnel, particularly switchboard operator, typing and bookkeeping departments

Exhibit and/or Explain:
Time report form
Expense report form
Office hours
Vacation policy
Supper money allowance
Filing system
Mail boxes

Issue to new employee:
Personnel list
Firm's report manual   No.___
Key to office   No.___

Staff bulletins

Brief case, if necessary   No.___

Business cards, if the employee is at least a senior accountant

The new employee to read and study where necessary:
Manual of forms used by staff and explanation of their use.
Indexing of work papers, sets of work papers, headings, and cash reconcilements
Firm's report manual
Office memoranda file
Issues of house organ to date
Duties of Junior Accountant
Duties of Senior Accountant
Accounting Research and Terminology Bulletins, AICPA, Final ed., 1961
Statements on Auditing Procedure, AICPA
The Successful Practice of Accounting—Paul E. Bacas
Good book on business letter writing
Accounting Practice Management Handbook, AICPA, 1962

*Reprinted from the *CPA Handbook,* AICPA, 1952, Ch. 7, App. B, p. 11. (One of a co-ordinated set of forms for a public accountant's office.)

SELECTED LIST OF BOOKS FOR AN ACCOUNTANT'S LIBRARY*

Author	Title	Publisher
Accounting		
AICPA	Accountants' Index (supplements published biennially)	AICPA
AICPA	Accounting Research and Terminology Bulletins, 1961	AICPA
Anthony, Robert H.	Management Accounting, 1960	Richard D. Irwin, Inc.
Blough, Carman G.	Practical Applications of Accounting Standards, 1957	AICPA
Controllership Foundation, Inc.	Whole Dollar Accounting, 1957	Controllership Foundation, Inc.
Finney & Miller	Principles of Accounting— Introductory, 1957, 5th ed.	Prentice-Hall, Inc.
	Advanced, 1960, 5th ed. (also 3rd ed.)	Prentice-Hall, Inc.
	Intermediate, 1958, 5th ed.	Prentice-Hall, Inc.
Hill and Gordon	Accounting—A Management Approach, 1959	Richard D. Irwin, Inc.
Hills, George S.	Law of Accounting & Financial Statements, 1957	Little, Brown & Co.
Holmes & others	Intermediate Accounting, 1958	Richard D. Irwin, Inc.
Karrenbrock & Simons	Advanced Accounting— Comprehensive, 1961	Southwestern Pub. Co.
	Intermediate Accounting— Comprehensive, 1958	Southwestern Pub. Co.
Keller, I. Wayne	Management Accounting for Profit Control, 1957	McGraw-Hill Book Co.
Kohler, Eric	Dictionary for Accountants, 1957	Prentice-Hall, Inc.
May, George O.	Financial Accounting, 1946	The Macmillan Co.
Moonitz & Staehling	Accounting: An Analysis of Its Problems (Vols. 1 and 2), 1952	The Foundation Press, Inc.
Paton, W. A., Ed.	Accountants' Handbook, 1943, 3rd ed.	The Ronald Press Co.
Paton, W. A.	Advanced Accounting, 1941	The Macmillan Co.
Paton & Littleton	An Introduction to Corporate Accounting Standards, 1940	American Accounting Association
Paton & Paton	Asset Accounting, 1952	The Macmillan Co.
Wixon, Rufus, Ed.	Accountants' Handbook, 1956	The Ronald Press Co.
Auditing		
Holmes, Arthur W.	Auditing, 1959	Richard D. Irwin, Inc.
Jencks, W. B.	Auditing Principles, 1960	McGraw-Hill Book Co.
Lasser, J. K., Ed.	Handbook of Auditing Methods, 1953	D. Van Nostrand Co.
Meigs, W. B.	Principles of Auditing, 1959, rev. ed.	Richard D. Irwin, Inc.
Montgomery, Robert H.	Auditing, 1957, 8th ed. (also 7th ed.)	The Ronald Press Co.
Palmer & Bell	Accountants' Working Papers, (rev. by R. S. Johns), 1950	The Ronald Press Co.
Stettler, H. F.	Auditing Principles, 1961	Prentice-Hall, Inc.

*Suggested by the AICPA library staff, 1962.

Author	Title	Publisher

Budgeting

Heckert & Willson	Business Budgeting and Control, 1955	The Ronald Press Co.
Heiser, Herman C.	Budgeting, 1959	The Ronald Press Co.
Welsch, Glenn A.	Budgeting: Profit Planning and Financial Control, 1957	Prentice-Hall, Inc.

Commercial law

Bergh & Conyngton	Business Law, 1956	The Ronald Press Co.
Lavine, A. Lincoln	Modern Business Law	Prentice-Hall, Inc.

Corporations; Business organization and management

Anderson & Schmidt	Practical Controllership, 1961	Richard D. Irwin, Inc.
Bennet, C. L.	Defining the Manager's Job, 1959	American Management Association
Cornell & Madeheim	Organization and Management in Industry and Business, 1958	The Ronald Press Co.
Dewing, A. S.	Financial Policy of Corporations (2 vols.), 1953	The Ronald Press Co.
Doris, L., Ed.	Corporate Treasurer's and Controller's Encyclopedia (4 vols.), 1958	Prentice-Hall, Inc.
Gerstenberg, Charles W.	Financial Organization and Management of Business, 1959	Prentice-Hall, Inc.
Guthmann & Dougall	Corporate Financial Policy, 1955, 3rd ed.	Prentice-Hall, Inc.
Heckert & Willson	Controllership, 1952	The Ronald Press Co.
Pace & Koestler	Corporation Accounting, 1954	Pace & Pace
Paton & Paton	Corporation Accounts and Statements, 1955	The Macmillan Co.
Rohrlich, C.	Organizing Corporate and Other Business Enterprises, 1959	M. Bender & Co.
Terry, G. R.	Office Management and Control, 1958	Richard D. Irwin, Inc.
Villers, R.	Dynamic Management in Industry	Prentice-Hall, Inc.
Washington & Rothschild	Compensating the Corporate Executive, 1951, rev. ed.	The Ronald Press Co.
Wylie, Harry L.	Office Management Handbook, 1958	The Ronald Press Co.

Cost accounting

Bennett, Clinton W.	Standard Costs, 1957	Prentice-Hall, Inc.
Dickey, R. I., Ed.	Accountants' Cost Handbook, 1960	The Ronald Press Co.
Fiske & Beckett	Industrial Accountant's Handbook, 1954	Prentice-Hall, Inc.
Gillespie, Cecil M.	Accounting Procedure for Standard Costs, 1952, rev. ed.	The Ronald Press Co.
Gillespie, Cecil M.	Cost Accounting and Control, 1957	Prentice-Hall, Inc.
Heckert & Miner	Distribution Costs, 1953	The Ronald Press Co.
Henrici, Stanley B.	Standard Costs for Manufacturing, 1960	McGraw-Hill Book Co.

Author	Title	Publisher
Lang, McFarland, & Schiff	Cost Accounting, 1953	The Ronald Press Co.
Longman & Schiff	Practical Distribution Cost Analysis, 1955	Richard D. Irwin, Inc.
Matz, Curry, & Frank	Cost Accounting, 1957	Southwestern Pub. Co.
Vance, Lawrence L.	Theory and Technique of Cost Accounting, 1958, rev. ed.	Henry Holt & Co.

Depreciation

Grant & Norton	Depreciation, 1955	The Ronald Press Co.

Government accounting and finance

Kohler & Wright	Accounting for the Federal Government	Prentice-Hall, Inc.
Mikesell & Hay	Governmental Accounting, 1961	Richard D. Irwin, Inc.
Municipal Finance Officers Association	Simplified Municipal Accounting: A Manual for Smaller Governmental Units, 1950	Municipal Finance Officers Association
National Committee on Governmental Accounting	Municipal Accounting and Auditing, 1952	National Committee on Government Accounting
Tenner, Irving, & Lynn, Eds.	Municipal and Governmental Accounting, 1960, 4th ed.	Prentice-Hall, Inc.

Graphic methods and statistics

Schmid, Calvin F.	Handbook of Graphic Presentation, 1954	The Ronald Press Co.
Smart & Arnold	Graphic Presentation of Business Statistics, 1951	Bureau of Business Research, Ohio State University
Trueblood & Cyert	Sampling Techniques in Accounting	Prentice-Hall, Inc.
Vance & Neter	Statistical Sampling for Auditors and Accountants, 1956	John Wiley & Sons

Internal audit and control

Brink, Victor Z. (rev. by James A. Cashin)	Internal Auditing, 1958	The Ronald Press Co.
Cadmus & Child	Internal Control against Fraud and Waste, 1953	Prentice-Hall, Inc.
Lamperti & Thurston	Internal Auditing for Management, 1953	Prentice-Hall, Inc.

Inventory

Butters & Niland	Effects of Taxation; Inventory Accounting and Policies, 1949	Harvard University Graduate School of Business Administration

Author	Title	Publisher
McNair & Hersum	Retail Inventory Method & LIFO, 1952	McGraw-Hill Book Co.
Seidman, Walter S.	Accounts Receivable and Inventory Financing, 1957	Masterco Press

Investments and securities

Badger & Guthmann	Investment Principles and Practice, 1951	Prentice-Hall, Inc.
Graham & Dodd	Security Analysis, 1951	McGraw-Hill Book Co.
Pickett & Ketchum	Investment Principles and Policy, 1954	Harper & Bros.
Prime, John H.	Investment Analysis, 1959	Prentice-Hall, Inc.
Rappaport, Louis H.	SEC Accounting Practice and Procedure, 1959	The Ronald Press Co.

Mathematics and finance

Bogen, Jules I.	Financial Handbook, 1949	The Ronald Press Co.
Curtis & Cooper	Mathematics of Accounting, 1947, 3rd ed.	Prentice-Hall, Inc.
Hummel & Seabeck	Mathematics of Finance, 1956	McGraw-Hill Book Co.
Trefftzs & Hills	Mathematics of Business, Accounting and Finance, 1956	Harper & Bros.

Professional problems

Carey, John L.	Professional Ethics of Certified Public Accountants, 1956	AICPA
Isaacson, Bernard	Guides to Successful Accounting Practice	AICPA
Lasser, J. K., Ed.	Standard Handbook for Accountants, 1956	McGraw-Hill Book Co.
Levy, Saul	Accountants' Legal Responsibility, 1954	AICPA
Rockey, Chas.	Accountants Office Manual, 1952	Prentice-Hall, Inc.

Reports and statements

Foulke, Roy A.	Practical Financial Statement Analysis, 1961	McGraw-Hill Book Co.
Greidinger, B. B.	Preparation and Certification of Financial Statements, 1950	The Ronald Press Co.
Guthmann, Harry G.	Analysis of Financial Statements, 1953, 4th ed.	Prentice-Hall, Inc.
Kennedy & McMullen	Financial Statements, 1957	Richard D. Irwin, Inc.
Palen, Jennie	Report Writing for Accountants, 1956	Prentice-Hall, Inc.

Selected specialized accounting

American Council on Education	College and University Business Administration (Vol. 1, 1952; Vol. 2, 1955)	American Council on Education

Author	Title	Publisher
American Hospital Association	Uniform Chart of Accounts and Definitions for Hospitals, 1959	American Hospital Association
Coombs, W. E.	Construction Accounting and Financial Management, 1958	F. W. Dodge Corp.
Grange, Staub, & Blackford	Wills, Executors and Trustees, 1950	The Ronald Press Co.
Harris, H. I.	Estates Practice Guide (2 vols.), 1954	Baker, Voorhis & Co.
Insurance Accounting & Statistical Association	Insurance Accounting, Fire & Casualty, 1954	Spectator
Martin, T. L.	Hospital Accounting, 1958	Physician's Record Co.
Pace, H. S.	Insurance Organization and Accounting, 1948	Pace & Pace
Seawell, L. Vann	Principles of Hospital Accounting, 1960	Physician's Record Co.
Walker, Frank	Practical Accounting and Cost Keeping for Contractors, 1957	F. R. Walker Co.
Wightman, E. C.	Life Insurance Statements and Accountants, 1952	Life Office Management Association
Willcox, Frank	Mine Accounting and Financial Administration, 1949	Pitman Publishing Corp.

System building

Gillespie, Cecil	Accounting Systems, 1961	Prentice-Hall, Inc.
Heckert & Kerrigan	Accounting Systems, 1953	The Ronald Press Co.
Lasser, J. K., Ed.	Handbook of Accounting Methods, 1954	D. Van Nostrand Co.
Lasser, J. K., Ed.	Handbook of Cost Accounting Methods, 1949	D. Van Nostrand Co.
Thompson, W. R.	Accounting Systems, 1953	LaSalle Extension University
Williams & Doris	Encyclopedia of Accounting Systems (5 vols.)	Prentice-Hall, Inc.

Taxation

Balter, H. G.	Fraud under Federal Tax Law, 1957	Commerce Clearing House Inc.
Bardes, Philip, et al.	Montgomery's Federal Taxes, 1961, 38th ed.	The Ronald Press Co.
Roberts, Schultz, & Mayer	Handbook of Annotated Forms for Tax Practice, 1959	Prentice-Hall, Inc.
Stanley & Kilcullen	Federal Income Tax, 1955	Tax Club Press

Valuation

McMichael, Stanley L.	McMichael's Appraising Manual, 1950	Prentice-Hall, Inc.
Marston, Winfrey, & Hempstead	Engineering Valuation and Depreciation, 1953	McGraw-Hill Book Co.

Directory of publishers

American Accounting Association	College of Commerce & Business Administration, University of Illinois, Urbana
American Council on Education	1785 Massachusetts Ave., N.W., Washington 6, D.C.
American Hospital Association	840 North Lake Shore Drive, Chicago 11, Ill.
American Institute of Certified Public Accountants	270 Madison Ave., New York 16, N.Y.
American Management Association	1515 Broadway, New York 36, N.Y.
Baker, Voorhis & Co., Inc.	30 Smith Ave., Mt. Kisco, N.Y.
Bender, Matthew & Co.	255 Orange St., Albany 10, N.Y.
Commerce Clearing House, Inc.	4025 W. Peterson Ave., Chicago 46, Ill.
Controllership Foundation, Inc.	2 Park Ave., New York 16, N.Y.
Dodge, F. W., Corp.	119 West 40th St., New York 18, N.Y.
Harper & Bros.	49 East 33rd St., New York 16, N.Y.
Harvard University, Graduate School of Business Administration	Boston 63, Mass.
Henry Holt & Co.	383 Madison Ave., New York 17, N.Y.
Irwin, R. D., Inc.	1818 Ridge Rd., Homewood, Ill.
LaSalle Extension University	417 S. Dearborn St., Chicago 5, Ill.
Life Office Management Association	110 E. 42nd St., New York 17, N.Y.
Little, Brown & Co.	34 Beacon St., Boston 6, Mass.
McGraw-Hill Book Co.	330 West 42nd St., New York 36, N.Y.
Macmillan Co.	60 Fifth Ave., New York 11, N.Y.
Masterco Press	1608 Morton Ave., Ann Arbor, Mich.
Municipal Finance Officers Association of the U.S. and Canada	1313 E. 60th St., Chicago 37, Ill.
National Committee on Governmental Accounting (formerly National Committee on Municipal Accounting	1313 E. 60th St., Chicago 37, Ill.
Ohio State University, Bureau of Business Research	Columbus 10, Ohio
Pace & Pace	296 Broadway, New York 7, N.Y.
Physicians' Record Co.	3000 S. Ridgeland Ave., Berwyn, Ill.
Pitman Publishing Corp.	2 W. 45th St., New York 36, N.Y.
Prentice-Hall, Inc.	Englewood Cliffs, N.J.
Ronald Press Co.	15 East 26th St., New York 10, N.Y.
Southwestern Publishing Co., Inc.	5101 Madison Rd., Cincinnati 27, Ohio
Spectator	Chestnut & 56th Sts., Philadelphia 39, Pa.
Tax Club Press	233 Broadway, New York 7, N.Y.
Van Nostrand, D., Co.	120 Alexander St., Princeton, N.J.
Walker, Frank R., Co.	173 West Madison St., Chicago 2, Ill.
Wiley, John & Sons, Inc.	440 Park Ave. South, New York 16, N.Y.

ACCOUNTANTS' PROFESSIONAL LIABILITY INSURANCE POLICY*

The basic policy provisions of most of the American companies are similar. Among the broader policies is the New York State Society Plan, which is summarized here.

The most important part of the policy is the Insuring Agreement in which the company agrees:

1. To pay, on behalf of the insured, all sums which the insured shall become legally obligated to pay for damages caused or alleged to have been caused by the insured, any accountant or accounting organization acting under contract with the insured or any partner or employee of any of the foregoing, in the performance of professional services for others, including but not limited to breach of contract
   a. Through neglect, error or omission
   b. Through dishonesty, misrepresentation, or fraud, except if made or committed by or at the direction of the insured, any officer or partner of the insured with affirmative dishonesty or actual intent to deceive or defraud
   c. Through civil libel or slander or defamation of character, except if committed in bad faith by the insured, or by any partner, officer or employee of the insured, and except loss and expense due to criminal libel or criminal slander by the insured, or by any partner, officer, or employee of the insured.
2. Moreover, the policy states that the company shall, as respects the insurance afforded by the policy, defend in his name and behalf any action or suit against the insured alleging negligence, error, or omission, etc., even if such action is groundless, false, or fraudulent. This, perhaps, is more important to a professional man, whose professional reputation may be at stake, than the payment of such claims.
3. The policy contains a broad definition of the scope of the insured's duties. They are defined to mean professional services performed by and advice given by the insured in the conduct of his practice, including, without limitation, duties performed or advices given in relation to matters of taxation, whether or not any claim or suit refers to the insured's professional status as an accountant.
4. The policy covers claims or suits against any employee, charging neglect, error or omission, while acting within the scope of his employment as an employee of the insured, in the performance of professional services for others.
5. On bonds to release attachments and on appeal bonds the insured is relieved of providing indemnity to the surety up to the limit of liability under the policy.
6. Coverage is afforded the insured where he would be obligated to pay damages because of professional acts of any predecessor in business.
7. The policy remains in effect when there is a change among the partners

*Reprinted from Economics of Accounting Practice Bulletin 10, *Insurance for Accounting Firms and Practitioners*, AICPA, 1959 (revised, 1962), pp. 42-43.

of the named insured even though it results in changes in the name or business style of the firm. Notice of changes are required to be given to the company.

8. Retired partners covered for pre-retirement acts under firm's policy at no charge.
9. The estate of deceased principal or partner is covered.
10. The insured shall not be required to contest any legal proceedings unless counsel, to be mutually agreed upon by the insured and the company, shall advise that such claim should be contested.
11. The policy affords coverage even if there is other insurance applicable to an occurrence covered by this policy. In that event the coverage under this policy becomes excess over the limits of such other insurance.
12. The company must give thirty days' notice of cancellation.
    a. If the company cancels, the thirty-day period for reporting claim may be extended for two years at reasonable cost.
    b. If the insured does not renew, the thirty-day period for reporting claims may be extended up to six years at reasonable cost.

SUGGESTED INSURANCE PROGRAMS*

Office Furniture, Equipment and Supplies, Office Contents Special Form or Fire and Extended Coverages .... Note: If leases make tenants responsible for redecorating and repairs to air conditioning, etc., put in by them—value of same should be included in insurance amount.	At least 90% of present insurable value
Valuable Papers and Records—All Risks	$5,000 minimum
Accountants' Professional Liability	$100/200,000
General Public Liability—Comprehensive Form	
Bodily injury—Occurrence basis	$100/200,000
Property damage	$10,000
Automobile—Firm-owned or Employee-used cars	
Bodily injury	$100/200,000
Property damage .... (Should be combined with comprehensive general liability)	$25,000
Workmen's Compensation	As per law of states from which employees are hired
Employers' liability if in "$25,000 limit" states	$100,000
Statutory Sickness or Nonoccupational Accidents (N.Y., N.J., Calif. and R.I.)	As per law
Dishonesty—Comprehensive 3-D form Fidelity	{ $5,000 position form or $25,000 commercial
Damage and destruction of money, etc. Check alteration and forgery	Maximum average exposure $5,000
Employee Benefits (a) Life	{ (AICPA plan (Approx. one year's earnings)
(b) Accident and sickness (nonstatutory)	Immediate benefits—accident; 7-day waiting—sickness
(c) Hospitalization	Blue Cross, or similar plan
(d) Surgical	Blue Shield, or similar plan
(e) Major medical (catastrophe)	$5,000

Death or Disability of Practitioner

	(a) Life	AICPA plan
	(b) Business Expense Disability	50% of overhead as minimum
Best coverage and rates usually under State Society of CPAs Plans, where available	(c) Weekly indemnity for time lost on account of:	
	Accident	$25 to $100 up to 5 years
	Sickness	$25 to $100 up to 2 years
	(d) Hospitalization	$8 to $12 a day
	(e) Surgical	$150 to $225
	(f) Major medical	$10,000

Travel Accident All modes of travel or at least business trips by air	$25,000

*Reprinted from Economics of Accounting Practice Bulletin 10, *Insurance for Accounting Firms and Practitioners*, AICPA, 1959, pp. 30-31.

3 Partners 10 Employees	6 Partners 35 Employees	100 Staff
At least 90% of present insurable value	At least 90% of present insurable value	At least 90% of present insurable value
$10,000 minimum	$20,000 minimum	$25,000 minimum
$150/300,000	$250/500,000	$500/1,000,000
$150/300,000	$250/500,000	$500/1,000,000
$20,000	$25,000	$50,000
$150/300,000	$250/500,000	$500/1,000,000
$25,000	$25,000	$25,000
As per law of states from which employees are hired.	As per law of states from which employees are hired.	As per law of states from which employees are hired.
$100,000	$100,000	$100,000
As per law	As per law	As per law
$10,000 position form or $50,000 commercial	$10,000 position form or $100,000 commercial	$10,000 position form or $100,000 commercial
Maximum average exposure $10,000	Maximum average exposure $15,000	Maximum average exposure $25,000
AICPA plan (Approx. one year's earnings)	AICPA plan (Approx. one year's earnings)	AICPA plan (Approx. one year's earnings)
Immed. benefits—accident 7-day waiting—sickness	Immed. benefits—accident 7-day waiting—sickness	Immed. benefits—accident 7-day waiting—sickness
Blue Cross, or similar plan	Blue Cross, or similar plan	Blue Cross, or similar plan
Blue Shield, or similar plan	Blue Shield, or similar plan	Blue Shield, or similar plan
$5,000	$7,500	$10,000
AICPA Plan None	AICPA Plan None	AICPA Plan None
$25 to $100 up to 5 years $25 to $100 up to 2 years $8 to $12 a day $150 to $225 $10,000	$25 to $100 up to 5 years $25 to $100 up to 2 years $8 to $12 a day $150 to $225 $10,000	$25 to $100 up to 5 years $25 to $100 up to 2 years $8 to $12 a day $150 to $225 $10,000
$25,000	$50,000	$50,000 staff travelers $100,000—partners

INCOME AND EXPENSE DISTRIBUTION (as a Percentage of Gross Fees)†

ALL OFFICES	Sole practitioner (no staff)			Sole practitioner (1 to 4 staff)			Sole practitioner (5 or more staff)		
	Me-dian	Middle 50% range		Me-dian	Middle 50% range		Me-dian	Middle 50% range	
		From	To		From	To		From	To
Fee Production	%	%	%	%	%	%	%	%	%
By partners	98.8	86.2	100.0	46.7	33.6	64.1	20.0	15.0	30.0
By staff accountants	0.0	0.0	0.0	44.1	30.2	57.7	70.0	60.5	79.8
By office staff	0.7	0.0	8.3	5.0	2.2	9.9	5.0	0.0	10.0
Expense Items									
Salaries, staff accountants	0.0	0.0	0.0	25.1	19.6	32.0	41.9	36.0	45.0
Salaries, office staff	5.9	1.0	14.0	8.6	5.1	11.3	8.0	6.0	11.0
Employee benefits	0.0	0.0	0.0	8.4	0.0	8.9	0.8	0.0	1.1
Payroll taxes and other costs	0.1	0.0	0.4	1.0	0.6	1.9	1.3	1.0	2.0
Total payroll and benefits	7.3	0.2	17.2	35.5	28.9	43.6	52.0	47.9	57.0
Professional dues and meetings	0.9	0.5	1.3	0.6	0.4	1.0	0.4	0.2	0.7
Tax services, subscriptions, etc.	1.6	1.0	2.6	1.1	0.8	1.7	1.0	0.6	1.2
Staff training, special study, etc.	0.0	0.0	0.0	0.0	0.0	0.1	0.0	0.0	0.5
Total professional development	2.7	1.8	4.1	2.0	1.3	2.9	1.7	1.0	2.0
Entertainment and other client and public relations	2.3	0.8	4.7	1.9	0.9	3.6	1.6	1.0	3.0
Occupancy	5.9	3.8	8.4	4.8	3.5	6.2	4.9	3.2	6.0
Office supplies	2.4	1.6	3.7	2.2	1.6	3.0	2.0	1.4	3.3
Telephone and telegraph	1.8	1.1	2.7	1.3	1.0	1.9	1.3	1.0	1.5
Equipment maintenance	0.1	0.0	0.4	0.2	0.1	0.5	0.3	0.1	0.5
Automobile (including depreciation)	5.9	3.9	8.9	3.4	2.2	5.0	1.7	1.0	2.5
Travel	0.3	0.0	1.0	0.3	0.0	1.2	0.9	0.1	1.5
Depreciation	1.0	0.3	1.9	1.3	0.7	1.6	1.0	0.5	2.0
Taxes (excluding income and payroll)	0.1	0.0	0.4	0.1	0.0	0.3	0.1	0.0	0.4
Insurance	0.4	0.0	1.0	0.5	0.1	1.1	0.5	0.3	0.7
Outside services	0.0	0.0	0.1	0.0	0.0	0.2	0.0	0.0	0.3
Other office expense	0.6	0.3	1.9	0.7	0.1	1.7	1.0	0.4	2.5
Total office and administrative expense	22.4	16.4	27.1	17.1	13.5	21.0	16.1	14.0	19.4
Net Income									
Net income	61.4	50.8	69.0	41.0	35.0	48.6	25.7	21.3	31.0
Partners' salaries									
Net income available for profit sharing									

†Condensation of Tables 1-8, pp. 26-39, Economics of Accounting Practice Bulletin 8, *Survey of Accounting Office Expenses*, AICPA, 1959.
*Before partners' salaries

Two/three partners (less than 5 staff)			Two/three partners (5 or more staff)			Four/six partners (less than 20 staff)			Four/six partners (20 or more staff)			Over six partners		
Me-dian	Middle 50% range		Me-dian	Middle 50% range		Me-dian	Middle 50% range		Me-dian	Middle 50% range		Me-dian	Middle 50% range	
	From	To		From	To		From	To		From	To		From	To
%	%	%	%	%	%	%	%	%	%	%	%	%	%	%
64.9	51.5	81.3	34.7	23.3	45.7	53.5	38.3	70.0	27.5	22.5	34.5	33.4	25.3	35.9
27.9	13.3	40.8	57.9	47.2	69.8	40.5	24.7	59.3	70.7	64.4	76.4	64.3	57.7	72.6
5.5	1.2	9.7	4.9	2.2	8.8	5.0	0.0	8.0	3.5	0.0	5.0	3.7	1.2	6.1
17.4	7.6	24.0	33.0	27.3	37.9	23.6	17.0	33.6	36.2	33.7	38.5	34.0	27.4	37.9
7.7	5.6	10.6	7.6	5.5	9.4	7.8	6.1	9.1	8.2	7.4	10.2	8.2	6.5	9.7
0.3	0.0	0.7	0.6	0.3	1.2	0.7	0.3	1.0	1.1	0.8	1.3	0.7	0.4	1.3
0.9	0.5	1.1	1.1	0.9	1.4	0.9	0.6	1.2	1.0	0.9	1.2	0.9	0.8	1.0
27.0	17.8	35.3	43.2	35.6	47.2	33.1	26.4	44.4	45.3	43.8	51.2	45.8	37.0	48.1
0.6	0.4	1.1	0.4	0.2	0.7	0.6	0.4	1.0	0.3	0.2	0.5	0.7	0.4	1.2
1.0	0.7	1.4	0.7	0.4	1.0	0.8	0.5	1.1	0.4	0.3	0.6	0.5	0.3	0.9
0.0	0.0	0.1	0.0	0.0	0.2	0.0	0.0	0.1	0.3	0.0	0.9	0.1	0.0	0.5
1.8	1.2	2.4	1.1	0.9	1.9	1.5	1.1	2.2	1.0	0.8	2.3	1.5	0.9	2.4
1.4	0.6	2.6	1.3	0.5	2.5	1.2	0.5	1.8	1.8	1.0	3.0	1.1	0.3	2.1
4.6	3.1	5.9	4.1	3.2	5.5	4.5	3.1	5.5	4.0	3.1	4.9	3.8	3.3	4.2
2.3	1.7	3.1	2.0	1.5	2.8	2.1	1.7	2.9	1.8	1.3	2.5	2.1	1.4	2.7
1.3	1.0	1.9	1.0	0.7	1.3	1.1	0.9	1.5	0.9	0.7	1.1	0.7	0.5	1.0
0.1	0.0	0.4	0.2	0.0	0.3	0.3	0.1	0.5	0.2	0.2	0.3	0.2	0.1	0.3
2.7	0.9	4.7	1.4	0.0	2.6	0.9	0.0	2.5	0.3	0.0	1.8	0.0	0.0	0.2
0.3	0.0	1.3	0.8	0.1	2.0	0.5	0.0	1.3	0.3	0.0	0.9	0.3	0.2	1.1
1.0	0.5	1.5	0.8	0.5	1.4	1.0	0.6	1.3	1.2	0.7	1.5	0.7	0.4	1.1
0.1	0.0	0.4	0.1	0.0	0.3	0.1	0.0	0.2	0.1	0.1	0.2	0.2	0.1	0.3
0.4	0.1	0.8	0.4	0.2	0.6	0.3	0.1	0.4	0.3	0.3	0.6	0.3	0.2	0.5
0.0	0.0	0.1	0.0	0.0	0.1	0.0	0.0	0.1	0.1	0.0	0.4	0.0	0.0	0.1
0.5	0.1	1.4	0.5	0.1	1.1	0.8	0.3	2.0	0.9	0.3	1.8	1.1	0.3	3.4
15.3	12.2	19.2	13.1	10.7	16.0	14.3	10.7	16.4	12.3	10.3	14.0	11.0	8.7	12.6
54.0*	46.7*	61.3*	41.3*	35.8*	47.5*	47.6*	40.2*	57.6*	37.0*	32.3*	42.0*	40.6*	36.4*	49.3*
37.2	28.4	45.9	21.6	16.8	30.0	27.5	21.6	35.2	22.5	15.1	23.5	18.0	12.1	21.7
13.7	8.4	23.4	17.1	8.0	25.7	19.1	11.0	27.6	18.9	8.7	21.4	22.1	14.4	30.7

Index

Administrative expenses
See Accounting and recordkeeping—
Expenses

Advancement
Budgeting time
Individual advancement, 328
Professional advancement, 327-8
CPA certificate, upon obtaining, 207
Career plateaus, remedies, 208
Opportunities, practices of firms, 208-
10
Partner status, achieving, 207-8
Permitting staff members to deal with
clients, 207
Policy, 206
Timing of, 206
Uneven progress of staff member, 207

"Afterthought" audit, 552-3

Agricultural equipment industry
Study by security analysts, 289-90

American academy of general practice
Continuing education program, 382

American accounting association
See also American institute of certified
public accountants and Amer-
ican accounting association
Activities and objectives, 392-3
Professional literature for accountants'
libraries, 636

American arbitration association
Disagreements between partners submitted to, 486

American bar association
Continuing education programs, 382

**American institute of certified public
accountants**
See also Municipal finance officers as-
sociation and American in-
stitute of certified public ac-
countants
Activities and objectives, 385-90
Accounting education, 389
Accounting research, 388
CPA certificate, standards for, 387
Library facilities, 389
Professional standards, 387
Relations among accountants, 389-90
Safeguarding the interest of CPAs,
387-8
Technical information service, 389
Unity of the profession, 386-7
Agreements with surety companies re-
garding AICPA members,
292-3
*Audits by certified public accountants:
their nature and significance*
(pamphlet), 249

**American institute of certified public
accountants** (*Continued*)
Code of professional ethics
See Code of professional ethics
(AICPA)
*Codification of statements on auditing
procedure* (pamphlet), 560
Community service activities, survey
of members, 298-9
Continuing education program, 383
*Insurance for accounting firms and
practitioners* (pamphlet)
Liability insurance policy, 914-15
Suggested insurance program, 916-17
Personnel testing program, 116-23
Professional literature for accountants'
libraries, 633-6, 640, 908-13
Public relations program, 221-2
*Report of the Committee on account-
ing and office equipment
1960-61*, 582
Survey of accounting office expenses
(pamphlet), 918

————**Committee on professional ethics**
Numbered opinions
See Professional ethics

————**and American accounting association**
*Statement of standards and responsibil-
ities under public accounting
internship programs*, 127-31

————**and Surety association of America**
*Safeguards against employee dishon-
esty in business* (booklet),
293

American law institute
Continuing education programs, 382

American management association
Continuing education programs, 382

Announcements
See Professional ethics

Application form for job, 115, 787-9

Aptitude testing
See Personnel testing

Arbitration
Disagreements between partners settled
by, 486

Aspley, J. C.
How to sell quality (book), 327

Audit programs
Review procedures, 550-1
Use of, effectiveness in staff utiliza-
tion, 203

Audit working papers
See Working papers

Auditing
Cash accounts, staff training, 162-3
Class program in staff training, 162-4
Correspondent audits, fees, 32
First audits, cost of, 270-1
Procedure manuals, 162
Texts for study in staff training, 162
Verification procedures, staff training, 162-3

Auditing standards
Staff training program, 161

Audits by certified public accountants: their nature and significance (pamphlet)
By American institute of CPAs, 249

Automobile expense
Percentage of gross fees, 723

Automobile liability insurance
See Insurance, Liability

B

Bailey vs. Lynch
See *Lynch vs. Bailey,* 470

Balance sheet
Accountant's office
See Accounting and recordkeeping
—Statements and statistics

Bank reconciliations
Adding machine, use of, 663
Utilizing client's staff, 253-4

Bankers and credit men
Accounting firm's qualifications, determination of, 278-9
Bank customers' opinions of CPA services, 283-4
CPA as a source of bank business, 284
CPA reports, bankers opinions, 281-2
Critical comments, 281-2
Favorable comments, 281
CPA reports, suggestions for improving, 282-3
CPA's importance, views on, 284
Changing accountants, recommendations to borrowers, 277-8
Consultations with accountant on borrower's statement, 280
Credit negotiations, CPA's role, 279-81
Criticisms of CPAs, 272-3, 285-6
Desirability of frequent contact with CPA, 285
Improving relations with, examples, 286-7

Bankers and credit men
(*Continued*)
Opinions on financial statements, importance, 275-7
Policies on audit requests, 273-5
Size of loan requiring audits, 274-5
Rating of CPAs with, 272-3
Reliance on CPA's findings in making loans, comments, 280

Barr, Andrew
SEC filings, 368

Belo-type plan
Overtime pay, 146

Benge clerical test D, 620

Billing
Advantages of well-planned system, 55
Client complaints, 67-8
Collection and follow-up, 65-7
Collections, legal action, 68-9
Conferences with clients, 71
Consultation charges, 257
Determining amount of bill, hints, 61-2
Items included, 59,63
Partners' responsibility for, 56-7
Pitfalls in wording, 63
Practitioners' discussions, 69-73
Preprinted invoices, 65
Rates
Office and clerical assistants, 718-19
Chart of median fees billed, 720
Partners and individual practitioners, 717-18
Chart of median fees billed, 719
Staff accountants, 718
Chart of median fees billed, 719
Research time, 59
Senior staff member on job, consultations with, 58
Separating expenses from "services rendered", 65
Summary of billings by partners, 58-9
Supporting records, 62
Telephone calls, 59
Texts of bills, samples, 64-5
Timing the bill, 60-1
Traveling time, 59
Visits to client, 59
Who should handle, 56

Blackstone stenographic proficiency test, 620

Block, Max
Valuation of goodwill in an accounting practice (article), 478

Blough, Carman G.
Internal rotation of auditors, 270

Blue cross and Blue shield insurance
See Insurance, Hospitalization

Clerical work
By CPAs, avoidance, 250
Clients
See also Engagements
Accountant's office location and appearance, effect on, 233-4
Accounting procedures, persuading the client to accept different, 228
Billing
See Billing
CPA staff members and clients, relations between, 212
CPA's value, comments by, 245-6
"Client survey" forms, 352, 817-21
Communicating results of engagement to, 228-30
Conduct in office of, 234-5, 250-2
Avoiding disruption, 250-2
Complaints about accountants, 250-1
Junior accountants, 213
Conference reports, use of, 71
Confidential relations, 261-2
Consultations with CPA, clients' reluctance to, 257-8
Practitioners' comments, 258
Contact with, during engagement, 237
Continual service
Failure to provide, dangers, 259-60
Value of, 258-60
Continuity of service to, in partnership dissolution, 465
Contracts with, 669
Creating the professional image among clients, 231-5
Decisions between partners and clients, informing seniors of, 238
Division of clientele, in partnership dissolution, 464-5
Fees
See Fees
Going public, advice to clients, 268
Greeting cards to, 267
Long-form reports, delivering and discussing with, 229-30
Loss of, 271-2
Management memorandum to, 229
Management services
Acquainting clients with
Methods, 247-8
Misconceptions of clients, 248-50
Value to client, 230, 243-6
Mergers of accounting firms, effect on, 366
New, junior partner's compensation for, 444
New, preparing for, 668-9
"New client data sheet", 668

Clients (*Continued*)
Obtaining, in starting a practice, 323-6
Sources, 324-5
Performing efficiently for, 227-8
Personal touch, 263-7
Advantages of the fresh reaction, 267
Getting the feel of client's affairs, 263-4
Keeping client informed, 266-7
Keeping up with client's affairs, 264-6
Personnel
Appraisal of, 252
Utilizing in audit, 252-7
Accounts receivable, aging, 254
Accounts receivable, confirmation, 254
Bank-account reconciliations, 253-4
Confirmation letters and forms, 255
Criticism of, 255-6
Fixed assets, 255
Government securities, 254
Insurance, 254
Inventories, 254
Investments, 254
Notes payable, 255
Petty cash funds, 253
Practitioners' experiences, 256-7
Profit and loss, 255
Savings in audit time, 257
Work outlines, 253
Pre-engagement conferences, 235-6
Professional service to, elements, 227
Profits, accountant's contribution, 243-6
Specific suggestions, 243-4
Relations with, 225-72
Personal, 232-3, 267-8
Points for improving, 225-7
Responsibility to all partners of, 262-3
Reviewer's report of client's affairs, 265-6
Rotation of auditors
See Rotation of auditors
Simultaneous demands of, handling, 260-1
Staff
See Clients—Personnel
Staff members dealing with, 207
Tax returns, 566-81
Value of service in relation to cost, suggestions for achieving maximum benefit, 227
Welfare, accountant's concern for, 231-2

Clients (*Continued*)

Withdrawal of, by resigning partner, 456-7

Year-round contact with, 232

Clippings

Periodical and tax service, of interest to client, 266-7

Code of professional ethics (AICPA)

Article 1—Relations with clients and public, 821-2

Rule 1.01—Financial interest in client's affairs, 821

Rule 1.02—Act discreditable to the profession, 822

Rule 1.03—Confidential relationship between client and accountant, 822

Rule 1.04—Contingent fees, 822

Article 2—Technical standards, 822-3

Rule 2.01—Certifying to statements audited by others, 822

Rule 2.02—False and misleading statements, 822

Rule 2.03—Expression of opinion on financial statements, 822-3

Rule 2.04—Forecasts, 823

Article 3—Promotional practices, 823

Rule 3.01—Advertising, 823

Rule 3.02—Solicitation, 823

Rule 3.03—Competitive bidding, 823

Rule 3.04—Commissions, brokerage, and fee-splitting, 823

Article 4—Operating practices, 823-4

Rule 4.01—Designation of Institute membership, 823

Rule 4.02—Use of accountant's name, 823

Rule 4.03—Services performed by employees, 823-4

Rule 4.04—Occupations incompatible, 824

Rule 4.05—Simultaneous occupations, 824

Rule 4.06—Practice by corporations, 824

Article 5—Relations with fellow members, 824

Rule 5.01—Encroaching on practice of another accountant, 824

Rule 5.02—Referrals, 824

Rule 5.03—Employees of other accountants, 824

Codification of statements on auditing procedures (pamphlet)

By American institute of CPAs, 560

Collections

See Billing

Collective bargaining

See Labor-management relations

College placement council

Salary survey, 142-3

Commissions

See Professional ethics

Communication

See also Reports
Speaking
Writing

Ability to communicate, 338-9

Community service

AICPA members engaged in, survey, 298

Age of CPA and activity engaged in, 300

Budgeting time for, 328

Capacities in which CPAs serve, 299

Desire to serve, 299-301

Encouraging employees to participate, 300

Factor in professional development, 379

Profile of a participant, 301

Compensation

See also specific type, e.g., Overtime

Advances and loans on salary, 152

Incentive and morale, 139-41

Per-diem basis, 144-5

Plans in general, 141-2

Policies of selected firms, 153-4

Professional expenses, 152

Temporary employees, 144-5

Competitive bidding

See Professional ethics

Conferences with clients

Pre-engagement conference, 235-6
Presence of senior, 238

Reports of, 71

Confirmations

See also Accounts receivable

Audit information from attorneys, form, 659-60

Bank, 660-1

Utilizing client's staff to prepare, 255

Written, for audit engagement, 236
Example, 237

Constructive ownership

Tax aspects, 504-5

Consultation program

Michigan association of CPAs, 302-3

Consultations

With other accounting firms, 302-3

Contingent fees

See Professional ethics

Continuing education

See Education

Contractors
Underwriting bonds for, 295-6

Contracts
Disposition of, in partnership dissolution, 465-6
Employment
    See Personnel
With clients, 669

Contributions
See also Capital contributions
Percentage of gross fees for, 721

Controllers institute of America
Activities and objectives, 394-5
Professional literature for accountants' libraries, 636

Copying equipment
See Duplicating and copying equipment

Correspondence
See also Style manual
File copies, 627-8
Form letters, use of, 627
Signing, 627
Storage and disposal, 608

Correspondent audits
See Auditing

Cost flow principle
Fees, 19-21

"Costing" method
Fees, 21-2

Costs
See also Accounting and recordkeeping—Time and cost control records
Allocation of, 713-15
Fee setting, factor in, 18
Standard, illustration of use, 703-7

Covenants not to compete
See Noncompetition clauses

Credit and credit men
Reports
    See Bankers and credit men

Current legal forms with tax analysis (book)
By Rabkin and Johnson, 830
Specimen form of partnership agreement, 830-3

Curse of balancing (article)
By Robert H. Montgomery, 551

D

DAT clerical speed and accuracy test, 620

Data processing service centers
See also Write-ups—Punched card accounting

Data processing service centers
(*Continued*)
AICPA committee recommendations, 736-7
Client resistance, 733
Ethics in establishment of service centers by CPAs, 734-5, 827
Quality of work by, 732
Selection of a service bureau, 734

Defalcations
See Fraud

Delegating
Importance, 330

Dentists
Income, 78-80

Depreciation
Percentage of gross fees, 723-4

Developing a practice
See Practice development

Diazo method
See Duplicating and copying equipment
—Kinds

Dictating machines
See Office management—Office machines

Disability benefits insurance
See Insurance, Liability

Disclaimers
See Opinion

Discrimination
Laws relating to, 217-18

Dishonesty insurance
See Insurance, Dishonesty

Dissolution of partnership
See Partnerships—Dissolution

Division of a practice
Tax aspects, 508

Doctors
See Dentists
Physicians

Doctor's bill (book)
By Hugh Cabot

Dues
Professional societies, payment by firms, 152, 168, 379

Duplicating and copying equipment
Audit reports, 584-5
    Diazo method, 585
    Electrostatic method, 585
    Offset method, 584-5
Commercial reproduction service, 594
Kinds, 582-4, 902-3
    Comparison of processes, 902-3
    Diazo method, 582-3
    Dye-transfer method, 583

Duplicating and copying equipment
(*Continued*)
Kinds (*Continued*)
Electrostatic method, 584
Heat-transfer method, 583
Offset methods, 583-4
Photocopy methods, 582
Spirit-duplicating method, 583
Stencil-duplicating method, 583
Tax returns, 586-8, 590, 904-6
Utilizing, 589-94
Audit reports, 584-5
Client's reaction, 590
Inter- and intra-office communication, 589
Monthly jobs, 590-1
Paper saving suggestion, 594
Reports, newsletters, forms, 591-2
Staff training, 588
Strip statements, 592-4
Tax returns, 586-8, 590
Work-paper duplications, 588-9

Dye-transfer method
See Duplicating and copying equipment—Kinds

E

Eaton, Marquis G.
Accountant's own evaluation of his worth, 3
Financial soundness of the professional man, 1
Income goal in terms of achievement, 3

Education
Continuing
See also Professional development
AICPA program, 383
Address by Earl J. McGrath, 382
American academy of general practice program, 382
American bar association programs, 382
American law institute programs, 382
American management association programs, 382
Requirements in starting a practice, 307

Educational records bureau, 620

Electronic data processing
See Data processing service centers

Electrostatic method
See Duplicating and copying equipment—Kinds

Embezzlement
See Fraud

Emergency assistance
See also Transferring a practice
Bridgeport plan, 371
Illinois plan, 371-2

Employment
Fair employment practices, 217-18
Part-time, while starting a practice, 318-20

Employment contracts
See Personnel

Engagements
See also Clients
Preliminary surveys, charging for, 236
Winding up procedures, 532-3
Written confirmation of, 236

Errors
Correction of, in review procedures, 557
Uncovering, CPA's role, 249-50

Ethics
See Professional ethics

Expense reports
See Accounting and recordkeeping—Time and cost control records

Expenses
See Accounting and recordkeeping
also under specific expense, e.g., Traveling expenses

Expenses and income
Distribution of, as percentage of gross fees, 918-19

F

Fagerberg, Dixon
Fees, variable scale, 24-5

Family
Activities, budgeting time for, 328

Fees
See also Billing
Income
Ability to pay, 15-16
Acceptability to client, 16-17
Adjustments for types of services, 25-6
Adjustments of "standard" fees, 47-9
Automobile expense, percentage of gross fees, 723
Billing rates
Office and clerical assistants, 718-19
Chart of median fees billed, 720
Partners and individual practitioners, 717-18
Chart of median fees billed, 719
Staff accountants, 718
Chart of median fees billed, 719
Brokerage
See Professional ethics

Forms (*Continued*)

Operations card—tax work, 753

Personnel rating sheet, staff, 794-5

Productivity record for billing by time and services rendered, 69

Progress report, junior accountant, 793

Rate and time statistics (monthly and cumulative), 703

Recruiting

Evaluation sheet, 786

Letter to student describing advantages of employment with firm, 783-4

Student information blank, 785

Reminder list for special services, 817-21

Report review checklist, 899-901

Review questionnaire for in-charge accountant, 894-6

Review questionnaire, office, 896-8

Staff income and production data, 705

Staff location record, 679, 770

Tax calendar for individuals, 573

Tax questionnaire (individual), 576

Tax return transmittal letter, 579

Tax returns follow-up, 755

Tickler card, 754

Time and expense report, 757-8

Time and expense report (weekly), 763-4

Time report (daily), 762

Time report (weekly), 761

Time sheet using units and variable rates, 682

Time, summary classification of, 777

Time tickets (envelope system), 688

Work analysis schedule (daily), 776

Work forecast (long-range), 771

Forwarding fees

See Professional ethics

Fraud

CPA and defalcations, suits by surety companies, 292

CPA's role in discovering, 249-50, 292

Free time budgeting

See Time budgets

Fringe benefits 139-54

See also under specific type of benefit, e.g., Pension plans

Frisbee, Ira N.

Organizing and perpetuating an accounting partnership (article), 414, 480

From the executive director's desk (article)

By John L. Carey, 243

G

Gains and losses

See Partnerships—Tax problems

Garrison, Lloyd K.

Fee schedules, 17

General electric company

How managers are made and how you can grow your own executives (study), 378

Gilman, Stephen

Accounting concepts of profit (book), 709

Going public

Advice to small corporation clients, 268

Goodwill

See also Purchase and sale of a practice

Computation, 408

Existence of, 473-5

Payment of, and withdrawal of clients by resigning partner, 456-7

Recognition, 475-7

Provisions in partnership agreement, 475-6

Tax aspects, 509-11, 518-19

Transferring, tax aspects, 509-11

Valuation methods, 477-80

Government agencies

Competitive bidding for audit services

Joint statement by Municipal finance officers association and American institute of CPAs, 781-2

Greeting cards

To clients, 267, 668

Group life insurance

See Insurance, Group

Guide to a practical staff training program (pamphlet)

By Michigan association of CPAs, 174-83

H

Heat transfer method

See Duplicating and copying equipment—Kinds

Hiring

See Personnel

Horton vs. commissioner, 510

Hospitalization insurance

See Insurance, Hospitalization

Hours of labor 197-8, 628-9

See also Overtime

Conformance with client's hours, 198

Mergers (*Continued*)
Effects
On clients of local firm, 366
On partners, 364-5
On public, 367
On staffs of local firms, 365-6
On the practice, 366-7
Future of local firms, 368
Management services as factor, 360-1
Number of, 361
Patterns, 367-8
Reasons for merging
Viewpoint of local firm, 362-3
Viewpoint of national firm, 361-2
Reasons for not merging, 363-4
Referrals, extent of, 369
Small firms merging, 369
Source of partners, 403
Tax aspects, 508

Metropolitan New York college placement officers association
Survey of salary offers, table, 143

Michigan association of certified public accountants
Consultation program, 302-3
Guide to a practical staff training program (pamphlet), 174-83

Microfilming
See Office management—Office machines

Military service
Effect on students, 110
In partnership agreements, 439

Minnesota clerical test, 620

Montgomery, Robert H.
Curse of balancing (article), 551

Municipal audits
Competitive bidding, 35
Joint statement by Municipal finance officers association and the American institute of CPAs, 781-2

Municipal finance officers association and American institute of certified public accountants
Joint statement on competitive bidding, 781-2

N

National association of accountants
Activities and objectives, 393-4
Literature for accountants' libraries, 636

National federation of financial analysts societies
Committee on corporate information, 289

Natural business year, 711

Needle-sorted punch cards
See Accounting and recordkeeping—Tickler and follow-up files

"New client data sheet," 668

New York state society of certified public accountants
Accountants' professional liability insurance policy, 914-15

Noncertified accountants
Certified public accountants, distinction between, 224-5

Noncompetition clauses
Withdrawal of partner, 456-7, 469-70
Lynch vs. Bailey, 470
Tax aspects, 509-11

Notes payable
Utilizing client's staff to detail, 255

Numbered opinions
By American institute of CPAs, Committee on professional ethics
See Professional ethics

O

Occupancy expense
See Accounting and recordkeeping—Expenses

Office contents insurance
See Insurance, Property

Office equipment
Investment in starting a practice, 314-15

Office expenses
See Accounting and recordkeeping—Expenses

Office layout
See Office management—Layout and furnishings

Office location and appearance
Accounting firm's, effect on client, 233-4
Obtaining space in starting a practice, 313-14

Office machines
See Duplicating and copying equipment
Office management—Office machines

Office management
Administration of the CPA's office, 234
Branches, 655-7
Interchange of field workers, 657

Personnel

See also Clients—Personnel
Achieving partner status, 207-8
Advancement, 206-10
  Allowing staff members to deal with clients, 207
  Basic policy and authority, 206
  CPA certificate, upon obtaining, 207
  Career plateaus, remedies, 208
  Current practices, 208-10
  Partner status, achieving, 207-8
  Timing, 206
  Uneven progress of staff member, 207
Appearance, 212
Application blanks for employment, 787-9
Classification of accounting staff, 93-4
Clients', utilization of, 252-7
Compensation, 139-54
  See also under specific type, e.g., Salaries
Conduct of employees, 212, 234-5, 629, 802-4
Discharging staff member, 215-16
Discrimination, laws relating to, 217-18
Distribution of, in dissolution of partnership, 465
Employment by small firm, advantages, 102-4
Employment contracts
  Audit staff, 211
  Forms, 796-9
  Office help, 621
Experienced, reasons for hiring, 94-5
Fair employment practices, 217-18
File-room, 604
Incentive and morale, 139-41
Inexperienced, reasons for hiring, 94
Insurance
  See Insurance, Employees
    Insurance, Partners
Internship
  See Internship
Job interviews
  Application form, 115, 787-9
  Interviewer's record, 790
  Procedure, 114-15
  Recruiting, 104-5
    Student reaction, 108-9
  Systematic approach, 90
  Training in, 112-13
Junior accountants
  See Junior accountants
Loyalty, 171
Medical examinations, 152-3
Mergers, effect of, 365-6

Personnel (*Continued*)

Morale, developing, 171
Non-economic motivations, 86-7
Objectives of the firm, management's career goals, 87
Obtaining and keeping, methods, 89-91
Office help
  Employee relations, factors, 623-4
  Employment application form, 787, 789
  Receptionist, 625
  Selection, 618-21
    Hiring, responsibility for, 619
    Screening applicants, 620-1
    Sources of personnel, 619
  Supplying personnel for clients, 621
  Training employees, 621-3
    Manuals and instructions, 621-3
  Utilization, 624
Older men, reasons for hiring, 95
Organization chart, 92-3
Organization of the firm, 88-9, 92-4
Outside employment offers, 214
Performance ratings, 204-5
  Forms, 791-5
  Interpretation, 205
Policies, 87-8, 211-18
Procedures and practices, 89-91
Progress discussions with staff members, 205-6
Recruiting
  See Recruiting
Rehiring staff member, 214-15
Released staff member, assistance in placing, 216
Retaining staff members, comments and attitudes, 196
Retaining young people in the profession, 192-6
Rewarding progress, 204-10
Salaries
  See Salaries
Seasonal problems
  Peak-season remedies, 96
  Slack-season remedies, 96-7
Secrecy regarding firm's business, 213
Selection
  See Personnel selection
Social activities, 174
Sick leave
  See Sick leave
Staff development responsibility
  Partners, 88
  Senior accountants, 88
  Staff members, 89
  Supervisors, 88
Staff location records, 678
  Illustration, 679

Practice development (*Continued*)
Starting a practice, 305-23
  Additional occupations, engaging in, 318-20
  Announcements, 315-17
    Examples, 316-17
  Appraising the community, 310-13
    First CPA in community, 313
    Survey and formula, 310-13
  Associates or partners, starting with, 317-18
  Decision to take the step, 306
  Desire to serve, 306-7
  Educational requirements, 307
  Equipment, investment in, 314-15
  Experience in public accounting, 308
  Financial requirements, 309-10
  Getting an early start, 306
  Office space, 313-14
  Personality as factor, 306
  Reputation, developing a, 320-2
  Small community versus large city, 311-12
  Success story, 322-3
  Time of year to start, 315
  Volume, concentrating on, 320
Transferring a practice
  See Transferring a practice

Preparing for the auditor
Utilizing client's staff, 252-7

Production records
See Accounting and recordkeeping—Time and cost control records

Professional development
AICPA courses, 384
Continuing education
  See Education
Financial assistance by firm, 379-80
Firm's obligation to the profession, 380-1
Management training for staff men, 377-8
Percentage of gross fees for, survey, 719-21
Professional activities, 378-9
Professional organizations, 385-96
Recognition of staff man by client, 377

Professional ethics
See also Code of professional ethics (AICPA)
Announcements in starting a practice, 315-17
  Examples, 316-17
Brokerage fees, 35-6
  AICPA rule, 35
Commissions, 35-6
  AICPA rule, 35

Professional ethics (*Continued*)
Competitive bidding, 34-5
  AICPA rule, 34
  Joint statement by Municipal finance officers association and American institute of CPAs, 781-2
  Municipal audits, 35
  Objections to, 34
Confidential papers, clients', 357
Confidential relations between accountant and client, 261-2
Contingent fees, 30-1
  AICPA rule, 30
  Treasury department requirements, 30
Data processing service bureaus, 734-5, 827
Forwarding fees, 35-6
  AICPA rule, 35
Independence
  See Independence
Letterheads, 611-12
Maintaining standards, 329-30
Management services and independence, 261
Numbered opinions, 824-9
  No. 1—Newsletters, publications, 824
  No. 2—Responsibility of member for acts of third parties on his behalf, 825
  No. 3—Confidence of client, 825
  No. 4—Authorship—propriety of showing firm affiliation of author, 825-6
  No. 5—Prohibited self-designations—Use of title "tax consultant," "tax specialist" or similar designation forbidden, 826
  No. 6—Concept of "laity" in sharing of fees, 826-7
  No. 7—Statistical tabulating services, 827
  No. 8—Denial of opinion does not discharge responsibility in all cases, 827-8
  No. 9—Distribution of literature, 828
  No. 10—Responsibility of members for pro forma statements and forecasts under rule 2.04, 828-9
Part-time employment, while starting a practice, 319-20
Referrals
  See Referrals
Working papers
  See Working papers

Professional ethics of certified public accountants (book)
By John L. Carey, 228, 357

Professional expenses
Financial assistance by firms, 152, 379-80
Percentage of gross fees for, survey, 719-21

Professional goodwill (article)
By W. G. Rodger, 479

Professional image
Creating, 231-5

Professional men
See also under specific type, e.g., Physicians
Financial soundness, 1
Obligation to the profession, 380-1

Professional societies
American accounting association, 392-3
American institute of CPAs, 385-90
Controllers institute of America, 394-5
Financial assistance by firms for dues and expenses, 152, 168, 379-80
Institute of internal auditors, 395-6
Membership in, banker's interest in CPA's, 278
National association of accountants, 393-4
Participation in activities, 168, 182, 378, 379
State societies of CPAs, 390-1

Profit and loss
Utilizing client's staff to prepare analyses of items, 255

Profit sharing plans
Computation of "profits," 149
Employees participating, 148-9
Retirement provisions, 149
Size of firm as factor, 149
Types, 148-9

Profits
Client's, accountant's contribution, 243-6
Division of, in partnership, 412-25

Proofreading
See also Style manual
Reports, 542-3

Property insurance
See Insurance, Property

Proprietorships
Advantages, 398
Tickler and follow-up files, 672
Where the fee dollar goes, charts, 727

Psychological corporation
Tests of clerical aptitude, 620

Public officials
Claims against, under surety bonds, 294-5

Public relations
AICPA program and the state societies, 221-2
Attitudes toward CPAs, opinion surveys, 220
Distinguishing the CPA from other groups performing accounting services, 224-5
Expenses, percentage of income, 721
Financial reporting, survey by Elmo Roper, 221
Need for, 221
Professional status of CPAs, 220, 222-3
Recruiting as opportunity to firms, 106-7
Reputation of CPA, 219-20
Tax practice problem, 223-4
Value of CPA, survey, 222
Years of accomplishment, 221-2

Public service
See Community service

Punched-card accounting
See Mechanization

Punctuation
See Style manual

Purchase and sale of a practice
See also Goodwill
Client's position in sale, 356-7
Fees, character of, 357-8
Future profits, basing price on, 359
Making the transition, 360
Net-profit approach, 358
Purchase price, 355-6
Sale on retirement of practitioner, 372-3
Special points for consideration, 358-9
Valuation of practice, computing, 355-6
Working papers, transferring
Professional ethics rule, 357

Purdue clerical adaptability test, 620

R

Rabkin and Johnson
Current legal forms with tax analysis (book)
Form of partnership agreement, 830-3

Rating personnel
See Personnel—Performance ratings

Records

See also Accounting and recordkeeping

Branch office, 657

Retention and destruction, 605-6, 608-9

Recreation

Budgeting time for, 328

Recruiting

Aids and pitfalls, 104-6

Application form of prospect, 115, 787-8

Attitude of staff toward prospect, 105-6

College, 98-9

Colleges, cooperating with, 107

Competition for accounting graduates, 99-100

Conduct of recruiter, 105

Evaluation sheet, 105, 786

Hiring criteria, 111

Improving, 110-13

  Firms' programs, 111

Initial contact, 104

Job interviews

See Personnel

Joint advisory councils for developing student interest in accounting, 107

Letter describing advantages of employment with firm, 783-4

Military service, effect on students, 110

Offer, handling the, 106

Public relations for the firm, 106-7

Publications for use, 107

Representatives, training of, 112-13

Sales appeal, 107-8

  Examples, 108

Small practitioners, advantages of employment with, 102-4

Small practitioners, disadvantages in recruiting, 102

Small practitioners, techniques used by, 101-2

Sources of personnel, 98

Student information blank, 105

Time for, 100-1

Visits to firm by prospect, 105-6

Working with representatives of accounting societies, 107

Referrals

Advantages and disadvantages, 302

Extent of, 369

Fees, 35

Obtaining clients through, 324-5

Registration statements

See Securities and exchange commission

Report of the Committee on accounting and office equipment 1960-61

By American institute of CPAs, 582

Reports

See also Financial statements

Audit, misconceptions of clients, 248-9

Branch office, preparation and signing, 656-7

Communicating results to client, 228-30

Covers and envelopes, 613-15

Duplicating machines in preparing, 584-5

For credit purposes

See Bankers and credit men

Internal control reports to management, 536

Long-form, delivering and discussing with client, 229-30

Long-form, staff training, 164-5

Management memorandum to client, 229

Number of copies, 542

Opinion on

See Opinion

Paper used for, 612-13

Preparation, 533-6

Processing, 537-45

Proofreading, 542-3

Review procedures, 557-9

Review questionnaire, 560-1

Reviewer's, of client affairs, 265-6

Security analysts

See Security analysts

Setting up in advance of audit, 658

Staff training, 164-5

Statistical, use of punched tape, 730

Storage and disposal, 608

Style manual, 533-5, 834-93

To SEC

See Securities and exchange commission

Typing, 539-41

Writing, communicating results to clients, 228-30

Writing, staff training course, 166-8

  Clarity, 167-8

  Subject matter, 167

  Teaching the course, 167

Reputation

Developing, in starting a practice, 320-2

Research
Time spent in, factor in fees, billing,
7-8, 59

Retainer contracts
See Fees

Retention of records
See Records

Retirement plans
See also Pension plans
Transferring a practice
Partners', 449-54
Age for retirement, 450-1
Amount of retirement provision,
452-4
Limitations on retirements, 454
Need for a plan, 450
Notice of intention to retire, 454
Problems involved, 451
Tax problems, 515-23

Review procedures
Errors, correction of, 557
Field review
Audit program, 550-1
Audit report, 552
Closing the audit, 550
Internal control, degree of, 549-50
Reliance on staff, 550
Time for review, 548-9
Working papers, 551-2
Field work, 545-57
Flexibility of approach, 555-6
Informing staff man of results of re-
view, 564-5
Levels of responsibility, 548
Need for review, 546-7
Office review, 553-5
Absence of field review, 555
Following field review, 554-5
Questionnaire, 896-8
Responsibility for reviewing, 553
Reviewer's approach, 553-4
Questionnaire, 559-61
Audit working papers and reports,
560-1
Basic data, 560
Checklist for report review, 899-
901
In-charge accountant's, 894-6
Office review, 896-8
Report release, 561
Representations by client, 560
Report review, 557-9
Clerical review, 557
Long-form report, 558-9
Objective review, 558
Responsibility for, 558
Subjective review, 559
Responsibilities of firm, 545

Review procedures (*Continued*)
Scope of review, 547-8
Minimum review for small firm,
547-8
Special investigations, 563
Statements and adjustments, review
of, with client, 556-7
System installation, 562-3
Tax returns, 567-9

"Reviewer's report"
Of client's affairs, 265-6

Robert Morris associates, 272

Rockey, Charles S.
Accountant's relations with his client
(article), 230

Rodger, W. G.
Professional goodwill (article), 479

Roper, Elmo
Survey on financial reporting, 221

Rotation of assignments, 169-70

Rotation of auditors
Arguments for, 268-70
Expense factor, 270-1
Internal rotation, 270
Interval of rotation, 271

S

SRA tests of clerical aptitude, 620

Safe-deposit box insurance
See Insurance, Dishonesty

*Safeguards against employee dishonesty
in business* (booklet)
By American institute of CPAs and
Surety association of America, 293

Salaries
Advances and loans, 152
Fees, relation between, 239
Increases, methods, 143-4
Offers to college seniors, table, 142-3
Starting rate, 142-3
Survey of College placement council,
142-3
Survey of Metropolitan New York
college placement officers as-
sociation, 143

Sale of a practice
See Purchase and sale of a practice

Salesmanship
Psychology, 340-3
Sales techniques, 339-40
Selling oneself to the client, 337-43
Ability to communicate, 338-9

**Seashore-Bennett stenographic profi-
ciency test,** 620

Valuation of a practice
See Goodwill
　　Purchase and sale of a practice
*Valuation of goodwill in an accounting
　　practice* (article)
　　By Max Block, 478
*Value of partnership interests and
　　changes in partnership* (ar-
　　ticle)
　　By Lorin A. Torrey, 407
Variable scale
Fees, 24-6

W

Wage negotiations
Accountant's role, 296-8
Whole-dollar accounting
Advantages, 535
Williams, T. Dwight
Fees, adjustments for types of services,
　　25
Withdrawal of partner
See Partnerships
Women accountants
On audit staffs, 94
Work forecasts
See Accounting and recordkeeping
Work in process
Valuation, in accounting partnership,
　　471-3
Work schedules, 201
Delays, reasons for, 202-3
Working papers
Destruction, 605-6, 608-9
Duplicating equipment, use of, 588-9
Forms, making up, 610-11
Managing and identifying, 658-9
Review, field review, 551-2
Review, on-the-job training, 157-8
Review, questionnaire, 560-1
Setting up in advance of audit, 658
Transferring, to purchaser of practice,
　　357
Use of, in staff training, 161-2
Workmen's compensation insurance
See Insurance, Liability

Write-ups
AICPA survey on firms performing,
　　334-5
Advantages and disadvantages in start-
　　ing a practice, 333
CPAs role, 250
Guide for handling, 336-7
Methods used, 337
Prestige of CPA in performing, 333-4
Punched-card accounting, 729-46
　　Converting to, 732-6
　　　Auditing and tax work, 735-6
　　　Client resistance, 733
　　　Costs, 733
　　　Ethics, 734-5, 827
　　　Selecting a service bureau, 734
　　　Time saved, 734
　　Data processing service centers,
　　　AICPA committee recom-
　　　mendations, 736-7
　　Experiences of practitioners, 741-6
　　　Discontinuance of punched-tape
　　　　method, 744-5
　　　Small firm's use of punched tape,
　　　　741-3
　　　Use of computer, 743-4
　　　Use of single tape-punching ma-
　　　　chine, 746
　　Input data, 730-2
　　Processing, 731-2
　　Source-data method, 737-41
　　　Accounting records design, 737-8
　　　Advantages, 740-1
　　　Cash disbursements method, 738
　　　Cash receipts journal, 738
　　　Cumulative earnings records, 740
　　　General ledger and statements,
　　　　739-40
　　　Monthly adjustments, 739
　　　Payroll journal, 738
　　　Preliminary trial balance and
　　　　payroll register, 739
　　　Preparing the punched cards, 739
　　　Review of client's work, 738
　　　Statistical reports to management,
　　　　730
　　Services included in, 334
　　Usefulness and desirability, 335-6
Writing
See also Reports
Developing ability, 177
Wyler vs. commissioner, 357, 510

952